LEARNING
CANADIAN
CRIMINAL LAW

Eighth Edition

LEARNING CANADIAN CRIMINAL LAW

Eighth Edition

by

DON STUART
B.A., LL.B., Dip. Crim., D. Phil.
Faculty of Law
Queen's University

and

RONALD JOSEPH DELISLE
B.Sc., LL.B., LL.M.
Faculty of Law
Queen's University

CARSWELL
A THOMSON COMPANY

Canadian Cataloguing in Publication Data

Main entry under title:
Learning Canadian criminal law

8th ed.
ISBN 0-459-26115-0

1. Criminal law — Canada — Cases. I. Stuart, Don, 1943- .
II. Delisle, R.J.

KE8809.L43 2001   345.71   C2001-930213-4
KF9219.A2L42 2001

CARSWELL

A THOMSON COMPANY

One Corporate Plaza
2075 Kennedy Road
Scarborough, Ontario
M1T 3V4

Customer Relations:
Toronto 1-416-609-3800
Elsewhere in Canada/U.S. 1-800-387-5164
Fax 1-416-298-5094
World Wide Web: http://www.carswell.com
E-mail: orders@carswell.com

PREFACE TO THE EIGHTH EDITION

We think that the major focus for studying criminal law in first year law school should be on the tools which lawyers and Judges must know and use in the daily business of the conduct of a criminal trial. It is obvious that law students, teachers and lawyers can better understand criminal law if they seek help from the many disciplines that now offer insights into the criminal justice system. However, time and energy are limited and choices have to be made. It is also quite impossible to properly address all the basic legal principles of the substantive, procedural, evidentiary and sentencing aspects of the criminal justice system in one first-year course. Such a survey would belittle the worth of each. Our choice is to concentrate on substantive principles and the trial context: the adversary system, how the elements of crime are proved, punishment theories and sentencing practices. We promote a full inquiry into the methods of determining legal guilt and the major legal justifications and excuses.

With the arrival of an entrenched *Charter of Rights and Freedoms* in 1982, the subject of teaching the criminal justice system has become even more demanding and complex. In order to leave the task manageable, we leave the detailed study of police powers under the *Charter*, concerning such important matters as search and seizure, arrest, right to counsel and right to silence, to more specialist upper-year courses. To that end, we have published a separate casebook, *Learning Canadian Criminal Procedure* (6th ed., 2000). Likewise, our students are left to study the law of evidence and more technical aspects of sentencing and release from prison in other courses.

Although the development of a critical perspective is key to any university environment, we believe it essential to ensure that we first provide a full and complete analysis of the existing laws before we turn to critical analysis. Our students need to be informed before they can be truly critical.

Criminal law teachers should encourage a learning process rather than just lecture. Our approach throughout has been to concentrate on the major sources: the *Criminal Code* itself, key judicial decisions and critical review. Increasingly, major decisions, especially those from the Supreme Court of Canada, tend to be long. Although we have had to resort to editing, we have tried not to be too intrusive. We try to pose questions rather than provide answers. We have also used the device of problems, sometimes based on actual decisions, sometimes to provoke thought on current social problems. We have also included general review questions. On occasion, we have suggested teaching exercises, as in our suggestion to hold a mock obscenity trial.

Our materials have evolved from the first edition in several important ways. We still see our lengthy introductory section as vitally important as a carefully selected set of materials designed to quickly equip the new student with the proper legal tools and context by which to study the criminal trial process. Over the years, we have added and refined sections dealing with ethical obligations of Crown and defence counsel and also the new reality of the possibility of exclusion of evidence obtained in violation of the *Charter*. We now include materials to introduce the student to feminist perspectives, issues of victims' rights and also to gain insight into the plea that the present system ignores aboriginal values.

We have always stressed the importance of a logical order that builds on understanding. In early editions we began the subject of fault by a chapter entitled "The Aware State of Mind (Mens Rea)" and followed it by a chapter on "Departures from the Subjective Mens Rea Principle", where we addressed public welfare offences and negligence offences. We made a major structural change with the 5th edition to reflect the Supreme Court's major decision on fault in *Creighton*. Chapter 3 now amalgamates these chapters into one entitled "The Fault Requirement (Mens Rea or Negligence)". This starts with an introductory analysis of the distinction between subjective and objective standards as outlined by Supreme Court judgments, still using the infamous U.K. case of *D.P.P. v. Smith* as a test case. We then move to public welfare offences, reviewing the due diligence compromise of *Sault Ste. Marie* and how this became a *Charter* standard for any offence which threatens the liberty interest. We then turn to *Criminal Code* offences and first examine how the Supreme Court decided that subjective awareness would only be constitutionally required for a few crimes such as murder. Then, following the dictates of *Creighton*, we analyze in detail the three types of crimes the Court envisages: those of subjective *mens rea*, objective crimes requiring a marked departure from the norm and, finally, those based on predicate offences, which have a much reduced fault requirement. This allows us to postpone to the end consideration of the difficult decisions in *DeSousa*, *Creighton* (respecting unlawful act manslaughter), and *Godin* (aggravated assault). Over these past few years we have found that this structure works well.

This new strategy absorbed our separate chapters on homicide and theft. However we kept our separate chapter on Rape and Sexual Assault to allow consideration of that controversial subject in context, the 1982 change from rape to sexual assault and the 1992 Bill C-49 changes respecting the mistaken belief in consent defence and consent. In this edition we have included the blockbuster ruling of the Supreme Court in *Ewanchuk* on the issue of consent and imposing new limits on the defence of mistaken belief in consent. We have constructed problems, including the facts of the recent ruling of the Supreme Court on *O. (M.)*, so that the impact of *Ewanchuk* can be better assessed in less emotive contexts. We also include the Supreme Court's latest ruling on air of reality in *Davis*, its upholding of the "new" rape shield provisions in *Darrach* and the attempt by the Manitoba Court of Appeal in *Malcolm* to interpret the statutory duty to take reasonable steps. The Supreme Court's controversial and complex rulings in *O'Connor*, *Carosella* and *Mills*, respecting discovery of medical and counselling records of complainants in sexual assault cases, are mentioned but full treatment is left to Criminal Procedure and Evidence courses. We do assess the determination in *Mills* that complainants in sexual assault cases have enforceable equality rights under s. 15 of the *Charter*.

In this edition there are no structural changes but we have updated throughout and added new problems to test comprehension. In the introductory chapter we have, in recent editions, used both *Verrette* and *Jobidon* for the first major case briefing assignments. This edition uses instead the decision of the Ontario Court of Appeal in *Jacob*, which concerns a charge of an indecent act laid against a woman walking topless about the streets of Guelph. We decided that *Jobidon* is too important to address so early so we moved it to be considered with other consent cases in the Actus Reus section. There are now notes to consider recent unsuccessful general challenges to marihuana laws based on the assertion of a harm principle under s. 7 in British Columbia, *Malmo-Levine*, and in Ontario, *Parker*. We also refer to the medical exemption recognized by the Ontario Court of Appeal in *Clay*. In the section on ethics we added the *Murray* case, respecting a defence lawyer's conduct in retrieving videotapes in the *Bernardo* case. In our lengthy section on fault we have added Ontario Court of Appeal decisions on wilful blindness for accessories after the fact, *Duong*, and the *mens rea* required for criminal harassment, *Krushel*. We have a new note on the definitional confusion there now exists respecting the *mens rea* required for assault causing bodily harm. We consider the important ruling of the Supreme Court in *Stone* in three places: voluntariness, sane automatism and the partial defence of provocation. We note the effect of the ruling of the Supreme Court in *Winko* as to the disposition of those found not criminally responsible on account of mental disorder. We draw attention to conflicting lower court decisions on the constitutionality of s. 33.1, where Parliament purports to abolish the extreme intoxication defence to general intent crimes asserted in *Daviault*. We have added the controversial mercy killing decision of *Latimer* to the consideration of the defence of necessity and refer to the *Conjoined Twins* decision of the U.K. Court of Appeal of September, 2000. We have shortened the section on attempting to commit the impossible to reflect the pre-emptive decision of the Supreme Court in *Dynar*.

To aid discussions on law reform we have included in the Appendices two recent proposals for General Parts.

We usually distribute edited crime statistics to our classes. We consulted on this issue with fellow teachers and decided not to put them in the book itself. They tend to date and come out every year in any event.

We are grateful to Jilean Bell at Carswell for her continuing support. We are especially indebted to Dennis Brennan, whose meticulous work at the production stage much improved our manuscript.

Don Stuart
R.J. Delisle
January 1, 2001

ACKNOWLEDGMENTS

We gratefully thank the following authors, publishers or organizations for permission to reproduce excerpts from the material listed below.

Aboriginal Peoples and Criminal Justice
Law Reform Commission of Canada

Acts of Will and Responsibility
H.L.A. Hart
Oxford University Press

Adversary System Excuse
Rowman and Allanheld

Burdens of Proof and Presumptions
Law Reform Commission of Canada

Case for the Defence
E. Greenspan and Macmillan of Canada

The Charter, the Supreme Court and the Invisible Politics of Fault
Rosemary Cairns Way

Code of Professional Conduct
Canadian Bar Association

Comment
Cambridge Law Journal
Cambridge University Press
Glanville L. Williams

Comment
Canadian Bar Review
J. Willis

Crime and Punishment in Britain
Edinburgh University Press
N.D. Walker

Criminal Law. The General Part
Glanville L. Williams
Stevens and Sons Ltd.
Sweet and Maxwell Ltd.

Criminal Responsibility for Ommissions
H.R.S. Ryan

Culpable Mistakes and Rape: Harsh Words on Pappajohn
T. Pickard
University of Toronto Law Journal
University of Toronto Press

Dancing with a Ghost
Rupert Ross

Diagnostic and Statistical Manual of Mental Disorders
American Psychiatric Association

Dimensions of Criminal Law
Toni Pickard and Phil Goldman

Error Juris: A Comparative Study
The University of Chicago

False Memory Syndrome
Nicholas Bala
Queen's Law Journal

The Insanity Defence Since Schwartz v. R.
S.N. Verdun-Jones

The Intoxicated Offender — A Problem of Responsibility
S.M. Beck
Canadian Bar Review
G.E. Parker

The Jury in Criminal Trials
Law Reform Commission of Canada

Our Criminal Law
Law Reform Commission of Canada

Portia in a Different Voice
Berkeley Women's Law Journal

Principles of Criminal Liability
Canadian Bar Association

Psychiatry, Ethics and the Criminal Law
Columbia Law Review
T. Szasz

Public Opinion, Aggressive Soliciting Force Crackdown on B.C. Prostitutes
The Canadian Press

Punishment and Responsibility
H.L.A. Hart
Oxford University Press

Recodifying Criminal Law
Law Reform Commission of Canada

Re-Thinking Criminal Law
G.P. Fletcher

Report of the Committee on Mentally Abnormal Offenders
Her Majesty's Stationery Office

Sentencing Reform: A Canadian Approach
Minister of Supply and Services, Canada

Soliciting Law a Bust
The Canadian Press

Teaching Rape Law
Susan Estrich
Yale Law Journal

Textbook of Criminal Law
Glanville L. Williams
Stevens and Sons Ltd.
Sweet and Maxwell Ltd.

Towards Unity: Criminal Justice and Correction
Solicitor General, Canada

When Titans Clash
Alan N. Young

Will Women Judges Really Make a Difference?
Madame Justice Bertha Wilson
Osgoode Hall Law Journal

TABLE OF CONTENTS

TABLE OF CASES

The bold entries reflect those cases where the text of the judgment is given.

Chapter 1

INTRODUCTION

Sources

R. v. SEDLEY

(1663) as described in Curll, *Cobbett's Complete Collection of State Trials*, Vol. 17 (1727), 155

Sir Charles Sedley was indicted at common law for several misdemeanors against the King's peace, and which were to the great scandal of Christianity; and the cause was, for that he shewed his naked body in a balcony in Covent Garden to a great multitude of people, and there did such things, and spoke such words, & c. mentioning some particulars of his misbehaviour, as throwing down bottles (pissed in) *vi et armis* among the people. Fortescue's Reports, 99, 100. And this indictment was openly read to him in court; and the justices told him, that notwithstanding there was not then any Star-chamber, yet they would have him know, that the Court of King's bench was the custos morum of all the king's subjects; and that it was then high time to punish such profane actions, committed against all modesty, which were as frequent, as if not only Christianity, but morality also had been neglected. After he had been kept in court by recognizance from Trinity term to the end of Michaelmas term, the Court required him to take his trial at bar: but being advised, he submitted himself to the Court, and confessed the indictment. The Michaelmas term following, the Court considered what judgment to give; and inasmuch as he was a gentleman of a very ancient family (in Kent) and his estate incumbered, (not intending his ruin, but his reformation) they fined him only 2,000 marks, and to be imprisoned a week without bail, and to be of good behaviour for three years.

THE CONSTITUTION ACT, 1867
(formerly the British North America Act)

1867, 30 and 31 Vic., c. 3

VI.—DISTRIBUTION OF LEGISLATIVE POWERS.

Powers of the Parliament.

91. It shall be lawful for the Queen, by and with the Advice and Consent of the Senate and House of Commons, to make Laws for the Peace, Order, and good Government of Canada, in relation to all Matters not coming within the Classes of Subjects by this Act assigned exclusively to the Legislatures of the Provinces; and for greater Certainty, but not so as to restrict the Generality of the foregoing Terms of this Section, it is hereby declared that (notwithstanding anything in this Act) the exclusive Legislative Authority of the Parliament of Canada extends to all Matters coming within the Classes of Subjects next hereinafter enumerated; that is to say,—

. . . .

27. The Criminal Law, except the Constitution of Courts of Criminal Jurisdiction, but including the Procedure in Criminal Matters.
28. The Establishment, Maintenance, and Management of Penitentiaries.

. . . .

Exclusive Powers of Provincial Legislatures.

92. In each Province the Legislature may exclusively make Laws in relation to Matters coming within the Classes of Subject next herein-after enumerated; that is to say,—

. . . .

6. The Establishment, Maintenance, and Management of Public and Reformatory Prisons in and for the Province.

. . . .

13. Property and Civil Rights in the Province.
14. The Administration of Justice in the Province, including the Constitution, Maintenance, and Organization of Provincial Courts, both of Civil and of Criminal Jurisdiction, and including Procedure in Civil Matters in those Courts.
15. The Imposition of Punishment by Fine, Penalty, or Imprisonment for enforcing any Law of the Province made in relation to any Matter coming within any of the Classes of Subjects enumerated in this Section.

In 1892 Parliament enacted Canada's first *Criminal Code*. It was modelled on the English Draft Code of 1879 which in turn was primarily the work of Sir James Stephen, a remarkable English jurist. The English Draft Code was rejected in England and there is still no *Criminal Code* there. Most U.S. states have a *Criminal Code*. Criminal law there differs from state to state. Our *Criminal Code* is federal and applies across Canada. It declares offences and defences and also procedure. There are also a number of other federal offences declared in other federal statutes and regulations and also provincial offences such as driving and liquor offences declared in provincial statutes and regulations.

Can you guess how many offences exist in law in Canada?

FREY v. FEDORUK

[1950] S.C.R. 517, 10 C.R. 26, 97 C.C.C. 1

Frey had been seen on Fedoruk's property looking into a lighted side window of the house where Fedoruk's mother was preparing for bed. Fedoruk chased him brandishing a butcher's knife. He caught and detained him. A policeman, Stone, was called and, after some investigation, arrested Frey without warrant. Frey sued for damages for malicious prosecution and for false imprisonment. The suit was dismissed by the trial Judge and this was affirmed by a majority in the British Columbia Court of Appeal on the ground that Frey had been guilty of a criminal offence at common law and therefore that there had been legal justification for the arrest without warrant. The appeal to the Supreme Court was concerned only with the claim for false imprisonment. The Court decided that criminal offences were to be found in the *Criminal Code* and established common law. Since being a "peeping tom" was not an offence known to the law, there was no justification in law for Fedoruk and Stone to have imprisoned Frey, and Frey was entitled to succeed against both of them.

CARTWRIGHT J.: —

. . . .

I do not think that it is safe to hold as a matter of law, that conduct, not otherwise criminal and not falling within any category of offences defined by the criminal law, becomes criminal because a natural and probable result thereof will be to provoke others to violent retributive action. If such a principle were admitted, it seems to me that many courses of conduct which it is well settled are not criminal could be made the subject of indictment by setting out the facts and concluding with the words that such conduct was likely to cause a breach of the peace. Two examples may be mentioned. The speaking of insulting words unaccompanied by any threat of violence undoubtedly may and sometimes does produce violent retributive action, but is not criminal. The commission of adultery has, in many recorded cases, when unexpectedly discovered, resulted in homicide; but, except where expressly made so by statute, adultery is not a crime.

If it should be admitted as a principle that conduct may be treated as criminal because, although not otherwise criminal, it has a natural tendency to provoke violence by way of retribution, it seems to me that great uncertainty would result.

. . . .

I do not understand O'Halloran J.A. to suggest in his elaborate reasons that there is precedent for the view that the plaintiff's conduct in this case was criminal. Rather he appears to support the finding of the trial Judge to that effect on the grounds stated in the following paragraph:

> Criminal responsibility at common law is primarily not a matter of precedent, but of application of generic principle to the differing facts of each case. It is for the jury to apply to

the facts of the case as they find them, the generic principle the Judge gives them. Thus by their general verdict the jury in practical effect decide both the law and the facts in the particular case, and have consistently done so over the centuries, and *cf.* Coke on Littleton (1832 ed.) vol. 1, note 5, para. 155(*b*). The fact-finding Judge in this case, as the record shows, had not the slightest doubt on the evidence before him that what the appellant had been accused of was a criminal offence at common law.

In my opinion when it is read against the background of the rest of the reasons of O'Halloran J.A., it appears that, in relation to the facts of this case, the "generic principle" which the learned Judge has in mind is too wide to have any value as a definition. The genus appears to be a "breach of the King's Peace" in the wider signification which is attached to that expression elsewhere in the reasons.

It appears to me that so understood, the genus is wide enough to include the whole field of the criminal law. As it is put in Pollock and Maitland, History of English Law (1895), vol. 1, p. 22: "all criminal offences have long been said to be committed against the King's peace." And in vol. 2 of the same work at p. 452, it is stated: "to us a breach of the King's peace may seem to cover every possible crime."

Once the expression "a breach of the King's peace" is interpreted, as O'Halloran J.A. undoubtedly does interpret it, not to require as an essential ingredient anything in the nature of "riots, tumults, or actual physical violence" on the part of the offender, it would appear to become wide enough to include any conduct which in the view of the fact-finding tribunal is so injurious to the public as to merit punishment. If, on the other hand, O'Halloran J.A. intended to give to the expression a more limited meaning so that it would include only conduct of a nature likely to lead to a breach of the peace in the narrower sense of which he speaks, the authorities referred to elsewhere in this judgment seem to me to show that this is not an offence known to the law.

I am of opinion that the proposition implicit in the paragraph quoted above ought not to be accepted. I think that if adopted, it would introduce great uncertainty into the administration of the criminal law, leaving it to the judicial officer trying any particular charge to decide that the acts proved constituted a crime or otherwise, not by reference to any defined standard to be found in the *Code* or in reported decisions, but according to his individual view as to whether such acts were a disturbance of the tranquillity of people tending to provoke physical reprisal.

To so hold would, it seems to me, be to assert the existence of what is referred to in Stephen's History of the Criminal Law of England, vol. 2, p. 190, as:

the power which has in some instances been claimed for the judges of declaring anything to be an offence which is injurious to the public although it may not have been previously regarded as such.

The writer continues: "this power, if it exists at all, exists at common law."

In my opinion, this power has not been held and should not be held to exist in Canada. I think it safer to hold that no one shall be convicted of a crime unless the offence with which he is charged is recognized as such in the provisions of the *Criminal Code*, or can be established by the authority of some reported case as an offence known to the law. I think that if any course of conduct is now to be declared criminal, which has not up to the present time been so regarded, such declaration should be made by Parliament and not by the Courts.

. . . .

J. WILLIS, COMMENT

(1950), 28 Can. Bar Rev. 1023 at 1024-1025

Where do we stand now with peeping toms? This is a comparatively unimportant question; for if Parliament doesn't like the law as laid down by the Supreme Court of Canada, it can, of course, change it. The conduct of a peeping tom is not prohibited by any section in the *Code* and is not a criminal offence at common law. So there is no point, as heretofore, in quietly ringing up the police and asking them to cart the fellow away in the patrol wagon; the fellow has not committed any Criminal offence at all, let alone an offence for which he may be arrested without warrant. What you must do is ask him politely for his name and address and then request the police to find him at that address and have him "bound to his good behaviour for causes of scandal *contra bonos mores*"; the fellow's "conduct in peeping through the window was *contra bonos mores*", as Cartwright J. admits. Or, more sensibly, and more naturally, and this is just what O'Halloran J.A. was afraid of as he went through intellectual contortions to create the new criminal offence out of thin air, just creep up behind him and, if you are bigger than he is, beat him up.

Much more important, where do we stand with common law offences? It has always been a fundamental principle of the Canadian *Criminal Code* that the common law was not superseded, and the reason for leaving it in existence was to allow the judges to meet new needs with new criminal law. The Stephen Draft Code expressly abrogated all common law offences not embodied in some statute and was sharply criticized by some of the English judges for so doing. Baron Parke said:

> My objection to the proposed measure is founded on the danger of confining provisions against crimes to enactments and repealing in this respect the rules of the common law, which are clear and well understood and have the incalculable advantage of being capable of application to new combinations of circumstances, perpetually recurring, which are decided, when they arise, by inference and analogy to them and upon the principles on which they rest.

And it was with this in mind that Sir John Thompson said when introducing the *Criminal Code* Bill into the House of Commons: "The common law will still exist and be referred to, and in that respect the code . . . will have that elasticity which has been so much desired by those who are opposed to codification on general principles". But elasticity is just what Cartwright J. does not want; his ideal is certainty in the administration of criminal law. What is happening is that the Supreme Court of Canada is introducing into the *Code* through the backdoor of interpretation a principle that the sponsors of the *Code* rejected in favour of elasticity, the principle of *nullum crimen, nulla poena, sine lege*, no one shall be punished for anything that is not expressly forbidden by law. In the eternal conflict of values Baron Parke and, following him, Sir John Thompson, placed the protection of the state from the risk of disorder above the protection of the individual from the risk of oppression; the Supreme Court of Canada has reversed that order.

In the 1955 Revision of the *Criminal Code* (see below), Parliament went further than the Supreme Court and, in s. 9, abolished common-law offences but in s. 8 preserved all common defences. It also enacted what is now section 177 which provides:

> Everyone who, without lawful excuse, the proof of which lies upon him, loiters or prowls at night upon the property of another person near a dwelling house situated on that property is guilty of an offence punishable on summary conviction.

In 1993 Parliament enacted a new crime of criminal harassment. See s. 264.

Have Professor Willis's fears been satisfied by legislative action?

THE CRIMINAL CODE

R.S.C. 1985, c. C-46

8. (1) The provisions of this Act apply throughout Canada except

(*a*) in the Northwest Territories, in so far as they are inconsistent with the *Northwest Territories Act*, and

(*b*) in the Yukon Territory, in so far as they are inconsistent with the *Yukon Act*.

(2) The criminal law of England that was in force in a province immediately before the 1st day of April 1955 continues in force in the province except as altered, varied, modified or affected by this Act or any other Act of the Parliament of Canada.

(3) Every rule and principle of the common law that renders any circumstance a justification or excuse for an act or a defence to a charge continues in force and applies in respect of proceedings for an offence under this Act or any other Act of the Parliament of Canada, except in so far as they are altered by or are inconsistent with this Act or any other Act of the Parliament of Canada.

9. Notwithstanding anything in this Act or any other Act no person shall be convicted or discharged under section 736

(*a*) of an offence at common law,

(*b*) of an offence under an Act of the Parliament of England, or of Great Britain, or of the, United Kingdom of Great Britain and Ireland, or

(*c*) of an offence under an Act or ordinance in force in any province, territory or place before that province, territory or place became a province of Canada,

but nothing in this section affects the power, jurisdiction or authority that a Court, Judge, justice or magistrate had, immediately before the 1st day of April 1955, to impose punishment for contempt of Court.

While at the time of *Sedley's* trial it fell to the Judges to punish those activities which they believed violated contemporary community morals, we see that in Canada today the pre-eminent source of criminal law is legislation. The judges are given the task of interpreting the legislation and applying it to the activities in their particular case. In interpreting the law, is there room for creativity? To what extent are they restricted by the words of statutes and the doctrine of precedent? In considering the next case, ask whether our criminal courts have greatly advanced from the position taken in *Sedley*.

R. v. JACOB

(1996), 4 C.R. (5th) 86, 112 C.C.C. (3d) 1 (Ont. C.A.)

WEILER J.A. (concurring in the result): — The issue in this appeal is whether the appellant's display of her breasts in public was an indecent act. On a hot summer day, between five and seven p.m., the appellant walked about the streets of Guelph barebreasted. On one of Guelph's main streets, a police officer asked the appellant to put on a top and to cover her breasts. The appellant explained that she felt it was her constitutional right to go topless; it was all right for men to go topless and women should be allowed the same right. The police officer allowed the appellant to proceed on her way. The appellant walked to a residential area and then paused to talk to a man working on his lawn in front of his residence. Young children at play across the street saw the appellant's exposed breasts and ran to tell their mothers. One mother requested that the appellant cover up; when she refused to do so, the mother complained to the police.

The appellant was charged with committing an indecent act by exposing her breasts in a public place contrary to s. 173(1)(a) of the *Criminal Code*, R.S.C. 1985, c. C-46. The provincial court judge found that the appellant's act was beyond the community standard of tolerance, convicted her of committing an indecent act and sentenced her to pay a fine of $75. She appealed her conviction to the Ontario Court (General Division). The appeal judge found that the trial judge's decision was not unreasonable, that it could be supported on the evidence, and that he had not erred in law. He dismissed the appeal. The appellant now seeks to appeal to this court.

. . . .

In reaching the conclusion that the appellant's act was indecent, the trial judge did not consider the wording of s. 173(1)(a) as it contrasts with the wording in s. 173(1)(b). It is a canon of statutory interpretation that in interpreting one part of a section regard should be had to its context within the section as a whole. For ease of reference s. 173(1) is reproduced below.

> Everyone who wilfully does an indecent act
>
> (a) in a public place in the presence of one or more persons, or
>
> (b) in any place, with intent thereby to insult or offend any person,
>
> is guilty of an offence punishable on summary conviction.

Section 173(1) provides that an indecent act may be a crime in one of two ways. The mental element of "wilfully" applies to both subsections (a) and (b). No further mental element is required under subsection (a). The intention of the actor does not determine the indecent quality of the act. The subsecton also requires that the act occur in a public place. The test used to determine whether the act is indecent under subsection (a) is the community standard of tolerance. This is an objective measure.

In contrast, subsection (b) requires a mental element in addition to wilfulness. The act must be done with the intention to insult or offend another person. It may take place either in public or in private. The intention of the actor to insult or offend determines the indecent quality of the act. This is a subjective standard. Here, even if the act was beyond the community standard of tolerance, if there is no intention to insult or offend, the criminal nature of the act would not have been made out. Conversely, if an act was not beyond the community standard of tolerance but it was done with the intent to insult or offend, it could be an indecent act.

To illustrate the differences between the two subsections, suppose that it is not beyond the community standard of tolerance for a woman to expose her breasts. However, it is a tenet of a certain religion that, in the presence of others, a woman's bare skin be exposed as little as possible. In an attempt to insult those who accept this faith, a female opponent of the dress restrictions imposed on women of this faith decides to expose her breasts to both the religious leader and the congregation. She does this by walking back and forth on the street in front of their place of worship. The religious leader and members of the congregation are shocked and insulted. The woman is charged under subsection (b). It seems to me that, because the woman intended to insult or offend, her act would be considered indecent despite the fact that the community at large might tolerate the public exposure of a woman's breasts. By considering the exposure of a woman's breasts to be indecent in these circumstances and criminalizing this behaviour, the court would be protecting the underlying value of respect for the religion of others which is at the heart of the *Charter* value of freedom of religion. Under subsection (b) the community standard of tolerance does not have a role to play in determining whether an act is indecent. Paragraph (b) enables the court to punish a person whose act is intended to show disrespect for the rights and freedoms of others.

Subsection (a), on the other hand, is different. Its underlying purpose is to recognize those values which are considered to be essential for people to exist with each other when they are together in a public place.

. . . .

[Weiler J. then reviewed the jurisprudence regarding the meaning of the word "obscenity" in the *Criminal Code*. The *Code* provided that obscenity was "the undue exploitation of sex". She noted that the test for that phrase was whether the matter went beyond "the commuity standard of tolerance". She then noted that that test was later applied to determine the meaning of "indecent" in the *Criminal Code*. From this review she drew a certain conclusion with respect to which her colleagues disagreed.]

Thus, in applying the community standard of tolerance to determine whether an act is obscene or indecent, the court is determining whether there has been an undue exploitation of sex. . . . Not all conduct which is beyond the community standard of tolerance is indecent. For example, if a woman stood at the corner of Queen and Yonge in Toronto and produced a hypodermic needle full of heroin and shot it into her arm, she would not be guilty of an indecent act even though the community is not prepared to tolerate this harmful conduct. She would, however, be guilty of the illegal act of possession of heroin under the *Narcotics Control Act*, R.S.C. 1985, c. N-1. An act which is beyond the community standard of tolerance because it is harmful is not necessarily an indecent act. A sexual context is required for the standard to be applied.

. . . .

If the content of the conduct is ignored and regard is had only to community standards there is a danger of a majority deciding what values are important and coercing minorities to conform to those values on the basis of avoiding perceived harm to society from non-conformity. If resort is had only to the community standard of tolerance test without there being a context-based prerequisite, then it is possible that discrimination arising from social stereotyping will be legitimized. In so far as community standards of tolerance are to be applied under s. 173(1)(a), therefore, an essential element is that the context of the conduct must first be sexual.

. . . .

How does one determine when conduct has a sexual context? The matter was considered in *R. v. Chase*, [1987] 2 S.C.R. 293, 37 C.C.C. (3d) 97. In that case, McIntyre J., on behalf of the court at p. 299 S.C.R., p. 101 C.C.C., adopted the position of Martin J.A. in *R. v. Alderton* (1985), 17 C.C.C. (3d) 204 (C.A.), and Laycraft C.J.A. in *R. v. Taylor* (1985), 19 C.C.C. (3d) 156, 44 C.R. (3d) 263 (Alta. C.A.), to the effect that it is an act which, viewed objectively in all the circumstances, is done for sexual gratification.

. . . .

As applied to this case, the question is, would a reasonable bystander, fully apprised of all the circumstances, have considered the appellant's act was sexual in the sense that she was exposing her breasts for the sexual gratification of herself or someone else? The exposure today of a woman's breasts in public does not automatically import a conclusion that this act is being done for the sexual gratification of the actor or the audience. For example, the exposure of a woman's breasts in public in order to breastfeed a child is not done for the sexual gratification of the woman or anyone else. It affords women, who choose to nourish a child by breastfeeding, mobility. This example illustrates the importance of the circumstances in determining whether an act is sexual. Consideration of the circumstances, according to McIntyre J. at pp. 301-02 S.C.R., p. 103 C.C.C., includes consideration of any part of the body touched, words and gestures accompanying the act, and the intent or purpose of the person committing the act, to the extent that this may appear from the evidence. While the motive of the accused person is but one factor to consider, its importance will vary depending on the circumstances. Here, Ms. Jacob did not touch or stroke her breasts. With respect to words, I consider that underlying the remarks of the police officers and the mother who spoke to Ms. Jacob was a concern that Ms. Jacob was degrading the essential human dignity of herself and the members of her sex by exposing her breasts. The rude remarks made by some men upon seeing Ms. Jacob barebreasted would tend to support this view. But the reasonable bystander would not be fully informed without also considering Ms. Jacob's reply to the police officer protesting against what she viewed as discrimination, her conversation with the man working on his front lawn which was unremarkable, and her reply to the mother who spoke to her. Having regard to these conversations and weighing them in all the circumstances, the reasonable bystander would not, in my opinion, conclude beyond a reasonable doubt that the appellant was exposing her breasts for the sexual gratification of herself or someone else. As a result, the appellant's conduct lacks the sexual context for being an indecent act within the meaning of s. 173(1)(a).

. . . .

The trial judge's task was not an easy one. Given the paucity of guidance on the subject of indecency, it is perhaps not surprising that he erred in his interpretation of s. 173(1)(a). The trial judge concluded that the appellant's act in exposing her breasts went beyond the community standard of tolerance and it was for this reason that he convicted her. The trial judge erred in that he did not determine whether the appellant's act had a sexual context before applying the community standard of tolerance test. The trial judge also erred in the manner in which he applied the community standard of tolerance test.

The trial judge observed that the fact women do not go about with their chests bare was an indication that they did not approve of such conduct for themselves. He concluded that the appellant had offended the community standard of tolerance and convicted.

Although the fact that women do not go about with their chests bare is an indication that they do not approve of such conduct for themselves, it does not follow that such conduct is beyond the commnunity standard of tolerance. The community standard of tolerance means allowing what is not actually approved: *Towne Cinema Theatres, supra*, per Wilson J. at p. 522. What is beyond the community standard of tolerance is what Canadians will not abide other Canadians seeing, in the case of a performance or exhibition . . . or doing, in the case of gross indecency or an indecent act. . . .

. . . .

Conclusion

In applying the community standard of tolerance test under s. 173(1)(a), one must bear in mind that this test is not an end in itself. If the term indecent were to mean whatever the community will not tolerate, there is a danger that discrimination by the community will be seen as harmful and legitimized. The community standard of tolerance is a measure of whether conduct is unduly sexual. In order for an act to be an indecent act under s. 173(1)(a), the act must be a sexual act in the sense that the act is done for the sexual gratification of the accused or others. In this case, a reasonable bystander, fully informed of all the circumstances, would not conclude that this was the case. Secondly, the trial judge erred in the manner in which he applied the community standard of tolerance test. For these reasons I would grant leave to appeal, allow the appeal and order that an acquittal be entered.

. . . .

OSBORNE J.A. (AUSTIN J.A. concurring): —

. . . .

Analysis

(i) *Does an act have to have a sexual context to be an indecent act?*

My colleague refers to legislation proscribing indecency, obscenity and nudity, some of the relevant case law and the history of the community standard of tolerance test in support of her conclusion that an indecent act requires a sexual context. I will discuss the relevant provisions of the *Criminal Code* and the case law in dealing with the sexual context issue. I will then address the community standard of tolerance test and set out the basis of my conclusion that that test is the exclusive measure in determining whether the appellant committed an indecent act on July 19, 1991.

For convenience, I set out below ss. 173 and 174 (the indecency and nudity sections) of the *Code*:

173.(1) Every one who wilfully does an indecent act

(a) in a public place in the presence of one or more persons, or

(b) in any place, with intent thereby to insult or offend any person,

is guilty of an offence punishable on summary conviction.

(2) Every person who, in any place, for a sexual purpose, exposes his or her genital organs to a person who is under the age of fourteen years is guilty of an offence punishable on summary conviction.

174.(1) Every one who, without lawful excuse,

(a) is nude in a public place, or

(b) is nude and exposed to public view while on private property, whether or not the property is his own,

is guilty of an offence punishable on summary conviction.

While I agree with my colleague that in interpreting s. 173(1)(a) regard must be had for the sections as a whole, I do not agree with her interpretation of s. 173(1)(a) or (b). I do not think that the language of s. 173(1)(a) (the section under which the appellant was charged) requires that an indecent act must have a sexual context. There is no reference to sexual context in s. 173(1)(a). Moreover, I see nothing in s. 173(1) that would reduce the scope or meaning of "indecent" for purposes of the section.

In my view, to import a sexual context requirement into s. 173(1) would unduly limit the scope of the section in a manner inconsistent with Parliament's intention.

In contrast, s. 173(2), which deals with the exposure of genital organs to a person under 14 years of age, explicitly requires that the exposure be for a sexual purpose. This suggests that Parliament was alert to the prospect that some, but I would suggest not all, indecent acts have a sexual purpose. Parliament did not use similar language in respect of the purpose of the acts targeted in s. 173(1)(a) or (b). It seems to me that if Parliament had intended to limit the application of s. 173(1)(a) to acts that are in substance sexual, it would have said so.

My colleague has also referred to the difference between s. 173(1)(a) and s. 173(1)(b). In my opinion, subsection (1)(b) (the real target of which is indecent acts committed on private property but within the public's view) adds another element that the Crown must establish — the accused's intent to insult or offend. I agree that if that intent is not established there cannot be a conviction under subsection (1)(b). In my view, to secure a conviction under subsection (1)(b), the act must be done wilfully, with the intent to insult or offend *and* it must be "indecent", that is it must exceed the community standard of tolerance. Thus, I do not agree that an act that does not exceed the community standard of tolerance may, nonetheless, be a subsection (1)(b) indecent act because it was done wilfully with the intent to insult or offend. Whether my colleague's example of breast exposure proximate to a place of worship with intent to insult would constitute an indecent act would depend upon whether the trier of fact concluded that, in all the circumstances, the intentionally insulting behaviour exceeded the community standard of tolerance.

In summary, I think that the community standard of tolerance test is relevant to acts alleged to be criminally indecent under both subsections (1)(a) and (b). In any case, I see nothing in the language of subsections (1)(a) and (b) that would suggest a subsection (1)(a) act must have a sexual context to be indecent.

. . . .

All obscenity prosecutions and most acts that are the basis of criminal prosecutions alleging the commission of an "indecent act" or an "indecent performance" involve conduct that has a sexual element. It was in that context in *R. v. Mara* (1996), 27 O.R. (3d) 643 at p. 648, 105 C.C.C. (3d) 147 (C.A.), that Dubin C.J.O., quoting with approval Boilard J.'s statement in *R. v. Pelletier* (1985), 27 C.C.C. (3d) 77 at p. 89, 49 C.R. (3d) 253 (Que. S.C.), said:

> . . . Indecency *"concerns sexual behaviour or its representation* which is neither obscene nor immoral but inappropriate according to the Canadian standards of tolerance because of the context in which it takes place. In other words, indecency is not a function of the behaviour itself but rather of the circumstances in which it takes place". [Emphasis added.]

I readily accept that indecency "concerns" sexual behaviour but that does not mean it cannot concern other objectionable behaviour. Because "indecent" is not defined in the *Criminal Code*, I see nothing wrong with considering dictionary definitions for assistance as the trial judge did in this case. This is consistent with this court's judgment in *R. v. St. Pierre* (1974), 17 C.C.C. (2d) 489. In that case in issue was whether an admitted act (cunnilingus) constituted gross indecency. Dubin J.A. noted with approval at p. 645 that in an earlier appeal by the same accused, the court had said that "it would have been much better in this case, had the trial Judge given to the jury the dictionary definition of gross and the definition of indecency, there being no definition in the *Criminal Code*, and then left the matter to the jury to determine whether the acts which were committed here fell within the provisions of the section of the *Criminal Code*". The dictionary definitions of indecent and indecency (including those referred to by the trial judge) do not suggest that to be indecent, an act requires some sexual context.

The Federal Court of Appeal in *Luscher v. Deputy Minister of National Revenue (Customs & Excise)* (1985), 17 D.L.R. (4th) 503, considered what was meant by immoral and indecent. In that case a magazine had been classified under the *Customs Act*, R.S.C. 1970, c. C-40, as "immoral" or "indecent". It was submitted that the words immoral and indecent were impermissibly vague. Hugessen J. said at pp. 509-10 D.L.R.:

> [T]he words "immoral" and "indecent" are nowhere defined in the legislation. This at once serves to distinguish the provisions . . . from the obscenity provisions of the *Criminal Code*. . . . While obscenity under the *Criminal Code* is, by statutory definition, limited to matters predominantly sexual, *there is no such limitation upon the concepts of immorality or indecency, and this is so notwithstanding the judicial gloss which has carried over into the test for immorality or indecency of community standards of tolerance.* As was stated by Lord Reid in *R. v. Knuller (Publishing, Printing & Promotions) Ltd. et al.*, [1973] A.C. 435 at p. 458:
>
>> *Indecency is not confined to sexual indecency*: Indeed it is difficult to find any limit short of saying that *it includes anything which an ordinary decent man or woman would find to be shocking, disgusting and revolting.* [Emphasis added.]

I agree with Hugessen J.'s comments. If an indecent act requires a sexual context, there would be no difference between that which is obscene and that which is indecent.

. . . .

[Osborne J. then reviewed the jurisprudence surrounding the community standard of tolerance test and concluded.]

I cannot agree that because the community standard of tolerance test is used to determine whether conduct was obscene (that is whether it involved the "undue" exploitation of sex) that it should, or does, follow that the use of the same test to determine whether conduct is indecent means the conduct must as a matter of law have a sexual context. The community standard of tolerance test is a general test that has been held to be relevant to the determination whether conduct is obscene and in other cases whether conduct is indecent. I do not see the logic in concluding that the use of a constant test for two different purposes should result in giving the word "indecent", as it appears in s. 173(1), the same meaning as Parliament gave the word "obscene" when s. 163(8) was added to the *Criminal Code* in 1959.

This brings me to the trial judge's reasons in this case and the test for indecency that he applied to determine if the appellant's conduct constituted an indecent act . . . . After reviewing the evidence, the trial judge referred to a number of dictionary definitions of indecent and some of the case law. Weiler

J.A. is correct in stating that the trial judge gave no consideration to the issue whether the appellant's conduct had a sexual context.

The trial judge stated at p. 112 of his reasons that the determination whether conduct is indecent ". . . . must be made in the context of the general community standards as defined by the Court. Accordingly, as a preliminary step, the Court must ascertain the general community standard." It is not clear to me what the trial judge meant by "community standard". He then reviewed some of the literature filed by the Crown and concluded at p. 120 of his reasons:

> . . . It is clear to me, therefore, that the female breast constitutes a very personal and responsive part of the female anatomy and is a part of the female body that is sexually stimulating to men, both by sight and touch, and is not, therefore, a part of the body that ought to be flagrantly exposed to public view.

In his determination of the "community standard", the trial judge attached significance to the fact that women generally have chosen not to be seen publicly with their breasts exposed. He said at p. 121 of his reasons:

> . . . If public exposure of breasts is generally acceptable, then one has to consider that it is acceptable for all women in all circumstances, and if a particular employer imposes a dress code on his employees, this obviously would be doing so in response for what he believed to be an acceptable standard of conduct that his customers would expect him to meet.

The trial judge then noted that neither the *Guelph Mercury* nor the *Toronto Star* printed a picture of the appellant with her breasts exposed. At p. 121 of his reasons he asked the question:

> . . . Is it because they thought it might be in bad taste? Or indecent? This course of conduct speaks more eloquently of community standards than any editorial.

The summary conviction appeal court judge did not address the issue of the test to be applied in determining whether the appellant's activities on July 19, 1991 constituted an indecent act within the meaning of s. 173(1)(a) of the *Code*. He simply concluded that the trial judge's judgment was not unreasonable and that it could be supported by the evidence. He thus dismissed the appeal.

On the basis of the trial judge's reasons, which as I have said were accepted by the summary conviction appeal court judge, I think that Ms. Buist is correct in her submission that what the trial judge did was measure the appellant's choice of apparel and conduct against what the trial judge concluded Guelph women would deem to be appropriate for themselves. . . .

In my opinion, both the trial judge and the summary conviction appeal court judge erred in law in applying the wrong test to determine whether the appellant's conduct was indecent. They used a test of acceptance based upon the trial judge's assessment of how women choose to act, as opposed to what the contemporary national community would tolerate.

. . . .

Accordingly, I would allow the appeal, set aside the appellant's conviction and direct that she be acquitted. The fine should be remitted to her.

POUND, THE DEVELOPMENT OF AMERICAN LAW AND ITS DEVIATION FROM ENGLISH LAW

(1951), 67 L.Q.R. 49 at 49-50

In the first place, the common law is characteristically judicial. In England, America, and the British Dominions characteristically the prestige of the judge is very great. In the English or the American *Who's Who* one will find the names of the judges of the higher courts. Continental law is characteristically administrative. The judges have no special prestige. In the Continental equivalents of *Who's Who* one will scarcely ever find the name of a judge. Again, the Anglo-American common law is a law of the courts. Its oracles are judges. It was taught in the Inns of Court, societies of lawyers, by practising lawyers and was developed in the courts. The Continental law is a law of the universities. Its oracles are professors. It has been taught and developed in the universities from the Middle Ages. In consequence, the common law is little systematised. Principles are cautiously and tentatively derived from details. On the other hand, Continental law is highly systematised. Details are subordinated to broad principles. The law books of Anglo-American common law are typically alphabetical abridgments, digests and cyclopaedias. The law books of the Continental law are systematic treatises.

. . . .

In particular, there is a marked difference in the attitude of the two systems as to legislation. The common-law lawyer thinks of a body of law as characteristically customary or traditional. He is at his best in developing a decision from a body of decided cases, thinking of a statute as only fixing a rule for defined situations of fact but not as something to be reasoned from by analogy. He is not at his best in dealing with legislative texts. On the other hand, the Continental lawyer thinks of a body of law as characteristically legislative. He is at his best in developing and applying legislative texts, reasoning from them by analogy as one might say, as formulations of natural law. He does not think of judgments as the basis of analogical reasoning. Judicial decision may fix the rule of law on some parlicular point. To him it does not lay down general principles.

Precedent

Swift, in *Gulliver's Travels* (1977 ed. O.U.P.) p. 249 has Gulliver say:

It is a maxim among these lawyers, that whatever hath been done before, may legally be done again: and therefore they take special care to record all the decisions formerly made against common justice and the general reason of mankind. These under the name of precedents, they produce as authorities, to justify the most iniquitous opinions; and the Judges never fail of decreeing accordingly.

Jerome Frank, *Law and the Modern Mind* (1949) p. 48 is even more sceptical:

Lawyers and Judges purport to make large use of precedents; that is, they purport to rely on the conduct of judges in past cases as a means of procuring analogies for action in new cases. But since what was actually decided in the earlier cases is seldom revealed, it is impossible, in a real sense, to rely on these precedents. What the Courts in fact do is to manipulate the language of former decisions. They could approximate a system of real precedents only if the judges, in rendering those former decisions, had reported with fidelity the precise steps by which they arrived at their decisions. The paradox of the situation is that, granting there is a value in a system of precedents, our present use of illusory precedents makes the employment of real precedents impossible.

The decision of a Judge after trying a case is the product of a unique experience . . . [The] *"decision is reached after an emotive experience in which principles and logic play a secondary part".*

While Gulliver's view that precedent is a slavish adherence to bad rules and Frank's view that no credence can be put on what Judges say they are doing are both overstatements, they point to the ideal. It is widely accepted that the doctrine of precedent is a working ingredient of the judicial function and achieves a compromise between a goal of certainty and predictability and one of flexibility. It is recognized that there are indeed several powerful devices with which to manipulate rules. An unwelcome precedent can be distinguished on its facts and the proposition or propositions of law involved can be restated at a different level of generality, consigned to mere *obiter dicta* (*i.e.*, not logically necessary for the decision) or qualified by reference to other precedent. Few would be content to see the judicial function as a mere exercise of these linguistic skills. Surely our Judges should do more than search for and then assert rules espoused by other Judges. Each rule or principle, if not absolutely binding (and few are) should be independently evaluated for its soundness in respect of the particular case and for other cases as well. Although this is a much more intellectually demanding mandate upon Judges, it is only by a frank discussion of these factors of justification that a sound approach to the law can be developed.

Compare the approaches to statutory interpretation in the following three judgments of the same Judge, Mr. Justice Dickson, later the Chief Justice of Canada:

R. v. HEFFER

10 C.R.N.S. 103, [1970] 4 C.C.C. 104 (Man. C.A.)

DICKSON J.A.: — Mr. Heffer is 24 years of age. Earlier this year, after employment in Vancouver as part-time longshoreman, he hitch-hiked to Winnipeg, arriving July 9. He had four dollars in his pocket. He went directly to the unemployment insurance office where he obtained a pink card and a piece of paper containing the address of a casual employment firm in the city. He then went to an organization known as C.R.Y.P.T. (Committee Representing Youth Problems Today) and was directed to St. Gerard Church where he would receive free lodging for that night. He spent the night there with several other young people, strangers to him. About 8:30 a.m. next morning he walked to downtown Winnipeg intending, as he said, to register for employment. He was accompanied by another youth. The two sat down on the steps of the Centennial Centre to rest and smoke a cigarette. They were joined by three other youths whom Mr. Heffer recognized as having spent the night at St. Gerard Church. One of them showed Mr. Heffer a 25-cent piece and said something to the effect it was his lucky day. It was not, for at that moment the group was arrested by a detective of the city of Winnipeg police department and taken into custody. Shortly before the arrest the detective, patrolling in a police car, had observed a youth begging nearby, on Disraeli Bridge. The detective was unable to question the youth, but later observed him with Mr. Heffer and three others on the steps of the Centennial Centre. No questions were asked at this time; the youths were simply told to get into the police car and were taken to the nearby public safety building.

On July 11, 1969, Mr. Heffer was charged with vagrancy. He pleaded not guilty and was released on his own recognizance until the date of his trial.

On July 15, 1969, the trial took place before Baryluk P.M. The witnesses were the arresting detective and Mr. Heffer. Mr. Heffer testified that at the public safety building he attempted to show the detective the pink unemployment insurance card and the other piece of paper obtained by him at the unemployment insurance office but the detective refused to look at either paper. The detective admitted Mr. Heffer may have produced those pieces of paper but said he was sceptical of the pink cards because they are easy to obtain, and could not recall the other piece of paper. Mr. Heffer explained, if explanation were necessary, his lack of employment from the date of his release on bail Friday noon (July 11, 1969) until trial the following Tuesday (July 15, 1969). He said he arrived at the employment office to find it closed, regular closing hour being 1:00 p.m. The office was not open on Saturday and Sunday. He did not attend on Monday because he had an afternoon appointment with a lawyer and his trial was set for 9:30 a.m. on Tuesday.

The magistrate convicted. Imposition of sentence was suspended for three months.

Mr. Heffer questioned the validity of the conviction.

. . . .

I am in no doubt that upon the stated facts the magistrate erred in finding Mr. Heffer guilty of the offence charged. Mr. Heffer had just arrived in the city the previous day. He had been employed in Vancouver. Immediately upon arrival in Winnipeg he sought employment. He had no criminal record. He had done nothing to suggest criminal activity or tendency. There is lacking here proof of a course of conduct within the mischief aimed at by the section; there is missing the "repeated acts or some single act, omission or manner of living of a certain duration or continuity" mentioned by Prendergast C.J.M. in *Rex v. Oiseberg*, [1931] 3 W.W.R. 507, at 509, 56 C.C.C. 385. There was no evidence of discreditable conduct on the day of, or anterior to, the arrest. Heffer simply took advantage of free lodging by a reputable organization to persons such as he. There is nothing untoward about resting on the steps of a public building. If this case had reached us by way of appeal nothing more would need be said. But it has come to us by way of stated case and certain questions are asked. We are told it is a test case and we are asked to deal with it on the footing that Mr. Heffer is one of those young people, of substantial number, including adherents of what is sometimes termed the "hippie sub-culture," who wander from place to place across Canada maintaining themselves as best they can without crime. Therefore some further observations would seem to be required.

The charge was laid under sec. 164(1)(*a*) [since repealed] of the *Criminal Code*, reading:

> 164. (1) Every one commits vagrancy who
>
>> (*a*) not having any apparent means of support is found wandering abroad or trespassing and does not, when required, justify his presence in the place where he is found.

Sec. 164 provides further that a person may commit vagrancy by begging or by living by gaming or crime. A prostitute who fails to give a good account of herself commits vagrancy. So does a sexual offender who loiters near a schoolground or playground. However, no aged or infirm person is liable to conviction under sec. 164(1)(*a*).

Sec. 164(1)(*a*) came into effect at the time of the revision of the *Criminal Code* effected by 1953-54, ch. 51. The subsection formerly read:

> 238. Every one is a loose, idle or disorderly person or vagrant who:
>
>> (*a*) not having any visible means of subsistence, is found wandering abroad or lodging in any barn or outhouse, or in any deserted or unoccupied building, or in any car or wagon, or in any railway carriage or freight car, or in any railway building, and not giving a good account of himself, or who, not having any visible means of maintaining himself, lives without employment.

A number of important changes were effected by the revision, including:

(i) The words "loose, idle or disorderly person" were removed.

(ii) The words "apparent means of support" were substituted for "visible means of subsistence." If any change was thereby effected it would seem to have been in broadening the field of inquiry, that is to say, a person might visibly seem to be without means of support but further inquiry would make it apparent that from family or other lawful source he had ample means with which to support himself.

(iii) Reference to lodging in barns, unoccupied buildings, and railway property, is deleted. The word "trespassing" is new. "Wandering abroad" is still an essential element.

(iv) The concept of "lives without employment" has been deleted. In present context this deletion is worthy of note.

(v) The alleged offender must now justify his presence "when required." This raises the question, with which I will presently deal, whether the suspect must be asked, and fail, before arrest, to justify his presence where found.

It would seem important, if one is properly to understand and apply s. 164, to have regard not only to the earlier s. 238, but also to the English legislation and mores from which that earlier section sprang. In *Ledwith v. Roberts*, [1936] 3 All E.R. 570, at 594, Scott L.J. traces the history of the vagrancy Acts from as far back as 1494, 11 Henry VII, ch. 2, and the attempts made to deal with those who through "the gradual decay of the feudal system under which the labouring classes had been anchored to the soil" lost employment and took to the roads in a vagrant way of life, creating a serious threat to public peace.

The vagrancy laws were originally directed against such people. The vagrancy laws presently in force in England are based upon the *Vagrancy Act, 1824*, 5 Geo. IV, ch. 83. That Act set up three classes, idle and disorderly persons, rogues and vagabonds, and incorrigible rogues. Section 238 of our *Code* embodied *verbatim* much of the language of s. 4 of the *Vagrancy Act, 1824*. Although our *Code* did not divide offenders into three arbitrary classes, the classification is not without interest. Comprised within those classes are to be found pedlars, prostitutes, beggars, disorderly persons, persons wandering abroad and failing to give a good account of themselves, persons exposing obscene prints, procurers, fortune tellers and palmists. Implicit in all of this is the recognition, within the community, of a body of persons, distinguished by the epithet "vagrant," having the common characteristic of preying upon the public. The word "vagrant" is open to two meanings — the *Shorter Oxford English Dictionary* says it can mean "One of a class of persons who, having no settled home or regular work, wander from place to place, and maintain themselves by begging or in some disreputable or dishonest way." Or it can mean "One who leads a wandering life; a rover." It is the first class with which the vagrancy laws are, and have throughout, been concerned.

It now falls to apply the vague and, in some respects, archaic language of s. 164(l)(*a*), in the mores of today, to the facts of the present case.

The sociological phenomenon of peregrinating youth is of relatively recent origin in Canada but not in Europe where it has long since been the custom of many young people of little means to roam from place to place, aided in some countries by the provision of youth hostels where bed and breakfast can be had at little cost.

It cannot be the intent of s. 164(l)(*a*) to stigmatize as criminal every young person who travels across the country without employment and with little money in his pocket.

There are three ingredients of the offence.

(1) *Not Having any Apparent Means of Support*

The true principle is that stated in *Reg. v. Riley* (1898), 2 C.C.C. 128, where Wurtele J. said at p. 129:

> The mere fact of living without employment is not an offence against the law, if the person living without employment is able to do so, because he has sufficient means either belonging to himself or which are provided for him in a legitimate way.

This language was quoted with approval by Boyd C. in *Rex v. Munroe* (1911), 19 C.C.C. 86 (C.A.).

In *Rex v. Fleury* (1933), 60 C.C.C. 32, the facts were, briefly, these: Fleury was an inmate of a hostel at Oshawa, receiving public relief in the form of food and shelter. He declined an offer of employment, saying that the pay, 20 cents a working day, was insufficient. Thereupon a vagrancy charge was laid. Garrow, J. quashed a conviction, rejecting the implication (at p. 33) that "any unfortunate receiving relief who declines to accept the first job offered thereby becomes liable to conviction as a vagrant."

In *Rex v. Zelky*, [1939] 1 W.W.R. 305, replacing the judgment as reported in (1938), 71 C.C.C. 143, Martin C.J.B.C. interpreted the principle laid down in *Rex v. Munroe*, *supra*, in this manner:

> the question as to what is "visible means" depends upon all the circumstances of each case, including the state of the times in which that adjudication must be made.

One statement by O' Halloran J.A.in *Rex v. Konkin*, [1949] 2 W.W.R. 1225, 9 C.R. 59, 95 C.C.C. 373 (B.C. C.A.), would seem to run counter to the burden of the cases which I have mentioned. He said at p. 1229:

> Moreover, visible means of subsistence in the case of a healthy adult does not include living on the generosity or charity of others; see *Rex v. Munroe, supra*.

It is questionable whether *Rex v. Munroe*, a beggar case, is authority for the principle enunciated. In any event, with respect, I am unable to agree that a person living on the generosity or charity of others is without apparent means of support. There is nothing unlawful about it. Nor can it be said that it is subject to condemnation by contemporary standards of the community.

(2) *Found Wandering Abroad or Trespassing*

The phrase "wandering abroad" was considered in *Rex v. Konkin, supra*, where O'Halloran J.A. said at p. 1230:

> It seems to me that "wandering abroad" as it appears in s. 238(*a*) embraces two concepts not capable of being defined with mathematical exactitude, viz., (*a*) a departure from one's own room, house, or abode, coupled with (*b*) a condition of aimlessness ordinarily associated with the lack of a legal occupation or pursuit.

In *Pedersen v. Hansen and Reid*, [1963] 2 C.C.C. 348 (B.C.) Verchere J., at p. 355, speaks of the conduct of the person affording "in the circumstances then present an indication of the lack of a legal occupation or pursuit on his part."

(3) *Does not, when required, justify his presence in the place where he is found*

The judgment in *Rex v. Konkin, supra,* contains this statement at p. 1230:

> The three elements of wandering abroad, lack of any visible means of subsistence, and failure to give a good account of oneself, are essential ingredients of the offence. As such they must all be present together at the one time.

It is not a crime to be without apparent means of support. Nor is it a crime to wander abroad. Vagrancy status is established only when these two ingredients are present in combination with a third, namely, failure of the suspect to justify his presence in the place where he is found, when required to do so. Unless and until those three ingredients conjoin, no crime has been committed and the suspect is not liable to arrest. It is not enough to afford an accused an opportunity during his trial to justify his presence in the place where he was found. Such opportunity must be given before the arrest and before he is charged: See *Re Brady* (1912-13), 21 C.C.C. 123; *Pedersen v. Hansen and Reid, supra,* and the recent decision of Wootton J. in *Reg. v. Petryshen* (1969), 8 C.R.N.S. 224 (B.C.).

. . . .

The appeal is allowed and the conviction quashed.

HARRISON v. CARSWELL

[1976] 2 S.C.R. 200, 25 C.C.C. (2d) 186

DICKSON J. (MARTLAND, JUDSON, RITCHIE, PIGEON and DE GRANDPRE JJ. concurring): — The respondent, Sophie Carswell, was charged under the *Petty Trespasses Act,* R.S.M. 1970, c. P-50, with four offences (one on each of four days) of unlawfully trespassing upon the premises of the Fairview Corporation Limited, trading under the firm name and style of Polo Park Shopping Centre, located in the City of Winnipeg, after having been requested by the owner not to enter on or come upon the premises. The appellant, Peter Harrison, manager of Polo Park Shopping Centre, swore the informations. The charges were dismissed by the Provincial Judge, but on a trial *de novo* in the County Court, Mrs. Carswell was convicted and fined $10 on each of the charges. The convictions were set aside by the Manitoba Court of Appeal (Freedman C.J.M., and Matas J.A., with Guy J.A., dissenting) [17 C.C.C. (2d) 521] and the present appeal followed, by leave of this Court.

With great respect, I am unable to agree with the majority reasons, delivered in the Court of Appeal by Chief Justice Freedman, for I find it difficult, indeed impossible, to make any well-founded distinction between this case and *R. v. Peters* (1971), 17 D.L.R. (3d) 128*n*, decided by this Court four years ago in a unanimous decision of the full Bench. The constitutional issue raised in *Peters* no longer concerns us; the only other issue was whether the owner of a shopping plaza had sufficient control or possession of the common areas, having regard to the unrestricted invitation to the public to enter upon the premises, as to enable it to invoke the remedy of trespass. The Court decided it did. That case and the present case came to us on much the same facts, picketing within a shopping centre in connection with a labour dispute. In *Peters*, the picketing was carried out by the president of the Brampton Labour Council and seven other persons, carrying placards and distributing leaflets in front of a Safeway store, seeking a boycott of Safeway for selling California grapes. In the present case, the picketing was carried out by Mrs. Carswell and 11 other persons, carrying placards and distributing leaflets, in front of the premises of their employer, Dominion Stores. In both instances the picketing was peaceful. Although the question posed in *Peters* did not recite the facts upon which the case rested, the question was worded thus:

> Did the learned Judges in appeal err in law in determining that *the* owner of *the* property had sufficient possession of *the* shopping plaza sidewalk to be capable of availing itself of the remedy for trespass under the Petty Trespass Act, R.S.O. 1960, Chapter 294, Section 1(1)?

(italics are my own) and in my view is so expressed, with repeated use of the definite article, as to relate the question to the circumstances in respect of which the Judges made their determination.

The judgment of the Ontario Court of Appeal in *R. v. Peters* (1971), 2 C.C.C. (2d) 336, was delivered by Chief Justice Gale who said, at p. 338 C.C.C.:

> With respect to the first ground of appeal, it is our opinion that an owner who has granted a right of entry to a particular class of the public has not thereby relinquished his or its right to withdraw its invitation to the general public or any particular member thereof, and that if a member of the public whose invitation to enter has been withdrawn refuses to leave, he thereby becomes a trespasser and may be prosecuted under the *Petty Trespass Act*. Here, the invitation extended by the owner was of a general nature and included tenants, employees, agents and all persons having or seeking business relations with the tenants. However, notwithstanding the general nature of the invitation, the owner did not thereby lose its right to withdraw the invitation from the general public or any particular member thereof. In addition, it is also our view with respect to trespass that possession does not cease to be exclusive so long as there is the right to control entry of the general public, and here the owner had not relinquished that right of control.

The brief judgment in this Court, answering in the negative the question asked, neither adopted nor repudiated the reasons delivered in the Court of Appeal, but it should not be overlooked that when the *Peters* case was before the Ontario Court of Appeal, counsel for Peters relied upon the decision of the Court of Appeal for Saskatchewan in *Grosvenor Park Shopping Centre Ltd. v. Waloshin et al.* (1964), 46 D.L.R. (2d) 750. That case arose out of injunction proceedings during a strike of employees of Loblaw Groceterias Co. Ltd., in Saskatoon, who were picketing with placards on the sidewalk adjacent to store premises located in a shopping centre. The pertinent part of the judgment of the Saskatchewan Court of Appeal reads [at p. 755]:

Learned counsel for the appellant argued that the respondent did not have that degree of possession essential to an action in trespass.

> The area upon which it is alleged the appellants have trespassed is part of what is well known as a shopping centre. While legal title to the area is in the respondent, it admits in its pleadings that it has granted easements to the many tenants. The evidence also establishes that the respondent has extended an unrestricted invitation to the public to enter upon the premises. The very nature of the operation is one in which the respondent, both in its own interests and in the interests of its tenants, could not do otherwise. Under the circumstances, it cannot be said that the respondent is in actual possession. The most that can be said is that the respondent exercises control over the premises but does not exercise that control to the exclusion of other persons. For that reason, therefore, the respondent cannot maintain an action in trespass against the appellants: *vide* 38 Hals., 3rd ed., p. 743, para. 1212. Support, too, for this view may be found in *Zeller's (Western) Ltd. v. Retail Food & Drug Clerks Union, Local 1518* (1963), 42 D.L.R. (2d) 582, 45 W.W.R. 337.

Chief Justice Gale, in *Peters*, offered this observation with respect to *Grosvenor Park* [at pp. 338-9 C.C.C.]:

> The solicitor for the appellant relied very heavily upon a decision of the Court of Appeal for Saskatchewan in *Grosvenor Park Shopping Centre Ltd. v. Waloshin et al.* (1964), 46 D.L.R. (2d) 750, 49 W.W.R. 237. If our view in this appeal does not harmonize with the reasoning of the Court in the *Grosvenor Park* case we must respectfully disagree with that reasoning.

So when the *Peters* case came to this Court for consideration, the Court had before it the reasoning of the Court of Appeal for Ontario in that case and the reasoning, difficult to reconcile, of the Court of Appeal for Saskatchewan in *Grosvenor Park*; the reasoning of the Ontario Court prevailed. There has been no suggestion that Peters was wrongly decided; therefore, I would think it must be regarded as controlling unless it can properly be distinguished from the case at bar. No distinction can be made on the ground of contract; there is a copy of the lease from Fairview to Dominion Stores, among the papers, but it would not appear, nor has it been argued, that any distinction can rest on that document. As to a possible statutory distinction, the petty trespass acts of Manitoba and Ontario do not differ in any material respect and indeed s. 24 of the *Labour Relations Act*, 1972 (Man.), c. 75 (continuing consolidation, c. L10), specifically preserves rights against trespassers. Therefore it would seem the appeal must succeed unless a valid distinction can be drawn on the ground that the president of the Brampton Labour Council, in *Peters*, was a mere member of the general public from whom permission to remain on the premises could be withdrawn at will, whereas Mrs. Carswell was an employee of one of the tenants of the shopping centre on strike in support of a current labour dispute, from whom permission to remain on the premises could not, as a matter of law, be withdrawn. I find myself unable to accept that any ground in law supports such a distinction.

The evidence discloses that distribution of pamphlets or leaflets in the mall of Polo Park Shopping Centre or on the parking lot, has never been pemitted by the management of the centre and that this prohibition has extended to tenants of the centre. The centre as a matter of policy has not permitted any person to walk in the mall carrying placards. There is nothing in the evidence supporting the view that in the present case the owner of the centre was acting out of caprice or whimsy or *mala fides*. In a comment entitled *Labour Law - Picketing in Shopping Centres*, 43 Can. Bar. Rev. 357 at p. 362 (1965), H.W. Arthurs referred to the following as one of the legitimate concerns of the landlord of a shopping centre:

> While public authorities may, on behalf of the community, strike a reasonable balance between traffic and picketing on public sidewalks and streets, the shopping centre owner can hardly be expected to make such a choice: he has no authority to speak for the community; to grant picketing or parading privileges to all would invite chaos, while to do so selectively would invite commercial reprisals. He is thus driven to adopt a highly restrictive approach to granting permission to groups who wish to parade or picket in the shopping centre.

It is urged on behalf of Mrs. Carswell that the right of a person to picket peacefully in support of a lawful strike is of greater social significance than the proprietary rights of an owner of a shopping centre, and that the rights of the owner must yield to those of the picketer. The American example has been cited, but I cannot say that I find the American cases to which we have been referred of great help. The facts in *Schwartz-Torrance Investment Corp. v. Bakery and Confectionery Workers' Union, Local 31* (1964), 394 P. 2d 921, decided by the Supreme Court of California are almost identical with those in *Grosvenor Park*, but I think it not unimportant to note that in *Schwartz-Torrance*, Justice Tobriner, early in his judgment, drew attention to the fact that the Legislature of the State of California had expressly declared that the public policy of the State favoured concerted activities of employees for the purpose of collective bargaining and had enacted the policy into an exception to the criminal trespass law. Construing that exception, the California Supreme Court in a case antedating *Schwartz-Torrance* had concluded that the Legislature, in dealing with trespasses, had specifically subordinated the rights of the property owner to those of persons engaged in lawful labour activities. *Schwartz-Torrance* is, therefore, of small aid in this case and indeed can be said to support, in a negative sense, a position inimical to that of Mrs. Carswell. And one need only read *Amalgamated Food Employees' Union, Local 590 v. Logan Valley Plaza Inc.* (1968), 391 U.S. 308, and then read *Lloyd Corp. Ltd. v. Tanner* (1972), 407 U.S. 551, to apprehend the uncertainties and very real difficulties which emerge when a Court essays to legislate as to what is and what is not a permissible activity within a shopping centre.

The submission that this Court should weigh and determine the respective values to society of the right to property and the right to picket raises important and difficult political and socio-economic issues, the resolution of which must, by their very nature, be arbitrary and embody personal economic and social beliefs. It raises also fundamental questions as to the role of this Court under the Canadian Constitution. The duty of the Court, as I envisage it, is to proceed in the discharge of its adjudicative function in a reasoned way from principled decision and established concepts. I do not for a moment doubt the power of the Court to act creatively — it has done so on countless occasions; but manifestly one must ask — what are the limits of the judicial function? There are many and varied answers to this question. Holmes J. said in *Southern Pacific Co. v. Jensen* (1917), 244 U.S. 205 at p. 221: "I recognize without hesitation that judges do and must legislate, but they can do it only interstitially; they are confined from molar to molecular actions". Cardozo, *The Nature of the Judicial Process* (1921), p. 141, recognized that the freedom of the Judge is not absolute in this expression of his view:

> This judge, even when he is free, is still not wholly free. He is not to innovate at pleasure. He is not a knight-errant, roaming at will in pursuit of his own ideal of beauty or of goodness. He is to draw his inspiration from consecrated principles.

The former Chief Justice of the Australian High Court, Sir Owen Dixon, in an address delivered at Yale University in September, 1955, "Concerning Judicial Method", had this to say:

> But in our Australian High Court we have had as yet no deliberate innovators bent on express change of acknowledged doctrine. It is one thing for a court to seek to extend the application of accepted principles to new cases or to reason from the more fundamental of settled legal principles to new conclusions or to decide that a category is not closed against unforeseen instances which in reason might be subsumed thereunder. It is an entirely different thing for a Judge, who is discontented with a result held to flow from a long accepted legal principle, deliberately to abandon the principle in the name of justice or of social necessity or of social convenience. The former accords with the technique of the common law and amounts to no more than an enlightened application of modes of reasoning traditionally respected in the courts. It is a process by the repeated use of which the law is developed, is adapted to new conditions, and is improved in content. The latter means an abrupt and almost arbitrary change.

See also: Jaffe, *English and American Judges as Lawmakers* (1969); McWhinney, *Canadian Jurisprudence* (1958) pp. 1-23; Friedmann, *Law in a Changing Society*, 2nd ed. (1972), pp. 49-90; and Allen, *Law in the Making*, 7th ed. (1964), pp. 302-11.

Society has long since acknowledged that a public interest is served by permitting union members to bring economic pressure to bear upon their respective employers through peaceful picketing, but the right has been exercisable in some locations and not in others and to the extent that picketing has been permitted on private property the right hitherto has been accorded by statute. For example, s. 87 [since rep. & sub. 1975, c. 33, s. 21] of the *Labour Code of British Columbia Act*, 1973 (B.C.) (2nd Sess.), c. 122, provides that no action lies in respect of picketing permitted under the Act for trespass to real property to which a member of the public ordinarily has access.

Anglo-Canadian jurisprudence has traditionally recognized, as a fundamental freedom, the right of the individual to the enjoyment of property and the right not to be deprived thereof, or any interest therein, save by due process of law. The Legislature of Manitoba has declared in the *Petty Trespasses Act* that any person who trespasses upon land, the property of another, upon or through which he has been requested by the owner not to enter, is guilty of an offence. If there is to be any change in this statute law, if A is to be given the right to enter and remain on the land of B against the will of B, it would seem to me that such a change must be made by the enacting institution, the Legislature, which is representative of the people and designed to manifest the political will, and not by this Court.

I would allow the appeal, set aside the judgment of the Court of Appeal for Manitoba and restore the judgment of the County Court Judge.

LASKIN C.J.C. (dissenting) (SPENCE and BEETZ JJ. concurring): — I would be content to adopt the reasons of Freedman, C.J.M., and, accordingly, to dismiss this appeal without more if I did not feel compelled, in view of the course of argument, to add some observations bearing on the decision of this Court in *R. v. Peters* (1971), 17 D.L.R. (3d) 128*n*, dismissing an appeal from the judgment of the Ontario Court of Appeal, 2 C.C.C. (2d) 336. The observations I am about to make about the *Peters* case carry into two areas of concern respecting the role of this Court as the final Court in this country in both civil and criminal causes. Those areas are, first, whether this Court must pay mechanical deference to *stare decisis* and, second, whether this Court has a balancing role to play, without yielding place to the Legislature, where an ancient doctrine, in this case trespass, is invoked in a new setting to suppress a lawful activity supported both by legislation and by a well-understood legislative policy.

.   .   .   .

The first question put to this Court in the *Peters* case was framed as follows:

> Did the learned Judges in appeal err in law in determining that the owner of the property had sufficient possession of the shopping plaza sidewalk to be capable of availing itself of the remedy for trespass under the Petty Trespass Act, R.S.O. 1960, Chapter 294, section 1(1)?

This question, a strictly legal one without any context of fact, was answered unanimously in the negative by the full Court of which I was a member. The Court gave the briefest of oral reasons (see 17 D.L.R. (3d) 128*n*), and I regarded the answer as a response to a narrow question of whether a shopping centre owner can have sufficient possession of a sidewalk therein to support a charge of trespass under the provincial Act. The question, to me, was whether the owner had divested itself of possession so as to make the shopping centre sidewalk a public way upon which there could be no trespass as against such owner in any circumstances.

It is, of course, open to others to read this Court's disposition of the *Peters* case differently, but I can say for myself that the brief reasons would not have sufficed had the question that was asked been put in a factual frame as is often done when questions are formulated for the consideration of this Court. For me, it follows that the *Peters* case is neither in law, nor in fact a controlling authority for the present case which came to this Court not upon specific questions of fact, but at large so as to enable this Court to consider both law and fact as they bear on the position *inter se* of the shopping centre owner and of the lawful picketer in a legal strike.

My brother, Spence, who also sat as a member of this Court in the *Peters* case, associates himself with me in the view of it that I have put forward, and I would think that this should give pause to any suggestion that the *Peters* case has concluded the issue now before us, an issue arising on different facts and on a broader question of law than that to which an answer was sought and given in the *Peters* case.

This Court, above all others in this country, cannot be simply mechanistic about previous decisions, whatever be the respect it would pay to such decisions. What we would be doing here, if we were to say that the *Peters* case, because it was so recently decided, has concluded the present case for us, would be to take merely one side of a debatable issue and say that it concludes the debate without the need to hear the other side.

I do not have to call upon pronouncements of members of this Court that we are free to depart from previous decisions in order to support the pressing need to examine the present case on its merits. Pressing, because there are probably many hundreds of shopping centres in this country where similar issues have arisen and will arise.

. . . .

I come then to those issues, and they can only be understood if we look at the present case not only from the position asserted by the shopping centre owner, but as well from the position asserted by the lawful picketer. An ancient legal concept, trespass, is urged here in all its pristine force by a shopping centre owner in respect of areas of the shopping centre which have been opened by him to public use, and necessarily so because of the commercial character of the enterprise based on tenancies by operators of a variety of businesses. To say in such circumstances that the shopping centre owner may, at his whim, order any member of the public out of the shopping centre on penalty or liability for trespass if he refuses to leave, does not make sense if there is no proper reason in that member's conduct or activity to justify the order to leave.

Trespass in its civil law sense, and in its penal sense too, connotes unjustified invasion of another's possession. Where a dwelling-house is concerned, the privacy associated with that kind of land-holding makes any unjustified or unprivileged entry a trespass, technically so even if no damage occurs. A Court, however, would be likely to award only nominal damages for mere unprivileged entry upon another's private premises where no injury occurs, and it is probable that the plaintiff would be ordered to pay costs for seeking empty vindication. If the trespasser refuses to leave when ordered, he could be forcibly removed, but, more likely, the police would be called and the issue would be resolved at that point, or a basis for an action or for a penal charge would arise. In short, apart from privileged entry, a matter to which I will return in these reasons, there is a significant element of protection of privacy in resort to trespass to exclude or remove persons from private dwellings.

The considerations which underlie the protection of private residences cannot apply to the same degree to a shopping centre in respect of its parking areas, roads and sidewalks. Those amenities are closer in character to public roads and sidewalks than to a private dwelling. All that can be urged from a theoretical point of view to assimilate them to private dwellings is to urge that if property is privately owned, no matter the use to which it is put, trespass is as appropriate in the one case as in the other and it does not matter that possession, the invasion of which is basic to trespass, is recognizable in the one case but not in the other. There is here, on this assimilation, a legal injury albeit no actual injury. This is a use of theory which does not square with economic or social fact under the circumstances of the present case.

What does a shopping centre owner protect, for what invaded interest of his does he seek vindication in ousting members of the public from sidewalks and roadways and parking areas in the shopping centre? There is no challenge to his title and none to his possession nor to his privacy when members of the public use those amenities. Should he be allowed to choose what members of the public come into those areas when they have been opened to all without discrimination? Human rights legislation would prevent him from discriminating on account of race, colour or creed or national origin, but counsel for the appellant would have it that members of the public can otherwise be excluded or ordered to leave by mere whim. It is contended that it is unnecessary that there be a reason that can stand rational assessment. Disapproval of the owner, in assertion of a remote control over the "public" areas of the shopping centre, whether it be disapproval of picketing or disapproval of the wearing of hats or anything equally innocent, may be converted (so it is argued) into a basis of ouster of members of the public. Can the common law be so devoid of reason as to tolerate this kind of whimsy where public areas of a shopping centre are concerned?

If it was necessary to categorize the legal situation which, in my view, arises upon the opening of a shopping centre, with public areas of the kind I have mentioned (at least where the opening is not accompanied by an announced limitation on the classes of public entrants), I would say that the members of the public are privileged visitors whose privilege is revocable only upon misbehaviour (and I need not spell out here what this embraces) or by reason of unlawful activity. Such a view reconciles both the interests of the shopping centre owner and of the members of the public, doing violence to neither and recognizing the mutual or reciprocal commercial interests of shopping centre owner, business tenants and members of the public upon which the shopping centre is based.

The respondent picketer in the present case is entitled to the privilege of entry and to remain in the public areas to carry on as she did (without obstruction of the sidewalk or incommoding of others) as being not only a member of the public but being as well, in relation to her peaceful picketing, an employee involved in a labour dispute with a tenant of the shopping centre, and hence having an interest, sanctioned by the law, in pursuing legitimate claims against her employer through the peaceful picketing in furtherance of a lawful strike.

The civil law doctrine of abusive exercise of rights provides, in my opinion, an apt analogue for the present case. I do not press it as having precise application, but in so far as it embraces a balancing of rights, a consideration of the relativity of rights involving advertence to social purpose as well as to personal advantage, it is the peaceful picketer who has cause for complaint against interference with her, rather than the shopping centre owner having a legally cognizable complaint: see, generally, Gutteridge, "Abuse of Rights" 5 Camb. L.J. 22 (1933-35); Castel, *The Civil Law System of the Province of Quebec* (1962), pp. 409*ff*. The shopping centre owner has no overriding or even coequal interest to serve in intervening in the labour dispute, and, if anything, is acting as surrogate of the struck tenant in a situation where the latter has not and probably could not claim redress or relief.

It seems to me that the present case involves a search for an appropriate legal framework for new social facts which show up the inaptness of an old doctrine developed upon a completely different social foundation. The history of trespass indicates that its introduction as a private means of redress was directed to breaches of the peace or to acts likely to provoke such breaches. Its subsequent enlargement beyond these concerns does not mean that it must be taken as incapable of further adaptation, but must be applied on what I can only characterize as a level of abstraction which ignores the facts. Neither logic nor experience (to borrow from Holmes' opening sentence in his classic *The Common Law*) supports such a conclusion.

Recognition of the need for balancing the interests of the shopping centre owner with competing interests of members of the public when in or on the public areas of the shopping centre, engaged Courts in the United States a little earlier than it did the Courts in this country. Making every allowance for any constitutional basis upon which Courts there grappled with this problem, their analyses are helpful because they arise out of the same economic and social setting in which the problem arises here. Thus, there is emphasis on unrestricted access to shopping centres from public streets, and on the fact that access by the public is the very reason for the existence of shopping centres; there is the comparison drawn between the public markets of long ago and the shopping centre as a modern market place; there is the appreciation that in the light of the interests involved there can be no solution to their reconciliation by positing a flat all or nothing approach. The cases in the United States, and I cite a few of them here without further elaboration, appear to me to reject the appellant's proposition that (as his counsel put it) "the issue is trespass, not picketing" because that, in my opinion, involves a predetermination without regard to the issues of fact: see *Schwartz-Torrance Investment Corp. v. Bakery & Confectionery Workers' Union, Local 31* (1964), 394 P. 2d 921 (Calif.); *Amalgamated Clothing Workers of America v. Wonderland Shopping Center, Inc.* (1963), 122 N.W. 2d 785 (Mich.); *Amalgamated Food Employees' Union, Local 590 v. Logan Valley Plaza Inc.* (1968), 391 U.S. 308; *Lloyd Corp. Ltd. v. Tanner* (1972), 407 U.S. 551.

A more appropriate approach, to which I adverted earlier, is to recognize a continuing privilege in using the areas of the shopping centre provided for public passage subject to limitations arising out of the nature of the activity thereon and to the object pursued thereby, and subject as well to a limitation against material damage. There is analogy in existing conceptions of privilege as an answer to intentional torts, such as trespass. The principle is expressed in Prosser, *Handbook of the Law of Torts*, 4th ed. (1971), at pp. 98-9 as follows:

> "Privilege" is the modern term applied to those considerations which avoid liability where it might otherwise follow. In its broader sense, it is applied to any immunity which prevents the existence of a tort; but in its more common usage, it signifies that the defendant has acted to further an interest of such social importance that it is entitled to protection, even at the expense of damage to the plaintiff. He is allowed freedom of action because his own interests, or those of the public require it, and social policy will best be served by permitting it. The boundaries of the privilege are marked out by current ideas of what will most effectively promote the general welfare.

> The question of "privilege" arises almost exclusively in connection with intentional torts. Much the same considerations have weight in negligence cases, in determining whether the defendant's conduct is reasonable under the circumstances. Negligence, however, is a matter of risk and probability of harm; and where the likelihood of injury to the plaintiff is relatively slight, the defendant will necessarily be allowed greater latitude than where the harm is intended, or substantially certain to follow.

> As the defendant's interest gains weight in the scale of social values, his privilege becomes greater. It may be absolute, in the sense that there is immunity from all liability, regardless of the motive or purpose for which he acts. The acts of judicial officers, done under authority of law, for example, are absolutely privileged, even though malicious or corrupt. It may be conditioned upon a proper motive and reasonable behavior, as in the case of the privilege of self-defense. It may be limited, in the sense that the defendant may not be restrained in advance from acting, and is not liable for any mere technical tort, but is still liable for any substantial damage that he may cause. The sliding scale by which the law balances the interests of the parties to accomplish a social purpose is nowhere better illustrated than in the field of privilege.

See also, Bohlen, "Incomplete Privilege to Inflict Intentional Invasions of Interests of Property and Personality", 39 Har. L. Rev. 307 (1926), where it is said, at pp. 319-20:

> The liability for harmless invasion of either an interest of personality or property is either punitive or compensatory. In so far as it is punitive, there is no reason why, if the good likely to result from an act is greater than the harm it is intended to cause, the actor should be punished either criminally by fine or imprisonment, or by damages, whether labelled punitive or not, imposed in a civil action. And clearly there is no more reason for imposing either punishment because the harm intended and done is a harmless invasion of a dignitary interest of personality rather than a harmless invasion of a similar interest of property.

Illustrations were given during the course of argument of situations which might put the respondent's activity in a different light relative to the place of picketing and to the object of picketing and which, correlatively, might provide some redeeming interest of the shopping centre owner in exercising control over the public areas. The character of a shopping centre, such as the one involved here, is one thing, and the nature and place of activities carried on there are something else. I would agree that it does not follow that because unrestricted access is given to members of the public to certain areas of the shopping centre during business hours, those areas are available at all times during those hours and in all circumstances to any kind of peaceful activity by members of the public, regardless of the interest being prompted by that activity and regardless of the numbers of members of the public who are involved. The Court will draw lines here as it does in other branches of the law as may be appropriate in the light of the legal principle and particular facts. In the present case it is the respondent who has been injured rather than the shopping centre owner.

I would dismiss the appeal.

Appeal allowed; conviction restored.

HUNTER v. SOUTHAM INC.

(1984), 41 C.R. (3d) 97, [1984] 2 S.C.R. 145, 14 C.C.C. (3d) 97

DICKSON J.: — . . . The task of expounding a constitution is crucially different from that of construing a statute. A statute defines present rights and obligations. It is easily enacted and as easily repealed. A constitution, by contrast, is drafted with an eye to the future. Its function is to provide a continuing framework for the legitimate exercise of governmental power and, when joined by a bill or a charter of rights, for the unremitting protection of individual rights and liberties. Once enacted, its provisions cannot easily be repealed or amended. It must therefore be capable of growth and development over time to meet new social, political and historical realities often unimagined by its framers. The judiciary is the guardian of the constitution and must, in interpreting its provisions, bear these considerations in mind. Professor Paul Freund expressed this idea aptly when he admonished the American courts "not to read the provisions of the Constitution like a last will and testament lest it become one".

The need for a broad perspective in approaching constitutional documents is a familiar theme in Canadian constitutional jurisprudence. It is contained in Viscount Sankey L.C.'s classic formulation in *Edwards v. A.G. Can.*, [1930] A.C. 124 at 136-37, (P.C.), cited and applied in countless Canadian cases:

"The British North America Act planted in Canada a living tree capable of growth and expansion within its natural limits. The object of the Act was to grant a Constitution to Canada . . .

"Their Lordships do not conceive it to be the duty of this Board — it is certainly not their desire — to cut down the provisions of the Act by a narrow and technical construction, but rather to give it a large and liberal interpretation."

More recently, in *Min. of Home Affairs v. Fisher*, [1980] A.C. 319 (P.C.), dealing with the Bermudian constitution, Lord Wilberforce reiterated at p. 329 that a constitution is a document "sui generis, calling for principles of interpretation of its own, suitable to its character", and that as such a constitution incorporating a bill of rights calls for [p. 328]:

". . . a generous interpretation avoiding what has been called 'the austerity of tabulated legalism', suitable to give individuals the full measure of the fundamental rights and freedoms referred to."

Such a broad, purposive analysis, which interprets specific provisions of a constitutional document in the light of its larger objects, is also consonant with the classical principles of American constitutional construction enunciated by Marshall C.J. in *McCulloch v. Maryland*, 17 U.S. (4 Wheat.) 316, 4 L. Ed. 870 (1819). It is, as well, the approach I intend to take in the present case.

I begin with the obvious. The Canadian *Charter of Rights and Freedoms* is a purposive document. Its purpose is to guarantee and to protect, within the limits of reason, the enjoyment of the rights and freedoms it enshrines. It is intended to constrain governmental action inconsistent with those rights and freedoms; it is not in itself an authorization for governmental action.

Another potential source of substantive criminal law is the *Canadian Charter of Rights and Freedoms, 1982*, entrenched by the *Constitution Act* of December 8, 1981 [en. by the *Canada Act, 1982* (U.K.), c. 11, Sched. B], Pt. 1. Unlike its predecessor, the *Canadian Bill of Rights*, R.S.C. 1970, App. III, it applies to provincial as well as federal laws by virtue of s. 32. Furthermore s. 52(1) reads:

> The Constitution of Canada is the supreme law of Canada, and any law that is inconsistent with the provisions of the Constitution is, to the extent of the inconsistency, of no force or effect.

This provision is a significant inroad on the principle of parliamentary supremacy and grants to the courts the power to measure legislation against a now entrenched yardstick of human rights and freedoms. Arguments against such a judicial function (for example, that it constitutes an unjustifiable transfer of legislative power to the courts, that the courts are not democratically elected and should not therefore be ruling on such value questions, and that Judges, particularly at the lower levels are not sufficiently equipped to handle these large questions) are now at an end. The courts have the power and arguments such as these can only be made in seeking to persuade Judges to exercise their power with restraint.

The *Charter* has had a considerable impact on the criminal courts. In literally hundreds of cases judges at all levels are grappling with the meaning of various aspects of the *Charter*. The impact of the *Charter* has been most marked on procedural law. It enshrines several procedural rights quite specific to the criminal trial. Most are to be found under the heading of "Legal Rights" — the protection against unreasonable search or seizure (s. 8), the right not to be arbitrarily detained (s. 9), the right on arrest or detention to be informed promptly of the reasons (s. 10(*a*)), the right to retain and instruct counsel without delay and to be informed of that right (s. 10(*b*)), the right of an accused not to be compelled to be a witness (s. 11 (*c*)) and the protection against self-crimination (s. 13). Such purely procedural topics will not be considered here. This book is primarily concerned with substantive criminal law and not procedure. This material is concerned with examining the elements of a crime (what has to be proved) and not with how the crime will be investigated or prosecuted. However we will consider the already broadly interpreted s. 7, which reads:

> Everyone has the right to life, liberty and security of the person and the right not to be deprived thereof except in accordance with the principles of fundamental justice.

We shall also deal with the presumption of innocence under s. 11(*d*), the remedy of exclusion of evidence under s. 24(2) and with what constitutes a demonstrably justified reasonable limit under s. 1.

By s.1 the rights set out in the *Charter* are subject to " such reasonable limits prescribed by law as can be demonstrably justified in a free and democratic society."

For a review of the impact of the *Charter* on all aspects of the criminal justice system, see Stuart, *Charter Justice in Canadian Criminal Law* (3rd ed., 2001, Carswell).

Void for Vagueness and Overbreadth

Before the advent of the *Charter*, void for uncertainty was a well-recognized ground of challenge to by-law offences (see, *e.g.*, *Harrison v. Toronto* (1982), 31 C.R. (3d) 244, (H.C.)), but our courts had recoiled from its availability in the case of other types of criminal sanction. In *R. v. Pink Triangle Press* (1979), 45 C.C.C. (2d) 385 (Ont. Prov. Ct.), Harris Prov. J. held that the undefined term "immoral" in s. 164 of the *Criminal Code* was so "ambiguous and indefinite" (p. 407) that it had "no legally enforceable meaning" (p. 408). This decision was, however, soon reversed (51 C.C.C. (2d) 485 (Co. Ct.)) and on further appeal the Ontario Court of Appeal (19 C.R. (3d) 393 (sub nom. *Popert v. R.*), 58 C.C.C. (2d) 505) confirmed that the trial Judge had erred. On behalf of the Court Zuber J.A. agreed that the meaning of "immoral" was imprecise but, observing that the Courts often had to interpret imprecise terms such as "reasonable", "undue" and "dangerous", held at p. 398 that the Courts had "to work as best they can with the tools in hand".

Since the *Charter*, the Supreme Court of Canada has determined, in a series of decisions, that any penal law should be declared unconstitutional if it is too vague. A challenge should normally be brought under s. 7 on the basis that it is a principle of fundamental justice that laws may not be too vague. Sometimes the issue will arise where there has been a breach of a *Charter* right such as freedom of expression; then the issue is whether that violation is a demonstrably justified reasonable limit prescribed by law under s. 1. The Court has confirmed that a law that is too vague cannot be "prescribed by law". Although the Court has thus recognized a constitutional doctrine of void for vagueness, the Supreme Court has been most reluctant to strike down penal law. It has, for example, dismissed vagueness challenges against the *Criminal Code* offences of keeping a common bawdy house (s. 193) and communicating for the purposes of prostitution (s. 195.1(1)(c)) (*Prostitution Reference* (1990), 77 C.R. (3d) 1 (S.C.C.), see below under "Commission of Unlawful Act") and against the obscenity definition in s. 163(8) of an undue exploitation of sex or of sex and violence (*Butler* (1992), 11 C.R. (4th) 137 (S.C.C.), see below under "Obscenity: A Test Case").

R. v. PHARMACEUTICAL SOCIETY (NOVA SCOTIA)

[1992] 2 S.C.R. 606, 15 C.R. (4th) 1, 74 C.C.C. (3d) 289

Twelve accused were charged with conspiracy to prevent or lessen competition unduly, contrary to what is now s. 45(1)(c) of the *Competition Act*, R.S.C., 1985, c. C-34, relating to the sale and offering for sale of prescription drugs and pharmacists' dispensing services. A Judge of the Nova Scotia Supreme Court quashed the charge on the basis that the use of the word "unduly" made the law too vague. However, this ruling was overturned by the Nova Scotia Appeal Division and the Supreme Court dismissed the appeal.

GONTHIER J. [having summarized the previous decisions of the Supreme Court, went on]: —

The foregoing may be summarized by way of the following propositions:

1. Vagueness can be raised under s. 7 of the *Charter*, since it is a principle of fundamental justice that laws may not be too vague. It can also be raised under s. 1 of the *Charter in limine*, on the basis that an enactment is so vague as not to satisfy the requirement that a limitation on *Charter* rights be "prescribed by law". Furthermore, vagueness is also relevant to the "minimal impairment" stage of the *Oakes* test (*Morgentaler, Irwin Toy, Prostitution Reference*).

2. The "doctrine of vagueness" is founded on the rule of law, particularly on the principles of fair notice to citizens and limitation of enforcement discretion (*Prostitution Reference, Committee for the Commonwealth of Canada*).

3. Factors to be considered in determining whether a law is too vague include (a) the need for flexibility and the interpretative role of the Courts, (b) the impossibility of achieving absolute certainty, a standard of intelligibility being more appropriate and (c) the possibility that many varying judicial interpretations of a given disposition may exist and perhaps coexist (*Morgentaler, Irwin Toy, Prostitution Reference, Taylor, Osborne*).

4. Vagueness, when raised under s. 7 or under s. 1 in limine, involves similar considerations (*Prostitution Reference, Committee for the Commonwealth of Canada*). On the other hand, vagueness as it relates to the "minimal impairment" branch of s. 1 merges with the related concept of overbreadth (*Committee for the Commonwealth of Canada, Osborne*).

5. The Court will be reluctant to find a disposition so vague as not to qualify as "law" under s. 1 in limine, and will rather consider the scope of the disposition under the "minimal impairment" test (*Taylor, Osborne*).

. . . .

2. The Proper Place of the Doctrine of Vagueness in Charter Adjudication

Vagueness is often mingled and confused with overbreadth, possibly because of the influence of American authorities. From a review of American law, it will appear that overbreadth is not an autonomous notion in Canadian law, and that, contrary to the position of U.S. constitutional law, vagueness should have a constant meaning in Canadian law. Overbreadth in American law is tied to the First Amendment.

. . . .

Overbreadth ties in to the taxonomy of protected and unprotected conduct and expression developed by American courts under the First Amendment. Some conduct or expression receives First Amendment protection and some does not, and to the extent that a statute substantially touches upon protected conduct and cannot be severed or read down, it will be declared void.

This distinction between protected and unprotected conduct or expression is typical of American law, since the American Constitution does not contain a general balancing clause similar to s. 1 of the *Charter*. Balancing must be done within the First Amendment itself. In this respect, it can be seen that the doctrine of overbreadth in American law involves an element of balancing, since the aims and scope of the statute must be compared with the range of protection of the First Amendment. This court has repeatedly emphasized the numerous differences which exist between the *Charter* and the *American Constitution*. In particular, in the interpretation of s. 2 of the Charter, this court has taken a route completely different from that of U.S. courts. In cases starting with *Irwin Toy* up to *Butler*, including the *Prostitution Reference* and *Keegstra*, this court has given a wide ambit to the freedoms guaranteed by s. 2 of the *Charter*, on the basis that balancing between the objectives of the state and the violation of a right or freedom should occur at the s. 1 stage. Other sections of the *Charter*, such as ss. 7 and 8, do however incorporate some element of balancing, as a limitation within the definition of the protected right, with respect to other notions such as principles of fundamental justice or reasonableness.

A notion tied to balancing such as overbreadth finds its proper place in sections of the *Charter* which involve a balancing process. Consequently, I cannot but agree with the opinion expressed by L'Heureux-Dube, J. in Committee for the Commonwealth of Canada that overbreadth is subsumed under the "minimal impairment branch" of the *Oakes* test, under s. 1 of the *Charter*. This is also in accordance with the trend evidenced in *Osborne* and *Butler*. . . . . In all these cases, however, overbreadth remains no more than an analytical tool. The alleged overbreadth is always related to some limitation under the *Charter*. It is always established by comparing the ambit of the provision touching upon a protected right with such concepts as the objectives of the state, the principles of fundamental justice, the proportionality of punishment or the reasonableness of searches and seizures, to name a few. There is no such thing as overbreadth in the abstract. Overbreadth has no autonomous value under the *Charter*. As will be seen below, overbreadth is not at the heart of this case, although it has been invoked in argument.

. . . .

A vague law may also constitute an excessive impairment of Charter rights under the *Oakes* test. This court recognized this, when it mentioned the two aspects of vagueness under s. 1 of the *Charter*, in *Osborne* and *Butler*. For the sake of clarity, I would prefer to reserve the term "vagueness" for the most serious degree of vagueness, where a law is so vague as not to constitute a "limit prescribed by law" under s. 1 *in limine*. The other aspect of vagueness, being an instance of overbreadth, should be considered as such. . . . . Under the *Charter*, however, given the statements of Lamer J. in the Prostitution Reference, at p. 1155 [S.C.R.], I would consider that the "doctrine of vagueness" is a single concept, whether invoked as a principle of fundamental justice under s. 7 of the *Charter* or as part of s. 1 of the *Charter*, *in limine*. Indeed from a practical point of view this makes little difference in the analysis, since a consideration of s. 1 *in limine* would follow immediately the determination of whether s. 7 has been violated. No intermediate step is lost. From a theoretical perspective, the justifications invoked for the doctrine of vagueness under both s. 7 and s. 1 are similar. A reading of the aforementioned cases shows that the rationales of fair notice to the citizen and limitation of enforcement discretion are put forward in every discussion of vagueness, irrespective of where it occurs in the *Charter* analysis. I see no ground for distinguishing them.

Vagueness may be raised under the substantive sections of the *Charter* whenever these sections comprise some internal limitation. For example, under s. 7, it may be that the limitation on life, liberty and security of the person would not otherwise be objectionable, but for the vagueness of the impugned law. The doctrine of vagueness would then rank among the principles of fundamental justice. Outside of these cases, the proper place of a vagueness argument is under s. 1 *in limine*.

I would therefore conclude that:

1. What is referred to as "overbreadth", whether it stems from the vagueness of a law or from another source, remains no more than an analytical tool to establish a violation of a *Charter* right. Overbreadth has no independent existence. References to a "doctrine of overbreadth" are superfluous.

2. The "doctrine of vagueness", the content of which will be developed shortly, is a principle of fundamental justice under s. 7 and it is also part of s. 1 in limine ("prescribed by law").

3. The Content of the "Doctrine of Vagueness"

As was said by this Court in *Osborne* and *Butler*, the threshold for finding a law vague is relatively high. So far discussion of the content of the notion has evolved around intelligibility.

The two rationales of fair notice to the citizen and limitation of enforcement discretion have been adopted as the theoretical foundations of the doctrine of vagueness, here *(Prostitution Reference, Committee for the Commonwealth of Canada)* as well as in the United States (see *Grayned v. Rockford (City)*, 408 U.S. 104 (1972), at pp. 108-109) and in Europe, as will be seen later. These two rationales have been broadly linked with the corpus of principles of government known as the "rule of law", which lies at the core of our political and constitutional tradition.

a. *Fair Notice to the Citizen*

Fair notice to the citizen, as a guide to conduct and a contributing element to a full answer and defence, comprises two aspects.

First of all, there is the more formal aspect of notice, that is acquaintance with the actual text of a statute. In the criminal context, this concern has more or less been set aside by the common law maxim "Ignorance of the law is no excuse", embodied in s. 19 of the *Criminal Code* (see *R. v. MacDougall*, [1982] 2 S.C.R. 605, 31 C.R. (3d) 1, 1 C.C.C. (3d) 65). In the civil context, the maxim does not apply with equal force (see J.-L. Baudouin, *Les obligations* 3d ed. (Cowansville, Que.: Yvon Blais, 1989), at p. 122, and *Chitty on Contracts* 25th ed. (London: Sweet & Maxwell, 1983), at paras. 314 and 353). Some authors have expressed the opinion that this maxim contradicts the rule of law, and should be revised in the light of the growing quantity and complexity of penal legislation (see E. Colvin, "Criminal Law and The Rule of Law", in P. Fitzgerald, ed., *Crime, Justice & Codification* (Toronto: Carswell, 1986) 125 at p. 151, and J. C. Jeffries, Jr., "Legality, Vagueness, and the Construction of Penal Statutes" (1985), 71 Va. L. Rev. 189, at p. 209). Since this argument was not raised in this case, I will refrain from ruling on this issue. In any event, given that, as this Court has already recognized, case law applying and interpreting a particular section is relevant in determining whether the section is vague, formal notice is not a central concern in a vagueness analysis.

. . . .

Fair notice may not have been given when enactments are in somewhat general terms, in a way that does not readily permit citizens to be aware of their substance, when they do not relate to any element of the substratum of values held by society. It is no coincidence that these enactments are often found vague. For instance, the vagrancy ordinance invalidated by the United States Supreme Court in *Papachristou v. Jacksonville*, 405 U.S. 156 (1972), or the compulsory identification statute struck down in *Kolender v. Lawson*, 461 U.S. 352 (1983), fall in this group.

Hence, aside from a formal aspect which is in our current system often presumed, fair notice to the citizen comprises a substantive aspect, that is an understanding that certain conduct is the subject of legal restrictions.

b. *Limitation of Law Enforcement Discretion*

Lamer J. in the *Prostitution Reference* used the phrase "standardless sweep", first coined by the United States Supreme Court in *Smith v. Goguen*, 415 U.S. 566 (1974), at p. 575, to describe the limitation of enforcement discretion rationale for the doctrine of vagueness. It has become the prime concern in American constitutional law (*Kolender*, at pp. 357-358). Indeed today it has become paramount, given the considerable expansion in the discretionary powers of enforcement agencies that has followed the creation of the modern welfare state.

A law must not be so devoid of precision in its content that a conviction will automatically flow from the decision to prosecute. Such is the crux of the concern for limitation of enforcement discretion. When the power to decide whether a charge will lead to conviction or acquittal, normally the preserve of the judiciary, becomes fused with the power to prosecute because of the wording of the law, then a law will be unconstitutionally vague.

For instance, the wording of the vagrancy ordinance invalidated by the United States Supreme Court in *Papachristou* and quoted at length in the *Prostitution Reference* at pp. 1152-1153 [S.C.R.], was so general and so lacked precision in its content that a conviction would ensue every time the law enforcer decided to charge someone with the offence of vagrancy. The words of the ordinance had no substance to them, and they indicated no particular legislative purpose. They left the accused completely in the dark, with no possible way of defending himself before the Court.

c. *European Court of Human Rights Case Law*

I would also note that the European Court of Human Rights (hereinafter "E.C.H.R.") has adopted the same approach to issues of vagueness, in the course of its treatment of words such as "prescribed by law", found in many limitation clauses of the *European Convention for the Protection of Human Rights and Fundamental Freedoms*, 213 U.N.T.S. 222 (hereinafter the "convention"), such as arts. 8(2), 9(2), 10(2), 11(2) or art. 2(3) of Protocol No. 4 to the Convention, Europ. T.S. No. 46. The E.C.H.R. gave this phrase a substantive content, which went beyond a mere inquiry as to whether a law existed or not.

The E.C.H.R. developed its conception of "prescribed by law" in the course of two famous cases, the *Sunday Times Case*, (1979), Ser. A, No. 30, and the *Malone Case*, judgment of (August 2, 1984), Ser. A, No. 82. In the former, the E.C.H.R. drew attention to the two aspects of fair notice, namely formal notice ("accessibility") and substantive notice ("foreseeability"). It wrote at p. 31:

> In the Court's opinion, the following are two of the requirements that flow from the expression "prescribed by law". Firstly, the law must be adequately accessible: the citizen must be able to have an indication that is adequate in the circumstances of the legal rules applicable to a given case. Secondly, a norm cannot be regarded as a "law" unless it is formulated with sufficient precision to enable the citizen to regulate his conduct: he must be able — if need be with appropriate advice — to foresee, to a degree that is reasonable in the

circumstances, the consequences which a given action may entail. Those consequences need not be foreseeable with absolute certainty: experience shows this to be unattainable. Again, whilst certainty is highly desirable, it may bring in its train excessive rigidity and the law must be able to keep pace with changing circumstances. Accordingly, many laws are inevitably couched in terms which, to a greater or lesser extent, are vague and whose interpretation and application are questions of practice.

In the latter, the E.C.H.R. added the limitation of enforcement discretion to the range of interests underpinning its interpretation of "prescribed by law" at p. 32:

The phrase thus implies . . . that there must be a measure of legal protection in domestic law against arbitrary interferences by public authorities with the rights safeguarded by paragraph 1 [of article 8 of the Convention].

(See also the *Kruslin* Case, judgment of (April 24, 1990), Ser. A, No. 176-A, at pp. 24-25, and the *Huvig Case*, judgment of (April 24, 1990), Ser. A, No. 176-B, at p. 56.)

In my opinion, the case law of the E.C.H.R. is a very valuable guide on this issue, and it will be relied on further below.

d. *The scope of precision*

This leads me to synthesize these remarks about vagueness. The substantive notice and limitation of enforcement discretion rationales point in the same direction: an unintelligible provision gives insufficient guidance for legal debate and is therefore unconstitutionally vague.

. . . .

Legal rules only provide a framework, a guide as to how one may behave, but certainty is only reached in instant cases, where law is actualized by a competent authority. In the meanwhile, conduct is guided by approximation. The process of approximation sometimes results in quite a narrow set of options, sometimes in a broader one. Legal dispositions therefore delineate a risk zone, and cannot hope to do more, unless they are directed at individual instances.

By setting out the boundaries of permissible and non-permissible conduct, these norms give rise to legal debate. They bear substance, and they allow for a discussion as to their actualization. They therefore limit enforcement discretion by introducing boundaries, and they also sufficiently delineate an area of risk to allow for substantive notice to citizens.

Indeed no higher requirement as to certainty can be imposed on law in our modern state. Semantic arguments, based on a perception of language as an unequivocal medium, are unrealistic. Language is not the exact tool some may think it is. It cannot be argued that an enactment can and must provide enough guidance to predict the legal consequences of any given course of conduct in advance. All it can do is enunciate some boundaries, which create an area of risk. But it is inherent to our legal system that some conduct will fall along the boundaries of the area of risk; no definite prediction can then be made.

Guidance, not direction, of conduct is a more realistic objective. The E.C.H.R. has repeatedly warned against a quest for certainty and adopted this "area of risk" approach in *Sunday Times, supra*, and especially the case of *Silver Case*, judgment of (March 25, 1983), Ser. A, No. 61, (sub nom. *Silver v. United Kingdom*) 3 E.H.R.R. 475, at pp. 33-34, and *Malone, supra*, at pp. 32-33.

A vague provision does not provide an adequate basis for legal debate, that is, for reaching a conclusion as to its meaning by reasoned analysis applying legal criteria. It does not sufficiently delineate any area of risk, and thus can provide neither fair notice to the citizen nor a limitation of enforcement discretion. Such a provision is not intelligible, to use the terminology of previous decisions of this Court, and therefore it fails to give sufficient indications that could fuel a legal debate. It offers no grasp to the judiciary. This is an exacting standard, going beyond semantics. The term "legal debate" is used here not to express a new standard or one departing from that previously outlined by this court. It is rather intended to reflect and encompass the same standard and criteria of fair notice and limitation of enforcement discretion viewed in the fuller context of an analysis of the quality and limits of human knowledge and understanding in the operation of the law.

. . . .

One must be wary of using the doctrine of vagueness to prevent or impede State action in furtherance of valid social objectives, by requiring the law to achieve a degree of precision to which the subject-matter does not lend itself. A delicate balance must be maintained between societal interests and individual rights. A measure of generality also sometimes allows for greater respect for fundamental rights, since circumstances that would not justify the invalidation of a more precise enactment may be accommodated through the application of a more general one.

What becomes more problematic is not so much general terms conferring broad discretion, but terms failing to give direction as to how to exercise this discretion, so that this exercise may be controlled. Once more, an unpermissibly vague law will not provide a sufficient basis for legal debate; it will not give a sufficient indication as to how decisions must be reached, such as factors to be considered or determinative elements. In giving unfettered discretion, it will deprive the judiciary of means of controlling the exercise of this discretion. The need to provide guidelines for the exercise of discretion was at the centre of the E.C.H.R. reasons in *Malone, supra*, at pp. 32-33, and the *Leander Case*, judgment of (March 27, 1987), Ser. A, No. 116, at p. 23.

Finally, I also wish to point out that the standard I have outlined applies to all enactments, irrespective of whether they are civil, criminal, administrative or other. The citizen is entitled to have the state abide by constitutional standards of precision whenever it enacts legal dispositions. In the criminal field, it may be thought that the terms of the legal debate should be outlined with special care by the state.

. . . .

The doctrine of vagueness can therefore be summed up in this proposition: a law will be found unconstitutionally vague if it so lacks in precision as not to give sufficient guidance for legal debate. This statement of the doctrine best conforms to the dictates of the rule of law in the modern state, and it reflects the prevailing argumentative, adversarial framework for the administration of justice.

For an application of *Pharmaceutical Society* see *R. v. Haldenby* (1994), 93 C.C.C. (3d) 249 (Ont. Prov. Div.).

R. v. HEYWOOD

[1994] 3 S.C.R. 761

The accused was convicted in 1987 of two counts of sexual assault. In 1989 he was charged with two offences of committing vagrancy by being a person who had been convicted of a sexual offence, and "found loitering at or near a school ground, playground, public park or bathing area" contrary to s. 179(1)(*b*) of the *Criminal Code*. He had been observed carrying a camera with a telephoto lens near children's playground areas in parks and, in one case, had been seen taking photographs. One of the pictures and several found in his residence showed the crotch areas of young girls.

The accused was convicted. The trial judge ruled that although s. 179(1)(*b*) of the *Criminal Code* was contrary to ss. 7 and 11(*d*) of the *Charter* it was demonstrably justified as a reasonable limit under s. 1. The British Columbia Court of Appeal declared s. 179(1)(*b*) unconstitutional and allowed the appeal.

The majority of the Supreme Court dismissed the Crown's further appeal, confirming that s. 179(1)(*b*) was unconstitutional. By the time of the appeal Parliament had already replaced the provision with a more narrowly worded s. 161.

Section 179(1)(*b*) provided that:

179.(1) Every one commits vagrancy who

(*b*) having at any time been convicted of an offence under section 151, 152 or 153, subsection 160(3) or 173(2) or section 271, 272 or 273, or of an offence under a provision referred to in paragraph (*b*) of the definition "serious personal injury offence" in section 687 of the *Criminal Code*, chapter C-34 of the Revised Statutes of Canada, 1970, as it read before January 4, 1983, is found loitering in or near a school ground, playground, public park or bathing area.

"serious personal injury offence" in s. 687 of the *Criminal Code*, as it read before January 4, 1983, was rape, attempted rape, sexual intercourse with a female under fourteen or between fourteen and sixteen, indecent assault or gross indecency.

CORY J. (LAMER C.J. and SOPINKA, IACOBUCCI and MAJOR JJ. concurring): — Section 179(1)(*b*) of the *Criminal Code*, R.S.C., 1985, c. C-46, as amended, makes it a crime for persons convicted of specified offences to be "found loitering in or near a school ground, playground, public park or bathing area". It must be determined whether the section infringes ss. 7 or 11(*d*) of the *Canadian Charter of Rights and Freedoms*.

. . . .

What then is the ordinary meaning of the word "loiter"? The *Oxford English Dictionary* (2nd ed. 1989), defines "loiter" in this manner:

> 1. In early use: To idle, waste one's time in idleness. Now only with more specific meaning: To linger indolently on the way when sent on an errand or when making a journey; to linger idly about a place; to waste time when engaged in some particular task, to dawdle. Freq. in legal phr. to loiter with intent (to commit a felony).

Similarly, *Black's Law Dictionary* (5th ed. 1979), defines "loiter" as follows:

> To be dilatory; to be slow in movement; to stand around or move slowly about; to stand idly around; to spend time idly; to saunter; to delay; to idle; to linger; to lag behind.

None of these definitions requires a malevolent intent or makes any reference to such a requirement. Cases which have considered the meaning of "loiter" in other sections of the Code support the use of the ordinary meaning of "loiter" in s. 179(1)(*b*). . . . . The ordinary definition of "loiter" is also consistent with the purpose of s. 179(1)(*b*). The section is aimed at protecting children from becoming victims of sexual offences. This is apparent from the places to which the prohibition of loitering applies. School grounds, playgrounds, public parks and public bathing areas are typically places where children are likely to congregate. The purpose of the prohibition on loitering is to keep people who are likely to pose a risk to children away from places where they are likely to be found. Prohibiting any prolonged attendance in these areas, which is what the ordinary definition of "loiter" does, achieves this goal.

There can be no question that s. 179(1)(*b*) restricts the liberty of those to whom it applies. Indeed, the appellant made no argument to the contrary. The section prohibits convicted sex offenders from attending (except perhaps to quickly walk through on their way to another location) at school grounds, playgrounds, public parks or bathing areas — places where the rest of the public is free to roam. The breach of this prohibition is punishable on summary conviction and, as this case demonstrates, imprisonment is the consequence.

The question this Court must decide is whether this restriction on liberty is in accordance with the principles of fundamental justice. The respondent conceded in oral argument that a prohibition for the purpose of protecting the public does not per se infringe the principles of fundamental justice. *R. v. Lyons*, [1987] 2 S.C.R. 309, at pp. 327-34, held that the indeterminate detention of a dangerous offender, the purpose of which was the protection of the public, did not per se violate s. 7. . . . . The question, then, is whether some other aspect of the prohibition contained in s. 179(1)(B) violates the principles of fundamental justice. In my opinion it does. It applies without prior notice to the accused, to too many places, to too many people, for an indefinite period with no possibility of review. It restricts liberty far more than is necessary to accomplish its goal.

A. Overbreadth

This Court considered the issue of overbreadth as a principle of fundamental justice in *R. v. Nova Scotia Pharmaceutical Society*, [1992] 2 S.C.R. 606. Writing for the Court, Gonthier J. discussed the relationship between overbreadth and vagueness at pp. 627-31.

Overbreadth and vagueness are different concepts, but are sometimes related in particular cases. As the Ontario Court of Appeal observed in *R. v. Zundel* (1987), 58 O.R. (2d) 129, at pp. 157-58, cited with approval by Gonthier J. in *R. v. Nova Scotia Pharmaceutical Society*, *supra*, the meaning of a law may be unambiguous and thus the law will not be vague; however, it may still be overly broad. Where a law is vague, it may also be overly broad, to the extent that the ambit of its application is difficult to define. Overbreadth and vagueness are related in that both are the result of a lack of sufficient precision by a legislature in the means used to accomplish an objective. In the case of vagueness, the means are not clearly defined. In the case of overbreadth the means are too sweeping in relation to the objective.

Overbreadth analysis looks at the means chosen by the state in relation to its purpose. In considering whether a legislative provision is overbroad, a court must ask the question: are those means necessary to achieve the State objective? If the State, in pursuing a legitimate objective, uses means which are broader than is necessary to accomplish that objective, the principles of fundamental justice will be violated because the individual's rights will have been limited for no reason. The effect of overbreadth is that in some applications the law is arbitrary or disproportionate.

Reviewing legislation for overbreadth as a principle of fundamental justice is simply an example of the balancing of the State interest against that of the individual. .... However, where an independent principle of fundamental justice is violated, such as the requirement of *mens rea* for penal liability, or of the right to natural justice, any balancing of the public interest must take place under s. 1 of the *Charter*: *Re B.C. Motor Vehicle Act*, *supra*, at p. 517; *R. v. Swain*, [1991] 1 S.C.R. 933, at p. 977.

In analyzing a statutory provision to determine if it is overbroad, a measure of deference must be paid to the means selected by the legislature. While the courts have a constitutional duty to ensure that legislation conforms with the *Charter*, legislatures must have the power to make policy choices. A court should not interfere with legislation merely because a judge might have chosen a different means of accomplishing the objective if he or she had been the legislator. .... However, before it can be found that an enactment is so broad that it infringes s. 7 of the *Charter*, it must be clear that the legislation infringes life, liberty or security of the person in a manner that is unnecessarily broad, going beyond what is needed to accomplish the governmental objective.

The purpose of s. 179(1)(*b*) is to protect children from becoming victims of sexual offences. This is apparent from the prohibition which applies to places where children are very likely to be found. In determining whether s. 179(1)(*b*) is overly broad and not in accordance with the principles of fundamental justice, it must be determined whether the means chosen to accomplish this objective are reasonably tailored to effect this purpose. In those situations where legislation limits the liberty of an individual in order to protect the public, that limitation should not go beyond what is necessary to accomplish that goal. .... In my opinion, s. 179(1)(*b*) suffers from overbreadth and thus the deprivation of liberty it entails is not in accordance with the principles of fundamental justice.

The section is overly broad in its geographical ambit. It applies not only to school grounds and playgrounds, but also to all public parks and bathing areas. Its application to schools and playgrounds is appropriate, as these are the very places children are likely to congregate. But its application to all public parks and bathing areas is overly broad because not all such places are places where children are likely to be found. Public parks include the vast and remote wilderness parks. Bathing areas would include all the lakes in Canada with public beaches. Prohibiting individuals from loitering in all places in all parks is a significant limit on freedom of movement. Parks are places which are specifically designed to foster relaxation, indolent contemplation and strolling; in fact it may be assumed that "hanging around" and "idling" is encouraged in parks. .... Section 179(1)(*b*) is also overly broad in another aspect. It applies for life, with no possibility of review. The absence of review means that a person who has ceased to be a danger to children (or who indeed never was a danger to children), is subject to the prohibition in s. 179(1)(*b*). .... Section 179(1)(*b*) is overly broad in respect to the people to whom it applies. It applies to all persons convicted of the listed offences, without regard to whether they constitute a danger to children. .... A new s. 161 was passed following the decision of the British Columbia Court of Appeal in this case and is set out later in these reasons. It is significant and telling that the new section only applies to persons who have committed the listed offences in respect of a person who is under the age of 14 years. In addition, under the new section, the order is discretionary, so that only those offenders who constitute a danger to children will be subject to a prohibition. I would add that in certain circumstances, legislative provisions for notice and for review of the prohibition may reduce the significance of the factor of overbreadth in the application of one impugned provision. It is noteworthy that the new s. 161 provides for both notice and review of the prohibition. These provisions are absent in s. 179(1)(B). In summary, s. 179(1)(*b*) is overly broad to an extent that it violates the right to liberty proclaimed by s. 7 of the *Charter* for a number of reasons. First, it is overly broad in its geographical scope embracing as it does all public parks and beaches no matter how remote and devoid of children they may be. Secondly, it is overly broad in its temporal aspect with the prohibition applying for life without any process for review. Thirdly, it is too broad in the number of persons it encompasses.

The violation of s. 7 of the *Charter* is thus established. It is now necessary to consider whether the section may be saved by the provisions of s. 1 of the *Charter*.

This Court has expressed doubt about whether a violation of the right to life, liberty or security of the person which is not in accordance with the principles of fundamental justice can ever be justified, except perhaps in times of war or national emergencies: *Re B.C. Motor Vehicle Act*. In a case where the violation of the principles of fundamental justice is as a result of overbreadth, it is even more difficult to see how the limit can be justified. Overbroad legislation which infringes s. 7 of the *Charter* would appear to be incapable of passing the minimal impairment branch of the s. 1 analysis.

The objective of s. 179(1)(*b*) is certainly pressing and substantial. The protection of children from sexual offences is obviously very important to society. Furthermore, at least in some of their applications, the means employed in s. 179(1)(*b*) are rationally connected to the objective. However, for the same reasons that s. 179(1)(*b*) is overly broad, it fails the minimal impairment branch of the s. 1 analysis. . . . . Section 179(1)(*b*) cannot be justified under s. 1 of the Charter.

Counsel for the appellant argued that even if s. 179(1)(*b*) of the *Criminal Code* is so overbroad as to result in a violation of s. 7 which cannot be saved by s. 1, rather than striking the section down in its entirety, the section should be read down so as to come within constitutional limits. In my opinion reading down is not appropriate in this case. The changes which would be required to make s. 179(1)(*b*) constitutional would not constitute reading down or reading in; rather, they would amount to judicial rewriting of the legislation.

GONTHIER J. (LA FOREST, L'HEUREUX-DUBÉ and MCLACHLIN JJ. concurring): —

. . . .

In my view s. 179(1)(*b*) should be interpreted as prohibiting the persons affected from being in one of the enumerated places for a malevolent or ulterior purpose related to the predicate offences. My reasons for favouring this interpretation are drawn from the purpose and legislative history of s. 179(1)(*b*) as well as precedent and statutory context.

. . . .

My review of the legislative history, purpose and context of s. 179(1)(*b*) thus leads to the conclusion that the offence should be interpreted as lingering or hanging about the enumerated areas for a malevolent or ulterior purpose related to any of the predicate offences. This interpretation is suggested by the terms of the offence and general desire to limit the intrusiveness of the prohibition while still achieving the objectives of public safety and offender treatment. As will be seen in the next section, this interpretation is also consistent with the *Charter*.

C. Section 179(1)(*b*) and Its Conformity with the *Charter*

The two primary *Charter* concerns raised by s. 179(1)(*b*) pertain to vagueness and overbreadth. Cory J.'s broader interpretation of s. 179(1)(*b*) eliminates any vagueness problem, but, in his view, leads to a prohibition which is unjustifiably overbroad. The interpretation I have adopted avoids both these problems.

As discussed in *R. v. Nova Scotia Pharmaceutical Society*, [1992] 2 S.C.R. 606, at p. 643, a provision which is unconstitutionally vague provides an intolerable level of prosecutorial discretion and fails to give those subject to the provision notice of its content. Put in its most simplistic form, what is prohibited will be what those charged with law enforcement decide at any given moment should be prohibited. Interpreting s. 179(1)(*b*) to prohibit lingering with an "untoward or improper motive" would arguably be an example of an unconstitutionally vague restriction on liberty. "Untoward or improper motive" gives little basis for legal debate within the terms of *Nova Scotia Pharmaceutical Society*. It is difficult to identify the factors to be considered or the determinative elements in ascertaining whether a motive is untoward or improper. Qualifying malevolent or ulterior purposes by reference to the predicate offences, however, eliminates any concerns as to vagueness. The enumerated offences provide a clear basis for legal debate and narrow the scope of potential liability. The persons affected would thus have notice of what is prohibited and prosecutorial discretion would be sufficiently restricted.

Cory J., however, suggests that the prohibition created by s. 179(1)(*b*) is overbroad in terms of the persons, places and time period to which it applies. I express no opinion on the soundness of this analysis of liberty because it is not necessary in this case to decide the issue. The interpretation I advocate eliminates Cory J.'s concern that the prohibition is overbroad. A lifetime prohibition of activities with a malevolent or ulterior purpose related to re-offending is in no way objectionable or overbroad. Such a prohibition would impose a restriction on the liberty of the affected individuals to which ordinary citizens are not subject, but that restriction is directly related to preventing re-offending. The affected persons' history of offending, the uncertainties prevalent in treating offenders and a desire to disrupt the cycle of re-offending justify what is in effect a minor intrusion which does not breach the principles of fundamental justice.

That restraint of the affected persons' liberty is minor and easily illustrated. As noted above, use of public parks for the legitimate purposes for which they are intended would not be caught. Furthermore, though trite, it must be remembered that the Crown will bear the burden of proving all elements of the offence beyond a reasonable doubt. This burden guarantees that only loitering which can be proven to be related to one of the predicate offences will be subject to the criminal prohibition. I recognize that this formulation of the offence will likely lead to certain evidentiary presumptions which, absent a satisfactory explanation, may cause a judge to draw an adverse inference. Take for example a person with a history of offences in relation to children who is observed hanging around a playground and offering children candy. Similarly, as discussed above, just lingering about a school yard with no apparent purpose, as distinct from a public park, would give rise to legitimate suspicions. Such presumptions, however, in no way reverse the burden of proof, nor do they violate the accused's right to silence.

Prohibiting lingering or hanging about the enumerated areas for a malevolent or ulterior purpose related to one of the predicate offences thus survives *Charter* scrutiny. The predicate offences provide an ample basis for limiting prosecutorial discretion and giving guidance as to what is prohibited to those affected. Furthermore, prohibiting only conduct which can be demonstrated to be part of the cycle of re-offending carefully balances the objectives of public safety and offender treatment with a desire to limit the intrusiveness of the prohibition.

From the point of view of defence counsel is an overbreadth argument easier to win on the current law than one of vagueness? Was it wise for the Supreme Court to establish constitutional doctrines of vagueness and overbreadth?

The Supreme Court has already served notice that it may reconsider or at least qualify the *Heywood* doctrine of overbreadth. In *Canadian Pacific Ltd.* (1995), 41 C.R. (4th) 147 (S.C.C.), the Court was unanimous in deciding that an offence under a provincial *Environmental Protection Act* prohibiting any use of the natural environment was not too vague or overbroad. Properly interpreted the provision provided a basis for legal debate and did not capture pollution with only a trivial or minimal impact. The Court saw the need to allow legislators considerable room to manoeuvre in the field of environmental regulation. Gonthier J. for the majority added a caveat to his analysis that the provision was not overbroad. Since *Heywood* had not been argued his reasons should not be taken to endorse the view that the independent principle of overbreadth recognized in *Heywood* was available in the circumstances of this case.

A citizen complains that he ought to be able to bring into the country a magazine which the Customs people have refused because the Deputy Minister has classified it as immoral and indecent and therefore falling under the prohibition pursuant to s. 14 of the *Customs Tariff*, which prohibits the importation of:

Books, printed paper, drawings, paintings,prints photographs or representations of ant kind of a treasonable or seditious, or of an immoral or indecent character.

Given the approach of the Supreme Court in *Nova Scotia Pharmaceutical Society* how do you think that a Court would respond? Compare *Luscher* v. *Dep. M.N.R. (Customs & Excise)* (1985), 45 C.R. (3d) 81 (Fed. C.A.)). What of the *Criminal Code* offence under s. 163(2)(*b*) of exhibiting a disgusting object? Compare *Glassman* (1986), 53 C.R. (3d) 164 (Ont. Prov. Ct.).

For views critical of the Court's approach to the issue of void for vagueness, see Gary T. Trotter "LeBeau: Toward a Canadian Vagueness Doctrine" (1988), 62 C.R. (3d) 157 and Stuart, *Charter Justice in Canadian Criminal Law* (3rd ed., 2001) Chapter 2.

In *R. v. Sharpe* (2000), 39 C.R. (5th) 72, the Supreme Court upheld the validity of the prohibition against child pornography in s. 163.1(4) of the *Criminal Code*. McLachlin C.J., writing for six justices, concluded that the prohibition was a demonstrably justified reasonable limit on freedom of expression guaranteed in s. 2(*b*) of the *Charter*. However, the Court identified a problem of overbreadth and, apart from making careful clarification of many of the provisions, found it necessary to read in two exclusions dealing with self-authored works of imagination and visual representation of sexual activity by teenagers for private use. The Court makes no mention of the doctrines of vagueness under *Nova Scotia Pharmaceutical Society* or overbreadth under *Heywood*.

Strict Construction

Do Canadian Courts construe penal statutes "strictly"? Should they?

Interpretation Act, R.S.C. 1985, c. I-21, s. 12:

> Every enactment shall be deemed remedial, and shall be given such fair, large and liberal construction and interpretation as best ensures the attainment of its objects.

Interpretation Act, R.S.O. 1980, c. 219, s. 10:

> Every Act shall be deemed to be remedial, whether its immediate purport is to direct the doing of anything that the Legislature deems to be for the public good or to prevent or punish the doing of anything that it deems to be contrary to the public good, and shall accordingly receive such fair, large and liberal construction and interpretation as will best ensure the attainment of the object of the Act according to its true intent, meaning and spirit.

RE XEROX OF CANADA LTD. AND REGIONAL ASSESSMENT COMMISSIONER REGION NO. 10

(1980), 30 O.R. (2d) 90 (C.A.), at 95, reversed on other grounds [1981] 2 S.C.R. 137

JESSUP J.A.: —

. . . .

In the *Reference re Certain Titles in Ontario*, which as a reference is not binding on this or any Court, it was said at p. 643 O.R., p. 40 D.L.R.:

> In our reasons for judgment herein we have cited many English authorities relating to statutory construction. The English *Interpretation Act* does not appear to contain a provision

similar to s. 10 of the Ontario *Interpretation Act*, R.S.O. 1970, c. 225, but it would not appear that the absence of such a provision from the English Act has deterred our Courts from applying substantially the same principles of statutory interpretation as those recognized and applied in England.

It is certainly correct as noted in *North York Steel Fabricators* that ss. 10 and 11 of the respective *Interpretation Acts* have been largely disregarded by the Courts of this Province. Professor Arthurs notes that disregard at p. 20 of (1979), 17 Osgoode Hall L.J. A survey, undertaken by law clerk Donna Morgan, of reports of 410 cases in this Province decided in the past 15 years and dealing with questions of statutory interpretation shows that only 45 have an explicit reference to either s. 10 or s. 11 or to any of the language of either section as being the governing principle: 255 of the cases surveyed rely on common law principles; in 110 of the cases it does not appear what principle, if any, was applied. New Zealand, which has a section similar to ss. 10 and 11 in its *Interpretation Act*, has had a similar experience as noted at p. 161 by Sir Rupert Cross in his text on *Statutory Interpretation* (1976). The resulting judicial chaos is noted by D.A.S. Ward in [1973] 1 N.Z.L.R. 293.

The disregard by our Courts, in my opinion, has been an affront to our Legislatures and has probably frustrated many a legislative intent. I have been as guilty as any. Perhaps we can all be forgiven; we were nurtured uncritically on the good old English common law principles and over the years they have become our security blanket that we are loath to part with.

R. v. BUDGET CAR RENTALS (TORONTO) LTD.

(1981), 57 C.C.C (2d) 201, 20 C.R. (3d) 66 (Ont. C.A.), at 207-8 (C.C.C.)

The defendant was charged in an information as the owner of a motor vehicle unlawfully parked, in violation of a municipal by-law passed pursuant to s. 460(8)(*b*) of the *Municipal Act*. That section provided that the owner, as well as the driver, was "liable to a penalty unless at the time the offence was committed the vehicle was in the possession of a person . . . without the owner's consent". The defendant argued that the section didn't create an offence. The defendant's position was that the municipality should first prosecute the driver and only after the driver was convicted should the defendant, as owner, be "liable to a penalty". The Court of Appeal disagreed and gave a meaning "to attain the object of the legislation according to its true intent, meaning and spirit".

HOWLAND C.J.O. [for a unanimous five judge court]: —

. . . .

In the course of argument, counsel for the respondent has directed us to a principle governing the construction and interpretation of statutes which, he argued, supported his contention that the legislation in question ought not to be construed as creating an offence by the owner of a vehicle for which, upon proof that the vehicle has been parked in contravention of the by-law made pursuant to the legislation, the owner will be answerable, subject, of course, to the statutory defence available to him.

Among these principles is the often-quoted principle that a penal statute must be construed "strictly". That this is so is surely beyond dispute, but it is important that it should be clear what the principle really means and what it does not mean. What it does mean is that, where a person is charged with an offence created by a statute, the conduct of that person which gives rise to the charge, or the conduct of someone for which that person may be held answerable, must be such as can be clearly and unmistakably demonstrated to fall within the kind of conduct which is proscribed by the statute. What the principle does *not* mean is that, because a statute is "penal", or contains provisions to which penal consequences for breaches are attached, the meaning that is to be given to language used in the statute is to be determined in accordance with a rule of construction that is somehow "stricter" than, or is to be applied more stringently than, the ordinary rules which apply to determine the meaning to be given to language used in statutes.

A person who is charged with, or sought to be made answerable for, conduct to which penal consequences are attached by a statute is therefore entitled to insist that the impugned conduct be shown to the required degree of certainty to be conduct which, in fact and in law, renders him liable under the statute to the penalty prescribed therefor. In my view, however, he is not entitled to insist that, merely because the statute can accordingly be described as "penal", its true meaning and intent must be ascertained by applying to it different (*i.e.*, "stricter") principles ot construction and interpretation than those which govern the construction and interpretation of statutes generally.

At one time, as remarked by E.A. Driedger in his recent work entitled the Construction Of Statutes (1974), p. 148, statutes were regarded as falling into one of two broad classes, "penal" and "remedial". On this basis, penal statutes (which were taken to include not only statutes imposing penalties for violations but also revenue statutes and statutes interfering with the liberty or property of the subject) were to be construed strictly, and remedial statutes were to be construed liberally. Against this background, the language used in s. 10 of the *Interpretation Act of Ontario* and in s. 11 of the *Interpretation Act of Canada*, R.S.C. 1970, c. 1-23, deeming every Act or enactment to be remedial, takes on a special and obvious significance.

I think it is worth repeating here the words of Lord Russell C.J. in *A.G. v. Carlton Bank*, [1899] 2 Q.B. 158 at 164:

> I see no reason why special canons of construction should be applied to any Act of Parliament, and I know of no authority for saying that a taxing Act is to be construed differently from any other Act. The duty of the Court is, in my opinion, in all cases the same, whether the Act to be construed relates to taxation or to any other subject, namely, to give effect to the intention of the Legislature as that intention is to be gathered from the language employed having regard to the context in connection with which it is employed.

Where the Court is concerned with a penal statute, it has been said that the defendant in the proceedings will not be liable to a penalty if, upon one of two equally reasonable readings of the statute, the penalty is incurred but on the other reading he is "let out". This has been expressed in another way by Wright J. in *London County Council v. Aylesbury Dairy Co.*, [1898] 1 Q.B. 106 at 109 (D.C.), where he stated his understanding of the rule to be that:

> where there is an enactment which may entail penal consequences, you ought not to do violence to its language in order to bring people within it.

Again, as Driedger stated at p. 154:

> One might ask whether one ought ever "to do violence" to language, but, in any case, "doing violence" would be placing an unreasonable construction on language, and, clearly, a reasonable construction that does not impose a penalty is preferred to an unreasonable construction that does.

R. v. GOULIS

(1981), 20 C.R. (3d) 360 (Ont. C.A.), at 365

MARTIN J.A.: —

. . . .

This Court has on many occasions applied the well-known rule of statutory construction that if a penal provision is reasonably capable of two interpretations that interpretation which is the more favourable to the accused must be adopted: see, for example, *Cheetham v. R.* (1980), 17 C.R. (3d) 1, 53 C.C.C. (2d) 109; *Negridge v. R.* (1980), 17 C.R. (3d) 14. I do not think, however, that this principle always requires a word which has two accepted meanings to be given the more restrictive meaning. Where a word used in a statute has two accepted meanings, then either or both meanings may apply. The Court is first required to endeavour to determine the sense in which Parliament used the word from the context in which it appears. It is only in the case of an ambiguity which still exists after the full context is considered, where it is uncertain in which sense Parliament used the word, that the above rule of statutory construction requires the interpretation which is the more favourable to the defendant to be adopted. This is merely another way of stating the principle that the conduct alleged against the accused must be clearly brought within the proscription.

For an extreme example of strict construction, see *R. v. Steer* (1982), 30 C.R. (3d) 269 (B.C. Prov. Ct.). On a charge of leaving the scene of an accident, the accused was acquitted since the trial Judge found that the accused had deliberately rammed the other vehicle in a fit of temper and thus was not leaving an accident.

R. v. PARÉ

[1987] 2 S.C.R. 618, 60 C.R. (3d) 346, 38 C.C.C. (3d) 97

The accused, aged 17, lured a seven-year-old boy to a place under a bridge, where he indecently assaulted him. When the boy told the accused that he would tell his mother, the accused threatened to kill him if he did. When the accused became certain that the boy would nevertheless tell, he held the boy down on his back for two minutes and then killed him through strangulation and hitting him with an oil filter. The accused was charged with and convicted of first degree murder on the basis of s. 214(5) [now s. 231(5)] of the *Criminal Code*, in that "murder is first degree murder . . . when the death is caused . . . *while committing*" an indecent assault (now sexual assault).

WILSON J.: —

. . . .

(iii) Strict Construction

Counsel for the respondent argue that the doctrine of strict construction of criminal statutes requires that this Court adopt the interpretation most favourable to the accused. According to this argument the words "while committing" must be narrowly construed so as to elevate murder to first degree only when the death and the underlying offence occur simultaneously. In order to assess the validity of this position we must examine the doctrine of strict construction.

The doctrine is one of ancient lineage. It reached its pinnacle of importance in a former age when the death penalty attached to a vast array of offences. As Stephen Kloepfer points out in his article "The Status of Strict Construction in Canadian Criminal Law" (1983), 15 Ottawa L. Rev. 553, at pp. 556-60, the doctrine was one of many tools employed by the judiciary to soften the impact of the Draconian penal provisions of the time. Over the past two centuries criminal law penalties have become far less severe. Criminal law remains, however, the most dramatic and important incursion that the state makes into individual liberty. Thus, while the original justification for the doctrine has been substantially eroded, the seriousness of imposing criminal penalties of any sort demands that reasonable doubts be resolved in favour of the accused.

This point was underlined by Dickson J. (as he then was) in *Marcotte v. Deputy Attorney General for Canada*, [1976] 1 S.C.R. 108, at p. 115:

> It is unnecessary to emphasize the importance of clarity and certainty when freedom is at stake. No authority is needed for the proposition that if real ambiguities are found, or doubts of substance arise, in the construction and application of a statute affecting the liberty of a subject, then that statute should be applied in such a manner as to favour the person against whom it is sought to be enforced. If one is to be incarcerated, one should at least know that some Act of Parliament requires it in express terms, and not, at most, by implication.

The continued vitality of the doctrine is further evidenced by the decisions in *R. v. Goulis* (1981), 60 C.C.C. (2d) 347 (Ont. C.A.), and *Paul v. The Queen*, [1982] 1 S.C.R. 621. The question, therefore, is not whether the doctrine of strict construction exists but what its implications are for this case.

(iv) Applying the Doctrine

As we have noted above, it is clearly grammatically possible to construe the words "while committing" in s. 214(5) as requiring murder to be classified as first degree only if it is exactly coincidental with the underlying offence. This, however, does not end the question. We still have to determine whether the narrow interpretation of "while committing" is a reasonable one, given the scheme and purpose of the legislation.

In my view, the construction that counsel for the respondent would have us place on these words is not one that could reasonably be attributed to Parliament. The first problem with the exactly simultaneous approach flows from the difficulty in defining the beginning and end of an indecent assault. In this case, for example, after ejaculation the respondent sat up and put his pants back on. But for the next two minutes he kept his hand on his victim's chest. Was this continued contact part of the assault? It does not seem to me that important issues of criminal law should be allowed to hinge upon this kind of distinction. An approach that depends on this kind of distinction should be avoided if possible.

A second difficulty with the exactly simultaneous approach is that it leads to distinctions that are arbitrary and irrational. In the present case, had the respondent strangled his victim two minutes earlier than he did, his guilt of first degree murder would be beyond dispute. The exactly simultaneous approach would have us conclude that the two minutes he spent contemplating his next move had the effect of reducing his offence to one of second degree murder. This would be a strange result. The crime is no less serious in the latter case than in the former; indeed, if anything, the latter crime is more serious since it involves some element of deliberation. An interpretation of s. 214(5) that runs contrary to common sense is not to be adopted if a reasonable alternative is available.

In my view, such an interpretation has been provided by Martin J.A. in *Stevens, supra*. As noted above, Martin J.A. suggested that "where the act causing death and the acts constituting the rape, attempted rape, indecent assault or an attempt to commit indecent assault, as the case may be, all form part of one continuous sequence of events forming a single transaction" the death was caused "while committing" an offence for the purposes of s. 214(5). This interpretation eliminates the need to draw artificial lines to separate the commission and the aftermath of an indecent assault. Further, it eliminates the arbitrariness inherent in the exactly simultaneous approach. I would, therefore, respectfully adopt Martin J.A.'s single transaction analysis as the proper construction of s. 214(5).

This approach, it seems to me, best expresses the policy considerations that underlie the provision. Section 214, as we have seen, classifies murder as either first or second degree. All murders are serious crimes. Some murders, however, are so threatening to the public that Parliament has chosen to impose exceptional penalties on the perpetrators. One such class of murders is that found in s. 214(5), murders done while committing a hijacking, a kidnapping and forcible confinement, a rape, or an indecent assault. An understanding of why this class of murder is elevated to murder in the first degree is a helpful guide to the interpretation of the language.

The Law Reform Commission of Canada addressed this issue in its paper on Homicide (Working Paper 33, 1984). At page 79, the paper states:

> . . . there is a lack of rationale in the law. Subsection 214(5) provides that, whether planned and deliberate or not, murder is first degree murder when committed in the course of certain listed offences. It is curious that the list there given is considerably shorter than that given in section 213 which makes killing murder if done in the commission of certain specified offences. Inspection and comparision of the two lists, however, reveal no organizing principle in either of them and no rationale for the difference between them.

With respect, I disagree. The offences listed in s. 214(5) are all offences involving the unlawful domination of people by other people. Thus an organizing principle for s. 214(5) can be found. This principle is that where a murder is committed by someone already abusing his power by illegally dominating another, the murder should be treated as an exceptionally serious crime. Parliament has chosen to treat these murders as murders in the first degree.

Refining then on the concept of the "single transaction" referred to by Martin J.A. in *Stevens, supra,* it is the continuing illegal domination of the victim which gives continuity to the sequence of events culminating in the murder. The murder represents an exploitation of the position of power created by the underlying crime and makes the entire course of conduct a "single transaction". This approach, in my view, best gives effect to the philosophy underlying s. 214(5).

. . . .

4. Conclusion

The respondent murdered Steve Duranleau minutes after indecently assaulting him. The killing was motivated by fear that the boy would tell his mother about the indecent assault. The jury found the respondent guilty of first degree murder. They were entitled to do so. The murder was temporally and causally connected to the underlying offence. It formed part of one continuous sequence of events. It was part of the same transaction.

I would allow the appeal and restore the conviction of first degree murder.

In *R. v. McIntosh* (1995), 36 C.R. (4th) 171 (S.C.C.) Chief Justice Lamer confirmed for the majority that

It is a principle of statutory interpretation that where two interpretations of a provision which affects the liberty of a subject are available, one of which is more favourable to an accused, then the court should adopt this favourable provision.

Lamer C.J. went as far as to add that this should be so even if this led to absurdity or illogicality. *McIntosh* is considered later under Self-defence. For competing views on strict construction see *Scott* (2000), 34 C.R. (5th) 322, 145 C.C.C. (3d) 52 (B.C. C.A.).

The Adversary System

The method of inquiry in our courts is quite distinct from the scientific method; the method of ascertaining the facts at common law is known as adversarial while the scientific might be labelled inquisitorial. The principal distinguishing characteristic between the two methods resides in the relative passivity of the Judge in the adversarial method. The Judge's function is to make the ultimate finding of facts but not to personally investigate; rather, to judge the merits of two positions. The tradition in the English-speaking world is to regard the "over-speaking 'Judge as no well-tuned cymbal' " (Bacon L.C. as quoted by Lord Denning in *Jones v. National Coal Board*, [1957] 2 Q.B. 55 (C.A.) at 64 (Q.B.)) and should a trial Judge intervene too frequently during the trial he or she runs the risk of being reversed on appeal and a new trial ordered. A frank description of our method of inquiry by the Ontario Court of Appeal appears in *Phillips v. Ford Motor Co.* (1971), 18 D.L.R. (3d) 641 at 657 (Ont. C.A.) where Evans J.A. wrote:

> Our mode of trial procedure is based upon the adversarial system in which the contestants seek to establish through relevant supporting evidence, before an impartial trier of facts, those events or happenings which form the bases of their allegations. This procedure assumes that the litigants, assisted by their counsel, will fully and diligently present all the material facts which have evidentiary value in support of their respective positions and that these disputed facts will receive from a trial Judge a dispassionate and impartial consideration in order to arrive at the truth of the matters in controversy. A trial is not intended to be a scientific exploration with the presiding Judge assuming the role of a research director; it is a forum established for the purpose of providing justice for the litigants. Undoubtedly a Court must be concerned with truth, in the sense that it accepts as true certain sworn evidence and rejects other testimony as unworthy of belief, but it cannot embark upon a quest for the "scientific" or "technological" truth when such an adventure does violence to the primary function of the Court, which has always been to do justice, according to law.

The adversary method, however, has been justified over the years by many lawyers as capable of promoting the finest approximation to the truth. As Jerome Frank said:

> They think that the best way for the Court to discover the facts in a suit is to have each side strive as hard as it can, in a keenly partisan spirit, to bring to the Court's attention the evidence favourable to that side. Macauley said that we obtain the fairest decision "when two men argue, as unfairly as possible, on opposite sides" for then "it is certain that no important consideration will altogether escape notice". (*Courts on Trial*, (1949), p. 80.)

The diligence of the parties in ferreting out evidence favourable to their side and the vigour with which they attack their opponent's case are seen as finer guarantees of approximating the historical truth than giving the problem for resolution to some government official whose motivation can rarely be of the magnitude of the parties. Also, it is believed that the bias of the decision-maker can be minimized if played to a much less active role than is demanded in the inquisitorial method. The Judge who conducts the examination of witnesses is seen as "descend[ing] into the arena and is liable to have his vision clouded by the dust of the conflict. Unconsciously he deprives himself of the advantage of calm and dispassionate observation". (Lord Green M.R. in *Yuill v. Yuill*, [1945] 1 All E.R. 183 (C.A.) at 189.)

Whether the adversary method will more closely approximate truth is certainly open to question. The lawyer is trained to seek success for the client, to win the game. The goal is to present the best picture of the client's position and not the most complete picture. Also, the adversary system presupposes for success some equality between the parties and when this is lacking the "truth" becomes too often simply the view of the more powerful. Most Judges will confess to the frequent temptation to reach out and "even the match" but the system cautions against such practice. Perhaps most importantly, while it may be true that in deciding between the validity of two competing theories the decision-maker may be considerably aided by advocates on each side presenting their respective position in the strongest arguments possible, it is certainly questionable whether such a technique is valuable in ensuring that all of the available evidence has been presented by the parties for examination. As Professor Peter Brett has noted:

> observe the practice of scientists and historians in carrying out their investigations. . . . [A] lengthy search will fail to reveal one competent practitioner in either discipline who will willingly and in advance confine himself, in deciding any question involving factual data, to a choice between two sets of existing data proffered to him by rival claimants. In short, the inquisitorial method is the one used by every genuine seeker of the truth in every walk of life (not merely scientific and historical investigations) with only one exception . . . the trial system in the common-law world. (Brett, "Legal Decision-Making Bias: A Critique" (1973), 45 U. Col. L. Rev. 1.)

One large impediment to our search for truth is that the facts to be discovered by our Courts are almost always past facts. Our method of discovering them is normally through the oral testimony of witnesses who have personal knowledge about what happened. This personal "knowledge" might perhaps better be described as personal beliefs about what they now remember of facts which they believe they observed. The trier of fact then has regard to what the witness says and, based on observations of what the witness said and of the manner of saying it, comes to an own opinion as to whether that is an honest belief. One can do no more. One cannot, as the scientist might, duplicate in the laboratory the actual facts and test the hypothesis proposed. Facts as found by the Court are really then only guesses about the actual facts. "Subjectivity piled on subjectivity . . . a trial Court's finding of fact is, then, at best, its belief or opinion about someone else's belief or opinion". (Frank, *Courts on Trial*, p. 22). Recently Mr. Justice Haines of the Ontario Supreme Court described it this way:

> A trial is not a faithful reconstruction of the events as if recorded on some giant television screen. It is an historical recall of that part of the events to which witnesses may be found and presented in an intensely adversary system where the object is quantum of proof. Truth may be only incidental. (*R. v. Lalonde* (1972), 15 C.R.N.S. 1, 5 C.C.C (2d) 168 (H.C.), at 4 (C.R.N.S.) emphasis added.)

Besides searching for a different truth than the scientist our methods are circumscribed by other considerations which require our fact-finding to be done in a way which is acceptable to the parties and to society. Our Courts provide a forum for the purpose of resolving disputes between parties which they themselves have been unable to resolve in any other way. Our modern form of trial began simply as a substitute for private (duels and feuds which had later been dignified by the process of trial by battle. The resolution of the conflict must be done in a way which ensures social tranquillity generally and is also acceptable to the individual parties. The parties should be able to leave the Court feeling that they have had their say, that their case has been presented in the best possible light and that they have been judged by an impartial trier. In judging the efficacy of the legal system's method of fact-finding we must remember that:

> A contested law suit is society's last line of defense in the indispensable effort to secure the peaceful settlement of social conflicts — it is a last-ditch process in which something more is at stake than the truth only of the specific matter in contest. There is at stake also that confidence of the public generally in the impartiality and fairness of public settlement and disputes which is essential if the ditch is to be held and the settlements accepted peaceably. . . . While it is important that the Court be right . . . a decision must be made now, one way or the other;. . . to require certainty . . . would be impracticable and undesirable. The law thus compromises. (Hart and McNaughton, *Evidence and Inference in the Law*, D. Lerner, ed., (1958), p. 57.)

With these thoughts in mind we might better understand, and even accept, some of the rules and procedures at work in a criminal trial. For additional thoughts along this line see Brooks, "The Judge and the Adversary System," *The Canadian Judiciary*, A. Linden, ed., (1976).

It would be quite misleading to view the criminal justice system as always leading to an adversarial contest at trial. A large percentage of accused plead guilty. Estimates as to the number of accused charged with criminal offences who plead guilty range between 70 and 90 percent. A large number of guilty pleas are reached as a result of a plea bargain where there is an agreement by the accused to plead guilty with a view to some consideration, usually relating to charge or sentence. The agreement may be reached quite formally after protracted discussion or it may involve a hurried hallway discussion. Usually the plea bargain is entered into following a discussion between the Crown Attorney and the defence counsel but sometimes, although less frequently in Canada, the judge is involved. Sometimes the reality is that the plea bargain can be traced to a discussion between the accused and the police without any lawyer being involved. See generally Klein, *Let's Make A Deal* (1976), Erikson and Bayanek, *The Ordering Of Justice: A Study of Persons as Dependants in the Criminal Process (1982)* and Warner and Renner, "The Bureaucratic and Adversary Models of the Criminal Courts: The Criminal Sentencing Process", (1981) 1 *Windsor Yearbook of Access to Justice* 81.

In a criminal trial the prosecution has the burden at the outset to lead sufficient evidence to warrant calling on the accused for a defence; since the prosecution alleges certain wrongful activity on the part of the accused it seems logical that the prosecution should follow its allegation with proof. The prosecution satisfies this evidential burden if there is sufficient evidence that the Judge can conclude that a trier of fact properly instructed could rationally conclude guilt, (see Delisle, "Sufficiency of Evidence" (1978), 4 Queen's L.J. 111). Only after the trial Judge has decided this issue in favour of the prosecution will the accused be put to his election of whether he will call evidence. The accused is not obliged to lead evidence and he cannot be compelled to testify; his privilege against self-incrimination guarantees his right to remain silent. Aside from its evidential burden the prosecution has the persuasive burden of establishing all essential ingredients in the case; it should be obvious from the above that we cannot insist that the prosecution prove these matters to an absolute certainty and we are therefore satisfied if he proves them "beyond a reasonable doubt". At times a statutory provision may fix the accused with a persuasive burden and at other times with an evidential burden; these burdens differ in kind and not just degree. A persuasive burden arises for resolution only at the end of the case when the trier of fact is called on to decide whether the proponent of a fact in issue has established its existence. An evidential burden entertained by the accused with respect to a fact in issue requires that there be evidence in the case, led by the prosecution or the defence, which can support a reasonable doubt as to its existence; if there is not such evidence then the trier of fact would be speculating on its existence rather than rationally concluding on the possibility of its existence.

Is the adversary system and the criminal-law precept that the State must prove guilt beyond reasonable doubt compatible with values of women and aboriginal people? In arriving at your opinion consider the following views:

CARRIE MENKEL-MEADOW, PORTIA IN A DIFFERENT VOICE: SPECULATION ON A WOMEN'S LAWYERING PROCESS

(1985), 1 Berkeley Women's L.J. 39, at pp. 44-55

In her book, *In a Different Voice: Psychological Theory and Women's Development*, Gilligan observes that much of what has been written about human psychological development has been based on studies of male subjects exclusively. As a consequence, girls and women have either not been described, or they are said to have "failed" to develop on measurement scales based on male norms. Just as Gilligan has observed that studies of human psychological development have been centred on males, feminists have observed the law to be based on male values and behaviours. As Frances Olsen notes:

> Law is supposed to be rational, objective, abstract and principled, like men; it is not supposed to be irrational, subjective, contextualized or personalized like women. The social, political and intellectual practices that constitute "law" were for many years carried out almost exclusively by men. Given that women were long excluded from the practice of law, it should not be surprising that the traits associated with women are not greatly valued by law. Moreover, in a kind of vicious cycle, the "maleness" of law was used as a justification for excluding women from practicing law. While the number of women in law has been rapidly increasing, the field continues to be heavily male dominated.

The male-derived model of moral reasoning and psychological development described by Gilligan values hierarchical thinking based on the logic of reasoning from abstract, universal principles. Gilligan measures her findings against the work of her colleague, Lawrence Kohlberg. His theory of moral development comprised of six "universal" stages is based on a study of 84 *boys* from childhood through adulthood. Gilligan explains that when Kohlberg's model is applied to women, they tend to score at a stage three, a stage characterized by seeing morality as a question of interpersonal relations and caring for and pleasing others. In looking at moral judgments and hearing the "women's voice," Gilligan discovered that:

> When one begins with the study of women and derives developmental constructs from their lives, the outline of a moral conception different from that described by Freud, Piaget, or Kohlberg begins to emerge and informs a different description of development. In this conception, the moral problem arises from conflicting responsibilities rather than from competing rights and requires for its resolution a mode of thinking that is contextual and narrative rather than formal and abstract.

An example drawn from Gilligan's work best illustrates the duality of girls' and boys' moral development. In one of the three studies on which her book is based, a group of children are asked to solve Heinz's dilemma, a hypothetical moral reasoning problem used by Kohlberg to rate moral development on his six-stage scale. The dilemma is that Heinz's wife is dying of cancer and requires a drug which the local pharmacist has priced beyond's Heinz's means. The question is posed: should Heinz steal the drug?

To illustrate and explain the differences between the ways boys and girls approached this problem, Gilligan quotes from two members of her sample, Jake and Amy. Jake, an 11-year-old boy, sees the problem as one of "balancing rights," like a judge who must make a decision or a mathematician who must solve an algebraic equation. Life is worth more than property, therefore Heinz should steal the drug. For Amy, an 11-year-old girl, the problem is different. Like a "bad" law student she "fights the hypo"; she wants to know more facts: Have Heinz and the druggist explored other possibilities, like a loan or credit transaction? Why couldn't Heinz and the druggist simply sit down and talk it out so that the druggist would come to see the importance of Heinz's wife's life? In Gilligan's terms, Jake explores the Heinz dilemma with "the logic of justice" while Amy uses the "ethic of care." Amy scores lower on the Kohlberg scale because she sees the problem rooted in the persons involved rather than in the larger universal issues posed by the dilemma.

In conventional terms Jake would make a good lawyer because he spots the legal issues of excuse and justification, balances the rights, and reaches a decision, while considering implicitly, if not explicitly, the precedential effect of his decision. But as Gilligan argues, and as I develop more fully below, Amy's approach is also plausible and legitimate, both as a style of moral reasoning and as a style of lawyering. Amy seeks to keep the people engaged; she holds the needs of the parties and their relationships constant and hopes to satisfy them all (as in a negotiation), rather than selecting a winner (as in a lawsuit). If one must be hurt, she attempts to find a resolution that will hurt least the one who can least bear the hurt. (Is she engaged in a "deep pocket" policy analysis?) She looks beyond the "immediate lawsuit" to see how the "judgment" will affect the parties. If Heinz steals the drug and goes to jail, who will take care of his wife? Furthermore, Amy is concerned with *how* the dilemma is resolved; the process by which the parties communicate may be crucial to the outcome. (Amy cares as much about procedure as about substance.) And she is being a good lawyer when she inquires whether all the facts have been discovered and considered.

The point here is not that Amy's method of moral reasoning is better than Jake's, nor that she is a better lawyer than Jake. (Some have read Gilligan to argue that the women's voice is better. I don't read her that way.) The point is that Amy does some things differently from Jake when she resolves this dilemma, and these things have useful analogies to lawyering and may not have been sufficiently credited as useful lawyering skills. Jake and Amy have something to learn from one another.

Thus, although a "choice of rights" conception (life v. property) of solving human problems may be important, it is not the only or the best way. Responsibilities to self and to others may be equally important in measuring moral, as well as legal decision making, but have thus far been largely ignored. For example, a lawyer who feels responsible for the decisions she makes with her client may be more inclined to think about how those decisions will hurt other people and how the lawyer and client feel about making such decisions. (Amy thinks about Heinz, the druggist, and Heinz's wife at all times in reaching her decision; Jake makes a choice in abstract terms without worrying as much about the people it affects.)

. . . .

III. THE ADVOCACY-ADVERSARIAL MODEL

The basic structure of our legal system is premised on the adversarial model, which involves two advocates who present their cases to a disinterested third party who listens to evidence and argument and declares one party a winner. In this simplified description of the Anglo-American model of litigation, we can identify some of the basic concepts and values which underlie this choice of arrangements: advocacy, persuasion, hierarchy, competition, and binary results (win/lose). The conduct of litigation is relatively similar (not coincidentally, I suspect) to a sporting event — there are rules, a referee, an object to the game, and a winner is declared after the play is over. As I have argued elsewhere, this conception of the dispute resolution process is applied more broadly than just in the conventional courtroom. The adversarial model affects the way in which lawyers advise their clients ("get as much as you can"), negotiate disputes ("we can really get them on that") and plan transactions ("let's be sure to draft this to your advantage"). All of these activities in lawyering assume competition over the same limited and equally valued items (usually money) and assume that success is measured by maximizing individual gain. Would Gilligan's Amy create a different model?

By returning to Heniz's dilemma we see some hints about what Amy might do. Instead of concluding that a choice must be made between life and property, in resolving the conflict between parties as Jake does, Amy sees no need to hierarchically order the claims. Instead, she tries to account for all the parties' needs, and searches for a way to find a solution that satisfies the needs of both. In her view, Heinz should be able to obtain the drug for his wife and the pharmacist should still receive payment. So Amy suggests a loan, credit arrangement, or a discussion of other ways to structure the transaction. In short, she won't play by the adversarial rules. She searches outside the system for a way to solve the problem, trying to keep both parties in mind. Her methods substantiate Gilligan's observations that women will try to change the rules to preserve the relationships.

Furthermore, in addition to looking for more substantive solutions to the problem (i.e., not accepting the binary win/lose conception of the problem), Amy also wants to change the process. Amy sees no reason why she must act as a neutral arbiter of a dispute and make a decision based only on the information she has. She "belie[ves] in communication as the mode of conflict resolution and [is convinced] that the solution to the dilemma will follow from its compelling representation. . . ." If the parties talk directly to each other, they will be more likely to appreciate the importance of each other's needs. Thus, she believes direct communication, rather than third party mediated debate, might solve the problem, recognizing that two apparently conflicting positions can both be simultaneously legitimate, and there need not be a single victor.

The notion that women might have more difficulty with full-commitment-to-one-side model of the adversary system is graphically illustrated by Hilary, one of the women lawyers in Gilligan's study. This lawyer finds herself in one of the classic moral dilemmas of the adversary system: she sees that her opponent has failed to make use of a document that is helpful to his case and harmful to hers. In deciding not to tell him about the document because of what she sees as her "professional vunerability" in the male adversary system, she concludes that "the adversary system of justice impedes not only the supposed search for truth (the conventional criticism), but also *the expression of concern for the person on the other side.*" Gilligan describes Hilary's tension between her concept of rights (learned through legal training) and her female ethic of care as a sign of her socialization in the male world of lawyering. Thus, the advocacy model, with its commitment to one-side advocacy, seems somehow contrary to "apprehending the reality of the other" which lawyers like Hilary experience. Even the continental inquisitorial model, frequently offered as an alternative to the adversarial model, includes most of these elements of the male system — hierarchy, advocacy, competition and binary results.

So what kind of legal system would Amy and Hilary create if left to their own devices? They might look for ways to alter the harshness of win/lose results; they might alter the rules of the game (or make it less like a game); and they might alter the very structures and forms themselves. Thus, in a sense Amy and Hilary's approach can already be found in some of the current alternatives to the adversary model such as mediation. Much of the current interest in alternative dispute resolution is an attempt to modify the harshness of the adversarial process and expand the kinds of solutions available, in order to respond the better to the varied needs of the parties. Amy's desire to engage the parties in direct communication with each other is reflected in mediation models where the parties talk directly to each other and forge their own solutions. The work of Gilligan and Noddings, demonstrating an ethic of care and a heightened sense of empathy in women, suggests that women lawyers may be particularly interested in mediation as an alternative to litigation as a method of resolving disputes.

Even within the present adversarial model, Amy and Hilary might, in their concern for others, want to provide for a broader conception of interested parties, permitting participation by those who might be affected by the dispute (an ethic of inclusion). In addition, like judges who increasingly are managing more of the details of their cases, Amy and Hilary might seek a more active role in settlement processes and rely less on Court-ordered relief. Amy and Hilary might look for other ways to construct their lawsuits and remedies in much the same ways as Courts of equity mitigated the harshness of the law Court's very limited array of remedies by expanding the conception of what was possible.

The process and rules of the adversary system itself might look different if there were more female voices in the legal profession. If Amy is less likely than Jake to make assertive, rights-based statements, is she less likely to adapt to the male-created advocacy mode? In my experience as a trial lawyer, I observed that some women had difficulty with the "macho" ethic of the courtroom battle. Even those who did successfully adapt to the male model often confronted a dilemma because women were less likely to be perceived as behaving properly when engaged in strong adversarial conduct. It is important to be "strong" in the courtroom, according to the stereotypic conception of appropriate trial behavior. The woman who conforms to the female stereotype by being "soft" or "weak" is a bad trial lawyer, but if a woman is "tough" or "strong" in the courtroom, she is seen as acting inappropriately for a woman. Note, however, that this stereotyping is contextual: the same woman acting as a "strong" or "tough" mother with difficult children would be praised for that conduct. Women's strength is approved of with the proviso that it be exerted in appropriately female spheres.

Amy and Hilary might create a different form of advocacy, one resembling a "conversation" with the fact finder, relying on the creation of a relationship with the jury for its effectiveness, rather than on persuasive intimidation. There is some anecdotal evidence that this is happening already. Recently, several women prosecutors described their styles of trial advocacy as the creation of a personal relationship with the jury in which they urge jurors to examine their own perceptions and values and encourage them to think for themselves, rather than "buying" the arguments of one of the advocates. This is a conception of the relationship between the lawyer and the fact-finder which is based on trust and mutual respect rather than on dramatics, intimidation and power, the male mode in which these women had been trained and which they found unsatisfactory.

In sum, the growing strength of women's voice in the legal profession may change the adversarial system into a more cooperative, less war-like system of communication between disputants in which solutions are mutually agreed upon rather than dictated by an outsider, won by the victor, and imposed upon the loser. Some seeds of change may already be found in existing alternatives to the litigation model, such as mediation. It remains to be seen what further changes Portia's voice may make.

Compare D.L. Rhode, "The Woman's Point of View" (1988), 38 J. Leg. Ed. 39.

MADAM JUSTICE BERTHA WILSON,* WILL WOMEN JUDGES REALLY MAKE A DIFFERENCE?

(1990), 28 Osgoode Hall L.J. 507

. . . .

In the literature which is required reading for every newly appointed Judge, it is repeatedly stated that Judges must be both independent and impartial, that these qualities are basic to the proper administration of justice and fundamental to the legitimacy of the judicial role. The Judge must not approach his or her task with preconceived notions about law or policy, with personal prejudice against parties or issues, or with bias toward a particular outcome of a case. Socrates defined the essential qualities of a Judge in the following manner: "Four things belong to a Judge: to hear courteously, to answer wisely, to consider soberly, and to decide impartially."

. . . .

Many have criticized as totally unreal the concept that Judges are somehow superhuman, neutral, above politics and unbiased, and are able to completely separate themselves from their personal opinions and predispositions when exercising their judicial function.

. . . .

Judge Rosalie Abella (Chair of the Ontario Law Reform Commission) also doubts that judicial impartiality is a realistic requirement. In her article "The Dynamic Nature of Equality," she emphasizes that "[e]very decisionmaker who walks into a courtroom to hear a case is armed not only with the relevant legal texts, but with a set of values, experiences and assumptions that are thoroughly embedded."

. . . .

But what has all this got to do with the subject: Will women Judges really make a difference?" It has a great deal to do with it, and whether you agree or not will probably depend on your perception of the degree to which the existing

---

* This paper was presented by Madam Justice Wilson at the Fourth Annual Barbara Betcherman Memorial Lecture, Osgoode Hall Law School, 8 February 1990. Copyright, 1990, Madam Justice Bertha Wilson.

law reflects the judicial neutrality or impartiality we have been discussing. If the existing law can be viewed as the product of judicial neutrality or impartiality, even although the judiciary has been very substantially male, then you may conclude that the advent of increased numbers of women Judges should make no difference, assuming, that is, that these women judges will bring to bear the same neutrality and impartiality. However, if you conclude that the existing law, in some areas at least, cannot be viewed as the product of judicial, neutrality then your answer may be very different.

. . . .

Talking from my own experience as a Judge of 14 years' standing, working closely with my male colleagues on the bench, there are probably whole areas of the law on which there is no uniquely feminine perspective. This is not to say that the development of the law in these areas has not been influenced by the fact that lawyers and Judges have all been men. Rather, the principles and the underlying premises are so firmly entrenched and so fundamentally sound that no good would be achieved by attempting to re-invent the wheel, even if the revised version did have a few more spokes in it. I have in mind areas such as the law of contract, the law of real property, and the law applicable to corporations. In some other areas of the law, however, a distinctly male perspective is clearly discernible. It has resulted in legal principles that are not fundamentally sound and that should be revisited when the opportunity presents itself. Canadian feminist scholarship has done an excellent job of identifying those areas and making suggestions for reform. Some aspects of the criminal law in particular cry out for change; they are based on presuppositions about the nature of women and women's sexuality that, in this day and age, are little short of ludicrous.

But how do we handle the problem that women Judges, just as much as their male counterparts, are subject to the duty of impartiality? As was said at the outset, Judges must not approach their task with preconceived notions about law and policy. They must approach it with detachment and, as Lord MacMillan said, purge their minds "not only of partiality to persons, but of partiality to arguments." Does this then foreclose any kind of "judicial affirmative action" to counteract the influence of the dominant male perspective of the past and establish judicial neutrality through a countervailing female perspective? Is Karen Selick, writing recently in the *Lawyers Weekly*, correct when she argues that offsetting male bias with female bias would only be compounding the injustice? Does the nature of the judicial process itself present an insuperable hurdle so that the legislatures rather than the Courts must be looked to for any significant legal change?

In part this may be so. Certainly, the Legislature is the more effective instrument for rapid or radical change. But there is no reason why the judiciary cannot exercise some modest degree of creativity in areas where modern insights and life's experience have indicated that the law has gone awry. However, and this is extremely important, it will be a Pyrrhic victory for women and for the justice system as a whole if changes in the law come only through the efforts of women lawyers and women Judges. The Americans were smart to realize that courses and workshops on gender bias for Judges, male and female, are an essential follow-up to scholarly research and learned writing. In Canada, we are just beginning to touch the fringes.

. . . .

I return, then, to the question of whether the appointment of more women Judges will make a difference. Because the entry of women into the judiciary is so recent, few studies have been done on the subject. Current statistics show that just over 9 percent of federally appointed Judges are women; it is reasonable to assume that more women will be appointed to the Bench as more women become licensed to practise law. Will this growing number of women Judges by itself make a difference?

The expectation is that it will, that the mere presence of women on the bench will make a difference. In her article "The Gender of Judges," Suzanna Sherry (an Associate Law Professor at the University of Minnesota) suggests that the mere fact that women are judges serves an educative function; it helps to shatter stereotypes about the role of women in society that are held by male Judges and lawyers, as well as by litigants, jurors, and witnesses.

Judge Gladys Kessler (former President of the National Association of Women Judges in the United States) defends the search for competent women appointees to the bench. She says: "But the ultimate justification for deliberately seeking Judges of both sexes and all colors and backgrounds is to keep the public's trust. The public must perceive its judges as fair, impartial and representative of the diversity of those who are being judged." Justice Wald has expressed similar sentiments. She believes that women judges are indispensable to the public's confidence in the ability of the courts to respond to the legal problems of all classes of citizens.

. . . .

Some feminist writers are persuaded that the appointment of more women Judges will have an impact on the process of judicial decision-making itself and on the development of the substantive law. As was mentioned earlier, this flows from the belief that women view the world and what goes on in it from a different perspective from men. Some define the difference in perspective solely in terms that women do not accept male perceptions and interpretations of events as the norm or as objective reality. Carol Gilligan (a Professor of Education at Harvard University) sees the difference as going much deeper than that. In her view, women think differently from men, particularly in responding to moral dilemmas. They have, she says, different ways of thinking about themselves and their relationships to others.

. . . .

Gilligan's work on conceptions of morality among adults suggests that women's ethical sense is significantly different from men's. Men see moral problems as arising from competing rights; the adversarial process comes easily to them. Women see moral problems as arising from competing obligations, the one to the other; the important thing is to preserve relationships, to develop an ethic of caring. The goal, according to women's ethical sense, is not seen in terms of winning or losing but, rather, in terms of achieving an optimum outcome for all individuals involved in the moral dilemma. It is not difficult to see how this contrast in thinking might form the basis of different perceptions of justice.

There is merit in Gilligan's analysis. In part, it may explain the traditional reluctance of courts to get too deeply into the circumstances of a case, their anxiety to reduce the context of the dispute to its bare bones through a complex system of exclusionary evidentiary rules. This is one of the characteristic features of the adversarial process. We are all familiar with the witness on cross-examination who wants to explain his or her answer, who feels that a simple yes or no is not an adequate response, and who is frustrated and angry at being cut off with a half-truth. It is so much easier to come up with a black and white answer if you are unencumbered by a broader context which might prompt you, in Lord MacMillan's words, to temper the cold light of reason with the warmer tints of imagination and sympathy.

. . .

Professor Patricia Cain, in her article "Good and Bad Bias: A Comment on Feminist Theory and Judging," says:

> What we want, it seems to me, are lawyers who can tell their clients' story, lawyers who can help Judges to see the parties as human beings, and who can help remove the separation between Judge and litigant. And, then, what we want from our Judges is a special ability to listen with connection before engaging in the separation that accompanies judgment.

Obviously, this is not an easy role for the Judge — to enter into the skin of the litigant and make his or her experience part of your experience and only when you have done that, to judge. But we have to do it; or at least make an earnest attempt to do it. Whether the criticism of the justice system comes to us through Royal Commissions, through the media, or just through our own personal friends, we cannot escape the conclusion that, in some respects, our existing system of justice has been found wanting. And as Mr. Justice Rothman says, the time to do something about it is *now*.

One of the important conclusions emerging from the Council of Europe's Seminar on Equality between Men and Women held in Strasbourg last November is that the universalist doctrine of human rights must include a realistic concept of masculine and feminine humanity regarded as a whole, that human kind *is* dual and must be represented in its dual form if the trap of an asexual abstraction in which *human being* is always declined in the masculine is to be avoided. If women lawyers and women Judges through their differing perspectives on life can bring a new humanity to bear on the decision-making process, perhaps they *will* make a difference. Perhaps they will succeed in infusing the law with an understanding of what it means to be fully human.

ABORIGINAL PEOPLES AND CRIMINAL JUSTICE

Law Reform Commission of Canada, Report No. 34: (1991), 5-7

The Aboriginal Perspective on Criminal Justice

Aboriginal communities number in the several hundreds and each has had a distinctive experience of the Canadian criminal justice system. Given this diversity, there is necessarily some oversimplification in the following general description of Aboriginal perceptions and aspirations. Nevertheless, we have been struck by the remarkably uniform picture of the system that has been drawn by Aboriginal speakers and writers.

I. Aboriginal Perceptions

From the Aboriginal perspective, the criminal justice system is an alien one, imposed by the dominant white society. Wherever they turn or are shuttled throughout the system, Aboriginal offenders, victims or witnesses encounter a sea of white faces. Not surprisingly, they regard the system as deeply insensitive to their traditions and values: many view it as unremittingly racist.

Abuse of power and the distorted exercise of discretion are identified time and again as principal defects of the system. The police are often seen by Aboriginal people as a foreign, military presence descending on communities to wreak havoc and take people away. Far from being a source of stability and security, the force is feared by them even when its services are necessary to restore a modicum of social peace to the community.

For those living in remote and reserve communities, the entire court apparatus, quite literally, appears to descend from the sky — an impression that serves to magnify their feelings of isolation and erects barriers to their attaining an understanding of the system.

The process is in reality incomprehensible to those who speak only Aboriginal languages, especially where little or no effort is made to provide adequate interpretation services. Even the English- or French-speaking inhabitants of these communities find the language of the Courts and lawyers difficult to understand. Understanding is more than a problem of mere language. Aboriginal persons contend that virtually all of the primary actors in the process (police, lawyers, Judges, correctional personnel) patronize them and consistently fail to explain adequately what the process requires of them or what is going to happen to them. Even those who are prepared to acknowledge certain well-intentioned aspects of the present system nevertheless conclude that the system has utterly failed.

Such efforts as have been made to involve the community in the administration of justice are seen as puny and insignificant, and there is little optimism about the future. Elders see the community's young people as the primary victims of the system — cut adrift by it and removed from the community's support as well as from its spiritual and cultural traditions. They recount experiences of children taken from their communities at an early age who later emerge, hardened from the court and correctional processes and ultimately beyond the reach of even imaginative initiatives designed to promote rehabilitation.

Evident and understandable weariness and frustration attend any discussion of approaches to fixing the system or setting it right. For Aboriginal persons, the system presents an unending course of barriers and obstacles, with no avenues of effective complaint or redress. Their sense of injustice is bottomless. They have little or no confidence in the legal profession or in the judiciary to bring about justice or to effect a just resolution of any particular dispute in which they are involved. If the truth be told, most have given up on the criminal justice system.

II. Aboriginal Aspirations

Aboriginal people have a vision of a justice system that is sensitive to their customs, traditions and beliefs. This vision is a natural outgrowth of their aspirations to self-government and sovereignty. They desire a criminal justice system that is Aboriginal-designed, -run and -populated, from top to bottom.

Undoubtedly there are many contrasting visions as to what constitutes an Aboriginal justice system, but fundamental is the belief that the system must be faithful to Aboriginal traditions and cultural values, while adapting them to modern society. Hence, a formal Aboriginal justice system would evince appropriate respect for community Elders and leaders, give heed to the requirements of Aboriginal spirituality and pay homage to the relation of humankind to the land and to nature.

The Aboriginal vision of justice gives pre-eminence to the interests of the collectivity, its overall orientation being holistic and integrative. Thus, it is community-based, stressing mediation and conciliation while seeking an acknowledgment of responsibility from those who transgress the norms of their society. While working toward a reconciliation between the offender and the victim, an Aboriginal justice system would pursue the larger objective of reintegrating the offender into the community as a whole.

The Aboriginal vision challenges both common and civil law concepts. Statute law becomes less important. Within an Aboriginal justice system, laws would not be uniform or homogeneous; they would vary from community to community, depending on customary practices. Customary law would be the binding force promoting harmony within the community.

While possessing common general characteristics, an Aboriginal justice system would of necessity be pluralistic. What such a system would actually look like is unclear. This haziness is a source of frustration. Much essential detail is missing, and Aboriginal people are hesitant to provide that detail, not because they are incapable of providing it — some communities have well-developed and well-articulated models — but because, in their view, they should not have to do so. They aspire to local control. Their contention is essentially: "Give us the keys. Let us control the system. We can hardly do worse than you have."

For accounts of one Judge's struggle to deal with cultural diversity in the Yukon Territory, see H. Lilles, "Some Problems in the Administration of Justice in Remote and Isolated Communities" (1990), 15 Queen's L.J. 327 and "A Plea for More Human Values in Our Justice System" (1992), 17 Queen's L.J. 328. For an attempt in the Yukon to further involve the community in the sentencing process, see *Moses*, later under Sentencing, concerning "Circle Sentencing".

RUPERT ROSS, DANCING WITH A GHOST
Exploring Indian Reality
(Octopus Publishing, 1992), 41-46

[Rupert Ross is an assistant Crown Attorney for the District of Kenora, Ontario, where he works closely with the Ojibway and Cree peoples to make the Court system more responsive to the needs of their communities.]

. . . .

Gradually, though, I began to see and hear things which made me suspect that there might exist a whole range of different explanations where Native people are concerned. One young victim of a rape refused to testify because, as she put it, "It's not right to do this after so much time. He should be finished with it now and getting on with his life." She was 16 years old.

Another woman, the victim of a violent assault by her dangerous nephew, went over her evidence with me in great detail just before Court. She insisted (uncharacteristically, I should add) that I do whatever I could to send this uncontrollably violent young man out of the community for as long as possible so that she and her children could live in peace. When she took the witness stand minutes later, however, her refusal to say anything at all about the attack led to his acquittal.

In another case, after a lengthy review of her evidence, the victim, a 15-year-old who had been sexually assaulted by her former boyfriend, told me she thought she could repeat her story in Court. As we walked into the courtroom, though, she tugged at my sleeve and asked, "Should I say these things in court? Is it right?"

"Is it right?" That was a dumbfounding question for me. I knew of many significant reasons which made it difficult for people to testify, but it had never occurred to me that in their eyes it might not be the *right* thing to do. I had always assumed that even the most frightened and reluctant witness shared my conviction that testifying was what they should do, even if competing concerns made it impossible for them to go through with it.

What, I asked myself, if we are wrong in that assumption when we deal with Native people? Could they actually believe that coming forward in this fashion was an improper thing to do? If that was the case, then factors such as fear or embarrassment only reinforced the basic disinclination.

It was not until 1986, at a conference in Whitehorse dealing with Native justice issues, that I began to see a little further into the dynamics of such reluctance. It was commonly agreed by the conference participants that Native people, with their belief in consensus decision-making, might find our adversarial system foreign and inappropriate. To explore alternate forms of dealing with social disruption we play-acted a more informal mediation process. In this exercise we devised a scenario in which a youth had broken into the community store and vandalized it. We selected some volunteers from the audience to act as the boy, the store manager and the mediation panel. That panel then asked them both about the break-in, the value of the damage, about how they felt towards each other, and about what could be done to set matters straight between them. It seemed a sensible alternative approach.

One of the mediators, however, was Charlie Fisher, whom I mentioned in Chapter 1. He was asked if such a technique bore any resemblance to what might have been done at Whitedog in more traditional times. His response was a very vehement "no". He then volunteered to make the appropriate changes.

He began by getting rid of the chairs and tables, everyone sat on the floor in a circle, as equals. He then asked for two other people to act as "Representing Elders", one each for the boy and the store manager. As he continued, it became clear that our little experiment in non-adversarial mediation was flawed in virtually every respect. In Charlie's version, the boy and the store manager never spoke in the presence of the panel of Elders. There was no discussion whatever about the break-in, the damage, the feelings of the disputants, or what might be done to set matters straight. There was no *talk* of compensation or restitution, much less the actual imposition of such measures.

Once we understood what was *not* going to take place, we had only one question left: "Why, then, is there a panel at all?"

Charlie Fisher tried to answer us in this way. The duty of each Representing Elder, he explained, was not to speak for the young man or the store manager, but to counsel them in private. That counselling was intended to help each person "rid himself of his bad feelings". Such counselling would continue until the Elder was satisfied that "the person's spirit had been cleansed and made whole again". When the panel convened, an Elder could signify that such cleansing had taken place by touching the ceremonial pipe. The panel would continue to meet until both Elders so signified. At that point, the pipe would be lit and passed to all. As far as the community was concerned, that would be the end of the matter. Whether the two disputants later arranged recompense of some sort was entirely up to them. Passing the pipe signified, as Charlie phrased it, that each had been "restored to the community and to himself".

What was going on here? No fact finding? No allocation of responsibility? No imposition of consequences? Weren't these the very things our courts were created to do? Why didn't the Whitedog people do them in traditional times?

. . . .

I suggest that we must react differently than we have in the past when we find ourselves puzzled by something a Native person has done or, more importantly, when we are about to come to a negative conclusion about it. Rather than assuming that their behaviour stems from principles similar to ours, and then judging that behaviour badly because it does not conform to our own typical behaviour, we must realize that their behaviour is different because it flows from different basic principles. We are not seeing, despite what we *seem* to be seeing, a people who don't care if their friends make dangerous mistakes or if their loved ones fall into self-destructive habits, who don't care about the peace, health and security of their communities. We are instead seeing people whose traditional commandments require that they demonstrate their care in two ways which are fundamentally different from our ways: by conferring virtually absolute freedom on everyone and, when damaging events do occur, by doing whatever is possible to put those events behind them, to let bygones be bygones and to restore essential harmony.

Until we realize that Native people have a highly developed, formal, but radically different set of cultural imperatives, we are likely to continue misinterpreting their acts, misperceiving the real problems they face and imposing, through government policies, potentially harmful "remedies".

We also need to realize that these ethics and attitudes are not necessarily seen as "rules" by Native people themselves, just as we are often unaware that vigorous introspection is an acquired cultural trait with us. These sorts of habits represent, to each group respectively, the way they assume all people are naturally. We are seldom conscious of the fact that at some time we *learned* them, and that we could just as easily have learned different approaches instead.

. . . .

It is also clear that at this stage in history Native people are declaring that they have had enough. After putting up politely with our all-encompassing interference for so long, they are asking us to leave them alone, for in many spheres they have seen only negative results.

The Court system is one clear example. The function of traditional Native dispute-resolution systems was the real resolution of disputes. They hoped that at the end of their process the parties would be returned to cooperative co-existence, to real interpersonal harmony. Naturally, they expected that our Courts would have the same goal. Little did they know that we do not even pretend to that goal. Our society is a society of strangers. Our judicial processes do not aim at restoring friendship or harmony, if only because between strangers these qualities do not exist in the first place. Instead, we aim at deterring harmful *activity* so that each stranger can continue to follow his private path without interference.

It is little wonder that one Chief recently complained that the court doesn't do what it should do. As he put it, "your Court only comes in here to take money in fines and to take our people out to jail, leaving us with the problem." That problem, needless to say, was the unresolved original dispute between people, or the uncorrected dysfunction within an individual accused. Until recently, Native people have been willing to endure many of the traditionally unethical requirements of our legal system in the belief that we too aimed at restoring interpersonal harmony and individual mental health. That belief was mistaken, for our Courts focus primarily on the preservation of public peace. They are concerned not with what people are, but with what they do. The Native approach essentially ignores what was done and concentrates instead upon the personal or interpersonal dysfunctions which caused the problem in the first place. Their first priority lies in trying to correct those dysfunctions rather than in trying to keep those continuing dysfunctions from erupting into further harmful or illegal acts.

It is now the judgment of many bands that our system is inappropriate both in its processes and in its goals. If we are not even going to attempt to do what they believe should be done, they don't want us, for our processes themselves are harmful, involving as they do confrontation and the perpetuation of disruptive issues.

Victims' Rights

It is clear that victims have in the past been ignored and sometimes denigrated by the criminal justice system. Abuses have included unwarranted humiliation on cross-examination, especially in sexual assault trials, the trauma of endless Court appearances and delays often without proper explanation, and no consideration in sentencing of the impact of the offence on the victim. Clearly victims have a right to be treated with respect. Legislative changes to better protect interests of victims have included rape shield laws, greater restitution provisions, fine surcharge programs to support victim services, and provisions for bans on publicity of the identity of victims, written victim impact statements on sentencing and victim input into parole decisions.

Although there are often now calls to recognize new legal and constitutional rights for victims and complaints that accused have too many rights, there is room for considerable caution and concern. A criminal trial is about determining guilt and just punishment of an accused, not about personal redress for victims. What, for example, if the input of victims were to be determinative on the issue of sentence? Would it be just to have the length of a prison sentence determined by whether the victim wants revenge or compassion? Wouldn't a general right of representation of victims at trial, even on the determination of guilt, hopelessly burden and confuse an already overtaxed and under-resourced criminal justice system?

Constitutional rights for those alleging crimes were directly recognized by the Supreme Court for the first time in its controversial decision in *R. v. O'Connor* (1996) 44 C.R. (4th) 1 (S.C.C.). The Court adopted a special balancing procedure respecting discovery of medical records in the possession of third parties. L'Heureux-Dubé, J., with La Forest, Gonthier and McLachlin JJ. concurring, saw the need to balance the accused's right to a fair trial and full answer and defence with the complainant's rights to privacy and to equality without discrimination. The majority, through a joint judgment by Lamer C.J. and Sopinka J., with Cory, Iacobucci and Major JJ. concurring, determined that the accused's right to full answer and defence should be balanced against the complainant's rights to privacy under ss. 7 and 8. However the majority, in not referring to a section 15 equality right for complainants, although it was fully argued, implicitly reject it.

The question of whether the Court should recognize equality rights for those alleging crimes is posed in Chapter 4 in the context of sexual assault.

For full discussion of issues of criminal trials and victims' rights, see Paciocco, *Getting Away With Murder*, (1999) pp. 351-382.

What Is Evidence?

The Crown, we have seen, has the obligation of proving the allegations. How do we prove things? By evidence. What is evidence? Evidence may take the form of oral testimony, I saw the accused stab the victim, or real evidence, clothes belonging to the accused with bloodstains matching the victim's bloodtype. Whatever the form of the evidence it must be relevant. To understand the meaning of relevance and the reason for its necessity we should first trace briefly the developments of our fact-finding process.

The methods employed by the Anglo-Saxons at the time of the Conquest involved the invocation of the Deity. One method was known as compurgation or wager of law. The litigants would assemble specified numbers of oath-takers who would swear to their belief in the correctness of "their" litigant's claim or defence or to his trustworthiness; these oath-takers would have no personal knowledge of the facts of the case. The supernatural sanction for a false oath was seen as assuring the correctness of the decision. Another method of fact-finding was known as trial by ordeal. The litigant would grasp a hot iron and God would directly indicate the litigant's righteousness by producing a clean, healed wound after three days. The accused would be bound and thrown into a body of water; if the water accepted him and he sank he was innocent. Trial by ordeal ended in the early 13th century when the Pope forbade participation by the clergy. The early Anglo-Norman technique of fact-finding, trial by combat, was based on the belief that God would assist the innocent and the honest.

By the late 13th century the Norman Inquest had largely supplanted the earlier modes of fact-finding. The Inquest was revolutionary in its emphasis on a *rational* inquiry and consisted of sworn investigators, or jurors, who undertook to discover the facts and relate the same to the Judge who would pass judgment thereon. Gradually these jurors came to rely on sworn witnesses to the facts in question and by the 17th century the functions of jurors and witnesses were formally separated.

The fact-finding process has developed into a system of inquiry which is *considered* to be rational. There must therefore be a rational connection between the evidence tendered and the proposition sought to be established. This connection is labelled relevance.

When evidence about a material proposition is led, the proponent seeks to persuade the trier to draw the inference from the fact led to the proposition. If there is a rational connection between them, if the fact will, according to reason and experience, support the inference, the fact will be adjudged relevant and received. The facts tendered in evidence are normally classified as either testimonial or circumstantial, but in each case inferences are necessary and problems of relevancy therefore occur. With testimonial evidence, sometimes called direct evidence, the trier is asked to infer from the fact that the witness made a statement to the truth of the matter stated. If the witness is seen to be sincere and possessed of an ability to observe and accurately recall, and it is clear that he had the opportunity to see the matter in issue, there will be reason to draw the inference and his testimony will be credited. Though a true problem of relevance exists, it is more common, however, to examine and discuss the probative worth of such evidence under the heads of Testimonial Qualifications and Credibility. Commonly we reserve the concept of relevancy for discussions involving circumstantial evidence. In cases of circumstantial evidence certain facts connected with the material fact are proved and the trier is asked to infer from these facts that the material fact exists. If reason and experience support the connection the evidence led is relevant.

If a witness is willing to testify that she saw the accused shoot the deceased, this is direct evidence of that fact. The trial Judge will first ensure the witness's competence to speak, then the evidence may be evaluated according to the trier of fact's assessment of the witness's credibility. If a witness is willing to testify that she heard the deceased scream and moments later saw the accused standing over the body holding a smoking gun this is circumstantial evidence of the accused shooting the deceased. The trial Judge will assess the relevance of the evidence led; if received the trier of fact will then assess its sufficiency.

Having said that evidence must be relevant it is important to emphasize the requirement of materiality. The concept of materiality demands a rational connection between the tendered evidence and a fact in issue. The trial of an action or a criminal allegation is not designed to review all that has occurred between the parties or all of the accused's past delinquencies, but rather a particular section of that history. A particular slice of life is to be examined and that slice is dictated by the substantive law and the pleadings of the parties. In the criminal area the "pleadings" of the parties are confined to the information and particulars ordered by the Court; sometimes the issues are narrowed by formal admissions made by the accused.

For evidence to be received it must then be relevant to a material issue. We have seen that relevancy and materiality are not dictated by the laws of evidence. The laws of evidence are concerned with canons of exclusion which render inadmissible evidence which is both relevant and material. For a variety of policies the law of evidence excludes material which might aid in the search for truth. Some of these rules are due to a concern regarding the ability of the trier of fact to adequately assess the evidence, some out of concern for values inherent in the adversary system, and some to protect certain relationships in society as we recognize the competition with values other than truth. Evidence, then, is information which clears all three hurdles and is therefore receivable.

Presumption of Innocence

The cornerstone precepts of the presumption of innocence and that the Crown must normally prove to a standard of proof beyond a reasonable doubt were asserted by the House of Lords relatively recently.

WOOLMINGTON v. D.P.P.

[1935] A.C. 462 (H.L.)

May 23. VISCOUNT SANKEY L.C.: — My Lords, the appellant, Reginald Woolmington, after a trial at the Somerset Assizes at Taunton on January 23, at which, after an absence of one hour and twenty-five minutes, the jury disagreed, was convicted at the Bristol Assizes on February 14 of the wilful murder of his wife on December 10, 1934, and was sentenced to death.

. . . .

The facts are as follows. Reginald Woolmington is 21-1/2 years old. His wife, who was killed, was 17-1/2 years old last December. They had known each other for some time and upon August 25 they were married. Upon October 14 she gave birth to a child. Shortly after that there appears to have been some quarrelling between them and she left him upon November 22 and went to live with her mother. Woolmington apparently was anxious to get her to come back, but she did not come. The prosecution proved that at about 9.15 in the morning of the 10th Mrs. Daisy Brine was hanging out her washing at the back of her house at 25 Newtown, Milborne Port. While she was engaged in that occupation, she heard voices from the next door house, No. 24. She knew that in that house her niece, Reginald Woolmington's wife, was living. She heard and could recognize the voice of Reginald Woolmington saying something to the effect "are you going to come back home?" She could not hear the answer. Then the back door in No. 24 was slammed. She heard a voice in the kitchen but could not tell what it said. Then she heard the sound of a gun. Upon that she looked out of the front window and she saw Reginald Woolmington, whose voice she had heard just before speaking in the kitchen, go out and get upon his bicycle, which had been left or was standing against the wall of her house, No. 25. She called out to him but he gave no reply. He looked at her hard and then he rode away.

According to Reginald Woolmington's own story, having brooded over and deliberated upon the position all through the night of December 9, he went on the morning of the 10th in the usual way to the milking at his employer's farm, and while milking conceived this idea that he would take the old gun which was in the barn and he would take it up that morning to his wife's mother's house where she was living, and that he would show her that gun and tell her that he was going to commit suicide if she did not come back. He would take the gun up for the purpose of frightening her into coming back to him by causing her to think that he was going to commit suicide. He finished his milking, went back to his father's house, had breakfast and then left, taking with him a hack saw. He returned to the farm, went into the barn, got the gun, which had been used for rook shooting, sawed off the barrels of it, then took the only two cartridges which were there and put them into the gun. He took the two pieces of the barrel which he had sawn off and the hack saw, crossed a field about 60 yards wide and dropped them into the brook. Having done that, he returned on his bicycle, with the gun in his overcoat pocket, to his father's house and changed his clothes. Then he got a piece of wire flex which he attached to the gun so that he could suspend it from his shoulder underneath his coat, and so went off to the house where his wife was living. He knocked at the door, went into the kitchen and asked her: "Are you coming back?" She made no answer. She came into the parlour, and on his asking her whether she would come back she replied she was going into service. He then, so he says, threatened he would shoot himself, and went on to show her the gun and brought it across his waist, when it somehow went off and his wife fell down and he went out of the house. He told the jury that it was an accident, that it was a pure accident; that whilst he was getting the gun from under his shoulder and was drawing it across his breast it accidentally went off and he was doing nothing unlawful, nothing wrong, and this was a pure accident. There was considerable controversy as to whether a letter in which he set out his grievances was written before or after the above events. But when he was arrested at 7.30 on the evening of the 10th and charged with having committed murder he said: "I want to say nothing, except I done it, and they can do what they like with me. It was jealousy I suppose. Her mother enticed her away from me. I done all I could to get her back. That's all."

The learned Judge in summing-up the case to the jury said:—

> If you accept his evidence, you will have little doubt that she died in consequence of a gunshot wound which was inflicted by a gun which he had taken to this house, and which was in his hands, or in his possession, at the time that it exploded. If you come to the conclusion that she died in consequence of injuries from the gun which he was carrying, you are put by the law of this country into this position: The killing of a human being is homicide, however he may be killed, and all homicide is presumed to be malicious and murder, unless the contrary appears from circumstances of alleviation, excuse, or justification. "In every charge of murder, the fact of killing being first proved, all the circumstances of accident, necessity, or infirmity are to be satisfactorily proved by the prisoner, unless they arise out of the evidence produced against him: for the law will presume the fact to have been founded in malice until the contrary appeareth." That has been the law of this country for all time since we had law. Once it is shown to a jury that somebody has died through the act of another, that is presumed to be murder, unless the person who has been guilty of the act which causes the death can satisfy a jury that what happened was something less, something which might be alleviated, something which might be reduced to a charge of manslaughter, or was something which was accidental, or was something which could be justified.

At the end of his summing-up he added:

> The Crown has got to satisfy you that this woman, Violet Woolmington, died at the prisoner's hands. They must satisfy you of that beyond any reasonable doubt. If they satisfy you of that, then he has to show that there are circumstances to be found in the evidence which

has been given from the witness-box in this case which alleviate the crime so that it is only manslaughter or which excuse the homicide altogether by showing that it was a pure accident.

In the argument before the Court of Criminal Appeal cases were cited by the learned counsel on either side and textbooks of authority were referrcd to, but the learned Judges contented themselves with saying "there can be no question to start with that the learned Judge laid down the law applicable to a case of murder in the way in which it is to be found in the old authorities." They repeated the learned Judge's words and said: "No doubt there is ample authority for that statement of the law." They then relied, as I have already mentioned, upon the proviso to s. 4 of the *Criminal Appeal Act, 1907*, and dismissed the appeal.

It is true as stated by the Court of Appeal that there is apparent authority for the law as laid down by the learned Judge. But your Lordships' House has had the advantage of a prolonged and exhaustive inquiry dealing with the matter in debate from the earliest times, an advantage which was not shared by either of the Courts below. Indeed your Lordships were referred to legal propositions dating as far back as the reign of King Canute (994-1035). But I do not think it is necessary for the purpose of this opinion to go as far back as that. Rather would I invite your Lordships to begin by considering the proposition of law which is contained in Foster's Crown Law, written in 1762, and which appears to be the foundation for the law as laid down by the learned judge in this case. It must be remembered that Sir Michael Foster, although a distinguished Judge, is for this purpose to be regarded as a textbook writer, for he did not lay down the doctrine in any case before him, but in an article which is described as the "Introduction to the Discourse of Homicide." In the folio edition, published at Oxford at the Clarendon Press in 1762, at p. 255, he states:

> In every charge of murder, the fact of killing being first proved, all the circumstances of accident, necessity, or infirmity, are to be satisfactorily proved by the prisoner, unless they arise out of the evidence produced against him; for the law presumeth the fact to have been founded in malice, until the contrary appeareth. And very right it is, that the law should so presume. The defendant in this instance standeth upon just the same foot that every other defendant doth: the matters tending, to justify, excuse, or alleviate, must appear in evidence before he can avail himself of them.

Now the first part of this passage appears in nearly every textbook or abridgment which has been since written. To come down to modern times, the passage appears in Stephen's Digest of the Criminal Law; also in the well-known treatise of Archbold, Criminal Pleading, Evidence and Practice, which is the companion of lawyers who practise in the criminal Courts. It also appears most textually in Russell on Crimes and in the second edition of Halsbury's Laws of England, which purports to state the law as on May 1, 1933, where it is said:

> When it has been proved that one person's death has been caused by another, there is a *prima facie* presumption of law that the act of the person causing the death is murder, unless the contrary appears from the evidence either for the prosecution or for the defence. The onus is upon such person when accused to show that his act did not amount to murder.

The authority for that proposition is given as Foster, pp. 255, 290, and also the case of *Rex v. Greenacre*.

The question arises, Is that statement correct law? Is it correct to say, and does Sir Michael Foster mean to lay down, that there may arise in the course of a criminal trial a situation at which it is incumbent upon the accused to prove his innocence? To begin with, if that is what Sir Michael Foster meant, there is no previous authority for his proposition, and I am confirmed in this opinion by the fact that in all the textbooks no earlier authority is cited for it. Before, however, one considers the earlier criminal law several facts have to be remembered.

First, it was not till 1907 that the Court of Criminal Appeal was set up. It is perfectly true that from time to time there have been famous occasions on which the Judges and Barons were called together to give their opinion upon the law bearing on murder. Examples of this will be found; in the year 1611, in the case of *Mackalley*, all the Judges and Barons were moved to give their opinion; in 1706, in the case of *Reg. v. Mawgridge*, which case was argued before all the Judges and all of them except Lord Chief Justice Trevor were of opinion that Mawgridge was guilty of murder; and in 1843 in the case of *Reg. v. M'Naghten*, where all the Judges gave answers to your Lordships' House upon the test of insanity.

M'Naghten's case stands by itself. It is the famous pronouncement on the law bearing on the question of insanity in cases of murder. It is quite exceptional and has nothing to do with the present circumstances. In *M'Naghten's* case the onus is definitely and exceptionally placed upon the accused to establish such a defence. See *Rex v. Oliver Smith*, where it is stated that the only general rule that can be laid down as to the evidence in such a case is that insanity, if relied upon as a defence, must be established by the defendant. But it was added that all the Judges had met and resolved that it was not proper for the Crown to call evidence of insanity, but that any evidence in the possession of the Crown should be placed at the disposal of the prisoner's counsel to be used by him if he thought fit. See also Archbold, 29th Edition. It is not necessary to refer to *M'Naghten's* case again in this judgment, for it has nothing to do with it.

It is true that at a later period certain cases were reserved by the Judges for the consideration of the Court of Crown Cases Reserved, but many of the propositions with regard to criminal law are contained either in the summing-up of the Judges or in text-books of authority as distinguished from a Court sitting in banc.

The learned author of Stephen's Digest of the Criminal Law has an interesting note on the definition of murder and manslaughter. But his remarks are rather directed to the ingredients of the crime than to the proof of it. None the less, the author does not hesitate to tread a path of very robust criticism of the previous authorities. He speaks of the "intricacy, confusion and uncertainty of this branch of the law." He refers to the definition of Coke (1552-1623) and says "these passages, overloaded as Coke's manner is, with a quantity of loose, rambling gossip, form the essence of his account of murder." He describes Coke's chapter on manslaughter as "bewildering" and adds that Hale (1609-1676) treats manslaughter in a manner so meagre and yet so confused that no opinion of it can be obtained except by reading through chapters 38 to 40 and trying to make sense of them, and concludes by saying (p. 466) that Sir Michael Foster "to some extent mitigates the barbarous rule laid down by Coke as to unintentional personal violence."

Next it must be remembered that prisoners were not entitled to be represented by counsel, except in cases of felony, where counsel might argue the law on their behalf.

Thirdly, it must not be forgotten that the prisoner himself was not allowed to give evidence before the Act passed in 1898.

Bearing these considerations in mind, I now turn to some of the cases cited to us.

. . . .

The case of *Rex v. Greenacre* was certainly heard by a very distinguished Judge, Tindal, C.J. But it is to be observed that the dictum relied upon by the prosecution in this case — namely:

> that where it appears that one person's death has been occasioned by the hand of another, it behoves that other to show from evidence, or by inference from the circumstances of the case, that the offence is of a mitigated character, and does not amount to the crime of murder,

was contained in the summing-up of the learned Judge to the jury. It is the passage in Sir Michael Foster and this summing-up which are usually relied on as the authority for the proposition that at some particular time of a criminal case the burden of proof lies on the prisoner to prove his innocence. The presumption of innocence in a criminal case is strong: see Taylor On Evidence, and it is doubtful whether either of these passages means any such thing. Rather do I think they simply refer to stages in the trial of a case. All that is meant is that if it is proved that the conscious act of the prisoner killed a man and nothing else appears in the case, there is evidence upon which the jury may, not must, find him guilty of murder. It is difficult to conceive so bare and meagre a case, but that does not mean that the onus is not still on the prosecution.

If at any period of a trial it was permissible for the Judge to rule that the prosecution had established its case and that the onus was shifted on the prisoner to prove that he was not guilty, and that unless he discharged that onus the prosecution was entitled to succeed, it would be enabling the Judge in such a case to say that the jury must in law find the prisoner guilty and so make the Judge decide the case and not the jury, which is not the common law. It would be an entirely different case from those exceptional instances of special verdicts where a Judge asks the jury to find certain facts and directs them that on such facts the prosecution is entitled to succeed. Indeed, a consideration of such special verdicts shows that it is not till the end of the evidence that a verdict can properly be found and that at the end of the evidence it is not for the prisoner to establish his innocence, but for the prosecution to establish his guilt. Just as there is evidence on behalf of the prosecution so there may be evidence on behalf of the prisoner which may cause a doubt as to his guilt. In either case, he is entitled to the benefit of the doubt. But while the prosecution must prove the guilt of the prisoner, there is no such burden laid on the prisoner to prove his innocence and it is sufficient for him to raise a doubt as to his guilt; he is not bound to satisfy the jury of his innocence.

This is the real result of the perplexing case of *Rex v. Abramovitch*, which lays down the same proposition, although perhaps in somewhat involved language. Juries are always told that, if conviction there is to be, the prosecution must prove the case beyond reasonable doubt. This statement cannot mean that in order to be acquitted the prisoner must "satisfy" the jury. This is the law as laid down in the Court of Criminal Appeal in *Rex v. Davies*, the headnote of which correctly states that where intent is an ingredient of a crime there is no onus on the defendant to prove that the act alleged was accidental. Throughout the web of the English Criminal Law one golden thread is always to be seen, that it is the duty of the prosecution to prove the prisoner's guilt subject to what I have already said as to the defence of insanity and subject also to any statutory exception. If, at the end of and on the whole of the case, there is a reasonable doubt, created by the evidence given by either the prosecution or the prisoner, as to whether the prisoner killed the deceased with a malicious intention, the prosecution has not made out the case and the prisoner is entitled to an acquittal. No matter what the charge or where the trial, the principle that the prosecution must prove the guilt of the prisoner is part of the common law of England and no attempt to whittle it down can be entertained. When dealing with a murder case the Crown must prove (*a*) death as the result of a voluntary act of the accused and (*b*) malice of the accused. It may prove malice either expressly or by implication. For malice may be implied where death occurs as the result of a voluntary act of the accused which is (i.) intentional and (ii.) unprovoked. When evidence of death and malice has been given (this is a question for the jury) the accused is entitled to show, by evidence or by examination of the circumstances adduced by the Crown that the act on his part which caused death was either unintentional or provoked. If the jury are either satisfied with his explanation or, upon a review of all the evidence, are left in reasonable doubt whether, even if his explanation be not accepted, the act was unintentional or provoked, the prisoner is entitled to be acquitted. It is not the law of England to say, as was said in the summing-up in the present case:

> if the Crown satisfy you that this woman died at the prisoner's hands then he has to show that there are circumstances to be found in the evidence which has been given from the witness-box in this case which alleviate the crime so that it is only manslaughter or which excuse the homicide altogether by showing it was a pure accident.

If the proposition laid down by Sir Michael Foster or in the summing-up in *Rex v. Greenacre* means this, those authorities are wrong.

We were then asked to follow the Court of Criminal Appeal and to apply the proviso of s. 4 of the *Criminal Appeal Act, 1907*, which says:

> the Court may, notwithstanding that they are of opinion that the point raised in the appeal might be decided in favour of the appellant, dismiss the appeal if they consider that no substantial miscarriage of justice has actually occurred.

There is no doubt that there is ample jurisdiction to apply that proviso in a case of murder. The Act makes no distinction between a capital case and any other case, but we think it impossible to apply it in the present case. We cannot say that if the jury had been properly directed they would have inevitably come to the same conclusion.

In the result we decline to apply the proviso and, as already stated, we order that the appeal should be allowed and the conviction quashed.

While the prosecution must satisfy the trier of all ingredients of the offence, and thus negative all possible defences, a defence is not properly in the case unless there is evidence capable of supporting it.

R. v. OSOLIN

[1993] 4 S.C.R. 595

The accused was charged with sexual assault. At the trial, the accused testified that the complainant was an eager although not active participant in all the acts leading up to and including sexual intercourse. The trial judge declined to charge the jury with respect to the defence of honest but mistaken belief in consent. He ruled that in this case there was no "air of reality" to the defence. The accused was found guilty.

CORY J.: —

. . . .

The second position put forward by the appellant is that s. 265(4) violates the rights of an accused under ss. 11(d) (the presumption of innocence) and 11(f) (the right to trial by jury). Section 265(4) of the *Criminal Code* is applicable to all assaults, not just sexual assaults. It appears to be no more than the codification of the common law defence of mistake of fact. In my view the section simply sets out the basic requirements which are applicable to all defences. Namely, that a defence should not be put to the jury if a reasonable jury properly instructed would have been unable to acquit on the basis of the evidence tendered in support of that defence. On the other hand, if a reasonable jury properly instructed could acquit on the basis of the evidence tendered with regard to that defence, then it must be put to the jury. It is for the trial judge to decide whether the evidence is sufficient to warrant putting a defence to a jury as this is a question of law alone. There is thus a two step procedure which must be followed. First, the trial judge must review all the evidence and decide if it is sufficient to warrant putting the defence to the jury. Second, if the evidence meets that threshold, the trial judge must put the defence to the jury, which in turn will weigh it and decide whether it raises a reasonable doubt. I take this to be the meaning of the words "sufficient evidence" as they appear in s. 265(4).

It is trite law that a trial judge must instruct the jury only upon those defences for which there is a real factual basis. A defence for which there is no evidentiary foundation should not be put to the jury. This rule extends well beyond the defence of mistaken belief in consent and is of long standing. . . . . The question is not whether there is some evidence, but rather, whether there is some evidence capable of supporting the particular defence alleged by the accused. . . . . It can be seen that this Court has consistently held that the defence of mistake of fact in a sexual assault trial will be put to the jury so long as it meets the same threshold requirement as that demanded of all defences. The term "air of reality" simply means that the trial judge must determine if the evidence put forward is such that, if believed, a reasonable jury properly charged could have acquitted. If the evidence meets that test then the defence must be put to the jury. This is no more than an example of the basic division of tasks between judge and jury. It is the judge who must determine if evidence sought to be adduced is relevant and admissible. In the same way, it is the judge who determines if there is sufficient evidence adduced to give rise to the defence. If there has been sufficient evidence put forward, then the jury must be given the opportunity to consider that defence along with all the other evidence and other defences left with them in coming to their verdict.

Why do we presume innocence in criminal law?

C.K. ALLEN, LEGAL DUTIES AND OTHER ESSAYS IN JURISPRUDENCE

(1931), 286-288

Again, 'it is better that ten guilty persons should be acquitted than that one innocent person should be convicted'. As Stephen dryly observes, it all depends on what the guilty persons have been doing. It also depends on the general social conditions in which they have been doing it. I have already called attention to the vague fluctuations in the proverbial ratio between the guilty and the innocent; and I have done so in no spirit of levity, for the ratio which it assumes is not without significance. I dare say some sentimentalists would assent to the proposition that it is better that a thousand, or even a million, guilty persons should escape than that one innocent person should suffer; but no sensible and practical person would accept such a view. For it is obvious that if our ratio is extended indefinitely, there comes a point when the whole system of justice has broken down and society is in a state of chaos. In short, it is only when there is a reasonable and uniform probability of guilty persons being detected and convicted that we can allow humane doubt to prevail over security. But we must never forget that ideally the acquittal of ten guilty persons is exactly ten times as great a failure of *justice* as the conviction of one innocent person.

Again, 'in a civil case a preponderance of probabilities is sufficient, but in a criminal case the prisoner's guilt must be proved beyond all reasonable doubt.

This statement is constantly repeated in the textbooks, but very little authority is cited for it, and it is difficult to know what real meaning is to be attached to it. Certainly it cannot mean that there is any substantive difference (except perhaps in certain offences where corroboration is required) between the methods of proof in civil and criminal cases, for it is laid down again and again that this is not the law. Is there any true difference between a preponderance of probabilities and a reasonable certainty (the converse of *reasonable* doubt)? 'Probability' may mean different things. It is often loosely used to indicate mere conjecture or plausibility. Neither in civil nor in criminal cases is a jury entitled to consider an averment established by conjecture or plausibility. But 'probability' may also mean the utmost degree of certainty or conviction which, upon the evidence of circumstances, things and statements, can be attained by our limited powers of reasoning and observation. That degree of certainty or conviction exists, or ought to exist, in the decision of any legal issue. It is difficult to see how men and women, called upon to weigh evidence either in civil or criminal matters, can bring to bear anything more than Pollock C.B. requires of them — *i.e.* 'that degree of certainty that you would act upon in your own grave and important concerns'; for indeed they have no other means of reasoning. The principle of 'reasonable doubt' therefore seems to be little more than a counsel of prudence; and there is considerable judicial authority for this view. The warning is not so frequently uttered in civil cases, because the occasion is not so solemn; but does it follow that the same degree of care and certainty is not as necessary, or at least as desirable, in the one case as in the other? I apprehend that a Judge who directed a jury in an action for damages, 'You need not be as careful in arriving at your conclusions as if you were trying a criminal case', would considerably startle the legal world and the public; and though there is a good reason for reminding juries of the necessity for caution in criminal cases, I know of no authority for the proposition that their duty is any less when property, and not life or liberty, is at stake.

What is a reasonable doubt? Can we define it? Is this standard of proof different from that of proof on a balance of probabilities in civil cases?

LAW REFORM COMMISSION OF CANADA, BURDENS OF PROOF AND PRESUMPTIONS

S.P. No. 8, (1973), 52-53

A high standard of proof is now required in criminal cases and is justified by the purposes for which the criminal sanction is used, the seriousness of depriving someone of his liberty, the stigmatization of the accused that results from a criminal conviction, and the other economic and social consequences that a criminal conviction entails.

We concluded that no better formula could be devised than "proof beyond a reasonable doubt" to express the burden of persuasion in criminal cases.

Unlike the formula now used in civil cases, "the preponderance of evidence", the phrase correctly directs the fact-finders' attention to the degree of belief they must have in order to find for the prosecution, rather than the amount of evidence that the prosecution must produce. It is a phrase that is well-known among laymen and has acquired an important meaning for them. Moreover, by itself the phrase is perfectly intelligible. If the Judge explains to the jury that the Crown does not satisfy its burden of proof unless the evidence convinces them beyond a reasonable doubt of the existence of all the facts the Crown must prove, there would appear to be little danger that the average juror would fail to understand. Reasonable doubt is doubt which is reasonable; it is difficult to see how such a formula could be simplifed or amplified to advantage. Indeed, amplifications or paraphrases of it probably only confuse the jury, and on many occasions have led to appeals and reversals.

In addition to the necessary direction concerning "reasonable doubt", a few appellate courts have insisted that the trial Judge should instruct the jury that the accused is presumed innocent until proved guilty. The assumption of innocence is specifically mentioned in the section to clarify the meaning of that assumption and to remind the jury and others of its vital importance. The word "assumed" is substituted in the section for the more commonly used word "presumed" in the phrase "presumed to be innocent", since a person's innocence is not "presumed" as that word is properly used in law, *i.e.*, to describe a fact that is inferred from certain basic facts proved at trial. Rather, as a matter of social policy, a person's innocence is "assumed" from the outset of the case.

Professor Wigmore thought that the term "presumption of innocence" was only another way of articulating the burden of proof upon the prosecution, but he did say,

> the term does convey a special and perhaps useful hint . . . in that it cautions the jury to put away from their minds all the suspicions that arise from the arrest, the indictment, and the arraignment, and to reach their conclusion solely from the legal evidence adduced. (9 Wigmore, *Evidence* s. 251 at 507 (3d ed., 1940).)

For the reason given by Wigmore, the Project concluded that as an important addition to the charge to the jury, and as a reminder to all persons, the sentence, "The trier of fact shall draw no inferences of guilt from the accused person's arrest or detention nor from his having been charged with the offence being tried", should be added to the section.

R. v. W. (D.)

[1991] 1 S.C.R. 742, 3 C.R. (4th) 302, 63 C.C.C. (3d) 397

The accused was convicted of sexual assault after a trial that pitted the credibility of the accused against that of the complainant. The main charge was relatively short and was correct and fair. In a short recharge the trial Judge characterized the core issue to be determined by the jury as whether they believed the complainant or whether they believed the appellant. When counsel for the accused objected to the recharge, the trial judge responded that he did not feel that he left the jury with the impression that they must accept the accused's evidence in order to acquit him. An appeal to the Court of Appeal was dismissed. On further appeal to the Supreme Court, all five justices agreed that the trial Judge erred in his recharge; the majority decided that looking at the charge as a whole the jury would not have been misled.

CORY J. (GONTHIER and IACOBUICCI JJ. concurring): —

. . . .

It is clear that the trial Judge erred in his recharge. It is incorrect to instruct a jury in a criminal case that, in order to render a verdict, they must decide whether they believe the defence evidence or the Crown's evidence. Putting this either/or proposition to the jury excludes the third alternative; namely, that the jury, without believing the accused, after considering the accused's evidence in the context of the evidence as a whole, may still have a reasonable doubt as to his guilt.

In a case where credibility is important, the trial Judge must instruct the jury that the rule of reasonable doubt applies to that issue. The trial Judge should instruct the jury that they need not firmly believe or disbelieve any witness or set of witnesses. Specifically, the trial Judge is required to instruct the jury that they must acquit the accused in two situations. First, if they believe the accused. Second, if they do not believe the accused's evidence but still have a reasonable doubt as to his guilt after considering the accused's evidence in the context of the evidence as a whole.

. . . .

Ideally, appropriate instructions on the issue of credibility should be given, not only during the main charge, but on any recharge. A trial Judge might well instruct the jury on the question of credibility along these lines:

First, if you believe the evidence of the accused, obviously you must acquit.

Second, if you do not believe the testimony of the accused but you are left in reasonable doubt by it, you must acquit.

Third, even if you are not left in doubt by the evidence of the accused, you must ask yourself whether, on the basis of the evidence which you do accept, you are convinced beyond a reasonable doubt by that evidence of the guilt of the accused.

If that formula were followed, the oft-repeated error which appears in the recharge in this case would be avoided. The requirement that the Crown prove the guilt of the accused beyond a reasonable doubt is fundamental in our system of criminal law. Every effort should be made to avoid mistakes in charging the jury on this basic principle.

SOPINKA J. (dissenting): —

. . . .

In my opinion, in this case credibility was a fundamental issue and the case fell to be decided on the basis of the evidence of the complainant versus the evidence of the accused. ... First, they were told that in dealing with the credibility of the accused the Crown would fail to prove the case beyond a reasonable doubt, if the jury had a doubt about the credibility of the accused's story. On the recharge, they were told that this would only be the case if they believed the evidence of the accused. ... at the very least the jury would be uncertain as to which version was correct and it is pure speculation that they would have accepted the first version rather than the second version.

. . . .

When dealing with the burden of proof, the trial Judge is dealing with the most fundamental rule of the game. It is particularly important in a case in which the prosecution depends on the credibility of the complainant and the accused testifies, that it be very clear and unequivocal that the prosecution has not proved its case beyond a reasonable doubt if, after considering the evidence of the accused and the complainant together with any other evidence, there is a doubt. I cannot say with confidence that this charge made this clear to the jury in this case, and therefore I would direct a new trial.

McLachlin J. (dissenting): — I agree with the conclusion of Sopinka J. and Brooke J.A., in the Court of Appeal, that the error in the charge may have misled the jury. I would allow the appeal.

Are you satisfied with the formula asserted by Cory J.? If not, what is wrong with it?

R. v. LIFCHUS

[1997] 3 S.C.R. 320, 9 C.R. (5th) 1, 118 C.C.C. (3d) 1

The accused was charged with fraud. The trial judge told the jury in her charge on the burden of proof that she used the words "proof beyond a reasonable doubt' . . . in their ordinary, natural every day sense", and that the words "doubt" and "reasonable" are "ordinary, every day words that . . . you understand". The accused was convicted of fraud. On appeal, he contended that the trial judge had erred in instructing the jury on the meaning of the expression "proof beyond a reasonable doubt". The Court of Appeal allowed the appeal and ordered a new trial. The Supreme Court dismissed the Crown's appeal.

Cory J. (Lamer C.J., Sopinka, McLachlin, Iacobucci and Major JJ. concurring): —

. . . .

The phrase "beyond a reasonable doubt", is composed of words which are commonly used in everyday speech. Yet, these words have a specific meaning in the legal context. This special meaning of the words "reasonable doubt" may not correspond precisely to the meaning ordinarily attributed to them. In criminal proceedings, where the liberty of the subject is at stake, it is of fundamental importance that jurors fully understand the nature of the burden of proof that the law requires them to apply. An explanation of the meaning of proof beyond a reasonable doubt is an essential element of the instructions that must be given to a jury. That a definition is necessary can be readily deduced from the frequency with which juries ask for guidance with regard to its meaning. It is therefore essential that the trial judge provide the jury with an explanation of the expression.

. . . .

Perhaps a brief summary of what the definition should and should not contain may be helpful. It should be explained that:

- the standard of proof beyond a reasonable doubt is inextricably intertwined with that principle fundamental to all criminal trials, the presumption of innocence;
- the burden of proof rests on the prosecution throughout the trial and never shifts to the accused;
- a reasonable doubt is not a doubt based upon sympathy or prejudice;
- rather, it is based upon reason and common sense;
- it is logically connected to the evidence or absence of evidence;
- it does not involve proof to an absolute certainty; it is not proof beyond <u>any</u> doubt nor is it an imaginary or frivolous doubt; and
- more is required than proof that the accused is probably guilty — a jury which concludes only that the accused is probably guilty must acquit.

On the other hand, certain references to the required standard of proof should be avoided. For example:

- describing the term "reasonable doubt" as an ordinary expression which has no special meaning in the criminal law context;
- inviting jurors to apply to the task before them the same standard of proof that they apply to important, or even the most important, decisions in their own lives;
- equating proof "beyond a reasonable doubt" to proof "to a moral certainty";
- qualifying the word "doubt" with adjectives other than "reasonable", such as "serious", "substantial" or "haunting", which may mislead the jury; and
- instructing jurors that they may convict if they are "sure" that the accused is guilty, before providing them with a proper definition as to the meaning of the words "beyond a reasonable doubt".

A charge which is consistent with the principles set out in these reasons will suffice regardless of the particular words used by the trial judge. Nevertheless, it may . . . be useful to set out a "model charge" which could provide the necessary instructions as to the meaning of the phrase beyond a reasonable doubt.

Suggested Charge

Instructions pertaining to the requisite standard of proof in a criminal trial of proof beyond a reasonable doubt might be given along these lines:

The accused enters these proceedings presumed to be innocent. That presumption of innocence remains throughout the case until such time as the Crown has on the evidence put before you satisfied you beyond a reasonable doubt that the accused is guilty.

What does the expression "beyond a reasonable doubt" mean?

The term "beyond a reasonable doubt" has been used for a very long time and is a part of our history and traditions of justice. It is so engrained in our criminal law that some think it needs no explanation, yet something must be said regarding its meaning.

A reasonable doubt is not an imaginary or frivolous doubt. It must not be based upon sympathy or prejudice. Rather, it is based on reason and common sense. It is logically derived from the evidence or absence of evidence.

Even if you believe the accused is probably guilty or likely guilty, that is not sufficient. In those circumstances you must give the benefit of the doubt to the accused and acquit because the Crown has failed to satisfy you of the guilt of the accused beyond a reasonable doubt.

On the other hand you must remember that it is virtually impossible to prove anything to an absolute certainty and the Crown is not required to do so. Such a standard of proof is impossibly high.

In short if, based upon the evidence before the court, you are sure that the accused committed the offence you should convict since this demonstrates that you are satisfied of his guilt beyond a reasonable doubt.

This is not a magic incantation that needs to be repeated word for word. It is nothing more than a suggested form that would not be faulted if it were used . . .

Further, it is possible that an error in the instructions as to the standard of proof may not constitute a reversible error. It was observed in *R. v. W. (D.)*, [1991] 1 S.C.R. 742, at p. 758, that the verdict ought not be disturbed "if the charge, when read as a whole, makes it clear that the jury could not have been under any misapprehension as to the correct burden and standard of proof to apply". On the other hand, if the charge as a whole gives rise to the reasonable likelihood that the jury misapprehended the standard of proof, then as a general rule the verdict will have to be set aside and a new trial directed.

R. v. R.D.S.

[1997] 3 S.C.R. 484, 118 C.C.C. (3d) 353, 10 C.R. (5th) 1

The accused, a black 15-year-old, was charged with a series of offences arising out of an incident wherein a white police officer had arrested the accused for interfering with the arrest of another youth. The police officer and the accused were the only witnesses at trial. Their accounts of the relevant events differed widely. The trial judge weighed the evidence and determined that the accused should be acquitted. While delivering her oral reasons, the trial judge remarked:

> The Crown says, well, why would the officer say that events occurred the way in which he has relayed them to the Court this morning. I am not saying that the Constable has misled the court, although police officers have been known to do that in the past. I am not saying that the officer overreacted, but certainly police officers do overreact, particularly when they are dealing with non-white groups. That to me indicates a state of mind right there that is questionable. I believe that probably the situation in this particular case is the case of a young police officer who overreacted. I do accept the evidence of [R.D.S.] that he was told to shut up or he would be under arrest. It seems to be in keeping with the prevalent attitude of the day. At any rate, based upon my comments and based upon all the evidence before the court I have no other choice but to acquit.

The Crown challenged these comments as raising a reasonable apprehension of bias. The Crown's appeal was allowed and a new trial ordered. This judgment was upheld by a majority of the Nova Scotia Court of Appeal. The accused appealed further.

The Supreme Court allowed the appeal and restored the acquittals. There was a complex division of opinion.

CORY J. (IACOBUCCI J. concurring): —

. . . .

In some circumstances it may be acceptable for a judge to acknowledge that racism in society might be, for example, the motive for the overreaction of a police officer. This may be necessary in order to refute a submission that invites the judge as trier of fact to presume truthfulness or untruthfulness of a category of witnesses, or to adopt some other form of stereotypical thinking. Yet it would not be acceptable for a judge to go further and suggest that all police officers should therefore not be believed or should be viewed with suspicion where they are dealing with accused persons who are members of a different race. Similarly, it is dangerous for a judge to suggest that a particular person overreacted because of racism unless there is evidence adduced to sustain this finding. It would be equally inappropriate to suggest that female complainants, in sexual assault cases, ought to be believed more readily than male accused persons solely because of the history of sexual violence by men against women.

If there is no evidence linking the generalization to the particular witness, these situations might leave the judge open to allegations of bias on the basis that the credibility of the individual witness was prejudged according to stereotypical generalizations. This does not mean that the particular generalization — that police officers have historically discriminated against visible minorities or that women have historically been abused by men — is not true, or is without foundation. The difficulty is that reasonable and informed people may perceive that the judge has used this information as a basis for assessing credibility instead of making a genuine evaluation of the evidence of the particular witness' credibility. As a general rule, judges should avoid placing themselves in this position.

. . . .

The Crown contended that the real problem arising from Judge Sparks' remarks was the inability of the Crown and Constable Stienburg to respond to the remarks. In other words, the Crown attempted to put forward an argument that the trial was rendered unfair for failure to comply with "natural justice". This cannot be accepted. Neither Constable Stienburg nor the Crown was on trial. Rather, it is essential to consider whether the remarks of Judge Sparks gave rise to a reasonable apprehension of bias. This is the only basis on which this trial could be considered unfair.

. . . .

However, there was no evidence before Judge Sparks that would suggest that anti-black bias influenced this particular police officer's reactions. Thus, although it may be incontrovertible that there is a history of racial tension between police officers and visible minorities, there was no evidence to link that generalization to the actions of Constable Stienburg. The reference to the fact that police officers may overreact in dealing with non-white groups may therefore be perfectly supportable, but it is nonetheless unfortunate in the circumstances of this case because of its potential to associate Judge Sparks' findings with the generalization, rather than the specific evidence. This effect is reinforced by the statement "[t]hat to me indicates a state of mind right there that is questionable" which immediately follows her observation.

There is a further troubling comment. After accepting R.D.S.'s evidence that he was told to shut up, Judge Sparks added that "[i]t seems to be in keeping with the prevalent attitude of the day". Again, this comment may create a perception that the findings of credibility have been made on the basis of generalizations, rather than the conduct of the particular police officer. Indeed these comments standing alone come very close to indicating that Judge Sparks predetermined the issue of credibility of Constable Stienburg on the basis of her general perception of racist police attitudes, rather than on the basis of his demeanour and the substance of his testimony.

The remarks are worrisome and come very close to the line. Yet, however troubling these comments are when read individually, it is vital to note that the comments were not made in isolation. It is necessary to read all of the comments in the context of the whole proceeding, with an awareness of all the circumstances that a reasonable observer would be deemed to know.

The reasonable and informed observer at the trial would be aware that the Crown had made the submission to Judge Sparks that "there's absolutely no reason to attack the credibility of the officer". She had already made a finding that she preferred the evidence of R.D.S. to that of Constable Stienburg. She gave reasons for these findings that could appropriately be made based on the evidence adduced. A reasonable and informed person hearing her subsequent remarks would conclude that she was exploring the possible reasons why Constable Stienburg had a different perception of events than R.D.S. Specifically, she was rebutting the unfounded suggestion of the Crown that a police officer by virtue of his occupation should be more readily believed than the accused. Although her remarks were inappropriate they did not give rise to a reasonable apprehension of bias.

. . . .

A high standard must be met before a finding of reasonable apprehension of bias can be made. Troubling as Judge Sparks' remarks may be, the Crown has not satisfied its onus to provide the cogent evidence needed to impugn the impartiality of Judge Sparks. Although her comments, viewed in isolation, were unfortunate and unnecessary, a reasonable, informed person, aware of all the circumstances, would not conclude that they gave rise to a reasonable apprehension of bias. Her remarks, viewed in their context, do not give rise to a perception that she prejudged the issue of credibility on the basis of generalizations, and they do not taint her earlier findings of credibility.

. . . .

I must add that since writing these reasons I have had the opportunity of reading those of Major J. It is readily apparent that we are in agreement as to the nature of bias and the test to be applied in order to determine whether the words or actions of a trial judge raise a reasonable apprehension of bias. The differences in our reasons lies in the application of the principles and test we both rely upon to the words of the trial judge in this case. The principles and the test we have both put forward and relied upon are different from and incompatible with those set out by Justices L'Heureux-Dubé and McLachlin.

MAJOR J. (LAMER C.J. and SOPINKA J. concurring): — The trial judge stated that "police officers have been known to [mislead the court] in the past" and that "police officers do overreact, particularly when they are dealing with non-white groups" and went on to say "[t]hat to me indicates a state of mind right there that is questionable." She in effect was saying, "sometimes police lie and overreact in dealing with non-whites, therefore I have a suspicion that this police officer may have lied and overreacted in dealing with this non-white accused." This was stereotyping all police officers as liars and racists, and applied this stereotype to the police officer in the present case. The trial judge might be perceived as assigning less weight to the police officer's evidence because he is testifying in the prosecution of an accused who is of a different race. Whether racism exists in our society is not the issue. The issue is whether there was evidence before the court upon which to base a finding that this particular police officer's actions were motivated by racism. There was no evidence of this presented at the trial.

. . . .

Trial judges have to base their findings on the evidence before them. It was open to the appellant to introduce evidence that this police officer was racist and that racism motivated his actions or that he lied. This was not done. For the trial judge to infer that based on her general view of the police or society is an error of law. For this reason there should be a new trial.

. . . .

The life experience of this trial judge, as with all trial judges, is an important ingredient in the ability to understand human behaviour, to weigh the evidence, and to determine credibility. It helps in making a myriad of decisions arising during the course of most trials. It is of no value, however, in reaching conclusions for which there is no evidence. The fact that on some other occasions police officers have lied or overreacted is irrelevant. Life experience is not a substitute for evidence. There was no evidence before the trial judge to support the conclusions she reached.

. . . .

Canadian courts have, in recent years, criticized the stereotyping of people into what is said to be predictable behaviour patterns. If a judge in a sexual assault case instructed the jury or him- or herself that because the complainant was a prostitute he or she probably consented, or that prostitutes are likely to lie about such things as sexual assault, that decision would be reversed. Such presumptions have no place in a system of justice that treats all witnesses equally. Our jurisprudence prohibits tying credibility to something as irrelevant as gender, occupation or perceived group predisposition.

. . . .

It can hardly be seen as progress to stereotype police officer witnesses as likely to lie when dealing with non-whites. This would return us to a time in the history of the Canadian justice system that many thought had past. This reasoning, with respect to police officers, is no more legitimate than the stereotyping of women, children or minorities.

. . . .

I agree with the approach taken by Cory J. with respect to the nature of bias and the test to be used to determine if the words or actions of a judge give rise to apprehension of bias. However, I come to a different conclusion in the application of the test to the words of the trial judge in this case. It follows that I disagree with the approach to reasonable apprehension of bias put forward by Justices L'Heureux-Dubé and McLachlin.

L'HEUREUX-DUBÉ J. (MCLACHLIN J. concurring): —

. . . .

In our view, the test for reasonable apprehension of bias established in the jurisprudence is reflective of the reality that while judges can never be neutral, in the sense of purely objective, they can and must strive for impartiality. It therefore recognizes as inevitable and appropriate that the differing experiences of judges assist them in their decision-making process and will be reflected in their judgments, so long as those experiences are relevant to the cases, are not based on inappropriate stereotypes, and do not prevent a fair and just determination of the cases based on the facts in evidence.

We find that on the basis of these principles, there is no reasonable apprehension of bias in the case at bar. Like Cory J. we would, therefore, overturn the findings by the Nova Scotia Supreme Court (Trial Division) and the majority of the Nova Scotia Court of Appeal that a reasonable apprehension of bias arises in this case, and restore the acquittal of R.D.S. This said, we disagree with Cory J.'s position that the comments of Judge Sparks were unfortunate, unnecessary, or close to the line. Rather, we find them to reflect an entirely appropriate recognition of the facts in evidence in this case and of the context within which this case arose — a context known to Judge Sparks and to any well-informed member of the community.

. . . .

Cardozo recognized that objectivity was an impossibility because judges, like all other humans, operate from their own perspectives. As the Canadian Judicial Council noted in *Commentaries on Judicial Conduct* (1991), at p. 12, "[t]here is no human being who is not the product of every social experience, every process of education, and every human contact". What is possible and desirable, they note, is impartiality:

> . . . [T]he wisdom required of a judge is to recognize, consciously allow for, and perhaps to question, all the baggage of past attitudes and sympathies that fellow citizens are free to carry, untested, to the grave.

> True impartiality does not require that the judge have no sympathies or opinions; it requires that the judge nevertheless be free to entertain and act upon different points of view with an open mind.

. . . .

As discussed above, judges in a bilingual, multiracial and multicultural society will undoubtedly approach the task of judging from their varied perspectives. They will certainly have been shaped by, and have gained insight from, their different experiences, and cannot be expected to divorce themselves from these experiences on the occasion of their appointment to the bench. In fact, such a transformation would deny society the benefit of the valuable knowledge gained by the judiciary while they were members of the Bar. As well, it would preclude the achievement of a diversity of backgrounds in the judiciary. The reasonable person does not expect that judges will function as neutral ciphers; however, the reasonable person does demand that judges achieve impartiality in their judging.

. . . .

An understanding of the context or background essential to judging may be gained from testimony from expert witnesses in order to put the case in context: *R. v. Lavallee,* . . . *R. v. Parks,* . . . and *Moge v. Moge,* . . . from academic studies properly placed before the Court; and from the judge's personal understanding and experience of the society in which the judge lives and works. This process of enlargement is not only consistent with impartiality; it may also be seen as its essential precondition.

A reasonable person far from being troubled by this process, would see it as an important aid to judicial impartiality.

. . . .

It is important to note that having already found R.D.S. to be credible, and having accepted a sufficient portion of his evidence to leave her with a reasonable doubt as to his guilt, Judge Sparks necessarily disbelieved at least a portion of the conflicting evidence of Constable Stienburg. At that point, Judge Sparks made reference to the submissions of the Crown that "there's absolutely no reason to attack the credibility of the officer", and then addressed herself to why there might, in fact, be a reason to attack the credibility of the officer in this case. It is in this context that Judge Sparks made the statements which have prompted this appeal.

[The trial judge's] remarks do not support the conclusion that Judge Sparks found Constable Stienburg to have lied. In fact, Judge Sparks did quite the opposite. She noted firstly, that she was <u>not</u> saying Constable Stienburg had misled the court, although that could be an explanation for his evidence. She then went on to remark that she was *not* saying that Constable Stienburg had overreacted, though she was alive to that possibility given that it had happened with police officers in the past, and in particular, it had happened when police officers were dealing with non-white groups. Finally, Judge Sparks concluded that, though she was not willing to say that Constable Stienburg did overreact, it was her belief that he <u>probably</u> overreacted. And, in support of that finding, she noted that she accepted the evidence of R.D.S. that "he was told to shut up or he would be under arrest".

At no time did Judge Sparks rule that the probable overreaction by Constable Stienburg was motivated by racism. Rather, she tied her finding of probable overreaction to the evidence that Constable Stienburg had threatened to arrest the appellant R.D.S. for speaking to his cousin. At the same time, there was evidence capable of supporting a finding of racially motivated overreaction. At an earlier point in the proceedings, she had accepted the evidence that the other youth arrested that day, was handcuffed and thus secured when R.D.S. approached. This constitutes evidence which could lead one to question why it was necessary for both boys to be placed in choke holds by Constable Stienburg, purportedly to secure them. In the face of such evidence, we respectfully disagree with the views of our colleagues Cory and Major JJ. that there was no evidence on which Judge Sparks could have found "racially motivated" overreaction by the police officer.

While it seems clear that Judge Sparks <u>did not in fact</u> relate the officer's probable overreaction to the race of the appellant R.D.S., it should be noted that if Judge Sparks <u>had</u> chosen to attribute the behaviour of Constable Stienburg to the racial dynamics of the situation, she would not necessarily have erred. As a member of the community, it was open to her to take into account the well-known presence of racism in that community and to evaluate the evidence as to what occurred against that background.

That Judge Sparks recognized that police officers <u>sometimes</u> overreact when dealing with non-white groups simply demonstrates that in making her determination in this case, she was alive to the well-known racial dynamics that may exist in interactions between police officers and visible minorities.

. . . .

Judge Sparks' oral reasons show that she approached the case with an open mind, used her experience and knowledge of the community to achieve an understanding of the reality of the case, and applied the fundamental principle of proof beyond a reasonable doubt. Her comments were based entirely on the case before her, were made after a consideration of the conflicting testimony of the two witnesses and in response to the Crown's submissions, and were entirely supported by the evidence. In alerting herself to the racial dynamic in the case, she was simply engaging in the process of contextualized judging which, in our view, was entirely proper and conducive to a fair and just resolution of the case before her.

GONTHIER J. (LA FOREST J. concurring): — . . . I agree with Cory J. and L'Heureux-Dubé and McLachlin JJ. as to the disposition of the appeal and with their exposition of the law on bias and impartiality and the relevance of context. However, I am in agreement with and adopt the joint reasons of L'Heureux-Dubé and McLachlin JJ. in their treatment of social context and the manner in which it may appropriately enter the decision-making process as well as their assessment of the trial judge's reasons and comments in the present case.

For competing views on *R.D.S.*, see Archibald, "The Lessons of the Sphinx: Avoiding Apprehensions of Judicial Bias in a Multi-racial, Multi-cultural Society" (1998), 10 C.R. (5th) 54; Delisle, "An Annotation to R.D.S." (1998), 10 C.R. (5th) 7 and Paciocco, "The Promise of R.D.S.: Integrating the Law of Judicial Notice and Apprehension of Bias" (1998), 3 Can. Crim. L.R. 319.

With the advent of the *Canadian Charter of Rights and Freedoms*, the presumption of innocence has taken on a constitutional dimension. The *Charter* provides in section 11:

11. Any person charged with an offence has the right

. . . .

(*d*) to be presumed innocent until proven guilty according to law in a fair and public hearing by an independent and impartial tribunal.

R. v. OAKES

(1986), 50 C.R. (3d) 1 (S.C.C.)

DICKSON C.J.C. (CHOUINARD, LAMER, WILSON and LE DAIN JJ. concurring):

This appeal concerns the constitutionality of s. 8 of the *Narcotic Control Act*, R.S.C. 1970, c. N-1. The section provides, in brief, that if the Court finds the accused in possession of a narcotic, he is presumed to be in possession for the purpose of trafficking. Unless the accused can establish the contrary, he must be convicted of trafficking. The Ontario Court of Appeal held that this provision constitutes a "reverse onus" clause and is unconstitutional because it violates one of the core values of our criminal justice system, the presumption of innocence, now entrenched in s. 11 (*d*) of the *Canadian Charter of Rights and Freedoms*. The Crown has appealed.

. . . .

The respondent, David Edwin Oakes, was charged with unlawful possession of a narcotic for the purpose of trafficking, contrary to s. 4(2) of the *Narcotic Control Act*. He elected trial by magistrate without a jury. At trial, the Crown adduced evidence to establish that Mr. Oakes was found in possession of eight one gram vials of *cannabis* resin in the form of hashish oil. Upon a further search conducted at the police station, $619.45 was located. Mr. Oakes told the police that he had bought ten vials of hashish oil for $150 for his own use, and that the $619.45 was from a workers' compensation cheque. He elected not to call evidence as to possession of the narcotic. Pursuant to the procedural provisions of s. 8 of the *Narcotic Control Act*, the trial judge proceeded to make a finding that it was beyond a reasonable doubt that Mr. Oakes was in possession of the narcotic.

Following this finding, Mr. Oakes brought a motion to challenge the constitutional validity of s. 8 of the *Narcotic Control Act*, which he maintained imposes a burden on an accused to prove that he or she was not in possession for the purpose of trafficking. He argued that s. 8 violates the presumption of innocence contained in s. 11(*d*) of the *Charter*.

[The trial judge found s. 8 to be inoperative as in conflict with s. 11(*d*). He afforded the Crown an opportunity to adduce further evidence and the Crown declined. The trial Judge acquitted on the offence charged and found the accused guilty of possession only.]

. . . .

To interpret the meaning of s. 11(*d*), it is important to adopt a purposive approach. As this Court stated in *R. v. Big M Drug Mart Ltd.*, [1985] 1 S.C.R. 295 at p. 344:

> The meaning of a right or freedom guaranteed by the *Charter* was to be ascertained by an analysis of the *purpose* of such a guarantee; it was to be understood, in other words, in the light of the interests it was meant to protect.
>
> In my view this analysis is to be undertaken, and the purpose of the right or freedom in question is to be sought by reference to the character and the larger objects of the *Charter* itself, to the language chosen to articulate the specific right or freedom, to the historical origins of the concepts enshrined, and where applicable to the meaning and purpose of the other specific rights and freedoms.

To identify the underlying purpose of the *Charter* right in question, therefore, it is important to begin by understanding the cardinal values it embodies.

The presumption of innocence is a hallowed principle lying at the very heart of criminal law. Although protected expressly in s. 11(*d*) of the *Charter*, the presumption of innocence is referable and integral to the general protection of life, liberty and security of the person contained in s. 7 of the *Charter* (see *Reference re s. 94(2) of the Motor Vehicle Act*, December 17, 1985, unreported, per Lamer J.). The presumption of innocence protects the fundamental liberty and human dignity of any and every person accused by the State of criminal conduct. An individual charged with a criminal offence faces grave social and personal consequences, including potential loss of physicial liberty, subjection to social stigma and ostracism from the community, as well as other social, psychological and economic harms. In light of the gravity of these consequences, the presumption of innocence is crucial. It ensures that until the State proves an accused's guilt beyond all reasonable doubt, he or she is innocent. This is essential in a society committed to fairness and social justice. The presumption of innocence confirms our faith in humankind; it reflects our belief that individuals are decent and law-abiding members of the community until proven otherwise.

The presumption of innocence has enjoyed longstanding recognition at common law. In the leading case, *Woolmington v. Director of Public Prosecutions*, [1935] A.C. 462 (H.L.), Viscount Sankey wrote at pp. 481-482:

> Throughout the web of the English Criminal Law one golden thread is always to be seen, that it is the duty of the prosecution to prove the prisoner's guilt subject to what I have already said as to the defence of insanity and subject also to any statutory exception. If, at the end of and on the whole of the case, there is a reasonable doubt, created by the evidence given by either the prosecution or the prisoner, as to whether the prisoner killed the deceased with a malicious intention, the prosecution has not made out the case and the prisoner is entitled to an acquittal. No matter what the charge or where thc trial, the principle that the prosecution must prove the guilt of the prisoner is part of the common law of England and no attempt to whittle it down can be entertained.

Subsequent Canadian cases have cited the *Woolmington* principle with approval (see, for example, *Manchuk v. The King*, [1938] S.C.R. 341, at p. 349; *R. v. City of Sault Ste. Marie*, [1978] 2 S.C.R. 1299, at p. 1316).

Further evidence of the widespread acceptance of the principle of the presumption of innocence is its inclusion in the major international human rights documents. Article 11(1) of the *Universal Declaration of Human Rights*, adopted December 10, 1948 by the General Assembly of the United Nations, provides:

> Art. 11(1) Everyone charged with a penal offence has the right to be presumed innocent until proved guilty according to law in a public trial at which he has had all the guarantees necessary for his defence.

In the *International Convenant on Civil and Political Rights*, 1966, art. 14(2) states:

> Art. 14(2) Everyone charged with a criminal offence shall have the right to be presumed innocent until proved guilty according to law.

Canada acceded to this Covenant, and the Optional Protocol which sets up machinery for implementing the Covenant, on May 19, 1976. Both came into effect on August 19, 1976.

In light of the above, the right to be presumed innocent until proven guilty requires that s. 11(*d*) have, at a minimum, the following content. First, an individual must be proven guilty beyond a reasonable doubt. Second, it is the State which must bear the burden of proof. As Mr. Justice Lamer stated in *Dubois v. The Queen* (November 21, 1985, unreported) at p. 6:

> Section 11 (*d*) imposes upon the Crown the burden of proving the accused's guilt beyond reasonable doubt as well as that of making out the case against the accused before he or she need respond, either by testifying or calling other evidence.

Third, criminal prosecutions must be carried out in accordance with lawful procedures and fairness. The latter part of s. 11(*d*), which requires the proof of guilt "according to law in a fair and public hearing by an independent and impartial tribunal", underlines the importance of this procedural requirement.

. . . .

The *Woolmington* case was decided in the context of a legal system with no constitutionally entrenched human rights document. In Canada, we have tempered parliamentary supremacy by entrenching important rights and freedoms in the Constitution. Viscount Sankey's statutory exception proviso is clearly not applicable in this context and would subvert the very purpose of the entrenchment of the presumption of innocence in the *Charter*. . . . Section 8 of the *Narcotic Control Act* is not rendered constitutionally valid simply by virtue of the fact that it is a statutory provision.

. . . .

In general one must, I think, conclude that a provision which requires an accused to disprove on a balance of probabilities the existence of a presumed fact, which is an important element of the offence in question, violates the presumption of innocence in s. 11(*d*). If an accused bears the burden of disproving on a balance of probabilities an essential element of an offence, it would be possible for a conviction to occur despite the existence of a reasonable doubt. This would arise if the accused adduced sufficient evidence to raise a reasonable doubt as to his or her innocence but did not convince the jury on a balance of probabilities that the presumed fact was untrue.

The fact that the standard is only the civil one does not render a reverse onus clause constitutional. As Sir Rupert Cross commented in the *Rede Lectures*, "The Golden Thread of the English Criminal Law: The Burden of Proof", delivered in 1976 at the University of Toronto, at pp. 11-13:

> It is sometimes said that exceptions to the Woolmington rule are acceptable because, whenever the burden of proof on any issue in a criminal case is borne by the accused, he only has to satisfy the jury on the balance of probabilities, whereas on issues on which the Crown bears the burden of proof the jury must be satisfied beyond a reasonable doubt. . . . The fact that the standard is lower when the accused bears the burden of proof than it is when the burden of proof is borne by the prosecution is no answer to my objection to the existence of exceptions to the Woolmington rule as it does not alter the fact that a jury or bench of Magistrates may have to convict the accused although they are far from sure of his guilt.

As we have seen, the potential for a rational connection between the basic fact and the presumed fact to justify a reverse onus provision has been elaborated in some of the cases discussed above and is now known as the "rational connection test". In the context of s. 11(*d*), however, the following question arises: if we apply the rational connection test to the consideration of whether s. 11(*d*) has been violated, are we adequately protecting the constitutional principle of the presumption of innocence? As Professors MacKay and Cromwell point out in their article "Oakes: A Bold Initiative" (1983), 32 C.R. (3d) 221, at p. 233:

> The rational connection test approves a provision that *forces* the trier to infer a fact that may be simply rationally, connected to the proved fact. Why does it follow that such a provision does not offend the constitutional right to be proved guilty beyond a reasonable doubt?

A basic fact may rationally tend to prove a presumed fact, but not prove its existence beyond a reasonable doubt. An accused person could thereby be convicted despite the presence of a reasonable doubt. This would violate the presumption of innocence.

I should add that this questioning of the constitutionality of the "rational connection test" as a guide to interpreting s. 11(*d*) does not minimize its importance. The appropriate stage for invoking the rational connection test, however, is under s. 1 of the *Charter*. This consideration did not arise under the *Canadian Bill of Rights* because of the absence of an equivalent to s. 1. At the Court of Appeal level in the present case, Martin J.A. sought to combine the analysis of s. 11(*d*) and s. 1 to overcome the limitations of the *Canadian Bill of Rights* jurisprudence. To my mind, it is highly desirable to keep s. 1 and s. 11(*d*) analytically distinct. Separating the analysis into two components is consistent with the approach this Court has taken to the *Charter* to date (see *R. v. Big M Drug Mart Ltd., supra; Hunter v. Southam Inc.*, [1984] 2 S.C.R. 145; *Law Society of Upper Canada v. Skapinker*, [1984] 1 S.C.R. 357).

To return to s. 8 of the *Narcotic Control Act*, I am in no doubt whatsoever that it violates s. 11(*d*) of the *Charter* by requiring the accused to prove on a balance of probabilitics that he was not in possession of the narcotic for the purpose of trafficking. Mr. Oakes is compelled by s. 8 to prove he is *not* guilty of the offence of trafficking. He is thus denied his right to be presumed innoccent and subjected to the potential penalty of life imprisonment unless he can rebut the presumption. This is radically and fundamentally inconsistent with the societal values of human dignity and liberty which we espouse, and is directly contrary to the presumption of innocence enshrined in s. 11(*d*). Let us turn now to s. 1 of the *Charter*.

. . . .

It is important to observe at the outset that s. 1 has two functions: first, it constiutionally guarantees the rights and freedoms set out in the provisions which follow; and, second, it states explicitly the exclusive justificatory criteria (outside of s. 33 of the *Constitution Act, 1982*) against which limitations on those rights and freedoms must be measured. Accordingly, any s. 1 inquiry must be premised on an understanding that the impugned limit violates constitutional rights and freedoms — rights and freedoms which are part of the supreme law of Canada. As Madam Justice Wilson stated in *Singh et al. v. Ministry of Employment and Immigration, supra*, at pp. 218-19: ". . . it is important to remember that the Courts are conducting this inquiry in light of a commitment to uphold the rights and freedoms set out in the other sections of the *Charter*."

A second contextual element of interpretation of s. 1 is provided by the words "free and democratic society". Inclusion of these words as the final standard of justification for limits on rights and freedoms refers the Court to the very purpose for which the *Charter* was originally entrenched in the Constitution: Canadian society is to be free and democratic. The Court must be guided by the values and principles essential to a free and democratic society which I believe embody, to name but a few, respect for the inherent dignity of the human person, commitment to social justice and equality, accommodation of a wide variety of beliefs, respect for cultural and group identity, and faith in social and political institutions which enhance the participation of individuals and groups in society. The underlying values and principles of a free and democratic society are the genesis of the rights and freedoms guaranteed by the *Charter* and the ultimate standard against which a limit on a right or freedom must be shown, despite its effect, to be reasonable and demonstrably justified.

The rights and freedoms guaranteed by the *Charter* are not, however, absolute. It may become necessary to limit rights and freedoms in circumstances where their exercise would be inimical to the realization of collective goals of fundamental importance. For this reason, s. 1 provides criteria of justification for limits on the rights and freedoms guaranteed by the *Charter*. These criteria impose a stringent standard of justification, especially when understood in terms of the two contextual considerations discussed above, namely, the violation of a constitutionally guaranteed right or freedom and the fundamental principles of a free and democratic society.

The onus of proving that a limit on a right or freedom guaranteed by the *Charter* is reasonable and demonstrably justified in a free and democratic society rests upon the party seeking to uphold the limitation. It is clear from the text of s. 1 that limits on the rights and freedoms enumerated in the *Charter* are exceptions to their general guarantee. The presumption is that the rights and freedoms are guaranteed unless the party invoking s. 1 can bring itself within the exceptional criteria which justify their being limited. This is further substantiated by the use of the word "demonstrably" which clearly indicates that the onus of justification is on the party seeking to limit: *Hunter v. Southam Inc., supra.*

The standard of proof under s. 1 is the civil standard, namely, proof by a preponderance of probability. The alternative criminal standard, proof beyond a reasonable doubt, would, in my view, be unduly onerous on the party seeking to limit. Concepts such as "reasonableness", "justifiability" and "free and democratic society" are simply not amenable to such a standard. Nevertheless, the preponderance of probability test must be applied rigorously. Indeed, the phrase "demonstrably justified" in s. 1 of the *Charter* supports this conclusion. Within the broad category of the civil standard, there exist different degrees of probability depending on the nature of the case: see Sopinka and Lederman, *The Law of Evidence in Civil Cases* (Toronto: 1974) at p. 385. As Lord Denning explained in *Bater v. Bater*, [1950] 2 All E.R. 458 (C.A.) at p. 459:

> The case may be proved by a preponderance probability, but there may be degrees of probability within that standard. The degree depends on the subject-matter. A civil Court, when considering a charge of fraud, will naturally require a higher degree of probability than that which it would require if considering whether negligence were established. It does not adopt so high a standard as a criminal Court, even when considering a charge of a criminal nature, but still it does require a degree of probability which is commensurate with the occasion.

This passage was cited with approval in *Hanes v. Wawanesa Mutual Insurance Co.*, [1963] S.C.R. 154 at p. 161. A similar approach was put forward by Cartwright J. in *Smith v. Smith & Smedman*, [1952] 2 S.C.R. 312 at pp. 331-32:

> I wish, however, to emphasize that in every civil action before the tribunal can safely find the affirmative of an issue of fact required to be proved it must be satisfied, and that whether or not it will be so satisfied must depend on the totality of the circumstances on which its judgment is formed including the gravity of the consequences.

Having regard to the fact that s. 1 is being invoked for the purpose of justifying a violation of the constitutional rights and freedoms the *Charter* was designed to protect, a very high degree of probability will be, in the words of Lord Denning, "commensurate with the occasion". Where evidence is required in order to prove the constituent elements of a s. 1 inquiry, and this will generally be the case, it should be cogent and persuasive and make clear to the Court the consequences of imposing or not imposing the limit. See: *Law Society of Upper Canada v. Skapinker, supra,* at p. 384; *Singh et al. v. Ministry of Employment and Immigration, supra,* at p. 217. A Court will also need to know what alternative measures for implementing the objective were available to the legislators when they made their decisions. I should add, however, that there may be cases where certain elements of the s. 1 analysis are obvious or self-evident.

To establish that a limit is reasonable and demonstrably justified in a free and democratic society, two central criteria must be satisfied. First, the objective, which the measures responsible for a limit on a *Charter* right or freedom are designed to serve, must be "of sufficient importance to warrant overriding a constitutionally protected right or freedom": *R. v. Big M Drug Mart Ltd.*, *supra*, at p. 352. The standard must be high in order to ensure that objectives which are trivial or discordant with the principles integral to a free and democratic society do not gain s. 1 protection. It is necessary, at a minimum, that an objective relate to concerns which are pressing and substantial in a free and democratic society before it can be characterized as sufficiently important.

Second, once a sufficiently significant objective is recognized, then the party invoking s. 1 must show that the means chosen are reasonable and demonstrably justified. This involves "a form of proportionality test": *R. v. Big M Drug Mart Ltd.*, *supra*, at p. 352. Although the nature of the proportionality test will vary depending on the circumstances, in each case Courts will be required to balance the interests of society with those of individuals and groups. There are, in my view, three important components of a proportionality test. First, the measures adopted must be carefully designed to achieve the objective in question. They must not be arbitrary, unfair or based on irrational considerations. In short, they must be rationally connected to the objective. Second, the means, even if rationally connected to the objective in this first sense, should impair "as little as possible" the right or freedom in question: *R. v. Big M Drug Mart Ltd.*, *supra*, at p. 352. Third, there must be a proportionality between the *effects* of the measures which are responsible for limiting the *Charter* right or freedom, and the objective which has been identified as of "sufficient importance".

With respect to the third component, it is clear that the general effect of any measure impugned under s. 1 will be the infringement of a right or freedom guaranteed by the *Charter*; this is the reason why resort to s. 1 is necessary. The inquiry into effects must, however, go further. A wide range of rights and freedoms are guaranteed by the *Charter*, and an almost infinite number of factual situations may arise in respect of these. Some limits on rights and freedoms protected by the *Charter* will be more serious than others in terms of the nature of the right or freedom violated, the extent of the violation, and the degree to which the measures which impose the limit trench upon the integral principles of a free and democratic society. Even if an objective is of sufficient importance, and the first two elements of the proportionality test are satisfied, it is still possible that, because of the severity of the deleterious effects of a measure on individuals or groups, the measure will not be justified by the purposes it is intended to serve . The more severe the deleterious effects of a measure, the more important the objective must be if the measure is to be reasonable and demonstrably justified in a free and democratic society.

Having outlined the general principles of a s. 1 inquiry, we must apply them to s. 8 of the *Narcotic Control Act*. Is the reverse onus provision in s. 8 a reasonable limit on the right to be presumed innocent until proven guilty, beyond a reasonable doubt as can be demonstrably, justified in a free and democratic society?

The starting point for formulating a response to this question is, as stated above, the nature of Parliament's interest or objective which accounts for the passage of s. 8 of the *Narcotic Control Act*. According to the Crown, s. 8 of the *Narcotic Control Act* is aimed at curbing drug trafficking by facilitating the conviction of drug traffickers. In my opinion, Parliament's concern with decreasing drug trafficking can be characterized as substantial and pressing. The problem of drug trafficking has been increasing since thc 1950's at which time there was already considerable concern. (See *Report of the Special Committee on Traffic in Narcotic Drugs*, Appendix to Debates of the Senate, Canada, Session 1955, pp. 690-700; see also *Final Report, Commission of Inquiry into the Non-Medical Use of Drugs* (Ottawa, 1973)). Throughout this period, numerous measures were adopted by free and democratic societies, at both the international and national levels.

At the international level, on June 23, 1953, the Protocol for Limiting and Regulating the Cultivation of the Poppy Plant, the Production of, International and Wholesale Trade in, and Use of Opium, to which Canada is a signatory, was adopted by the United Nations Opium Conference held in New York. The *Single Convention on Narcotic Drugs, 1961*, was acceded to in New York on March 30, 1961. This treaty was signed by Canada on March 30, 1961. It entered into force on December 13, 1964. As stated in the Preamble, "addiction to narcotic drugs constitutes a serious evil for the individual and is fraught with social and economic danger to mankind . . ."

At the national level, statutory provisions have been enacted by numerous countries which, *inter alia*, attempt to deter drug trafficking by imposing criminal sanctions (see, for example, *Misuse of Drugs Act*, 1975, No. 116 (New Zealand); *Misuse of Drugs Act*, 1971, c. 38 (United Kingdom)).

The objective of protecting our society from the grave ills associated with drug trafficking, is, in my view, one of sufficient importance to warrant overriding a constitutionally protected right or freedom in certain cases. Moreover, the degree of seriousness of drug trafficking makes its acknowledgement as a sufficiently important objective for the purposes of s. 1, to a large extent, self-evident. The first criterion of a s. 1 inquiry, therefore, has been satisfied by the Crown.

The next stage of inquiry is a consideration of the means chosen by Parliament to achieve its objective. The means must be reasonable and demonstrably justified in a free and democratic society. As outlined above, this proportionality test should begin with a consideration of the rationality of the provision: is the reverse onus clause in s. 8 rationally related to the objective of curbing drug trafficking? At a minimum, this requires that s. 8 be internally rational; there must be a rational connection between the basic fact of possession and the presumed fact of possession for the purpose of trafficking. Otherwise, the reverse onus clause could give rise to unjustified and erroneous convictions for drug trafficking of persons guilty only of possession of narcotics.

In my view, s. 8 does not survive this rational connection test. As Martin J.A. of the Ontario Court of Appeal concluded, possession of a small or negligible quantity of narcotics does not support the inference of trafficking. In other words, it would be irrational to infer that a person had an intent to traffic on the basis of his or her possession of a very small quantity of narcotics. The presumption required under s. 8 of the *Narcotic Control Act* is overinclusive and could lead to results in certain cases which would defy both rationality and fairness. In light of the seriousness of the offence in question, which carries with it the possibility of imprisonment for life, I am further convinced that the first component of the proportionality test has not been satisfied by the Crown.

Having concluded that s. 8 does not satisfy this first component of proportionality, it is unnecessary to consider the other two components.

. . . .

The Ontario Court of Appeal was correct in holding that s. 8 of the *Narcotic Control Act* violates the *Canadian Charter of Rights and Freedoms* and is therefore of no force or effect. Section 8 imposes a limit on the right guaranteed by s. 11(*d*) of the *Charter* which is not reasonable and is not demonstrably justified in a free and democratic society for the purpose of s. 1.

Estey J. (McIntyre J. concurring) delivered a short concurring judgment.

R. v. WHYTE

[1988] 2 S.C.R. 3, 64 C.R. (3d) 123, 42 C.C.C. (3d) 97

The accused was charged with having the care or control of a motor-vehicle while his ability was impaired. He argued that the presumptive device in s. 237(1)(*a*) (now s. 258(1)(*a*)) violated s. 11(*c*) and (*d*) of the *Charter*. The trial judge rejected the argument saying that he was bound by the Supreme Court's decision in *Appleby* which had interpreted the same language in the *Canadian Bill of Rights* and had held that the presumption of innocence was not violated by the provision. The trial judge convicted the accused although he did say that but for the presumption he would have acquitted. The District Court and the British Columbia Court of Appeal dismissed his appeals.

DICKSON C.J.C.: — Section 234(1) of the *Criminal Code*, R.S.C. 1970, c. C-34, provides that everyone who drives a motor vehicle or has the care or control of a motor vehicle, whether it is in motion or not, while his ability to drive a motor vehicle is impaired by alcohol or a drug, is guilty of an indictable offence, or an offence punishable on summary conviction. Section 237(1)(*a*) then legislates a presumption against an accused to the following effect:

> 237. (1) In any proceedings under section 234 or 236,
>
> (a) where it is proved that the accused occupied the seat ordinarily occupied by the driver of a motor vehicle, he shall be deemed to have had the care or control of the vehicle unless he establishes that he did not enter or mount the vehicle for the purpose of setting it in motion . . .

The issue in this appeal is whether this provision infringes the rights of the accused under the *Canadian Charter of Rights and Freedoms*.

. . . .

Later, pursuant to R. 32 of the Rules of the Supreme Court of Canada, SOR/83-74, the following constitutional questions were stated for consideration by this court:

> 1. Does s. 237(1)(a) of the *Criminal Code* of Canada, R.S.C. 1970, c. C-34 infringe or deny the rights and freedoms guaranteed by s. 11(d) of the *Canadian Charter of Rights and Freedoms*?
>
> 2. If s. 237(1)(a) of the *Criminal Code* infringes or denies the rights and freedoms guaranteed by s. 11(d) of the *Charter*, is this section justified by s. 1 of the *Charter*, and therefore not inconsistent with the *Constitution Act, 1982*?

. . . .

The Facts

The evidence disclosed that when the investigating constables came upon the appellant's vehicle, it was in a parked position along the roadside, its hood was warm, the dashboard ignition light was on, keys were in the ignition, but the engine was not running. The applicant was seated in the driver's seat with his body slumped over the steering wheel. Counsel for the defence concedes that the appellant's ability to operate a motor vehicle was impaired by alcohol when he was found by the police.

A. *Canadian Bill of Rights*

As I have indicated, the British Columbia Courts placed heavy reliance on the decision of this court in *Appleby*, which held that s. 237(1)(a) (then s. 224A(1)(a)) was not inconsistent with s. 2(f) of the *Canadian Bill of Rights*.

The first aspect of the *Appleby* decision continues to be relevant under the *Charter*, namely, the characterization of the legal effect of the presumption contained in s. 224A(1)(a), now s. 237(1)(a). Ritchie J. concluded that the presumption places an onus on the accused to prove on a balance of probabilities that he or she did not enter the vehicle with the intention of setting it in motion. Since Laskin J. agreed with Ritchie J. on this point, this Court was unanimous on the interpretation of the provision.

Ritchie J. reached this conclusion for two reasons. The first of these was based on the word "establishes" in the section. He held that as a matter of statutory interpretation, the word "establishes" requires the accused to prove the necessary fact on the balance of probabilities, and cannot be read as equivalent to "raises a reasonable doubt." The meaning of the words "establishes" and "proves" are well defined in the criminal law. They require convincing proof, at least on the balance of probabilities. This meaning of the words "establishes" and "proves" had been set out earlier in *Latour v. R.*, [1951] S.C.R. 19, 11 C.R. 1, 98 C.C.C. 258 [Ont.], and *Tupper v. R.*, [1967] S.C.R. 589, 2 C.R.N.S. 35, [1968] 1 C.C.C. 253 [Ont.]. Pigeon J. reaffirmed this meaning in the majority decision in *R. v. Proudlock*, [1979] 1 S.C.R. 525, 5 C.R. (3d) 21, 43 C.C.C. (2d) 321 [B.C.].

The second reason given by Ritchie J. for concluding that the provision places an onus of proof on the accused was that the section would otherwise be meaningless. The presumption was included to allow the Crown to prove care or control by proving beyond a reasonable doubt that the accused occupied the driver's seat. If the accused could rebut the presumption simply by raising a reasonable doubt, then the Crown would be required to prove the fact of care or control beyond a reasonable doubt, even though the statute deems that care or control is shown upon proof beyond a reasonable doubt that the accused occupied the driver's seat. This is exactly the same onus that the Crown would have to satisfy if the presumption were not included in the section. To interpret the section in this way would make the presumption ineffective and the section meaningless.

The second aspect of *Appleby* was the contention that even though s. 237(1)(*a*) created a reverse onus, it was not consistent with s. 2(*f*) of the *Canadian Bill of Rights*. Writing for the majority on this point, Ritchie J. observed [at p. 315] that s. 2(*f*) gave statutory approval to the principle enunciated by Viscount Sankey L.C. in *Woolmington v. D.P.P.*, [1935] A.C. 462 at 481, 25 Cr. App. R. 72 (H.L.):

> "Throughout the web of the English Criminal Law one golden threat is always to be seen, that it is the duty of the prosecution to prove the prisoner's guilt subject to what I have already said as to the defence of insanity *and subject also to any statutory exception*." [emphasis added by Ritchie J.]

Ritchie J. went on to hold as follows (at p. 316):

> ... the words "presumed innocent until proved guilty according to law ..." as they appear in s. 2(*f*) of the *Bill of Rights*, must be taken to envisage a law which recognizes the existence of statutory exceptions reversing the onus of proof with respect to one or more ingredients of an offence in cases where certain specific facts have been proved by the Crown in relation to such ingredients.

In my view, the reasoning of the Court in *Appleby* was manifestly influenced by the limited extent to which the court considered the *Canadian Bill of Rights* could override otherwise valid legislation which conflict with its terms. The interpretation accorded to s. 2(*f*) effectively eliminated any need to assess the validity of legislative derogation from the guarantee of the presumption of innocence. It is clear from the case law that it is appropriate for this Court to reassess the meaning of words borrowed in the *Charter* from the *Canadian Bill of Rights*; see *R. v. Big M Drug Mart Ltd.*, [1985] 1 S.C.R. 295 at 333-34, 18 C.C.C. (3d) 385, overruling *Robertson v. R.*, [1963] S.C.R. 651, 41 C.R. 392, [1964] 1 C.C.C. 1, [Ont.], on the meaning of "freedom of religion"; *R. v. Therens*, [1985] 1 S.C.R. 613 at 639-40, 45 C.R. (3d) 97, 18 C.C.C. (3d) 481, overruling *Chromiak v. R.*, [1980] 1 S.C.R. 471, 12 C.R. (3d) 300, 14 C.R. (3d) 393, 49 C.C.C. (2d) 257, on the meaning of "detention"; *Re B.C. Motor Vehicle Act*, [1985] 2 S.C.R. 486, 48 C.R. (3d) 289, 23 C.C.C. (3d) 289, departing from *Duke v. R.*, [1972] S.C.R. 917, 18 C.R.N.S. 302, 7 C.C.C. (2d) 474 [Ont.], on the meaning of "fundamental justice"; *R. v. Smith*, [1987] 1 S.C.R. 1045, 58 C.R. (3d) 193, 34 C.C.C. (3d) 97, adopting the minority opinion in *Miller v. R.*, [1977] 2 S.C.R. 680, 38 C.R.N.S. 139, 31 C.C.C. (2d) 177 [B.C.], in preference to that of the majority.

Although the principles set out in the *Canadian Bill of Rights* are of great importance (many of them having been re-enacted in the *Charter*), a constitutional document is fundamentally different from a statute. The purpose of the *Charter* is to entrench certain basic rights and freedoms and immunize them from legislative encroachments. Ordinary legislation must conform to the constitutional requirements. An interpretation of s. 11(*d*) that would make the presumption of innocence subject to legislative exceptions would run directly contrary to the overall purpose of an entrenched constitutional document. Although the same important principle is involved, it is the nature of the two documents which gives the presumption of innocence different effects under the *Canadian Bill of Rights* and the *Charter*.

I conclude, therefore, that despite the holding in *Appleby* that s. 237(1)(*a*) does not infringe the presumption of innocence, the question of the validity of s. 237(1)(*a*) in the face of s. 11(*d*) of the *Charter* is still an open one.

B. *General Charter Principles*

The Supreme Court has considered the presumption of innocence guaranteed by the *Charter* in several recent cases: *Dubois v. R.*, [1985] 2 S.C.R. 350,   48 C.R. (3d) 193, 22 C.C.C. (3d) 513; *R. v. Oakes, supra*; *R. v. Vaillancourt*, [1987] 2 S.C.R. 636, 60 C.R. (3d) 289, 39 C.C.C. (3d) 118 [Que.]; and *R. v. Holmes*, 26th May 1988 [now reported ante, p. 97, also 27 O.A.C. 321]. These cases set out the basic principles of the presumption of innocence and have started to explore its application to particular statutory provisions. It is not necessary to review these cases in depth; a brief summary will suffice.

In *Oakes*, the majority relied on the earlier decision in *Dubois* to conclude that the presumption of innocence has at least three components. First, an individual must be proven guilty beyond a reasonable doubt. Second, the Crown must bear the onus of proof. Third, criminal prosecutions must be carried out in accordance with lawful procedures and principles of fairness (*Oakes*, at p. 121). As Lamer J. stated for the majority in *Dubois*, the Crown must make out the case against the accused before he or she need respond (*Dubois*, at p. 357). Applying these principles to a statutory provision that required the accused to disprove an essential element of the offence, the majority in *Oakes* held (at pp. 132-33) that:

> In general one must, I think, conclude that a provision which requires an accused to disprove on a balance of probabilities the existence of a presumed fact, which is an important element of the offence in question, violates the presumption of innocence in s. 11(*d*). If an accused bears the burden of disproving on a balance of probabilities an essential element of an offence, *it would be possible for a conviction to occur despite the existence of a reasonable doubt.* This would arise if the accused adduced sufficient evidence to raise a reasonable doubt as to his or her innocence but did not convince the jury on a balance of probabilities that the presumed fact was untrue. [emphasis added]

In *Vaillancourt* Lamer J., for the majority on that point, again considered s. 11(*d*). He confirmed that the presumption of innocence requires that the trier of fact be convinced beyond a reasonable doubt of the existence of all the essential elements of the offence. A provision that permits or requires a conviction in spite of a reasonable doubt as to the existence of one or more of the elements of the offence violates the presumption of innocence. Lamer J. recognized that Parliament can in some cases permit proof of a substituted fact to be taken as proof of an essential element of the offence, but that there are limitations on the scope of such substitutions (at p. 656):

> Finally, the Legislature, rather than simply eliminating any need to prove the essential element, may substitute proof of a different element. In my view, this will be constitutionally valid only if upon proof beyond reasonable doubt of the substituted element it would be unreasonable for the trier of fact not to be satisfied beyond reasonable doubt of the existence of the essential element. If the trier of fact may have a reasonable doubt as to the essential element notwithstanding proof beyond a reasonable doubt of the substituted element, then the substitution infringes ss. 7 and 11(*d*).

The next stage in the development of these principles occurred in *Holmes*, which raised the question whether a requirement that the accused prove a lawful excuse, rather than disprove an essential element of the offence, violated the presumption of innocence. Two members of the Court held that a requirement of this sort would offend s. 11(*d*):

> Any burden on an accused which has the effect of dictating a conviction despite the presence of reasonable doubt, whether that burden relates to proof of an essential element of the offence or some element extraneous to the offence but nonetheless essential to verdict, contravenes s. 11(*d*) of the *Charter*. An accused must not be placed in the position of being required to do more than raise a reasonable doubt as to his or her guilt, regardless of whether that doubt arises from uncertainty as to the sufficiency of Crown evidence supporting the constituent elements of the offence or from uncertainty as to criminal culpability in general.

C. *Section 237(1)(a) and the Charter*

Is s. 237(1)(*a*) consistent with these principles? The basic fact which the Crown must prove to invoke the section is that the accused occupied the seat normally occupied by the driver of the motor vehicle. The presumed fact is that the accused had the care or control of the vehicle. To rebut this presumption, the accused must "establish" the absence of intention to set the vehicle in motion. As I have already indicated, *Appleby*, *supra*, and other decisions of this Court make it clear that the word "establishes" requires the accused to prove lack of intention on a balance of probabilities.

The exact relationship between s. 237(1)(*a*) and the *mens rea* requirement of s. 234 was the subject of uncertainty for some time. Is the intention to set the vehicle in motion an ingredient of the offence of having care or control of a motor vehicle while impaired or is the absence of such intention simply a way for an accused to rebut the presumption of care or control? This Court settled the question in *Ford v. R.*, [1982] 1 S.C.R. 231, 65 C.C.C. (2d) 392 [P.E.I.], when Ritchie J. for the majority held that the intention to set the vehicle in motion is not an element of the offence. Proof of lack of intention is simply an evidentiary point that rebuts the presumption of care or control of the vehicle established by s. 237(1) (*a*). The court recently reaffirmed *Ford* in *R. v. Toews*, [1985] 2 S.C.R. 119, 47 C.R. (3d) 213, 21 C.C.C. (3d) 24 [B.C.].

In the case at bar, the Attorney General of Canada argued that since the intention to set the vehicle in motion is not an element of the offence, s. 237(1)(*a*) does not infringe the presumption of innocence. Counsel relied on the passage from *Oakes* quoted above, with its reference to an "essential element", to support this argument. The accused here is required to disprove a fact collateral to the substantive offence, unlike *Oakes*, where the accused was required to disprove an element of the offence.

The short answer to this argument is that the distinction between elements of the offence and other aspects of the charge is irrelevant to the s. 11(*d*) inquiry. The real concern is not whether the accused must disprove an element or prove an excuse, but that an accused may be convicted while a reasonable doubt exists. When that possibility exists, there is a breach of the presumption of innocence.

The exact characterization of a factor as an essential element, a collateral factor, an excuse, or a defence should not affect the analysis of the presumption of innocence. It is the final effect of a provision on the verdict that is decisive. If an accused is required to prove some fact on the balance of probabilities to avoid conviction, the provision violates the presumption of innocence because it permits a conviction in spite of a reasonable doubt in the mind of the trier of fact as to the guilt of the accused. The trial of an accused in a criminal matter cannot be divided neatly into stages, with the onus of proof on the accused at an intermediate stage and the ultimate onus on the Crown. Section 237(1)(*a*) requires the accused to prove lack of intent on a balance of probabilities. If an accused does not meet this requirement the trier of fact is required by law to accept that the accused had care or control and to convict. But of course it does not follow that the trier of fact is convinced beyond a reasonable doubt that the accused had care or control of the vehicle. Indeed, in this case, as in *Appleby*, the trier of fact stated that he convicted the accused despite the existence of a reasonable doubt as to care or control, an element of the offence.

In the passage from *Vaillancourt* quoted earlier, Lamer J. recognized that in some cases substituting proof of one element for proof of an essential element will not infringe the presumption of innocence if, upon proof of the substituted element, it would be unreasonable for the trier of fact not to be satisfied beyond a reasonable doubt of the existence of the essential element. This is another way of saying that a statutory presumption infringes the presumption of innocence if it requires the trier of fact to convict in spite of a reasonable doubt. Only if the existence of the substituted fact leads inexorably to the conclusion that the essential element exists, with no other reasonable possibilities, will the statutory presumption be constitutionally valid.

The presumption in s. 237(1)(*a*) does not have this inexorable character, as the section itself recognizes. A person can be seated in the driver's seat without an intention to assume care or control of the vehicle within the meaning of s. 234. *Appleby* provides an illustration: the accused in that case explained that he sat in the driver's seat of a taxi to use the radio to report an accident, and for no other purpose. The accused failed to convince the trial Judge on a balance of probabilities, but the Judge admitted that he had a reasonable doubt about the explanation. Other reasonable explanations for sitting in the driver's seat can readily be imagined. It cannot be said that proof of occupancy of the driver's seat leads inexorably to the conclusion that the essential element of care or control exists and, therefore, s. 237(1)(*a*) does not meet the test set out by Lamer J. in *Vaillancourt*.

Section 237(1)(*a*) requires the trier of fact to accept as proven that an accused had care or control of a vehicle, an essential element of the offence, in spite of a reasonable doubt about the existence of the element. The section therefore breaches the presumption of innocence guaranteed by s. 11(*d*) of the *Charter*.

VI

SECTION 1 OF THE *CHARTER*

The respondent and the Attorney General of Canada argue that even if s. 237(1)(*a*) infringes the presumption of innocence, the infringement is salvaged by s. 1 of the *Charter*, which reads:

> 1. The *Canadian Charter of Rights and Freedoms* guarantees the rights and freedoms set out in it subject only to such reasonable limits prescribed by law as can be demonstrably justified in a free and democratic society.

To decide this point, it is necessary to apply the s. 1 analysis set out by the majority in *Oakes*. There are two major criteria. First, the objective which the measure responsible for the limit on a right or freedom is designed to serve must be sufficiently important to permit overriding the constitutionally protected right or freedom (*Oakes*, at p. 138). Second, to show that the measures are reasonable and demonstrably justified requires an analysis of the proportionality of the measures (*Oakes*, at p. 139). There are three components to the proportionality test: the measures must be carefully designed to achieve the objective of the legislation, with a rational connection to the objective. The second component is that the measure should impair the right or freedom as little as possible. Finally, there must be proportionality between the effects of the impugned measures on the protected right and the attainment of the objective.

The respondent Crown and the Attorney General of Canada argued strongly that the objective of s. 237(1)(a) is sufficiently important to warrant overriding a *Charter* right. The section, along with the related sections concerning the use, care or control of a motor vehicle while the ability to drive is impaired by alcohol or while the proportion of alcohol in the blood exceeds certain limits, is a response to a major social problem. Counsel for the respondent submitted affidavit evidence outlining the number of people charged annually with these offences, the number of fatalities and injuries caused by impaired drivers, the number of accidents where alcohol is a factor, and the cost to the public through insurance, hospital care and the operation of the justice system. Counsel for the Attorney General referred the Court to the debates in the House of Commons when the predecessor of s. 237(1)(a) was first introduced in 1947, and also to the debates on the 1985 amendments. The Court was also referred to its own past decisions in *Saunders v. R.*, [1967] S.C.R. 284, 1 C.R.N.S. 249, [1967] 3 C.C.C. 278, [Sask.], and *Curr v. R.*, [1972] S.C.R. 889, 18 C.R.N.S. 281, 7 C.C.C. (2d) 181 [Ont.], where the severity of the problems caused by impaired drivers was recognized. Reference should also be made to the recent decisions of this Court in *R. v. Hufsky*, [1988] 1 S.C.R. 621, 63 C.R. (3d) 14 [Ont.], and *R. v. Thomsen*, [1988] 1 S.C.R. 640, 63 C.R. (3d) 1 [Ont.].

It is not necessary to go into these submissions in detail, since the appellant conceded that the objective of s. 237(1)(a) was sufficiently important to warrant overriding a constitutionally protected right. He did note, however, that s. 237(1)(a) is intended to assist the Crown to prove the offence of care or control of a motor vehicle while impaired, where the risk is that the occupant will put the vehicle in motion. The presumption does not address the more prevalent problem of those who actually operate the vehicle while their ability to do so is impaired.

In light of the submissions by the respondent and the Attorney General and the concession by the appellant, I accept that there is a valid objective for s. 237(1)(a) and that the first criterion of the *Oakes* test is met.

The first component of the proportionality inquiry is the requirement that the provision be carefully drawn and have a rational connection to the objective. Section 237(1)(a) creates a presumption that a person in the driver's seat of a vehicle has the care or control of the vehicle, one of the elements of the offences under ss. 234 and 236. In my view, there is plainly a rational connection between the proved fact and the fact to be presumed. There is every reason to believe the person in the driver's seat has the care or control of the vehicle. The driver's seat is designed to give the occupant access to all the controls of the car, to be able to operate it. It is true that a vehicle can be occupied by one who does not assume care or control, but a person in this state of mind is likely to assume a position in the vehicle intended for a passenger rather than the driver. In my view, the relationship between the proved fact and the presumed fact under s. 237(1)(a) is direct and self-evident, quite unlike that which confronted the court in *Oakes*.

Since s. 237(1)(*a*) is intended to achieve the objective identified and is not arbitrary, unfair or based on irrational considerations, it passes this stage of the proportionality test.

The next stage of the proportionality inquiry is to ask whether the impugned measure impairs the right or freedom as little as possible. With respect to s. 237(1)(*a*), this is the most crucial and difficult aspect of s. 1 analysis. In my view, we must recognize that Parliament was faced with a difficult task in defining drinking and driving offences. The very fact that consumption of alcohol is an element of these offences renders problematic the element of intention. Justice precludes undue emphasis upon the mental element to these offences. Parliament has decided to define the offence in terms of "care or control". As I have already noted, this court has held that the Crown need not prove that the accused had an intention to drive or set the vehicle in motion in order to secure a conviction for "care or control". The *mens rea* requirement for the offence of care or control is a minimal one and it has not been argued here that this constitutes a departure from the requirements of s. 7 or 11(*d*) of the *Charter*.

Criminal legislation relating to the use of a motor vehicle while impaired dates back some 67 years.

. . . .

This history shows that there is a serious problem with the mental element of this offence, because the fact of intoxication itself raises doubts about the accused's mental state and ability to form an intention. The presumption was created by Parliament in response to that history. On the one hand, it was repugnant to theories of criminal liability that a person could be convicted of an absolute liability crime, with no possibility of a defence based on the mental state of the accused. On the other hand, as the Minister of Justice commented, it is shocking to hear that an accused could be acquitted of an offence for which consumption of alcohol is a required element, because he was too intoxicated to be guilty. The presumption was added to resolve the problems caused by both of these alternatives. Parliament wished to discourage intoxicated people from even placing themselves in a position where they could set a vehicle in motion, while at the same time providing a way for a person to avoid liability when there was a reason for entering the vehicle other than to set it in motion. The position adopted is admittedly a compromise. It is an attempt to balance the dangers posed by a person whose abilities to reason are impaired by alcohol with the desire to avoid absolute liability offences. It is an attempt by Parliament to recognize that alcohol, because of its effects on the reasoning process, may in some cases require a special treatment, while avoiding absolute liability offences.

The facts of the present case indicate that the problem identified by the Minister of Justice in 1947 could well recur today, absent s. 237(1)(*a*). Although the accused was found slumped over the steering wheel in a vehicle with the lights on, keys in the ignition and engine warm, the trial Judge found that, in the absence of the presumption, there would be a reasonable doubt as to guilt.

In my view, viewed in this context, s. 237(1)(*a*) represents a restrained Parliamentary response to a pressing social problem. It is important for the purposes of the s. 1 analysis to view s. 237(1)(*a*) in the context of its overall statutory setting. Parliament has attempted to strike a balance. On the one hand, the Crown need only prove a minimal level of intent on account of the fact that consumption of alcohol is itself an ingredient of the offence. On the other hand, where an accused can show that he or she had some reason for entering the vehicle and occupying the driver's seat other than to drive the vehicle, the accused will escape conviction. Viewed in this light, s. 237(1)(*a*) constitutes a minimal interference with the presumption of innocence guaranteed by s. 11(*d*) of the *Charter*.

The final stage of the *Oakes* test is to ask whether there is proportionality between the effects of the impugned measure and the objective being advanced. In my view, s. 237(1)(*a*) satisfies this final element in s. 1 analysis. The threat to public safety posed by drinking and driving has been established by evidence in this case and recognized by this court in others. While s. 237(1)(*a*) does infringe the right guaranteed by s. 11(*d*) of the *Charter*, it does so in the context of a statutory setting which makes it impracticable to require the Crown to prove an intention to drive. The reverse onus provision, in effect, affords a defence to an accused which could not otherwise be made available.

In *Whyte*, Dickson C.J. applies the Court's decisions in *Ford* and *Toews* respecting the offence of having care or control while impaired. The majority in *Ford*, with Justice Dickson dissenting, somehow interpreted the presumption in what is now s. 258(1)(*a*) to not involve the proof of an intent to set the vehicle in motion. *Toews* speaks of an element of intent to exert control over the vehicle. *Toews* has frequently been applied to convict an accused who has pulled over to sleep off his drunkenness, for example in *Hatfield* (1997), 115 C.C.C. (3d) 47 (Ont. C.A.), even if the keys are on the floor of the vehicle, *Pilon* (1998), 131 C.C.C. (3d) 236 (Ont. C.A.). However, the accused was found not guilty where the vehicle was in a ditch and immovable and the accused had got into the car to keep warm: *Wren* (2000), 34 C.R. (5th) 81, 144 C.C.C. (3d) 374 (Ont. C.A.), leave to appeal refused (October 12, 2000), Doc. 27912 (S.C.C.).

A review of many decisions in the Supreme Court applying the *Oakes* blueprint to s. 1 shows that the *Oakes* test is formalistic. Whether a limit can be demonstrably justified under s. 1 almost always turns on what has become known as the "minimum intrusion" test of whether the limitation restricts the *Charter* right as little as possible. Even in the context of criminal law, there seems to be a trend towards judicial deference to legislative choices, as evidenced in *Whyte*.

Oakes Test for Section 1

In *R. v. Edwards Books & Art Ltd.*, [1986] 2 S.C.R. 713, the issue was whether a Sunday observance law was unconstitutional through a violation of the freedom of religion guaranteed by s. 2(*a*) of the *Charter*. In applying his *Oakes* test, Chief Justice Dickson stated that the nature of the proportionality test would "vary depending on the circumstances" and that, both in the articulation of the standard of proof and in the applicable criteria, the Court had been "careful to avoid rigid and inflexible standards". The Chief Justice saw the question as whether the Act abridged freedom of religion as "little as is reasonably possible". Was there "some reasonable alternative scheme which would allow the province to achieve its objective with fewer detrimental effects on religious freedom?"

In *R. v. Chaulk*, [1990] 3 S.C.R. 1303, it was argued that the presumption of sanity then contained in s. 16(4) of the *Criminal Code*, placing the onus of proving the defence of insanity on the accused, was an unconstitutional violation of the presumption of innocence in s. 11(*d*). Chief Justice Lamer, writing for himself and four other judges, held that there had been a violation but it could be justified under s. 1. The objective of the presumption was to "avoid placing an impossible burden of proof on the Crown". Citing recent judgments of the Court, indicating that Parliament was not required to adopt the absolutely least intrusive means, Chief Justice Lamer saw the issue as "whether a less intrusive means would achieve the same objective or would achieve the same objective as effectively". The Chief Justice concluded that the alternative of an evidentiary burden requiring that the accused merely raise a reasonable doubt would not be as effective, accepting arguments by Attorneys General that it would be very easy for accused persons to "fake" such a defence.

The sole dissent on this point in *Chaulk* was Madam Justice Wilson, who held that this was not a case for relaxing the minimum impairment test. This might be done where a legislature, mediating between competing groups of citizens or allocating scarce resources, had to compromise on the basis of conflicting evidence. But in *Chaulk* the state was acting as "singular antagonists" of a very basic legal right of an accused and the strict standard of review in *Oakes* should be applied. The government's objective could be quite readily met by a mere burden on the accused to adduce evidence that made insanity "a live issue fit and proper to be left to the jury".

In the decade of jurisprudence since *Oakes*, section 1 consideration has invariably started with a recitation of the *Oakes* approach, almost as if it were a legislative replacement of the words of section 1. In *RJR-MacDonald Inc. v. Canada (Attorney General)* [1995] 3 S.C.R. 199, a recent major decision on section 1, McLachlin J. reasserts for the majority that:

> The factors generally relevant to determining whether a violative law is reasonably and demonstrably justified in a free and democratic society remain those set out in *Oakes*. The first requirement is that the objective of the law limiting the Charter right or freedom must be of sufficient importance to warrant overriding it. The second is that the means chosen to achieve the objective must be proportional to the objective and the effect of the law — proportionate, in short, to the good which it may produce. Three matters are considered in determining proportionality: the measures chosen must be rationally connected to the objective; they must impair the guaranteed right or freedom as little as reasonably possible (minimal impairment); and there must be overall proportionality between the deleterious effects of the measures and the salutary effects of the law.

In *R. v. Laba* (1994) 34 C.R. (4th) 360 (S.C.C.) the issue was the constitutionality of a provision under s. 394(1)(*b*) of the *Criminal Code* requiring a person charged with possessing or selling minerals to establish the defence of ownership or lawful authority. Sopinka J., for a Court unanimous on this point, held that the *Crown* could not demonstrably justify this persuasive burden on an accused given a reasonable legislative alternative of an evidentiary burden. In the course of the judgment a reference to *Chaulk* is followed by the remark that:

> it is also important to remember that this is not a case in which the legislature has attempted to strike a balance between the interests of competing individuals or groups. Rather it is a case in which the government (as opposed to other individuals or groups) can be characterised as the singular antagonist of an individual attempting to assert a legal right which is fundamental to our system of criminal justice (at 392).

This appears to endorse the minority Wilson position in *Chaulk*. Since the Court has changed its basic premise, previous section 1 rulings justifying various *Charter* violations in criminal cases, especially but not only those concerning reverse onus clauses, may well have to be revisited and/or properly distinguished on fresh challenges.

In its very lengthy judgment in *RJR-MacDonald* the Supreme Court held that a federal ban on advertising and promotion of tobacco without health warnings under the *Tobacco Products Act* violated freedom of expression guaranteed by section 2(*b*) of the *Charter*. The Court further held, 5-4, that the violation could not be saved under section 1. The judgment turns on section 1 with the degree of deference to be paid to Parliament being the pivotal issue. The majority finds it crucial that the federal government did not tender evidence in support of the need for a total ban. The minority through Mr. Justice La Forest would have allowed Parliament considerable latitude in its decision that a total ban was appropriate. On minimum intrusion the Court again seems agreed that the issue is whether the measure restricted as little as reasonably possible.

One of the majority judgments, by Madam Justice McLachlin, Major and Sopinka JJ. concurring, engages in the most wide-ranging and thoughtful consideration of *Oakes* since that decision. Unfortunately the extent to which she is speaking for the Court is unclear given a much shorter concurring judgement by Justice Iacobucci, Lamer C.J. concurring, which indicates that he differs "somewhat" with McLachlin J.'s section 1 analysis. The extent of the disagreement is left unclear.

McLachlin J. calls for a new stress by courts on the words "reasonable" and "demonstrably justified":

> While remaining sensitive to the social and political context of the impugned law and allowing for difficulties of proof inherent in that context, the courts must nevertheless insist that before the state can override constitutional rights, there must be a reasoned demonstration of the good which the law may achieve in relation to the seriousness of the infringement. It is the task of the courts to maintain this bottom line if the rights conferred by our constitutional are to have force and meaning. The task is not easily discharged, and may require the courts to confront the tide of popular public opinion.

McLachlin J. agrees with La Forest J. that the *Oakes* test, being a fact-specific inquiry, must be applied flexibly having regard to the factual and social context of each case. However she warns that this should not undercut the obligation of Parliament to justify limitations on *Charter* rights by reasoned demonstration. Her Ladyship later warns that care must be taken not to overstate the objective of the measure under challenge:

> The objective relevant to the s. 1 analysis is *the objective of the infringing measure*, since it is the infringing measure and nothing else which is sought to be justified. If the objective is stated too broadly, its importance may be exaggerated and the analysis compromised.

On the degree of deference courts should show Parliament McLachlin J. accepts that context is relevant. She gives a qualified answer to the question of whether a tougher approach should always be demanded in criminal law:

> It has been suggested that greater deference to Parliament or the legislature may be appropriate if the law is concerned with competing rights between different sections of society than if it is a contest between the individual and the state. . . . However, such distinctions may not always be easy to apply. For example, the criminal law is generally seen as involving a contest between the state and the accused, but it also involves an allocation of priorities between the accused and the victim, actual or potential.

McLachlin J. also suggests that care should be taken not to extend the notion of deference to the point of relieving the government of its burden of demonstrating reasonable and justified limits:

> Parliament has its role: to choose the appropriate response to social problems within the limiting framework of the constitutional. But the courts also have a role: to determine, objectively and impartially, whether Parliament's choice falls within the limiting framework of the constitution.

For McLachlin J. the standard of proof is not to the standard required by science nor proof beyond reasonable doubt. The standard of proof on a balance of probabilities may be established by the application of common sense to what is known. However she determines that this standard must be applied at all stages of the proportionality analysis, including the demonstration of a rational connection.

Her final general point relates to deference by appeal courts to findings by trial judges. There should be more deference to findings based on evidence of a purely factual nature but less where the trial judge has considered social science and other policy oriented evidence.

Do you think that the minimum intrusion test for s. 1 should, in the context of criminal law, be (a) does the limit restrict as little as possible (*Oakes*) or (b) does it restrict as little as reasonably possible (*Edwards Books*) or (c) does it achieve the same objective as effectively (*Chaulk*)? The Supreme Court still appears inconsistent in which test it applies. However there would appear to be a trend towards the *Edwards Books* approach.

For further consideration of this controversial jurisprudence on the s. 1 test, see Stuart, *Charter Justice in Canadian Criminal Law* (Toronto: Carswell, 3rd ed., 2001) Chapter 1.

Exclusion of Evidence Obtained Contrary to the *Charter*

Introduction

The *Charter* contains a provision which specifically equips a court with power to exclude evidence if the evidence was obtained in a manner that infringed or denied any rights or freedoms guaranteed by the *Charter*. However, an understanding of the present Canadian approach to the admissibility of illegally obtained evidence begins with *R. v. Wray*.[1] John Wray was charged with murder. He gave an incriminatory statement to police officers under circumstances that rendered it inadmissible pursuant to the classic rule that statements of an accused must be proved voluntary in the sense that they were not obtained by fear of prejudice or hope of advantage held out by a person in authority.[2] In the statement, Wray apparently admitted that he had disposed of the murder weapon and later actually directed the police to the spot where it was found. Ballistic evidence matched the bullet from the victim's body to the gun. The prosecution sought to introduce into evidence both the gun and the accused's involvement in its discovery. The Crown relied on the *St. Lawrence* rule:

> Where the discovery of the fact confirms the confession — that is, where the confession must be taken to be true by reason of the discovery of the fact — then that part of the confession that is confirmed by the discovery of the fact is admissible, but further than that no part of the confession is admissible.[3]

The trial Judge however disallowed the evidence, deciding that, given all the circumstances, the strict legal rule should not be applied.

To fully appreciate the trial Judge's ruling in *Wray*, some facts about the case are necessary. The murder occurred in Peterborough on March 23,1968. Ballistics identified the murder weapon as a Winchester 1892-44-40 rifle. On June 2 the O.P.P. went to Wray's home in search of such a weapon. With Wray's permission, his house and car were searched. Nothing was found. On June 4 Wray was asked if he'd take a lie-detector test. Wray agreed and he was transported to Toronto for the test. The interrogation, before Wray had been permitted to speak with a lawyer, by the polygraph analyst, Jurems, lasted from 2:35 p.m. to 7:10 p.m. The police waited in the next room listening and tape-recording the proceedings. The transcript occupied 60 pages. Portions of that transcript are reproduced in the Report on the Law of Evidence, Ontario Law Reform Commission, 1976, pp.74-90. The following excerpt gives a bit of the flavour:

(b) *The Interrogation of Wray*

JUREMS: Well this is a release form, John, that you have to sign to give me permission to examine you, see, because to put some attachments on you I have to have your permission. Right.

WRAY: Yes. If the test is negative or positive it wouldn't be used in evidence against me?

JUREMS: No, not necessarily, used as evidence against you.

WRAY: Or as evidence for them?

JUREMS: No, it's just to see John, we want to know. Let us assume that you're telling the truth?

WRAY: Yes.

---

1   [1971] S.C.R. 272, 11 C.R.N.S. 235, [1970] 4 C.C.C. 1.

2   This formula, stated in *Ibrahim v. R.*, [1914] A.C. 599 (P.C.), was first accepted in Canada as "correctly stating the rule" in *Prosko v. R.* (1922), 63 S.C.R. 226, 37 C.C.C. 199, 66 D.L.R. 340. The interrogation of Wray was recorded and lengthy portions of the transcript, showing the pressure that was brought to bear, are reproduced in the *Report on the Law of Evidence*, Ontario Law Reform Commission, 1976.

3   *R. v. St. Lawrence*, [1949] O.R. 215 at 228, 7 C.R. 464, 93 C.C.C. 376, (H.C.).

JUREMS: The machine will show that you're telling the truth and that will be the end of that. That will take the policemen off your back. Is that what you want?

WRAY: Yes.

JUREMS: So, if you would print your name on top and sign it here.

WRAY: Uh, yes.

The release was signed and Wray was questioned concerning the 44-40 rifle and a direct question was put, "Did you shoot a man at the Shell Station on March 23?" The answer was "No."

JUREMS: John, now listen to me good. Now I was through the war, see, and I've been around. Now remember this and remember it good. Have you ever seen rubby dubbies, winos?

WRAY: Yes.

JUREMS: Have you ever seen the alcoholics?

WRAY: Yes.

JUREMS: Do you know why they go that way. Have you got a clue?

WRAY: No. I have an idea.

JUREMS: I'll explain you something. You have the cerebreal [sic], cerebreal [sic] and then you have the tholmus [sic] and the hipatholmus [sic]. Now, a person is going to blot out something he doesn't like, see, but you just can't do it, John. You just no can do, because the subconscious mind takes over and you never live it down. Every time you want to do something you think of it. Now here's this poor joker, he's in the grave, oh, yes, now you can never go to him and explain to him, say I'm sorry I did it. He won't understand you. Do you believe in E.S.P., Extra Sensory Perception?

WRAY: I don't understand it too much, but I know it exists.

JUREMS: All right. All right, do you know what happens when they're dead. The spirit takes off.

WRAY: Yes.

JUREMS: The body's spirit takes off. Now his body's lying there in the grave. Now for Christ sake, John, if you did it, see, if you did it and if you think for one goddamn minute you can live with this all your life without telling you'll never make it. You'll never ever make it. It will haunt you and in about five years time you will be in the goddamn with the rubby dubs trying to hide it, you'll be trying to get in behind some curtains, you'll be trying to pull a shroud around you but you'll never make it, see. You get half a dozen of those rubby dubs and you bring them in here and I'll put them on the machine and they tell me why they're like that. You know why? They're trying to forget something. They're trying to forget something they did that was very goddamn serious, very bad, see, but they never make it. They go rubby dub, they go here, they steal here, they do every goddamn thing wrong, all their life, eh. Now, if you committed this goddamn thing, see, tell them, tell the cops. What the hell can you get? They're not going to hang you. That's out. There is no capital murder. They're not going to hang you. What do you do. You get in there for seven or eight years and you're out. But at least you've got it and after that you can live with your conscience. But how the hell are you going to go to the grave and explain? You can't, and if you think for one minute, John, remember this that that boy has relatives, that boy has mother and brothers and sisters and do you know what a vindictive person is? Eh? They'll go for you and maybe a year, maybe five years from now you'll be going down the road and some son of a bitch will run you off the road. You'll never know why, but you'll guess why. See. Now, you were there, see. You were in the goddamn service station. Now when I asked you whether it was an accident you said, yes, and it was an accident, see. There's extenuating circumstances because a person goes in there you didn't go in — you don't go in the — there to shoot the fellow. When a fellow goes in there, sure, what happened to this — look at that goofy one that came here from Montreal, he shot three people in a bank robbery, what did he get, he's out now. He didn't even serve ten years. Three people in a bank robbery. See. So you went in there. You didn't go in there to shoot the guy, but the gun went off. It was at close range. What did he do, grab the gun from you. Did he grab the rifle from you? Eh?

WRAY: No.

JUREMS: What happened? Well, get it off your chest man, you're young, but in a few years you'll be out. But if you think that you're going to live with this, laddie, you'll never ever never make it. It's going to bug you for the rest of your goddamn life. And you try and sleep, that's the kicker, you try and lay down and go to sleep. Now what the hell happened there. Did you get in a tussle with him — what happened. Well, spit it out. Your mother knows, your brother knows, your sisters know, your uncle knows. Do you think you can kid your mother for one minute — never! Your mother knows. That's why she tried to protect you. You know. Now what the hell happened, eh? Will you tell us what happened?

WRAY: Yes.

JUREMS: Okay, tell us what happened.

WRAY: I went in. . .

JUREMS: You went in, talk a little louder, John.

WRAY: I went in there.

JUREMS: Yeah.

WRAY: To Knoll's.

JUREMS: Yeah, you went in to Knoll's, yeah.

WRAY: And the boy —

JUREMS: Which boy?

WRAY: There's only one boy.

JUREMS: Just the boy that was shot. Yeah, what happened?

WRAY: He came out.

JUREMS: Talk a little louder, John.

WRAY: He came out.

JUREMS: Yeah.

WRAY: And asked me what I wanted.

JUREMS: He asked you what you wanted.

WRAY: And I told him to open the till.

JUREMS: And told him to open the till. Was it closed?

WRAY: Yes.

JUREMS: And what did he say?

WRAY: He said, all right.

JUREMS: He opened the till, yeah.

WRAY: And then he — he gave me the money.

JUREMS: He gave you the money. Well, what the hell did you shoot him for?

WRAY: It was an accident.

JUREMS: What?

WRAY: It was an accident.

JUREMS: It was an accident. Sure, you showed it on your check it was an accident. All the reactions you gave me when I asked you was the shooting an accident, you said, yes, and it's an accident. Well, what the hell is wrong with that. All they are going to charge you with. You went in there, your intentions weren't to do any harm to the man. Where is the gun now?

WRAY: I don't know exactly.

JUREMS: Well, where did you drop it, on the way home?

WRAY: No, eh?

JUREMS: On the way to Toronto?

WRAY: Yes.

JUREMS: Around Oshawa?

WRAY: No.

JUREMS: Where?

WRAY: Near Omemee someplace.

JUREMS: Where?

WRAY: Omemee.

JUREMS: Omemee, in the ditch?

WRAY: No.

JUREMS: Where?

WRAY: In the swamp.

JUREMS: In the swamp. Could you, could you show the police where it is?

WRAY:	Yes.
JUREMS:	Now you're talking like a man. Jesus Christ, John, because you got to live with it all your life, man, oh, man, you'll never make it if you a person sleeps, hasn't it been bothering you?
WRAY:	Yes.
JUREMS:	Have you been sleeping well?
WRAY:	Yes, fairly well.
JUREMS:	But it bothers you. A person never lives it down. Now when, now I'll call in the — the Inspector there and you tell him what happened, okay. Will you tell him?
WRAY:	Yes.
LIDSTONE:	Now, John, you will be charged with the non-capital murder of Donald Comrie on the 23rd day of March, 1968, at Otonabee Township. You are not required to say anything in answer to the charge, but what you do say will be given in evidence. Do you understand that?
WRAY:	Yes.

Following the interrogation by Jurems and the Inspector a statement was prepared by the officers and signed by Wray. It read:

John Wray

You are charged with the non-capital murder of Donald Comrie on the 23rd of March, 1968 at Otonabee Twp. You are not required to say anything or answer to the charge but what you do say will be given in evidence.

Q. Do you understand that?
A. Yes. Well I went into the station and asked him for the money and he gave it to me. I told him to back away and he did and I backed away and the gun went off. It was an accident. I didn't mean to shoot him. . . I didn't even know I had the gun pointed in his direction. Then I went out and ran back to my car and went to the garage. That was it. I didn't mean to hurt him.
Q. What happened to the gun?
A. I threw it in the swamp.
Q. Where?
A. Near Omemee.
Q. Will you try and show us the spot?
A. Yes.
Q. Is there anything else you want to add to this John?
A. Not now, thank you.

"John Wray"

"J.W. Lidstone"
"D.O. Woodbeck"   7:18 p.m.

After this statement was signed the officers drove with the accused to the swamp to search for the rifle. They did not find it the first night. The next day they found it a short distance from where the accused said he had thrown it.

The Court of Appeal agreed with the trial Judge's ruling and explained:

> In our view, a trial Judge has a discretion to reject evidence, even of substantial weight, if he considers that its admission would be unjust or unfair to the accused or calculated to bring the administration of justice into disrepute, the exercise of such discretion, of course, to depend upon the particular facts before him.[4]

---

4 [1970] 2 O.R. 3 at 4, 3 C.C.C. (2d) 122, 123.

The majority of the Supreme Court of Canada however voted to reverse and ordered a new trial, clearly rejecting any notion that a trial Judge should be concerned with how the evidence was obtained:

> This development of the idea of a general discretion to exclude admissible evidence is not warranted by the authority on which it purports to be based. . .the exercise of a discretion by the trial Judge arises only if the admission of the evidence would operate unfairly. The allowance of admissible evidence relevant to the issue before the Court and of substantial probative value may operate unfortunately for the accused, but not unfairly. It is only the allowance of evidence gravely prejudicial to the accused, the admissibility of which is tenuous, and whose probative force in relation to the main issue before the court is trifling, which can be said to operate unfairly.[5]

In a separate concurring opinion, Justice Judson upheld the admissibility of evidence of the accused's involvement in finding the murder weapon by distinguishing between statements and things:

> The theory for the rejection of confessions is that if they are obtained under certain conditions, they are untrustworthy. This theory has no application whatever to incontrovertible facts, such as the finding of articles. . .[6]

The majority of the Supreme Court of Canada in *Wray* expressly limited the rationale of the confession rule to ensuring trustworthiness. The minority however saw another reason:

> If, on the other hand, the exclusion of an involuntary confession is based also on the maxim *nemo tenetur seipsum accusare* the truth or falsity of the confession does become logically irrelevant. It would indeed be a strange result if, it being the law that no accused is bound to incriminate himself and that he is to be protected from having to testify at an inquest, a preliminary hearing or a trial, he could none the less be forced by the police or others in authority to make a statement which could then be given in evidence against him. The result which would seem to follow if the exclusion is based on the maxim would be that the involuntary confession even if verified by subsequently discovered evidence could not be referred to in any way.[7]

Competing views have always existed in Canadian jurisprudence: is the confession rule based solely on a concern for trustworthiness or is it also based on the notion that it is unfair to make use of an accused for the purposes of his own destruction.[8] Although that tension continued to exist in judicial views

---

5 Supra, n. 2 at S.C.R. 293, C.C.C. 17, Martland, J.

6 Ibid, at S.C.R. 296, C.C.C. 20.

7 Ibid, at S.C.R. 280, C.C.C. 7, per Cartwright, J.

8 See e.g. *Piche v. R.*, [1971] S.C.R. 23, 12 C.R.N.S. 222, [1970] 4 C.C.C. 27, where, in a decision handed down on the same day as *Wray*, the majority decided that an accused's earlier exculpatory statement, tendered by the Crown, not for its truth but as a false statement impacting on credibility, must nevertheless be proved voluntary. See also *DeClercq v. R.*, [1968] S.C.R. 902, 4 C.R.N.S. 205, [1969] 1 C.C.C. 197, 70 D.L.R. (2d) 530, where the Court held it permissible to ask an accused, during the *voir dire* held to determine voluntariness, whether the statement was true; the Court believed truth was relevant to voluntariness. Even if truth is relevant to voluntariness, no one would suggest it was conclusive and therefore, by implication, the Court was holding that a statement, admitted to be true by the accused, could nevertheless be excluded as involuntary. See also the opinions in *Rothman v. R.*, [1981] 1 S.C.R. 640, 20 C.R. (3d) 97, 59 C.C.C. (2d) 30. In *Rothman* the accused's statement was gained by an undercover officer and the majority voted to receive since the accused did not know that his confidant was a "person in authority." In dissent, Estey, J. argued that the basic reason for the rule was concern for the integrity of the criminal justice system and he would exclude lest the administration of justice be brought into disrepute. The Court has also held however that a statement might be involuntary because of circumstances in the case other than a peace officer's holding out advantage or prejudice: see, e.g. *Ward v. R.*, [1979] 2 S.C.R. 30, 7 C.R. (3d) 153, 44 C.C.C. (2d) 498 and *Horvath v. R.* (1979), 7 C.R. (3d) 97, 44 C.C.C. (2d) 385.

expressed after *Wray*, the majority viewpoint in the Supreme court of Canada in 1982 is that, aside from confessions, the Court should not be concerned with how the evidence was obtained. Then came the *Charter*!

Section 24 of the *Charter* provides:

> 24. (1) Anyone whose rights or freedoms, as guaranteed by this *Charter*, have been infringed or denied may apply to a court of competent jurisdiction to obtain such remedy as the Court considers appropriate and just in the circumstances.
>
> (2) Where, in proceedings under subsection (1), a court concludes that evidence was obtained in a manner that infringed or denied any rights or freedoms guaranteed by this charter, the evidence shall be excluded if it is established that, having regard to all the circumstances, the admission of it in the proceedings would bring the administration of justice into disrepute.

Although it was at one time thought[9] that s. 24(1) might also empower exclusion, the Supreme Court of Canada has now decided that the power to exclude evidence is to be found solely in s. 24(2).[10] The language of s. 24(2) specifically denies an automatic rule of exclusion; even though a constitutional right has been infringed evidence obtained as a result is to be excluded only if the accused establishes that admission "would bring the administration of justice into disrepute".

The first Supreme Court of Canada decision to interpret s. 24 of the *Charter* was, ironically, a breathalyzer case, *R. v. Therens*.[11] The accused's motor-vehicle was involved in a collision. A police officer demanded that the accused accompany him to the station for the purpose of obtaining breath samples. The accused accompanied the officer and supplied the required breath samples. At no time was the accused informed of the right to retain and instruct counsel. The trial Judge, finding a violation of the accused's constitutional rights in s. 10(*b*), acted pursuant to s. 24 and excluded evidence of the breathalyzer readings. Since there was a lack of other evidence of blood-alcohol level he dismissed the charge. Appeals by the Crown were dismissed.[12] The Supreme Court in *Therens* thus signalled to the country that the *Charter of Rights and Freedoms* was not going to follow the earlier path chartered by the *Canadian Bill of Rights*.[13] The *Charter* was a constitutional document. The Bill of Rights, a statute of the federal parliament, embodying many of the same rights as the *Charter*, confronted a series of breathalyzer cases in its infancy,[14] and the spectre of carnage on the highways caused the Supreme Court to narrowly interpret the Bill and so denude it of much of its authority. The Court in *Therens* decided to exclude the evidence, finding the police officer's conduct to be a "flagrant" violation of the accused's *Charter* right, although, on the facts, and according to the then interpretation of

---

9 *R. v. Therens*, 33 C.R. (3d) 204, 5 C.C.C. (3d) 409 (Sask. C.A.).

10 *R. v. Therens*, [1985] 1 S.C.R. 613, 45 C.R. (3d) 97, 18 C.C.C. (3d) 481 (S.C.C.).

11 [1985] 1 S.C.R. 613, 18 C.C.C. (3d) 481.

12 *Supra*, notes 8 and 9.

13 *An Act for the Recognition and Protection of Human Rights and Fundamental Freedoms*, S.C. 1960, c. 44.

14 See *Brownridge v. R.*, [1972] S.C.R. 926, 18 C.R.N.S. 308, 7 C.C.C. (2d) 417; *Curr v. R.*, [1972] S.C.R. 889, 18 C.R.N.S. 281, 7 C.C.C. (2d) 181 and *R. v. Appleby*, [1972] S.C.R. 303, 16 C.R.N.S. 35, 3 C.C.C. (2d) 354.

the word "detention",[15] a compelling argument could be made that the officer had acted in good faith.[16]

Therens is also noteworthy for the opinion of Justice Le Dain, suggesting for the first time a hierarchy in the legal rights listed in the *Charter* which would influence the approach to the exclusion of illegally obtained evidence. In his view:

> . . . the right to counsel is of such fundamental importance that its denial in a criminal law context must prima facie discredit the administration of justice. That effect is not diminished but, if anything, increased by the relative seriousness of the possible criminal law liability.[17]

He did not explain why a person's right to counsel is necessarily more important than, for example, his right to be secure against an unreasonable search or an arbitrary detention but, as we will see, this seed, here planted, does grow in later cases.

In *Clarkson v. R.*[18] the accused was charged with murder. Arrested at the scene, she was given the customary police warning regarding her right to remain silent and duly informed of the right to retain and instruct counsel. She was then transported from the scene of the murder to a hospital where she was physically examined. A blood-test showed her to be highly intoxicated. She was then taken to the police station and again advised of her right to counsel. A relative, present during the interrogation, tried to dissuade the police from any questioning, and the accused from answering, until a lawyer was present. The police relied on the fact that they had advised the accused of her rights and that the accused had waived off her friend's advice, saying that there was "no point" and that she did not need the help of a lawyer. The trial judge excluded her statements on the basis that, in her intoxicated state she did not appreciate the consequences of making the statements. The jury acquitted. The Court of Appeal reversed saying that the proper test, in applying the confession rule, was to ask simply whether the accused's mind was in a sufficiently functional state to give probative value to her words. The Supreme Court restored the acquittal on the ground that, aside from the common law confession rule, it had not been shown that the accused had voluntary waived her right to counsel:

> . . . it is clear that the waiver of the s. 10(*b*) right by an intoxicated accused must pass some form of "awareness of the consequences" test. Unlike the confession itself, there is no room for an argument that the Court in assessing such a waiver should be concerned only with the probative value of the evidence so as to restrict the test to the accused's mere comprehension of his or her own words. Rather, the purpose of the right, as indicated by each of the members of this Court writing in *Therens*, is to ensure that the accused is treated fairly in the criminal process. While this constitutional guarantee cannot be forced upon an unwilling accused, any voluntary waiver, in order to be valid and effective, must be premised on a true appreciation of the consequences of giving up the right.[19]

---

15 In *R. v. Chromiak*, [1980] 15 C.R. 471 the Court unanimously held that a person who complied with a demand to accompany an officer and submit to a roadside test was not "detained" within the meaning of s. 2(*c*) of the *Canadian Bill of Rights* so as to trigger his right to counsel. For the Court in that case "detained" meant "detained by due process of law" and did not necessarily include arrest.

16 Le Dain J., (McIntyre J. concurring) would have received the evidence because of the officer's good faith reliance on the Court's previous judgment.

17 45 C.R. (3d) 97 at 133.

18 [1986] 1 S.C.R. 383, 50 C.R. (3d) 289, 25 C.C.C. (3d) 207.

19 Per Wilson J. at 302. For a criticism see Duncan, "Clarkson: Some Unanswered Questions" (1986), 60 C.R. (3d) 305.

The majority found that the police acted deliberately, knowing that the accused was forfeiting a valuable protection, at a time when there was no urgency in the gathering of evidence. For the majority this added up to a "flagrant" breach. Allowing the accused's confession into evidence would necessarily bring the administration of justice into disrepute.

The most important Supreme Court decision to date on the question of illegally obtained evidence is *R. v. Collins*.

R. v. COLLINS

[1987] 1 S.C.R. 265, 56 C.R. (3d) 193, 33 C.C.C. (3d) 1

Collins was charged with possession of heroin for the purpose of trafficking. The police were conducting a surveillance of a tavern in connection with a heroin investigation. When the accused's husband left the premises the police followed, searched his car, and found heroin. The police returned to the tavern, an officer seized the accused by the throat and pulled her to the ground. In her hand he discovered a green balloon containing a substance that later analyzed as heroin. At the beginning of her trial, counsel sought a *voir dire* to determine whether the evidence was receivable pursuant to s. 24. The trial Judge concluded that the officer had only a suspicion that the accused was carrying drugs and did not have a belief based on reasonable grounds. The search was accordingly unlawful and therefore unreasonable in violation of the appellant's rights under s. 8 of the *Charter*. Nevertheless the trial judge held that the accused had failed to satisfy him that the evidence should be excluded under s. 24. The Court of Appeal dismissed the accused's appeal but the Supreme Court reversed.

LAMER J. (DICKSON C.J.C., WILSON and LAFOREST JJ. concurring): —

The appellant, Ruby Collins, was seated in a pub in the town of Gibsons when she was suddenly seized by the throat and pulled down to the floor by a man who said to her "police officer". The police officer, then noticing that she had her hand clenched around an object, instructed her to let go of the object. As it turned out, she had a green balloon containing heroin.

It is common knowledge that drug traffickers often keep their drugs in balloons or condoms in their mouths so that they may, when approached by the Narcotics Control Agent, swallow the drugs without harm and recoup them subsequently. The "throat hold" is used to prevent them from swallowing the drugs.

The issue is whether the evidence obtained under these circumstances is to be excluded under s. 24(2) of the *Charter*.

. . . .

Legislation

The search of Ruby Collins was purportedly authorized by s. 10(1) of the *Narcotic Control Act*, R.S.C. 1970, c. N-1, as amended, as that section read prior to the amendments of December 1985:

10. (1) A peace officer may, at any time,

(a) without a warrant enter and search any place other than a dwelling-house, and under the authority of a writ of assistance or a warrant issued under this section, enter and search any dwelling-house in which he reasonably believes there is a narcotic by means of or in respect of which an offence under this Act has been committed;

(b) search any person found in such place; and

(c) seize and take away any narcotic found in such place, any thing in such place in which he reasonably suspects a narcotic is contained or concealed, or any other thing by means of or in respect of which he reasonably believes an offence under this Act has been committed or that may be evidence of the commission of such an offence.

. . . .

The Law

The appellant seeks the exclusion of evidence that she was in possession of heroin, alleging that the heroin was discovered pursuant to a search which was unreasonable under s. 8 of the *Charter*. This Court in *Therens, supra,* held that evidence cannot be excluded as a remedy under s. 24(1) of the *Charter*, but must meet the test of exclusion under s. 24(2). At first glance, the wording of s. 24 leads one to conclude that there are three prerequisites to the exclusion of evidence under s. 24(2) of the *Charter*:

1) that the applicant's rights or freedoms, as guaranteed by the *Charter*, have been infringed or denied,
2) that the evidence was obtained in a manner that infringed or denied any rights or freedoms guaranteed by the *Charter*, and
3) that, having regard to all the circumstances, the admission of the evidence in the proceedings would bring the administration of justice into disrepute.

The Reasonableness of the Search

The appellant, in my view, bears the burden of persuading the Court that her *Charter* rights or freedoms have been infringed or denied. That appears from the wording of s. 24(1) and (2), and most Courts which have considered the issue have come to that conclusion (see *R. v. Lundrigan* (1985), 19 C.C.C. (3d) 499 (Man. C.A.), and the cases cited therein, Gibson, The Law of the *Charter*: General Principles (1986), p. 278). The appellant also bears the initial burden of presenting evidence. The standard of persuasion required is only the civil standard of the balance of probabilities and, because of this, the allocation of the burden of persuasion means only that, in a case where the evidence does not establish whether or not the appellant's rights were infringed, the court must conclude that they were not.

The Courts have also developed certain presumptions. In particular, this Court held in *Hunter v. Southam Inc.*, [1984] 2 S.C.R. 145, at p. 161:

In *United States v. Rabinowitz*, 339 U.S. 56 (1950), the Supreme Court of the United States had held that a search without warrant was not *ipso facto* unreasonable. Seventeen years later, however, in *Katz*, Stewart J. concluded that a warrantless search was *prima facie* "unreasonable" under the Fourth Amendment. The terms of the Fourth Amendment are not identical to those of s. 8 and American decisions can be transplanted to the Canadian context only with the greatest caution. Nevertheless, I would in the present instance respectfully adopt Stewart J.'s formulation as equally applicable to the concept of "unreasonableness" under s. 8, and would require the party seeking to justify a warrantless search to rebut this presumption of unreasonableness.

This shifts the burden of persuasion from the appellant to the Crown. As a result, once the appellant has demonstrated that the search was a warrantless one, the Crown has the burden of showing that the search was, on a balance of probabilities, reasonable.

A search will be reasonable if it is authorized by law, if the law itself is reasonable and if the manner in which the search was carried out is reasonable. In this case, the Crown argued that the search was carried out under s. 10(1) of the *Narcotic Control Act, supra.* As the appellant has not challenged the constitutionality of s. 10(1) of the Act, the issues that remain to be decided here are whether the search was unreasonable because the officer did not come within s. 10 of the Act, or whether, while being within s. 10, he carried out the search in a manner that made the search unreasonable.

For the search to be lawful under s. 10, the Crown must establish that the officer believed on reasonable grounds that there was a narcotic in the place where the person searched was found. The nature of the belief will also determine whether the manner in which the search was carried out was reasonable. For example, if a police officer is told by a reliable source that there are persons in possession of drugs in a certain place, the officer may, depending on the circumstances and the nature and precision of the information given by that source, search persons found in that place under s. 10, but surely, without very specific information, a seizure by the throat, as in this case, would be unreasonable. Of course, if he is lawfully searching a person whom he believes on reasonable grounds to be a "drug handler", then the "throat hold" would not be unreasonable.

Because of the presumption of unreasonableness, the Crown in this case had to present evidence of the officer's belief and the reasonable grounds for that belief. It may be surmised that there were reasonable grounds based on information received from the local police. However, the Crown failed to establish such reasonable grounds in the examination-in-chief of Constable Woods, and, as set out earlier, when it attempted to do so on its re-examination, the appellant's counsel objected. As a result, the Crown never did establish the constable's reasonable grounds. Without such evidence, it is clear that the trial Judge was correct in concluding that the search was unreasonable because unlawful and carried out with unnecessary violence.

However, the problem is that the objection raised by the appellant's counsel was groundless: this Court has held that reasonable grounds can be based on information received from third parties without infringing the hearsay rule (*Eccles v. Bourque, supra*), and the question put to the constable in this case was not outside the ambit of the ground covered in cross-examination. A further problem is that the record does not disclose why the question was not answered: it is not clear whether the trial Judge maintained the objection or whether the Crown had reacted to the objection by withdrawing the question. It is worthy of mention that, because a conviction was entered, the Crown could not in any event appeal against the decision.

This Court has two options. We could resolve the doubt against the Crown, which had the burden of persuasion, and simply proceed on the basis that there was no such evidence. Alternatively, we could order a new trial. I would order a new trial on the basis that the trial Judge either made an incorrect ruling or failed to make a ruling, and, in any event, the appellant should not, in the particular circumstances of this case, be allowed to benefit from her counsel's unfounded objection.

However, before ordering a new trial, we must decide whether we agree with the trial judge and the Court of Appeal that the evidence of the heroin would be admissible regardless of the constable's grounds for the search, for there then would be no point in a new trial and we should dismiss the appeal. As a result, I must determine whether I would exclude the evidence under s. 24(2) on the assumption that Constable Woods testifies that he had not received any further information, thereby leaving matters in that regard as they stand at present on the record.

Bringing the Administration of Justice into Disrepute

On the record as it now stands, the appellant has established that the search was unreasonable and violated her rights under s. 8 of the *Charter*. As Seaton J.A. pointed out in the Court of Appeal, s. 24(2) has adopted an intermediate position with respect to the exclusion of evidence obtained in violation of the *Charter*. It rejected the American rule excluding all evidence obtained in violation of the *Bill of Rights* and the common law rule that all relevant evidence was admissible regardless of the means by which it was obtained. Section 24(2) requires the exclusion of the evidence "if it is established that, having regard to all the circumstances, the admission of it in the proceedings would bring the administration of justice into disrepute".

At the outset, it should be noted that the use of the phrase "if it is established that" places the burden of persuasion on the applicant, for it is the position which he maintains which must be established. Again, the standard of persuasion required can only be the civil standard of the balance of probabilities. Thus, the applicant must make it more probable than not that the admission of the evidence would bring the administration of justice into disrepute.

It is whether the admission of the evidence would bring the administration of justice into disrepute that is the applicable test. Misconduct by the police in the investigatory process often has some effect on the repute of the administration of justice, but s. 24(2) is not a remedy for police misconduct, requiring the exclusion of the evidence if, because of this misconduct, the administration of justice was brought into disrepute. Section 24(2) could well have been drafted in that way, but it was not. Rather, the drafters of the *Charter* proceedings, and the purpose of s. 24(2) is to prevent having the administration of justice brought into further disrepute by the admission of the evidence in the proceedings. This further disrepute will result from the admission of evidence that would deprive the accused of a fair hearing, or from judicial condonation of unacceptable conduct by the investigatory and prosecutorial agencies. It will also be necessary to consider any disrepute that may result from the exclusion of the evidence. It would be inconsistent with the purpose of s. 24(2) to exclude evidence if its exclusion would bring the administration of justice into greater disrepute then would its admission. Finally, it must be emphasized that even though the inquiry under s. 24(2) will necessarily focus on the specific prosecution, it is the long-term consequences of regular admission or exclusion of the type of evidence on the repute of the administration of justice which must be considered (see on this point Gibson, *supra*, p. 245).

The concept of disrepute necessarily involves some element of community views, and the determination of disrepute thus requires the Judge to refer to what he conceives to be the views of the community at large. This does not mean that evidence of the public's perception of the repute of the administration of justice, which Professor Gibson suggested could be presented in the form of public opinion polls (*supra*, pp. 236-47), will be determinative of the issue (see Therens, *supra*, pp. 653-54). The position is different with respect to obscenity, for example, where the Court must assess the level of tolerance of the community, whether or not it is reasonable, and may consider public opinion polls (*R. v. Prairie Schooner News Ltd. and Powers* (1970), 1 C.C.C. (2d) 251 (Man. C.A.), at p. 266, cited in *Towne Cinema Theatres Ltd. v. The Queen* [1985] 1 S.C.R. 494, at p. 513). It would be unwise, in my respectful view, to adopt a similar attitude with respect to the *Charter*. Members of the public generally become conscious of the importance of protecting the rights and freedoms of accused only when they are in some way brought closer to the system either personally or through the experience of friends or family. Professor Gibson recognized the danger of leaving the exclusion of evidence to uninformed members of the public when he stated at p. 246:

> The ultimate determination must be with the Courts, because they provide what is often the only effective shelter for individuals and unpopular minorities from the shifting winds of public passion.

The *Charter* is designed to protect the accused from the majority, so the enforcement of the *Charter* must not be left to that majority.

The approach I adopt may be put figuratively in terms of the reasonable person test proposed by Professor Yves-Marie Morissette in his article "The Exclusion of Evidence under the *Canadian Charter of Rights and Freedoms*: What to Do and What Not to Do" (1984), 29 McGill L.J. 521, at p. 538. In applying s. 24(2), he suggested that the relevant question is: " 'Would the admission of the evidence bring the administration of justice into disrepute in the eyes of the reasonable man, dispassionate and fully apprised of the circumstances of the case?" The reasonable person is usually the average person in the community, but only when that community's current mood is reasonable.

The decision is thus not left to the untramelled discretion of the Judge. In practice, as Professor Morissette wrote, the reasonable person test is there to require of Judges that they "concentrate on what they do best: finding within themselves, with cautiousness and impartiality, a basis for their own decisions, articulating their reasons carefully and accepting review by a higher Court where it occurs." It serves as a reminder to each individual Judge that his discretion is grounded in community values, and, in particular, long term community values. He should not render a decision that would be unacceptable to the community when that community is not being wrought with passion or otherwise under passing stress due to current events. In effect, the Judge will decline to interfere with his decision, even though they might have decided the matter differently, using the well-known statements that they are of the view that the decision was not unreasonable.

In determining whether the admission of evidence would bring the administration of justice into disrepute, the Judge is directed by s. 24(2) to consider "all the circumstances". The factors which are to be considered and balanced have been listed by many Courts in the country. . . . The factors that the Courts have most frequently considered include:

-what kind of evidence was obtained?
-what *Charter* right was infringed?
-was the *Charter* violation serious or was it of a merely technical nature?
-was it deliberate, wilful or flagrant, or was it inadvertent or committed in good faith?
-did it occur in circumstances of urgency or necessity?
-were there other investigatory techniques available?
-would the evidence have been obtained in any event?
-is the offence serious?
-is the evidence essential to substantiate the charge?
-are other remedies available?

I do not wish to be seen as approving this as an exhaustive list of the relevant factors, and I would like to make some general comments as regards these factors.

As a matter of personal preference, I find it useful to group the factors according to the way in which they affect the repute of the administration of justice. Certain of the factors listed are relevant in determining the effect of the admission of the evidence on the fairness of the trial. The trial is a key part of the administration of justice, and the fairness of Canadian trials is a major source of the repute of the system and is now a right guaranteed by s. 11(*d*) of the *Charter*. If the admission of the evidence in some way affects the fairness of the trial, then the admission of the evidence would tend to bring the administration of justice into disrepute and, subject to a consideration of the other factors, the evidence generally should be excluded.

It is clear to me that the factors relevant to this determination will include the nature of the evidence obtained as a result of the violation and the nature of the right violated and not so much the manner in which the right was violated. Real evidence that was obtained in a manner that violated the *Charter* will rarely operate unfairly for that reason alone. The real evidence existed irrespective of the violation of the *Charter* and its use does not render the trial unfair. However, the situation is very different with respect to cases where, after a violation of the *Charter*, the accused is conscripted against himself through a confession or other evidence emanating from him. The use of such evidence would render the trial unfair, for it did not exist prior to the violation and it strikes at one of the fundamental tenets of a fair trial, the right against self-incrimination. Such evidence will generally arise in the context of an infringement of the right to counsel. Our decisions in *Therens, supra*, and *Clarkson v. The Queen*, [1986] 1 S.C.R. 383, are illustrative of this. The use of self-incriminating evidence obtained following a denial of the right to counsel will generally go to the very fairness of the trial and should generally be excluded. Several Courts of Appeal have also emphasized this distinction between pre-existing real evidence and self-incriminatory evidence created following a breach of the *Charter* (see *R. v. Dumas* (1985), 23 C.C.C. (3d) 366 (Alta. C.A.), *R. v. Strachan* (1986), 24 C.C.C. (3d) 205 (B.C. C.A.), *R. v. Dairy Supplies Ltd.* (Man. C.A., January 13, 1987, unreported)). It may also be relevant, in certain circumstances, that the evidence would have been obtained in any event without the violation of the *Charter*.

There are other factors which are relevant to the seriousness of the *Charter* violation and thus to the disrepute that will result from judicial acceptance of evidence obtained through that violation. As Le Dain J. wrote in *Therens, supra*, at p. 652:

> The relative seriousness of the constitutional violation has been assessed in the light of whether it was committed in good faith, or was inadvertent or of a merely technical nature, or whether it was deliberate, wilful or flagrant. Another relevant consideration is whether the action which constituted the constitutional violation was motivated by urgency or necessity to prevent the loss or destruction of the evidence.

I should add that the availability of other investigatory techniques and the fact that the evidence could have been obtained without the violation of the *Charter* tend to render the *Charter* violation more serious. We are considering the actual conduct of the authorities and the evidence must not be admitted on the basis that they could have proceeded otherwise and obtained the evidence properly. In fact, their failure to proceed properly when that option was open to them tends to indicate a blatant disregard for the *Charter*, which is a factor supporting the exclusion of the evidence.

The final relevant group of factors consists of those that relate to the effect of excluding the evidence. The question under s. 24(2) is whether the system's repute will be better served by the admission or the exclusion of the evidence, and it is thus necessary to consider any disrepute that may result from the exclusion of the evidence. In my view, the administration of justice would be brought into disrepute by the exclusion of evidence essential to substantiate the charge, and thus the acquittal of the accused, because of a trivial breach of the *Charter*. Such disrepute would be greater if the offence was more serious. I would thus agree with Professor Morissette that evidence is more likely to be excluded if the offence is less serious (*supra*, pp. 529-31). I hasten to add, however, that if the admission of the evidence would result in an unfair trial, the seriousness of the offence could not render that evidence admissible. If any relevance is to be given to the seriousness of the offence in the context of the fairness of the trial, it operates in the opposite sense: the more serious the offence, the more damaging to the system's repute would be an unfair trial.

Finally, a factor which, in my view, is irrelevant is the availability of other remedies. Once it has been decided that the administration of justice would be brought into disrepute by the admission of the evidence, the disrepute will not be lessened by the existence of some ancillary remedy (see Gibson, *supra*, at p. 261).

I would agree with Howland C.J.O. in *Simmons*, *supra*, that we should not gloss over the words of s. 24(2) or attempt to substitute any other test for s. 24(2). At least at this early stage of the *Charter's* development, the guidelines set out are sufficient and the actual decision to admit or exclude is as important as the statement of any test. Indeed, the test will only take on concrete meaning through our disposition of cases. However, I should at this point add some comparative comment as regards the test I enunciated in *Rothman*, *supra*, a pre-*Charter* confession case dealing with the resort to "tricks", which was coined in the profession as the "community shock test". That test has been applied to s. 24(2) by many Courts, including the lower Courts in this case. I still am of the view that the resort to tricks that are not in the least unlawful let alone in violation of the *Charter* to obtain a statement should not result in the exclusion of a free and voluntary statement unless the trick resorted to is a dirty trick, one that shocks the community. That is a very high threshold, higher, in my view, than that to be attained to bring the administration of justice into disrepute in the context of a violation of the *Charter*.

There are two reasons why the threshold for exclusion under s. 24(2) is lower. The first, an obvious one, is that, under s. 24(2), there will have been a violation of the most important law in the land, as opposed to the absence of any unlawful behaviour as a result of the resort to tricks in Rothman.

The second reason is based on the language of s. 24(2). Indeed, while both the English text of s. 24(2) and Rothman use the words "*would* bring the administration of justice into disrepute", the French versions are very different. The French text of s. 24(2) provides "*est susceptible de* déconsidérer l'administration de la justice", which I would translate as "*could* bring the administration of justice into disrepute". This is supportive of a somewhat lower threshold than the English text. As Dickson J. (as he then was) wrote in *Hunter v. Southam Inc.*, *supra*, at p. 157:

> Since the proper approach to the interpretation of the *Charter of Rights and Freedoms* is a purposive one, before it is possible to assess the reasonableness or unreasonableness of the impact of a search or of a statute authorizing a search, it is first necessary to specify the

purpose underlying s. 8; in other words, to delineate the nature of the interests it is meant to protect.

As one of the purposes of s. 24(2) is to protect the right to a fair trial, I would favour the interpretation of s. 24(2) which better protects that right, the less onerous French text. Most Courts which have considered the issue have also come to this conclusion (see Gibson, *supra*, at pp. 63 and 234-35). Section 24(2) should thus be read as "the evidence shall be excluded if it is established that, having regard to all the circumstances, the admission of it in the proceedings *could* bring the administration of justice into disrepute". This is a less onerous test than Rothman, where the French translation of the test in our reports, "ternirait l'image de la justice", clearly indicates that the resort to the word "would" in the test "would bring the administration of justice into disrepute" means just that.

Conclusion

As discussed above, we must determine in this case whether the evidence should be excluded on the record as it stands at present.

The evidence obtained as a result of the search was real evidence, and, while prejudicial to the accused as evidence tendered by the Crown usually is, there is nothing to suggest that its use at the trial would render the trial unfair. In addition, it is true that the cost of excluding the evidence would be high: someone who was found guilty at trial of a relatively serious offence will evade conviction. Such a result could bring the administration of justice into disrepute. However, the administration of justice would be brought into greater disrepute, at least in my respectful view, if this Court did not exclude the evidence and dissociate itself from the conduct of the police in this case which, always on the assumption that the officer merely had suspicions, was a flagrant and serious violation of the rights of an individual. Indeed, we cannot accept that police officers take flying tackles at people and seize them by the throat when they do not have reasonable and probable grounds to believe that those people are either dangerous or handlers of drugs. Of course, matters might well be clarified in this case if and when the police officer is offered at a new trial an opportunity to explain the grounds, if any, that he had for doing what he did. But if the police officer does not then disclose additional grounds for his behaviour, the evidence must be excluded.

I would allow the appeal and order a trial.

McIntyre J. (dissenting) — I have had the advantage of reading the reasons for judgment prepared in this appeal by my colleague Justice Lamer. I accept and adopt his statement of facts. I accept as well his statement of the question for decision, that is, was the search conducted by the police officer unreasonable and, if so, having regard to all the circumstances, would the admission of the evidence bring the administration of justice into disrepute? I am unable, however, with deference to my colleague's views, to reach the same conclusion.

. . . .

I do not suggest that we should adopt the "community shock" test or that we should have recourse to public opinion polls and other devices for the sampling of public opinion. I do not suggest that we should seek to discover some theoretical concept of community views or standards on this question. I do suggest that we should adopt a method long employed in the common law Courts and, by whatever name it may be called, apply the standard of the reasonable man. The question should be as stated by Yves-Marie Morissette, *supra*, "Would the admission of the evidence bring the administration of justice into disrepute in the eyes of a reasonable man, dispassionate and fully apprised of the circumstances of the case?"

. . . .

Applying this test to the case at bar, I am led to the conclusion that the administration of justice would not fall into disrepute by the admission of this evidence. This is not a case where the search revealed a concealed capsule or two of heroin, such as one might have for personal use. Here, the appellant, with heroin in her hand contained in a balloon, was found in a public bar among other people. In my view, the admission of this evidence on a trial for possession of narcotics for the purpose of trafficking would not — in the eyes of a reasonable man, dispassionate and fully apprised of the circumstances of the case — bring the administration of justice into disrepute. The circumstances of the case include the events described by Nemetz C.J.B.C., at p. 143:

> The facts are not in dispute. Constables Rodine and Woods of the drug section of the R.C.M.P. were on duty at Gibsons, a small community near Vancouver. They took up a surveillance-post near a pub in the village. There they saw the appellant and another woman seated at a table. A short time later the pair were joined by Richard Collins and another man. About 15 minutes later, Collins and the stranger left the pub and drove in a car to a trailer-park a short distance from the pub. The police followed them. They searched the car and there found heroin, some multicoloured balloons and other paraphernalia. Richard Collins was arrested. At 4.15 p.m., Constables Rodine and Woods returned to the pub. The appellant and her companion were still there.

The police then entered the bar and found heroin in the possession of the appellant, not concealed but in her hand in a public place. I express no view as to the cogency or weight of this evidence but, in my view, a reasonable man would not be offended at the thought that on the issue of possession for the purpose of trafficking the trier of fact should be permitted to consider it. I would dismiss the appeal.

LE DAIN J. — I agree with Justice Lamer that the appeal should be allowed and a new trial ordered. Assuming, as we must on the present record, that the police officer did not have grounds for a reasonable belief that the accused was in possession of a narcotic, I am in agreement with the conclusion that, having regard to all the circumstances, and in particular the relative seriousness of the violation of the right guaranteed by s. 8 of the *Charter* to be secure against unreasonable search, the admission of the evidence would bring the administration of justice into disrepute. I am also in general agreement with what Lamer J. says concerning the nature of the test under s. 24(2) of the *Charter* and the factors to be weighed, but I do not wish to be understood as necessarily subscribing to what is said concerning the nature and relative importance under s. 24(2) of the factor which he refers to as the effect of the admission of the evidence on the fairness of the trial. Since, as Lamer J. indicates, it is not necessary to consider this factor in the present case, I prefer to reserve my opinion with respect to it. I am concerned about the possible implications for such matters as self-incrimination and confession, aspects of fairness to which Lamer J. refers and which are the subject of special provision in the *Charter* or in well established rules of law. I am also concerned as to whether there is a basis in s. 24(2) for the view that, to the extent this factor is relevant, it should generally lead to the exclusion of the evidence.

Appeal allowed and a new trial ordered.

For criticism of the distinction drawn in *Collins* based on the type of evidence obtained see Delisle, "Collins: An Unjustified Distinction" (1987), 56 C.R. (3d) 216. However, the *Collins* approach is now thoroughly entrenched. For reviews of the history of s. 24(2) and recent decisions of the Supreme Court see Stuart, *Charter Justice in Canadian Criminal Law* (3rd ed., 2001) Chapter 11 and "Eight Plus Twenty-Four Two Equals Zero" (1998), 13 C.R. (5th) 50.

Prior to the Supreme Court's decisions on s. 24(2) the policy issues were perhaps most clearly joined in the division in the Ontario Court of Appeal in *R. v. Duguay*.

R. v. DUGUAY

(1985), 45 C.R. (3d) 140, 18 C.C.C. (3d) 289 (Ont. C.A.)

Between 8:00 p.m. on June 25, 1982, and 3:00 a.m. on June 26, 1982, there was a break and entry in the home of Mr. and Mrs. Laframboise, in the City of Windsor, while the occupants were away. A stereo set, a wrist-watch and some liquor were stolen. On the morning following the theft, Detectives Reaume and Chevalier were dispatched to the Laframboise residence. Upon their arrival, the detectives were informed by a constable already on the scene that prior to leaving their home, the Laframboises had noticed three young men drinking beer in the Grummetts' back yard, which bordered their own property to the north. This information was thereafter confirmed in a discussion with Mrs. Laframboise, who recalled having already seen one of the youths there on a number of occasions. She added that there was a short conversation between one of the youths and Mr. Laframboise: as the latter was putting his dog in the garage before leaving the house, one of the three men inquired as to whether he always put his dog there. The detectives then met with the neighbour on the southern side of the property who informed them that the yard lights in the Laframboise residence went out at around 10:00 p.m., two hours after the occupants had left. The neighbour did not see anyone in the residence at the time. The detectives then returned to the Grummett residence and questioned a boarder who lived there, Mr. Dura. He told the detectives that he had not seen anybody in the Grummetts' back yard the previous evening.

While the detectives were receiving Mr. Dura's information, a car pulled up in the Grummetts' driveway. Mr. Grummett was returning from an out-of-town trip. The detectives went to meet him and informed him of the break-in and investigation. As he had been away, he could not confirm the presence of the youths in his back yard the preceding evening. Nevertheless, on the basis of the description of the young men given to him by the detectives, he recognized "the Murphy lad". He then went into his home to call the Murphy residence and asked Murphy to come over with his friends who were with him the night before. Detective Chevalier was informed by Mr. Grummett that three young men were on their way over. Both officers went back to the front porch of the Laframboise residence to wait for them.

The young men arrived a short while later, accompanied by the Grummetts' son, who left the group to enter into his parents' house. The Laframboises, who were with the detectives at the time, recognized Murphy and Sevigny as two of the youths in the Grummetts' backyard the previous evening. Detective Reaume went to meet the respondents at the Grummetts' driveway, while Detective Chevalier went back into the Laframboise residence with the couple. Detective Reaume identified himself to the youths and asked them their names, addresses and dates of birth. He then asked the respondents: "You guys want to have a seat in our car? — We want to talk to you." All three complied and sat in the back seat of the car. Detective Reaume sat in the front. It was an unmarked patrol car. As the youths were seated, Detective Reaume asked them: "You guys save me a trip back, and tell me where the stereo is?" One of them, Murphy, spontaneously answered and, while the content of his reply was not disclosed in evidence, both counsel agreed in their oral pleadings that it was an incriminating reply. At this time, Detective Chevalier returned to the patrol car and Detective Reaume formally placed the three respondents under arrest on a charge of break and enter and theft. The youths were given the customary caution and read their rights to counsel pursuant to the then newly-enacted *Canadian Charter of Rights and Freedoms*. All replied that they understood their rights. The events in the patrol car lasted only a few minutes. The youths were then driven to the police station and put in separate interview rooms. An inculpatory statement was obtained form each of them. Their fingerprints were taken. Later that evening, Murphy led the policemen to the crawl-space under his house, where the stereo set was recovered. The fingerprints of Duguay and Murphy were eventually matched to the fingerprints found on the stereo, and Duguay's fingerprints were also matched to those found on the window through which access to the Laframboise residence was gained.

MacKinnon A.C.J.O. (Martin J.A. concurring): —

. . . .

Section 9 of the Canadian Charter of Rights and Freedoms

Having found the arrest to be unlawful, the trial Judge concluded that the detention was "arbitrary" within the meaning of that word as found in s. 9 of the *Canadian Charter of Rights and Freedoms*. He stated:

> An unlawful arrest, as it occurred in the circumstances of this case is, in the opinion of this Court, a blatant violation of the rights and freedoms of these accused as protected by the supreme law of our country. There is no doubt that our recently enacted constitutional rights have made police investigations somewhat more difficult than previously, but whether they like it or not, they now have to live with it and govern themselves accordingly.

It cannot be that every unlawful arrest necessarily falls within the words "arbitrarily detained". The grounds upon which an arrest was made may fall "just short" of constituting reasonable and probable cause. The person making the arrest may honestly, though mistakenly, believe that reasonable and probable grounds for the arrest exist and there may be some basis for that belief. In those circumstances the arrest, though subsequently found to be unlawful, could not be said to be capricious or arbitrary. On the other hand, the entire absence of reasonable and probable grounds for the arrest could support an inference that no reasonable person could have genuinely believed that such grounds existed. In such cases, the conclusion would be that the person arrested was arbitrarily detained. Between these two ends of the spectrum, shading from white to grey to black, the issue of whether an accused was arbitrarily detained will depend, basically, on two considerations: first, the particular facts of the case, and secondly, the view taken by the Court with respect to the extent of the departure from the standard of reasonable and probable grounds and the honesty of the belief and basis for the belief in the existence of reasonable and probable grounds on the part of the person making the arrest.

In my view, on the facts as found by the trial Judge, the arrest or detention was arbitrary, being for quite an improper purpose — namely, to assist in the investigation. This conclusion does not minimize the significance or importance of an experienced detective's "hunch" or intuition. Such "hunch" must, however, have some reasonable basis. It cannot be used as a defence and explanation without examination, for irrational and high-handed actions.

Martin J.A. stated the legal position in *R. v. Dedman* (1981), 59 C.C.C. (2d) 97 at p. 109. Although that case is under appeal [39 N.R. 449n] I do not understand that any issue arises with respect to this:

> . . . a police officer has no right to detain a person for questioning or for further investigation. No one is entitled to impose any physical restraint upon the citizen except as authorized by law, and this principle applies as much to police officers as to anyone else. Although a police officer may approach a person on the street and ask him questions, if the person refuses to answer the police must allow him to proceed on his way, unless, of course, the officer arrests him on a specific charge or arrests him pursuant to s. 450 of the *Code* where the officer has reasonable and probable grounds to believe that he is about to commit an indictable offence: see the Judges Rules, [1964] 1 W.L.R. 153; *Bales et al. v. Parmeter* (1935), 35 S.R.N.S.W. 182; *Rice v. Connolly*, [1966] 2 Q.B. 414; *Koechlin v. Waugh and Hamilton* (1957), 118 C.C.C. 24 (C.A.); "Arrest, Detention and Compulsion", [1974] *Crim. L. Rev.* 288, by David Lanham; J.L. Lambert, "Police Powers of Stop and Search" (1974), 124 N.L.J. 476.

It was clearly the trial Judge's view that the officers were not speaking truthfully when they said they believed they had reasonable and probable grounds for arresting the accused. They had neither grounds nor an honest belief that they had the necessary grounds. These being the findings of fact, I cannot see that there was any error in law in the finding made by the trial Judge with relation to s. 9.

Section 24(2) of the Canadian Charter of Rights and Freedoms

Section 24(2) reads:

> 24(2) Where, in proceedings under subsection (1), a Court concludes that evidence was obtained in a manner that infringed or denied any rights or freedoms guaranteed by this *Charter*, the evidence shall be excluded if it is established that, having regard to all the circumstances, the admission of it in the proceedings would bring the administration of justice into disrepute.

This is a more difficult issue to determine. It is agreed that the onus was on the respondents to establish that the admission of their statements and their fingerprints, and the fact that the stereo was recovered as a direct result of Murphy's statement, would, under the circumstances, bring the administration of justice into disrepute.

After quoting from Mr. Justice Lamer's statement in *Rothman v. The Queen*, [1981] 1 S.C.R. 640 at p. 696, 59 C.C.C. (2d) 30 at p. 74, the trial Judge went on to say on the point:

> Other than some actual form of torture, I cannot think of anything more shocking to the right-thinking member of the community that the courts would allow police officers to introduce evidence which they have obtained through the nefarious means of an unlawful arrest. To admit such evidence would, in effect mean, that the court sanctions unlawful arrests by the police. Far be it from this court to give that blessing. I therefore rule as inadmissible any utterances or statements made by the accused in this case. I further rule inadmissible, any evidence which the police might have obtained as a result of such utterances or statements. Fingerprint evidence which arises out of the fact that these accused were fingerprinted following their arrest is also ruled inadmissible.

Although the trial Judge's language is somewhat excessive in condemning the action of the two detectives, and his statement is too general, in my view, without becoming too overblown in my own language, the manner in which the police proceeded suggested a somewhat incipient Star Chamber attitude.

There are cases where the circumstances satisfy that even if the evidence is "tainted" by some breach of *Charter* rights the refusal to admit that evidence may cause greater injury to the State and society and to the administration of justice than its admission. In other words, in such cases the refusal to admit the evidence may be more likely to bring the administration of justice into disrepute. But that is not this case. As already indicated, there will also be cases where the breach is a "slight" one and the admission of the evidence would have no effect on the reputation of the administration of justice.

It is repugnant to our concept of the administration of criminal justice and to the rights of citizens in a free and democratic society, to make them subject to arbitrary arrest for investigation purposes. The arbitrary quality of the act with the resultant breach of a *Charter* right has already been determined in the instant case. The question to be determined is: whether, "having regard to the circumstances", the admission of the inculpatory statements, the evidence of the fingerprints and their evidence relative to the recovery of the stereo set would bring the administration of justice into disrepute?

Counsel for the Crown argued that there had to be a "causal connection" established between the breach of the *Charter* right and the securing of the evidence before one could enter upon a consideration of s. 24(2). He submitted that there was no such causal connection here. The language of s. 24(2) has been described as broad enough to encompass circumstances in which the violation is not a necessary condition to the obtaining of the evidence. Be that as it may, in my view there is in this case a simple, understandable causal connection between the breach of the *Charter* right and the obtaining of the evidence. The inculpatory statements were a direct result of the illegal arrest — indeed the hoped for result and purpose of the arrest. The location of the stereo set flowed directly from the respondent Murphy's statement. The securing of the respondent's fingerprints (which were not otherwise available) was under the compulsion of the *Identification of Criminals Act*, R.S.C. 1970, c. I-1, s. 2, which only came into play on the arrest (presumed legal at the time) of the respondents: *Davis v. State of Mississippi* (1969), 89 S. Ct. 1394, 394 U.S. 721.

As there is no suggestion that the police had or would necessarily have discovered the evidence without the breach of the *Charter* the significance of the breach is great, the evidence being necessary for a successful prosecution.

Counsel for the Crown argues that the trial Judge erred in that he considered only the controlling of police conduct and failed to assess other criteria in determining whether the admission of the evidence would bring the administration of justice into disrepute. On a careful reading of the trial Judge's analysis of the evidence, however, in my opinion he did balance various factors in considering this issue, and earlier made his findings of fact for that purpose.

What are the factors in this case that need to be considered? First, the finding of fact that, in effect, the arrest was not made in good faith. The trial Judge held that these experienced officers could not have believed that they had reasonable and probable grounds for the arrest. There was found to be a deliberate breach of the *Charter* right for an illegal purpose. Secondly, the offence was not a serious one. As MacDonald J.A. put it in *R. v. Stevens* (1983), 7 C.C.C. (3d) 260 at p. 264, 35 C.R. (3d) 1:

> In a relatively minor case like the present the violation of the individual's right to privacy might, to some jurists, be considered shocking. In a far more serious case the interests of society might well dictate that similar conduct was not so shocking as to bring the administration of justice into disrepute.

Thirdly, there was no question of urgency which might not excuse but could explain the conduct of the police. Fourthly, the respondents were three 17-year-olds, whose names and addresses were known. They had no criminal record. Indeed, one of them (Duguay) was not even identified as being in the neighbour's backyard on the night of the break-in. Finally, there was clearly no fear of the respondents fleeing the jurisdiction or going into hiding. When these facts are added to the arbitrary actions of the police — which facts I suppose, in part, underline the arbitrary conduct — I conclude that the trial Judge was entitled to hold that the admission of the evidence would bring the administration of justice into disrepute and that he made no error in law in so finding.

It has been suggested that the victim of such a crime may wonder why the admitted perpetrator is allowed to go free and that this reaction may very well bring the administration of justice into disrepute. But that is not the test. One could as well ask what the victim's attitude would be if it were his child's *Charter* rights that were infringed. Long before the *Charter* there existed the possibility that a guilty person might go free if an inculpatory statement, truthful or not, were held not to be a voluntary one; or if some procedural defect existed in a wiretap resulting in the exclusion of evidence obtained thereby. The integrity of the criminal justice system demands these results. Under the *Charter*, if to the average citizen interested in the administration of justice and the protection of the *Charter* rights, the admission of the objected-to evidence, *under all the circumstances*, would bring the administration of justice into disrepute then it must be excluded: *Davis v. State of Mississippi, supra.*

If the Court should turn a blind eye to this kind of conduct, then the police may assume that they have the Court's tacit approval of it. I do not view the exclusion of the evidence as a punishment of the police for their conduct, although it is to be hoped that it will act as a future deterrent. It is rather an affirmation of fundamental values of our society, and the only means in this case of ensuring that the individual's *Charter* rights are not illusory. I agree with the conclusion of the trial Judge and would have reached the same conclusion that, on the facts as found by him, the respondents have satisfied the burden of establishing that the admission of the evidence would bring the administration of justice into disrepute.

. . . .

Zuber J.A. (dissenting): —

. . . .

The Charter violation

The learned trial Judge found that at the time Detectives Reaume and Chevalier arrested the three accused, they did not on reasonable and probable grounds believe that the three accused had committed the indictable offence with which they were charged. He went on to find that the accused were therefore arbitrarily detained contrary to s. 9 of the *Charter*.

It is clear that when Mark Laframboise closed up his home and with his wife prepared to leave for the evening, the three accused were drinking in a yard abutting the Laframboise property and saw the fact that Laframboise and his wife were leaving. When Laframboise put his dog in the garage, one of the accused inquired if this was his customary practice. Laframboise and his wife departed at about 8:00 p.m. A rear light of the Laframboise home was seen to go out at 10:00 p.m. and it is more than likely that the break-in was, in my view, more than a pure flight of fancy. To believe on reasonable and probable grounds that a person has committed an indictable offence does not require that the grounds be made up of evidence that can later be adduced in a court-room. Nevertheless, the trial Judge could not accept the fact that anyone could believe, based on reasonable and probable grounds composed only of the foregoing facts, that the accused had committed this indictable offence. As a result of this conclusion, he did not believe the two detectives. In his reasons for judgment, he said: "I find as a fact that there was absolutely no basis for Detective Chevalier's opinion that the three youths were the culprits." This is a conclusion that I do not share.

In any event, even if the grounds upon which the two detectives acted fell short of reasonable and probable grounds, does it necessarily follow that the detention was arbitrary? In my view, the detention that follows an arrest based on something less than reasonable and probable grounds is not necessarily arbitrary. The arrest in this case was neither capricious nor random. I have very serious doubts as to these two conclusions reached by the trial Judge but since they are bound up with issues of fact and since the appeal by the Crown is dependent upon an issue of law alone, I am content to accept his conclusions on these two issues and rest my judgment entirely on the third and last issue, *i.e.*, the propriety of excluding the evidence.

Excluding the evidence

Assuming that there was a violation of the *Charter* in this case, the problem remains whether or not the evidence obtained as a result should be excluded. Section 24(2) of the *Charter* provides as follows:

> 24(2) Where, in proceedings under subsection (1), a court concludes that evidence was obtained in a manner that infringed or denied any rights or freedoms guaranteed by this *Charter*, the evidence shall be excluded if it is established that, having regard to all the circumstances, the admission of it in the proceedings would bring the administration of justice into disrepute.

It is apparent from the wording of the section itself that the critical question is whether or not the admission of the evidence in question would bring the administration of justice into disrepute. It is further apparent from the words of the section that all of the circumstances must be considered.

In a pre-*Charter* case, *Rothman v. The Queen*, [1981] 1 S.C.R. 640, 59 C.C.C. (2d) 30, dealing with the admissibility of a statement, Lamer J. dealt with the concept of "bringing the administration of justice into disrepute" and provided some helpful comments and also identified some of the circumstances which should be considered. He said at p. 697 S.C.R., pp. 74-5 C.C.C.:

> The Judge, in determining whether under the circumstances the use of the statements in the proceedings would bring the administration of justice into disrepute, should consider all of the circumstances of the proceedings, the manner in which the statement was obtained, the degree to which there was a breach of social values, the seriousness of the charge, the effect the exclusion would have on the result of the proceedings. It must also be borne in mind that the investigation of crime and the detection of criminals is not a game to be governed by the Marquis of Queensberry rules. The authorities, in dealing with shrewd and often sophisticated criminals, must sometimes of necessity resort to tricks or other forms of deceit and should not through the rule be hampered in their work. What should be repressed vigorously is conduct on their part that shocks the community. That a police officer pretend to be a lock-up chaplain and hear a suspect's confession is conduct that shocks the community; so is pretending to be the duty legal-aid lawyer eliciting in that way incriminating statements from suspects or the accused; injecting Pentothal into a diabetic suspect pretending it is his daily shot of insulin and using his statement in evidence would also shock the community; but generally speaking, pretending to be a hard drug addict to break a drug ring would not shock the community; nor would, as in this case, pretending to be a truck driver to secure the conviction of a trafficker; in fact, what would shock the community would be preventing the police from resorting to such a trick.

This statement is the origin of what is referred to in later cases dealing with s. 24(2) as the "community shock test".

In *R. v. Simmons* (1984), 11 C.C.C. (3d) 193, 39 C.R. (3d) 223, Howland C.J.O. dealt with the question of what would bring the administration of justice into disrepute and also addressed the community shock test. At p. 218 C.C.C., p. 252 C.R., he said:

> In my opinion, in determining whether the administration of justice has been brought into disrepute within s. 24(2), the following matters are of importance: the nature and extent of the illegality, the manner in which the evidence was obtained, the good faith or the lack of good faith of the persons who obtained the evidence, whether the accused's rights under the *Charter* were knowingly infringed, and the seriousness of the charge. This list is not intended to be all-inclusive. There may be other matters of importance which should be considered.
>
> If the evidence is obtained in such a manner as to shock the Canadian community as a whole, it would no doubt be inadmissible as bringing the administration of justice into disrepute. There may, however, be instances where the administration of justice is brought into disrepute within s. 24(2) without necessarily shocking the Canadian community as a whole. In my opinion, it is preferable to consider every case on its merits as to whether it satisfies the requirements of s. 24(2) of the *Charter* and not to substitute a "community shock" or any other test for the plain words of the statute.

I agree with the Chief Justice of Ontario that Courts should not, by a process of redefinition and by the formulation of tests, make the *Charter* into something that it is not. However, in my respectful opinion, the formulation of a judgment premised on s. 24(2) of the *Charter* requires more than a recitation of all of the circumstances followed by a selection of the result — admission or exclusion. If this is done by a trial court, it is difficult for an appellate Court to know the real reason for the decision. On the other hand, if this process is followed by an appellate Court, it is of very little guidance to trial Courts.

Bound up in the evaluation of all of the circumstances and the determination of whether the administration of justice will be brought into disrepute are the principles that one brings to the evaluation process. Without a clear appreciation of what these principles are, the evaluation process will become far too subjective and, as a result, the treatment of evidentiary matters pursuant to s. 24(2) will become unacceptably inconsistent. In my view, the Chief Justice of Ontario in *Simmons*, in telling us that we should not substitute tests for the clear words of the *Charter*, did not exclude the identification of the principles that we bring to the process of evaluation.

I wish, then, to turn to the principles that underlie this process of evaluation and, of course, I cannot pretend that the following is an exhaustive list of such principles.

First, s. 24(2) represents a compromise between the American exclusionary rule and our own pre-*Charter* law that, generally speaking, evidence illegally obtained was nevertheless admissible. In my view, however, the position arrived at is not a middle position equidistant between the two competing positions. Evidence obtained as a result of a *Charter* violation is, as a general rule, admissible. The exception to this general rule arises only when the admission of such evidence will bring the administration of justice into disrepute. I agree with the comment of Ewaschuk J., who said in *R. v. Gibson* (1984), 37 C.R. (3d) 175 at p. 185:

> As a result of that compromise, s. 24(2) of the *Charter* tilts the balance in favour of truth, so that evidence, even though obtained as a result of constitutional violation, is *prima facie* admissible. However, the evidence may nonetheless be excluded where an applicant for its exclusion establishes on a balance of probabilities that, having regard to all the circumstances of the individual case, the admission of the evidence would bring the administration of justice into disrepute: see *R. v. Collins* [(1983), 5 C.C.C. (3d) 141, 33 C.R. (3d) 130, and *R. v. Chapin* (1983), 43 O.R. (2d) 458 (C.A.).

Section 24(2) is premised on a *Charter* violation. It is therefore inappropriate to say that Courts cannot turn a blind eye to *Charter* violations or cannot sanction violations by admitting the evidence. The *Charter* itself contemplates the admission of evidence obtained as a result of a *Charter* violation. Further, it is not necessary that courts sanction or turn a blind eye to *Charter* violations. Section 24(1) permits courts to use a wide range of remedies other than the exclusion of evidence to uphold the value of *Charter* rights.

The logical extension of the blind-eye argument leads to the exclusion of evidence almost automatically and will inevitably lead us to a position very close to the exclusionary rule as it exists in the United States. This would be a result which is clearly inconsistent with the compromise position taken by s. 24(2) itself. On wider grounds, and as a matter of principle, we should be very wary of moving in the direction of an exclusionary rule. The American experience with the exclusionary rule should dampen the ardour of anyone ready to follow that course.

Second, it is important that we understand clearly what is being done when evidence is sought to be excluded pursuant to s. 24(2). Courts are being asked to suppress the truth. Most evidentiary rules of exclusion are based upon the lack of relevance, unreliability or the confusion that could be caused by admission.

In the case of exclusion pursuant to s. 24(2), none of these frailities exist. The case at hand is a good example. Evidence in this case is clear, cogent and reliable and is sought to be excluded.

Obviously, the reliability of the evidence is not a reason which, by itself, can defeat the effect of s. 24(2) but it is an important consideration when we come to consider the issue of "bringing the administration of justice into disrepute". The question becomes whether the admission of the truth (albeit discovered as a result of a *Charter* violation) will bring the administration of justice into disrepute. The converse question is, what will the suppression of the truth do to the repute of the administration of justice?

Section 24(2) of the *Charter* entitles courts to say that at a certain point the price of truth is too high. When the *Charter* violation by which the evidence is obtained does more damage to the fabric of society than the crime which is being investigated, then reasonable men will say that the admission of such evidence will bring the administration of justice into disrepute.

Third, in approaching the issue of the repute of the administration of justice, it is of some significance to keep in mind that our criminal justice system from its beginnings until 1982 regularly admitted evidence despite the fact that it was illegally obtained. Had this case taken place prior to 1982, all of the evidence excluded by the trial judge would have been admitted without exciting any notice whatever.

Granted that the *Charter* has changed the law but it has not, overnight, transformed the healthy repute of the administration of justice into a fragile flower ready to wilt because of the admission of evidence obtained as a result of a violation of the *Charter* rights of an accused. The regard of the Canadian public for the administration of justice prior to the *Charter*, despite the fact that evidence illegally obtained was admitted as a matter of course, was, in my view, very high. The repute of the administration of justice has not now suddenly become highly vulnerable.

Fourth, control of the police has no place in the application of s. 24(2). Prior to the enactment of the *Charter* and when evidence illegally obtained was freely admitted, misconduct of the police could be dealt with either by prosecution or by civil action. Section 24(1) expands this notion and provides courts with a large armoury of remedies whereby *Charter* violations can be dealt with apart from the exclusion of evidence. Even in the United States, control of the police is not regarded as a strong argument for upholding the exclusionary rule. On a more mundane level, there is no satisfactory evidence that the exclusion of evidence is effective as a mechanism for control of police methods. Whatever penalty there may be in excluding the evidence in a given case does not fall on the police. It falls on the public.

Fifth, it is, I think, obvious that disrepute must rest on the view of the whole community and not just the view of the few no matter how knowledgeable or expert the few may be.

I conclude from all of the foregoing that evidence will be excluded pursuant to s. 24(2) on the grounds that the administration of justice will be brought into disrepute only in highly exceptional cases. As mentioned above, Howland

C.J.O. in *Simmons*, has told us that the community shock test should not displace the plain words of the statute. In my view, Lamer J. in *Rothman*, in enunciating the community shock test, did not mean it to be definitive. However, the community shock test retains value as a convenient way of expressing the exceptional quality of the circumstances that will lead to the conclusion that the administration of justice will be brought into disrepute.

Frequent resort to the exclusion of evidence will create a perception by the public that the criminal justice system is a sort of legalistic game in which a misstep by the police confers immunity upon the accused. This perception will most certainly bring the administration of justice into disrepute.

In all of the foregoing, to a large extent I have repeated concepts earlier expressed by Seaton J.A. in *R. v. Collins* (1983), 5 C.C.C. (3d) 141, 33 C.R. (3d) 130, and Esson J.A. in *R. v. Hamill* (1984), 14 C.C.C. (3d) 338, 41 C.R. (3d) 123. By repetition I express my agreement.

The facts of this case.

I turn now to the circumstances to be considered pursuant to s. 24(2).

Accepting the trial Judge's findings that the two detectives did not believe on reasonable and probable grounds that the three accused were the authors of the break-in, there was nevertheless a basis in fact for their arrest. As mentioned earlier, the arrest was neither random nor capricious. Their following detention was neither oppressive nor inhumane. Nothing in the trial record suggests that the detectives were acting in bad faith. The principle criticism of the procedure followed by the two detectives is that they arrested first and took the statements thereafter. Had it been the other way around, there seems to be be little doubt that the statements would have been the same and, rather obviously, the rest of the evidence would have been the same.

The crime with which these three accused are charged is a serious one. The break and entry of a dwelling carries a maximum penalty of life imprisonment. In *Colet v. The Queen*, [1981] 1 S.C.R. 2, 57 C.C.C. (2d) 105, the Supreme Court of Canada was concerned with police powers of search of a dwelling. Ritchie J. said at p. 8 S.C.R., p. 110 C.C.C.:

> . . . what is involved here is the longstanding right of a citizen of this country to the control and enjoyment of his own property, including the right to determine who shall and who shall not be permitted to invade it. The common law principle has been firmly engrafted in our law since *Semayne's Case*, 77 E.R. 194, 5 Co. Rep. 91a, in 1604 where it was said "That the house of every one is to him as his castle and fortress, as well for his defence against injury and violence, as for his repose. . .". This famous dictum was cited by my brother Dickson in the case of *Eccles v. Bourque*, [1975] 2 S.C.R. 739, in which he made an extensive review of many of the relevant authorities.

It seems to me that the law of this country which protects a citizen's dwelling against unauthorized police entry should be equally solicitous with respect to a break-in of a dwelling by thieves.

In excluding the evidence, the learned trial Judge treated all of the evidence as having been obtained in a manner that infringed or denied *Charter* rights. In a mechanical way there is a causal link between the arrest and the three accused and all of the evidence that followed. However, in my view, the casual link becomes much weaker with respect to the finding of the stolen goods and very much weaker with respect to the fingerprint evidence. It is argued that without the arrest the sample prints would not have been taken from the three accused. However, this was only the mechanism of identification. The Laframboise premises and the stolen goods bore the fingerprints. Two of the accused had hands and fingers with prints that matched. The procedural act of causing the accused to place their prints on a card to provide the connective link was obtained through a *Charter* violation only in the most technical sense.

In my view, the plight of the victim is also a relevant circumstance within s. 24(2). His dwelling was broken into and his possessions were stolen. He expended his time and energy by reporting the matter to the police, testifying at the preliminary hearing and apparently by attending at the trial ready to testify again. However, his recourse to the law has yielded him nothing. He, no doubt, has some interesting impressions as to the course of these proceedings.

The last circumstance to be considered is the effect of the exclusion of the evidence and, in this case, it is obvious that the exclusion of the evidence in question led to the collapse of the Crown's case.

The foregoing circumstances evaluated against a background of the principles earlier set out lead me to the conclusion that the respondents fall far short of establishing that the admission of the evidence in this case would bring the administration of justice into disrepute. It is likely not accurate to speak of the burden resting on those who seek to exclude evidence as an onus of proof. In most cases, no evidence will be called respecting the issue of disrepute. This burden may be more aptly referred to as a burden of persuasion and, in my view, this burden was not discharged. On the contrary, I think it more likely that the exclusion of the evidence in this case will bring the administration of justice into disrepute.

Which position do you prefer? Which position do you think found favour in the Supreme Court of Canada? See *R. v. Duguay*, [1989] 1 S.C.R. 93, 67 C.R. (3d) 252, 46 C.C.C. (3d) 1.

In *R. v. Stillman*, [1997] 5 C.R. (5th) 1 (S.C.C.), the Court provided its latest "definitive word" on the approach to be taken to s. 24(2). The accused, 17 at the time, was arrested for the brutal murder of a teenage girl. He was the last person seen with the victim. The victim died from wounds to the head. Semen was found in her vagina and a human bite mark had been left on her abdomen. At the police station, the accused's lawyers informed the police by letter that the accused was not consenting to provide any bodily samples, including hair and teeth imprints, nor to give any statements. When the lawyers left, police officers took, under threat of force, scalp hair, buccal swabs and he was made to pull some of his own pubic hair. Plasticine teeth impressions were also taken. The trial judge found that the hair samples, buccal swabs and teeth impressions had been obtained in violation of s. 8 of the *Charter* but concluded that the evidence was nevertheless admissible. The accused was later convicted by a jury of first degree murder. The majority of the Court of Appeal upheld the trial judge's ruling and affirmed the verdict. A 6-3 majority of the Supreme Court of Canada allowed the appeal and a new trial was ordered at which the hair samples, buccal swabs and dental impressions are to be excluded.

The majority said the primary aim of considering the trial fairness factor in the s. 24(2) analysis was to prevent an accused person whose *Charter* rights have been infringed from being forced or conscripted to provide evidence in the form of confessions, statements or bodily samples for the benefit of the state. Thus, when the trial fairness factor was being considered, it was necessary to classify the evidence as conscriptive or non-conscriptive based upon the manner in which the evidence was obtained. If the accused was not compelled to participate in the creation or discovery of the evidence, the evidence would be classified as non-conscriptive. Its admission would not render the trial unfair and the court would then proceed to consider the seriousness of the breach and the effect of exclusion on the repute of the administration of justice. If the evidence is found to be conscriptive evidence, which in the case of statements includes derivative evidence, and the *Crown* demonstrates on a balance of probabilities that it would have been discovered by alternative non-conscriptive means — where an independent source exists or discovery was inevitable — then its admission would generally not render the trial unfair. However, the seriousness of the *Charter* breach and the effect of exclusion on the repute of the administration of justice would still have to be considered. If the evidence is conscriptive and the *Crown* fails to demonstrate on a balance of probabilities that the evidence would have been discovered by alternative non-conscriptive means, then its admission would render the trial unfair. The court, as a general rule, will exclude the evidence without considering the seriousness of the breach or the effect of exclusion on the repute of the administration of justice. This, the majority said, must be the result since an unfair trial would necessarily bring the administration of justice into disrepute.

The majority in *Stillman* decided that, in considering how the admission of the evidence would affect the fairness of the trial, the trial judge erred in concluding that the hair samples, saliva and dental impressions existed independently of any *Charter* breach and were thus admissible. The accused's bodily samples and impressions existed as "real" evidence but the police, by their words and actions, compelled the accused to provide evidence from his body. This evidence constituted conscriptive evidence. The impugned evidence would not have been discovered had it not been for the conscription of the accused in violation of his *Charter* rights and no independent source existed by which the police could have obtained the evidence. For the majority it followed that its admission would render the trial unfair and that finding was sufficient to resolve the s. 24(2) issue as the evidence had to be excluded.

Assuming *Charter* violations in the following problems, should the evidence be excluded?

1. The accused was arrested for armed robbery of a convenience store. He was advised of his right to remain silent and of his right to

counsel. The accused told the police he didn't want to say anything until he had seen his lawyer but the constable questioned him as follows:

Q.   What is your full name? A. Ronald Charles Manninen.

Q.   Where is your address? A. Ain't got one.

Q.   Where is the knife that you had along with this [showing Manninen the CO gun found in the car] when you ripped off the Mac's Milk on Wilson Avenue? A. He's lying. When I was in the store I only had the gun. The knife was in the tool box in the car.

The last answer was relied on by the trial Judge in convicting the accused of the robbery charge. Compare *R. v. Manninen*, [1987] 1 S.C.R. 1233, 58 C.R. (3d) 97, 34 C.C.C. (3d) 385.

2. The accused was charged with possession of a stolen auto. Following his arrest and the usual police cautions he was asked regarding the whereabouts of the keys to the car. He professed ignorance. The police threatened him that he would be kept in custody until the keys were found. The prosecution did not seek to introduce any statements which may have been made following this exchange. The prosecution did, however, lead evidence of the accused taking the police to the place where the keys were hidden. The trial Judge excluded the evidence of the accused's involvement in the finding of the keys. The accused was acquitted.

Compare *R. v. Woolley* (1988), 63 C.R. (3d) 333, 40 C.C.C. (3d) 531 (Ont. C.A.) and *R. v. Black*, [1989] 2 S.C.R. 138, 70 C.R. (3d) 97, 50 C.C.C. (3d) 1.

Ethical Obligations of Crown and Defence Counsel

CANADIAN BAR ASSOCIATION'S
CODE OF PROFESSIONAL CONDUCT (1987)

CONFIDENTIAL INFORMATION

RULE

The lawyer has a duty to hold in strict confidence all information concerning the business and affairs of the client acquired in the course of the professional relationship, and should not divulge such information unless disclosure is expressly or impliedly authorized by the client, required by law or otherwise permitted or required by this Code.

Commentary

Guiding Principles

1. The lawyer cannot render effective professional service to the client unless there is full and unreserved communication between them. At the same time the client must feel completely secure and entitled to proceed on the basis that without any express request or stipulation on the client's part, matters disclosed to or discussed with the lawyer will be held secret and confidential.

. . . .

Disclosure to Prevent a Crime

11. Disclosure of information necessary to prevent a crime will be justified if the lawyer has reasonable grounds for believing that a crime is likely to be committed and will be mandatory when the anticipated crime is one involving violence.

. . . .

13. When disclosure is required by law or by order of a Court of competent jurisdiction, the lawyer should always be careful not to divulge more information than is required.

THE LAWYER AS ADVOCATE

RULE

When acting as an advocate, the lawyer must treat the tribunal with courtesy and respect and must represent the client resolutely, honourably and within the limits of the law.

Commentary

Guiding Principles

1. The advocate's duty to the client "fearlessly to raise every issue, advance every argument, and ask every question, however distasteful, which he thinks will help his client's case" and to endeavour "to obtain for his client the benefit of any and every remedy and defence which is authorized by law" must always be discharged by fair and honourable means, without illegality and in a manner consistent with the lawyer's duty to treat the Court with candour, fairness, courtesy and respect.

Prohibited Conduct

2. The lawyer must not, for example:

. . . .

(b) knowingly assist or permit the client to do anything that the lawyer considers to be dishonest or dishonourable;

. . . .

(e) knowingly attempt to deceive or participate in the deception of a tribunal or influence the course of justice by offering false evidence, misstating facts or law, presenting or relying upon a false or deceptive affidavit, suppressing what ought to be disclosed or otherwise assisting in any fraud, crime or illegal conduct.

. . . .

Duties of Prosecutor

9. When engaged as a prosecutor, the lawyer's prime duty is not to seek a conviction, but to present before the trial Court all available credible evidence relevant to the alleged crime in order that justice may be done through a fair trial upon the merits. The prosecutor exercises a public function involving much discretion and power and must act fairly and dispassionately. The prosecutor should not do anything that might prevent the accused from being represented by counsel or communicating with counsel and, to the extent required by law and accepted practice, should make timely disclosure to the accused or defence counsel (or to the court if the accused is not represented) of all relevant facts and known witnesses, whether tending to show guilt or innocence, or that would affect the punishment of the accused.

Duties of Defence Counsel

10. When defending an accused person, the lawyer's duty is to protect the client as far as possible from being convicted except by a court of competent jurisdiction and upon legal evidence sufficient to support a conviction for the offence charged. Accordingly, and notwithstanding the lawyer's private opinion as to credibility or merits, the lawyer may properly rely upon all available evidence or defences including so-called technicalities not known to be false or fraudulent.

11. Admissions made by the accused to the lawyer may impose strict limitations on the conduct of the defence and the accused should be made aware of this. For example, if the accused clearly admits to the lawyer the factual and mental elements necessary to constitute the offence, the lawyer, if convinced that the admissions are true and voluntary, may properly take objection to the jurisdiction of the court, or to the form of the indictment, or to the admissibility or sufficiency of the evidence, but must not suggest that some other person

committed the offence, or call any evidence that, by reason of the admissions, the lawyer believes to be false. Nor may the lawyer set up an affirmative case inconsistent with such admissions, for example, by calling evidence in support of an alibi intended to show that the accused could not have done, or in fact had not done, the act. Such admissions will also impose a limit upon the extent to which the lawyer may attack the evidence for the prosecution. The lawyer is entitled to test the evidence given by each individual witness for the prosecution and argue that the evidence taken as a whole is insufficient to amount to proof that the accused is guilty of the offence charged, but the lawyer should go no further than that.

R. v. STINCHCOMBE

[1991] 3 S.C.R. 326, 8 C.R. (4th) 277, 68 C.C.C. (3d) 1

The accused, a lawyer, was charged with breach of trust, theft and fraud. His former secretary was a Crown witness at the preliminary inquiry, where she gave evidence apparently favourable to the defence. After the preliminary inquiry but prior to trial, the witness was interviewed by an R.C.M.P. officer and a tape-recorded statement was taken. Later, during the course of the trial, the witness was again interviewed by a police officer and a written statement was taken. Defence counsel was informed of the existence but not of the content of the statements. His requests for disclosure were refused. During the trial defence counsel learned that the witness would not be called by the Crown. The defence sought an order that the witness be called or that the Crown disclose the contents of the statements to the defence. In support of this motion defence counsel indicated that the witness refused to speak to him or his staff when they attempted to interview her about the contents of the statements. The trial Judge dismissed the application. The trial proceeded and the accused was convicted of breach of trust and fraud. The Court of Appeal affirmed the convictions without giving reasons. The Supreme Court ordered a new trial.

SOPINKA J.: —

. . . .

Production and discovery were foreign to the adversary process of adjudication in its earlier history when the element of surprise was one of the accepted weapons in the arsenal of the adversaries. This applied to both criminal and civil proceedings. Significantly, in civil proceedings this aspect of the adversary process has long since disappeared, and full discovery of documents and oral examination of parties and even witnesses are familiar features of the practice. This change resulted from acceptance of the principle that justice was better served when the element of surprise was eliminated from the trial and the parties were prepared to address issues on the basis of complete information of the case to be met. Surprisingly, in criminal cases in which the liberty of the subject is usually at stake, this aspect of the adversary system has lingered on.

While the prosecution bar has generally co-operated in making disclosure on a voluntary basis, there has been considerable resistance to the enactment of comprehensive rules which would make the practice mandatory. This may be attributed to the fact that proposals for reform in this regard do not provide for reciprocal disclosure by the defence.

. . . .

It is difficult to justify the position which clings to the notion that the Crown has no legal duty to disclose all relevant information. The arguments against the existence of such a duty are groundless while those in favour are, in my view, overwhelming. The suggestion that the duty should be reciprocal may deserve consideration by this court in the future but is not a valid reason for absolving the Crown of its duty. The contrary contention fails to take account of the fundamental difference in the respective roles of the prosecution and the defence. In *Boucher v. R.*, [1955] S.C.R. 16, 20 C.R. 1, 110 C.C.C. 263, Rand J. states at (pp. 23-24) [S.C.R.]:

> It cannot be over-emphasized that the purpose of a criminal prosecution is not to obtain a conviction, it is to lay before a jury what the Crown considers to be credible evidence relevant to what is alleged to be a crime. Counsel have a duty to see that all available legal proof of the facts is presented: it should be done firmly and pressed to its legitimate strength but it must also be done fairly. The role of prosecutor excludes any notion of winning or losing; his function is a matter of public duty than which in civil life there can be none charged with greater personal responsibility. It is to be efficiently performed with an ingrained sense of the dignity, the seriousness and the justness of judicial proceedings.

I would add that the fruits of the investigation which are in the possession of counsel for the Crown are not the property of the Crown for use in securing a conviction but the property of the public to be used to ensure that justice is done. In contrast, the defence has no obligation to assist the prosecution and is entitled to assume a purely adversarial role toward the prosecution. The absence of a duty to disclose can, therefore, be justified as being consistent with this role.

. . . .

The right to make full answer and defence is one of the pillars of criminal justice on which we heavily depend to ensure that the innocent are not convicted. Recent events have demonstrated that the erosion of this right due to non-disclosure was an important factor in the conviction and incarceration of an innocent person. In the *Royal Commission on the Donald Marshall, Jr., Prosecution*, vol. 1: Findings and Recommendations (1989) (the "Marshall Commission Report"), the commissioners found that prior inconsistent statements were not disclosed to the defence. This was an important contributing factor in the miscarriage of justice which occurred and led the commission to state that "anything less than complete disclosure by the Crown falls short of decency and fair play" (vol. 1 at p. 238). The commission recommended an extensive regime of disclosure.

. . . .

[The] obligation to disclose is not absolute. It is subject to the discretion of counsel for the Crown. This discretion extends both to the withholding of information and to the timing of disclosure. For example, counsel for the Crown has a duty to respect the rules of privilege. In the case of informers the Crown has a duty to protect their identity. In some cases serious prejudice or even harm may result to a person who has supplied evidence or information to the investigation. While it is a harsh reality of justice that ultimately any person with relevant evidence must appear to testify, the discretion extends to the timing and manner of disclosure in such circumstances. A discretion must also be exercised with respect to the relevance of information. While the Crown must err on the side of inclusion, it need not produce what is clearly irrelevant. The experience to be gained from the civil side of the practice is that counsel, as officers of the Court and acting responsibly, can be relied upon not to withhold pertinent information. Transgressions with respect to this duty constitute a very serious breach of legal ethics. The initial obligation to separate "the wheat from the chaff" must therefore rest with Crown counsel. There may also be situations in which early disclosure may impede completion of an investigation. Delayed disclosure on this account is not to be encouraged and should be rare. Completion of the investigation before proceeding with the prosecution of a charge or charges is very much within the control of the Crown. Nevertheless, it is not always possible to predict events which may require an investigation to be reopened and the Crown must have some discretion to delay disclosure in these circumstances.

The discretion of Crown counsel is, however, reviewable by the trial judge. Counsel for the defence can initiate a review when an issue arises with respect to the exercise of the Crown's discretion. On a review the Crown must justify its refusal to disclose. Inasmuch as disclosure of all relevant information is the general rule, the Crown must bring itself within an exception to that rule.

. . . .

With respect to timing, I agree with the recommendation of the Law Reform Commission of Canada in both of its reports that initial disclosure should occur before the accused is called upon to elect the mode of trial or to plead. These are crucial steps which the accused must take which affect his or her rights in a fundamental way. It will be of great assistance to the accused to know what are the strengths and weaknesses of the Crown's case before committing on these issues.

. . . .

With respect to what should be disclosed, the general principle to which I have referred is that all relevant information must be disclosed subject to the reviewable discretion of the Crown. The material must include not only that which the Crown intends to introduce into evidence but also that which it does not. No distinction should be made between inculpatory and exculpatory evidence.

LUBAN, THE ADVERSARY SYSTEM EXCUSE

The Good Lawyer: Lawyers' Rules and Lawyers' Ethics (Rowman and
Allenheld, 1984), 84-88

On February 7, 1973, Richard Helms, the former director of the Central Intelligence Agency, lied to a Senate committee about American involvement in the overthrow of the Allende government in Chile. Santiago proved to be Helms's Waterloo: he was caught out in his perjury and prosecuted. Helms claimed that requirements of national security led him to lie to Congress. We can only speculate, however, on how the Court would have viewed this excuse, for in fact the case never came to trial; Helm's lawyer, the redoubtable Edward Bennett Williams, found an ingenious way to back the government down. He argued that national security information was relevant to Helms's defense and must be turned over to Helms, thereby confronting the government with the unpleasant choice of dropping the action or making public classified and presumably vital information. The government chose the first option and allowed Helms to plead guilty to a misdemeanor charge.

I don't know if anyone ever asked Williams to justify his actions; had anyone attempted to do so, they would presumably have been told that Williams was simply doing his job as a criminal defense attorney. The parallel with Helms's own excuse is clear — he was doing his job, Williams was doing his — but it is hard to miss the irony. Helms tried to conceal national security information; therefore he lied. Williams, acting on Helms's behalf, threatened to reveal national security information as part of a tactic that has come to be called "graymailing." One man's ends are another man's means. Neither lying nor graymailing (to say nothing of destabilizing elected regimes) are morally pretty, but a job is a job and that was the job that was. So, at any rate, runs the excuse.

We may want to reject these "good soldier" excuses or we may find them valid and persuasive. That is the issue I shall address here. A second graymailing example will warm us to our topic:

> In instances [of merger cases involving firms in competition with each other] in which the [Federal Trade] commission's legal case looked particularly good and none of the usual defenses appeared likely to work, the staff was confronted several times with the argument that if they did not refrain from prosecution and allow the merger, one of the proposed merger partners would close down its operations and dismiss its employees.
>
> . . . Of course, the mere announcement of the threat to close the plant generates enormous political pressure on the prosecutor not to go forward. Ought lawyers to be engaged in such strategies for the purpose of consummating an otherwise anticompetitive and illegal transaction involving the joinder of two substantial competitors?

On the lawyers' advice, the firms played a nice game of chicken: closing down by stages, they laid off a few workers each day until the FTC cried uncle.

What could justify the conduct of these lawyers? A famous answer is the following statement of Lord Henry Brougham:

> An advocate, in the discharge of his duty, knows but one person in all the world, and that person is his client. To save that client by all means and expedients, and at all hazards and costs

to other persons, and, amongst them to himself, is his first and only duty; and in performing this duty he must not regard the alarm, the torments, the destruction which he may bring upon others. Separating the duty of a patriot from that of an advocate, he must go on reckless of consequences, though it should be his unhappy fate to involve his country in confusion.

This speech, made in his 1820 defense of Queen Caroline against King George IV's charge of adultery, was itself an act of graymail. Reminiscing years later, Brougham said that the king would recognize in it a tacit threat to reveal his secret marriage to a Catholic, a marriage that, were it to become public knowledge, would cost him his crown. Knowing this background of Brougham's oft-quoted statement might make us take a dim view of it; it has, nevertheless, frequently been admired as the most eloquent encapsulation of the advocate's job.

Brougham's statement invites philosophical reflection for at first blush it is equally baffling to utilitarianism, and moral rights theory, and Kantianism. The client's utility matters more than that of the rest of the world put together. No one else's moral rights matter. Other people are merely means to the client's ends. Moral theory seems simply to reject Brougham's imperatives.

They are, however, universalizable over lawyers, or so it is claimed. The idea seems to be that the role of lawyer, hence the social institutions that set up this role, reparse the Moral Law, relaxing some moral obligations and imposing new ones. In the words of an Australian appellate Court, "Our system of administering justice necessarily imposes upon those who practice advocacy duties which have no analogies, and the system cannot dispense with their strict observance."

The system of which the Court speaks is the so-called "adversary system of justice." My main question is this: does the adversary system really justify Brougham's position? I hope that the example of Helms and his lawyers has convinced you that a more general issue is lurking here, the issue of what I shall call *institutional excuses*. We can state the main question in full generality in this way: can a person appeal to a social institution in which he or she occupies a role in order to excuse conduct that would be morally culpable were anyone else to do it? Plausibly, examples exist in which the answer is yes: we do not call it murder when a soldier kills a sleeping enemy, although it is surely immoral for you or me to do it. There are also cases where the answer is no, as in the job "concentration camp commandant" or "professional strikebreaker." Here, we feel, the immorality of the job is so great that it accuses, not excuses, the person who holds it.

This suggests that an important feature of a successful institutional excuse is that the institution is itself justified. I think that is partly right, but I do not think it is the whole story: I shall argue that the *kind* of justification that can be offered of the institution is germane to the success of the excuses it provides.

GEOFFREY HAZARD ETHICS IN THE PRACTICE OF LAW

(1978), 128

There are several escapes [from moral responsibility]. It is said that no client is guilty until so found by a court; therefore one cannot know what the truth is until then; therefore, one cannot conclude that a client's testimony will constitute perjury. This is pure casuistry. Of course there are doubtful situations, but there are also ones that are not doubtful. A thing is not made true or not by a Court's pronouncing on it, and a lawyer can reach conclusions about an issue without having a Judge tell him what to think.

GREENSPAN AND JONAS, GREENSPAN: THE CASE FOR THE DEFENCE

(1987), 260-265

Whenever a crime is committed (or whenever some people in the community suspect that an act may amount to a crime), a large, impersonal machinery goes into motion. Its initial purpose is to determine if some act or event was, in fact, a crime — and if it concludes that it was, to find the individual (or group of individuals) responsible for it.

Once this appears to be accomplished, the machinery shifts into second gear. It tries to establish the accused individual's *degree* of responsibility. Then, in third gear, his or her appropriate punishment. Sometimes there is a fourth gear: the machinery may turn its attention to some social or legal condition in the hope of making it easier to define, prevent, or detect such crimes in the future.

This process can involve dozens and dozens of people in its various stages. Ideally — and often in actual fact — they are highly trained, intelligent, dedicated, and hard-working human beings: people of great personal integrity. They are police officers, forensic experts, medical doctors, prosecuting attorneys, Court officials, Judges, jurors, parole officials, prison administrators, and lawmakers. Except for the jurors, they are all professionals. Many of them have the authority to knock on anybody's door and ask for information and assistance. Even when they cannot compel people's co-operation by law, they can expect people to co-operate with them as a civic or moral duty. They also have at their disposal support personnel and sophisticated, expensive equipment, the best society can provide, to help them in their work.

There is nothing wrong with any of this, of course. Crime cannot go undetected, undefined, or unpunished. No community could function without protecting itself from crime.

However, this great, impersonal, awesome machinery has one built-in bias. It is an unconscious, functional bias, somewhat like an aircraft's bias for leaving the ground as soon as it has attained a certain speed. The bias of the justice system is to find guilt. That is, first, to define any human act that comes to its attention as a crime; then, to define any suspect as a person who has probably committed such an act; and finally, to define any human being who has committed such an act as a criminal. That's the way the justice system flies.

Everyone knows that in a given individual case none of this may be true — yet the great machine of the criminal justice system may thunder down the runway and take off regardless.

. . . .

Our justice system has tried to counteract this potential by two remedies.

First, on an abstract level, the remedy is the law's presumption that every person is innocent until proven guilty on relevant evidence beyond a reasonable doubt.

By saying "on an abstract level" I don't mean to imply that this presumption is unimportant. On the contrary, it is vital and fundamental. Everything else flows from the presumption of innocence. However, without a second remedy on a concrete level, it could remain as ineffectual as a sheathed sword. Or, to use a more up-to-date metaphor, as an engine without a driver.

This second, concrete remedy is the lawyer for the defence. He drives the abstract engine of the presumption of innocence. He is the one person in the entire world, apart from the accused person's mother, who *starts* with the assumption that the authorities must be mistaken.

To balance the awe-inspiring machinery of the criminal-justice system, the law permits one individual to be the accused person's friend. He is, as the legal expression goes, to be "of counsel" to him. Simply put, his job is to "believe" the accused —— or at least not to disbelieve him. His job is to look at every circumstance surrounding the allegations against a defendant with the assumption that they prove, or are consistent with, his innocence.

The defence lawyer is to balance the dozens of powerful professionals whose task is to investigate and prosecute an accused person. We give the defence lawyer this task in the knowledge that a defendant may *be* innocent. Innocent, not just as an abstract legal idea (because in that sense he is innocent anyway until found guilty), but as a matter of plain, actual fact. What he is accused of may not amount to a crime, or he may not have committed it. If it is a crime and he did commit it, it may not be as serious a crime as his adversary, the prosecutor, suggests. And even if it is as serious, there may be something about the circumstances, or about the defendant as a human being, that makes him something else than a criminal deserving the worst punishment.

Since this may be so, our system has decided that there must be one person in the defendant's community who acts as if it were so. One man or woman who is not the defendant's inquisitor, accuser, or Judge. One who doesn't merely keep an open mind about him. One person who is the defendant's advocate.

Society assigns this role to the defence lawyer. He is the one person whose duty is to assume the best about a defendant at every step of the way. The defence lawyer alone, among all the defendant's fellow citizens and neighbours, must act on the assumption that whatever the defendant says is true. He must act on the assumption that the defendant's accusers are mistaken. Mistaken — or possibly malicious. They may have their own axe to grind. The defence lawyer must put everything they say about the defendant to the strictest test of proof. In so far as the law permits, he must put the accusers on trial.

This is the defence lawyer's duty. It's a duty not just to his client, but to his society. It is not something the defence lawyer decides in his own mind: it is an obligation the community places on him. The defence lawyer chooses his occupation voluntarily, but he does not choose his role: his society defines his role for him. The moral essence of this role has been distilled by the common experience of our legal tradition over the centuries. It is that a community can retain justice and freedom only as long as it gives standing to one person to take, within the limits of the law, the defendant's side in Court.

. . . .

The defence lawyer, as many people have pointed out, only defends a client (or a client's act) and not a crime. Central to any defence, other than a submission in mitigation of sentence, is the position that the client didn't do something. Or that whatever he did was not wrong in law, or at least not as wrong as the prosecution contends. If a lawyer suggested that yes, my client did shoot this man deliberately and in cold blood, but the victim was a nasty fellow who deserved to be shot, *then* he would be defending a crime — but no lawyer does that. (The only exceptions in our times have been some "activist" lawyers who attempted to gain the acquittal of murderers on the basis of some "higher" political or social motive.)

But these are only aberrations — albeit dangerous ones — and we need not concern ourselves with them here. Like most criminal lawyers, I defend clients, not crimes. Which is why I find questions like: "How can you defend those people?" or Is there any kind of crime at which you'd draw a line?" meaningless.

I haven't the slightest moral conflict defending people accused of homicide, sexual assault, business fraud, environmental offences, or even crimes against humanity. I don't "draw the line" at anything. If I defended *crimes*, maybe I would — but I don't defend crimes. I only defend innocent people. Until they are found guilty there are no other kinds of people for me to defend, and what difference does it make what an innocent person is accused of?

Would you represent any and all accused?

It has been said that there are broadly two models of the practice of criminal law as a defence counsel. Some defence counsel start by advising potential clients that everything told to them will be kept in strictest confidence but that, having heard the full story, the defence counsel may be limited in the ability to present a defence. The client is told that the lawyer cannot participate in perjured testimony. Subject to these limits, the accused is encouraged to tell the defence counsel everything about the case. On the other model, sometimes called "blind person's bluff" the lawyer remains purposefully ignorant about potentially embarrassing facts and discourages the client from telling everything. The accused is never directly asked for his or her version of the facts. Instead, the questions are entirely limited to such questions as whether the accused gave a statement to the police, which witnesses could be of assistance to the defence and what else is known by the police or the Crown Attorney.

What advantages do you see in these models of practice. Which would you follow?

---

1. John Smith has been charged with assault. He asks you to represent him and you agree. He tells you that he beat on the victim during a drunken rage. He imagines that it was because he has never cared for his manner. He knows that he started this particular fracas but also advises you that the victim himself has two previous convictions of common assault, which, he suggests, could be fertile ground for cross-examination. The victim describes the beating in some detail. When he finishes his examination in chief you turn to your client who advises "That's exactly what happened. Now go get him. Destroy his credibility." What do you do?

Your client is convicted. Would you inform the Crown about two other assault convictions registered against your client under another name?

2. Your client is prosecuted for robbery. He committed the crime at 10:45 and has admitted the same to you. The sole prosecution witness identified your client as the robber but mistakenly placed the time at 10:15. Your client has an airtight alibi for 10:00 to 10:30. Will you present the alibi?

3. You have been assigned to prosecute a case of domestic assault. The police laid the charge after they had been called to investigate a disturbance. The wife told the police that her husband had beaten her and that this was not the first time. The trial is to take place tomorrow, three months after the alleged incident. The woman approaches you and wants to withdraw the charge. She tells you that her husband has returned to Alcoholics Anonymous and is participating with her in a marriage-counselling program. The incidence of domestic violence in your community is very high. Will you withdraw?

4. Mr. Murray is a member of the Ontario Bar and certified as a specialist in criminal litigation by the Law Society of Upper Canada. He was retained by Paul Bernardo initially in February 1993 in regard to the "Scarborough Rapes" and on May 18, 1993, in connection with the murders of L.M. and K.F. and additional related offences.

On May 6, 1993, he went to the Bernardo home after the search warrant for those premises had expired to retrieve personal possessions and evidence that might be helpful to the defence. He had a letter from his client with written instructions that he was only to open it once inside the house. Once inside he opened the sealed envelope, which contained a map and directions to assist in locating six eight-millimetre videotapes from above a pot light. He did so and removed them to his office. Bernardo's written instructions were for his counsel not to view them. The videotapes depicted gross sexual abuse of K.F., L.M., Jane Doe and T.H. by Bernardo and his co-accused Karla Homolka. Without disclosing their existence to the Crown, he retained the tapes for 17 months. He only viewed them at the instruction of Bernardo after he and Bernardo learned of a deal under which Karla Homolka agreed to plead guilty to two counts of manslaughter, with a joint submission to be made for a sentence of 12 years in exchange for her testifying for the Crown in the first degree murder trial of Bernardo. The tapes would be used to aid the defence that Bernardo was guilty of sexual assault but not murder. The Crown was going to portray Homolka as an abused, manipulated victim, while the tapes showed the reverse: that she was not afraid and was an enthusiastic participant in the sexual crimes. He felt obliged to keep the existence of the tapes secret so that the Crown could not prepare Homolka for defence cross-examination.

Trial motions were to begin on September 12, 1994. On September 2, 1994, the accused, through his counsel, applied to the Law Society of Upper Canada for advice. He was advised the tapes should be turned over to the judge and that he should withdraw from the case. Accepting that advice he appeared before the trial judge, who directed that the tapes, their integrity protected by suitable undertakings, go to John Rosen, new counsel for Bernardo, at which time the accused was given leave to withdraw as counsel. Rosen, on September 22, 1994, turned the tapes over to the police and they were used by Crown counsel at the trial. A jury found Bernardo guilty on all charges.

Murray was later charged with wilfully attempting to obstruct justice contrary to s. 139(2) of the *Criminal Code* by concealment of the videotapes. Did he do anything ethically wrong? If so what precisely? Should he be convicted? Compare *R. v. Murray* (2000), 34 C.R. (5th) 290, 144 C.C.C. (3d) 289 (Ont. S.C.J.), and Annotation to that case by Stuart.

5. Your client says that he is innocent, but that he wants to plead guilty "to get it over with". He is tired of the court delay and does not want to lose any more time off work. The offence is a minor one. Would you assist him in entering his guilty plea? Would you advise him to indicate remorse to secure a minimal penalty?

6. John is observed slipping a box of mints, value $1.75, into his jacket. He is arrested by store security and, following store policy, a charge is laid. John is in his second year of university and hopes to go to law school. He has no prior record. Your brief indicates that he was co-operative during the investigation. He had told the security officer, "I'm dumbfounded. I don't know why I took them". You are approached by a senior defence counsel, acting for John. He's also a friend of John's family. He tells you that John has been going through some rough times of late. John's older brother was recently killed in a car accident and John has just broken up with his girl friend. He tells you that John is basically a "good kid" but he's under a lot of pressure because exams are just around the corner. Counsel asks if you'll withdraw the charges. Will you?

Suppose that you decide not to withdraw the charge but just as the case is being called by the Court clerk you are advised that the store security officer is not present. You can't prove the charge and the trial Judge is known not to grant adjournments in such cases. You know that John is about to plead guilty. What do you do?

Procedural Classification of Offences

At common law a distinction was drawn between indictable offences (treason, felonies and misdemeanours) triable only by Judge and jury and offences triable only summarily by justices of the peace sitting without a jury. The distinction between felonies and misdemeanours was important in that the former (*e.g.*, murder, burglary and rape) were punishable by death and resulted in forfeiture of the felon's property while the latter never involved the death penalty and only rarely forfeiture. It is still maintained in the United States, but was abolished in England in 1967 and in Canada by the *Criminal Code* as early as the nineteenth century.

In Canada today the *Code* distinguishes between indictable offences, those triable only by way of summary conviction proceedings and those triable on indictment or by way of summary conviction proceedings. The designation not only affects trial and appeal procedures but also many pre-trial rights and responsibilities. There are therefore only two modes of procedure. The section which creates the offence and specifies its punishment also states the manner in which it is to be tried.

(a) Offences triable only on indictment

Indictable offences are divided into three categories. The most serious offences are given into the exclusive jurisdiction of the superior Court of criminal jurisdiction, in Ontario, the Court of Justice, General Division (see ss. 468 and 469). The least serious indictable offences are absolutely within the jurisdiction of a Magistrate, in Ontario, a Judge of the Court of Justice, Provincial Division (see s. 553). For the great bulk of the indictable offences remaining, the accused is entitled to choose his mode of trial. Under s. 536(2), the accused will be put to his election and he will be asked to choose whether he wishes to be tried by a provincial Court Judge without a jury, a Judge without a jury or a Court composed of a Judge and jury. If the accused does not elect a mode of trial he will be deemed to have elected trial by Judge and jury (s. 565(l)(c)). It is important to note the difference between the *exclusive* jurisdiction of the superior Court at one end of the scale and the *absolute* jurisdiction of the Magistrate at the other. The superior Court has exclusive jurisdiction: no other Court can try these offences. The Magistrate has absolute jurisdiction: the Magistrate is absolutely entitled to try these offences in the sense that he is not dependent on the accused's electing to be so tried. Other Courts of criminal jurisdiction are nevertheless entitled to try the accused for offences within the Magistrate's absolute jurisdiction should the matter come before them (see *R. v. Holliday*, 26 C.R.N.S. 279, 12 C.C.C. (2d) 56 (Alta. C.A.)).

Notwithstanding that the accused has elected trial by Magistrate, the Magistrate may decide that the matter should be proceeded with by a Judge or jury (s. 555), and the Attorney General may also override an accused's decision and compel a jury trial where the offence is punishable by more than five years (s. 568).

There are detailed, recently-amended provisions which allow the accused to change his mind and to re-elect his mode of trial (ss. 560-565).

(b) Summary conviction offences

Part XXVII of the *Criminal Code* sets out the procedure for the trial of summary conviction offences (*i.e.*, trial before a provincial judge without a jury and without a preliminary inquiry). The maximum penalty for any summary conviction offence unless otherwise provided is $2000 or six months' imprisonment or both (s. 787(l)).

(c) Hybrid offences

In some instances the legislation makes the offence punishable on indictment or on summary conviction at the option of the Crown. In 1994 Parliament increased the maximum penalty for several hybrid offences when proceeded against by way of summary conviction to 18 months: see, eg. assault causing bodily harm (s. 267) and sexual assault (s. 271). Only when the prosecutor elects to proceed by indictment does the accused have the choice under s. 464. The prosecutor should indicate the nature of the proceeding prior to trial.

How are the following *Criminal Code* offences classified? What options for trial will an accused have in each case? What factors will you as counsel take into account in determining how to exercise your options?

1. **frightening the Queen**
2. **murder**
3. **impaired driving**
4. **shoplifting**
5. **robbery**
6. **assault**
7. **assault causing bodily harm**
8. **sexual assault**
9. **causing a disturbance in a public place**

LAW REFORM COMMISSION OF CANADA, THE JURY IN CRIMINAL TRIALS

W.P. No. 27, (1980), 76-77

Questions of law are decided by the judge; questions of fact are decided by the jury. This well-known dichotomy of functions raises the problem of who applies the law to the facts. Because the jury in criminal cases returns a general verdict of guilty or not-guilty, it must discharge this responsibility. Thus, to enable the jury to carry out its duties, the Judge instructs the jury on the law which governs the case. In reaching a verdict the jury must then apply those instructions to the facts as it finds them.

Jury instructions must, therefore, satisfy two conflicting requirements: the need to state accurately the relevant law and the need to state the law so that the jury understands it. The need to state the law accurately is, of course, an obvious requirement. If the case is appealed, counsel will scrutinize the charge for all possible errors in the statement of law. The Court of Appeal will hold the instructions to be in error unless the Judge has correctly stated the law in all respects. (Of course, not every error causes a substantial wrong or miscarriage of justice.) Because strict legal correctness is the primary concern of the appellate Courts, it is naturally the concern of trial Judges as well. Indeed, to eliminate the possibility of error from their statements of the law, trial Judges will sometimes include long quotations from appellate Court judgments in their instructions and in other ways generally attempt to "boiler-plate" them. This often results in instructions which are long, repetitive, and disjointed.

The need to state the law correctly may thus often conflict with the other important requirement of jury instructions: that they be understandable to the jury. The allocation of responsibility between the Judge and jury is premised on the jury's ability to understand and apply the law. It is often alleged that one of the most serious deficiencies of trial by jury, and indeed an aspect of it which is sometimes said to place the institution of the jury in jeopardy, is the jury's inability to follow and comprehend the instructions given by the Judge. If jurors are confused about the law they are to apply, they cannot perform their function properly, and a just verdict will be reached only by chance.

Our survey of Judges also led us to the conclusion that something to improve the quality of jury instructions ought to be attempted. Only 23 percent of the Judges were quite certain that juries generally understand the Judge's instructions. And while most (82 percent) felt that it was at least probable that juries understood what was being told to them, a significant minority (18 percent) felt that it was probable that juries did not understand what was being told them.

Truths of Criminology

Many disciplines other than law have devoted considerable time and energy to a serious study of the causes, nature, punishment or treatment of criminal behaviour. Are there truths of criminological research that should be taken into account in the development of substantive criminal law principles?

Few researchers now attempt to explain "crime". Even assuming that an inquiry into legally-defined criminality is adequate, there is the Barbara Wootton contention[1] that criminal behaviour covers too large a range of human behaviour to be classified and analysed, a miscellaneous aggregate of quite different kinds of action.

> It seems time that we recognised that delinquency or criminality (even with its major motoring component left out) is not a rational field of discourse. . . . The inherent stupidity of treating criminals, delinquents, or prisoners, even of a given sex and age group, as sufficiently homogeneous for rational study had been repeatedly demonstrated.[2]

1 *Social Science and Social Pathology*, (1959).
2 At 306.

Even if one could reject this view, a researcher into criminality must look wider than officially recorded crime. It is universally accepted that the figures often represent the "tip of the iceberg", due to such factors as police discretion, the low reporting of some crimes and the vagaries of recording practices. The researcher must also contend with the observation, stemming from the controversial study by Sutherland of "white-collar" criminality,[3] that conduct which is not officially criminal sometimes appears similar. In the Canadian context we could not ignore motoring offenders on the legalistic basis that they, were mostly provincial offences,[4] that false advertising by companies which looks like fraud is not a *Criminal Code* offence[5] and that the distinction between tax evasion which is an offence and tax avoidance which is not is sometimes fudgy.[6]

Even if an acceptable typology of conduct is arrived at most researchers now agree that any attempt to seek a mono-causal theory is doomed to failure and that the best we can do is to suggest that there are a host of interacting predisposing factors — biological, psychological and sociological. The invariable problem with a monolithic theory such as "'poverty causes crime" is that it does not explain the exceptions. David Matza[7] has used the phrase "embarrassment of riches" to describe this deficiency. Why do so many poor people not commit crimes? The modern approach of avoiding extravagant claims characterizes the recent Senate Report, *Child at Risk* (1980).[8] For example, it firmly rejects the concept of a "natural born criminal" in these terms:

> Some individuals may be more likely than others to become criminal or violent as a result of inheritence, but it is never inevitable that they will become so. At most, genetic make-up must be considered as one factor, among many others, that can place a child at risk.[9]

Thus no magic answers exist, or are ever likely to exist, on the question of what causes crime. We should thus retain a healthy scepticism of claims that the explanation is to be found in the "extra Y chromosome,"[10] "brain dysfunction,"[11] or in the rational challenge to inequities in the structure of ownership and the distribution of wealth.[12] Social labelling theorists[13] who assert that it is the quality

---

3   "Is 'White Collar Crime' Crime?" (1945), 10 Am. Soc. Rev. 132.

4   T.C. Willett, *Criminal on the Road*, (1964).

5   Cf. C. Goff and C.E. Reasons, "Corporations in Canada: A Study of Crime and Punishment" (1976), 18 Crim. L.Q. 468, who survey prosecution statistics under the Combines Investigation Act and conclude that the Federal Government is devoting less effort to proceed against Canada's largest companies. See now their book *Corporate Crime in Canada: A Criticial Analysis of Anti-Combines Legislation*, (1978). See too, L. Snider, "Corporate Crime in Canada: A Preliminary Report" (1978), 20 Can. J. of Crim. 142.

6   See R.S. Rice, "Judicial Techniques in Combating Tax Avoidance" (1953), 51 Mich. L. Rev. 1021.

7   *Delinquency and Drift*, (1964).

8   3, 8-9, 60, 50-2.

9   At 9.

10 N. Wade, "Born Criminals" New Society, December 19, 1968 made the monstrous suggestion that once computer methods made it feasible to culture the blood cells of all new-born babies it may not be "ethically" correct to let XYY babies live. Researchers are now extremely cautious: see especially H.A. Witkin *et al*, "Criminality in XYY and XXY Men" (1976), 193 Scienice 547.

11 M. Yeudall, "Neuropsychological Assessment of Forensic Disorders" (1977), 25 Canada's Mental Health 7.

12 See L. McDonald, *The Sociology of Law and Order*, (1976) for a description of "conflict theories" stemming from the work of I. Taylor, P. Walton, and J. Young, *The New Criminology*, (1973) and *Critical Criminology*, (1975). See also A.E.C. Antony, "Radical Criminology" in R.A. Silverman and J.J. Teevan Jr., eds., *Crime in Canadian Society*, 2nd ed., (1980), 234.

13 E.M. Lemert, *Social Pathology*, (1951), H.S. Becker *Outsiders*, (1963) and generally E. Rubington and M.S. Weinberg, *Deviance: The Interactionist Perspective*, (1968). In Canada, see R.V. Ericson, *Criminal Reactions: The Labelling Perspective*, (1975).

of societal reaction to deviancy rather than the quality of the act or actor himself that determines criminality have a point — decriminalizing everything would "solve" crime — but it is a limited truth. What initiates the act?

This marshy base leads to the conclusion that human behaviour is so complex that we should be careful about generalizing, let alone talking about an individual case which is what concerns a criminal trial. It is not surprising that the truths from what may be called applied criminology are equally guarded and limited.

Research has been undertaken on the effectiveness of different forms of punishment or treatment, predictions of dangerousness, and the notion of general deterrence.

Research on the effectiveness of punishments and treatments almost inevitably encounters grave methodological problems. Not the least of these is the widely perceived unethical nature of the best research model of experimentation with a controlled group. Yet even the most sophisticated research[14] has produced very pessimistic results, particularly if we are concerned with the acid test: the rate of recidivism. Different forms of punishment or treatment seem equally ineffective, even if we compare such markedly different punishments as long- and short-term prison sentences, probation and institutional punishments, and authoritarian institutions and therapeutic communities. The greatest hope is with the first offenders but it does not seem to matter what the disposition is. The gloom is so pervasive that Dr. Fattah's conclusion[15] appears optimistic:

> Recidivism rates appear to vary greatly for different types of crime and for different types of offenders. More research is needed to establish what types of offences or what types ot offenders are relatively immune to the influence of intimidation.
>
> On the basis of existing evidence it appears that there are persistent offenders who are very likely to be reconvicted whatever is done to them. On the other hand there are offenders who have relatively good chances of avoiding reconviction no matter what penal measure they were subjected to. Between these two extremes there is a group of offenders, probably the largest group, for whom differential sentencing is needed and for whom the choice of sentence makes a difference. . . .
>
> The development of a typology of crime and of the criminal would, no doubt, be very useful in selecting appropriate deterrent measures.[16]

The difficulty with putting our hope in typologies is that no one has yet been able to develop them. Although accurate figures in respect of recidivism rates of those sent to Canadian prisons and penitentiaries are not available, few would doubt that the rates are not very high.[17]

---

14 R. Hood, "Research on the Effectiveness of Punishments and Treatments" (1967), 1 Collected Studies in Criminological Research 73; W. Outerbridge, "The Tyranny of Treatment?" (1968), 10 Can. J. of Corr. 378; R. Martinson, "What Works? Questions and Answers About Prison Reform" (1974), 35 The Public Interest 22; N. Morris, The Future of Imprisonment (1974); K. Jobson, "Reforming Sentencing Laws: A Canadian Perspective", in B. Grossman, (ed.), New Directions in Sentencing (1980), p. 73 at 75-76. Before his death, Martinson however reversed his "nothing works" stance: R. Martinson, "New Findings, New Views: A Note of Caution Regarding Sentencing Reform" (1979), 7 Hofstra L. Rev. 243. See also P. Gendreau and B. Ross, "Effective Correctional Treatment: Bibliography for Cynics" (1979), 25 Crime & Deliquency 463.
15 "Deterrence: A Review of the Literature" in L.R.C., Fear of Punishment, (1976).
16 At 97.
17 See I. Waller, Men Released from Prison, (1974) and see, as to parole, P. Macnaughton-Smith, Permission to be Slightly Free, L.R.C. (1976). The most optimistic findings are by R.B. Cormier, "Canadian Recidivism Index" (1981), 23 Can. J. Crim. 103.

On the topic of prediction of dangerousness there is now strong evidence denying the expertise of psychiatrists or anybody else to make reasonably accurate predictions. Clinical analysis is as ineffective as an examination of past behaviour. After their exhaustive review of research findings, Ennis and Litwack[18] conclude:

> Whatever may be said for the reliability and validity of psychiatric judgments in general, there is literally no evidence that psychiatrists reliably and accurately can predict dangerous behaviour. To the contrary, such predictions are wrong more often than they are right. It is inconceivable that a judgment could be considered an "expert" judgment when it is less accurate than the flip of a coin."[19]

Research on the general deterrent effect of penalties[20] faces tremendous methodological barriers. Again the greatest barrier is that ethical considerations strongly militate against experimentation with real subjects in the criminal justice system. Most researchers now go out of their way to emphasize how complex the issue of general deterrence is and how little we know. The most authoritative recent study was by a panel on the National Research Council of the United States who concluded that the deterrence effect was not yet proven but also not disproven:

> Our reluctance to assert that the evidence warrants an affirmative conclusion regarding deterrence derives from the limited validity of the available evidence and the number of competing explanations for the results.
> It is also important to recognise that our reluctance to draw stronger conclusions does not imply support tor a position that there are no deterrent effects; the evidence certainly favours a proposition supporting deterrence more than it favours one asserting that deterrence is absent. Furthermore, the Panel is convinced on *a priori* grounds that criminal sanctions do influence at least some criminal behaviour by some individuals.[21]

---

18 "Psychiatry and the Presumption of Expertise: Flipping Coins in the Courtroom" (1974), 62 Cal. L. Rev. 693, discussed in the Canadian context by N. Boyd, "Ontario's Treatment of the 'Criminally Insane' and the Potentially Dangerous: The Questionable Wisdom of Procedural Reform" (1980), 22 Can. J. of Crim. 151. See also, for example, R. Price, "Psychiatry, Criminal Law Reform and the Mythophilic Impulse: on Canadian Proposals for the Control of the Dangerous Offender" (1970), 4 Ottawa L. Rev.; J. Klein, "Habitual Offender Legislation and the Bargaining Process" (1973), 15 Crim. L.Q. 417; "The Dangerousness of Dangerous Offender Legislation: Forensic Folklore Revisited" (1976), 18 Can. J. of Crim. and Corr. 109; R. Price and A. Gold, "Legal Controls for the Dangerous Offender" in L.R.C., *Studies on Imprisonment*, (1976), 153; More recent studies in the United States are discussed by Jobson, note 14 above at 78-80; and see T.P. Thornberry and J.E. Jacoby, *The Criminally Insane: A Community Follow-Up of Mentally Ill Offenders*, (1979). See, however, Canadian claims for risk assessment based on a combination of actuarial and clinical assessment: C.D. Webster, G.T. Harris, M.E. Rice, C. Cormier and V.L. Quinsey, *The Violence Prediction Scheme: Assessing Dangerousness in High Risk Men* (1994). The authors are themselves cautious: "No one claims that its use will guarantee 'fairness', 'accuracy' and 'absence of bias' in each and every case" (at p. 65).

19 At 737. See, however, Canadian claims for risk assessment based on a combination of actuarial and clinical assessment: C.D. Webster, G.T. Harris, M.E. Rice, C. Cormier and V.L. Quinsey, *The Violence Prediction Scheme: Assessing Dangerousness in High Risk Men* (1994). The authors are themselves cautious: "No one claims that its use will guarantee 'fairness', 'accuracy' and 'absence of bias' in each and every case" (at p. 65).

20 See the careful assessment by Fattah, note 15 above. See also F. Henry, "Imprisonment as a General Deterrent" (1978), 21 Crim L.Q 69 and C.T. Griffiths, J F. Klein, and S.N. Verdun-Jones, *Criminal Justice in Canada*, (1980), 179-82.

21 *Panel on Research on Deterrent and Incapacitative Effects*, (1978), p. 47, quoted and discussed by Jobson, note 14 above at 76-7, 92-3.

The Canadian Sentencing Commission[22] relies on the sceptical conclusion of Professor Douglas Cousineau:

Drawing upon some nine bodies of research addressing the deterrence question, we contend that there is little or no evidence to sustain an empirically justified belief in the deterrent efficacy of legal sanctions. However, we go beyond a review of this literature and set out several argument which document the mitigation of deterrent oriented legal sanctions.

Our thesis, however, is not confined to deterrence oriented legal sanctions. We suggest that many factors mitigate the effects of *any* legal sanctions intended to produce specific uniform outcomes.[23]

There is research indicating that any deterrent effect or penalty depends more on its certainty than its severity. There is evidence that certainty of detection is even more important, while there is research, and indeed common sense would indicate the same, that what will act as a deterrent is likely to differ markedly from crime to crime. Thus traffic offences including drunken driving or parking violations might be responsive to changes in law enforcement or penalty. Although the question is particularly controversial, there would seem to be no evidence that an extreme penalty such as death or a long maximum prison sentence deters murder. The crime is typically committed in volatile and emotional circumstances in which there is little time for reason.

The truths of criminology are limited. There are no clear explanations, definitions or answers. We can no longer develop our substantive law principles without taking this reality into account.

Scope

"There are acts of wickedness so gross and outrageous that self-protection apart they must be prevented as far as possible at any cost to the offender and punished if they occur with exemplary severity." (J.F. Stephen, *Liberty, Fraternity and Equality*, 2nd ed., (1874), p. 178.)

"The only purpose for which power can rightfully be exercised over any member of a civilized community against his will is to prevent harm to others." (John Stuart Mill, *On Liberty*, (1859), Chapter 1.)

CANADIAN COMMITTEE ON CORRECTIONS, TOWARDS UNITY: CRIMINAL JUSTICE AND CORRECTIONS (OUIMET REPORT)

(1969), 12-13

1. No act should be criminally proscribed unless its incidence, actual or potential, is *substantially damaging to society*.

---

22 Report of the Canadian Sentencing Commission, *Sentencing Reform: A Canadian Approach* (1987).
23 At 136.

2. No act should be criminally prohibited where its incidence may adequately be controlled by social forces other than the criminal process. Public opinion may be enough to curtail certain kinds of behaviour. Other kinds of behaviour may be more appropriately dealt with by non-criminal legal processes, *e.g.* by legislation relating to mental health or social and economic condition.

3. No law should give rise to social or personal damage greater than that it was designed to prevent.

To designate certain conduct as criminal in an attempt to control anti-social behaviour should be a last step. Criminal law traditionally, and perhaps inherently, has involved the imposition of a sanction. This sanction, whether in the form of arrest, summons, trial, conviction, punishment or publicity is, in the view of the Committee, to be employed only as an unavoidable necessity. Men and women may have their lives, public and private, destroyed; families may be broken up; the state may be put to considerable expense: all these consequences are to be taken into account when determining whether a particular kind of conduct is so obnoxious to social values that it is to be included in the catalogue of crimes. If there is any other course open to society when threatened, then that course is to be preferred. The deliberate infliction of punishment or any other state interference with human freedom is to be justified only where manifest evil would result from failure to interfere.

LAW REFORM COMMISSION OF CANADA, STUDIES ON STRICT LIABILITY

(1974), 56

Total Numbers: Federal and Provincial

Total number of offences — Federal Statutes. 3,582

Federal Regulations. 19,460

Provincial Statutes 4,420

Provincial Regulations . . 14,120

Total 41,582

Strict liability offences — Federal Statutes. 1,587 (44%)

Federal Regulations. 18,820 (96%)

Provincial Statutes 3,640 (82%)

Provincial Regulations . . 13,920 (98%)

Total 37,967

LAW REFORM COMMISSION OF CANADA, REPORT:
OUR CRIMINAL LAW

(1976), 27-28

But criminal law is not the only means of bolstering values. Nor is it necessarily always the best means. The fact is, criminal law is a blunt and costly instrument — blunt because it cannot have the human sensitivity of institutions like the family, the school, the church or the community, and costly since it imposes suffering, loss of liberty and great expense.

So criminal law must be an instrument of last resort. It must be used as little as possible. The message must not be diluted by overkill — too many laws and offences and charges and trials and prison sentences. Society's ultimate weapon must stay sheathed as long as possible. The watchword is restraint — restraint applying to the scope of criminal law, to the meaning of criminal guilt, to the use of the criminal trial and to the criminal sentence.

1. Scope of Criminal Law

In re-affirming values criminal law denounces acts considered wrong. Accordingly it has to stick to really wrongful acts. It must not overextend itself and make crimes out of things most people reckon not really wrong or, if wrong, merely trivial. Only those acts thought seriously wrong by our society should count as crimes.

Not all such acts, however, should be crimes. Wrongfulness is a necessary, not a sufficient condition of criminality. Before an act should count as a crime, three further conditions must be fulfilled. First, it must cause harm to other people, to society or, in special cases to those needing protection from themselves. Second, it must cause harm that is serious both in nature and degree. And third, it must cause harm that is best dealt with through the mechanism of the criminal law. These conditions would confine the criminal law to crimes of violence, dishonesty and other offences traditionally in the centre of the stage. Any other offences, not really wrong but penally prohibited because this is the most convenient way of dealing with them, must stay outside the *Criminal Code* and qualify merely as quasi-crimes or violations.

1. **Are there dangers in the Commission's last recommendation?**
2. **Are the proposed criteria of crime helpful?**
3. **Which of the following crimes listed by Dr. Walker meet the Commission's criteria?**

N.D. WALKER, CRIME AND PUNISHMENT IN BRITAIN

Rev. ed. (1968), 5-7

Borderline Offences. It is noticeable, however, that the boundary between the criminal and the civil law, and the boundary between the criminal law and mere discouragement by social disapproval, are drawn at slightly different points in different penal systems. All civilised and most primitive codes prohibit homicide, unjustifiable personal violence, rape, theft, and the intentional destruction of another's property. Civilised societies also use criminal procedure to enforce taxation and discourage behaviour which obstructs roads, or endangers life or health. But there are some types of behaviour which in some countries are criminal, and in others merely civil wrongs or simply matters of private morals.

Most of these involve, directly or indirectly, sexual conduct:

1. Extra-marital intercourse. In some American states the crimes created by the Puritans of fornication between unmarried persons, or adultery between a married person and someone other than his or her spouse, are still on the statute book, although seldom prosecuted. Adultery by a wife is a crime which is still prosecuted in France and Italy, and in France a husband who imports his mistress into the marital home can be convicted of concubinage. In Britain adultery by either spouse is not criminal, although it is a ground for a matrimonial suit, and a husband may sometimes seek damages at civil law from a co-respondent.

2. Homosexual acts. In a diminishing number of countries, including Western Germany and most states of the U.S.A., a homosexual act between males but not between females is an offence. This was the position in Britain until recently. The Wolfenden Committee recommended in 1957 that homosexual acts in private between consenting males over the age of 21 should no longer be criminal. Although the recommendation was too controversial for the Government of the day, prosecutions were gradually restricted, and eventually a Private Member's Bill which implemented the recommendation was passed in 1967.

3. Abortion. In some countries abortion is criminal only if performed by unauthorised persons. But in most Western countries, including Britain, it is criminal unless there is a special justification for it. In this country the special justifications are that the continuance of pregnancy would involve risk to the woman's life, or injury to her physical or mental health or that of her existing children; or that there is substantial risk that if the child were born it would suffer from such physical or mental abnormalities as to be seriously handicapped.

4. Prostitution. In some states of the U.S.A. this is a crime, although seldom prosecuted unless the authorities have special reasons for wishing to do so. In most other countries, including Britain, it is not of itself a crime, but certain methods of practising it are: for example, soliciting in the street, brothel-keeping, or living on the earnings of prostitution. Proposals that it

should be made possible to prosecute the clients of prostitutes have been made — for example by the Archbishop of Canterbury in 1957 — but were not seriously considered by the Legislature.

There are a few "borderline crimes", however, which are not sexual:

5. Attempted suicide. From 1854 until 1961 attempted suicide was prosecuted as a crime in England but not in Scotland, although even in that country a person who unsuccessfully but publicly attempted to kill himself has been prosecutcd for a breach of the peace. As a result of the Suicide Act, 1961, this form of behaviour is no longer a crime in England.
6. Negligent injury. In some countries, for example Canada, a person whose negligence causes injury to another person can be convicted of a crime. In Britain, if the injury is fatal and the negligence gross, the person may be charged with manslaughter. If the injury is caused by a moving vehicle the driver may be charged with careless or dangerous driving, but these charges could be brought even if no injury resulted. Yet a person who negligently cripples someone for life by driving into him at golf, demolishing a building or cutting down a branch of a tree, can be sued at civil law but not charged with a crime.

There are other offences which, though they appear in almost all civilised criminal codes, have recently been criticised in England as unnecessary:

7. Incest. Until 1908 this was not a criminal offence, although until 1857 it had been punishable under ecclesiastical law and — more important — was strongly discouraged by social pressure. A growing acquaintance with ways of life other than those of the middle and upper classes brought it home to the Church of England that social and religious sanctions were not completely effective, and they persuaded a private member of Parliament to introduce a Bill to make incest criminal. After several sessions of resistance the Government eventually complied. It has been argued that while children certainly need protection against incestuous adults, this protection is already provided by other statutes; and that incest between consenting adults in private, like homosexual acts in similar circumstances, is not a proper subject for the criminal law.
8. Euthanasia. The general abhorrence of the deliberate taking of human life is so strong that civilised criminal codes permit very few exceptions. They include in this prohibition even the killing of sane adults who have good reasons — such as a painful, fatal and incurable disease — for wanting to die. It has been argued that with suitable safeguards such cases should be excluded from the definition of murder.
9. Bigamy. The felony of bigamy, created in 1603, is no longer punishable by death, but has nevertheless been criticised even by 19th-century Judges. A married man who leaves his wife to live with another woman commits only a matrimonial offence, even if they pretend to be married; but if they go through a ceremony of marriage he commits a crime punishable with seven

years' imprisonment. This is so even if he wrongly believes himself to be divorced, or even if his new "wife" knows him to be married. Glanville Williams has argued that in many cases the only anti-social consequences of bigamy are the waste of the time of the minister (or registrar) and the falsification of official records. He points out that similar consequences would result if a man contracted several "marriages" with his adult nieces, one after another. None of them would be valid, and none would be criminal; but there would be a similar waste of time and falsification of records.

Other prohibitions are criticised as too wide in their scope. For example:

10. The use of narcotic and other addictive drugs without medical prescription is prohibited in most civilised countries (with the notable exception of alcohol and nicotine), and is the subject of increasing efforts by police and other social services. It is often argued, however, that some drugs — especially marihuana — should not be subject to this strict control, on the grounds that they are neither addictive nor harmful. A more extreme section of opinion argues that even heroin and other "hard" drugs would be less of a menace if their use were controlled in non-penal ways.

There have also been unsuccessful agitations for the creation of new crimes. A recent example, again concerned with sexual behaviour, is

11. Artificial insemination. In 1958, after the Scots Judge, Lord Wheatley, had ruled in a divorce case that artificial insemination was not adultery, some members of the House of Lords, led by the Archbishop of Canterbury, urged that it should be made a crime. Instead the Government appointed the Feversham Committee, which preferred the *status quo*.

1. The population is aging. Statistics show that 40 percent of hospital beds are occupied by geriatric patients and that 30 percent of the intensive care space is used for the treatment of geriatric patients, many of whom are on life support systems.

Medical science prides itself on its ability to prolong life. But at what cost? Many members have received mail urging legislation to give patients the right to die with dignity; to give patients and their families the right to determine treatment and the right to decline treatment. The Netherlands now recognizes a limited form of mercy killing conducted under medical supervision. Within this context a private member's bill is before the committee to legalize euthanasia or mercy killing. Under the present law such killing is culpable homicide, likely first or second degree murder resulting in minimum sentences of 25 years and 10 years respectively.

In *Rodriguez v. B.C. (A.G.)*, [1993] 3 S.C.R. 519, 24 C.R. (4th) 281, 85 C.C.C. (3d) 15, the majority of the Court held that the *Criminal Code* offence under s. 241 (*b*) of the *Criminal Code*, forbidding counselling or aiding and abetting suicide, did not violate *Charter* guarantees of principles of fundamental justice under s. 7, protection against cruel and unusual treatment under s. 12 nor equality before the law under s. 15.

The Law Reform Commission of Canada addressed this issue and concluded:

> The Commission recommends against legalizing or decriminalizing voluntary active euthanasia in any form and is in favour of continuing to treat it as culpable homicide.

> The Commission recommends that mercy killing not be made an offence separate from homicide and that there be no formal provision for special modes of sentencing for this type of homicide other than what is already provided for homicide.

Two sub-committees were appointed by the committee to consider the issue: the first advocates the legalization of euthanasia or mercy killing under prescribed conditions, and the second urges the retention of the law as it stands — culpable homicide.

Prepare your arguments for submission before the full committee. The committee may well vote on the proposal at the next meeting. Therefore, your presentation is critical to sway "undecided" members.

2. The incidence of AIDS in Canada has reached epidemic proportions. One in every fifty persons is infected and the consequence is always fatal.

Research indicates that in 80 percent of the cases the virus is caused by acts of buggery between human beings. Many groups are lobbying the government to make buggery a crime, whether it be consensual or not.

Buggery is a crime:

> Section 155. Every one who commits buggery or bestiality is guilty of an indictable offence and is liable to imprisonment for fourteen years.

However, since 1968-69 the *Criminal Code* makes exception for consensual acts of buggery committed in private between husband and wife or between any two persons of 21 years of age or more (section 158).

You are duly elected members of Parliament and are sitting on a Parliamentary committee to study this matter. After due consideration of the question, two sub-committees are created: the first, in answer to the AIDS crisis, wishes that buggery becomes a crime in all circumstances, and the second is in favour of maintaining the status quo. The remainder of the committee members are undecided.

Prepare your arguments for submission before the full committee. The committee may well vote on the proposal at the next meeting, therefore, your presentation is critical to sway "undecided" members.

Obscenity: A Test Case

R. v. BUTLER

[1992] 1 S.C.R. 452, 11 C.R. (4th) 137, 70 C.C.C. (3d) 129

The accused owned a shop selling and renting "hard core" videotapes and magazines as well as sexual paraphernalia. He was charged with over 200 counts of selling obscene material, possessing obscene material for the purpose of distribution or sale, and exposing obscene material to public view, contrary to s. 159 (now 163) of the *Criminal Code*. Section 163(8) of the *Code* provides that "any publication a dominant characteristic of which is the undue exploitation of sex, or of sex and any one or more of . . . crime, horror, cruelty and violence, shall be deemed to be obscene". The trial Judge concluded that all of the material before him was obscene but that most of the obscene material was protected by the guarantee of freedom of expression in s. 2(*b*) of *Charter*. He decided that only those materials which contained scenes involving violence or cruelty intermingled with sexual activity or depicted lack of consent to sexual contact or otherwise could be said to dehumanize men or women in a sexual context were legitimately proscribed under s. 1. He convicted the accused on eight counts relating to eight films and entered acquittals on the remaining charges. The Crown appealed the acquittals. The Court of Appeal, in a majority decision, allowed the appeal and entered convictions with respect to all the counts. The majority concluded that the materials in question fell outside the protection of the *Charter* since they constituted purely physical activity and involved the undue exploitation of sex and the degradation of human sexuality. The accused appealed. The Supreme Court allowed the accused's further appeal and ordered a new trial to determine whether all of the materials were obscene. In the course of the ruling, the Supreme Court held that, although the obscenity provisions of the *Criminal Code* violated the freedom of expression guaranteed by s. 2(*b*), that violation could be demonstrably justified as a reasonable limit under s. 1. Before determining the constitutional issue, the Court first restated and clarified its approach to the meaning of obscenity under s. 163(8).

SOPINKA J. (LAMER C.J.C. and LA FOREST, CORY, MCLACHLIN, STEVENSON and IACOBUCCI JJ. concurring): —

. . . .

Parliament's first attempt to criminalize obscenity was in s. 179 of the *Criminal Code*, S.C. 1892, c. 29, which provided in part as follows:

> **179.** Every one is guilty of an indictable offence and liable to two years' imprisonment who knowingly, without lawful justification or excuse
>
> (*a*) publicly sells, or exposes for public sale or to public view, any *obscene* book, or other printed or written matter, or any picture, photograph, model or other object, *tending to corrupt morals*; or
>
> (*b*) publicly exhibits any *disgusting object or indecent show*;

(c) offers to sell, advertises, publishes an advertisement of or has for sale or disposal any medicine, drug or article intended or represented as a means of preventing conception or causing abortion. [Emphasis added.]

In 1949, Parliament repealed the successor to s. 179 [*Criminal Code, R.S.C.* 1927, c. 36, s. 207] and substituted it with the following provision:

207. (1) Every one who is guilty of an indictable offence and liable to two years' imprisonment who

(a) makes, prints, publishes, distributes, circulates, or has in possession for any such purpose any obscene written matter, picture, model or other thing whatsoever; or

(b) makes, prints, publishes, distributes, sells or has in possession for any such purpose, any crime comic.

(2) Every one is guilty of an indictable offence and liable to two years' imprisonment who knowingly, without lawful justification or excuse

(a) sells, exposes to public view or has in possession for any such purpose any obscene written matter, picture, model or other thing whatsoever;

(b) publicly exhibits any disgusting object or any indecent show; or

(c) offers to sell, advertises, publishes an advertisement of, or has for sale or disposal any means, instructions, medicine, drug or article intended or represented as a means of preventing conception or causing abortion or miscarriage or advertises or publishes an advertisement of any means, instructions, medicine, drug or article for restoring sexual virility or curing venereal diseases or diseases of the generative organs.

The *Criminal Code* did not provide a definition of any of the operative terms, "obscene", "indecent" or "disgusting". The notion of obscenity embodied in these provisions was based on the test formulated by Cockburn C.J. in *R. v. Hicklin* (1868), L.R. 3 Q.B. 360 [at p. 371]:

. . . I think the test of obscenity is this, whether the tendency of the matter charged as obscenity is to deprave and corrupt those whose minds are open to such immoral influences, and into whose hands a publication of this sort may fall.

The focus on the "corruption of morals" in the earlier legislation grew out of the English obscenity law which made the Court the "guardian of public morals". As Charron D.C.J. stated in *R. v. Fringe Product Inc.* (1990), 53 C.C.C. (3d) 422 (Ont. Dist. Ct.) [at pp. 441-442 C.C.C.]:

When one looks at the legislative history of the obscenity provisions of the *Code*, it is clear that when the English Court of King's Bench first asserted itself in this field following the demise of the Star Chamber in 1641, it did so as the guardian of public morals: *R. v. Sidley* (1663), 1 Sid. 168, 82 E.R. 1036. The crime of publishing an obscene libel was created in 1727 in the case of *R. v. Curl* (1727), 2 Stra. 788, 93 E.R. 849, when the Court accepted the argument that publishing an obscene libel tended to corrupt the morals of the King's subjects and as such was against the peace of the King and government.

The current provision, which is the subject of this appeal, entered into force in 1959 in response to the much criticized former version (*Criminal Code*, S.C. 1953-54, c. 51, s. 150). Unlike the previous statutes, subs. (8) provided a statutory definition of "obscene":

150. . . .

(8) For the purposes of this Act, any publication a dominant characteristic of which is the undue exploitation of sex, or of sex and any one or more of the following subjects, namely, crime, horror, cruelty and violence, shall be deemed to be obscene.

As will be discussed further, the introduction of the statutory definition had the effect of replacing the *Hicklin* test with a series of rules developed by the courts. The provision must be considered in light of these tests.

B. Judicial Interpretation of s. 163(8)

The first case to consider the current provision was *Brodie v. R.*, [1962] S.C.R. 681, 37 C.R. 120, 132 C.C.C. 161. The majority of this Court found in that case that D. H. Lawrence's novel, *Lady Chatterley's Lover*, was not obscene within the meaning of the Code. The *Brodie* case lay the groundwork for the interpretation of s. 163(8) by setting out the principal tests which should govern the determination of what is obscene for the purposes of criminal prosecution. The first step was to discard the *Hicklin* test.

(a) Section 163(8) to be Exclusive Test

In examining the definition provided by subs. (8), the majority of this Court was of the view that the new provision provided a clean slate and had the effect of bringing in an "objective standard of obscenity" which rendered all the urisprudence under the *Hicklin* definition obsolete. In the words of Judson J. [at p. 702 S.C.R.]:

. . . I think that the new statutory definition does give the Court an opportunity to apply tests which have some certainty of meaning and are capable of objective application and which do not so much depend as before upon the idiosyncrasies and sensitivities of the tribunal of fact, whether Judge or jury. We are now concerned with a Canadian statute which is exclusive of all others.

Any doubt that s. 163(8) was intended to provide an exhaustive test of obscenity was settled in *R. v. Dechow, supra*. Laskin C.J.C stated [at p. 962 S.C.R.]:

I am not only satisfied to regard s. 159(8) [now s. 163(8)] as prescribing an exhaustive test of obscenity in respect of a publication which has sex as a theme or characteristic but I am also of the opinion that this Court should apply that test in respect of other provisions of the *Code*, such as ss. 163 and 164, in cases in which the allegation of obscenity revolves around sex considerations. Since the view that I take, in line with that expressed by Judson J. in the *Brodie* case, is that the *Hicklin* rule has been displaced by s. 159(8) in respect of publications, I would not bring it back under any other sections of the *Code*, such as ss. 159, 163, 164, to provide a back-up where a sexual theme or sexual factors are the basis upon which obscenity charges are laid and the charges fail because the test prescribed by s. 159(8) has not been met.

In the *Dechow* case, the majority ascribed a liberal meaning to the term "publication", and found that the sex devices in question were "publications" as the accused had made such objects "publicly known" and had produced and issued such articles for public sale. Furthermore in *Germain v. R.*, *supra*, La Forest J., with whom a majority of the Court agreed on this point, held that the word "obscene" must be given the same meaning whether the articles are publications under s. 159(1) (now s. 163(1)) or matter covered by s. 159(2)(*a*) (now s. 163(2)(*a*)). As a consequence, it is now beyond dispute that s. 163(8) provides the exhaustive test of obscenity with respect to publications and objects which exploit sex as a dominant characteristic and that the common law test of obscenity found in the *Hicklin* decision is no longer applicable.

(b) *Tests of "Undue Exploitation of Sex"*

In order for the work or material to qualify as "obscene", the exploitation of sex must not only be its dominant characteristic, but such exploitation must be "undue". In determining when the exploitation of sex will be considered "undue", the courts have attempted to formulate workable tests. The most important of these is the "community standard of tolerance" test.

i) "Community Standard of Tolerance" Test

In *Brodie*, Judson J. accepted the view espoused notably by the Australian and New Zealand Courts that obscenity is to be measured against "community standards". He cited the following passage in the judgment of Fullagar J. in *R. v. Close*, [1948] V.L.R. 445 [at pp. 705-706 S.C.R.]:

> There does exist in any community at all times — however the standard may vary from time to time — a general instinctive sense of what is decent and what is indecent, of what is clean and what is dirty, and when the distinction has to be drawn, I do not know that today there is any better tribunal than a jury to draw it . . . I am very far from attempting to lay down a model direction, but a Judge might perhaps, in the case of a novel, say something like this: "It would not be true to say that any publication dealing with sexual relations is obscene. The relations of the sexes are, of course, legitimate matters for discussion everywhere . . . There are certain standards of decency which prevail in the community, and you are really called upon to try this case because you are regarded as representing, and capable of justly applying, those standards. What is obscene is something which offends against those standards."

The community standards test has been the subject of extensive judicial analysis. It is the standards of the community as a whole which must be considered and not the standards of a small segment of that community such as the university community where a film was shown (*R. v. Goldberg* (1971), 4 C.C.C. (2d) 187 (C.A.)) or a city where a picture was exposed (*R. v. Kiverago* (1973), 11 C.C.C. (2d) 463 (Ont. C.A.)). The standard to be applied is a national one (*R. v. Cameron*, 49 C.R. 49, [1966] 4 C.C.C. 273 (Ont. C.A.); *R. v. Duthie Books Ltd.* (1966), 50 C.R. 55, [1967] 1 C.C.C. 254 (B.C.C.A.); *R. v. Ariadne Developments Ltd.* (1974), 19 C.C.C. (2d) 49 (N.S.C.A.), at p. 59). With respect to expert evidence, it is not necessary and is not a fact which the Crown is obliged to prove as part of its case (*R. v. Sudbury News Service Ltd.* (1978), 39 C.C.C. (2d) 1 (C.A.); *R. v. Prairie Schooner News Ltd.* (1970), 1 C.C.C. (2d) 251 (Man. C.A.); *R. v. Great West News Ltd.*, 10 C.R.N.S. 42, [1970] 4 C.C.C. 307 (Man. C.A.)). In *Dominion News & Gifts (1962) Ltd. v. R.*, 40 C.R. 109, [1963] 2 C.C.C. 103 (Man. C.A.), Freedman J.A. (dissenting) emphasized that the community standards test must necessarily respond to changing mores [at pp. 116-117 C.C.C., pp. 126-127 C.R.]:

> Community standards must be contemporary. Times change, and ideas change with them. Compared to the Victorian era this is a liberal age in which we live. One manifestation of it is the relative freedom with which the whole question of sex is discussed. In books, magazines, movies, television, and sometimes even in parlour conversation, various aspects of sex are made the subject of comment, with a candour that in an earlier day would have been regarded as indecent and intolerable. We cannot and should not ignore these present-day attitudes when we face the question whether [the subject materials] are obscene according to our criminal law.

Our Court was called upon to elaborate the community standards test in *Towne Cinema Theatres Ltd. v. R.*, [1985] 1 S.C.R. 494, 45 C.R. (3d) 1, 18 C.C.C. (3d) 193. Dickson C.J.C. reviewed the case law and found [at pp. 508-509 S.C.R.]:

> The cases all emphasize that it is a standard of *tolerance*, not taste, that is relevant. What matters is not what Canadians think is right for themselves to see. What matters is what Canadians would not abide other Canadians seeing because it would be beyond the contemporary Canadian standard of tolerance to allow them to see it.

> Since the standard is tolerance, I think the audience to which the allegedly obscene material is targeted must be relevant. The operative standards are those of the Canadian community as a whole, but since what matters is what other people may see, it is quite conceivable that the Canadian community would tolerate varying degrees of explicitness depending upon the audience and the circumstances. [Emphasis in original.]

Therefore, the community standards test is concerned not with what Canadians would not tolerate being exposed to themselves, but what they would not tolerate *other* Canadians being exposed to. The minority view was that the tolerance level will vary depending on the manner, time and place in which the material is presented as well as the audience to whom it is directed. The majority opinion on this point was expressed by Wilson J. in the following passage [at p. 521]:

> It is not, in my opinion, open to the courts under s. 159(8) of the *Criminal Code* to characterize a movie as obscene if shown to one constituency but not if shown to another . . . In my view, a movie is either obscene under the *Code* based on a national community standard of tolerance or it is not. If it is not, it may still be the subject of provincial regulatory control.

ii) "Degradation or Dehumanization" Test

There has been a growing recognition in recent cases that material which may be said to exploit sex in a "degrading or dehumanizing" manner will necessarily fail the community standards test. Borins Co. Ct. J. expressed this view in *R. v. Doug Rankine Co.* (1983), 36 C.R. (3d) 154, 9 C.C.C. (3d) 53 (Ont. Co. Ct.) [at p. 70 C.C.C., p. 173 C.R.]:

> [F]ilms which consist substantially or partially of scenes which portray violence and cruelty in conjunction with sex, particularly where the performance of indignities degrade and dehumanize the people upon whom they are performed, exceed the level of community tolerance.

Subsequent decisions, such as *R. v. Ramsingh* (1984), 14 C.C.C. (3d) 230 (Q.B.) and in *R. v. Wagner* (1985), 43 C.R. (3d) 318 (Q.B.) held that material that "degraded" or "dehumanized" any of the participants would exceed community standards even in the absence of cruelty and violence. In *R. v. Ramsingh*, supra, Ferg J. described in graphic terms the type of material that qualified for this label. He states on p. 239 [C.C.C.]:

> They are exploited, portrayed as desiring pleasure from pain, by being humiliated and treated only as an object of male domination sexually, or in cruel or violent bondage. Women are portrayed in these films as pining away their lives waiting for a huge male penis to come along, on the person of a so-called sex therapist, or window washer, supposedly to transport them into complete sexual ecstasy. Or even more false and degrading one is led to believe their raison d'être is to savour semen as a life elixir, or that they secretly desire to be forcefully taken by a male.

Among other things, degrading or dehumanizing materials place women (and sometimes men) in positions of subordination, servile submission or humiliation. They run against the principles of equality and dignity of all human beings. In the appreciation of whether material is degrading or dehumanizing, the appearance of consent is not necessarily determinative. Consent cannot save materials that otherwise contain degrading or dehumanizing scenes. Sometimes the very appearance of consent makes the depicted acts even more degrading or dehumanizing.

This type of material would, apparently, fail the community standards test not because it offends against morals but because it is perceived by public opinion to be harmful to society, particularly to women. While the accuracy of this perception is not susceptible of exact proof, there is a substantial body of opinion that holds that the portrayal of persons being subjected to degrading or dehumanizing sexual treatment results in harm, particularly to women and therefore to society as a whole. See *Wagner*, supra, at p. 336 [C.R.]; see also: Attorney General's Commission on Pornography (the "Meese Commission"), *Final Report* (United States, 1986), vol. 1, at pp. 938-1035; Metro Toronto Task Force on Public Violence Against Women and Children, *Final Report* (1984), at p. 66; *Report of the Joint Select Committee on Video Material* (Australia, 1988), at pp. 185-230; *Pornography: Report of the Ministerial Committee of Inquiry into Pornography* (New Zealand, 1988), at pp. 38-45. It would be reasonable to conclude that there is an appreciable risk of harm to society in the portrayal of such material. The effect of the evidence on public opinion was summed up by Wilson J. in *Towne Cinema*, supra, as follows [at p. 524 S.C.R.]:

> The most that can be said, I think, is that the public has concluded that exposure to material which degrades the human dimensions of life to a subhuman or merely physical dimension and thereby contributes to a process of moral desensitization must be harmful in some way.

In *Towne Cinema*, Dickson C.J.C. considered the "degradation" or "dehumanization" test to be the principal indicator of "undueness" without specifying what role the community tolerance test plays in respect of this issue. He did observe, however, that the community might tolerate some forms of exploitation that caused harm that were nevertheless undue. The relevant passages appear at p. 505 [S.C.R.]:

> There are other ways in which exploitation of sex might be "undue". Ours is not a perfect society and it is unfortunate but true that the community may tolerate publications that cause harm to members of society and therefore to society as a whole. Even if, at certain times, there is a coincidence between what is not tolerated and what is harmful to society, there is no necessary connection between these two concepts. Thus, a legal definition of "undue" must also encompass publications harmful to members of society and, therefore, to society as a whole.

> Sex related publications which portray persons in a degrading manner as objects of violence, cruelty or other forms of dehumanizing treatment, may be "undue" for the purpose of s. 159(8). No one should be subject to the degradation and humiliation inherent in publications which link sex with violence, cruelty, and other forms of dehumanizing treatment. It is not likely that at a given moment in a society's history, such publications will be tolerated.

. . . .

> However, as I have noted above, there is no *necessary* coincidence between the undueness of publications which degrade people by linking violence, cruelty or other forms of dehumanizing treatment with sex, and the community standard of tolerance. Even if certain sex related materials were found to be within the standard of tolerance of the community, it would still be necessary to ensure that they were not "undue" in some other sense, for example in the sense that they portray persons in a degrading manner as objects of violence, cruelty, or other forms of dehumanizing treatment. [Emphasis in original.]

In the reasons of Wilson J. concurring in the result, the line between the mere portrayal of sex and the dehumanization of people is drawn by the "undueness" concept. The community is the arbiter as to what is harmful to it. She states [at p. 524 S.C.R.]:

> As I see it, the essential difficulty with the definition of obscenity is that "undueness" must presumably be assessed in relation to consequences. It is implicit in the definition that at some point the exploitation of sex becomes harmful to the public or at least the public believes that to be so. It is therefore necessary for the protection of the public to put limits on the degree of exploitation and, through the application of the community standard test, the public is made the arbiter of what is harmful to it and what is not. The problem is that we know so little of the consequences we are seeking to avoid. Do obscene movies spawn immoral conduct? Do they degrade women? Do they promote violence? The most that can be said, I think, is that the public has concluded that exposure to material which degrades the human dimensions of life to a subhuman or merely physical dimension and thereby contributes to a process of moral desensitization must be harmful in some way. It must therefore be controlled when it gets out of hand, when it becomes "undue".

iii) "Internal Necessities Test" or "Artistic Defence"

In determining whether the exploitation of sex is "undue", Judson J. set out the test of "internal necessities" in *Brodie*, supra [at pp. 704-705 S.C.R.]:

> What I think is aimed at is excessive emphasis on the theme for a base purpose. But I do not think that there is undue exploitation if there is no more emphasis on the theme than is required in the serious treatment of the theme of a novel with honesty and uprightness. That the work under attack is a serious work of fiction is to me beyond question. It has none of the characteristics that are often described in judgments dealing with obscenity — dirt for dirt's sake, the leer of the sensualist, depravity in the mind of an author with an obsession for dirt, pornography, an appeal to a prurient interest, etc. The section recognizes that the serious-minded author must have freedom in the production of a work of genuine artistic and literary merit and the quality of the work, as the witnesses point out and common sense indicates, must have real relevance in determining not only a dominant characteristic but also whether there is undue exploitation.

As counsel for the Crown pointed out in his oral submissions, the artistic defence is the last step in the analysis of whether the exploitation of sex is undue. Even material which by itself offends community standards will not be considered "undue", if it is required for the serious treatment of a theme. For example, in *R. v. Odeon Morton Theatres Ltd.* (1974), 16 C.C.C. (2d) 185, the majority of the Manitoba Court of Appeal held that the film "Last Tango in Paris" was not obscene within the meaning of the *Code*. To determine whether a dominant characteristic of the film is the undue exploitation of sex, Freedman C.J.M. noted that the courts must have regard to various things — the author's artistic purpose, the manner in which he or she has portrayed and developed the story, the depiction and interplay of character and the creation of visual effect through skilful camera techniques (at p. 194) [C.C.C.]. Freedman C.J.M. stated that the issue of whether the film is obscene must be determined according to contemporary community standards in Canada. Relevant to that determination were several factors: the testimony of experts, the classification of "Restricted" which made the film unavailable to persons under 18 years of age and the fact that the film had passed the scrutiny of the censor boards of several provinces.

Accordingly, the "internal necessities" test, or what has been referred to as the "artistic defence", has been interpreted to assess whether the exploitation of sex has a justifiable role in advancing the plot or the theme, and in considering the work as a whole, does not merely represent "dirt for dirt's sake" but has a legitimate role when measured by the internal necessities of the work itself.

iv) The relationship of the tests to each other

This review of jurisprudence shows that it fails to specify the relationship of the tests one to another. Failure to do so with respect to the community standards test and the degrading or dehumanizing test, for example, raises a serious question as to the basis on which the community acts in determining whether the impugned material will be tolerated. With both these tests being applied to the same material and apparently independently, we do not know whether the community found the material to be intolerable because it was degrading or dehumanizing, because it offended against morals or on some other basis. In some circumstances a finding that the material is tolerable can be overruled by the conclusion by the Court that it causes harm and is therefore undue. Moreover, is the internal necessities test dominant so that it will redeem material that would otherwise be undue or is it just one factor? Is this test applied by the community or is it determined by the Court without regard for the community? This hiatus in the jurisprudence has left the legislation open to attack on the ground of vagueness and uncertainty. That attack is made in this case. This lacuna in the interpretation of the legislation must, if possible, be filled before subjecting the legislation to *Charter* scrutiny. The necessity to do so was foreseen by Wilson J. in *Towne Cinema, supra,* when she stated [at p. 525 S.C.R.]:

> The test of the community standard is helpful to the extent that it provides a norm against which impugned material may be assessed but it does little to elucidate the underlying question as to why some exploitation of sex falls on the permitted side of the line under s. 159(8) and some on the prohibited side. No doubt this question will have to be addressed when the validity of the obscenity provisions of the *Code* is subjected to attack as an infringement on freedom of speech and the infringement is sought to be justified as reasonable.

Pornography can be usefully divided into three categories: (1) explicit sex with violence, (2) explicit sex without violence but which subjects people to treatment that is degrading or dehumanizing, and (3) explicit sex without violence that is neither degrading nor dehumanizing. Violence in this context includes both actual physical violence and threats of physical violence. Relating these three categories to the terms of s. 163(8) of the *Code*, the first, explicit sex coupled with violence, is expressly mentioned. Sex coupled with crime, horror or cruelty will sometimes involve violence. Cruelty, for instance, will usually do so. But, even in the absence of violence, sex coupled with crime, horror or cruelty may fall within the second category. As for category (3), subject to the exception referred to below, it is not covered.

Some segments of society would consider that all three categories of pornography cause harm to society because they tend to undermine its moral fibre. Others would contend that none of the categories cause harm. Furthermore there is a range of opinion as to what is degrading or dehumanizing. See *Pornography and Prostitution in Canada: Report of the Special Committee on Pornography and Prostitution* (1985) (the Fraser Report), Vol. 1, at p. 51. Because this is not a matter that is susceptible of proof in the traditional way and because we do not wish to leave it to the individual tastes of judges, we must have a norm that will serve as an arbiter in determining what amounts to an undue exploitation of sex. That arbiter is the community as a whole.

The Courts must determine as best they can what the community would tolerate others being exposed to on the basis of the degree of harm that may flow from such exposure. Harm in this context means that it predisposes persons to act in an anti-social manner as, for example, the physical or mental mistreatment of women by men, or, what is perhaps debatable, the reverse. Anti-social conduct for this purpose is conduct which society formally recognizes as incompatible with its proper functioning. The stronger the inference of a risk of harm the lesser the likelihood of tolerance. The inference may be drawn from the material itself or from the material and other evidence. Similarly evidence as to the community standards is desirable but not essential.

In making this determination with respect to the three categories of pornography referred to above, the portrayal of sex coupled with violence will almost always constitute the undue exploitation of sex. Explicit sex which is degrading or dehumanizing may be undue if the risk of harm is substantial. Finally, explicit sex that is not violent and neither degrading nor dehumanizing is generally tolerated in our society and will not qualify as the undue exploitation of sex unless it employs children in its production.

If material is not obscene under this framework, it does not become so by reason of the person to whom it is or may be shown or exposed nor by reason of the place or manner in which it is shown. The availability of sexually explicit materials in theatres and other public places is subject to regulation by competent provincial legislation. Typically such legislation imposes restrictions on the material available to children. See *McNeil v. Nova Scotia (Board of Censors)*, [1978] 2 S.C.R. 662, 25 N.S.R. (2d) 128, 36 A.P.R. 128, 19 N.R. 570, 84 D.L.R. (3d) 1, 44 C.C.C. (2d) 316.

The foregoing deals with the interrelationship of the "community standards test" and "the degrading or dehumanizing" test. How does the "internal necessities" test fit into this scheme? The need to apply this test only arises if a work contains sexually explicit material that by itself would constitute the undue exploitation of sex. The portrayal of sex must then be viewed in context to determine whether that is the dominant theme of the work as a whole. Put another way, is undue exploitation of sex the main object of the work or is this portrayal of sex essential to a wider artistic, literary, or other similar purpose? Since the threshold determination must be made on the basis of community standards, that is, whether the sexually explicit aspect is undue, its impact when considered in context must be determined on the same basis. The Court must determine whether the sexually explicit material when viewed in the context of the whole work would be tolerated by the community as a whole. Artistic expression rests at the heart of freedom of expression values and any doubt in this regard must be resolved in favour of freedom of expression.

GONTHIER J. (L'HEUREUX-DUBÉ J. concurring) delivered a separate concurring judgment.

In *R. v. Jorgensen* (1996), 43 C.R. (4th) 137 (S.C.C.) J was the sole officer of a company which owns and operates an adult video store in Scarborough, Ontario. Undercover police officers bought eight videotapes from that store. Although the Ontario Film Review Board (OFRB) had approved all of them, officers of the Pornography and Hate Literature Section viewed them and concluded that they were obscene. Jorgensen and the company were charged with eight counts of knowingly selling obscene material without lawful justification or excuse contrary to s. 163(2)(*a*) of the *Criminal Code*. The trial judge found that three of the eight videos were obscene within the meaning of s. 163(8) of the *Criminal Code* due to their portrayal of sex coupled with violence and coercion, or subordination which created the risk of harm. The Ontario Court of Appeal upheld the convictions: (1993) 26 C.R. (4th) 75 (Ont. C.A.) (reported *sub. nom. R. v. Ronish*). The trial judge had not erred. The Crown need only show that the retailer was aware of the videos and the nature of the subject matter. The OFRB approval was not relevant to *mens rea* and only related to the community standard of tolerance. It also did not amount to a lawful justification or excuse.

On appeal the Supreme Court substituted an acquittal. Sopinka J. spoke for the Court on the issue of *mens rea*. For a conviction of "knowingly" selling obscene material contrary to s. 163 (2)(*a*) of the *Criminal Code* the *Crown* must prove not only that the accused was aware that the subject matter had as its dominant characteristic the exploitation of sex but that the accused knew of the presence of the ingredients of the subject matter which as a matter of law rendered the exploitation of sex undue. This may require knowledge of specific acts or sets of facts or in some cases of the overall nature of the film. Knowledge does not require proof that the retailer actually watched the video. Knowledge can also be proved by evidence of warnings, directions from external sources or circumstances directly linked to the context of the retailer's activity. In appropriate circumstances the *Crown* may rely on proof of wilful blindness where the question to be determined from all the circumstances is "Did the accused shut his eyes because he knew or strongly suspected that looking would fix him with knowledge?" Here there was no evidence to suggest any knowledge on the part of the accused beyond the fact that the videos in question were sex films in the general sense that they involved the exploitation of sex. This did not satisfy the *mens rea* requirement and the accused should be acquitted.

Sopinka J. further held that the approval of the subject matter by a provincial censor board may be relevant to the determination of community standards of tolerance and on the issue of wilful blindness. It was not relevant to the issue of the accused's knowledge and the *Crown* need not prove that the accused knew that the subject matter of the charge exceeded community standards.

According to Sopinka J. approval by a provincial censor board does not constitute a justification or excuse. One level of government cannot delegate its legislative power to another. Approval by a provincial body cannot as a matter of constitutional law preclude the prosecution of a charge under the *Criminal Code*. Parliament could not have intended that conduct criminalised by s. 163(2) be rendered lawful or the person engaging in it excused as a result of a decision of a provincial body.

Later in Chapter 5 on Mistake we shall consider Chief Justice Lamer's view that the proceedings should be stayed as a result of officially induced error. The majority left this issue open as the matter had not been raised in the Supreme Court or the courts below.

Chapter 2

guilty act

THE ACT REQUIREMENT (ACTUS REUS)

Introduction

C. HOWARD, CRIMINAL LAW

3rd ed. (1977), 9-10

The traditional analysis of a crime at common law is into *actus reus*, or guilty act, and *mens rea*, or guilty mind, but the codes use neither these expressions nor any exact synonyms for them. A writer on the criminal law in Australia therefore has to decide between using different terms according as he is talking about common law or code rules and abandoning the traditional common law terminology altogether. The opinion acted on in this book is that the expressions *actus reus* and *mens rea* are too obscure to be of practical utility in an exposition of the modern law in any context. They therefore do not justify adopting the otherwise disadvantageous course of discussing the principles of the criminal law at common law and under the codes in different language, especially since the principles themselves are the same in all significant respects in both contexts.

The words *actus reus* and *mens rea* are taken from the maxim, *actus non facit reum nisi mens sit rea*, there is no guilty act without a guilty mind. An alternative statement of this principle in English which stresses the implication that the guilty act must be coincidental in time with the guilty mind is, "The intent and the Act must both concur to constitute the crime". The argument in favour of keeping the terms *actus reus* and *mens rea* in common use is that they are the customary language of the Courts and that since in themselves they have no special significance, their content being "only one of legal arrangement", there is no point in replacing them with unfamiliar terminology which can be no less arbitrary. Nevertheless there are reasons for thinking that at the present day these particular expressions are responsible for much confusion of thought and should be abandoned in favour of any language which accurately conveys the effect of the law without in itself imposing an unnecessary burden of translation and explanation.

Why require an act?

E.M. BURCHELL, P.M.A. HUNT and J.M. BURCHELL, SOUTH AFRICAN CRIMINAL LAW AND PROCEDURE

2nd ed. (1983), 106

The reason for requiring an *actus reus* is usually said to be the impossibility of proving a purely mental state. "The thought of man is not triable, for the devil himself knoweth not the thought of man", said Brian C.J. But Glanville Williams draws attention to the fallacy of this argument, and suggests two better reasons for the requirement of *actus reus*:

> (1) the difficulty of distinguishing between day-dream and fixed intention in the absence of behaviour tending towards the crime intended, and (2) the undesirability of spreading the criminal law so wide as to cover a mental state that the accused might be too irresolute even to begin to translate into action.

The invariable rule is then that criminal liability is dependent upon proof of an *actus reus* on the part of the accused. Where *mens rea* is required, there must be some act which puts the accused's guilty mind into action or at least goes part of the way towards doing so.

J.F. STEPHEN, A HISTORY OF THE CRIMINAL LAW OF ENGLAND

Vol. 2, (1883), 78-9

No temper of mind, no habit of life, however pernicious, has ever been treated as a crime, unless it displayed itself in some definite overt act. It never entered into the head of any English legislator to enact, or of any English Court, to hold, that a man could be indicted and punished for ingratitude, for hardheartedness, for the absence of natural affection, for habitual idleness, for avarice, sensuality, pride, or, in a word, for any vice whatever as such. Even for purposes of ecclesiastical censure some definite act of immorality was required. Sinful thoughts and dispositions of mind might be the subject of confession and of penance, but they were never punished in this country by ecclesiastical criminal proceedings.

The reasons for imposing this great leading restriction upon the sphere of criminal law are obvious. If it were not so restricted it would be utterly intolerable; all mankind would be criminals, and most of their lives would be passed in trying and punishing each other for offences which could never be proved.

Criminal law, then, must be confined within narrow limits, and can be applied only to definite overt acts or omissions capable of being distinctly proved, which acts or omissions inflict definite evils, either on specific persons or on the community at large.

Commission of an Unlawful Act

In many, if not most crimes, the act requirement is self-evident. Stealing requires taking something belonging to someone else, assault is a positive act of applying force, etc. In some instances, however, the law's description of the necessary external circumstance of the offence requires careful judicial analysis because it is vague or involves what appears to be a most minimal form of an act. What follows in this section is a selection of a number of different offences where the definition of the act requirement is difficult and often controversial.

HUTT v. R.

[1978] 2 S.C.R. 476, 1 C.R. (3d) 164, 38 C.C.C. (2d) 418

RITCHIE J. (PIGEON, BEETZ and PRATTE JJ. concurring): — I have had the advantage of reading the reasons for judgment prepared for delivery by my brother Spence in which he has reviewed the facts giving rise to this appeal and has also made reference to the question of law upon which leave to appeal was granted which is:

> Whether the Court of Appeal erred in law in interpreting the meaning of the word "solicit" in s. 195.1 of the *Criminal Code*.

I have concluded that the Court of Appeal did err in law in interpreting the word "solicit" as used in s. 195.1 [enacted 1972, c. 13, s. 15] in such manner as to be descriptive of the behaviour of the appellant as disclosed by the evidence in this case. In this regard I am in accord with my brother Spence, but as the appeal, in my opinion, falls to be determined within the limits of the question upon which leave to appeal was granted I prefer to base my conclusion on somewhat narrower grounds than those which he has adopted.

I subscribe to the opinion that the word "solicit" as used in the section in question carries with it an element of persistence and pressure and I find no evidence of the existence of such an element in the description of the appellant's activities as contained in the evidence. I am, on the other hand, of the opinion that the police officer's own testimony to the effect that "one of his duties was to appear as if he wanted a girl for sex" is such as to make it more appropriate to characterize the appellant's conduct as "co-operation" rather than "solicitation".

For these reasons, I would allow this appeal, but I do not find it necessary to express any view on the other points referred to by Mr. Justice Spence.

SPENCE J. (LASKIN C.J.C., MARTLAND, DICKSON and ESTEY JJ. concurring): — This is an appeal, by leave, from the judgment of the Court of Appeal of British Columbia pronounced on May 19, 1976. By that judgment, the Court of Appeal allowed an appeal from the judgment of His Honour Judge Macdonnell pronounced on December 5, 1975. By the latter judgment, His Honour Judge

Macdonnell had allowed an appeal from the conviction of the appellant by a Provincial Court Judge on the charge that

> at the City of Vancouver, Province of British Columbia, on the 8th day of May A.D., 1975 unlawfully did solicit a person, in a public place, to wit, 700 block Helmcken for the purpose of prostitution.

JUL 18 1975

That charge was laid under the provisions of s. 195.1 of the *Criminal Code* which provides:

> 195.1 Every person who solicits any person in a public place for the purpose of prostitution is guilty of an offence punishable on summary conviction.

His Honour Judge Macdonnell outlined a statement of facts which was adopted by Robertson J.A., in the Court of Appeal for British Columbia which I set out hereunder [32 C.C.C. (2d) 99 at pp. 102-3, [1976] 4 W.W.R. 690, 36 C.R.N.S. 139]:

> "On the appeal, the Crown called one witness, Detective Barclay of the Vancouver City Police, who gave evidence that at approximately 9:25 p.m. on May 8, 1975, while on duty and casually dressed, he drove his unmarked standard passenger car along Helmcken St. and came to a stop at the intersection of Granville Street and Helmcken Street in Vancouver. The officer was alone in the car. The officer believed that he saw the accused before he stopped the car but in any event, as he pulled up and stopped, he saw the accused almost immediately standing on the sidewalk of Helmcken Street approximately one car length from the stop line adjacent to the stop sign. He had a good look at the appellant and from this look he was able to describe what she was wearing. While looking at her, the accused smiled at him and he smiled in return. The appellant then approached the passenger side of the car, opened the door and got in. Either while she was getting in or when she had got in the car, the officer again smiled at her. The appellant then sat in the front seat and closed the door behind her. The conversation that then took place between them was as follows:
>
> 'Appellant: Hi.
> 'Officer: Hi.
> 'Appellant: Do you want a girl?
> 'Officer: What do you mean?
> 'Appellant: Do you want to go out?
> 'Officer: Okay.
> 'Appellant: It's $30.00.
> 'Officer: Oh, gosh, what will we do,
> 'Appellant: I am a working girl.
> 'Officer: Oh, what's that?
> 'Appellant: Do you want a girl?
> 'Officer: Okay, yes.
> 'Appellant: I am a working girl, I am a prostitute.
> 'Officer: Oh, I've never done this before.
> 'Appellantt: Oh.
> 'Officer: I'm staying at the Dufferin.
> 'Appellant: Okay.
> 'Officer: Will you do oral sex?
> 'Appellant: You mean a french?
> 'Officer: Yeah.
> 'Appellant: Oh, yes.

in a public place

'Officer: Okay.
'Appellant: Let's go.'

"Some further conversation then took place with respect to going to the Dufferin Hotel followed by the arrest of the appellant when the officer's car was parked at the rear of the Dufferin Hotel. Officer Barclay testified that the word 'french' meant an act of fellatio, that the expression 'working girl' was a word used by prostitutes to identify themselves to male customers.
"On cross-examination, the officer agreed that one of his duties was to make it appear as if he wanted a girl for sex and that the reason he immediately returned the smile was to encourage her to solicit him (for the purpose of prostitution)."

The order of this Court granting leave to appeal provided that:

IT IS ORDERED that Leave to Appeal be granted on the following question of law:
Whether the Court of Appeal erred in law in interpreting the meaning of the word "solicit" in Section 195.1 of the *Criminal Code*.

The charge which I have recited above was that the accused did solicit "in a public place, to wit, 700 block Helmcken" and s. 195.1, which I have quoted above, makes it an offence to solicit "in a public place". The learned County Court Judge, in his reasons for judgment, said: "The officer's car where it was located was clearly a public place."

In view of the limitation of the question upon which leave to appeal was granted, the issue of whether or not the officer's car was a "public place" was not referred to in the factums filed on this appeal. "Public place" [enacted 1972, c. 13, s. 13] is defined for the purpose of Part V of the *Criminal Code* in s. 179(1) as follows:

"public place" includes any place to which the public have access as of right or by invitation, express or implied.

I am most strongly of the opinion that this officer's automobile was not such a public place but was, on the other hand, a private place of which he had the sole control. To interpret the words otherwise would mean that if I were to invite anyone to enter my own home then that home would be a public place. In my view, the determination that the officer's car was not a public place would have been sufficient to dispose of the appeal and it must be allowed.

The facts which I have recited above show that there was not one word spoken until the appellant had entered the automobile and had closed the door. Even if one were to give to the word "solicit" the widest possible definition, there was, until the time that automobile door was closed, no demonstration that the intention of the appellant was to make herself available for prostitution. I suppose that in Vancouver there are hundreds of pedestrians every day who request free rides in automobiles, and it would appear ridiculous and abhorrent to say that every one of them who was female and who did so was guilty of soliciting within the provisions of this section of the *Criminal Code*. Since, however, the issue of whether or not the officer's automobile was a "public place" was not before the Court upon this appeal, I shall proceed to dispose of the appeal as if it had been a "public place".

It is evident, of course, that the sole issue before the learned County Court Judge and before the Court of Appeal for British Columbia was whether the circumstances in this case, so accurately outlined by the learned County Court Judge, fall within the prohibition of the *Code*, that is, did the appellant solicit? It must be noted, and it has been noted below, that the word "solicit" is not defined in the *Criminal Code*, therefore, the Courts below have taken what I am of the opinion was a proper course and have turned to established English dictionaries for the purpose of defining the word. The natural choice, of course, is the Shorter Oxford Dictionary. There, as has been said, the definition is exact and I quote it; "c. of women; to accost and importune (men) for immoral purposes". Of course, that definition requires, in turn, the definition of the words "accost" and "importune" and it is noted that the definition used those two verbs conjunctively and not alternatively. "Accost" in the same dictionary, is defined: "3. *trans.*, to approach for any purpose; to face; to make up to; 4. to address; 5. to solicit in the street for an "improper purpose". I think I might summarize those definitions by saying "to confront".

"Importune", again in the Shorter Oxford Dictionary, is variously defined and I choose the following: "3. To solicit pressingly or persistently; to beset with petitions."

It was the view of the Courts below that the definition of "importune" as "to burden; to trouble; worry, pester, annoy" was obsolete and I am quite ready to agree that "importune" does not import the element of pestering or annoying but I am of the opinion that it still maintains the meaning of "pressing or persisting".

Robertson J.A., in giving his reasons in the Court of Appeal for British Columbia, found that there must be "something more" than the demonstration of intention to make herself available for prostitution but that "something more" did not necessarily have to be conduct that is "pressing, persistent, troublesome, worrying, pestering or annoying". In using those various adjectives, Robertson J.A., was combining two alternative definitions of "importune" in the Shorter Oxford Dictionary. As I have said, I agree that as to the adjectives "troublesome, worrying, pestering or annoying" modern usage does not require the conduct to amount to compliance therewith but I am of the opinion that the "something else" is to be "pressing or persistent" within the definition which I have quoted above.

After having discussed various cases, and set out the statement of facts which I have cited above, Robertson J.A., said [at p. 103]:

> It appears to me that these facts provide in abundance the something-in-addition that is necessary to constitute the offence. I refer particularly to the accused getting into the man's car uninvited, and to her asking him "Do you want a girl?", followed by the statement "I am a working girl, I am a prostitute".

In the first place, the appellant did not enter the officer's car uninvited. The officer returned her smile and, in the last paragraph of the statement of facts, there is recited the admission of the officer that one of his duties was to make it appear that he wanted a girl for sex and that the reason he immediately returned the smile was to encourage her to solicit him. We are not, however, in this case concerned with any defence of entrapment. To continue reference to the facts and Robertson J.A.'s characterization of them, I can find nothing more than the demonstration that the appellant was available for prostitution in either her question "Do you want a girl?" or her further statement "I am a working girl. I am a prostitute" which followed the officer's reply to her question which was "Okay, yes". Therefore, I can find nothing in that conversation which would comply with even the indefinite "something else" which Robertson J.A., required and certainly I can find nothing pressing or persistent as I am of the opinion is required.

I am strengthened in this view of the appeal by considering the changes in the legislation. From 1869 until 1972, there appeared in penal statutes in Canada as one of the kinds of "vagrancy" the offence in the *Criminal Code* as it appeared in R.S.C. 1970, c. C-34, s. 175(1)(*c*):

> (*c*) being a common prostitute or night walker is found in a public place and does not, when required, give a good account of herself;

That provision was repealed by 1972, c. 13, s. 12(1). Prostitution itself was not then an offence. The offences of keeping a common bawdy-house and of being an inmate of a common bawdy-house were retained by s. 193(1) and (2). At the same time, s. 195.1 was enacted. The comparison between the old s. 175(1)(*c*) and s. 195.1 is informative. Firstly, s. 175(1)(*c*) applied only to common prostitutes or night walkers. Section 195.1 applies to "every person". Secondly, s. 175(1)(*c*) made it an offence for such common prostitute to be in a public place even if absolutely immobile and silent unless she could give a good account of herself, while s. 195.1 requires the person to solicit. I am of the opinion that this history of the legislation indicates that Parliament wished to require some acts on the part of the person which would contribute to public inconvenience, and certainly the acts of the present appellant were not such as would so contribute. In fact, when one reads the statement of facts, one wonders whether the appellant solicited any more than the complaining officer.

Section 195.1 is enacted in Part V which is entitled "Disorderly Houses, Gaming and Betting". Offences in reference to all three of these subject-matters are offences which do contribute to public inconvenience or unrest and again I am of the opinion that Parliament was indicating that what it desired to prohibit was a contribution to public inconvenience or unrest. The conduct of the appellant in this case cannot be so characterized.

It would appear that the complaining police officer, on instructions, was attempting to enforce the provisions of the *Criminal Code* as if they still contained s. 175(1)(*c*).

I note that my conclusion accords with that of the Court of Appeal for Ontario in *R. v. Rolland* (1975), 27 C.C.C. (2d) 485, 31 C.R.N.S. 68, and I adopt the judgment of Jessup J.A.

For the above reasons, I am of the opinion that the appeal must be allowed and the conviction quashed.

. . . .

Appeal allowed; conviction quashed.

PUBLIC OPINION, AGGRESSIVE SOLICITING FORCE CRACKDOWN ON B.C. PROSTITUTES

The Globe and Mail, June 30, 1979, p. 12, col. 1

VANCOUVER (CP) — Ladies of the night in Vancouver are working mainly afternoon shifts to avoid a recent police crackdown aimed at ending the confusion that has left prostitutes virtually free to ply their trade for more than a year.

The main target of a 30-man police task force are street prostitutes, the most visible of the 800 women and 150 men believed to work as prostitutes in Vancouver.

In the last month, at least 20 women have been charged with soliciting. The charges are the first since a Supreme Court of Canada decision in February, 1978, which police and prosecutors said tied their hands in the fight against prostitution.

Bail for the women has included the condition that they stay away from well-known prostitutes' haunts. Two men, both potential customers, also have been charged.

Police won't talk about their current campaign, but its effects are obvious.

The usual line of ladies has disappeared in front of Air Canada's downtown office, within a block of half a dozen major hotels.

Beat officers and unmarked cars prowl the West End's residential side streets, replacing the prostitutes and cruising clients that used to crowd the corners.

Transvestites, teen-age boys and prostitutes still flaunt themselves in the area most afternoons, but police are planning to put more men on day shift to curb that as well.

Police say they lost their most valuable weapon when the vagrancy section of the *Criminal Code*, allowing easy detention of a suspected common prostitute, was repealed in 1972.

The soliciting clause that replaced it, they argue, was undermined when a charge against 23-year-old Debra Hutt went to the Supreme Court of Canada early last year.

Miss Hutt, now serving eight months for welfare fraud and heroin possession, had smiled at a Vancouver policeman in an unmarked car. He smiled back, she jumped in, and they agreed on $30 as a fair price for services to be rendered. She was arrested.

The Court restored her original acquittal, saying that an unmarked car is not a public place and that Miss Hutt's overtures were not as pressing and persistent as the court decided soliciting must be.

Police and prosecutors stopped going after soliciting convictions. They also refused to lay the loitering charges that Montreal and Toronto police say have allowed them to maintain some control since the Hutt decision.

The Vancouver street scene flourished and the push for police action increased with publicity surrounding the investigation of a Provincial Court Judge and the resignation of the head of the B.C. Court of Appeal.

Both were alleged to have consorted with prostitutes.

But authorities said they couldn't do anything until loopholes in the law were plugged.

Police and prosecutors say public pressure and more aggressive soliciting forced them to come up with a new strategy. That, apparently, will involve arguing in court that a prostitute is just as pressing and persistent in approaching ten men as in approaching one man ten times.

However, some observers say that the police only want to clean up the streets for the summer tourist trade, which will include a police convention in August. Others say Vancouver police could no longer refuse to act while colleagues in the east made arrests.

"The most interesting thing is how suddenly they've changed their approach," says lawyer Tony Serka, who represented Miss Hutt. "I think it's because of pressure from Ontario.

"It's funny that Ontario has been doing so well while we've been crying the blues."

But assistant Attorney-General Neil McDiarmid says some loitering charges were thrown out of court in Toronto, reinforcing British Columbia's decision "not to grasp at straws.

"It's become a game and it shouldn't be," he says. "It should be easy for us to get them off the streets."

Mr. McDiarmid says the province will continue to press for *Criminal Code* amendments that would be even more effective than the ones which died on the order paper when the federal election was called.

The definition of soliciting, he says, "should be clear, simple and easy to understand.

"If a person offers to sell sexual services in a public place, that would constitute an offence. If a person agrees to buy those services, that's an offence."

Mr. Serka, however, says authorities have been pressing a political point by refusing to use the legislation at hand.

"They haven't been moving with the times," he says. "They haven't been responsible enough to try to enforce a new law."

They're trying now, and local nightclub owners, residents, merchants and even the prostitutes say they can see the effects. Some U.S. prostitutes, who called this a safe haven, have gone home — many were deported and some part-timers, out for a lucrative weekend fling, have given up as the risk increased.

Other prostitutes are reported to have moved into clubs.

However, Penthouse club owner Joe Philippone says prostitutes haven't flocked back to his place as he expected they might.

"If they come, I let them in," he says. "We'll take their money as long as they behave themselves."

Police officials won't comment on their plans and probably will remain silent until the current charges go to Court in the fall. Officers on the street, however, say the crackdown is a drain on manpower and some prostitutes couldn't agree more.

"Police are wasting so much time when there are robbers and murderers," says one woman. "They're too busy trying to babysit us. Let's face it, prostitution is the oldest thing going."

The *Criminal Code* was amended in December 1985 (S.C. 1985, c. 50, s. 1) to provide:

213.(1) Every person who in a public place or in any place open to public view
    (a) stops or attempts to stop any motor vehicle,
    (b) impedes the free flow of pedestrian or vehicular traffic or ingress to or egress from premises adjacent to that place, or
    (c) stops or attempts to stop any person or in any manner communicates or attempts to communicate with any person
for the purpose of engaging in prostitution or of obtaining the sexual services of a prostitute is guilty of an offence punishable on summary conviction.

(2) In this section, "public place" includes any place to which the public have access as of right or by invitation, express or implied, and any motor vehicle located in a public place or in any place open to public view.

Has Parliament solved the problem of *Hutt*? Has it created new problems?

STEPHEN BINDMAN, "SOLICITING LAW A BUST IN MOST CITIES: STUDY", OTTAWA CITIZEN, AUGUST 1, 1989

Ottawa is one of the few Canadian cities which has benefited from a tough anti-soliciting law introduced by the federal government in 1985, a new study has found.

The study, obtained by Southam News under access-to-information legislation, concludes Bill C-49 has not succeeded in deterring either prostitutes or their customers in most Canadian cities.

"In most of the cities included in the study, street prostitution was as prevalent as it was before the new law," says the 120-page report, entitled *Street Prostitution: Assessing the impact of the law.*

"Perhaps the clearest conclusion of this evaluation is that police enforcement of the new (section of the *Criminal Code*) did not suppress the street prostitution trade in most cities. The main effect was to move street prostitutes from one downtown area to another, thereby displacing the problem."

The main exception was Ottawa where, police told researchers, the number of prostitutes in the Byward Market area dropped from "some 50 to 75 female prostitutes (in 1984 to) 10 to 12" in 1987.

"According to police, C-49 contributed to a substantial reduction in street prostitution in Ottawa," notes the report by Justice Department researcher John Fleischman. "In addition, police reported that complaints from businesses and residents had decreased."

Police speculated prostitutes moved either to escort services or to other cities such as Montreal or Toronto.

The report is a compilation of five studies done for the government by private researchers in 1987 and 1988 into the situation in Vancouver, Calgary, Toronto, Montreal and Halifax.

Smaller studies were also done in Regina, Winnipeg, London, Niagara Falls, Ottawa, Trois-Rivières and Quebec City.

The 1985 law makes it illegal to communicate or attempt to communicate in a public place for the purpose of prostitution. It was passed in response to a growing furore in a number of cities over the prevalence of hookers and their clients in certain neighborhoods.

The law, which provides for a maximum penalty of six months in jail and a $2,000 fine for both prostitutes and their customers, is to be reviewed later this year by a Commons committee.

The Supreme Court of Canada is also expected to rule on several challenges to the constitutionality of the legislation.

Although appeal Courts in Ontario, Manitoba and Alberta have upheld it, Nova Scotia's top court has ruled the law violates the guarantee of freedom of expression in the *Charter of Rights and Freedoms*. It has not been enforced in Nova Scotia since the 1987 ruling.

When then-justice minister John Crosbie first introduced the law, he said it would result in the "streets being reclaimed for the citizens."

But although almost 12,000 charges were laid in the law's first two years, the $275,000 study concludes there are now no fewer prostitutes working the streets of Toronto, Vancouver, Winnipeg, Regina and Calgary.

In Toronto and Vancouver, where the problem was the worst, the legislation "had virtually no success in moving prostitutes off the street. At best, prostitutes were simply displaced to new areas."

The number of streetwalkers does appear to have fallen in Quebec City, Niagara Falls and London as well as Ottawa, so "the problem appears to be under control."

In Montreal and Halifax, the situation has improved because "some women appear to have left the street trade and the concentration in certain areas was lower," the study says.

Most sex-for-sale still takes place in cars, the study says, even though the legislation specifically includes the inside of an automobile within its definition of a "public place."

Nor has the type of women who are street prostitutes changed much since the law took effect, says the study, they merely have "longer criminal records."

Among the report's other findings:

• Prostitutes are charged much more often than their customers, except in Toronto and London. In Vancouver, Calgary, Ottawa and Halifax, customers represented one-quarter or less of the charges laid.

• Very few male prostitutes and almost none of their customers are ever charged. Police interviewed said the male hooker trade is "smaller, generally less of a nuisance and more difficult to infiltrate" than the female trade.

• Prostitutes were generally sentenced more severely than their customers, although this was partly because of their prior criminal records.

REFERENCE RE SS. 193 & 195.1(1)(c) OF THE *CRIMINAL CODE* (CANADA) (PROSTITUTION REFERENCE)

[1990] 1 S.C.R. 1123, 77 C.R. (3d) 1, 56 C.C.C. (3d) 65

The Supreme Court rejected a *Charter* challenge to the offence of communicating for the purpose of prostitution. The Court agreed that the provision, now s. 213(1)(*c*), infringed the guarantee of freedom of expression in s. 2(*b*) of the *Charter* but was divided on the question of whether that provision was a demonstrably justified limit on that freedom within the meaning of s. 1. The justices were in agreement that the provision was not too vague. The division of opinion occurred over the issue of whether the provision was overly broad such that it could not meet the minimum intrusion test of *Oakes*.

DICKSON C.J.C. (LAFOREST and SOPINKA JJ. concurring): —

. . . .

The first step in the analysis, established in *R. v. Oakes*, [1986] 1 S.C.R. 103, 50 C.R. (3d) 1, 24 C.C.C. (3d) 321, to assess the justification pursuant to s. 1 for a *Charter* violation is to characterize the legislative objective of the impugned provision. Like Wilson J., I would characterize the legislative objective of s. 195.1(1)(*c*) in the following manner: the provision is meant to address solicitation in public places and, to that end, seeks to eradicate the various forms of social nuisance arising from the public display of the sale of sex. My colleague Lamer J. finds that s. 195.1(1)(*c*) is truly directed towards curbing the exposure of prostitution and related violence, drugs and crime to potentially vulnerable young people, and towards eliminating the victimization and economic disadvantage that prostitution, and especially street soliciting, represents for women. I do not share the view that the legislative objective can be characterized so broadly. In prohibiting sales of sexual services in public, the legislation does not attempt, at least in any direct manner, to address the exploitation, degradation and subordination of women that are part of the contemporary reality of prostitution. Rather, in my view, the legislation is aimed at taking solicitation for the purposes of prostitution off the streets and out of public view.

The *Criminal Code* provision subject to attack in these proceedings clearly responds to the concerns of home-owners, businesses, and the residents of urban neighbourhoods. Public solicitation for the purposes of prostitution is closely associated with street congestion and noise, oral harassment of non-participants and general detrimental effects on passers-by or bystanders, especially children. In my opinion, the eradication of the nuisance-related problems caused by street solicitation is a pressing and substantial concern. I find, therefore, that sending the message that street solicitation for the purposes of prostitution is not to be tolerated constitutes a valid legislative aim.

I turn now to the issue of proportionality. With respect to the question of rational connection between the impugned legislation and the prevention of the social nuisance associated with the public display of the sale of sex, I agree with Wilson J. that such a connection exists. The next step is to determine whether the means embodied in this legislation are appropriately tailored to meet the objective. Is it reasonable and justifiable to limit freedom of expression according to the terms of s. 195.1(1)(c) in order to eliminate street solicitation and the social nuisance which it creates? The answer to this question requires an analysis of whether the means impair the right as little as possible and of the effects and reasonableness of the limits imposed.

I start by considering the nature of the expression and the nature of the infringing legislation. Freedom of expression is fundamental to a democratic society. Parliament, through s. 195.1(1)(c) of the *Criminal Code*, has chosen to use the criminal justice system to prosecute individuals on the basis of the exercise of their freedom of expression. When a *Charter* freedom has been infringed by state action that takes the form of criminalization, the Crown bears the heavy burden of justifying that infringement. Yet the expressive activity, as with any infringed *Charter* right, should also be analyzed in the particular context of the case. Here, the activity to which the impugned legislation is directed is expression with an economic purpose. It can hardly be said that communications regarding an economic transaction of sex for money lie at, or even near, the core of the guarantee of freedom of expression.

The legislation aims at restraining communication or attempts at communication for the purpose of engaging in prostitution. That communication must occur in "a public place or in any place open to public view". It is argued that the legislation is overbroad because it is not confined to places where there will *necessarily* be many people, or in fact *any* people, who will be offended by the activity. The objective of this provision, however, is not restricted to the control of actual disturbances or nuisances. It is broader, in the sense that it is directed at controlling, in general, the nuisance-related problems identified above that stem from street soliciting. Much street soliciting occurs in specified areas where the congregation of prostitutes and their customers amounts to a nuisance. In effect, the legislation discourages prostitutes and customers from concentrating their activities in any particular location. While it is the cumulative impact of individual transactions concentrated in a public area that effectively produces the social nuisance at which the legislation in part aims, Parliament can only act by focusing on individual transactions. The notion of nuisance in connection with street soliciting extends beyond interference with the individual citizen to interference with the public at large, that is with the environment represented by streets, public places and neighbouring premises.

The appellants' argument that the provision is too broad and therefore cannot be found to be appropriately tailored also focuses on the phrase "in any manner communicate or attempt to communicate". The communication in question cannot be read without the phrase "for the purpose of engaging in prostitution, or of obtaining the sexual services of a prostitute", which follows and qualifies it. In my opinion, the definition of communication may be, and indeed is, very wide, but the need for flexibility on the part of Parliament in this regard must be taken into account. Certain acts or gestures in addition to certain words can reasonably be interpreted as attracting customers for the purposes of prostitution or as indicating a desire to procure the services of a prostitute. This provides the necessary delineation of the scope of the communication that may be criminalized by s. 195.1(1)(c). This Court, in *Hutt v. R.*, [1978] 2 S.C.R. 476, 1 C.R. (3d) 164, 38 C.C.C. (2d) 418 [B.C.], interpreted the meaning of solicitation in keeping with the purposes of the provision. In that case, the actions of a prostitute who had engaged in conversation regarding the sale of sexual services for a fee with an undercover police officer in his car were found not to constitute "solicitation". In a similar vein, the Courts are capable of restricting the meaning of "communication" in this context by reference to the purpose of the impugned legislation.

Can effective yet less intrusive legislation be imagined? The means used to attain the objective of the legislation may well be broader than would be appropriate were actual street nuisance the only focus. However, as I find the objective to extend to the general curtailment of visible solicitation for the purposes of prostitution, it is my view that the legislation is not unduly intrusive.

It is legitimate to take into account the fact that earlier laws and considered alternatives were thought to be less effective than the legislation that is presently being challenged. When Parliament began its examination of the subject of street soliciting, it was presented with a spectrum of views and possible approaches by both the Fraser Committee and the Justice and Legal Affairs Committee. In making a choice to enact s. 195.1(1)(c) as it now reads, Parliament had to try to balance its decision to criminalize the nuisance aspects of street soliciting and its desire to take into account the policy arguments regarding the effects of criminalization of any aspect of prostitution. The legislative history of the present provision and, in general, of legislation directed to street solicitation is both long and complicated. The legislative scheme that was eventually implemented and has now been challenged need not be the "perfect" scheme that could be imagined by this Court or any other Court. Rather, it is sufficient if it is appropriately and carefully tailored in the context of the infringed right. I find that this legislation meets the test of minimum impairment of the right in question.

In this regard, I find my words in *R. v. Edwards Books & Art Ltd.*, [1986] 2 S.C.R. 713 at 783, 55 C.R. (3d) 193 (sub nom. *R. v. Videoflicks Ltd.*), 30 C.C.C. (3d) 385, to be applicable:

> I should emphasize that it is not the role of this Court to devise legislation that is constitutionally valid, or to pass on the validity of schemes which are not directly before it or to consider what legislation might be the most desirable. The discussion of alternative legislative schemes that I have undertaken is directed to one end only, that is, to address the issue whether the existing scheme meets the requirements of the second limb of the test for the application of s. 1 of the *Charter* as set down in *Oakes*.

The final question to be answered under the *Oakes* test is whether the effects of the law so severely trench on a protected right that the legislative objective is outweighed by the infringement. I have already found that the objective of the legislation to which these intended effects are linked is of pressing and substantial importance in the free and democratic society that Canada represents. Because the impugned *Criminal Code* provision prohibits legitimate expression in the form of communication for the purposes of a commercial agreement exchanging sex for money, and therefore violates a protected right, the justification of that *Charter* infringement must be in keeping with the principles of a democratic society and the rights, freedoms and interests of its members. Here, the legislation limits the conditions under which communication between prostitutes and customers can take place. In thereby moving toward the eradication of public communication with respect to prostitution, it addresses itself precisely to the objective it seeks to achieve. The curtailment of street solicitation is in keeping with the interests of many in our society for whom the nuisance-related aspects of solicitation constitute serious problems. I find that the obtrusiveness linked to the enforcement of the provision, when weighed against the resulting decrease in the social nuisance associated with street solicitation, can be justified in accordance with s. 1.

I wish to add here that other attempts at legislation in this area have failed for various reasons. This is not to say that the Crown can discharge its burden under s. 1 simply by saying that it is difficult to find a legislative solution in the area of prostitution and that the Courts should therefore be ready to accept the enactment under challenge. Rather it is to point out that a legislative scheme aimed at street solicitation must be of a criminal law nature after this Court's decision in *Westendorp v. R.*, [1983] 1 S.C.R. 43, 32 C.R. (3d) 97, 2 C.C.C. (3d) 330. In that case, the city of Calgary enacted a by-law that prohibited the use of city streets by those approaching or being approached by others for the purpose of prostitution. Laskin C.J.C., for the Court, found the challenged by-law to be *ultra vires* as invading federal powers in relation to the criminal law. A province or municipality may not "translate a direct attack on prostitution into street control through reliance on public nuisance" (p. 53). Only Parliament can attack prostitution through the use of criminal measures, and legislation seeking to eradicate street solicitation cannot originate with the individual municipalities. The restriction on the activities of prostitutes effected by s. 195.1(1)(*c*) of the *Criminal Code*, at stake in these proceedings, must be assessed accordingly.

In conclusion, with respect to the s. 1 justification of the infringement of freedom of expression, I find that s. 195.1(1) (*c*) is valid legislation aimed at the curtailment of street solicitation. After taking into consideration the nature of the expression and the nature of the infringing legislation, and the issue of whether a free and democratic society can countenance legislation aimed at the social nuisance of street solicitation and at its eventual elimination, I conclude that the impugned provision is saved by s. 1.

. . . .

WILSON J. (dissenting) (L'HEUREUX-DUBÉ J. concurring): —

. . . .

(ii) *Parliament's objective in passing s. 195.1(1)(c)*

The parties and interveners in this appeal and the related appeals in *R. v. Stagnitta*, S.C.C. No. 20497, 31st May 1990 (not yet reported) [Alta.] [noted 76 C.R. (3d) xxix], and *R. v. Skinner*, S.C.C., No. 20428, 31st May 1990 [post, p. 84] [N.S.], made a number of submissions with respect to the legislative objective underlying s. 195.1 in general and s. 195.1(1)(c) in particular. These may be grouped into three categories of gradually widening scope.

(1) Nuisance in the Streets

The appellant Stagnitta and the respondent Skinner give s. 195.1(1)(c) its narrowest interpretation. They submit that the objective underlying the legislation is the protection of the public's right to the unobstructed use of the streets and sidewalks. They do, however, acknowledge that the legislation may also be designed to prevent citizens from being disrupted in their enjoyment of public residential areas by activities incidental to street soliciting.

(2) Social Nuisance

In the overwhelming majority of submissions made to the Court it was claimed that the objective of the legislation was the control of a "social" nuisance. The Attorney General of Canada submitted that s. 195.1 as a whole was designed, not just to deal with the interference by prostitutes and their customers of the citizens' use of public places, but also to address the secondary effects of street soliciting. These secondary effects, which were in his view the primary motivation for the legislation, included "all night noise, traffic congestion, trespass, reduced property values and other adverse consequences". The specific focus of s. 195.1(1)(c), on the other hand, was to deal with the "precise activity from which all the harm flows", namely, street solicitation. The appellants and the respondent in this appeal are all in substantial agreement with this submission, although they obviously differ with respect to whether the impugned provision is an acceptable way in which to achieve the stated objective.

The Attorneys General for Alberta and Saskatchewan cover similar ground. They agree that "The objective of s. 195.1(1) of the *Criminal Code* is to deal with the problem of bartering for sexual services in public places" and they point to a list of "harms" which they say the legislation seeks to prevent — the harassment of women, street congestion, noise, decreased property values, adverse effects on businesses, increased incidents of violence, and the impact of street soliciting on children who cannot avoid seeing what goes on.

The Attorney General of British Columbia also submits that s. 195.1(1)(c) is specifically designed to deal with the harms caused by the "act of the prostitute in conveying his or her message". The provision seeks to prevent neighbourhoods lapsing into "total disintegration". The Attorney General of Nova Scotia states that Parliament wished to protect the public from "impeded pedestrian and vehicular traffic, the indignity of being propositioned, exposure of children to the vices of adults, viewing the actions and hearing the communications related to prostitution in "a public place".

I think it important to emphasize, however, that those whose submissions fall into this broader category of "social" nuisance do not claim that the aim of the legislation is to prohibit prostitution. Rather, they submit that it seeks to prohibit sales of sexual services from taking place in the public domain. The Attorney General of Manitoba, the respondent in this appeal, notes that the legislation does not purport to prevent prostitution-related activities in circumstances where no public nuisance is created. The Attorney General of Canada states that "Parliament did not seek to suppress solicitation, but only to remove it from the public areas where it was creating the obvious harm". The Attorney General of Nova Scotia acknowledges that prostitution is not a criminal offence and that "s. 195.1(1)(c) is not intended to eradicate prostitution but focuses on the undesirability of bringing prostitution into the public forum". Hence the characterization of the legislative objective as a "social" rather than a strictly legal nuisance.

(3) Prostitution-Related Activities

The Attorney General for Ontario goes further than any other Attorney General who presented submissions in this appeal and in *Stagnitta* and *Skinner*, both *supra*. He submits that s. 195.1 is designed to deal with a much wider array of problems associated with prostitution, including violence, drug addiction, crime and juvenile prostitution. While he agrees that the legislation is aimed at many of the aspects of public nuisance discussed by his colleagues, he points out that the legislation is also directed to drug addiction and juvenile prostitution because of the risk that young children who are exposed to street soliciting will be drawn into the world of drugs and prostitution.

Which characterization of Parliament's objective seems most accurate? Lamer J. appears to have been persuaded by the position taken by the Attorney General for Ontario. He concludes that the legislation is an attack on prostitution, albeit an indirect one, and that part of the legislative objective sought to be achieved through s. 195.1(1)(c) was to give law enforcement officials a way of controlling prostitution in the streets. He points out [at p. 539] that "The streets provide an environment for pimps and procurers to attract adults (usually, as the data shows, women) and adolescents into the trade by befriending them and often offering them short term affection and economic assistance". He agrees with the Attorney General for Ontario's submission that it is the young who are most desirable to pimps, as they bring in the most money and are the easiest to control. Young girls become dependent on pimps and are often manipulated through the use of drugs. Physical violence may result. My colleague concludes that prostitution is degrading to the individual dignity of the prostitute and a vehicle for pimps and customers to exploit the disadvantaged position of women in our society. Thus Lamer J. finds that the Legislature's objective goes beyond preventing congestion in the streets and sidewalks; it has the additional objective of restricting the entry of young girls into an activity that is degrading to women and is associated with drugs, crime and physical abuse.

While I do not disagree with my colleague that prostitution is, for the reasons he gives, a degrading way for women to earn a living, I cannot agree with his conclusion that s. 195.1(1)(c) of the *Code* attempts to address that problem. With the exception of the Attorney General for Ontario, the parties and interveners in this appeal and in *Skinner* and *Stagnitta* were unanimously of the view that the legislation does not seek to deal with prostitution *per se* but is directed only at the public or social nuisance aspect of the sale of sexual services in public. Indeed, the Attorneys General of Canada, Nova Scotia and Manitoba went out of their way to emphasize that s. 195.1(1) does not prohibit prostitution, which remains a perfectly legal activity. It does not even prohibit solicitation; it only prohibits solicitation in public places. In my view, the wording of s. 195.1(1) in general and s. 195.1(1)(c) in particular supports that view.

But, if the legislative objective was not to criminalize prostitution per se, which of the narrower objectives did Parliament have in mind? In my view, it is once again important to look to the wording of the impugned section. While s. 195.1(1)(a) and (b) refer to activities that "stop any motor vehicle" or that impede "the free flow of pedestrian or vehicular traffic", s. 195.1(1)(c) refers not just to stopping persons (although it does include that) but to communicating or attempting to communicate with persons. Accordingly, activities caught by s. 195.1(1)(c) need not result in the kinds of problems addressed in s. 195.1(1)(a) and (b). It was not alleged, for example, in either *Stagnitta* or *Skinner* that the accused's activities had impeded traffic or led to congestion. The accused were simply charged with communicating in a public place for the purpose of engaging in prostitution or of obtaining the sexual services of a prostitute. While the circumstances in which charges are laid under the section are obviously not determinative of the objective sought to be achieved by the legislation, they do reveal how the law enforcement agencies are interpreting and applying it. They clearly interpreted s. 195.1(1)(c) in *Stagnitta* and *Skinner* as intended to do more than keep the streets and sidewalks free of congestion. In my view, they were not mistaken in this regard. Indeed, this is why s. 195.1(1)(c) was considered a necessary addition to s. 195.1(1) (a) and (b). The difficulty, however, is to determine just how much more the impugned provision was intended to catch.

I have concluded that the submissions made to the Court by the majority of counsel are correct and that the fundamental concern attempted to be addressed in s. 195.1(1)(c) is the social nuisance arising from the public display of the sale of sex. I believe this is clear from the requirement that the communication or attempted communication be for the purchase or sale of sexual services and that such communication occur in a public place or in a place open to public view. Parliament's concern, I believe, goes beyond street or sidewalk congestion, which is dealt with in paras. (a) and (b). The legislature clearly believes that public sensitivities are offended by the sight of prostitutes negotiating openly for the sale of their bodies and customers negotiating, perhaps somewhat less openly, for their purchase. The reality, in other words, is accepted and permitted. Neither prostitution nor solicitation is made illegal. But the high visibility of these activities is offensive and has harmful effects on those compelled to witness it, especially children. This being the legislative approach to prostitution, it forecloses, in my view, any suggestion that in s. 195.1(1)(c) Parliament intended to stamp out all the ills and vices that my colleague sees as flowing from prostitution. The provision addresses only one narrow aspect of prostitution, namely solicitation in public places.

Given, then, that s. 195.1(1)(c) infringes upon freedom of expression under s. 2(b) of the *Charter* and that the legislative objective in passing it is the one we have identified, does the provision constitute a reasonable limit on the freedom which is justifiable in a free and democratic society? Does it, in other words, meet the tests laid down by this court in *R. v. Oakes*, [1986] 1 S.C.R. 103, 50 C.R. (3d) 1, 24 C.C.C. (3d) 321?

(iii) *Section 1 of the Charter*

None of the counsel appearing before us on this appeal seriously argued that the nuisance caused by street solicitation, at least in the major centres of population in the country, was not a pressing and substantial concern. Indeed, most acknowledged it to be so, and I agree. The first test in *Oakes* is therefore met.

The next question under *Oakes* is whether s. 195.1(1)(c) is rationally connected to the prevention of the nuisance. I believe it is. The logical way to prevent the public display of the sale of sex and any harmful consequences that flow from it is through the twofold step of prohibiting the prostitute from soliciting prospective customers in places open to public view and prohibiting the customer from propositioning the prostitute likewise in places open to public view. If communication for this purpose or attempts to communicate for this purpose are criminalized, it must surely be a powerful deterrent to those engaging in such conduct.

But is the legislation proportionate to the objective sought to be achieved? To answer this we must direct our attention to the scope of the legislation.

On 9th September 1985, when the present s. 195.1 was introduced in the House of Commons, the then Minister of Justice stated (Debates of the House of Commons (1985), vol. 5, p. 6374):

> The legislation does not attempt to deal with all of the problems that prostitution creates or with the problems of prostitution generally, which of course is the sale of sexual favours or sexual services for pay. *It only purports to deal with one aspect of the problems that prostitution can create, which is the nuisance to others created by street soliciting not only by the prostitute but by the customers of the prostitute.* [Emphasis added.]

The Attorney General of Canada, adverting to the minister's statement, submitted that the purpose of s. 195.1 was to prevent prostitutes and their customers from congregating and concentrating their activities in any particular location. He pointed out that prostitutes go where they can expect to find customers and customers go where they can expect to find prostitutes, and the more widely such an area becomes known for what it is the more it will attract prostitutes and customers and the more nuisance will be created. The problem, in other words, feeds upon itself.

The Attorney General of Canada described the legislation as "time and place regulation" and emphasized that many trades and businesses are subject to government regulation in the public interest. He argued that the net effect of the legislation is merely to remove the transaction of the business of prostitution from public places. It is no different, he submitted, from regulating the conditions under which other businesses must operate. The Attorney General further submitted that no business enterprise should be free to pre-empt a public place for its own commercial gain without regard to the nuisance it may create for the surrounding community. The Attorney General submitted (rather surprisingly, I think, in light of the impact of s. 193 of the *Criminal Code* on attempts to engage in prostitution from private premises) that one of the purposes of s. 195.1 is to diffuse the activities associated with prostitution and ensure that prostitutes, like retailers and consumers, conduct their activities on private premises and in a way which will avoid the creation of a nuisance to others.

I believe, with respect, that the Attorney General has overlooked a number of significant aspects of the impugned legislation which go directly to the question of its proportionality. The first is that it criminalizes communication or attempted communication for the prohibited purpose in any public place or place open to public view. "Public place" is then expanded in subs. (2) to include any place to which the public have access as of right or by invitation, express or implied. In other words, the prohibition is not confined to places where there will necessarily be lots of people to be offended or inconvenienced by it. The prohibited communication may be taking place in a secluded area of a park where there is no one to see or hear it. It will still be a criminal offence under the section. Such a broad prohibition as to the locale of the communication would seem to go far beyond a genuine concern over the nuisance caused by street solicitation in Canada's major centres of population. It enables the police to arrest citizens who are disturbing no one solely because they are engaged in communicative acts concerning something not prohibited by the *Code*. It is not reasonable, in my view, to prohibit *all* expressive activity conveying a certain meaning that takes place in public simply because in *some* circumstances and in *some* areas that activity *may* give rise to a public or social nuisance.

I note also the broad scope of the phrase "in any manner communicates or attempts to communicate". It would seem to encompass every conceivable method of human expression. Indeed, it may not be necessary for the prostitute to say anything at all in order to be found to be "communicating" or "attempting to communicate" for the purpose of prostitution. The proverbial nod or wink may be enough. Perhaps more serious, a hapless citizen may be picked up for soliciting when he or she has nothing more pressing in mind than hailing a taxi! While it is true that he or she may subsequently be let go as lacking the necessary intent for the offence, the experience of being arrested is not something the ordinary citizen would welcome. Some definitional limits would appear to be desirable in any activity labelled as criminal.

Directly relevant to the issue of proportionality, it seems to me, is the fact already referred to that under para. (*c*) no nuisance or adverse impact of any kind on other people need be shown, or even be shown to be a possibility, in order that the offence be complete. Yet communicating or attempting to communicate with someone in a public place with respect to the sale of sexual services does not automatically create a nuisance, any more than communicating or attempting to communicate with someone on the sidewalk to promote a candidate for municipal election. Moreover, as already mentioned, prostitution is itself a perfectly legal activity, and the avowed objective of the legislature was not to make it illegal but only, as the Minister of Justice emphasized at the time, to deal with the nuisance created by street solicitation. It seems to me that to render criminal the communicative acts of persons engaged in a lawful activity which is not shown to be harming anybody cannot be justified by the legislative objective advanced in its support. The impugned provision is not sufficiently tailored to that objective and constitutes a more serious impairment of the individual's freedom than the avowed legislative objective would warrant. Section 195.1(1) (c) therefore fails to meet the proportionality test in *Oakes*.

The concurring opinion of Lamer J. is omitted. As reflected in the judgments of Dickson C.J.C. and Wilson J., the major difference between Justice Lamer's approach and that of the Chief Justice is that Justice Lamer saw the communicating offence as addressing problems associated with prostitution wider than that of a street nuisance. The further objective was "minimizing the public exposure of an activity that is degrading to women with the hope that potential entrants in the trade can be deflected at an early stage, and to restrict the blight that is associated with public solicitation for the purposes of prostitution".

In view of the definition of possession in s. 4(3) of the *Criminal Code*, as interpreted in the following three decisions, mount defences to charges of possession of marijuana against three partygoers. A passed on a joint to C without herself smoking, knowing full well what it was. B did not touch the joint but joined the group in which the joint was being smoked, knowing full well what it was. D owned the apartment where the party was held and knew that some of her guests were smoking marijuana.

MARSHALL v. R.

[1969] 3 C.C.C. 149, 5 C.R.N.S. 348 (Alta. C.A.)

McDermid J.A.: — The appellant was charged jointly with three other persons that:

> Reginald James Smith, Roy Clare Jones, Daniel Joseph Marshall and Frank Nelson Brander stand charged that you on the 5th day of February, A.D. 1968 in the Province of Alberta, near the City of Calgary, in the said Province, were unlawfully in possession of a narcotic, to wit: Cannabis (Marihuana) for the purpose of trafficking, contrary to the provisions of Section 4, sub-section 2 of the *Narcotic Control Act*.

All of the accused were found guilty and the appellant Marshall has appealed against his conviction and sentence.

At the date of the offence the appellant was 16 years of age and was attending school in the city of Calgary. He decided to accompany his friend, one of the accused, Roy Clare Jones, who owned a car, to Vancouver for a short weekend holiday. Also accompanying them were the accused Brander and one, Wes. Cameron. The appellant Marshall did not know Wes. Cameron before the trip to Vancouver. The appellant Marshall only had $15 when he commenced the trip and upon arrival in Vancouver on Friday, February 2, he slept the first night in the car, but subsequently he slept in a suite of a friend of Cameron. Very early Monday morning, February 5, the four who were jointly charged and Wes. Cameron started driving back to Calgary. Shortly after leaving Vancouver the appellant discovered that there was *cannabis* (marijuana) in the car. On the trip marijuana was smoked in the car but not by Marshall.

At Golden, B.C., which is better than halfway on the Trans-Canada Highway to Calgary from Vancouver, while doing 95 m.p.h., the car was stopped by the R.C.M.P. The driver at the time was Cameron. As the highway does not go directly through Golden the police required the car to follow them into Golden. The marijuana was thrown out of the car, but not by the appellant. At Golden as Cameron did not have an identification or a driver's licence he was detained by the police but the other boys were allowed to proceed. Jones, the owner of the car, then drove it. They returned to where they had thrown out the marijuana and it was picked up by one of the boys but not the appellant. They then proceeded on to Calgary, picking up a hitchhiker east of Banff. On the outskirts of Calgary the boys were again stopped by the R.C.M.P. as they only had one light burning. This was in the evening of Monday, February 5. The appellant was sitting in the left rear seat of the car. The R.C.M.P. searched the car and found the marijuana, which was a kilogram or 2.2 lbs. It was on the floor of the rear seat on the right-hand side partially covered by a sweater which belonged to Wes. Cameron. Also in the sleeve of the sweater was found a bag containing additional marijuana.

The police also found a hookah pipe, which is a pipe used for smoking marijuana, the bowl of which was found in the glove compartment and the stem in the pocket of the sweater. With the exception of the hitchhiker all of the boys in the car were arrested and charged as aforesaid. The appellant, Marshall, gave evidence in his defence, and stated that he did not know the marijuana was in the car until they were about 30 miles out of Vancouver on their way home. When asked why he did not leave the car when he found out about the marijuana he said he had no money and he was just getting a ride back to Calgary as he had to get back to classes. He further testified that it was Cameron's marijuana, that he said he did not want to pick up the marijuana after it had been thrown out of the car at Golden, and that when asked by the police about the marijuana he said that whosoever it was would take him off the hook at the trial. When asked why he said that he answered, "Oh I didn't want to, I didn't actually want to tell, say whose it was at the time, what you say squeal on him."

Nowhere does the trial Judge throw any doubt on the credibility of the testimony given by Marshall and he did say that he believed that he (Marshall) "did not do anything to exercise control or take control of the marihuana." Such being the case I have accepted the evidence of Marshall even where there is conflict between it and the evidence of others.

Marshall was convicted along with the others by the learned trial Judge who stated:

> In the case of Marshall his role at this time was perhaps less of a participant in the sense that he did not drive the car, but certainly at that point he had an opportunity of leaving the car. He may or may not have had an opportunity before reaching Golden. I make no finding on that question but at Golden it is very clear that he had the opportunity of leaving the car, requesting the assistance of the police to get back to Calgary or simply leaving the car and hitch hiking himself if there were no other means.

> . . . .

> Although I believe the evidence of Marshall that he did not do anything to exercise control or take control of the marihuana, yet having ridden in the car as long as he did ride in the car, not having indicated in his evidence any protest or any act on his part separating himself from the actions of the others or from their company, and considering the length of time that transpired, which I think is quite a material consideration, I find that he acquiesced in what the others did, and I also find that in the meaning of the *Narcotic Control Act* and the *Criminal Code*, he was in possession.

The crown relies upon s. 3(4)(*b*) of the *Criminal Code*, 1953-54, ch. 51, to support the conviction of the appellant, Marshall, The *Narcotic Control Act*, 1960-61, ch. 35, provides that possession means possession as defined in the *Criminal Code*. Section 3(4)(*b*) of the *Criminal Code* provides:

> (4) For the purposes of this Act,

> . . . .

> (b) where one of two or more persons, with the knowledge and consent of the rest, has anything in his custody, it shall be deemed to be in the custody and possession of each and all of them.

There is no doubt that Marshall had knowledge of the marijuana being in the car so the question is did he consent to it being there.

The *Shorter Oxford Dictionary* defines "consent" as: "1. Voluntary agreement to or acquiescence in what another proposes or desires; compliance, concurrence, permission."

The meaning of s. 5(2) in the previous *Code*, which is in substantially the same terms as s. 3(4)(*b*) in the present *Code*, has been dealt with by the British Columbia and the Ontario Courts of Appeal in several cases.

. . . .

It was much pressed on us by counsel for the defence that there must be an element of control in order for there to be possession, and the statement of Cartwright J. (now C.J.) was quoted in *Beaver v. Reg.*, [1957] S.C.R. 531, at 541, 26 C.R. 193, 118 C.C.C. 129, reversing (1956), 25 C.R. 53, 116 C.C.C. 231:

In my view the law is correctly stated in the following passage in the judgment of O'Halloran J.A., with whom Robertson J.A. concurred, in *Rex. v. Hess* (1949), 8 C.R. 42, 94 C.C.C. 48, at 50-1 (B.C.):

"To constitute 'possession' within the meaning of the criminal law it is my judgment that where, as here, there is manual handling of a thing, it must be co-existent with knowledge of what the thing is, and both these elements must be co-existent with some act of control (outside public duty). When those three elements exist together, I think it must be conceded that under s. 4(1)(*d*) it does not then matter if the thing is retained for an innocent purpose."

However, in that case s. 5(2) was not being considered. The reference was to manual possession.

I find it unnecessary to decide in this case whether there must be some measure of control in order to find the "knowledge and consent" required by s. 3(4)(*b*) of the *Code*. In my opinion, although Marshall certainly had knowledge of the presence of the marijuana he had no control, right to control, nor did he consent to its presence.

The choice facing Marshall was to leave the car at Golden and run the risk of obtaining a ride to Calgary in time to attend his classes, or to stay with the car containing the marijuana. There can be no doubt that he would have been much wiser to have left the car and hitch-hiked to Calgary no matter how long it took him. But to say that a 16-year-old boy faced with this alternative, by choosing to continue his trip to Calgary has consented or agreed or acquiesced to the presence of marijuana in the car is not maintainable. It was certainly an error of judgment on his part to run the risk of being charged with possession of marijuana by being found as an occupant of the car. The trial Judge might not have believed his story but once it was believed his decision to continue the journey was consent to riding in the car, but such consent does not mean he consented to the marijuana being in the car. He said he objected to it being picked up again after it was thrown out at Golden. He did nothing to impede the police, although he did not volunteer any assistance to them.

Crown counsel argued that at the time it was stated to the police that Boltwood the hitchhiker had nothing to do with the marijuana that Marshall at that time should also have said he had nothing to do with it. This is, of course, a matter the trial Judge could take into consideration in deciding whether to believe Marshall or not. Marshall had no obligation to make a statement. His conduct in the whole matter was not only childish but silly but this does not make him guilty of the offence.

. . . .

In the circumstances of this case the appellant, Marshall, had no power to control the persons possessing the marijuana. He was not the owner of the car. In my opinion, he could not be found guilty of aiding and abetting.

I have been concerned as to the fact that although Marshall stated he did not smoke the marijuana when the pipe was passed to him, he did pass it on. This I think comes very close to a consent, but it could be due almost as a reflex action just as a lighted squib was passed on in the squib case, and in all of the circumstances I do not think constituted consent.

In my opinion, the learned trial Judge was in error in drawing the inferences from the facts which he found and he should not have inferred the appellant, Marshall, consented to the others having possession of the drug. Accordingly I would allow the appeal and quash the conviction.

R. v. TERRENCE

33 C.R. (3d) 193, [1983] 1 S.C.R. 357, 4 C.C.C. (3d) 193

RITCHIE J.: — This is an appeal brought with leave of this Court at the instance of the Attorney-General of Ontario, pursuant to s. 621(1)(b) of the Criminal Code, from a judgment of the Court of Appeal for Ontario whereby that Court allowed the appeal and quashed the conviction of the accused entered at trial before Judge P.H. Megginson in the Ontario Provincial Court (Criminal Division) for the County of Frontenac, Ontario, on a charge that he:

> . . . on or about the 30th day of January, 1980 at the Township of Kingston and elsewhere in the County of Frontenac, unlawfully did have in his possession one 1980 Chevrolet automobile, of a value exceeding $200.00, the property of Trudeau Motors, Belleville, Ontario which had been theretofore obtained by a person unknown by an offence committed in Canada punishable on indictment, to wit: theft, the said Kelly Brett Terrence, then knowing the said automobile to have been obtained and did thereby commit an indictable offence, contrary to s. 313(a) of the Criminal Code of Canada.

The important question raised by this appeal relates to the true meaning to be attached to the word "possession" as the same occurs in the context of s. 3(4)(b) of the Criminal Code and more particularly whether "possession" as there employed imports control as an essential element. Section 3(4)(b) reads as follows:

> 3(4) For the purposes of this Act

> . . . .

> (b) where one of two or more persons, with the knowledge and consent of the rest, has anything in his custody or possession, it shall be deemed to be in the custody and possession of each and all of them.

The only evidence in the record of this appeal which is in any way descriptive of the manner in which the respondent first became aware of the existence of the automobile in question is the evidence of the respondent himself which is, in my view, accurately summarized in the judgment of Mr. Justice MacKinnon at p. 64 of the case on appeal herein as follows [55 C.C.C. (2d) 183 at pp. 184-5, 17 C.R. (3d) 390]:

> The 17-year-old appellant testified at his trial. His evidence was that Bill Rorback, Rorback's brother and one Rick Hayes lives across the street from him in Belleville. He often went across to visit after dinner and he had done so on the evening of January 29, 1980. When he arrived Rick Hayes was not present and the appellant and the two Rorbacks watched

television. At about midnight Hayes drove up to the front of the house in a new Camaro automobile and asked if anybody wanted to go for a ride in his "brother-in-law's new car". The appellant said "sure" and went with Hayes.

According to the appellant's evidence, Hayes and the appellant drove around town for three quarters of an hour or so and then started east along Highway 401 towards Kingston. It was established that the Camaro had in fact been recently stolen and the licence plates it carried had recently been stolen from another Camaro in Belleville. The appellant knew that Hayes did not own his own motor vehicle but Hayes had, on previous occasions, borrowed his brother-in-law's car which the appellant described as "an old junker". He thought that it was probably time for Hayes' brother-in-law to acquire a new car and as Hayes had the keys to the car, he had no suspicion at the time that the car was stolen.

Hayes turned onto Highway 2 around Napanee and shortly thereafter an O.P.P. cruiser gave chase. Constable Mallock testified that the stolen vehicle, on being pursued, increased its speed to 150 km/h, although the appellant's evidence was that the vehicle did not speed up but rather continued at a constant pace. The car was finally stopped by an O.P.P. roadblock some time shortly after 2:30 a.m. The Camaro pulled over to the shoulder and was apparently slowing down to a stop when the appellant jumped from the moving vehicle, rolled onto the shoulder and ran into the adjoining field. The Camaro collided with a cruiser and then came to a stop . . .

As I have indicated, this was the account given by the respondent and it remains uncontradicted by any direct evidence; it accordingly appears to me that the only basis for doubting the accuracy of this account was the repeated assertion by the trial Judge that he "utterly" disbelieved it.

There is no doubt about the fact that the vehicle had been stolen from a garage in Belleville and, indeed, there was evidence to the effect that the theft occurred on the very night when the respondent accepted the invitation from Hayes to go for a ride "in his brother-in-law's car". It was this latter circumstance which permitted the trial Judge to say, ". . . this car was as hot as a car could be, having been taken by someone during the same night . . .".

There was, as I have said, no direct evidence to contradict the respondent's version of what occurred, but it is evident from his somewhat acid comments that the Judge's finding of "possession" is in great measure based on his disbelief of the respondent and it is apparent that the Judge proceeded on the assumption that the respondent's knowledge of the stolen character of the vehicle was a proven fact.

Based on the assumption that the respondent knew the car to be stolen property, the trial Judge went on to find that:

Even if the accused was not the operator of the vehicle and in that sense had the control of it, if the person who had control of the vehicle had it with his knowledge and consent and he is in the vehicle as well, in my view, that is sufficient to found the necessary conditions to constitute constructive possession under s. 3(4)(b) of the *Criminal Code* as defined.

In the course of his reasons for judgment rendered on behalf of the Court of Appeal, Mr. Justice MacKinnon reviewed the relevant cases concerning the ingredients of possession under s. 3(4)(b) of the *Criminal Code* and concluded that in order to establish "possession" under that section it was necessary that there should be evidence of control on the part of the accused. In the course of these reasons he said [p. 399]:

In my view, on the proven facts the necessary measure of control was not established beyond a reasonable doubt by the Crown, nor do those facts allow for the invocation of s. 21. If, by way of example only, it were established that the appellant had directed Hayes to drive to Kingston, that, in light of all the other proven facts, would, in my view, satisfy the requirement of some measure of control over the car. If, by way of further example, he had been seen handing the stolen licence plates to Hayes for them to be placed on the motor vehicle, that, once again in my view, would be sufficient to warrant the application of s. 21 and to establish constructive possession of the car by the appellant.

Section 21 of the *Criminal Code* defines the meaning of "parties" to an offence and involves the question of common intention. It will be remembered that in the present case there is no suggestion that the respondent participated in any way in the actual theft of the car by an unknown person, which took place some time before he was invited to drive in it, and there is nothing to support a finding of common intention in relation to the offence of "possession" with which the respondent is here charged.

The Court of Appeal had reference to the case of *R. v. Lou Hay Hung* (1946), 85 C.C.C. 308, which was a decision of its own court concerned with a charge under the *Opium and Narcotic Drug Act*, 1929 (Can.), c. 49, and in which Mr. Justice Roach in the course of his reasons for judgment, referred to and quoted s. 5(2) of the *Criminal Code*, the predecessor of s. 3(4)(*b*), in the following terms at p. 321 C.C.C.:

> Under s. 5(2), both "knowledge" and "consent" are necessary. I have already stated that, in my opinion, there is no doubt that the appellant knew that the accused Watson had opium in the premises. I have been more than a little concerned with the question whether or not, on the evidence, it should be held that he also consented.

In the same set of reasons, Mr. Justice Roach referred to the judgment of O'Halloran J.A. in *R. v. Colvin and Gladue* (1942), 78 C.C.C. 282 at p. 287, where he said: [at p. 322 C.C.C.]:

> " 'Knowledge and consent' which is an integral element of joint possession in s. 5(2) must be related to and read with the definition of 'possession' in the previous s. 5(1)(*b*). It follows that 'knowledge and consent' cannot exist without the co-existence of some measure of control over the subject-matter. If there is the power to consent there is equally the power to refuse and vice versa. They each signify the existence of some power or authority which is here called control, without which the need for their exercise could not arise or be invoked."

In the course of the reasons for judgment rendered by Mr. Justice MacKinnon on behalf of the Court of Appeal in the present case, he had occasion to say of the above passage from Mr. Justice O'Halloran's judgment [at pp. 188-9]:

> The judgment of O'Halloran J.A. in *R. v. Colvin and Gladue* (1942), 78 C.C.C. 282, the relevant passage of which for our purposes being the one quoted by Roach J.A., *supra*, to the effect that "knowledge and consent cannot exist without the co-existence of some measure of control over the subject-matter", has been followed by British Columbia Courts in subsequent decisions: *R. v. Sherman* (1929), 1 C.R. 153; *R. v. Bunyon* (1954), 110 C.C.C. 119; *R. v. Dick and Malley* (1969), 7 C.R.N.S. 75; *R. v. Baker* — May 21, 1976 (B.C. C.A.) (unreported as yet) [reported [1976] W.W.D. 132].

The Courts in Quebec have adopted the same reasoning as will be seen by reference to *R. v. Sigouin et al.* (1964) 43 C.R. 211, and *R. v. Fournier* (1979), 43 C.C.C. (2d) 468.

As I have indicated, I agree with the Court of Appeal that a constituent and essential element of possession under s. 3(4)(*b*) of the *Criminal Code* is a measure of control on the part of the person deemed to be in possession by that provision of the *Criminal Code* and, accordingly, I do not consider that the Court of Appeal for the Province of Ontario erred in this regard.

. . . .

Appeal dismissed.

RE CHAMBERS AND THE QUEEN

(1985), 20 C.C.C. (3d) 440 (Ont. C.A.)

MARTIN J.A. : — The respondent, Sandra Chambers, was jointly charged with Rafael Cardenas on count 1 in an information alleging that on February 24, 1984, they unlawfully had in their possession a narcotic, to wit, cocaine, for the purpose of trafficking. The respondent, following a preliminary hearing, was committed for trial on that charge. On October 9, 1984, Mr. Justice Gray quashed the respondent's committal for trial on the ground that there was no evidence that the applicant, Sandra Chambers, was in possession of the cocaine which was the subject of the charge, and that there was no evidence that she aided or abetted the possession of the cocaine by her co-accused, Rafael Cardenas.

. . . .

The Attorney-General of Canada now appeals pursuant to s. 719 of the *Criminal Code* from the order of Gray J., quashing the respondent's committal for trial.

I

The evidence

The Crown adduced the following evidence at the preliminary hearing. On Friday, February 24, 1984, at 7:15 p.m., Constable Ralph Brookes, assisted by other officers from Number 5 District Drug Squad, executed a warrant to search "the dwelling house of Ralph Cardines [*sic*] and person(s) unknown at 106 Rhodes Avenue, Toronto" for the narcotic cocaine. The execution of the warrant was preceded by observation of the premises for about 25 minutes during which the respondent was seen in an upstairs bedroom and, for part of that time, was seen near a shelf or wall unit.

The respondent opened the door in response to the officer's knock. She was shown the warrant which she appeared to read. Two of the officers, Valentine and Wretham, went upstairs and searched the front bedroom which faces on Rhodes Ave. The bedroom contained a double bed and a dresser. Constable Valentine found a plastic bag containing 104 grams of cocaine of 95% purity on the top shelf of an open closet, at the north end of the bedroom. The closet contained mostly women's clothing and the plastic bag containing the cocaine was underneath some women's sweaters. A number of photographs of the respondent, showing her modelling women's clothing, were also found underneath the sweaters. The dresser contained women's clothing and on the top of the dresser were lipstick, nail polish and other things of that kind. Constable Wretham also found on top of the dresser a drug debt list or a drug price list and an empty "deck", that is, a folded paper used for carrying drugs, such as cocaine. Men's clothing was scattered at the foot of the bed, and a rack hanger at the south end of the bedroom held men's clothing. The respondent's purse containing identification papers was found at the foot of the bed.

Constable Brookes, in the mean time, had a conversation in the living-room with the respondent. Defence counsel conceded for the purpose of the preliminary hearing that all statements made by the respondent to the police were voluntary, Constable Brookes asked the respondent who else lived on the premises and she replied, "Just my roommate". He then asked her who the person named in the warrant was and she said that he was her boy-friend. In response to further questions, the respondent said that her boy-friend came from Detroit and was visiting her, but he had not arrived home yet. She said that he had been there for a week, that he was staying with her and that he stored his clothes in her bedroom. Constable Brookes asked the respondent where her boyfriend slept, and she replied, "In my bedroom". Constable Brookes heard a soft knocking on the door, and the respondent indicated that it should be her boyfriend. Constable Brookes went to the door and brought Cardenas into the house. Constable Brookes advised him of the search warrant and when Constable Brookes asked him if he had any drugs on him, he replied, "Just this" and pulled some marijuana out of his pocket. He was then arrested and cautioned on a charge of possession of marijuana. Cardenas said he had been on the premises a day and a half. Cardenas then said that he felt ill and was taken to the wash-room, but he did not appear to be ill and he was taken from the washroom to the kitchen where the respondent was seated. From the top of the refrigerator Constable Brookes seized a set of scales described as standard drug scales, capable of weighing as little as two grams.

After finding the cocaine in the bedroom closet, Constables Valentine and Wretham went downstairs where they found the respondent and Cardenas seated in the kitchen. Constable Valentine asked the following questions: "Where do you two sleep?" The respondent replied, "In the front bedroom" and Cardenas replied, "I stay with her when I visit". Constable Valentine then showed the respondent and Cardenas the plastic baggie containing cocaine found in the closet and asked, "What is this?", but neither the respondent nor Cardenas made any reply. They likewise made no response when Constable Valentine asked them who owned it.

Constable Wretham conducted a further search of the front bedroom, and found at the south end of the bedroom a gym bag containing men's clothing. He found in the gym bag a "deck" with the writing "1/2" on it containing a small quantity of cocaine. Cardenas admitted that the gym bag belonged to him.

II

Whether there was any evidence upon which to commit the respondent for trial

Mr. Justice Gray, in quashing the respondent's committal for trial, held that the occupancy of the room by the respondent was not *per se* evidence of possession. He also held that even if there was some slight evidence that the respondent knew of the presence of the cocaine, the necessary measure of control over the drug was lacking. There was, in our view, some evidence from which it could be inferred that the respondent knew that the cocaine was in her room and, indeed, this was conceded by the respondent's experienced and able counsel before the Provincial Court Judge and before us.

It is well-established that on a motion to quash a committal for trial the reviewing Court is not empowered to determine whether in its opinion there is any evidence upon which a properly instructed jury could convict, but is confined to considering whether there is any evidence before the committing justice upon which acting judicially he could form an opinion that the evidence is sufficient to put the accused on trial: see *Re Martin, Simard and Desjardins and The Queen* (1977), 41 C.C.C. (2d) 308 at p. 340; *R. v. Kendall* (1984), 3 O.A.C. 294.

Mr. Justice Gray enunciated the correct test, but, with the greatest deference, we have reached a different conclusion from that which he reached. Section 3(4)(*b*) of the *Criminal Code* reads:

> 3(4) For the purposes of this Act,
>
> . . . .
>
> (*b*) where one of two or more persons, with the knowledge and consent of the rest, has anything in his custody or possession, it shall be deemed to be in the custody and possession of each and all of them.

The law is now settled that "consent" within s. 3(4)(*b*) of the *Code* requires a measure of control over the subject-matter: see *R. v. Terrence* (1983), 4 C.C.C. (3d) 193, [1983] 1 S.C.R. 357 (S.C.C.); affirming 55 C.C.C. (2d) 183, 17 C.R. (3d) 390 (Ont. C.A.).

There was evidence that the room in which the drug was found was the respondent's room and, consequently, she could give or withhold her consent to the drug being in her room. Mr. Code contended, however, that the respondent's control over the room where the cocaine was found cannot be equated with a measure of control over the drug itself which he said imports the right to the benefit of the drug or its proceeds. We disagree. In our view, the respondent's right to grant or withhold her consent to the drug being stored in her room gave her the necessary measure of control over the drug essential to constitute "consent" within s. 3(4)(b) of the *Code*. Mr. Code's argument, if pressed to its logical conclusion, leads to the startling result that a warehouseman who knowingly stores on his premises drugs for drug traffickers is not in possession of the drugs in his warehouse, since he has no right to the benefit of the drugs themselves.

The foundation of the modern law that "consent" under s. 3(4)(b) of the *Code* requires a measure of control over the subject-matter is the judgment of O'Halloran J.A., of the British Columbia Court of Appeal, in *R. v. Colvin and Gladue* (1942), 78 C.C.C. 282 (B.C. C.A.).

It is helpful to examine the circumstances which gave rise to the much-quoted judgment of Mr. Justice O'Halloran. In *R. v. Colvin and Gladue*, *supra*, the Crown appealed against the respondents' acquittal on a charge of unlawful possession of a drug, morphine. One Harmann Singh was the tenant of a room in which he had morphine and the respondents were visiting Singh in his room. The magistrate found that the respondents had knowledge of Singh's possession of the morphine, but was of the opinion that that evidence did not establish "consent" within then s. 5(2) of the *Code* (the predecessor of present s. 3(4)(b) of the *Code*) in the absence of evidence of control.

The British Columbia Court of Appeal, by a majority of three judges to two, dismissed the Crown's appeal from the acquittal. Mr. Justice O'Halloran stated that if consorting with one who is in physical possession of a drug, or who has it in his control or has the right to its custody is to be regarded by itself as "knowledge and consent" sufficient to constitute joint possession, then one would expect unequivocal authority for it in the *Opium and Narcotic Drug Act* (the predecessor of the *Narcotic Control Act*). Mr. Justice O'Halloran then went on to say at p. 287:

> The "knowledge and consent" which is an integral element of joint possession in s. 5(2) must be related to and read with the definition of "possession" in the previous s. 5(1)(b). It follows that "knowledge and consent" cannot exist without the co-existence of some measure of control over the subject-matter. *If there is the power to consent there is equally the power to refuse and vice versa. They each signify the existence of some power or authority which is here called control, without which the need for their exercise could not arise or be invoked. The principle of "sufficient reason" applies. For example it would be an irrational act for A to attempt to consent to or refuse B the use of C's motorcar unless A has some measure of control over it.*

(Emphasis added.)

This passage in the judgment of Mr. Justice O'Halloran was quoted by Mr. Justice Roach in *R. v. Lou Hay Hung* (1946), 85 C.C.C. 308 at p. 322 (Ont. C.A.), which in turn was quoted with approval by Mr. Justice Ritchie, speaking for the Supreme Court of Canada, in *R. v. Terrence*, *supra*, at p. 198. The respondents in *R. v. Colvin and Gladue*, *supra*, being mere visitors, had no power to withhold their consent to Harmann Singh, the tenant, having the morphine in his possession. The mere consorting with Singh knowing that he had possession of morphine did not constitute "consent" within s. 5(2) of the

Code. In contrast, the respondent in the present case had the power to either consent or withhold her consent to her room being used to store cocaine.

In holding that the respondent's occupancy of the room did not constitute any evidence that the respondent was in possession of the cocaine found therein, Mr. Justice Gray placed considerable emphasis on the fact that s. 17 of the *Opium and Narcotic Drug Act*, R.S.C. 1952, c. 201 (as amended by 1953-54, c. 38, s. 8), is not found in the *Narcotic Control Act*, R.S.C. 1970, c. N-1. Section 17(1) read:

> 17(1) Without limiting the generality of subsection (1) or paragraph (*b*) of subsection (3) of section 4, any person who occupies, controls, or is in possession of any building, room, vessel, vehicle, enclosure or place in or upon which any drug is found shall be deemed to be in possession thereof unless he proves that the drug was there without his authority, knowledge or consent.

Section 17 was held to be inapplicable where the accused has no control over that part of the premises where the drugs were found: *R. v. Lou Hay Hung, supra.* Where s. 17 was applicable the accused was deemed to be in possession of a drug found in premises over which he had the necessary control unless he or she proved on a balance of probabilities that the drug was there without his or her authority, knowledge or consent. The fact that this provision was not introduced into the present Act has the effect only of requiring the prosecution on a charge of unlawful possession to prove in the ordinary way without the aid of a deeming provision that the accused was in possession of the drug even though the drug is found in premises subject to his control. The failure of Parliament to enact in the present Act a provision similar to s. 17 does not, however, preclude a Court from drawing appropriate inferences from evidence that a prohibited drug is found in a room under the control of an accused where there is also evidence from which an inference may properly be drawn that the accused was aware of the presence of the drug.

Mr. Code contended that the Provincial Court Judge committed the respondent for trial on the basis that she was a party to Cardenas' possession under s. 21 of the *Code.* He strongly argued that the respondent's mere omission to remove the drugs did not provide a basis for liability under s. 21. He said that it would be absurd to hold that a household, because he failed to eject a guest who was smoking a marijuana cigarette was a party under s. 21 of the *Code* to the guest's possession of marijuana. Be that as it may, those are not the facts of the present case. It is not entirely clear that the Provincial Court Judge committed the respondent for trial on the basis that by allowing Cardenas to store the cocaine for his own purposes, there was evidence of her being a party under s. 21 to Cardenas' possession, rather than on the basis that permitting Cardenas to use her room to store the cocaine was evidence of "consent" within s. 3(4)(*b*).

Crown counsel submitted before the Provincial Court Judge that the test was whether the respondent had authority real or potential over the drug, that the respondent had authority to remove the drugs and she chose to leave them in her room which constituted a measure of control over the drug. The Provincial Court Judge said:

I agree with what you say. The reason succinctly on that basis and the fact that she allowed this man to have the drugs in her place and keep them there for his purposes. That was her control and assisting him in the control. That's where it comes in. She doesn't have to take the stuff herself.

MR. CODE: I quite agree, but she's got to do something. You can't commit her for trial on the basis of an omission. There's got to be some positive act.

THE COURT: The positive act is allowing him to keep those drugs in her room for the purpose of selling them, or whatever he was going to do with them.

Anyway, it's going to be left to a jury on that basis.

There is sufficient evidence that a jury properly instructed could bring in a verdict of guilt.

One reading of the Judge's reasons for committing the respondent for trial is that he found the necessary measure of control in the respondent permitting Cardenas to store the cocaine in her room. In my view, there was some evidence upon which the Provincial Court Judge could commit the respondent for trial either on the basis that there was evidence that she had the necessary measure of control over the cocaine or that there was evidence upon which a jury properly instructed could find that she was a party under s. 21 of the *Code*. I think I should add that the appeal was argued on the basis that the cocaine belonged to Cardenas and that the respondent had no interest in the drug or its proceeds. Although it appears likely that the drug belonged to Cardenas, I do not think it can be assumed on this record that the respondent had no interest in the drug. However, even if it be assumed that the cocaine belonged to Cardenas, there was, as I have previously stated, some evidence upon which a reasonable jury properly instructed could find that the respondent had possession of the drug under s. 3(4)(*b*) of the *Code* or was a party under s. 21 to Cardenas' possession by allowing him to store the cocaine in her room.

It is scarcely necessary to add that the Provincial Court Judge was not trying the respondent and determining her guilt. That, of course, was not his function. He decided only that there was some evidence upon which a properly instructed jury *could* convict. A jury might, of course, entertain a reasonable doubt as to the respondent's guilt, and, indeed, additional facts might cast a different light on the case.

. . . .

Accordingly, I would allow the appeal, set aside the order of Gray J. quashing the respondent's committal for trial and restore the committal for trial.

Appeal allowed.

The ruling in *Chambers* was distinguished on the facts in *Escoffery* (1996), 47 C.R. (4th) 40 (Ont. C.A.), on the issue of knowledge. Unlike *Chambers* this was a trial requiring proof beyond reasonable doubt. No witnesses had testified that the accused knew about the crack cocaine hidden in his girlfriend's apartment. Knowledge would have to be inferred from his regular occupancy of her apartment, usually at weekends. However, the apartment was rented by his girlfriend, a co-accused, and others frequented the apartment. The trial judge had accepted that his scales found in the apartment were to weigh ingredients in the restaurant where he worked. The finding of proof of possession was unreasonable. The accused was acquitted.

In *Chambers*, the Court recognized the possibility of liability under s. 21 for aiding and abetting a principal offender: see below, Chapter 10, Parties to an Offence. This further widens the net of constructive possession. In *Williams* (1998), 17 C.R. (5th) 75, 125 C.C.C. (3d) 552 (Ont. C.A.), the Ontario Court of Appeal, however, held that a trial judge should have instructed the jury that mere passive acquiescence on the part of a passenger in a vehicle being used to transport drugs cannot, without more, support a conviction for importing. A new trial was ordered. The constructive possession provision in s. 4(3)(*b*) could be challenged under s. 7 of the *Charter* on the alternative grounds of violations of the requirements of a meaningful act, see *Burt*, below, or overbreadth, see *Heywood*, above.

A powerful new constitutional standard may have emerged in recent unsuccessful general challenges to marihuana possession laws before the B.C. Court of Appeal in *Malmo-Levine* (2000), 34 C.R. (5th) 91, 145 C.C.C. (3d) 225 (B.C. C.A.) and the Ontario Court of Appeal in *Clay* (2000), 37 C.R. (5th) 170, 146 C.C.C. (3d) 276 (Ont. C.A.). In *Malmo-Levine*, Justice Braidwood for the majority, Rowles J.A. concurring, accepted, after a detailed analysis of the common law, Law Reform Commission recommendations and federalism and *Charter* cases, that principles of fundamental justice under s. 7 include a harm principle:

> It is a legal principle and it is concise. Moreover, there is a consensus among reasonable people that it is vital to our system of justice. Indeed, I think that it is common sense that you don't go to jail unless there is a potential that your activities will cause harm to others. (C.R., para. 134)

The test is

> whether the prohibited activities hold a "reasoned apprehension of harm" to other individuals or society. . . . The degree of harm must be neither insignificant nor trivial. (C.R., para. 138)

The majority found that the prohibition against marihuana did not offend this harm test as there was some harm involved. Any change in the law should be left for Parliament.

In dissent Prowse J.A. preferred a higher threshold test of reasonable apprehension of harm that was of a "serious, substantial or significant nature", (C.R., para. 171), relying on *Butler*, [1992] 1 S.C.R. 452, 11 C.R. (4th) 137, 70 C.C.C. (3d) 129 (S.C.C.), reconsideration refused [1993] 2 W.W.R. lxi (S.C.C.). Marihuana possession laws did not meet this standard.

In *Clay*, Justice Rosenberg for the Ontario Court of Appeal reached the same conclusion as the majority in *Malmo-Levine*. For the purposes of the decision, the Court accepted the majority view as to the harm principle. It dismissed the Prowse approach as one that could lead to an unjustifiable intrusion into the legislative sphere (C.R., paras. 26-28). Referring to Sopinka J.'s opinion in *Rodriguez*, Rosenberg J.A. expressed doubts about the harm principle as a constitutional standard:

> While it is a good basis for legislative policy, a helpful guide for the exercise of discretion by prosecutions and an important principle for judges in exercising discretion in sentencing, it is a difficult principle to translate into a means of measuring the constitutionality of legislation. For

example, how much harm is sufficient to warrant legislative action? And, can the harm principle be applied outside the *mens rea* area in a manner that yields an understandable result? (C.R., para. 25)

In a companion case of *Parker*, Justice Rosenberg for the same Court declared the law inoperative in not providing a medical exemption. The harm principle awaits the imprimatur of the Supreme Court. If accepted, it would introduce a new vehicle for restraint and give teeth to years of rhetoric about the need to use the criminal sanction with caution. The Braidwood test appears as workable as presently accepted *Charter* grounds of challenge under principles of vagueness and overbreadth. Indeed it may be easier to apply. The resolution of the harm principle issue will provide a good barometer of how activist the present Supreme Court chooses to be. **Do you think the Court should be activist in this respect?**

———————————

A consent will often negate the *actus reus*. Whether the consent was genuine was at issue in the following controversial case.

R. v. JOBIDON

[1991] 2 S.C.R. 714, 7 C.R. (4th) 233, 66 C.C.C. (3d) 454

The accused was tried by Judge alone on a charge of manslaughter. A fight had begun in a bar. It was stopped by the bar's owner and the two men agreed it was not over. Outside, the accused struck the victim with his fist. The victim was knocked backwards onto the hood of a car. The trial Judge found that the victim had been rendered unconscious by this punch. In a brief flurry lasting no more than a few seconds, the accused struck the unconscious victim a further four to six times on the head. There was one single continuing exchange until the victim rolled off the hood and lay limp. He later died of contusions to the head. The trial Judge found as a fact that the accused and the victim had consented to a fair fist fight, and that physical injury was intended. He also found that there was no intent to kill or cause serious bodily harm. He further found that the accused did not intentionally exceed the consent that was given and that he struck the last blows under a reasonable but mistaken apprehension that the victim was still capable of returning the fight and was trying to do so. The victim had died of severe contusions to the head. The cause of death was one or more of the punches thrown by the accused in the parking lot. The trial judge acquitted. He decided that there was no unlawful act which could form the basis for a manslaughter conviction. The connection between the two offences of assault and manslaughter is found in s. 222 of the *Code*. The section provides that culpable homicide is either murder or manslaughter and that a person commits culpable homicide when he causes the death of a human being by means of an unlawful act. Since there was a consent to a fair fist fight there was no assault within the meaning of s. 265 of the *Criminal Code* and therefore no unlawful act. The Crown's appeal to the Ontario Court of Appeal was allowed and a conviction of manslaughter substituted. That Court decided that the word "consent" in s. 265 of the *Criminal Code*, defining the crime of assault, should be construed subject to common law limits under which consent to a fight in private or public is not a defence to a charge of assault if actual bodily harm is intended and/or caused. The accused appealed. The Supreme Court dismissed the appeal.

GONTHIER J. (LA FOREST, L'HEUREUX-DUBÉ, CORY and IACOBUCCI JJ. concurring): —

. . . .

There is one principal issue raised in this appeal. The principal issue is whether absence of consent is a material element which must be proved by the Crown in all cases of assault or whether there are common law limitations which restrict or negate the legal effectiveness of consent in certain types of cases.

. . . .

Section 265(1)(*a*) states that an assault occurs when, "without the consent of another person, he applies force intentionally to that other person, directly or indirectly". . . . In the appellant's opinion, the trial Judge's finding of consent meant that all the elements of the offence of assault had not been proved. The appellant should therefore have been acquitted on that basis, since the Legislature intended that consent should serve as a bar to conviction.

According to the appellant, the Legislature could have specified that in certain situations, or in respect of certain forms of conduct, absence of consent would not be an operative element of the offence. It has done so with other offences. Parliament has provided that no person is entitled to consent to have death inflicted on him (s. 14). It restricted the concept in ss. 150.1 and 159 of the *Code* by denying defences to sexual offences based on a child's consent. It also did this in s. 286 by negating the validity of a young person's consent to abduction. But with the assault provisions in s. 265, it chose not to insert policy-based limitations on the role of consent.

. . . .

The appellant further observed that, in England, the crime of assault is not defined in a *Criminal Code* but in the common law, to which common law limitations and exceptions more naturally apply. In Canada, we have a code of general principles by which, it is presumed, ambiguity is to be construed in favour of the liberty of the subject.

. . . .

There is no indication in s. 265 that the jurisprudence of the criminal common law was to be undermined by its enactment. There was no hint that traditional policy limits on consent, described below in greater detail, were to be ousted by s. 258 of the first *Criminal Code* of 1892, nor by enactment of its successor provision in s. 244 (now s. 265). This should not be surprising. As the foregoing sketch of the history of the offence demonstrates, far from intending to curtail the authority of that law, the *Code* was a partial expression of it.

All criminal offences in Canada are now defined in the *Code* (s. 9). But that does not mean the common law no longer illuminates these definitions nor gives content to the various principles of criminal responsibility those definitions draw from. As the Law Reform Commission of Canada has noted in its 31st report on recodification, the basic premises of our criminal law—the necessary conditions for criminal liability —are at present left to the common law (*Recodifying Criminal Law*, op. cit., at pp. 17, 28 and 34. Reference may also be made to Eric Colvin, *Principles of Criminal Law* (Toronto: Carswell, 1986), at pp. 16-17). The *Code* itself, in s. 8, explicitly acknowledges the ongoing common law influence.

. . . .

Section 8 expressly indicates that the common law rules and principles continue to apply, but only to the extent that they are not inconsistent with the *Code* or other Act of Parliament and have not been altered by them. While little judicial analysis of this section of the *Code* has been undertaken, the references made to it have predominantly concerned exceptional circumstances which provide defences or which deny certain features of an offence. (See Colvin, op. cit., at pp. 16-17.) This Court's leading interpretation of s. 8(3) is found in *R. v. Kirzner*, [1978] 2 S.C.R. 487, 1 C.R. (3d) 138, 38 C.C.C. (2d) 131. Chief Justice Laskin expressly rejected a static view of the common law under s. 8(3) (formerly s. 7(3)). Though speaking in the context of alleged prosecutorial impropriety, and a claimed defence of entrapment, Laskin C.J.C. offered an expansive, developmental view, at p. 496 [S.C.R.]:

> There are good reasons for leaving the question open [re: application of an entrapment defence]. Indeed, if that position is based on a static view of s. 7(3) of the *Criminal Code* I find it unacceptable. I do not think that s. 7(3) should be regarded as having frozen the power of the Courts to enlarge the content of the common law by way of recognizing new defences.

The approach of the Chief Justice in *Kirzner* was later reinforced in *R. v. Amato*, [1982] 2 S.C.R. 418, 29 C.R. (3d) 1, 69 C.C.C. (2d) 31. Writing in dissent, on behalf of Laskin C.J.C., McIntyre and Lamer JJ., Estey J. applied what he termed the "ordinary rule of construction where statutes and common law meet" to conclude that "s. 7(3) is the authority for the Courts of criminal jurisdiction to adopt, if appropriate in the view of the Court, defences including the defence of entrapment" (p. 445 [S.C.R.]). The Court's majority did not disagree with this determination.

. . . .

In light of this communicated understanding of the antecedents and purpose of s. 8(3), it can hardly be said that the common law's developed approach to the role and scope of consent as a defence to assault has no place in our criminal law. If s. 8(3) and its interaction with the common law can be used to develop entirely new defences not inconsistent with the *Code*, it surely authorizes the Courts to look to preexisting common law rules and principles to give meaning to, and explain the outlines and boundaries of, an existing defence or justification, indicating where they will not be recognized as legally effective—provided of course that there is no *clear* language in the *Code* which indicates that the *Code* has displaced the common law. That sort of language cannot be found in the *Code*.(As such, the common law legitimately serves in this appeal as an archive in which one may locate situations or forms of conduct to which the law will not allow a person to consent.)

. . . .

We have observed from the general analysis of the *Code* and common law that, in the history of our criminal law, codification did not replace common law principles of criminal responsibility, but in fact reflected them. That history also reveals that policy-based limitations of the sort at issue here boast a lineage in the common law equally as long as the factors which vitiate involuntary consent. Since these policy-based limitations also existed before the codification of Canada's criminal law, there is no reason to think they have been ousted by statutory revisions and amendments made to the *Code* along the way.

. . . .

Furthermore, since s. 8(3) of the *Code* expressly confirms the common law's continued authority and provides that exculpatory defences not expressly struck down by the *Code* continue to operate to exclude criminal liability, in this appeal, where the *Code* has not erased the common law limit in fist fights, it must continue to define the scope of legally effective consent. Some may object that s. 8(3) cannot be used to support this interpretation because consent is not really a defence, but instead forms part of the offence; indeed it is the absence of consent that is relevant as an element of the offence of assault. For example, Mewett and Manning, op. cit., at p. 567, write that "Real consent is therefore an essential element of assault going to the *actus reus* in the sense that if consent is present no offence can have been committed." Yet while that objection may have some relevance from a strictly formalistic perspective, it is of little consequence from a substantive point of view. Moreover it conflicts with the spirit of this court's previously expressed understanding of s. 8(3).

Whether consent is formally categorized as part of the *actus reus* of the offence, or as a defence, its essential function remains unaltered—if consent is proved, or if absence of consent is not proved, an individual accused of assault will *generally* be able to rely on the consent of the complainant to bar a conviction. He will be able to lean on the consent as a defence to liability. This basic reality has been widely recognized. English and Canadian Courts widely refer to consent as being in the nature of a defence. Leading treatises on criminal law conceive it this way. See Watt, op. cit., at p. 216; Clarkson and Keating, op. cit., at pp. 283-292; Glanville Williams, *Textbook of Criminal Law*, 2nd ed. (London: Steven & Sons, 1983), at pp. 549 and 576-578; and Law Reform Commission of Canada, *Assault*, op. cit., at p. 24. We have also observed, in the general interpretive section above, that the law confers on s. 8(3) an open and developmental view of the common law's role. Section 8(3) strongly suggests preservation of the common law approach to consent in assault.

Assault has been given a very encompassing definition in s. 265. It arises whenever a person intentionally applies force to a person "directly or indirectly", without the other's consent. The definition says nothing about the degree of harm which must be sustained. Nor does it refer to the motives for the touching. If taken at face value, this formulation would mean that the most trivial intended touching would constitute assault. As just one of many possible examples, a father would assault his daughter if he attempted to place a scarf around her neck to protect her from the cold but she did not consent to that touching, thinking the scarf ugly or undesirable. (Even an argument for implied consent would not seem to apply in a case like this.) That absurd consequence could not have been intended by Parliament. Rather its intention must have been for the courts to explain the content of the offence, incrementally and over the course of time.

Furthermore, whereas the factors specified in s. 265(3) are readily identifiable, and are generally applicable to all sorts of situations, that is inherently not true of limitations based on policy considerations, which are fact-specific by nature. It would have been quite impractical, if not impossible, for Parliament to establish an adequate list of exceptions to apply to all situations, old and new. Policy-based limits are almost always the product of a balancing of individual autonomy (the freedom to choose to have force intentionally applied to oneself) and some larger societal interest. That balancing may be better performed in the light of actual situations, rather than in the abstract, as Parliament would be compelled to do.

With the offence of assault, that kind of balancing is a function the courts are well-suited to perform. They will continue to be faced with real situations in which complicated actions and motivations interact, as they have in the past. I do not accept the argument that by failing to enact a list of *objects or forms of conduct* to which one could not validly consent, Parliament intended to eliminate their role in the offence of assault and to rely only on the four factors specified in s. 265(3). Such a major departure from well-established policy calls for more than mere silence, particularly as such a list would have been unduly difficult and impractical to prescribe, and was unnecessary given their existing entrenchment in the common law. The common law is the register of the balancing function of the courts — a register Parliament has authorized the courts to administer in respect of policy-based limits on the role and scope of consent in s. 265 of the *Code*.

. . . .

Limits on consent to assault have long been recognized by English and Canadian courts. . . . In present times as well, the English courts have on the whole been very consistent when confronted by assaults arising from fist fights and brawls. Since the English cases have set the overall direction for the Canadian common law in the assault context, and apparently continues to do so, it is of particular relevance in the circumstances of this case. The Canadian authorities also favour limits on consent. However, in recent years there has evolved a mixed record across provincial courts of appeal. This appeal therefore presents a timely opportunity for clarification.

[The Court then reviewed a number of English decisions.]

Finally, in 1980, the English Court of Appeal was asked to state the law in *Attorney General's Reference* (No. 6 of 1980), [1981] 2 All E.R. 1057. It was a reference prompted by a street fight between two young men who, in a relatively calm fashion, had decided to settle differences between them by resorting to their fists. One suffered a bleeding nose and some bruises. The other was charged with assault, but acquitted. The question put to the appellate court was, at p. 1058:

> Where two persons fight (otherwise than in the course of sport) in a public place can it be a defence for one of those persons to a charge of assault arising out of the fight that the other consented to fight?

The court held that because it is not in the public interest that people should cause each other bodily harm for no good reason, consent is no answer to a charge of assault when "actual bodily harm is intended and/or caused" (p. 1059). This meant that most fights would be unlawful regardless of consent. Only minor struggles, or rough but properly conducted sporting events, which may have some positive social value, were combative activities where consent would be an effective bar to a charge of assault. Of course lawful chastisement and reasonable surgical interference were also activities in which the public interest does not require nullification of consent. In such cases the general rule applies: the Crown must prove absence of consent to get a conviction for assault. The English Court of Appeal added that the public nature of the forum in which the fight occurs is not determinative of the effectiveness of consent. Private fights deserved no more protection than public ones.

If determinative of this appeal, the English authorities would undoubtedly support the decision of the court below. Here the assault occurred in circumstances which appear very nearly to have amounted to a disturbance of the peace. And there is no question that the punches thrown by Jobidon were intentional applications of force intended to cause the deceased bodily harm. Rodney Haggart's apparent consent would provide no defence to Jobidon in England.

(ii) The Canadian Authorities

. . . .

Ontario's appellate court joined New Brunswick's approach in *R. v. Dix, supra*. The court faced a situation partly similar to the one here. A scuffle occurred in a beverage room. The two men went outside the premises to fight, with the consequence that the complainant was severely injured. The trial Judge convicted the accused of assault causing bodily harm.

The Court of Appeal stated its legal opinion in unequivocal terms, at p. 325 [10 C.C.C. (2d)]:

> There is no doubt that the Crown proved that the accused intentionally applied force to his victim, and thereby caused bodily harm to him, but the intentional application of force does not amount to an assault unless the force was applied without the victim's consent. The Judge found that there was consent, in the sense that the two persons involved agreed to fight. The onus then was on the Crown, as it seems to us, to satisfy the Judge that what the appellant did was beyond the scope of the consent that had been given.

The appellate Court overturned the conviction on the ground stated by Gale C.J.O., at pp. 325-326, that: "the Crown failed to prove the necessary element of lack of consent to that which was done. The two parties consented to a fight and the fight was had in a normal manner, if I might use that phrase."

. . . .

A fourth province added its voice to this developing chorus in *R. v. Setrum* (1976), 32 C.C.C. (2d) 109. The Saskatchewan Court of Appeal confronted a situation in which a fight had erupted between two men outside the residence in which they had been drinking. As in the case at bar, the fight ended in the death of one of them. The trial judge had . . . to hold that a fight by consenting parties was unlawful assault per se, regardless of consent. The Saskatchewan Court of Appeal directly rejected the interpretation after a close examination of the terms of s. 244 of the *Code* and after reviewing and agreeing with the author of *Tremeear's Annotated Criminal Code* (6th ed. 1964), who, following an exposition of the English cases, concluded:

> It is, however, very doubtful in view of the wording of the *Code*, whether there can in any circumstances be an assault where the person assaulted has consented, unless that consent has been obtained by fraud.

Finally, drawing on *Dix* and *Abraham*, the Court had this to say, at p. 114:

> The language defining assault makes it absolutely clear that the proof of lack of consent to the assault is an essential element which must be proved if a conviction is to be found. . . . The instruction that a fight by consent, *per se*, was an unlawful act, was wrong in law.

With this interpretation in hand, the Saskatchewan court allowed Setrum's appeal of the conviction for manslaughter, and ordered a new trial. *Setrum* was followed by Creaghan J. of the New Brunswick Court of Queen's Bench in *R. v. Crouse* (1982), 39 N.B.R. (2d) 1.

If the preceding line of authority were singularly determinative of the common law binding this court, there should be little question about the result called for here. Given the finding of consent by the trial judge, Jobidon would not have committed the offence of assault. But the path is by no means as straight and clear as these cases seem to indicate. Since *Setrum, supra,* certain decisions have in varying degrees pulled away from that bright-line, absolutist approach which more or less ignores the traditional view of consent in fist fight cases. The respondent relies on some of these more recent decisions when claiming that the *MacTavish - Dix - Abraham - Setrum* line should not be followed.

While some of the most recent decisions are consistent with that chain of cases, others take due note of the established common law policy to insist that fist fights are special situations which call for *some* limits on the effectiveness of the element of consent in s. 265. There are of course shades of opinion as to the most appropriate place to draw protective lines in different situations.

Although dealing with homicide and the defence of provocation, the Ontario Court of Appeal in *R. v. Squire* (1975), 31 C.R.N.S. 314, 26 C.C.C. (2d) 219, (reversed on other grounds, [1977] 2 S.C.R. 13, 29 C.C.C. (2d) 497), found occasion to rely on both *Coney* and *Donovan* (omitting reference to *R. v. Dix, supra*) to conclude that the mere fact of consent between two persons to administer blows to one another did not of itself make such blows lawful, as per Martin J.A., at p. 230 [26 C.C.C. (2d)]:

> Where two persons engage in a fight in anger by mutual consent the blows struck by each constitute an assault on the other, unless justifiable in self-defence in accordance with the provisions of the *Code*.

. . . .

The Nova Scotia Court of Appeal supported these views in *R. v. Gur* (1986), 27 C.C.C. (3d) 511. There, the accused and the victim had been armed with knives and fought with them in the victim's house. The complainant sustained serious cuts to his hands. *Inter alia*, the accused was charged with unlawfully using a weapon in committing an assault contrary to (then) s. 245.1 of the *Code*. The accused invoked the consent of the victim as his primary defence. After stating that the *Code* had not negated the applicability of the common law in the assault context, and relying on the trio of English cases, the Court distinguished *MacTavish, Dix, Abraham* and *Setrum, supra*, on the basis that they dealt with assault charges arising out of fist fights, not the use of dangerous weapons. In coming to its conclusion that the trial Judge had erred in instructing the jury that consent was a defence to the charge, and relying heavily on the *Attorney General's Reference, supra*, the Nova Scotia Court stated its interpretation of the law in direct and open-ended terms, per Jones J.A., at p. 518 [C.C.C.]:

> As it is an offence to commit an assault where bodily harm is intended or caused then consent cannot be a defence to using a weapon for the purpose of committing an assault. . . . *I cannot agree that a person can consent to the infliction of bodily harm that results in death.* [Emphasis added.]

This approach was more broadly applied by the Nova Scotia Supreme Court, Appeal Division in *R. v. McIntosh* (1991), 64 C.C.C. (3d) 294. The sole issue in that appeal was whether a participant in a fist fight can give a legally effective consent to the intentional infliction of bodily harm upon himself. After reviewing the relevant jurisprudence, the unanimous court, speaking through Macdonald J.A., concluded that because it was not in the public interest that people should try to cause each other actual bodily harm for no good reason, most fights would be unlawful regardless of consent.

In fairly quick succession, the Alberta Court of Appeal was thrice required to grapple with this issue, first in *R. v. Carriere* (1987), 56 C.R. (3d) 257, 35 C.C.C. (3d) 276, then in *R. v. Bergner* (1987), 58 C.R. (3d) 281, 36 C.C.C. (3d) 25, and most recently in *R. v. Loonskin* (1990), 103 A.R. 193.

In *R. v. Carriere*, two women engaged in a fist fight in the lobby of a hotel. Stopped briefly, and moved outdoors, the fight was renewed in a parking lot, this time with knives. The victim sustained a stab wound in her abdomen. The accused was charged and convicted of aggravated assault contrary to (then) s. 245.2 of the *Code*. The Court of Appeal upheld that conviction. In delivering the judgment of the Court, Laycraft C.J.A. stated unequivocally that the English cases demonstrated a definite rule that a victim's consent provides no defence "where the assault maimed the victim". He noted that Professor Williams, op. cit., at p. 585, has suggested that in modern times the rationale of the rule may be that the victim will likely become a public charge, contrary to the public interest.

With lesser forms of bodily harm, Laycraft C.J.A. conceded that Canadian authorities reflect a considerable diversity of opinion. So, although he acknowledged that "fists are not insignificant weapons" and that fist fights often end in serious injury or death, he restricted his holding to the narrower issue before the Court, concluding, at p. 269 [C.R.]:

> I have, however, no doubt of the answer which the law must reach in a fight with knives where the charge is under one of the assault sections. One cannot consent to be stabbed. The public policy of the law intervenes to nullify the apparent consent of each of the combatants.

Before completing his judgment, Laycraft C.J.A. commented, in passing, that some cases dealt with under the assault sections of the *Criminal Code* might be better handled by charges of criminal negligence.

In *R. v. Bergner* [(1987), 58 C.R. (3d) 281], heard later the same year, the court was given the chance to decide the issue of fist fights on which it had refrained from commenting in *Carriere*. The accused, Bergner, had been charged with assault causing bodily harm, arising from a fight initiated in a hotel bar and continued outside on the street. Bergner hit the inebriated complainant repeatedly in the stomach and face with his fist, and then kicked the complainant's face and ribs with his boots. The complainant suffered a fractured nose and cheek-bone, as well as damage to an optic nerve which left him blind in one eye.

The trial judge held that it was a consensual fist fight and on that basis acquitted Bergner of assault causing bodily harm. Laycraft C.J.A. again noted that in Canada cases of consensual fist fights show considerable variation in both result and rationale. Due to that indeterminacy, Laycraft C.J.A. thought himself obliged to allow policy considerations to decide the issue. In the end, he determined that consent to fist fights should not be nullified on the basis of the tests of "blow[s] struck in anger" (*Buchanan*, *Squire*) and where "actual bodily harm is intended and/or caused" (Attorney General's Reference), even when intentional bodily harm was caused. In his opinion, the extent of such nullification would be overly encompassing, it would invalidate too many consents, in numerous activities, at p. 31:

> If anger, or the intention to do corporal hurt or to truly injure or to cause actual bodily harm is to trigger the intervention of public policy and so nullify consent, it is difficult to imagine the case in which there would be no such intervention. School boys in disagreement, with or without boxing-gloves, intend and strive mightily to injury or cause bodily harm; they are certainly angry. Even professional boxers fighting for money may not be able to resist the onset of a certain choler. The contestants in fights in hockey or football also meet all the criteria. The friendly fight is a rare phenomenon. . . .

> The expressed tests do not, in my respectful opinion, focus on one of the elements which should even more quickly induce the public policy of the law to nullify consent [the fact that in most fist fights challengers are often large, trained bullies, and the genuine consent of the other person is dubious at best].

Having rejected these tests for fist fight cases, Laycraft C.J.A. stated that once consent to a fist fight is truly established, it will preclude conviction for assault. Unlike fights with weapons, it would be too difficult, and bordering on judicial usurpation of political authority, to formulate a code of tests for nullifying the consent of weaponless fighters based on anger or intent to cause bodily harm. Thus, even though it disagreed with the trial judge's factual finding of consent, the Court of Appeal regretfully dismissed the Crown's appeal. Provincial appellate courts have thrice been asked to interpret the role of consent in assault based offences after *Bergner*.

In *R. v. Loonskin, supra*, the Alberta Court of Appeal followed the approach it established in Bergner. It held that, while the Crown was required by s. 265 to prove absence of consent to ground a conviction of aggravated assault, on the facts of the case before it where one of the combatants in a fist fight had bitten off part of the other's ear, consent had in fact not been given. Any consent to a fight, in general, was exceeded by the extent and force of the accused's harmful conduct.

The court took the opportunity to emphasize that while a legal defence of consent exists, nevertheless truly consensual fights would be very rare: "[w]here . . . one person attacks and another defends, and even in many cases where a challenge is met by a defence, it is not realistic to speak of a consensual fight" (p. 194). In overturning the acquittal, the Court of Appeal distinguished *Bergner* on the ground that in *Bergner* it was easier to find as a matter of fact that the combatants had consented to fight, because they deliberately moved from one place to another with the express intention of settling their differences by combat; not so in *Loonskin* where the fight had erupted rather spontaneously and without agreement that bites would be involved.

Having not faced this issue of consent since its decision in *Setrum, supra*, the Saskatchewan Court of Appeal returned to it in *R. v. Cey* (1989), 48 C.C.C. (3d) 480, apparently with a very different mindset. *Cey* involved a charge of assault causing severe bodily harm under s. 245.1 of the *Code* for injuries sustained in a hockey game when the accused stick-checked the complainant in the neck and face. The complainant suffered injuries to his head and was found to have sustained a concussion and a whiplash, keeping him hospitalized for three days. The trial judge found that the accused had not intended to injure the complainant, nor had he intended to apply any greater force to the victim than was customary in the game. Since the complainant had continued to play the game after he received the injuries, the trial judge held that that willingness amounted to an implied consent to the bodily contact which had occurred, and used that finding as a basis for acquitting the accused. The Crown appealed on the partial ground that the trial judge had misdirected himself on the issue of consent.

Without referring to *Setrum*, the majority in *Cey* came to its conclusion by relying on *Attorney General's Reference*, supra, and on the Ontario Court of Appeal's decision in the case at bar; both cases having been decided subsequent to its earlier decision in *Setrum*. To that extent, the reasoning in *Cey* is as much at stake in this appeal as that of the Ontario Court of Appeal below. The Saskatchewan Court of Appeal held that, although consent to the application of force may be implied, and *may* thereby constitute a valid and effective consent, nonetheless its effective scope is limited, not only by circumstance, but also by the law, at pp. 492-493 [48 C.C.C.]:

> The trial judge, if he found either express or implied consent, was in my view *required to consider whether the nature of the act was such that the victim could in law consent to it.* I am in agreement with the analysis of the term "assault" and the limits for a victim to consent thereof in the decision of the Ontario Court of Appeal in *R. v. Jobidon.* . . . While the *Jobidon* case dealt with a consensual fight outside a bar and while the English reference case referred to activity outside of sport, I see no reason in principle why the consent, express or implied, to assault in the context of a sporting event should not be considered similarly. That is in sporting events as well the mere fact that a type of assault occurs with some frequency does not necessarily mean that it is not of such a severe nature that consent thereto is precluded. In a sport such as hockey, however, I believe the test may be more limited than in the *Attorney General's Reference* case — that is, I think the alternate reference to "caused" to be inappropriate where actions to which there is implied consent may in extraordinary circumstances cause harm. [Emphasis added.]

Since the trial Judge had not directed himself to the nature of the act impliedly consented to, the acquittal was set aside.

. . . .

(d)   *Summary of the Common Law*

(i)   The English Position

Attorney General's Reference makes it clear that a conviction of assault will not be barred if "bodily harm is intended *and/or* caused". Since this test is framed in the alternative, consent could be nullified even in situations where the assailant did not intend to cause the injured person bodily harm but did so inadvertently. In Canada, however, this very broad formulation cannot strictly apply, since the definition of assault in s. 265 is explicitly restricted to *intentional* application of force. Any test in our law which incorporated the

English perspective would of necessity have to confine itself to bodily harm intended *and* caused.

(ii)   The Canadian Position

The preceding analysis reveals division in the Canadian jurisprudence. Decisions by courts of appeal in Manitoba, Ontario, Nova Scotia and (lately) Saskatchewan would nullify consent to intentionally inflicted bodily harm arising from a fist fight. Their approach is contained, respectively, in *Buchanan* (1898), *Cullen* (1948), *Squire* (1975), *Jobidon* (1988), *Gur* (1986), *McIntosh* (1991), and *Cey* (1989). (There is of course general support for the idea of policy-based nullification in the Alberta Court of Appeal; witness the language of Laycraft C.J.A. in *R. v. Carriere, supra.*) On the other side are decisions of appellate Courts in New Brunswick (*MacTavish* (1972)), Quebec (*Abraham* (1974)), Saskatchewan (*Setrum* (1976)), and Alberta (*Bergner* (1987) and *Loonskin* (1990)).

Although there is certainly no crystal-clear position in the modern Canadian common law, still, when one takes into account the combined English and Canadian jurisprudence, when one keeps sight of the common law's centuries-old persistence to limit the legal effectiveness of consent to a fist fight, and when one understands that s. 265 has always incorporated that persistence, the scale tips rather heavily against the validity of a person's consent to the infliction of bodily injury in a fight.

The thrust of the English common law is particularly important in this regard because it has been consistent for many decades, indeed, centuries. It became an integral component of the Canadian common law and has remained so to this day. Many of the seemingly pivotal pro-consent decisions made by courts in the 1970s were either obiter or were pronounced upon insufficient consideration of the important role of the traditional common law. Moreover they were decided prior to the decision in *Attorney General's Reference* (1980), which offered a very authoritative pronouncement of the common law position. The significance of that decision is perhaps best indicated in the instant appeal, for it provided the basis used by the Ontario Court of Appeal to overrule its decision in *R. v. Dix, supra.* The *Attorney General's Reference* case was again observed to be pivotal in the recent decision of the Appeal Court in Saskatchewan, in *R. v. Cey.* In light of these many considerations, I am of the view that the Canadian position is not as opaque or bifurcated as one might initially think.

Notwithstanding this conclusion, given the residual indeterminacy which admittedly lingers in the recent Canadian cases, it is useful to canvass policy considerations which exert a strong influence in this appeal, for they rather decisively support the respondent, bringing down the scales even more surely in support of the decision in the court below.

e) *Policy considerations*

Foremost among the policy considerations supporting the Crown is the social uselessness of fist fights. As the English Court of Appeal noted in the *Attorney General's Reference*, it is not in the public interest that adults should willingly cause harm to one another without a good reason. There is precious little utility in fist fights or street brawls. These events are motivated by unchecked passion. They so often result in serious injury to the participants. Here it resulted in a tragic death to a young man on his wedding day.

There was a time when pugilism was sheltered by the notion of "chivalry". Duelling was an activity not only condoned, but required by honour. Those days are fortunately long past. Our social norms no longer correlate strength of character with prowess at fisticuffs. Indeed, when we pride ourselves for making positive ethical and social strides, it tends to be on the basis of our developing reason. This is particularly true of the law, where reason is cast in a privileged light. Erasing longstanding limits on consent to assault would be a regressive step, one which would retard the advance of civilized norms of conduct.

Quite apart from the valueless nature of fist fights from the combatants' perspective, it should also be recognized that consensual fights may sometimes lead to larger brawls and to serious breaches of the public peace. In the instant case, this tendency was openly observable. At the prospect of a fight between Jobidon and the deceased, in a truly macabre fashion many patrons of the hotel deliberately moved to the parking lot to witness the gruesome event. That scene easily could have erupted in more widespread aggression between allies of the respective combatants. Indeed it happened that the brothers of Jobidon and Haggart also took to each other with their fists.

Given the spontaneous, often drunken nature of many fist fights, I would not wish to push a deterrence rationale too far. Nonetheless, it seems reasonable to think that, in some cases, common law limitations on consent might serve some degree of deterrence to these sorts of activities.

. . . .

Wholly apart from deterrence, it is most unseemly from a moral point of view that the law would countenance, much less provide a backhanded sanction to the sort of interaction displayed by the facts of this appeal. The sanctity of the human body should militate against the validity of consent to bodily harm inflicted in a fight.

. . . .

Some may see limiting the freedom of an adult to consent to applications of force in a fist fight as unduly paternalistic; a violation of individual self-rule. Yet while that view may commend itself to some, those persons cannot reasonably claim that the law does not know such limitations. All criminal law is "paternalistic" to some degree — top-down guidance is inherent in any prohibitive rule. That the common law has developed a strong resistance to recognizing the validity of consent to intentional applications of force in fist fights and brawls is merely one instance of the criminal law's concern that Canadian citizens treat each other humanely and with respect.

Finally, it must not be thought that by giving the green light to the common law, and a red light to consent to fights, this court is thereby negating the role of consent in all situations or activities in which people willingly expose themselves to intentionally applied force. No such sweeping conclusion is entailed. The determination being made is much narrower in scope.

f) *Conclusion*

How, and to what extent is consent limited?

The law's willingness to vitiate consent on policy grounds is significantly limited. Common law cases restrict the extent to which consent may be nullified; as do the relevant policy considerations. The unique situation under examination in this case, a weaponless fist fight between two adults, provides another important boundary.

The limitation demanded by s. 265 as it applies to the circumstances of this appeal is one which *vitiates consent between adults intentionally to apply force causing serious hurt or non-trivial bodily harm to each other in the course of a fist fight or brawl.* (This test entails that a minor's apparent consent to an adult's intentional application of force in a fight would also be negated.) This is the extent of the limit which the common law requires in the factual circumstances of this appeal. It may be that further limitations will be found to apply in other circumstances. But such limits, if any, are better developed on a case-by-case basis, so that the unique features of the situation may exert a rational influence on the extent of the limit and on the justification for it.

Stated in this way, the policy of the common law will not affect the validity or effectiveness of freely given consent to participate in rough sporting activities, so long as the intentional applications of force to which one consents are within the customary norms and rules of the game. Unlike fist fights, sporting activities and games usually have a significant social value; they are worthwhile. In this regard the holding of the Saskatchewan Court of Appeal in *R. v. Cey, supra*, is apposite.

The court's majority determined that some forms of intentionally applied force will clearly fall within the scope of the rules of the game, and will therefore readily ground a finding of implied consent, to which effect should be given. On the other hand, very violent forms of force which clearly extend beyond the ordinary norms of conduct will not be recognized as legitimate conduct to which one can validly consent.

There is also nothing in the preceding formulation which would prevent a person from consenting to medical treatment or appropriate surgical interventions. Nor, for example, would it necessarily nullify consent between stuntmen who agree in advance to perform risky sparring or daredevil activities in the creation of a socially valuable cultural product. A charge of assault would be barred if the Crown failed to prove absence of consent in these situations, insofar as the activities have a positive social value and the intent of the actors is to produce a social benefit for the good of the people involved, and often for a wider group of people as well. This is a far cry from the situation presented in this appeal, where Jobidon's sole objective was to strike the deceased as hard as he physically could, until his opponent either gave up or retreated. Fist fights are worlds apart from these other forms of conduct.

Finally, the preceding formulation avoids nullification of consent to intentional applications of force which cause only minor hurt or trivial bodily harm. The bodily harm contemplated by the test is essentially equivalent to that contemplated by the definition found in s. 267(2) of the *Code*, dealing with the offence of assault causing bodily harm. The section defines bodily harm as "any hurt or injury to the complainant that interferes with the health or comfort of the complainant and that is more than merely transient or trifling in nature".

On this definition, combined with the fact that the test is restricted to cases involving adults, the phenomenon of the "ordinary" schoolyard scuffle, where boys or girls immaturely seek to resolve differences with their hands, will not come within the scope of the limitation. That has never been the policy of the law and I do not intend to disrupt the status quo. However, I would leave open the question as to whether boys or girls under the age of 18 who truly intend to harm one another, and ultimately cause more than trivial bodily harm, would be afforded the protection of a defence of consent. (As was the accused in *R. v. Barron* (1985), 48 C.R. (3d) 334, 23 C.C.C. (3d) 544 (Ont. C.A.), in which a boy was charged with manslaughter, via assault, for pushing another boy down a flight of stairs thereby causing the boy's death. The trial judge held that the deceased boy had impliedly consented to rough-housing on the stairs as they descended.) The appropriate result will undoubtedly depend on the peculiar circumstances of each case.

. . . .

I would uphold the decision of the Court of Appeal. The appeal is dismissed.

SOPINKA J. (STEVENSON J. concurring): —

I have had the advantage of reading the reasons of Gonthier J., and while I agree with his disposition of the matter I am unable to agree with his reasons. This appeal involves the role that consent plays in the offence of criminal assault. Unlike my colleague I am of the view that consent cannot be read out of the offence.

. . . .

While the consent of the victim cannot transform a crime into lawful conduct, it is a vital element in determining what conduct constitutes a crime. It is a well-accepted principle of the criminal law that the absence of consent is an essential ingredient of the actus reus. Thus it is not theft to steal if the owner consents and consensual intercourse is not sexual assault. In Don Stuart,

Canadian Criminal Law: A Treatise 2d ed. (Toronto: Carswell, 1987), the author states [at p. 469]:

> The general principle, to which there are exceptions, that the true consent of the victim is always a defence to criminal responsibility is a fundamental principle of the criminal law.

. . . .

In *R. v. Lemieux*, [1967] S.C.R. 492, 2 C.R.N.S. 1, [1968] 1 C.C.C. 187, this court held that the offence of breaking and entering was not made out when it was carried out by pre-arrangement with the agent of the owner. The consent of the owner deprived the activity of an essential feature of the *actus reus*.

. . . .

There is, moreover, no generally accepted exception to this principle with respect to the intentional infliction of physical harm. There are many activities in society which involve the intentional application of force which may result in serious bodily harm but which are not criminal. Surgical operations and sporting events are examples. It was no doubt the absence of an exception to this principle that led Parliament to enact s. 14 of the *Criminal Code*, R.S.C., 1985, c. C-46, which creates an exception for the most serious of assaults, the intentional infliction of death.

In my view, Parliament has chosen to extend this principle to all assaults save murder in the interests of making this aspect of the criminal law certain. I see no evidence in the clear and simple language of s. 265 that it intended to outlaw consensual fighting in the interests of avoiding breaches of the peace or to allow it if a judge thought that it occurred in circumstances that were socially useful. Rather, the policy reflected in s. 265 is to make the absence of consent a requirement in the definition of the offence, but to restrict consent to those intentional applications of force in respect of which there is a clear and effective consent by a victim who is free of coercion or misrepresentation. Instead of reading the words "without the consent of another person" out of s. 265, I am of the opinion that the intention of Parliament is respected by close scrutiny of the scope of consent to an assault. Instead of attempting to evaluate the utility of the activity, the trial judge will scrutinize the consent to determine whether it applied to the very activity which is the subject of the charge. The more serious the assault, the more difficult it should be to establish consent.

2. Interpretation of Section 265

Section 265 states that "[a] person commits an assault when *without the consent of another person*, he applies force intentionally to that other person. . . ." (emphasis added). My colleague Gonthier J. concludes that on the basis of cases which applied the common law, that section should be interpreted as excluding the absence of consent as an element of the *actus reus* in respect of an assault with intent to commit intentional bodily harm. In coming to his conclusion my colleague relies on a number of English authorities. The issue was not finally resolved in England until the decision of the English Court of Appeal on a reference to it by the Attorney General in 1980. See *Attorney General's Reference (No. 6 of 1980)*, [1981] 2 All E.R. 1057. Unconstrained by the expression of legislative policy, the Court moulded the common law to accord with the Court's view of what was in the public interest. On this basis the Court discarded the absence of consent as an element in assaults in which actual bodily harm was either caused or intended. Exceptions were created for assaults that have some positive social value such as sporting events. In Canada, the criminal law has been codified and the judiciary is constrained by the wording of sections defining criminal offences. The Courts' application of public policy is governed by the expression of public policy in the *Criminal Code*. If Parliament intended to adopt the public policy which the English Court of Appeal developed it used singularly inappropriate language. It made the absence of consent a specific requirement and provided that this applied to *all* assaults without exception. The conflict in the Canadian cases which my colleague's review discloses is largely due to the application of these two disparate strains of public policy.

In my opinion the above observations as to the appropriate use of public policy are sufficient to conclude that the absence of consent cannot be swept away by a robust application of judge-made policy. This proposition is strengthened and confirmed by the specific dictates of the *Code* with reference to the essential elements of a criminal offence. Section 9(*a*) of the *Code* provides that "[n]otwithstanding anything in this Act or any other Act, no person shall be convicted . . . (a) of an offence at common law." The effect of my colleague's approach is to create an offence where one does not exist under the terms of the *Code* by application of the common law. The offence created is the intentional application of force with the consent of the victim. I appreciate that my colleague's approach is to interpret the section in light of the common law but, in my view, use of the common law to eliminate an element of the offence that is required by statute is more than interpretation and is contrary to not only the spirit but also the letter of s. 9(*a*). One of the basic reasons for s. 9(*a*) is the importance of certainty in determining what conduct constitutes a criminal offence. That is the reason we have codified the offences in the *Criminal Code*. An accused should not have to search the books to discover the common law in order to determine if the offence charged is indeed an offence at law. Where does one search to determine the social utility of a fight during a hockey game to take one example? There are those that would argue that it is an important part of the attraction. Judges may not agree. Is this a matter for judicial notice or does it require evidence? The problem of uncertainty which the social utility test creates is greater than searching out the common law, a problem which lead to the prohibition in s. 9(*a*).

· · · ·

It appears clear from the findings of the trial Judge that the accused had an honest belief in consent, but that consent extended only until Haggart "gave up or retreated". The extent of the consent given by Haggart did not, therefore, extend to being struck once he had been knocked unconscious. The accused knew that Haggart's consent did not extend beyond consciousness.

In my opinion, based on his own findings, the trial Judge misconstrued the evidence with respect to the accused's belief that all the blows were struck prior to Haggart losing consciousness.

. . . .

Having found that the accused committed an assault, and given that Mr. Haggart died as a result of that unlawful act, the accused is therefore guilty of manslaughter via *Criminal Code* ss. 222(5)(*a*) and 234. I would therefore dispose of the appeal as proposed by Gonthier J.

For a criticism of the majority's position see Upsrich (1992), 7 C.R. (4th) 235.

Problem

John Jones came into your law office yesterday. He's a man aged 52 who has a son Bill, who is 19. Mr. Jones advised you that his son was involved yesterday in an incident at his school. He says that his son was not the instigator but did respond to taunts from a schoolmate, Spike O'Toole. All of Bill's friends were present in the schoolyard when Spike challenged him to a fight. Bill is a karate expert who is schooled that retreat is always to be preferred but the pressure of the situation got to him and he took up the challenge. In the result Spike went to the hospital with a broken jaw. Mr. Jones has asked you for advice as to Bill's position.

Compare *R. v. W. (G.)* (1994), 30 C.R. (4th) 393, 90 C.C.C. (3d) 139 (C.A.) and *R. v. B. (T.B.)* (1994), 34 C.R. (4th) 241 (P.E.I. C.A.).

BOLDUC AND BIRD v. R.

[1967] S.C.R. 677, 2 C.R.N.S. 40, [1967] 3 C.C.C. 294

SPENCE J. (dissenting): — These are appeals by each accused from the judgment of the Court of Appeal of British Columbia pronounced on February 6, 1967 whereby that Court dismissed the appeals of the accused from their convictions by His Honour Judge Ladner on November 24, 1966, of charges of indecent assault contrary to the provisions of s. 141 [repealed, 1985, c. 19] of the *Criminal Code*. The appeals were argued together.

The circumstances are as follows. Bolduc was a physician and surgeon licensed to practice in the Province of British Columbia. In the course of such practice he was treating the complainant Diana Elizabeth Osborne for an erosion of the cervic uteri. During the course of treatment, after necessary examinations, he had on several occasions cauterized the affected parts. On a Saturday morning in the month of October or November 1965, Mrs. Osborne attended Dr.

Bolduc's office for another examination and treatment, if the latter were required.

The accused Bird was a professional musician in a night club. He had been for some time a personal friend of the accused Bolduc. He had obtained an honours degree in chemistry from the university and he swore that "I was very seriously considering returning to university to go to medical school".

On Mrs. Osborne's attendance at the office, the receptionist prepared her for the examination and/or treatment and then attended the accused Bolduc in his office to inform him that his patient was ready. Present in the office with Bolduc was the accused Bird and upon noticing that Bolduc was not alone the receptionist simply informed Bolduc that his patient had been prepared and requested him to notify her when he was ready to proceed. In a few moments the receptionist was recalled into the office and Bolduc instructed her to get a white lab coat, such as commonly worn by doctors, so that Bird might use the same stating to her that Bird was an intelligent young man and that he intended to pass Bird off as a doctor or medical intern, adding "this was a good way to learn the facts of life". The receptionist protested at what she considered such unethical conduct and declined to bring the lab coat. Bolduc himself obtained the coat for Bird and requested that the receptionist give her stethoscope to Bird. The receptionist simply dropped the instrument in the office and returned to the examining room.

Bolduc and Bird then entered the room together. Bird was wearing the white lab coat and had in his possession a stethoscope. Bolduc introduced Bird to Mrs. Osborne as "Dr. Bird", told Mrs. Osborne that Bird was a medical intern who had not obtained practical experience of this type of thing during his internship and asked if she would mind if Dr. Bird were present during the examination. Mrs. Osborne replied in the negative because he was an intern, that she didn't mind — "this is fine".

I have above summarized the evidence of the receptionist which was accepted by the learned trial Judge.

The examination proceeded with Bolduc, the physician, sitting on a stool at the end of the examining table. He then proceeded to examine carefully and to touch Mrs. Osborne's private parts, and during the course of the treatment he inserted a speculum in the vaginal canal. Throughout this, the accused Bird stood to one side of Bolduc about a foot or 18 inches away from him and Bolduc made comments as to the patient's treatment, progress, her condition, and also on the prevalence of such condition amongst female patients, Bird simply answered by nods and did not touch the patient at all. It is, of course, the question for decision whether or not the conduct of Bolduc in the circumstances constituted the offence of indecent assault.

Before the Court of Appeal and in this Court, it was immediately admitted, and it could not be otherwise, that if Bolduc's conduct did amount to indecent assault Bird was also guilty under the provisions of s. 21 of the *Criminal Code* despite the fact that he did not touch the patient at any time. Section 141(1) of the *Criminal Code* provides:

141.(1) Every one who indecently assaults a female person is guilty of an indictable offence and is liable to imprisonment for five years and to be whipped.

Section 230 [now s. 244] of the *Criminal Code* provides:

230. A person commits an assault when, without the consent of another person or with consent, where it is obtained by fraud,
(a) he applies force intentionally to the person of the other, directly or indirectly.

It is, of course, trite law that the force applied may be of very slight degree, in fact, may be mere touching.

The Courts below were concerned with the provisions of s. 141(2) of the *Criminal Code* which provides:

(2) An accused who is charged with an offence under subsection (1) may be convicted if the evidence establishes that the accused did anything to the female person with her consent that, but for her consent, would have been an indecent assault, if her consent was obtained by false and fraudulent representations as to the nature and quality of the act.

Much argument was directed in this Court to whether the admittedly fraudulent and false representation made to Mrs. Osborne was as to "the nature and character of the act" so that the consent would be vitiated by the provisions of the said subsection.

I am of the opinion that this Court need not be concerned directly with the provisions of s. 141(2). Under s. 230 the application of force, however slight, is an assault when it is "without the consent of another person or with consent when it is obtained by fraud". Let us examine for a moment what was the consent obtained from Mrs. Osborne. Surely upon the evidence to which I have referred above, it was a consent to the examination by Bolduc of her private parts and the touching of them in the course of treatment in the presence of a doctor, and not a mere medical student or a mere layman who was in some vague fashion considering becoming a medical student.

There was no evidence whatsoever that Mrs. Osborne knew the accused Bird at all. The name Bird meant nothing to her. She only gave this consent to such a serious invasion of her privacy on the basis that Bird was a doctor intending to commence practice and who desired practical experience in such matters as Bolduc was proposing to engage in. That was the consent which Mrs. Osborne granted. The indecent assault upon her was not the act to which she consented and therefore I am of the opinion that the two accused were guilty under the provisions of s. 141(1) when considered with s. 230 and s. 21 of the *Criminal Code* without recourse to the provisions of s. 141(2). This makes it unnecessary, in my view, to consider the many authorities cited in the most able argument of counsel for the accused and which dealt with the problem of the nature and character of the act under the provisions of the latter subsection.

I would dismiss both appeals.

HALL J. (CARTWRIGHT, FAUTEUX and RITCHIE JJ. concurring): — The facts and circumstances relative to this appeal are fully set out in the judgment of my brother Spence. The question for decision is whether on those facts and in the circumstances so described the appellants Bolduc and Bird were guilty of an indecent assault upon the person of the complainant contrary to s. 141 of the *Criminal Code* which reads:

> 141. (1) Every one who indecently assaults a female person is guilty of an indictable offence and is liable to imprisonment for five years and to be whipped.
>
> (2) An accused who is charged with an offence under subsection (1) may be convicted if the evidence establishes that the accused did anything to the female person with her consent that, but for her consent, would have been an indecent assault, if her consent was obtained by false and fraudulent representations as to the nature and quality of the act.

With respect, I do not agree that an indecent assault was committed within the meaning of this section. What Bolduc did was unethical and reprehensible in the extreme and was something no reputable medical practitioner would have countenanced. However, Bolduc's unethical conduct and the fraud practised upon the complainant do not of themselves necessarily imply an infraction of s. 141, *supra*. It is common ground that the examination and treatment, including the insertion of the speculum were consented to by the complainant. The question is: "Was her consent obtained by false and fraudulent representations as to the nature and quality of the act?" Bolduc did exactly what the complainant understood he would do and intended that he should do, namely, to examine the vaginal tract and to cauterize the affected parts. Inserting the speculum was necessary for these purposes. There was no fraud on his part as to what he was supposed to do and in what he actually did. The complainant knew that Bird was present and consented to his presence. The fraud that was practised on her was not as to the nature and quality of what was to be done but was as to Bird's identity as a medical intern. His presence as distinct from some overt act by him was not an assault. However, any overt act either alone or in common with Bolduc would have transposed the situation into an unlawful assault, but Bird did not touch the complainant; he merely looked on and listened to Bolduc's comments on what was being done because of the condition then apparent in the vaginal tract. Bird was in a sense a "peeping tom". Conduct popularly described as that of a "peeping tom" was not an offence under the *Criminal Code* nor was it an offence at common law: *Frey v. Fedoruk et al.* Since the decision in *Frey v. Fedoruk, supra*, the *Code* was amended by the inclusion of s. 162 which first appeared in the 1955 *Code*. That section reads:

> 162. Every one who, without lawful excuse, the proof of which lies upon him, loiters or prowls at night upon the property of another person near a dwelling house situated on that property is guilty of an offence punishable on summary conviction.

The act of "peeping" is not of itself made an offence, but it is the loitering or prowling at night near a dwelling house without lawful excuse that is made unlawful.

This case differs from *Rex v. Harms* where the accused was charged with rape following carnal knowledge of an Indian girl, her consent to the intercourse having been obtained by false and fraudulent misrepresentations as to the nature and quality of the act. In that case Harms falsely represented himself to be a medical doctor, and although the complainant in that case knew that he was proposing sexual intercourse, she consented thereto because of his representations that the intercourse was in the nature of a medical treatment necessitated by a condition which he said he had diagnosed. Harms was not a medical man at all. He had no medical qualifications. The Court of Appeal affirmed the conviction by the jury that the Indian girl's consent had been obtained by false and fraudulent representations as to the nature and quality of the act.

The question of fraud vitiating a woman's consent in the case of rape or indecent assault was fully canvassed by Stephen J. in *The Queen v. Clarence* and by the High Court of Australia in *Papadimitropoulos v. The Queen* where the Court, in concluding a full review of the relevant law and cases decided up to that time, including the *Harms* case, *supra*, said:

> To return to the central point; rape is carnal knowledge of a woman without her consent: carnal knowledge is the physical fact of penetration; it is the consent to that which is in question; such a consent demands a perception as to what is about to take place, as to the identity of the man and the character of what he is doing. But once the consent is comprehending and actual the inducing causes cannot destroy its reality.

The complainant here knew what Bolduc was proposing to do to her, for this was one in a series of such treatments. Her consent to the examination and treatment was real and comprehending and it cannot, therefore, be said that her consent was obtained by false or fraudulent representations as to the nature and quality of the act to be done, for that was not the fraud practised on her. The fraud was as to Bird being a medical intern and it was not represented that he would do anything but observe. It was intended that the examination and treatment would be done by Bolduc and this he did without assistance or participation by Bird.

I would, accordingly, allow the appeal, quash the conviction and direct that a verdict of acquittal be entered for both appellants.

In 1983, the law relating to coerced consent was changed. Now, under s. 265(3), applying to all forms of assault and sexual assault,

No consent is obtained where the complainant submits or does not resist by reason of

a) the application of force to the complainant or to a person other than the complainant;
b) threats or fear of the application of force to the complainant or to a person other than the complainant;
c) fraud; or
d) the exercise of authority.

R. v. CUERRIER

(1998), 18 C.R. (5th) 1, 127 C.C.C. (3d) 1

The accused was charged with two counts of aggravated assault pursuant to s. 268 of the *Criminal Code*. The accused had tested positive for HIV in August 1992. At that time a public health nurse explicitly instructed him to use condoms every time he engaged in sexual intercourse and to inform all prospective sexual partners that he was HIV-positive. The accused angrily rejected this advice. He complained that he would never be able to have a sex life if he told anyone that he was HIV-positive. The accused had unprotected sexual relations with the two complainants without informing them he was HIV-positive. The complainants had consented to unprotected sexual intercourse with the accused, but they testified at trial that if they had known that he was HIV-positive they would never have engaged in unprotected intercourse with him.

The trial judge entered a directed verdict acquitting the accused. The Court of Appeal upheld the acquittals. The Supreme Court was unanimous in allowing the appeal and ordering a new trial. The Court was divided in its reasons.

CORY J. (MAJOR, BASTARACHE and BINNIE JJ. concurring): —

. . . .

In 1983, the Criminal Code was amended. The rape and indecent assault provisions were replaced by the offence of sexual assault. The s. 265 assault provision was enacted in its present form, and it, by the terms of s. 265(2), applies to all forms of assault, including sexual assault.

Section 265(3)(c) simply states that no consent is obtained where the complainant submits or does not resist by reason of "fraud". There are no limitations or qualifications on the term "fraud". It is no longer necessary when examining whether consent in assault or sexual assault cases was vitiated by fraud to consider whether the fraud related to the "nature and quality of the act".

. . . .

. . . A principled approach consistent with the plain language of the section and an appropriate approach to consent in sexual assault matters is preferable. To that end, there is no reason why, with appropriate modifications, the principles which have historically been applied in relation to fraud in criminal law cannot be used.

In criminal law cases dealing with commercial transactions, it has been held that mere negligent misrepresentation would not amount to a fraudulent act. However, deliberately practised fraudulent acts which, in the knowledge of the accused, actually put the property of others at risk is subject to criminal sanction. Non-disclosure can constitute fraud where it would be viewed by the reasonable person as dishonest. The essential elements of fraud then are dishonesty, which can include non-disclosure of important facts, and deprivation or risk of deprivation.

It is now necessary to consider the nature of fraud and how it should be applied in the context of the wording of the present s. 265.

. . . .

At the outset it can be accepted that fraud pertaining to the nature and quality of the act or the identity of the partner will still constitute fraud which can be found to vitiate consent. What other acts of dishonesty which give rise to the risk of deprivation can have the same effect?

. . . .

The deadly consequences that non-disclosure of the risk of HIV infection can have on an unknowing victim, make it imperative that as a policy a broad view of fraud vitiating consent . . . should be adopted. . . . [I]t should now be taken that for the accused to conceal or fail to disclose that he is HIV-positive can constitute fraud which may vitiate consent to sexual intercourse.

Persons knowing that they are HIV-positive who engage in sexual intercourse without advising their partner of the disease may be found to fulfil the traditional requirements for fraud namely dishonesty and deprivation. That fraud may vitiate a partner's consent to engage in sexual intercourse.
invalidate

. . . .

Without disclosure of HIV status there cannot be a true consent. The consent cannot simply be to have sexual intercourse. Rather it must be consent to have intercourse with a partner who is HIV-positive. True consent cannot be given if there has not been a disclosure by the accused of his HIV-positive status. A consent that is not based upon knowledge of the significant relevant factors is not a valid consent. The extent of the duty to disclose will increase with the risks attendant upon the act of intercourse. To put it in the context of fraud the greater the risk of deprivation the higher the duty of disclosure. The failure to disclose HIV-positive status can lead to a devastating illness with fatal consequences. In those circumstances, there exists a positive duty to disclose. The nature and extent of the duty to disclose, if any, will always have to be considered in the context of the particular facts presented. . . . [T]he Crown will have to establish that the dishonest act . . . had the effect of exposing the person consenting to a significant risk of serious bodily harm. The risk of contracting AIDS as a result of engaging in unprotected intercourse would clearly meet that test.

A position that any fraud that is designed to induce the complainant to submit to the act will vitiate consent and constitute an assault would trivialize the criminal process by leading to a proliferation of petty prosecutions instituted without judicial guidelines or directions. To say that any fraud which induces consent will vitiate consent would bring within the sexual assault provisions of the *Code* behaviour which lacks the reprehensible character of criminal acts. . . . [S]ome limitations on the concept of fraud as it applies to s. 265(3)(c) are clearly necessary or the courts would be overwhelmed and convictions under the sections would defy common sense. The existence of fraud should not vitiate consent unless there is a significant risk of serious harm.

. . . .

It was contended that criminalization would further stigmatize all persons with HIV/AIDS. However it cannot be forgotten that the further stigmatization arises as a result of a sexual assault and not because of the disease. Just as an HIV-positive individual convicted of armed robbery will be further stigmatized but it will not be related to the status of his health. To proceed by way of a criminal charge for assault is not to "criminalize" the accused's activities. Rather, it is simply to apply the provisions of the *Code* to conduct which could constitute the crime of assault and thereby infringe s. 265.

L'HEUREUX-DUBÉ J.: — . . . [T]he 1983 amendment to the *Criminal Code*, in which the rape and indecent assault provisions were reconstituted as the offence of sexual assault, and the words "false and fraudulent representations as to the nature and quality of the act" were removed, evidences Parliament's intention to move away from the unreasonably strict common law approach to the vitiation of consent by fraud.

. . . Parliament has recognized with s. 265(3), that in order to maximize the protection of physical integrity and personal autonomy, only consent obtained without negating the voluntary agency of the person being touched, is legally valid. . . . [F]raud is simply about whether the dishonest act in question induced another to consent to the ensuing physical act, whether or not that act was particularly risky and dangerous. The focus of the inquiry into whether fraud vitiated consent so as to make certain physical contact non-consensual should be on whether the nature and execution of the deceit deprived the complainant of the ability to exercise his or her will in relation to his or her physical integrity with respect to the activity in question.

. . . .

An interpretation of fraud that focuses only on the sexual assault context, and which limits it only to those situations where a "significant risk of serious bodily harm" is evident, is unjustifiably restrictive. Such a particularization and limitation is nowhere present in the assault scheme, because Parliament removed any qualifications to the fraud provision as it relates to sexual assault.

McLACHLIN J. (GONTHIER J. concurring): — For more than a century, the law has been settled; fraud does not vitiate consent to assault unless the mistake goes to the nature of the act or the identity of the partner. Fraud as to collateral aspects of a consensual encounter, like the possibility of contracting serious venereal disease, does not vitiate consent. Parliament did not intend to remove the common law limitations on fraud for assault by amending s. 265(3) of the Criminal Code in 1983.

. . . [T]he criminalization of conduct is a serious matter. Clear language is required to create crimes . . . When courts approach the definition of elements of old crimes, they must be cautious not to broaden them in a way that in effect creates a new crime. Only Parliament can create new crimes and turn lawful conduct into criminal conduct . . . [T]he *Interpretation Act*, . . . s. 45(2), . . . provides that an amending enactment shall not be deemed to involve a declaration of a change in the existing law . . . As such, the 1983 amendment of the assault provisions, which removed the qualifier "nature and quality of the act" from the type of fraud sufficient to vitiate consent, should not, in the absence of evidence to the contrary, be taken as a change in the law of assault.

This conclusion is also supported by the rule that where a criminal statute is ambiguous, the interpretation that favours the accused is preferred . . .

. . . [T]he 1983 amendments to the *Criminal Code* did not oust the common law governing fraud in relation to assault. The common law continues to inform the concept of fraud in s. 265(3)(c) of the *Criminal Code*.

. . . .

However, it does not follow that all change to the law of assault is barred. It is open to courts to make incremental changes by extending the common law concepts of nature of the act and identity, provided the ramifications of the changes are not overly complex.

. . . .

It is the proper role of the courts to update the common law from time to time to bring it into harmony with the changing needs and mores of society . . . This applies to the common law concept of fraud in relation to assault.

. . . .

The basic precondition of such change is that it is required to bring the law into step with the changing needs of society.

. . . .

In the case at bar . . . the current state of the law does not reflect the values of Canadian society. It is unrealistic, indeed shocking, to think that consent given to sex on the basis that one's partner is HIV-free stands unaffected by blatant deception on that matter . . . [The] common law [earlier] recognized that deception as to sexually transmitted disease carrying a high risk of infection, constituted fraud vitiating consent to sexual intercourse. Returning the law to this position would represent an incremental change to the law.

. . . .

The final and most difficult question is whether the change would introduce complex and unforeseeable changes of the sort better left to Parliament . . .

[O]nce the law leaves the certainty of the dual criteria of nature of the act in the sense of whether it was sexual or non-sexual, and the identity of the perpetrator, the argument is made that to go beyond these criteria would be to open the door to convictions for assault in the case, for example, where a man promises a woman a fur coat in return for sexual intercourse . . . This difficulty is a serious one. The courts should not broaden the criminal law to catch conduct that society generally views as non-criminal. If that is to be done, Parliament must do it. Furthermore, the criminal law must be clear. I agree with the fundamental principle . . . that it is imperative that there be a clear line between criminal and non-criminal conduct. Absent this, the criminal law loses its deterrent effect and becomes unjust.

. . . . .

The question is whether a narrower increment is feasible that catches only harm of the sort at issue in this appeal and draws the required bright line . . . [A] return to the [earlier] common law would draw a clear line between criminal conduct and non-criminal conduct . . . [T]he [earlier] law permitted fraud to vitiate consent to contact where there was (a) a deception as to the sexual character of the act; (b) deception as to the identity of the perpetrator; or (c) deception as to the presence of a sexually transmitted disease giving rise to serious risk or probability of infecting the complainant. This rule is clear and contained. It would catch the conduct here at issue, without permitting people to be convicted of assault for inducements like false promises of marriage or fur coats. The test for deception would be objective, focussing on whether the accused falsely represented to the complainant that he or she was disease-free when he knew or ought to have known that there was a high risk of infecting his partner. The test for inducement would be subjective, in the sense that the judge or jury must be satisfied beyond a reasonable doubt that the fraud actually induced the consent.

. . . .

. . . [A]n explanation may be suggested for why deceit as to venereal disease may vitiate consent while deceit as to other inducements, like promises of marriage or fur coats, does not. Consent to unprotected sexual intercourse is consent to sexual congress with a certain person and to the transmission of bodily fluids from that person. Where the person represents that he or she is disease-free, and consent is given on that basis, deception on that matter goes to the very act of assault. The complainant does not consent to the transmission of diseased fluid into his or her body. This deception in a very real sense goes to the nature of the sexual act, changing it from an act that has certain natural consequences (whether pleasure, pain or pregnancy), to a potential sentence of disease or death. It differs fundamentally from deception as to the consideration that will be given for consent, like marriage, money or a fur coat, in that it relates to the physical act itself. It differs, moreover, in a profoundly serious way that merits the criminal sanction.

The accused is charged with sexual assault. He testified that he met the complainant on a street corner in the early morning hours and had agreed to pay her $100 for sexual intercourse. He conceded that he had driven the complainant to an underground parking lot and that he had sexual relations with her to which she consented. In the course of his testimony he stated that he never had intended to pay her $100 for sexual services and that he had offered to pay $100 only because he wanted to have some sexual activity. Result? Compare *R. v. P.* (1987), 58 C.R. (3d) 320, 35 C.C.C. (3d) 528 (B.C. C.A.).

LEMIEUX v. R.

[1967] S.C.R. 492, 2 C.R.N.S. 1, [1968] 1 C.C.C. 187

JUDSON J: — In October of 1964, the appellant, Florian Lemieux, was tried before a Judge and jury on an indictment charging that he did

> On the 17th day of November, A.D. 1963, at the City of Ottawa in the County of Carleton, unlawfully break and enter the dwelling house of Benjamin Achbar situated at premises numbered 905 Killeen Avenue in the said City of Ottawa, with intent to commit an indictable offence therein, contrary to Section 282(l)(a) [now s. 348(1)(a)] of the *Criminal Code.*

He was found guilty and sentenced to three years' imprisonment. His appeal to the Court of Appeal was dismissed on February 24, 1965. His appeal to this Court, pursuant to leave granted under s. 597(l)(*b*) [am. 1956, c. 48, s. 19; 1960-61, c. 43, s. 27(1)] of the *Criminal Code* is on the following question of law:

> Did the learned trial Judge err in law in not charging the jury as to whether there was a consent to the breaking and entering?

The facts of the case which give rise to this suggested defence are very unusual. In November of 1963, the Ottawa police were very anxious to arrest the members of a gang which was known as the "hooded gang" and which was engaged in a series of break-ins in the Ottawa area. On November 16, 1963, one R. D. Bard telephoned an officer of the Ottawa Police Department to inform him that he had information about this gang. The officer immediately visited Bard at his house and Bard told him that he wanted money for his information. The officer then summoned another officer, who came to Bard's house. Then all three went to see an inspector of the Ottawa Police Department.

Bard and the first two mentioned officers next drove to the west end of the City of Ottawa to look for a house where a feigned break-in could be staged. They went to the neighbourhood of Killeen Ave. and Lenester St. where Bard pointed out a house at 905 Killeen Ave. belonging to Mr. Benjamin Achbar. Bard knew this house because some time before he had paved the laneway. The police obtained the key to Achbar's house from Achbar himself and then staked out the premises.

On November 17, 1963, at 7:30 p.m., a car owned by Florian Lemieux drove past the house. There were three men in the car. Lemieux was driving under the direction of Bard. The third man was Jean Guindon. The car circled the block and was then parked near the house. Guindon and Bard got out of the car. Lemieux remained behind the wheel. Guindon and Bard went to the side door and Guindon did the actual breaking with a screwdriver. The police were waiting inside. Bard was arrested on the spot. Lemieux was arrested in the car. Guindon escaped and was arrested a short time later.

Bard was called at trial as a witness for the Crown. On cross-examination he did not remember what was discussed with the police on November 16, 1963; did not remember if he agreed to take part in the break-in; did not remember if the matter of a reward was discussed and did not remember that he had picked out the Achbar house for the purpose of breaking and entering.

Guindon was also called as a Crown witness and testified that Lemieux knew nothing about the break-in and that he thought that he was driving Bard to the house for the purpose of enabling Bard to collect money owing to him. Guindon was declared a hostile witness and a previous inconsistent statement was put to him in which he had said that he had asked Lemieux to drive him to the house because he and Bard were going to break in. Guindon sought to minimize the effect of this statement by pleading lack of understanding of the contents because of language difficulties, but the two police officers who took the statement both said that Guindon had spoken to them in English that night.

Both Guindon and Lemieux were convicted by the jury. Their appeals to the Court of Appeal were also dismissed. Bard, the informer, pleaded guilty and received a heavy sentence. His appeal to the Court of Appeal was allowed and he was acquitted.

Lemieux's appeal to this Court was argued on the basis that he knew that he was acting as a driver to take Bard and Guindon to a house that he had never seen and that these two were going to break in. What he did not know, however, was that he, along with Guindon, was being led into a trap, It is quite clear that he and Guindon were solicited by Bard, the informer, to undertake this break-in. The police had secured the key from the owner of the house, who was willing to co-operate in this scheme. In the present case Lemieux had no thought of breaking and entering this house until he was approached by Bard, who was acting under police instruction. The police had obtained the consent of the owner to use the premises in the hope that they would be able to arrest certain criminals.

The case is very different from *R. v. Chandler*, [1913] 1 K.B. 125 at p. 127, where an accused who intended to break into a shop sought a key from the servant of the owner of the shop. This servant informed his master. The key was supplied and the police were waiting for the shop-breaker when he arrived. The key in this case was supplied by the servant only for the purpose that the criminal might be detected in the commission of the offence. The criminal was guilty of shop-breaking.

But in Lemieux's case, the facts are not at all similar. The police set the whole scheme in motion through Bard. He was to lead a man who at first had no intention of breaking and entering, who went to the scene of the crime at Bard's instigation and who was led into the trap by Bard.

On the evidence it was open to the jury to find that the owner of the house had placed the police officers in possession of it giving them authority to deal with it as they pleased and that they had not merely consented to Bard breaking into it with the assistance of others, but had urged him to do so. To break into a house in these circumstances is not an offence.

For Lemieux to be guilty of the offence with which he was charged, it was necessary that two elements should co-exist, (i) that he had committed the forbidden act, and (ii) that he had the wrongful intention of so doing. On the assumption on which the appeal was argued *mens rea* was clearly established but it was open to the jury to find that, notwithstanding the guilty intention of the appellant, the *actus* which was in fact committed, was no crime at all.

In my opinion, if the jury had been properly charged on this aspect of the matter and had taken the view of the facts which it has been pointed out above it was open to them to take, they would have acquitted the appellant.

Had Lemieux in fact committed the offence with which he was charged, the circumstance that he had done the forbidden act at the solicitation of an *agent provocateur* would have been irrelevant to the question of his guilt or innocence. The reason that this conviction cannot stand is that the jury were not properly instructed on a question vital to the issue whether any offence had been committed.

I would allow the appeal, quash the conviction and direct that a verdict of acquittal be entered.

Appeal allowed; accused acquitted.

JOHNSON v. R.

[1977] 2 S.C.R. 646, 37 C.R.N.S. 370, 34 C.C.C. (2d) 12

DICKSON J.: — The question raised in this appeal is not novel. It was current in the time of Lord Hale, in the 18th century. The question is whether an intruder can be convicted of breaking and entering premises without actual breaking. Hale (Pleas of the Crown, vol. 1, p. 551) writing in 1778, delineates two forms of breaking:

> 1. In law, and thus every one that enters into another's house against his will, or to commit a felony, tho the doors be open, does in law break the house. 2. There is a breaking in fact an actual force upon the house, as by opening a door, breaking a window. etc.

Today, (1) would be regarded as a constructive breaking and (2) as an actual breaking. Hale recounts how an earlier jurist had held breaking in law sufficient to constitute burglary if a man entered the house by the doors open in the night and stole goods, but, Hale adds: "yet the law is, that a bare breaking in law, *viz*. as entry by the doors or windows open is not sufficient to make burglary without an actual breaking". There was an exception: if a thief went down a chimney to steal, that was breaking and entering. The distinction between actual and constructive breaking endures to this day.

At common law an actual breaking occurred whenever any part of the building or its closed fastenings was displaced as, for example, by drawing a bolt, turning a key or lifting a latch: Kenney's Outlines of Criminal Law, 17th ed., para. 311. The opening of a closed but unlocked bedroom window was a breaking while the further opening of a window already partly opened was not. The reason suggested for this precious distinction was that when a householder left a window or a door partly open he offered a visible invitation to enter.

Constructive breaking, in the absence of actual breaking, extended at common law to cases in which the intruder entered the premises by some aperture which, by necessity, was left permanently open, such as a chimney. In 1892 that concept found its way into the *Canadian Criminal Code* (1892 (Can.) c. 29, s. 407(*b*)(ii)). It was repeated in the Codes of 1906 (R.S.C. 1906, c. 146, s. 340) and 1927 (R.S.C., c. 36, s. 340(2)) in these words:

> Every one who obtains entrance into any building by any threat or artifice used for that purpose, or by collusion with any person in the building, or who enters any chimney or other aperture of the building, permanently left open for any necessary purpose, shall be deemed to have broken and entered that building.

The wording was substantially altered and extended by 1953-54, c. 51, s. 294(*b*), and now appears as s. 308(*b*) [now s. 350(*b*)], reading:

> 308. For the purpose of sections 306 and 307 . . .
>
> (*b*) a person shall be deemed to have broken and entered if
> (i) he obtained entrance by a threat or artifice or by collusion with a person within, or
> (ii) he entered without lawful justification or excuse, the proof of which lies upon him, by a permanent or temporary opening.

Central to this appeal is the scope to be given to s. 308(*b*)(ii).

The definition of "break" is found in s. 282 [now s. 321] of the *Code* reading:

> 282. In this Part
> "break" means
> (*a*) to break any part internal or external, or
> (*b*) to open any thing that is used or intended to be used to close or to cover an internal or external opening.

The facts in the present case are unexceptional, The accused entered a partly constructed unoccupied dwelling house at 3:30 a.m. through an open doorway leading into the house from a carport. The door had not yet been installed. The owner, as a temporary measure, had nailed a sheet of plywood over the opening, but it would appear that someone had removed it as it was lying on the ground at the time of entry by the accused and a companion. The accused was convicted on a charge that he did unlawfully break and enter a place, to wit, a dwelling house under construction, and did commit the indictable offence of theft therein. It was common ground that the building was, by definition, a "place" but that it was not a dwelling house. There was no suggestion that the accused had any lawful justification of excuse for entering the building. In dismissing an appeal by the accused the British Columbia Court of Appeal, speaking through McFarlane J.A., held that the language of s. 308(b) (ii) was clear and unambiguous and sufficient to support the conviction. The reasoning of the same Court in the earlier case of *Regina v. Sutherland*, 50 C.R. 197, [1967] 2 C.C.C. 84, was applied rather than that of the Ontario Court of Appeal in *Regina v. Jewell* (1974), 28 C.R.N.S. 331, 22 C.C.C. (2d) 252.

In the *Sutherland* case the accused was charged with unlawfully breaking and entering a garage and committing an indictable offence therein. The garage was enclosed on three sides and open at one end for the entrance of a car. It was through this entrance that the accused entered to steal gasoline. McFarlane J.A. delivered the judgment of the Court.

Regina v. Sutherland was decided on the narrow ground that the open end of a garage would be described as an entrance and not an opening. In the reasons for judgment delivered in the case at bar, McFarlane J.A. had this to say respecting the *Sutherland* case:

> In my opinion the basis of the decision in *Regina v. Sutherland* was the interpretation of the words "permanent or temporary opening" in s. 308(b) (ii). I think it is clearly implicit in the judgment that if the entrance to the garage had been held to be a permanent or temporary opening within the meaning of the statute, Sutherland's conviction would have been upheld although the breaking was constructive only and not actual. It was decided that 308(b) (ii) did not apply because the entry was not by a permanent or temporary opening.

In *Regina v. Bargiamis*, 10 C.R.N.S. 129, [1970] 4 C.C.C. 358 (Ont. C.A.), the accused induced the assistant night manager to leave open the doors of a restaurant. It was understood that the accused would enter the restaurant and through it reach an adjacent drug store for the purpose of stealing a safe. The store manager advised his employer and the police were notified. The accused on a Sunday evening entered and went downstairs and through another door into the restaurant, where he was arrested. Gale C.J.O. delivering the judgment of the Ontario Court of Appeal, dismissing an appeal had this to say, p. 132:

> In our view, the accused entered the Zumburger "without lawful justification or excuse . . . by a permanent or temporary opening". As the subsection qualifies the terms "opening" by using both "permanent" and "temporary", it matters not, as it seems to us, whether one considers the opening of the door that was ajar in the laneway or the opening of the door into the Zumburger as the opening through which the accused entered without lawful justification or excuse. Mr. Levy relied upon the case of *Regina v. Sutherland* [supra], a decision of the Court of Appeal of British Columbia. If the facts were the same we would, of course, be very much inclined to follow the *Sutherland* judgment. However, in our view, that case does not in any sense inhibit us in upholding the conviction here. In the *Sutherland* case the accused entered a three-sided garage at the point where there was no wall and the Court of Appeal of British Columbia held that where there was no wall or other structure surrounding an open space, the "opening" was not regarded as coming within the subsection. In our view that is quite correct. In other words, there has to be something in which an opening exists and in the *Sutherland* case there was nothing to sustain the opening. Here, of course, both doorways constitute openings, the one at the lane in the outside wall of the building and the one into the Zumburger's basement in an

inside wall of the building. Accordingly, the provisions of subs. (*b*)(ii) cover the situation precisely. In this connection, reference should also be had to the case of *Regina v. Corkum* (1969), 7 C.R.N.S. 61, where McLellan Co. Ct. J. of the Nova Scotia County Court also distinguished the situation before him from that which prevailed in the *Sutherland* case.

In *Regina v. Bargiamis* doorways were held to constitute openings. The Court relied upon para. (*b*)(ii) of s. 308 because of the argument advanced by counsel for the accused that para. (*b*)(i) did not apply. The argument was based on the submission that there was no collusion because the employee was merely pretending to agree to a collusive agreement and was not in fact doing so.

I come now to *Regina v. Jewell, supra.* The accused in that case entered an unoccupied dilapidated dwelling house through a screen door and an inner door, both of which were open wide enough to permit the accused to enter without further opening the doors. The Court held that entry through the open door in the circumstances of the case did not constitute a breaking of the premises. The judgment notes that at common law and under s. 340(2) (the section referring to chimneys or other apertures permanently left open) entry through a temporary opening such as a hole in the roof or a wall in the building did not constitute a breaking of the building; nor did further opening a door or window which was already open. With respect, I disagree. It is then stated that s. 294 (now s. 308) of the *Code* had effected a change in the Canadian law, and the following note to s. 294 from Martin's *Criminal Code*, 1955, p. 517, was quoted and relied upon:

> This comes from the former s. 340, altered by addition of the words "or temporary" in clause (*b*). The purpose of the addition is to meet decisions that the raising of a window that was partly open did not constitute a breaking: *Rex. v. Burns* (1903), 36 N.S.R. 257, 7 C.C.C. 95; *Rex. v. Miller*, 5 C.R. 415, [1948] 1 W.W.R. 1093, 91 C.C.C. 270 (Alta. C.A.); *Regina v. Dolbec*, [1950] R.L. 193, 98 C.C.C. 62.

The change may well have been prompted by decisions which had held that raising a partly opened window did not constitute a breaking, as the learned author of Martin's *Criminal Code* suggests, but it is clear that the language which Parliament used in changing the law embraced far more than partly opened windows. It broadened the reference to permanent apertures by removing the requirement that they be "left open for any necessary purpose". It extended constructive breaking to include entry by any temporary opening. In addition, the burden of proof that he had lawful justification or excuse for entry was placed upon the person who enters.

If I understand that judgment in *Regina v. Jewell* correctly, it would have the effect of limiting s. 308(*b*)(ii) to those situations in which a would-be intruder found a door or window partly ajar and opened it further in order to gain entry. A partly opened door would be an opening but a fully open door would not be so regarded. There is nothing in the language of the section to connote such a result. A distinction of the kind suggested would differentiate between doors open wide enough to permit an intruder to slip around them and those so narrowly ajar as to require a push in order to enter; it would also distinguish, as one of my colleagues was moved to observe during argument, between fat burglars and thin ones. Such an interpretation of the section would also do away with constructive entry through chimneys, perhaps not a daily occurrence but conceptually imbedded in common law and statute for centuries.

Parliament has extended the limits of constructive breaking. Parliament, for the purpose of the *Criminal Code*, has given the word "break" an artificial construction that would not otherwise prevail. The notion that a person has broken and entered if he obtains entrance by threat or artifice or collusion is equally a fiction, long recognized at common law and now codified in s. 308(*b*)(i). It is within Parliamentary competence to extend constructive entry from "any chimney or other aperture permanently left open for any necessary purpose", as stated in s. 304(2), and in the common law, to "a permanent or temporary opening". These are plain words which must be given effect according to their ordinary meaning. There are many other "deeming" sections in the *Criminal Code*. Some of them were noted in the judgment of Ritchie J. in *Brodie v. The Queen*, 37 C.R. 120, [1962] S.C.R. 681, 132 C.C.C. 161. This court had occasion to say in *Regina v. Maroney*, 27 C.R.N.S. 185 at 188, [1975] 2 S.C.R. 306, 18 C.C.C. (2d) 257:

> We are not concerned with larceny here but with theft by conversion as defined by the *Criminal Code* of Canada. Smith and Hogan, *Criminal Law*, 3rd ed., p. 396, point out that the 1916 Larceny Act [1916 (U.K.), c. 50] was often construed on the tacit assumption that there was no intention to alter the previous law and the earlier case law had lost little or no authority. We are concerned here with a *Code*. We start with the *Code* and not with the previous state of the law for the purpose of inquiring whether the *Code* has made any change. On the plain meaning of our *Code* the facts of this case show the commission of an indictable offence — theft.

The argument was advanced that the distinction between ss. 306 [now 348] and 307 [now 349] of the *Code* would be extinguished if entry through an open door constituted breaking. There can be no doubt that the effect of the amendment was to narrow the gap between the two sections. They overlap but some differences remain. Section 307 is concerned only with dwelling houses, s. 306 with "places" which, in addition to dwellings, includes other buildings or structures, railway vehicles, vessels, aircraft and trailers. Section 307 speaks also of a person who is "in" a dwelling house with intent. Section 306 does not, though it provides for the situation in which a person "breaks out" of a place after committing an indictable offence therein. Thus, certain factual situations will call for a charge under s. 306, others under s. 307. In some cases of dwelling house entry the prosecutor may have the alternative of charging under one section or the other, but this is not uncommon. A stabbing, for example, may give rise to a nice question of whether to charge attempted murder, or causing bodily harm with intent to maim, or some lesser charge. It remains for the prosecutor in the circumstances of the particular case to decide which charge is appropriate.

I would dismiss the appeal.

R. v. LOHNES

[1992] 1 S.C.R. 167, 10 C.R. (4th) 125, 69 C.C.C. (3d) 289

McLACHLIN J.: — This case requires this Court for the first time to consider what constitutes a public disturbance under s. 175(1)(a) of the *Criminal Code*, R.S.C. 1985, c. C-46, which makes it an offence to cause a disturbance in or near a public place by, inter alia, fighting, screaming, shouting, swearing, singing or using insulting or obscene language. Shouting or swearing or singing are not in themselves criminal offences. They become criminal only when they cause a disturbance in or near a public place. What constitutes such a disturbance? For example, does mere annoyance or emotional disturbance of the complainant suffice? Or is something more required?

The Facts

The case began as a disagreement between two neighbours in the town of Milton, Nova Scotia. The appellant, Donald Lohnes, lived across the street from a certain Mr. Porter. Mr. Porter, it seems, was given to collecting equipment on his premises and running motors which made loud noises. This disturbed Mr. Lohnes. It disturbed him so much that on two occasions a year apart he went onto the veranda of his house and shouted obscenities at Mr. Porter. The essence of Mr. Lohnes's remarks was that he did not want Mr. Porter "to run that chain saw or that lawn mower or to leave that or have that God-damned junk heap". This was embellished by a string of epithets revealing an impressive command of the obscene vernacular. On the second occasion Mr. Lohnes concluded his oration with the assertion that he would shoot Mr. Porter if he had a gun.

Mr. Porter filed a complaint. He was the only Crown witness. There was no evidence that anyone else heard Mr. Lohnes's statements or that Mr. Porter's conduct was affected by them.

Mr. Lohnes was convicted on the ground that his conduct in itself constituted a disturbance within s. 175(1)(a) of the *Criminal Code*; the trial Judge found, as well, that Mr. Porter was "disturbed" by the impugned conduct. The convictions were upheld by the Summary Convictions Appeal Court. The Nova Scotia Supreme Court, Appeal Division refused leave from that decision: (1990), 100 N.S.R. (2d) 268. He now appeals to this Court.

Legislation

Section 175 of the *Criminal Code* states:

175. (1) Every one who

> (a) not being in a dwelling house, causes a disturbance in or near a public place,

(i) by fighting, screaming, shouting, swearing, singing or using insulting or obscene language,

. . .

is guilty of an offence punishable on summary conviction.

(2) In the absence of other evidence, or by way of corroboration of other evidence, a summary conviction Court may infer from the evidence of a peace officer relating to the conduct of a person or persons, whether ascertained or not, that a disturbance described in paragraph (1)(a) or (d) was caused or occurred.

Analysis

Section 175(1)(a) creates a two-element offence consisting of: (1) commission of one of the enumerated acts; which, (2) causes a disturbance in or near a public place. There is no doubt on the facts of this case that one of the enumerated acts was committed. The only question is whether the evidence establishes that it caused a disturbance in or near a public place.

The word "disturbance" encompasses a broad range of meanings. At one extreme, it may be something as innocuous as a false note or a jarring colour; something which disturbs in the sense of annoyance or disruption. At the other end of the spectrum are incidents of violence, inducing disquiet, fear and apprehension for physical safety. Between these extremes lies a vast variety of disruptive conduct. The question before us is whether all conduct within this broad spectrum elicits criminal liability under s. 175(1), and if not, where the line should be drawn.

The Nova Scotia Supreme Court, Appeal Division, in dismissing Mr. Lohnes's application for leave to appeal, agreed with the finding implicit to the judgments below: all that is required to establish an offence under s. 175(1)(a) is one of the forms of prohibited conduct (fighting, screaming, shouting, swearing, singing or using insulting or obscene language) which one ought to know would disturb others. The appellant contends that this interpretation is too broad; there must be some overtly manifested disturbance of the public's use and enjoyment of the public place where the act takes place. The main issue thus turns on how "disturbance" in s. 175(1)(a) is defined; does foreseeable emotional upset suffice, or must there be an externally manifested disturbance of a public nature? The appeal, like the judgments below, focuses upon the requisite *actus reus* of the offence, although the issue of *mens rea*, as recognized by the respondent, flows necessarily from a discussion of "disturbance". A subsidiary issue concerns whether the act itself may constitute the disturbance, or whether a secondary disturbance is required.

The values at stake on this appeal are readily discerned. On the one hand lies the freedom of the individual to shout, sing or otherwise express himself or herself. On the other lies the collective right of every subject to peace and tranquillity. Neither right is absolute. The individual right of expression must at some point give way to the collective interest in peace and tranquillity, and the collective right in peace and tranquillity must be based on recognition that in a society where people live together some degree of disruption must be tolerated. The question is where the line is to be drawn.

I propose to consider these issues from the perspectives of the authorities, the principles of statutory construction, and the underlying policy issues. On my reading, these considerations point to the conclusion that s. 175(1)(a) of the *Criminal Code* requires an externally manifested disturbance in or near a public place, consisting either in the act itself or in a secondary disturbance.

The Authorities

The offence created by s. 175(1)(a) finds its origins in the common law of vagrancy, an "offence against public convenience", which proscribed certain behaviour in order to preserve peace and order in the community: see, for example, *An Act Respecting Vagrants*, S.C. 1869, c. 28. In 1947, the *Criminal Code* created a new and distinct offence of causing a disturbance; the offence was moved from the section of the *Code* entitled "Vagrancy" to the nuisance offences falling under Part V labelled "Offences Against Religion, Morals and Public Convenience", S.C. 1947, c. 55, s. 3. Upon the *Code's* revision in 1955, S.C. 1953-54, c. 51, the offence was included in Part IV, renamed "Sexual Offenses, Public Morals and Disorderly Conduct", as s. 160 under the section entitled "Disorderly Conduct".

Our jurisprudence has exhibited two different doctrinal approaches to the offence dating to the first federal vagrancy enactments. The first line of authority adopts an expansive approach to "disturbance"; the second a narrower approach which would limit "disturbance" by requiring external manifestations of disturbance.

. . . .

Whatever their theoretical pronouncements, Canadian Courts have entered few if any convictions under (what is now) s. 175(1)(a) absent an overtly manifested disturbance which affected people's conduct, be it found in the act itself or in its effect. In *Swinimer* the accused's fighting, shouting and obscene language in front of his residence interfered with the usual activities of a neighbour as well as her children, to judge from her testimony that she had to return to the bedroom during the episode to calm the children down. The conviction in *R. v. Allick* (February 20, 1976), Munroe J. (B.C. S.C.) [unreported] (cited in *R. v. Peters*, *supra*, at p. 90 [C.C.C., p. 256 C.R.]), arose from a spirited barroom brawl. In *R. v. Chikoski* (1973), 14 C.C.C. (2d) 38 (Ont. Prov. Ct.), the police officer testified that the obscenities which the accused had shouted at him not only offended and disturbed him, but caused a group of men working in a field some 200 feet away to stop their work and look up towards the place where the police officer and the accused were standing. In *R. v. D. (C.)*, the trial Judge found that the accused caused an affray in the street by shouting and ramming his car into the back of another car, reducing the wife of the owner to tears. Yet, the Court of Appeal overturned even this conviction, finding that the interruption of "tranquillity" of mind or the "emotional upset" caused the owner and his wife was insufficient to constitute a "disturbance". Shouting abusive language without more was held not to trigger the section in *R. v. Eyre* (1972), 10 C.C.C. (2d) 236 (B.C. S.C.) and *R. v. Peters*. In *R. v. Wolgram, supra*, shouting obscenities at police in a barroom was similarly held not to offend the section because "[i]t was not made to appear that any person or persons were so disturbed by what occurred as to cause some disorder or agitation to ensue or that there was any interference with the ordinary and customary use by the public of a public place" (p. 537 [C.C.C.]).

I conclude that the weight of the authority, whether viewed from the point of view of theory or result, suggests that before an offence can arise under s. 175(1) of the *Criminal Code*, the enumerated conduct must cause an overtly manifested disturbance which constitutes an interference with the ordinary and customary use by the public of the place in question. This may be proved by direct evidence or inferred under s. 175(2). It is not necessary that there be a separate disturbance secondary to the disturbing act; the act itself may in some cases amount to a disturbance and "cause" it in this sense. Finally, the principle of legality, alluded to in the judgment of Wilson J. in *Skoke-Graham* suggests that only conduct which may reasonably be expected to cause such a disturbance in the particular circumstances of the case falls within s. 175(1)(*a*) (see p. 14, below).

Principles of Statutory Construction

The word "disturbance" is capable of many meanings. The task is to choose the meaning which best accords with the intention of Parliament.

The following arguments support the conclusion that "disturbance" in s. 175(1)(*a*) involves more than mere mental or emotional annoyance or disruption.

First, the noun "disturbance" may have a different connotation than the verb "to disturb". Not everything that disturbs people results in a disturbance (*e.g.*, smoking). A definition which posits identity between "disturb" and "disturbance" is contrary to ordinary usage, the most fundamental principle of statutory construction. This is not to say that one cannot speak of a purely emotional disturbance, but rather that "disturbance" has a secondary meaning which "disturb" does not possess; a meaning which suggests interference with an ordinary and customary conduct or use.

Second, the context of "disturbance" in s. 175(1)(*a*) suggests that Parliament did not intend to protect society from mere emotional disturbance. Had Parliament sought to protect society from annoyance and anxiety, the section would not be confined to acts occurring in or near a public place, nor would it single out particular forms of objectionable conduct — many other types of conduct disturb us. Parliament could have expressly protected against emotional disturbance, as was done in the *Public Order Act 1986* (U.K.), 1986, c. 64. But, to borrow the language of MacKeigan C.J.N.S. in *Swinimer, supra*, Parliament chose to speak of a disturbance in or near a public place, not in someone's mind. By addressing "disturbance" in the public context, Parliament signalled that its objective was not the protection of individuals from emotional upset, but the protection of the public from disorder calculated to interfere with the public's normal activities.

Third, interpretative aids suggest that s. 175(1)(*a*) is directed at publicly exhibited disorder. As noted in *Skoke-Graham, supra*, headings and preambles may be used as intrinsic aids in interpreting ambiguous statutes. Section 175(1)(*a*) appears under the section "Disorderly Conduct". Without elevating headings to determinative status, the heading under which s. 175(1)(*a*) appears supports the view that Parliament had in mind, not the emotional upset or annoyance of individuals, but disorder and agitation which interferes with the ordinary use of a place.

Fourth, the word used for disturbance in the French version of s. 175(1), "tapage", connotes an externally manifested disturbance involving violent noise or confusion disrupting the tranquillity of those using the area in question. For example, Le Petit Robert 1 (Paris: Le Robert, 1990) defines the term as: "10 Bruit violent, confus, désordonné produit par un groupe de personnes; ... *Tapage injurieux ou nocturne*: consistant à troubler la tranquillité des habitants en faisant du bruit, sans motif légitime". [Emphasis in original.]

Finally, it can be argued that the reference in s. 175(2) to an inference of disturbance from evidence "relating to the *conduct* of a person *or persons*" is consistent with the finding that Parliament had in mind the effect of the shouting, swearing or singing, for example, on the conduct of persons other than the accused. In short, Parliament was concerned with how members of the public other than the accused may have been affected by the impugned act.

Policy

Considerations pertaining to the practical application of the criminal law suggest that the narrower "public disturbance" interpretation of s. 175(1)(*a*) is preferable to the broader "emotional disturbance" standard.

The first consideration pertains to fundamental justice, and in particular, the principle of legality, which affirms the entitlement of every person to know in advance whether their conduct is illegal. As Wilson J. points out in *Skoke-Graham, supra*, application of the internal test would mean that "anyone in any given situation would act at the risk of causing some unmanifested emotional upset or 'disturbance' to another person" (p. 131 S.C.R.). Read thus, s. 175(1)(*a*) imposes a duty to ascertain whether one's conduct disturbs or can reasonably be expected to disturb the "mental" or "emotional" tranquillity of others. Such a burden, dependent as it is on time, place, circumstance and the sensitivities of others, verges on the capricious. It may well be questioned whether it could ever be discharged with certainty.

The second consideration is that the narrower "public disturbance" test permits a more sensitive balancing between the countervailing interests at stake. As MacKeigan C.J.N.S. points out in *Swinimer*, the test for a disturbance in or near a public place under s. 175(1)(*a*) should permit the Court to weigh the degree and intensity of the conduct complained of against the degree and nature of the peace which can be expected to prevail in a given place at a given time. A test which accepts mental or emotional disturbance as sufficient to establish the offence does not permit such balancing; all that is required is that the accused should have known that someone might be internally disturbed. A test, on the other hand, which turns on whether the effect of the conduct was such as to interfere with the ordinary and customary use of the premises at the time and place in question, permits the countervailing factors to be weighed and balanced. As such, it arguably strikes a more sensitive balance between the individual interest in liberty and the public interest in going about its affairs in peace and tranquillity.

The final policy consideration takes us into the more precarious terrain of pondering the proper goals and limits of the criminal law. The *Swinimer* standard, adopted by the Courts below, would make it a criminal offence to sing or shout in circumstances where a person has reason to believe that his or her conduct might annoy or upset someone else, even though no one may have heard the sound, much less have been affected by it. In support of this interpretation, it was argued that such a stringent standard is necessary in order to nip disturbances in the bud before they become truly disruptive to the public. But it is far from self-evident that the goal of peace and order in our public places requires the criminal law to step in at the stage of foreseeability of mental annoyance. Indeed, our society has traditionally tolerated a great deal of activity in our streets and byways which can and does disturb and annoy others sharing the public space. Given the intrusion on public liberty and the uncertainty in the criminal law which such a rule would introduce, it is arguable that some external manifestation of disorder in the sense of interference with the normal use of the affected place should be required to transform lawful conduct into an unlawful criminal offence.

Conclusion on the Ambit of s. 175(1)(a)

The weight of the authorities, the principles of statutory construction and policy considerations, taken together, lead me to the conclusion that the disturbance contemplated by s. 175(1)(*a*) is something more than mere emotional upset. There must be an externally manifested disturbance of the public peace, in the sense of interference with the ordinary and customary use of the premises by the public. There may be direct evidence of such an effect or interference, or it may be inferred from the evidence of a police officer as to the conduct of a person or persons under s. 175(2). The disturbance may consist of the impugned act itself, as in the case of a fight interfering with the peaceful use of a barroom, or it may flow as a consequence of the impugned act, as where shouting and swearing produce a scuffle. As the cases illustrate, the interference with the ordinary and customary conduct in or near the public place may consist in something as small as being distracted from one's work. But it must be present and it must be externally manifested. In accordance with the principle of legality, the disturbance must be one which may reasonably have been foreseen in the particular circumstances of time and place.

Disposition of the Appeal

There was no evidence of a disturbance of the use of the premises in question by anyone in the case at bar. The trial Judge applied a mental disturbance test, convicting on the basis that an "ordinary reasonable individual would be disturbed by language of that nature being shouted in a public area". The convictions were upheld. In denying leave to appeal, the Court of Appeal agreed that language such as that used by the accused was "inherently disturbing and was of itself a disturbance" (p. 270 [N.S.R.]). There was no finding that the conduct of the complainant or anyone else was affected or disturbed by the language. In the absence of such findings, the convictions cannot stand.

I would allow the appeal, quash the convictions, and substitute acquittals in their place.

———————

Under a doctrine of vicarious responsibility, one person is automatically responsible for the wrongdoing of another solely on the basis of a relationship between the parties, irrespective of whether that person was at fault or even acted. In the law of torts it has long been clear common-law doctrine that a "master" may be vicariously liable for a tort committed by his "servant" acting in the course and scope of his employment. Given that the purpose of torts is compensation, the doctrine has a pragmatic rationale: a master is likely to be in a better position to compensate the victim and an employer profits through his employee's work. In this way the employer also bears the risk of employing a bad worker. In the criminal law where the purpose is just punishment, the emphasis is usually on an individual's own act and fault. Our courts have accordingly been reluctant to impose vicarious responsibility. They have generally done so in the past only where there is an express statutory provision. One such statutory provision has now been held to be unconstitutional.

R. v. BURT

(1985), 47 C.R. (3d) 49, 21 C.C.C. (3d) 138 (Sask. Q.B.).

GEREIN J.: — The accused was charged that he did contrary to "s. 141 via s. 253 [of the Vehicles Act] as registered owner allow someone to operate vehicle and cause excessive noise in its operation". After a trial which proceeded on the basis of an agreed statement of facts, the learned trial Judge concluded that s. 253 contravened the *Canadian Charter of Rights and Freedoms* and entered an acquittal. From said decision the Crown has appealed.

The agreed facts giving rise to the charge were as follows:

> 1. THAT on the 4th day of September, 1983 at approximately 2:45 a.m. a Ford pick-up truck, being a motor vehicle registered in the name of the defendant, was operated within the Town of Kindersley, in the Province of Saskatchewan on a public highway.
>
> 2. THAT the vehicle was operated in a manner which created excessive or unusual noise, contrary to Section 141 of *The Vehicle* [sic] *Act* for the Province of Saskatchewan. The vehicle left approximately 25 feet of tire marks while crossing Main Street.
>
> 3. THAT the Royal Canadian Mounted Police constable on patrol pursued the vehicle, which was approximately two blocks ahead of the police car when it pulled to the right and stopped. As the police vehicle approached the registered owner was observed standing next to the vehicle. The police car stopped and the officer called to the owner who ignored the officer and continued walking into his residence.
>
> 4. THAT the driver of the motor vehicle was not identified and the accused is charged as the registered owner of the motor vehicle under the provisions of Section 253 of *The Vehicles Act* for the Province of Saskatchewan.

Section 253 (now s. 169(1)) of the *Vehicles Act*, R.S.S. 1978, c. V-3 (since replaced by the *Vehicles Act, 1983* (Sask.), c. V-3.1), provided:

> 253. The owner of a motor vehicle, tractor or trailer, other than a public service vehicle, is liable for violation of any Provision of this Act in connection with the operation of the motor vehicle, tractor or trailer, unless he proves to the satisfaction of the provincial magistrate or justice of the peace trying the case that at the time of the offence the vehicle, tractor or trailer was not being operated by him, nor by any other person with his consent, express or implied.

The trial Judge held that s. 253 contravened s. 7 of the *Canadian Charter of Rights and Freedoms*, which provides:

> 7. Everyone has the right to life, liberty and security of the person and the right not to be deprived thereof except in accordance with the principles of fundamental justice.

By reason of s. 253 of the *Vehicles Act* an owner of a motor vehicle became vicariously liable for any violation of the Act in which the motor vehicle was involved: see *R. v. Grant* (1957), 29 C.R. 229, 122 C.C.C. 261 (Sask. Police Ct.); *R. v. Davlyn Corp.*, 8 C.R.N.S. 219, [1970] 3 C.C.C. 115 (Alta. C.A.); and *R. v. Budget Car Rentals (Toronto) Ltd.* (1981), 20 C.R. (3d) 66 (C.A.). Thus an owner became liable to be convicted of the substantive violation and not simply of lending or permitting the use of his motor vehicle. On conviction he was subject to punishment, which could be a fine of up to $1,000, imprisonment, suspension of licence or a combination thereof. A person could be asleep at home when events transpire which ultimately result in that person's imprisonment. This could occur even though the person took no part in the violation, even in the sense of aiding or abetting. Thus an owner could be convicted in the absence of *both mens rea* and *actus reus*.

Does this absence of *actus reus* render the legislation invalid? In my opinion it does.

. . . .

Throughout the history of the common law the conduct of the wrongdoer had to compromise the prohibited act. The *actus reus* had to be present. Thus, in *Fowler v. Padget* (1798), 101 E.R. 1103 at 1106, Lord Kenyon C.J. stated:

> . . . it is a principle of natural justice, and of our law, that *actus non facit reum nisi mens sit rea*. The intent and the act must both concur to constitute the crime . . .

In Russell on Crime, 12th ed. (1964), vol. 1, at p. 22, the learned author states:

> The new conception that merely to bring about a prohibited harm should not involve a man in liability to punishment unless in addition he could be regarded as morally blameworthy came to be enshrined in the well-known maxim *actus non facit reum nisi mens sit rea*. This ancient maxim has remained unchallenged as a declaration of principle at common law throughout the centuries up to the present day. So long therefore as it remains unchallenged no man should be convicted of a crime at common law unless the two requirements which it envisages are satisfied, namely, that there must be both a physical element and a mental element in every crime.

Then, at p. 26:

> We may repeat, then, that to constitute a crime at common law there must always be a result brought about by human conduct, a physical event, which the law prohibits, for example the death of a man who is under the Queen's peace; and that it has for some time past been the custom to employ the term *actus reus* to denote a deed so prohibited.

In the text Criminal Law, 4th ed. (1978), by Smith and Hogan, the learned authors state at p. 31:

> Before a man can be convicted of a crime it is usually necessary for the prosecution to prove (a) that a certain event or a certain state of affairs, which is forbidden by the criminal law, has been caused by his conduct and (b) that this conduct was accompanied by a prescribed state of mind. The event, or state of affairs, is usually called the *actus reus* and the state of mind the *mens rea* of the crime. Both these elements must be proved beyond reasonable doubt by the prosecution.

From my reading, I conclude that traditionally a person was not to be convicted of an offence unless he committed the prohibited act.

The legislative tradition has been more mixed. That a person should not be convicted of an offence committed by someone else unless he has assisted, encouraged, counselled or participated in the offence was enunciated as long ago as *R. v. Huggins* (1730), 92 E.R. 518. However, three exceptions were early recognized, namely: (1) public nuisance committed by an employee; (2) criminal libel; and (3) criminal contempt of Court: see *Upholsterers Int. Union of N. Amer., Loc. I v. Hankin & Struck Furniture Ltd.*, [1965] 1 C.C.C. 110 (B.C. C.A.), particularly at p. 40. Then, over the years, other instances of vicarious liability have been created by statute and approved by the Courts. By way of example see *Barker v. Levinson*, [1950] 2 All E.R. 825 (Div. Ct.); *R. v. Piggly Wiggly Can. Ltd.* (1933), 60 C.C.C. 104 (C.A.); and *R. v. Kiewel Brewing Co.*(1930), 53 C.C.C. 56 (C.A.). Thus for some considerable time our society has lived with vicarious liability in the field of criminal or quasi-criminal law. Put otherwise, there is a certain legislative tradition of vicarious liability in this country.

Yet instances of vicarious liability have remained the exception rather than the rule. Usually such an approach appears to have been adopted to regulate situations where substantial control over the conduct being regulated and an effective means of enforcing same has reposed in one of the parties, *e.g.,* employment situations: again see *Barker v. Levinson* and *R. v. Kiewel Brewing Co.*

In any event the legislative tradition must be looked at in the light of the then prevailing jurisprudence. More particularly, one must remember that prior to the *Charter* the law was that Parliament and Legislatures were supreme and could enact legislation as they saw fit, subject only to the division of powers as set out in the *British North America Act* [now the *Constitution Act, 1867*]. Thus, it was futile to resist legislation even if it did offend principles of fundamental justice. This situation undoubtedly caused the Courts to try to temper certain legislation by resorting to the concept of *mens rea* and implying the requirement of same as often as possible. However, this has now changed. Legislation must now conform to the requirements of the *Charter*.

To ascertain community standards as to *actus reus* is exceedingly difficult. Not only have lay members of society failed to discuss the matter, but the same can be said of the legal community. To my mind this dearth of comment is significant. It suggests that it is generally assumed or taken for granted that actus reus will be present when a charge is preferred.

In my opinion, fundamental justice encompasses the concept that a person should not be punished in the absence of a wrongful act. I am satisfied that this is the prevailing view in our society. In speaking about mens rea in *R. v. Sault Ste. Marie, supra*, Dickson J. (now C.J.C.) said at pp. 362-63:

> Public welfare offences obviously lie in a field of conflicting values. It is essential for society to maintain, through effective enforcement, high standards of public health and safety. Potential victims of those who carry on latently pernicious activities have a strong claim to consideration. On the other hand, there is a generally held revulsion against punishment of the morally innocent.

Surely no less revulsion is held when the person has not even committed the act.

I return now to a consideration of s. 253 itself and in doing so I bear in mind the statement of Dickson J., at p. 51 of *R. v. Big M Drug Mart Ltd.*, supra:

> In short, I agree with the respondent that the legislation's purpose is the initial test of constitutional validity and its effects are to be considered when the law under review has passed or, at least, has purportedly passed the purpose test. If the legislation fails the purpose test, there is no need to consider further its effects, since it has already been demonstrated to be invalid. Thus, if a law with a valid purpose interferes by its impact with rights or freedoms, a litigant could still argue the effects of the legislation as a means to defeat its applicability and possibly its validity. In short, the effects test will only be necessary to defeat legislation with a valid purpose; effects can never be relied upon to save legislation with an invalid purpose.

The purpose of the *Vehicles Act* as it existed in 1983, and indeed as it presently exists, was to achieve safe and orderly operation of motor vehicles on public highways. To this end various types of conduct are prohibited and sanctions are provided for any breach thereof. No criticism can be made of the Act as a whole.

The purpose of s. 253 is not so clear. It could not have been enacted to ensure that the owner operates his vehicle in a safe manner. The section itself anticipates that he will not be operating the vehicle and in any event the sections which explicitly govern the operation of a vehicle would cover the situation. I do not think the section was intended to regulate the lending of a motor vehicle. The very wording of the section does not suggest this. Were it otherwise the Legislature could have so stated. It seems to me that the real purpose of the section is to provide a means whereby a form of coercion can be brought to bear upon the owner of a vehicle to disclose who was driving his vehicle or had possession of it at the time when a violation occurred but the actual malefactor was not apprehended or ascertained. In short, it is a device to facilitate enforcement of the provisions of the Act.

It is of interest to note that s. 231 (now s. 172) required an owner, upon request, to furnish a police officer "with such information as he requires in the fulfilment of his duties". However, I am unable to say that the purpose of the section contravenes the *Charter*.

The result is different when one looks at the effect of the legislation. The owner would not be convicted of having improperly permitted the use of his vehicle by another or refusing to provide information. Rather, he would be convicted of the substantive offence or actual violation; in this case, causing excessive noise. As stated earlier, the owner plays no part in the violation of the Act which gives rise to the charge which is preferred. The result is that the owner becomes subject to punishment for the misconduct of another. As I have earlier concluded that this is contrary to principles of fundamental justice, it follows that s. 253 of the Vehicles Act has contravened s. 7 of the *Charter*. I use the past tense as I am concerned only with the former section.

Further, it is my opinion that s. 1 of the *Charter* cannot be utilized to maintain the impugned section. I accept that the *Vehicles Act* has the public welfare as its object and to that end seeks to achieve safe and orderly operation of motor vehicles. I also recognize that motor vehicles are numerous and, by their very nature, highly mobile. Difficulties in enforcement of the provisions of the *Vehicles Act* may result therefrom. While the object is laudable and the difficulties unfortunate, the provisions of s. 253 go beyond the reasonable limits envisaged by s. 1 of the *Charter*.

Appeal dismissed.

The decision in *Burt* was confirmed on appeal by the Saskatchewan Court of Appeal, the majority on the basis that there was no requirement of fault. For discussion of this ruling and other decisions see Lee Stuesser, "Convicting The Innocent Owner: Vicarious Liability Under Highway Traffic Legislation" (1989), 67 C.R. (3d) 316.

A car rental company disputes its responsibility for a municipal by-law parking offence arising from a parking meter violation by a lessee of one of its cars. The by-law declares that a driver of a vehicle who was not the owner is liable to any penalty exacted for a parking by-law offence, but that

the owner of the vehicle is also liable "to such a penalty unless at the time the offence was committed the vehicle was in the possession of a person other than the owner or his chauffeur without the owner's consent". Do you think that a constitutional defence along the lines of *Burt* should succeed?

Compare *R. v. Budget Car Rentals (Toronto) Ltd.* (1981), 20 C.R. (3d) 66, 57 C.C.C. (2d) 201 (C.A.).

Should such a constitutional defence bar enforcement of speeding laws through means of photo radar equipment? Would it be material that the scheme of automatically charging the owner of the vehicle involved fines but no demerit points?

Omissions

The general common-law principle is that criminal responsibility for omissions is limited to cases where there is a legal and not merely a moral duty to act. A failure to fulfil the moral duty to stop a blind man walking over a cliff, or an animal drowning in a pool, or a person from being stabbed is therefore insufficient to attract the criminal sanction. The vital question of whether there is a legal duty to act is, however, a difficult one to answer with any precision.

THE NEW TESTAMENT

Luke 10:30-37

A certain man went down from Jerusalem to Jericho, and fell among thieves, which stripped him of his raiment, and wounded him, and departed, leaving him half dead.

And by chance there came down a certain priest that way; and when he saw him, he passed by on the other side.

And likewise a Levite, when he was at the place, came and looked on him, and passed by on the other side.

But a certain Samaritan, as he journeyed, came where he was: and when he saw him, he had compassion on him,

And went to him, and bound up his wounds, pouring in oil and wine, and set him on his own beast, and brought him to an inn, and took care of him.

And on the morrow when he departed, he took out two pence, and gave them to the host, and said unto him, "Take care of him; and whatsoever thou spendest more, when I come again, I will repay thee."

Which now of these three, thinkest thou, was neighbour unto him that fell among the thieves?

And he said, "He that shewed mercy on him." Then said Jesus to him. "Go, and do thou likewise."

BUCH v. AMORY MORTGAGE CO.

(1898), 44 A. 809 at 810 (N.H. S.C.)

CARPENTER C.J.: —

. . . .

With purely moral obligations the law does not deal. For example, the priest and Levite who passed by on the other side were not, it is supposed, liable at law for the continued suffering of the man who fell among thieves, which they might, and morally ought to have, prevented or relieved. Suppose A., standing close by a railroad, sees a two year old babe on the track, and a car approaching. He can easily rescue the child, with entire safety to himself, and the instincts of humanity require him to do so. If he does not, he may, perhaps, justly be styled a ruthless savage and a moral monster; but he is not liable in damages for the child's injury, or indictable under the statute for its death.

H.R.S. RYAN, CRIMINAL RESPONSIBILITY FOR OMISSIONS

(1967), Study Note

In the debate between Bentham and Macaulay — at long range, at the distance of two generations — the former would impose on everybody a duty to act to save another from harm when he can do so without prejudicing himself. So, we may note, would Bracton, writing in mid-13th century.

Bentham used the following examples:

(1) A woman's headdress catches fire;
(2) A drunken man falls face down into a puddle of water;
(3) A man with a lighted candle in his hand is about to enter a room in which gunpowder is lying scattered about.

In each case, somebody who is present and aware of the danger can easily prevent harm without the slightest danger to himself but omits to act and harm follows as a consequence.

"Who is there," asks Bentham, "That in these cases would think punishment misapplied?"

Livingstone, the American early 19th-century theorist and code maker, in his draft *Criminal Code* for Louisiana, proposed to constitute an offence of criminal homicide consisting of death following upon an omission to save life if the accused could have saved the life without personal danger or pecuniary loss.

But Macaulay, the draftsman of the *Indian Penal Code*, rejected this theory and the proposals based on it. He based his rejection on the great difficulty, if not impossibility of defining the conditions and limitations of guilt. His reasoning followed these lines:

(a) Suppose I have refused food to a beggar who must die unless I gave it to him and who has died. Am I guilty of criminal homicide? You cannot answer, "Yes", in all circumstances.

What if I myself am a beggar and have barely a crust between me and starvation?

What if my wife and children are hungry and wish to eat the food?

Are these two cases the same as if I am rich and need too much?

It may seem clear that I am not guilty in the first case. What about the second?

You can imagine an infinite number of readily possible cases in which the answer must be in doubt.

(b) Again, suppose I am a physician coming upon the scene of an accident and finding a victim bleeding to death and refuse to look after him. Am I guilty of criminal homicide?

What if I am on my way to treat a family all of whom are in danger of death from poison accidently taken?

What if I have been on duty for 48 hours at the scene of a disaster and am exhausted?

(c) If I am a surgeon and refuse to operate to save a life, will it make a difference whether I would have to walk a block to do it, or go to Barrifield? Or to Napanee? Or Belleville? Or Windsor?

(d) How far should I travel to give warning of an impending flood? 50 yards? Half a mile? Ten miles?

Many of Macaulay's examples clearly fall outside Bentham's limitation "without prejudicing himself" and Livingstone's "without personal danger or pecuniary loss" but he demonstrates the difficulty in practice of defining the limits of an offence based on an omission. It is, however, arguable that the offence could be so defined as to include only situations in which it is clearly demonstrated beyond question that the actor could have acted without in any way prejudicing himself personally or in property.

In Macaulay's draft *Code*, it was provided that an omission should be illegal if it had caused and had been intended to cause harm or was known to be likely to cause harm or was on other grounds illegal, that is, an offence in itself or a breach of some direction of law, or such a wrong as would be a good ground for a civil action.

He said that any further duty to act must be moral and not legal, enforced by public opinion and by teaching precepts of religion and morality.

As Jerome Hall points out, Macaulay and the English courts of the 18th and early 19th century had reached the same position.

Stephen, the draftsman of the *English Draft Code of 1878* on which the departmental draftsmen of the *Canadian Criminal Code of 1892* drew heavily, accepted Macaulay's position, and it appears in our present *Code*.

How would Bentham and Macaulay have reacted to the uncertain trend in Canada, as shown by the following recent provincial legislation, towards the creation of crimes of
   1. failing to report suspected child abuse, and
   2. not acting as the good Samaritan?

CHILD AND FAMILY SERVICES ACT

R.S.O. 1990, c. 11

72. *Interpretation.* — (1) In this section and in sections 73, 74 and 75, "to suffer abuse", when used in reference to a child, means to be in need of protection within the meaning of clause 37(2)(a), (c), (e), (f) or (h).

(2) *Duty to report that child in need of protection.* — A person who believes on reasonable grounds that a child is or may be in need of protection shall forthwith report the belief and the information upon which it is based to a society.

(3) *Idem: professional or official duties, suspicion of abuse.* — Despite the provisions of any other Act, a person referred to in subsection (4) who, in the course of his or her professional or official duties, has reasonable grounds to suspect that a child is or may be suffering or may have suffered abuse shall forthwith report the suspicion and the information on which it is based to a society.

(4) *Application of subs. (3).* — Subsection (3) applies to every person who performs professional or official duties with respect to a child, including,

(a) a health care professional, including a physician, nurse, dentist, pharmacist and psychologist;

(b) a teacher, school principal, social worker, family counsellor, priest, rabbi, clergyman, operator or employee of a day nursery and youth and recreation worker;

(c) a peace officer and a coroner;

(d) a solicitor; and

(e) a service provider and an employee of a service provider.

(5) *Interpretation.* — In clause (4)(b), "youth and recreation worker" does not include a volunteer.

(6) *Duty of society.* — A society that obtains information that a child in its care and custody is or may be suffering or may have suffered abuse shall forthwith report the information to a Director.

(7) *Section overrides privilege.* — This section applies although the information reported may be confidential or privileged, and no action for making the report shall be instituted against a person who acts in accordance with subsection (2) or (3) unless the person acts maliciously or without reasonable grounds for the belief or suspicion, as the case may be.

(8) *Exception: solicitor client privilege.* — Nothing in this section abrogates any privilege that may exist between a solicitor and his or her client.

_____

Note that s. 85(1)(*b*) creates a provincial offence for a breach of s. 72(3) but *not* respecting s. 72(2).

QUEBEC CHARTER OF HUMAN RIGHTS AND FREEDOMS

R.S.Q. 1980, c. C-12

2. Every human being whose life is in peril has a right to assistance. Every person must come to the aid of anyone whose life is in peril either personally or calling for aid, by giving him the necessary and immediate physical assistance, unless it involves danger to himself or a third person, or he has another valid reason.

For an assertion that this provision in the Quebec *Charter* has had a marked educative effect on the medical profession see S. Rodgers, "The Right to Emergency Medical Assistance in the Province of Quebec" (1980), 40 R. du B. 373.

FRENCH PENAL CODE

Article 63, translated by G. Hughes in "Criminal Omissions" (1958), 67 Yale L.J. 590 at 632

Whoever is able to prevent by his immediate action, without risk to himself or others, the commission of a serious crime or offence against the person, and voluntarily neglects to do so shall be liable to imprisonment from one month to three years and a fine of 24,000 to 1,000,000 francs, or one of these penalties only.

The same punishments are applicable to one who voluntarily neglects to give to a person in peril assistance which he could render without risk to himself or others whether by his personal action or by procuring aid.

What is an omission? How does one characterize conduct?

O.W. HOLMES, THE COMMON LAW

Howe, ed., (1963), 218-219

Although a man has a perfect right to stand by and see his neighbor's property destroyed, or, for the matter of that, to watch his neighbor perish for want of his help, yet if he once intermeddles he has no longer the same freedom. He cannot withdraw at will. To give a more specific example, if a surgeon from benevolence cuts the umbilical cord of a newly-born child, he cannot stop there and watch the patient bleed to death. It would be murder wilfully to allow death to come to pass in that way, as much as if the intention had been entertained at the time of cutting the cord. It would not matter whether the wickedness began with the act, or with the subsequent omission.

FAGAN v. COMMISSIONER OF METROPOLITAN POLICE

[1968] 3 All E.R. 442 (C.A.)

July 31. LORD PARKER C.J.: — I will ask James J. to read the judgment which he has prepared, and with which I entirely agree.

JAMES J.: — The appellant, Vincent Martel Fagan, was convicted by the Willesden magistrates of assaulting David Morris, a police constable, in the execution of his duty on August 31, 1967. He appealed to quarter sessions. On October 25, 1967, his appeal was heard by Middlesex Quarter Sessions and was dismissed. This matter now comes before the Court on appeal by way of case stated from that decision of quarter sessions.

The sole question is whether the prosecution proved facts which in law amounted to an assault.

On August 31, 1967, the appellant was reversing a motor car in Fortunegate Road, London, N.W.10, when Police Constable Morris directed him to drive the car forwards to the kerbside and standing in front of the car pointed out a suitable place in which to park. At first the appellant stopped the car too far from the kerb for the officer's liking. Morris asked him to park closer and indicated a precise spot. The appellant drove forward towards him and stopped it with the offside wheel on Morris's left foot. "Get off my foot," said the officer. "Fuck you, you can wait," said the appellant. The engine of the car stopped running. Morris repeated several times "Get off my foot." The appellant said reluctantly "Okay man, okay," and then slowly turned on the ignition of the vehicle and reversed it off the officer's foot. The appellant had either turned the ignition off to stop the engine or turned it off after the engine had stopped running.

The justices at quarter sessions on those facts were left in doubt as to whether the mounting of the wheel on the officer's foot was deliberate or accidental. They were satisfied, however, beyond all reasonable doubt that the appellant "knowingly, provocatively and unnecessarily allowed the wheel to remain on the foot after the officer said 'Get off, you are on my foot'." They found that on those facts an assault was proved.

Mr. Abbas for the appellant relied upon the passage in Stone's Justices' Manual (1968), Vol. 1, p. 651, where assault is defined. He contends that on the finding of the justices the initial mounting of the wheel could not be an assault and that the act of the wheel mounting the foot came to an end without there being any *mens rea*. It is argued that thereafter there was no act on the part of the appellant which could constitute an *actus reus* but only the omission or failure to remove the wheel as soon as he was asked. That failure, it is said, could not in law be an assault, nor could it in law provide the necessary *mens rea* to convert the original act of mounting the foot into an assault.

Mr. Rant for the respondent argues that the first mounting of the foot was an *actus reus* which act continued until the moment of time at which the wheel was removed. During that continuing act, it is said, the appellant formed the necessary intention to constitute the element of *mens rea* and once that element was added to the continuing act, an assault took place. In the alternative, Mr. Rant argues that there can be situations in which there is a duty to act and that in such situations an omission to act in breach of duty would in law amount to an assault. It is unnecessary to formulate any concluded views on this alternative.

In our judgment the question arising, which has been argued on general principles, falls to be decided on the facts of the particular case. An assault is any act which intentionally — or possibly recklessly — causes another person to apprehend immediate and unlawful personal violence. An assault may be committed by the laying of a hand upon another, and the action does not cease to be an assault if it is a stick held in the hand and not the hand itself which is laid on the person of the victim. So for our part we see no difference in principle between the action of stepping on to a person's toe and maintaining that position and the action of driving a car on to a person's foot and sitting in the car whilst its position on the foot is maintained.

To constitute the offence of assault some intentional act must have been performed: a mere omission to act cannot amount to an assault. Without going into the question whether words alone can constitute an assault, it is clear that the words spoken by the appellant could not alone amount to an assault: they can only shed a light on the appellant's action. For our part we think the crucial question is whether in this case the act of the appellant can be said to be complete and spent at the moment of time when the car wheel came to rest on the foot or whether his act is to be regarded as a continuing act operating until the wheel was removed. In our judgment a distinction is to be drawn between acts which are complete — though results may continue to flow — and those acts which are continuing. Once the act is complete it cannot thereafter be said to be a threat to inflict unlawful force upon the victim. If the act, as distinct from the results thereof, is a continuing act there is a continuing threat to inflict unlawful force.

For an assault to be committed both the elements of *actus reus* and *mens rea* must be present at the same time. The "*actus reus*" is the action causing the effect on the victim's mind (see the observations of Park B. in *Regina v. St. George*). The "*mens rea*" is the intention to cause that effect. It is not necessary that *mens rea* should be present at the inception of the *actus reus*; it can be superimposed upon an existing act. On the other hand the subsequent inception of *mens rea* cannot convert an act which has been completed without *mens rea* into an assault.

In our judgment the Willesden magistrates and quarter sessions were right in law. On the facts found the action of the appellant may have been initially unintentional, but the time came when knowing that the wheel was on the officer's foot the appellant (1) remained seated in the car so that his body through the medium of the car was in contact with the officer, (2) switched off the ignition of the car, (3) maintained the wheel of the car on the foot and (4) used words indicating the intention of keeping the wheel in that position. For our part we cannot regard such conduct as mere omission or inactivity.

There was an act constituting a battery which at its inception was not criminal because there was no element of intention but which became criminal from the moment the intention was formed to produce the apprehension which was flowing from the continuing act. The fallacy of the appellant's argument is that it seeks to equate the facts of this case with such a case as where a motorist has accidentally run over a person and, that action having been completed, fails to assist the victim with the intent that the victim should suffer.

We would dismiss this appeal.

BRIDGE J.: — I fully agree with my Lords as to the relevant principles to be applied. No mere omission to act can amount to an assault. Both the elements of *actus reus* and *mens rea* must be present at the same time, but the one may be superimposed on the other. It is in the application of these principles to the highly unusual facts of this case that I have, with regret, reached a different conclusion from the majority of the Court. I have no sympathy at all for the appellant, who behaved disgracefully. But I have been unable to find any way of regarding the facts which satisfies me that they amounted to the crime of assault. This has not been for want of trying. But at every attempt I have encountered the inescapable question: after the wheel of the appellant's car had accidentally come to rest on the constable's foot, what was it that the appellant did which constituted the act of assault? However the question is approached, the answer I feel obliged to give is: precisely nothing. The car rested on the foot by its own weight and remained stationary by its own inertia. The appellant's fault was that he omitted to manipulate the controls to set it in motion again.

Neither the fact that the appellant remained in the driver's seat nor that he switched off the ignition seem to me to be of any relevance. The constable's plight would have been no better, but might well have been worse, if the appellant had alighted from the car leaving the ignition switched on. Similarly I can get no help from the suggested analogies. If one man accidentally treads on another's toe or touches him with a stick, but deliberately maintains pressure with foot or stick after the victim protests, there is clearly an assault. But there is no true parallel between such cases and the present case. It is not, to my mind, a legitimate use of language to speak of the appellant "holding" or "maintaining" the car wheel on the constable's foot. The expression which corresponds to the reality is that used by the justices in the case stated. They say, quite rightly, that he "allowed" the wheel to remain.

With a reluctantly dissenting voice I would allow this appeal and quash the appellant's conviction.

Appeal dismissed.

How Do Legal Duties Arise?

Sometimes by statute. For example consider these provisions of the *Criminal Code*:

215. (1) Every one is under a legal duty
  (a) as a parent, foster parent, guardian or head of a family, to provide necessaries of life for a child under the age of 16 years;
  (b) as a married person, to provide necessaries of life to his spouse; and
  (c) to provide necessaries of life to a person under his charge if that person
      (i) is unable, by reason of detention, age, illness, mental disorder or other cause, to withdraw himself from that charge, and
      (ii) is unable to provide himself with necessaries of life.

216. Every one who undertakes to administer surgical or medical treatment to another person or to do any other lawful act that may endanger the life of another person is, except in cases of necessity, under a legal duty to have and to use reasonable knowledge, skill and care in so doing.

217. Every one who undertakes to do an act is under a legal duty to do it if an omission to do the act is or may be dangerous to life.

Can the Courts create legal duties? Is this desirable? Remember s. 9 of the *Criminal Code*.

R. v. MILLER

[1983] 1 All E.R. 978, [1983] A.C. 161 (H.L.)

LORD DIPLOCK: — My Lords, the facts which give rise to this appeal are sufficiently narrated in the written statement made to the police by the appellant Miller. That statement, subject to two minor orthographical corrections, reads:

> Last night I went out for a few drinks and at closing time I went back to the house where I have been kipping for a couple of weeks. I went upstairs into the back bedroom where I've been sleeping. I lay on my mattress and lit a cigarette. I must have fell to sleep because I woke up to find the mattress on fire. I just got up and went into the next room and went back to sleep. Then the next thing I remember was the police and fire people arriving. I hadn't got anything to put the fire out with so I just left it.

He was charged on indictment with the offence of 'arson contrary to s. 1(1) and (3) of the *Criminal Damage Act, 1971*'; the particulars of offence were that he —

> on a date unknown between the 13th and 16th days of August 1980, without lawful excuse damaged by fire a house known as No. 9 Grantham Road, Sparkbrook, intending to do damage to such property or recklessly as to whether such property would be damaged.

He was tried in the Crown Court at Leicester before a recorder and a jury. He did not give evidence, and the facts as set out in his statement were not disputed. He was found guilty and sentenced to six months' imprisonment.

From his conviction he appealed to the Court of Appeal on the ground, which is one of law alone, that the undisputed facts did not disclose any offence under s. 1 of the *Criminal Damage Act 1971*. The appeal was dismissed (see [1982] 2 All E.R. 386), but leave to appeal to your Lordships' House was granted by the Court of Appeal, which certified that the following question of law of general public importance was involved:

> Whether the *actus reus* of the offence of arson is present when a Defendant accidentally starts a fire and thereafter, intending to destroy or damage property belonging to another or being reckless as to whether any such property would be destroyed or damaged, fails to take any steps to extinguish the fire or prevent damage to such property by that fire?

The question speaks of '*actus reus*'. This expression is derived from Coke's brocard (3 Co. Inst. ch. 1, fo. 10), '*Actus non facit reum, nisi mens sit rea*,' by converting incorrectly into an adjective the word *reus* which was there used correctly in the accusative case as a noun. As long ago as 1889 in *R. v. Tolson*, [1886-90] All E.R. Rep. 26 at 36-37 Stephen J. when dealing with a statutory offence, as are your Lordships in the instant case, condemned the phrase as likely to mislead, though his criticism in that case was primarily directed to the use of the expression '*mens rea*'. In the instant case, as the argument before this House has in my view demonstrated, it is the use of the expression '*actus reus*' that is liable to mislead, since it suggests that some positive act on the part of the accused is needed to make him guilty of a crime and that a failure or omission to act is insufficient to give rise to criminal liability unless some express provision in the statute that creates the offence so provides.

My Lords, it would I think be conducive to clarity of analysis of the ingredients of a crime that is created by statute, as are the great majority of criminal offences today, if we were to avoid bad Latin and instead to think and speak (as did Stephen J. in those parts of his judgment in *R. v. Tolson* to which I referred at greater length in *Sweet v. Parsley* [1969] 1 All E.R. 347 at 361) about the conduct of the accused and his state of mind at the time of that conduct, instead of speaking of *actus reus* and *mens rea*.

. . . .

The recorder, in his lucid summing up to the jury (they took 22 minutes only to reach their verdict), told them that the accused, having by his own act started a fire in the mattress which, when he became aware of its existence, presented an obvious risk of damaging the house, became under a duty to take some action to put it out. The Court of Appeal upheld the conviction, but its ratio *decidendi* appears to be somewhat different from that of the recorder. As I understand the judgment, in effect it treats the whole course of conduct of the accused, from the moment at which he fell asleep and dropped the cigarette onto the mattress until the time the damage to the house by fire was complete, as a continuous act of the accused, and holds that it is sufficient to constitute the statutory offence of arson if at any stage in that course of conduct the state of mind of the accused, when he fails to try to prevent or minimise the damage which will result from his initial act, although it lies within his power to do so, is that of being reckless whether property belonging to another would be damaged.

My Lords, these alternative ways of analysing the legal theory that justifies a decision which has received nothing but commendation for its accord with common sense and justice have, since the publication of the judgment of the Court of Appeal in the instant case, provoked academic controversy. Each theory has distinguished support. Professor J.C. Smith espouses the 'duty theory' (see [1982] Crim. L.R. 526 at 528); Professor Glanville Williams who, after the decision of the Divisional Court in *Fagan v. Metropolitan Police Comr.*, [1968] 3 All E.R. 442 appears to have been attracted by the duty theory, now prefers that of the continuous act (see: [1982] Crim. L.R. 773). When applied to cases where a person has unknowingly done an act which sets in train events that, when he becomes aware of them, present an obvious risk that property belonging to another will be damaged, both theories lead to an identical result; and, since what your Lordships are concerned with is to give guidance to trial Judges in their task of summing up to juries, I would for this purpose adopt the duty theory as being the easier to explain to a jury; though I would commend the use of the word 'responsibility', rather than 'duty' which is more appropriate to civil than to criminal law since it suggests an obligation owed to another person, *i.e.*, the person to whom the endangered property belongs, whereas a criminal statute defines combinations of conduct and state of mind which render a person liable to punishment by the state itself.

While, in the general run of cases of destruction or damage to property belonging to another by fire (or other means) where the prosecution relies on the recklessness of the accused, the direction recommended by this House in *R. v. Caldwell* is appropriate, in the exceptional case (which is most likely to be one of arson and of which the instant appeal affords a striking example), where the accused is initially unaware that he has done an act that in fact sets in train events which, by the time the accused becomes aware of them, would make it obvious to anyone who troubled to give his mind to them that they present a risk that property belonging to another would be damaged, a suitable direction to the jury would be that the accused is guilty of the offence under s. 1(1) of the 1971 Act if, when he does become aware that the events in question have happened as a result of his own act, he does not try to prevent or reduce the risk of damage by his own efforts or if necessary by sending for help from the fire brigade and the reason why he does not is either because he has not given any thought to the possibility of there being any such risk or because having recognized that there was some risk involved he has decided not to try to prevent or reduce it.

So, while deprecating the use of the expression '*actus reus*' in the certified question, I would answer that question Yes and would dismiss the appeal.

MOORE v. R.

[1979] 1 S.C.R. 195, 2 C.R. (3d) 289, 43 C.C.C. (2d) 83

SPENCE J. (MARTLAND, RITCHIE, PIGEON and BEETZ JJ. concurring): — This is an appeal from the judgment of the Court of Appeal for British Columbia pronounced on June 7, 1977.

The appellant had been acquitted after his trial before His Honour Judge Millward and a jury upon an indictment charging him:

> THAT at the City of Victoria, County of Victoria, Province of British Columbia, on the 19th day of April, 1976, he did unlawfully and wilfully obstruct a Peace Officer, to wit, Constable Sutherland, in the execution of his duty as such Peace Officer, contrary to the *Criminal Code* of Canada.

The appellant was acquitted by a verdict directed by the learned trial Judge at the close of the Crown's case. The facts are outlined in an admission by counsel for Moore which I quote:

> If it please, your Honour, I have certain admission of facts to make to expedite matters. Firstly, I am instructed to admit that on or about the 19th of April 1976, at or about 9:10 a.m., the Accused, Richard Harvey Moore, was southbound on Government Street at Pandora and

at that intersection proceeded through a light which had not yet turned green and was, in fact red when he proceeded through on his ten-speed bicycle. That is the extent of my admission of fact.

and are further dealt with by Carrothers J.A., in his reasons for judgment as follows [36 C.C.C. (2d) 481 at p. 489, 40 C.R.N.S. 93]:

> Constable Sutherland, a peace officer with the Victoria City Police, in uniform and on a motorcycle, observed this infraction on the part of Moore and set about to "ticket" Moore. The constable and Moore proceeded side by side on their respective cycles, with Moore sometime taking elusive action by riding his bicycle on the sidewalk, with the constable repeatedly requesting Moore to "pull over and stop" and Moore lewdly rebuffing each such request with an obscene demand to leave him alone as he was in a hurry. I attach no importance to the particular salacious vulgarity used by Moore in rejecting the policeman's request to stop as it has been used by the unimaginative so excessively and indiscriminately as to have lost its literal quality, but there is no doubt that it constituted flat refusals on the part of Moore to stop as requested by the policeman.

As a result of this occurrence, Moore was charged upon an indictment, as I have said above, but he was not charged with failing to stop at a stop light only with obstructing a peace officer in the performance of his duty. The obstruction which the Crown put forward as constituting the offence was the failure of the appellant to give his name when requested to do so by the police constable.

The relevant sections of the provincial statutes with which I shall deal hereafter are as follows: first, the *Motor-vehicle Act*, R.S.B.C. 1960, c. 253. Section 2 contains definitions of "motor-vehicle" and "vehicle", as follows:

> "motor-vehicle" means a vehicle, not run upon rails, that is designed to be self-propelled or propelled by electric power obtained from overhead trolley-wires;

> . . . .

> "vehicle" means a device in, upon, or by which a person or thing is or may be transported or drawn upon a highway, except a device designed to be moved by human power or used exclusively upon stationary rails or tracks. [enacted 1963, c. 27, s. 2(c)]

Section 58 of the said *Motor-vehicle Act* provides:

> 58. Every person driving or operating or in charge of a motor-vehicle on any highway who refuses or fails
>
> (a) to stop his motor-vehicle when signalled or requested to stop by any police officer or constable who is in uniform or who displays his police badge conspicuously on the outside of his outer coat; or
>
> (b) to state correctly his name and address and the name and address of the owner of the motor-vehicle when requested by any peace officer or constable to state the same is guilty of an offence.

It will be seen plainly that a bicycle is neither a "motor-vehicle" nor a "vehicle" of any kind under the provisions of the aforesaid definition. A bicycle is plainly not self-propelled and, therefore, cannot be a "motor-vehicle" and it is a device designed to be moved by human power and, therefore, it cannot be a "vehicle" at all. Much argument was spent in the Court of Appeal for British

Columbia and in this Court in an attempt to say that although a bicycle was neither a "motor-vehicle" nor a "vehicle" s. 58 of the *Motor-vehicle Act* applied thereto because of other sections with which I shall deal hereafter. As the Courts below, I am quite unable to accept any such submission and I have come to the conclusion, with respect, that the Court of Appeal for British Columbia was quite correct in holding that the respondent was not in breach of s. 58 of the *Motor-vehicle Act* when he refused to give his name to the constable.

. . . .

After detailed consideration of statutory powers, Spence J. continued:

The constable, therefore, in requesting the appellant Moore to identify himself, was carrying out the duty of enforcing the law of the Province in this summary conviction matter by attempting to identify the accused person so that he might proceed to lay an information or take the more modern form permitted under the said *Summary Convictions Act* of British Columbia of issuing a ticket.

I am of the opinion that the Court of Appeal of British Columbia was correct in finding that when the appellant Moore refused to accede to the constable's request for his identification he was obstructing that constable in the performance of his duties. As did the members of the Court of Appeal, I am confining my consideration of this matter to the actual circumstances which occurred, that is, that a constable on duty observed the appellant in the act of committing an infraction of the statute and that that constable had no power to arrest the accused for such offence unless and until he had attempted to identify the accused so that he might be the subject of summary conviction proceedings.

I also agree, with respect, with the learned members of the Court of Appeal that this conclusion in no way opposes or ignores the judgment of the Queen's Bench in *Rice v. Connolly*, [1966] 2 All E.R. 649. In that case, the appellant was seen by police officers behaving suspiciously. On being questioned, he refused to say where he was going or where he had come from. He refused to give his full name and address, although he did give a name and the name of a road which were not untrue. He refused to accompany the police to a police box for identification purposes saying, "if you want me, you will have to arrest me". He was acquitted by the Court of Appeal upon a charge of obstructing the police. It is paramount to note that the appellant there had not committed any offence in the presence or view of a police officer. He had simply been acting in what the constable regarded as a suspicious manner. I view the situation very differently when a person is actually seen by the constable committing an offence.

Therefore, for the reasons which I have outlined above, I am of the opinion that the officer was under a duty to attempt to identify the wrongdoer and the failure to identify himself by the wrongdoer did constitute an obstruction of the police officer in the performance of his duties.

I add that in coming to this conclusion I have not forgotten the provisions of the *Canadian Bill of Rights* nor the topic of individual freedom generally but I am of the opinion that there is not even minimal interference with any freedom of a citizen who is seen committing an infraction by a police constable in the police constable simply requesting his name and address without any attempt to obtain from that person any admission of fault or any comment whatsoever. On the other hand, the refusal of a citizen to identify himself under such circumstances causes a major inconvenience and obstruction to the police in carrying out their proper duties. So that if anyone were engaged in any balancing of interest, there could be no doubt that the conclusion to which I have come would be that supported by the overwhelming public interest.

I would dismiss the appeal.

DICKSON J. (dissenting) (ESTEY J. concurring): — These proceedings originated in a minor traffic infraction in the City of Victoria, British Columbia. The issue raised, however, is an important one having to do with police power of interrogation and the right of citizens to remain silent. That right has always been regarded as absolute and as being firmly anchored to two fundamental common-law principles: the presumption of innocence and the privilege against self-incrimination. Explicit statutory provisions may impose a duty upon a person to identify himself to police officers in certain situations, but in this appeal the Court is being asked to impose such a duty in the absence of any statutory underpinning whatever. In more stark terms, the question is whether a person committing a petty traffic offence exposes himself to a criminal charge of "obstructing" and a maximum penalty of two years' imprisonment, if he refuses to give his name and address to a police officer.

. . . .

The general principle

Any duty to identify oneself must be found in either common law or statute, quite apart from the duties of the police. A person is not guilty of the offence of obstructing a police officer merely by doing nothing, unless there is legal duty to act. Omission to act in a particular way will give rise to criminal liability only where a duty to act arises at common law or is imposed by statute: 11 Hals., 4th ed., p. 15, para. 9. This idea was expressed by Mr. Justice Schroeder in *R. v. Patrick*, 128 C.C.C. 263 at p. 267, [1960] O.W.N. 206, 32 C.R. 338 at p. 343 (Ont. C.A.):

> Counsel for the appellant submitted that to sustain a charge of obstructing a peace officer in the execution of his duty, it was necessary for the Crown to prove either a positive act of interference, or a refusal to perform some act required to be done by a statute. . . . It not having been shown that the appellant was under any duty or obligation to communicate to the peace officer the information required of him under the provisions of either s. 221(2) of the *Cr. Code*, or s. 110(1) of the *Highway Traffic Act*, the Crown has failed to bring home to the appellant the commission of a criminal offence. This is sufficient to dispose of the appeal.
> . . .

The point under discussion is dealt with at some length by Dr. Glanville Williams in an article entitled "Demanding Name and Address" appearing in 66 *L.Q.R.* 465 (1950). The general principle of the common law is stated:

neither a private person nor a constable has any effective power to demand the name and address of a person on the ground that he has committed an offence or is under a civil liability.

Dr. Williams refers to the case of *Hatton v. Treeby*, [1897] 2 Q.B. 452 as an illustration of this principle. The head note reads:

A constable who sees a person riding a bicycle at night without a proper light, contrary to the provisions of s. 85 of the *Local Government Act, 1888*, has no power to stop him for the purpose of ascertaining his name and address.

The constable in that case called on the rider to stop, in order to ascertain his name and address. On the rider failing to do so, the constable caught hold of the handlebar of the bicycle, whereby the rider was thrown to the ground. The rider summoned the constable for assault. The Justices found that the constable did not know the name or address of the rider, and could not have ascertained his name or address in any other way than by stopping him, and that in so stopping him he used no more force than was necessary. They were of opinion that, as the rider was committing an offence punishable on summary conviction within view of the constable, the latter was justified in stopping him as he did in order to prevent a continuance of the offence and to ascertain his name and address. They accordingly dismissed the complaint, subject to a case for the opinion of the Court. The appellate Court held that the constable had no power to stop the bicycle rider at common law and the only question was whether he had statutory authority to do so. It was found that there was no statutory authority for the constable acting as he did. In the result the constable was convicted of assault.

No statutory duty

It appears to me impossible to extract from the statutory provisions of the British Columbia *Motor-vehicle Act*, R.S.B.C. 1960, c. 253, a duty on a cyclist, caught riding through a red light, to identify himself. Section 58 of the Act specifically places a duty on a person driving a "motor-vehicle" to state correctly his name and address when requested to do so by a peace officer. This in itself appears to recognize the absence of any such duty where there is no statutory requirement. Section 58 does not apply to persons operating either "vehicles" (as defined in s. 2) or bicycles, and there is no other provision in the *Motor-vehicle Act*, or any other relevant statute, placing such a duty on a cyclist caught committing a summary conviction offence under the *Motor-vehicle Act*.

I have had the advantage of reading the reasons of Mr. Justice Spence and I am in full agreement, for the reasons stated by him and by the Court of Appeal of British Columbia, that the accused was not in breach of s. 58 of the *Motor-vehicle Act*, when he refused to give his name and address to the constable.

. . . .

Power of arrest

. . . .

Constable Sutherland could have arrested the accused for the offence of proceeding against a red light if it were necessary to establish his identity. However, with great respect, I cannot agree that, as a consequence, the accused was guilty of the further, and much more serious, offence of obstructing the constable in the performance of his duties by refusing to divulge his name and address.

No common law duty

There is no duty at common law to identify oneself to police. As was stated by Lord Parker in *Rice v. Connolly*, [1966] 2 All E.R. 649 at p. 652 (Q.B.D.):

> It seems to me quite clear that though every citizen has a moral duty or, if you like, a social duty to assist the police, there is no legal duty to that effect, and indeed the whole basis of the common law is the right of the individual to refuse to answer questions put to him by persons in authority, and a refusal to accompany those in authority to any particular place, short, of course, of arrest.

The case stands for the proposition that refusal to identify oneself to the police could not constitute obstruction of the police. The Court distinguished a refusal to answer, which is legal, from a "cock and bull" story to the police, which might constitute obstruction. No other distinction was made. Lord Parker said:

> In my judgment there is all the difference in the world between deliberately telling a false story, something which on no view a citizen has a right to do, and silence or refusing to answer, something which he has every right to do.

In *Ingleton v. Dibble*, [1972] 1 All E.R. 275 (Q.B.D.), a distinction was drawn between a refusal to act, on the one hand, and the doing of some positive act, on the other. Bridge J. (with whom Lord Widgery C.J. and Ashworth J. concurred), said, at p. 279:

> In a case, as in *Rice v. Connolly*, where the obstruction alleged consists of a refusal by the defendant to do the act which the police constable has asked him to do — to give information, it might be, or to give assistance to the police constable — one can see readily the soundness of the principle, if I may say so with respect, applied in *Rice v. Connolly*, that such a refusal to act cannot amount to a wilful obstruction under s. 51 unless the law imposes on the person concerned some obligation in the circumstances to act in the manner requested by the police officer.

The legal position in England and Wales has been described in these terms in *Police Powers in England and Wales* (1975), by Leigh, at p. 195:

> and in general it still remains the rule that a citizen has a right to be as unco-operative as he pleases, provided that he does not impede the course of justice by knowingly giving false information to the police.

In the Ontario case of *R. v. Carroll* (1959), 126 C.C.C. 19, 31 C.R. 315 (Ont. C.A.), the facts, as disclosed in the headnote, were these. The accused was charged with unlawfully and wilfully obstructing a police constable while engaged in his duties as a peace officer, contrary to s. 110(*a*) of the *Criminal Code*, 1953-54 (Can.), c. 51. The accused, in company with three other men, was proceeding along a highway at an early hour in the morning. The constable heard them whistling and yelling and he advised them to be quiet and go home. Three of the party followed his advice. The accused remained. The constable asked him to produce his identification but the accused refused to do so and proceeded on his way. The constable caught up to him and again asked accused to identify himself. An argument and struggle followed and the accused was arrested. He was later charged with obstructing a police officer and was convicted. He appealed. The conviction was quashed. It was held that under the circumstances, the accused was not under any duty to identify himself as requested.

The Crown conceded in this Court that no such obligation was to be found in the common law. From whence then comes such a duty? Where does one find the legal compulsion to answer? A person cannot "obstruct" by refusing to answer a question unless he is under a legal duty to answer.

An "implied" or "reciprocal" duty?

It was strongly urged in argument before us that because a duty rested upon constables to investigate crime and enforce provincial laws, an "implied" or "reciprocal" duty rested upon a person, suspected of an infraction, to give his name and address, and refusal to do so amounted to such frustration as to constitute the offence of obstructing the police in the execution of their duty.

The Crown perforce had to fall back upon the proposition that because there was a duty upon the police officer to enquire before exercising the power to arrest under s. 450 [rep. & sub. R.S.C. 1970, c. 2, (2nd Supp.), s. 5] of the *Code*, there was a reciprocal duty upon the alleged culprit to respond. The alleged duty, as I understand the argument, is to be limited to divulging name and address, when caught in the commission of an offence and prior to arrest.

. . . .

A limited obligation to respond, effective only when the policeman is an eye witness, introduces into the criminal law, which should rest upon "broad, plain, intelligible" principles a qualification unsound in principle and unworkable in practice.

The fact that a police officer has a duty to identify a person suspected of, or seen committing, an offence says nothing about whether the person has the duty to identify himself on being asked. Each duty is entirely independent. Only if the police have a lawful claim to demand that a person identify himself, does the person have a corresponding duty to do so. As McFarlane J.A. said in *R. v. Bonnycastle*, [1969] 4 C.C.C. 198 at p. 201, 7 C.R.N.S. 37 (B.C. C.A.), the duty of a peace officer to make enquiries must not be confused with the right of a person to refuse to answer questions in circumstances where the law does not require him to answer.

The Legislature deliberately imposed a duty to identify upon the drivers of motor vehicles — perhaps because of their more lethal nature — but chose not to impose such duty on the drivers of other vehicles such as bicycles. The Legislature must be taken to have intended to relieve bicycle riders of the duty. To require the riders of bicycles to give their names and addresses would be tantamount to amending the *Motor-Vehicle Act*. It would also appear that Parliament, in providing in ss. 450(2) and 452(1)(*f*)(i) [rep. & sub. R.S.C. 1970, c. 2 (2nd Supp.), s. 5] of the *Criminal Code* for arrest and detention for the purpose of establishing identity, did not recognize a duty to identify oneself existing apart from statute, breach of which would expose the offender to a charge of "obstructing". Examples from English legislation of statutory obligation to disclose identity to police constables, unnecessary if the obligation existed otherwise, are to be found in the *Protection of Birds Act*, 1954 (U.K.), c. 30, s. 12(i)(*a*); *Dangerous Drugs Act*, 1965 (U.K.), c. 15, s. 15; *Representation of the People Act*, 1949 (U.K.), c. 68, s. 84(3); *Road Traffic Act*, 1960 (U.K.), c. 16, s. 228; *Prevention of Crime Act*, 1953 (U.K.), c. 14, s. 1(3).

The criminal law is no place within which to introduce implied duties, unknown to statute and common law, breach of which subjects a person to arrest and imprisonment.

The "reciprocal duty" argument advanced by the Crown in this case was considered by Dr. Glanville Williams in the article to which I have referred. Dr. Williams effectively disposed of the argument in words which I should like to adopt, pp. 473-4:

> The question may be asked whether the power of the police to demand name and address is in effect generalised by the statutes creating the offence of obstructing the police in the execution of their duty — so that refusal to comply with the demand amounts to an obstruction. At first sight it would seem that a good case could be made out for an affirmative answer. Although it is not the duty of the police to prosecute every crime, it can be said to be their duty to make inquiries into crimes with a view to prosecution. The Courts have held that interference with the police when they are collecting evidence of an offence constitutes an obstruction. Moreover, it has been decided that an obstruction may take place merely by a nonfeasance, where there is a refusal to comply with the lawful orders of the police. Notwithstanding these authorities, it is submitted that the refusal by an offender to give his name and address does not constitute an obstruction, for at least two reasons. First, if it were an obstruction, all the statutes making it an offence to refuse to give name and address in specific situations would have been unnecessary. When, for example, Parliament passed the *Public Order Act* in 1936, it must have been thought that the police had no general power to demand name and address. Secondly, it is a fundamental principle of English law that an accused person cannot be interrogated or at least cannot be forced to answer questions under a legal penalty if he refuses; this principle is absolute, and does not admit of exception even for a demand of name and address, unless a statute has expressly created an exception. To say that the police have a duty to gather evidence, and therefore that a criminal's refusal to give his name and address is an obstruction, is far too wide, because the same premise would yield the conclusion that a criminal's refusal to confess to the crime is an obstruction.

The views expressed by Dr. Williams were adopted in the New Zealand case of *Elder v. Evans*, [1951] N.Z.L.R. 801 at p. 806 (N.Z.S.C.).

I would allow the appeal, set aside the judgment of the Court of Appeal and restore the judgment at trial.

Appeal dismissed.

R. v. THORNTON

(1991), 3 C.R. (4th) 381 (Ont. C.A.)

The accused donated blood to the Red Cross. At that time the accused knew that he had twice tested positive for HIV antibodies and that he was therefore infectious. The Red Cross screening process detected the contaminated blood and it was put aside. The accused was charged that he did commit a common nuisance contrary to s. 180 of the *Criminal Code.* This section provides that every one commits a common nuisance who does an unlawful act or fails to discharge a legal duty and thereby endangers the lives, safety or health of the public. He was convicted and sentenced to a term of 15 months' imprisonment. At the trial the Crown did not argue an unlawful act but rather a failure to discharge a legal duty. The trial judge expressed concern with the Crown's position because it seemed to the Court that the facts in the case might define and constitute an unlawful act. The trial judge said the conduct of the accused was conduct evidencing marked disregard for safety of others. Nevertheless the trial judge proceeded on the basis that there was an omission. The trial judge found a duty within s. 216 of the *Criminal Code* which provides:

> Everyone who undertakes to administer surgical or medical treatment to another person or to do any other lawful act that may endanger the life of another person is, except in cases of necessity, under a legal duty to have and to use reasonable knowledge, skill and care in so doing.

The trial judge decided that by donating blood to the Red Cross and knowing the purpose for which such donations are collected the accused was involved in a medical procedure. The accused appealed conviction and sentence. One of the grounds of appeal was that the accused's conduct, though reprehensible, did not amount to an offence known to the law. The appeals from conviction and sentence were dismissed.

GALLIGAN J.A. (BROOKE and DOHERTY JJ.A. concurring): —

. . . For the purposes of this appeal, I am prepared to assume the correctness of Mr. Greenspon's cogent argument that the words "unlawful act" must be taken to mean conduct which is specifically proscribed by legislation. The *Code* does not make it an offence to donate contaminated blood. Counsel were unable to refer the Court to any other statutory provision, federal or provincial, which does so. On the assumption, therefore, that the appellant's conduct could not constitute an "unlawful act", I will examine whether it amounted to a failure to discharge a "legal duty".

I am unable to find any provision in the *Code*, or any other statute which I can read, as specifically imposing a legal duty upon a person to refrain from donating contaminated blood. The immediate issue therefore is two-fold. Can a "legal duty" within the meaning of s. 180(2) be one which arises at common-law, or must it be one found in a statute? Is there a "legal duty" arising at common law the breach of which, assuming the other essential elements of the offence were proved, could be the basis of an offence under s. 180?

There are no cases deciding whether the "legal duty" in s. 180(2) must be a duty imposed by statute or whether it can be a duty according to common law. However, the "duty imposed by law" which forms part of the definition of criminal negligence set out in s. 219 of the *Code* has been held to be either a duty imposed by statute or a duty arising at common law.

. . . .

In *R. v. Coyne* (1958), 31 C.R. 335, 124 C.C.C. 176, the New Brunswick Supreme Court, Appeal Division, considered the criminal negligence provisions of the *Code* in relation to a hunting accident. Speaking for that Court, Ritchie J.A. held at pp. 179-180 [C.C.C., p. 338 C.R.]:

> The "duty imposed by law" may be a duty arising by virtue of either the common law or by statute. Use of a firearm, in the absence of proper caution, may readily endanger the lives or safety of others. Under the common law anyone carrying such a dangerous weapon as a rifle is under the duty to take such precaution in its use as, in the circumstances, would be observed by a reasonably careful man. If he fails in that duty and his behaviour is of such a character as to show or display a wanton or reckless disregard for the lives or safety of other persons, then, by virtue of s. 191, his conduct amounts to criminal negligence.

In *R. v. Popen* (1981), 60 C.C.C. (2d) 232, this Court also had occasion to consider the nature of the "duty imposed by law" contained in the definition of criminal negligence. It was a child abuse case. In giving the judgment of the Court, Martin J.A. said at p. 240 [C.C.C.]:

> [A] parent is under a legal duty at common law to take reasonable steps to protect his or her child from illegal violence used by the other parent or by a third person towards the child which the parent foresees or ought to foresee.

The effect of that judgment is to hold that the common law duty, which was there described, was a "duty imposed by law" within the meaning of s. 219 because the Court held that its breach could amount to criminal negligence.

These decisions lead me to the opinion that it is well settled that, for the purpose of defining criminal negligence, a "duty imposed by law" includes a duty which arises at common law.

While the words "legal duty" in s. 180(2) are not the same as a "duty imposed by law" used in s. 219, they have exactly the same meaning. It follows therefore that the meaning given to a "duty imposed by law" in s. 219 should also be given to the "legal duty" contained in s. 180(2). Thus, I am of the opinion that the legal duty referred to in s. 180(2) is a duty which is imposed by statute or which arises at common law. It becomes necessary, then, to decide whether at common law there is a duty which would prohibit the donating of blood known to be HIV-contaminated to the Red Cross.

While this is not a civil case and the principles of tort law are not directly applicable to it, the jurisprudence on that subject is replete with discussions about the legal duties of one person to another which arise at common law. The jurisprudence is constant that those duties are legal ones: that is, they are ones which are imposed by law. Throughout this century and indeed since much earlier times, the common law has recognized a very fundamental duty, which while it has many qualifications, can be summed up as being a duty to refrain from conduct which could cause injury to another person.

This is not the place to make a detailed examination of the jurisprudence on the subject of tort law but a few references to authority are in order.

. . . .

In the course of his oft-quoted speech in the famous case of *M'Alister or (Donoghue) v. Stevenson*, [1932] A.C. 562 (H.L.), Lord Atkin said at p. 580 [A.C.]:

> The rule that you are to love your neighbour becomes, in law, you must not injure your neighbour.

. . . .

That brief reference to jurisprudence in civil matters shows that there is deeply embedded in the common law a broad fundamental duty which, although subject to many qualifications, requires everyone to refrain from conduct which could injure another. It is not necessary to decide in this case how far that duty extends. At the very least, however, it requires everyone to refrain from conduct which it is reasonably foreseeable could cause serious harm to other persons. Accepting, as I have said, that a "legal duty" within the meaning of that term in s. 180(2) includes a duty arising at common law, I think that the common law duty to refrain from conduct which it is reasonably foreseeable could cause serious harm to other persons is a "legal duty" within the meaning of that term in s. 180(2).

Donating blood which one knows to be HIV-contaminated to an organization whose purpose is to make the blood available for transfusion to other persons, clearly constitutes a breach of the common law duty to refrain from conduct which one foresees could cause serious harm to another person. It is thus a failure to discharge a "legal duty" within the contemplation of s. 180(2). It is therefore my conclusion that the indictment which alleges the commission of a nuisance by the donation of blood which the appellant knew to be HIV-contaminated does allege an offence known to law. The first argument made by counsel for the appellant cannot be accepted.

. . . .

In the light of the findings of the trial Judge on the issue of credibility, and in the light of all of the other evidence, there can be no doubt that this appellant had personal knowledge that he should not donate his blood, that it was possible for it to get through the testing screen, and that it could cause serious damage to the life and health of members of the public. It follows that he knew that, by giving his blood to the Red Cross, he was endangering the lives and health of other members of the public. . . . This appellant knew personally the danger to which the public was subjected by his donation of blood. He clearly had *mens rea*. . . .

It is my opinion that the appellant was properly convicted of the offence under s. 180. Accordingly, I would dismiss the appeal from conviction.

With respect to sentence, the trial Judge did not impose the maximum sentence prescribed by law. The maximum sentence must be reserved for the worst offender committing the worst category of the offence. The sentence imposed took into account that, because of his prior good record, the appellant would not fall into the category of the worst offender. The offence, however, can certainly be categorized as among the worst offences. The appellant's conduct verges on the unspeakable. It cried out for a sentence which would act as a deterrent to others and which would express society's repudiation of what he did. One must have great compassion for this man. He faces a terrible future. Nevertheless, the sentence demonstrates no error in principle and is one that is eminently fit.

The important issue of principle of whether a criminal omission can be based on a common-law duty, in apparent violation of s. 9(*a*) of the *Criminal Code*, was unfortunately avoided when *Thornton* reached the Supreme Court.

THORNTON v. R.

[1993] 2 S.C.R. 445, 21 C.R. (4th) 215, 82 C.C.C. (3d) 530

LAMER C.J. (for a unanimous nine-person court, orally): — Section 216 imposed upon the [accused] a duty of care in giving his blood to the Red Cross. This duty of care was breached by not disclosing that his blood contained HIV antibodies. This common nuisance obviously endangered the life, safety and health of the public.

The above is the complete judgment of the Court. The Court appears to read s. 216 literally to impose a duty of care on those doing lawful acts which endanger others' lives. This seems to establish a new wide measure of criminal responsibility for omissions.

Do you prefer the interpretation of the trial Judge, the Court of Appeal or the Supreme Court? Justify your preference.

See, more generally, Winnie Holland, "HIV/AIDS and the Criminal Law" (1994), 36 Crim. L.Q. 279.

R. v. BROWNE

(1997), 116 C.C.C. (3d) 183 (Ont. C.A.), leave to appeal refused (1997), 225 N.R. 396 (note) (S.C.C.)

The accused and the deceased were partners in drug dealing. The deceased swallowed a plastic bag of crack cocaine to avoid detection when they were strip-searched by police. She tried unsuccessfully to vomit it up. Later that night the accused found her shaking and sweating. He said he would take her to hospital. He called for a cab which took ten minutes to arrive and a further 15 minutes to get her to hospital. She had no pulse or heartbeat and was pronounced dead shortly after arrival.

ABELLA J.A. (CATZMAN and LABROSSE JJ.A. concurring): —

. . . .

The statement found by the trial judge to constitute an "undertaking" by Browne is underlined.

> He called her name a couple of times and she did not answer at first, but then she said yes. He said, "I'm going to take you to the hospital." He helped her up the stairs. He asked her if she could get up and there was no response. She sat up and she put her arm around him and he put his arm around her waist and they walked up the stairs. She could not walk on her own. He called a taxi. He testified she got heavy and he laid her on the floor by the front door and waited 10 to 15 minutes for the taxi. She was still sweating, shaking, and was mumbling. The taxi arrived and he could not pick her up and asked his brother to help him take her to the taxi.

. . . .

On her arrival at the hospital, Greiner had no pulse and no heartbeat. She was pronounced dead at 3:10 a.m.

The trial judge found that the appellant told Ms. Greiner at about 2:00 a.m. that he would take her to the hospital and "immediately thereafter embarked on that act". She concluded that this statement was an "undertaking" within the meaning of s. 217 of the *Criminal Code*.

The circumstances giving rise to a legal duty were summarized by the trial judge in the following passages:

> By taking charge of Audrey Greiner after he knew that she had ingested crack, Dexter Browne undertook to care for her while the crack was in her body. That undertaking included rendering assistance to her which required taking her to the hospital immediately. On this basis, the legal duty to Audrey Greiner within the meaning of section 217 arose just after 11:30 when the accused knew that Audrey Greiner had not vomited the crack cocaine.

> Although Dexter Browne testified that he did not say to Audrey Greiner that he would take care of her if something bad happened, he did admit that he would take care of her if she sold to someone who tried to rob her or anything like that.

. . . .

Using a taxi instead of calling 911 reflected, according to the trial judge, a "wanton and reckless disregard" for Audrey Greiner's life contrary to s. 219(1) of the *Criminal Code*.

Analysis

The charge of criminal negligence against the appellant was particularized as follows, mirroring the language found in s. 217 of the *Criminal Code*:

> . . . that he . . . failed to render assistance to Audrey Greiner by failing to take her immediately to the hospital after undertaking to render such assistance and did thereby cause the death of Audrey Greiner . . .

The particularization of the charge in this way meant that to find a legal duty, there had first to be a finding of an undertaking. This flows from the language of s. 217 which states that everyone "who *undertakes* to do an act is under a legal duty to do it if an omission to do the act is or may be dangerous to life". In other words, the legal duty does not flow from the relationship between the parties, as it does in s. 215, which creates legal duties between spouses, between parents and children, and between dependants and their caregivers. Under s. 217, there is no pre-existing relationship or situation that creates a legal duty; there must be an undertaking before a legal duty is introduced into the relationship. The relationship or context is relevant only to the determination of whether the breach reflected a "wanton or reckless disregard" under s. 219(1), not to whether there was an undertaking under s. 217.

What kind of an undertaking gives rise to a legal duty within the meaning of s. 217, the breach of which can result in criminal culpability? In my view, the ordinary dictionary definition of "undertaking" is of little assistance. There is no doubt that the definition embraces an interpretive continuum ranging from an assertion to a promise. But it seems to me that when we are deciding whether conduct is caught by the web of criminal liability, the threshold definition we apply must justify penal sanctions. A conviction for criminal negligence causing death carries a maximum penalty of life imprisonment. The word "undertaking" in s. 217 must be interpreted in this context. The threshold definition must be sufficiently high to justify such serious penal consequences. The mere expression of words indicating a willingness to do an act cannot trigger the legal duty. There must be something in the nature of a commitment, generally, though not necessarily, upon which reliance can reasonably be said to have been placed.

Any other interpretation of "undertaking" imports theories of civil negligence, rendering individuals who breach civil standards of care susceptible to imprisonment. The criminal standard must be — and is — different and higher. Before someone is convicted of recklessly breaching a legal duty generated by his or her undertaking, that undertaking must have been clearly made, and with binding intent. Nothing short of such a binding commitment can give rise to the legal duty contemplated by s. 217.

The trial judge found that the relationship between Dexter Browne and Audrey Greiner as partners in drug dealing gave rise to an implicit undertaking by Browne that he would take Audrey Greiner to the hospital whenever she swallowed cocaine. The fundamental error made by the trial judge was in reversing the analytical steps under s. 217 by starting her analysis with whether a duty of care existed, finding that it did, and then basing her finding of an undertaking on the existence of a legal duty. The inquiry should have begun with whether there was an undertaking. Only if there was an undertaking in the nature of a binding commitment could a legal duty have arisen under s. 217, regardless of the nature of the relationship between the appellant and Audrey Greiner.

In my view, the evidence does not disclose any undertaking of a binding nature. These were two drug dealers who were used to swallowing bags of drugs to avoid detection by the police. There was no evidence that the appellant knew that Audrey Greiner was in a life-threatening situation until 2:00 a.m., when he immediately phoned for a taxi. His words to her at that time — "I'll take you to the hospital" — hardly constitute an undertaking creating a legal duty under s. 217. He said he would take her to the hospital when he saw the severity of her symptoms, and he did. There is no evidence either that a 911 call would have resulted in a significantly quicker arrival at the hospital at that hour, or even that had she arrived earlier, Audrey Greiner's life could have been saved.

There being no undertaking within the meaning of s. 217 of the *Criminal Code*, there can be no finding of a legal duty. There being no duty, there can be no breach contrary to s. 219 of the *Code*.

. . . .

Accordingly, I would allow the appeal, set aside the conviction, and enter an acquittal.

PEOPLE v. BEARDSLEY

(1907), 113 N.W. 1128 (Mich. S.C.)

MCALVAY C.J.: — Respondent was convicted of manslaughter before the circuit Court for Oakland county, and was sentenced to the State prison at Jackson for a minimum term of one year and a maximum term not to exceed five years. He was a married man living at Pontiac, and at the time the facts herein narrated occurred, he was working as a bartender and clerk at the Columbia Hotel. He lived with his wife in Pontiac, occupying two rooms on the ground floor of a house. Other rooms were rented to tenants, as was also one living room in the basement. His wife being temporarily absent from the city, respondent arranged with a woman named Blanche Burns, who at the time was working at another hotel, to go to his apartments with him. He had been acquainted with her for some time. They knew each other's habits and character. . . . On the evening of Saturday, March 18, 1905, he met her at the place where she worked, and they went together to his place of residence. They at once began to drink and continued to drink steadily, and remained together, day and night, from that time until the afternoon of the Monday following, except when respondent went to his work on Sunday afternoon. There was liquor at these rooms, and when it was all used they were served with bottles of whiskey and beer by a young man who worked at the Columbia Hotel, and who also attended respondent's fires at the house. . . . On Monday afternoon, about one o'clock, the young man went to the house to see if anything was wanted. . . . During this visit to the house the woman sent the young man to a drug store to purchase, with money she gave him, camphor and morphine tablets. He procured both articles. There were six grains of morphine in quarter-grain tablets. She concealed the morphine from respondent's notice, and was discovered putting something into her mouth by him and the young man as they were returning from the other room after taking a drink of beer. She in fact was taking morphine. Respondent struck the box from her hand. Some of the tablets fell on the floor, and of these, respondent crushed several with his foot. She picked up and swallowed two of them, and the young man put two of them in the spittoon. Altogether it is probable she took from three to four grains of morphine. The young man went away soon after this. Respondent called him by telephone about an hour later, and after he came to the house requested him to take the woman into the room in the basement which was occupied by a Mr. Skoba. She was in a stupor and did not rouse when spoken to. Respondent was too intoxicated to be of any assistance and the young man proceeded to take her downstairs. While doing this Skoba arrived, and together they put her in his room on the bed. Respondent requested Skoba to look after her and let her out the back way when she waked up. Between nine and ten o'clock in the evening Skoba became alarmed at her condition. He at once called the city marshal and a doctor. An examination by them disclosed that she was dead.

. . . The principal assignments of error are based upon the charge of the Court, and refusal to give certain requests to charge, and are upon the theory that under the undisputed evidence in the case, as claimed by the people and detailed by the people's witnesses, the respondent should have been acquitted and discharged. In the brief of the prosecutor his position is stated as follows:

> It is the theory of the prosecution that the facts and circumstances attending the death of Blanche Burns in the house of respondent were such as to lay upon him a duty to care for her, and the duty to take steps for her protection, the failure to take which, was sufficient to constitute such an omission as would render him legally responsible for her death. . . . There is no claim on the part of the people that the respondent . . . was in any way an active agent in bringing about the death of Blanche Burns, but simply, that he owed her a duty which he failed to perform, and that in consequence of such failure on his part she came to her death.

Upon this theory a conviction was asked and secured.

The law recognizes that under some circumstances the omission of a duty owed by one individual to another, where such omission results in the death of the one to whom the duty is owing, will make the other chargeable with manslaughter. . . . This rule of law is always based upon the proposition that the duty neglected must be a legal duty, and not a mere moral obligation. It must be a duty imposed by law or by contract, and the omission to perform the duty must be the immediate and direct cause of death. . . .

One authority has briefly and correctly stated the rule, which the prosecution claims should be applied to the case at bar, as follows:

If a person who sustains to another the legal relation of protector, as husband to wife, parent to child, master to seaman, etc., knowing such person to be in peril of life, willfully or negligently fails to make such reasonable and proper efforts to rescue him as he might have done without jeopardizing his own life or the lives of others, he is guilty of manslaughter at least, if by reason of his omission of duty the dependent person dies.

So one who from domestic relationship, public duty, voluntary choice, or otherwise, has the custody and care of a human being, helpless either from imprisonment, infancy, sickness, age, imbecility, or other incapacity of mind or body, is bound to execute the charge with proper diligence and will be held guilty of manslaughter, if by culpable negligence he lets the helpless creature die. 21 Am. & Eng. Enc. Law (2d Ed.), p. 197, notes and cases cited.

. . . Another English case decided in the appellate Court, Lord Coleridge, C.J., delivering the opinion, is *Reg. v. Instan*, 17 Cox Crim. Cas. 602. An unmarried woman without means lived with and was maintained by her aged aunt. The aunt suddenly became very sick, and for ten days before her death was unable to attend to herself, to move about, or to do anything to procure assistance. Before her death no one but the prisoner had any knowledge of her condition. The prisoner continued to live in the house at the cost of the deceased and took in the food supplied by the tradespeople. The prisoner did not give food to the deceased, or give or procure any medical or nursing attendance for her; nor did she give notice to any neighbor of her condition or wants, although she had abundant opportunity and occasion to do so. In the opinion, Lord Coleridge, speaking for the Court, said:

It is not correct to say that every moral obligation is a legal duty; but every legal duty is founded upon a moral obligation. In this case, as in most cases, the legal duty can be nothing else than taking upon one's self the performance of the moral obligation. There is no question whatever that it was this woman's clear duty to impart to the deceased so much of that food, which was taken into the house for both and paid for by the deceased, as was necessary to sustain her life. The deceased could not get it for herself. She could only get it through the prisoner. It was the prisoner's clear duty at common law to supply it to the deceased, and that duty she did not perform. Nor is there any question that the prisoner's failure to discharge her legal duty, if it did not directly cause, at any rate accelerated, the death of the deceased. There is no case directly on the point; but it would be a slur and a stigma upon our law if there could be any doubt as to the law to be derived from the principle of decided cases, if cases were necessary. There was a clear moral obligation, and a legal duty founded upon it; a duty willfully disregarded and the death was at least accelerated, if not caused, by the nonperformance of the legal duty.

. . . We do not understand from this opinion that the Court held that there was a legal duty founded solely upon a moral obligation. The Court indicated that the law applied in the case was derived from the principles of decided cases. It was held that the prisoner had omitted to perform that which was a clear duty at the common law. The prisoner had wrongfully appropriated the food of the deceased and withheld it from her. She was the only other person in the house, and had assumed charge of her helpless relative. She was under a clear legal duty to give her the food she withheld, and under an implied legal duty by reason of her assumption of charge and care. . . .

Seeking for a proper determination of the case at bar by the application of the legal principles involved, we must eliminate from the case all consideration of mere moral obligation, and discover whether respondent was under a legal duty towards Blanche Burns at the time of her death, knowing her to be in peril of her life, which required him to make all reasonable and proper effort to save her; the omission to perform which duty would make him responsible for her death. This is the important and determining question in this case. If we hold that such legal duty rested upon respondent it must arise by implication from the facts and circumstances already recited. The record in this case discloses that the deceased was a woman past 30 years of age. She had been twice married. She was accustomed to visiting saloons and to the use of intoxicants. She previously had made assignations with this man in Detroit at least twice. There is no evidence or claim from this record that any duress, fraud, or deceit had been practiced upon her. On the contrary it appears that she went upon this carouse with respondent voluntarily and so continued to remain with him. Her entire conduct indicates that she had ample experience in such affairs.

It is urged by the prosecutor that the respondent "stood towards this woman for the time being in the place of her natural guardian and protector, and as such owed her a clear legal duty which he completely failed to perform." The cases cited and digested establish that no such legal duty is created based upon a mere moral obligation. The fact that this woman was in his house created no such legal duty as exists in law and is due from a husband towards his wife, as seems to be intimated by the prosecutor's brief. Such an inference would be very repugnant to our moral sense. Respondent had assumed either in fact or by implication no care or control over his companion. Had this been a case where two men under like circumstances had voluntarily gone on a debauch together and one had attempted suicide, no one would claim that this doctrine of legal duty could be invoked to hold the other criminally responsible for omitting to make effort to rescue his companion. How can the fact that in this case one of the parties was a woman, change the principle of law applicable to it? Deriving and applying the law in this case from the principle of decided cases, we do not find that such legal duty as is contended for existed in fact or by implication on the part of respondent towards the deceased, the omission of which involved criminal liability. We find no more apt words to apply to this case than those used by Mr. Justice Field in *United States v. Knowles* (4 Sawy 517, 519):

> In the absence of such obligations, it is undoubtedly the moral duty of every person to extend to others assistance when in danger; . . . and if such efforts should be omitted by any one when they could be made without imperiling his own life, he would, by his conduct, draw upon himself the just censure and reproach of good men; but this is the only punishment to which he would be subjected by society.

Other questions discussed in the briefs need not be considered. The conviction is set aside, and respondent is ordered discharged.

G. HUGHES, CRIMINAL OMISSIONS

(1957-58), 67 Yale L.J. 590 at 624

To be temperate about such a decision is difficult. In its savage proclamation that the wages of sin is death, it ignores any impulse of charity and compassion. It proclaims a morality which is smug, ignorant and vindictive. In a civilized society, a man who finds himself with a helplessly ill person who has no other source of aid should be under a duty to summon help, whether the person is his wife, his mistress, a prostitute or a Chief Justice. The *Beardsley* decision deserves emphatic repudiation by the jurisdiction which was responsible.

Do you agree? How would *Beardsley* be decided under current Canadian law?

Voluntariness

R. v. KING

[1962] S.C.R. 746, 38 C.R. 52, 133 C.C.C. 1,
at 749 (S.C.R.)

TASCHEREAU J.: — It is my view that there can be no *actus reus* unless it is the result of a willing mind at liberty to make a definite choice or decision, or in other words, there must be a willpower to do an act whether the accused knew or not that it was prohibited by law.

RABEY v. R.

[1980] 2 S.C.R. 513, 54 C.C.C. (2d) 1, 15 C.R. (3d) 225,
at 232, 235, 255 (C.R.)

RITCHIE J.: —

. . . .

Automatism is a term used to describe unconscious, involuntary behaviour, the state of a person who, though capable of action, is not conscious of what he is doing. It means an unconscious involuntary act, where the mind does not go with what is being done.

DICKSON J.: —

. . . .

Although the word "automatism" made its way but lately to the legal state, it is basic principle that absence of volition in respect of the act involved is always a defence to a crime. A defence that the act is involuntary entitles the accused to a complete and unqualified acquittal. That the defence of automatism exists as a middle ground between criminal responsibility and legal insanity is beyond question. Although spoken of as a defence, in the sense that it is raised by the accused, the Crown always bears the burden of proving a voluntary act. . . . [A] . . . principle, fundamental to our criminal law, which governs this appeal is that no act can be a criminal offence unless it is done voluntarily. Consciousness is a *sine qua non* to criminal liability.

R. v. PARKS

[1992] 2 S.C.R. 871, 15 C.R. (4th) 289, 75 C.C.C. (3d) 287

LA FOREST J.: —

Automatism occupies a unique place in our criminal law system. Although spoken of as a "defence", it is conceptually a subset of the voluntariness requirement, which in turn is part of the *actus reus* component of criminal liability.

R. v. STONE

[1999] 2 S.C.R. 290, 24 C.R. (5th) 1, 134 C.C.C. (3d) 353

BASTARACHE J.: I . . . prefer to define automatism as a state of impaired consciousness, rather than unconsciousness, in which an individual, though capable of action, has no voluntary control over that action. . . .

. . . .

[V]oluntariness, rather than consciousness, is the key legal element of automatistic behaviour since a defence of automatism amounts to a denial of the voluntariness component of the *actus reus*.

In *Stone*, Bastarache, for a 5-4 majority, also held that accused had to prove any defence of automatism on a balance of probabilities.

The leading decisions in *Rabey* (disassociated state), *Parks* (sleepwalking) and *Stone* will be considered much later after a consideration of the defence of insanity when voluntariness is re-visited under the heading of automatism.

COBB, FOUNDATIONS OF NEUROPSYCHIATRY

(1958), 117-18, quoted by S.J. Fox, "Physical Disorder Consciousness and Criminal Liability" (1963), 63 Col. L. Rev. 645 at 651

When the human organism is working well, functioning as a whole, there is probably the highest degree of consciousness, and a feeling of well being and capability. In such a state attention is usually directed to certain objects with neglect of others. Therefore there is never a state that could be called full consciousness. . . . When tired, bored, or slightly poisoned by alcohol, we are suffering from a partial loss of consciousness. From the excited state of great efficiency under stress, through normal work-a-day moods, to states of dullness, coma and stupor, there is a continuous series of states where consciousness is less and less active. . . . Only in deep sleep is the cortex inactive, as judged by the electroencephalograph. There are different degrees of consciousness in sleep. Persons lightly asleep can differentiate between ordinary noises and sounds that may mean danger. Dreaming is a form of consciousness. A sense of time may be carried through hours of sleep, allowing one to wake at a desired hour.

H.L.A. HART, ACTS OF WILL AND RESPONSIBILITY

Punishment and Responsibility, (1968), 104-106

The General Doctrine Reconstructed.

Most people, lawyers and laymen alike, would I think agree that in our list of examples of involuntary conduct (conscious and unconscious), some radical defect is present, and some vital component of normal action is absent, even if Austin's terminology of "desire" or muscular movement or volitions misdescribes it. For the cases do not seem to be a *mere* list without any unifying feature to justify treating them alike as cases where conduct is not voluntary. If it is the policy of the law to mark these cases off, there seems some good factual basis for this policy. Is it then possible to give a more adequate account than that of the traditional theory? Or must we leave the dark phrases "not governed by the will", "no act of will", "involuntary", "no operation of the will" etc. unexplained?

In fact, I think it would not be difficult to construct an account which would explain and justify the intuitive feeling that, in all these cases, there is some more fundamental defect than lack of knowledge or foresight. By a "more adequate" account I mean one which involves no fictions; which is better fitted to the facts of ordinary experience; and which could be used by the Courts in order to identify a range of cases where the minimum mental element required for responsibility is not satisfied. Such an account could cover both the conscious and unconscious examples suggested in the books, but it would necessarily differ from the kind of general explanation given there in two main ways. First it would be disassociated from any claim that the ordinary way of talking about actions was inferior, or less accurate than the definition of acts as muscular contractions. Secondly, omissions would have to be treated separately from positive interventions. Granted these two things, we could then characterise involuntary movements such as those made in epilepsy, or in a stroke, or mere reflex actions to blows or stings, as movements of the body which occurred although they were not appropriate, *i.e.* required for any action (in the ordinary sense of action) which the agent believed himself to be doing. This, I think, reproduces what is in fact meant by ordinary people when they say a man's bodily movements are uncontrolled, as in the case of a reflex or St. Vitus dance. Such movements are "wild" or not "governed by the will" in the sense that they are not subordinated to the agent's conscious plans of action: they do not occur as part of anything the agent takes himself to be doing. This is the feature which the Austinian theory represents in a distorted form by identifying the involuntary movements as those which are not caused by a desire for them.

In the unconscious cases, *e.g.* of epilepsy, automatism, etc. the same test can be used. Here too, the movements which we call involuntary are not part of any action the agent takes himself to be doing, because, being unconscious, he does not take himself to be doing any action. This test, it should be noted, preserves the distinction between involuntary conduct and mere lack of knowledge of circumstances or foresight of consequences, and so reproduces the sense that we have in involuntary movements a different and more fundamental defect. For one who merely fails to foresee that the gun he fires will harm someone still makes voluntary muscular movements, *i.e.* movements appropriate to the action of firing the gun, which he knows he is doing; whereas the involuntary tremors of the palsied man, who breaks a glass, are appropriate to no action which he believes himself to be doing.

Omissions must, I think, be catered for separately, though this can and should be done in a way which reveals that their voluntary or involuntary character depends on the same general principle as positive interventions. When a man fails to do some positive action demanded by the law, his failure to act is involuntary if he is unconscious and so *unable* to do any conscious action, or if, though conscious, he is *unable* to make the particular muscular movements required for the performance of actions demanded by the law.

Why have a voluntary requirement of the *actus reus*?

I.H. PATIENT, SOME REMARKS ABOUT THE ELEMENT OF VOLUNTARINESS IN OFFENCES OF ABSOLUTE LIABILITY

(1968), Crim. L. Rev. 23 at 25-26

It is important at this stage to stress that involuntariness goes beyond lack of *mens rea*. A series of examples may show this.

Case 1: A shoots B meaning to kill him and B is indeed killed. A kills intentionally.

Case 2: A is not sure whether the shape in the distance is a human being or a tree, he nevertheless shoots. It was in fact B, who was killed by the shot. A kills recklessly.

Case 3: A is convinced he is shooting at a tree trunk. In fact it is B. A reasonable man would have realised it was a human being. B is killed by A's shot. A kills negligently.

Case 4: A shoots in a pistol club at a target. Suddenly B falls from the spectator's gallery into A's line of fire. He is killed. Even a reasonable man could not foresee this. A kills with blameless inadvertence, *i.e.*, accidentally.

[handwritten: actus reus but no mens rea]

In all four cases A's shooting was voluntary.

Case 5: A has an epileptic fit. One of his movements causes a gun which is lying beside him on a table to go off and kill B.
or:
A is aiming at a target. The physically stronger X takes hold of A's hand and forces him to point the gun at B and to pull the trigger. B is hit and killed.
or:
A is aiming at a target. He is attacked by a swarm of bees. His defensive reflect movement causes the gun to go off in B's direction and B is killed.

[handwritten: No actus reus or mens reus]

In all these cases there was a lack of voluntariness. There was no act on A's part. A cannot be said to have "shot" B. He caused his death, just as lightning can cause a man's death. Since there was no act neither was there an *actus reus*. To bring out the difference between involuntariness and *mens rea*, cases 4 and 5 have to be compared. In case 4, A kills accidentally, *i.e.*, without *mens rea*. Though there was no *mens rea* with regard to the killing, there was nonetheless a voluntary act. A did shoot. Moreover, he implemented the full *actus reus* of homicide, he killed a human being. If homicide were an offence of strict liability, *i.e.*, an offence which makes you liable even without *mens rea*, then A would be guilty of homicide in case 4. As the law stands he luckily will not be so liable. In case 5, however, there is not even an *actus reus*. An *actus reus* presupposes an act. There was no such act. A's movements were causal in bringing about B's death, but A did not "shoot" B. The defect in case 5 is therefore more fundamental than the defect in case 4. Even if homicide were an offence of strict liability, A would nevertheless not be liable in case 5. For strict [absolute] liability means liability without *mens rea*. In case 5 there is more than lack of *mens rea*. There is not even an *actus reus*.

O.W. HOLMES, THE COMMON LAW

Howe, ed., (1963), 46

The reason for requiring an act is, that an act implies a choice, and that it is felt to be impolitic and unjust to make a man answerable for harm, unless he might have chosen otherwise. But the choice must be made with a chance of contemplating the consequence complained of, or else it has no bearing on responsibility for that consequence. If this were not true, a man might be held answerable for everything which would not have happened but for his choice at some past time. For instance, for having in a fit fallen on a man, which he would not have done had he not chosen to come to the city where he was taken ill.

H.L. PACKER, THE LIMITS OF THE CRIMINAL SANCTION

(1968), 76-77

Conduct must be, as the law's confusing term has it, "voluntary." The term is one that will immediately raise the hackles of the determinist, of whatever persuasion. But, once again, the law's language should not be read as plunging into the deep waters of free will vs. determinism, Cartesian duality, or any of a half-dozen other philosophic controversies that might appear to be invoked by the use of the term "voluntary" in relation to conduct. The law is not affirming that some conduct is the product of the free exercise of conscious volition; it is excluding, in a crude kind of way, conduct that in any view is not. And it does so primarily in response to the simple intuition that nothing would more surely undermine the individual's sense of autonomy and security than to hold him to account for conduct that *he* does not think he can control. He may be deluded, if the determinists are right, in his belief that such conduct differs significantly from any other conduct in which he engages. But that is beside the point. *He* thinks there is a difference, and that is what the law acts upon.

R. v. LUCKI

No mens rea
Not guilty

(1955), 17 W.W.R. 446 (Sask. Pol. Ct.)

GOLDENBERG Q.C. P.M.: — The charge against the accused is as follows:

[O]n the 22nd day of November, A.D., 1955, at the City of Saskatoon in the said Province did operate a motor vehicle, to wit, an automobile bearing Saskatchewan License Number 139-212 on a public highway in the said City of Saskatoon, to wit, Saskatchewan Crescent, and did fail to keep to the right half of the said highway, and did thereby inconvenience other persons using the said highway, contrary to the provisions of Section 125 (9) of *The Vehicles Act* of the Province of Saskatchewan.

The facts are not in dispute. The accused operated a car on 17th Street in the city of Saskatoon at a speed of from 10 to 15 miles per hour. He had proceeded on 17th Street a distance of only about 150 feet, and made a right turn onto Saskatchewan Crescent East. While doing so, his car skidded over onto the left or north side of the road, and as a result he collided with another car which was proceeding in an opposite direction.

It is clear that his car was not on the right half of the road and that another car was inconvenienced thereby. It is clear to me that he got onto the wrong side of the road by an involuntary act, caused by the condition of the road, and I cannot say upon the evidence before me that it was his faulty driving that placed him in the position where he ended up. I think it was an involuntary act, for which he is not to blame.

Do these facts render him guilty of an offence under sec. 125 (9) of *The Vehicles Act*, R.S.S., 1953, ch. 344 [amended by 1955, ch. 82, sec. 27 (3)]? There are many sections under that Act that require no *mens rea*. Is this one of them? I do not think so. Were it otherwise some grave injustices would arise.

I can think of a case where a person drives a car carefully and a drunken driver runs into him and pushes his car over on to the left side of the road. I do not believe that the legislature intended such a person to be convicted under the section in question. And yet, if *mens rea* was not an essential ingredient of this offence, he would be guilty of it, since he did drive on the left side of the road.

No general rule can be formulated beyond stating that a person who by an involuntary act for which he is not to blame gets onto the wrong side of the road is not guilty under the section in question.

I find the accused not guilty.

R. v. WOLFE

(1975), 20 C.C.C. (2d) 382 (Ont. C.A.)

The judgment of the Court was delivered orally by

GALE C.J.O.: — The appellant was found guilty following a trial on a charge of assault causing bodily harm. After the finding of guilt was registered, the trial Judge granted the appellant a conditional discharge. The appellant now appeals from the finding of guilt and this Court is unanimously of the opinion that the appeal ought to be allowed, the finding of guilt set aside and a verdict of acquittal entered.

The appellant is a part-owner of a hotel in Kingston. On previous occasions, the complainant had been told, for good reason, that he was not to enter the hotel premises. On the evening in question, despite that prohibition, he entered the hotel. The appellant, using discretion and restraint, ordered him to leave. The complainant would not leave. The appellant then went to the telephone and while he was calling the police for the purpose of having him removed, the complainant punched the appellant who turned quickly and hit the complainant on the head with the telephone receiver. The complainant had a rather serious cut on his forehead, but that was really all that happened.

In giving judgment the learned trial Judge said:

Now, there is evidence that Mr. Brown-Keay hit the accused Mr. Wolfe and then in a reflex action (if you can call it that) Mr. Wolfe, who was calling the police, hit Mr. Brown-Keay on the forehead and caused a four-inch cut on his forehead. . . .

If, as it would seem to us, the trial Judge regarded the action by the accused as being the result of a reflex action then no offence was committed because some intent is a necessary ingredient in an assault occasioning bodily harm.

Mr. Campbell argues, not very vigorously, however, that, because of the limitation in brackets in the above quotation, the trial Judge did not regard the action of the appellant as resulting from his reflexes. However, that was in fact what the Judge said and we see no reason to depart from his conclusion.

In any event, the encounter was a trifling one and we have come to the conclusion that the appeal ought to be allowed and the finding of guilt set aside, as I have already indicated. The appeal will therefore be allowed.

Appeal allowed.

R. v. RYAN

(1967), 40 A.L.J.R. 488 (Aus. H.C.)

The accused, aged 20, read a novel in which the hero, feeling obliged to his parents, decided to rob a service station to obtain money to "invest" in the Irish sweepstake. In the book the hero, armed with a gun, tied up the garage attendant's hands behind his back after having obtained his money. He subsequently won the lottery, repaid the owner of the service station handsomely and gave the balance of his winnings to his parents.

The accused, as an act of bravado and for excitement and self-aggrandizement, decided to emulate his hero. On arrival at the service station where he intended the drama to occur he left his companion outside and went in armed with a sawn-off rifle, loaded and cocked. He demanded money from the sole attendant, threatening him with the weapon. The attendant produced some money. The accused then told him to put his hands behind his back, and went to tie them together with a piece of cord he had brought with him for the purpose. At this point, according to the accused, the attendant made a sudden movement and the gun accidentally discharged, killing the attendant. It was clear that slight pressure by the accused's finger had caused the gun to discharge. The jury dismissed the defence of accident and convicted of murder. The accused was sentenced to life imprisonment.

On appeal the accused argued that the jury ought to have been instructed on the issue of involuntariness which, if accepted, would have resulted in an acquittal. The firing of the gun was a reflex response to a sudden movement by the victim and was unwilled action on his part. The police had conducted several re-enactments of this scenario and on each occasion the actor had pulled the trigger. However the Australian High Court unanimously rejected the view that the jury ought to have been so instructed.

WINDEYER J. (one of four judgments delivered): —

The essential that the act be a voluntary act is . . . . is generally spoken of as a necessary quality of a criminal act; but it is perhaps more accurately regarded as a mental quality or attribute of the actor. . . .

That an act is only punishable as a crime when it is the voluntary act of the accused is a statement satisfying in its simplicity. But what does it mean? What is a voluntary act? The answer is far from simple, partly because of ambiguities in the word "voluntary" and its supposed synonyms, partly because of imprecise, but inveterate, distinctions which have long dominated men's ideas concerning the working of the human mind. These distinctions, between will and intellect, between voluntary and involuntary action, may be unscientific and too simple for philosophy and psychology today. However that may be, the difficulty of expressing them in language is obvious and may be illustrated. The word "involuntary" is sometimes used as meaning an act done seemingly without the conscious exercise of the will, an "unwilled" act: sometimes as meaning an act done "unwillingly", that is by the conscious exercise of the will, but reluctantly or under duress so that it was not a "wilful" act. Words and phrases such as involuntary, unintentional, inadvertent, accidental, unmeditated, unthinking, not deliberate, unwilled and so forth are used by different writers. Their connotations often depend upon their context, and they are used in discussions which seem to drift easily off into psychological questions of consciousness, sanity and insanity and philosophical doctrines of free-will and of events uncontrolled by will. There is a discussion of some aspects of this subject in the American work, *Reflex Action, a Study in the History of Physiological Psychology*. I mention it, not because I profess any knowledge in this field, but because of the readiness with which the phrase "reflex action" was used in the course of the argument as a presumably exculpatory description of the act of the applicant when he pressed the trigger of the firearm.

The conduct which caused the death was of course a complex of acts all done by the applicant — loading the rifle, cocking it, presenting it, pressing the trigger. But it was the final act, pressing the trigger of the loaded and levelled rifle, which made the conduct lethal. When this was said to be a reflex action, the word "reflex" was not used strictly in the sense it ordinarily has in neurology as denoting a specific muscular reaction to a particular stimulus of a physical character. The phrase was, as I understood the argument, used to denote rather the probable but unpredictable reaction of a man when startled. He starts. In doing so he may drop something which he is holding, or grasp it more firmly. Doctor Johnson in his Dictionary — and his definition has been in substance repeated by others — said that "to start" means "to feel a sudden and involuntary twitch or motion of the animal frame on the apprehension of danger". The Oxford Dictionary speaks of a start as "a sudden involuntary movement of the body occasioned by surpise, terror, joy or grief . . . ". But assume that the applicant's act was involuntary, in the sense in which the lexicographers use the word, would that, as a matter of law, absolve him from criminal responsibility for its consequences? I do not think so. I do not think that, for present purposes, such an act bears any true analogy to one done under duress, which, although done by an exercise of the will, is said to be involuntary because it was compelled. Neither does it, I think, bear any true analogy to an act done in convulsions or an epileptic seizure, which is said to be involuntary because by no exercise of the will could the actor refrain from doing it. Neither does it, I think, bear any true analogy to an act done by a sleepwalker or a person for some other reason rendered unconscious whose action is said to be involuntary because he knew not what he was doing.

Such phrases as "reflex action" and "automatic reaction" can, if used imprecisely and unscientifically, be, like "blackout", mere excuses. They seem to me to have no real application to the case of a fully conscious man who has put himself in a situation in which he has his finger on the trigger of a loaded rifle levelled at another man. If he then presses the trigger in immediate response to a sudden threat or apprehension of danger, as is said to have occurred in this case, his doing so is, it seems to me, a consequence probable and foreseeable of a conscious apprehension of danger, and in that sense a voluntary act. The latent time is no doubt barely appreciable, and what was done might not have been done had the actor had time to think. But is an act to be called involuntary merely because the mind worked quickly and impulsively? I have misgivings in using any language descriptive of psychological processes and phenomena, especially as I doubt whether all those skilled in this field employ their descriptive terms uniformly. Guided however by what has been said in other cases and by writers on criminal law whose works I have read, and especially by the judgments in the House of Lords in *Bratty v. Attorney-General for Northern Ireland*, [1963] A.C. 386, I have come to the conclusion that if the applicant, being conscious of the situation in which he had put himself, pressed the trigger as a result, however spontaneous, of the man whom he was threatening making some sudden movement, it could not be said that his action was involuntary so as to make the homicide guiltless. The act which caused the death was. . . . an act of the accused. The question for the jury was whether it was an act done by him in such a way as to make the resulting homicide murder. This was the issue submitted to the jury. The application for special leave to appeal must I consider be refused.

KILBRIDE v. LAKE

[1962] N.Z.L.R. 590 (S.C.)

WOODHOUSE J.: — On Thursday, 15 June 1961, the appellant drove his wife's car into Queen Street in the City of Auckland where he left it parked. He returned to it a short time later to find stuck to the inside of the windscreen a traffic offence notice drawing his attention to the fact that a current warrant of fitness was not displayed in terms of Reg. 52 of the Traffic Regulations 1956 (S.R. 1956/217). It was agreed before me that the warrant had been in its correct position when he left the vehicle, but that it could not be found upon his return. It was further agreed that during the period of his absence from the car the warrant had become detached from the windscreen in some way and been lost, or it had been removed by some person unknown. The fact that it was a current warrant was proved conclusively by records showing that on 13 April it had been issued by the Auckland Municipal Motor Vehicle Testing Station under No. 4513, and in respect of voucher No. 115456. Thus it had been issued for only two months, and four months would elapse before it required to be renewed. Despite a written explanation to this general effect which he had forwarded on the same day, a prosecution followed and he was convicted before Justices on an information alleging that he "did operate a motor vehicle . . . and did fail to display in the prescribed manner a current warrant of fitness". The proceedings were defended, but no note of the evidence was taken and no reasons for the decision were given. In these circumstances the appeal was argued on agreed facts as I have summarised them.

So far as it is applicable the Regulation reads:

> (1) . . . No person shall operate a motor vehicle . . . unless there is carried on the vehicle a current warrant of fitness as described in subclause (2) of this Regulation.

Subclause (2) provides that in the case of a vehicle fitted with a windscreen the warrant shall be affixed to the inside of the windscreen. The word "operate" is defined in Reg. 3 as meaning

> to use or drive or ride, or cause or permit to be driven or ridden, or to permit to be on any road whether the person operating is present in person or not.

The appeal was argued on the basis that the appellant operated the vehicle by permitting it to be on the road, and the facts do not support any wider application of the word "operate". Accordingly the regulation under review may be written, for the present purpose, as follows:

> No person shall permit a motor vehicle to be on a road whether the person operating it is present or not unless there is carried on the vehicle a current warrant of fitness.

The case for the appellant was that if he could show an absence of *mens rea*, then he could not be convicted, and he had succeeded in doing this as the warrant had disappeared without his knowledge during his absence from the car. On the other hand it was claimed for the respondent that this statutory offence was one which excluded *mens rea* as an ingredient to be proved. On this basis it was submitted that the offence was one of strict liability, and therefore the knowledge or the intention of the appellant was irrelevant. The issue thus raised on these simple facts directly poses the important question as to whether something done perfectly lawfully by the appellant could become an offence on his part by reason of an intervening cause beyond his influence or control, and which produced an effect entirely outside his means of knowledge.

It has long been established, of course, that if there is an absolute prohibition, and the prohibited act is done by the defendant, then the absence of *mens rea* affords no defence. This principle derives its justification from the general public interest, and any consequential injustice which might seem to follow in individual cases has necessarily been accepted. In the present case the respondent has conceded that the appellant had no opportunity of dealing with the situation which arose. But, it is said, however unfair a conviction might be to him personally, this offence has been made one of absolute liability as it is essential to put strong pressure on drivers of motor vehicles to do their whole duty. He permitted the car to be on the road, it was found there without a warrant, and accordingly he is guilty of the offence. With all respect to the arguments of both counsel, however, I am of the opinion that the emphasis which has been put on the matter of *mens rea* has obscured the real issue in this case.

It is fundamental that quite apart from any need there might be to prove *mens rea*,

> a person cannot be convicted of any crime unless he has committed an overt act prohibited by the law, or has made default in doing some act which there was a legal obligation upon him to do. The act or omission must be voluntary. (*10 Halsbury's Laws of England*, 3rd ed., 272.)

He must be shown to be responsible for the physical ingredient of the crime or offence. This elementary principle obviously involves the proof of something which goes behind any subsequent and additional inquiry that might become necessary as to whether *mens rea* must be proved as well. Until that initial proof exists arguments concerning *mens rea* are premature. If the first decision to be made is that the offence excludes *mens rea*, then that finding is likely to disguise the fact that there is an absence of proof showing that the accused has done all that is charged against him, should this in fact be the case. The missing link in the chain of causation, if it is noticed at all, appears to be provided by notions of absolute liability. But it is impossible, of course, to prove the one ingredient by eliminating the need to prove another. It appears to me that this confusion has arisen in this case. The primary question arising on this appeal, in my opinion, is whether or not the physical element in the offence was produced by the appellant. This physical element may be described by the convenient term *actus reus*, in contrast to the mental element or *mens rea* which is also an ingredient of a crime or offence, unless expressly excluded by its statutory definition.

In considering whether the *actus reus* can be attributed to a defendant, it is important to recognize that this is something which occurs following acts or omissions. It is not the line of conduct which produces the prohibited event, but it is the event itself. It is an occurrence brought about by some activity or inactivity, or by both. The crime therefore (excluding for the moment the possible ingredient of *mens rea*) is constituted by the event, and not by the discrete acts or omissions which preceded it: *Russell on Crime*, 11th ed., pp. 25, *et seq.* Accordingly it is not sufficient to show by some single act or omission that the accused produced the event. It is this fact which produces difficulties of causation when attempting to attribute responsibility for the *actus reus* to a given person. It is easy to do this when the *actus reus* can result from a single act, as, for example, a death by shooting. When it depends, however, upon supervening acts, and particularly when omissions are added to them, then the difficulties tend to multiply. Of course, when *mens rea* is an ingredient to be proved against an accused person, all these difficulties disappear as soon as they arise, because he usually cannot be proved to have intended acts done by others. He is thereupon acquitted on that ground. As *mens rea* is so frequently an ingredient of crimes and offences, this is a problem which rarely arises, and for that reason is not always recognized.

In the present case the definition of the offence takes the form of a prohibition followed by an exception. The prohibited event, however, in the sense of the term *actus reus* is not merely to permit a vehicle to be on a road. It is the doing of that act accompanied by an omission to observe the obligation to carry the current warrant of fitness. The *actus reus* occurs only when the second of these factual ingredients co-exists with the first. There must be the presence of the car combined with the absence of the warrant. Did this appellant produce that prohibited event, or did he merely set the stage?

There can be no doubt that the appellant permitted the vehicle to be on the road, and his conduct in this respect was a continuing act which did not end when he left the vehicle. Nevertheless, at this latter point of time the warrant was on the car, and there was no unlawful situation. Only when some extraneous cause subsequently removed the warrant did the event occur which the regulation is directed to prevent. If he is to be regarded as responsible for that *actus reus*, therefore, the decision must be made on the basis that he omitted immediately to replace the warrant.

It is, of course, difficult to demonstrate that an omission to act was not, in a causal sense, an omission which produced some event. All omissions result from inactivity, and in this matter of the warrant the appellant was necessarily inactive. But, in my opinion, it is a cardinal principle that, altogether apart from the mental element of intention or knowledge of the circumstances, a person cannot be made criminally responsible for an act or omission unless it was done or omitted in circumstances where there was some other course open to him. If this condition is absent, any act or omission must be involuntary, or unconscious, or unrelated to the forbidden event in any causal sense regarded by the law as involving responsibility. See for example *Salmond on Jurisprudence*, 11th ed. 401, *Causation in the Law* by Hart and Honore 292, *et seq.*, and the passage in *10 Halsbury's Laws of England*, 3rd ed., 272 cited above. In my opinion a correct emphasis is now given by this last paragraph to the need for the act or omission making up the *actus reus* to be voluntary, whereas in the corresponding paragraph of the second edition this distinction was blurred in discussion of *mens rea*. Naturally the condition that there must be freedom to take one course or another involves free and conscious exercise of will in the case of an act, or the opportunity to choose to behave differently in the case of omissions. But this mental stimulus required to promote acts or available to promote omissions if the matter is adverted to, and consequently able to produce some forbidden condition, is entirely distinct from the mental element contained in the concept of *mens rea*. The latter is the intention or the knowledge behind or accompanying the exercise of will, while the former is simply the spark without which the *actus reus* cannot be produced at all. In the present case there was no opportunity at all to take a different course, and any inactivity on the part of the appellant after the warrant was removed was involuntary and unrelated to the offence. In these circumstances I do not think it can be said that the *actus reus* was in any sense the result of his conduct, whether intended or accidental. There was an act of the appellant which led up to the prohibited event (the *actus reus*), and that was to permit the car to be on the road. The second factual ingredient was not satisfied until the warrant disappeared during his absence. The resulting omission to carry the warrant was not within his conduct, knowledge, or control: on these facts the chain of causation was broken.

For the foregoing reasons I am of the opinion that the physical ingredient of this charge was not proved against the appellant. Accordingly, I express no opinion on the submission that *mens rea* is excluded as an ingredient of the offence. On the view I have taken of the case the point does not arise.

Before I part with this appeal I think it should be said that the true purpose of the regulation is to ensure that motor vehicles are kept off the highway unless they are shown to be roadworthy by means of a current warrant of fitness. The additional requirement that the current warrant be displayed in a particular manner is, of course, an effective and sensible means of promoting that purpose. It keeps the matter before the notice of the driver, and also it enables traffic officers to check the position regularly, and with a minimum of difficulty. This latter fact, however, should not be elevated to such a level that charges are laid almost automatically against ordinary folk who have shown promptly and conclusively that a missing warrant was in fact current, and that there was an acceptable and proper explanation for its absence from the windscreen. As I have already stated, this appellant provided the Traffic Department of the Corporation concerned with a written explanation of the whole position on the day of the alleged offence, and he included in his letter all the numerical details concerning the issue of the warrant to which I have referred. I was informed by counsel that if he had also enclosed the voucher itself, his explanation would probably have been accepted and no further action would have been taken. If there was any real doubt in the mind of the officer concerned as to the currency of the warrant, it is a pity that he did not check with the Municipal Testing Station, or invite the appellant to produce the voucher. To the extent that this is a mandatory requirement it is a weapon intended to put appropriate pressure on people to do their duty. This general purpose is not likely to be promoted by prosecuting people who cannot reasonably be expected to do more than in fact they have done. It seems a proper case to award costs against the respondent, and accordingly I allow the appellant 10 guineas and disbursements. The appeal is allowed and the conviction quashed.

Appeal allowed.

Causation

In the case of some but not all offences the *actus reus* requires the causing of certain consequences. These offences include all homicides (s. 222), wilful damage to property (s. 430), arson (s. 433), and causing bodily harm (s. 221) or death (s. 220) by criminal negligence. The latter two offences illustrate that graver consequences may attract a higher maximum penalty — life imprisonment in the case of death and ten years imprisonment in the case of bodily harm. Since 1985 the maximum penalty of five years for the offence of dangerous operation of a vehicle increases to ten years where that conduct causes bodily harm and to 14 years where death results (s. 249 (3) and (4) and see similarly for impaired driving (s. 255 (2) and (3)).

Our *Code* contains no general principles concerning causation but only a number of special rules concerning homicide: see ss. 222 and 224-228.

B.C. ELECTRIC RY. v. LOACH

[1916] 1 A.C. 719 at 727-728 (P.C.)

LORD SUMNER: —

. . . .

It is surprising how many epithets eminent judges have applied to the cause, which has to be ascertained for this judicial purpose of determining liability, and how many more to other acts and incidents, which for this purpose are not the cause at all. "Efficient or effective cause," "real cause," "proximate cause," "direct cause," "decisive cause," "immediate cause," "causa causans," on the one hand, as against, on the other, "causa sine qua non," "occasional cause," "remote cause," "contributory cause," "inducing cause," "condition," and so on. No doubt in the particular cases in which they occur they were thought to be useful or they would not have been used, but the repetition of terms without examination in other cases has often led to confusion, and it might be better, after pointing out that the inquiry is an investigation into responsibility, to be content with speaking of the cause of the injury simply and without qualification.

PROXIMATE AND REMOTE CAUSE

(1870), 4 Am. L. Rev. 201 at 211-214

There is but one view of causation which can be of practical service. To every event, there are certain antecedents, never a single antecedent, but always a set of antecedents, which bring given the effect is sure to follow, unless some new thing intervenes to frustrate such result. It is not any one of this set of antecedents taken by itself which is the cause. No one by itself would produce the effect. The true cause is the whole set of antecedents taken together. Sometimes also it becomes necessary to take into account, as a part of the set of antecedents, the fact that nothing intervened to prevent the antecedents from being followed by the effect. But when a cause is to be investigated for any practical purpose, the antecedent which is within the scope of that purpose is singled out and called the cause, to the neglect of the antecedents which are of no importance to the matter in hand. These last antecedents, if mentioned at all in the inquiry, are called conditions. Suppose a man to have been drowned. What was the cause of his death? There must have been a man, and there must have been water, and there must have been a coming together of the man and the water under certain circumstances. The fact of there being a man, and the fact of there being water, and each and every attending circumstance, without the presence of which circumstance the death would not have taken place, together with the fact that there was nothing intervening to prevent, constitute the true cause.

What one of the various circumstances necessary to the death we shall single out as the cause, to the neglect of the other circumstances, depends upon the question for what purpose we are investigating the death. For each different purpose with which we investigate we shall find a different circumstance, which we shall then intelligibly and properly call the cause. The man may have committed suicide; we say he himself was the cause of his death. He may have been pushed into the water by another; we say that other person was the cause. The drowned man may have been blind, and have fallen in while his attendant was wrongfully absent; we say the negligence of his attendant was the cause. Suppose him to have been drowned at a ford which was unexpectedly swollen by rain; we may properly say that the height of the water was the cause of his death. A medical man may say that the cause of his death was suffocation by water entering the lungs. A comparative anatomist may say that the cause of his death was the fact that he had lungs instead of gills like a fish. The illustration might be carried to an indefinite extent. From every point of view from which we look at the facts, a new cause appears. . . . These separate causes are not causes which stand to each other in the relation of proximate and remote, in any intelligible sense in which those words can be used.

. . . .

In the physical science there is a search for what may with some propriety, perhaps, be called the proximate cause. It is a search for the conditions immediately antecedent to and concomitant with the effect. . . . It signifies the nearest known cause considered in relation to the effect, and in contrast to some more distant cause.

In the law there is no such investigation as this. The law, in the application of this maxim [in jure non remota causa, sed proxima, spectatur], is not concerned with philosophical or logical views of causation. When the maxim is applied, the whole body of facts has been ascertained by testimony. The facts are the subject of inquiry for a single purpose. That purpose is to determine the rights and liabilities of the respective parties to the proceedings. Those facts are alone viewed as causes and effects which have a direct bearing upon those rights and liabilities. . . . The inquiry is often one of difficulty. The difficulty is not owing to any great ambiguity in the meaning of the word cause. That word is used in its popular signification. One difficulty is, that philosophy and metaphysics are sometimes brought into a discussion to which they do not belong. Another is, that cause and effect are often viewed as parts of a "chain of causation", and the discussion thus becomes meaningless. The chief difficulty, however, is that the term proximate and the term remote have no clear, distinct, and definable significations. . . . The division is neither scientific nor logical. . . . Above all, it is not fixed and constant division. . . . The meaning of the terms . . . is contracted or enlarged, according to what is the subject-matter of the inquiry.

R. v. MICHAEL

(1840), 9 C. & P. 356 (C.C.C.R.)

The prisoner was indicted for the wilful murder of George Michael. She was also charged on the coroner's inquisition with the same offence.

The indictment stated, that the prisoner, contriving and intending to kill and murder George Michael on the 31st day of March, in the third year of the reign of her present Majesty, upon the said George Michael feloniously, &c., did make an assault, and that the prisoner, a large quantity, to wit, half an ounce weight, of a certain deadly poison called laudanum, feloniously, &c., did give and administer unto the said George Michael, with intent that he should take and swallow the same down into his body (she then and there well knowing the said laudanum to be a deadly poison), and the said George Michael the said laudanum so given and administered unto him by the said Catherine Michael as aforesaid, did take and swallow down into his body; by reason and by means of which said taking and swallowing down the said laudanum into his body, as aforesaid, the said George Michael became and was mortally sick and distempered in his body, of which said mortal sickness and distemper the said George Michael from &c. till &c. did languish, &c., and died; and concluding in the usual form, as in cases of murder.

It appeared that the deceased was a child between nine and ten months old, and that the prisoner was its mother, and was a single woman living in service as wet nurse at Mrs. Kelly's, in Hunter Street, Brunswick Square. The child was taken care of by a woman named Stevens, living at Paddington, who received five shillings a week from the prisoner for its support. A few days before its death the prisoner told Mrs. Stevens that she had an old frock for the child, and a bottle of medicine, which she gave her, telling her it would do the baby's bowels good. Mrs. Stevens said the baby was very well, and did not want medicine; but the prisoner said it had done her mistress's baby good, and it would do her baby good, and desired Mrs. Stevens to give it one teaspoonful every night. Mrs. Stevens did not open the bottle, or give the child any of its contents, but put the bottle on the mantel-piece, where it remained till Tuesday, the 31st of March, on which day, about half-past four in the afternoon, Mrs. Stevens went out, leaving the prisoner's child playing on the floor with her children, one of whom, about five years of age, during the absence for about ten minutes of his elder sister, gave the prisoner's child about half the contents of the bottle, which made it extremely ill, and in the course of a few hours it died. The bottle was found to contain laudanum. The prisoner said that a young man, an assistant of Dr. Reid's, had given the bottle by mistake. This was proved to be untrue; and Dr. Reid stated, that in the course of a conversation he had with the prisoner, she used these remarkable words, speaking of the death of the child, and the probability of an inquest being held upon the body: — "If I am hanged for it, I could not support the child on my wages." It was also proved that the prisoner purchased the laudanum at the chemist's in Tavistock Place, Russell Square, saying that it was for her mistress, Mrs. Kelly, who was in the habit of taking it, being a bad sleeper. One of the medical men examined at the trial said, that a teaspoonful administered to a child of the age of the deceased would be sure to destroy life.

Alderson, B., in his summing up, told the jury, that if the prisoner delivered the laudanum to Sarah Stevens with the intention that she should administer it to the child, and thereby produce its death, and the quantity so directed to be administered was sufficient to cause death, and while the prisoner's original intention continued, the laudanum was administered by an unconscious agent, the death of the child, under such circumstances, would sustain the charge of murder against the prisoner. His Lordship added, that if the teaspoonful of laudanum was sufficient to produce death, the administration by the little boy of a much larger quantity would make no difference.

The jury found the prisoner guilty. The judgment was respited, that the opinion of the Judges might be taken, whether the facts above stated constituted an administering of the poison by the prisoner to the deceased child.

Ryland, for the prosecution.

Ballantine, for the prisoner.

At a subsequent Session, Mr. Baron Alderson, in passing sentence upon the prisoner, said, that the Judges were of opinion that the administering of the poison by the child of Mrs. Stevens, was, under the circumstances of the case, as much, in point of law, an administering by the prisoner as if the prisoner had actually administered it with her own hand. They therefore held that she was rightly convicted.

Would it have made any difference if the laudanum had been administered by a conscious agent who acted for his own purposes?

For Canadian authority applying the "doctrine of acting through an innocent agent" see *R. v. MacFadden* (1971), 5 C.C.C. (2d) 204, 16 C.R.N.S. 251 at 253 (N.B. C.A.); *R. v. Berryman* (1990), 78 C.R. (3d) 376, 57 C.C.C. (3d) 375, (B.C. C.A.); *R. v. Ali* (1990), 79 C.R. (3d) 382 (Ont. Prov. Ct.) and *Toma* (2000), 147 C.C.C. (3d) 252 (B.C. C.A.).

SMITHERS v. R.

[1978] 1 S.C.R. 506, 40 C.R.N.S. 79, 34 C.C.C. (2d) 427

DICKSON J.: — This is an appeal from a judgment of the Court of Appeal for Ontario dismissing an appeal brought by the appellant from his conviction by Judge and jury on a charge of manslaughter. The indictment alleges that the appellant did unlawfully kill Barrie Ross Cobby by kicking him.

On February 18, 1973, a hockey game was played between the Applewood Midget Team and the Cooksville Midget Team at the Cawthra Park Arena in the Town of Mississauga. The leading player on the Applewood team was the deceased, Barrie Cobby, 16 years of age; the leading player on the Cooksville team was the appellant. The game was rough, the players were aggressive and feelings ran high. The appellant, who is black, was subjected to racial insults by Cobby and other members of the Applewood team. Following a heated and abusive exchange of profanities, the appellant and Cobby were both ejected from the game. The appellant made repeated threats that he was going to "get" Cobby. Cobby was very apprehensive and left the arena at the end of the game, some 45 minutes later, accompanied by eight or ten persons including friends, players, his coach and the team's manager. The appellant repeated his threats and challenges to fight as the group departed. Cobby did not take up the challenge. Instead, he hurried toward a waiting car. The appellant caught up with him at the bottom of the outside steps and directed one or two punches to Cobby's head. Several of Cobby's team mates grabbed the appellant and held him. Cobby, who had taken no steps to defend himself, was observed to double up and stand back while the appellant struggled to free himself from those holding him. While Cobby was thus bent over, and approximately two to four feet from the appellant, the appellant delivered what was described as a hard, fast kick to Cobby's stomach area. Only seconds elapsed between the punching and the kick. Following the kick, Cobby groaned, staggered towards his car, fell to the ground on his back, and gasped for air. Within five minutes he appeared to stop breathing. He was dead upon arrival at the Mississauga General Hospital.

Doctor David Brunsdon, who performed an autopsy, testified that in his opinion death was due to the aspiration of foreign materials present from vomiting. He defined aspiration as the breathing, or taking in, or foreign material through the windpipe into the lungs. It appears from the medical evidence that aspiration is generally due to barbiturate overdosage, alcohol intoxication, motor vehicle accidents or epilepsy. One medical witness testified to the possibility of spontaneous aspiration, whereby foreign material may be aspirated without any precipitating cause. This witness had seen three such cases out of the 900 to 1,000 cases of aspiration which he had experienced. In none of the three cases was the aspiration preceded by a blow. The consensus among the doctors was that spontaneous aspiration was a rare and unusual cause of death in the case of a healthy teenager such as Cobby. Normally, when a person vomits the epiglottis folds over to prevent the regurgitated stomach contents from entering the air passage. In the instant case this protective mechanism failed.

. . . .

The ground of dissent in the Ontario Appeal Court forms the first ground of appeal in this Court. Counsel for the appellant submits that the trial Judge, in emphasizing the act of assault as a constituent element in the crime of manslaughter, did not make it clear to the jury that the act of assault must also cause the death of the deceased and, secondly, that in giving his summation of the Crown and defence theories, the trial Judge referred to the issue of causation as defence counsel's argument that the cause of death had not been proven beyond a reasonable doubt. It is contended that the effect of these remarks was to minimize this issue in the minds of the jury. The jury was never instructed, it is said, that as a matter of law one of the issues on which they had to be satisfied beyond a reasonable doubt was that the kick caused the vomiting.

. . . .

I agree with the majority view in the Ontario Court of Appeal that the issue as to the cause of death was properly and sufficiently delineated by the trial Judge. It was not an unduly complicated issue. The assault by the appellant upon the deceased boy was undoubtedly an unlawful act. The principal issue was whether the appellant had committed homicide by directly or indirectly, by any means, causing the death of Cobby and whether such homicide was culpable for the reason that it was caused by an unlawful act. The Crown quite properly chose to establish causation principally through medical evidence and the doctors, men of high professional standing, understandably were disinclined to speak in absolute terms.

Doctor Brunsdon testified as to the effect of a sudden blow in the abdominal area. He said:

> I couldn't say always, but it certainly I think, would be predisposed to regurgitation. I am certainly not going to say it would happen in every case, but I think it could be predisposed to.

During cross-examination, Dr. Brunsdon used the expressions "very possible" and "very probable" to describe the cause and effect of the kick and the vomiting. As to the relationship of the kick and aspiration, he said: "I can amplify that a bit. It is a rare condition, but the kick would have made it more likely to aspirate." The following passage appears in the testimony of Dr. Hillsdon Smith, Professor of Forensic Pathology at the University of Toronto:

> I have already given in evidence that fear by itself can cause vomiting, a kick by itself can cause vomiting. The two together have simply a greater effect than either of those singly.

The jury was not limited to the evidence of the medical experts. In considering the issue of causation the jury had the benefit of uncontradicted evidence of a number of lay witnesses to the effect that the appellant kicked the deceased boy in the stomach area, that the kick was followed by immediate distress, and that the death occurred within minutes. This was cogent evidence to which the jury could apply common sense in considering the issue of causality. In my opinion, the first ground of appeal cannot be maintained.

The second ground, not unrelated to the first ground, is that the Court of Appeal erred in holding that there was evidence on the basis of which the jury was entitled to find that it had been established beyond a reasonable doubt that the kick caused the death. This broad question is unfortunately phrased, in that it leaves doubt whether the issue raised is one of sufficiency of evidence, a question of fact to which the jurisdiction of this Court does not extend, or an entire absence of evidence upon which a finding could be made that the kick caused the death, a question of law. The appellant's factum tends to remove the uncertainty by subsuming, within the broad question, three narrower questions. The first of these is whether the jury was restricted to a consideration of the expert medical evidence in making its determination on the issue of causation. It is conceded that the jury was entitled to consider all of the evidence, expert and lay, in its deliberations with respect to the issue of causation but on the precise question of whether or not the kick caused the vomiting or the aspiration, it is contended the jury was restricted to the medical evidence. It seems to me to be a novel proposition, subversive of the usual jury procedure, that on a particular issue the jury should be denied the evidence of certain witnesses. I have difficulty also in reconciling the concession that the jury is entitled to consider all of the evidence on the issue of causation but something less than all the evidence when considering the only causative questions in the case, namely, whether the kick caused the vomiting and whether the kick caused the aspiration. In support of his submission counsel cited *Walker v. Bedard and Snelling*, [1945] 1 D.L.R. 529. That was a civil case tried by LeBel J., without a jury in which damages were claimed against a surgeon and an an anaesthetist for the death of a patient following the injection of nupercaine into the spinal canal. LeBel J., quoted with approval a passage from the American decision in *Ewing v. Goode* (1897), 78 Fed. Rep. 442 at p. 444, in which the following words appear [p. 536 D.L.R.]:

> "But when a case concerns the highly specialized art of treating an eye for cataract, or for the mysterious and dread disease of glaucoma, with respect to which a layman can have no knowledge at all, the Court and jury must be dependant on expert evidence. There can be no other guide, and, where want of skill or attention is not thus shown by expert evidence applied to the facts, there is no evidence of it proper to be submitted to the jury."

The other case cited was *State v. Minton* (1952), 68 S.E. 2d 844, in which the death of the deceased was caused by a pistol bullet fired by one of the defendants, and a resulting haemorrhage. The judgment contains these words:

> The State did not undertake to show any causal relation between the wound and the death by a medical expert. For this reason, the question arises whether the cause of death may be established in a prosecution for unlawful homicide without the use of expert medical testimony. The law is realistic when it fashions rules of evidence for use in the search for truth. The cause of death may be established in a prosecution for unlawful homicide without the use of expert medical testimony where the facts in evidence are such that every person of average intelligence would know from his own experience or knowledge that the wound was mortal in character.
>
> There is no proper foundation, however, for a finding by the jury as to the cause of death without expert medical testimony where the cause of death is obscure and an average layman could have no well grounded opinion as to the cause.

In my opinion, neither of the cases cited lends any support to the proposition sought to be advanced by the appellant. No useful comparison is possible between an operation for glaucoma and the circumstances in the case at bar. In *Minton's* case the causal relation between the wound and the death was established without medical evidence.

It is important in considering the issue of causation in homicide to distinguish between causation as a question of fact and causation as a question of law. The factual determination is whether A caused B. The answer to the factual question can only come from the evidence of witnesses. It has nothing to do with intention, foresight or risk. In certain types of homicide jurors need little help from medical experts. Thus, if D shoots P or stabs him and death follows within moments, there being no intervening cause, jurors would have little difficulty in resolving the issue of causality from their own experience and knowledge.

Expert evidence is admissible, of course, to establish factual cause. The work of expert witnesses in an issue of this sort, as Glanville Williams has pointed out ("Causation in Homicide", [1957] *Crim. L.R.* 429 at p. 431), is "purely diagnostic and does not involve them in metaphysical subtleties"; it does not require them to distinguish between what is a "cause", *i.e.*, a real and contributing cause of death, and what is merely a "condition", *i.e.*, part of the background of the death. Nor should they be expected to say, where two or more causes combine to produce a result, which of these causes contributes the more.

In the case at bar, the Crown had the burden of showing factual causation, that beyond a reasonable doubt the kick caused the death. In my view, the trial Judge did not err in failing to instruct the jury that in determining that issue they could consider only the medical evidence. The issue of causation is for the jury and not the experts. The weight to be given to the evidence of the experts was entirely for the jury. In the search for truth, the jury was entitled to consider all of the evidence, expert and lay, and accept or reject any part of it. Non-medical testimony is available to both the Crown and the accused, and in the instant case, lay evidence was vital to the defence raised by the appellant. That evidence tended to show that all the circumstances preceding the kick were such as to create in the deceased boy a highly emotional state which might well have given rise to spontaneous vomiting, unassociated with the kick.

The second sub-question raised is whether there was evidence on the basis of which the jury was entitled to find that it had been established beyond a reasonable doubt that the kick caused the death. In answer to this question it may shortly be said that there was a very substantial body of evidence, both expert and lay, before the jury indicating that the kick was at least a contributing cause of death, outside the *de minimis* range, and that is all that the Crown was required to establish. It is immaterial that the death was in part caused by a malfunctioning epiglottis to which malfunction the appellant may, or may not, have contributed. No question of remoteness or of incorrect treatment arises in this case.

I should like to adopt two short passages from a case note on *R. v. Larkin* (1942), 29 Cr. App. R. 18, by G.A. Martin, as he then was, which appeared in 21 *Can. Bar Rev.* 503 at pp. 504-5 (1943):

There are many unlawful acts which are not dangerous in themselves and are not likely to cause injury which, nevertheless if they cause death, render the actor guilty of culpable homicide, *e.g.*, the most trivial assault, if it should, through some unforeseen weakness in the deceased, cause death, will render the actor guilty of culpable homicide.

. . . .

In the case of so-called intentional crimes where death is an unintended consequence the actor is always guilty of manslaughter at least. The act of the accused in *R. v. Larkin* fell within the class of intentional crimes because he was engaged in committing an assault upon Nielsen, and the fact that he caused a different type of harm to that which he intended did not free him from criminal responsibility.

The Crown was under no burden of proving intention to cause death or injury. The only intention necessary was that of delivering the kick to Cobby. Nor was foreseeability in issue. It is no defence to a manslaughter charge that the fatality was not anticipated or that death ordinarily would not result from the unlawful act.*

In *R. v. Cato et al.* (1975), 62 Cr. App. R. 41, the act supporting the manslaughter conviction was the injection by the accused into another person of morphine which the accused had unlawfully taken into his possession. Attention was directed to causation, and the link alleged to exist between the injection of morphine and the death. The appellant's argument based on the medical evidence of causation and the rejection of that argument by the Court of Appeal are to be found in the following passage, pp. 44-5:

First of all, he invited us to look at the evidence of causation, and he pointed out that the medical evidence did not at any point say "This morphine killed Farmer"; the actual link of that kind was not present. The witnesses were hesitant to express such a view and often recoiled from it, saying it was not for them to state the cause of death. It is perfectly true, as Mr. Blom-Cooper says, that the expert evidence did not in positive terms provide a link, but it was never intended to do so. The expert witnesses here spoke to factual situations, and the conclusions and deductions therefore were for the jury. The first question was: was there sufficient evidence upon which the jury could conclude, as they must have concluded, that adequate causation was present?

The third sub-question is whether there was evidence from which the jury was entitled to find that it had been established beyond a reasonable doubt that the kick caused the aspiration. It is contended that the burden on the Crown was to prove beyond a reasonable doubt that the kick caused both the vomiting and the aggravated condition of aspiration. I do not agree. A person commits homicide, according to s. 205(1) of the *Code*, when directly or indirectly, by any means, he causes the death of a human being. Once evidence had been led concerning the relationship between the kick and the vomiting, leading to aspiration of stomach contents and asphyxia, the contributing condition of a malfunctioning epiglottis would not prevent conviction for manslaughter. Death may have been unexpected,

---

* This statement of the fault requirement for manslaughter was expressly overruled in *DeSousa*, followed by the full Court in *Creighton*, a case we consider later in Chapter 3, "The Fault Requirement (*Mens Rea* or Negligence)".

and the physical reactions of the victim unforeseen, but that does not relieve the appellant.

In *R. v. Garforth*, [1954] Crim. L.R. 936, a decision of the Court of Criminal Appeal of England, the accused, aged 16, and another young man, S, quarrelled with the deceased, aged 18, outside a dance-hall. S kicked the deceased and when he doubled up stabbed him in the neck and heart, then the accused kicked him on the body and legs and S kicked him on the head. S was found guilty of murder and the accused was found guilty of manslaughter. The accused appealed against his conviction on the ground there was no evidence that what he did was a cause of death. It was held, dismissing the appeal, that there was clear evidence that the accused unlawfully assaulted the deceased and inflicted minor injuries which contributed to the death. Had the jury found that the accused intended to do grievous bodily harm, he would have been guilty of murder.

It is a well-recognized principle that one who assaults another must take his victim as he finds him. An extreme example of the application of the principle will be found in the English case of *R. v. Blaue*, [1975] 1 W.L.R. 1411, in which the Court upheld a conviction for manslaughter where the victim's wounds were only fatal because of her refusal, on religious grounds, to accept a blood transfusion. The Court rejected the argument that the victim's refusal had broken the chain of causation between the stabbing and the death.

Although causation in civil cases differs from that in a criminal case, the "thin skulled man" may appear in the criminal law as in the civil law. The case of *R. v. Nicholson* (1926), 47 C.C.C. 113, 59 N.S.R. 323, will serve as an illustration. In that case, the accused dealt the deceased man two heavy blows. The man who was struck was in poor physical condition. His heart was abnormally small and he was suffering from Bright's disease. An eminent medical specialist was asked if the blow or blows could cause death, given the condition of the body which was described, and he said it was possible. The blow might be one of the causes. Over-indulgence in alcohol, bad health, and the blow and tussle combined, in his opinion, to account for the result. The appeal from conviction was dismissed. Even if the unlawful act, alone, would not have *Rub* caused the death, it was still a legal cause so long as it contributed in some way to the death. I myself presided at a jury trial in which the accused, one Alan Canada, following an argument, struck his brother lightly on the head with a piece of firewood as a result of which the brother died some time later without regaining consciousness. The medical evidence showed that the bony structure of his skull was unusually thin and fragile. The accused, on the advice of counsel, pleaded guilty to a charge of manslaughter and I have never considered that he was wrong in doing so.

I would conclude this point by saying that although Dr. Hillsdon Smith thought that once vomiting had been induced, aspiration in these circumstances was no more than an accident, both Dr. Brunsdon and Dr. Butt acknowledged that the kick may have contributed to the epiglottal malfunction.

That brings me to the third and final ground of appeal, namely, whether the trial Judge's charge to the jury on the issue of self-defence amounted to misdirection. Although undoubtedly much upset by the actions and language of Cobby during the first ten minutes of play, thereafter the appellant alone was the aggressor. He relentlessly pursued Cobby some 45 minutes later for the purpose of carrying out his threats to "get" Cobby. Despite the frail factual underpinning for such a defence, the trial Judge charged fully on self-defence and in a manner which, in my opinion, was not open to criticism.

I would dismiss the appeal.

Appeal dismissed.

Problem

At 9:30 p.m. the accused went to the nearby residence of the deceased, angry that his cat had apparently been injured by the deceased's cat. The accused stood on the porch of the deceased's residence and threatened the cat and the deceased, provoking the deceased into agreeing to fight with the accused outside. The deceased was barefoot and went downstairs to get his shoes. The deceased's wife asked the accused to stop and twice pointed out that her husband had had strokes. The deceased, who appeared emotionally upset, fetched his shoes and ran or walked quickly some sixty five feet to the sidewalk in front of his house. In a very brief physical encounter, the deceased was put or thrown down to the ground by the accused. A short while later that evening the deceased suffered an acute heart attack and died at about 11:30 p.m.

The deceased had a long history of medical illness. He had diabetes, high blood pressure, a history of strokes, and had suffered at least one prior heart attack. He had triple coronary decease, with high grade calcification and obstruction in all three arteries. He was on disability leave, was inactive and overweight. A stress test had revealed that he was unable to do fundamental tasks such as vacuuming or taking out the garbage.

At the accused's trial on a charge of manslaughter before judge alone, prosecution medical evidence was led that an acute plaque rupture in the right coronary artery ultimately led to the blockage of blood to the deceased's heart and, as a result, his death. According to the medical evidence emotional or physical stress or a combination of both may trigger a plaque rupture. It is often difficult to isolate specific triggering events. In cross-examination the cardiologist testified that there was an 80 to 90 per cent probability that the plaque rupture may have occurred even if the physical assault had never taken place. As he put it "I don't think that the actual dropping of the body, the actual fall, the trauma of the fall, had much bearing on the matter".

The trial judge found the accused guilty of unlawful act manslaughter. He found beyond a reasonable doubt that the unlawful act of physical assault, alone, was a contributing cause of death outside the *de minimis* range. The trial judge imposed a sentence of six years imprisonment, emphasizing the need for specific and general deterrence. Do you agree

with this ruling and sentence? Compare *R. v. Shanks* (1997), 4 C.R. (5th) 79 (Ont. C.A.) and accompanying annotation by David Tanovich.

R. v. BLAUE

[1975] 1 W.L.R. 1411 (C.A.)

July 16. LAWTON L.J. read the following judgment of the Court. On October 17, 1974, at Teesside Crown Court after a trial before Mocatta J. the defendant was acquitted of the murder of Jacolyn Woodhead but was convicted of her manslaughter on the ground of diminished responsibility (count 1). He was also convicted of wounding her with intent to do her grievous bodily harm (count 2) and of indecently assaulting her (count 3). He pleaded guilty to indecently assaulting two other women (counts 4 and 5). He was sentenced to life imprisonment on counts 1 and 2 and to concurrent sentences of 12 months' imprisonment on counts 3, 4 and 5.

The defendant appeals with the leave of this Court against his conviction on count 1 and, if his appeal is successful, he applies for leave to appeal against his sentence on count 2.

The victim was aged 18. She was a Jehovah's Witness. She professed the tenets of that sect and lived her life by them. During the late afternoon of May 3, 1974, the defendant came into her house and asked her for sexual intercourse. She refused. He then attacked her with a knife inflicting four serious wounds. One pierced her lung. The defendant ran away. She staggered out into the road. She collapsed outside a neighbour's house. An ambulance took her to hospital, where she arrived at about 7.30 p.m. Soon after she was admitted to the intensive care ward. At about 8.30 p.m. she was examined by the surgical registrar who quickly decided that serious injury had been caused which would require surgery. As she had lost a lot of blood, before there could be an operation there would have to be a blood transfusion. As soon as the girl appreciated that the surgeon was thinking of organising a blood transfusion for her, she said that she should not be given one and that she would not have one. To have one, she said, would be contrary to her religious beliefs as a Jehovah's Witness. She was told that if she did not have a blood transfusion she would die. She said that she did not care if she did die. She was asked to acknowledge in writing that she had refused to have a blood transfusion under any circumstances. She did so. The prosecution admitted at the trial that had she had a blood transfusion when advised to have one she would not have died. She did so at 12.45 a.m. the next day. The evidence called by the prosecution proved that at all relevant times she was conscious and decided as she did deliberately, and knowing what the consequences of her decision would be. In his final speech to the jury, Mr. Herrod for the prosecution accepted that her refusal to have a blood transfusion was *a* cause of her death. The prosecution did not challenge the defence evidence that the defendant was suffering from diminished responsibility.

Towards the end of the trial and before the summing up started counsel on both sides made submissions as to how the case should be put to the jury. Counsel then appearing for the defendant invited the Judge to direct the jury to acquit the defendant generally on the count of murder. His argument was that her refusal to have a blood transfusion had broken the chain of causation between the stabbing and her death. As an alternative he submitted that the jury should be left to decide whether the chain of causation had been broken. Mr. Herrod submitted that the Judge should direct the jury to convict, because no facts were in issue and when the law was applied to the facts there was only one possible verdict, namely, manslaughter by reason of diminished responsibility.

When the Judge came to direct the jury on this issue he did so by telling them that they should apply their common sense. He then went on to tell them they would get some help from the cases to which counsel had referred in their speeches. He reminded them of what Lord Parker C.J. had said in *Reg. v. Smith*, [1959] 2 Q.B. 35, 42 and what Maule J. had said 133 years before in *Reg. v. Holland* (1841), 2 Mood. & R. 351, 352. He placed particular reliance on what Maule J. had said. The jury, he said, might find it "most material and most helpful." He continued:

> This is one of those relatively rare cases, you may think, with very little option open to you but to reach the conclusion that was reached by your predecessors as members of the jury in *Reg. v. Holland*, namely, "yes" to the question of causation that the stab was still, at the time of this girl's death, the operative cause of death — or a substantial cause of death. However, that is a matter for you to determine after you have withdrawn to consider your verdict.

Mr. Comyn has criticized that direction on three grounds: first, because *Reg. v. Holland* should no longer be considered good law; secondly, because *Reg. v. Smith*, when rightly understood, does envisage the possibility of unreasonable conduct on the part of the victim breaking the chain of causation; and thirdly, because the Judge in reality directed the jury to find causation proved although he used words which seemed to leave the issue open for them to decide.

In *Reg. v. Holland*, 2 Mood. & R. 351, the defendant in the course of a violent assault, had injured one of his victim's fingers. A surgeon had advised amputation because of the danger to life through complications developing. The advice was rejected. A fortnight later the victim died of lockjaw. Maule J. said, at p. 352: "the real question is, whether in the end the wound inflicted by the prisoner was the cause of death." That distinguished Judge left the jury to decide that question as did the Judge in this case. They had to decide it as juries always do, by pooling their experience of life and using their common sense. They would not have been handicapped by a lack of training in dialectic or moral theology.

Maule J.'s direction to the jury reflected the common-law's answer to the problem. He who inflicted an injury which resulted in death could not excuse himself by pleading that his victim could have avoided death by taking greater care of himself: see *Hale's Pleas of the Crown* (1800 ed.), pp. 427-428. The common-law in Sir Matthew Hale's time probably was in line with contemporary concepts of ethics. A man who did a wrongful act was deemed *morally* responsible for the natural and probable consequences of that act. Mr. Comyn asked us to remember that since Sir Matthew Hale's day the rigour of the law relating to homicide has been eased in favour of the accused. It has been — but this has come about through the development of the concept of intent, not by reason of a different view of causation. Well known practitioner's textbooks, such as *Halsbury's Law's of England*, 3rd ed., vol. 10 (1955), p. 706 and *Russell on Crime*, 12th ed. (1964), vol. 1, p. 30 continue to reflect the common-law approach. Textbooks intended for students in jurisprudence have queried the common-law rule: see Hart and Honoré, *Causation in Law* (1959), pp. 320-321 and Smith and Hogan, *Criminal Law*, 3rd ed. (1973), p. 214.

. . . .

Mr. Comyn tried to overcome this line of reasoning by submitting that the jury should have been directed that if they thought the deceased's decision not to have a blood transfusion was an unreasonable one, then the chain of causation would have been broken. At once the question arises — reasonable by whose standards? Those of Jehovah's Witnesses? Humanists? Roman Catholics? Protestants of Anglo-Saxon descent? The man on the Clapham omnibus? But he might well be an admirer of Eleazar who suffered death rather than eat the flesh of swine (2 Maccabees, ch. 6, vv. 18-31) or of Sir Thomas More who, unlike nearly all his contemporaries, was unwilling to accept Henry VIII as Head of the Church in England. Those brought up in the Hebraic and Christian traditions would probably be reluctant to accept that these martyrs caused their own deaths.

As was pointed out to Mr. Comyn in the course of argument, two cases, each raising the same issue of reasonableness because of religious beliefs, could produce different verdicts depending on where the cases were tried. A jury drawn from Preston, sometimes said to be the most Catholic town in England, might have different views about martyrdom to one drawn from the inner suburbs of London. Mr. Comyn accepted that this might be so: it was, he said, inherent in trial by jury. It is not inherent in the common law as expounded by Sir Matthew Hale and Maule J. It has long been the policy of the law that those who use violence on other people must take their victims as they find them. This in our judgment means the whole man, not just the physical man. It does not lie in the mouth of the assailant to say that his victim's religious beliefs which inhibited him from accepting certain kinds of treatment were unreasonable. The question for decision is what caused her death. The answer is the stab wound. The fact that the victim refused to stop this end coming about did not break the casual connection between the act and death.

If a victim's personal representatives claim compensation for his death the concept of foreseeability can operate in favour of the wrongdoer in the assessment of such compensation: the wrongdoer is entitled to expect his victim to mitigate his damage by accepting treatment of a normal kind: see *Steele v. R. George & Co. (1937) Ltd.*, [1942] A.C. 497. As Mr. Herrod pointed out, the criminal law is concerned with the maintenance of law and order and the protection of the public generally. A policy of the common law applicable to the settlement of tortious liability between subjects may not be, and in our judgment is not, appropriate for the criminal law.

The issue of the cause of death in a trial for either murder or manslaughter is one of fact for the jury to decide. But if, as in this case, there is no conflict of evidence and all the jury has to do is to apply the law to the admitted facts, the Judge is entitled to tell the jury what the result of that application will be. In this case the Judge would have been entitled to have told the jury that the defendant's stab wound was an operative cause of death. The appeal fails.

Appeal dismissed.

Application to certify point of law of general public importance involved refused.

Although *Smithers* is a wide-reaching ruling on causation, it expressly leaves open questions of "remoteness or of incorrect treatment". What then of more difficult causation issues where, although the accused was a contributing cause outside the *de minimis* range to the consequence complained of, the consequence seems more attributable to a later intervening cause?

Note should first be taken of four specific statutory homicide rules where certain intervening causes are held not to break the chain of causation. See ss. 222(5)(c), 224, 225 and 226.

In situations where a statutory rule or *Smithers* seems to point to an unfair result, the accused may have to resort to a *Charter* argument.

R. v. F. (D.L.)

(1989), 73 C.R. (3d) 391 (Alta. C.A.)

McClung J.A.: — As a result of a pedestrian injury accident in Calgary on December 2, 1986, the respondent, a youth, was tried on a multiple count information which included allegations that he:

1. Did unlawfully operate a motor vehicle within the said city while his ability to operate a motor vehicle was impaired by alcohol or a drug and did thereby cause bodily harm to Alex Primeau, contrary to the *Criminal Code*.
2. Having consumed alcohol in such a quantity that the concentration thereof in his blood exceeded 80 milligrams of alcohol in 100 millilitres of blood, did unlawfully operate a motor vehicle, contrary to the *Criminal Code*.
3. Did unlawfully operate a motor vehicle on a highway within the said city in a manner dangerous to the public, having regard to all the circumstances including the nature, condition and use of such place and the amount of traffic that at the time was or might reasonably be expected to be on such place, and did thereby cause bodily harm to Alex Primeau, contrary to the *Criminal Code*.

D.L.F. was acquitted on all counts by the trial Judge after his review of the blameworthy aspects of D.L.F.'s driving was well as his physical condition. That review, which need not be set out in full, satisfied the trial Judge that the driving pattern of the accused was dangerous within the meaning assigned by s. 249(1) of the *Code*. However, he was acquitted. The acquittal was gained, and this appeal taken, from the Judge's conclusion that there was no culpable connection established between D.L.F.'s driving deficiencies and the bodily harm sustained by a pedestrian who was injured when he was struck by D.L.F.'s vehicle. The acquittal on the count alleging dangerous driving causing bodily harm is all that is under appeal by the Crown.

The trial Judge felt that he was obligated to analyze each circumstance alleged by the Crown which, in their totality, were said to establish dangerous driving. The Judge did so under the focus of what acts of negligence could be said to be traceable, and therefore contributory to, the bodily harm suffered by the pedestrian. The Judge refused any connection arising from the accused's failure to wear corrective lenses to help his driving vision. He rejected any causal relationship arising from speed in excess of the posted limit and the accident. He rejected evidence of inefficient brakes. He rejected the failure of the accused to accommodate his driving to a narrowing of the road at the point of impact. The Judge concluded that none of these facts were instrumental in the collision and the injuries that were suffered. He held that the sole factual connection joining the driving conduct and the accident was D.L.F.'s failure to see the pedestrian, who was jaywalking, before the impact. The Judge credited this to inattention, not to dangerous driving.

. . . .

We think we are not only bound by, but fully agree with, the trial Judge's finding that the driving pattern disclosed in the evidence was dangerous within the prohibition of s. 249(1), the definition section. The nature, condition and use of the highway by the accused and the pedestrian traffic that should have been anticipated, all support the Judge's conclusion. However, the trial Judge seems to have erred in attempting to analyze each blameworthy facet of the accused's driving pattern and attempting to determine whether those individual components, under separate examination, were an effective cause of the accident.

. . . .

Under the additional responsibility of determining whether bodily injury was *thereby caused* to any person by the dangerous driving (s. 249(3)), other considerations arise. Sections 249(3) and 249(4) codify aggravated acts of dangerous driving. That aggravation is supplied by proof that the accused's unlawful driving caused harm or death to others. The offence becomes indictable and the exposure to gaol, in the case of s. 249(3), is doubled as the maximum sentence becomes ten years. The words "thereby causes" demand some examination of the factual connection between the dangerous driving and the injury or fatality. That, of course, is an inquiry that is not required in prosecutions brought under s. 249(1), a lesser and included offence.

The approach suggested by Rick Libman of the Ontario Crown Attorney Office in his article, "The Requirements of Causation in the New Offences of Impaired Driving Causing Bodily Harm or Death" (1985), 48 M.V.R. 21, in terms of simplicity, has proved to be a useful and orderly guide for the trial of these aggravated driving cases. Mr. Libman suggests that in cases under s. 249(3) and s. 249(4), the trial Court should:

1. Determine whether the driving conduct in question has been proven to be driving in a dangerous manner within the definition assigned by s. 249(1).
2. Determine whether the injuries complained of meet the test of "bodily harm" defined by s. 267(2) — ". . . bodily harm means any hurt or injury to the complainant that interferes with his or her health or comfort and that is more than merely transient or trifling in nature".
3. Where the preceding questions have been answered adversely to the accused, determine what correlative link exists between the dangerous driving and the bodily harm proven.

The difficult question remains: when is bodily harm or death "*thereby caused*" in s. 249(3) or s. 249(4) prosecutions? In my view the words "*thereby caused*" must demand, at least, that the unlawful operation of the accused's vehicle be proven to be a real and truly contributing cause of any ensuing injury or death and the trial court should be chary of allowing speculative inferences alone to stand as the causative link between the driving and the injury accident solely because of the target of the statute. The unlawful driving must still demonstrably influence the actual injury accident beyond serving as its backdrop. Mr. Libman (and Mr. MacDonald for the Crown here), invokes *R. v. Smithers*, [1978] 1 S.C.R. 506, 34 C.C.C. (2d) 427, and urges that the level of proof is "did the activities of the accused contribute in some way to the injury?" That was the Crown's proof commitment in culpable homicide cases, now statutorily defined by s. 222(*a*) of the *Criminal Code*. In *Smithers*, a kicking-death manslaughter prosecution demanding proof of general intent alone, the causation hurdle was described as proof that the unlawful act ". . . was at least a contributing cause of death, outside the *de minimis* range". The "outside *de minimis*" test has been recited in at least four appellate aggravated driving cases since and is now authoritative. *R. v. Laroque* (1988), 5 M.V.R. (2d) 221 (Ont. C.A.); *R. v. Singhal* (1988), 5 M.V.R. (2d) 172 (B.C. C.A.); *R. v. Halkert*, unreported, December 15/88, #4281 (Sask. C.A.) and *R. v. Pinske* (1988), 6 M.V.R. (2d) 19, appeal to S.C.C. dismissed October 12, 1989. Nonetheless, I confess to some difficulty with its fairness in all aggravated driving prosecutions.

I do not wish to founder in semantics but the application of the "outside *de minimis*" test, as proposed by Mr. Libman, is not easily reconciled with the common understanding of the statutory words "thereby cause". In everyday usage, the latter words convey "resulting in" or "create by that means" — something more, and more onerous, than a mere identifiable contribution which I understand the "outside *de minimis*" test to imply.

The difficulty is twofold; the verb "cause" is particularly troublesome when found in penal statutes requiring full *mens rea* or even none at all. *R. v. Sault Ste. Marie* (1978), 85 D.L.R. (3d) 161, 183 (S.C.C.). Beyond that, a standard of proof related at all to the concept of "*de minimis*" would normally find little philosophical communion within the criminal law.

The distinction would not be a real issue in the majority of s. 249(3) or 249(4) prosecutions but in cases involving parallel or competing causes of an injury accident, one of which may be quite external to the conduct of the accused, it can arise. Two or three car collisions come to mind. See *R. v. Ewart*, Appeal No. 8803-0334-A (Alta. C.A.). Where the facts disclose the preponderant cause of an accident to be divorced from the conduct of the accused, the accused may be substantially blameless for that accident but snared under the criminality of the "outside *de minimis*" rule. In such cases, a finding that the accident which resulted in injury or death was inevitable, whatever the driving deficiencies of the accused, has been taken. *Singhal (supra)*.

With all respect, there will be cases where it could be argued that the "outside *de minimis*" test is in conflict with the fundamental justice predicate of s. 7 of the *Canadian Charter of Rights and Freedoms*. It is a test of sweeping accountability. In *Smithers* the unlawful link that caused death involved nothing, on even a standard of objective awareness, suggesting the foreseeability of the victim's death. Statutory interpretations, at least those guiding the criminal process, that align with *Charter* values should now prevail. *Hills v. Atty. Gen. of Canada*, [1988] 1 S.C.R. 513. Nonetheless until the Supreme Court chooses to reconsider the matter the broader "outside *de minimis*" rule will govern. For this Court the matter is presently resolved by *R. v. Pinske (supra)*.

These concerns do not arise under the facts of this case and I do not apply them to resolve this appeal. They are only raised under a review of the stages of the approach suggested by Mr. Libman. This prosecution is, I think, determined by the Judge's conclusion that there was dangerous driving including the fact that while the pedestrian was jaywalking, D.L.F. should have seen him but did not. In Judge Fitch's assessment of the evidence:

> He should have seen him, and there certainly is a direct causal connection between failing to observe the pedestrian jaywalking and the accident.

> If the charge before me was merely dangerous driving, the section in the *Code* prior to the 1985 amendments, and in the absence of the case law connecting dangerous driving and consequences, my conclusion would be, yes the accused's driving was dangerous within the meaning of the *Code*.

Under those findings a s. 249(3) offence was proven. I would allow the Crown's appeal and direct the entry of a conviction under the third Count of the Information which alleged dangerous driving causing bodily harm contrary to s. 249(3). The respondent is directed to appear, on a date to be forthwith fixed, for sentencing, before the Family and Youth Division of the Provincial Court of Alberta at Calgary.

R. v. HARBOTTLE

[1993] 3 S.C.R. 306, 24 C.R. (4th) 137, 84 C.C.C. (3d) 1

The accused together with a companion forcibly confined a young woman. After his companion brutally sexually assaulted her while the accused watched, the accused and his companion discussed ways of killing her. The accused held the victim's legs to prevent her from continuing to kick and struggle while his companion strangled her. The accused was convicted of murder in the first degree. The conviction was upheld at the Court of Appeal where it was conceded that accused was a party to the murder while participating in her forcible confinement and sexual assault. At issue in the Supreme Court of Canada was whether accused's participation was such that he could be found guilty of first degree murder pursuant to s. 214(5) [s. 231(5)] of the *Criminal Code*. The Court dismissed the accused's appeal.

CORY J.: —

. . . .

Object of the Section

In order to provide the appropriate distinctions pertaining to causation that must exist for the different homicide offences, it is necessary to examine the sections in their context while taking into account their aim and object.

At the outset, it is important to remember that when s. 214(5) comes into play it is in essence a sentencing provision. First degree murder is an aggravated form of murder and not a distinct substantive offence. See *R. v. Farrant*, [1983] 1 S.C.R. 124. It is only to be considered after the jury has concluded that the accused is guilty of murder by causing the death of the victim. An accused found guilty of second degree murder will receive a mandatory life sentence. What the jury must then determine is whether such aggravating circumstances exist that they justify ineligibility for parole for a quarter of a century. It is at this point that the requirement of causation set out in s. 214(5) comes into play. The gravity of the crime and the severity of the sentence both indicate that a *substantial and high* degree of blameworthiness, above and beyond that of murder, must be established in order to convict an accused of first degree murder.

Substantial Cause Test

Accordingly, I suggest a restrictive test of substantial cause should be applied under s. 214(5). That test will take into account the consequences of a conviction, the present wording of the section, its history and its aim to protect society from the most heinous murderers.

The consequences of a conviction for first degree murder and the wording of the section are such that the test of causation for s. 214(5) must be a strict one. In my view, an accused may only be convicted under the subsection if the Crown establishes that the accused has committed an act or series of acts which are of such a nature that they must be regarded as a substantial and integral cause of the death. A case which considered and applied a substantial cause test from Australia is *R. v. Hallett*, [1969] S.A.S.R. 141 (S.C. In Banco). In that case, the victim was left beaten and unconscious by the sea and was drowned by the incoming tide. The Court formulated the following test of causation, at p. 149, which I find apposite:

> The question to be asked is whether an act or a series of acts (in exceptional cases an omission or series of omissions) consciously performed by the accused is or are so connected with the event that it or they must be regarded as having a sufficiently substantial causal effect which subsisted up to the happening of the event, without being spent or without being in the eyes of the law sufficiently interrupted by some other act or event.

The substantial causation test requires that the accused play a very active role — usually a physical role — in the killing. Under s. 214(5), the actions of the accused must form an essential, substantial and integral part of the killing of the victim. Obviously, this requirement is much higher than that described in *Smithers v. The Queen*, [1978] 1 S.C.R. 506, which dealt with the offence of manslaughter. There it was held at p. 519 that sufficient causation existed where the actions of the accused were "a contributing cause of death, outside the *de minimis* range". That case demonstrates the distinctions in the degree of causation required for the different homicide offences.

The majority of the Court of Appeal below expressed the view that the acts of the accused must physically result in death. In most cases, to cause physically the death of the victim will undoubtedly be required to obtain a conviction under s. 214(5). However, while the intervening act of another will often mean that the accused is no longer the substantial cause of the death under s. 214(5), there will be instances where an accused could well be the substantial cause of the death without physically causing it. For example, if one accused with intent to kill locked the victim in a cupboard while the other set fire to that cupboard, then the accused who confined the victim might be found to have caused the death of the victim pursuant to the provisions of s. 214(5). Similarly an accused who fought off rescuers in order to allow his accomplice to complete the strangulation of the victim might also be found to have been a substantial cause of the death.

Therefore, an accused may be found guilty of first degree murder pursuant to s. 214(5) if the Crown has established beyond a reasonable doubt that:

(1) the accused was guilty of the underlying crime of domination or of attempting to commit that crime;
(2) the accused was guilty of the murder of the victim;
(3) the accused participated in the murder in such a manner that he was a substantial cause of the death of the victim;
(4) there was no intervening act of another which resulted in the accused no longer being substantially connected to the death of the victim; and
(5) the crimes of domination and murder were part of the same transaction; that is to say, the death was caused while committing the offence of domination as part of the same series of events.

It would be appropriate to charge a jury in those terms.

For a comment on *Harbottle* see Allan Manson, "Rethinking Causation: The Implications of Harbottle" (1994), 24 C.R. (4th) 153-165.

R. v. CRIBBIN

(1994), 28 C.R. (4th) 137, 89 C.C.C. (3d) 67 (Ont. C.A.)

The accused had punched and kicked the victim first before a more vicious attack by the accused's companion. The injuries were not life-threatening but when the accused and his companion abandoned the unconscious victim, the victim drowned in his own blood. The jury convicted the accused of manslaughter. The trial Judge was found to have erred in his instructions relating to party liability and a new trial was ordered. The Court of Appeal decided that it was appropriate to give some guidance with respect to the issue of causation.

ARBOUR J.A.: —

. . . .

The only reference to causation in the Judge's instructions to the jury is as follows:

> If the Crown has failed to satisfy you beyond a reasonable doubt *that the assault by the accused contributed to the death of the deceased*, the accused committed culpable homicide, you must find the accused not guilty for he has committed no crime. If the Crown has failed to prove beyond a reasonable doubt *that Cribbin did anything which contributed to the death of Ginell*, then the accused is to be found not guilty and the homicide has not been proved. (Emphasis added.)

Appellant's counsel submits that the jury should have been told that the Crown must prove beyond a reasonable doubt that the assault by the appellant was an operative cause of the deceased's death, and not merely one of the circumstances in which the killing took place. Moreover, counsel contends that the jury should have been instructed that they could only convict if they found that the appellant's assault substantially contributed to the death, and that no intervening cause, such as Reid's actions, interrupted the chain of causation linking the appellant's assault to the victim's death.

. . . .

Leaving aside for the moment the appellant's contention as to the constitutional inadequacy of the *Smithers* test, I agree with counsel for the Crown that the trial Judge was not required to instruct the jury that they could convict only if they found that the appellant's assault substantially contributed to the victim's death. The requirement of "substantial causation", necessary to establish liability for first degree murder under s. 231(5) of the *Code*, was recently contrasted with the *Smithers* test in *R. v. Harbottle*.

. . . .

Had the trial Judge properly distinguished between Cribbin's potential liability for the homicide as a principal offender, on the basis of his own assault on the deceased, and his potential liability as an accessory to Reid's murder, it would have been unnecessary to burden the jury with distinctions between intervening and supervening causes capable or not, in law, of interrupting the chain of causation. The question of intervening cause would only arise if the jury were to conclude that the appellant and Reid were truly independent actors, which was a somewhat remote possibility despite the jury's apparent rejection of the robbery theory in so far as Cribbin was concerned. On any realistic view of the facts, Reid and Cribbin were either co-perpetrators or accomplices. If the jury were to reject the appellant's contention that he struck Ginell in self-defence, as this jury obviously did, the appellant's unlawful assault on the victim could hardly be said to be merely part of the history of the setting in which Reid inflicted the fatal blows to Ginell: see *R. v. Smith* (1959), 43 Cr. App. R. 121 at p. 131 (C.A.). The appellant admitted in cross-examination that he had hit the victim with sufficient force that he thought afterwards that his hand was broken. He struck the deceased on the cheek with a closed fist and his hand was still swollen and sore a few days later. He left with the others, abandoning the victim after having witnessed, if not participated in, the vicious attack inflicted by Reid on the deceased immediately after he, Cribbin, had initiated the assault.

Cribbin's own assaultive acts need not have been the medical cause of death. They were not, and neither were Reid's. The medical cause of death was anoxia. On the facts of this case, it cannot be said that the acts of Reid, which may have been the more immediate and the more severe factor in causing the unconsciousness from which the victim did not recover, operated as a supervening cause such as to insulate the appellant from the legal consequences flowing from Ginell's death. No useful purpose would have been served in instructing the jury further on that point. In my opinion, the charge was sufficient even though it did not invite the jury to examine whether Cribbin's contribution to Ginell's death was beyond the *de minimis* range.

(2) The Constitutionality of the *Smithers* Test

(a) *Introduction*

The appellant submits that the test in *Smithers* sets the causation threshold in homicide so low as to infringe upon the principles of fundamental justice in s. 7 of the *Charter*. In *Smithers*, Dickson J. held that on a charge of manslaughter, all the Crown has to establish is that the assault inflicted upon the victim "was at least a contributing cause of death, outside the *de minimis* range".

. . . . .

As I understand it, the constitutional argument advanced by the appellant is a two-pronged proposition. First, it is argued that the articulation of a legal causation rule involves a moral judgment as to blameworthiness, rather than a scientific inquiry, and that the principles of fundamental justice require that the rule triggering criminal responsibility, in this case the causation rule, be

propor tion
commensurate with the moral blameworthiness of the conduct that it prohibits. Under this argument, it is said to be unfair to punish for manslaughter one whose moral blameworthiness, reflected by both his conduct and his intention, never went beyond a simple assault. In short, the *de minimis* test is said to be too remote to satisfy the requirements of s. 7. Second, it is argued that the present law defining causation is void for vagueness.

(b) *Is the de minimis test too vague?*

In my opinion, the vagueness point can be summarily dismissed as the appellant has not demonstrated in what way a different causation test, such as the substantial connection test, the "but for", or the "*causa causans*" test, to refer only to a few that are well-known in the legal literature, would add any precision to the rule such as to give better guidance to citizens as to how to conduct their affairs in order to avoid criminal liability, and so as to properly curtail the discretionary powers of law enforcement officials. Even though analytical rules have evolved which are as rigorous as the methodologies commonly employed in many of the social sciences, whichever test is adopted, one has to recognize that causation in criminal law, as in other branches of the law, cannot be articulated with mathematical precision. The constitutional standard of precision which defeats the doctrine of vagueness was expressed by the Supreme Court as one which provides guidance to legal debate: *R. v. Nova Scotia Pharmaceutical Society*, [1992] 2 S.C.R. 606, 74 C.C.C. (3d) 289. The criminal law of causation, both in Canada and throughout the Anglo-American system, has a long and reputable history of doctrinal debate, the aim of which is to bring that concept within the boundaries that delineate criminal responsibility. The *de minimis* test, under attack as unduly vague, is indistinguishable, on a vagueness standard alone, from the more stringent test of substantial cause which the appellant says should be substituted for it.

(c) *Is the de minimis test too remote?*

(i) *The meaning of the de minimis test*

The remaining constitutional argument suggests that the *de minimis* test is too remote to engage criminal responsibility for homicide. In *R. v. Harbottle, supra*, the Supreme Court considered the causation requirements which had to be met before a person guilty of murder could be found guilty of first degree murder under s. 231(5) of the *Criminal Code*, which provides that murder is first degree in respect of a person when death is caused by that person in the commission of certain enumerated offences. In light of the language of the section, its legislative history and its purpose, Cory J. concluded that a narrower test of substantial cause should be applied. Cory J. specifically contrasted that test with the *de minimis* test applicable in the case of manslaughter, remarking that there were distinctions in the degree of causation required for the different homicide offences.

The *de minimis* test was enunciated in *Smithers, supra,* in the context of a charge of manslaughter. However, it must be taken to apply to murder in the same way. The *actus reus* of murder is indistinguishable from that of manslaughter. What distinguishes the two forms of culpable homicide is the different degree of fault represented by the constitutional requirement of subjective foresight in the case of murder, in contrast to the objective foreseeability of serious bodily harm which suffices for a conviction for manslaughter. Causation is a legal concept that addresses an aspect of the prohibited conduct and, as such, has significance only in crimes where consequences must flow from acts or omissions.

Specific causation rules are contained in various provisions of the *Code* dealing with homicide, such as s. 222(1) and (6), and ss. 223 to 228. The common law provides the guiding principles. Issues of causation rarely arise in murder cases, probably because the requirement that the Crown prove beyond a reasonable doubt the mental element related to the bringing about of the consequence, *i.e.,* the death of the victim, overshadows any concern that the consequence may not have been caused by the accused. In other words, if the jury is satisfied that the accused, in assaulting the deceased, intended to kill or intended to cause bodily harm that he knew was likely to cause death and was reckless as to that consequence, it will be rare for the jury to have a doubt as to whether the accused actually caused the death that he intended. In such a rare case, of course, a proper verdict could be attempted murder, assuming that the acts of the accused were not too remote: see Hart and Honore, *Causation in the Law,* 2nd ed. (Oxford: Clarendon Press, 1985), pp. 390-91.

Causation, on the other hand, is central to the law of manslaughter. It is essentially the vehicle by which the same act or omission of the accused will be defined as an assault, or some other appropriate offence depending on the circumstances, or as a homicide.

Before embarking upon an analysis of the constitutional argument as such, it is useful to examine more closely the meaning of the *Smithers* test. The appellant contends that the case of Smithers has set a causation requirement in manslaughter lower than its equivalent in England or Australia. For example, counsel points out that in *R. v. Harbottle, supra,* Cory J. adopted the definition of substantial cause from the Australian case of *R. v. Hallett,* [1969] S.A.S.R. 141 (S.C. In Banco), as the applicable causation test for first degree murder only, while *Hallett* was a murder case setting out the basic principle of causation applicable in homicide generally (see also *R. v. Jackson* (1989), 44 A. Crim. R. 320 (Qd. C.A.) at p. 327, where the Court followed the English case of *R. v. Pagett* (1983), 76 Cr. App. R. 279 (C.A.)).

In *Pagett,* the Court of Appeal noted that it is rarely necessary in homicide cases to give any direction to the jury on causation. Goff L.J., speaking for the Court, added, at p. 288:

> Even where it is necessary to direct the jury's minds to the question of causation, it is usually enough to direct them simply that in law the accused's act need not be the sole cause, or even the main cause, of the victim's death, it being enough that his act contributed significantly to that result.

More recently, in *R. v. Cheshire*, [1991] 3 All E.R. 670 (C.A.), the Court, per Beldam L.J., reiterated that test of "significant contribution" in the following terms, at p. 677:

> It is not the function of the jury to evaluate competing causes or to choose which is dominant provided they are satisfied that the accused's acts can fairly be said to have made a significant contribution to the victim's death. We think the word "significant" conveys the necessary substance of a contribution made to the death which is more than negligible.

This is consistent with the articulation of the substantial cause test in *R. v. Hennigan*, [1971] 3 All E.R. 133 (C.A.), which does not appear to mean anything different than the *Smithers* test of "beyond *de minimis*". In *Hennigan*, when dealing with the offence of dangerous driving causing death, Lord Chief Justice Parker said, at p. 135:

> The Court would like to emphasize this, that there is of course nothing in s. 1 of the *Road Traffic Act 1960* which requires the manner of the driving to be a substantial cause, or a major cause, or any other description of cause, of the accident. So long as the dangerous driving is a cause and something more than *de minimis*, the statute operates. What has happened in the past is that Judges have found it convenient to direct the jury in the form that it must be, as in one case it was put, the substantial cause. That was the case in which Finnemore J. gave a direction to the jury, in *R. v. Curphey*. That, in the opinion of this Court, clearly went too far, and Brabin J. in a later case of *R. v. Gould*, left it to the jury in the form of "a substantial cause".
>
> Although the word does not appear in the statute, it is clearly a convenient word to use to indicate to the jury that it must be something more than *de minimis*, and also to avoid possibly having to go into details of legal causation, remoteness and the like.

I am not persuaded that, even when the terminology used is slightly different, the Canadian standard by which causation is established in homicide differs from the English or Australian standard such as to present an anomaly which might suggest that it is set too low. *Harbottle* is clear in holding that s. 231(5) of the *Criminal Code* imposes a higher degree of causation for first degree murder than is required merely to establish the homicide. Cory J. referred to a substantial and integral cause of death, requiring that the accused play a very active role — usually a physical role — in the killing. He used the expression "the actions of the accused must form an essential, substantial and integral part of the killing". This test is not the same as the sometimes-called "substantial cause test" referred to in the English authorities dealing with causation in homicide, where the standard contemplated, in my view, is akin to the one in *Smithers*.

Finally, I add that the *Smithers* test is not an exhaustive statement of all the criminal causation rules which have a bearing on liability for homicide. Other rules, some provided for in the *Code*, some at common law, complement the general test of attributable cause which is at issue in this appeal (see, for example, the legislative choice to curtail liability expressed in s. 227 which restricts the applicability of the law of homicide to cases where death occurred within a year and a day).

(ii) *The constitutionality of the de minimis test*

As I see it, the appellant's argument raises two issues: Whether the criminal law of causation amounts to a principle of fundamental justice within the meaning of s. 7 of the *Charter*, and, if so, whether the *de minimis* standard applicable in homicides infringes upon that principle of fundamental justice. Causation as a constitutional standard has not been addressed directly by the Supreme Court of Canada. However, in *R. v. Creighton, supra,* the Court held that the offence of unlawful act manslaughter requires objective foreseeability of bodily harm which is neither trivial nor transitory, arising from a dangerous act. The Crown relies on the following statement by McLachlin J., at pp. 40-41:

> In my view, the offence by unlawful act manslaughter, as defined by our Courts and those in other jurisdictions for many centuries, is entirely consistent with the principles of fundamental justice. There is no need to read up its requirements; as it stands, it conforms to the *Charter*.

Although the constitutionality of the *de minimis* test was not at issue in *Creighton, supra,* the entire focus of the analysis in that case was on the required element of fault with respect to death having ensued from the unlawful act of the accused. McLachlin J. expressed the view that, in light of the "thin-skull" rule, the distinction between foreseeability of death and foreseeability of bodily harm in manslaughter largely disappears. In expanding on that idea, she referred to *R. v. Smithers, supra,* in the following terms (p. 52):

> In *Smithers v. The Queen,* [1978] 1 S.C.R. 506] at pp. 521-22, Dickson J., writing for a unanimous Court, confirmed this principle:

> It is a well-recognized principle that one who assaults another must take his victim as he finds him. . . .

> Although causation in civil cases differs from that in a criminal case, the "thin-skulled man" may appear in the criminal law as in the civil law. . . . Even if the unlawful act, alone, would not have caused the death, it was still a legal cause so long as it contributed in some way to the death.

> The thin-skull rule is a good and useful principle. It requires aggressors, once embarked on their dangerous course of conduct which may foreseeably injure others, to take responsibility for all the consequences that ensue, even to death. That is not, in my view, contrary to fundamental justice.

The idea of taking responsibility for the consequences of one's actions expresses a link between causation and fault. Cory J. noted in *R. v. Harbottle, supra,* at pp. 320-21, the tendency of the Courts to elevate the causation requirement when the *mens rea* for a form of murder was statutorily reduced. He referred to *R. v. Black,* [1966] 3 C.C.C. 187 (C.A.); *R. v. Gourgon (No. 1)* (1979), 9 C.R. (3d) 313 (B.C. S.C.), affirmed (1979), 19 C.R. (3d) 272 (B.C. C.A.); *R. v. Dollan* (1980), 53 C.C.C. (2d) 146 (Ont. H.C.), affirmed (1982), 65 C.C.C. (2d) 240 (C.A.); and *R. v. Woods* (1980), 57 C.C.C. (2d) 220, 19 C.R. (3d) 136 (Ont. C.A.), as examples of Courts requiring a high level of causation for first degree murder at a time when it was possible to convict for murder on the basis of objective foresight alone. The fact that a more stringent causation requirement was used in these first degree murder cases demonstrated, in Cory J.'s opinion, an understandable attempt by the Courts to impose an appropriate limitation to the reach of the first degree murder section because of the possibility of convicting of murder persons who had no intention to kill. Cory J. then noted that many of the concerns previously expressed by the Courts have disappeared in light of the Supreme Court constitutional jurisprudence imposing a subjective *mens rea* for murder.

I refer to the link between causation and the fault element in crime, represented in homicide by foresight of death or bodily harm, whether subjective or objective, because it serves to confirm that the law of causation must be considered to be a principle of fundamental justice akin to the doctrine of *mens rea*. The principle of fundamental justice which is at stake in the jurisprudence dealing with the fault element in crime is the rule that the morally innocent should not be punished. This was the premise acceptable to all the Judges in *Creighton*. McLachlin J. said, at pp. 60-61:

> I agree with the Chief Justice that the rule that the morally innocent not be punished in the context of the objective test requires that the law refrain from holding a person criminally responsible if he or she is not capable of appreciating the risk.

In my opinion, causation is embodied in the same principle of fundamental justice and it requires that the law should refrain from holding a person criminally responsible for consequences that should not be attributed to him or her. This is so because criminal causation as a legal rule is based on concepts of moral responsibility, rather than on demonstrable mechanical or scientific formulas. This is expressed by Glanville Williams in the following terms:

> When one has settled the question of but-for causation, the further test to be applied to the but-for cause in order to qualify it for legal recognition is not a test of causation but a moral reaction. The question is whether the result can fairly be said to be imputable to the defendant . . . If the term "cause" must be used, it can best be distinguished in this meaning as the "imputable" or "responsible" or "blamable" cause, to indicate the value-judgment involved. The word "imputable" is here chosen as best representing the idea. Whereas the but-for cause can generally be demonstrated scientifically, no experiment can be devised to show that one of a number of concurring but-for causes is more substantial or important than another, or that one person who is involved in the causal chain is more blameworthy than another.

(Williams, *Textbook of Criminal Law*, 2nd ed. (1983), at pp. 381-82.)

This finds support in Hart and Honore, *supra*, in the chapters dealing with causation and responsibility, and causation and the principles of punishment. Moral judgment is engaged when causation is used not merely as an explanation for the unfolding of events, but as a way of making people account for their contribution to a result. The morally innocent could be wrongly punished if criminal causation was reduced to a simple *sine qua non* requirement.

This link between causation and the fault element, both being based on the same notion of moral responsibility, leads me to conclude that the appellant's argument cannot succeed in light of Creighton. Not only must I consider that the approval of Smithers by McLachlin J., although *obiter*, disposes of the issue; more importantly, I think that the articulation of the fault element in unlawful act manslaughter in *Creighton* removes any danger that the *de minimis* causation test casts the net so broadly as to risk punishing the morally innocent. As the law of manslaughter stands, if a person commits an unlawful dangerous act, in circumstances where a reasonable person would have foreseen the risk of bodily harm which is neither trivial nor transitory, and the unlawful act is at least a contributing cause of the victim's death, outside the *de minimis* range, then the person is guilty of manslaughter. Both causation and the fault element must be proved beyond a reasonable doubt before the prosecution can succeed. Combined in that fashion, both requirements satisfy the principles of fundamental justice in that any risk that the *de minimis* test could engage the criminal responsibility of the morally innocent is removed by the additional requirement of objective foresight.

Therefore, in my opinion, the appellant's constitutional challenge fails on the basis of the Supreme Court decision in *R. v. Creighton*, *supra*, and the application of s. 1 of the *Charter* does not arise.

See comment on *Cribbin* by Jill Presser, "All for a Good Cause: The Need for Overhaul of the *Smithers* Test of Causation" (1994), 28 C.R. (4th) 178, who argues that *Cribbin* sets the constitutional standard too low. See, too, Tanovich and Lockyer, "Revisiting Harbottle: Does the Substantial Cause Test Apply to All Murder Offences?" (1996), 38 Crim. L.Q. 322.

Do you think that the *Harbottle* test should also apply to second degree murder?

Post-*Cribbin* authority is still content to apply the *Smithers* test. See *Meiler* (1999), 25 C.R. (5th) 161, 136 C.C.C. (3d) 11 (Ont. C.A.), criticized by Ron Delisle in "Unlawful Object Murder is Alive and Well" (1999), 25 C.R. (5th) 179 at 180-183: "It is the context. Murder is murder". See, too, *Nette* (1999), 29 C.R. (5th) 195, 141 C.C.C. (3d) 130 (B.C. C.A.), leave to appeal allowed (2000), 257 N.R. 198 (note) (S.C.C.), where there was a dissent by McEachern C.J.B.C. See comments by Stanley Yeo, "Giving Substance to Legal Causation" (2000), 29 C.R. (5th) 215 and Michael Plaxton, "Imputable Causation as *Mens Rea*: A Reply to Professor Yeo" (2000), 33 C.R. (5th) 78.

R. v. SMITH

[1959] 2 All E.R. 193 (Cts.-Man. App. Ct.)

THE LORD CHIEF JUSTICE: — The appellant in this case was convicted by a General Court-Martial in Germany of murder and was sentenced to imprisonment for life. The matter arose in this way: the appellant was a private soldier in the King's Regiment. At the material time a company of the King's Regiment was sharing barracks with a company of the Gloucestershire Regiment, and on the night of April 13, 1958, a fight developed. As a result of that fight three members of the Gloucesters were stabbed with a bayonet and one of them, Private Creed, subsequently died. It was for his murder that the appellant was convicted.

. . . .

The second ground concerns a question of causation. The deceased man in fact received two bayonet wounds, one in the arm and one in the back. The one in the back, unknown to anybody, had pierced the lung and caused haemorrhage. There followed a series of unfortunate occurrences. A fellow member of his company tried to carry him to the medical reception station. On the way he tripped over a wire and dropped the deceased man. He picked him up again, went a little further, and fell apparently a second time causing the deceased man to be dropped on the ground. Thereafter he did not try a third time, but went for help and ultimately the deceased man was brought into the reception station. There, the medical officer, Captain Millward, and his orderly were trying to cope with a number of other cases, two serious stabbings and some minor injuries, and it is clear that they did not appreciate the seriousness of the deceased man's condition or exactly what had happened. A transfusion of saline solution was attempted and failed. When his breathing seemed impaired, he was given oxygen and artificial respiration was applied, and in fact he died after he had been in the station about an hour, which was about two hours after the original stabbing. It is now known that, having regard to the injuries which the man had in fact suffered, his lung being pierced, the treatment that he was given was thoroughly bad and might well have affected his chances of recovery. There was evidence that there is a tendency for a wound of this sort to heal and for the haemorrhage to stop. No doubt his being dropped on the ground and having artificial respiration applied would halt or at any rate impede the chances of healing. Further, there were no facilities whatsoever for blood transfusion, which would have been the best possible treatment. There was evidence that, if he had received immediate and different treatment, he might not have died. Indeed, had facilities for blood transfusion been available and been administered, Dr. Camps, who gave evidence for the defence, said that his chances of recovery were as high as 75 percent.

In these circumstances Mr. Bowen urges that not only was a careful summing-up required, but that a correct direction to the Court would have been that they must be satisfied that the death of Private Creed was a natural consequence and the sole consequence of the wound sustained by him and flowed directly from it. If there was, says Mr. Bowen, any other cause whether resulting from negligence or not, or if, as he contends here, something happened which impeded the chance of the deceased recovering, then the death did not result from the wound. The Court is quite unable to accept that contention. It seems to the Court that if at the time of death the original wound is still an operating cause and a substantial cause, then the death can properly be said to be the result of the wound, albeit that some other cause of death is also operating. Only if it can be said that the original wounding is merely the setting in which another cause operates can it be said that the death does not result from the wound. Putting it in another way, only if the second cause is so overwhelming as to make the original wound merely part of the history can it be said that the death does not flow from the wound.

There are a number of cases in the law of contract and tort on these matters of causation, and it is always difficult to find a form of words when directing a jury or, as here, a Court, which will convey in simple language the principle of causation. It seems to the Court enough for this purpose to refer to one passage in the judgment of Lord Wright in *The Oropesa*, reported in [1943] P. 32, where he says (at p. 39):

> To break the chain of causation it must be shown that there is something which I will call ultroneous, something unwarrantable, a new cause which disturbs the sequence of events, something which can be described as either unreasonable or extraneous or extrinsic.

To much the same effect was a judgment on the question of causation given by Denning J., as he then was, in *Minister of Pensions v. Chennel* in [1947] K.B. 250.

Mr. Bowen placed great reliance on a case decided in this Court, *Jordan* (1956), 40 Cr. App. R. 152, and in particular on a passage in the headnote which says:

> *Semble*, that death resulting from any normal treatment employed to deal with a felonious injury may be regarded as caused by the felonious injury, but that the same principle does not apply where the treatment employed is abnormal.

Reading those words into the present case, Mr. Bowen says that the treatment that this unfortunate man received from the moment that he was struck to the time of his death was abnormal. The Court is satisfied that *Jordan* (*supra*) was a very particular case depending upon its exact facts. It incidentally arose in this Court on the grant of an application to call further evidence, and, leave having been obtained, two well-known medical experts gave evidence that in their opinion death had not been caused by the stabbing, but by the introduction of terramycin after the deceased had shown that he was intolerant to it and by the intravenous introduction of abnormal quantities of liquid. It also appears that at the time when that was done the stab wound which had penetrated the intestine in two places had mainly healed. In those circumstances the Court felt bound to quash the conviction, because they could not say that a reasonable jury, properly directed, would not have been able on that to say that there had been a break in the chain of causation; the court could only uphold the conviction in that case if they were satisfied that no reasonable jury could have come to that conclusion.

In the present case it is true that the Judge-Advocate did not, in his summing-up, go into the refinements of causation. Indeed, in the opinion of this Court, he was probably wise to refrain from doing so. He did leave the broad question to the Court whether they were satisfied that the wound had caused the death in the sense that the death flowed from the wound, albeit that the treatment he received was in the light of after-knowledge a bad thing. In the opinion of this Court, that was on the facts of the case a perfectly adequate summing-up on causation; I say "on the facts of the case," because in the opinion of the Court they can only lead to one conclusion. A man is stabbed in the back, his lung is pierced and haemorrhage results; two hours later he dies of haemorrhage from that wound; in the interval there is no time for a careful examination and the treatment given turns out in the light of subsequent knowledge to have been inappropriate and, indeed, harmful. In those circumstances no reasonable jury or Court could, properly directed, in our view possibly come to any other conclusion than that the death resulted from the original wound. Accordingly, the Court dismisses this appeal.

Appeal dismissed.

THE QUEEN v. BINGAPORE

(1974-5), 11 S.A.S.R. 469 (S. Aus. S.C.)

The Court (BRIGHT, SANGSTER and JACOBS JJ.) delivered the following judgment: —

This is in part an appeal as of right pursuant to s. 352(*a*) of the *Criminal Law Consolidation Act* 1935-1972 and in part an application for leave to appeal pursuant to placitum (*c*) of the same section and is wholly against the appellant's conviction for murder.

. . . .

The appellant was, admittedly, involved in an assault on the victim, McMillan.

About 11.45 a.m. a business man parked his car in Angas Street near the unoccupied premises; he noticed a man, slumped against the railings outside the unoccupied premises, appearing to be dazed and holding what appeared to be a red coloured rag against his head; that man then moved off towards Police Headquarters further west along Angas Street. Somewhere about that time McMillan arrived at Police Headquarters, was seen to be bleeding profusely, an ambulance was called and McMillan was taken to the Royal Adelaide Hospital and admitted.

. . . .

At the Royal Adelaide Hospital, McMillan's condition was found to include a profusely bleeding wound to the head and, after some trouble, an artery was sutured and the bleeding stopped; internal head injuries were suspected; he was kept at the hospital overnight. On the Saturday at about 12.30 p.m. conversations took place between a resident medical officer, McMillan, and Mrs. McMillan, the brief effect of which was that the medical officer warned both the McMillans of the danger involved in McMillan leaving the hospital, namely the danger of death, notwithstanding which McMillan signed a "risk form" and the McMillans left the hospital. They walked to the new lodgings at

McLaren Street and some six hours or thereabouts later Mr. McMillan was brought back to the Royal Adelaide Hospital by ambulance, was seen to be in need of urgent attention, and within four and a half hours was operated on, but unsuccessfully, and he died the next day from brain damage caused by subdural haemorrhage which, in turn, was described in evidence as consistent with trauma to the head within a range of times which included the Friday morning.

. . . .

Three challenges were made to the learned trial Judge's directions on causation. On causation we need look no further than *Reg. v. Bristow*, at p. 217 (citing *Reg. v. Smith*) and, in turn, cited with approval in *Reg. v. Hallett*: —

> It seems to the Court that, if at the time of death the original wound is still an operating cause and a substantial cause, then the death can properly be said to be the result of the wound, albeit that some other cause of death is also operating. Only if it can be said that the original wounding is merely the setting in which another cause operates can it be said that the death does not result from the wound.

Counsel for the appellant contended that we should add to the law (as it is at present found in the authorities) a new proposition that where the gross negligence/unreasonable conduct/some degree of negligence more than mere negligence, (counsel used all three expressions without limiting his contentions to any one of them) contributed to the death of the victim, the chain of causation was broken. Alternatively, he contended, the learned trial Judge's direction that causation was sufficiently established if the acts of the accused was "a" cause, should have been cut down to "the" cause, or alternatively "the most substantial" cause. In so far as we are able to follow his contentions we do not agree with them. In any case, on the evidence as the jury must have viewed it, the chain of causation was violence by the appellant to the victim, subdural haemorrhage from that violence, and death from that subdural haemorrhage, a short and direct chain. The appellant's only complaint is that had an operation on the victim been performed earlier it might have saved him, and that the victim's wanton departure from hospital (to which he was returned at his wife's instance about six hours later) denied him any opportunity for such an earlier operation. That complaint, of course, relates not to a break in the chain of causation, not to a new cause, but to the loss of a possible opportunity of avoiding death from a still operating cause, namely the violence inflicted by the appellant. The act of the appellant causing injuries from which the victim dies does not cease to be a causative act because the victim thereafter acts to his detriment or because some third party is negligent. The case of *Reg. v. Jordan* to which we were referred, is clearly distinguishable, for there the victim did not die from injuries caused by the act of the prisoner, but from some other cause for which the prisoner could not be held responsible.

. . . .

Appeal dismissed.

COMMONWEALTH v. ROOT

(1961), 170 A. 2d 310 (Pa. S.C.)

CHARLES ALVIN JONES, CHIEF JUSTICE: —

The appellant was found guilty of involuntary manslaughter for the death of his competitor in the course of an automobile race between them on a highway. The trial Court overruled the defendant's demurrer to the Commonwealth's evidence and, after verdict, denied his motion in arrest of judgment. On appeal from the judgment of sentence entered on the jury's verdict, the Superior Court affirmed. We granted allocatur because of the important question present as to whether the defendant's unlawful and reckless conduct was a sufficiently direct cause of the death to warrant his being charged with criminal homicide.

The testimony, which is uncontradicted in material part, discloses that, on the night of the fatal accident, the defendant accepted the deceased's challenge to engage in an automobile race; that the racing took place on a rural three-lane highway; that the night was clear and dry, and traffic light; that the speed limit on the highway was 50 miles per hour; that, immediately prior to the accident, the two automobiles were being operated at varying speeds of from 70 to 90 miles per hour; that the accident occurred in a no-passing zone on the approach to a bridge where the highway narrowed to two directionally-opposite lanes; that, at the time of the accident, the defendant was in the lead and was proceeding in his right hand lane of travel; that the deceased, in an attempt to pass the defendant's automobile, when a truck was closely approaching from the opposite direction, swerved his car to the left, crossed the highway's white dividing line and drove his automobile on the wrong side of the highway head-on into the oncoming truck with resultant fatal effect to himself.

This evidence would of course amply support a conviction of the defendant for speeding, reckless driving and, perhaps, other violations of The Vehicle Code of May 1, 1929, P.L. 905, as amended. In fact, it may be noted, in passing, that the Act of January 8, 1960, P.L. (1959) 2118, Sec. 3, 75 P.S. 1041, amending The Vehicle Code of April 29, 1959, P.L. 58, 75 P.S. 101 et seq., makes automobile racing on a highway an independent crime punishable by fine or imprisonment or both up to $500 and three years in jail. As the highway racing in the instant case occurred prior to the enactment of the Act of 1960, cit. *supra*, that statute is, of course, not presently applicable. In any event, unlawful or reckless conduct is only one ingredient of the crime of involuntary manslaughter. Another essential and distinctly separate element of the crime is that the unlawful or reckless conduct charged to the defendant was the *direct* cause of the death in issue. The first ingredient is obviously present in this case but, just as plainly, the second is not.

While precedent is to be found for application of the tort law concept of "proximate cause" in fixing responsibility for criminal homicide, the want of any rational basis for its use in determining criminal liability can no longer be properly disregarded. When proximate cause was first borrowed from the field of tort law and applied to homicide prosecutions in Pennsylvania, the concept connoted a much more direct causal relation in producing the alleged culpable result than it does today. Proximate cause, as an essential element of a tort founded in negligence, has undergone in recent times, and is still undergoing, a marked extension. More specifically, this area of civil law has been progressively liberalized in favor of claims for damages for personal injuries to which careless conduct of others can in some way be associated. To persist in applying the tort liability concept of proximate cause to prosecutions for criminal homicide after the marked expansion of *civil* liability of defendants in tort actions for negligence would be to extend possible *criminal* liability to persons chargeable with unlawful or reckless conduct in circumstances not generally considered to present the likelihood of a resultant death.

In this very case (*Commonwealth v. Root*, 191 Pa. Super. 238, 245, 156 A. 2d 895, 900) the Superior Court mistakenly opined that:

> The concept of proximate cause as applied in tort cases is applicable to similar problems of causation in criminal cases. *Commonwealth v. Almeida*, 1949, 362 Pa. 596, 603, 611, 68 A. 2d. 595, 12 A.L.R. 2d 183.

It is indeed strange that the *Almeida* case should have been cited as authority for the above quoted statement: the rationale of the *Almeida* case was flatly rejected by this court in *Commonwealth v. Redline*, 1958, 391 Pa. 486, 504-505, 137 A. 2d 472 where we held that the tort liability concept of proximate cause is not a proper criterion of causation in a criminal homicide case. True enough, *Commonwealth v. Redline* was a murder case, but the distinction between murder and involuntary manslaughter does not rest upon a differentiation in causation; it lies in the state of mind of the offender. If one kills with malice aforethought, he is chargeable with murder; and if death, though unintentional, results directly from his unlawful or reckless conduct, he is chargeable with involuntary manslaughter. In either event, the accused is not guilty unless his conduct was a cause of death sufficiently direct as to meet the requirements of the *criminal*, and not the *tort*, law.

. . . .

Legal theory which makes guilt or innocence of criminal homicide depend upon such accidental and fortuitous circumstances as are now embraced by modern tort law's encompassing concept of proximate cause is too harsh to be just. A few illustrations should suffice to so demonstrate.

In *Mautino v. Piercedale Supply Co.*, 1940, 338 Pa. 435, 12 A. 2d 51, — a civil action for damages — we held that where a man sold a cartridge to a person under 16 years of age in violation of a State statute and the recipient subsequently procured a gun from which he fired the cartridge injuring someone, the injury was proximately caused by the act of the man who sold the cartridge to the underage person. If proximate cause were the test for criminal liability and the injury to the plaintiff in the *Mautino* case had been fatal, the man who sold the bullet to the underage person (even though the boy had the appearance of an adult) would have been guilty of involuntary manslaughter, for his unlawful act would, according to the tort law standard, have been the proximate cause of the death.

In *Schelin v. Goldberg*, 1958, 188 Pa. Super. 341, 146 A. 2d 648, it was held that the plaintiff, who was injured in a fight, could recover in tort against the defendants, the owners of a taproom who prior to the fight had unlawfully served the plaintiff drinks while he was in a visibly intoxicated condition, the unlawful action of the defendants being held to be the proximate cause of the plaintiff's injuries. Here, again, if proximate cause were the test for criminal liability and the plaintiff had been fatally injured in the fight, the taproom owners would have been guilty of involuntary manslaughter, for their unlawful act would have been no less the proximate cause of death.

In *Marchl v. Dowling & Company*, 1945, 157 Pa. Super. 91, 41 A. 2d 427, it was held that where a truck driver had double parked his truck and the minor plaintiff was struck by a passing car when she walked around the double parked truck, the truck driver's employer was held liable in tort for the plaintiff's injuries on the ground that the truck driver's act of double parking, which violated both a State statute and a city ordinance, was the proximate cause of the plaintiff's injuries. Here, also, if proximate cause were the test for criminal liability and the plaintiff's injuries had been fatal, the truck driver would have been guilty of involuntary manslaughter since his unlawful act would have been the proximate cause of the death for which his employer was held liable in damages under *respondeat superior*. To be guilty of involuntary manslaughter for double parking would, of course, be unthinkable, yet if proximate cause were to determine criminal liability, such a result would indeed be a possibility.

Even if the tort liability concept of proximate cause were to be deemed applicable, the defendant's conviction of involuntary manslaughter in the instant case could not be sustained under the evidence. The operative effect of a supervening cause would have to be taken into consideration, *Commonwealth v. Redline, supra*, 391 Pa. at page 505, 137 A. 2d at page 481. But, the trial Judge refused the defendant's point for charge to such effect and erroneously instructed the jury that "negligence or want of care on the part of [the deceased] is no defense to the criminal responsibility of the defendant. . . ."

The Superior Court, in affirming the defendant's conviction in this case, approved the charge above mentioned, despite a number of decisions in involuntary manslaughter cases holding that the conduct of the deceased victim must be considered in order to determine whether the defendant's reckless acts were the proximate (*i.e.*, sufficiently direct) cause of his death. See *Commonwealth v. Amecca*, 1947, 160 Pa. Super. 257, 260, 263, 50 A. 2d 725; *Commonwealth v. Hatch*, 1942, 149 Pa. Super. 289, 292, 27 A. 2d 742; *Commonwealth v. Aurick*, 1939, 138 Pa. Super. 180, 187, 10 A. 2d 22. The Superior Court dispensed with this decisional authority (see *Commonwealth v. Root, supra*, 191 Pa. Super. at page 252, 156 A. 2d at page 903) by expressly overruling *Commonwealth v. Amecca, supra*, and by impliedly overruling each of the other cases immediately above cited. It did so on the ground that there can be more than one proximate cause of death. The point is wholly irrelevant. Of course there can be more than one proximate cause of death just as there can also be more than one *direct* cause of death. For example, in the so-called "shield" cases where a felon interposes the person of an innocent victim between himself and a pursuing officer, if the officer should fire his gun at the felon to prevent his escape and fatally wound the person used as a shield, the different acts of the policeman and the felon would each be a direct cause of the victim's death.

If the tort liability concept of proximate cause were to be applied in a criminal homicide prosecution, then the conduct of the person whose death is the basis of the indictment would have to be considered, not to prove that it was merely an *additional* proximate cause of the death, but to determine, under fundamental and long recognized law applicable to proximate cause, whether the subsequent wrongful act *superseded* the original conduct chargeable to the defendant. If it did in fact supervene, then the original act is so insulated from the ensuing death as not to be its proximate cause.

[1] Under the uncontradicted evidence in this case, the conduct of the defendant was not the proximate cause of the decedent's death as a matter of law. In *Kline v. Moyer and Albert*, 1937, 325 Pa. 357, 364, 191 A. 43, 46, 111 A.L.R. 406, the rule is stated as follows:

> Where a second actor has become aware of the existence of a potential danger created by the negligence of an original tort-feasor, and thereafter, by an independent act of negligence, brings about an accident, the first tort-feasor is relieved of liability, because the condition created by him was merely a circumstance of the accident and not its proximate cause.

. . . .

In the case now before us, the deceased was aware of the dangerous condition created by the defendant's reckless conduct in driving his automobile at an excessive rate of speed along the highway but, despite such knowledge, he recklessly chose to swerve his car to the left and into the path of an oncoming truck, thereby bringing about the head-on collision which caused his own death.

[2] To summarize, the tort liability concept of proximate cause has no proper place in prosecutions for criminal homicide and more direct causal connection is required for conviction, *Commonwealth v. Redline*, supra, 391, Pa. at pages 504-505, 137 A. 2d at page 480. In the instant case, the defendant's reckless conduct was not a sufficiently direct cause of the competing driver's death to make him criminally liable therefor.

The judgment of sentence is reversed and the defendant's motion in arrest of judgment granted.

EAGEN, JUSTICE (dissenting): —

The opinion of the learned Chief Justice admits, under the uncontradicted facts, that the defendant, at the time of the fatal accident involved, was engaged in an unlawful and reckless course of conduct. Racing an automobile at 90 miles per hour, trying to prevent another automobile going in the same direction from passing him, in a no-passing zone on a two-lane public highway, is certainly all of that. Admittedly also, there can be more than one direct cause of an unlawful death. To me, this is self-evident. But, says the majority opinion, the defendant's recklessness was not a direct cause of the death. With this, I cannot agree.

If the defendant did not engage in the unlawful race and so operate his automobile in such a reckless manner, this accident would never have occurred. He helped create the dangerous event. He was a vital part of it. The victim's acts were a natural reaction to the stimulus of the situation. The race, the attempt to pass the other car and forge ahead, the reckless speed, all of these factors the defendant himself helped create. He was part and parcel of them. That the victim's response was normal under the circumstances, that his reaction should have been expected and was clearly foreseeable, is to me beyond argument. That the defendant's recklessness, was a substantial factor is obvious. All of this, in my opinion, makes his unlawful conduct a direct cause of the resulting collision.

. . . .

1 Wharton, Criminal Law and Procedure 68 (1957), speaking of causal connections, says:

> A person is only criminally liable for what he was caused, that is, there must be a causal relationship between his act and harm sustained for which he is prosecuted. It is not essential to the existence of a causal relationship that the ultimate harm which has resulted was foreseen or intended by the actor. It is sufficient that the ultimate harm is one which a reasonable man would foresee as being reasonably related to the acts of the defendant.

Section 295, in speaking about manslaughter, says:

> When homicide is predicated upon the negligence of the defendant, it must be shown that his negligence was the proximate cause or a contributing cause of the victim's death. It must appear that the death was not the result of misadventure, but the natural and probable result of a reckless or culpably negligent act. To render a person criminally liable for negligent homicide, the duty omitted or improperly performed must have been his personal duty, and the negligent act from which death resulted must have been his personal act, and not the act of another. But he is not excused because the negligence of someone else contributed to the result, when his act was the primary or proximate cause and the negligence of the other did not intervene between his act and the result.

Professor Joseph Beale, late renowned member of the Harvard Law School faculty, in an article entitled, The Proximate Consequence of an Act, 33 Harv. L. Rev. 633, 646, said,

> Though there is an active force intervening after defendant's act, the result will nevertheless be proximate if the defendant's act actually caused the intervening force. In such a case the defendant's force is really continuing in active operation *by means of the force it stimulated into activity.*

Professor Beale, at 658, sums up the requirements of proximity of result in this manner:

> 1. The defendant must have acted (or failed to act in violation of a duty). 2. The force thus created must (a) have remained active itself or created another *force* which remained active until it directly caused the result; or (b) have created a new active *risk* of being acted upon by the active force that caused the result.

2 Bishop, New Criminal Law 121 (1913), says:

> He whose act causes in any way, directly or indirectly, the death of another, kills him, within the meaning of felonious homicide. It is a rule of both reason and the law that whenever one's will contributes to impel a physical force, whether another's, his own, or a combined force, proceeding from whatever different sources, he is responsible for the result, the same as though his hand, unaided had produced it.

But says the majority opinion, these are principles of tort law and should not in these days be applied to the criminal law. But such has been the case since the time of Blackstone. These same principles have always been germane to both crimes and tort. See, Beale, Recovery for Consequence of an Act, 9 Harv. L. Rev. 80; Greene, Rationale of Proximate Cause, 132-133 (1927); Frederick C. Moesel, Jr., A Survey of Felony Murder, 28 Temp. L.Q. 453, 459-466.

While the victim's foolhardiness in this case contributed to his own death, he was not the only one responsible and it is not he alone with whom we are concerned. It is the people of the Commonwealth who are harmed by the kind of conduct the defendant pursued. Their interests must be kept in mind.

I, therefore, dissent and would accordingly affirm the judgment of conviction.

The concurring judgment of Bell J. is omitted.

Problems

1. An accused is driving with excessive alcohol in his blood but is driving normally. A pedestrian comes out of nowhere and walks into the path of the vehicle. He is killed. The accused is charged with impaired driving causing death. Is there any argument that he did not cause the death?

Compare *Wilmot* (1940), 74 C.C.C. 1 (Alta. C.A.), affirmed (1940), [1941] S.C.R. 53, 75 C.C.C. 161 (S.C.C.); *Fisher* (1992), 13 C.R. (4th) 222 (B.C. C.A.) and *White* (1994), 28 C.R. (4th) 160, 89 C.C.C. (3d) 336 (N.S. C.A.).

2. The accused, the victim and two others, all aged 17, decided to play Russian roulette. A single cartridge was placed in the revolver. The accused spun the chamber, pointed the gun to his head and pulled the trigger. Nothing happened. He handed the gun to the victim, who spun it, put it to his head, then pulled the trigger. The cartridge exploded, and he fell over dead. The accused is charged with manslaughter. What result? How about the others? Suppose the game was played where each participant directed the gun not at himself but at another player?

Compare *Commonwealth v. Atencio* (1963), 189 N.E. (2d) 223 (Mass. S.C.).

3. The accused operated a corner store in a run-down area of a large city. One item he stocked was Sterno, a canned heat containing methanol. The label read "Danger. Poison. For use only as a fuel". The accused sold large quantities of Sterno to derelicts who lived in the neighbourhood. Two of them died. As Crown Attorney, you have been asked by the police whether charges should be laid. Advise.

Compare *Commonwealth v. Feinberg* (1969), 253 A. 2d 636 (Pa. S.C.).

4. The accused owns a tavern at a crossroads in the country. He recognizes that a customer is badly impaired but continues to serve him as he "doesn't want any trouble". After a few more drinks the customer leaves. Shortly thereafter there is the noise of squealing tires and thrown gravel and a collision. The owner rushes to the parking lot where he finds the customer behind the steering wheel of his car, dead. Can the owner be successfully prosecuted for manslaughter? Can the owner be sued civilly?

Respecting civil liability of a tavern owner for injuries caused to a third party by a patron who was intoxicated, see the *Liquor Licence Act*, R.S.O. 1980, c. 244, s. 53, *Barsalou v. Wolf* (1985), 48 C.P.C. 294 (Ont. H.C.) and *Jordan House Ltd. v. Menow*, [1974] S.C.R. 239 and *Stewart v. Pettie*, [1995] 3 W.W.R. 1 (S.C.C.).

Chapter 3

THE FAULT REQUIREMENT
(MENS REA OR NEGLIGENCE)

Introduction

J.F. STEPHEN, A HISTORY OF THE CRIMINAL LAW OF ENGLAND

Vol. 2, (1883), 94-95

The maxim, *actus non facit reum nisi mens sit rea*, is sometimes said to be the fundamental maxim of the whole criminal law; but I think that, like many other Latin sentences supposed to form part of the Roman law, the maxim not only looks more instructive than it really is, but suggests fallacies which it does not precisely state.

It is frequently though ignorantly supposed to mean that there cannot be such a thing as legal guilt where there is no moral guilt, which is obviously untrue, as there is always a possibility of a conflict between law and morals.

It also suggests the notion that there is some state of mind called a *mens rea*, the absence of which, on any particular occasion, deprives what would otherwise be a crime of its criminal character. This also is untrue. There is no one such state of mind, as any one may convince himself by considering the definitions of dissimilar crimes. A pointsman falls asleep, and thereby causes a railway accident and the death of a passenger; he is guilty of manslaughter. He deliberately and by elaborate devices produces the same result; he is guilty of murder; if in each case there is a *mens rea*, as the maxim seems to imply, *mens rea* must be a name for two states of mind, not merely differing from but opposed to each other, for what two states of mind can resemble each other less than indolence and an active desire to kill?

The truth is that the maxim about *mens rea* means no more than that the definition of all or nearly all crimes contains not only an outward and visible element, but a mental element, varying according to the different nature of different crimes. Thus, in reference to murder, the *mens rea* is any state of mind which comes within the description of malice aforethought. In reference to theft the *mens rea* is an intention to deprive the owner of his property permanently, fraudulently and without claim of right. In reference to forgery the *mens rea* is anything which can be described as an intent to defraud. Hence the only means of arriving at a full comprehension of the expression *mens rea* is by a detailed examination of the definitions of particular crimes, and therefore the expression itself is unmeaning.

W.S. GILBERT, THE MIKADO, (1885)

That's the pathetic part of it. Unfortunately the fool of an Act says, 'Compassing the death of the heir apparent.' There's not a word about mistake, or not knowing, or having no notion, or not being there. There should be, of course, but there isn't. That's the slovenly way in which these Acts are drawn.

G. MUELLER, ON COMMON LAW MENS REA

(1957-58), 42 Minn. L. Rev. 1043 at 1055, 1061

There has crept into our thinking the idea that there is no singular concept of *mens rea* but that, since every crime has a different *mens rea* requirement, one should talk of *mentes reae* rather than *mens rea*. This is a misconception and it is false to conclude, as some do, that there is no unifying *mens rea* concept. Just as all cars have different wheels, little cars little wheels and big cars big wheels, and we are justified in referring to them collectively under the unifying concept wheels, so all crimes have a different *mens rea* and yet the concept of *mens rea* must be regarded as a unifying concept of various possible frames of mind.

Mens rea, then, is not the mere psychic relation between act and actor, it is, rather, the ethico-legal *negative* value of the deed (appearing in various legally prescribed forms), i.e., it is a *community value of which the perpetrator at the time of the deed knows the existence and that it will materialize when the deed becomes known.*

G.L. WILLIAMS, CRIMINAL LAW: THE GENERAL PART

2nd ed. (1961), 30-31

It may be said that any theory of criminal punishment leads to a requirement of some kind of *mens rea*. The deterrent theory is workable only if the culprit has knowledge of the legal sanction; and if a man does not foresee the consequence of his act he cannot appreciate that punishment lies in store for him if he does it. The retributive theory presupposes moral guilt; incapacitation supposes social danger; and the reformative aim is out of place if the offender's sense of values is not warped.

However, the requirement as we have it in the law does not harmonise perfectly with any of these theories. It does not quite fit the deterrent theory, because a man may have *mens rea* although he is ignorant of the law, . . . Again, the requirement does not quite conform to the retributive theory, because the *mens rea* of English law does not necessarily connote an intention to engage in moral wrongdoing. . . . There are similar difficulties with incapacitation and reform.

What, then, does legal *mens rea* mean? It refers to the mental element necessary for the particular crime, and this mental element may be either *intention* to do the immediate act or bring about the consequence or (in some crimes) *recklessness* as to such act or consequence. . . . Some crimes require intention and nothing else will do, but most can be committed either intentionally or recklessly. Some crimes require particular kinds of intention or knowledge.

Outside the class of crimes requiring *mens rea* there are some that do not require any particular state of mind but do require negligence. Negligence in law is not necessarily a state of mind; and thus these crimes are best regarded as not requiring *mens rea*. However, negligence is a kind of legal fault, and in that respect they are akin to crimes requiring *mens rea*.

Yet other crimes do not even require negligence. They are crimes of strict or vicarious responsibility, and, like crimes of negligence, they constitute exceptions to the adage *Actus non facit reum nisi mens sit rea*.

G.H. GORDON, THE CRIMINAL LAW OF SCOTLAND

2nd ed. (1978), 219, 268

The basic common law principle. Although it is true that *mens rea* in the sense of one state of mind required for all forms of criminal responsibility does not exist, and that instead there are only a number of *mentes reae* varying from crime to crime and from material element to material element, the maxim *actus non facit reum nisi mens sit rea* is still of paramount importance. It serves as a reminder of the moral nature of the criminal law and also offers an ideal against which particular rules of that law can be measured. There is a presumption that criminal guilt involves moral blame, and it is for those who wish to impose punishment in the absence of such blame to show good reason for displacing the presumption.

. . . .

In dealing with statutory offences it is particularly necessary to bear in mind that each offence consists of different elements so that *mens rea* must be considered with regard to each element separately. Failure to do so may lead to the common mistake of asking whether a particular statutory offence, viewed as a unitary whole, either does or does not require *mens rea* for its commission, instead of asking whether a particular element of the offence must be committed intentionally, or whether knowledge of a particular element is necessary. There is also a tendency to concede that a particular offence does require *mens rea*, and then to nullify the concession by saying that the requirement of *mens rea* is satisfied by "an intention to do the act prohibited," by which is meant an intention regarding what is taken to be the central element of the offence. This works in the following way: suppose it is an offence for A to sell silk stockings but lawful for him to sell stockings of any other kind and that he does in fact sell B a particular pair of stockings which unknown to A are silk — if, then, A intended to sell these particular stockings to B and did not, for example, mistakenly put in B's parcel a pair of stockings he had set aside with the intention of dealing with them otherwise than by sale, A can be said to have *mens rea*, to act intentionally, although he lacked *mens rea* regarding the one circumstance which rendered his act illegal. To adopt this attitude is to pay lip service to the rule that even in statutory offences there is a presumption in favour of *mens rea*, while imposing in practice what is virtually strict responsibility.

Consider the material read into the record in connection with the testimony of Dr. Bernard Diamond, Psychiatrist, in the following action.

PEOPLE v. GORSHEN

(1959), 336 P. 2d 492, (Cal. S.C.) at 497

[T]he central issue [in a psychiatric evaluation of malice aforethought], that of the age-old philosophical abstraction of free will vs. determinism, is itself undetermined. Freud, in 1904, brilliantly demonstrated by analysis of slips of the tongue, forgetting, and trains of association that what we call free will or voluntary choice is merely the conscious rationalization of a chain of unconsciously determined processes. Each act of will, each choice presumedly made on a random basis, turns out to be as rigidly determined as any other physiological process of the human body. Yet all of us continue to live our lives, make our choices, exercise our free will, and obey or disobey the law as if we actually had something to say about what we are doing. Criminal law could not exist were it not for this posit that each normal person intends to do the act which he does do and that such intention is based upon the exercise of free will.

Medical psychology has embarrassingly few answers to this one question which the criminal law is most interested in. It does no good to proclaim to the jurist that scientific evidence proves that there is no such thing as free will. There is a subjective phenomenon which the normal individual experiences as free will. Illusory or not, free will remains the basis of all criminal law simply because free will is the basis of all normal social behavior.

In truth, today, *we do not have a sufficient foundation of scientific knowledge about the ego functions of decision, choice, and determination of action to justify the formulation of any general principles which could be applied to the law. . . .*

The task then becomes to understand the motivations, intent, and actions of the individual who deviates from the common-sense posit of free will. This can be accomplished without specious generalizations which would attack the very structure of the law itself and would compel non-acceptance by the juridical mind. (Italics added.)

In the Canadian context, we shall discover that there is a constitutional requirement of fault for any offence threatening the liberty interest. Almost always the only real issue is what the fault requirement actually entails. Jurisprudence on fault is a matter of common law, statutory interpretation and

Charter standards and is still in a state of flux. There is considerable ambiguity and confusion about definition. A central issue continues to be whether the approach is subjective or objective.

Subjective/Objective Distinction

The Supreme Court of Canada judgments in *R. v. Creighton*, [1993] 3 S.C.R. 3, 23 C.R. (4th) 189, 83 C.C.C. (3d) 346 and *R. v. Hundal*, [1993] 1 S.C.R. 867, 19 C.R. (4th) 169, 79 C.C.C. (3d) 97, accept that there should be a clear distinction between the subjective standard of whether the accused was actually aware of a risk and the objective standard of whether the accused failed to measure up to the external standard of the reasonable person, irrespective of awareness. On the subjective standard all of the accused's individual factors are taken into account. The objective standard is now clearly much tougher given the ruling by the majority in *Creighton*, to be fully discussed later, that on the objective standard no personal factors, such as age, race, gender, poverty and experience, can be taken into account except where they relate to incapacity. Should such factors be considered before State punishment?

F.M. DOSTOEVSKY, THE BROTHERS KARAMAZOV

Book 5, Chapter 4, as Quoted in Brett and Waller,
Cases and Materials in Criminal Law, (1962), 713

Tell me. I challenge you to give me a straight answer yourself. Imagine that you yourself are building an edifice of human destiny that has the ultimate aim of making people happy and giving them finally peace and rest, but that to achieve this you are faced inevitably and inescapably with torturing just one tiny baby, say that small fellow just now who was beating his little fists on his chest, so that you would be building your edifice on his unrequited tears — would you agree to be its architect under these conditions? Tell me and don't lie.

O.W. HOLMES, THE COMMON LAW

Howe, ed., (1963), 37, 45

No society has ever admitted that it could not sacrifice individual welfare to its own existence. If conscripts are necessary for its army, it seizes them, and marches them, with bayonets in their rear, to death.

How do we determine the accused's state of mind?

"The thought of man is not triable for the devil alone knoweth the thought of man." (Brian C.J., (1477), Year Books, Pasch Ed. IV Fi pl.2.)

"The state of man's mind is as much a fact as the state of his digestion." (Bowen L.J. in *Edington v. Fitzmaurice* (1885), 29 Ch.D. 459.)

The important distinction between a subjective substantive standard and the objective approach to proof is emphasized in the following judgments:

R. v. HUNDAL

[1993] 1 S.C.R. 867, 19 C.R. (4th) 169, 79 C.C.C. (3d) 97

The Court was called on to determine the fault requirement for the crime of dangerous driving.

CORY J. (for the majority): —

A truly subjective test seeks to determine what was actually in the mind of the particular accused at the moment the offence is alleged to have been committed. In his very useful text, Professor Stuart puts it in this way in *Canadian Criminal Law* (2nd ed.) at pp. 123-24 and at p. 125:

> What is vital is that *this accused* given his personality, situation and circumstances, actually intended, knew or foresaw the consequence and/or circumstance as the case may be. Whether he "could", "ought" or "should" have foreseen or whether a reasonable person would have foreseen is not the relevant criterion of liability.

. . .

> In trying to ascertain what was going on in the accused's mind, as the subjective approach demands, the trier of fact may draw reasonable inferences from the accused's actions or words at the time of his act or in the witness box. The accused may or may not be believed. To conclude that, considering all the evidence, the Crown has proved beyond a reasonable doubt that the accused "must" have thought in the penalized way is no departure from the subjective substantive standard. Resort to an objective substantive standard would only occur if the reasoning became that the accused "must have realized it if he had thought about it". [Emphasis in original.]

On the other hand, the test for negligence is an objective one requiring a marked departure from the standard of care of a reasonable person. There is no need to establish the intention of the particular accused. The question to be answered under the objective test concerns what the accused "should" have known. The potential harshness of the objective standard may be lessened by the consideration of certain personal factors as well as the consideration of a defence of mistake of fact. See McIntyre J. and Lamer J., as he then was, in *R. v. Tutton*, [1989] 1 S.C.R. 1392, and *R. v. Waite*, [1989] 1 S.C.R. 1436). Nevertheless, there should be a clear distinction in the law between one who was aware (pure subjective intent) and one who should have taken care irrespective of awareness (pure objective intent).

R. v. THÉROUX

[1993] 2 S.C.R. 5, 19 C.R. (4th) 194, 79 C.C.C. (3d) 499

The Court was called on to discuss the fault requirement for the crime of fraud. Justice McLachlin spoke for the majority:

This brings us to the *mens rea* of fraud. What is the guilty mind of fraud? At this point, certain confusions inherent in the concept of *mens rea* itself become apparent. It is useful initially to distinguish between the mental element or elements of a crime and the *mens rea*. The term *mens rea*, properly understood, does not encompass all of the mental elements of a crime. The *actus reus* has its own mental element; the act must be the voluntary act of the accused for the *actus reus* to exist. *Mens rea*, on the other hand, refers to the guilty mind, the wrongful intention, of the accused. Its function in criminal law is to prevent the conviction of the morally innocent — those who do not understand or intend the consequences of their acts. Typically, *mens rea* is concerned with the consequences of the prohibited *actus reus*. Thus in the crimes of homicide, we speak of the consequences of the voluntary act — intention to cause death, or reckless and wilfully blind persistence in conduct which one knows is likely to cause death. In other offences, such as dangerous driving, the *mens rea* may relate to the failure to consider the consequences of inadvertence.

This brings me to the question of whether the test for *mens rea* is subjective or objective. Most scholars and jurists agree that, leaving aside offences where the *actus reus* is negligence or inadvertence and offences of absolute liability, the test for *mens rea* is subjective. The test is not whether a reasonable person would have foreseen the consequences of the prohibited act, but whether the accused subjectively appreciated those consequences at least as a possibility. In applying the subjective test, the Court looks to the accused's intention and the facts as the accused believed them to be: G. Williams, *Textbook of Criminal Law* (2nd ed. 1983), at pp. 727-28.

Two collateral points must be made at this juncture. First, as Williams underlines, this inquiry has nothing to do with the accused's system of values. A person is not saved from conviction because he or she believes there is nothing wrong with what he or she is doing. The question is whether the accused subjectively appreciated that certain consequences would follow from his or her acts, not whether the accused believed the acts or their consequences to be moral. Just as the pathological killer would not be acquitted on the mere ground that he failed to see his act as morally reprehensible, so the defrauder will not be acquitted because he believed that what he was doing was honest.

The second collateral point is the oft-made observation that the Crown need not, in every case, show precisely what thought was in the accused's mind at the time of the criminal act. In certain cases, subjective awareness of the consequences can be inferred from the act itself, barring some explanation casting doubt on such inference. The fact that such an inference is made does not detract from the subjectivity of the test.

R. v. MULLIGAN

(1976), 26 C.R.N.S. 179, 18 C.C.C. (2d) 270 (Ont. C.A.)

Martin J.A.: —

. . . .

The central issue in this case was whether the accused, when he caused the death of his wife by repeatedly stabbing her, meant to cause her death or meant to cause her bodily harm that he knew was likely to cause her death, and was reckless whether death ensued and thereby committed the crime of murder as defined by the *Criminal Code*, R.S.C. 1970, c. C-34, s. 212(*a*)(i), (ii). The accused's intention was a fact in issue and like any other fact in issue it fell to be determined by a consideration of all the evidence including his acts, his utterances and any other circumstances which might shed light on his state of mind. As previously observed, the accused did not testify with respect to his state of mind at the relevant time. Such evidence would have been relevant and admissible. *Rex v. Fitzpartrick* (1926), 19 Cr. App. R. 91; Wigmore on Evidence, 3rd ed., Vol. II, pp. 714-15.

The jury would, of course have been entitled to reject his evidence and conclude that the circumstances were consistent only with the existence of the necessary intent. Although the accused did not testify on his own behalf, the statements made by him to the police contained an assertion that he did not mean to kill the deceased. The jury was properly charged with respect to the use that they could make of those statements and it is perhaps unnecessary to add that the jury was entitled, if it saw fit, to reject his assertion that he did not mean to kill the deceased.

In *Vallance v. The Queen*, [1961] 108 C.L.R. 56, Windeyer J. said at pp. 82-83:

> What a man does is often the best evidence of the purpose he had in mind. The probability that harm will result from a man's act may be so great, and so apparent, that it compels an inference that he actually intended to do that harm. Nevertheless, intention is a state of mind. The circumstances and probable consequences of a man's act are no more than evidence of his intention. For this reason this Court has often said that it is misleading to speak of a man being presumed always to intend the natural and probable consequences of his acts. And this, I do not doubt is so.

and at p. 83 said:

> A man's own intention is for him a subjective state, just as are his sensations of pleasure or of pain. But the state of another man's mind, or of his digestion, is an objective fact. When it has to be proved, it is to be probed in the same way as other objective facts are proved. A jury must consider the whole of the evidence relevant to it as a fact in issue. If an accused gives evidence of what his intentions were, the jury must weigh his testimony along with whatever inference as to his intentions can be drawn from his conduct or from other relevant facts. References to a "subjective test" could lead to an idea that the evidence of an accused man as to his intent is more credible than his evidence of other matters. It is not: he may or may not be believed by the jury. Whatever he says, they may be able to conclude from the

whole of the evidence that beyond doubt he had a guilty mind and a guilty purpose. But always the questions are what did *he* in fact know, foresee, expect, intend.

In the United Kingdom a decision that the intent required for murder had to be determined objectively both as a matter of substance and proof led to judicial revolt in Australia and legislative intervention in England.

D.P.P. v. SMITH

[1960] 3 All E.R. 161, [1961] A.C. 290 (H.L.)

Smith stole some stacks of scaffolding clips and placed them in the back of a car which he was driving. A Police constable who knew Smith ordered him to pull in to the side of the road. Smith thereupon accelerated and the constable held on to the side of the car which proceeded to zig-zag through the traffic. After 130 yards the constable was thrown off and was crushed to death under the wheels of an oncoming bubble car. Smith then turned into a side street, dumped the sacks of clips and returned to the scene. On being told the constable was dead Smith stated: "I knew the man. I wouldn't do that for the world. I only wanted to shake him off". On being arrested and cautioned he said: "I didn't mean to kill him, but I didn't want him to find the gear." At the trial the accused stated that when the constable jumped on the side of the car his foot went down on the accelerator and he was scared. He did not take his foot off the accelerator because when the constable jumped on he was frightened, and "it happened in a matter of seconds".

Smith was convicted of capital murder, but on appeal the Court of Criminal Appeal quashed this conviction and substituted a verdict of manslaughter. The Crown appealed to the House of Lords.

Viscount Kilmuir gave the unanimous judgment of the House:

[His Lordship stated the facts and continued:] In this state of the evidence the defence was twofold: (1) That he did not realise the officer was hanging on to the car until the officer fell off and that he could not keep a straight course having regard to the weight of metal in the back. In other words, he raised the defence of accident. (2) Alternatively, that it was a case of manslaughter and not murder in that he had no intent to kill or to do grievous bodily harm.

As regards the defence of accident, the learned Judge went through the relevant evidence and ended by saying this:

> There is a limit, is there not, members of the jury, to human credulity, and you may think that the accused man's unsupported assertion on this part of the case goes well past it, that the evidence is overwhelming, and he knew his car was carrying the officer up the road? The matter is one for you, but if you arrive at the conclusion that, of course, he knew, it is one which I would regard as abundantly right. Indeed, on the evidence I do not see how you could properly arrive at any other conclusion. If that be so the defence of pure accident goes.

My Lords, it would seem that this observation was fully justified on the evidence, and the jury by their verdict must have rejected the possibility of accident. Indeed, the defence of accident was never suggested either in the Court of Criminal Appeal or in your Lordships' House.

It is in regard to the second defence that the summing-up of the learned Judge has been criticised, and indeed has been held to amount to a misdirection, by the Court of Criminal Appeal. It is said that the jury were misdirected as to the intent which has to be proved in order to constitute the necessary ingredient of malice. The passages complained of are these:

> The intention with which a man did something can usually be determined by a jury only by inference from the surrounding circumstances including the presumption of law that a man intends the natural and probable consequences of his acts.
>
> If you feel yourselves bound to conclude from the evidence that the accused's purpose was to dislodge the officer, then you ask yourselves this question: Could any reasonable person fail to appreciate that the likely result would be at least serious harm to the officer? If you answer that question by saying that the reasonable person would certainly appreciate that, then you may infer that that was the accused's intention, and that would lead to a verdict of guilty on the charge of capital murder.
>
> Now the only part of that evidence of Police Constable Weatherill which the accused challenges is the part that incriminates him, namely, "I only wanted to shake him off." He says he did not say that. Well, you may think it is a curious thing to imagine, and further it may well be the truth — he did only want to shake him off; but if the reasonable man would realise that the effect of doing that might well be to cause serious harm to this officer, then, as I say, you would be entitled to impute such an intent to the accused, and, therefore, to sum up the matter as between murder and manslaughter, if you are satisfied that when he drove his car erractically up the street, close to the traffic on the other side, he must as a reasonable man have contemplated that grievous bodily harm was likely to result to that officer still clinging on, and that such harm did happen and the officer died in consequence, then the accused is guilty of capital murder, and you should not shrink from such a verdict because of its possible consequences. On the other hand, if you are not satisfied that he intended to inflict grievous bodily harm upon the officer — in other words, if you think he could not as a reasonable man have contemplated that grievous bodily harm would result to the officer in consequence of his actions — well, then, the verdict would be guilty of manslaughter.

The main complaint is that the learned Judge was there applying what is referred to as an objective test, namely, the test of what a reasonable man would contemplate as the probable result of his acts, and therefore would intend, whereas the question for the jury, it is said, was what the respondent himself intended. This, indeed, was the view of the Court of Criminal Appeal, who said:

> Once mere accident was excluded, the present case became one in which the degree of likelihood of serious injury to the police officer depended on which of the not always consistent versions of the facts given by witnesses for the prosecution was accepted. It was one in which it could not be said that there was a certainty that such injury would result; and it was one in which there always remained the question whether the appellant really did during the relevant ten seconds realise what was the degree of likelihood of serious injury. If the jury took the view that the appellant deliberately tried to drive the body of the police officer against oncoming cars, the obvious inference was open to them that the appellant intended serious injury to result; if, however, they concluded he merely swerved or zigzagged to shake off that officer, or if they concluded that for any reason he may not have realised the degree of danger to which he was exposing the police officer, a different situation would arise with regard to the inferences to be drawn. In the former case the jury might well have felt they were dealing with consequences that were certain; in the latter only with degrees of likelihood.

Putting aside for a moment the distinction which the Court of Criminal Appeal were seeking to draw between results which were "certain" and those which were "likely," they were saying that it was for the jury to decide whether, having regard to the panic in which he said he was, the respondent in fact at the time contemplated that grievous bodily harm would result from his actions or, indeed, whether he contemplated anything at all. Unless the jury were satisfied that he in fact had such contemplation, the necessary intent to constitute malice would not, in their view, have been proved. This purely subjective approach involves this, that if an accused said that he did not in fact think of the consequences, and the jury considered that that might well be true, he would be entitled to be acquitted of murder.

My Lords, the proposition has only to be stated thus to make one realise what a departure it is from that upon which the Courts have always acted. The jury must, of course, in such a case as the present make up their minds the evidence whether on the accused was unlawfully and voluntarily doing something to someone. The unlawful and voluntary act must clearly be aimed at someone in order to eliminate cases of negligence or of careless or dangerous driving. Once, however, the jury are satisfied as to that, it matters not what the accused in fact contemplated as the probable result or whether he ever contemplated at all, provided he was in law responsible and accountable for his actions, that is, was a man capable of forming an intent, not insane within the M'Naghten Rules and not suffering from diminished responsibility. On the assumption that he is so accountable for his actions, the sole question is whether the unlawful and voluntary act was of such a kind that grievous bodily harm was the natural and probable result. The only test available for this is what the ordinary responsible man would, in all the circumstances of the case, have contemplated as the natural and probable result. That, indeed, has always been the law, and I would only make a few citations.

The true principle is well set out in that persuasive authority "The Common Law" by Holmes J. After referring to Stephens' Digest of the Criminal Law and the statement that foresight of the consequence of the act is enough, he says at pp. 53-54:

> But again, What is foresight of consequences? It is a picture of a future state of things called up by knowledge of the present state of things, the future being viewed as standing to the present in the relation of effect to cause. Again, we must seek a reduction to lower terms. If the known present state of things is such that the act done will very certainly cause death, and the probability is a matter of common knowledge, one who does the act, knowing the present state of things, is guilty of murder, and the law will not inquire whether he did actually foresee the consequences or not. The test of foresight is not what this very criminal foresaw, but what a man of reasonable prudence would have foreseen.

[A]nd again at p. 56:

> But furthermore, on the same principle, the danger which in fact exists under the known circumstances ought to be of a class which a man of reasonable prudence could foresee. Ignorance of a fact and inability to foresee a consequence have the same effect on blameworthiness. If a consequence cannot be foreseen, it cannot be avoided. But there is this practical difference, that whereas, in most cases, the question of knowledge is a question of

the actual condition of the defendant's consciousness, the question of what he might have foreseen is determined by the standard of the prudent man, that is, by general experience.

. . . .

My Lords, the law being as I have endeavoured to define it, there seems to be no ground upon which the approach by the trial Judge in the present case can be criticised. Having excluded the suggestion of accident, he asked the jury to consider what were the exact circumstances at the time as known to the respondent, and what were the unlawful and voluntary acts which he did towards the police officer. The learned Judge then prefaced the passages of which complaint is made by saying, in effect, that if in doing what he did he must as a reasonable man have contemplated that serious harm was likely to occur then he was guilty of murder.

My only doubt concerns the use of the expression "a reasonable man," since this to lawyers connotes the man on the Clapham omnibus by reference to whom a standard of care in civil cases is ascertained. In judging of intent, however, it really denotes an ordinary man capable of reasoning who is responsible and accountable for his actions, and this would be the sense in which it would be understood by a jury.

Another criticism of the summing-up and one which found favour in the Court of Criminal Appeal concerned the manner in which the trial Judge dealt with the presumption that a man intends the natural and probable consequences of his acts. I will cite the passage again:

> The intention with which a man did something can usually be determined by a jury only by inference from the surrounding circumstances including the presumption of law that a man intends the natural and probable consequences of his acts.

It is said that the reference to this being a presumption of law without explaining that it was rebuttable amounted to a misdirection. Whether the presumption is one of law or of fact or, as has been said, of common sense, matters not for this purpose. The real question is whether the jury should have been told that it was rebuttable. In truth, however, as I see it, this is merely another way of applying the test of the reasonable man. Provided that the presumption is applied, once the accused's knowledge of the circumstances and the nature of his acts has been ascertained, the only thing that could rebut the presumption would be proof of incapacity to form an intent, insanity or diminished responsibility. In the present case, therefore, there was no need to explain to the jury that the presumption was rebuttable.

Strong reliance was, however, placed on the case of *Rex v. Steane*, in which Lord Goddard C.J. said:

> No doubt, if the prosecution prove an act the natural consequence of which would be a certain result and no evidence or explanation is given, then a jury may, on a proper direction, find that the prisoner is guilty of doing the act with the intent alleged, but if on the totality of the evidence there is room for more than one view as to the intent of the prisoner, the jury should be directed that it is for the prosecution to prove the intent to the jury's satisfaction, and if, on a review of the whole evidence, they either think that the intent did not exist or they are left in doubt as to the intent, the prisoner is entitled to be acquitted.

That, however, was a very special case. The appellant had been charged and convicted of doing acts likely to assist the enemy, with intent to assist the enemy. His case was that while he might have done acts likely to assist the enemy he had only done so out of duress and in order to save his wife and children. Accordingly, this was a case where over and above the presumed intent there had to be proved an actual intent or, it might be said, a desire by the appellant to assist the enemy.

It was also said that the Court of Criminal Appeal were right in stating the law thus:

> The law on this point as it stands today is that this presumption of intention means this: that, as a man is usually able to foresee what are the natural consequences of his acts, so it is, as a rule, reasonable to infer that he did foresee them and intend them. But, while that is an inference which may be drawn, and on the facts in certain circumstances must inevitably be drawn, yet if on all the facts of the particular case it is not the correct inference, then it should not be drawn.

This passage in the judgment of the Court of Criminal Appeal seems to have been lifted verbatim from the judgment of Denning L.J. in *Hosegood v. Hosegood*, a case dealing with proof of constructive desertion. In that case, my noble and learned friend, Lord Denning, was approving the school of thought which said that a husband is not to be found guilty of constructive desertion, however bad his conduct, unless he had in fact an intention to bring the married life to an end. Accordingly, the words in that passage were being used in connection with a case where an actual or overall intent or desire was involved. No such overall intent or desire is involved in the consideration of intent to kill or to do grievous bodily harm. Thus an overall intent or desire, for example, an intent or desire to escape, could not afford any defence.

While, however, I can see no possible criticism of the trial Judge in regard to the use he made of the presumption in the present case, I cannot help feeling that it is a matter which might well be omitted in summing up to a jury. The phrase "presumption of law" and the reference, if it has to be made, to the presumption being "rebuttable" are only apt to confuse a jury. In my opinion, the test of the reasonable man, properly understood, is a simpler criterion. It should present no difficulty to a jury and contains all the necessary ingredients of malice aforethought.

. . . .

In the result the appeal should, in my opinion, be allowed and the conviction of capital murder restored.

LORD GODDARD: — My Lords, I agree with the opinion which has just been pronounced.

LORD TUCKER: — My Lords, I also agree.

LORD DENNING: — My Lords, I agree.

LORD PARKER OF WADDINGTON: — My Lords, I also agree.

PARKER v. THE QUEEN

(1963), 111 C.L.R. 610 (Aust. H.C.) at 632

DIXON C.J.: —

. . . .

In *Stapleton v. The Queen* we said: "The introduction of the maxim or statement that a man is presumed to intend the reasonable consequences of his act is seldom helpful and always dangerous." That was some years before the decision in *Director of Public Prosecutions v. Smith*, which seems only too unfortunately to confirm the observation. I say too unfortunately for I think it forces a critical situation in our (Dominion) relation to the judicial authority as precedents of decisions in England. Hitherto I have thought that we ought to follow decisions of the House of Lords, at the expense of our own opinions and cases decided here, but having carefully studied *Smith's Case* I think that we cannot adhere to that view or policy. There are propositions laid down in the judgment which I believe to be misconceived and wrong. They are fundamental and they are propositions which I could never bring myself to accept. I shall not discuss the case. There has been enough discussion and, perhaps I may add, explanation, to make it unnecessary to go over the ground once more. I do not think that this present case really involves any of the so-called presumptions but I do think that the summing-up drew the topic into the matter even if somewhat unnecessarily and therefore if I left it on one side some misunderstanding might arise. I wish there to be no misunderstanding on the subject. I shall not depart from the law on the matter as we had long since laid it down in this Court and I think *Smith's Case* should not be used as authority in Australia at all.

After much criticism (see, for example, J.C. Smith and B. Hogan, *Criminal Law*, 4th ed. (1978), 289-91) and distinguishing by subsequent cases (R.J. Buxton, "The Retreat from Smith" (1966), Crim. L. Rev. 195), the objective test of *D.P.P. v. Smith* was abandoned in England by the *Criminal Justice Act*.

CRIMINAL JUSTICE ACT

1967 (U.K.), c. 80, s. 8

A Court or jury, in determining whether a person has committed an offence

—

(a) shall not be bound in law to infer that he intended or foresaw a result of his action by reason only of its being a natural and probable consequence of those actions; but
(b) shall decide whether he did intend or foresee that result by reference to all the evidence, drawing such inferences from the evidence as appear proper in the circumstances.

R. v. ORTT

(1969), 6 C.R.N.S. 233, [1970] 1 C.C.C. 223 (Ont. C.A.)

On appeal from a conviction of non-capital murder, the main ground was that the charge of the trial Judge suggested there was an onus on the accused to prove his incapacity to have the specific intent necessary. A passage from the charge follows.

The intention of a person *can* be judged by what he says or what he does. *In our law a person is presumed to have intended the natural consequences of his act.* Where a person deliberately strikes another with a lethal weapon an intention to kill will be *presumed* or, at least, an intention to cause bodily harm which is likely to result in death will be *presumed*. If a person strikes another with a knife in the region of the heart, in the region of the abdomen, various parts of the body, as was done to this woman, there would be a *presumption* that the person inflicting those wounds intended to cause the death of that woman or intended to cause bodily harm to her which he knew was likely to cause death and that he was reckless whether death would ensue or not. Where a person does acts calculated to kill a person and does kill that person, that is evidence of intent.

While the appeal was dismissed on the basis that the charge as a whole made it clear that the Crown had the onus of proof on the issue of intent, the Court noted:

It has been held by this Court that it is error in law to tell a jury it is a presumption of law that a person intends the natural consequences of his acts: *R. v. Giannotti* (1956), 115 C.C.C. 203, 23 C.R. 259. Moreover the word "presumption" alone creates a difficulty in that it may suggest an onus on the accused. I agree with the comment of the authors of *Martin's Annual Criminal Code* (1968), p. 195:

> The difficulty would not arise if the use of the word "presumption" were avoided. A presumption requires that a certain conclusion must be drawn, unless the accused takes steps to make that conclusion unwarranted. An inference, however, is no more than a matter of common sense and merely indicates that a certain conclusion may be drawn if warranted by the evidence.

As was said by Denning L.J. in *Hosegood v. Hosegood* (1950), 66 T.L.R. 735 at p. 738:

> The presumption of intention is not a proposition of law but a proposition of ordinary good sense. It means this: that, as a man is usually able to foresee what are the natural consequences of his acts, so it is, as a rule, reasonable to infer that he did foresee them and intend them. But, while that is an inference which may be drawn, it is not one which must be drawn. If on all the facts of the case it is not the correct inference, then it should not be drawn.

In my opinion, therefore, the word "presumption" is to be avoided in this context and juries simply told that generally it is a reasonable inference that a man intends the natural consequences of his acts so that when, for instance, a man points a gun at another and fires it the jury may reasonably infer that he meant either to cause his death or to cause him bodily harm that he knew was likely to cause death reckless of whether death ensued or not.

_____

The following detailed consideration of the current law on fault will reveal that a low level objective standard is pervasive for public welfare offences and that, while the subjective approach is still required for many crimes, for a significant number of crimes there are now less demanding standards of fault.

Fault for Public Welfare or Regulatory Offences

(a) Common Law

Until the pivotal decision in *Sault Ste. Marie*, in the case of some offences that were argued to be not truly criminal the choice for the Courts was between requiring the Crown to establish full subjective *mens rea* in the actor or absolute liability. Absolute liability, at that time also called strict liability, rested merely on proof of an act with no requirement of any form of fault. Consider how the Supreme Court made this choice in the following two leading cases:

BEAVER v. R.

[1957] S.C.R. 531, 26 C.R. 193, 118 C.C.C. 129

The accused was appealing convictions on counts of selling and possessing diacetylmorphine.

CARTWRIGHT J. (RAND and LOCKE JJ. concurring): —

. . . .

It is not necessary to set out the facts in detail. There was evidence on which it was open to the jury to find (i) that Max Beaver sold to a police officer, who was working under cover, a package which in fact contained diacetylmorphine, (ii) that the appellant was a party to the sale of the package, (iii) that while the appellant did not have the package on his person or in his physical possession he and Max Beaver were acting jointly in such circumstances that the possession which the latter had of the package was the possession of both of the accused, and (iv) that the appellant had no knowledge that the substance contained in the package was diacetylmorphine and believed it to be sugar of milk.

I do not mean to suggest that the jury would necessarily have made the fourth finding but there was evidence on which they might have done so, or which might have left them in a state of doubt as to whether or not the appellant knew that the package contained anything other than sugar of milk.

The learned trial Judge, against the protest of the appellant, charged the jury, in effect, that if they were satisfied that the appellant had in his possession a package and sold it, then, if in fact the substance contained in the package was diacetylmorphine, the appellant was guilty on both counts, and that the questions (i) whether he had any knowledge of what the substance was, or (ii) whether he entertained the honest but mistaken belief that it was a harmless substance were irrelevant and must not be considered. Laidlaw J.A. who delivered the unanimous judgment of the Court of Appeal, [116 Can. C.C. 231], was of opinion that this charge was right in law and that the learned trial Judge was bound by the decision in *R. v. Lawrence*, 102 Can. C.C. 121, to direct the jury as he did. The main question on this appeal is whether this view of the law is correct.

The problem is one of construction of the *Opium and Narcotic Drug Act*, R.S.C. 1952, c. 201, and particularly the following sections, which at the date of the offences charged read as follows:

> 4(1) Every, person who . . .
>
> (*d*) has in his possession any drug save and except under the authority of a licence from the Minister first had and obtained, or other lawful authority; . . .
>
> (*f*) manufactures, sells, gives away, delivers or distributes or makes any offer in respect of any drug, or any substance represented or held out by such person to be a drug, to any person without first obtaining a licence from the Minister, or without other lawful authority;
> . . .
> is guilty of an offence, and is liable
>
> (i) upon indictment, to imprisonment for any term not exceeding seven years and not less than six months, and to a fine not exceeding one thousand dollars and not less than two hundred dollars, and, in addition, at the discretion of the Judge, to be whipped; or
>
> (ii) upon summary conviction, to imprisonment with or without hard labour for any term not exceeding 18 months and not less than six months, and to a fine not exceeding one thousand dollars and not less than two hundred dollars.

· · · ·

The judgment in appeal is supported by earlier decisions of Appellate Courts in Ontario, Quebec and Nova Scotia, but a directly contrary view has been expressed by the Court of Appeal for British Columbia. While this conflict has existed since 1948, this is the first occasion on which the question has been brought before this Court.

It may be of assistance in examining the problem to use a simple illustration. Suppose X goes to the shop of Y, a druggist, and asks Y to sell him some baking soda. Y hands him a sealed packet which he tells him contains baking soda and charges him a few cents. X honestly believes that the packet contains baking soda but in fact it contains heroin. X puts the package in his pocket, takes it home and later puts it in a cupboard in his bathroom. There would seem to be no doubt that X has had actual manual and physical possession of the package and that he continues to have possession of the package while it is in his cupboard. The main question raised on this appeal is whether, in the supposed circumstances, X would be guilty of the crime of having heroin in his possession?

· · · ·

In *Reynolds v. G.H. Austin & Sons Ltd.*, [1951] 2 K.B. 135, Devlin J. says at pp. 147-8:

It has always been a principle of the common law that *mens rea* is an essential element in the commission of any criminal offence against the common law. In the case of statutory offences it depends on the effect of the statute. In *Sherras v. De Rutzen*, [1895] 1 Q.B. 918, 921, Wright, J., in his well-known judgment, laid it down that there was a presumption that *mens rea* was an essential ingredient in a statutory offence, but that that presumption was liable to be displaced either by the words of the statute creating the offence or by the subject-matter with which it dealt. . . . Kennedy, L.J., in *Hobbs v. Winchester Corporation*, [1910] 2 K.B. 471, 483, thought that in construing a modern statute this presumption as to *mens rea* did not exist. In this respect, as he said, he differed from Channell, J., in the court below. But the view of Wright, J., in *Sherras v. De Rutzen* has consistently been followed. I need refer only to the dictum of Lord Goddard, C.J., in *Harding v. Price*, [1948] 1 K.B. 695, 700, "The general rule applicable to criminal cases is *actus non facit reum nisi mens sit rea*, and I venture to repeat what I said in *Brend v. Wood* (1946), 62 T.L.R. 462, 463, 'It is of the utmost importance for the protection of the liberty of the subject that a court should always bear in mind that, unless a statute either clearly or by necessary implication rules out *mens rea* as a constituent part of a crime, the Court should not find a man guilty of an offence against the criminal law unless he has a guilty mind.' "

In *R. v. Tolson* (1889), 23 Q.B.D. 168 at p. 188, Stephen J. says:

"I think it may be laid down as a general rule that an alleged offender is deemed to have acted under that state of facts which he in good faith and on reasonable grounds believed to exist when he did the act alleged to be an offence. I am unable to suggest any real exception to this rule, nor has one ever been suggested to me.

And adds at p. 189:

Of course, it would be competent to the legislature to define a crime in such a way as to make the existence of any state of mind immaterial. The question is solely whether it has actually done so in this case.

I adhere to the opinion which, with the concurrence of my brother Nolan, I expressed in *R. v. Rees*, 115 Can. C.C. 1 at p. 11, [1956] S.C.R. 640 at p. 651 that the first of the statements of Stephen J. quoted above should now be read in the light of the judgment of Lord Goddard C.J., concurred in by Lynskey and Devlin JJ. in *Wilson v. Inyang*, [1951] 2 All E.R. 237, which, in my opinion, rightly decides that the essential question is whether the belief entertained by the accused is an honest one and that the existence or non-existence of reasonable grounds for such belief is merely relevant evidence to be weighed by the tribunal of fact in determining that essential question.

In *Watts & Gaunt v. The Queen*, 105 Can. C.C. 193 at p. 199, [1953], 1 S.C.R. 505 at p. 511, Estey J. says:

While an offence of which *mens rea* is not an essential ingredient may be created by legislation, in view of the general rule a section creating an offence ought not to be so construed unless Parliament has, by express language or necessary implication, disclosed such an intention.

. . . .

When the decisions as to the construction of the *Opium and Narcotic Drug Act* on which the respondent relies are examined it appears that two main reasons are assigned for holding that *mens rea* is not an essential ingredient of the offence created by s. 4(1)(*d*), these being (i) the assumption that the subject-matter with which the Act deals is of the kind dealt with in the cases of which *Hobbs v. Winchester Corp.*, [1910] 2 K.B. 471, is typical and which are sometimes referred to as "public welfare offence cases", and (ii) by implication from the wording of s. 17 of the Act.

As to the first of these reasons, I can discern little similarity between a statute designed, by forbidding the sale of unsound meat, to ensure that the supply available to the public shall be wholesome, and a statute making it a serious crime to possess or deal in narcotics; the one is to ensure that a lawful and necessary trade shall be carried on in a manner not to endanger the public health, the other to forbid altogether conduct regarded as harmful in itself. As a necessary feature of his trade, the butcher holds himself out as selling meat fit for consumption; he warrants that quality; and it is part of his duty as trader to see that the merchandise is wholesome. The statute simply converts that civil personal duty into a public duty.

. . . .

Has X possession of heroin when he has in his hand or in his pocket or in his cupboard a package which in fact contains heroin but which he honestly believes contains only baking soda? In my opinion that question must be answered in the negative. The essence of the crime is the possession of the forbidden substance and in a criminal case there is in law no possession without knowledge of the character of the forbidden substance. Just as in *R. v. Ashwell* (1885), 16 Q.B.D. 190, the accused did not in law have possession of the complainant's sovereign so long as he honestly believed it to be a shilling so in my illustration X did not have possession of heroin so long as he honestly believed the package to contain baking soda. The words of Lord Coleridge C.J. in *R. v. Ashwell* at p. 225, quoted by Charles J. delivering the unanimous judgment of the Court of Criminal Appeal in *R. v. Hudson* (1943), 29 Cr. App. R. 65 at p. 71:

> "In good sense it seems to me he did not take it till he knew what he had got; and when he knew what he had got, that same instant he stole it."

might well be adapted to my illustration to read: "In good sense it seems to me he did not have possession of heroin till he knew what he had got."

. . . .

If the matter were otherwise doubtful I would be drawn to the conclusion that Parliament did not intend to enact that *mens rea* should not be an essential ingredient of the offence created by s. 4(1)(*d*) by the circumstance that on conviction a minimum sentence of six months' imprisonment plus a fine of $200 must be imposed. Counsel informed us that they have found no other statutory provision which has been held to create a crime of strict responsibility, that is to say, one in which the necessity for *mens rea* is excluded, on conviction for which a sentence of imprisonment is mandatory. The legislation dealt with in *Hobbs v. Winchester, supra*, provided that a sentence of imprisonment might, not must, be imposed on a convicted person.

. . . .

It would, of course, be within the power of Parliament to enact that a person who, without any guilty knowledge, had in his physical possession a package which he honestly believed to contain a harmless substance such as baking soda but which in fact contained heroin, must on proof of such facts be convicted of a crime and sentenced to at least six months' imprisonment; but I would refuse to impute such an intention to Parliament unless the words of the statute were clear and admitted of no other interpretation. To borrow the words of Lord Kenyon in *Fowler v. Padget* (1798), 7 Term R. 509 at p. 514, 101 E.R. 1103: "I would adopt any construction of the statute that the words will bear, in order to avoid such monstrous consequences as would manifestly ensue from the construction contended for by the defendant."

The conclusion which I have reached on the main question as to the proper construction of the word possession makes it unnecessary for me to consider the other points raised by Mr. Dubin in his argument as to the construction of s. 4(1)(*d*). For the above reasons I would quash the conviction on the charge of having possession of a drug.

As to the charge of selling, as is pointed out by my brother Fauteux, the appellant's version of the facts brings his actions within the provisions of s. 4(1)(*f*) since he and his brother jointly sold a substance represented or held out by them to be heroin; and I agree with the conclusion of my brother Fauteux that the conviction on the charge of selling must be affirmed.

. . . .

FAUTEUX J. (dissenting), ABBOTT J. (concurring): —

. . . .

The plain and apparent object of the Act is to prevent, by a rigid control of the possession of drugs, the danger to public health, and to guard society against the social evils which an uncontrolled traffic in drugs is bound to generate. The scheme of the Act is this: The importation, exportation, sale, manufacture, production and distribution of drugs are subject to the obtention of a licence which the Minister of National Health and Welfare may issue, with the approval of the Governor-General in Council, and in which the place where such operations may be carried on is stated. Under the same authority are indicated ports and places in Canada where drugs may be exported or imported, the manner in which they are to be packed and marked for export, the records to be kept for such export, import, receipt, sale, disposal and distribution. The Act also provides for the establishment of all other convenient and necessary regulations with respect to duration, terms and forms of the several licences therein provided. Without a licence, it is an offence to import or export from Canada and an offence for any one who, not being a common carrier, takes or carries, or causes to be taken or carried from any place in Canada to any other place in Canada, any drug. Druggists, physicians, dentists and veterinary surgeons stand, of course, in a privileged class; but even their dealings in drugs for medicinal purposes are the object of a particular control. Under penalties of the law, some of them have to keep records of their operations, while others have the obligation to answer inquiries in respect thereto. Having in one's possession drugs without a licence or other lawful authority, is an offence. In brief, the principle underlying the Act is that possession of drugs covered by it is unlawful; and where any exception is made to the principle, the exceptions themselves are attended with particular controlling provisions and conditions.

The enforcement sections of the Act manifest the exceptional vigilance and firmness which Parliament thought of the essence to forestall the unlawful traffic in narcotic drugs and cope effectively with the unusual difficulties standing in the way of the realization of the object of the statute. Substantive and procedural principles generally prevailing under the *Criminal Code* in favour of the subject are being restricted or excepted. The power to search by day or by night, either premises or the person, is largely extended under s. 19. Special writs of assistance are provided for under s. 22. The consideration of the provisions of ss. 4 and 17 being deferred for the moment, the burden of proof is either alleviated or shifted to persons charged with violations under ss. 6, 11, 13, 16 and 18. Minimum sentences are provided or are made mandatory, under ss. 4 and 6. Deportation of aliens found guilty is also mandatory and this notwithstanding the provisions of the *Immigration Act* [R.S.C. 1952, c. 325] or any other Act, under s. 26. And the application of the *Identification of Criminals Act* [R.S.C. 1952, c. 144], ordinarily limited to the case of indictable offences, is, by s. 27, extended to any offence under the Act.

All of these provisions are indicative of the will of Parliament to give the most efficient protection to public health against the danger attending the uncontrolled use of drugs as well as against the social evils incidental thereto, by measures generally centred and directed to possession itself of the drugs covered by the Act. The subject-matter, the purpose and the scope of the Act are such that to subject its provisions to the narrow construction suggested on behalf of appellant would defeat the very object of the Act.

. . . .

This case, amongst others, such as *R. v. Thomas Wheat, R. v. Marion Stocks*, [1921] 2 K.B. 119, is a clear authority supporting the proposition that the presumption that *mens rea* is an ingredient to an offence, as well as the defence flowing from an honest belief as to the existence of a state of facts may, by reason of the subject-matter of the Act or of the language of its provisions, or of both, cease to obtain. The *Opium and Narcotic Drug Act* comes, in my view, within these classes of Acts referred to by Wright J. in *Sherras v. De Rutzen*, *supra*.

. . . .

On the plain, literal and grammatical meaning of the words of this section, there is an absolute prohibition to be in possession of drugs, whatever be the various meanings of which the word possession may be susceptible, unless the possession is under the authority of a licence from the Minister, first had and obtained, or under other lawful authority. . . . .

Appeal from conviction for possession of drug allowed; appeals from conviction for sale of a drug and finding of being an habitual criminal dismissed.

R. v. PIERCE FISHERIES LTD.

[1969] 4 C.C.C. 163 (N.S. C.A.)

McKINNON C.J.N.S.: — This is an appeal brought by the Crown by way of stated case from an acquittal by C. Roger Rand Q.C., a Provincial Magistrate in and for the Magisterial District of the Province of Nova Scotia, wherein the respondent, Pierce Fisheries Limited, was charged that the said company

at or near Lockeport in the County of Shelburne in the Magisterial District of the Province of Nova Scotia on or about the 29th day of April A.D. 1968 in Lobster Fishing District No. 4 did without lawful excuse have in possession lobsters of a length less than three and three-sixteenths (3 3/16) inches, the minimum length specified in the schedule for that district contrary to Subsection (1)(b) of Section 3 of the *Lobster Fishery Regulations*, P.C. 19630745 as amended made pursuant to Section 34 of the *Fisheries Act*.

. . . .

The questions submitted for the judgment of the Court are as follows:

1. Is *mens rea* an essential ingredient to be established by evidence on a charge of violating Sub-Section (1)(b) of Section 3 of the *Lobster Fisheries Regulations*?

. . . .

Subsection (1)(*b*) of s. 3 of the *Lobster Fishery Regulations*, being P.C. 1963-745 [SOR/63-173], as amended, made in pursuance of s. 34 of the *Fisheries Act*, stated above, is as follows:

3(1) No person shall, in any district or portion of a district,
    (*b*) at any time fish for, catch, kill or have in possession any lobster of a length less than
       that specified in the Schedule of that district or that portion of a district.

The Schedule to the *Lobster Fishery Regulations*, being P.C. 1963-745, provides by s-s.(2) of s. 1 (am. P.C. 1964-1845, SOR/64-478), that in a part of Digby County, Yarmouth, Shelburne, Queens, Lunenburg Counties, and a part of Halifax County, all in the Province of Nova Scotia, the prohibition applies to lobsters of a length less than 3 3/16 inches.

By s. 2(1) of the Regulations (P.C. 1963-745), length, used in reference to a lobster, means the distance from the rear of either eye socket to the rear end of the body shell measured along a line parallel to the centre line of the body shell.

. . . .

There appear to be two main arguments in support of the doctrine of strict liability, one, that in certain fields the law cannot afford to entertain pleas of no fault, for only strict liability is sufficient to enforce the extremely high standards required; and two, that strict liability is the only practical means of enforcing standards in areas where it would be too difficult, time consuming and expensive to prove fault. The argument against the application of the doctrine would seem to be that if there has been no fault, it cannot even act as a meaningful encouragement towards greater care, and it is harmful because it brings blameless people, and the law, into disrepute.

In *R. v. V.K. Mason Construction Ltd.*, [1968] 3 C.C.C. 62 at p. 67, Lieff J., states that most statutes creating strict liability fall into three classes:

1. Where the act is not criminal in any real sense but is prohibited under a penalty in the public interest. Instances of this class have arisen on legislation concerning food, drugs, liquor licensing, the operation of motor vehicles, etc.
2. Where the act is in the nature of a public nuisance.
3. Where the proceeding is criminal in form, but it is really a summary mode of enforcing a civil right. (See *Sherras v. De Rutzen, supra* [[1895] 1 Q.B. 918].)

It is argued by the appellant here that the *Lobster Fishery Regulations* fall within the first class, above. Also that the Regulations are obviously intended to protect the lobster beds from depletion and are for the protection of the Maritime fishing industry in which the State has an obvious interest. It is also argued that widespread fishing for short lobsters will eventually cause the extinction of the industry, and as there is no efficient method of checking lobsters for size, "the inference is irresistible from the subject matter of the legislation that absolute prohibition was intended".

. . . .

To read strict liability into the wording of s. 3(1)(*b*), would be to provide that every lobster fisherman who had undersized lobsters in his boat would be in contravention of the Regulations, and this could have the effect of making it virtually impossible for lobster fishermen to carry out their work without violating the law. It is a notorious fact in the lobster fishing industry, of which this Court may take judicial notice, that fishermen, particularly those fishing alone, may have to haul a number of traps before they can find an opportunity to measure and cull the short lobsters which they then have in possession. If the boat is inspected before there is time to return the short lobsters to the water, and if s. 3(1)(*b*) is interpreted as one of strict liability, they are liable to prosecution under the Regulations.

. . . .

Appeal dismissed.

R. v. PIERCE FISHERIES LTD.

[1971] S.C.R. 5, 12 C.R.N.S. 272, [1970] 5 C.C.C. 193

RITCHIE J. (FAUTEUX, ABBOTT, MARTLAND, JUDSON JJ., HALL, SPENCE and PIGEON JJ. concurring): —

. . . .

Generally speaking, there is a presumption at common law that *mens rea* is an essential ingredient of all cases that are criminal in the true sense, but a consideration of a considerable body of case law on the subject satisfies me that there is a wide category of offences created by statutes enacted for the regulation of individual conduct in the interests of health, convenience, safety and the general welfare of the public which are not subject to any such presumption. Whether the presumption arises in the latter type of cases is dependent upon the words of the statute creating the offence and the subject-matter with which it deals.

In the case of *Cundy v. Le Cocq* (1884), 13 Q.B.D. 207, the appellant had been convicted of selling liquor to a person who was drunk, contrary to s. 13 of the *Licensing Act, 1872*, although he was unaware of the drunkenness. In affirming this conviction, Stephen J., clearly indicated that in 1884 the presumption of *mens rea* had already ceased to have general application in statutory offences. At p. 210 he said:

> In old time, and as applicable to the common law or to earlier statutes, the maxim may have been of general application; but a difference has arisen owing to the greater precision of modern statutes. It is impossible now, as illustrated by the cases of *Reg. v. Prince*, Law Rep. 2 C.C.R. 154, and *Reg. v. Bishop*, 5 Q.B.D. 259, to apply the maxim generally to all statutes, and the substance of all the reported cases is that it is necessary to look at the object of each Act that is under consideration to see whether and how far knowledge is of the essence of the offence created.

The case most frequently cited as illustrating the limits of the presumption that *mens rea* is an essential ingredient in all offences and the exceptions to it, is *Sherras v. De Rutzen*, [1895] 1 Q.B. 918, where Wright J., said, at p. 921:

> There is a presumption that *mens rea*, an evil intention, or a knowledge of the wrongfulness of the act, is an essential ingredient in every offence; but that presumption is liable to be displaced either by the words of the statute creating the offence or by the subject-matter with which it deals, and both must be considered.

The learned Judge then went on to say:

> the principal of classes of exceptions may perhaps be reduced to three. One is a class of acts which, in the language of Lush, J. in *Davies v. Harvey*, L.R. 9 Q.B. 433, are not criminal in any real sense, *but are acts which in the public interest are prohibited under a penalty.*

The italics are my own.

The two other classes of exceptions to which Wright J., referred were public nuisances and proceedings which, although criminal in form, are really only a summary mode of enforcing a civil right.

In considering the full effect to be given to Wright J.'s definition of the first class of exception, *i.e.*, acts which are not criminal in any real sense but rather "acts which in the public interest are prohibited under a penalty", I derive great assistance from the dictum of Dixon J., in the High Court of Australia in *Proudman v. Dayman* (1941), 67 C.L.R. 536 at p. 540, to which reference was made in this Court in *R. v. King,* 133 C.C.C. 1 at p. 17, [1962] S.C.R. 746, where he said of the presumption of the existence of *mens rea* as an essential ingredient in criminal offences:

> The strength of the presumption that the rule applies to a statutory offence newly created varies with the nature of the offence and the scope of the statute. *If the purpose of the statute is to add a new crime to the general criminal law, it is natural to suppose that it is to be read subject to the general principles according to which that law is administered.* But other considerations arise where in matters of police, of health, of safety or the like the legislature adopts penal measures in order to cast on the individual the responsibility of so conducting his affairs that the general welfare will not be prejudiced. In such cases there is less ground, either in reason or in actual probability, for presuming an intention that the general rule should apply making honest and reasonable mistake a ground of exoneration, and the presumption is but a weak one.

The italics are my own.

The same thought was expressed by Lord Reid in the recent case of *Sweet v. Parsley*, [1969] 2 W.L.R. 470, where he said at p. 474 speaking of the first class of exception referred to by Wright J., in *Sherras v. De Rutzen, supra*:

> It has long been the practice to recognize absolute offences in this class of quasi-criminal acts, and one can safely assume that, when Parliament is passing new legislation dealing with this class of offences, its silence as to *mens rea* means that the old practice is to apply. But when one comes to acts of a truly criminal character, it appears to me that there are at least two other factors which any reasonable legislator would have in mind. In the first place a stigma still attaches to any person convicted of a truly criminal offence, and the more serious or more disgraceful the offence the greater the stigma.

In the case of *R. v. King, supra*, this Court found that the enactment of s. 223 of the *Criminal Code* did "add a new crime to the general criminal law" and I think it must be assumed that in the case of *Beaver v. The Queen*, 118 C.C.C. 129, [1957] S.C.R. 531, 26 C.R. 193, the Court considered that the offence created by s. 4(1)(*d*) of the *Opium and Narcotic Drug Act*, R.S.C. 1952, c. 201, also constituted a crime in the "real sense". In the course of the reasons for judgment which he delivered on behalf of the majority of the Court in that case, Cartwright J. (as he then was), had occasion to say [at p. 138 C.C.C.]:

> I can discern little similarity between a statute designed, by forbidding the sale of unsound meat, to ensure that the supply available to the public shall be wholesome, and a statute making it a *serious crime to possess or deal in narcotics*; the one is to ensure that a lawful and necessary trade shall be carried on in a manner not to endanger the public health, the other to forbid altogether conduct regarded as harmful in itself.

The italics are my own.

The scope and purpose of the Regulations here at issue are in my view to be determined by a consideration of the provisions of s. 34 of the *Fisheries Act*, R.S.C. 1952, c. 119, as amended by 1960-61, c. 23, s. 5 which provide that:

> 34. The Governor in Council may make regulations for carrying out the purposes and provisions of this Act and in particular, but without restricting the generality of the foregoing, may make regulations
>
> (a) for the proper management and control of the seacoast and inland fisheries;
>
> (b) respecting the conservation and protection of fish;
>
> (c) respecting the catching, loading, landing, handling, transporting, possession and disposal of fish;

I agree with the submission made on behalf of the appellant, which appears to have received qualified approval in the reasons for judgment rendered on behalf of the Appeal Division by the Chief Justice of Nova Scotia, that the *Lobster Fishery Regulations* are obviously intended for the purpose of protecting lobster beds from depletion and thus conserving the source of supply for an important fishing industry which is of general public interest.

I do not think that a new crime was added to our criminal law by making regulations which prohibit persons from having undersized lobsters in their possession, nor do I think that the stigma of having been convicted of a criminal offence would attach to a person found to have been in breach of these regulations. The case of *Beaver v. The Queen*, *supra*, affords an example of provisions of a federal statute other than the *Criminal Code* which were found to have created a truly criminal offence, but in the present case, to paraphrase the language used by the majority of this Court in the *Beaver* case, I can discern little similarity between a statute designed, by forbidding the possession of undersized lobsters, to protect the lobster industry, and a statute making it a serious crime to possess or deal in narcotics.

In view of the above, it will be seen that I am of opinion that the offence created by s. 3(1)(b) of the Regulations falls within the first class of exceptions referred to by Wright J., in *Sherras v. De Rutzen, supra*, and that it should be construed in accordance with the language in which it was enacted, free from any presumption as to the requirement of *mens rea*.

In considering the language of the Regulation, s. 3(i)(b), it is significant, though not conclusive, that it contains no such words as "knowingly", "wilfully", "with intent" or "without lawful excuse", whereas such words occur in a number of sections of the *Fisheries Act* itself which create offences for which *mens rea* is made an essential ingredient.

In this latter regard, the outstanding example is s. 55(1) of which it is made an offence for any person who has not got a licence from the Minister (a) to leave any port or place in Canada, "with intent to fish" or "to cause any other person to fish with a vessel that uses an 'otter' or other trawl of a similar nature" and (b) [rep. & sub. 1964-65, c. 22, s. 12(5)] to "knowingly" bring into Canada any fish caught beyond the territorial waters of Canada with any vessel that uses an "otter" or other trawl of a similar nature. Finally, s. 55(6) provides that "The burden of proving absence of intent or knowledge, when intent or knowledge is necessary to constitute an offence under this section, lies upon the person accused, and intent or knowledge shall be presumed unless negatived by proof".

This appears to me to be a clear indication of the fact that in making provision for offences under the *Fisheries Act*, Parliament was careful to specify those of which it intended that guilty knowledge should be an essential ingredient.

The learned Chief Justice of Nova Scotia adopted the view that the governing intention of the *Fisheries Act* was to be found in s. 18 thereof which reads:

> 18. No one, without lawful excuse, the proof whereof lies on him, shall fish for, buy, sell or have in his possession any fish, or portion of any fish, at a place where *at that time fishing for such fish is prohibited by law.*

(The italics are my own.) It is significant, however, as has been pointed out in the reasons for judgment of Cartwright C.J.C., that the words "lawful excuse" are given a very limited meaning by s. 2(*g*) of the *Fisheries Act* which reads:

> 2. In this Act,
>   (*g*) "lawful excuse" means
>   (i) ability to prove that fish in possession *during the close time* therefor at the place of possession, were legally caught; or
>   (ii) the unintentional or incidental catching of any fish that may not *then* be taken, when legally fishing for other fish;

The italics are my own.

Section 18 appears to be the only section of the *Fisheries Act* itself in which the words "lawful excuse" occur and I think that when that section and the definition section are read together, there is a clear inference that they refer to fish caught during the close season.

This appears to me to be borne out by the provisions of s. 3(1)(*a*) of the *Lobster Fishery Regulations* which immediately precede the regulation here in question and read:

> 3(1) No person shall in any district or portion of a district,
>   (*a*) during the closed season specified in the Schedule for that district or that portion of a district
>   (i) fish for, catch or kill any lobster, or
>   (ii) have any lobster in possession *without lawful excuse*; or
>   (iii) leave lobster pots in the water on lobster fishing grounds.

The italics are my own.

The offence of violating the prohibition contained in s. 3(1)(*a*)(ii) is therefore not one of strict liability, in that proof of lawful excuse in the limited sense defined in the Act constitutes a defence and the fact that there is no provision for such a defence in the subsection which immediately follows (*i.e.*, s. 3(1)(*b*)) is, in my view, another strong indication of the fact that the offence here charged is one of strict liability.

It is said, however, that all enactments which make "possession" of a forbidden substance an offence are to be construed in accordance with the view adopted by a majority of this Court in the *Beaver* case, *supra*, at p. 140 [118 C.C.C.] where it was said:

> The essence of the crime is the possession of the forbidden substance and in a criminal case there is in law no possession without knowledge of the character of the forbidden substance.

This appears to me to be another way of saying that guilty knowledge is an essential ingredient wherever possession is made the essence of an offence, but it is to be remembered that the statement was made in relation to what was found in that case to be a truly criminal offence and I do not think that it applies to statutory offences which are not "criminal in any real sense".

In the present appeal we are, of course, bound by the facts as set forth in the case stated.

. . . .

These circumstances, taken together with the first of the three "main facts" stated by the learned Magistrate, make it clear beyond any question that the respondent was in physical possession of 50,000 to 60,000 lbs. of lobsters, some of which were undersized, but it is contended that because there was no evidence to show that "any officer or responsible employee" of the Company had any knowledge of the presence of these undersized lobsters, they were therefore not in the respondent's possession as a matter of law.

This is not a case where a quantity of lobsters, some of which turned out to be undersized, was "planted" on the premises of Pierce Fisheries Limited by a trick, nor did the 50,000 or 60,000 lbs. of lobsters come to the respondent's plant by mistake or otherwise without its knowledge. The respondent was a dealer in lobsters and it purchased this great quantity in the course of its business. It cannot be suggested that no officer or responsible employee of Pierce Fisheries Ltd. had knowledge of the fact that a big shipment of lobsters was being packaged on the premises on the day in question, but it was not proved that any of these people knew that there were any undersized lobsters in the shipment. As employees of the company working on the premises in the shed "where fish is weighed and packed" were taking lobsters from boxes "preparatory for packing" in crates, and as some of the undersized lobsters were found "in crates ready for shipment", it would not appear to have been a difficult matter for some "officer or responsible employee" to acquire knowledge of their presence on the premises.

This case appears to me to fall into the same category as that of *R. v. Woodrow* (1846), 15 M.&W. 403, to which Wright J., referred in the *Sherras* case, where the accused, a dealer in tobacco, was charged with having adulterated tobacco in his possession. He had a quantity of tobacco on his premises but he did not know that any of it was adulterated. In the course of his reasons for judgment Chief Baron Pollock observed at p. 415:

> It appears to me, that, in this case, it being within the personal knowledge of the party that he was in possession of the tobacco, (indeed, a man can hardly be said to be in possession of anything without knowing it), it is not necessary that he should know that the tobacco was adulterated; for reasons probably very sound, and not applicable to this case only, but to many

other branches of the law, persons who deal in an article are made responsible for its being of a certain quality.

. . . .

In this case the respondent knew that it had upwards of 60,000 lbs. of lobsters on its premises; it only lacked knowledge as to the small size of some of them, and I do not think that the failure of any of its responsible employees to acquire this knowledge affords any defence to a charge of violating the provisions of s. 3(1)(b) of the *Lobster Fishery Regulations*.

If lack of knowledge by any responsible employee constituted a defence for a limited company to a charge under s. 3(1)(b) of the Regulations, then I think it would in many cases be virtually impossible to secure a conviction.

The language used by Mr. Justice Roach in *R. v. Pee-Kay Smallwares Ltd.*, 90 C.C.C. 129 at p. 137, 6 C.R. 28, appears to me to be pertinent in this regard. The learned Judge there said:

> If on a prosecution for the offences created by the Act, the Crown had to prove the evil intent of the accused, or if the accused could escape by denying such evil intent, the statute, by which it was obviously intended that there should be complete control without the possibility of any leaks, would have so many holes in it that in truth it would be nothing more than a legislative sieve.

With the greatest respect for those who may hold a different view, I am of opinion that the offence of violating s. 3(1)(b) of the *Lobster Fishery Regulations* is an offence of strict liability of which *mens rea* is not an essential ingredient.

I would accordingly allow this appeal and direct that the question of law stated by the learned Provincial Magistrate, upon which leave to appeal to this Court was granted, be answered in the negative and that the case be remitted to the Provincial Magistrate to be dealt with in accordance herewith.

Under the circumstances there will be no order as to costs.

CARTWRIGHT C.J.C. (dissenting): —

. . . .

On the facts as found by the learned Magistrate the question is whether, it being proved that amongst 50,000 to 60,000 lbs. of lobsters purchased by and on the premises and under the control of the respondent there were 26 short lobsters, it must be convicted of the offence charged although none of its officers or responsible employees had any knowledge of that fact and specific instructions had been given to its officers, responsible employees and dealers not to buy undersized lobsters.

. . . .

In my view a principle of construction of a statute which makes possession of a forbidden substance an offence was laid down by this Court in *Beaver v. The Queen*, 118 C.C.C. 129, [1957] S.C.R. 531, 26 C.R. 193, where it was said by the majority at p. 140:

The essence of the crime is the possession of the forbidden substance and in a criminal case there is in law no possession without knowledge of the character of the forbidden substance.

Applying this principle to the words of the charge against the respondent in the case at bar, it appears to me that the express finding of fact that the respondent had no knowledge, factually or inferentially, that any of the lobsters on its premises and under its control were undersized necessarily leads to a finding of not guilty.

. . . .

There is no evidence before the Court as to whether a dealer in lobsters in the position of the defendant having occasionally, without fault or knowledge on its part, undersized lobsters on its premises and under its control would create so serious a danger of the destruction of the lobster-catching industry as to render it necessary in the public interest that, on the facts as found in this case, one blameless of any intentional wrongdoing and without any guilty mind must be convicted of a criminal offence albeit not one involving grave moral turpitude. Assuming that the case of *R. v. Pee-Kay Smallwares Ltd.* (1948), 90 C.C.C. 129, 6 C.R. 28, was rightly decided it does not appear to me to govern the case before us.

Parliament could, of course, provide by apt words that anyone having in fact an undersized lobster on his premises and under his control should be guilty of an offence although he had no knowledge that such lobster was undersized but, in my opinion, no such words have been used, and no such intention can be implied from the words which have been used considered in the light of all relevant circumstances.

The argument in the appellant's factum concludes with the following paragraph:

> It is submitted that, if this case is not one where strict liability was intended, it is unlikely that such a case can be found in the absence of the legislators saying so specifically.

This suggests the question whether it would not indeed be in the public interest that whenever it is intended to create an offence of absolute liability the enacting provision should declare that intention in specific and unequivocal words.

I would dismiss the appeal with costs in this Court; I would not interfere with the decision of the Appeal Division not to award costs of the proceedings in that Court.

R. v. HICKEY

(1976), 29 C.C.C. (2d) 23 (Ont. H.C.)

The accused, a truck driver, offered in defence to a charge of speeding his honest belief that he had not been exceeding the speed limit. He had relied on his speedometer, and had no reason to suspect a malfunction, which was subsequently proved to have been the case.

GALLIGAN J. (REID J. concurring): —

. . . .

The second ground of appeal raises the issue of whether a mistake of fact upon the part of the accused can ever in law amount to a valid defence to a charge of an offence of strict liability. There is a strong body of legal opinion (which has its roots in Australia), that holds in cases charging an accused with an offence for which there is strict liability that there is a valid legal defence to such a charge if the accused proves on the balance of probabilities that he honestly believed on reasonable grounds in a mistaken set of facts which if true would render his act an innocent one.

That defence appears to have been rejected in at least two Canadian cases which arose under circumstances not dissimilar to those in the case at bar. The first is *R. v. Gillis* (1974), 18 C.C.C. (2d) 190, a decision of the Nova Scotia Supreme Court, Appeal Division. The second is *R. v. Rendall* (1975), 21 C.C.C. (2d) 253, which was a judgment of His Honour Judge Vannini of the Algoma District Court. The defence was also rejected by the Manitoba Court of Appeal in *R. v. Brydon*, 21 C.C.C. (2d) 513. On the other hand, the defence has been specifically allowed in other strict liability offences in Canada. One of those is *R. v. V.K. Mason Construction Ltd.*, [1968] 3 C.C.C. 62, which is a decision of my brother Lieff, in a case involving the Ontario *Construction Safety Act*. Another is *R. v. A.O. Pope Ltd.* (1973), 20 C.R.N.S. 159 [affirmed 10 C.C.C. (2d) 430], which is a judgment of His Honour Judge Keirstead in the New Brunswick County Court and was a decision involving the New Brunswick *Industrial Safety Act*.

The availability of the defence of honest belief upon reasonable grounds in a state of facts which if true would have rendered the accused's act an innocent one, as a defence in Ontario has been stated by the Court of Appeal for Ontario on more than one occasion.

In *R. v. McIver, supra*, four of the five Judges of that Court who decided that case said that the defence was available. The Court was composed of Porter C.J.O., Roach, Gibson, MacKay and Kelly JJ.A. The case was a significant one involving important principles of law and for that reason it was decided by a five-man Court. Among other issues, the Court had to determine whether the offence of careless driving, which was then contained in s. 60 of the *Highway Traffic Act*, R.S.O. 1960, c. 162, was an offence of strict liability. Porter C.J.O., wrote the judgment of the Court which held that the offence of careless driving was one of strict liability. MacKay J.A., wrote a judgment with which the other three Judges agreed. He expressed agreement with the reasons and conclusions of the Chief Justice on the issue of strict liability.

I pause here to mention that while one's first impression might be that the judgment of MacKay J.A., was *obiter dicta*, on more careful consideration, I am of the opinion that it was not intended to be mere *obiter dicta*. While it may be that his judgment was not the *ratio decidendi* of the case, it clearly was intended to be an important pronouncement on the law of careless driving in this Province. Up until that decision it had not been the general opinion of members of the profession that the offence of careless driving was one of strict liability.

Since the offence was one that was frequently before the Courts in Ontario, I am certain that MacKay, Roach, Gibson and Kelly JJ.A., intended to outline the law of strict liability for the guidance of those members of the profession who would be prosecuting or defending such charges and for the guidance of the Courts that would be adjudicating upon them. Their judgment was a vitally important declaration of the law to enable the Courts and the profession to know what types of defences would still be legally available to the offence of careless driving which was now judicially determined to be one of strict liability. For these reasons, it appears to me that the judgment of MacKay J.A., is not mere *obiter dicta*, but is a pronouncement of the law of the Province of Ontario which this Court ought to follow.

. . . .

While that excerpt relates principally to the onus of proof which rests upon an accused of establishing a defence to a strict liability offence, I note that the Australian cases to which he refers with approval are those which are the foundation of the defence of honest mistake upon reasonable grounds. It also is clear that the Court pronounced that in the case of the strict liability offence there under consideration the defence of absence of negligence was specifically held to be open to an accused. It also appears to me implicit in that excerpt that MacKay J.A., and those Judges on whose behalf he spoke considered that the defence of honest mistake on reasonabie grounds was a valid legal defence to a charge of an offence of strict liability.

A few years after *R. v. McIver, supra*, MacKay J.A., speaking for the Ontario Court of Appeal had further opportunity to comment upon the defence of honest mistake on reasonable grounds. In *R. v. Custeau*, 6 C.C.C. (2d) 179, 17 C.R.N.S. 127, when giving the judgment of the Court, he said at p. 180 C.C.C.:

> In the case of an offence of strict liability (sometimes referred to as absolute liability), it has been held to be a defence if it is found that the defendant honestly believed on reasonable grounds in a state of facts which if true would render his act an innocent one.

. . . It is my view that it is appropriate that this Court be very strongly guided by the strong statements relating to this defence made by the Ontario Court of Appeal.

In *R. v. Gillis* (1974), 18 C.C.C. (2d) 190, the Nova Scotia Supreme Court Appeal Division was of the opinion that the issue had been conclusively decided by the Supreme Court of Canada in *Hill v. The Queen*, 14 C.C.C. (2d) 505, [1975] 2 S.C.R. 402. If the matter is conclusively determined by *Hill*, then of course this Court must follow that decision.

. . . .

In my opinion, that case does not decide the issue of whether that defence is or is not available as a matter of law in strict liability cases. I do not think that the Supreme Court of Canada has considered what the result in the *Hill* case would have been had Mrs. Hill had an honest belief on reasonable grounds that she had not in fact been involved in an accident. If that had been the issue before the Supreme Court of Canada and the statement of Dickson J., quoted above had been made by the majority, then, in my opinion, the defence of honest mistake on reasonable grounds would not be available as a defence to a charge involving an offence of strict liability. However, that not being the issue before that Court, in my opinion that defence is not foreclosed by that decision.

Submissions were made to this Court about the difficulties involved in the prosecution of speeding cases and other strict liability offences if this defence is a valid one in law. In my opinion, the availability of the defence as a matter of law should make no unreasonable burden upon the prosecution or the Courts. It is clear from the Australian authorities that not only is the burden of proving such a defence upon the accused, he must prove it upon a balance of probabilities. It is not sufficient merely to raise a reasonable doubt. In this respect, the defence of mistake when raised as a defence to an offence of strict liability is very different than is the defence of mistake of fact when it is raised in a case involving *mens rea* as an essential ingredient of the offence. In the former case, the mistake of fact must not only be an honest one, but it must be based on reasonable grounds and it must be proved by the accused on the balance of probabilities. In the latter case the defence need only be an honest one and need not necessarily be based upon reasonable grounds and it need only cause the Court to have a reasonable doubt: see *R. v. Morgan et al.*, [1975] 2 W.L.R. 913 (H.L.) and *Beaver v. The Queen*, 118 C.C.C. 129, [1957] S.C.R. 531, 26 C.R. 193.

In strict liability cases such as this, it will be the duty of the trial Court, assuming the essential factual elements of the Crown's case are proved, to determine whether on the balance of probabilities the accused has satisfied it that he honestly and upon reasonable grounds believed in a state of facts which if they had been true would have made his conduct innocent. The resolution of that kind of factual problem is made all the time by trial Courts and should give no particular difficulty to a Court or prosecutor.

Accordingly, I am of the opinion that the appellant legally had available to him the defence that he honestly believed on reasonable grounds in a state of facts which if true would have rendered his act an innocent one and that he was entitled to have that defence adjudicated upon. The failure of the learned trial Judge to adjudicate upon that defence amounted to an error in law.

The application for leave is therefore granted. The appeal is allowed. The conviction is set aside and the case is remitted to Judge Campbell to adjudicate upon the defence of honest mistake of fact based upon reasonable grounds.

ESTEY C.J.H.C. (dissenting): —

. . . .

The authorities which are said to support the majority view stem from some Australian decisions which appear to classify offence-creating statutes into three categories:

(a) *Group 1*: Those statutes which require the prosecutor to prove affirmatively beyond a reasonable doubt a *mens rea*, that is an attempt to commit the offence.

(b) *Group 2*: Those statutes which prohibit a specified act or omission but which are interpreted to permit the accused a complete defence if he can prove on the balance of probabilities an honest belief, held on reasonable grounds, in a mistaken set of facts which, if true, would render his act or omission innocent. This midway point is sometimes referred to as "strict liability".

(c) *Group 3*: Those statutes creating offences of strict liability where it is not open to the defendant to exculpate himself by showing that he acted reasonably and without any blameworthy state of mind.

The Courts and authors in discussing these issues appear to have divided "strict liability" into categories (b) and (c) above. It might lead to less misunderstanding and more certainty if category (c) above were described as "absolute liability".

. . . .

The *Highway Traffic Act* evidences the clearest legislative intent and purpose of establishing a simple code of rules for the conduct of people who by their own volition take recourse to the highways in motor vehicles. The statute imposes precise speed limitations for varying types of highway, road conditions and other express considerations. The statute does not require the user of a vehicle, except a bus, on the highway to equip himself with any particular device to assist in the determination of his speed. The driver is left to make that determination on his own. He may proceed by instinct, by instruments, or by any way he chooses. Furthermore, other members of the public using the highway at the same time must be entitled to confidently rely upon the adherence by all highway travellers to this simple code of conduct. The specific offence is created by the words "no person shall drive a motor vehicle at a greater speed than . . . 50 miles per hour . . . 30 miles per hour . . . 15 miles per hour . . ." depending upon either the type of highway, its location with reference to built-up areas, the presence of railway crossings and other works, the nature of the vehicle itself or other considerations. The language could not be more precise or, indeed, more abrupt unless the Legislature, in order to create an offence of the third category, were to go to the extent of adding at the end of such a clause words to the effect "and there shall be no defence available to any person who exceeds the aforementioned speed limits".

The activities regulated by this statute generally, and s. 82 in particular, are commonplace actions undertaken by the populous generally and daily. The general public has at great expense created the highway system for the purpose of safe and convenient inter-communication and transportation. Effective and simple regulation is necessary in order to achieve intensive, economic and efficient use of the road system; hence the precise prescription of a scale of speed limits.

Apart from all other considerations this code of conduct for the use of highways reveals a constant realization on the part of the Legislature of the need for strict regulation for the purposes of safety. Indeed, a perusal of the statute reveals that safety is the most pervasive characteristic in all the Regulations found in the statute for the use of highways. The safety of other users of the highway can hardly be promoted by a subjective test of the propriety of the conduct of an individual in violation of a clearly proscribed act. There is, of course, in this day and age no stigma whatever attached to the violation of the simplest speed limits and, perhaps the only stigma which can be associated with convictions under s. 82 would be those associated with acts of gross misconduct such as high speed escapes from police, or gross speed violations in built-up areas. The violations of the limited magnitude which would support the argument of honest and reasonable mistake of fact would not on conviction, in my view, attract any stigma in the present day community. What may be of consideration, however, is the position of the law in the eyes of the community, which would include all those involved in the regular administration of justice as it applies to highway traffic offences, of simple speeding offences encumbered by the creation of a defence of honest and reasonable belief where the limits have been so clearly and precisely imposed because of the needs of the community as expressed in detail in the offence creating provision.

For all these reasons I reach the conclusion in this alternative course of examination of the statute that s. 82 creates a strict liability affording no defence of honest and reasonable mistake of fact or, in other terminology, an absolute liability. It is interesting to note that while category (b) seems to have originated in Australia some time ago, there are no reported cases where such a defence has been recognized by the Australian Courts in proceedings under speed regulation statutes.

Therefore, in my view, the law of this Province, interpreted in *Hill v. The Queen*, recognizes no midway point or second category of offences in the field of strict liability and, alternatively, if such a concept has been imported into our law, then the statutory provision in question has not established or given rise to any such defence. I would therefore dismiss the appeal.

Appeal allowed; conviction set aside.

After this extensive litigation and difference of opinion, the Ontario Court of Appeal literally took a few sentences to dispose of the defence in the case of speeding.

R. v. HICKEY

(1976), 30 C.C.C. (2d) 416 (Ont. C.A.)

JESSUP J.A.: — Assuming, without deciding, that statutory offences can be classified into one of three groups as mentioned by Estey C.J.H.C., in his judgment given in the Divisional Court, we are of the opinion that the offence here in question, of speeding, under the *Highway Traffic Act*, R.S.O. 1970, c. 202, is a statutory offence within the third group mentioned by Estey C.J.H.C.; that is one of absolute liability in the sense that reasonable mistake of fact is not a defence.

Accordingly, on any view of the law, we think that the conviction was properly entered by the learned Judge of first instance. In the result the appeal is allowed, the judgment of the Divisional Court is set aside and the conviction registered is restored.

R. v. CITY OF SAULT STE. MARIE

[1978] 2 S.C.R. 1299, 3 C.R. (3d) 30, 40 C.C.C. (2d) 353

DICKSON J.: — In the present appeal the Court is concerned with offences variously referred to as "statutory", "public welfare", "regulatory", "absolute liability", or "strict responsibility", which are not criminal in any real sense, but are prohibited in the public interest: *Sherras v. De Rutzen*, [1895] 1 Q.B. 918. Although enforced as penal laws through the utilization of the machinery of the criminal law, the offences are in substance of a civil nature and might well be regarded as a branch of administrative law to which traditional principles of criminal law have but limited application. They relate to such everyday matters as traffic infractions, sales of impure food, violations of liquor laws, and the like. In this appeal we are concerned with pollution.

The doctrine of the guilty mind expressed in terms of intention or recklessness, but not negligence, is at the foundation of the law of crimes. In the case of true crimes there is a presumption that a person should not be held liable for the wrongfulness of his act if that act is without *mens rea*: *R. v. Prince* (1875), L.R. 2 C.C.R. 154; *R. v. Tolson* (1889), 23 Q.B.D. 168; *R. v. Rees*, 115 C.C.C. 1, [1956] S.C.R. 640; *Beaver v. The Queen*, 118 C.C.C. 129, [1957] S.C.R. 531, 26 C.R. 193; *R. v. King*, 133 C.C.C. 1, [1962] S.C.R. 746. Blackstone made the point over two hundred years ago in words still apt: "to constitute a crime against human laws, there must be, first, a vicious will; and secondly, an unlawful act consequent upon such vicious will . . .": see *Commentaries on the Laws of England* (1809), Book IV, 15th ed., c. 15, p. 21. I would emphasize at the outset that nothing in the discussion which follows is intended to dilute or erode that basic principle.

. . . .

The City of Sault Ste. Marie was charged that it did discharge, or cause to be discharged, or permitted to be discharged, or deposited materials into Cannon Creek and Root River, or on the shore or bank thereof, or in such place along the side that might impair the quality of the water in Cannon Creek and Root River, between March 13, 1972 and September 11, 1972. The charge was laid under s.

32(1) of the *Ontario Water Resources Act*, R.S.O. 1970, c. 332, [formerly *Ontario Water Resources Commission Act*, renamed by 1972, c. 1, s. 70(1)] which provides, so far as relevant, that every municipality or person that discharges, or deposits, or causes, or permits the discharge or deposit of any material of any kind into any water course, or on any shore or bank thereof, or in any place that may impair the quality of water, is guilty of an offence and, on summary conviction, is liable on first conviction to a fine of not more than $5,000 and on each subsequent conviction to a fine of not more than $10,000, or to imprisonment for a term of not more than one year, or to both fine and imprisonment.

Although the facts do not rise above the routine, the proceedings have to date had the anxious consideration of five Courts. The City was acquitted in Provincial Court (Criminal Division), but convicted following a trial *de novo* on a Crown appeal. A further appeal, by the City, to the Divisional Court was allowed and the conviction quashed. The Court of Appeal for Ontario on yet another appeal directed a new trial. Because of the importance of the legal issues, this Court granted leave to the Crown to appeal and leave to the City to cross-appeal.

To relate briefly the facts, the City on November 18, 1970, entered into an agreement with Cherokee Disposal and Construction Co. Ltd., for the disposal of all refuse originating in the City. Under the terms of the agreement, Cherokee became obligated to furnish a site and adequate labour, material and equipment. The site selected bordered Cannon Creek which, it would appear, runs into the Root River. The method of disposal adopted is known as the "area", or "continuous slope" method of sanitary land fill, whereby garbage is compacted in layers which are covered each day by natural sand or gravel.

Prior to 1970, the site had been covered with a number of fresh-water springs that flowed into Cannon Creek. Cherokee dumped material to cover and submerge these springs and then placed garbage and wastes over such material. The garbage and wastes in due course formed a high mound sloping steeply toward, and within 20 ft. of, the creek. Pollution resulted. Cherokee was convicted of a breach of s. 32(1) of the *Ontario Water Resources Act*, the section under which the City has been charged. The question now before the Court is whether the City is also guilty of an offence under that section.

In dismissing the charge at first instance, the Judge found that the City had had nothing to do with the actual disposal operations, that Cherokee was an independent contractor and its employees were not employees of the City. On the appeal *de novo* Judge Vannini found the offence to be one of strict liability and he convicted. The Divisional Court in setting aside the judgment found that the charge was duplicitous. As a secondary point, the Divisional Court also held that the charge required *mens rea* with respect to causing or permitting a discharge. When the case reached the Court of Appeal that Court held that the conviction could not be quashed on the ground of duplicity, because there had been no challenge to the information at trial. The Court of Appeal agreed, however, that the charge was one requiring proof of *mens rea*. A majority of the Court (Brooke and Howland JJ.A.) held there was not sufficient evidence to establish *mens rea* and ordered a new trial. In the view of Mr. Justice Lacourcière, dissenting, the inescapable inference to be drawn from the findings of fact of Judge Vannini was that the City had known of the potential impairment of waters of Cannon Creek and Root River and had failed to exercise its clear powers of control.

The divers, and diverse, judicial opinions to date on the points under consideration reflect the dubiety in these branches of the law.

. . . .

The mens rea point

The distinction between the true criminal offence and the public welfare offence is one of prime importance. Where the offence is criminal, the Crown must establish a mental element, namely, that the accused who committed the prohibited act did so intentionally or recklessly, with knowledge of the facts constituting the offence, or with wilful blindness toward them. Mere negligence is excluded from the concept of the mental element required for conviction. Within the context of a criminal prosecution a person who fails to make such inquiries as a reasonable and prudent person would make, or who fails to know facts he should have known, is innocent in the eyes of the law.

In sharp contrast, "absolute liability" entails conviction on proof merely that the defendant committed the prohibited act constituting the *actus reus* of the offence. There is no relevant mental element. It is no defence that the accused was entirely without fault. He may be morally innocent in every sense, yet be branded as a malefactor and punished as such.

Public welfare offences obviously lie in a field of conflicting values. It is essential for society to maintain, through effective enforcement, high standards of public health and safety. Potential victims of those who carry on latently pernicious activities have a strong claim to consideration. On the other hand, there is a generally held revulsion against punishment of the morally innocent.

Public welfare offences evolved in mid-19th century Britain (*R. v. Woodrow* (1846), 15 M. & W. 404, and *R. v. Stephens* (1866), L.R. 1 Q.B. 702) as a means of doing away with the requirement of *mens rea* for petty police offences. The concept was a judicial creation, founded on expediency. That concept is now firmly embedded in the concrete of Anglo-American and Canadian jurisprudence, its importance heightened by the ever-increasing complexities of modern society.

Various arguments are advanced in justification of absolute liability in public welfare offences. Two predominate. Firstly, it is argued that the protection of social interests requires a high standard of care and attention on the part of those who follow certain pursuits and such persons are more likely to be stimulated to maintain those standards if they know that ignorance or mistake will not excuse them. The removal of any possible loophole acts, it is said, as an incentive to take precautionary measures beyond what would otherwise be taken, in order that mistakes and mishaps be avoided. The second main argument is one based on administrative efficiency. Having regard to both the difficulty of proving mental culpability and the number of petty cases which daily come before the Courts, proof of fault is just too great a burden in time and money to place upon the prosecution. To require proof of each person's individual intent would allow almost every violator to escape. This, together with the glut of work entailed in proving *mens rea* in every case would clutter the docket and impede adequate enforcement as virtually to nullify the regulatory acts statutes. In short, absolute liability, it is contended, is the most efficient and effective way of ensuring compliance with minor regulatory legislation and the social ends to be achieved are of such importance as to override the unfortunate by-product of punishing those who may be free of moral turpitude. In further justification, it is urged that slight penalties are usually imposed and that conviction for breach of a public welfare offence does not carry the stigma associated with conviction for a criminal offence.

Arguments of greater force are advanced against absolute liability. The most telling is that it violates fundamental principles of penal liability. It also rests upon assumptions which have not been, and cannot be, empirically established. There is no evidence that a higher standard of care results from absolute liability. If a person is already taking every reasonable precautionary measure, is he likely to take additional measures, knowing that however much care he takes, it will not serve as a defence in the event of breach? If he has exercised care and skill, will conviction have a deterrent effect upon him or others? Will the injustice of conviction lead to cynicism and disrespect for the law, on his part and on the part of others? These are among the questions asked. The argument that no stigma attaches does not withstand analysis, for the accused will have suffered loss of time, legal costs, exposure to the processes of the criminal law at trial and, however one may downplay it, the opprobrium of conviction. It is not sufficient to say that the public interest is engaged and, therefore, liability may be imposed without fault. In serious crimes, the public interest is involved and *mens rea* must be proven. The administrative argument has little force. In sentencing, evidence of due diligence is admissible and therefore the evidence might just as well be heard when considering guilt. Additionally, it may be noted that s. 198 of the *Alberta Highway Traffic Act*, R.S.A. 1970, c. 169, provides that upon a person being charged with an offence under this Act, if the Judge trying the case is of the opinion that the offence (a) was committed wholly by accident or misadventure and without negligence, and (b) could not by the exercise of reasonable care or precaution have been avoided, the Judge may dismiss the case. See also s. 230(2) [am. 1976, c. 62, s. 48] of the Manitoba *Highway Traffic Act*, R.S.M. 1970, c. H60, which has a similar effect. In these instances at least, the Legislature has indicated that administrative efficiency does not foreclose inquiry as to fault. It is also worthy of note that historically the penalty for breach of statutes enacted for the regulation of individual conduct in the interests of health and safety was minor, $20 or $25; today, it may amount to thousands of dollars and entail the possibility of imprisonment for a second conviction. The present case is an example.

Public welfare offences involve a shift of emphasis from the protection of individual interests to the protection of public and social interests: see F.B. Sayre, "Public Welfare Offenses", 33 *Columbia Law Rev.* 55 (1933); Hall, *General Principles of Criminal Law* (1947), c. 13, p. 427; R.M. Perkins, "Civil Offense", 100 *U. of Pa. L. Rev.* 832 (1952); Jobson, "Far From Clear", 18 *Crim. L.Q.* 294 (1975-76). The unfortunate tendency in many past cases has been to see the choice as between two stark alternatives: (i) full *mens rea*; or (ii) absolute liability. In respect of public welfare offences (within which category pollution offences fall) where full *mens rea* is not required, absolute liability has often been imposed. English jurisprudence has consistently maintained this dichotomy: see "Criminal Law, Evidence and Procedure", 11 Hals., 4th ed., pp. 20-2, para. 18. There has, however, been an attempt in Australia, in many Canadian Courts, and indeed in England, to seek a middle position, fulfilling the goals of public welfare offences while still not punishing the entirely blameless. There is an increasing and impressive stream of authority which holds that where an offence does not require full *mens rea*, it is nevertheless a good defence for the defendant to prove that he was not negligent.

Dr. Glanville Williams has written: "There is a half-way house between *mens rea* and strict responsibility which has not yet been properly utilized, and that is responsibility for negligence" (*Criminal Law: General Part*, 2nd ed. (1961), p. 262.) Morris and Howard, in *Studies in Criminal Law* (1964), p. 200, suggest that strict responsibility might with advantage be replaced by a doctrine of responsibility for negligence strengthened by a shift in the burden of proof. The defendant would be allowed to exculpate himself by proving affirmatively that he was not negligent. Professor Howard ("Strict Responsibility in the High Court of Australia", 76 *L.Q.R.* 547 (1960)) offers the comment that English law of strict responsibility in minor statutory offences is distinguished only by its irrationality, and then has this to say in support of the position taken by the Australian High Court, at p. 548:

> Over a period of nearly sixty years since its inception the High Court has adhered with consistency to the principle that there should be no criminal responsibility without fault, however minor the offence. It has done so by utilizing the very half-way house to which Dr. Williams refers, responsibility for negligence.

In his work, "Public Welfare Offenses", at p. 78, Professor Sayre suggests that if the penalty is really slight involving, for instance, a maximum fine of $25, particularly if adequate enforcement depends upon wholesale prosecution, or if the social danger arising from violation is serious, the doctrine of basing liability upon mere activity rather than fault, is sound. He continues, however, at p. 79:

> On the other hand, some public welfare offenses involve a possible penalty of imprisonment or heavy fine. In such cases it would seem sounder policy to maintain the orthodox requirement of a guilty mind but to shift the burden of proof to the shoulders of the defendant to establish his lack of a guilty intent if he can. For public welfare offenses defendants may be convicted by proof of the mere act of violation; but, if the offense involves a possible prison penalty, the defendant should not be denied the right of bringing forward affirmative evidence to prove that the violation was the result of no fault on his part.

and at p. 82:

> It is fundamentally unsound to convict a defendant for a crime involving a substantial term of imprisonment without giving him the opportunity to prove that his action was due to an honest and reasonable mistake of fact or that he acted without guilty intent. If the public danger is widespread and serious, the practical situation can be met by shifting to the shoulders of the defendant the burden of proving a lack of guilty intent.

The doctrine proceeds on the assumption that the defendant could have avoided the *prima facie* offence through the exercise of reasonable care and he is given the opportunity of establishing, if he can, that he did in fact exercise such care.

The case which gave the lead in this branch of the law is the Australian case of *Proudman v. Dayman* (1941), 67 C.L.R. 536, where Dixon J., said, at p. 540:

> It is one thing to deny that a necessary ingredient of the offence is positive knowledge of the fact that the driver holds no subsisting licence. It is another to say that an honest belief founded on reasonable grounds that he is licensed cannot exculpate a person who permits him to drive. As a general rule an honest and reasonable belief in a state of facts which, if they existed, would make the defendant's act innocent affords an excuse for doing what would otherwise be an offence.

This case, and several others like it, speak of the defence as being that of reasonable mistake of fact. The reason is that the offences in question have generally turned on the possession by a person or place of an unlawful status, and the accused's defence was that he reasonably did not know of this status: *e.g.*, permitting an unlicensed person to drive, or lacking a valid licence oneself, or being the owner of property in a dangerous condition. In such cases, negligence consists of an unreasonable failure to know the facts which constitute the offence. It is clear, however, that in principle the defence is that all reasonable care was taken. In other circumstances, the issue will be whether the accused's behaviour was negligent in bringing about the forbidden event when he knew the relevant facts. Once the defence of reasonable mistake of fact is accepted, there is no barrier to acceptance of the other constituent part of a defence of due diligence.

The principle which has found acceptance in Australia since *Proudman v. Dayman, supra,* has a place also in the jurisprudence of New Zealand: see *The Queen v. Strawbridge*, [1970] N.Z.L.R. 909; *The King v. Ewart* (1905), 25 N.Z.L.R. 709.

In the House of Lords case of *Sweet v. Parsley*, [1970] A.C. 132, Lord Reid noted the difficulty presented by the simplistic choice between *mens rea* in the full sense and an absolute offence. He looked approvingly at attempts to find a middle ground, Lord Pearce, in the same case, referred to the "sensible half-way house" which he thought the Courts should take in some so-called absolute offences. The difficulty, as Lord Pearce saw it, lay in the opinion of Viscount Sankey L.C. in *Woolmington v. Director of Public Prosecutions*, [1935] A.C. 462, if the full width of that opinion were maintained. Lord Diplock, however, took a different and, in my opinion, a preferable view, at p. 164:

> *Woolmington's* case did not decide anything so irrational as that the prosecution must call evidence to prove the absence of any mistaken belief by the accused in the existence of facts which, if true, would make the act innocent, any more than it decided that the prosecution must

call evidence to prove the absence of any claim of right in charge of larceny. The jury is entitled to presume that the accused acted with knowledge of the facts, unless there is some evidence to the contrary originating from the accused who alone can know on what belief he acted and on what ground the belief, if mistaken, was held.

In *Woolmington's* case the question was whether the trial Judge was correct in directing the jury that the accused was required to prove his innocence. Viscount Sankey L.C. referred to the strength of the presumption of innocence in a criminal case and then made the statement, universally accepted in this country, that there is no burden on the prisoner to prove his innocence; it is sufficient for him to raise a doubt as to his guilt. I do not understand the case as standing for anything more than that. It is to be noted that the case is concerned with criminal offences in the true sense; it is not concerned with public welfare offences. It is somewhat ironic that *Woolmington's* case, which embodies a principle for the benefit of the accused, should be used to justify the rejection of a defence of reasonable care for public welfare offences and the retention of absolute liability, which affords the accused no defence at all. There is nothing in *Woolmington's* case, as I comprehend it, which stands in the way of adoption, in respect of regulatory offences, of a defence of due care, with burden of proof resting on the accused to establish the defence on the balance of probabilities.

There have been several cases in Ontario which open the way to acceptance of a defence of due diligence. In *R. v. McIver*, [1965] 4 C.C.C. 182, 45 C.R. 401, the Court of Appeal held that the offence charged, namely, careless driving, was one of strict liability, but that it was open to an accused to show that he had a reasonable belief in facts which, if true, would have rendered the act innocent. MacKay J.A., who wrote for the Court, relied upon *Sherras v. De Rutzen*, [1895] 1 Q.B. 918; *Proudman v. Dayman, supra*; *Maher v. Musson* (1934), 52 C.L.R. 100, and *R. v. Patterson*, [1962] 1 All E.R. 340, in availing an accused the opportunity of explanation in the case of statutory offences that do not by their terms require proof of intent. The following two short passages from the judgment might be quoted (at pp. 189-90 C.C.C.):

> On a charge laid under s. 60 of the *Highway Traffic Act*, it is open to the accused as a defence, to show an absence of negligence on his part. For example, that his conduct was caused by the negligence of some other person, or by showing that the cause was a mechanical failure, or other circumstance, that he could not reasonably have foreseen.

> . . . .

> In the present case it was open to the accused to show, if he could, that the collision of his car with the car parked on the shoulder of the road, occurred without fault or negligence on his part. He having failed to do so was properly convicted.

An appeal to this Court was dismissed, [1966] 2 C.C.C. 289n, [1966] S.C.R. 254, 48 C.R. 4, on other grounds.

Later, in *R. v. Custeau*, 6 C.C.C. (2d) 179, 17 C.R.N.S. 127, MacKay J.A., again speaking for the Court, returned to the same point, at p. 180 C.C.C.:

> In the case of an offence of strict liability (sometimes referred to as absolute liability), it has been held to be a defence if it is found that the defendant honestly believed on reasonable grounds in a state of facts which if true would render his act an innocent one.

In the British Columbia Court of Appeal the concept of reasonable care was discussed in *R. v. Laroque* (1958), 120 C.C.C. 246, 28 C.R. 331 (selling liquor to an interdicted person contrary to a provincial statute) by Mr. Justice Sheppard, speaking for the Court, at p. 247:

> That test has been defined in *Bank of New South Wales v. Piper*, [1897] A.C. 383 at pp. 389-90 as follows: "On the other hand, the absence of *mens rea* really consists in an honest and reasonable belief entertained by the accused of the existence of facts which, if true, would make the act charged against him innocent."
>
> The onus would therefore be upon the accused to show not merely that he did not know that Pierre was an interdicted person but also that he, the accused, had used honest and reasonable efforts to become acquainted with the information supplied by the Department and to comply therewith and that notwithstanding such efforts he had an honest and reasonable belief that Pierre was not an interdicted person.

In an early Saskatchewan Court of Appeal decision in *R. v. Regina Cold Storage & Forwarding Co. Ltd.*, 41 C.C.C. 21 (unlawful possession of liquor) it was held that *mens rea* was an essential element for conviction and that element was absent. Chief Justice Haultain appears to have conceptualized absence of *mens rea*, not as lack of knowledge or intent but rather in terms of reasonable care in an offence of strict liability. He said, at p. 23 C.C.C.: "Absence of *mens rea* means an honest and reasonable belief by the accused in the existence of facts which, if true, would make the charge against him innocent".

In the New Brunswick case of *R. v. A.O. Pope Ltd.* (1972), 20 C.R.N.S. 159 (failing to provide properly fitted goggles contrary to the *Industrial Safety Act, 1964* (N.B.), c. 5) Keirstead Co. Ct. J. held that the offence was one of strict but not absolute liability, and a defence of reasonable care was open to the accused to prove that the act was done without negligence or fault on his part. An appeal to the New Brunswick Supreme Court, Appeal Division, was dismissed (10 C.C.C. (2d) 430) without, however, any discussion of this issue.

Two more recent cases, one being from the Province of Ontario and the other from the Province of Alberta, deserve attention. In *R. v. Hickey* (1976), 29 C.C.C. (2d) 23 (speeding), the Divisional Court held that the offence was one of strict liability, but that the accused would have a valid defence if he proved on the balance of probabilities that he honestly believed on reasonable grounds in a mistaken set of facts which, if true, would have made his conduct innocent. The accused had testified that he honestly believed because of the speedometer reading that he was not exceeding the speed limit. A test conducted by a police officer at the scene showed that the speedometer was, in fact, not working properly. The majority of the Court, therefore, set aside the conviction. Mr. Justice Galligan made the following comment, at pp. 36-7 C.C.C.:

> Submissions were made to this Court about the difficulties involved in the prosecution of speeding cases and other strict liability offences if this defence is a valid one in law. In my opinion, the availability of the defence as a matter of law should make no unreasonable burden upon the prosecution or the Courts. It is clear from the Australian authorities that not only is the burden of proving such a defence upon the accused, he must prove it upon a balance of probabilities. It is not sufficient merely to raise a reasonable doubt. In this respect, the defence of mistake when raised as a defence to an offence of strict liability is very different than is the

defence of mistake of fact when it is raised in a case involving *mens rea* as an essential ingredient of the offence. In the former case, the mistake of fact must not only be an honest one, but it must be based on reasonable grounds and it must be proved by the accused on the balance of probabilities. In the latter case the defence need only be an honest one and need not necessarily be based upon reasonable grounds and it need only cause the Court to have a reasonable doubt: see *R. v. Morgan et al.*, [1975] 2 W.L.R. 913 (H.L.) and *Beaver v. The Queen*, 118 C.C.C. 129, [1957] S.C.R. 531, 26 C.R. 193.

The decision in *Hickey* was subsequently appealed to the Court of Appeal, 30 C.C.C. (2d) 416. The Court allowed the appeal and restored the conviction. Mr. Justice Jessup, in giving judgment for the Court, said [*loc. cit.* (C.C.C.]:

> Assuming, without deciding, that statutory offences can be classified into one of three groups mentioned by Estey C.J.H.C., in his judgment given in the Divisional Court, we are of the opinion that the offence here in question, of speeding, under the *Highway Traffic Act*, R.S.O. 1970, c. 202, is a statutory offence within the third group mentioned by Estey C.J.H.C.; that is one of absolute liability in the sense that reasonable mistake of fact is not a defence.

No reasons were given for the identification of the offence as one of absolute liability once the three groups of statutory offences were assumed to exist.

In the Appellate Division of the Alberta Supreme Court, the defence of reasonable care for an offence of strict liability was accepted after full consideration of the issues involved, in the recent case of *R. v. Servico Ltd.* (1977), 2 Alta. L.R. (2d) 388. The offence in question was that an employer "shall not permit a person under the full age of 18 years to work during the period of time prohibited by this section." Mr. Justice Morrow, writing for the majority of the Court, said, at p. 397:

> While the language of the particular regulation under review does in my view come within the category of absolute or strict liability offences, I am also of the opinion that the general language used — particularly with the inclusion of the word "permit", which has a connotation suggesting some intent is to be considered — brings this section into what probably can be described as the exception to the rule of absoluteness as suggested by Estey C.J.H.C. in his dissenting judgment in *Regina v. Hickey* (1976), 29 C.C.C. (2d) 63, reversed 30 C.C.C. (2d) 416 (C.A.), where at p. 580 he describes statutes which prohibit a specified act or omission but which are interpreted to permit the defence of an honest belief held on reasonable grounds in a mistaken set of facts which if true would render the act or omission innocent.
>
> The above exception or type of defence has long been recognized in Australia.

It is interesting to note the recommendations made by the Law Reform Commission to the Minister of Justice (*Our Criminal Law*) in March, 1976. The Commission advises (p. 32) that (i) every offence outside the *Criminal Code* be recognized as admitting of a defence of due diligence; (ii) in the case of any such offence for which intent or recklessness is not specifically required the onus of proof should lie on the defendant to establish such defence; (iii) the defendant would have to prove this on the preponderance or balance of probabilities. The recommendation endorsed a working paper (*Meaning of Guilt: Strict Liability*, June 20, 1974), in which it was stated that negligence should be the minimum standard of liability in regulatory offences, that such offences were (p. 32):

to promote higher standards of care in business, trade and industry, higher standards of
honesty in commerce and advertising, higher standards of respect for the . . . environment
and [therefore] the . . . offence is basically and typically an offence of negligence;

that an accused should never be convicted of a regulatory offence if he
establishes that he acted with due diligence, that is, that he was not negligent. In
the working paper, the Commission further stated (p. 33), ". . . let us recognize
the regulatory offence for what it is — an offence of negligence — and frame
the law to ensure that guilt depends upon lack of reasonable care". The view is
expressed that in regulatory law, to make the defendant disprove negligence —
prove due diligence — would be both justifiable and desirable.

In an interesting article on the matter now under discussion, "Far From
Clear", *supra*, Professor Jobson refers to a series of recent cases, arising
principally under s. 32(1) of the *Ontario Water Resources Act*, the section at
issue in the present proceedings, which [at p. 297] "openly acknowledged a
defence based on lack of fault or neglect: these cases require proof of the *actus
reus* but then permit the accused to show that he was without fault or had no
opportunity to prevent the harm." The paramount case in the series is *R. v.
Industrial Tankers Ltd.*, [1968] 4 C.C.C. 81, 10 *Crim. L.Q.* 346, in which Judge
Sprague, relying upon *R. v. Hawinda Taverns Ltd.* (1955), 112 C.C.C. 361, and
R. v. Bruin Hotel Co. Ltd. (1954), 109 C.C.C. 174, 19 C.R. 107, held that the
Crown did not need to prove that the accused had *mens rea*, but it did have to
show that the accused had the power and authority to prevent the pollution, and
could have prevented it, but did not do so. Liability rests upon control and the
opportunity to prevent, *i.e.*, that the accused could have and should have
prevented the pollution. In *Industrial Tankers*, the burden was placed on the
Crown to prove lack of reasonable care. To that extent *Industrial Tankers* and s.
32(1) cases which followed it, such as *R. v. Sheridan*, 10 C.C.C. (2d) 545, differ
from other authorities on s. 32(1) which would place upon the accused the
burden of showing as a defence that he did not have control or otherwise could
not have prevented the impairment: see *R. v. Cherokee Disposals &
Construction Ltd.*, 13 C.C.C. (2d) 87; *R. v. Liquid Cargo Lines Ltd.* (1974), 18
C.C.C. (2d) 428, and *R. v. North Canadian Enterprises Ltd.* (1974), 20 C.C.C.
(2d) 242.

The element of control, particularly by those in charge of business activities
which may endanger the public, is vital to promote the observance of regulations
designed to avoid that danger. This control may be exercised by "supervision or
inspection, by improvement of his business methods or by exhorting those
whom he may be expected to influence or control": Lord Evershed in *Lim Chin
Aik v. The Queen*, [1963] A.C. 160 at p. 174. The purpose, Dean Roscoe Pound
has said (*Spirit of the Common Law* (1906)), is to "put pressure upon the
thoughtless and inefficient to do their whole duty in the interest of public health
or safety or morale". As Devlin J. noted in *Reynolds v. G.H. Austin & Sons Ltd.*,
[1951] 2 K.B. 135 at p. 149:

a man may be made responsible for the acts of his servants, or even for defects in his business
arrangements, because it can fairly be said that by such sanctions citizens are induced to keep
themselves and their organizations up to the mark.

Devlin J. added, however:

> if a man is punished because of an act done by another, whom he cannot reasonably be
> expected to influence or control, the law is engaged, not in punishing thoughtlessness or
> inefficiency, and thereby promoting the welfare of the community, but in pouncing on the
> most convenient victim.

The decision of this Court in *The Queen v. Pierce Fisheries Ltd.*, [1970] 5
C.C.C. 193 [1971] S.C.R. 5, is not inconsistent with the concept of a "half-way
house" between *mens rea* and absolute liability. In *Pierce Fisheries* the charge
was that of having possession of undersized lobsters contrary to the Regulations
under the *Fisheries Act*, R.S.C. 1952, c. 119. Two points arise in connection
with the judgment of Ritchie J., who wrote for the majority of the Court. First,
the adoption of what had been said by the Ontario Court of Appeal in *R. v. Pee-
Kay Smallwares Ltd.*, 90 C.C.C. 129 at p. 137, 6 C.R. 28:

> If on a prosecution for the offences created by the Act, the Crown had to prove the evil intent
> of the accused, or if the accused could escape by denying such evil intent, the statute, by which
> it was obviously intended that there should be complete control without the possibility of any
> leaks, would have so many holes in it that in truth it would be nothing more than a legislative
> sieve.

Ritchie J. held that the offence was one in which the Crown, for the reason
indicated in the *Pee-Kay Smallwares* case, did not have to prove *mens rea* in
order to obtain a conviction. This, in my opinion, is the *ratio decidendi* of the
case. Secondly, Ritchie J. did not, however, foreclose the possibility of a
defence. The following passage from the judgment (at p. 205 C.C.C., p. 21
S.C.R.) suggests that a defence of reasonable care might have been open to the
accused, but that in that case care had not been taken to acquire the knowledge
of the facts constituting the offence:

> As employees of the company working on the premises in the shed "where fish is weighed
> and packed" were taking lobsters from boxes "preparatory for packing" in crates, and as some
> of the undersized lobsters were found "in crates ready for shipment", it would not appear to
> have been a difficult matter for some "officer or responsible employee" to acquire knowledge
> of their presence on the premises.

In a later passage Ritchie J. added (at pp. 205-6 C.C.C., p. 22 S.C.R.):

> In this case the respondent knew that it had upwards of 60,000 lbs. of lobsters on its
> premises; it only lacked knowledge as to the small size of some of them, and I do not think
> that the failure of any of its responsible employees to acquire this knowledge affords any
> defence to a charge of violating the provisions of s. 3(1)(*b*) of the *Lobster Fishery Regulations*.

I do not read *Pierce Fisheries* as denying the accused all defences, in particular
the defence that the company had done everything possible to acquire
knowledge of the undersized lobsters. Ritchie J. concluded merely that the
Crown did not have to prove knowledge.

The judgment of this Court in *Hill v. The Queen*, 14 C.C.C. (2d) 505,
[1975] 2 S.C.R. 402, has been interpreted (*R. v. Gillis* (1974), 18 C.C.C. (2d)
190) as imposing absolute liability and denying the driver of a motor vehicle the
right to plead in defence an honest and reasonable belief in a state of facts which,
if true, would have made the act non-culpable. In *Hill*, the appellant was charged

under the *Highway Traffic Act* with failing to remain at the scene of an accident. Her car had "touched" the rear of another vehicle. She did not stop, but drove off, believing no damage had been done. This Court affirmed the conviction, holding that the offence was not one requiring *mens rea*. In that case the essential fact was that an accident had occurred, to the knowledge of Mrs. Hill. Any belief that she might have held as to the extent of the damage could not obliterate that fact, or make it appear that she had reasonable grounds for believing in a state of facts which, if true, would have constituted a defence to the charge. The case does not stand in the way of a defence of reasonable care in a proper case.

We have the situation therefore in which many Courts of this country, at all levels, dealing with public welfare offences favour (i) *not* requiring the Crown to prove *mens rea*, (ii) rejecting the notion that liability inexorably follows upon mere proof of the *actus reus*, excluding any possible defence. The Courts are following the lead set in Australia many years ago and tentatively broached by several English Courts in recent years.

It may be suggested that the introduction of a defence based on due diligence and the shifting of the burden of proof might better be implemented by legislative act. In answer, it should be recalled that the concept of absolute liability and the creation of a jural category of public welfare offences are both the product of the judiciary and not of the Legislature. The development to date of this defence, in the numerous decisions I have referred to, of Courts in this country as well as in Australia and New Zealand, has also been the work of Judges. The present case offers the opportunity of consolidating and clarifying the doctrine.

The correct approach, in my opinion, is to relieve the Crown of the burden of proving *mens rea*, having regard to *Pierce Fisheries* and to the virtual impossibility in most regulatory cases of proving wrongful intention. In a normal case, the accused alone will have knowledge of what he has done to avoid the breach and it is not improper to expect him to come forward with the evidence of due diligence. This is particularly so when it is alleged, for example, that pollution was caused by the activities of a large and complex corporation. Equally, there is nothing wrong with rejecting absolute liability and admitting the defence of reasonable care.

In this doctrine it is not up to the prosecution to prove negligence. Instead, it is open to the defendant to prove that all due care has been taken. This burden falls upon the defendant as he is the only one who will generally have the means of proof. This would not seem unfair as the alternative is absolute liability which denies an accused any defence whatsoever. While the prosecution must prove beyond a reasonable doubt that the defendant committed the prohibited act, the defendant must only establish on the balance of probabilities that he has a defence of reasonable care.

I conclude, for the reasons which I have sought to express, that there are compelling grounds for the recognition of three categories of offences rather than the traditional two:

1. Offences in which *mens rea*, consisting of some positive state of mind such as intent, knowledge, or recklessness, must be proved by the prosecution either as an inference from the nature of the act committed, or by additional evidence.

2. Offences in which there is no necessity for the prosecution to prove the existence of *mens rea*; the doing of the prohibited act *prima facie* imports the offence, leaving it open to the accused to avoid liability by proving that he took all reasonable care. This involves consideration of what a reasonable man would have done in the circumstances. The defence will be available if the accused reasonably believed in a mistaken set of facts which, if true, would render the act or omission innocent, or if he took all reasonable steps to avoid the particular event. These offences may properly be called offences of strict liability. Mr. Justice Estey so referred to them in *Hickey's* case.

3. Offences of absolute liability where it is not open to the accused to exculpate himself by showing that he was free of fault.

Offences which are criminal in the true sense fall in the first category. Public welfare offences would, *prima facie*, be in the second category. They are not subject to the presumption of full *mens rea*. An offence of this type would fall in the first category only if such words as "wilfully", "with intent", "knowingly", or "intentionally" are contained in the statutory provision creating the offence. On the other hand, the principle that punishment should in general not be inflicted on those without fault applies. Offences of absolute liability would be those in respect of which the Legislature had made it clear that guilt would follow proof merely of the proscribed act. The over-all regulatory pattern adopted by the Legislature, the subject-matter of the legislation, the importance of the penalty, and the precision of the language used will be primary considerations in determining whether the offence falls into the third category.

Ontario Water Resources Act, s. 32(1)

Turning to the subject-matter of s. 32(1) — the prevention of pollution of lakes, rivers and streams — it is patent that this is of great public concern. Pollution has always been unlawful and, in itself, a nuisance: *Groat v. City of Edmonton*, [1928] 3 D.L.R. 725, [1928] S.C.R. 522. A riparian owner has an inherent right to have a stream of water "come to him in its natural state, in flow, quantity and quality": *Chasemore v. Richards* (1859), 7 H.L. Cas. 349 at p. 382. Natural streams which formerly afforded "pure and healthy" water for drinking or swimming purposes become little more than cesspools when riparian factory owners and municipal corporations discharge into them filth of all descriptions. Pollution offences are undoubtedly public welfare offences enacted in the interests of public health. There is thus no presumption of a full *mens rea*.

There is another reason, however, why this offence is not subject to a presumption of *mens rea*. The presumption applies only to offences which are "criminal in the true sense", as Ritchie J., said in *the Queen v. Pierce Fisheries, supra*, at p. 199 C.C.C., p. 597 D.L.R., p. 13 S.C.R. The *Ontario Water*

Resources Act is a provincial statute. If it is valid provincial legislation (and no suggestion was made to the contrary), then it cannot possibly create an offence which is criminal in the true sense.

The present case concerns the interpretation of two troublesome words frequently found in public welfare statutes: "cause" and "permit". These two words are troublesome because neither denotes clearly either full *mens rea* nor absolute liability. It is said that a person could not be said to be permitting something unless he knew what he was permitting. This is an over-simplification. There is authority both ways, indicating that the Courts are uneasy with the traditional dichotomy. Some authorities favour the position that "permit" does not import *mens rea*; see *Millar v. The Queen* (1954), 107 C.C.C. 321, 17 C.R. 293; *R. v. Royal Canadian Legion* (1971), 4 C.C.C. (2d) 196; *R. v. Teperman & Sons Ltd.*, [1968] 4 C.C.C. 67; *R. v. Jack Cewe Ltd.* (1975), 23 C.C.C. (2d) 237; *Browning v. J.W.H. Watson (Rochester) Ltd.*, [1953] 1 W.L.R. 1172; *Lyons v. May*, [1948] 2 All E.R. 1062; *Korten v. West Sussex County Council* (1903) , 72 L.J.K.B. 514. For a *mens rea* construction see *James & Son Ltd. v. Smee*, [1955] 1 Q.B. 78; *Somerset v. Hart* (1884), 12 Q.B.C. 360; *Grays Haulage Co. Ltd. v. Arnold*, [1966] 1 All E.R. 896; Smith & Hogan, *Criminal Law*, 3rd ed. (1973), p. 87; Edwards, *Mens Rea and Statutory Offences* (1955), pp. 98-119. The same is true of "cause". For a non-*mens rea* construction, see *R. v. Peconi* (1907), 1 C.C.C. (2d) 213; *Alphacell Ltd. v. Woodward*, [1972] A.C. 824; *Sopp v. Long*, (1969) 1 All E.R. 855; *Laird v. Dobell*, [1906] 1 K.B. 131; *Korten v. West Sussex County Council*, *supra*; *Shave v. Rosner*, [1954] 2 W.L.R. 1057. Others say that "cause" imports a requirement for a *mens rea*: see *Lovelace v. D.P.P.*, [1954] 3 All E.R. 481; *Ross Hillman Ltd. v. Bond*, [1974] 2 All E.R. 287; Smith and Hogan, *Criminal Law*, pp, 89-90.

The Divisional Court of Ontario relied on these latter authorities in concluding that s. 32(1) created a *mens rea* offence.

The conflict in the above authorities, however, shows that in themselves the words "cause" and "permit" fit much better into an offence of strict liability than either full *mens rea* or absolute liability. Since s. 32(1) creates a public welfare offence, without a clear indication that liability is absolute, and without any words such as "knowingly" or "wilfully" expressly to import *mens rea*, application of the criteria which I have outlined above undoubtedly places the offence in the category of strict liability.

Proof of the prohibited act *prima facie* imports the offence, but the accused may avoid liability by proving that he took reasonable care. I am strengthened in this view by the recent case of *R. v. Servico Ltd.* (1977), 2 Alta. L.R. (2d) 388, in which the Appellate Division of the Alberta Supreme Court held that an offence of "permitting" a person under 18 years to work during prohibited hours was an offence of strict liability in the sense which I have described. It also will be recalled that the decisions of many lower Courts which have considered s. 32(1) have rejected absolute liability as the basis for the offence of causing or permitting pollution, and have equally rejected full *mens rea* as an ingredient of the offence.

The present case

As I am of the view that a new trial is necessary, it would be inappropriate to discuss at this time the facts of the present case. It may be helpful, however, to consider in a general way the principles to be applied in determining whether a person or municipality has committed the *actus reus* of discharging, causing, or permitting pollution within the terms of s. 32(1), in particular in connection with pollution from garbage disposal. The prohibited act would, in my opinion, be committed by those who undertake the collection and disposal of garbage, who are in a position to exercise continued control of this activity and prevent the pollution from occurring, but fail to do so. The "discharging" aspect of the offence centres on direct acts of pollution. The "causing" aspect centres on the defendant's active undertaking of something which it is in a position to control and which results in pollution. The "permitting" aspect of the offence centres on the defendant's passive lack of interference or, in other words, its failure to prevent an occurrence which it ought to have foreseen. The close interweaving of the meanings of these terms emphasizes again that s. 32(1) deals with only one generic offence.

When the defendant is a municipality, it is of no avail to it in law that it had no duty to pick up the garbage, s. 354(1), para. 76 of the *Municipal Act*, R.S.O. 1970, c. 284, merely providing that it "may" do so. The law is replete with instances where a person has no duty to act, but where he is subject to certain duties if he does act. The duty here is imposed by s. 32(1) of the *Ontario Water Resources Act*. The position in this respect is no different from that of private persons, corporate or individual, who have no duty to dispose of garbage, but who will incur liability under s. 32(1) if they do so and thereby discharge, cause, or permit pollution.

Nor does liability rest solely on the terms of any agreement by which a defendant arranges for eventual disposal. The test is a factual one, based on an assessment of the defendant's position with respect to the activity which it undertakes and which causes pollution. If it can and should control the activity at the point where pollution occurs, then it is responsible for the pollution. Whether it "discharges", "causes", or "permits" the pollution will be a question of degree, depending on whether it is actively involved at the point where pollution occurs, or whether it merely passively fails to prevent the pollution. In some cases the contract may expressly provide the defendant with the power and authority to control the activity. In such a case the factual assessment will be straightforward. *Prima facie*, liability will be incurred where the defendant could have prevented the impairment by intervening pursuant to its right to do so under the contract, but failed to do so. Where there is no such express provision in the contract, other factors will come into greater prominence. In every instance the question will depend on an assessment of all the circumstances of the case. Whether an "independent contractor" rather than an "employee" is hired will not be decisive. A homeowner who pays a fee for the collection of his garbage by a business which services the area could probably not be said to have caused or permitted the pollution if the collector dumps the garbage in the river. His position would be analagous to a householder in Sault

Ste. Marie, who could not be said to have caused or permitted the pollution here. A large corporation which arranges for the nearby disposal of industrial pollutants by a small local independent contractor with no experience in this matter would probably be in an entirely different position.

It must be recognized, however, that a municipality is in a somewhat different position by virtue of the legislative power which it possesses and which others lack. This is important in the assessment of whether the defendant was in a position to control the activity which it undertook and which caused the pollution. A municipality cannot slough off responsibility by contracting out the work. It is in a position to control those whom it hires to carry out garbage disposal operations, and to supervise the activity, either through the provisions of the contract or by municipal by-laws. It fails to do so at its peril.

One comment on the defence of reasonable care in this context should be added. Since the issue is whether the defendant is guilty of an offence, the doctrine of *respondeat superior* has no application. The due diligence which must be established is that of the accused alone. Where an employer is charged in respect of an act committed by an employee acting in the course of employment, the question will be whether the act took place without the accused's direction or approval, thus negating wilful involvement of the accused, and whether the accused exercised all reasonable care by establishing a proper system to prevent commission of the offence and by taking reasonable steps to ensure the effective operation of the system. The availability of the defence to a corporation will depend on whether such due diligence was taken by those who are the directing mind and will of the corporation, whose acts are therefore in law the acts of the corporation itself. For a useful discussion of this matter in the context of a statutory defence of due diligence see *Tesco Supermarkets Ltd. v. Nattrass*, [1972] A.C. 153.

The majority of the Ontario Court of Appeal directed a new trial as, in the opinion of that Court, the findings of the trial Judge were not sufficient to establish actual knowledge on the part of the City. I share the view that there should be a new trial, but for a different reason. The City did not lead evidence directed to a defence of due diligence, nor did the trial Judge address himself to the availability of such a defence. In these circumstances, it would not be fair for this Court to determine, upon findings of fact directed toward other ends, whether the City was without fault.

I would dismiss the appeal and direct a new trial. I would dismiss the cross-appeal. There should be no costs.

Appeal dismissed; cross-appeal dismissed.

The distinction between crimes and regulatory offences was central to the decision in *Sault Ste. Marie (City)*. It has recently been revisited by Mr. Justice Cory in a minority concurring judgment in *Wholesale Travel Group Inc.* That decision's complex rulings on the issue of fault and reverse onus for regulatory offences will soon be re-visited in these materials.

R. v. WHOLESALE TRAVEL GROUP INC.

[1991] 3 S.C.R. 154, 8 C.R. (4th) 145, 67 C.C.C. (3d) 193

The accused corporation, a travel agency, was charged with various counts of misleading advertising contrary to what is now s. 60(2) of the *Competition Act.* Although that offence carries a sentence on conviction on indictment to a fine in the discretion of the Court and to imprisonment for five years or to both and on summary conviction to a fine of $25,000 or to imprisonment for one year or both, Mr. Justice Cory nevertheless characterized it as a regulatory offence as follows:

CORY J. (L'HEUREUX-DUBÉ J. concurring): —

. . . .

The Rationale for the Distinction

It has always been thought that there is a rational basis for distinguishing between crimes and regulatory offences. Acts or actions are criminal when they constitute conduct that is, in itself, so abhorrent to the basic values of human society that it ought to be prohibited completely. Murder, sexual assault, fraud, robbery and theft are all so repugnant to society that they are universally recognized as crimes. At the same time, some conduct is prohibited, not because it is inherently wrongful, but because unregulated activity would result in dangerous conditions being imposed upon members of society, especially those who are particularly vulnerable.

The objective of regulatory legislation is to protect the public or broad segments of the public (such as employees, consumers and motorists, to name but a few) from the potentially adverse effects of otherwise lawful activity. Regulatory legislation involves a shift of emphasis from the protection of individual interests and the deterrence and punishment of acts involving moral fault to the protection of public and societal interests. While criminal offences are usually designed to condemn and punish past, inherently wrongful conduct, regulatory measures are generally directed to the prevention of future harm through the enforcement of minimum standards of conduct and care.

It follows that regulatory offences and crimes embody different concepts of fault. Since regulatory offences are directed primarily not to conduct itself but to the consequences of conduct, conviction of a regulatory offence may be thought to import a significantly lesser degree of culpability than conviction of a true crime. The concept of fault in regulatory offences is based upon a reasonable care standard and, as such, does not imply moral blameworthiness in the same manner as criminal fault. Conviction for breach of a regulatory offence suggests nothing more than that the defendant has failed to meet a prescribed standard of care.

That is the theory, but, like all theories, its application is difficult. For example, is the single mother who steals a loaf of bread to sustain her family more blameworthy than the employer who, through negligence, breaches regulations and thereby exposes his employees to dangerous working conditions, or the manufacturer who, as a result of negligence, sells dangerous products or pollutes the air and waters by its plant? At this stage it is sufficient to bear in mind that those who breach regulations may inflict serious harm on large segments of society. Therefore, the characterization of an offence as regulatory should not be thought to make light of either the potential harm to the vulnerable or the responsibility of those subject to regulation to ensure that the proscribed harm does not occur. It should also be remembered that, as social values change, the degree of moral blameworthiness attaching to certain conduct may change as well.

Nevertheless there remains, in my view, a sound basis for distinguishing between regulatory and criminal offences. The distinction has concrete theoretical and practical underpinnings and has proven to be a necessary and workable concept in our law. Since *Sault Ste. Marie*, this Court has reaffirmed the distinction. Most recently, in *Thomson Newspapers Ltd. v. Canada (Director of Investigation and Research*, [1990] 1 S.C.R. 425, 76 C.R. (3d) 129, 54 C.C.C. (3d) 417, at pp. 510-511 [S.C.R., p. 209 C.R.], Justice La Forest adopted the following statement of the Law Reform Commission of Canada (Criminal Responsibility for Group Action, Working Paper No. 16 1976, at p. 12):

> [The regulatory offence] is not primarily concerned with values, but with results. While values necessarily underlie all legal prescriptions, the regulatory offence really gives expression to the view that it is expedient for the protection of society and for the orderly use and sharing of society's resources that people act in a prescribed manner in prescribed situations, or that people take prescribed standards of care to avoid risks of injury. The object is to induce compliance with rules for the overall benefit of society.

B. The Fundamental Importance of Regulatory Offences in Canadian Society

Regulatory measures are the primary mechanisms employed by governments in Canada to implement public policy objectives. What is ultimately at stake in this appeal is the ability of federal and provincial governments to pursue social ends through the enactment and enforcement of public welfare legislation.

Some indication of the prevalence of regulatory offences in Canada is provided by a 1974 estimate by the Law Reform Commission of Canada. The commission estimated that there were, at that time, approximately 20,000 regulatory offences in an average province, plus an additional 20,000 regulatory offences at the federal level. By 1983, the commission's estimate of the federal total had reached 97,000. There is every reason to believe that the number of public welfare offences at both levels of government has continued to increase.

Statistics such as these make it obvious that government policy in Canada is pursued principally through regulation. It is through regulatory legislation that the community seeks to implement its larger objectives and to govern itself and the conduct of its members. The ability of the government effectively to regulate potentially harmful conduct must be maintained.

It is difficult to think of an aspect of our lives that is not regulated for our benefit and for the protection of society as a whole. From cradle to grave, we are protected by regulations; they apply to the doctors attending our entry into this world and to the morticians present at our departure. Every day, from waking to sleeping, we profit from regulatory measures which we often take for granted. On rising, we use various forms of energy whose safe distribution and use are governed by regulation. The trains, buses and other vehicles that get us to work are regulated for our safety. The food we eat and the beverages we drink are subject to regulation for the protection of our health.

In short, regulation is absolutely essential for our protection and well-being as individuals, and for the effective functioning of society. It is properly present throughout our lives. The more complex the activity, the greater the need for and the greater our reliance upon regulation and its enforcement. For example, most people would have no idea what regulations are required for air transport or how they should be enforced. Of necessity, society relies on government regulation for its safety.

II. The Offence in the Present Case

Competition legislation generally

The offence of misleading advertising with which Wholesale Travel is charged is found in the *Competition Act* (the "Act"). This Act, like its predecessor, the *Combines Investigation Act*, is aimed at regulating unacceptable business activity. In *General Motors of Canada Ltd. v. City National Leasing Ltd.*, [1989] 1 S.C.R. 641, Dickson C.J.C. held that the Act embodied a complex scheme of economic regulation, the purpose of which is to eliminate activities that reduce competition in the marketplace.

The nature and purpose of the Act was considered in greater detail in *Thomson Newspapers, supra*. La Forest J. pointed out that the Act is aimed at regulating the economy and business with a view to preserving competitive conditions which are crucial to the operation of a free market economy. He observed that the Act was not concerned with "real crimes" but with regulatory or public welfare offences. He put the position this way, at p. 510 [S.C.R., pp. 199-200 C.R.]:

> At bottom, the Act is really aimed at the regulation of the economy and business, with a view to the preservation of the competitive conditions which are crucial to the operation of a free market economy. This goal has obvious implications for Canada's material prosperity. It also has broad political overtones in that it is aimed at preventing concentration of power . . . It must be remembered that private organizations can be just as oppressive as the state when they gain such a dominant position within their sphere of operations that they can effectively force their will upon others.
>
> *The conduct regulated or prohibited by the Act is not conduct which is by its very nature morally or socially reprehensible. It is instead conduct we wish to discourage because of our desire to maintain an economic system which is at once productive and consistent with our values of individual liberty. It is, in short, not conduct which would be generally regarded as by its very nature criminal and worthy of criminal sanction. It is conduct which is only criminal in the sense that it is in fact prohibited by law.* One's view of whether it should be so proscribed is likely to be functional or utilitarian, in the sense that it will be based on an assessment of the desirability of the economic goals to which combines legislation is directed

or its potential effectiveness in achieving those goals. *It is conduct which is made criminal for strictly instrumental reasons.* [Emphasis added.]

These decisions make it clear that the *Competition Act* in all its aspects is regulatory in character.

The Offence of False or Misleading Advertising

Is the offence of false or misleading advertising regulatory in nature? It seems to me that the fact that the provision is located within a comprehensive regulatory framework would ordinarily be sufficient to demonstrate its regulatory nature. Several other considerations point to the same conclusion.

The offence of misleading advertising has existed in Canada since 1914. It is not without significance that it was, in 1969, transferred from the *Criminal Code* to the *Combines Investigation Act*, a step which confirms the regulatory nature of the offence. The provision was amended in 1975 to provide for a defence of due diligence, converting the offence from absolute to strict liability.

It is true that the availability of imprisonment as a sanction for breach of a statute might be taken to indicate that the provision is criminal in nature. However, this fact is not itself dispositive of the character of an offence. Rather, one must consider the conduct addressed by the legislation and the purposes for which such conduct is regulated. This view was most recently expressed by La Forest J. in *Thomson Newspapers, supra,* at p. 509 [S.C.R., p. 129 C.R.]. He noted that many regulatory offences provide for imprisonment in order to ensure compliance with the terms of the statute and thereby achieve the regulatory goal.

The appellant has argued that conviction for the offence of false advertising carries a stigma of dishonesty, with the inference that the accused falsely advertised for the purposes of obtaining economic advantage. It is said that nothing could be more damaging to a business than the implication that it has made dishonest representations. In my view, however, the offence does not focus on dishonesty but rather on the harmful consequences of otherwise lawful conduct. Conviction suggests only that the defendant has made a representation to the public which was in fact misleading, and that the defendant was unable to establish the exercise of due diligence in preventing the error. This connotes a fault element of negligence rather than one involving moral turpitude. Thus, any stigma that might flow from a conviction is very considerably diminished.

In summary, the offence of false advertising possesses the essential characteristics which distinguish regulatory offences from those which are truly criminal. Accordingly, it should be considered to be a regulatory offence rather than a crime in the ordinary sense.

. . . .

[His Lordship further held that the contextual approach to *Charter* interpretation required that regulatory and criminal offences be treated differently for the purposes of *Charter* review.]

Before proceeding to the substantive analysis, however, it is necessary to consider the justifications for differential treatment. They are two-fold: the first relates to the distinctive nature of regulatory activity, while the second acknowledges the fundamental need to protect the vulnerable through regulatory legislation.

1. The Licensing Justification

Those who argue against differential treatment for regulatory offences assert that there is no valid reason to distinguish between the criminal and regulatory accused. Each, it is said, is entitled in law to the same procedural and substantive protections. This view assumes equality of position between criminal and regulatory defendants; that is to say, it assumes that each starts out from a position of equal knowledge, volition and "innocence". The argument against differential treatment further suggests that differentiating between the regulatory and criminal defendants implies the subordination and sacrifice of the regulatory accused to the interests of the community at large. Such a position, it is argued, contravenes our basic concern for individual dignity and our fundamental belief in the importance of the individual. It is these assumptions which the licensing justification challenges.

Criminal law is rooted in the concepts of individual autonomy and free will and the corollary that each individual is responsible for his or her conduct. It assumes that all persons are free actors, at liberty to choose how to regulate their own actions in relation to others. The criminal law fixes the outer limits of acceptable conduct, constraining individual freedom to a limited degree in order to preserve the freedom of others. Thus, the basis of criminal responsibility is that the accused person has made a deliberate and conscious choice to engage in activity prohibited by the *Criminal Code*. The accused person who is convicted of an offence will be held responsible for his or her actions, with the result that the opprobrium of society will attach to those acts and any punishment imposed will be considered to be deserved.

The licensing argument is directed to this question of choice. Thus, while in the criminal context, the essential question to be determined is whether the accused has made the choice to act in the manner alleged in the indictment, the regulated defendant is, by virtue of the licensing argument, assumed to have made the choice to engage in the regulated activity. The question then becomes not whether the defendant chose to enter the regulated sphere but whether, having done so, the defendant has fulfilled the responsibilities attending that decision. Professor Genevra Richardson puts the position this way in "Strict Liability for Regulatory Crime: the Empirical Research," [1987] Crim. L. R. 295, at pp. 295-296:

> [I]t can be argued that the strict liability regulatory offender is not a "blameless innocent". By indulging in the regulated activity she has voluntary adopted the risks of regulatory infraction and her supposed "innocence" flows from the law's traditional tendency to view the criminal act "only in the context of its immediate past".

The licensing concept rests on the view that those who choose to participate in regulated activities have, in doing so, placed themselves in a responsible relationship to the public generally and must accept the consequences of that responsibility. Therefore, it is said, those who engage in regulated activity should, as part of the burden of responsible conduct attending participation in the regulated field, be deemed to have accepted certain terms and conditions applicable to those who act within the regulated sphere. Foremost among these implied terms is an undertaking that the conduct of the regulated actor will comply with and maintain a certain minimum standard of care.

The licensing justification is based not only on the idea of a conscious choice being made to enter a regulated field, but also on the concept of control. The concept is that those persons who enter a regulated field are in the best position to control the harm which may result, and that they should therefore be held responsible for it. A compelling statement of this view is found in the decision of the United States Supreme Court in *Morissette v. United States*, 342 U.S. 246, 72 S.Ct. 240 (Mich., 1952), where the court stated, at p. 256 [U.S.]:

> The accused, if he does not will the violation, usually is in a position to prevent it with no more care than society might reasonably expect and no more exertion than it might reasonably exact from one who assumed his responsibilities.

The licensing justification may not apply in all circumstances to all offenders. That is, there are some cases in which the licensing argument may not apply so as to permit the imputation to an accused of choice, knowledge and implied acceptance of regulatory terms and conditions. This may occur, for instance, where the nature of the regulated conduct is so innocuous that it would not trigger in the mind of a reasonable person the possibility that the conduct was regulated.

The nature of the regulated conduct will itself go far to determining whether the licensing argument applies. It is useful to distinguish between conduct which, by virtue of its inherent danger or the risk it engenders for others, would generally alert a reasonable person to the probability that the conduct would be regulated, from that conduct which is so mundane and apparently harmless that no thought would ordinarily be given to its potentially regulated nature. In the latter circumstances, the licensing argument would not apply.

. . . .

2. *The Vulnerability Justification*

The realities and complexities of a modern industrial society, coupled with the very real need to protect all of society and particularly its vulnerable members, emphasize the critical importance of regulatory offences in Canada today. Our country simply could not function without extensive regulatory legislation. The protection provided by such measures constitutes a second justification for the differential treatment, for *Charter* purposes, of regulatory and criminal offences.

This court has on several occasions observed that the *Charter* is not an instrument to be used by the well-positioned to roll back legislative protections enacted on behalf of the vulnerable. This principle was first enunciated by Dickson C.J.C. for the majority in *R. v. Videoflicks Ltd.*, (sub nom. *R. v. Edwards Books & Art Ltd.*), [hereinafter "Edwards Books"], [1986] 2 S.C.R. 713, 55 C.R. (3d) 193, 30 C.C.C. (3d) 385. He wrote, at p. 779 [S.C.R., p. 241 C.R.]:

> In interpreting and applying the *Charter* I believe that the Courts must be cautious to ensure that it does not simply become an instrument of better situated individuals to roll back legislation which has as its object the improvement of the condition of less advantaged persons.

The same principle has been repeated and emphasized in *Irwin Toy Ltd. v. Quebec (Attorney General)*, [1989] 1 S.C.R. 927, at p. 993, and in *Slaight Communications Inc. v. Davidson*, [1989] 1 S.C.R. 1038, at p. 1051. This principle recognizes that much government regulation is designed to protect the vulnerable. It would be unfortunate indeed if the *Charter* were used as a weapon to attack measures intended to protect the disadvantaged and comparatively powerless members of society. It is interesting to observe that in the United States, Courts struck down important components of the program of regulatory legislation known as "the New Deal". This so-called "*Lochner* era" is now almost universally regarded by academic writers as a dark age in the history of the American Constitution.

Regulatory legislation is essential to the operation of our complex industrial society; it plays a legitimate and vital role in protecting those who are most vulnerable and least able to protect themselves. The extent and importance of that role has increased continuously since the onset of the Industrial Revolution. Before effective workplace legislation was enacted, labourers — including children — worked unconscionably long hours in dangerous and unhealthy surroundings that evoke visions of Dante's *Inferno*. It was regulatory legislation with its enforcement provisions which brought to an end the shameful situation that existed in mines, factories and workshops in the nineteenth century. The differential treatment of regulatory offences is justified by their common goal of protecting the vulnerable.

The importance of the vulnerability concept as a component of the contextual approach to *Charter* interpretation has been recognized in the employer/employee field in *Edwards Books*, *supra*, and *Slaight Communications*, *supra*, and in the sphere of commercial advertising in *Irwin Toy*, *supra*. The same considerations should apply whenever regulatory legislation is subject to *Charter* challenge.

Do you find Mr. Justice Cory's approach to distinguishing regulatory offences persuasive?

R. v. CHAPIN

[1979] 2 S.C.R. 121, 7 C.R. (3d) 225, 45 C.C.C. (2d) 333

DICKSON J.: —

The Facts

Mrs. Loise Chapin went duck hunting in the Balmoral marsh, near Chatham, one windy afternoon in mid-October 1976. She was accompanied by a friend whom she had not seen for some time. As they walked through the marsh they were, she testified, talking a lot and not paying attention to anything but the beautiful day. They reached a dyke road and walked along it a short distance, then along some "duck boards", five or six inches in width, placed over water and leading to a duck blind from which Mrs. Chapin intended to shoot.

Some time, and two ducks, later, Mrs. Chapin was arrested by a conservation officer of the Ontario Ministry of Natural Resources. He had been in the area and heard shots. Leaving his car, he proceeded on foot through two gates, down through a small canal gully, over scrub land and across a corn field, and finally arrived at a road leading to a small pond. The road over which Mrs. Chapin and her friend had passed earlier was approximately 12 feet in width and composed of a mixture of mud and gravel. As the conservation officer approached the pond, he observed, in the centre of the road and about ten feet from the water's edge, a small pile of soy beans, weed seeds and wheat, like the gleanings from a harvesting operation on a farm. The officer said that he was practically on top of the pile before he noticed it. It was a small pile, about a foot to a foot and a half in length, three inches wide and approximately two inches in depth. The blind from which Mrs. Chapin had been shooting was located some distance out from the edge of the pond and about 50 yards from the pile. The officer also noted grain in the water on either side of the boardwalk.

Mrs. Chapin testified that she was unaware of the presence of the grain. It was a very windy day and many things were flying around the marsh. When she walked along the duck boards, in hip waders and carrying a gun, her sole concern was to avoid falling into the water. It seems to be generally accepted that Mrs. Chapin did not know that the grain was there until it was pointed out to her by the conservation officer. Even then, she did not know what it was. She was shooting on private property belonging to the Balmoral Hunt Club, of which her husband was part owner. During the trial, there was vague reference by defence counsel to "spite baiting", but no evidence adduced to indicate by whom or in what circumstances the grain had been deposited.

The Migratory Birds Regulations

Now, it is unlawful to hunt for migratory birds within 1/4 mile of a place where bait has been deposited. Section 14 [am. SOR/73-509; SOR/75-436] of the *Migratory Birds Regulations*, SOR/71-376, reads:

14. (1) Subject to subsection (2), no person shall hunt for migratory game birds within one-quarter mile of any place where bait has been deposited.

(2) Subsection (1) does not apply to a place where bait had been deposited, if

(a) a game officer inspects that place and declares that it is clear of bait, and

(b) seven days have elapsed since the inspection referred to in paragraph (a).

(3) Where bait is deposited in a place after an inspection referred to in subsection (2), that subsection ceases to apply to that place for the remainder of the open season.

(4) No person shall deposit bait in any place during the period commencing seven days before the open season applicable in that place and ending on the day immediately following the last day of the open season in that place unless that person, at least thirty days prior to placing the bait,

(a) obtains the consent in writing of

(i) every landowner and every lessee or tenant whose land is located within one-quarter mile of that place, and

(ii) the Director and the Chief Game Officer of a province, and

(b) posts in that place signs of a type and wording satisfactory to, and in a location designated by, the Director,

(5) A consent obtained pursuant to paragraph (4)(a) is valid only in respect of the open season in respect of which it was obtained.

(6) Subsection (4) does not apply to the holder of a permit referred to in section 19 or 20 who places bait

(a) in a confined area specified in his permit, or

(b) at a distance of not less than one-quarter mile from an area where the hunting of migratory birds is permitted for the sole purpose of feeding migratory birds lawfully in his possession.

(7) For the purpose of subsection (1), any area

(a) of standing crops, whether flooded or not,

(b) of harvested crop land that is flooded,

(c) where crops are properly shocked in the field where they grow, or

(d) where grain is scattered solely as a result of normal agricultural or harvesting operations shall not be regarded as a place where bait has been deposited.

Section 12(1) of the *Migratory Birds Convention Act*, R.S.C. 1970, c. M-12, provides:

12. (1) Every person who violates this Act or any regulation is, for each offence, liable upon summary conviction to a fine of not more than three hundred dollars and not less than ten dollars, or to imprisonment for a term not exceeding six months, or to both fine and imprisonment.

· · · ·

The case has now, by leave, reached this Court. There are two preliminary observations. First, the judicial history of the case, all before the judgment of this Court in *R. v. Sault Ste. Marie* (1978), 3 C.R. (3d) 30, 40 C.C.C. (2d) 353, provides an interesting example of the Courts attempting to come to grips with the classic sort of regulatory offence. The three Courts which have dealt with the matter to date have characterized the offence in three different ways. Walker J. P. treated it as an offence of strict liability, to which the accused could plead that she committed the offence under an honest and reasonable mistake of fact. Beardall Co. Ct. J. considered it to be one of absolute liability. The Court of Appeal majority regarded it as a *mens rea* offence, while Houlden J.A. regarded it as one of absolute liability.

In *Sault Ste. Marie* at pp. 53-54, this Court recognized three categories of offences.

. . . .

The Crown argues that the offence is one of absolute liability or, in the alternative, strict liability. The respondent contends that it is one requiring full *mens rea* or, if not, a strict liability offence.

Not a Mens Rea Offence

One would be hard pressed to characterize the offence created by s. 14(1) of the *Migratory Birds Regulations* as a "crime in the true sense". Violation is punishable upon summary conviction, and not by indictment. One must note the absence of the usual signals connoting *mens rea*, such as "wilfully" or "with intent". In contrast, to take an example, s. 10 of the *Migratory Birds Convention Act* commences:

> 10. Any person who wilfully refuses to furnish information or wilfully furnishes false information to a game officer. . . .

The *Migratory Birds Convention Act* is a regulatory statute enacted by the Parliament of Canada for the general welfare of the Canadian public, not to mention the welfare of the ducks. The purpose of the legislation is expressed in the preamble to the Migratory Birds Convention, which has been sanctioned, ratified and confirmed by s. 2 of the Act, and which reads in part as follows:

> Whereas many species of birds in the course of their annual migrations traverse certain parts of the Dominion of Canada and the United States; and
> Whereas many of these species are of great value as a source of food or in destroying insects which are injurious to forests and forage plants on the public domain, as well as to agricultural crops, in both Canada and the United States, but are nevertheless in danger of extermination through lack of adequate protection during the nesting season or while on their way to and from their breeding grounds:
> His Majesty the King of the United Kingdom of Great Britain and Ireland and of the British dominions beyond the seas, Emperor of India, and the United States of America, being desirous of saving from indiscriminate slaughter and of insuring the preservation of such migratory birds as are either useful to man or are harmless, have resolved to adopt some uniform system of protection which shall effectively accomplish such objects.

Article I of the Convention, attached as a schedule to the Act, describes the migratory game birds included in the terms of the Convention. Article II provides for closed seasons, "during which no hunting shall be done except for scientific or propagating purposes under permits issued by proper authorities". Article III provides for a continuous close season on certain migratory game birds. Article IV provides for special protection to be given the wood duck and the eider duck. Article V provides for the prohibition of the taking of nests or eggs, and Art. VI for the prohibition of the shipment or export of migratory birds or their eggs during the continuance of the close season. Finally, Art. VII provides for the issuance of permits to kill migratory birds which, under extraordinary conditions, may become seriously injurious to the agricultural or other interests in any particular community.

The *Migratory Birds Convention Act* authorizes the making of *Migratory Birds Regulations* for the purpose of effecting the public welfare goals of the Migratory Birds Convention. Section 4 of the Act provides, in part:

> 4.(1) The Governor in Council may make such regulations as are deemed expedient to protect the migratory game, migratory insectivorous and migratory nongame birds that inhabit Canada during the whole or any part of the year.
>
> (2) Subject to the provisions of the Convention, the regulations may provide . . .
>
> (*b*) for limiting the number of migratory game birds that may be taken by a person in any specified time during the season when the taking of such birds is legal, and providing the manner in which such birds may then be taken and the appliances that may be used therefor.

It seems clear that the offence of hunting for migratory game birds within 1/4 mile of any place where bait has been deposited contrary to s. 14(1) of the *Migratory Birds Regulations* and s. 12(1) of the *Migratory Birds Convention Act* is legislation designed to protect migratory birds from indiscriminate slaughter for the general welfare of the public. It seems equally clear that s. 14(1) of the *Migratory Birds Regulations* creates a public welfare offence which is not criminal in the true sense, and it is therefore not subject to the presumption of full *mens rea*. Section 14(1) is thus not creating a new crime, but in the public interest is prohibiting an act under a penalty: *Sherras v. De Rutzen*, [1895] 1 Q.B. 918 (D.C.).

Not an Absolute Liability Offence

The language of the offence is straightforward: "No person shall. . . ." Yet there is not a strict prohibition on hunting, rather a hunt controlled within certain limits as to season, methods, and types and numbers of species taken. Nor can one ignore the controls on shipment and export of game, not the stricter controls in certain prescribed geographic areas "for the control and management of such area".

Accepting that this is a public welfare or regulatory offence, neither party mentions the approach taken by this Court in *Sault Ste. Marie, supra*, that "public welfare offences would *prima facie* be in the second category" of strict liability. The Crown merely lists the factors suggested as relevant in *Sault Ste. Marie, viz.*, the overall regulatory pattern, the subject matter of the legislation, the importance of the penalty and the precision of the language, in order to move the offence out of the second category and into the third.

The Crown suggests that "the summary conviction nature of the penalty" should carry some weight. Summary conviction it may be, but one could hardly term the penalties minimal. Rather than a "small monetary fine" alone, we find a number of serious consequences upon conviction. Section 12(1) of the Act lays down a minimum fine of $10 and a maximum fine of $300, or up to six months' imprisonment, or both. (The County Court Judge imposed a fine of $100 in this case.) Other serious consequences ensue. Section 22(1) provides for a mandatory prohibition upon conviction of either holding or applying for a migratory game bird hunting permit for a period of one year from date of conviction. Further, as the respondent points out, the Court may, under s. 88(2) of the *Game and Fish Act*, R.S.O. 1970, c. 186, cancel "any licence to hunt" — not just a game bird licence — and may further order no obtaining of, or application for, a hunting licence "during the period stated in the order". Nor is that all. The most serious potential consequence comes in s. 7 of the *Migratory Birds Act* itself, permitting the justice of the peace to make an order of forfeiture of the gun and any other equipment used in violation of the Act or Regulations. While the respondent employs these penalties in support of her full *mens rea* position, they certainly support the *prima facie* classification of strict liability.

The best the Crown can do to shift this offence into the category of absolute liability is to suggest that the availability of a defence of reasonable care would considerably weaken the enforcement of the legislation. This may be true, but, as Weatherston J.A. observed, the problems that may be encountered in the administration of a statute or regulation are a very unsure guide to its proper interpretation. Difficulty of enforcement is hardly enough to dislodge the offence from the category of strict liability, particularly when regard is had to the penalties that may ensue from conviction. I do not think that the public interest, as expressed in the Convention, requires that s. 14 of the Regulations be interpreted so that an innocent person should be convicted and fined and also suffer the mandatory loss of his hunting permit and the possible forfeiture of his hunting equipment, merely in order to facilitate prosecution.

The Crown contends that a person found hunting within 1/4 mile of a place where bait is deposited is guilty of an offence, to which no defence is available. On the Crown's submission, proof of making all *reasonable* efforts to ascertain the presence of the bait would be unavailing, as would proof of all *possible* efforts. This, in my view, is an untenable position. Hunting being a permitted sport, it would be a practical impossibility for a hunter to search a circular area having a diameter of 1/2 mile for the presence of illegally deposited bait before hunting. One must bear in mind the nature of the terrain over which hunting is done, as the evidence in this case discloses, and the fact that many hunters hope to get into position before first light. Is one first expected to search through swamp, bog, creeks, corn fields, over land and in water in search of illegal bait?

The case of *R. v. Pierce Fisheries Ltd.*, [1971] S.C.R. 5, 12 C.R.N.S. 272, [1970] 5 C.C.C. 193, was cited, but I do not believe that it assists the Crown. In that case, care had not been taken to acquire knowledge of the facts constituting the offence. Ritchie J. said that it would not have been a difficult matter for some officer or responsible person of the accused company to acquire knowledge of the undersize lobsters, and failure to acquire that knowledge did not afford a defence. Nor does the decision of the Ontario Court of Appeal in *R. v. Hickey*, supra, assist, having regard to the many differences between the *Ontario Highway Traffic Act*, R.S.O. 1970, c. 202, and the legislation here under consideration.

In my view, subs. (1) and (4) of s. 14 of the Regulations must be read together. Together they speak of legal baiting, the obtaining of written consents and the posting of signs to give notice of the presence of bait. Anyone who hunts within such a posted area may be more readily taken to be knowingly or recklessly in breach of the Regulations. The Regulations do not seek to impose an absolute obligation upon a hunter who innocently hunts in an unposted area within 1/4 mile of bait which has been placed illegally by a person unknown. Parliament could not have intended to afford a person hunting within 1/4 mile of an illegally baited area any less protection than that afforded a person hunting within 1/4 mile of a legally baited area. Otherwise, as counsel for Mrs. Chapin argues, an activity which is legal is rendered illegal by the illegal act of someone over whom the accused has no control. We should not assume that punishment is to be imposed without fault.

These considerations incline me to the view that the offence here under study is not one of absolute liability.

Strict Liability Offence

In my view, the offence created by s. 14(1) is one of strict liability. It is a classic example of an offence in the second category delineated in the *Sault Ste. Marie* case, *supra*. An accused may absolve himself on proof that he took all the care which a reasonable man might have been expected to take in all the circumstances or, in other words, that he was in no way negligent.

Conclusion

It remains to consider whether to dispose of the case in this Court or send it back for a new trial. The respondent has to date been subjected to two trials and two appeals. She lost her hunting privileges from April to November 1977. Her gun was seized and held under seizure for some time.

The following evidence is undisputed. The hunting was done at a private club, of which the husband of the respondent was part owner and to which she had been going for some eight years. The club had a permit from the Canadian Wildlife Service to bait at the proper season, but the club had never baited ponds. The respondent played no part in the management of the marsh. The day was windy, with matter of all kinds flying about. The pile of grain was not large. It looked like a gleaning after harvesting. It lay on a mud and gravel road. Mrs. Chapin had no reason to be looking down. The conservation officer did not notice the grain until he was practically on top of it. The other grain was in the water on either side of a narrow duck walk which Mrs. Chapin had to navigate to get to the blind. There were no signs indicating that this was a baited area.

After careful reading of all the evidence, I have arrived at the conclusion reached by this count in *Thibodeau v. R.*, [1955] S.C.R. 646, 21 C.R. 265, namely, that on the evidence in the record it would have been unreasonable to convict the respondent, and that we ought not to direct a new trial.

I would accordingly dismiss the appeal. Pursuant to the terms under which leave to appeal was granted, the respondent is entitled to costs on a solicitor-and-client basis.

Appeal dismissed.

(b) Charter Standards

Within a mere five years from the date of the entrenchment of the *Canadian Charter of Rights and Freedoms* the *Sault Ste. Marie* compromise of allowing a due diligence defence for regulatory offences with a reverse onus became a minimum constitutional standard of fault for any offence which threatens the liberty interest.

REFERENCE RE SECTION 94(2) OF THE MOTOR VEHICLE ACT (B.C.)

(1986), 48 C.R. (3d) 289 (S.C.C.)

LAMER J. (DICKSON C.J.C., BEETZ, CHOUINARD and LE DAIN JJ. concurring): —

The Facts

On August 16, 1982, the Lieutenant-Governor in Council of British Columbia referred the following question to the Court of Appeal of that province, by virtue of s. 1 of the *Constitutional Question Act*, R.S.B.C. 1979, c. 63.:

> Is s. 94(2) of the *Motor Vehicle Act*, R.S.B.C. 1979, as amended by the *Motor Vehicle Amendment Act*, 1982, consistent with the *Canadian Charter of Rights and Freedoms*?

On February 3, 1983, the Court of Appeal handed down reasons in answer to the question in which it stated that s. 94(2) of the Act is inconsistent with the *Canadian Charter of Rights and Freedoms*: (1983), 4 C.C.C. (3d) 243, 33 C.R. (3d) 22. The Attorney General for British Columbia launched an appeal to this Court.

The Legislation

Motor Vehicle Act, R.S.B.C. 1979, c. 288, s. 94, as amended by the *Motor Vehicle Act Amendment Act, 1982*, S.B.C. 1982 c. 36, s. 19:

> 94.(1) A person who drives a motor vehicle on a highway or industrial road while
> (a) he is prohibited from driving a motor vehicle under sections 90, 91, 92 or 92.1, or
> (b) his driver's licence or his right to apply for or obtain a driver's licence is suspended under s. 82 or 92 as it was before its repeal and replacement came into force pursuant to the *Motor Vehicle Amendment Act*, 1982,
> commits an offence and is liable,
> (c) on a first conviction, to a fine of not less than $300 and not more than $2000 and to imprisonment for not less than seven days and not more than six months, and
> (d) on a subsequent conviction, regardless of when the contravention occurred, to a fine of not less than $300 and not more than $2000 and to imprisonment for not less than 14 days and not more than one year.

(2) Subsection (1) creates an absolute liability offence on which guilt is established by proof of driving, whether or not the defendant knew of the prohibition or suspension.

Canadian Charter of Rights and Freedoms: Constitution Act 1982:
S.1 The *Canadian Charter of Rights and Freedoms* guarantees the rights and freedoms set out in it subject only to such reasonable limits prescribed by law as can be demonstrably justified in a free and democratic society.
S.7 Everyone has the right to life, liberty and security of the person and the right not to be deprived thereof except in accordance with the principles of fundamental justice.

. . . .

The judgment of the Court of Appeal of British Columbia

The Court was of the view that the phrase "principles of fundamental justice" was not restricted to matters of procedure, but extended to substantive law, and that the Courts were "therefore called upon, in construing the provisions of s. 7 of the *Charter*, to have regard to the content of legislation".

Relying on the decision of this Court in *R. v. City of Sault Ste-Marie*, [1978] 2 S.C.R. 1299, the Court of Appeal found "that s. 94(2) of the *Motor Vehicle Act* is inconsistent with the principles of fundamental justice." They did not heed the invitation of counsel opposing the validity of s. 94(2) to declare that, as a result of that decision by our Court, all absolute liability offences violated s. 7 of the *Charter* and could not be salvaged under s. 1. Quite the contrary, the Court of Appeal said that "there are, and will remain, certain public welfare offences, *e.g.* air and water pollution offences, where the public interest requires that the offences be absolute liability offences." Their finding was predicated on the following reasoning:

The effect of s. 94(2) is to transform the offence from a mens rea offence to an absolute liability offence hence giving the defendant no opportunity to prove that his action was due to an honest and reasonable mistake of fact or that he acted without guilty intent. Rather than placing the burden to establish such facts on the defendant and thus making the offence a strict liability offence, the legislature has seen fit to make it an absolute liability offence coupled with a mandatory term of imprisonment.

It can therefore be inferred with certainty that, in the Court's view, the combination of mandatory imprisonment and absolute liability was offensive to s. 7. It cannot however be ascertained from their judgment whether the violation was triggered by the requirement of minimum imprisonment or solely by the availability of imprisonment as a sentence.

Section 7

[I]n the context of s. 7, and in particular of the interpretation of "principles of fundamental justice" there has prevailed in certain quarters an assumption that all but a narrow construction of s. 7 will inexorably lead the Courts to "question the wisdom of enactments", to adjudicate upon the merits of public policy.

From this have sprung warnings of the dangers of a judicial "super-legislature" beyond the reach of Parliament, the provincial Legislatures and the electorate.

. . . .

This is an argument which was heard countless times prior to the entrenchment of the *Charter* but which has in truth, for better or for worse, been settled by the very coming into force of the *Constitution Act, 1982.*

. . . .

The concerns with the bounds of constitutional adjudication explain the characterization of the issue in a narrow and restrictive fashion, *i.e.*, whether the terms "principles of fundamental justice" have a substantive or merely procedural content. In my view, the characterization of the issue in such fashion preempts an open-minded approach to determining the meaning of "principles of fundamental justice".

The substantive/procedural dichotomy narrows the issue almost to an all-or-nothing proposition. Moreover, it is largely bound up in the American experience with substantive and procedural due process. It imports into the Canadian context American concepts, terminology and jurisprudence, all of which are inextricably linked to problems concerning the nature and legitimacy of adjudication under the U.S. Constitution. That Constitution, it must be remembered, has no s. 52 nor has it the internal checks and balances of sections 1 and 33. We would, in my view, do our own Constitution a disservice to simply allow the American debate to define the issue for us, all the while ignoring the truly fundamental structural differences between the two constitutions. Finally, the dichotomy creates its own set of difficulties by the attempt to distinguish between two concepts whose outer boundaries are not always clear and often tend to overlap. Such difficulties can and should, when possible, be avoided.

. . . .

The task of the Court is not to choose between substantive or procedural content *per se* but to secure for persons "the full benefit of the *Charter's* protection" (Dickson C.J.C. in *R. v. Big M Drug Mart Ltd.*, [1985] 1 S.C.R. 295 at 344), under s. 7, while avoiding adjudication of the merits of public policy. This can only be accomplished by a purposive analysis and the articulation (to use the words in *Curr v. The Queen*, [1972] S.C.R. 889, at p. 899) of "objective and manageable standards" for the operation of the section within such a framework.

A number of Courts have placed emphasis upon the Minutes of the Proceedings and Evidence of the Special Joint Committee of the Senate and of the House of Commons on the Constitution in the interpretation of "principles of fundamental justice". . .

In particular, the following passages dealing with the testimony of federal civil servants from the Department of Justice have been relied upon:

Mr. Strayer (Assistant Deputy Minister, Public Law):

Mr. Chairman, it was our belief that the words "fundamental justice" would cover the same thing as what is called procedural due process, that is the meaning of due process in relation to requiring fair procedure. However, it in our view does not cover the concept of what is called substantive due process, which would impose substantive requirements as to policy of the law in question.

This has been most clearly demonstrated in the United States in the area of property, but also in other areas such as the right to life. The term due process has been given the broader concept of meaning both the procedure and substance. Natural justice or fundamental justice in our view does not go beyond the procedural requirements of fairness.

. . . .

Mr. Strayer: The term "fundamental justice" appears to us to be essentially the same thing as natural justice.

Mr. Tassé (Deputy Minister) also said of the phrase "principles of fundamental justice" in testimony before the committee:

We assume that the Court would look at that much like a Court would look at the requirements of natural justice, and the concept of natural justice is quite familiar to Courts and they have given a good deal of specific meaning to the concept of natural justice. We would think that the Court would find in that phraseology principles of fundamental justice a meaning somewhat like natural justice or inherent fairness.

Courts have been developing the concept of administrative fairness in recent years and they have been able to give a good deal of consideration, certainly to these sorts of concepts and we would expect they could do the same with this.

The Honourable Jean Chrétien, then federal Minister of Justice, also indicated to the Committee that, while he thought "fundamental justice marginally more appropriate than natural justice" in s. 7, either term was acceptable to the government.

. . . .

[T]he simple fact remains that the *Charter* is not the product of a few individual public servants, however distinguished, but of a multiplicity of individuals who played major roles in the negotiating, drafting and adoption of the *Charter*. How can one say with any confidence that within this enormous multiplicity of actors, without forgetting the role of the provinces, the comments of a few federal civil servants can in any way be determinative?

. . . .

Another danger with casting the interpretation of s. 7 in terms of the comments made by those heard at the Special Joint Committee Proceedings is that, in so doing, the rights, freedoms and values embodied in the *Charter* in effect become frozen in time to the moment of adoption with little or no possibility of growth, development and adjustment to changing societal needs.

. . . .

The main sources of support for the argument that "fundamental justice" is simply synonymous with natural justice have been the Minutes of the Proceedings and Evidence of the Special Joint Committee on the Constitution and the *Bill of Rights* jurisprudence. In my view, neither the Minutes nor the *Bill of Rights* jurisprudence are persuasive or of any great force. The historical usage of the term "fundamental justice" is, on the other hand, shrouded in ambiguity. Moreover, not any one of these arguments, taken singly or as a whole, manages to overcome in my respectful view the textual and contextual analyses.

Consequently, my conclusion may be summarized as follows:

The term "principles of fundamental justice" is not a right, but a qualifier of the right not to be deprived of life, liberty and security of the person; its function is to set the parameters of that right.

Sections 8 to 14 address specific deprivations of the "right" to life, liberty and security of the person in breach of the principles of fundamental justice, and as such, violations of s. 7. They are therefore illustrative of the meaning, in criminal or penal law, of "principles of fundamental justice"; they represent principles which have been recognized by the common law, the international conventions and by the very fact of entrenchment in the *Charter*, as essential elements of a system for the administration of justice which is founded upon a belief in the dignity and worth of the human person and the rule of law.

Consequently, the principles of fundamental justice are to be found in the basic tenets and principles, not only of our judicial process, but also of the other components of our legal system.

We should not be surprised to find that many of the principles of fundamental justice are procedural in nature. Our common law has largely been a law of remedies and procedures and, as Frankfurter J. wrote in *McNabb v. U.S.* 318 U.S. 332 (1942) at p. 347, "the history of liberty has largely been the history of observance of procedural safeguards". This is not to say, however, that the principles of fundamental justice are limited solely to procedural guarantees. Rather, the proper approach to the determination of the principles of fundamental justice is quite simply one in which, as Professor Tremblay has written, "future growth will be based on historical roots". ((1984), 18 U.B.C.L. Rev. 201 at 254).

Whether any given principle may be said to be a principle of fundamental justice within the meaning of s. 7 will rest upon an analysis of the nature, sources, rationale and essential role of that principle within the judicial process and in our legal system, as it evolves.

Consequently, those words cannot be given any exhaustive content or simple enumerative definition, but will take on concrete meaning as the courts address alleged violations of s. 7.

I now turn to such an analysis of the principle of *mens rea* and absolute liability offences in order to determine the question which has been put to the Court in the present Reference.

Absolute Liability and Fundamental Justice in Penal Law

It has from time immemorial been part of our system of laws that the innocent not be punished. This principle has long been recognized as an essential element of a system for the administration of justice which is founded upon a belief in the dignity and worth of the human person and on the rule of law. It is so old that its first enunciation was in Latin *actus non facit reum nisi mens sit rea.*

As Glanville Williams said:

> There is no need here to go into the remote history of *mens rea*; suffice it to say that the requirement of a guilty state of mind (at least for the more serious crimes) had been developed by the time of Coke, which is as far back as the modern lawyer needs to go. "If one shoot at any wild fowl upon a tree, and the arrow killeth any reasonable creature afar off, without any evil intent in him, this is *per infortunium.*"

(Glanville Williams, *Criminal Law, The General Part*, Second Edition, London, Stevens and Sons Limited, 1961, p. 30.)

One of the many judicial statements on the subject worth mentioning is of the highest authority, *per* Goddard C.J. in *Harding v. Price*, [1948] 1 K.B. 695 at p. 700, where he said:

> The general rule applicable to criminal cases is *actus non facit reum nisi mens sit rea*, and I venture to repeat what I said in *Brend v. Wood* (1946), 62 T.L.R. 462, 463: 'It is of the utmost importance for the protection of the liberty of the subject that a Court should always bear in mind that, unless a statute either clearly or by necessary implication rules out *mens rea* as a constituent part of a crime, the Court should not find a man guilty of an offence against the criminal law unless he has a guilty mind'.

This view has been adopted by this Court in unmistakable terms in many cases, amongst which the better known are *Beaver v. The Queen*, [1957] S.C.R. 531, and the most recent and often quoted judgment of Dickson J. (as he then was), writing for the Court in *R. v. City of Sault Ste. Marie, supra.*

This Court's decision in the latter case is predicated upon a certain number of postulates one of which, given the nature of the rules it elaborates, has to be to the effect that absolute liability in penal law offends the principles of fundamental justice. Those principles are, to use the words of Dickson J., to the effect that "there is a generally held revulsion against punishment of the morally innocent". He also stated that the argument that absolute liability "violates fundamental principles of penal liability" was the most telling argument against absolute liability and one of greater force than those advanced in support thereof.

In my view it is because absolute liability offends the principles of fundamental justice that this Court created presumptions against Legislatures having intended to enact offences of a regulatory nature falling within that category. This is not to say, however, and to that extent I am in agreement with the Court of Appeal, that, as a result, absolute liability *per se* offends s. 7 of the *Charter.*

A law enacting an absolute liability offence will violate s. 7 of the *Charter* only if and to the extent that it has the potential of depriving of life, liberty, or security of the person.

Obviously, imprisonment (including probation orders) deprives persons of their liberty. An offence has that potential as of the moment it is open to the judge to impose imprisonment. There is no need that imprisonment, as in s. 94(2), be made mandatory.

I am therefore of the view that the combination of imprisonment and of absolute liability violates s. 7 of the *Charter* and can only be salvaged if the authorities demonstrate under s. 1 that such a deprivation of liberty in breach of those principles of fundamental justice is, in a free and democratic society, under the circumstances, a justified reasonable limit to one's rights under s. 7.

As no one has addressed imprisonment as an alternative to the non-payment of a fine, I prefer not to express any views in relation to s. 7 as regards that eventuality as a result of a conviction for an absolute liability offence; nor do I need to address here, given the scope of my finding and the nature of this appeal, minimum imprisonment, whether it offends the *Charter per se* or whether such violation, if any, is dependent upon whether it be for a *mens rea* or strict liability offence. Those issues were not addressed by the Court below and it would be unwise to attempt to address them here. It is sufficient and desirable for this appeal to make the findings I have and no more, that is, that no imprisonment may be imposed for an absolute liability offence, and, consequently, given the question put to us, an offence punishable by imprisonment cannot be an absolute liability offence.

. . . .

Administrative expediency, absolute liability's main supportive argument, will undoubtedly under s. 1 be invoked and occasionally succeed. Indeed, administrative expediency certainly has its place in administrative law. But when administrative law chooses to call in aid imprisonment through penal law, indeed sometimes criminal law and the added stigma attached to a conviction, exceptional, in my view, will be the case where the liberty or even the security of the person guaranteed under s. 7 should be sacrificed to administrative expediency. Section 1 may, for reasons of administrative expediency, successfully come to the rescue of an otherwise violation of s. 7, but only in cases arising out of exceptional conditions, such as natural disasters, the outbreak of war, epidemics, and the like.

Of course I understand the concern of many as regards corporate offences, specially, as was mentioned by the Court of Appeal, in certain sensitive areas such as the preservation of our vital environment and our natural resources. This concern might well be dispelled were it to be decided, given the proper case, that s. 7 affords protection to human persons only and does not extend to corporations.

Even if it be decided that s. 7 does extend to corporations, I think the balancing under s. 1 of the public interest against the financial interests of a corporation would give very different results from that of balancing public interest and the liberty or security of the person of a human being.

Indeed, the public interest as regards "air and water pollution offences" requires that the guilty be dealt with firmly, but the seriousness of the offence does not in my respectful view support the proposition that the innocent *human* person be open to conviction, quite the contrary.

Section 94(2)

I do not take issue with the fact that it is highly desirable that "bad drivers" be kept off the road. I do not take issue either with the desirability of punishing severely bad drivers who are in contempt of prohibitions against driving. The bottom line of the question to be addressed here is: whether the Government of British Columbia has demonstrated as justifiable that the risk of imprisonment of a few innocent is, given the desirability of ridding the roads of British Columbia of bad drivers, a reasonable limit in a free and democratic society. That result is to be measured against the offence being one of strict liability open to a defence of due diligence, the success of which does nothing more than let those few who did nothing wrong remain free.

As did the Court of Appeal, I find that this demonstration has not been satisfied, indeed, not in the least.

McIntyre and Wilson JJ. gave separate concurring judgments.

In *R. v. Pontes* (1995), 41 C.R. (4th) 201, 100 C.C.C. (3d) 353, [1995] 3 S.C.R. 44, the Supreme Court reconsidered the constitutionality of the offence of driving while prohibited under s. 94 of the B.C. *Motor Vehicle Act*. This time the Court held that the offence was constitutional. A 5-4 majority classified the offence as one of absolute liability but held there was no violation of the right to life, liberty and security of the person as there was no longer any risk of imprisonment. By amendments to the B.C. *Offence Act* a person is no longer liable to imprisonment and non-payment of a fine would not result in imprisonment. For a critical review of this complex decision see Anne-Marie Boisvert, "Innocence Morale, Diligence Raisonnable et Erreur de Droit" (1995), 41 C.R. (4th) 243 and Jill Presser, "Absolute Liability and Mistakes of Law in the Regulatory Context: Pontes Disappoints and Confuses" (1995), 41 C.R. (4th) 249.

R. v. CANCOIL THERMAL CORP.

(1986), 52 C.R. (3d) 188 (Ont. C.A.)

LACOURCIÈRE J.A. (MARTIN and GOODMAN JJ.A. concurring): — The Crown appeals by leave, on a pure question of law, against the order of the Honourable Judge Alan R. Campbell in the District Court of Ontario at Kingston dismissing two appeals from the judgment of His Honour Judge Baker acquitting the respondents. On January 10, 1985, the respondents had pleaded not guilty to the following charges:

> . . . Cancoil Thermal Corporation . . . as Employer on or about the 20th day of March, 1984 at the Township of Pittsburg in the County of Frontenac and Province of Ontario, did commit the offence of failing to ensure that the measures and procedures prescribed by section 28 of *Revised Regulations of Ontario, 1980*, Regulation 692 were carried out in the work place in an industrial establishment, to wit, a factory located at Kingston Mills Road East. Contrary to section 14(1)(c), the *Occupational Health and Safety Act*, R.S.O. 1980, c. 321.
>
> Particulars: A machine having an exposed moving part that endangered the safety of a worker was not equipped with and guarded by a guard or other device which prevented access to the moving part. Stewart Pare was injured as a result.
>
> (2) and further that Cancoil Thermal Corporation, Part Lot 41, Conc. 4, Pittsburg Township, as Employer, on or about the 20rh day of March, 1984, at the Township of Pittsburg in the County of Frontenac and Province of Ontario, did commit the offence of failing to ensure that the equipment, materials and protective devices prescribed by section 28 of *Revised Regulations of Ontario, 1980*, Regulation 692 were provided in an industrial establishment, to wit, a factory located at Kingston Mills Road East. Contrary to section 14(1)(a), the *Occupational Health and Safety Act*, R.S.O. 1980, c. 321.

Particulars: [same as above]

I. *The Facts*

The respondent corporation is in the business of manufacturing heat transfer coils at a factory located outside of Kingston. In December, 1983, the company took delivery of a large metal shearing machine, known as a "Newton Shear", which was needed to cut the metal used in the production of the casings for the coils. The blade of this "Newton Shear" was operated by means of a "foot pedal" located 7 1/2 inches from the floor. When this foot pedal was depressed, the clutch would engage, the "hold down" mechanism would clamp the inserted piece of metal in place, and the blade would come down and cut the metal. When the foot pedal was not depressed, the blade was in the up position and was not in motion. Needless to say, when the shearing mechanism was engaged by the depression of the foot pedal, the blade of the machine became dangerous to its operator.

When the respondent corporation took delivery of the Newton Shear, the machine was equipped with a "guard" which had been installed by its manufacturer to prevent access to the blade area of the machine by the operator during its operation. However, the respondent Parkinson, who was the supervisor and foreman of the factory, and Mr. Datta, its general manager, felt that the guard created a hazard in that its presence made it more difficult for the operator to clear away pieces of scrap metal. Accordingly, they decided to remove the guard from the machine. No other guard or similar safety device was installed on the machine as a replacement. It was felt that the hold down device provided sufficient safety to the operator of the machine. However, there were openings in the hold down mechanism which permitted physical access to the blade area of the machine. With the guard removed, there was nothing on the machine to prevent physical access to the blade.

On March 20, 1984, a 26 year old employee, Stuart Bradford Pare, while engaged in the operation of the metal shearing machine, accidentally cut off the tips of six of his fingers (three fingers of each hand) down to approximately the first joint. After cutting large pieces of metal into smaller pieces of a specified size, Mr. Pare, following what he described as the accepted procedure, had used his fingers to push a small piece of scrap metal through the machine and onto the floor. In the process of doing this he accidentally depressed the foot pedal on the machine, activating the blade mechanism.

There can be no doubt that the guard which came installed on the machine would have prevented this accident, acting as a barrier to prevent the operator's hands or fingers from going into the area of the cutting blade. Mr. Pare had been employed by the respondent as a machine operator for seven or eight months. Before March 20, 1984, he had operated the machine on one occasion and only for a short period; there was a conflict of evidence at trial as to the specific instructions given to him on safety precaution in the operation of the machine. Mr. Pare had helped Mr. Parkinson to modify the machine by removing the guard.

It will be more convenient to detail later the inspection of this machine made by an inspector of the Ministry of Labour before the accident, in January, 1984, and on the day after the accident when he made an order that the machine could not be used until the guard was replaced.

II. *The Statutory Provisions*

Generally, the *Occupational Health and Safety Act*, R.S.O. 1980, c. 321 is designed to protect the health and safety of workers in Ontario and is administered and enforced by the Ministry of Labour. Part VIII of the Act deals with enforcement. Inspectors are given broad powers to inspect the work place and to make orders, without the requirement of a hearing, where they find that a contravention of the Act or regulation creates a danger or hazard to the health or safety of a worker. Part IX deals with offences and penalties. The general penalty section is s. 37(1) which provides as follows:

37. — (1) Every person who contravenes or fails to comply with,
(a) a provision of this Act or the regulations;
(b) an order or requirement of an inspector or a Director; or
(c) an order of the Minister,

is guilty of an offence and on conviction is liable to a fine of not more than $25,000 or to imprisonment for a term of not more than twelve months, or to both.

The information alleged that the respondent corporation had breached s. 14(1)(a) and (c) which provide:

> 14. — (1) An employer shall ensure that,
> (a) the equipment, materials and protective devices as prescribed are provided;
> . . . .
>
> (c) the measures and procedures prescribed are carried out in the work place;

It was alleged that the respondent was in breach of s. 28 of the Regulations, R.R.O. 1980, Regulation 692 which provides:

> 28. Where a machine or prime mover or transmission equipment has an exposed moving part that may endanger the safety of any worker, the machine or prime mover or transmission equipment shall be equipped with and guarded by a guard or other device that prevents access to the moving part.

I should note at this time that the Act provides a statutory equivalent of the defence of due diligence. This provision does not apply to the offence charged against the respondent corporation under s. 14(1)(a). Section 37(2) of the Act provides as follows:

> (2) On a prosecution for a failure to comply with,
> (a) subsection 13(1);
> (b) clause 14(1)(b), (c) or (d); or
> (c) subsection 16(1),
>
> it shall be a defence for the accused to prove that every precaution reasonable in the circumstances was taken.

The specific exclusion of this statutory defence in the case of offences under s. 14(1)(a) would suggest that the Legislature, as a matter of policy, had determined that the subsection creates an offence of absolute liability, as defined in *The Queen v. City of Sault Ste. Marie*, [1978] 2 S.C.R. 1299. However, if s. 14(1)(a) were treated as creating an absolute liability offence, it would offend s. 7 of the *Charter*, the right to life, liberty and security of the person and the right not to be deprived thereof except in accordance with the principles of fundamental justice. Under s. 37(1), a violation of s. 14(1)(a) may attract a term of imprisonment. In *Reference re Section 94(2) of the Motor Vehicle Act*, [1985] 2 S.C.R. 486, the Supreme Court of Canada held that the combination of absolute liability and the potential penalty of imprisonment was a violation of s. 7 of the *Charter*. In the words of Lamer J. at p. 515:

> A law enacting an absolute liability offence will violate s. 7 of the *Charter* only if and to the extent that it has the potential of depriving of life, liberty, or security of the person.
> Obviously, imprisonment (including probation orders) deprives persons of their liberty. An offence has that potential as of the moment it is open to the Judge to impose imprisonment. There is no need that imprisonment, as in s. 94(2), be made mandatory.

> I am therefore of the view that the combination of imprisonment and of absolute liability
> violates s. 7 of the *Charter*. . . .

To avoid a violation of s. 7 of the *Charter*, s. 14(1)(*a*) must be treated as creating a strict liability offence. The defence of due diligence was available to the respondents.

III. *The Judgments Below*

The trial Judge considered the question before him to be whether the cutting blade of the machine was an exposed moving part that was unguarded. He found, in effect, that the "hold down" device and the foot pedal could be regarded as "two types of guard". Responding to a question of Crown counsel, he referred to the foot pedal as a protective measure within the meaning of s. 16(1), the section under which the individual respondent had been charged. In his conclusion, the trial Judge indicated that he was not satisfied beyond a reasonable doubt that the removal of the original guard left the blade unguarded. In the result, he found the respondents not guilty on each count.

The learned Judge, in the summary appeal, quoted and stressed the words "other device that prevents access to the moving part" which follows the requirement of a guard in s. 28 of the Regulation. He found that the hold down device "vitiated any significant guarding" but quoted with approval the trial Judge's subsequent discussion and concluded that the machine did "have a guard as required in the form of the foot pedal".

IV. *The Error of Law*

I agree with counsel for the appellant that both the learned Provincial Judge and the learned District Court Judge erred in law in holding that the legal definition of a "guard or other device that prevents access to the moving part" could possibly include the foot pedal. A guard is a protective device designed to prevent personal injury to the operator of a machine which is potentially dangerous because of the presence of an exposed moving part. Such a guard or protective device must be capable of preventing any intentional or inadvertent physical access to the potentially dangerous moving part, which, in the case of the Newton Shear, is the moving cutting blade. The device installed by the manufacturer and intentionally removed by the respondents came within the definition. The foot pedal is a device which activates the blade mechanism. It is incapable of preventing access to the moving blade.

The trial Judge erred in his interpretation of the relevant statutory regulation and found that the metal shearing machine was equipped with the protective device required by the regulation. The meaning of a word in a statute or a statutory regulation is question of law. There is no evidence upon which the Court could find that the foot pedal was a guard. The acquittals were therefore based on an error of law.

V. *The Disposition*

Having concluded that the acquittals should be set aside, the question now arises whether the Court should register a conviction against both respondents and remit the matters for sentencing or whether the Court should order a new trial.

It was conceded by the Crown that the courts below, having made the error of law, did not consider any defences that might be available to the respondents. It was open to the trier of fact, on this record, to find that the respondents took all reasonable care:

> This involves consideration of what a reasonable man would have done in the circumstances. The defence will be available if the accused reasonably believed in a mistaken set of facts which, if true, would render the act or omission innocent, or if he took all reasonable steps to avoid the particular event. (*The Queen v. City of Sault Ste. Marie, supra*, at p. 1326.)

I would, accordingly, direct a new trial. The onus then would be on the respondents to show, by a preponderance of evidence, that they acted with due diligence.

R. v. WHOLESALE TRAVEL GROUP INC.

[1991] 3 S.C.R. 154, 8 C.R. (4th) 145, 67 C.C.C. (3d) 193

In a most complex ruling the Court determined that a due diligence defence was all that could constitutionally be required in the case of the offence of false advertising under what is now s. 52(1)(*a*) of the *Competition Act*, R.S.C. 1985, c. C-34.

The Court also unanimously ruled that the due diligence defence could not be watered down by a more rigorous requirement than that of reasonable care. The Court struck down the *Competition Act's* express requirement that there had to have been a prompt retraction of the advertisement before an accused could subsequently successfully rely on the due diligence defence.

By a narrow majority of 5-4, the Supreme Court further held that placing the persuasive burden of proof on the accused was constitutional. The majority of the Court rejected a compromise proposal of the Ontario Law Reform Commission that a more principled solution to strict responsibility offences would be to presume negligence such that the accused would merely have an evidentiary burden. On this issue the following opinions were expressed.

LAMER C.J.C. (SOPINKA, McLACHLIN and LaFOREST JJ. concurring) (dissenting on this point): —

. . . .

Proportionality test

1. *Rational Connection*

Convicting all those who are unable to establish due diligence on a balance of probabilities, including those who were duly diligent, is one way of ensuring that all those guilty of false/misleading advertising are convicted, and is therefore one way of ensuring that the overall goal of ensuring fair and vigorous competition is attained. While this method of achieving the objective may raise certain problems and may not be the preferred method of achieving the objective, it is nonetheless a *logical* means of achieving the desired objective.

Thus, in my view, there is a rational connection between the objectives and the means chosen to attain the objectives, and the persuasive burden embodied in the words "he establishes that" in s. 37.3(2) therefore passes the first part of the proportionality test in *Oakes*.

2. *As Little as Possible*

While the imposition of a persuasive burden is rationally connected to the objective, it does not, in my view, infringe constitutionally protected rights as little as is reasonably possible. The Crown has not established that it is necessary to convict those who were duly diligent in order to "catch" those accused who were *not* duly diligent.

Parliament clearly had the option of employing a mandatory presumption of negligence (following from proof of the *actus reus*) which could be rebutted by something *less* than an accused's establishing due diligence on a balance of probabilities. This option was, in fact, recommended by the Ontario Law Reform Commission in its *Report on the Basis of Liability for Provincial Offences* (Toronto, 1990). The Commission stated (at p. 48):

> With respect to the burden of proof for strict liability offences, the Commission proposes a compromise solution that balances the fundamental rights of the accused with the need for effective law enforcement. We recommend the enactment of a mandatory presumption rather than a reverse onus. In other words, *in the absence of evidence to the contrary, negligence will be presumed. The Crown will continue to bear the burden of establishing the physical element or actus reus beyond a reasonable doubt. However, in a strict liability case, it will be necessary that evidence of conduct capable of amounting to reasonable care be adduced, either by the testimony of the accused, through the examination or cross-examination of a Crown or defence witness, or in some other way. The accused will merely have an evidentiary burden and will no longer be required to satisfy the persuasive burden of establishing, on a balance of probabilities, that he was not negligent. Where evidence of reasonable care has been adduced, thereby rebutting the presumption, in order to secure a conviction the prosecution should be required to establish the accused's negligence beyond a reasonable doubt.* [Emphasis added.]

I note that the presence of such a mandatory presumption alongside the accused's evidentiary burden would, in effect, require the accused to adduce evidence capable of amounting to evidence of due diligence, either through the testimony of the accused or that of other witnesses, including the cross-examination of Crown witnesses or by other means. It goes without saying that if the Crown has adduced such evidence, the accused can rely on it in discharge of the evidentiary burden. This will ensure that the information as to what steps, if any, were taken to avoid the occurrence of the prohibited act is in the record, and will relieve the Crown of the obligation to bring forward evidence on a matter that is exclusively in the possession of the accused. On the other hand, the Crown will bear the risk of non-persuasion if the conclusions and inferences to be drawn from such information leave the trier of fact in a state of reasonable doubt on the issue of due diligence.

In view of the foregoing, this alternative would not raise the problem discussed in *R. v. Chaulk, supra*, of imposing an "impossibly onerous burden" on the Crown. A requirement that the Crown prove lack of due diligence (negligence) beyond a reasonable doubt once an accused has rebutted a mandatory presumption is not akin to a requirement that the Crown prove an accused's sanity once the accused has raised a reasonable doubt about his or her sanity. In *R. v. Chaulk*, I indicated that the tremendous difficulties which would be faced by the Crown in proving sanity beyond a reasonable doubt flowed largely from the uncertainty of our scientific knowledge in this area. In my view, these difficulties are qualitatively different than the kinds of evidentiary difficulties which would be faced by the Crown in proving lack of due diligence beyond a reasonable doubt (once the accused has discharged the evidentiary burden).

The use of such a mandatory presumption in s. 37.3(2) would be less intrusive on s. 11(*d*) and would go a long way in achieving the objective: namely, ensuring that those who are *not* duly diligent are convicted (either because those accused would be unable to rebut the mandatory presumption or because the Crown would be able to prove a lack of due diligence). While the over-inclusive persuasive burden may bring about *more* convictions than would an evidentiary burden, the general objective of convicting the guilty would be attained by a less intrusive, evidentiary burden.

While a mandatory presumption with an evidentiary burden on the accused would be far less intrusive on s. 11(*d*) than would the existing persuasive burden, it must be recognized that a mandatory presumption would itself to some degree infringe the presumption of innocence. As discussed above, this court stated in *Oakes, supra*, that the presumption of innocence includes both the right of an accused to be presumed innocent until proven guilty, and the right to have the *state bear the burden* of proving guilt beyond a reasonable doubt. Unless it can be said that proof of the *actus reus* of false/misleading advertising, in and of itself and in all cases, leads inexorably to the conclusion that the accused was *negligent* in carrying out that *actus reus*, a mandatory presumption of negligence leaves open the possibility that the accused will be convicted despite the fact that the Crown's evidence leaves a reasonable doubt about the accused's negligence.

In the absence of a mandatory presumption, the Crown would be required to raise some evidence of negligence in order to secure a conviction. If the Crown failed to address the element of negligence, the accused could successfully raise a "no evidence motion" or (in a jury trial) a motion for a "directed verdict". The presence of a mandatory presumption means that the usual requirement for Crown evidence has been replaced by a presumption of negligence (which can only be rebutted if the accused can point to some evidence capable of raising a reasonable doubt about negligence). It follows from this that an accused who chose to remain silent and lead no defence evidence would, in the absence of some other evidence capable of raising a reasonable doubt, be deemed to have been negligent (a fault requirement which I have just concluded is constitutionally required), and would, therefore, be convicted. *Such would not be the case in the absence of a mandatory presumption and evidentiary burden.* It can be seen from the above discussion that a mandatory presumption can operate so as to indirectly force an accused into the stand in order to avoid being convicted. If proof of the *actus reus* itself necessarily established negligence in all cases, this would not conflict with the presumption of innocence because the accused would then be "forced" into the stand only as a result of the Crown's evidence of *actus reus* effectively constituting evidence of negligence (the necessary inference of negligence being drawn from the Crown's evidence of *actus reus*). However, mere proof of the *actus reus* of false advertising does *not* inexorably lead to the conclusion that the accused was negligent in committing the *actus reus*. Thus, the indirect compulsion of an accused into the stand which arises from a mandatory presumption of negligence infringes on an accused's s. 11(*d*) right to have the Crown prove his or her guilt beyond a reasonable doubt.

At the same time, it is my view that any such infringement of s. 11(*d*) would be clearly justified as a reasonable limit prescribed by law under s. 1 of the *Charter*. The objective of incorporating a mandatory presumption and evidentiary burden into s. 37.3(2) would be to avoid placing an impossible burden on the Crown. Like most public welfare offences, false/misleading advertising is of such a nature that the accused will be in the best position to garner evidence of due diligence. In the absence of *some* explanation by the accused, it will nearly always be impossible for the Crown to prove the absence of due diligence. Indeed, without an evidentiary burden on the accused, the Crown may well be put in the difficult situation which was addressed in *R. v. Chaulk, supra*, whereby the burden of adducing evidence of negligence on an ongoing basis could give rise to intrusions of other *Charter* rights, such as the right to be free from unreasonable search and seizure (s. 8). Thus, the use of a mandatory presumption in s. 37.3(2) would be rationally connected to avoiding this impossible burden, would fall well within the range of means which impair *Charter* rights as little as is reasonably possible, and would be proportional in its effect on the presumption of innocence.

In summary, while the use of a mandatory presumption in s. 37.3(2) would also infringe s. 11(*d*), it constitutes a less intrusive alternative which would not violate the *Charter* (in that it would constitute a justifiable limit under s. 1).

In light of this alternative, it is my view that the words "he establishes that" do not limit constitutionally protected rights as little as is reasonably possible, and that the persuasive burden cannot, therefore, be upheld as a reasonable limit under s. 1. However, even if it can be said that a mandatory presumption along with an evidentiary burden would not attain the objective *as effectively* as a persuasive burden and that the words in question therefore *do* limit *Charter* rights as little as is reasonably possible, it is my view that any marginal increase in the obtaining of the objective (via a persuasive burden on the accused) would be clearly outweighed by the detrimental effect on the presumption of innocence. In other words, if I am wrong in finding that the words in question do not pass the second branch of the proportionality test in *Oakes*, it is my view that the persuasive burden does not pass the third branch of the proportionality test in *Oakes* because the effect of the means chosen on *Charter* rights and freedoms is *not* proportional to the objective. Indeed, here we are postulating legislation enabling the imprisonment of those who were duly diligent but could not prove it on a balance of probabilities, even though there might well have existed a reasonable doubt thereof. Sending the innocent to jail is too high a price.

I also wish to point out that Parliament had the further option of maintaining the persuasive burden on the accused but removing the possibility of imprisonment. The use of a persuasive burden in circumstances where imprisonment was not a possible punishment would be far less intrusive on constitutional rights.

In light of the alternative means open to Parliament, I am of the view that the use of a persuasive burden in s. 37.3(2) cannot be justified under the proportionality part of the *Oakes* test.

In summary, it is my view that the words "he establishes that" contained in s. 37.3(2) limit s. 11(*d*) of the *Charter* and cannot be upheld as a reasonable limit under s. 1. Consequently, the words "he establishes that" must be held to be of no force or effect, pursuant to s. 52(1) of the *Constitution Act, 1982*.

Once the words "he establishes that" are deleted from s. 37.3(2), the question becomes, who proves what under the remaining provision? Parliament may well choose to re-enact the offence of false/misleading advertising within constitutionally acceptable parameters but, until such time, how is this offence to be proven? In my opinion, the answer to this question requires the court to consider this court's judgment in *R. v. Sault Ste. Marie (City)*, *supra*, but this time in light of the *Charter*.

In *R. v. Sault Ste. Marie (City)*, *supra*, this court set out a classification of offences to be followed where the Legislature had not expressly addressed the requirement of fault. The court drew a general distinction between "true crimes" and "public welfare offences". While the court contemplated public welfare offences which carried relatively light sentences, it would seem that the offence of false/misleading advertising would be one which would fall within the "public welfare" classification in *Sault Ste. Marie*. For "public welfare offences", the court held that the standard of fault was that of "strict liability". This meant that conviction would follow proof (by the Crown) of the actus reus, unless the accused proved, on a balance of probabilities, that he or she took all reasonable care and was duly diligent.

It is clear to me from the foregoing discussion of this court's judgments in *Oakes*, *Wigglesworth*, *Vaillancourt*, *Whyte*, and *Chaulk*, *supra*, that where an accused faces imprisonment upon conviction, the presence of the persuasive burden in the *Sault Ste. Marie* category of "strict liability" is inconsistent with the principles of fundamental justice. The previous judgments of this court make clear that, to the extent that imprisonment is a possible penalty, this category of "strict liability", placing a persuasive burden on the accused, cannot withstand *Charter* scrutiny. It follows from this that when imprisonment is a possible punishment for the commission of a "public welfare offence", the persuasive burden contemplated by this court in *R. v. Sault Ste. Marie (City)* cannot be operative; in this sense, the developing *Charter* jurisprudence of this court has, over the last five years, been modifying this holding in *Sault Ste. Marie*. At the same time, the reasons for not imposing a fault requirement of subjective mens rea for "public welfare offences", which were discussed at length in *Sault Ste. Marie*, are still compelling. Therefore, I would characterize the modification of *Sault Ste. Marie* as follows: where the Legislature has not expressly addressed the requirement of fault (or where, as here, it has done so in a manner which violates the Constitution), a "public welfare offence" (such as false/misleading advertising) which carries the possibility of imprisonment will be construed as setting up a rebuttable mandatory presumption of negligence. Once the Crown proves the *actus reus*, the accused will carry the evidentiary burden of pointing to some evidence (led either by the Crown or the defence) which is capable of raising a reasonable doubt as to his or her negligence, short of which a conviction will properly ensue.

CORY J. (L'HEUREUX-DUBÉ J. concurring): —

. . . .

In *Sault Ste. Marie*, Dickson J. carefully considered the basic principles of criminal liability, including the presumption of innocence, and balanced them against the public goals sought to be achieved through regulatory measures. He determined that strict liability represented an appropriate compromise between the competing interests involved. This conclusion is no less valid today. The *Charter* was not enacted in a vacuum. The presumption of innocence which it guarantees had long been established and was well recognized at common law. The due diligence defence recognized in *Sault Ste. Marie*, which is the target of the present challenge, was itself a function of the presumption of innocence.

The reasons for ascribing a different content to the presumption of innocence in the regulatory context are persuasive and compelling. As with the *mens rea* issue, if regulatory mechanisms are to operate effectively, the Crown cannot be required to disprove due diligence beyond a reasonable doubt. Such a requirement would make it virtually impossible for the Crown to prove regulatory offences, and would effectively prevent governments from seeking to implement public policy through regulatory means.

It has been suggested that requiring the Crown to prove negligence beyond a reasonable doubt, either as part of its case or after the accused adduces some evidence raising a reasonable doubt as to due diligence, would represent an acceptable compromise: it would, it is said, lessen the burden on the accused while still allowing for the effective pursuit of the regulatory objective. I cannot accept this contention. While such an approach would undoubtedly be beneficial to the accused, it would effectively eviscerate the regulatory power of government by rendering the enforcement of regulatory offences impossible in practical terms. Under this approach, the Crown would be forced to prove lack of reasonable care where the accused raises a reasonable doubt as to the possibility of due diligence.

It is difficult to conceive of a situation in which a regulated accused would not be able to adduce *some* evidence giving rise to the possibility that due diligence was exercised. For instance, an environmental polluter would often be able to point to *some* measures it had adopted in order to prevent the type of harm which ultimately resulted. This might raise a reasonable doubt that it had acted with due diligence, no matter how inadequate those measures were for the control of a dangerous situation. Similarly, a wholly inadequate effort to ensure that an advertisement was true might nevertheless succeed in raising a reasonable doubt as to due diligence.

To impose such a limited onus is inappropriate and insufficient in the regulatory context. Criminal offences have always required proof of guilt beyond a reasonable doubt; the accused cannot, therefore, be convicted where there is a reasonable doubt as to guilt. This is not so with regulatory offences, where a conviction will lie if the accused has failed to meet the standard of care required. Thus, the question is not whether the accused has exercised *some* care, but whether the degree of care exercised was sufficient to meet the standard imposed. If the false advertiser, the corporate polluter and the manufacturer of noxious goods are to be effectively controlled, it is necessary to require them to show on a balance of probabilities that they took reasonable precautions to avoid the harm which actually resulted. In the regulatory context, there is nothing unfair about imposing that onus; indeed, it is essential for the protection of our vulnerable society.

. . . .

Nor can I accept the contention that there is little practical difference between requiring the accused to prove due diligence on a balance of probabilities and requiring only that the accused raise a reasonable doubt as to the exercise of due diligence. Professor Webb, in his article, *supra*, deals with this argument in the following terms, at p. 467 [21 Ottawa L. Rev.]:

> Some might argue that in practice there is no workable distinction between an offence which requires the accused to prove due diligence on the balance of probabilities to avoid conviction, and one that permits the accused to raise a reasonable doubt as to the existence of due diligence. Trial Judges will find a way to convict those whom they feel are guilty of negligence, the argument would go, and they will acquit those whom they feel have exercised due diligence, regardless of burdens of proof. This type of reasoning certainly contradicts the statement of the trial Judge in *Whyte*, [*supra*], who contended that in the absence of a balance of probability presumption, he would have found reasonable doubt as to whether the accused had "care and control" of a motor vehicle.

Webb then goes on, at p. 467, to identify the deleterious effects on prosecution of regulatory offences which would result from requiring the Crown to prove negligence:

> The "there is no difference in practice anyway" argument also fails to recognize the different quantity and quality of evidence which administrators would be forced to provide to prosecutors in preparation for a case. If an evidential rather than a persuasive burden is adopted, merely raising a reasonable doubt as to the existence of due diligence would then shift the burden of proof to the prosecutors to *prove negligence*. Prior to any case reaching the prosecution stage, administrators would be under an obligation to collect all the evidence necessary to prove negligence. In effect, prosecutors would be more likely to turn down a request from administrators for a prosecution unless proof of negligence could be established. Given the difficulty in accumulating such information, it is not unlikely that there would be a chilling effect on use of the prosecution mechanism. Once it became noticeable that less cases were reaching the Courts, it is possible that regulatees would receive the signal that, in most circumstances, the offence of negligence was not enforceable. [Emphasis in original.]

I agree with these conclusions of Professor Webb. To reduce the onus on the accused would, from a practical point of view, raise insurmountable barriers for the Crown seeking to enforce a regulatory scheme.

In these circumstances, it cannot be contended that requiring the prosecution to prove negligence beyond a reasonable doubt would still allow for the effective achievement of regulatory objectives. To the contrary, its effect would be, in practical terms, to render the regulatory power of governments ineffectual.

Nor can it be argued that other solutions would be satisfactory; there is simply no other practical solution. Both with respect to the consumption of government resources and the intrusiveness of regulatory measures, the consequences of a finding that the due diligence defence violates s. 11(*d*) of the *Charter* would be extremely severe. Governments would be forced to devote tremendous expenditure, in terms of monetary and human resources, to regulatory enforcement mechanisms. Armies of investigators and experts would be required in order to garner sufficient evidence to establish negligence or disprove due diligence beyond a reasonable doubt.

Further, a marked expansion in enforcement mechanisms by definition implies an escalation in the intrusiveness of regulatory measures. The greater the burden of proof on the Crown, the greater the likelihood that those charged with the enforcement of regulatory measures would have to resort to legislation authorizing search and surveillance in order to gather sufficient evidence to discharge that onus.

As with the s. 7 challenge, licensing considerations support the conclusion that strict liability does not violate s. 11(*d*) of the *Charter*. The licensing argument attributes to the regulated actor knowledge and acceptance, not only of the standard of reasonable care itself, but also of the responsibility to establish on a balance of probabilities the exercise of reasonable care. Acceptance of this burden is an implied term and a precondition of being allowed to engage in activity falling within the regulated sphere. Regulated actors are taken to understand that, should they be unable to discharge this burden, an inference of negligence will be drawn from the fact that the proscribed result has occurred.

I wish to emphasize, however, that the difference in the scope and meaning of s. 11(d) in the regulatory context does not imply that the presumption of innocence is meaningless for a regulated accused. The Crown must still prove the actus reus of regulatory offences beyond a reasonable doubt. Thus, the Crown must prove that the accused polluted the river, sold adulterated food, or published a false advertisement. However, once having established this beyond a reasonable doubt, the Crown is presumptively relieved of having to prove anything further. Fault is presumed from the bringing about of the proscribed result, and the onus shifts to the defendant to establish reasonable care on a balance of probabilities.

For these reasons, I conclude that the presumption of innocence as guaranteed in s. 11(d) of the *Charter* is not violated by strict liability offences as defined in *Sault Ste. Marie*. The imposition of a reverse persuasive onus on the accused to establish due diligence on a balance of probabilities does not run counter to the presumption of innocence, notwithstanding the fact that the same reversal of onus would violate s. 11(d) in the criminal context.

IACOBUCCI J. (GONTHIER and STEVENSON JJ. concurring): — [Agreeing with the result of Justice Cory's judgment, and therefore making up the majority judgment.]

. . . .

With respect to the second requirement of *Oakes*, I agree that there is a rational connection between the desired objective and the means chosen to attain the objective. Removing the burden on the Crown to prove lack of due diligence beyond a reasonable doubt, and instead requiring the accused to establish due diligence on a balance of probabilities, is without a doubt a rational and logical way of attaining the legislative objective.

However, it is with respect to the third requirement of the *Oakes* analysis, that I respectfully disagree with the conclusions of Lamer C.J.C. This step requires a consideration of whether the means chosen impair the right or freedom in question *no more than is necessary to accomplish the desired objective*. Lamer C.J.C. is of the opinion that the use of a persuasive burden in s. 37.3(2) of the *Competition Act* cannot pass this third step of the *Oakes* analysis because of the presence of an alternative means open to Parliament that would be less intrusive on s. 11(d) of the *Charter* and would "go a long way" in achieving the objective. The alternative in question is the use of a "mandatory presumption of negligence" (following from the proof of the actus reus) which could be rebutted by something less than an accused establishing due diligence on a balance of probabilities, *i.e.*, by raising a reasonable doubt as to due diligence. With respect, I cannot agree that such a means would achieve the stated objective as effectively, nor would it go a long way in achieving it. Such a means would shift to the accused the burden of simply raising a reasonable doubt as to due diligence, and would not thereby allow the effective pursuit of the regulatory objective. It would leave the Crown the legal burden of proving facts largely within the peculiar knowledge of the accused.

For the reasons given by Cory J. in the context of his s. 11(*d*) analysis, such an alternative would in practice make it virtually impossible for the Crown to prove public welfare offences such as the one in question, and would effectively prevent governments from seeking to implement public policy through prosecution. It would also not provide effective inducement for those engaged in regulated activity to comply strictly with the regulatory scheme, including adopting proper procedures and record-keeping and might even have a contrary effect. Though such a result would be clearly advantageous to an accused, it would not be effective in avoiding the loss of convictions because the Crown could not prove facts within the particular knowledge of the accused. In sum, taking into account the particular circumstances described by Cory J. in his reasons, Parliament could *not* "reasonably have chosen an alternative means which would have achieved the identified objective as effectively": *R. v. Chaulk*, [1990] 3 S.C.R. 1303, 2 C.R. (4th) 1, 62 C.C.C. (3d) 193, at p. 1341, [S.C.R., p. 31 C.R.] per Lamer C.J.C. for the majority.

As for the final requirement of the *Oakes* analysis, I would also respectfully disagree with the conclusions of Lamer C.J.C. As noted by Cory J. in his reasons, regulated activity and public welfare offences are a fundamental part of Canadian society. Those who choose to participate in regulated activities must be taken to have accepted the consequential responsibilities and their penal enforcement. One of these consequences is that they should be held responsible for the harm that may result from their lack of due diligence. Unless they can prove on a balance of probabilities that they exercised due diligence, they shall be convicted and in some cases face a possible prison term. These participants are in the best position to prove due diligence, since they possess in most cases the required information. Viewed in this context, and taking into account the fundamental importance of the legislative objective as stated and the fact that the means chosen impair the right guaranteed by s. 11(*d*) as little as is reasonably possible, the effects of the reverse onus on the presumption of innocence are proportional to the objective.

Having found that the reverse onus on the accused to establish due diligence on a balance of probabilities (via the words "he establishes that" in s. 37.3(2) of the *Competition Act*) satisfies all four requirements of the *Oakes* analysis, I conclude that such an onus is saved under s. 1 of the *Charter* as a reasonable limit in a free and democratic society. Accordingly, I would dispose of the appeal in the manner suggested by Cory J.

It has not yet been determined whether the majority's ruling on the question of onus can also apply to the burden of proving due diligence defences in the case of some *Criminal Code* offences. In the context of the following regulatory offence, which was accepted to be one of strict liability, consider whether it was wise that the Supreme Court decided that the accused should bear a persuasive and not merely evidentiary burden of proving due diligence:

An elevator installation worker, employed by the elevator installation subcontractor, fell down an elevator shaft to his death at a building under construction. He had apparently arrived earlier than expected, unfastened a barrier to the shaft, and either climbed or jumped down to a wooden structure a few feet below the level of the 13th floor. The structure had been temporarily supported but was not sufficiently strong to support a person's weight. Charges were laid under the *Occupational Health and Safety Act*, R.S.O. 1980, c. 321, against the general contractor for failing to ensure that the safety measures set out in the regulations were carried out on its project, and also against the project's superintendent for failing to ensure that workers acted in accordance with the safety measures.

Compare *R. v. Ellis-Don Ltd.* (1990), 2 C.R. (4th) 118 (Ont. C.A.), in which the majority held that the accused should merely have an evidentiary burden. This ruling was reversed without full reasons by the Supreme Court of Canada, applying *Wholesale Travel* (1992), 71 C.C.C. (3d) 63 (S.C.C.). Unlike *Wholesale Travel*, the Court had here been presented with full evidence of enforcement patterns seeking to show that the reverse onus was unnecessary.

---

1. The accused shot and killed a black bear and three grizzly bears. They had obtained the appropriate hunting licence for each type of bear. A week earlier, after an abortive hunt, they had shot and killed an ailing horse and left it in the area. The bears had been attracted to the carcass. The accused were charged with the offence of using bait for the purpose of hunting big game, contrary to s. 50(1)(*b*) of the *Alberta Wildlife Act*, R.S.A. 1980, c. W-9, which reads: "No person shall for the purpose of hunting or taking big game set out, use or employ . . . any bait of any kind". The penalty is a fine of not less than $100 and not more than $1,500 and, in default of payment, imprisonment for a term of not more than six months.
How should the offence be classified?
Compare *R. v. Brown* (1982), 29 C.R. (3d) 107, 69 C.C.C. (2d) 301, (Alta. C.A.), leave to appeal to S.C.C. refused (1982), 46 N.R. 85.

2. The accused was charged with wilfully having evaded or attempted to evade the payment of moneys, contrary to s. 62(*d*) of the *Quebec Revenue Department Act*, S.O. 1972, c. 22. At trial, counsel for the accused admitted all the facts charged except that he had acted "wilfully". The prosecution then declared its case closed. Counsel for the accused moved for non-suit, alleging absence of proof of intent, this being a *mens rea* offence.
Rule on the motion
(1) where "wilfully" appears in the section, and
(2) where it does not.
Compare *Pichette v. Dep. in Revenue of Que.* (1982), 29 C.R. (3d) 129 (Que. C.A.).

3. The accused, while hunting, shot a deer, then realized that he had left his deer tag at home. He returned home to get his deer tag, but in the meantime a Lands and Forests Officer found the untagged deer. The accused was charged with failing to tag deer contrary to the Deer Regulations made pursuant to the *Nova Scotia Lands and Forests Act*, R.S.N.S. 1967, c. 163. The regulations declare that a licensed hunter on

killing a deer "shall immediately affix and securely lock" his tag to the carcass. The penalty is a fine of not less than $100 nor more than $300.

Is the offence absolute or strict? Is it constitutional?

Compare *R. v. Maidment* (1984), 37 C.R. (3d) 387, 10 C.C.C. (3d) 512 (N.S. C.A.).

4. Your client is faced with a speeding charge with a fixed $200 fine. He is bankrupt and will be sent to gaol in default.

Is the offence absolute or strict? Is it constitutional?

Compare *R. v. Lemieux* (1978), 3 C.R. (3d) 284, 41 C.C.C. (2d) 33 (Que. C.A.); *R. v. Naugler* (1981), 25 C.R. (3d) 392, 65 C.C.C. (2d) 25 (N.S. C.A.); *R. v. Burt* (1987), 60 C.R. (3d) 372, 38 C.C.C. (3d) 299 (Sask. C.A.) and *R. v. Williams* (1992), 14 C.R. (4th) 218, 74 C.C.C. (3d) 160 (N.S. C.A.).

5. The accused was charged under s. 5(1) of the *Food and Drugs Act*, R.S.C. 1970, c. F-27, which provides:

> 5.(1) No person shall label, package, treat, process, sell or advertise any food in a manner that is false, misleading or deceptive or is likely to create an erroneous impression regarding its character, value, quantity, composition, merit or safety.

An inspector of the Federal Department of Consumer and Corporate Affairs went to the accused's meat market to discuss the purchase of a side of beef. He requested that, after packaging, all bone and trim be returned to him. Subsequent analysis indicated a weight discrepancy of some 15 pounds. Reconstructing the hide of beef indicated both the sirloin tip and a sirloin steak were missing. Also, extraneous portions of bone and fat were found that could not have been part of the side purchased. The accused testified that he was not in the store on the day the side was butchered. His employee, who could not specifically recollect the sale, stated that the store was very busy that day. The employee and the accused both testified that no meat was ever deliberately left out of an order but occasionally meat was forgotten or inadvertently left in the freezer. When those incidents occurred and the store was notified the mistakes were always rectified. Section 29 of the Act only provides a defence to any individual dealing with *pre-packaged* material if he can establish that he could not with reasonable diligence ascertain the quality of the goods. Give judgment. Compare *R. v. Grottoli* (1978), 43 C.C.C. (2d) 158 (Ont. C.A.).

Summary: Regulatory Offences

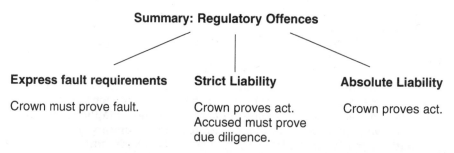

Express fault requirements	Strict Liability	Absolute Liability
Crown must prove fault.	Crown proves act. Accused must prove due diligence.	Crown proves act.

It would appear that all provincial offences, and federal offences which do not incorporate *Criminal Code* standards, may be safely characterized as regulatory. In such cases the approach to fault seems clear. Courts should give full expression to any express legislative fault requirement whether this be subjective *mens rea*, negligence or statutory due diligence defences. In the case of all other regulatory offences, as a matter of common-law presumption or constitutional requirement, where the liberty interest is engaged, the Court should read in a defence of due diligence. Under this state of the law absolute liability offences should be very rare.

An example of an express fault requirement in a regulatory statute is the objective test required for provincial offences of careless driving. Typical wording is that found in the *Highway Traffic Act*, R.S.O. 1990, c. H.8, s. 130:

> Every person is guilty of an offence of driving carelessly who drives a vehicle or street car on a highway without due care and attention and without reasonable consideration for other persons using the highway and on conviction is liable to a fine of not less than $100 and not more than $500 or to imprisonment for a term of not more than six months, or to both, and in addition his licence or permit may be suspended for a period of not more than two years.

R. v. BEAUCHAMP

(1953), 16 C.R. 270, 106 C.C.C. 6 (Ont. C.A.)

The accused was convicted of careless driving. The accused had driven his bus out onto the street from the parking garage. At this time there were no other cars on the street. The accused waited for another bus to leave the garage and then proceeded to back very slowly into a parking position on the street. Unfortunately, in the interim, another car had come down the street and parked in that position. The accused testified he checked his inside mirror, also looked through the back window, but found his outside mirror was loose and, because of the vibration, of no use. The bus crumpled the other car's bumper, grille and fender. The Court of Appeal allowed the accused's appeal.

MacKay J.A.: —

. . . .

My conclusions are that, while the same facts may, and in many cases do, give rise to both civil and criminal proceedings, nevertheless there is no necessity, in dealing with criminal or quasi-criminal conduct in relation to the operation of motor vehicles, for entering into a discussion or consideration of the negligence that would support a civil action. It is also clear that there are different degrees of criminal or quasi-criminal negligence.

Section 29(1) of *The Highway Traffic Act* creates a statutory offence that is quasi-criminal in its nature: *Rex v. Van Leishout* (1943), 80 C.C.C. 361.

A crime is defined in 9 Halsbury, 2nd ed. 1933, p. 9, para. 1, as follows:

> A crime is an unlawful act or default which is an offence against the public, and renders the person guilty of the act or default liable to legal punishment. While a crime is often also an injury to a private person, who has remedy in a civil action, it is as an act or default contrary

to the order, peace, and well-being of society that a crime is punishable by the State. A civil proceeding has for its object the recovery of money or other property, or the enforcement of a right for the advantage of the person suing, while a criminal proceeding has for its object the punishment of a public offence.

To support a charge under s. 29(1) of *The Highway Traffic Act*, the evidence must be such as to prove beyond reasonable doubt that the accused drove in the manner prohibited by the subsection, namely, without due care and attention or without reasonable consideration for others. The standard of care and skill to be applied has been long established and is not that of perfection. It is, I think, correctly stated in Mazengarb, *op cit.*, at pp. 176-7, as follows:

> The law does not require of any driver that he should exhibit "perfect nerve and presence of mind, enabling him to do the best thing possible." It does not expect men to be more than ordinary men. Drivers of vehicles cannot be required to regulate their driving as if in constant fear that other drivers who are under observation, and apparently acting reasonably and properly, may possibly act at a critical moment in disregard of the safety of themselves and other users of the road.

> But the law does insist upon a reasonable amount of skill in the handling of a vehicle which is a potential source of danger to other users of the road. . . . The question always is "What would an ordinary prudent person in the position of the plaintiff have done in relation to the event complained of?" (Pollock on Torts uses the term "average man".)

Motor vehicles are now in general use as a common means of transportation and pleasure. If too high a standard of care and skill were demanded, those people who are not capable of attaining such a standard would be deprived of the privilege of driving motor vehicles, and their use would be confined to experts, and even persons who might become experts might well be prevented from qualifying as such by experience. It must also be borne in mind that the test, where an accident has occurred, is not whether, if the accused had used greater care or skill, the accident would not have happened. It is whether it is proved beyond reasonable doubt that this accused, in the light of existing circumstances of which he was aware or of which a driver exercising ordinary care should have been aware, failed to use the care and attention or to give to other persons using the highway the consideration that a driver of ordinary care would have used or given in the circumstances? The use of the term "due care", which means care owing in the circumstances, makes it quite clear that, while the legal standard of care remains the same in the sense that it is what the average careful man would have done in like circumstances, the factual standard is a constantly shifting one, depending on road, visibility, weather conditions, traffic conditions that exist or may reasonably be expected, and any other conditions that ordinary prudent drivers would take into consideration. It is a question of fact, depending on the circumstances in each case.

In this case, and in some of the cases to which I have referred, evidence has been admitted to show that the accused had a good record as a careful driver. Such evidence is not relevant on the issue of guilt or innocence. As was said by Lord Hewart C.J. in *McCrone v. Riding*, *supra*, at p. 158: "That standard is an objective standard, impersonal and universal, fixed in relation to the safety of other users of the highway. It is in no way related to the degree of proficiency or degree of experience attained by the individual driver."

There is a further important element that must also be considered, namely, that the conduct must be of such a nature that it can be considered a breach of duty to the public and deserving of punishment. This further step must be taken even if it is found that the conduct of the accused falls below the standard set out in the preceding paragraphs. This principle may be somewhat difficult to apply, but I think it might be illustrated by the common example of a motorist attempting to park at the curb in a space between two other parked vehicles. Frequently one or other of the parked vehicles is bumped in the process. Damage seldom arises, because cars are equipped with bumpers, but if damage were caused it might well give rise to a civil action for damages, but it could hardly be said to be such a lack of care or attention as would be considered to be deserving of punishment as a crime or quasi-crime.

Fault for Crimes

(a) Charter Standards

Once the Supreme Court decided in *Motor Vehicle Act Reference* that a due diligence defence was the minimum standard of fault required by the *Charter* for any type of offence threatening the liberty interest, it was only a matter of time before the Supreme Court would have to decide whether that standard or another was sufficient for *Criminal Code* offences. The first challenge came with respect to the law of murder.

Murder under ss. 229(a)(i) or (ii)

SIMPSON v. R.

(1981), 20 C.R. (3d) 36, 58 C.C.C. (2d) 122 (Ont. C.A.), at 61-64 (C.R.)

MARTIN J.A.: —

Following the argument of the appeal, and while the decision of the Court was under reserve, the Court requested counsel to submit argument with respect to the effect of a passage in the Judge's charge defining the intent requisite for attempted murder, to which no objection was taken at the trial and which was not a ground of appeal. The Court reconvened on 12th February 1981 and heard argument with respect to the passage in question.

The learned trial Judge charged the jury as follows:

> Under the *Criminal Code*, anyone who attempts by any means to commit murder is guilty of an indictable offence. In this case, neither victim died, most fortunately. So the charge isn't murder, but attempted murder. What is murder? It is defined in s. 212 of the *Criminal Code*, in part, as follows:

> "Culpable homicide is murder
>
> (a) where the person who causes the death of a human being
> (i) means to cause his death, or
> (ii) means to cause him bodily harm that he knows is likely to cause his death and is reckless whether death ensues or not".

Now, "culpable" means "blameworthy". Culpable homicide is death of a human being for which some person may be blamed in law. The definition that I have just read to you, then, is one of murder, and the charge we are dealing with here is attempt to murder. I have earlier told you that proof of the intention of the accused is an essential element in the offence of attempt to murder. The Crown must satisfy you beyond a reasonable doubt that the accused stabbed the victim and that he did so intending to cause the death, or intending to cause the victim bodily harm that he knew or ought to have known was likely to cause death and was reckless whether death ensued or not. I repeat the second part of that definition: If the Crown has, on the evidence, satisfied you beyond a reasonable doubt that the accused was the stabber and that in stabbing he intended to cause bodily harm that he knew or ought to have known was likely to cause death and was reckless whether death ensued or not, then the offence of attempted murder has been proved.

It has now been authoritatively decided that either of the intents specified in s. 212(a)(i) and (ii) [now ss. 229(a)(i) and (ii)] suffices to constitute the intent required for the offence of attempted murder: see *Lajoie v. R.*, [1974] S.C.R. 399, 20 C.R.N.S. 360; *R. v. Ritchie*, (1970), 16 C.R.N.S. 287, [1970] 5 C.C.C. 336 (C.A.). Unfortunately, the learned trial Judge, in paraphrasing the intent specified in s. 212(a)(ii) — namely, an intention to cause bodily harm that the offender *knows* is likely to cause death — substituted for the requisite intent an intention to cause bodily harm that the offender knows or *ought to know* is likely to cause death. This incorrect summary of the provision of s. 212(a)(ii) constituted a serious error. Liability under s. 212(a)(ii) is subjective, and the requisite *knowledge* that the intended injury is likely to cause death must be brought home to the accused subjectively. To substitute for that state of mind an intention to cause bodily harm that the accused knows or *ought* to know is likely to cause death is to impose liability on an objective basis. An intention to cause bodily harm that the offender *ought* to have known was likely to cause death is merely evidence from which, along with all the other circumstances, the jury *may* infer that the accused actually had the requisite intention and knowledge required by s. 212(a)(ii). It does not, however, constitute the requisite state of mind.

The effect of the misdirection is magnified by the fact that the incorrect statement of the intention required to be proved was repeated twice in the passage above reproduced. Although the learned trial Judge had read the provisions of s. 212(a)(i) and (ii) just before the impugned passage, the jury was more likely to remember his clear-cut summary than the provisions of the *Code*: see *R. v. Harrison* (1945), 84 C.C.C. 78 at 82-83 (C.A.).

The error was never corrected by the learned trial Judge. It is true that, in putting the case for the Crown, he said:

> The Crown suggests to you that, if you are satisfied that Simpson was the attacker, you should in the circumstances have no doubt that he intended to kill or cause bodily harm knowing that it might result in death and being reckless as to whether death ensued or not.

It is to be observed that even this passage is not entirely correct, as it refers to an intention to cause bodily harm knowing that it *might* result in death, as distinct from an intention to inflict bodily harm that the offender knows is *likely* to cause bodily harm. In any event, the jury would rely on the Judge's instruction, as they had previously been told they must, with respect to the elements of the offence of attempted murder.

In my view, the seriousness of the error requires a new trial, unless it is proper to invoke the curative provisions of s. 613(1)(*b*)(iii). In *R. v. Smith* (1977), 33 C.C.C. (2d) 172 (Ont. C.A.), the trial Judge, in instructing the jury as to the definition of murder, had on a number of occasions incorrectly summarized the provisions of s. 212(*a*)(ii) by omitting from the definition of the necessary intent the requirement that the person who means to cause bodily harm knows that the bodily harm is likely to cause death. The Court in that case was satisfied, in view of the clear direction with respect to this requirement by the trial Judge on so many occasions during his charge, that in the context in which the slips occurred they did not result in a substantial wrong or miscarriage of justice. In *R. v. Reynolds* (1978), 44 C.C.C. (2d) 129 (C.A.), the trial judge, in instructing the jury as to the elements of murder under s. 212(*a*)(ii), had made a similar error on a number of occasions in his charge, but on the error being brought to his attention he gave the jury an emphatic and correct instruction which, in the opinion of the court, nullified the earlier errors.

I have not been persuaded, even by Mr. Watt's able argument, that it is appropriate to invoke the provisions of s. 613(1)(*b*)(iii) in relation to the conviction of the appellant on count 2, relating to Cathy Wagenaar. I am not satisfied that a reasonable jury, properly instructed, having found that the appellant was Cathy Wagenaar's assailant, would inevitably have found that he intended to kill her or intended to inflict an injury upon her that he *knew* was likely to kill her. Although it would be open to a properly instructed jury to conclude that the requisite intent to constitute attempted murder had been established, the accompanying circumstances and the assailant's utterances are not such as to inevitably require a reasonable jury to reach that conclusion.

. . . .

New trial ordered.

Constructive Murder: ss. 229(c) and 230

VAILLANCOURT v. R.

[1987] 2 S.C.R. 636, 60 C.R. (3d) 289, 39 C.C.C. (3d) 118

LAMER J. (DICKSON C.J.C. and WILSON J. concurring): —

INTRODUCTION

Vaillancourt was convicted of second degree murder following a trial before a sessions Court Judge and jury in Montreal. He appealed to the Quebec Court of Appeal, arguing that the Judge's charge to the jury on the combined operation of ss. 213(d) [now s. 230(d)] and 21(2) of the *Criminal Code*, R.S.C. 1970, c. C-34, was incorrect. His appeal was dismissed and the conviction was affirmed [31 C.C.C. (3d) 75]. Before this Court, he has challenged the constitutional validity of s. 213(d), alone and in combination with s. 21(2), under the *Canadian Charter of Rights and Freedoms*.

THE FACTS

For the purposes of this appeal, the Crown does not contest the following statement of the facts.

The appellant and his accomplice committed an armed robbery in a pool hall. The appellant was armed with a knife and his accomplice with a gun. During the robbery, the appellant remained near the front of the hall while the accomplice went to the back. There was a struggle between the accomplice and a client. A shot was fired and the client was killed. The accomplice managed to escape and has never been found. The appellant was arrested at the scene.

In the course of his testimony, the appellant said that he and his accomplice had agreed to commit this robbery armed only with knives. On the night of the robbery, however, the accomplice arrived at their meeting place with a gun. The appellant said that he objected because on a previous armed robbery his gun had discharged accidentally, and he did not want that to happen again. He insisted that the gun be unloaded. The accomplice removed three bullets from the gun and gave them to the appellant. The appellant then went to the bathroom and placed the bullets in his glove. The glove was recovered by the police at the scene of the crime and was found at trial to contain three bullets. The appellant testified that at the time of the robbery he was certain that the gun was unloaded.

CONSTITUTIONAL QUESTIONS

Before this Court, the following constitutional questions were formulated:

> 1. Is s. 213(d) of the *Criminal Code* inconsistent with the provisions of either s. 7 or s. 11(d) of the *Canadian Charter of Rights and Freedoms* and, therefore, of no force or effect?

2. If not, is the combination of s. 21 and 213(*d*) of the *Criminal Code* inconsistent with the provisions of either s. 7 or s. 11(*d*) of the *Canadian Charter of Rights and Freedoms* and is s. 21 of the *Criminal Code* therefore of no force or effect in the case of a charge under s. 213(*d*) of the *Criminal Code*?

THE LAW

Narrowing the issue

The appellant has framed his attack on s. 213(*d*) of the *Code* in very wide terms. He has argued that the principles of fundamental justice require that, before Parliament can impose any criminal liability for causing a particular result, there must be some degree of subjective *mens rea* in respect of that result. This is a fundmental question with far-reaching consequences. If this case were decided on that basis, doubt would be cast on the constitutional validity of many provisions throughout our *Criminal Code*, in particular s. 205(5)(*a*) [now s. 222(5)(*a*)], whereby causing death by means of an unlawful act is culpable homicide, and s. 212(*c*) [now s. 229(*c*)], whereby objective foreseeability of the likelihood of death is sufficient for a murder conviction in certain circumstances.

However, the appellant was convicted under s. 213(*d*) and the constitutional question is limited to this provision. In my opinion, the validity of s. 213(*d*) can be decided on somewhat narrower grounds. In addition, the Attorney General of Canada has seen fit not to intervene to support the constitutionality of s. 213(*d*), which is clearly in jeopardy in this case, though he might have intervened to support ss. 205(5)(*a*) and 212(*c*) and other similar provisions. I will thus endeavour not to make pronouncements the effect of which will be to predispose in *obiter* of other issues more properly dealt with if and when the constitutionality of the other provisions is in issue. I do, however, find it virtually impossible to make comments as regards s. 213(*d*) that will not have some effect on the validity of the rest of s. 213 or that will not reveal to some extent my views as regards s. 212(*c*). However, the validity of those sections and of subs. (*a*) to (*c*) of s. 213 is not in issue here and I will attempt to limit my comments to s. 213(*d*).

The appellant has also challenged the combined operation of ss. 21(2) and 213(*d*). Given my decision on the validity of s. 213(*d*), and in view of the importance of s. 21(2) and the absence of the Attorney General of Canada, I do not find it necessary or advisable to deal with s. 21(2) in this appeal.

Analysis of s. 213(d)

Section 213(*d*) in the context of the murder provisions

It is first necessary to analyze s. 213(*d*) in the context of the other murder provisions in the *Code* in order to determine its true nature and scope. Murder is defined as a culpable homicide committed in the circumstances set out at ss. 212 and 213 of the *Code*. There is a very interesting progression through s. 212 to s. 213 with respect to the mental state that must be proven.

The starting point is s. 212(*a*)(i), which provides:

> 212. Culpable homicide is murder
>
> (*a*) where the person who causes the death of a human being
>
> (i) means to cause his death . . .

This clearly requires that the accused have actual subjective foresight of the likelihood of causing the death, coupled with the intention to cause that death. This is the most morally blameworthy state of mind in our system.

There is a slight relaxation of this requirement in s. 212(*a*)(ii), which provides:

> 212. Culpable homicide is murder
>
> (*a*) where the person who causes the death of a human being . . .
>
> (ii) means to cause him bodily harm that he knows is likely to cause his death, and is reckless whether death ensues or not   . . .

Here again the accused must have actual subjective foresight of the likelihood of death. However, the Crown need no longer prove that he intended to cause the death, but only that he was reckless whether death ensued or not. It should also be noted that s. 212(*a*)(ii) is limited to cases where the accused intended to cause bodily harm to the victim.

Section 212(*c*) provides:

> 212. Culpable homicide is murder. . .
>
> (*c*) where a person, for an unlawful object, does anything that he knows or ought to know is likely to cause death, and thereby causes death to a human being, notwithstanding that he desires to effect his object without causing death or bodily harm to any human being.

In part, this is simply a more general form of recklessness, and thus the logical extension of s. 212(*a*)(ii), in that it applies when the accused "does *anything* . . . he knows . . . is likely to cause death" (emphasis added). However, there is also a further relaxation of the mental element required for murder, in that it is also murder where the accused "does *anything that he . . . ought to know* is likely to cause death" (emphasis added). This eliminates the requirement of actual subjective foresight and replaces it with objective foreseeability or negligence.

The final relaxation in the definition of murder occurs at s. 213:

> 213. Culpable homicide is murder where a person causes the death of a human being while committing or attempting to commit high treason or treason or an offence mentioned in section 52 (sabotage), 76 (piratical acts), 76.1 (hijacking an aircraft), 132 or subsection 133(1) or sections 134 to 136 (escape or rescue from prison or lawful custody), 143 or 145 (rape or attempt to commit rape), 149 or 156 (indecent assault), subsection 246(2) (resisting lawful arrest), 247 (kidnapping and forcible confinement), 302 (robbery), 306 (breaking and entering) or 389 or 390 (arson), whether or not the person means to cause death to any human being and whether or not he knows that death is likely to be caused to any human being, if

(*a*) he means to cause bodily harm for the purpose of
(i) faclitating the commission of the offence, or
(ii) facilitating his flight after committing or attempting to commit the offence,
and the death ensues from the bodily harm;

(*b*) he administers a stupefying or overpowering thing for a purpose mentioned in paragraph (*a*), and the death ensues therefrom;

(*c*) he wilfully stops, by any means, the breath of a human being for a purpose mentioned in paragraph (*a*), and the death ensues therefrom; or

(*d*) he uses a weapon or has it upon his person
(i) during or at the time he commits or attempts to commit the offence, or
(ii) during or at the time of his flight after committing or attempting to commit the offence,
and the death ensues as a consequence.

Under this provision, it is murder if the accused causes the victim's death while committing or attempting to commit one of the enumerated offences if he performs one of the acts in subss. (*a*) to (*d*). Proof that the accused performed one of the acts in subss. (*a*) to (*d*) is substituted for proof of any subjective foresight, or even objective foreseeability, of the likelihood of death.

I should add that there appears to be a further relaxation of the mental state when the accused is a party to the murder through s. 21(2) of the *Code*, as in this case. However, as I have said, it is sufficient to deal with 213(*d*) in order to dispose of this appeal.

The historical development of s. 213

Although the concept of felony muder has a long history at common law, a brief review of the historical development of s. 213 indicates that its legitimacy is questionable.

In the early history of English criminal law, "murdrum", or murder, referred to a secret killing, or the killing of a Dane, or later a Norman, by an Englishman, and to the fine levied on the township where the killing occurred. By the early 14th century, the fines had been abandoned and murder had come to be the name used to describe the worst kind of homicide. The expression "malice aforethought" was subsequently adopted to distinguish murder from manslaughter, which denoted all culpable homicides other than murder. Malice aforethought was not limited to its natural and obvious sense of premeditation, but would be implied whenever the killing was intentional or reckless. In these instances, the malice was present and it is the premeditation which was implied by law.

Coke took this one step further and implied both the malice and the premeditation in cases where the death occurred in the commission of an unlawful act. He wrote in the Third Part of the Institutes of the Laws of England (1817), London, W. Clarke and Sons, at p. 56:

Unlawful. If the act be unlawful it is murder. As if A. meaning to steale a deere in the park of B., shooteth at the deer, and by the glance of the arrow killeth a boy that is hidden in a bush: this is murder, for that the act was unlawfull, although A. had no intent to hurt the boy, nor knew not of him. But if B. the owner of the park had shot at his own deer, and without any ill intent had killed the boy by the glance of his arrow, this had been homicide by misadventure and no felony.

So if one shoot at any wild fowle upon a tree, and the arrow killeth any reasonable creature afar off, without any evill intent in him, this is *per infortunium*: for it was not unlawfull to shoot at the wilde fowle: but if he had shot at a cock or hen, or any tame fowle of another mans, and the arrow by mischance had killed a man, this had been murder, for the act was unlawfull.

Coke's statement of the unlawful act murder rule has been much criticized. Stephen demonstrated that Coke's statement was not supported by the authorities cited: History of the Criminal Law of England (1883), vol. 3, pp. 57-58. Further, a recent author has suggested that Coke's statement was just "a slip of the quill" and that Coke intended to say that accidental killing by an unlawful act was manslaughter: see D. Lanham, "Felony Murder — Ancient and Modern" (1983), 7 Crim. L.J. 90, at pp. 92-94. Other 17th century writers (Dalton, Countrey Justice (1619), pp. 225-26, and Hale, History of the Pleas of the Crown (1736), vol. 1, at p. 475) and cases (*Chichester's Case* (1647), Aleyn 12, and *Hull's Case* (1664), Kel. 40) rejected the unlawful act murder rule as set out by Coke. Despite all of this, Coke's doctrine seems to have been accepted by the writers and the cases in the 18th century, and their only contribution was to limit it to killings in the course of felonies: see *R. v. Plummer* (1702), Kel. 109, 84 E.R. 1103 at 1107; Hawkins Pleas of the Crown (1716), vol. 1, c. 29, s. 11; *R. v. Woodburne* (1722), 16 St. Tr. 53; Foster, Crown Law (1762), p. 258; East, Pleas of the Crown (1803), vol. 1, at p. 255. Of course, at that time both the underlying felony and the murder were punishable by death, so the definition of a homicide in the course of a felony as a murder had little practical effect.

In the 19th century, the felony murder rule was accepted as part of the common law: see *Stephen's Digest of the Criminal Law*, 9th ed. (1950), art. 264(*c*). However, the rule was strongly criticized by Stephen, who labelled it "cruel" and "monstrous": *History of the Criminal Law*, vol. 3, p. 75.

Despite the rule's questionable origins and the subsequent criticisms, s. 175 of the *English Draft Code of 1879* included a restricted form of felony murder, which was subsequently adopted in the first *Canadian Criminal Code*, in 1892. Through subsequent amendments this provision has been widened, and it is now s. 213. It is more restricted than the common-law rule, in that it is limited to deaths occurring in the commission of certain enumerated offences and it requires that the accused have committed one of the acts set out in subss. (*a*) to (*d*).

Section 213 and its predecessors in the *Code* have long been subject to academic criticism: see J. Willis, Comment on *Rowe v. R.* (1951), 29 Can. Bar Rev. 784, at pp. 794-96; J. Ll. J. Edwards, "Constructive Murder in Canadian and English Law" (1961), 3 Cr. L.Q. 481, at pp. 506-509; A. Hooper, "Some Anomalies and Developments in the Law of Homicide" (1967), 3 Univ. of B.C. L. Rev. 55, at pp. 75-77; P. Burns and R.S. Reid, "From Felony Murder to

Accomplice Felony Attempted Murder: The Rake's Progress Compleat?" (1977), 55 Can. Bar Rev. 75, at pp. 103-105; G. Parker, An Introduction to Criminal Law (1977), pp. 145-48; D. Stuart, *Canadian Criminal Law: A Treatise* (1982), pp. 222-25; I. Grant and A.W. Mackay, "Constructive Murder and the Charter: In Search of Principle" (1987), 25 Alta. L. Rev. 129; cf. A.W. Mewett and M. Manning, Criminal Law, 2nd ed. (1985), p. 545. It has also been subject to judicial criticism. In *R. v. Farrant*, [1983] 1 S.C.R. 124, 32 C.R. (3d) 289, 4 C.C.C. (3d) 354, Dickson J. (as he then was) wrote that s. 213 seemed harsh (p. 130). In *R. v. Ancio*, [1984] 1 S.C.R. 225, 39 C.R. (3d) 1, 10 C.C.C. (3d) 385, dealing with the *mens rea* of attempted murder, McIntyre J. wrote at pp. 250-51 [S.C.R.]:

> It was argued, and it has been suggested in some of the cases and academic writings on the question, that it is illogical to insist upon a higher degree of *mens rea* for attempted murder, while accepting a lower degree amounting to recklessness for murder. I see no merit in this argument. The intent to kill is the highest intent in murder and there is no reason in logic why an attempt to murder, aimed at the completion of the full crime of murder, should have any lesser intent. *If there is any illogic in this matter, it is in the statutory characterization of unintentional killing as murder.* [Emphasis added.]

Finally, the Law Reform Commission of Canada criticized s. 213 in its working paper 33, Homicide (1984), at pp. 47-51, and excluded the notion of constructive murder from its *Draft Criminal Code* in its report 30, Recodifying Criminal Law (1986), s. 6(3), p. 54.

Felony murder in other jurisdictions

Felony murder is a peculiarly common-law concept which appears to be unknown outside a small circle of common-law jurisdictions, and it has not fared well in those jurisdictions. In the United Kingdom, where the rule originated, it was abolished by the Homicide Act, 1957 (5 & 6 Eliz. 2, c. 11). The rule is still quite widespread in the United States, though it is said to be in decline: R.W. Perkins and R.N. Boyce, *Criminal Law*, 3rd ed. (1982), p. 70. The rule has been abolished by statute or by the Courts in several jurisdictions (see *People v. Aaron; People v. Thompson; People v. Wright*, 299 N.W. 2d 304, 409 Mich. 672, 13 A.L.R. 4th 1180 (S.C. 1980), and *State v. Doucette*, 470 A. 2d 676 (S.C. Vt., 1983)), and it has been downgraded to manslaughter in others. In addition, the Courts and the Legislatures have limited the scope of the common-law rule by limiting the felonies to which it is applicable, requiring some degree of *mens rea* with respect to the death, establishing affirmative defences or limiting the punishments available. The rule also exists in New Zealand and certain Australian states, but it is narrower, and abolition has been recommended in some jurisdictions.

Section 213(d) and the Charter

This appeal calls into play two principles of fundamental justice.

The First Principle: The essential elements of certain crimes and s. 7 of the *Charter*

Prior to the enactment of the *Charter*, Parliament had full legislative power with respect to "The Criminal Law" (*Constitution Act, 1867*, s. 91(27)), including the determination of the essential elements of any given crime. It could prohibit any act and impose any penal consequences for infringing the prohibition, provided only that the prohibition served "a public purpose which can support it as being in relation to criminal law": *Ref. re S. 5(a) of the Dairy Indust. Act*, [1949] S.C.R. 1 at 50, affirmed (sub nom. *Cdn. Fed. of Agriculture v. Can. (A.G.)*) [1951] A.C. 179 (P.C.). Once the legislation was found to have met this test, the Courts had very little power to review the substance of the legislation. For example, in *R. v. Sault Ste. Marie (City)*, [1978] 2 S.C.R. 1299, 3 C.R. (3d) 30, 40 C.C.C. (2d) 353 [Ont.], Dickson J. (as he then was) held that, when an offence was criminal in the true sense, there was a presumption that the prosecution must prove the *mens rea*. However, it was always open to Parliament expressly to relieve the prosecution of its obligation to prove any part of the *mens rea*, as it is said to have done in s. 213 of the *Criminal Code* with respect to the foreseeability of the death of the victim. It is thus clear that, prior to the enactment of the *Charter*, the validity of s. 213 could not have been successfully challenged.

However, federal and provincial legislatures have chosen to restrict through the *Charter* this power with respect to criminal law. Under s. 7, if a conviction, given either the stigma attached to the offence or the available penalties, will result in a deprivation of the life, liberty or security of the person of the accused, then Parliament must respect the principles of fundamental justice. It has been argued that the principles of fundamental justice in s. 7 are only procedural guarantees. However, in *Ref. re S. 94(2) of Motor Vehicle Act*, [1985] 2 S.C.R. 486, 48 C.R. (3d) 289, 23 C.C.C. (3d) 289, this court rejected that argument and used s. 7 to review the substance of the legislation. As a result, while Parliament retains the power to define the elements of a crime, the courts now have the jurisdiction and, more important, the duty, when called upon to do so, to review that definition to ensure that it is in accordance with the principles of fundamental justice.

This Court's decision in *Re Motor Vehicle Act* stands for the proposition that absolute liability infringes the principles of fundamental justice, such that the combination of absolute liability and a deprivation of life, liberty or security of the person is a restriction on one's rights under s. 7 and is *prima facie* a violation thereof. In effect, *Re Motor Vehicle Act* acknowledges that, whenever the state resorts to the restriction of liberty, such as imprisonment, to assist in the enforcement of a law, even, as in *Re Motor Vehcle Act*, a mere provincial regulatory offence, there is, as a principle of fundamental justice, a minimum mental state which is an essential element of the offence. It thus elevated *mens rea* from a presumed element in *Sault Ste. Marie, supra*, to a constitutionally-required element. *Re Motor Vehicle Act* did not decide what level of *mens rea* was constitutionally required for each type of offence, but inferentially decided that even for a mere provincial regulatory offence *at least* negligence was required, in that *at least* a defence of due diligence must *always* be open to an accused who risks imprisonment upon conviction. In *Sault Ste. Marie*, Dickson J. stated at pp. 1309-10:

> Where the offence is criminal, the Crown must establish a mental element, namely, that the accused who committed the prohibited act did so intentionally or recklessly, with knowledge of the facts constituting the offence, or with wilful blindness toward them. Mere negligence is excluded from the concept of the mental element required for conviction. Within the context of a criminal prosecution a person who fails to make such enquiries as a reasonable and prudent person would make, or who fails to know facts he should have known, is innocent in the eyes of the law.

It may well be that, as a general rule, the principles of fundamental justice require proof of a subjective *mens rea* with respect to the prohibited act, in order to avoid punishing the "morally innocent". It must be remembered, however, that Dickson J. was dealing with the *mens rea* to be presumed in the absence of an express legislative disposition, and not the *mens rea* to be required in all legislation providing for a restriction on the accused's life, liberty or security of the person. In any event, this case involves criminal liability for the result of an intentional criminal act, and it is arguable that different considerations should apply to the mental element required with respect to that result. There are many provisions in the *Code* requiring only objective foreseeability of the result or even only a causal link between the act and the result. As I would prefer not to cast doubt on the validity of such provisions *in this case*, I will assume, but only for the purposes of this appeal, that something less than subjective foresight of the result may sometimes suffice for the imposition of criminal liability for causing that result through intentional criminal conduct.

But, whatever the minimum *mens rea* for the act or the result may be, there are, though very few in number, certain crimes where, because of the special nature of the stigma attached to a conviction therefor or the available penalties, the principles of fundamental justice require a *mens rea* reflecting the particular nature of that crime. Such is theft, where, in my view, a conviction requires proof of some dishonesty. Murder is another such offence. The punishment for murder is the most severe in our society, and the stigma that attaches to a conviction for murder is similarly extreme. In addition, murder is distinguished from manslaughter only by the mental element with respect to the death. It is thus clear that there must be some special mental element with respect to the death before a culpable homicide can be treated as a murder. That special mental element gives rise to the moral blameworthiness which justifies the stigma and sentence attached to a murder conviction. I am presently of the view that it is a principle of fundamental justice that a conviction for murder cannot rest on anything less than proof beyond a reasonable doubt of subjective foresight. Given the effect of this view on part of s. 212(*c*), for the reasons I have already given for deciding this case more narrowly, I need not and will not rest my finding that s. 213(*d*) violates the *Charter* on this view, because s. 213(*d*) does not, for reasons I will set out hereinafter, even meet the lower threshold test of objective foreseeability. I will therefore, for the sole purpose of this appeal, go no further than to say that it is a principle of fundamental justice that, absent proof beyond a reasonable doubt of at least objective foreseeability, that surely cannot be a murder conviction.

The Second Principle: Section 11(*d*) and the burden of persuasion

The presumption of innocence in s. 11(*d*) of the *Charter* requires at least that an accused be presumed innocent until his guilt has been proven beyond a reasonable doubt: *Dubois v. R.*, [1985] 2 S.C.R. 350 at 357, 48 C.R. (3d) 193, 22 C.C.C. (3d) 513; *R. v. Oakes*, [1986] 1 S.C.R. 103 at 120-21, 50 C.R. (3d) 1, 24 C.C.C. (3d) 321. This means that, before an accused can be convicted of an offence, the trier of fact must be satisfied beyond reasonable doubt of the existence of all of the essential elements of the offence. These essential elements include not only those set out by the Legislature in the provision creating the offence but also, those required by s. 7 of the *Charter*. Any provision creating an offence which allows for the conviction of an accused notwithstanding the existence of a reasonable doubt on any essential element infringes ss. 7 and 11(*d*).

. . . .

With respect, the Nova Scotia Supreme Court, Appeal Division, was thus clearly incorrect when it stated in *R. v. Bezanson* (1983), 8 C.C.C. (3d) 493 at 508:

> In my view, there was no attempt by Parliament to reverse the onus of proof under s. 213, and s. 11(*d*) of the *Charter* has no application. Parliament has not reversed the burden of proof, it has simply omitted what the appellant argues is an essential element from the definition of the offence so that no evidence is required at all on that issue.

The omission of an essential element does bring s. 11(*d*) into play.

Finally, the Legislature, rather than simply eliminating any need to prove the essential element, may substitute proof of a different element. In my view, this will be constitutionally valid only if upon proof beyond reasonable doubt of the substituted element it would be unreasonable for the trier of fact not to be satisfied beyond reasonable doubt of the existence of the essential element. If the trier of fact may have a reasonable doubt as to the essential element notwithstanding proof beyond a reasonable doubt of the substituted element, then the substitution infringes ss. 7 and 11(*d*).

Given the first principle I have enunciated earlier and my assumption for the sole purpose of disposing of this appeal with respect to objective foreseeability, an accused cannot be found guilty of murder absent proof beyond a reasonable doubt of that element, and a murder provision which allows a conviction in the absence of proof beyond reasonable doubt of at least that essential element infringes ss. 7 and 11(*d*).

Application of the principles to s. 213

The *mens rea* required for s. 213 consists of the *mens rea* for the underlying offence and the intent to commit one of the acts set forth in subss. (*a*) to (*d*): *Swietlinski v. R.*, [1980] 2 S.C.R. 956, 18 C.R. (3d) 231, 55 C.C.C. (2d) 481 [Ont.]. Section 213 does not impose on the accused the burden of disproving objective foreseeability. Further, it does not completely exclude the need to prove any objective foreseeability. Rather, s. 213 has substituted for proof beyond a reasonable doubt of objective foreseeability, if that is the essential element, proof beyond a reasonable doubt of certain forms of intentional dangerous conduct causing death.

The question is therefore: Can Parliament make this substitution without violating ss. 7 and 11(*d*)? As I have discussed earlier, if Parliament frames the section so that, upon proof of the conduct, it would be unreasonable for a jury not to conclude beyond a reasonable doubt that the accused ought to have known that death was likely to ensue, then I think that Parliament has enacted a crime which is tantamount to one which has objective foreseeability as an essential element, and, if objective foreseeability is sufficient, then it would not be in violtion of s. 7 or s. 11(*d*) in doing so in that way. The acid test of the constitutionality of s. 213 is this ultimate question: *Would it be possible for a conviction for murder to occur under s. 213 despite the jury having a reasonable doubt as to whether the accused ought to have known that death was likely to ensue?* If the answer is "Yes", then the section is prima facie in violation of ss. 7 and 11(*d*). I should add in passing that if the answer is "No" then it would be necessary to decide whether objective foreseeability is sufficient for a murder conviction. However, because in my view the answer is "Yes" and because I do not want to pass upon the constitutionality of s. 212(*c*) in this case, I will not address that issue.

To varying degrees it can be said that in almost any case a jury satisfied beyond a reasonable doubt that an accused has done one of the prohibited acts described in subss. (*a*) to (*d*) will be satisfied beyond a reasonable doubt that the accused ought to have known that death was likely to be caused. But not always. Indeed, as a first example, drunkenness would under certain circumstances leave the jury in doubt in that regard. The rule as regards the effect of drunkenness on objective foreseeability was unanimously laid down by this Court in *R. v. Vasil*, [1981] 1 S.C.R. 469, 20 C.R. (3d) 193, 58 C.C.C. (2d) 97 [Ont.], a murder prosecution under s. 212(*c*). This Court addressed the issue at some length and then summarized its conclusion as follows, per Lamer J. at pp. 500-501:

> (5) Whilst the test under [s.] 212(*c*) is objective and the behaviour of the accused is to be measured by that of the reasonable man, such a test must nevertheless be applied having regard, not to the knowledge a reasonable man would have had of the surrounding circumstances that allegedly made the accused's conduct dangerous to life, but to the knowledge the accused had of those circumstances;

(6) As a result, drunkenness, though not relevant in the determination of what a reasonable man, with the knowledge the accused had of those circumstances, would have anticipated, is relevant in the determination of the knowledge which the accused had of those circumstances.

It is clear to me that, under s. 213 as drafted, there will be cases where the effect of drunkenness on an accused's knowledge of the circumstances would leave a jury with a reasonable doubt as to whether the accused ought to have known of the likelihood of death ensuing even though it has been proven beyond a reasonable doubt that the accused actually did one of the acts described under subss. (*a*) to (*d*).

A second example, and this case amply illustrates the point, is the accused who is brought into s. 213 not as a principal but through the operation of s. 21(2) of the *Criminal Code*. In *R. v. Trinneer*, [1970] S.C.R. 638, 11 C.R.N.S. 110, [1970] 3 C.C.C. 289 [B.C.], this Court had the opportunity to consider the combined operation of ss. 21(2) and 213 (s. 202 [of the 1953-54 *Criminal Code*] at the time). Cartwright C.J.C., delivering the judgment of the Court, stated at pp. 645-46:

> At the risk of repetition, it is my opinion that on the true construction of s. 202 and s. 21(2) as applied to the circumstances of this case it was necessary to support a verdict of guilty against the respondent that the Crown should establish (i) that it was in fact a probable consequence of the prosecution of the common purpose of the respondent and Frank to rob Mrs. Vollet that Frank for the purpose of facilitating the commission of the robbery would intentionally cause bodily harm to Mrs. Vollet, (ii) that it was known or ought to have been known to the respondent that such consequence was probable and (iii) that in fact Mrs. Vollet's death ensued from the bodily harm. *It was not necessary for the Crown to establish that the respondent knew or ought to have known that it was probable that Mrs. Vollet's death would ensue.* [Emphasis added.]

It is clear that an accused can be convicted of murder under the combined operation of ss. 21(2) and 213 in circumstances where the death was not objectively foreseeable. As s. 21(2) requires proof of objective foreseeability, the culprit, in my view, must be s. 213.

These two examples suffice, in my view, for one to conclude that, notwithstanding proof beyond a reasonable doubt of the matters set forth in subss. (*a*) to (*d*), a jury could reasonably be left in doubt as regards objective foreseeability of the likelihood that death be caused. In other words, s. 213 will catch an accused who performs one of the acts in subss. (*a*) and (*d*) and thereby causes a death but who otherwise would have been acquitted of murder because he did not foresee and could not reasonably have foreseen that death would be likely to result. For that reason, s. 213 *prima facie* violates ss. 7 and 11(*d*). It is thus not necessary to decide whether objective foreseeability is sufficient for murder, as s. 213 does not even meet that standard. This takes us to s. 1 for the second phase of the constitutional inquiry.

Section 1

Finding that s. 213 of the *Criminal Code* infringes ss. 7 and 11(*d*) of the *Charter* does not end the inquiry on the constitutional validity of s. 213. Any or all of subss. (*a*) to (*d*) of s. 213 can still be upheld as a reasonable limit "demonstrably justified in a free and democratic society" under s. 1 of the *Charter.*

In this case and at this stage of the inquiry, we need only consider subs. (*d*) of s. 213. The criteria to be assessed under s. 1 have been set out by this Court in several cases, particularly *R. v. Big M Drug Mart Ltd.*, [1985] 1 S.C.R. 295, 18 C.C.C. (3d) 385, and *R. v. Oakes, supra.* First, the objective which the measures are designed to serve must be "of sufficient importance to warrant overriding a constitutionally protected right or freedom": *Big M Drug Mart*, at p. 352 [S.C.R.]. Through s. 213(*d*) of the *Code*, Parliament intended to deter the use or carrying of a weapon in the commission of certain offences, because of the increased risk of death. In my view, it is clear that this objective is sufficiently important.

In addition, the measures adopted must be reasonable and demonstrably justified. The measures adopted appear to be rationally connected to the objective: indiscriminately punishing for murder all those who cause a death by using or carrying a weapon, whether the death was intentional or accidental, might well be thought to discourage the use and the carrying of weapons. I believe, however, that the measures adopted would unduly impair the rights and freedoms in question: see *Big M Drug Mart* at p. 352 [S.C.R.]. It is not necessary to convict of murder persons who did not intend to foresee the death and who could not even have foreseen the death in order to deter others from using or carrying weapons. If Parliament wishes to deter the use or carrying of weapons, it should punish the use or carrying of weapons. A good example of this is the minimum imprisonment for using a firearm in the commission of an indictable offence under s. 83 of the *Criminal Code*. In any event, the conviction for manslaughter which would result instead of a conviction for murder is punishable by from a day in jail to confinement for life in a penitentiary. Very stiff sentences when weapons are involved in the commission of the crime of manslaughter would sufficiently deter the use or carrying of weapons in the commission of crimes. But stigmatizing the crime as murder unnecessarily impairs the *Charter* right.

In my view, therefore, s. 213(*d*) is not saved by s. 1.

CONCLUSION

As a result of the foregoing, I would answer the first constitutional question in the affirmative, as s. 213(*d*) violates both s. 7 and s. 11(*d*) of the *Charter*, and I would declare s. 213(*d*) of the *Criminal Code* to be of no force or effect. I would, for the reasons which I have given, decline to answer the second constitutional question. It follows that the appeal must be allowed, the appellant's conviction for murder set aside, and a new trial ordered.

LA FOREST J.: — I have had the advantage of reading the judgment of Lamer J. and would dispose of the appeal [from 31 C.C.C. (3d) 75] in the manner proposed by him. I am in agreement with him that because of the stigma attached to a conviction for murder the principles of fundamental justice require a mens rea reflecting the particular nature of that crime, namely, one referable to causing death. In addition to the intention to cause death, this can include a closely-related intention, such as intention to cause bodily harm likely to result in death combined with recklessness as to that result. Whether and how much further the intention can be extended it is not necessary to explore for the purposes of this case. It is sufficient to say that the mental element required by s. 213(*d*) of the *Criminal Code* is so remote from the intention specific to murder (which intention is what gives rise to the stigma attached to a conviction for that crime) that a conviction under that paragraph violates fundamental justice. All the provision requires is an intention to commit another crime and to possess a weapon while carrying out this intention or in fleeing afterwards. The provision is so broad that under it a person may be found guilty of murder even though the death was the result of an accident. This occurred in *Rowe v. R.*, [1951] S.C.R. 713, 12 C.R. 148, 100 C.C.C. 97 [Ont.], and more extreme examples can easily be imagined. The section thus not only is remote from the *mens rea* specific to murder, but even removes its *actus reus* as traditonally defined; see Isabel Grant and A. Wayne MacKay, "Constructive Murder and the Charter: In Search of Principle" (1987); 25 Alta. L. Rev. 129.

As my colleague notes, the objective of discouraging the use of weapons in the commission of crimes can be achieved by means other than attaching the stigma of a conviction for murder to a person who has caused death in the circumstances like those described in the provision.

BEETZ J. (LE DAIN concurring): — For the reasons given by Lamer J. and La Forest J., I agree that s. 213(*d*) of the *Criminal Code* does not conform to the principles of fundamental justice entrenched in the *Canadian Charter of Rights and Freedoms* and cannot be saved under s. 1. I also agree with Lamer J. that s. 213(*d*) of the *Criminal Code* violates s. 11(*d*) of the *Charter* and cannot be justified under s. 1 of the *Charter*.

Given these conclusions, I do not find it necessary to decide whether there exists a principle of fundamental justice that a conviction for murder cannot rest on anything less than proof beyond a reasonable doubt of subjective foresight.

I would dispose of the appeal [from 31 C.C.C. (3d) 75] in the manner proposed by Lamer J. and answer the first constitutional question as he does. I would also decline to answer the second constitutional question.

McINTYRE J. (dissenting): — I have had the advantage of reading the reasons for judgment in this appeal [from 31 C.C.C. (3d) 75] prepared by my colleague Lamer J. I find myself unable to agree with his disposition of the appeal and, with the greatest respect for his view on the matter, I would dismiss the appeal and answer both constituional questions in the negative.

My colleague has set out the facts of the case. They need not be repeated here. It is evident as well from his reasons that, save for the *Canadian Charter of Rights and Freedoms*, he is in agreement that the appellant would be properly convicted of murder under the combined effect of s. 21(2) and s. 213(*d*) of the

Criminal Code. He would allow the appeal essentially on the basis that a conviction for murder which will result in the deprivation of liberty or security of the person of the accused can be upheld only if, in accordance with the terms of s. 7 of the *Charter*, it is procured in accordance with the principles of fundamental justice. While Parliament has the power to define the elements of a crime, in his view the Courts must now review that definition to ensure that it is in accordance with the principles of fundamental justice. These principles would require that there be no murder conviction without proof of a *mens rea* of at least objective foreseeability of death. Such foreseeability is not a necessary requirement under s. 213(*d*) of the *Code.*

I am not prepared to accept the proposition that s. 213(*d*) of the *Criminal Code* admits of a conviction for murder without proof of objective foreseeability of death or the likelihood of death, but in the view I take of this case it is not necessary to reach a firm conclusion on that point. The Crown sought the conviction of Vaillancourt on the basis of the interaction of s. 21(2) and s. 213(*d*) of the *Code.* For the Crown to succeed in such a prosecution, it would be required to prove that the accused and another had formed an intention in common to carry out an unlawful purpose and to assist each other therein. In addition, in the circumstances of this case, the Crown would be required to prove that the appellant knew or ought to have known that his associate was armed with a pistol and would, if necessary, use it during the commission of the offence or the attempt to commit the offence, or during his flight after committing or attempting to commit the offence, and that as a consequence a death occurred: see *R. v. Munro* (1983), 36 C.R. (3d) 193, 8 C.C.C. (3d) 260 (Ont. C.A.), per Martin J.A. at p. 301, and the pre-*Charter* case in this Court in *R. v. Tinneer,* [1970] S.C.R. 638, 11 C.R.N.S. 110, [1970] 3 C.C.C. 289 [B.C.].

It must be recognized at the outset that Parliament has decided that the possession and use of weapons, particularly firearms, in the course of the commission of offences is a gravely aggravating factor. Experience has shown that the presence of firearms leads to personal injury and loss of life. Parliament has chosen to term a killing arising in the circumstances described here as "murder". In *R. v. Munro, supra,* Martin J.A., speaking for the Ontario Court of Appeal (Arnup, Martin and Houlden JJ.A.), said this, at p. 293:

> Under the provisions of s. 213(*d*) liability for murder attaches if death ensues as a consequence of the use of the weapon or as a consequence of the possession of a weapon which he has on his person. Manifestly, s. 213(*d*) is very stringent, but it is equally obvious that Parliament intended to create a stringent basis of liability where death ensued as a consequence of the use or possession of a weapon which the offender has upon his person during the commission or attempted commission of certain offences or the offender's flight after the commission or attempted commission of the offence. It is clear that Parliament intended to provide a strong deterrent to the carrying of weapons in the commission of certain crimes because of the high risk to life which experience has shown attends such conduct.

The principal complaint in this case is not that the accused should not have been convicted of a serious crime deserving of severe punishment, but simply that Parliament should not have chosen to call that crime "murder". No objection could be taken if Parliament classified the offence as manslaughter or a killing during the commission of an offence, or in some other manner. As I have observed before (see *R. v. Ancio*, [1984] 1 S.C.R. 225 at 251, 39 C.R. (3d) 1, 10 C.C.C. (3d) 385), while it may be illogical to characterize an unintentional killing as murder, no principle of fundamental justice is offended only because serious criminal conduct, involving the commission of a crime of violence resulting in the killing of a human being, is classified as murder and not in some other manner. As Martin J.A. said in *R. v. Munro, supra*, at p. 301:

> This legislation has frequently been critized as being harsh, but that is a matter for Parliament and not for the Courts.

I would refer as well to the words found in Mewett and Manning, *Criminal Law*, 2nd ed. (1985), at pp. 544-45:

> Section 213 and the concept of constructive murder have been much criticized and, in fact, abolished in many jurisdictions. The criticism is that it imposes liability for murder in situations where death was not intended nor even, in some cases, foreseen. But murder is a legal concept; it does not have to be defined in terms of intentional killing, and even under s. 212 the definition is not this narrow. The policy behind s. 213 is to put the risk of killing a victim during the course of the commision of certain offences upon the offender to a higher degree than if it were merely classified as manslaughter. In any case, with the present distinction between murder punishable by death and murder punishable by life imprisonment now abolished, much of the criticism loses its force. It was the thought of someone being executed for a non-intended homicide that led to the feeling that the definiton of murder should somehow be limited to the old common law concept of "murder with malice aforethought".

As has been noted, the appellant's conviction is based on a combination of s. 21(2) and s. 213(*d*) of the *Criminal Code*. There was in this case evidence of active participation in the commission of the robbery, the underlying offence, and the terms of s. 21(2) were fully met. It must be accepted that the section gives expression to a principle of joint criminal liability long accepted and applied in the criminal law. I am unable to say upon what basis one could exempt conduct which attracts criminal liability, under s. 213 of the *Criminal Code*, from the application of that principle. In *R. v. Munro, supra*, Martin J.A. said, at p. 301:

> Patently, Parliament has decided that the carrying of weapons during the commission of certain crimes, such as robbery, so manifestly endangers the lives of others, that one who joins a common purpose to commit one of the specified offences and who knows or ought to know that his accomplice has upon his person a weapon which he will use if needed, must bear the risk if death, in fact, ensues as a consequence of the use or possession of the weapon during the commission of one of the specified offences or during the flight of the offender after the commission or attempted commission of the underlying offence. . . .

In my view, Martin J.A. has stated the policy considerations which have motivated Parliament in this connection, and I would not interfere with the Parliamentary decision. I would therefore dismiss the appeal and answer the two constitutional questions in the negative.

For views on *Vaillancourt*, see the Criminal Reports Forum in 60 C.R. (3d) 332-345. See also Stuart, "Progress on the Constitutional Requirement of Fault", 64 C.R. (3d) 352.

R. v. MARTINEAU

[1990] 2 S.C.R. 633, 79 C.R. (3d) 129, 58 C.C.C. (3d) 353

The accused and a companion, armed with a pellet pistol and a rifle respectively, set out to commit a crime. The accused testified that he thought it would only be a break and enter. They forced their way into a trailer and tied up two of its occupants, James and Ann McLean. The companion shot and killed the two people after robbing them and their home. The accused testified that as soon as he heard the first shot, he realized that James McLean had been shot. He testified that he then said or thought, "Lady, say your prayers". As they left, the accused asked his companion why he killed them and the companion answered "They saw our faces". The accused responded "But they couldn't see mine 'cause I had a mask on". The accused was convicted of second degree murder. The trial Judge charged the jury on s. 213(*a*) and (*d*) (now s. 230(*a*) and (*d*) and on s. 21(1) and (2) of the *Criminal Code*. The Court of Appeal held that s. 213(*a*) was inconsistent with ss. 7 and 11(*d*) of the *Charter* for reasons given in *R. v. Vaillancourt* and that it was not saved by s. 1 of the *Charter*. The Court ordered a new trial and the Crown appealed.

Per LAMER C.J.C. (DICKSON C.J.C. and WILSON, GONTHIER and CORY JJ. concurring): —

This is the first of a series of appeals that raises the constitutionality of s. 213(*a*) of the *Criminal Code*, R.S.C. 1970, c. C-34, (now s. 230(*a*), *Criminal Code*, R.S.C., 1985, c. C-46).

. . . .

In *Vaillancourt* I analyzed a number of matters, including s. 213 of the *Code* in the context of the other murder provisions, the historical development of s. 213, felony murder provisions in other jurisdictions, the essential elements of certain crimes at common law, and the principles of fundamental justice under the *Charter* and their application to s. 213 of the *Code*. As a result of this analysis I concluded that objective foreseeability of death was the minimum threshold test before a conviction for murder could be sustained. I went on to state, however, that it was my view that the principles of fundamental justice require more; they demand that a conviction for murder requires proof beyond a reasonable doubt of subjective foresight of death. The Chief Justice, Estey and Wilson JJ. agreed with that position. I am still of that view today, and indeed, while I agree with the Alberta Court of Appeal and could dispose of this appeal on the basis of objective foreseeability, it is on the basis of the principle of subjective foresight of death that I choose to dispose of this appeal. I choose this route because I would not want this case, a very serious matter, to return to this

Court once again on the grounds that there is some doubt as to the validity of the portion of s. 212(c) of the *Code* that allows for a conviction for murder if the accused "ought to know" that death is likely to result. I need not, therefore, repeat the analysis from *Vaillancourt* here, except to add some brief observations as regards s. 213(a) and the principle of fundamental justice that subjective foresight of death is required before a conviction for murder can be sustained.

Section 213(a) of the *Code* defines culpable homicide as murder where a person causes the death of a human being while committing or attempting to commit a range of listed offences, whether or not the person means to cause death or whether or not he or she knows that death is likely to ensue if that person means to cause bodily harm for the purpose of facilitating the commission of the offence or flight after committing or attempting to commit the offence. The introductory paragraph of the section, therefore, expressly removes from the Crown the burden of proving beyond a reasonable doubt that the accused had subjective foresight of death. This section stands as an anomaly as regards the other murder provisions, especially in light of the common-law presumption against convicting a person of a true crime without proof of intent or recklessness: *R. v. Sault Ste. Marie (City)*, [1978] 2 S.C.R. 1299 at 1309-10, 3 C.R. (3d) 30, 40 C.C.C. (2d) 353, [Ont.], per Dickson J., (as he then was).

A conviction for murder carries with it the most severe stigma and punishment of any crime in our society. The principles of fundamental justice require, because of the special nature of the stigma attached to a conviction for murder, and the available penalties, a *mens rea* reflecting the particular nature of that crime. The effect of s. 213 is to violate the principle that punishment must be proportionate to the moral blameworthiness of the offender, or as Professor Hart puts it in *Punishment and Responsibility* (1968), at p. 162, the fundamental principle of a morally based system of law that those causing harm intentionally be punished more severely than those causing harm unintentionally. The rationale underlying the principle that subjective foresight of death is required before a person is labelled and punished as a murderer is linked to the more general principle that criminal liability for a particular result is not justified except where the actor possesses a culpable mental state in respect of that result: see *R. v. Bernard*, [1988] 2 S.C.R. 833, 67 C.R. (3d) 113, 45 C.C.C. (3d) 1, per McIntyre J.; and *R. v. Buzzanga* (1979), 49 C.C.C. (2d) 369 (C.A.), per Martin J.A. In my view, in a free and democratic society that values the autonomy and free will of the individual, the stigma and punishment attaching to the most serious of crimes, murder, should be reserved for those who choose to intentionally cause death or who choose to inflict bodily harm that they know is likely to cause death. The essential role of requiring subjective foresight of death in the context of murder is to maintain a proportionality between the stigma and punishment attached to a murder conviction and the moral blameworthiness of the offender. Murder has long been recognized as the "worst" and most heinous of peace time crimes. It is, therefore, essential that to satisfy the principles of fundamental justice, the stigma and punishment attaching to a murder conviction must be reserved for those who either intend to cause death or who intend to cause bodily harm that they know will likely cause death. In this regard, I refer to the following works as support for my position, in addition to those cited in *Vaillancourt*: Cross, "The Mental Element in Crime" (1967), 83 L.Q. Rev. 215; Ashworth, "The Elasticity of *Mens Rea*" in Crime, Proof and Punishment (1981); Williams, The Mental Element in Crime (1965); and Williams, "Convictions and Fair Labelling" [1983] 42 C.L.J. 85.

In sum then, I am of the view that a special mental element with respect to death is necessary before a culpable homicide can be treated as murder. That special mental element gives rise to the moral blameworthiness that justifies the stigma and punishment attaching to a murder conviction. For all the foregoing reasons, and for the reasons stated in *Vaillancourt*, I conclude that it is a principle of fundamental justice that a conviction for murder cannot rest on anything less than proof beyond a reasonable doubt of subjective foresight of death. That was my position when *Vaillancourt* was decided, and that is my position today. Therefore, since s. 213 of the *Code* expressly eliminates the requirement for proof of subjective foresight, it infringes ss. 7 and 11(*d*) of the *Charter*.

As regards s. 1 of the *Charter*, there is no doubt that the objective of deterring the infliction of bodily harm during the commission of certain offences because of the increased risk of death is of sufficient importance to warrant overriding a *Charter* right. Further, indiscriminately punishing for murder all those who cause death irrespective of whether they intended to cause death might well be thought to discourage the infliction of bodily harm during the commission of certain offences because of the increased risk of death. But it is not necessary in order to achieve this objective to convict of murder persons who do not intend or foresee the death. In this regard the section unduly impairs the *Charter* rights. If Parliament wishes to deter persons from causing bodily harm during certain offences, then it should punish persons for causing the bodily harm. Indeed, the conviction for manslaughter that would result instead of a conviction for murder is punishable by, from a day in jail, to confinement for life. Very stiff sentences for the infliction of bodily harm leading to death in appropriate cases would sufficiently meet any deterrence objective that Parliament might have in mind. The more flexible sentencing scheme under a conviction for manslaughter is in accord with the principle that punishment be meted out with regard to the level of moral blameworthiness of the offender. To label and punish a person as a murderer who did not intend or foresee death unnecessarily stigmatizes and punishes those whose moral blameworthiness is not that of a murderer, and thereby unnecessarily impairs the rights guaranteed by ss. 7 and 11(*d*) of the *Charter*. In my view then, s. 213(*a*), indeed all of s. 213, cannot be saved by s. 1 of the *Charter*.

The fact that I have based my reasons on the principle of subjective foresight casts serious if not fatal doubt on the constitutionality of part of s. 212(*c*) of the *Code*, specifically the words "ought to know is likely to cause death". The validity of s. 212(*c*) of the *Code* has not been directly attacked in this appeal, but the court has had the benefit of hearing argument from the Attorney General of Canada and from the Attorneys General for Alberta, British

Columbia, Ontario, Quebec, and Manitoba, who chose to intervene, on the issue of whether subjective foresight or objective foreseeability of death is the constitutionally required minimum *mens rea* for murder. In my view, subjective foresight of death must be proven beyond a reasonable doubt before a conviction for murder can be sustained, and as a result, it is obvious the part of s. 212(*c*) of the *Code* allowing for a conviction upon proof that the accused ought to have known that death was likely to result violates ss. 7 and 11(*d*) of the *Charter*. I find further support for this view in the following passage from Professor Stuart's treatise *Canadian Criminal Law: A Treatise*, at pp. 217-18, dealing specifically with the objective element of s. 212(*c*) of the *Code* and the principle of subjective foresight:

> This is a clear instance where our legislation has not kept up with developments in other jurisdictions. We have seen that a similar objective test for murder resorted to by the House of Lords in the notorious decision in *Director of Public Prosecutions v. Smith* (1960) [[1961] A.C. 290 (H.L.)] was rejected by the British Legislature and by the Australian High Court. Very few jurisdictions, including those in the United States, resort to anything but the subjective approach in defining murder. The only direct parallels to our section 212(*c*) are to be found in the codes of Queensland, Tasmania, and New Zealand. The wording in these provisions is almost identical to ours except that in New Zealand the words "or ought to have known" were deleted as a result of a quick and firm rejection of *Smith*. The New Zealand section now reads in part:

> . . . if the offender for any unlawful object does an act that he knows to be likely to cause death, and thereby kills any person, though he may have desired that his object should be effected without hurting anyone.

Indeed, Lord Goff in his article "The Mental Element in the Crime of Murder" (1988), 104 L.Q. Rev. 30, at p. 36, had this to say about the *Smith* decision and about objective foreseeability as a test for murder:

> This decision was very much criticised, by Judge and jurist alike. What they disliked about it was that it imposed an objective instead of a subjective test for ascertaining the existence of the relevant mental element for the crime of murder. In due course, it was reversed by statute; later, on an appeal from a jurisdiction where that statute did not apply at the relevant time, *Smith* was, in effect, held by the Judicial Committee of the Privy Council to have been wrongly decided (see *Frankland and Moore v. R.*), [[1987] 2 W.L.R. 1251]). *So the objective test was never part of the common law, properly understood; and we can now forget about it.* [Emphasis added.]

Although it would be open to save that part of s. 212(*c*) under s. 1 of the *Charter*, it seems to me that the attempt would fail for the reasons I have given in respect of the attempt to similarly save s. 213 of the *Code*. I would therefore answer the constitutional questions as follows:

> Q: Does s. 213(*a*) of the *Criminal Code* infringe or deny the rights or freedoms guaranteed by s. 7 and/or s. 11(*d*) of the *Canadian Charter of Rights and Freedoms*?

> A: Yes, the section infringes both ss. 7 and 11(*d*) of the *Charter*.

Q: If the answer to question 1 is affirmative, is s. 213(*a*) justified by s. 1 of the *Canadian Charter of Rights and Freedoms*, and therefore not inconsistent with the *Constitution Act, 1982*?

A: No.

The only remaining issue is the potential application of s. 613(1)(*b*)(iii) of the *Criminal Code*. The Court of Appeal for Alberta declined to invoke the section and enter a conviction for the following reason, at p. 279:

> The jury in this case was not instructed on any portion of s. 212. I am unable to say that a properly instructed jury must necessarily have found that the appellant had, at some point, the requisite intention under that section rather than being carried along by events.

I agree. In the present case, the respondent was convicted pursuant to a combination of ss. 213 and 21 of the *Code*. Since in this case the jury was left only with s. 213 which has been declared to be inoperative, a new trial must be ordered. Accordingly, the Court of Appeals decision quashing the convictions and directing a new trial is affirmed. The appeal is, therefore, dismissed.

L'HEUREUX-DUBÉ J. (dissenting): —

. . . .

My colleague concludes that s. 213(*a*) is unconstitutional because it violates ss. 7 and 11(*d*) of the *Charter* and cannot be saved by s. 1. In his opinion, the principles of fundamental justice demand that subjective foresight of death be proven beyond a reasonable doubt before a conviction for murder can be secured. I reach a contrary conclusion on the basis that subjective foresight is not the only appropriate standard that can be applied to conform to ss. 7 and 11(*d*) of the *Charter*. My reasons are as follows: the test of objective foreseeability of death for the crime of murder does not offend the principles of fundamental justice; this Court's decisions, including *R. v. Vaillancourt*, [1987] 2 S.C.R. 636, 60 C.R. (3d) 289, 39 C.C.C. (3d) 118 [Que.], do not commend such a result; the exclusive standard of subjective foresight of death for the crime of murder has found no parallel in other common law jurisdictions; and there are significant policy considerations in favour of upholding the existing legislation.

. . . .

The above analysis indicates that tests of subjective foresight and objective foreseeability cannot be seen as static or distinct concepts. They are certainly not mutually exclusive. In most instances, and certainly in those limited circumstances delineated by s. 213(*a*), discussed below, death will be both objectively and subjectively foreseeable. There is a profound interrelationship between the two, especially when dealing with a crime committed during the execution of a predicate crime. The validity of a provision should not be evaluated on a strict "either-or" approach, and a fastidious adherence to prescribed labels becomes particularly obdurate when gauging the constitutionality of Parliamentary legislation.

. . . .

Vaillancourt held that s. 213(*d*) of the *Criminal Code* violated ss. 7 and 11(*d*) of the *Canadian Charter of Rights and Freedoms*, and could not be saved by s. 1. Paragraph 213(*a*) of the *Criminal Code* is completely different — in its historical development, in its consistency with the objective foreseeability of death test established in *Vaillancourt*, and in the parallel provisions adopted in other common law jurisdictions.

. . . .

(b) *Section 213(a) Passes the Objective Foreseeability Test*

An exacting combination of factors *must* be proven, all beyond a reasonable doubt, before the accused can be found guilty of murder under this paragraph. The offender must:

(1) cause the death by means of the commission of a "culpable homicide";

(2) cause the death while committing or attempting to commit one of a limited number of very serious crimes all of which are, by their very nature, inherently dangerous;

(3) intentionally inflict bodily harm while committing one of these inherently dangerous offences, all of which are specific intent crimes;

(4) inflict the bodily harm purposefully in order to perpetrate the dangerous underlying crime or for the purpose of facilitating his flight; and

(5) the death must ensue from the bodily harm intentionally inflicted.

It should be noted that in the present case the underlying offence was committed, and the intent to inflict bodily harm was clear. Moreover, this amalgamation of indispensable prerequisites establishes that this crime, as phrased by Lamer J. in *Vaillancourt* is "tantamount to one which has objective foreseeability as an essential element, and, if objective foreseeability is sufficient, then it would not be in violation of s. 7 or s. 11(*d*) in doing so in that way". I am of the view that in light of these requirements, the test of objective foreseeability is sufficient, and that if that test has been met, then no *Charter* violation has taken place. The above list requires that the accused specifically intend to, and actually commit the underlying offence, and specifically intend to, and actually inflict bodily harm. In my view, the inexorable conclusion is that the resulting death is objectively foreseeable.

. . . .

(c) *A Comparative Analysis*

This sudden introduction of a subjective foresight standard for the crime of murder is most novel, and finds no parallel in Great Britain, Australia, New Zealand or the United States. While each of these jurisdictions imposes different requirements for the crime of murder, none has adopted the requirement of subjective foresight of death.

. . . .

IV. POLICY CONSIDERATIONS

During the 27-year period from 1961-87, the evidence reveals that 2,177 homicide offences occurred during the commission of another criminal act. The percentage of homicide offences committed during the commission of another criminal act has varied from 11.9 percent in 1965 to 28.4 percent in 1970. The annual average for the period was 16.7 percent. "Homicide in Canada: Offences Committed During the Commission of Another Criminal Act", statistics provided by R.C.M.P. for the period 1961-87. The homicide offences committed during another criminal act are divided into four categories:

Robbery: includes robbery, theft, and break and enter offences. 1315 victims; 61.7 percent of all homicide offences committed during another criminal act.

Sexual Assault & Rape: includes all sexual attacks on either males or females. 483 victims; 22.3 percent of all homicide offences committed during another criminal act.

Escape: involves attempts to escape from correctional institutions or lawful custody, to avoid arrest, or to escape detection as a parole or probation violator. 346 victims; 14.2 percent of all homicide offences committed during another criminal act.

Other: includes other types of criminal acts such as arson, assault, kidnapping, etc. 33 victims; 1.8 percent of all homicide offences committed during another criminal act.

These statistics reflect a matter of critical public concern, and sustain the Legislature's compulsion to deliver an appropriate response. It is constitutionally permissible under the *Canadian Charter of Rights and Freedoms* to define the mental element required for murder with reference to an intention by the perpetrator to harm or injure the victim, with death resulting. How that harm or injury is to be defined, and what level of harm or injury is required are matters for Parliament to consider and decide.

. . . .

The fact that the principles embraced by s. 213(*a*) have existed for over 300 years is in itself relevant, though not necessarily determinative, of whether or not a rule of "fundamental justice" has been breached by virtue of their adoption by the Parliament of Canada. In my view, while the guarantee entrenched in s. 7 of the *Charter* is to have broad application, it cannot go so far as to grant the courts judicial licence to modify or strike down legislation in the absence of a constitutional violation.

. . . .

Section 213(*a*) is intended to carve out certain killings and place them in a category of the most serious culpable homicides, murder. This is a designation which Parliament is entitled to ascribe pursuant to its responsibility for the protection of those under its dominion. This legislative objective can be anchored in Parliament's legitimate attempt to deter persons from conduct which falls within s. 213(*a*). In particular, Parliament is attempting to deter those who commit crimes from intentionally inflicting actual bodily harm on their victims in order to achieve their unlawful purpose. The killings subsumed within s. 213(*a*) are regarded as sufficiently heinous to warrant being placed in the category of the gravest culpable homicides. Parliament felt that this was the appropriate manner to ensure that the criminal law is in accordance with social values as to the gravity of such killings, and that this was an effective method to preserve the lives and safety of Canadians.

. . . .

In the present appeal, my colleague's justification for insisting on the narrowest of all possible definitions for the crime of murder is that [pp. 106-107]:

> A conviction for murder carries with it the most severe stigma and punishment of any crime in our society. . . . [and] should be reserved for those who choose to intentionally cause death or who choose to inflict bodily harm that they know is likely to cause death.

The menacing component of "stigma" was discussed in *Vaillancourt* as well. As Lindsay pointed out in "The Implications of *R. v. Vaillancourt*: Much Ado About Nothing?" (1989), 47 U. of Toronto Fac. L. Rev. 465, at p. 472:

> It should also be noted that Lamer J. justified a requirement of a "special mental element" based on *either* the stigma associated with a crime or the penalties available. A murder conviction qualified on both grounds. However, theft can involve penalties as low as an absolute discharge. *Thus, the inclusion of theft in Lamer J.'s list of crimes requiring a "special mental element" must have been based on stigma rather than available penalties.* [Emphasis added.]

I find this concentration on social "stigma" to be overemphasized, and in the great majority of cases, completely inapplicable. The facts in the present appeals reveal the truly heinous nature of the criminal acts at issue. The concern that these offenders not endure the Mark of Cain is, in my view, an egregious example of misplaced compassion. If the apprehension is that the offenders in question will suffer from their "murderer" label, I suspect they will fare little better tagged as "manslaughterers". Accidental killings cannot, after *Vaillancourt*, result in murder prosecutions. Only killings resulting from circumstances in which death is, at a minimum, objectively foreseeable will be prosecuted under s. 213(*a*). Furthermore, the duration of imprisonment, if at all different, will not attenuate the "stigma". To the extent that any such "stigma" can be said to exist, it is at least as palpable upon release to the outside world as it is within the prison environment itself.

. . . .

Section 213(*a*) does not deal with accidental killings, but rather with killings that are objectively foreseeable as a result of the abominable nature of the predicate crimes, committed with specific intent, coupled with the intentional infliction of bodily harm. Given the dual subjective requirement already in place, the deterrence factor is most cogent in these circumstances. Whatever the competing arguments may be with respect to deterring the merely negligent, here we are dealing with those who have already expressly acted with the intent to commit at least two underlying serious crimes. If deterrence is to ever have any application to the criminal law, and in my view it should, this is the place.

Deterrence can neither be analyzed in the abstract nor in isolation from the context of the provision in question. Section 213(*a*) deals with one who has already proven to be a "hijacker", a "kidnapper", a "rapist", or an "arsonist". Furthermore, this person has already proven willing to cause bodily harm to commit the offence or to enable himself to escape after having committed the offence. In these circumstances, it is certainly appropriate for Parliament to put this person on notice, that if these purposeful acts result in death, you will be charged as a "murderer" as well.

This notion of Parliamentary autonomy cannot be displaced unless a *Charter* violation has occurred. In my view that has not taken place here. Repeating my colleagues own test, as articulated in *Vaillancourt* at p. 657, if the legislation is "tantamount to one which has objective foreseeability as an essential element, and, if objective foreseeability is sufficient, then it would not be in violation of s. 7 or s. 11(*d*) in doing so in that way."

V. Conclusion

Policy considerations in Canada as well as in other jurisdictions have inspired legislation that considers objective foreseeability sufficient as the minimum *mens rea* requirement for murder. While it may not be the very best test for all cases, it is certainly a constitutionally valid one. Parliament did not have to enact s. 213(*a*), but that is not the question before this Court. The issue is whether it could. In my view, the answer rests on what level of foreseeability will be required before a conviction for murder can be returned. Based on this Court's precedents, and the principles of fundamental justice, I believe that the objective foreseeability of death test for the crime of murder is constitutionally valid. The additional mandatory elements demanded by s. 213(*a*) lend even greater force to this conclusion.

Striking down the legislation simply because some other scheme may be preferable would be an unwarranted intrusion into Parliament's prerogative, and would undermine the means it has chosen to protect its citizens. The *Charter* is not designed to allow this Court to substitute preferable provisions for those already in place in the absence of a clear constitutional violation. Such a task should be reserved for the Law Reform Commission or other advisory bodies. This Court's province is to pronounce upon the constitutionality of those provisions properly before it. The *Charter* does not infuse the Courts with the power to declare legislation to be of no force or effect on the basis that they believe the statute to be undesirable as a matter of criminal law policy. For the aforementioned reasons, I do not believe that s. 213(*a*) offends the *Canadian Charter of Rights and Freedoms*.

. . . .

SOPINKA J. (concurring in the result): — I have had the advantage of reading the reasons of Lamer C.J.C. and L'Heureux-Dubé J. [appeal from (1988), 43 C.C.C. (3d) 417]. I agree with Lamer C.J.C. that there must be a new trial in this case. I would give the same answers to the constitutional questions as Lamer C.J.C. but, with respect, I cannot agree with his reasons.

In my view, the issue of subjective foresight of death should be addressed only if it is necessary to do so in order to decide this case or if there is an overriding reason making it desirable to do so. Overbroad statements of principle are inimical to the tradition of incremental development of the common law. Likewise, the development of law under the *Canadian Charter of Rights and Freedoms* is best served by deciding cases before the Courts, not by anticipating the results of future cases.

The first inquiry is whether ruling on the issue of subjective foresight is necessary for the disposition of this case. In my view, the case at bar is governed by the reasons given in this Court's decision in *R. v. Vaillancourt*, [1987] 2 S.C.R. 636, 60 C.R. (3d) 289, 39 C.C.C. (3d) 118 [Que.]. The Court need go no further.

For diverging comments on *Martineau* see Stuart, "Further Progress on the Constitutional Requirement of Fault, But Stigma is not Enough" (1990), 79 C.R. (3d) 247 and Rosemary Cairns Way, "Constitutionalizing Subjectivism: Another View" (1990), 79 C.R. (3d) 260.

In *R. v. Sit* (1991), 9 C.R. (4th) 126 (S.C.C.), the Supreme Court made it clear that the constructive murder category under what was s. 213(*c*) [later s. 230(*c*)] was also unconstitutional since it resorts to a test of objective foresight and therefore does not involve proof beyond a reasonable doubt that the accused had subjective foresight of the death of the victim.

For over ten years after *Vaillancourt*, prosecutors appeared reluctant to test the possible interpretation that the unlawful object murder category under s. 229(*c*) was still partially constitutional. However, in *Meiler* (1999), 25 C.R. (5th) 161, 136 C.C.C. (3d) 11 (Ont. C.A.), the Ontario Court of Appeal confirmed a murder conviction where a trial judge had instructed the jury it could convict on the basis of s. 229(*c*) if it found that the accused for an unlawful object did anything knowing that it was likely to cause someone's death. The decision can be criticized for not adopting a narrower interpretation limiting s. 229(*c*) to a person who had a subjective awareness of the likelihood of the actual victim's death: see, further, R.J. Delisle, "Unlawful Object Murder Is Alive and Well" (1995), 25 C.R. (5th) 179. In *Meiler*, on the accused's evidence, he was carrying a loaded and cocked shotgun with intent to kill a particular person and the gun discharged during a struggle and accidentally killed another. The particular application of s. 229(*c*) in *Meiler* appears to resurrect a type of constructive murder the Supreme Court had declared unconstitutional. Any resort to s. 229(*c*) will also unfortunately return the law of murder to former common law complexities of trying to identify an unlawful object distinct from the immediate object accompanying the act of killing.

First Degree Murder

The punishment for both first and second degree murder is fixed at life imprisonment. The significance of the distinction relates to parole eligibility: see s. 745.

Planned and Deliberate: s. 231(2)

R. v. SMITH

(1979), 51 C.C.C. (2d) 381 (Sask. C.A.)

CULLITON C.J.S.: — Gerald Thomas Smith was charged that he, on July 9, 1978, at the Edenwold District, Saskatchewan, did cause the death of Darryl Wayne Skwarchuk and thereby commit first degree murder contrary to s. 218 [now s. 231] [rep. & sub. 1974-75-76, c. 93, s. 5] of the *Criminal Code*.

After a jury trial presided over by MacLeod J., he was found guilty as charged and was sentenced to life imprisonment without eligibility for parole until he has served 25 years of his sentence.

While he has appealed in respect of conviction and sentence, his counsel conceded both at the trial and on the appeal that there were only three verdicts open to the jury, namely, guilty of first degree murder, guilty of second degree murder or guilty of manslaughter. I am satisfied the evidence fully supported that position.

The argument that a verdict of manslaughter was open to the jury was founded on the plea of provocation. That defence was rejected by the jury and, in my view, rightly so. Thus, the sole question on the appeal is simply whether or not there was evidence of planning and deliberation upon which the jury could properly find the appellant guilty of first degree murder.

For the Court to consider this question, it is not necessary to review all of the evidence adduced at trial. The evidence upon which the Crown relied in its contention that a finding of first degree murder was a proper finding, was the evidence of William Mitchel Massier. I think it is evident the jury accepted his evidence and it is the only evidence in respect of the actual killing.

Massier was a young man 18 years of age, who, at the time he gave evidence, was also charged with the murder of Skwarchuk. He said he knew

Smith and first met him in October, 1977, while working at MacDonald's. He said, he also knew Skwarchuk and met him in November, 1977, while Skwarchuk was working at a laundromat. He said that he, Smith and Skwarchuk became friends. He said they partied together and jointly engaged in a number of breaking and entering offences in the spring of 1978. He said from time to time they went hunting together and probably did so some 20 or 25 times. They always went north of the city and usually had a rented car or Skwarchuk's car. On occasion he said they had a friend's car.

Massier said that on July 9, 1978, he had a .12 guage shot-gun. He said he had possessed that gun for three or four months having obtained it from an apartment which they broke and entered. He said Skwarchuk also had a .22 gun and that Smith owned a .22 semi-automatic rifle and a pellet gun.

Smith lived at 201 Branew Apts. at the corner of St. John St. and Victoria Ave. Massier testified they used to party there. These parties consisted of drinking liquor and at times smoking marijuana and taking pills. Skwarchuk lived on Osler St.

On Sunday, July 9, 1978, at about 11:00 or 11:30 a.m., Massier said Smith telephoned to him and asked if they should keep the rented cart that day. According to Massier, Smith had possession of a car which they had rented the previous day. He told Smith to keep the car.

About 12 noon, Smith arrived at Massier's place in the car accompanied by Skwarchuk. Massier said he went out and was told they were going hunting and he said he would go with them. They then went to Smith's apartment and picked up a .22 ruger with a scope, a .12 guage shot-gun and a pellet pistol. The shot-gun had been sawed off and was owned by Massier. Smith also brought some shot-gun shells. They then went to Skwarchuk's and obtained 50 rounds of .22 ammunition.

After this, they drove to MacDonald's where they had something to eat. According to Massier, Smith and Skwarchuk were taking valium pills. After eating, they returned to Massier's place and picked up some tools and a pair of gloves. According to Massier, they obtained the tools and gloves because Smith said he wanted to break into a drug store. At the same time, they picked up more .22 ammunition.

Following this, they drove north on Highway 6. After travelling some 10 or 15 miles they turned west off of the highway. Massier said, from time to time, thereafter, they stopped to shoot birds, ducks and mail boxes. Finally they arrived at an abandoned farmhouse and stopped there. Smith shot off the door knob with the shot-gun.

According to the evidence of Massier, while driving from Regina, Smith had consumed the best part of a mickey of rye. He said during the drive there was considerable conversation about girl friends but no unfriendliness was shown by anyone.

After Smith had shot off the door knob, Massier said he broke down the inside door and they all went into the house. He said Smith and Skwarchuk were shooting up the house and windows with the shot-gun and he smashed a couple of windows with a beer bottle. He said he also shot a few rounds with the .22.

Massier said after about 15 minutes, Smith and Skwarchuk said they wanted to leave. They then all left the house. He said they went to the car and there he obtained a pair of leather gloves. He said he put the gloves on and returned to the house and started smashing windows with a board. He said he smashed two front windows and then smashed a window on the west side. He jumped through this window and was then at the back of the house. He broke two more windows there and then went around the corner where he saw Smith and Skwarchuk and heard an argument between them.

Massier said he was some distance away and could not understand exactly what they were saying. He said it seemed to him Smith was telling Skwarchuk to put down his gun and he would do the same. He said Smith had the shot-gun and Skwarchuuk the .22 and they were pointing the guns at each other.

Massier said he did not think the situation was serious so he returned to his window breaking activity. He said he was on the east side of the house when he heard a shot. He testified he then immediately came to the front of the house and saw Smith standing at the front of the car, on the driver's side, and Skwarchuk was about three yards from the rear bumper on the passenger side. He saw Smith with the shot-gun in his hand and Skwarchuk's gun was on the ground. He said Skwarchuk had been shot in the left elbow, and his arm was hanging and blood was squirting on the ground. He said Skwarchuk was running away; that he ran some distance, stopped and faced the car. Massier testified Skwarchuk was screaming and yelling and said he was bleeding to death and should be taken to a hospital.

When Skwarchuk stopped, Massier said he went to the car and asked Smith what was going on and Smith told him to shut up. He said he asked Smith if he was going to shoot Skwarchuk and Smith did not answer. He said he then asked Smith if he was going to shoot him and Smith told him to shut up and get behind him. According to Massier, this episode lasted from one to three minutes. During this time, Smith reloaded the shot-gun. He put in five shells. According to Massier, Smith then called Skwarchuk's name. Following this Skwarchuk took a step towards the car and when Smith pumped the shell into the chambers of the gun, Skwarchuk turned and ran. He said Smith shot from long range and he could not tell whether Skwarchuk had been hit. He said Smith shot again. It appeared some pellets hit Skwarchuk in the back. Massier said Skwarchuk continued to run but before he stopped, Smith shot him again and he fell down and stayed down.

According to Massier, Smith then walked up to Skwarchuk who was sitting with his knees up and his head resting on his knees. He said Smith held the gun three or four inches from the back of Skwarchuk's head and then fired the same. Skwarchuk fell back and appeared to be dead. Massier said this episode took about 30 seconds.

After this, Massier said he asked Smith if he was going to shoot him, to which Smith replied: "No, you are my friend: don't worry about it". Massier testified Smith told him to go back to the car and get the .22. He said he went to the car and was followed by Smith. Massier said when he went to load the .22, the clip was not in the gun. He said Smith gave him the clip which he loaded with four shells and gave it to Smith. Smith put the clip in the gun. When asked by Massier what he was going to do, Smith answered he was going to shoot Skwarchuk with the .22 and that would be his insurance: if he got caught, he would say Massier shot him. Massier testified he followed Smith who went to where Skwarchuk was lying and shot him in the head three times.

According to Massier, he was told to take Skwarchuk's watch; that he did so and threw it into a pond. They heard a truck approach and Smith said that they should take off. Smith put the .22 and the shot-gun in the car and they returned to the city. They were subsequently arrested and charged with the murder of Skwarchuk.

Section 214(2) [rep. & sub. 1974-75-76, c. 105, s. 4] of the *Code* reads:

> 214(2) [now s. 231(2)] Murder is first degree murder when it is planned and deliberate.

In *More v. The Queen*, [1963] 3 C.C.C. 289, [1963] S.C.R. 522, the Supreme Court of Canada considered the meaning of the words "planned" and "deliberate". The Court made it clear that the accused could not be found guilty of first degree murder unless it was proved beyond a reasonable doubt, not only that the murder was planned but also that it was deliberate. Fauteux J. (later C.J.C.), accepted as a meaning of "planned" — "arranged beforehand".

In so far as the word "deliberate" is concerned Cartwright J. (later C.J.C.). said at p. 291 C.C.C., p. 534 S.C.R.:

> The learned trial Judge also rightly instructed the jury that the word "deliberate", as used in s. 202A(2)(*a*), means "considered, not impulsive".
>
> Other meanings of the adjective given in the Oxford Dictionary are "not hasty in decision", "slow in deciding" and "intentional". The word as used in the subsection cannot have simply the meaning "intentional" because it is only if the accused's act was intentional that he can be guilty of murder and the subsection is creating an additional ingredient to be proved as a condition of an accused being convicted of capital murder.

Similar views were expressed by the Supreme Court in *McMartin v. The Queen*, [1965] 1 C.C.C. 142, [1964] S.C.R. 484. In *R. v. Mitchell*, [1965] 1 C.C.C. 155, 43 C.R. 391, Spence J., in delivering the majority judgment of the Supreme Court, after referring to *More v. The Queen, supra*, and *McMartin v. The Queen, supra*, said at p. 162 C.C.C., pp. 393-4 C.R.:

> I am of the opinion that the judgment in these two cases have as their *ratio decidendi* the principle that in determining whether the accused committed the crime of capital murder in that it was "planned and deliberate on the part of such person" the jury should have available and should be directed to consider all the circumstances including not only the evidence of the accused's actions but also his condition, his state of mind as affected by either real or even imagined insults and provoking actions of the victim and by the accused's consumption of alcohol. There is no doubt this is a finding of fact. The questions which the jury must decide and decide beyond reasonable doubt before they may convict the accused of capital murder under the relevant subsection — s. 202A(2)(*a*) — are: Was the murder which he committed planned and was it deliberate? I separate the jury's problem in that form because I am in complete agreement with Whittaker J.A., when he said [[1964] 2 C.C.C. at p. 16]: "It is possible to imagine a murder to some degree planned and yet not deliberate." Therefore, to determine whether the charge to the jury delivered by the learned trial Judge was adequate in submitting to them the issue of planning and deliberation the charge must be examined with some care.

In *R. v. Widdifield*, Gale J. (later C.J.O.), in charging the jury on planned and deliberate, as reported in 6 *Crim. L.Q.* 152 at p. 153 (1963-64), said:

> I think that in the Code "planned" is to be assigned, I think, its natural meaning of a calculated scheme or design which has been carefully thought out, and the nature and consequences of which have been considered and weighed. But that does not mean, of course, to say that the plan need be a complicated one. It may be a very simple one, and the simpler it is perhaps the easier it is to formulate.

The foregoing direction was approved by the Ontario Court of Appeal in *R. v. Reynolds* (1978), 44 C.C.C. (2d) 129. See particulary the comments of Martin J.A., speaking for the Court at p. 137.

I realize it is both difficult and unwise to attempt to give an exhaustive meaning to the word "planned". It is a common word and to it should be attributed its meaning as understood in everyday life. Clearly, planning must not be confused with intention as the planning would only occur after the intent to murder had been formed. There must be some evidence the killing was the result of a scheme or design previously formulated or designed by the accused and the killing was the implementation of that scheme or design. It is obvious a murder committed on a sudden impulse and without prior consideration, even though the intent to kill is clearly proven, would not constitute a planned murder.

In the present case, there is not the slightest evidence the appellant had given any consideration to the murder of Skwarchuk until after he and Skwarchuk had left the house. In instructing the jury, the learned trial Judge said:

> So without beating it more than that, the Crown must establish to establish first degree murder that the accused caused the death, he intended to do so and that he planned and deliberated. Now, I think you can say without any doubt that there was no plan to kill prior to arriving at the farm. There's no evidence of that, nor any suggestion of that. Equally there was no plan or intention to kill the first while at the farm. If the accused planned to kill, deliberated this, it must have been started, at the earliest, about the time of the altercation. There is no evidence that it would have started earlier than that, and then the question that you must weigh and consider is did he have the time to deliberate under the circumstances; did he have time to plan, and if so, did he? If you can say beyond a reasonable doubt that from the circumstances that you see and the facts that you find that it was planned and deliberate, then you should return a verdict of guilty of first degree murder. If you have a reasonable doubt about any of those things, then you should not bring a verdict of first degree murder.

To the foregoing instruction, no objection was taken by counsel either for the Crown or for the appellant. As a matter of fact, learned counsel for the Crown, in his address to the jury relied entirely on the evidence of Massier to establish "planned" and "deliberate".

I am satisfied there was no evidence whatever to support the conclusion that the actions of the appellant, cruel and sadistic as they were, in killing Skwarchuk was the implementation of a previously determined design or scheme. I think it is obvious his actions were the result of a sudden impulse. It would be pure speculation to try and determine what triggered that impulse.

It may well be that the killing was deliberate. However, even if it was, there could only be a verdict of first degree murder if the evidence established as well that the murder was planned.

Whether or not there was evidence the murder was planned was a question of law for the Judge. In my respectful view, as there was no such evidence, the learned trial Judge erred in law in instructing the jury there was evidence upon which a verdict of first degree murder could be found. In these circumstances, therefore, I direct that the verdict of first degree murder be set aside and a conviction of second degree murder be substituted therefore.

R. v. NYGAARD AND SCHIMMENS

(1989), 72 C.R. (3d) 257, 51 C.C.C. (3d) 417 (S.C.C.)

M bought a car stereo from the accused N for $100. Payment was made by means of a cheque signed jointly by T. and H. The cheque bounced. N came to M's motel and told him that, if the matter was not cleared up that day, M could expect trouble. Later that day N, the accused S, and another man, went to the apartment. S struck M several times on the forehead with a baseball bat and broke his arm, which was raised to protect his face. S then asked who had signed the cheque. When told it was H, he proceeded to attack H with the bat, hitting him three times between the eyes with full two-handed swings. H died in hospital of multiple skull fractures. S and N were charged with first degree murder. Following trial before Judge and jury they were convicted.

When the matter reached the Supreme Court of Canada a new trial was ordered respecting a misdirection on a point of evidence. In the course of the judgment the Court unanimously held that the trial Judge had not erred in directing the jury that they could return a verdict of first degree murder on the basis of a combination of sections 229(*a*)(ii) and 231(2):

Cory J.: —

Throughout history the idea that one human being could cold-bloodedly plan and deliberate upon the killing of another has been repugnant to all civilized societies and has tended to be considered as the most reprehensible of violent crimes. In *Droste v. R.*, Dickson C.J.C. noted that it is the element of planning and deliberation of the murder which makes the crime of murder in the first degree more culpable and justifies the harsher sentence.

It remains then to consider what is the specific *mens rea* required by s. 212(*a*)(ii) to which the element of planning and deliberation must be related. The section requires that the Crown prove that the accused meant to cause the victim such bodily harm that he knew that it was likely to cause the death of the victim and was reckless whether death ensued or not as a result of causing that bodily harm. The essential element is that of intending to cause bodily harm of such a grave and serious nature that the accused knew that it was likely to result in the death of the victim. The aspect of recklessness is almost an afterthought insofar as the basic intent is concerned.

In *Sansregret v. R.*, [1985] 1 S.C.R. 570, 45 C.R. (3d) 193, 18 C.C.C. (3d) 223, recklessness was defined as being the attitude of one who was aware of the danger the prohibited conduct could bring about yet nevertheless persisted in that conduct despite the knowledge of the risk. Thus the section requires the accused to intend to cause the gravest of bodily harm that is so dangerous and serious that he knows it is likely to result in death and to persist in that conduct despite the knowledge of the risk.

In my view, the vital element of the requisite intent is that of causing such bodily harm that the perpetrator knows that it is likely to cause death and yet persists in the assault. There can be no doubt that a person can plan and deliberate to cause terrible bodily harm that he knows is likely to result in death. Nothing is added to the aspect of planning and deliberation by the requirement that the fatal assault be carried out in a reckless manner, that is to say, by heedlessly proceeding with the deadly assault in the face of the knowledge of the obvious risks. The planning and deliberation to cause the bodily harm which is likely to be fatal must of necessity include the planning and deliberating to continue and to persist in that conduct despite the knowledge of the risk. The element of recklessness does not exist in a vacuum as a sole *mens rea* requirement, but rather it must act in conjunction with the intentional infliction of terrible bodily harm. I therefore conclude that planning and deliberation may well be coupled with the *mens rea* requirements of s. 212(*a*)(ii) and that a first degree murder conviction can be sustained by virtue of the combined operation of ss. 214(2) and 212(*a*)(ii). This ground of appeal must therefore fail.

As well, the appellant argued it was wrong to label an offence under s. 212(*a*)(ii) as murder. It was said that the requisite *mens rea* is such that it is not as grave a crime as that defined in s. 212(*a*)(i), where the requisite intent is to cause the death of someone. I cannot accept that contention. The variation in the degree of culpability is too slight to take into account. Let us consider the gravity of the crime described by s. 212(*a*)(ii) in the light of three examples which, pursuant to the section, would be murder. First, an accused forms the intent to inflict multiple stab wounds in the abdomen and chest of a person knowing that the wounds are likely to kill the victim and, heedless of the known probable result, proceeds with the stabbing. Second, an accused forms the intent to shoot a former associate in the chest knowing that death is likely to ensue and, uncaring of the result, shoots the victim in the chest. Third, two accused form the intent to repeatedly and viciously strike a person in the head with a baseball bat realizing full well that the victim will probably die as a result. Nonetheless they continue with the bone-splintering, skull-shattering assault. The accused in all these examples must have committed as grave a crime as the accused who specifically intends to kill. Society would, I think, find the drawing of any differentiation in the degree of culpability an exercise in futility. The difference in the calibration on the scale of culpability is too minute to merit a distinction. I would conclude that the crime defined in s. 212(*a*)(ii) can properly be described as murder and on a "culpability scale" it varies so little from s. 212(*a*)(i) as to be indistinguishable.

I find some support for this position in *R. v. Vaillancourt*, [1987] 2 S.C.R. 636, 60 C.R. (3d) 289, 39 C.C.C. (3d) 118 [Que.]. There Lamer J., giving the reasons for the Court, stated at pp. 644-45:

> There is a very interesting progression through s. 212 to s. 213 with respect to the mental state that must be proven.
>
> The starting point is s. 212(*a*)(i) . . .
>
> This clearly requires that the accused have actual subjective foresight of the likelihood of causing the death coupled with the intention to cause that death. This is the most morally blameworthy state of mind in our system.
>
> There is a slight relaxation of this requirement in s. 212(*a*)(ii) . . .
>
> Here again the accused must have actual subjective foresight of the likelihood of death. However, the Crown need no longer prove that he intended to cause the death but only that he was reckless whether death ensued or not. It should also be noted that s. 212(*a*)(ii) is limited to cases where the accused intended to cause bodily harm to the victim.

He went on to note that there is still a greater relaxation of the requisite mental element in s. 212(*c*), a provision which "eliminates the requirement of actual subjective foresight and replaces it with objective foreseeability or negligence" (pp. 645-46). It is clear from these observations that the Court in that case concluded that there was but a slight relaxation of the requisite intent in s. 212(*a*)(ii) from that required by s. 212(*a*)(i). Section 212(*a*)(ii) demands a highly subjective mental element to be present, that of the intent to cause the gravest of bodily injuries that are known to the accused to be likely to cause death to the victim. It is to this intent that the s. 214(2) requirement of planning and deliberation can be properly applied.

For comment on *Nygaard* see Stuart (1989), 72 C.R. (3d) 259-261.

Murder of a Police Officer: s. 231(4)

R. v. MUNRO AND MUNRO

(1983), 36 C.R. (3d) 193, 8 C.C.C. (3d) 260 (Ont. C.A.), leave to appeal to
S.C.C. refused 56 N.R. 230n

MARTIN J.A.: —

. . . .

It is also open to serious question whether, under s. 214(4)(*a*) of the *Code*, where the person murdered is in fact a police officer acting in the course of his duties, it is necessary for the Crown to prove that the offender knew that he was shooting at a police officer who was acting in the course of his duties. The trial Judge, in charging the jury that in order to constitute first degree murder the prosecution must prove that Craig Munro knew that he was shooting at a police officer acting in the course of his duties, followed the judgment of the Manitoba Court of Appeal in *R. v. Shand* (1971), 3 C.C.C. (2d) 8, affirmed (1971), 4 C.C.C. (2d) 173 (S.C.C.). In that case, the Court stated by way of *obiter* that under the former s.202A [en. 1960-61, c.44, s. 1; am. 1967-68, c. 15, s. 1] of the *Code* knowledge on the part of the accused that the person he killed was a police officer or other person mentioned in the section was requisite for a conviction for capital murder.

Section 202A, in part, read:

"(2) Murder is capital murder, in respect of any person, where such person by his own act caused or assisted in causing the death of

"(*a*) a police officer . . . acting in the course of his duties".

The Court, in holding that knowledge by the accused that the person killed was a police officer was requisite to a conviction for capital murder, based its decision on the ground that there was a presumption that *mens rea* is an essential ingredient in all criminal cases. Freedman J.A. (later C.J.M.), delivering the judgment of the Court, said at pp. 14-15:

> "Nor should it be thought that the *mens rea* necessary to an act of murder carries over to make that act capital murder even if the accused did not know that his victim was a police officer. The crime of capital murder differs from that of non-capital murder in that an additional ingredient has been added to the former. Ought we to say that a person may be found guilty of capital murder even if he had no *mens rea* in relation to that additional ingredient? To do that would be to go counter to the historic presumption making *mens rea* essential to the proof of a crime — not part of a crime, not a lesser crime, but the whole crime as charged. Parliament could have declared in appropriate language that *mens rea* would not be required on the aspect of the crime we are here considering. Indeed, Crown counsel argues that Parliament has arrived at that end by another course. He suggests that the absence of any language in s. 202A(2) indicating a requirement of *mens rea* as regards the additional ingredient (*e.g.* 'knowing him to be such') has made proof of such *mens rea* unnecessary. But we prefer the view that the presumption is not to be displaced by mere silence; and that, least of all, in a capital case."

The trial Judge in that case, however, had charged the jury that knowledge by the accused that the person he killed was a police officer was an essential element of capital murder. The other grounds of appeal were rejected, and the appeal was accordingly dismissed. A further appeal by the accused to the Supreme Court of Canada was also dismissed. Fauteux C.J.C., delivering the brief oral judgment of the court dismissing the appeal, said that the Court agreed with the conclusion of the Manitoba Court of Appeal that the appeal must be dismissed and stated at p. 173 that the court found "it unnecessary to express any view on the *obiter dictum* in the Court below that proof of knowledge is an essential ingredient of the offence of capital murder".

Professor Alan W. Mewett argues persuasively that the *obiter dictum* in *R. v. Shand, supra*, is not correct, and that, given the requisite proof of murder, then all that s. 214 does is to require proof that, in fact, certain other elements are present: see Alan W. Mewett, "First Degree Murder" (1978), 21 Cr. L.Q. 82, at pp. 88-90. I find some difficulty in reconciling the reasoning of the Manitoba Court of Appeal with the analysis of s. 214 by Dickson J., delivering the majority judgment of the Supreme Court of Canada in *R. v. Farrant*, 32 C.R. (3d) 289.

In that case, Dickson J. said at pp. 301-302:

> "Section 214, however, is not the section which sets out the elements of the offence of murder. This is done in ss. 212 and 213 [am. 1974-75-76, c. 93, s. 13; c. 105, s. 29; since am. 1980-81-82-83, c. 125, s. 15]. *Section 214 does not create a distinct and independent substantive offence of first degree constructive murder pursuant to forcible confinement. The*

section is subservient to ss. 212 and 213 as either first or second degree murder. The importance of the distinction between first and second degree murder is that first degree murder carries with it a mandatory life sentence without eligibility for parole for 25 years (ss. 218 [re-en. 1974-76, c. 105, s. 5], 669(*a*) [re-en. 1974-75-76, c. 105, s. 21]). A conviction for second degree murder also carries with it a mandatory life sentence, but parole may be granted after ten years of imprisonment unless the jury recommends a greater number of years . . . "There is no distinction between ss. 214(5)(*a*) and 212 based upon intent. The presence or absence of intent is the distinction between ss. 212 and 213, not s. 214. Intent is an element of the offence of murder under s. 212, be it first or second degree. *The distinction between first and second degree murder in s. 214 is not based upon intent; it is based upon (1) the presence of planning and deliberation (s. 212(2)); (2) the identity of the victim (s. 214(4)); or (3) the nature of the offence being committed at the time of the murder (s. 214(5)).* The primary and essential determination for a jury to make is whether murder has been committed, either under s. 212 or, where the evidence warrants it, under s. 213. Considerations of the distinctions between first and second degree murder are irrelevant in making this preliminary determination. Once the offence has been found, it is then classified." (The italics are mine.)

Even if *mens rea* with respect to the identity of the victim is a requisite element of first degree murder under s. 244(4)(*a*), the ordinary *mens rea* which suffices where no mental element is specified in the definition of the offence is supplied by either intention or recklessness with respect to the material elements of the *actus reus*. In the present case, the appellant Craig Munro, on his own evidence, knew that there was a police officer at the back door attempting to enter the premises, and he had fired a shot at or through the door, knowing that there was a police officer outside, minutes before the fatal shooting of Constable Sweet. The only reasonable conclusion to which the jury could come on the evidence was that he realized that the police were also endeavouring to enter the premises by the front doors when he and his brother ran to the back of the premises and subsequently went downstairs to the basement. The appellant Craig Munro must, at the very least, have been conscious of the risk that he was firing at a police officer acting in the course of his duties, and no reasonable jury could, on the evidence, have reached any other conclusion. Accordingly, his recklessness with respect to whether he was shooting at a police officer acting in the course of his duties supplied the necessary *mens rea* for murder under s. 214(4)(*a*), if *mens rea* with respect to that element was necessary.

R. v. COLLINS

(1989), 69 C.R. (3d) 235, 48 C.C.C. (3d) 343 (Ont. C.A.)

GOODMAN J.A.: —

. . . .

There can be no doubt that the onus was on the Crown to establish beyond a reasonable doubt the *actus reus* and *mens rea* of the substantive offence of murder under s. 212. I am of the view, however, that under s. 214(4)(*a*) [now s. 231(4)(*a*)] there is an onus on the Crown to establish beyond a reasonable doubt that the victim was a person who falls within the designation of the occupations set forth in that subsection acting in the course of his duties to the knowledge of the accused or with recklessness on his part as to whether the victim was such a person so acting.

In my opinion there is no binding authority to the contrary. It seems clear to me that the object of the classification of first degree murder in s. 214 is to require a more severe punishment for the offence of murder in circumstances that involve an added degree of moral culpability or to act as a more effective deterrent in the prevention of the murder of persons engaged in the preservation, prevention of infringement and enforcement of the law or of persons who have fallen under the domination of an offender.

It is my view that s. 214(4)(a) should be interpreted in such a manner that requires proof of the facts which give rise to the added moral culpability or which would act as an additional deterrent. It is clear to me that to fulfil such interpretation it is necessary that the Crown prove that the murderer had knowledge of the identity of the victim as one of the persons designated in the subsection and that such person was acting in the course of his duties or was reckless as such identity and acts of the victim.

The section could, of course, be interpreted to simply require that the Crown prove that the occupation of the victim was one of those set forth in the subsection and that the person was acting in the course of his duties without proof of knowledge thereof on the part of the murderer. The subsection does not refer to proof of such knowledge.

I am satisfied that if the latter interpretation is adopted, it would offend s. 7 of the *Charter*: If, for example, a gunman sees two persons on the street dressed in plain clothes of whom one is a merchant walking home and the other is a detective on his way to investigate or in the process of investigating a break-in, and if the gunman decides without planning and deliberation to shoot and kill one of them and does, so he would be guilty of murder no matter which person he killed. In the case of the killing of the ordinary citizen he would be guilty of second degree murder with a sentence of life imprisonment with a possibility of parole eligibility after 10 years but in the case of the killing of the detective he would be guilty of first degree murder with a sentence of life imprisonment with a possibility of parole in no less than 25 years, being the minimum period before parole eligibility (subject of course to the provisions of s. 745 of the *Code* (formerly s. 672)).

Although the crime of murder is deserving of the heavy sentence involved, it seems to me that there would be no difference in moral culpability in the example set forth above no matter which person was the victim, nor would there be any additional deterrent provided under s. 214(4)(a) in those circumstances if proof of knowledge that the detective was indeed a detective acting in the course of his duty were not required. There would then be no rational or logical reason for imposing a heavier penalty in the case where the murderer killed the person whom he did not know and had no reason to know was a police officer acting in the course of his duties.

On the other hand, if s. 214(4)(a) is interpreted to require proof of such knowledge before the murder can be classified as first degree murder, then a heavier sentence can be justified on the basis of added moral culpability or as additional deterrent on the grounds of public policy. In such event, it is my opinion that the subsection would not contravene the provisions of s. 7 of the *Charter*.

I am of the opinion that, where a statutory provision is open to two interpretations, one of which will contravene the *Charter* and the other of which will not, the provision should be interpreted in such a manner as will not contravene the *Charter*: see *R. v. Corbett*, [1988] 1 S.C.R. 670, 64 C.R. (3d) 1 at 23, 41 C.C.C. (3d) 385, per Beetz J.

I conclude that the onus was on the Crown to prove that the appellant knew that the victim was a police officer who was acting in the course of his duty and I find, accordingly, that the provisions of s. 214(4)(*a*) do not contravene s. 7 of the *Charter*. In the present case the trial Judge charged the jury in accordance with this conclusion. There was evidence to support a finding of knowledge on the part of the appellant. (And see *R. v. Prevost* (1988), 64 C.R. (3d) 188, 42 C.C.C. (3d) 314 at 318 (C.A.).) This ground of appeal, therefore, fails.

Constructive First Degree Murder: s. 231(5)

R. v. ARKELL

[1990] 2 S.C.R. 695, 79 C.R. (3d) 207, 59 C.C.C. (3d) 65

The accused was convicted, pursuant to now s. 231(5), with first degree murder. It was the theory of the Crown that the victim was killed while he attempted to sexually assault her. One of the the constitutional questions for the Court was whether s. 231(5) contravened s. 7 of the *Charter*.

LAMER C.J.C. (DICKSON C.J.C. and WILSON, GONTHIER and CORY JJ. concurring): —

The main argument of the appellant, as regards his constitutional challenge of the section, is that it is arbitrary and irrational and thereby offends s. 7 of the *Charter*.

. . . .

The argument of the appellant suggests that the sentencing scheme is flawed and in violation of s. 7 of the *Charter* because it results in the punishment of individuals that is not proportionate to the seriousness of the offences giving rise to the sentences. First, I must note that as a result of this Court's decision in *Martineau*, released concurrently, it can no longer be said that s. 214(5) has the potential to classify unintentional killings as first degree murder. A conviction for murder requires proof beyond a reasonable doubt of subjective foresight of death. Therefore, when we reach the stage of classifying murders as either first or second degree, we are dealing with individuals who have committed the most serious crime in our *Criminal Code*, and who have been proven to have done so with the highest level of moral culpability, that of subjective foresight. Section

214(5) represents a decision by Parliament to impose a more serious punishment on those found guilty of murder while committing certain listed offences.

This leads me to a second point, namely, a consideration of the underlying rationale of s. 214(5). Again, I refer to the decision of this Court in *R. v. Paré*, [1987] 2 S.C.R. 618, at pp. 632-33:

> All murders are serious crimes. Some murders, however, are so threatening to the public that Parliament has chosen to impose exceptional penalties on the perpetrators. One such class of murders is that found in s. 214(5), murders done while committing a hijacking, a kidnapping and forcible confinement, a rape, or an indecent assault. . .

> The offences listed in s. 214(5) are all offences involving the unlawful domination of people by other people. Thus an organizing principle for s. 214(5) can be found. This principle is that where a murder is committed by someone already abusing his power by illegally dominating another, the murder should be treated as an exceptionally serious crime. Parliament has chosen to treat these murders as murders in the first degree.

I can find no principle of fundamental justice that prevents Parliament, guided by the organizing principle identified by this Court in *Paré*, from classifying murders done while committing certain underlying offences as more serious, and thereby attaching more serious penalties to them. In the case of the distinction between first and second degree murder, the difference is a maximum extra 15 years that must be served before one is eligible for parole. This distinction is neither arbitrary nor irrational. The section is based on an organizing principle that treats murders committed while the perpetrator is illegally dominating another person as more serious than other murders. Further, the relationship between the classification and the moral blameworthiness of the offender clearly exists. Section 214 only comes into play when murder has been proven beyond a reasonable doubt. In light of *Martineau*, this means that the offender has been proven to have had subjective foresight of death. Parliament's decision to treat more seriously murders that have been committed while the offender is exploiting a position of power through illegal domination of the victim accords with the principle that there must be a proportionality between a sentence and the moral blameworthiness of the offender and other considerations such as deterrence and societal condemnation of the acts of the offender. Therefore, I conclude that in so far as s. 214(5) is neither arbitrary nor irrational, it does not infringe upon s. 7 of the *Charter*.

L'HEUREUX-DUBÉ J. and SOPINKA J. concurred in the result.

For critical comments, see Allan Manson, "The Easy Acceptance of Long Term Confinement in Canada" (1990), 79 C.R. (3d) 265.

Subjective Awareness Required for Few Crimes

When the Supreme Court struck down the constructive murder rule in s. 230(*d*) of the *Criminal Code* in *Vaillancourt*, Justice Lamer left the impression that the Court might one day decide that subjective *mens rea* was constitutionally required for all crimes. It is now clear that the Supreme Court is only likely to declare such a requirement for a very few offences. At present the Supreme Court has required subjective fault for murder, *i.e.*, *Martineau*, attempted murder; *R. v. Logan*, [1990] 2 S.C.R. 731, 79 C.R. (3d) 169, 58 C.C.C. (3d) 391, accessory liability to an offence constitutionally requiring a subjective test, *Logan*; and war crimes and crimes against humanity, *R. v. Finta*, [1994] 1 S.C.R. 701, 28 C.R. (4th) 265, 88 C.C.C. (3d) 417. There is also *obiter* recognition in *Vaillancourt* and *Martineau* that theft requires subjective awareness.

The analysis is still turning on the unruly criterion of stigma criticized by most commentators as unreliable and potentially circular. See, for example, Isabel Grant and Christine Boyle, "Equality, Harm and Vulnerability: Homicide and Sexual Assault Post-*Creighton*" (1993), 23 C.R. (4th) 252 at 258-259 and Rosemary Cairns Way, "Constitutionalizing Subjectivism: Another View" (1990), 79 C.R. (3d) 260. The Supreme Court has decided that the stigma necessary to require subjective *mens rea* does not follow from a conviction of the *Criminal Code* offences of unlawful act causing bodily harm, *R. v. DeSousa*, [1992] 2 S.C.R. 944, 15 C.R. (4th) 66, 76 C.C.C. (3d) 124; dangerous driving, *R. v. Hundal*, [1993] 1 S.C.R. 867, 19 C.R. (4th) 169, 79 C.C.C. (3d) 97; manslaughter, *R. v. Creighton*, [1993] 3 S.C.R. 3, 23 C.R. (4th) 189, 83 C.C.C. (3d) 346; failing to provide necessaries of life, *R. v. Naglik*, [1993] 3 S.C.R. 122, 23 C.R. (4th) 335, 83 C.C.C. (3d) 526, and careless use of a firearm, *R. v. Finlay*, [1993] 3 S.C.R. 103, 23 C.R. (4th) 321, 83 C.C.C. (3d) 513 and *R. v. Gosset*, [1993] 3 S.C.R. 76, 23 C.R. (4th) 280, 83 C.C.C. (3d) 494.

Provincial Courts of Appeal have also been unreceptive to *Charter* arguments to entrench subjective tests. Challenges have been rejected for offences of causing bodily harm in committing assault, *R. v. Brooks* (1988), 64 C.R. (3d) 322, 41 C.C.C. (3d) 157 (B.C. C.A.); criminal negligence, *R. v. Nelson* (1990), 75 C.R. (4th) 70, 54 C.C.C. (3d) 285 (Ont. C.A.) and *R. v. Gingrich* (1991), 6 C.R. (4th) 197, 65 C.C.C. (3d) 188 (Ont. C.A.); and arson, *R. v. Peters* (1991), 11 C.R. (4th) 48, 69 C.C.C. (3d) 461 (B.C. C.A.).

(b) Three Types of Crimes since *Creighton*

Given *Creighton*, *Criminal Code* offences are, for the determination of fault, divided into three categories as follows:

Fault for Crimes

① Subjective *mens rea*	② Objective Negligence	③ Offences based on predicate offences
aware of risk, all individual factors	marked departure from objective norm, no individual factors short of incapacity	objective foresight of harm, no individual factors, no marked limit,except for predicate offences of negligence
e.g., murder, assault, break and enter, theft, possession offences	*e.g.*, dangerous driving careless firearms, failure to provide necessaries	*e.g.*, unlawful act man-slaughter, unlawfully causing bodily harm, aggravated assault

(1) Crimes Requiring Subjective *Mens Rea*

Where the *Criminal Code* definitions of an offence include a clear *mens rea* word, such as "intentionally", "wilfully", or "knowingly", Parliament has made its choice of the subjective test clear.

Where the definition of the crime contains no *mens rea* words, and there is no language indicating the crime is to be interpreted as one of objective negligence, it should be interpreted as an offence of subjective *mens rea*. Decisions reading in subjective fault requirements for drug offences, *R. v. Beaver*, [1957] S.C.R. 531, 26 C.R. 193 and the former offence of rape, *R. v. Pappajohn*, [1980] 2 S.C.R. 120, 52 C.C.C. (2d) 481 and *R. v. Sansregret*, [1985] 1 S.C.R. 570, 45 C.R. (3d) 193, are still authoritative. McLachlin J., who delivered the majority judgment in *R. v. Creighton*, also authored the majority judgment in *R. v. Théroux*, [1993] 2 S.C.R. 5, 19 C.R. (4th) 194, 79 C.C.C. (3d) 449, in which the Court interpreted the ambiguous word "fraudulent" to require a subjective *mens rea* requirement for theft and fraud. In *R. v. Clemente*, [1994] 2 S.C.R. 758, 31 C.R. (4th) 28, 91 C.C.C. (3d) 1, the Supreme Court read into the offence of threatening to cause death or serious harm the requirement of an intent to intimidate or instill fear or an intent to be taken seriously.

However, in *R. v. Hinchey* (1996), 3 C.R. (5th) 187, 111 C.C.C. (3d) 353 (S.C.C.), L'Heureux-Dube J., speaking for four of seven justices, appeared reluctant to adopt an approach of a common law presumption of subjective *mens rea*. Her Ladyship also noted that some offences have been interpreted to have both subjective and objective fault requirements. She gave *Lohnes* as an example. Her remarks are *obiter*, as she agreed that the crime in question, s.

121(1)(*c*) of the *Criminal Code* prohibiting the giving or receiving a benefit by a government official or employee, did require subjective *mens rea*. See the comment by Don Stuart, "Corruption in Hinchey: Scrambling Mens Rea Principles" (1997), 3 C.R. (5th) 238.

The most recent pronouncement from the Supreme Court of Canada asserts a common law presumption of subjective *mens rea*. In *Lucas*, [1998] 1 S.C.R. 439, 14 C.R. (5th) 237, 123 C.C.C. (3d) 97 (S.C.C.), the Court held that the crime of defamatory libel under ss. 298-300 of the *Criminal Code* was a demonstrably justified limit on the freedom of expression guaranteed by s. 2(*b*) of the *Charter*. Cory J., for a full Court unanimous on this point, declared the need for a requirement of an intent to defame based on the principle that:

> . . . in the absence of an express legislative provision, it should be presumed that proof of subjective *mens rea* is a requirement of criminal offences (C.R., para. 64).

The Court cited *City of Sault Ste. Marie* and, surprisingly, *Vaillancourt*. The Court went on to enunciate a test of whether the accused knew that the message, as it would be understood by a reasonable person, was false (C.R., para.102). Allan Manson, Annotation to *Lucas* (1998), 14 C.R. (5th) 237 at 241, argues that this wrongly incorporates an objective standard and that the test should be "whether the accused knows that the message, as he or she believes it will be understood, is false" (C.R. at 242).

Motive

THOMAS. Now is my way clear, now is the meaning plain:
    Temptation shall not come in this kind again.
    The last temptation is the greatest treason:
    To do the right deed for the wrong reason.
                  (T.S. Eliot, *Murder in the Cathedral*).

J. HALL, GENERAL PRINCIPLES OF CRIMINAL LAW

2nd ed. (1960), 104

. . . .

In sum: (1) the professional literature, especially beginning with Hale, distinguished *mens rea* from motive. *Mens rea*, a fusion of cognition and volition, is the mental state expressed in the *voluntary* commission of a proscribed harm. (2) The exclusion of motive, as not essential in *mens rea*, does not deny the importance of motive in determining the culpability ("guilt") of the defendant. Instead, the reason for doing that is the necessity to preserve the objectivity of the principle of *mens rea* and the principle of legality, *i.e.* to signify some degree of culpability regardless of how good the motive was. Thus questions of motivation and mitigating circumstances are allocated to administration which can explore such issues thoroughly. (3) Implied in the above conclusions is that the principle of *mens rea* must be given an objective ethical meaning — the premise being that actual harms (disvalues) are proscribed. Accordingly, neither the offender's conscience nor the personal code of ethics of the Judge or the jury can be substituted for the ethics of the penal law. The insistence that guilt should be personal must be interpreted to accord with the paramount value of the objectivity of the principle of *mens rea*.

LEWIS v. R.

[1979] 2 S.C.R. 821, 10 C.R. (3d) 299, 47 C.C.C. (2d) 24

The accused and one Tatlay were jointly charged with the murder of Tatlay's daughter and son-in-law. The accused admitted mailing a package to the victims on behalf of Tatlay but denied any knowledge that the package contained a bomb.

DICKSON J.: —

. . . .

During their deliberations, the jury asked to have read back: (i) the evidence of Brabant with regard to whether or not Lewis had written something down while in the telephone booth; and (ii) the cross-examination of Crown counsel dealing with the financial situation of Lewis. Defence counsel did not request that the judge at this time charge the jury on the concept of motive.

At the end of the day, the critical question in Lewis' case was whether or not at the time he mailed the package he knew that it contained a bomb.

Appeal

On appeal, a number of grounds were relied upon. All were rejected by a unanimous Court of Appeal. With respect to motive, the Court had this to say:

> Counsel for Lewis also submitted that the charge was deficient in failing to include a definition of "motive" and a direction regarding the absence of proof of motive on Lewis's part. There was some evidence, inconclusive, that Lewis' objective was money. In any event, the jury, as intelligent people, could not fail to consider the matter. That they were concerned is evidenced from the fact that they interrupted their deliberations to return to the courtroom and have read to them the cross-examination of Lewis dealing with his financial situation. This was done in a manner satisfactory to counsel. The defence of Lewis was, on the whole, adequately and fairly put before the jury by the Judge.

Motive in law

In ordinary parlance, the words "intent" and "motive" are frequently used interchangeably, but in the criminal law they are distinct. In most criminal trials the mental element, the *mens rea* with which the Court is concerned, relates to "intent", *i.e.*, the exercise of a free will to use particular means to produce a particular result, rather than with "motive", *i.e.*, that which precedes and induces the exercise of the will. The mental element of a crime ordinarily involves no reference to motive: 11 Hals. (4th) 17, para. 11.

. . . .

Accepting the term "motive" in a criminal law sense, as meaning "ulterior intention", it is possible, I think, upon the authorities, to formulate a number of propositions.

(1) As evidence, motive is always relevant and hence evidence of motive is admissible.

. . . .

(2) Motive is no part of the crime and is legally irrelevant to criminal responsibility. It is not an essential element of the prosecution's case as a matter of law

. . . .

(3) Proved absence of motive is always an important fact in favour of the accused and ordinarily worthy of note in a charge to the jury.

. . . .

(4) Conversely, proved presence of motive may be an important factual ingredient in the Crown's case, notably on the issues of identity and intention, when the evidence is purely circumstantial.

. . . .

(5) Motive is therefore always a question of fact and evidence and the necessity of referring to motive in the charge to the jury falls within the general duty of the trial Judge not only to outline the theories of the prosecution and defence but to give the jury matters of evidence essential in arriving at a just conclusion.

. . . .

(6) Each case will turn on its own unique set of circumstances. The issue of motive is always a matter of degree.

. . . .

The Present Case

In the light of the foregoing propositions, I examine the case at bar. One of the points to note is that the Crown put forward two alternative theories as to the transaction between Tatlay and Lewis. The dominant theory of the Crown was that Tatlay, enraged at his daughter's defiance, instigated Lewis to fashion and mail the kettle-bomb which killed the couple. Alternatively, the Crown suggested that Tatlay or some other person might have made the bomb, and that Lewis mailed the parcel, knowing it to contain a bomb. The broad theory related to both Tatlay and Lewis, the narrow theory related only to Lewis. Thus Lewis would stand convicted, as the trial Judge pointed out in his charge, if the jury accepted either theory:

> Now, it you were satisfied beyond a reasonable doubt that Lewis made this bomb and that Tatlay procured him to do it, that is, enlisted his services to do it, then I say — and I will tell you the law more particularly in a few moments — that you would have evidence upon which you could find — that you are satisfied beyond a reasonable doubt that these men were guilty of murder.

> Alternatively, it seems to me that even if you found that Lewis did not fashion the lethal weapon but he was the courier, that is, he is the one who mailed it, and that he mailed it with the realization of what he was mailing, again I would say that would be evidence if you are satisfied beyond a reasonable doubt of that fact, to justify finding that he was guilty of murder.

The *actus reus* of the narrow theory is identified by the Crown as the mailing of the parcel. This removes the materiality of motive as to proof of identity, and thus narrows the necessary mental element, or *mens rea*, to knowledge that the parcel contained a bomb, the requisite specific intent following as a matter of inference.

. . . .

Applying the propositions which I have outlined earlier, it will be seen that motive was not proven as part of the Crown's case, nor was absence of motive proven by the defence. There was therefore no clear obligation in law to charge on motive. Whether or not to charge became, therefore, a matter of judgment for the trial Judge, and his decision should not be lightly reversed. As Coyne J.A. said in *R. v. Malanik (No. 2)* (1951), 13 C.R. 160, 101 C.C.C. 182 (Man. C.A.), at p. 164:

> The summing-up must not be examined microscopically in a critical spirit to make *post facto* fault-finding (*R. v. Stoddart* (1909), 2 Cr. App. R. 217, approved in *Preston v. R.*, [1949] S.C.R. 156 at 162, 7 C.R. 72, 93 C.C.C. 81), but solely to determine whether the summing-up as a whole in the light of all the proceedings was such as to enable the jury to appreciate the case before them and their powers and duty and to afford some reasonable assistance to the exercise and performance of them in the case.

Every summing-up must be regarded in the light of the conduct of the trial and the questions which have been raised by the counsel for the prosecution and for the defence respectively: per Alverstone L.C.J. in *R. v. Stoddart, supra*, at p. 246.

Counsel at trial did not ask the Judge to instruct on motive, and the Judge obviously felt that such instruction was not called for in the light of the entire trial. Although evidence of Brabant was important to the case against Lewis, there was really very little conflict between the evidence of Brabant and that of Lewis.

. . . .

In the result, I am unable to find error on the part of the trial Judge and I therefore reach the same conclusion as the Court of Appeal of British Columbia.

I would accordingly dismiss the appeal.

Appeal dismissed.

Was the distinction between an intent and motive satisfactorily made in the following decision?

R. v. MATHE

(1973), 11 C.C.C. (2d) 427 (B.C. C.A.)

BRANCA J.A.: — The appellant was charged

for that he the said Eugene William Mathe on the 29th day of September 1972 at the City of Victoria, County aforesaid in the Province of British Columbia did unlawfully attempt to steal cash from Kathleen Hadley and at the time thereof did use threats of violence to the said Kathleen Hadley contrary to the *Criminal Code*.

The facts involved were very short and the material part of the narrative was testified to by Mrs. Hadley, a teller at the Canada Permanent Trust Company office at 1125 Douglas St. in the City of Victoria.

She stated that the appellant came into the building to her wicket at about 10:15 a.m. on September 29, 1972, alone, and said, "I have a 38 in my pocket. Hand over the cash." and then added, "Quickly hand over the cash." She went to her cash drawer and started getting out twenties at which time he said, "That's not what I want." and added that he was only joking and that he was a security guard and did not want the cash. He then shook her hand and left the building, walking north on Douglas St. in the company of a man named John Fuller, who was a customer of the bank and who was known to Mrs. Hadley.

She was very scared but when she took out the twenties from her cash drawer she set off a buzzer which was soundless and nothing went on which might indicate that fact to the appellant. He was apprehended later at 11:10 a.m. by the police, standing by the fountain at Centennial Square, only a couple of blocks from the police station in Victoria by Constable Dibden, who testified as follows:

I approached Mr. Mathe and asked him to accompany me to the City Police Station as he answered the description of a person of — who had earlier been broadcast by the Police Department. He agreed to go along with me, at this time I said, "Were you at Canada Trust

Building on Douglas Street this morning" and he stated he was. I said, "Did you tell the girl this was a holdup"? He stated, "I was only fooling, I didn't mean to hold the place up". I said, "Where's the gun that you told her you had"? He stated, "Did I say that, she'll have to prove that". By this time we approached on foot at the Police Station. I took him inside to the main floor of the Police Station where I turned him over to Detective Horsman.

The officer said the appellant had been drinking but did not believe he was intoxicated.

Horsman, a detective of the Victoria City Police Force, saw the appellant at 1:25 p.m. and charged and warned the appellant. He answered certain questions and the answers were at variance with what I have said. The detective said he felt that the appellant had been drinking excessively.

. . . .

It is true, as the learned trial Judge said, that his explanation might well yield an inference that the appellant at the time he uttered the words had a change of heart for some reason and decided to abandon the transaction or not to proceed with an apparent act of robbery. The action, however, plus the words were equally consistent with and confirmed a conclusion that the appellant very stupidly went into the office and uttered his words as a joke and then to show that, in fact it was a joke, he uttered the words, "That's not what I want" as she started sorting the twenties out and he added that he was only joking. The inference that the whole thing was a farce is as strong as the inference that it indicated a change of plan.

If, in fact, the transaction amounted to a joke, there was no crime. If on the other hand he was serious initially but decided to abandon the transaction, then there could be a crime. The accused was protected at all times by the presumption of innocence and by the fact that the Crown was under an obligation to prove guilt beyond a reasonable doubt.

The evidence, therefore, if it yields to an inference of guilt but likewise to an inference of innocence, cannot result in proof of the crime beyond a reasonable doubt.

In *R. v. Wilkins*, [1965] 2 C.C.C. 189, 44 C.R. 375, Wilkins was charged with the theft of a motor-cycle belonging to a policeman which was parked and running while the policeman was writing out a parking ticket. He took the motor-cycle to drive it for only a short distance and for the purpose of playing a joke on the policeman. He was convicted of theft and appealed.

The conviction was quashed on appeal and Roach J.A., who delivered a majority judgment stated at p. 195 as follows:

> In the instant case the facts could not possibly justify a conviction of theft. The accused did not intend to steal the vehicle, that is, to convert the property in it to his own use but only to drive it as contemplated by s. 281. His intention was merely to play a joke on Nichol and the Judge so found. The intention to perpetrate this joke, stupid though it was, is incompatible with the evil intent which is inherent in the crime of theft.

In *R. v. Kerr*, [1965] 4 C.C.C. 37, 47 C.R. 268, the accused was a prominent businessman, who with others was celebrating the winning of a dog trial championship show and while at the airport with his friends, being highly intoxicated, he behaved quite foolishly and made off with a 30-lb. ashtray, while the custodian was present and witnessing the whole transaction. The custodian notified the police, who then found it on Kerr's lawn in front of his house the next morning and Kerr then said to them that he was going to return it and was not aware, in fact, that he had taken it.

Miller C.J.M., with whom Guy J.A., concurred, stated at p. 41:

> In his reasons for judgment the learned Magistrate obviously thought that drunkenness was the main defence advanced, and he directed his mind almost entirely to the question of drunkenness and whether the accused was so drunk that he did not know what he was doing. The evidence as to drinking was led to show not only his condition but as an explanation of his mental attitude towards this silly, stupid, removal of the ashtray and in proof of the fact that it was a prank and not a theft. The learned Magistrate said taking the ashtray as a prank is not a defence to a charge of stealing. That may be so in some cases, but when all the circumstances of this case are considered it must be deemed that it was only a question of an ill-considered prank (if it were considered at all) and that the elements of intent and *animus furandi* were completely absent. Certainly, if the learned Magistrate had properly directed himself he would, in my opinion, have had at least a reasonable doubt as to the intent of the accused.

See also *Handfield v. The Queen* (1953), 109 C.C.C. 53, 17 C.R. 343, [1953] Que. Q.B. 584*n*, where a conviction dealing with the theft of an election banner belonging to one candidate was removed by the appellants and taken to a location down the road and placed on a tree in front of the home of the uncle of one of the accused who was not a political friend of the candidate from whom the banner was taken. The appellants were convicted and the conviction quashed in the Court of Appeal on the basis that it was done as a trick.

This Court, of course, is in as good a position to draw inferences from the uncontradicted facts proved in evidence by the Crown as was tbe trial Judge in the Court below: see *R. v. Rusnak (Alias Ross)*, [1963] 1 C.C.C. 143. In my judgment the evidence was such that it raised a substantial reasonable doubt in reference to the guilt of the appellant on the charge which should have been resolved in his favour and which I so resolve. The same reasoning would preclude a conviction for any included lesser offences.

The appeal must he allowed, the conviction quashed and a verdict of acquittal entered.

The concurring judgments of Maclean and Seaton JJ.A. are omitted.

Similar reasoning led to an acquittal on a charge of break, enter and theft in *R. v. Dewit and Sierens* (1981), 62 C.C.C. (2d) 176 (Man. Prov. Ct.). Sometimes a Court will reject "the defence of no *animus furandi*" and mitigate the penalty by imposing a light fine, *Paris v. R.* (1971), 15 C.R.N.S. 111 (Que. C.A.), or by granting a discharge, *Bogner v. R.* (1975), 33 C.R.N.S. 348 (Que. C.A.) and *R. v. Duggan* (1975), 38 C.R.N.S. 25 (N.S. Co. Ct.).

Which approach do you prefer?

Problem

The accused stopped his vehicle on a street corner and had a conversation with a female police officer, who was posing as a prostitute. He indicated he wanted a "lay" but that he only had $20 as he was a student. The officer agreed and asked him to pull around the block. The accused drove off in the opposite direction. On his arrest he was found to have only $14 in his possession. Charged with communicating for the purpose of obtaining the sexual services of a prostitute contrary to s. 213 of the *Criminal Code*, his defence is that he was merely "fooling around" to satisfy his curiosity. Give judgment. Compare *Pake* (1995), 45 C.R. (4th) 117, 103 C.C.C. (3d) 524 (Alta. C.A.).

Intention or Knowledge

R. v. STEANE

[1947] 1 K.B. 997, [1947] 1 All E.R. 813 (C.C.A.)

APPEAL from a conviction at the Central Criminal Court before Henn-Collins J. on an indictment charging the appellant with doing acts likely to assist the enemy with intent to assist the enemy contrary to reg. 2A of the Defence (General) Regulations, 1939. He was charged on the first count, with entering the service of the German Broadcasting System on a date in January, 1940 and the jury were discharged from returning a verdict in respect of eight other counts.

The appellant, a British subject, entered the service of the German broadcasting system, and on several occasions broadcast through that system. The evidence called by the prosecution was that of one witness who proved that the appellant did, in fact, so broadcast and said that he had seen a telegram, in the appellant's possession, signed Emmie Goering, which stated that he could expect to be released and be home very shortly. The principal evidence against him was a statement taken from him by an officer of the British Intelligence Service in October, 1945, purporting to give an account of his activities in the German broadcasting service, concluding with the words: "I have read this statement over and to the best of my knowledge and belief it is all true, and must request it to be used in conjunction with my written report dated July 5, 1945 to the American C.I.C. in Augsburg." This earlier report was not produced in evidence. Before the war, the appellant was employed in Germany as a film actor and was so engaged when the war broke out. His wife and two sons were living in Germany. On the outbreak of war the appellant was at once arrested, but his wife and two sons remained in Oberammergau.

The only other evidence was that of the appellant. He said that on his arrest he was questioned and that the interview ended with the order: "Say Heil Hitler, you dirty swine." He refused and was thereupon knocked down losing several teeth, and he was interned on September 11, 1939. Just before Christmas of that year he was sent for by Goebbels, who asked him to broadcast. He refused. He was thereupon warned that he was in an enemy country and that they had methods of making people do things. A week later an official named von Bockman saw him and dropped hints as to German methods of persuasion. A professor named Kossuth also warned him that these people could be dangerous to those who gave trouble. In consequence he submitted to a voice test, trying to perform as badly as he could. The next day he was ordered to read news three times a day, and did so until April, 1940. In that month he refused to do any more broadcasting. Two Gestapo men called on him. They said: "If you don't obey, your wife and children will be put in a concentration camp." In May three Gestapo men saw him and he was badly beaten up, one ear being partly torn off. He agreed to work for his old employers, helping to produce films. There was no evidence that the films he helped to produce were or could be of any assistance to the Germans or at all harmful to this country. He swore that he was in continual fear for his wife and children. He asserted, and said he had asserted, in his report of July 5, 1945, that he never had the slightest idea or intention of assisting the enemy, and that what he did was done to save his wife and children and that what he did could not have assisted the enemy except in a very technical sense. There was no record of the actual broadcasts made by the appellant.

· · · ·

The appellant was convicted and sentenced to three years penal servitude, but appealed.

May 1. LORD GODDARD C.J. read the judgment of the Court. The earlier statement made by the appellant to the American C.I.C. in Augsburg was not produced. That, no doubt, was inevitable, but, none the less, unfortunate, especially as the appellant in his evidence maintained that many matters were contained in that report which, accordingly, he did not restate in the statement which he made to the British Intelligence Officer. That a record of the appellant's broadcasts in Germany was not given in evidence again was, no doubt, inevitable, but unfortunate, as the actual tone of the broadcast might have thrown some light upon the motives and intentions of the appellant, but, in the opinion of the Court, there was undoubtedly evidence from which a jury could infer that the acts done by the appellant were acts likely to assist the enemy.

The far more difficult question that arises, however, is in connexion with the direction to the jury with regard to whether these acts were done with the intention of assisting the enemy. The case as opened, and indeed, as put by the learned Judge appears to this Court to be this: A man is taken to intend the natural consequences of his acts; if, therefore, he does an act which is likely to assist the enemy, it must be assumed that he did it with the intention of assisting the enemy. Now, the first thing which the Court would observe is that, where the essence of an offence or a necessary constituent of an offence is a particular intent, that intent must be proved by the Crown just as much as any other fact necessary to constitute the offence. The wording of the regulation itself shows that it is not enough merely to charge a prisoner with doing an act likely to assist the enemy; he must do it with the particular intent specified in the regulation.

While no doubt the motive of a man's act and his intention in doing the act are, in law, different things, it is, none the less, true that in many offences a specific intention is a necessary ingredient and the jury have to be satisfied that a particular act was done with that specific intent, although the natural consequences of the act might, if nothing else were proved, be said to show the intent for which it was done. To take a simple illustration, a man is charged with wounding with intent to do grievous bodily harm. It is proved that he did severely wound the prosecutor. Nevertheless, unless the Crown can prove that the intent was to do the prosecutor grievous bodily harm, he cannot be convicted of that felony. It is always open to the jury to negative by their verdict the intent and to convict only of the misdemeanor of unlawful wounding. Or again, a prisoner may be charged with shooting with intent to murder. Here again, the prosecution may fail to satisfy the jury of the intent, although the natural consequence of firing, perhaps at close range, would be to kill. The jury can find in such a case an intent to do grievous bodily harm or they might find that if the person shot at was a police constable, the prisoner was not guilty on the count charging intent to murder, but guilty of intent to avoid arrest. The important thing to notice in this respect is that where an intent is charged in the indictment, the burden of proving that intent remains throughout on the prosecution. No doubt, if the prosecution prove an act the natural consequence of which would be a certain result and no evidence or explanation is given, then a jury may, on a proper direction, find that the prisoner is guilty of doing the act with the intent alleged, but if on the totality of the evidence there is room for more than one view as to the intent of the prisoner, the jury should be directed that it is for the prosecution to prove the intent to the jury's satisfaction, and if, on a review of the whole evidence, they either think that the intent did not exist or they are left in doubt as to the intent, the prisoner is entitled to be acquitted. In many offences it is unnecessary to allege any particular intent. The commonest case is in larceny where the prisoner is simply charged with stealing. If the evidence shows that the prisoner picked a person's pocket, there is no necessity to prove that he intended to steal, although he may give some evidence in defence which would lead the jury to believe that he was not acting with a felonious intent. But, we repeat that where a particular intent must be laid and charged, that intent has to be proved. An illustration given by the learned Judge in the course of his rather brief summing-up, related to what are commonly called the black-out regulations. He pointed out to the jury that if a person accidentally omitted to put up his black-out curtains or left some gap in them, although he was doing an act likely to assist the enemy, as it was accidental, he would not be committing the offence with intent to assist the enemy. Matters which involve accidental acts are perhaps not altogether a happy illustration. A nearer case would be if a person deliberately took down his black-out curtains or shutters with the result that light appeared on the outside of his house, perhaps during an air raid; it might well be that if no evidence or explanation were given, and if all that was proved was that, during that raid the prisoner exposed lights by a deliberate act, a jury could infer that he intended to signal or assist the enemy. But, if the evidence in the case showed, for instance, that he or someone was overcome by heat and that he tore down the black-out to ventilate the room, the jury would certainly have to consider whether his act was done with intent to assist the enemy or with some other intent, so that, while he would be guilty of an offence against the black-out regulations, he would not be guilty of an offence with intent to assist the enemy.

In this case the Court cannot but feel that some confusion arose with regard to the question of intent by so much being said in the case with regard to the subject of duress. Duress is a matter of defence where a prisoner is forced by fear of violence or imprisonment to do an act which in itself is criminal. If the act is a criminal act, the prisoner may be able to show that he was forced into doing it by violence, actual or threatened, and to save himself from the consequences of that violence. There is very little learning to be found in any of the books or cases on the subject of duress and it is by no means certain how far the doctrine extends, though we have the authority both of Hale and of Fitzjames Stephen, that while it does not apply to treason, murder and some other felonies, it does apply to misdemeanors; and offences against these regulations are misdemeanors. But here again, before any question of duress arises, a jury must be satisfied that the prisoner had the intention which is laid in the indictment. Duress is a matter of defence and the onus of proving it is on the accused. As we have already said, where an intent is charged on the indictment, it is for the prosecution to prove it, so the onus is the other way.

Now, another matter which is of considerable importance in this case, but does not seem to have been brought directly to the attention of the jury, is that very different considerations may apply where the accused at the time he did the acts is in subjection to an enemy power and where he is not. British soldiers who were set to work on the Burma road or, if invasion had unhappily taken place, British subjects who might have been set to work by the enemy digging trenches would undoubtedly be doing acts likely to assist the enemy. It would be unnecessary surely in their cases to consider any of the niceties of the law relating to duress, because no jury would find that merely by doing this work they were intending to assist the enemy. In our opinion it is impossible to say that where an act was done by a person in subjection to the power of others, especially if that other be a brutal enemy, an inference that he intended the natural consequences of his act must be drawn merely from the fact that he did it. The guilty intent cannot be presumed and must be proved. The proper direction to the jury in this case would have been that it was for the prosecution to prove the criminal intent, and that while the jury would be entitled to presume that intent if they thought that the act was done as the result of the free uncontrolled action of the accused, they would not be entitled to presume it, if the circumstances showed that the act was done in subjection to the power of the enemy, or was as consistent with an innocent intent as with a criminal intent, for example, the innocent intent of a desire to save his wife and children from a concentration camp. They should only convict if satisfied by the evidence that the act complained of was in fact done to assist the enemy, and if there was doubt about the matter, the prisoner was entitled to be acquitted.

It is to be observed also in this case that in summing-up the learned Judge did not remind the jury of the various threats to which the prisoner swore he had been exposed. The jury might, of course, have disbelieved his evidence. The matters of these threats depended upon his evidence alone, and while it is fair to say that he does not appear to have been in any way shaken in cross-examination on these matters, the jury were not necessarily bound to believe it. But we do not think that the summing-up contained anything like a full enough direction as to the prisoner's defence. The defence must be fully put to the jury and we think they ought to have been reminded of various matters upon which the accused relied as negativing the intent. The jury may well have been left under the impression that, as they were told that a man must be taken to intend the natural consequences of his acts, these matters, as to which he had given evidence, were of no moment.

On both these grounds, therefore, we were of opinion that the conviction could not stand and accordingly quashed it.

Appeal allowed.
Conviction quashed.

R. v. HIBBERT

[1995] 2 S.C.R. 973, 40 C.R. (4th) 141, 99 C.C.C. (3d) 193 (S.C.C.)

In the context of a major ruling on duress, considered later, Chief Justice Lamer for the Court had to determine the meaning of "purpose" in the context of s. 21(1)(*b*) which imposes criminal liability as a party on anyone who does or omits to do anything for the purpose of aiding any person to commit an offence. The Court held that purpose was not the same as desire.

LAMER C.J.:—

. . . .

It is impossible to ascribe a single fixed meaning to the term "purpose". In ordinary usage, the word is employed in two distinct senses. One can speak of an actor doing something "on purpose" (as opposed to by accident) thereby equating purpose with "immediate intention". The term is also used, however, to indicate the ultimate ends an actor seeks to achieve, which imports the idea of "desire" into the definition. This dual sense is apparent in the word's dictionary definition. For instance, the Oxford English Dictionary (2nd ed., 1989), defines "purpose" alternatively as "[t]hat which one sets before oneself as a thing to be done or attained; the object which one has in view" and as "[t]he action or fact of intending or meaning to do something; intention, resolution, determination". The first of these definitions reflects the notion of one's "purpose" as relating to one's ultimate object or desire, while the latter conveys the notion of "purpose" as being synonymous with "intention".

Commentators who have considered the meaning of "purpose" in definitions of criminal offences have come to differing conclusions on the question of which of these alternate meanings is more appropriate in this context. Professor E. Colvin, for instance, argues on behalf of the "purpose as desire" interpretation in his text *Principles of Criminal Law*, 2nd ed. (Toronto: Carswell, 1991). He states (at pp. 121-22):

> The terms "direct intention" and "desire" are sometimes used instead of purpose. The latter term, however, best describes the relevant state of mind. In ordinary language descriptions of action, the concept of purpose usually refers to an actor's *reasons* for doing what he did . . . [Emphasis in original.]

According to Colvin, "an actor's purpose was to accomplish something if the prospect of its occurrence played a causal role in his decision to do what he did" (p. 122). The actor's knowledge that his actions will result in the occurrence, however, is not determinative. As Colvin states (at p. 123):

> If it is to be concluded that an actor's purpose in doing something did not include an outcome which was foreseen, then the actor must have been genuinely opposed or indifferent to it. Purpose is not negatived where an actor *chose* to bring about the outcome as a means of attaining some further objective. [Emphasis in original.]

Other commentators, however, have questioned this equation of "purpose" with "desire", arguing instead that a person who consciously performs an act knowing the consequences that will (with some degree of certainty) flow from it "intends" these consequences or causes them "on purpose", regardless of whether he or she *desired* them. As Mewett and Manning state:

> . . . the distinction between purpose/intent and knowledge/intent does not work, because if there is, given an awareness of the consequences of an act, a freedom of choice as to whether one acts or not, by choosing to act those consequences have been chosen. If intent is the choosing of consequences, it does not make any difference to the existence of the intent whether the accused wants those consequences to follow or merely knows that they will follow, without necessarily desiring them to do so.
>
> "Intent", is not a very descriptive word. *Mens rea* connotes volition on the part of the accused, that is to say, given an awareness that certain consequences will follow (or will probably follow) if he acts, an accused who chooses to act when he has the alternative of not acting "intends" those consequences in the sense of choosing to bring them about. It seems not only unnecessary but positively misleading to attempt to distinguish between purpose/intent and knowledge/intent.
>
> (*Criminal Law* (2nd ed., 1985), at p. 113.)

A similar argument is made by the English authors J. C. Smith and B. Hogan:

> . . . person may know that he cannot achieve his purpose, A, without bringing about some other result, B. If he is to bring about A, he knows he must also, at the same time or earlier, bring about B. It may be that, in any other circumstances, he would much rather B did not happen, indeed its occurrence may be abhorrent to him. But, the choice being between going without A and having A and B, he decides to have A and B. It seems fair to say that he intends to cause B as well as A.

(*Criminal Law* (7th ed., 1992), at p. 55.)

As this debate reveals, the term "purpose" is capable of bearing two distinct meanings, both of which can be supported by reasoned arguments. In a case, such as this one, where an interpretation of the term in a specific statutory context is required, the court's task is to determine which of the two possible meanings best accords with Parliament's intention in drafting the particular statutory provision at issue. In other words, our task in the present case is to consider the meaning of "purpose" as it is employed in s. 21(1)(*b*) of the Code in light of the Parliamentary objective underlying the subsection. It must be emphasized, however, that the word "purpose" is employed in many different sections of the *Criminal Code*, in a number of distinct contexts. My conclusions in the present case on the proper interpretation of the word "purpose" as it is employed in s. 21(1)(*b*) of the Code are thus restricted to this particular subsection. It may well be that in the context of some other statutory provision a different interpretation of the term will prove to be the most appropriate.

. . . As I will explain, I am of the view that in the context of s. 21(1)(*b*) of the Code, the second of the two meanings of "purpose" discussed above — that is, the interpretation that equates "purpose" with "intention" — best reflects the legislative intent underlying the subsection. In contrast, adopting the first interpretation of "purpose" (the "purpose" equals "desire" interpretation) to describe the mens rea for aiding in s. 21(1)(*b*) would, in my view, create a number of theoretical and practical difficulties that Parliament is unlikely to have envisioned or intended.

The problems associated with the "purpose equals desire" interpretation are several. First, incorporating the accused's feelings about the desirability of the commission of an offence by the principal into the definition of the mens rea for "aiding" can result in distinctions being made which appear arbitrary and unreasonable in light of the policy underlying s. 21(1)(*b*). As Professor Colvin notes, under the "purpose equals desire" interpretation a person would not be guilty of aiding in the commission of an offence if he or she were "genuinely opposed or indifferent to it" (p. 123). The reason for the aider's indifference or opposition would be immaterial. The perverse consequences that flow from this are clearly illustrated by the following hypothetical situation described by Mewett and Manning:

> If a man is approached by a friend who tells him that he is going to rob a bank and would like to use his car as the getaway vehicle for which he will pay him $100, when that person is . . . charged under s. 21 for doing something for the purpose of aiding his friend to commit the

offence, can he say "My purpose was not to aid the robbery but to make $100"? His argument would be that while he knew that he was helping the robbery, his desire was to obtain $100 and he did not care one way or the other whether the robbery was successful or not.

(*Criminal Law*, supra, at p. 112.)

I agree with the authors' conclusion that "[t]hat would seem an absurd result" (p. 112). As I noted in *McIntosh*, supra, at pp. 704-5, "[a]bsurdity is a factor to consider in the interpretation of ambiguous statutory provisions". That is, to quote the words of La Forest J.A. (as he then was) in *Re Estabrooks Pontiac Buick Ltd.* (1982), 44 N.B.R. (2d) 201, at p. 210, "[t]he fact that the words as interpreted would give an unreasonable result . . . is certainly ground for the courts to scrutinize a statute carefully to make abundantly certain that those words are not susceptible of another interpretation". In my view, the absurdity that would flow from the equation of "purpose" with "desire" cannot legitimately be ascribed to Parliamentary intention. This serves to cast considerable doubt on the correctness of this interpretation of the word "purpose" in this context, especially when one recalls that there exists an alternative interpretation of the word that can just as accurately be said to reflect its "plain meaning", under which this absurdity would be avoided.

. . . .

Finally, I am satisfied that the interpretation of the mens rea for liability under s. 21(1)(*b*) that I am proposing will not result in unjust convictions in cases involving coercion by threats of death or bodily harm, since in these cases the common law defence of duress will remain available to the accused. As I will explain shortly, this defence, properly understood, provides an excuse to persons who assist in the commission of offences as a result of threats of serious violence. On the other hand, interpreting "purpose" as equivalent to "desire" in s. 21(1)(*b*) would result in the introduction of unnecessary complication into the law. Under such an interpretation, juries in duress cases would have to be provided with extremely complex instructions that would, in the end, have very little, if any, impact on the final determination of guilt or innocence. As a matter of logic, the issue of whether an accused can invoke an excuse or justification arises only after the Crown has proven the existence of all the elements of the offence, including mens rea. Thus, if "purpose" were understood as incorporating "desire", and hence as being susceptible to "negation" by duress, trial judges would have to instruct juries accordingly. This would require judges, and juries, to delve into the arcane issue of whether a person who intentionally commits an offence in order to save his or her own skin commits the offence "on purpose" — a question of some philosophical significance, perhaps, but no easy matter for a judge to explain succinctly, or for a jury to comprehend readily.

R. v. BUZZANGA AND DUROCHER

(1979), 49 C.C.C. (2d) 369 (Ont. C.A.)

The defendants were active in promoting the construction of a French language high school in Essex County. They caused to be printed and circulated the following document:

WAKE UP CANADIANS

YOUR FUTURE IS AT STAKE!

IT IS YOUR TAX DOLLARS THAT SUBSIDIZE THE ACTIVITIES OF THE FRENCH MINORITY OF ESSEX COUNTY.

DID YOU KNOW THAT THE ASSOCIATION CANADIAN FRANCAIS DE L'ONTARIO HAS INVESTED SEVERAL HUNDREDS OF THOUSANDS OF DOLLARS OF YOUR TAX MONEY IN QUEBEC?

AND THAT NOW THEY ARE STILL DEMANDING 5 MILLION MORE OF YOUR TAX DOLLARS TO BUILD A FRENCH LANGUAGE HIGH SCHOOL?

YOU ARE SUBSIDIZING SEPARATISM WHETHER IN QUEBEC OR ESSEX COUNTY.

IF WE GIVE THEM A SCHOOL, WHAT WILL THEY DEMAND NEXT . . . INDEPENDENT CITY STATES? CONSIDER THE ETHNIC PROBLEM OF THE UNITED STATES AND TAKE HEED.

DID YOU KNOW THAT THOSE OF THE FRENCH MINORITY WHO SUPPORT THE BUILDING OF THE FRENCH LANGUAGE HIGH SCHOOL ARE IN FACT A SUBVERSIVE GROUP AND THAT MOST FRENCH CANADIANS OF ESSEX COUNTY ARE OPPOSED TO THE BUILDING OF THAT SCHOOL?

WHO WILL RID US OF THIS SUBVERSIVE GROUP IF NOT OURSELVES?

WE MUST STAMP OUT THE SUBVERSIVE ELEMENT WHICH USES HISTORY TO JUSTIFY ITS FREELOADING ON THE TAXPAYERS OF CANADA, NOW.

THE BRITISH SOLVED THIS PROBLEM ONCE BEFORE WITH THE ACADIANS, WHAT ARE WE WAITING FOR . . . ?

MARTIN J.A.: —

. . . .

The statement was composed by the appellant Durocher whose facility with the English language was greater than that of Buzzanga.

The appellant Durocher testified that the francophone community seemed to be "fed up" with the issue of the French-language high school and was becoming apathetic. He said that although economics was the stated reason for not building the school, this was merely an excuse and the real reason was prejudice. The appellant Buzzanga shared Durocher's feeling in this respect.

Both appellants testified as to their purpose in preparing and distributing the pamphlet. The appellant Durocher testified that his purpose was to show the prejudice directed towards French Canadians and expose the truth about the real problem that existed with respect to the French-language school. He said that the statement was largely composed from written material he had seen and from experiences he had had, although the paragraph: "WHO WILL RID US OF THIS SUBVERSIVE GROUP, IF NOT OURSELVES?" was pure theatrics and has its origin in the quotation "Who will rid me of this meddlesome priest", attributed to Henry

II. He testified in some detail as to the origin of various parts of the document and endeavoured to show that it reflected statements contained in such sources as letters to the editor of the Windsor Star, a document alleged to have been circulated by a member of the Essex County Ratepayers Association, a paid advertisement published in several newspapers, a book entitled "Bilingual Today, French Tomorrow", and the like. He said that he thought the pamphlet would be a catalyst that would bring a quick solution to the problem of the French-language school by provoking a Government reaction and thereby put pressure on the school board. He thought that by stating these things people would say: "This is ridiculous." A fair reading of his evidence is that he did not want to promote hatred against the "French people", for to do so would be to promote hatred against himself.

The appellant Buzzanga, too, said that he wanted to expose the situation, to show the things that were being said so that intelligent people could see how ridiculous they were. The pamphlet was intended as a satire. He wanted to create a furor that would reach the "House of Commons" and compel the Government to do something that would compel the opposing factions on the school question to reopen communications. He said it was not his intention "to raise hatred towards anyone".

The appellant Buzzanga arranged for the printing and distribution of the document. He placed the order for the printing of the document in the name of Wilfred Fortowsky, the president of the Essex County Ratepayers Association, but asked the printer to delete the name of Mr. Fortowsky when he picked up the material, leaving, however, the name of the Essex County Ratepayers Association on the order form. Neither Mr. Fortowsky nor the Essex County Ratepayers Association were, of course, aware that their names had been so used.

. . . .

The threshold question to be determined is the meaning of "wilfully" in the term "wilfully promotes hatred" in s. 281.2(2) [now s. 319(2)] of the *Criminal Code*. It will, of course, be observed that the word "wilfully" modifies the words "promotes hatred", rather than the words "communicating statements".

The word "wilfully" has not been uniformly interpreted and its meaning to some extent depends upon the context in which it is used. Its primary meaning is "intentionally", but it is also used to mean "recklessly": see Glanville Williams, *Criminal Law, The General Part*, 2nd ed. (1961), pp. 51-2; Glanville Williams, *Text book of Criminal Law* (1978), p. 87; Smith and Hogan, *Criminal Law*, 4th ed. (1978), pp. 104-5. The term "recklessly" is here used to denote the subjective state of mind of a person who foresees that his conduct may cause the prohibited result but, nevertheless, takes a deliberate and unjustifiable risk of bringing it about: see Glanville Williams, *Textbook of Criminal Law*, pp. 70 and 76; Smith and Hogan, *Criminal Law*, 4th ed., pp. 52-3.

The word "wilfully" has, however, also been held to mean no more than the accused's act is done intentionally and not accidentally. In *R. v. Senior*, [1899] 1 Q.B. 283, Lord Russell of Killowen C.J., in interpreting the meaning of the words "wilfully neglects" in s. 1 of the *Prevention of Cruelty to Children Act*, 1894 (U.K.), c. 41, said at pp. 290-1: " 'Wilfully' means that the act is done deliberately and intentionally, not by accident or inadvertence, but so that the mind of the person who does the act goes with it."

On the other hand, in *Rice v. Connolly*, [1966] 2 Q.B. 414, where the accused was charged with wilfully obstructing a constable in the execution of his duty, Lord Parker L.C.J., said at p. 419: "'Wilful' in this context not only in my judgment means 'intentional' but something which is done without lawful excuse. . .".

In *Willmott v. Atack*, [1976] 3 All E.R. 794, the appellant was convicted on a charge of wilfully obstructing a peace officer in the execution of his duty. A police officer, acting in the execution of his duty, arrested a motorist who struggled and resisted. The appellant, who knew the motorist, intervened with the intention of assisting the officer but, in fact, his conduct obstructed the officer. The Queen's Bench Divisional Court quashed the conviction and held that it was not sufficient to prove the appellant intended to do what he did, and which resulted in an obstruction, but that the prosecution must prove that the appellant intended to obstruct the officer.

The judgment of the Court of Criminal Appeal of Queensland in *R. v. Burnell*, [1966] Qd. R. 348, also illustrates that, depending on its context, the word "wilfully" may connote an intention to bring about a proscribed consequence. In that case the appellant was charged with arson in having set fire to a shed. Section 461 of the Queensland *Criminal Code* provides that ". . . any person who wilfully and unlawfully sets fire to . . . any building or structure is guilty of a crime. . .". The accused had deliberately set fire to some mattresses in a shed whereby the shed was set on fire. The trial Judge instructed the jury that "wilfully" connoted no more than a willed and voluntary act as distinguished from the result of an accident or mere negligence. The Queensland Court of Criminal Appeal, in setting aside the conviction, held that in the context of the section "wilfully" required proof that the accused did an act which resulted in setting fire to the building with the intention of bringing about that result. Gibbs J. (with whom Douglas J. concurred), said at p. 356:

> Under s. 461 it is not enough that the accused did the act which resulted in setting fire to the building foreseeing that his act might have that effect but recklessly taking the risk; it is necessary that the accused did the act which resulted in setting fire to the building with the intention of bringing about that result.

Mr. Manning conceded that in some cases the element of wilfulness is supplied by recklessness but he contended that in its context in s. 281.2(2) of the *Criminal Code* "wilfully" means with the intention of promoting hatred. In the course of his argument, Mr. Manning stressed the definition of "wilfully" contained in s. 386(1) [now s. 429(1)] of the *Code*, which reads:

> 386(1) Every one who causes the occurrence of an event by doing an act or by omitting to do an act that it is his duty to do, knowing that the act or omission will probably cause the occurrence of the event and being reckless whether the event occurs or not, shall be deemed, for the purposes of this Part, wilfully to have caused the occurrence of the event.

Mr. Manning emphasized that s. 386(1) provides that wilfully is to have the meaning specified in that section for the purposes of Part IX [now Part XI] of the *Code*. He argued with much force that the state of mind specified in s. 386(1) is recklessness and that where Parliament intends to extend the meaning of wilfully to include recklessness it does so expressly. In *R. v. Rese*, [1968] 1 C.C.C. 363 at p. 366, 2 C.R.N.S. 99, Laskin J.A. (as he then was), referred to the definition now contained in s. 386(1) as an extended meaning of "wilfully".

As previously indicated, the word "wilfully" does not have a fixed meaning, but I am satisfied that in the context of s. 281.2(2) it means with the intention of promoting hatred, and does not include recklessness. The arrangement of legislation proscribing the incitement of hatred, in my view, leads to that conclusion.

Section 281.2(1), unlike s. 281.2(2), is restricted to the incitement of hatred by communicating statements in a public place where such incitement is likely to lead to a breach of the peace. Although no mental element is expressly mentioned in s. 281.2(1), where the communication poses an immediate threat to public order, *mens rea* is, none the less, required since the inclusion of an offence in the *Criminal Code* must be taken to import *mens rea* in the absence of a clear intention to dispense with it: see *R. v. Prue; R. v. Baril* (1979), 46 C.C.C. (2d) 257 at pp. 260-1, 96 D.L.R. 577 at pp. 580-1, 8 C.R. (3d) 68 at p. 73. The general *mens rea* which is required and which suffices for most crimes where no mental element is mentioned in the definition of the crime, is either the intentional or reckless bringing about of the result which the law, in creating the offence, seeks to prevent and, hence, under s. 281.2(1) is either the intentional or reckless inciting of hatred in the specified circumstances.

The insertion of the word "wilfully" in s. 281.2(2) was not necessary to import *mens rea* since that requirement would be implied in any event because of the serious nature of the offence: see *R. v. Prue, supra*. The statements, the communication of which are proscribed by s. 281.2(2), are not confined to statements communicated in a public place in circumstances likely to lead to a breach of the peace and they, consequently, do not pose such an immediate threat to public order as those falling under s. 281.2(1); it is reasonable to assume, therefore, that Parliament intended to limit the offence under s. 281.2(2) to the intentional promotion of hatred. It is evident that the use of the word "wilfully" in s. 281.2(2), and not in s. 281.2(1), reflects Parliament's policy to strike a balance in protecting the competing social interests of freedom of expression on the one hand, and public order and group reputation on the other hand.

Having concluded that proof of an intention to promote hatred is essential to constitute the offence: under s. 281.2(2), it is necessary to consider the mental attitude which must be established to constitute an intention to promote hatred. The state of mind connoted by "intention", where an intention to bring about a certain result is an element of the offence, has been the subject of much discussion, and writers on jurisprudence, as well as Judges, have not always been in agreement as to its meaning. Some eminent legal scholars hold the view that a consequence is not intended unless it is desired, recognizing that a consequence may be desired not as an end in itself but desired in order to accomplish some other purpose: see *Salmond on Jurisprudence*, 8th ed. (1930), pp. 393-6 (but *cf.*, the view of P.J. Fitzgerald, the editor of the 12th edition, pp. 367-9; Holmes, *The Common Law*, pp. 52-3; Glanville Williams, *Textbook of Criminal Law*, p. 51). Other eminent legal scholars hold that the test of intention is not whether the actor desired the relevant consequence, but whether he decided or resolved to bring it about, even though it may have been distasteful to him: see Jerome Hall, *General Principles of Criminal Law*, 2nd ed. (1960), p. 112; *Russell on Crime*, 12th ed. (1964), vol. 1, p. 41. The latter description of intention is in accord with the views expressed by Lord Hailsham as to the meaning of intention in *Hyam v. Director of Public Prosecutions*, [1975] A.C. 55 at p. 74, and with those of the Court of Appeal (Criminal Division) in *R. v. Mohan* (1975), 60 Cr. App. R. 272 at pp. 276 and 278.

There are cases which appear to provide support for the proposition that where an intention to produce a particular consequence is essential to constitute the offence, an act is not done with intent to produce the prohibited consequence unless it is the actor's conscious purpose to bring it about, and that the actor's foresight of the certainty of the consequence is not synonymous with an intention to produce it: see *R. v. Miller* (1959), 125 C.C.C. 8 at p. 30, 31 C.R. 101; *R. v. Ahlers*, [1915] 1 K.B. 616; *Sinnasamy Selvanayagam v. The King*, [1951] A.C. 83; *R. v. Steane*, [1947] 1 K.B. 997. Most of these cases are subjected to critical examination by Dr. Glanville Williams in *Criminal Law, The General Part*, 2nd ed. (1961), pp. 40-2.

There is, however, substantial support for the proposition that in the criminal law a person intends a particular consequence not only when his conscious purpose is to bring it about, but also when he foresees that the consequence is certain or substantially certain to result from his conduct: see Glanville Williams, *Criminal Law, The General Part*, 2nd ed. (1961), p. 38; Walter Wheeler Cook, *Act, Intention, and Motive in the Criminal Law* (1916-17), 26 Yale L.J. 645 at pp. 654-8; Rollin Perkins, *A Rationale of Mens Rea*, 52 Harv. L. Rev. 905 at pp. 910-1 (1938-39).

Smith and Hogan, the learned authors of *Criminal Law*, 4th ed., state at p. 51, that the authorities referred to by them:

> suggest that in the criminal law generally, though not universally, a person intends a consequence if it is his purpose to achieve it or if he knows that the achievement of some other purpose is certain, or "morally" certain, to produce the consequence in question.

In *R. v. Lemon; R. v. Gay News Ltd.*, *supra*, Lord Diplock, however, defined intention in much wider terms. He said that where intention to produce a particular result is a necessary element of an offence, no distinction is to be drawn in law between the state of mind of one who does an act because he desires to produce that particular result, and the state of mind of one who, when he does the act, is aware that it is likely to produce that result but is prepared to take the risk that it may do so in order to achieve some other purpose. He considered that the law has been settled by *Hyam v. Director of Public*

Prosecutions, supra, "that both states of mind constitute 'intention' in the sense in which that expression is used in the definition of a crime whether at common law or in a statute" (at p. 905).

Hyam v. Director of Public Prosecutions, supra, was concerned with the mental element required to constitute "malice aforethought". It may well be that either an intention to kill or cause serious bodily harm, or foresight that death or serious bodily harm is a highly probable consequence of an act done for some other purpose, is a sufficient *mens rea* for murder at common law. I do not consider, however, that the actor's foresight that a consequence is highly probable, as opposed to substantially certain, is the same thing as an intention to bring it about: see *Hyam v. Director of Public Prosecutions, supra, per* Lord Hailsham at p. 75; *R. v. Belfon,* [1976] 3 All E.R. 46; Smith and Hogan, *Criminal Law,* 4th ed., pp. 47-51; Commentary on *R. v. Lemon et al.,* [1979] Crim. L.R. 311 at p. 314. In my view, the mental attitude described by Lord Diplock is a form of recklessness.

I agree, however (assuming without deciding that there may be cases in which intended consequences are confined to those which it is the actor's conscious purpose to bring about), that, as a general rule, a person who foresees that a consequence is certain or substantially certain to result from an act which he does in order to achieve some other purpose, intends that consequence. The actor's foresight of the certainty or moral certainty of the consequence resulting from his conduct compels a conclusion that if he, none the less, acted so as to produce it, then he decided to bring it about (albeit regretfully), in order to achieve his ultimate purpose. His intention encompasses the means as well as to his ultimate objective.

I conclude, therefore, that the appellants "wilfully" (intentionally) promoted hatred against the French Canadian community of Essex County only if: (a) their conscious purpose in distributing the document was to promote hatred against that group, or (b) they foresaw that the promotion of hatred against that group was certain or morally certain to result from the distribution of the pamphlet, but distributed it as means of achieving their purpose of obtaining the French-language high school.

Whether the trial Judge misdirected himself as to the meaning of wilfully?

The learned trial Judge in comprehensive reasons first considered whether the document objectively promoted hatred and concluded that the cumulative effect of the document rendered it a communication that promoted hatred against the French-speaking community of Essex County. He then said:

> It is, however, incumbent upon the Crown to prove beyond a reasonable doubt that the two accused wilfully promoted such hatred. In other words, has the Crown established the necessary element of *mens rea*. In considering the meaning to be given to the word "wilfully" in this section the Court must distinguish between what has been described by learned writers as primary and secondary intent; or to phrase it in a more understanding way, the distinction between intent and motive. I have earlier discussed the purpose or motive as explained by the

accused themselves. They wished to create a situation that would require the intervention of senior levels of Government and result in the construction of the high school. It is in evidence that the handbill was, in fact, shown to a mediator representing the Minister of Education who was in this area attempting to resolve the school issue. It is, of course, a matter of judicial notice that the Province did pass special legislation requiring the construction of the school. It is extremely doubtful, however, that this document played any part in the formulation of that decision. It was also their desire to unify the French Canadian community. As Father Vincent stated, opposition from outside often cements an ethnic group and tends to strengthen people rather than weaken them.

This is what the Court would refer to as the purpose or motive of the accused.

Wilful in this section, however, means intentional as opposed to accidental. Miss Susan Moylan who testified for the accused was involved in the early discussions between the accused in the preparation of the handbill. She testified that the document was not to create strong feelings but to create strong actions and strong reactions. How one can do the latter without the former is beyond the comprehension of this Court. The accused themselves testified they wished to create controversy, furor and an uproar. What better way of describing active dislike, detestation, enmity or ill will. The motives of the accused may or may not be laudable. The means chosen by the accused was the wilful promotion of hatred.

. . . .

I am not persuaded that the learned trial Judge fell into the error of detaching the word "wilfully" from the words "promotes hatred" and applied it only to the distribution of the pamphlet. I am of the view, however, that the learned trial Judge erred in holding that "wilfully" means only "intentional as opposed to accidental". Although, as previously indicated, "wilfully" has sometimes been used to mean that the accused's act, as distinct from its consequences, must be intended and not accidental (as in *R. v. Senior*, [1899] 1 Q.B. 283) , it does not have that meaning in the provisions under consideration.

The learned trial Judge's view of the meaning of "wilfully" inevitably caused him to focus attention on the intentional nature of the appellants' conduct, rather than on the question whether they actually intended to produce the consequence of promoting hatred. I observe that even if, contrary to the view which I have expressed, recklessness satisfies the mental element denoted by the word "wilfully", recklessness when used to denote the mental element attitude which suffices for the ordinary *mens rea*, requires actual foresight on the part of the accused that his conduct may bring about the prohibited consequence, although I am not unmindful that for some purposes recklessness may denote only a marked departure from objective standards. Where the prosecution, in order to establish the accused's guilt of the offence charged, is required to prove that he intended to bring about a particular consequence or foresaw a particular consequence, the question to be determined is what was in the mind of this particular accused, and the necessary intent or foresight must be brought home to him subjectively: see *R. v. Mulligan* (1974), 18 C.C.C. (2d) 270 at pp. 274-5, 26 C.R.N.S. 179; affirmed 28 C.C.C. (2d) 266, [1977] 1 S.C.R. 612.

What the accused intended or foresaw must be determined on a consideration of all the circumstances, as well as from his own evidence, if he testifies, as to what his state of mind or intention was.

Since people are usually able to foresee the consequences of their acts, if a person does an act likely to produce certain consequences it is, in general, reasonable to assume that the accused also foresaw the probable consequences of his act and if he, nevertheless, acted so as to produce those consequences, that he intended them. The greater the likelihood of the relevant consequences ensuing from the accused's act, the easier it is to draw the inference that he intended those consequences. The purpose of this process, however, is to determine what the particular accused intended, not to fix him with the intention that a reasonable person might be assumed to have in the circumstances, where doubt exists as to the actual intention of the accused. The accused's testimony, if he gives evidence as to what was in his mind, is important material to be weighed with the other evidence in determining whether the necessary intent has been established. Indeed, Mr. Justice Devlin, in his charge to the jury in *R. v. Adams* (The Times, April 10, 1957), said that where the accused testified as to what was in his mind and the jury "thought he might be telling the truth", they would "have the best evidence available on what was in his own mind". The background of the appellants and their commitment to preserving the French Canadian culture was, of course, relevant to the credibility of their denial that they intended to promote hatred against the French-speaking community of Essex County. The appellants' evidence as to their state of mind or intention is not, of course, conclusive.

In some cases the inference from the circumstances that the necessary intent existed may be so strong as to compel the rejection of the accused's evidence that he did not intend to bring about the prohibited consequence. The learned trial Judge did not, however, state that he disbelieved the appellants' evidence that they did not intend to promote hatred. He appears to have treated the appellants' testimony that they wished to create "controversy, furor and an uproar" as a virtual admission that they had the state of mind requisite for guilt.

I am, with deference to the learned trial Judge, of the view that an intention to create "controversy, furor and an uproar" is not the same thing as an intention to promote hatred, and it was an error to equate them. I would, of course, agree that if the appellants intentionally promoted hatred against the French-speaking community of Essex County as a means of obtaining the French-language high school, they committed the offence charged. The appellants' evidence, if believed, does not, however, as the learned trial Judge appears to have thought, inevitably lead to that conclusion. The learned trial Judge, not having disbelieved the appellants' evidence, failed to give appropriate consideration to their evidence on the issue of intent and, in the circumstances, his failure so to do constituted self-misdirection.

In view of the conclusion which I have reached it is necessary to refer only briefly to the other grounds of appeal which we regard as requiring discussion.

. . . .

Conclusion

I have concluded that the self-misdirection with respect to the meaning of the word "wilfully", and the failure to appreciate the significance of the appellants' evidence on the issue of intent requires a new trial. The outrageous conduct of the appellants in preparing and distributing this deplorable document was evidence to be weighed in determining their intent, but in the peculiar circumstances of this case I am not satisfied that the inferences to be drawn from it are such as to inevitably lead to a conclusion that they had the requisite intent or that the trial Judge would inevitably have reached that conclusion but for his self-misdirection.

In the result, I would allow the appeal, set aside the convictions and order new trials.

Appeal allowed; new trial ordered.

This interpretation was later adopted by the Supreme Court in *R. v. Keegstra*, [1990] 3 S.C.R. 697, 1 C.R. (4th) 129, 61 C.C.C. (3d) 1, a decision holding that s. 319(2) was constitutional. Although the offence violated freedom of expression guaranteed by s. 2 (*b*) of the *Charter* the limit was held to be demonstrably justified as a reasonable limit under s. 1. One of the reasons given by Chief Justice Dickson for the majority was that:

> The interpretation of "wilfully" in *Buzzanga* has great bearing upon the extent to which s. 319(2) limits the freedom of expression. This mental element, requiring more than merely negligence or recklessness as to result, significantly restricts the reach of the provision, and thereby reduces the scope of the targeted expression (at 193).

R. v. DOCHERTY

(1989), 72 C.R. (3d) 1, 51 C.C.C. (3d) 1 (S.C.C.)

The accused was found sitting in an automobile, apparently intoxicated. He later pleaded guilty to a charge of having care and control of a motor vehicle with excessive alcohol in his blood. He was then charged with wilful failure to comply with the terms of a previous probation order requiring him to keep the peace and be of good behaviour. The commission of the care and control offence was the basis relied on for the breach of s. 740(1) of the *Criminal Code*. When the matter reached the Supreme Court of Canada, the issue was *mens rea*.

WILSON J: —

. . . .

This case raises the important question whether an accused can be convicted of the summary conviction offence of wilfully breaching or refusing to comply with a probation order when, in the words of the trial Judge, the accused "had an honest belief, although you may be wrong, that you are not doing anything wrong". In other words, is s. 666(1) of the *Criminal Code* to be interpreted as an offence requiring its own *mens rea*, or is it to be interpreted as an offence which automatically follows upon a conviction for any *Criminal*

Code offence or other deliberate act which constitutes a violation of the conditions of a probation order? The respondent's case is particularly challenging in that the underlying *Criminal Code* offence, care or control of a motor vehicle "over 80 mg", was committed without proof or admission of *mens rea*, at least in the traditional sense. The respondent was simply found sitting in an intoxicated condition in a car which he thought (and the trial Judge believed him) would not start. At his trial the respondent testified that he did not think he was doing anything wrong, and this seems to have been accepted as a fact by the trial Judge.

The issue in the case is primarily one of statutory interpretation.

(a) *The literal interpretation*

Section 666(1) is clearly framed so as to require guilty knowledge in order to constitute a breach. The section prohibits an accused from *wifully* failing or *refusing* to comply with a probation order. The word "wilfully" is perhaps the archetypal word to denote a *mens rea* requirement. It stresses intention in relation to the achievement of a purpose. It can be contrasted with lesser forms of guilty knowledge, such as "negligently" or even "recklessly". In short, the use of the word "wilfully" denotes a legislative concern for a relatively high level of *mens rea*, requiring those subject to the probation order to have formed the intent to breach its terms and to have had that purpose in mind while doing so.

The requirement of "refusing" to comply with a probation order, although less obviously importing a *mens rea* element than the requirement of wilfully failing to comply, also denotes some form of guilty knowledge. In order to "refuse" to comply with something, it is necessary to know what you are not complying with. Only in that event can your actions constitute a "refusal". You know the strictures you are under, but deliberately flout them.

I would conclude, therefore, that on a literal construction of the section a relatively high level of *mens rea* is required for the offence.

(b) *The contextual interpretation*

Is the requirement of a relatively high level of *mens rea* under s. 666(1) consistent with the wider context of the legislation?

Since s. 666(1) creates a criminal offence, it should be presumed that some mental element is required, in the absence of clear words to the contrary. In the case of s. 666(1), far from having clear words to the contrary, we have clear words denoting a mental element. It would appear to be significant also in this connection that the general punishment provision, s. 722 [now s. 787] of the *Criminal Code*, applies in the case of a conviction under s. 666(1), and under that section imprisonment is a permitted sanction. Since s. 666(1) creates an offence under the *Criminal Code* for which imprisonment is a permitted sanction, it makes eminent good sense, in my opinion, to construe it as requiring a mental element.

Moreover, the purpose of s. 666(1) is clearly compliance with probation orders. Section 663(4) requires not only that a copy of the probation order be given to the accused but also that it be read to him or her. The accused must also be told that breach of it constitutes a distinct offence under s. 666(1). Lower Courts have held that the Crown must prove that this occurred before a conviction can be obtained under the section: *Piche v. R.* (1976), 31 C.C.C. (2d) 150 (Sask. Q.B.); *R. v. McNamara* (1982), 66 C.C.C. (2d) 24 (C.A.); *R. v. Bara* (1981), 58 C.C.C. (2d) 243 (C.A.). Indeed, the Courts in *Piche v. R.* and *R. v. Bara* also ruled that an accused is not "*bound* by a probation order" within the meaning of s. 666(1) unless and until the Court has complied with s. 663(4). Given the pains that Parliament has taken to ensure that the accused is fully aware of the terms of his or her probation order, it would be strange if an accused could be convicted under the section without knowing that he or she was violating it.

Other considerations seem to be relevant to the contextual approach to the interpretation of s. 666(1). For example, in *R. v. Sault Ste. Marie (City)*, [1978] 2 S.C.R. 1299, 3 C.R. (3d) 30, 40 C.C.C. (2d) 353 [Ont.], Dickson J. suggested that the deterrence rationale advanced in favour of absolute liability offences is in most cases overblown. Put simply, it makes little sense to think that a person will be deterred from wrongdoing in situations where that person does not believe and has no awareness that he or she is doing anything wrong. The appellant submitted to the Court, however, that the whole purpose of putting a person found guilty of criminal conduct on probation is to "heighten his or her awareness of the consequences of criminal activity". I am sure that is correct. However, in the context of this case the conviction of the accused under s. 666(1) would have little or no deterrent effect, given (as was accepted by the trial Judge) that the accused did not know he was doing anything wrong. A decision requiring a distinct *mens rea* element for the offence under s. 666(1) would not, in my view, undermine the effectiveness of probation orders, as the appellant alleges. The requirement that persons on probation keep the peace and be of good behaviour would still apply to those wilfully breaching their parole. It is, I think, consistent with the overall content and purpose of the probation provisions in the *Criminal Code* that those who unknowingly violate the terms of their parole not be convicted, but only those who wilfully breach such terms or deliberately refuse to obey them.

. . . .

As I have stated earlier, the *mens rea* of s. 666(1) requires that an accused intend to breach his probation order. This requires, at a minimum, proof that the accused knew that he was bound by the probation order and that there was a term in it which would be breached by his proposed conduct. The accused must be found to have gone ahead and engaged in the conduct regardless. The onus, of course, is on the Crown to prove that the accused had the requisite *mens rea*. To the extent that direct evidence of intent is almost always difficult to obtain, the Crown may ask the Court, absent any evidence to the contrary, to infer intent from the fact of the conduct. Any doubt, however, as to whether the accused intended to do what he did must be resolved in favour of the accused. The important point is that an intent to commit the underlying offence does not afford a basis for inferring the wholly distinct intent, *i.e.*, to breach one's probation order.

What then is the significance of the conviction for the underlying offence in relation to the undertaking in the probation order to be of good behaviour? It seems to me that it constitutes the *actus reus* under s. 666(1). It establishes that the accused has violated the terms of his parole through the commission of a criminal offence. But it is not, in my view, *prima facie* evidence of an intent to do so, still less a wilful intent to do so. This is a different intention to commit the *actus reus* of the underlying offence.

A full *mens rea* offence under the *Criminal Code* demands that the accused have an intent to perform the acts that constitute the *actus reus* of the offence. Section 666(1) is no different. In the circumstances of the present case the *actus reus* of the offence under s. 666(1) is the commission of the criminal offence under s. 236. Proof of the *mens rea* would therefore require that the respondent *intended to commit the criminal offence under s. 236* when he sat behind the wheel in an intoxicated condition. The respondent testified that he thought the automobile was not in an operating condition and for that reason he honestly believed he was not committing an offence by sitting behind the wheel while intoxicated. This testimony was accepted by the trial Judge. In my view, where the *actus reus* of s. 666(1) consists of the commission of a criminal offence, an honest belief on the part of the accused that he is not committing that offence means that the accused cannot be said to have *wilfully* failed or *refused* to comply with the probation order. He did not in these circumstances have the necessary *mens rea* for the offence under s. 666(1).

Does s. 19 of the *Criminal Code* prevent the respondent from relying on his honest belief to negate the *mens rea* requirement in s. 666(1)? The section provides:

> 19. Ignorance of the law by a person who commits an offence is not an excuse for committing that offence.

The respondent testified that he did not believe he was doing anything wrong when he got behind the wheel of the car while in an intoxicated condition. The trial Judge accepted that the respondent's belief was honestly held, and noted the existence of objective evidence in support of his contention.

It is beyond dispute that the respondent could not escape conviction for a violation of s. 236 of the *Criminal Code* on the ground that he did not know that having care and control of a motor vehicle with a blood alcohol level over .08 was against the law. That knowledge is not a component of the *mens rea* of s. 236. Neither could the respondent claim that he did not know that a wilful failure to be of good behaviour was a breach of probation, especially since s. 663(4) (now s. 737(3)) of the *Criminal Code* requires a Court, when it issues a probation order to ensure that the accused knows the terms and conditions of the order, the conduct that would constitute a breach and the consequences of such a breach, and the respondent has not alleged that this was not done.

Mewett and Manning in their text, *Criminal Law*, 2nd ed. (1985), discuss at p. 320 what is meant by the maxim "ignorance of the law is no excuse":

> It is often said that ignorance of the law is no excuse and as a general maxim — now incorporated in s. 19 of the *Code* — it is a harmless cliché. It is more accurate, however, to say that knowledge that one's act is contrary to the law is not one of the elements of the requisite *mens rea* and hence a mistake as to what the law is does not operate as a defence. That is to say, this belief that an act is lawful, however much it might affect sentence, does not affect liability.

While I agree with the authors' general proposition I believe that where the commission of a criminal offence is relied on as the *actus reus* of the offence under s. 666(1) (as in this case), knowledge that one's act is contrary to law (in this case, the law contained in s. 236 of the *Criminal Code*) *is* an element of the requisite mens rea of wilfully failing to comply with a probation order. I believe, in other words, that s. 666(1) constitutes an exception to the general rule expressed in s. 19 in a case where the commission of a criminal offence is relied on as the *actus reus* under the section. An accused cannot have wilfully breached his probation order through the commission of a criminal offence unless he knew that what he did constituted a criminal offence. However, the conviction is evidence of the *mens rea* under s. 666(1) only to the extent that wilfulness can be inferred from the actus reus as indicated above. Such *mens rea* must be proved and s. 19 of the *Code* does not preclude the respondent from relying on his honest belief that he was not doing anything wrong to negate its presence. Where knowledge is itself a component of the requisite *mens rea*, the absence of knowledge provides a good defence.

. . . .

Appeal dismissed.

For comment see Stuart (1989), 72 C.R. (3d) 2-3.

In 1995 Parliament removed the word "wilfully" from the offence of failing to comply with a probation order, now to be found in s. 733.1. *Docherty* appears to have been legislated away in this context. Do you agree with Parliament or the Supreme Court?

In *R. v. Gunn* (1997), 6 C.R. (5th) 405, 113 C.C.C. (3d) 174 (Alta. C.A.), leave to appeal to S.C.C. refused (1997), 212 A.R. 234 (S.C.C.), the Court distinguished *Docherty* in the course of determining that the offence of wilful obstruction of a police officer under s. 129(1) did not require proof of a specific intent.

However, in two recent high profile obstruction of justice charges, lack of proof of intent was the basis for acquittals. In *Kirkham* (1998), 17 C.R. (5th) 250, 126 C.C.C. (3d) 397 (Sask. Q.B.), a Crown Attorney had arranged for a police questionnaire to obtain information about the background of potential jurors for a mercy killing murder trial, *Latimer*, which he did not disclose to defence counsel. In *Murray* (2000), 34 C.R. (5th) 290, 144 C.C.C. (3d) 289 (Ont. S.C.J.), a defence counsel in the double murder case of *Bernardo* had withheld incriminating videotapes of sexual abuse of murder victims by his client and co-accused for 17 months. Such a definitional quagmire concerning so basic a crime as obstruction of justice speaks volumes about a need for a General Part with clear fault definitions.

R. v. Chartrand (1994), 31 C.R. (4th) 1 (S.C.C.), concerning the crime of abduction of a child under 14, is now strong authority for the view that where an offence has an express "with intent" element this requires proof of intent or actual foresight of certainty. Madam Justice L'Heureux-Dubé for the Court relied on *Buzzanga* but did not consider *Docherty*. The Court implicitly decided recklessness would not do but there is no discussion of why this should be so.

R. v. THÉROUX

[1993] 2 S.C.R. 5, 19 C.R. (4th) 194, 79 C.C.C. (3d) 449

The accused, the directing mind of a company involved in residential construction, was charged with fraud. The company entered into contracts and received deposits on the basis of a false representation by the company that the deposits were insured. The company became insolvent, the project was not completed and most of the depositors lost their money. The trial Judge found that the accused, as directing mind of the company, was responsible for the misrepresentations that the deposits were guaranteed. The accused knew at the time that the insurance was not in place but nevertheless made misrepresentations to induce potential home purchasers to sign a contract and give a deposit. The trial Judge also found that the accused sincerely believed that the residential project would be completed and hence that the deposits would not be lost. The accused was convicted of fraud pursuant to s. 380(1)(*a*) of the *Criminal Code* and the Court of Appeal upheld the conviction. The issue for the Supreme Court was whether the fact that the accused honestly believed that the project would be completed negated the *mens rea* of the offence of fraud.

McLachlin J.: —

There is no doubt that the appellant deliberately practised a deceitful act, constituting the *actus reus* of the offence of fraud. The issue is whether the fact that he honestly believed that the projects would be completed negates the guilty mind or *mens rea* of the offence. This requires this Court to examine the question of what constitutes the *mens rea* for the offence of fraud.

. . . .

The prohibited act is deceit, falsehood, or some other dishonest act. The prohibited consequence is depriving another of what is or should be his, which may, as we have seen, consist in merely placing another's property at risk. The *mens rea* would then consist in the subjective awareness that one was undertaking a prohibited act (the deceit, falsehood or other dishonest act) which could cause deprivation in the sense of depriving another of property or putting that property at risk. If this is shown, the crime is complete. The fact that the accused may have hoped the deprivation would not take place, or may have felt there was nothing wrong with what he or she was doing, provides no defence. To put it another way, following the traditional criminal-law principle that the mental state necessary to the offence must be determined by reference to the external acts which constitute the *actus* of the offence (see Williams, *supra*, c. 3), the proper focus in determining the *mens rea* of fraud is to ask whether the accused intentionally committed the prohibited acts (deceit, falsehood, or other dishonest act) knowing or desiring the consequences proscribed by the offence (deprivation, including the risk of deprivation). The personal feeling of the accused about the morality or honesty of the act or its consequences is no more relevant to the analysis than is the accused's awareness that the particular acts undertaken constitute a criminal offence.

This applies as much to the third head of fraud, "other fraudulent means", as to lies and acts of deceit. Although other fraudulent means have been broadly defined as means which are "dishonest", it is not necessary that an accused personally consider these means to be dishonest in order that he or she be convicted of fraud for having undertaken them. The "dishonesty" of the means is relevant to the determination whether the conduct falls within the type of conduct caught by the offence of fraud; what reasonable people consider dishonest assists in the determination whether the *actus reus* of the offence can be made out on particular facts. That established, it need only be determined that an accused knowingly undertook the acts in question, aware that deprivation, or risk of deprivation, could follow as a likely consequence.

I have spoken of knowledge of the consequences of the fraudulent act. There appears to be no reason, however, why recklessness as to consequences might not also attract criminal responsibility. Recklessness presupposes knowledge of the likelihood of the prohibited consequences. It is established when it is shown that the accused, with such knowledge, commits acts which may bring about these prohibited consequences, while being reckless as to whether or not they ensue.

These doctrinal observations suggest that the *actus reus* of the offence of fraud will be established by proof of:

1. the prohibited act, be it an act of deceit, a falsehood or some other fraudulent means; and

2. deprivation caused by the prohibited act, which may consist in actual loss or the placing of the victim's pecuniary interests at risk.

Correspondingly, the *mens rea* of fraud is established by proof of:

1. Subjective knowledge of the prohibited act; and

2. Subjective knowledge that the prohibited act could have as a consequence the deprivation of another (which deprivation may consist in knowledge that the victim's pecuniary interests are put at risk).

Where the conduct and knowledge required by these definitions are established, the accused is guilty whether he actually intended the prohibited consequence or was reckless as to whether it would occur.

The inclusion of *risk* of deprivation in the concept of deprivation in *Olan* requires specific comment. The accused must have subjective awareness, at the very least, that his or her conduct will put the property or economic expectations of others at risk. As noted above, this does not mean that the Crown must provide the trier of fact with a mental snapshot proving exactly what was in the accused's mind at the moment the dishonest act was committed. In certain cases, the inference of subjective knowledge of the risk may be drawn from the facts as the accused believed them to be. The accused may introduce evidence negating that inference, such as evidence that his deceit was part of an innocent prank, or evidence of circumstances which led him to believe that no one would act on his lie or deceitful or dishonest act. But in cases like the present one, where the accused tells a lie knowing others will act on it and thereby puts their property at risk, the inference of subjective knowledge that the property of another would be put at risk is clear.

Recklessness or Wilful Blindness

SANSREGRET v. R.

(1985), 45 C.R. (3d) 193 (S.C.C.)

Sansregret is a leading decision on the crime of rape, to be considered later in the chapter on "Sexual Assault". During the course of his unanimous judgment for the Supreme Court, Mr. Justice McIntyre authoritatively defined and distinguished the concepts of recklessness and wilful blindness as follows:

. . . .

The concept of recklessness as a basis for criminal liability has been the subject of much discussion. Negligence, the failure to take reasonable care, is a creature of the civil law and is not generally a concept having a place in determining criminal liability. Nevertheless, it is frequently confused with recklessness in the criminal sense and care should be taken to separate the two concepts. Negligence is tested by the objective standard of the reasonable man. A departure from his accustomed sober behaviour by an act or omission which reveals less than reasonable care will involve liability at civil law but forms no basis for the imposition of criminal penalties. In accordance with well-established principles for the determination of criminal liability, recklessness, to form a part of the criminal *mens rea*, must have an element of the subjective. It is found in the attitude of one who, aware that there is danger that his conduct could bring about the result prohibited by the criminal law, nevertheless persists, despite the risk. It is, in other words, the conduct of one who sees the risk and who takes the chance. It is in this sense that the term "recklessness" is used in the criminal law and it is clearly distinct from the concept of civil negligence.

. . . .

The idea of wilful blindness in circumstances such as this has been said to be an aspect of recklessness. While this may well be true, it is wise to keep the two concepts separate because they result from different mental attitudes and lead to different legal results. A finding of recklessness in this case could not override the defence of mistake of fact. The appellant asserts an honest belief that the consent of the complainant was not caused by fear and threats. The trial Judge found that such an honest belief existed. In the facts of this case, because of the reckless conduct of the appellant, it could not be said that such a belief was reasonable but, as held in *Pappajohn*, the mere honesty of the belief will support the "mistake of fact" defence, even where it is unreasonable. On the other hand, a finding of wilful blindness as to the very facts about which the honest belief is now asserted would leave no room for the application of the defence because, where wilful blindness is shown, the law presumes knowledge on the part of the accused, in this case knowledge that the consent had been induced by threats.

Wilful blindness is distinct from recklessness because, while recklessness involves knowledge of a danger or risk and persistence in a course of conduct which creates a risk that the prohibited result will occur, wilful blindness arises where a person who has become aware of the need for some inquiry declines to make the inquiry because he does not wish to know the truth. He would prefer to remain ignorant. The culpability in recklessness is justified by consciousness of the risk and by proceeding in the face of it, while in wilful blindness it is justified by the accused's fault in deliberately failing to inquire when he knows there is reason for inquiry. Cases such as *Wretham v. R.* (1971), 16 C.R.N.S. 124 (Ont. C.A.); *R. v. Blondin* (1971), 2 C.C.C. (2d) 118, affirmed [1971] S.C.R. v, 4 C.C.C. (2d) 566; *R. v. Currie* (1976), 24 C.C.C. (2d) 292 (Ont. C.A.); *R. v. McFall* (1976), 26 C.C.C. (2d) 181 (B.C. C.A.); *R. v. Aiello* (1978), 38 C.C.C. (2d) 485 (Ont. C.A.); *Taylor's Central Garages (Exeter) Ltd. v. Roper*, [1951] 2 T.L.R. 284 (Div. Ct.), among others, illustrate these principles. The textwriters have also dealt with the subject, particularly Glanville Williams, *Criminal Law: The General Part*, 2nd ed. (1961), at pp. 157-60. He says, at p. 157:

> Knowledge, then, means either personal knowledge or (in the licence cases) imputed knowledge. In either event there is someone with actual knowledge. To the requirement of actual knowledge there is one strictly limited exception. Men readily regard their suspicions as unworthy of them when it is to their advantage to do so. To meet this, the rule is that if a party has his suspicion aroused but then deliberately omits to make further enquiries, because he wishes to remain in ignorance, he is deemed to have knowledge.

He then referred to the words of Lord Sumner in *Re The Zamora*, [1921] 1 A.C. 801 at 811-12 (P.C.), which was a case wherein a ship and cargo were condemned in the Prize Court as contraband. The managing director of the shipping company denied knowledge of the contraband carried by the ship, and on this subject Lord Sumner said, at pp. 811-12:

Lord Sterndale [the president of the Prize Court] thus expressed his final conclusion: "I think the true inference is that, if Mr. Banck did not know this was a transaction in contraband, it was because he did not want to know, and that he has not rebutted the presumption arising from the fact of the whole cargo being contraband."

Their Lordships have been invited to read this as saying that Mr. Banck is not proved to have known the contraband character of the adventure; that if he did not know, because he did not want to know, he was within his rights and owed no duty to the belligerents to inform himself; and that the *Zamora* is condemned contrary to the passage above cited from *The Hakan* upon a legal presumption arising solely and arbitrarily from the fact that the whole cargo was contraband. It may be that in his anxiety not to state more than he found against Mr. Banck, the learned President appeared to state something less, but there are two senses in which a man is said not to know something because he does not want to know it. A thing may be troublesome to learn, and the knowledge of it, when acquired, may be uninteresting or distasteful. To refuse to know any more about the subject or anything at all is then a wilful but a real ignorance. On the other hand, a man is said not to know because he does not want to know, where the substance of the thing is borne in upon his mind with a conviction that full details or precise proof may be dangerous, because they may embarrass his denials or compromise his protests. In such a case he flatters himself that where ignorance is safe, 'tis folly to be wise, but there he is wrong, for he has been put upon notice and his further ignorance, even though actual and complete, is a mere affectation and disguise.

Glanville Williams, however, warns that the rule of deliberate blindness has its dangers and is of narrow application. He says, at p. 159:

The rule that wilful blindness is equivalent to knowledge is essential, and is found throughout the criminal law. It is, at the same time, an unstable rule, because Judges are apt to forget its very limited scope. A Court can properly find wilful blindness only where it can almost be said that the defendant actually knew. He suspected the fact; he realised its probability; but he refrained from obtaining the final confirmation because he wanted in the event to be able to deny knowledge. This, and this alone, is wilful blindness. It requires in effect a finding that the defendant intended to cheat the administration of justice. Any wider definition would make the doctrine of wilful blindness indistinguishable from the civil doctrine of negligence in not obtaining knowledge.

This subject is also dealt with by Professor Stuart in *Canadian Criminal Law* (1982), at p. 130 et seq., where its relationship to recklessness is discussed.

R. v. CURRIE

(1975), 24 C.C.C. (2d) 292 (Ont. C.A.)

The following judgments were delivered orally by

GALE C.J.O. (dissenting): — The accused was charged and convicted for uttering a forged document. I need not go into the circumstances of the case because it is my judgment that, although not expressing himself in his judgment as clearly as he might have, the Judge made sufficient findings to support the decision that the appellant was guilty on the ground of wilful blindness.

I base my conclusion on the finding of the Judge that the appellant "deliberately or knowingly" neglected to make the inquiries which he ought to have made. Such a finding plainly suggests that the Judge decided that the appellant was in fact suspicious of the authenticity of the cheque, for otherwise he could not have "deliberately" failed to make the necessary inquiries.

My brothers do not agree with me.

ARNUP J.A.: — I agree with the conclusions reached by my brother Martin. To his recitation of the facts I would add only two points. In his statement to the police, the accused said: "I didn't think anything was wrong." In his evidence at trial, he gave this evidence:

A. I didn't think I was going against the law, I thought I was helping somebody.
Q. Why did you feel this man needed help?
A. He'd been drinking a lot.
Q. Was he a clean cut fellow?
A. Yes.
Q. What was the impression he gave you?
A. Honest type, respectable person.
Q. Did you have any suspicion that that wasn't his cheque?
A. No.

The trial Judge did not, in his reasons for judgment, indicate that he declined to accept this evidence.

MARTIN J.A.: — The appellant appeals from his conviction before a Provincial Court Judge sitting under Part XVI of the *Criminal Code*, on December 5, 1974, on a charge that:

> on or about the 8th day of April, 1974, at the Regional Municipality of Niagara . . . did unlawfully and knowingly utter a forged document, to wit: a cheque payable to Edward Gerada in the amount ot $478.15 at the Canadian Imperial Bank of Canada, Main and Hellems in the City of Welland, with intent to use same as if it were genuine. Contrary to the provisions of the *Criminal Code of Canada.*

The appellant was 19 years of age at the time of the events giving rise to this charge. On April 8, 1974, he presented for payment, at a branch of the Canadian Imperial Bank of Commerce, at Welland, a cheque payable to one Edward Gerada, in the amount of $478.15. There was endorsed, on the back of the cheque at that time, a signature which purported to be that of the payee of the cheque, Edward Gerada. The cheque in fact had been stolen from Mr. Gerada's mailbox and the endorsement on the cheque was a forgery.

The appellant had a bank account at that branch with a small balance. He had had an account there for some months and was known to the teller of the bank. When he presented the cheque for payment he signed his own name on the back of the cheque, together with his address and telephone number.

When Mr. Gerada failed to receive the cheque which he was expecting, he communicated with the police who arrested the appellant. At that time the appellant made a statement to the police, which in substance was this: that he was sitting in the Reeta Hotel in Welland, having a beer with a friend of his, Mr. Gilbert Davidson, when a man whom he had never seen before asked him to cash the cheque for him, and said that he would pay the appellant $5 for cashing it. The appellant then took the cheque, cashed it and gave the proceeds to this unknown man.

The appellant gave evidence at his trial and he gave the same explanation as that contained in his statement to the police. His evidence on this point was confirmed by Mr. Davidson, who was with him.

The learned trial Judge did not reject the evidence of the appellant. However, he registered a conviction and based his finding of guilt upon his conclusion that the appellant was "wilfully blind" as to the forged nature of the endorsement. The trial Judge in convicting the appellant said:

> The Crown has submitted very strongly the doctrine of wilful blindness, said to be in this set of circumstances. [*sic*] That the accused must take on some responsibility, make some inquiries as to the validity of the cheque from whom he was obtaining it, before he voluntarily proceeded to cash that cheque through his bank. I am of the opinion that these responsibilities do fall upon the accused, that for some reason either deliberately or knowingly he neglected to make these inquiries which I believe he should have in the circumstances. And therefore that he wilfully blinded himself to the situation he was entering upon and he should have been suspicious of the circumstances, the manner in which the cheque was handed to him from an unknown person and he had a responsibility before his placing that cheque through his banking authorities to make some investigation as to the authenticity of the cheque and the person from whom he was receiving it from.

It is the view of my brother Arnup and myself, that this passage in the trial Judge's reasons for judgment is not free from ambiguity and is reasonably open to the conclusion that the learned trial Judge was of the view that the doctrine of wilful blindness applied because the accused should have been suspicious in all the circumstances of the forged endorsement on the cheque when he received it and should have made further inquiry.

This was a misconception on the part of the trial Judge as to the doctrine of wilful blindness, which he purported to apply. I accept the statements of that doctrine as set out in Williams on *Criminal Law, the General Part*, 2nd ed. (1961), at p. 157, where the following is stated:

> To meet this, the rule is that if a party has his suspicion aroused but then deliberately omits to make further enquiries, because he wishes to remain in ignorance, he is deemed to have knowledge.

He further states at p. 158:

> In other words, there is a suspicion which the defendant deliberately omits to turn into certain knowledge. This is frequently expressed by saying that he "shut his eyes" to the fact, or that he was "wilfully blind". Lord Hewart, C.J., expressed it by saying that "the respondent deliberately refrained from making inquiries the result of which he might not care to have".

I refer also to the judgment of this Court in *R. v. F.W. Woolworth Co. Ltd.* (1974), 18 C.C.C. (2d) 23, where Kelly J.A., speaking for the Court pointed out at p. 30 that, generally speaking, the doctrine of constructive knowledge has no application in criminal law. The fact that a person ought to have known that certain facts existed, while it may, for some purposes in civil proceedings, be equivalent to actual knowledge, does not constitute knowledge for the purpose of criminal liability, and does not by itself form a basis for the application of the doctrine of wilful blindness.

For these reasons we are of the opinion that the appeal must be allowed, the conviction quashed and a verdict of acquittal directed to be entered.

Appeal allowed.

R. v. BLONDIN

(1971), 2 C.C.C. (2d) 118 (B.C. C.A.)

ROBERTSON J.A.: — The respondent ("Blondin") was charged:

> that he . . . between the 27th day of August A.D. 1969 and the 29th day of August A.D. 1969, at the Municipality of Richmond, in the County of Vancouver, in the Province of British Columbia, did unlawfully import into Canada a narcotic, to wit: Cannabis resin, contrary to the provisions of the *Narcotic Control Act.*

He was tried by a Judge and jury in the County Court and was found not guilty. Against that acquittal the Crown has appealed. Blondin did not give evidence.

Having returned to Canada from Japan, Blondin went to the premises of Canadian Pacific Air Lines in the air terminal in Richmond to collect baggage that he had shipped from Japan, namely, a scuba-diving outfit. The weight of the tank that was part of the outfit aroused suspicion. At one time while it was being examined there were present, among others, Blondin, a Customs official named Montgomery and a constable of the R.C.M.P. named Kennedy. Kennedy was not in uniform and at that time did not identify himself to Blondin as a member of the R.C.M.P. Attempts to remove the valve stem from the tank having proved fruitless, Blondin voluntarily accompanied Montgomery and Kennedy to the Aquatic Shop in Vancouver to try to have the valve stem removed from the tank. At the Aquatic Shop the valve stem was removed, but not much could be seen inside the tank. In the course of the operation the harness was removed from the tank and this revealed that the tank had been cut in half and that the two halves had been put together again; they were kept together by a sleeve inside. When the two halves were separated, Kennedy saw inside a number of brown wafer-like objects; he immediately had the tank closed. Later analysis showed that the objects were cannabis resin, or hashish; they weighed about 23 lbs. After the tank was closed Kennedy, who had not yet made it known to Blondin that he was a police officer, approached Blondin. As Kennedy approached him, Blondin volunteered "I guess I am in for it". Kennedy then identified himself and gave the usual warning. I shall refer to these exchanges as the first conversation. Kennedy then took Blondin, Montgomery and the tank to the R.C.M.P. barracks in Montgomery's car. In the car what I shall call the second conversation occurred. Kennedy asked Blondin if he was aware of what was in the tank and

Blondin replied that he did not know. Blondin then asked Kennedy what was in the tank and Kennedy replied that it was hashish. Kennedy asked Blondin if he knew what hashish was and Blondin replied that he did not. On arrival at the barracks Blondin, Montgomery and Kennedy went upstairs to the drug squad office, where a third conversation took place. Kennedy asked Blondin if he was aware that the tank contained narcotics and Blondin said that he knew that there was something in the tank and that it was illegal. He went on to say that he had been paid to bring the tank over. Kennedy asked him who had paid him and Blondin replied that he did not think it was right for him to say. Kennedy asked Blondin to whom he was delivering the tank, and Blondin replied that he did not wish to say.

I am of the respectful opinion that the learned trial Judge erred when he instructed the jury that, in order to find Blondin guilty, they must find that he knew that the substance in the tank was cannabis resin. It would be sufficient to find, in relation to a narcotic, *mens rea* in its widest sense.

It remains to decide whether the Judge could properly instruct the jury that, if they were satisfied beyond a reasonable doubt that Blondin knew that it was illegal to import the substance in the tank, they might find him guilty, even though he did not know that the substance was a narcotic. I am not prepared so to hold. An essential ingredient of the offence is the importation of a narcotic and I do not consider that *mens rea qua* that offence is proven by an intention to commit an offence which, so far as Blondin's admitted knowledge went, might have been one against the *Customs Act*, R.S.C. 1952, c. 58.

These reasons will, I fear, dispose of this case inadequately if I do not indicate how I think the jury could properly have found *mens rea* in the circumstances of this case. They could have done so if they had found that Blondin had been paid to smuggle a substance illegally into Canada and either was reckless about what it was or wilfully shut his eyes to what it was, inferring therefrom that he suspected that it might be a narcotic. It follows that the learned Judge ought to have told the jury that they might convict if they found that Blondin brought the substance into Canada from Japan and knew that it was a narcotic. He should also have instructed the jury that they might convict if they found that he had brought the substance into Canada illegally and had either been reckless about what it was or wilfully shut his eyes to what it was, and then drew the inference that he suspected that it might be a narcotic.

I would allow the appeal, set aside the verdict and order a new trial.

DAVEY C.J.B.C.: — In the circumstances of this case I think the learned trial Judge ought to have instructed the jury that they should convict if they found beyond a reasonable doubt that Blondin brought the substance into Canada knowing that it was a narcotic, or being reckless about its nature, or wilfully shutting his eyes to what it was.

In other respects I agree with my brother Robertson, and would allow the appeal and direct a new trial.

McFARLANE J.A.: — I have the advantage of having read the reasons for judgment prepared by my brother Robertson.

. . . .

I agree with my brother Robertson that the learned trial Judge was wrong in instructing the jury that the Crown must prove beyond reasonable doubt that the respondent knew the substance was cannabis resin. I agree also it would be wrong to instruct the jury that proof of knowledge that the substance was one which it would be unlawful to import is itself sufficient to support a conviction. The offence of smuggling goods which may be imported lawfully on disclosure and payment of customs duty is, for this purpose, I think, essentially different from that of importing a narcotic, which Parliament has declared to be a serious offence. I refer to the statement by Cartwright J., as he then was, in *Beaver v. The Queen*, [1957] S.C.R. 531 at 539, 26 C.R. 193, 118 C.C.C. 129, that Parliament regards dealing in narcotics as conduct "harmful in itself". The importation of narcotics has been forbidden except by licence issued under authority of the Governor in Council pursuant to s. 12 of the statute [the *Narcotic Control Act*, 1960-61 (Can.), c. 35].

I therefore agree with my brother Robertson that the jury should have been instructed that the onus on the Crown was to prove beyond reasonable doubt that the respondent knew the substance was a narcotic, although not necessarily cannabis resin.

In *Beaver v. The Queen, supra*, the Supreme Court was dealing with a case of unlawful possession of a narcotic. Delivering the judgment of the majority of the Court, Cartwright J. (as he then was) said at p. 541:

> The essence of the crime is the possession of the forbidden substance and in a criminal case there is in law no possession without knowledge of the character of the forbidden substance. . . .
>
> In my view the law is correctly stated in the following passage in the judgment of O'Halloran J.A., with whom Robertson J.A. concurred, in *Rex v. Hess* (1949) 8 C.R. 42, 94 C.C.C. 48 at 50-1 (B.C. C.A.):
>
>> "To constitute 'possession' within the meaning of the criminal law it is my judgment that where, as here, there is manual handling of a thing, it must be co-existent with knowledge of what the thing is, and both these elements must be co-existent with some act of control (outside public duty). When those three elements exist together, I think it must be conceded that under sec. 4(1)(*d*) it does not then matter if the thing is retained for an innocent purpose."

I think that on a fair interpretation I must treat this decision as being applicable to a case of importing a narcotic. It follows that knowledge that the substance being imported is a narcotic is an essential ingredient of that offence.

As to proof of knowledge, I think the following extract from the speech of Lord Reid in *Warner v. Metropolitan Police Commissioner*, [1969] 2 A.C. 256 at 279-80 (a possession case) is apt and I respectfully adopt it:

> The object of this legislation is to penalise possession of certain drugs. So if mens rea has not been excluded what would be required would be the knowledge of the accused that he had prohibited drugs in his possession: it would be no defence, though it would be a mitigation, that he did not intend that they should be used improperly. And it is a commonplace that, if the accused had a suspicion but deliberately shut his eyes, the court or jury is well entitled to hold him guilty. Further it would be pedantic to hold that it must be shown that the accused

knew precisely which drug he had in his possession. Ignorance of the law is no defence and in fact virtually everyone knows that there are prohibited drugs. So it would be quite sufficient to prove facts from which it could properly be inferred that the accused knew that he had a prohibited drug in his possession. That would not lead to an unreasonable result. In a case like this Parliament, if consulted, might think it right to transfer the onus of proof so that an accused would have to prove that he neither knew nor had any reason to suspect that he had a prohibited drug in his possession. But I am unable to find sufficient grounds for imputing to Parliament an intention to deprive the accused of all right to show that he had no knowledge or reason to suspect that any prohibited drug was in his premises or in a container which was in his possession.

I accordingly agree that it would be correct to instruct a jury that the existence of that knowledge may be inferred as a fact, with due regard to all the circumstances, if the jury finds that the accused has recklessly or wilfully shut his eyes or refrained from inquiry as to the nature of the substance he imports.

I would, therefore, allow the appeal, set the verdict of acquittal aside and order a new trial.

A further appeal to the Supreme Court of Canada was dismissed without reasons, (1972), 4 C.C.C. (2d) 566 (S.C.C.).

R. v. SANDHU

(1989), 50 C.C.C. (3d) 492 (Ont. C.A.)

FINLAYSON J.A.: — This appeal is from convictions for importing heroin into Canada and for possession of heroin for the purposes of trafficking contrary to ss. 5(1) and 4(2) respectively of the *Narcotic Control Act*, R.S.C. 1985, c. N-1.

The two convictions arose from the same facts. On March 1, 1984, the appellant returned to Pearson International Airport from a trip to the Punjab in India. A search of his luggage by customs officials uncovered 93 packets of heroin weighing almost one pound sewn into the lining of two jackets. A search of his wallet revealed a packet containing two grams of heroin.

At trial, after the presiding Judge had made rulings with respect to the search and seizure of the heroin, trial counsel for the appellant formally admitted the following facts before the jury:

(1) that sometime around 7 p.m. on March 1, 1984, Mr. Sandhu arrived at Pearson International Airport on Canadian Pacific flight 215 connecting in Rome, from Alitalia's flight from New Delhi, India.
(2) that his luggage contained two similar green, winter type jackets and a matching pair of green pants, amongst other things.
(3) that discovered sewn under the linings of the jackets were a number of plastic bags containing a white powdery substance.
(4) that discovered in a compartment of Mr. Sandhu's wallet was a small packet containing a similar white powdery substance.

(5) that the powder was analyzed as heroin.

(6) that the powder was weighed and the weight was approximately 447 grams (about one pound).

(7) that if sold in Canada, it would fetch a street price in a range between approximately $120,000 and a million dollars.

There was then but one issue left to the jury and that was the knowledge of the appellant as to the narcotic found in his luggage and on his person.

In addition to the discovery of the heroin itself, the Crown relied upon a number of additional facts to bolster its case. They included the fact that the appellant had both an Indian and a Canadian passport. He presented the former at customs. It showed no previous trips to India whereas the Canadian passport showed two earlier trips. There was evidence of his modest financial circumstances and family obligations which were contrasted to the expense of his trip and the amount of cash in Canadian and American currency that he took to India. He had a receipt in his possession, issued in his name by the Bank of Nova Scotia, for the purchase of seven ounces of gold for $3,403.22. Much emphasis was laid on his movements and demeanour while in the customs area of the airport.

An extensive defence was called but, because of the disposition of this appeal that I propose, I do not think it appropriate to set it out in any detail. Suffice it to say that the appellant testified that while in India to settle up the details of family estate, he had an affair with a widow, one Amarjet Kaur, and became infatuated with her. On leaving for Canada he was persuaded to act as a courier for some gifts of clothing she wanted to give to relatives in Canada. He also entrusted her with his wallet so that she could pay for some drinks at the New Delhi airport prior to departure. Mrs. Kaur testified that the drugs were placed in the appellant's wallet without her knowledge by her paramour, Sucha Singh, upon whom she was dependent. He also gave her the clothing which she put in the appellant's luggage. She was not told by Singh about the heroin in the clothing or the wallet until after the appellant had left. Singh, we are told, was later killed by Indian soldiers in their attack on the Golden Temple.

As to what transpired at Pearson International Airport, the appellant testified that he was totally ignorant of the heroin he was carrying. His evidence of what transpired at customs is very different from that of the customs officers. In particular, he testified that when he was taken into the search room on his arrival in Toronto, the examination of his luggage initially failed to reveal anything. Inspector Donaldson told him he was free to go but he needed to sign some form of acknowledgment that his luggage was being returned intact. Donaldson allowed the appellant to leave the customs area unescorted to look for an English speaking Punjabi who could assist him in executing the acknowledgment. When he could not find anyone, he returned to the search room and it was thereafter that the first jacket was cut into and the heroin found. Donaldson specifically denied that any of this happened.

The most important issue argued before us was the charge on intent as it related to wilful blindness and recklessness, particularly recklessness. The trial Judge instructed the jury as follows:

To prove an intention to import a narcotic, the Crown must prove that Mr. Sandhu had knowledge of the fact that a narcotic was being imported. That narcotic did not necessarily have to be heroin. If, as alleged by Mr. Sandhu, he was unaware that there was a narcotic contained in the jackets in his baggage and/or in his wallet, then the knowledge necessary to constitute the offence of importing would not have been proved.

However, if you are satisfied beyond a reasonable doubt that Mr. Sandhu knew the jackets and wallet in this case contained a narcotic, or if you are satisfied beyond a reasonable doubt that he was wilfully blind whether any of these items contained a narcotic, or was reckless as to whether or not any of these items contained a narcotic, then the knowledge necessary to constitute the offence is established.

Wilful blindness is shutting one's eye to what is taking place. If a party has his suspicions aroused but then deliberately omits to make further enquiries because he wishes to remain in ignorance, he is deemed to have knowledge. It occurs when an accused person deliberately refrains from making enquiries, the results of which he might not choose to have.

The same instruction was given on the charge of possession. On a recharge the trial Judge stated:

You hopefully will remember that in dealing with the aspect of knowledge of the accused, as it relates to both of the counts and the fact that I said that the one issue is knowledge. I said to you: "If you are satisfied beyond a reasonable doubt that Mr. Sandhu knew that the jackets and wallet in this case contained a narcotic" and I mentioned that it did not matter what narcotic it contained, and I continued: "For if you are satified beyond a reasonable doubt that he was wilfully blind whether any of these items contained a narcotic, or was reckless as to whether or not any of these items contained a narcotic then the knowledge necessary to constitute the offence is established". I went on to explain to you what wilful blindness was.

It has been brought to my attention that I did not define for you what recklessness was and I think that I can best do it by stating to you that:

"Wilful blindness is distinct from recklessness because, while recklessness involves knowledge of a danger or risk and persistence in a course of conduct which creates a risk that the prohibited result will occur, wilful blindness arises where a person who has become aware of the need for some inquiry declines to make the inquiry because he does not wish to know the truth. He would prefer to remain ignorant. The culpability in recklessness is justified by consciousness of the risk and by proceeding in the face of it, while in wilful blindness it is justified by the accused's fault in deliberately failing to inquire when he knows there is reason for inquiry."

Now, as I say, I mentioned wilful blindness and recklessness on at least two occasions and possibly more than that, and I want you to know there is a distinction between wilful blindness and recklessness.

(The quotation is from *R. v. Sansregret* (1985), 18 C.C.C. (3d) 223 at p. 235, [1985] 1 S.C.R. 570 (S.C.C.)).

Unfortunately, the way the instruction was given, the jury was left with three bases upon which it could convict: actual knowledge *or* wilful blindness *or* recklessness. The jury was not told that wilful blindness is the equivalent of actual knowledge, but only that it is different from recklessness. Wilful blindness is imputed knowledge while recklessness is quite another thing. To compound the error, the trial Judge, in putting recklessness to the jury, did not instruct them that even if they considered the appellant's belief in what Mrs.

Kaur said and did was unreasonable, it did not follow that the belief was not honestly held.

In my opinion, it is now clear on the authority of *Sansregret, supra,* and *R. v. Zundel* (1987), 31 C.C.C. (3d) 97 (Ont. C.A.), that where an offence requires knowledge on the part of the accused, it is improper to instruct the jury that a finding of recklessness satisfies that requirement. It is an enlargement of the element of intent required by the *Narcotic Control Act* in both importing and possession offences. It is an expansion of the use of "knowingly" in the definition of "possession" in s. 4(3) of the *Criminal Code.*

Counsel for the respondent relied upon *R. v. Blondin* (1970), 2 C.C.C. (2d) 118 (B.C.C.A.); affirmed 4 C.C.C. (2d) 566*n*, [1971] S.C.R. v. (S.C.C.), and *R. v. Aiello* (1978), 38 C.C.C. (2d) 485 (Ont. C.A.), where language similar to that used in the charge in appeal was approved. In both cases, however, there was a strong evidentiary basis for the instruction on wilful blindness. The direction as to recklessness, used, as it was, in the context of wilful blindness, has been overtaken by the reasoning in both *Sansregret* and *Zundel*. Both *Blondin* and *Aiello* were referred to by McIntyre J. in *Sansregret* immediately following the quotation referred to above by the trial Judge. Martin J.A., who delivered the oral judgment in *Aiello*, was a member of the court in *Zundel* which unanimously endorsed McIntyre J.'s statement and enunciated this proposition as to knowledge at p. 157:

> The offence of knowingly publishing false statements under s. 177 of the *Code*, however, requires proof of actual knowledge of the falsity of the statements. Recklessness as to the truth or falsity of the statement is insufficient. Wilful blindness is, of course, the equivalent of actual knowledge.

The Court in *Zundel* went on to quote with approval the words of Ridley J., speaking for the English Court of Criminal Appeal in *R. v. Havard* (1914), 11 C.R. App. R. 2 at p. 3:

> ". . . it is not sufficient to say that if a man is reckless and does not care, he is just as guilty as if he received the property, knowing at the time that there was something wrong with it. We do not agree with that; the proper direction is that the jury must take into consideration all the circumstances in which the goods were received, and must say if the appellant, at the time when he received the goods, knew that they had been stolen."

The instruction to the jury as to recklessness in the case on appeal was particularly damaging in that the entire thrust of the defence was that the appellant was unwittingly duped into becoming a courier. The defence of honest belief was not put to the jury. This reinforces my concern that recklessness would be perceived by the jury as an extension of wilful blindness, which it is not. Recklessness imports an element of negligence into these two narcotic offences which was clearly not intended by the drafters of the *Narcotic Control Act*. The onus is on the Crown to prove knowledge. Recklessness is something less than that.

Appeal allowed; new trial ordered.

For comment see Stuart (1989), 73 C.R. (3d) 162-163.

Was it wise for the Court to exclude recklessness as a satisfactory fault requirement for importing narcotics? It is noteworthy that the *Blondin* decision, allowing that recklessness was sufficient, was seemingly approved by the Supreme Court of Canada in *R. v. Kundeus* (1976), 32 C.R.N.S. 129 (S.C.C.), discussed *infra*, in Chapter Five, Mistake of Fact. *Sandhu* was applied to reverse convictions for possession of stolen goods where the trial judge had said the three bases of knowledge, wilful blindness and recklessness were each sufficient: see *R. v. Anga*, [1991] O.J. No. 3167, (July 9, 1991), Doc. CA 563/89 (Ont. C.A.) and *R. v. Adams*, [1990] O.J. No. 692, 38 O.A.C. 166 (Ont. C.A.).

R. v. Oluwa (1996), 49 C.R. (4th) 40, 107 C.C.C. (3d) 236 (B.C. C.A.), additional reasons at (1996), 110 C.C.C. (3d) 95 (B.C. C.A.), dealt with a case of importing a narcotic. The accused was a passenger flying from Tokyo to Mexico City. He had swallowed drugs for the purposes of smuggling them into another country. On a scheduled but unannounced stopover in Canada the accused was searched and the drugs found. The accused was convicted of importing narcotics into Canada. His appeal was dismissed. The judges were divided. With whom do you agree?

McEACHERN C.J.B.C., with GOLDIE J.A. concurring: —

The *mens rea* of importing had been established. Absent any evidence to the contrary, it was permissible to infer that the accused, an experienced traveller, knew that his flight would make a scheduled stop in Vancouver. If he did not actually know of this stop, he was wilfully blind. His lack of knowledge, if any, resulted from his wilful failure to obtain information which was readily available to him. The accused was, at the very least, reckless in that he was aware of a risk that the plane would land in a place other than his final destination.

Donald J.A., citing *Sandhu*, dissenting: —

The trial judge erred in deeming knowledge on the part of the accused that he was coming to Canada. His intention was to take the narcotics to Mexico. Constructive knowledge has no place in the context of *mens rea*. Actual knowledge of a constituent fact of the offence must be shown or it can be imputed from wilful blindness. Recklessness has no application. Here there was no proof of actual knowledge that the flight would stop in Canada. It had not been established that the accused was essentially aware of upcoming stops and deliberately refrained from making inquiries in order to cheat the administration of justice.

R. v. DUONG

(1998), 15 C.R. (5th) 209, 124 C.C.C. (3d) 392 (Ont. C.A.)

The accused was charged with being an accessory after the fact to a murder committed by one L. Two people were killed in December 1993. There were reports in the newspapers and on television connecting L to the homicides. The accused and L had been friends for five or six years. L called the accused and asked if he could stay at the accused's apartment. L indicated he was in trouble for murder and had no place to go. The accused had seen the media reports of the homicides and knew that L was in trouble. The accused allowed L to hide in his apartment for about two weeks. The police raided the apartment and found L hiding in the bedroom. The accused was specifically asked by the police what L told him about the homicides and he replied that he had told him he was in trouble but that the accused said he didn't want to know anything more because he knew he would be in trouble for helping him hide.

L was charged with two counts of first degree murder and three counts of attempted murder. After a lengthy trial he was convicted of two counts of second degree murder and two counts of attempted murder. The accused was convicted and appealed.

Section 23(1) of the *Criminal Code* provides:

An "accessory after the fact" to an offence is one who, knowing that a person has been a party to the offence, receives, comforts or assists that person for the purpose of enabling that person to escape.

DOHERTY J.A. (CATZMAN and AUSTIN JJ.A. concurring): —

There is little Canadian case law dealing with the knowledge requirement in s. 23(1), perhaps because the language of s. 23(1) is unambiguous. In *R. v. Vinette* (1974), [1975] 2 S.C.R. 222, 19 C.C.C. (2d) 1 (S.C.C.), the accused was charged with being an accessory after the fact to manslaughter. Both the majority (per Pigeon J. at p. 231 S.C.R., p. 7 C.C.C.) and the dissent (per Laskin C.J.C. at pp. 225-26 S.C.R., pp. 2-3 C.C.C.) accepted that the Crown had to prove that an accused charged with being an accessory after the fact to a homicide had knowledge of "the unlawful killing." Similarly, in *R. v. A. (M.)*, released March 22, 1996, this court proceeded on the basis that knowledge of the offence committed by the person aided was an essential element of the charge of being an accessory after the fact. See, also, D. Watt, "Accesssoryship After the Fact: Substantive Procedural and Evidentiary Considerations" (1981), 21 C.R. (3d) 307 at pp. 308, 318-19; V. Rose, *Parties to an Offence* (1982) at pp. 164-66, 194.

In other jurisdictions where provisions like s. 23(1) were in effect, or the common law prevailed, courts required that the Crown prove that the accessory after the fact knew of the specific offence committed by the person assisted: *R. v. Levy*, [1912] 1 K.B. 158 (Eng. Ct. of Crim. App.) at p. 160; *R. v. Tevendale*,

[1955] V.L.R. 95 (Australia Vict. Sup. Ct.); *R. v. Carter* (1990), 47 A. Crim. R. 55 (Queensland C.A.) at p. 63; P. Gillies, *Criminal Law* (1990) at pp. 765-66. For example, in *R. v. Carter, supra,* Carter J. said at p. 63:

> It follows that in this case it was incumbent upon the Crown to establish the fact that the principal offender had done the acts said to constitute the offence of murder, that the accused knew that and, with that knowledge, received or assisted Carter in order to enable him to escape punishment.

The authorities referred to by Crown counsel rely on statutory language which is very different from that found in s. 23(1). These statutes create a more generic offence involving the hindering of an investigation, or interference with the apprehension or conviction of a person. For example, in *R. v. Morgan,* [1972] 1 Q.B. 436 (Eng. C.A.), the relevant statutory provision provided:

> Where a person has committed an arrestable offence, any other person who, *knowing or believing him to be guilty of the offence or of some other arrestable offence,* does without lawful authority or reasonable excuse any act with intent to impede his apprehension or prosecution shall be guilty of an offence. [Emphasis added.]

Parliament could have enacted similar legislation. It has not, however, done so and it is beyond the authority of the courts to enact such legislation by judicial fiat. I am not moved by the Crown's further contention that the requirement that the Crown prove that the accessory had knowledge of the offence committed by the person aided will allow individuals to escape justice when they aid someone believing that person has committed crime "x" when in fact the person has committed crime "y". If that is the effect of the present legislation, it is for Parliament to decide whether the statutory prohibition should be expanded. Moreover, it seems to me that the circumstances posited by the Crown would give rise to a charge of obstructing justice under s. 139(2) of the *Criminal Code.*

A charge laid under s. 23(1) must allege the commission of a specific offence (or offences) and the Crown must prove that the alleged accessory knew that the person assisted was a party to that offence. The Crown will meet its burden if it proves that the accused had actual knowledge of the offence committed. Whether wilful blindness will suffice is addressed below. The further question of whether recklessness as to the offence committed by the principal would be sufficient need not be decided in this case.

The appellant argues that wilful blindness can only be relied on by the Crown if the Crown proves that an accused whose suspicions were aroused had the means available to verify the accuracy of those suspicions. The appellant goes on to contend that he could have turned only to Lam to verify his suspicions and that the record does not suggest that Lam would have admitted his culpability in the murders. It follows, says the appellant, that he did not have the means available to him to verify his suspicions and should not, therefore, be held culpable on the basis of wilful blindness. The appellant cites no authority for this proposition.

Wilful blindness is explained in *Sansregret v. R.*, [1985] 1 S.C.R. 570 at p. 584, 18 C.C.C. (3d) 223 at p. 235:

> . . . wilful blindness arises where a person who has become aware of the need for some inquiry declines to make the inquiry because he does not wish to know the truth. He would prefer to remain ignorant. The culpability in recklessness is justified by consciousness of the risk and by proceeding in the face of it, *while in wilful blindness it is justified by the accused's fault in deliberately failing to inquire when he knows there is reason for inquiry.* [Emphasis added.]

More recently, in *R. v. Hawkins*, [1995] 4 S.C.R. 55 at pp. 110-11, (*sub. nom. R. v. Jorgesen*) 102 C.C.C. (3d) 97 at p. 135, Sopinka J. described wilful blindness in these terms in reference to a charge of selling obscene material:

> . . . *It is well established in criminal law that wilful blindness will also fulfil a mens rea requirement.* If the retailer becomes aware of the need to make further inquiries about the nature of the videos he was selling yet deliberately chooses to ignore these indications and does not make any further inquiries, then the retailer can be nonetheless charged under s. 163(2)(a) for "knowingly" selling obscene materials. *Deliberately choosing not to know something when given reason to believe further inquiry is necessary can satisfy the mental element of the offence. . . .*
>
> A finding of wilful blindness involves an affirmative answer to the question: Did the accused shut his eyes because he knew or strongly suspected that looking would fix him with knowledge? [Emphasis added.]

These authorities make it clear that where the Crown proves the existence of a fact in issue and knowledge of that fact is a component of the fault requirement of the crime charged, wilful blindness as to the existence of that fact is sufficient to establish a culpable state of mind. Liability based on wilful blindness is subjective. Wilful blindness refers to a state of mind which is aptly described as "deliberate ignorance" (Don Stuart, Canadian Criminal Law, 3rd ed. (1995), at p. 209). Actual suspicion, combined with a conscious decision not to make inquiries which could confirm that suspicion, is equated in the eyes of the criminal law with actual knowledge. Both are subjective and both are sufficiently blameworthy to justify the imposition of criminal liability.

The appellant's submission misunderstands the basis upon which liability is imposed where wilful blindness exists. Liability turns on the decision not to inquire once real suspicions arise and not on the hypothetical result of inquiries which were never made. Where an accused chooses to make no inquiries, preferring to remain "deliberately ignorant", speculation as to what the accused would have learned had he chosen to make the necessary inquiries is irrelevant to the determination of the blameworthiness of that accused's state of mind.

The appellant also submits that even if wilful blindness has application in the circumstances of this case, the trial judge erred in finding that the appellant was wilfully blind to the fact that Lam was a party to murder. This is in essence an argument that the trial judge's finding is unreasonable. It was urged that the appellant's statements to the police suggested only that he suspected that Lam had some connection, perhaps as a witness, to the homicides. The appellant submits that a finding of knowledge that Lam was a party to murder based on those statements was more speculation than reasonable inference.

It was certainly open to trial counsel to advance the argument now urged upon this court. I cannot say, however, that the trial judge's rejection of that argument and his conclusion that the appellant's suspicions extended to a suspicion that Lam had been a party to murder was unreasonable. It was open to him to infer that the appellant's statements revealed a state of mind which encompassed the suspicion that Lam was in trouble because he had been a party to murder. The fact that the appellant may have contemplated other possible connections between Lam and the murders afforded no bar to a finding that he was wilfully blind to the fact that Lam was a party to murder.

English Courts have taken a different approach.

R. v. PARKER

[1977] 2 All E.R. 37, 63 Cr. App. R. 211 (C.A.C.D.)

Appeal against conviction.

On February 6, 1976, at St. Alban's Crown Court, the appellant was convicted of criminal damage, was fined £10, ordered to pay £50 towards his legal aid costs and to pay 75p as compensation to the Post Office.

The facts of the case were these. Sometime between midnight and one o'clock in the morning of Saturday, January 11, 1975, two police officers in a police car drove into the forecourt of Baldock Railway Station in Hertfordshire. They saw the appellant in the telephone kiosk which stands outside that railway station and what they said they observed was this. They saw him raise the hand set of that telephone twice to head level and on each occasion bring the hand set down sharply — the words "smashing down" were used at one stage by the officers — on the dialing unit of the telephone.

The hand set and rest on which it should normally be situated were the older type made of some plastic material — probably Bakelite. One of the officers approached the telephone kiosk, opened the door and he saw that part of the telephone rest was broken and some of the pieces were on the floor. He said to the appellant: "What have you done this for?" The reply was: "I'm sorry." It then transpired that what had happened to lead up to this situation was as follows. The appellant had been to some function in London and he had arrived at King's Cross rather later than intended in order to catch a train to Stevenage. It was the last train of the evening. Unfortunately, he fell asleep in the train. Stevenage Station passed while he was still asleep and he did not wake up until Baldock. He then got out of the train and it seems he was charged the excess fare for having travelled beyond his proper destination. He asked if he might use the telephone in the station — that is the station's private telephone, so to speak — and that request was refused but he was given change in order to enable him to use the telephone outside.

For some reason which is not altogether clear, he was unable to get in touch with the taxi service to whom he was endeavouring to telephone. Whether that was because all telephones in Baldock at that stage were in the process of being altered or whether it was because it was an old type of box and he failed to insert coins in the box before he dialled is not altogether clear and it does not matter. The upshot was that quite plainly this man was in a great temper and quite plainly the explanation of the situation was partly his frustration at the series of events which had befallen him that evening and partly in anger at the telephone for failing to operate according to his wishes. The facts to that extent were not greatly in dispute.

What was in dispute was, first of all, whether it was this man who had caused the damage to the telephone receiver — he said it was not he who had caused the damage — and, secondly, the degree of force which he had used when bringing the hand set down on to the receiver. The way in which the appellant himself when giving evidence described the situation was this:

"I went to the telephone box to call a taxi. I put two pence on the slot — not in, but on — I picked up the headset;" (that must have been the hand set), "I heard a tone, I did not know it was necessary to put two pence in before dialling. I dialled two or three times without success. I put the headset down, hard. It did not fit on the cradle so I put it down hard again. I did not lift it before putting it down the first time. I must have missed the cradle the first time. I did not intend to damage it nor was I reckless as to whether I damaged it or not. It did not occur to me that what I was doing might damage it. I was simply reacting to the frustration which I felt. As I put the telephone down hard for the second time there were the police opening the door."

That was the way in which he put it.

The case is reported on the construction of s. 1(1) of the *Criminal Damage Act, 1971.*

. . . .

GEOFFREY LANE L.J.: — On February 6, 1976, at St. Alban's Crown Court, the applicant was convicted of criminal damage. He was fined £10 payable within seven days with 14 days' imprisonment in default. He was ordered to pay £50 towards his legal aid costs and 75p as compensation to the Post Office.

The application was out of time but this Court has given leave, nevertheless, for the application to be made and, now, with the agreement of Mr. Tager who appears on behalf of the applicant, we propose to grant the application for leave to appeal and to treat this hearing as the appeal.

[The learned Lord Justice stated the facts and continued:]

The complaint made by Mr. Tager on behalf of the appellant is that the learned Judge misdirected the jury in regard to the necessary mental element upon which the jury had to be satisfied before convicting. The section of the Act in question reads as follows. Section 1(1) of the *Criminal Damage Act, 1971* reads: "A person who, without lawful excuse, destroys or damages any property belonging to another intending to destroy or damage any such property or being reckless as to whether any such property would be destroyed or damaged shall be guilty of an offence." Mr. Tager complains that the directions given by the learned Judge to the jury on the meaning of the word "reckless" were incorrect directions and that they invalidate the summing-up and make the conviction unsafe or unsatisfactory.

This is the way in which the learned Judge dealt with the matter. There are, I should say in anticipation, two passages in the summing-up where the learned Judge deals with this definition. The first in the main body of the direction and the second when the jury came back and asked for further clarification about the meaning of the word "reckless." This is how the learned Judge dealt with the matter on the first occasion:

> Intentionally — I do not think needs any further explanation. You either do something intentionally or you do it accidentally. Recklessly — perhaps does need a word or two. It simply means in a frame of mind in which the consequences of an act deliberately done are ones which the doer of the act does not care about. If I can just put an example. If in the middle of a courtyard you throw a stone, that, if there are windows in the buildings round the courtyard, would be a reckless thing to do, would it not, because none of us are so accurate at stone throwing that we would miss a window and if we struck a window it would almost certainly be damaged. That is an example of the sort of thing that would be described as a reckless act.
>
> Here, what the prosecution say is that banging the telephone hand set down on the telephone instrument itself with the kind of force which appears from the evidence to have been used here was such an act. It was the act of a man who did not care whether or not damage resulted from what he did in the circumstances in which damage was likely.

Pausing there for a moment, Mr. Tager initially accepted that the final sentence was an accurate direction. On reflection, he withdrew that concession and he withdrew it because, he said, the learned Judge is there applying an objective test in order to determine recklessness or no and Mr. Tager says that the test is not an objective one but a subjective test as to what the defendant actually believed or knew. The further direction given, in answer to the jury's question: "Could we please have a further definition of what a reckless act is?", was as follows:

> Members of the jury, it is not an easy thing to formulate but I think I can put it in this way. A reckless act is an act done without thought for the consequence of it. In this context it is an act done without thought for the question of whether or not the telephone might suffer damage as a result of the doing of it. I do not think I can define it more closely or more clearly than that. That is the best definition that I can give you and I hope you find it helpful in your deliberations.

Mr. Tager complains that that passage is an even clearer example of the application of an objective rather than a subjective test. He draws support from a decision of this Court, that of *Briggs* [[1977] 1 W.L.R. 605 (C.A.)]. It was a case where the facts were very different from those in the instant case. In the course of the judgment the following passage is to be found:

A man is reckless in the sense required, [and that is dealing, of course, with the same section of the same statute], when he carries out a deliberate act knowing that there is some risk of damage resulting from that act, but nevertheless continues in the performance of that act. That being so, it is clear from the three passages to which I have in particular referred that the learned Judge did not give a correct direction to the jury on this aspect of the case. Using the words which he did, he might have cured the defect by explaining to the jury in clear terms that the test to be applied was the test of the state of this defendant's mind, but he did not put that anywhere in his summing-up.

We are bound by that decision, and, indeed, at least so far as the first sentence which I have read is concerned, we would not for one moment wish to disagree even if we were able to do so. The test is the test of the defendant's state of mind. But, and in the facts of the instant case it is a substantial "but," the circumstances of this case are that the appellant was plainly fully aware of all the circumstances of the case. He was fully aware that what he was handling was a telephone hand set made of Bakelite or some such material. He was well aware that the cradle on to which he admittedly brought down the hand set was made of similar material. He was well aware, of course, of the degree of force which he was using — a degree described by Mr. Tager before us as slamming the receiver down and a demonstration by Mr. Tager, whether wittingly or not, was given of a hand brought down from head-height on to whatever the receiving object was.

In those circumstances, it seems to this Court that if he did not know, as he said he did not, that there was some risk of damage, he was, in effect, deliberately closing his mind to the obvious — the obvious being that damage in these circumstances was inevitable.

In the view of this Court, that type of action, that type of deliberate closing of that mind, is the equivalent of knowledge and a man certainly cannot escape the consequences of his action in this particular set of circumstances by saying, "I never directed my mind to the obvious consequences because I was in a self-induced state of temper."

We, accordingly, do not differ from the views expressed in *Briggs* [above, at 215 (Cr. App. R.)] with the exception of adding to the definition these words: "A man is reckless in the sense required when he carries out a deliberate act knowing or closing his mind to the obvious fact that there is some risk of damage resulting from that act but nevertheless continuing in the performance of that act."

That being the way in which we consider the question of recklessness under this statute should be approached, the question remains whether the learned Judge at St. Albans Crown Court in his direction to the jury sufficiently and clearly made out to them what it was they had to determine. We think that he did. Certainly so far as the first passage was concerned to which reference has already been made, in the context of the case with which he was dealing, the direction that he gave to the jury was adequate.

So far as the second passage was concerned, that is the direction he gave to the jury in answer to their further question, when one reads that once again against the background of this case, against the fact that the defendant's prime defence was that he did not commit the damage at all and against the background of fact that the defendant knew of the circumstances which surrounded his act (and quite plainly had he directed his mind to the matter must have realised the likelihood, if not the inevitability of damage) we consider in the end that his direction has produced neither an unsafe nor unsatisfactory result and consequently we dismiss this appeal.

SCARMAN L.J.: — The Court was disturbed, in the course of the argument, by what you told us as to the possible attitude of the professional body which governs Mr. Parker's professional life and, as president of the Court, I wish to be on public record that we see in the facts of this case no reflection upon the integrity or honesty of Mr. Parker and that there is nothing here which would lead this Court to think that he is unfitted for his profession. We hope that these observations will be drawn to the attention of the professional body.

Appeal dismissed.

R. v. CALDWELL

[1981] 1 All E.R. 961 (H.L.)

The majority opinion was delivered by Lord Diplock:

LORD DIPLOCK: — My Lords, the facts that gave rise to this appeal are simple. The respondent had been doing work for the proprietor of a residential hotel. He considered that he had a grievance against the proprietor. One night he got very drunk and in the early hours of the morning he decided to revenge himself on the proprietor by setting fire to the hotel, in which some ten guests were living at the time. He broke a window and succeeded in starting a fire in a ground room floor; but fortunately it was discovered and the flames were extinguished before any serious damage was caused. At his trial he said that he was so drunk at the time that the thought that there might be people in the hotel whose lives might be endangered if it were set on fire had never crossed his mind.

He was indicted at the Central Criminal Court on two counts of arson under s. 1(1) and (2) respectively of the *Criminal Damage Act 1971*. That section reads as follows:

> (1) A person who without lawful excuse destroys or damages any property belonging to another intending to destroy or damage any such property or being reckless as to whether any such property would be destroyed or damaged shall be guilty of an offence.
> (2) A person who without lawful excuse destroys or damages any property, whether belonging to himself or another — (*a*) intending to destroy or damage any property or being reckless as to whether any property would be destroyed or damaged; and (*b*) intending by the destruction or damage to endanger the life of another or being reckless as to whether the life of another would be thereby endangered; shall be guilty of an offence.

(3) An offence committed under this section by destroying or damaging property by fire shall be charged as arson.

The respondent had pleaded not guilty to the more serious offence under subs. 2 relying on his drunkenness as negating the requisite mental state. The House of Lords concluded that the recorder was right in telling the jury that in deciding whether the respondent was reckless whether the lives of residents in the hotel would be endangered, the fact that, because of his drunkenness, he failed to give any thought to that risk was irrelevant. The question certified for the opinion of the House in this case called for their analysis of the meaning of the term reckless:

When cases under s. 1(1) of the new Act, in which the Crown's case was based on the accused having been "reckless as to whether . . . property would be destroyed or damaged", first came before the Court of Appeal, the question as to the meaning of the expression "reckless" in the context of that subsection appears to have been treated as soluble simply by posing and answering what had by then, unfortunately, become an obsessive question among English lawyers: is the test of recklessness subjective or objective? The first two reported cases, in both of which judgments were given off the cuff, are *R. v. Briggs*, [1977] 1 All E.R. 475 and *R. v. Parker*, [1977] 2 All E.R. 37. Both classified the test of recklessness as subjective. This led the Court in *R. v. Briggs*, [1977] 1 All E.R. 475 at 477-478 to say: "A man is reckless in the sense required when he carries out a deliberate act knowing that there is some risk of damage resulting from that act but nevertheless continues in the performance of that act." This leaves over the question whether the risk of damage may not be so slight that even the most prudent of men would feel justified in taking it, but it excludes that kind of recklessness that consists of acting without giving any thought at all to whether or not there is any risk of harmful consequences of one's act, even though the risk is great and would be obvious if any thought were given to the matter by the doer of the act. *R. v. Parker*, however, opened the door a chink by adding as an alternative to the actual knowledge of the accused that there is some risk of damage resulting from his act and his going on to take it, a mental state described as "closing his mind to the obvious fact" that there is such a risk (see [1977] 2 All E.R. 37 at 40).

R. v. Stephenson, [1979] 2 All E.R. 1198, [1979] Q.B. 695, the first case in which there was full argument, though only on one side, and a reserved judgment, slammed the door again on any less restricted interpretation of "reckless" whether particular consequences will occur than that originally approved in *Briggs*. The appellant, a tramp, intending to pass the night in a hollow in the side of a haystack, had lit a fire to keep himself warm; as a result of this the stack itself caught fire. At his trial, he was not himself called as a witness but a psychiatrist gave evidence on his behalf that he was schizophrenic and might not have had the same ability to foresee or appreciate risk as a mentally normal person. The Judge had given to the jury the direction on the meaning of reckless that had been approved in *R. v. Parker*. The argument for the appellant on the appeal was that this let in an objective test whereas the test should be entirely subjective. It was buttressed by copious citation from previous judgments in civil and criminal cases where the expressions "reckless" or "recklessness" had been used by Judges in various contexts. Counsel for the Crown expressed his agreement with the submissions for the appellant. The judgment of the Court contains an analysis of a number of the cited cases, mainly in the field of civil law. These cases do not disclose a uniform judicial use of the terms; and as respects judicial statements made before the current vogue for classifying all tests of legal liability as either objective or subjective they are not easily assignable to one of those categories rather than the other.

· · · ·

"Reckless" as used in the new statutory definition of the *mens rea* of these offences is an ordinary English word. It had not by 1971 become a term of legal art with some more limited esoteric meaning than that which it bore in ordinary speech, a meaning which surely includes not only deciding to ignore a risk of harmful consequences resulting from one's acts that one has recognised as existing, but also failing to give any thought to whether or not there is any such risk in circumstances where, if any thought were given to the matter, it would be obvious that there was.

If one is attaching labels, the latter state of mind is neither more nor less "subjective" than the first. But the label solves nothing. It is a statement of the obvious; *mens rea* is, by definition, a state of mind of the accused himself at the time he did the physical act that constitutes the *actus reus* of the offence; it cannot be the mental state of some non-existent, hypothetical person.

Nevertheless, to decide whether someone has been "reckless" whether harmful consequences of a particular kind will result from his act, as distinguished from his actually intending such harmful consequences to follow, does call for some consideration of how the mind of the ordinary prudent individual would have reacted to a similar situation. If there were nothing in the circumstances that ought to have drawn the attention of an ordinary prudent individual to the possibility of that kind of harmful consequence, the accused would not be described as "reckless" in the natural meaning of that word for failing to address his mind to the possibility; nor, if the risk of the harmful consequences was so slight that the ordinary prudent individual on due consideration of the risk would not be deterred from treating it as negligible, could the accused be described as "reckless" in its ordinary sense if, having considered the risk, he decided to ignore it. (In this connection the gravity of the possible harmful consequences would be an important factor. To endanger life must be one of the most grave.) So to this extent, even if one ascribes to "reckless" only the restricted meaning, adopted by the Court of Appeal in *Stephenson* and *Briggs*, of foreseeing that a particular kind of harm might happen and yet going on to take the risk of it, it involves a test that would be described in part as "objective" in current legal jargon. Questions of criminal liability are seldom solved by simply asking whether the test is subjective or objective.

In my opinion, a person charged with an offence under s. 1(1) of the 1971 Act is "reckless as to whether or not any property would be destroyed or damaged" if (1) he does an act which in fact creates an obvious risk that property will be destroyed or damaged and (2) when he does the act he either has not given any thought to the possibility of there being any such risk or has recognised that there was some risk involved and has none the less gone on to do it. That would be a proper direction to the jury; cases in the Court of Appeal which held otherwise should be regarded as overruled.

Where the charge is under s. 1(2) the question of the state of mind of the accused must be approached in stages, corresponding to paras. (*a*) and (*b*). The jury must be satisfied that what the accused did amounted to an offence under s. 1(1), either because he actually intended to destroy or damage the property or because he was reckless (in the sense that I have described) whether it might be destroyed or damaged. Only if they are so satisfied must the jury go on to consider whether the accused also either actually intended that the destruction or damage of the property should endanger someone's life or was reckless (in a similar sense) whether a human life might be endangered.

Lord Edmund-Davies (dissenting): —

I have to say that I am in respectful, but profound, disagreement. The law in action compiles its own dictionary. In time, what was originally the common coinage of speech acquires a different value in the pocket of the lawyer than when in the layman's purse. Professor Kenny used lawyers' words in a lawyers' sense to express his distillation of an important part of the established law relating to *mens rea*, and he did so in a manner accurate not only in respect of the law as it stood in 1902 but also as it has been applied in countless cases ever since, both in the United Kingdom and in other countries where the common law prevails: see, for example, in Western Australia, *Lederer v. Hitchins*, [1961] W.A.R. 99, and, in the United States of America, Jethro Brown's *General Principles of Criminal Law* (2nd Ed., 1960, p. 115). And it is well-known that the 1971 Act was in the main the work of the Law Commission, who defined recklessness by saying:

> A person is reckless if, (a) knowing that there is a risk that an event may result from his conduct or that a circumstances may exist, he takes that risk, and (b) it is unreasonable for him to take it, having regard to the degree and nature of the risk which he knows to be present.

(See Working Paper no. 31, Codification of the Criminal Law: General Principles: The Mental Element in Crime (16th June 1970).)

It was surely with this contemporaneous definition and the much respected decision of *R. v. Cunningham* in mind that the draftsman proceeded to his task of drafting the 1971 Act.

It has therefore to be said that, unlike negligence, which has to be judged objectively, recklessness involves foresight of consequences, combined with an objective judgment of the reasonableness of the risk taken. And recklessness in vacuo is an incomprehensible notion. It *must* relate to foresight of risk of the particular kind relevant to the charge preferred, which, for the purpose of s. 1(2), is the risk of endangering life and nothing other than that.

So, if a defendant says of a particular risk, "It never crossed my mind", a jury could not on those words alone properly convict him of recklessness simply because they considered that the risk *ought* to have crossed his mind, though his words might well lead to a finding of negligence. But a defendant's admission that he "closed his mind" to a particular risk could prove fatal, for "A person cannot, in any intelligible meaning of the words, close his mind to a risk unless he first realises that there is a risk; and if he realises that there is a risk, that is the end of the matter" (see Glanville Williams, *Textbook of Criminal Law* (1st Ed., 1978, p. 79)).

The *Caldwell* decision led two prominent English scholars to virulent criticism of this abandoning of the subjective awareness approach. They have pointed to a wealth of contrary authority, academic writings and recommendations of various law reform bodies. The strength of their concern is shown in their extraordinary joint call for the abolition of criminal appeals to the House of Lords, contained in a commentary in and a letter to the 1981 *Criminal Law Review* in part as follows:

Professor J.C. Smith (at 392):

The House of Lords has a dismal record in criminal cases. All too often their Lordships' decisions have to be reversed by legislation. *D.P.P. v. Smith* [1961] A.C. 290; *D.P.P. v. Sykes* [1962] A.C. 528; *D.P.P. v. Turner* [1974] A.C. 357, *Haughton v. Smith* [1975] A.C. 476 and *D.P.P. v. Nock* (see the Criminal Attempts Bill 1981) are obvious examples. The present decision could well be another, for it plainly defeats the intention of the Law Commission which was responsible for the drafting of the legislation and whose recommendations were accepted by Parliament; and it conflicts with the proposals of the Criminal Law Revision Committee in their report on the law of offences against the person. It sets back the law concerning the mental element in criminal damage, in theory to before 1861, and in practice probably to before Kenny formulated the law in the first edition of his *Outlines of Criminal Law* in 1902 and certainly to before the decision in *Cunningham* in 1957 ([1957] 2 Q.B. 396). Can we really afford the House of Lords as an appellate criminal Court? It has been frequently split three to two, in recent years and the fate of English criminal law depends on the chance of who happens to be sitting in the particular case. In the present case the opinion of two English and one Scottish Law Lords prevails not only over the weighty dissent of Lords Wilberforce and Edmund-Davies but also over the substantial body of judicial opinion in the cases of *Briggs*, *Stephenson*, and other cases in the Court of Appeal and the Divisional Court.

Professor Glanville Williams (at 581-82):

The further reflection prompted by the two cases is the extremely variable quality of the contribution made by the House of Lords to the development of a rational criminal law. Sometimes we are greatly indebted to their lordships, as we were for the decisions in *Sweet v. Parsley* [1970] A.C. 132 (though that did not make good all the damage done by *Warner* [1969] 2 A.C. 256); *Withers* [1975] A.C. 842; *Morgan* [1976] A.C. 182 (though the opinions in that case contained regrettable reservations), and *Camplin* [1978] A.C. 705. Against them must be set the bad reasoning in such cases as *D.P.P. v. Smith* [1961] A.C. 290 (reversed by a statute to which their majority lordships in the instant cases pay no attention), *Hyam* [1975] A.C. 55 (to be reversed if the latest report of the C.L.R.C. is put into effect), *Roger Smith* [1975] A.C. 476 (to be reversed in the forthcoming Criminal Attempts Act), *Charles* [1977] A.C. 177 (audaciously distinguished in *Lambie* [1981] 1 W.L.R. 78), *Majewski* [1977] A.C. 443 (perhaps right in policy but horrible in the means by which the policy was achieved), and now these two latest additions to the deplorable list. As Professor Smith points out, it is nice question whether, with this sort of balance-sheet, the appellate jurisdiction of the House of Lords in criminal cases is worth the expense to the community. It may be conceded that the House of Lords intended in the present two cases to change the law (as it thought) for the better, but even on the assumption that the enterprise was well undertaken, it is astonishing that their lordships failed to make a better job of drafting the new rule.

It would, to my mind, be a great improvement in our arrangements if the judicial strength of the Appellate Committee were used to augment the Court of Appeal on the criminal and civil sides, thus relieving the pressure on that Court and enabling it to hear more important cases at leisure with a Court of five. The objections to the House of Lords as a second appellate Court do not rest only on the fact that a double appeal is an unnecessary burden on litigants and the public purse. In the nature of things the average age of law lords is higher than that of members of the Court of Appeal. We all gain in wisdom from experience, but old men tend to be self-opinionated in two senses: they are often fixed in their opinions, and they tend to ignore the opinions of others. The latter tendency is particularly evident in the majority opinion in *Caldwell*, which, as Professor Smith points out, brushes aside the considerable body of opinion and argument in favour of the subjective definition of recklessness.

Another drawback to the House of Lords as an appellate Court is the breadth of its jurisdiction. Few lawyers, even the most competent, would care to be asked for opinions of momentous consequence on an absolutely unlimited range of legal problems. It is particularly inapt that a Chancery Judge should have the casting vote in the House of Lords in a criminal case, as Lord Cross did in *Hyam* [1975] A.C. 55.

All Judges fall into error from time to time, but, whatever the theory of precedent may say, the Court of Appeal is slightly better at correcting its mistakes than the House of Lords, about whose pronouncements there is an awful finality. Witness, for example, their lordships' refusal in *Nock* [1978] A.C. 979 to resile from their indefensible decision in *Roger Smith*. The assumption of almost papal infallibility is peculiar to the House of Lords. Quite apart from this, the Court of Appeal has far greater opportunity of correcting itself than the House of Lords, which hears comparatively few appeals, and is least likely to hear an appeal when the appeal seeks to question a decision of their lordships.

---

(2) Objective Crimes

The *Criminal Code* has long contained a wide variety of offences which expressly adopt an objective standard such as "ought to", "reasonable care", "good reason", "reasonable ground", "reasonably expected" or "reasonable steps". Such offences included, until declared unconstitutional by the Supreme Court, unlawful object murder. The current list includes the doctrine of common intent for accessories, s. 21(2), dangerous driving, s. 249(1)(a), careless use of firearms or ammunition, s. 86(2), and a strange assortment of other offences including alarming Her Majesty, s. 49(b), counselling another to be a party to an offence, s. 22(2), treason, s. 46(2)(b), forcible entry, s. 72(1), forcible detainer, s. 72(2), endangering aircraft safety, s. 77, failure to use reasonable care to prevent injury from an explosive substance, ss. 79-80, personating an officer, s. 130(b), importing gambling information, s. 202(g), abandoning a child, s. 218, not safeguarding an ice hole, s. 263(1), taking an unseaworthy ship to sea, s. 251, bigamy as a result of a mistaken and unreasonable belief that a spouse is dead, s. 290, publishing defamatory material, s. 303 and criminal breach of trust, s. 422. Another important recent example is Parliament's declaration that there can be no mistaken belief in consent defence to a sexual assault charge unless reasonable steps were taken: see below Chapter 4 "Rape and Sexual Assault". The anomalous list of offences clearly indicates a haphazard approach.

Sometimes our Courts have resorted to an objective standard for a *Criminal Code* offence where such an approach is not expressly required. This has long been the approach for unlawful act manslaughter, discussed *infra*, and also respecting offences requiring "criminal negligence". The jurisprudence respecting the latter has been conflicting and complex and requires separate treatment.

Criminal Negligence

The *Criminal Code* provides:

S. 219.(1) Every one is criminally negligent who
  (*a*) in doing anything, or
  (*b*) in omitting to do anything that it is his duty to do,
shows wanton or reckless disregard for the lives or safety of other persons.
(2) For the purposes of this section, "duty" means a duty imposed by law.

220. Every person who by criminal negligence causes death to another person is guilty of an indictable offence and liable
  (*a*) where a firearm is used in the commission of the offence, to imprisonment for life and to a minimum punishment of imprisonment for a term of four years; and
  (*b*) in any other case, to imprisonment for life.

221. Every one who by criminal negligence causes bodily harm to another person is guilty of an indictable offence and liable to imprisonment for a term not exceeding ten years.

222.(1) A person commits homicide when, directly or indirectly, by any means, he causes the death of a human being.
(2) Homicide is culpable or not culpable.
(3) Homicide that is not culpable is not an offence.
(4) Culpable homicide is murder or manslaughter or infanticide.
(5) A person commits culpable homicide when he causes the death of a human being,
  (*a*) by means of an unlawful act;
  (*b*) by criminal negligence;
  (*c*) by causing that human being, by threats or fear of violence or by deception, to do anything that causes his death; or
  (*d*) by wilfully frightening that human being, in the case of a child or sick person.

. . . .

234. Culpable homicide that is not murder or infanticide is manslaughter.

. . . .

236. Every person who commits manslaughter is guilty of an indictable offence and liable
  (*a*)   where a firearm is used in the commission of the offence, to imprisonment for life and to a minimum punishment of imprisonment for a term of four years; and
  (*b*)   in any other case, to imprisonment for life.

O'GRADY v. SPARLING

[1960] S.C.R. 804, 33 C.R. 293, 128 C.C.C. 1, at 808 (S.C.R.)

The appellant, charged with careless driving contrary to provincial legislation, argued that such legislation was inoperative as being in relation to criminal law and also because Parliament had occupied the field by its enactment (s. 233(1) of the *Criminal Code*, repealed in 1985) proscribing criminally negligent driving. For the majority, Judson J. dismissed the appeal, in part on the basis that criminal negligence according to what is now s. 219 of the *Criminal Code* is a form of recklessness which connotes advertence. The Court adopted the following passage from Kenny's *Outlines of Criminal Law*, 17th ed.:

> The difference between recklessness and negligence is the difference between advertence and inadvertence; they are opposed and it is a logical fallacy to suggest that recklessness is a degree of negligence. The common habit of lawyers to qualify the word "negligence" with some moral epithet such as "wicked", "gross", or "culpable" has been most unfortunate since it has inevitably led to great confusion of thought and of principle.

There was, however, an overwhelming tendency for provincial Courts to ignore *O'Grady* in adopting an objective standard for criminal negligence under s. 219. Many, however, assert a requirement of a gross departure from the objective norm.

R. v. TITCHNER

(1961), 35 C.R. 111, 131 C.C.C. 64 (Ont. C.A.)

MORDEN J.A.: — The accused was convicted on February 16, 1961, after trial at Woodstock before Landreville J. and a jury, of causing the death of Erika Jeske by criminal negligence in the operation of a motor vehicle. This Court heard her appeal from this conviction on April 19th and 20th and at the conclusion of the argument, allowed the appeal, quashed the conviction and ordered a new trial for the reasons which I am now delivering.

The appellant was driving an Oldsmobile car in an easterly direction on Provincial Highway 401 in the vicinity of Ingersoll at about 5 p.m. on September 21, 1960. The speed limit on this controlled access highway was 60 m.p.h. The deceased was driving a Mercedes-Benz car in the same direction. Prior to the accident, the appellant passed in the proper lane three other motor cars and while doing this, according to her evidence, she could have been travelling at 75 m.p.h. She then swung into the driving lane and began closing up on the Jeske car at which time she estimated her speed at about 70 m.p.h. and that of the Jeske car at 65 m.p.h. The appellant testified that when she was about three car lengths behind the Jeske car and was beginning to edge out towards the passing lane, the Jeske car started to move to the left "and then I saw her brake lights and the car seemed to slow down very quickly, so I slammed on my brakes, and I started skidding and I tried to swing around her, and instead of swinging around her, I guess I side-swiped it". The collision was violent and resulted in the death of Mrs. Jeske.

The several grounds of appeal argued before us related mainly to the learned trial Judge's charge. The first ground was that the trial Judge failed to instruct the jury properly upon what constitutes criminal negligence. In the course of his charge he read ss. 191 and 192 [now ss. 202 and 203] of the *Criminal Code*, 1953-54 (Can.), c. 51, and then proceeded to describe the type of negligence which found civil liability. He then told the jury that criminal negligence was a "higher type" and recalled to them the words "wanton" and "reckless" appearing in s. 191 and went on to say:

> In other words, it has been said that the negligence in a case to be such as to be under the *Criminal Code*, must be of a shocking character. It is shocking, and is so unexplainable and unreasonable and careless, utter carelessness, blank negligence, that is or has acquired a character of criminality.

After reading several pertinent sections of the *Highway Traffic Act*, R.S.O. 1950, c. 167 [now R.S.O. 1960, c. 172] and referring to the speed limit, he said:

> These laws and rules of the road are of importance, but I must tell you, that even if a person infringes or breaks one of these rules of the road, it does not mean automatically that it will make him liable or responsible for the crime or the offence alleged, because there must be the connection between these infractions of the law — of that rule of the road, or the law with the ultimate act complained of.

By way of illustration he pointed out that a failure to renew a driver's licence would not in itself found criminal or civil liability for an accident because there would be no causal connection in law between that breach of the Act and the accident. The learned trial Judge correctly drew to the jury's attention several sections of the Act and mentioned the speed limit. In the circumstances of this case, these sections did define the appellant's duty. But in my respectful opinion the jury at the end of the charge may very well have thought that if they found that the appellant was in breach of any of the pertinent sections of the Act, and there was no doubt that she was exceeding the speed limit, and that there was a causal connection between those infractions of the Act and the fatal collision, they could find her guilty of criminal negligence. In my view, this amounted to misdirection and I am unable to say that it was cured by the learned trial Judge's recharge. An accused's breach of duty whether imposed by statute or common law, which causes injury, is not by itself alone enough to found criminal liability.

Section 191 was first enacted by the new *Code* but has not changed the law. I agree with the following statement of Clinton J. Ford C.J.A. in *R. v. Savard* (1957), 119 Can. C.C. 92 at p. 93:

> It is evident that the new definition of criminal negligence if not derived from, is in accord with the leading decisions of *Andrews v. Director of Public Prosecutions*, [1937] A.C. 576; *R. v. Greisman*, 46 Can. C.C. 172; *R. v. Bateman* (1925), 19 Cr. App. R. 8 and others. In deciding if conduct in a case reaches the degree or is the kind of negligence to be criminal within the meaning of the definition, reference may usefully be made to what has been said in these decisions.

A Judge in explaining to a jury the meaning of criminal negligence would, of course, begin with s. 191. He would then in formulating a fuller explanation derive much help from the cases mentioned above. In *R. v. Bateman*, Lord Hewart C.J. said at pp. 11-12:

> In explaining to juries the test which they should apply to determine whether the negligence, in the particular case, amounted or did not amount to a crime, Judges have used many epithets, such as "culpable," "criminal," "gross," "wicked," "clear," "complete." But,

whatever epithet be used and whether an epithet be used or not, in order to establish criminal liability the facts must be such that, in the opinion of the jury, the negligence of the accused went beyond a mere matter of compensation between subjects and showed such disregard for the life and safety of others as to amount to a crime against the State and conduct deserving punishment.

In *Greisman*, Middleton J.A. used this language at pp. 177-8 Can. C.C.:

> I think the great weight of authority goes to show that there will be no criminal liability unless there is gross negligence, or wanton misconduct. To constitute crime there must be a certain moral quality carried into the act before it becomes culpable. In each case it is a question of fact, and it is the duty of the Court [the jury] to ascertain if there was such wanton and reckless negligence as in the eye of the law merits punishment. This may be found where a general intention to disregard the law is shown, or a reckless disregard of the rights of others.

I do not suggest that a trial Judge should read to the jury the extracts I have quoted. To the legal mind, they convey the elements essential to constitute a particular act or omission "criminal negligence". The very words "criminal negligence" may lead a jury to think that only a difference of degree distinguishes criminal from civil negligence. But as Middleton J.A. pointed out criminal negligence connotes a difference in quality as well as a difference in degree. ("A certain moral quality must be carried into the act.") The accused's state of mind immediately antecedent to or contemporaneous with his act or omission must be considered and, of course, this may be inferred from the conduct of the accused and the other circumstances. Before a jury can properly return a verdict of guilty, they should be satisfied beyond a reasonable doubt that the accused acted either (a) with the deliberate intention of doing or omitting to do something which it was his duty to do, the consequences of which he knew or should have known would endanger the lives or safety of others or (b) with such disregard for the lives and safety of others as would indicate that he was heedless of what the consequences of his conduct might be.

Appeal allowed;
new trial ordered.

R. v. ROGERS

4 C.R.N.S. 303, [1968] 4 C.C.C. 278 (B.C. C.A.)

NEMETZ J.A.: — After a lengthy trial at the Vancouver Assizes before Macdonald J. sitting with a jury, the accused, Dr. Everly Eldon Rogers, was found guilty of causing the death, by criminal negligence, of Leonidas Demosten, a child of about two years of age.

The following facts emerge from the evidence. The accused obtained the medical degrees of M.D. and C.M. from McGill University in 1917. At one time he was licensed to practise. He was, however, struck from the rolls of the

College of Physicians and Surgeons of this province in 1960. He also registered under The *Naturopathic Physicians Act*, R.S.B.C. 1960, c. 264, and practised "naturopathy" which is defined *inter alia* in that Act as "the art of healing by natural methods or therapeutics". In July 1967 he ceased to be a member of the Naturopathic Association since, as the accused explained it, he should not have been admitted because he had not studied at the Naturopathic School. On the door of his office, and on the diet instruction pamphlet he distributed, (ex. 1 at the trial) were inscribed the words "E.E. Rogers, M.D., C.M."

The child, Leonidas, had at age four months contracted chicken pox after which he had a continuing case of eczema. By June 1965 the child was hospitalized and treated for over two months by specialists who diagnosed the skin condition as exfoliative dermatitis. At this time the child was small but his weight and blood count were normal for his age and his kidneys functioned adequately. He had sufficient proteins to combat infection since he was then on a normal protein diet. The child was discharged from hospital on 29th August, 1965. At this time his skin condition had improved, although the skin was not completely clear. He weighed 20 pounds, a little underweight for a one year old child, but he was eating well, was not allergic to milk and could walk and run. On 17th April, 1966, the boy's skin condition had deteriorated somewhat from that obtaining in August 1965, but according to Dr. Yamanaka, the boy's doctor from the onset of the skin disease, the boy was otherwise physically quite well. His weight was 22 pounds, still somewhat underweight, but apart from the dermatitis he was a normal appearing child. Dr. Yamanaka said that the child's scrotum was not swelling.

Rogers testified as to the condition of the boy when he first saw him on or about 22nd April, 1966. His testimony is in conflict with that of Dr. Yamanaka. Rogers said that the skin condition was the colour of boiled lobster, crust over all of the body, the scrotum and glands of the groin enlarged. After examining the child, Rogers gave the father a pamphlet which contained a diet (ex. 1) which he prescribed for the child. It is an instructive document also setting out in part his own medical theories and was before the jury. I quote a portion of the document:

> FOODS YOU MAY HAVE (subject to individual instruction). All food is raw at first, with one exception, and the principal foods, "the staff of life", are the non-starchy or 10 to 15% vegetables. The foods we usually commence with are: carrots, celery, parsley, cabbage. These should be the basis of all salads, and are always available. In addition, any of the following, some of which are not always available, and some are seasonal: cress, either pepper grass or watercress, green pepper, green onions, radish, beets, turnips; a little garlic if one likes it; also cucumbers on the same basis; and if they do not cause gas. All these vegetables are used raw; cut, shredded or grated as required. One may also use home grown leaf lettuce, but not commercial head lettuce; also endive and romaine in season. One does not try to use all the above, but uses the first four, then one or two of the others according to availability, and for a change. There is no advantage in eating a lot, or more than one wants, and if one has no appetite for the above foods, he eats no food until he is hungry. He can NOT, at first substitute cooked or more appetizing foods.
>
> With the salad one has one half grapefruit, or if real grapefruit is not available, four ounces (no more) unsweetened grapefruit juice. Large amounts of juices must not be used. Also with the salad one may have one baked or one canned tomato (not tomato juice).

On the salad, for dressing, use sea salt, paprika, a little cayenne pepper, one teaspoonful of oil (olive, sunflower, peanut or soya), and a sprinkling of lemon juice.

The above constitute the entire meal, and nothing else must be used, but any item may be omitted. . . .

Everything will be fully explained to the co-operative patient; and do not forget: the first stage (this one) is the removal of poisons, which is usually accompanied by loss of weight and strength. Do not be alarmed. This first stage, or laying the foundation, is absolutely necessary, and health cannot be achieved without this stage. Weight and strength return after the poisons have been removed, and this is the start of the second stage — the building of health. Further instructions will be given then.

E.E. ROGERS, M.D., C.M.

All the physicians who testified declared this to be a low protein diet and contra-indicated for the child's condition. The child was under Rogers' care from 22nd April to 11th June. When the father reported difficulties the child was having in eating the prescribed foods, Rogers said: "Let him cry, he will eat when he is hungry." The child was then force fed with Rogers' authority and some milk allowed him. From this time on the child had three to four liquid bowel movements a day. On hearing this, Rogers told the father that this was poison working out of the child's system. A week later the skin began to peel in blotches. By the middle of May, for the first time since birth, pus was coming from the child's body. The father reported this to Rogers who again told him that this was poison working its way out. On 4th June Rogers stopped the giving of milk to the boy. By 9th June the father noticed swelling on the child's head, hands and legs. Again he reported, and again Rogers told him this was poison working its way out. On 10th June the child's stomach was swollen and the eyes were beginning to cloud over. On hearing this, Rogers said: "I have done all I could for him, I can't put life into him, take him to the hospital if you wish." The child died on 11th June.

. . . .

In essence it was submitted by counsel for the appellant that the element of *mens rea* that had to be proven in this case was recklessness. Recklessness, it was argued, entails the ability to foresee the consequences which would result. One cannot foresee those consequences (in this case death) if one has an honest belief that one's acts are beneficial. Accordingly, it was argued that the trial Judge should have directed the jury, and I quote counsel's suggested question: "Did Rogers in fact foresee that the course he pursued *i.e.* that prescribing the diet would have as a probable consequence the death of the child?" Accordingly, counsel contended that if the jury concluded that Rogers honestly believed that what he was doing was beneficial, he (Rogers) should be acquitted.

It is of interest to note that the necessary requisites of proof to support an indictment of manslaughter by negligence were set down by Hewart L.C.J. in *Regina v. Bateman* (1925), 19 Cr. App. R. 8. The rationale in *Bateman* was substantially accepted by the draftsmen of the 1953-54 revision of the *Criminal Code* of Canada, and I will now deal with ss. 187, 191, 192 [now ss. 216, 219 and 220] which were all read and explained to the jury. Section 187 states:

187. Every one who undertakes to administer surgical or medical treatment to another person or to do any other lawful act that may endanger the life of another person is, except in cases of necessity, under a legal duty to have and to use reasonable knowledge, skill and care in so doing.

Sections 191 and 192 state:

191. (1) Every one is criminally negligent who
(*a*) in doing anything, or
(*b*) in omitting to do anything that it is his duty to do, shows wanton or reckless disregard for the lives or safety of other persons.
(2) For the purposes of this section, "duty" means a duty imposed by law.
192. Every one who by criminal negligence causes death to another person is guilty of an indictable offence and is liable to imprisonment for life.

Section 191 has been repeatedly considered in cases where death ensues as a result of automobile accidents. There is no doubt that *mens rea* is an essential ingredient in the offence of criminal negligence. Ritchie J.A. speaking *per curiam* for the New Brunswick Supreme Court in *Regina v. Fortin* (1958), 29 C.R. 28, 121 C.C.C. 345 at 350-1, 9 Can. Abr. (2nd) 1786 said:

If the conduct of the accused comes within the language of s. 191, and there is no evidence such conduct may have been due to circumstances beyond his control, a blameworthy state of mind is imputed to him and criminal negligence, as an ingredient of the offence is established.

Section 191 has provided a definition upon which a Judge may fully rely when instructing a jury on the trial of an offence involving criminal negligence. It usually should suffice if the trial Judge, after reading the section and explaining what is meant by "a duty imposed by law" and the meaning of the words "wanton" and "reckless", direct the jury that the question to be determined in deciding the issue of criminal negligence is, as it was in [*Regina v. Savoie* (1956), 117 C.C.C. 327, 9 Can. Abr. (2nd) 1791 and *Stewart v. The Queen* (1956), 117 C.C.C. 346], whether the conduct of the accused was, in the circumstances disclosed by the evidence such as to show on his part a wanton or reckless disregard for the lives or safety of other persons. The important words requiring explanation are "wanton" and "reckless". It is only when explaining to the jury their meaning that the trial Judge may deem it necessary to refer to the state or attitude of mind of the accused. Any such reference, especially if lengthy, may tend to confuse rather than clarify the issue. The emphasis should be upon the conduct of the accused. If such conduct, on its face, indicates on the part of the accused, either in the operation of a dangerous agency, such as a motor vehicle, or otherwise, a wanton or reckless disregard for the lives or safety of others, and no exculpatory circumstances appear tending to show his conduct was due to causes beyond his control, then, without more, culpability may be inferred and the jury may convict.

. . . .

The paragraph which I have set out from the reasons for judgment of Ritchie J.A., *supra*, was quoted with approval by McKinnon J.A. in *Regina v. Belbeck*, 3 C.R.N.S. 173 at 183, [1968] 2 C.C.C. 331, where he also quoted the New Brunswick case of *Stewart v. The Queen*, *supra*, at p. 349 where it was said that:

Lack of intention to commit an offence is not an answer to a charge of criminal negligence. If there is conduct amounting to a wanton or reckless disregard for the lives or safety of other persons then such conduct alone amounts to criminal negligence regardless of intention, or absence of intention.

Again Evans J.A. in the recent Ontario case of *Regina v. Torrie* (1967), 50 C.R. 300, [1967] 3 C.C.C. 303 at 307 said:

> Section 191 has reference to *conduct* in the discharge of duties imposed by law. *Conduct* may be demonstrated by acts or omissions. If the *conduct, viewed objectively*, shows a wanton or reckless disregard for the lives and safety of others then it is criminal negligence. (The italics are mine.)

. . . .

In enacting s. 187, Parliament has imposed a legal duty upon every one who undertakes to administer medical treatment. Included in that legal duty is to "have reasonable knowledge" in so doing. The reasonableness of that knowledge can be, and was here, delineated by the testimony of every one of the medical witnesses except Rogers. The essence of that "reasonable knowledge" was that a physician (which Rogers was) should have foreseen the harmful consequences of depriving the child of proteins and calories in the circumstances. Regardless of his personal theories, Rogers was under a duty to have that foresight. It was, therefore, irrelevant for the jury to consider Rogers' own belief that his diet was a beneficial treatment. Rogers was fixed by law with the foresight of harmful consequences arising out of reasonable knowledge. In persisting with the administration of his dietary treatment he was reckless and brought about the unwished result of the death of the child. His honest belief that his diet was beneficial might exculpate him from the intention to cause the child's death, but intention was not the issue here. The duty imposed by law upon him was to have and use the reasonable knowledge of his peers. In deviating, he ought to have known the risks involved. Accordingly, the learned trial Judge did not err when he said:

> Now it is of course for you to say but I suggest you will find that Dr. Rogers knew very well that the view of the medical profession was that in a case like this one, the diet should provide calories and proteins in a high degree and if it did not the life of the patient would be in danger; that well knowing this, the Accused deliberately prescribed the diet given in evidence which he knew was extremely low in protein content because he thought that this diet was a better way of treating the patient.

In my view, even a definition of recklessness given by writers of such eminence as Professors Turner and Williams cannot be given, *in abstracto*, to a jury in cases falling under s. 191. Recklessness must be considered, as it was in this charge, in relation to all of what is said in this section. A consideration of the whole of s. 191 ineluctably leads one to the conclusion that Parliament intended the conduct of a person charged thereunder to be tested objectively.

In arguing against the objective test set out in the charge, emphasis was placed on a recent English case, *Regina v. Lamb*, [1967] 2 Q.B. 981. It seems to me the facts in that case are entirely different from those before us here. No duty existed for the accused Lamb to "have . . . reasonable knowledge . . ." in the operation of a revolver. In this case, however, Rogers was under a duty "to have . . . reasonable knowledge" when he undertook to administer medical treatment. Once all of the medical witnesses had testified that the possessors of reasonable medical knowledge would foresee that the taking away of proteins and calories (as was in fact done by Rogers) would probably result in death, it became irrelevant for the trial Judge to put Rogers' belief to the contrary to the jury. It was Rogers' duty to have the "reasonable knowledge" that was delineated and which represented the advances in scientific and medical knowledge to this day. If he persisted in his treatment notwithstanding that body of reasonable knowledge he ran the risk of bringing about the unwished result, namely, the death of the child. In my opinion, therefore, the learned trial Judge correctly charged the jury when he said:

> I want to make it clear to you that the standard of professional skill and care required of any person whatever his qualifications, who undertakes to administer medical treatment, is an objective standard. In other words, in a particular case it is entirely irrelevant, it does not matter at all, what the particular practitioner or person thinks is the level of skill, knowledge and care with which he gave treatment. The only test is whether in fact and regardless of what he may think about it, he did act with the competence the law requires of him. Failure to act with that degree of competence is negligence.

and in the further directions given when the jury asked for more assistance, when he said:

> whether you have been negligent or not, and whether your negligence is so great that it amounts to criminal negligence, in other words wanton or reckless disregard for the lives or safety of other persons, [it] isn't tested by what the person who is accused thinks about it, I would say for obvious reasons, it is tested objectively by the standards of reasonable people.

The distinguished American jurist, Oliver Wendell Holmes, when he served on the Supreme Judicial Court of Massachusetts, had occasion to consider a case in which the accused was charged with causing the death of a patient by prescribing that she wrap herself in kerosene soaked blankets. After reviewing the English authorities from ancient times, to 1884 he said: (*Commonwealth v. Pierce*, 138 Mass. 165 at 180)

> Common experience is necessary to the man of ordinary prudence, and a man who assumes to act as the defendant did must have it at his peril.

He further said in that case at p. 179:

> we cannot recognize a privilege to do acts manifestly endangering human life, on the ground of good intention alone.

It was open to the jury here, on the evidence before them, to consider whether Rogers in knowing the deteriorating condition of this child, yet obstinately continuing the administration of a diet based on his personal theory of medical treatment, was criminally negligent within the meaning of the *Criminal Code of Canada*.

Since, in my opinion, no error has been shown to exist in the charge, I would dismiss the appeal.

TYSOE J.A. (MACLEAN J.A. concurring) concurred in a separate judgment.

R. v. SHARP

(1984), 39 C.R. (3d) 367, 12 C.C.C. (3d) 428 (Ont. C.A.)

The accused was acquitted on four charges of criminal negligence causing death. The essence of the Crown's argument on appeal was that the trial judge erred in instructing the jury that the offence charged and the included offence of dangerous driving required a mental element of intent or knowledge on the part of the accused.

MORDEN J.A. (MacKinnon A.C.J.O. and Zuber J.A. concurring): —

. . . .

[The trial judge] dealt with what he called the "wrongful act" and the "wrongful mind" which had to be proven. In dealing with the former he said, after referring to "the standard to be expected of reasonable men and women in the operation of their motor vehicle", that the wrongful act should be "more than that" and that it:

> . . . must be conduct that in its physical description is a marked or significant departure from the standard of reasonable driver. The departure must be such that one would say that that conduct in terms of quantity represents a flagrant or a significant departure from what reasonable people have a right to expect, and indeed demand, of other people. So then, you look firstly in deciding this case — you look firstly at the physical driving, and you ask the question: is the conduct, is the driving here, viewed entirely in isolation from the driver, is that conduct such that I am sure it represents a significant, a very significant or marked departure from the standard of a reasonable driver?

No complaint is made on this part of the charge.

In dealing with the "wrongful mind" element of the offence he put a "fact situation" to the jury, which "viewed in isolation [showed] conduct [that] might well be a significant or marked departure from reasonable care". The following passage, which contains the fact situation, also sets forth the impugned definition of "criminal negligence", which was to be repeated in substantially the same words in the course of the judge's instructions to the jury:

> Suppose a busy street, traffic rush hour, rush hour traffic, 5:00 o'clock in the afternoon, everybody going everywhere, a car going 25 miles per hour drives through a red light without slowing and it strikes and kills a pedestrian who is lawfully in the crosswalk. Clearly, any jury would be entitled to say that that act is a very marked departure from reasonable care in all the circumstances. But suppose the driver failed to notice the red light because the passenger dropped a lighted cigarette down the driver's neck just at the time when he, the driver, would have ordinarily been directing his attention to the light. You would be hard put to label that criminal negligence, and why would you be hard put? The physical act hasn't changed, has it?

The same 25 miles an hour, it is the same going through a red light, it is the same rush hour, and on its face it is flagrant conduct. What would concern you is the mental element, however difficult it may be for you to precisely define in your own mind just what mental element you are thinking about. But my obligation is to attempt to define just exactly what mental element would bother you. And I say this in giving you that definition: before the act, which, viewed in isolation, in other words, before the driver [driving], which, viewed in isolation, does indeed represent a marked departure from reasonable care, before that driving becomes criminal negligence the driver of the car must have *deliberately* engaged in that wrongful act, either knowing in doing so an obvious danger to the lives or safety of others was thereby created, or without giving any thought to that danger, when, had he thought about it all, he would have realized that the *deliberate* pursuit of that conduct did in fact represent an obvious danger to the life or safety of others, not a fanciful or highly unlikely danger, but an obvious danger. [Emphasis added.]

. . . .

Both criminal negligence and dangerous driving are offences which require fault, in the sense of a blameworthy state of mind, to be proven, but in each case (assuming the criminal negligence to involve driving) it is open to a jury to find the required fault in the nature of the accused's driving if, objectively viewed, it amounts to that which is defined in the statute. A jury should not find fault, and hence that the accused is guilty, if there is an explanation which arises from the evidence that would account for the deviant conduct in a manner which would negative the element of fault. A cause resulting from circumstances beyond the accused's control, for example, a sudden malfunction of the steering mechanism, would afford such an explanation. In this case the real complaint is that the jury were being instructed that a kind of intention was required.

With respect to the charge, as I have said, substantially all of the difficulty arises from the use of "deliberate" (or "deliberately") in connection with the respondent's driving. If this word meant, in accordance with the usual dictionary meaning, "considered and not impulsive", then the charge in several places would have been in error in importing an element of intention and, indeed, a pronounced form of intention, that is not required for either of the offences charged. However, when the charge is read as a whole I think it is clear that the trial judge did not intend this meaning and, what is the relevant consideration, I do not think that this is the meaning that the jury would have understood to be intended.

It appears to me that, in giving the example at the outset of his charge of the effect of a passenger dropping a lighted cigarette down the driver's neck and in his final instruction on the effect of a bee sting "or . . . something . . . over which he had no control that . . . suddenly caused the bad driving", the trial judge has effectively indicated the intended meaning. I think that Mr. Greenspan is right in saying that the meaning of "deliberate" driving in the context of this definition and other parts of the charge is "conscious and volitional" driving. The other parts of the charge which I have in mind are not only passages where the trial judge quoted the statutory definitions of the offences, but also those that clearly stated the objective standard required by each of those provisions. At the very end of his instructions in answer to the jury's question, he said with respect to dangerous driving that if the accused "in fact" drove in a way that represented a danger to the public "it doesn't matter what he thought". With respect to criminal negligence he concluded by saying that even if the accused did not know that lives and safety would be endangered by his conduct he still would be liable if, applying that standard of "an ordinary sensible driver", it would have been "perfectly obvious to him had he thought about it."

. . . .

I think it is in order to make some general observations on the charge. The source of the term "deliberate" was probably the judgment of this court in *R. v. Titchner* (1961), 131 C.C.C. 64 at 68. The charge in the present case followed that in *Titchner* with some modification. As Laskin J. observed in *Arthurs v. R.* (1972), 7 C.C.C. (2d) 438 at 452-53 (in a dissenting judgment but not with respect to the point being made), the recommended instruction in *Titchner* has not been followed in other provincial jurisdictions and there has been a "recession" from it in this court, referring to *R. v. Torrie*, supra. The instruction gives the initial impression of a requirement not only of intent but also of a considered intent and, with respect, I suggest that it not be used as part of the definition of "criminal negligence" or "dangerous driving". In the present case it was of no practical assistance, even as narrowly defined, because no issue of unconscious or non-volitional driving was raised.

This was a case where the putting of the Code definition of "criminal negligence" to the jury with little more in the way of elaboration would have been sufficient. Proper elaboration would make clear to the jury the necessity for the driving to amount to a marked and substantial departure from the standard of a reasonable driver in the circumstances (which, as indicated earlier, was properly done in this case) and that the driver either recognized and ran an obvious and serious risk to the lives and safety of others or, alternatively, gave no thought to that risk.

. . . .

Appeal dismissed.

R. v. TUTTON AND TUTTON

[1989] 1 S.C.R. 1392, 69 C.R. (3d) 289, 48 C.C.C. (3d) 129

The accused were charged with manslaughter respecting the death of their five-year-old son. The charge and particulars alleged that they had caused the death of their son by criminal negligence through omitting to provide him necessaries of life, in failing to provide insulin and to obtain timely medical assistance. Their son had been diagnosed as a diabetic more than two years earlier. At the time, his parents were advised of his need to have insulin on a daily basis for the rest of his life and thorough instructions were given as to what was required for his care. For some time, both parents followed the instructions for the administration of insulin and observed the necessary dietary controls.

They were members of a religious sect which believed in faith healing, believing that God can perform miracles and cure ailments in response to prayer. The sect was not opposed to seeking medical advice and taking medicine, but believed that God can cure ailments which are beyond the purview of medical science. The parents' primary concern was for a cure for their son which would relieve him of the necessity of a lifetime daily intake of insulin. On one occasion the mother ceased administering insulin because she firmly believed that her son was being healed through the power of the Holy Spirit. His health immediately failed and he was taken to hospital, where the parents were strongly advised to continue with the insulin. They did so, but later the mother received a further vision from God which she believed advised her that her son was in fact cured of diabetes and no longer required insulin treatment. As a result of this the mother, with the agreement of the father, stopped the insulin "by God's authority". The son rapidly became ill. He died shortly after being admitted to hospital, his death being attributed to complications of diabetic hyperglycemia. Following a trial by Judge and jury, the accused were convicted of manslaughter. On appeal, the Ontario Court of Appeal set aside the conviction and ordered a new trial. The Court held that there had been a reversible error as the trial Judge had not clearly explained to the jury that the reverse onus in respect of proving a lawful excuse on a balance of probabilities applied only in the case of the included offence of failing to provide the necessaries of life under s. 197(2) [now s. 215(2)] of the *Criminal Code*. The Court further held that, although in some cases criminal negligence consisted of a marked and substantial departure from the standard of a reasonable person in the circumstances, in this case of criminal negligence through omission the jury had to be satisfied that the accused knew that there was a risk to the life or safety of their son and unjustifiably took that risk or closed their minds to any such risk with disregard for either his life or his safety. The Crown appealed.

After reserving for some 18 months, the Supreme Court of Canada unanimously confirmed the order of a new trial on the basis that there had been a reversible error in the charge respecting onus of proof. The Court also took the opportunity to consider the test for criminal negligence. On this issue, there was an inconclusive three-three split.

McINTYRE J. (L'HEUREUX-DUBÉ J. concurring): —

. . . .

In reaching a conclusion as to whether the conduct of an accused person has shown, within the meaning of s. 202 [now s. 219] of the *Criminal Code*, wanton or reckless disregard for the lives or safety of other persons, the authorities dictate an objective test: see the review of the authorities on this subject by Cory J.A. for the Court of Appeal in *R. v. Waite* (1986), 52 C.R. (3d) 355, 28 C.C.C. (3d) 326, approved in this Court (judgment given concurrently) [post, p. 323]. Indeed, in the Court of Appeal, Dubin J.A. accepted the objective test as one of general application, but made an exception in cases where the conduct complained of consisted of an act or acts of omission, as opposed to those of commission. In such cases, it was his view that occasions would arise where a subjective test would be required where acts of omission were under consideration. He considered that this was such a case. It is my view, however, that no such distinction as Dubin J.A. would adopt may be made. I am wholly unable to see any difference in principle between cases arising from an omission to act and those involving acts of commission. Indeed, the words of s. 202 of the *Criminal Code* make it clear that one is criminally negligent who, *in doing anything* or *in omitting to do anything* that it is his duty to do, shows wanton or reckless disregard for the lives or safety of other persons. The objective test must, therefore, be employed where criminal negligence is considered, for it is the conduct of the accused, as opposed to his intention or mental state, which is examined in this inquiry.

Our concept of criminal culpability relies primarily upon a consideration of the mental state which accompanies or initiates the wrongful act, and the attribution of criminal liability without proof of such a blameworthy mental state raises serious concerns. Nonetheless, negligence has become accepted as a factor which may lead to criminal liability and strong arguments can be raised in its favour. Section 202 of the *Criminal Code* affords an example of its adoption. In choosing the test to be applied in assessing conduct under s. 202 of the *Criminal Code*, it must be observed at once that what is made criminal is negligence. Negligence connotes the opposite of thought-directed action. In other words, its existence precludes the element of positive intent to achieve a given result. This leads to the conclusion that what is sought to be restrained by punishment under s. 202 of the *Code* is conduct, and its results. What is punished, in other words, is not the state of mind but the consequence of mindless action. This is apparent, I suggest, from the words of the section, which make criminal conduct which *shows* wanton or reckless disregard. It may be observed as well that the words "wanton or reckless" support this construction, denying as they do the existence of a directing mental state. Nor can it be said that criminal negligence, as defined in s. 202, imports in its terms some element of malice or intention. This point was made in the Crown's factum in para. 41, which provided, in part:

> The plain and ordinary meaning of the terms "wanton" and "reckless" when used in connection with the concept of negligence would seem to include a state of being heedless of apparent danger. Section 202(1) does not use the term "reckless" as an extended definition of intention or malice, but rather employs the term as part of a definition of conduct which amounts to "negligence" in a criminal context.

In my view, then, an objective standard must be applied in determining this question because of the difference between the ordinary criminal offence, which requires proof of a subjective state of mind, and that of criminal negligence. In criminal cases, generally, the act coupled with the mental state or intent is punished. In criminal negligence, the act which exhibits the requisite degree of negligence is punished. If this distinction is not kept clear, the dividing line between the traditional *mens rea* offence and the offence of criminal negligence becomes blurred. The difference, for example, between murder and manslaughter, both unlawful killings, is merely one of intent. If the question of an accused's intent had to be considered and separately proved in offences under s. 202 of the *Criminal Code*, the purpose of the section would be defeated because intentional conduct would perforce be considered under other sections of the *Code* and s. 202, aimed at mindless but socially dangerous conduct, would have no function. For these reasons, the objective test should be employed and, in my view, the Court of Appeal was in error in concluding in this case that a subjective test would be required. The test is that of reasonableness, and proof of conduct which reveals a marked and significant departure from the standard which could be expected of a reasonably prudent person in the circumstances will justify a conviction of criminal negligence.

In reaching this conclusion, I am not overlooking the comments I made in *Sansregret v. R.*, [1985] 1 S.C.R. 570 at 581-82, 45 C.R. (3d) 193, 23 C.C.C. (3d) 223, which were cited by counsel for the appellant. In *Sansregret*, I expressed the view that "recklessness, to form a part of the criminal *mens rea*, must have an element of the subjective." I then went on to say that "It is in this sense that the term 'recklessness' is used in the criminal law and it is clearly distinct from the concept of civil negligence." It was argued upon the basis of these words and later comments on the nature of negligence in relation to the criminal law that a subjective test should therefore be applied in considering the existence of criminal negligence under s. 202 of the *Code*. I would reject that argument on the basis that the concept of recklessness there described is not applicable in a case under s. 202 of the *Code*. Sansregret was charged with rape, a crime which involves positive mind-directed conduct on the part of the accused which aims at the accomplishment of a specific result. It is a traditional *mens rea* offence and a mental state must be proved, in that case an intention to persist with his purpose despite the fact that the complainant's consent has been extorted by threats and fear. Recklessness on his part forms a part of the *mens rea* (the blameworthy state of mind) and has to be proved on a subjective basis as part of the mental element of the offence. In this sense, the words in *Sansregret* are apposite. Section 202, on the other hand, has created a separate offence; an offence which makes negligence — the exhibition of wanton or reckless behaviour — a crime in itself and has thus defined its own terms. As noted by Cory J.A. in *R. v. Waite*, s. 202 of the *Criminal Code* was enacted in its present form as a codification of the offence which had emerged in Canadian jurisprudence, and in respect of which the necessary *mens rea* may be inferred on an objective basis from the acts of the accused.

The application of an objective test under s. 202 of the *Criminal Code*, however, may not be made in a vacuum. Events occur within the framework of other events and actions and, when deciding on the nature of the questioned conduct, surrounding circumstances must be considered. The decision must be made on a consideration of the facts existing at the time and in relation to the accused's perception of those facts. Since the test is objective, the accused's perception of the facts is not to be considered for the purpose of assessing malice or intention on the accused's part but only to form a basis for a conclusion as to whether or not the accused's conduct, in view of his perception of the facts, was reasonable. This is particularly true where, as here, the accused have raised the defence of mistake of fact. If an accused under s. 202 has an honest and reasonably held belief in the existence of certain facts, it may be a relevant consideration in assessing the reasonableness of his conduct. For example, a welder, who is engaged to work in a confined space, believing on the assurance of the owner of the premises that no combustible or explosive material is stored nearby, should be entitled to have his perception, as to the presence or absence of dangerous materials, before the jury on a charge of manslaughter when his welding torch causes an explosion and a consequent death.

As noted earlier, the Tuttons raised the defence of mistake of fact at trial. They argued that the failure to supply insulin was based upon the belief that the child had been cured by divine intervention and that the failure to provide medical care in timely fashion was based upon the belief that the child was not seriously ill, so medical assistance was not necessary. The trial Judge, it was argued, was in error in telling the jury that for any such belief to be effective as a defence it must have been reasonably held. It was held in this Court in *Pappajohn v. R.*, [1980] 2 S.C.R. 120, 14 C.R. (3d) 243, 19 C.R. (3d) 97, 52 C.C.C. (2d) 481 [B.C.], that an honest, though mistaken, belief in the existence of circumstances which, if present, would make the questioned conduct non-culpable would entitle an accused to an acquittal. It was also held in *Pappajohn* that the honest belief need not be reasonable, because its effect would be to deny the existence of the requisite mens rea. The situation would be different, however, where the offence charged rests upon the concept of negligence, as opposed to that of the guilty mind or blameworthy mental state. In such case, an unreasonable though honest belief on the part of the accused would be negligently held. The holding of such a belief could not afford a defence when culpability is based on negligent conduct. I would therefore conclude that the trial Judge made no error in charging the jury to the effect that any mistaken belief which could afford a defence in a charge of criminal negligence would have to be reasonable.

In the case at bar, then, the assertion of the Tuttons that they believed a cure had been effected by divine intervention and that insulin was not necessary for the preservation of the child's life would have to be considered by the jury. The jury would have to consider whether such belief was honest and whether it was reasonable. In this, they would be required to consider the whole background of the case. They would have to take into account the experience of the Tuttons with the child's illness; the fact that they had seen the result of the withdrawal of insulin on one occasion and that they had been informed of its necessity for the continued care of the child; and the fact that Mrs. Tutton had received some formal instruction or training in dealing with diabetes and diabetics. They would, as well, have to consider whether the belief in a miraculous cure leading to the conclusion that insulin and medical care were not required, though honest, was reasonable. Upon these facts and all others concerning the matter which were revealed in the evidence, the jury would be required to decide whether the refusal of insulin and medical attention represented a marked and significant departure from the standard to be observed by reasonably prudent parents.

I would dismiss the appeal and confirm the direction for a new trial.

LAMER J.: — I have read the reasons of my colleague, Mr. Justice McIntyre, and I am in agreement with them, subject to the following remarks. I am of the view that, when applying the objective norm set out by Parliament in s. 202 [now s. 219] of the *Criminal Code* [R.S.C. 1970, c. C-34; now R.S.C. 1985, c. C-46], there must be made "a generous allowance" for factors which are particular to the accused, such as youth, mental development and education: see Don Stuart, *Canadian Criminal Law: A Treatise*, 2nd ed. (1987), Toronto, Carswell, p. 194; see also Toni Pickard, "Culpable Mistakes and Rape: Relating *Mens Rea* to the Crime" (1980), 30 Univ. of Toronto L.J. 75. When this is done, as we are considering conduct which is likely to cause death, that is, high risk conduct, the adoption of the subjective or of an objective test will, in practice, nearly if not always produce the same result: see Eric Colvin, "Recklessness and Criminal Negligence" (1982), 32 Univ. of Toronto L.J. 345.

I should note that Parliament, when enacting s. 202, did not purport to determine the nature of the negligence which is required when grounding criminal liability thereupon. My understanding of s. 202 is that Parliament has in that section simply defined the expression "criminal negligence" whenever used in the *Criminal Code*.

I should finally mention that in this case the constitutionality of s. 205(5)(*b*) [now s. 222(5)(*b*)] was not in issue. Indeed, assuming without now deciding that it is a principle of fundamental justice that knowledge of a likely risk or deliberate ignorance thereof (foresight or wilful blindness) is an essential element of the offence of manslaughter, the issue as to whether proof of the substituted element of "criminal negligence" as defined by Parliament and interpreted by this Court satisfies the test set out in *R. v. Vaillancourt*, [1987] 2 S.C.R. 636, 60 C.R. (3d) 289, 39 C.C.C. (3d) 118 [Que.], does not arise. I therefore do not by my concurrence feel precluded or limited when addressing such a constitutional challenge, of course, if and when called upon to do so.

WILSON J. (DICKSON C.J.C. and LaFOREST J. concurring): —

. . . .

I do not, however, agree with my colleagues' conclusion that criminal negligence under s. 202 [now s. 219] of the *Criminal Code*, R.S.C. 1970, c. C-34 [now R.S.C. 1985, c. C-46], consists only of conduct in breach of an objective standard and does not require the Crown to prove that the accused had any degree of guilty knowledge. I also have reservations concerning the approach my colleagues suggest is available in order to relieve against the harshness of the objective standard of liability which they find in s. 202 and to ensure that the morally innocent are not punished for the commission of serious criminal offences committed through criminal negligence.

. . . .

I wish to deal first with the implications of my colleagues' approach in this case. By concluding that s. 202 of the *Criminal Code* prohibits conduct and the consequences of mindless action absent any blameworthy state of mind, they have, in effect, held that the crime of criminal negligence is an absolute liability offence. Conviction follows upon proof of conduct which reveals a marked and substantial departure from the standard expected of a reasonably prudent person in the circumstances regardless of what was actually in the accused's mind at the time the act was committed.

. . . .

This Court made clear in *Sault Ste. Marie* and other cases that the imposition of criminal liability in the absence of proof of a blameworthy state of mind, either as an inference from the nature of the act committed or by other evidence, is an anomaly which does not sit comfortably with the principles of penal liability and fundamental justice.

. . . .

This is particularly so in the case of offences carrying a substantial term of imprisonment which by their nature, severity and attendant stigma are true criminal offences aimed at punishing culpable behaviour as opposed to securing the public welfare. In the absence of clear statutory language and purpose to the contrary, this court should, in my view, be most reluctant to interpret a serious criminal offence as an absolute liability offence.

. . . .

In this case there can be no doubt that we are dealing with a serious criminal offence. The appellants are charged with committing manslaughter by criminal negligence. Under s. 219 [now s. 236] of the *Criminal Code* then in force they are liable to imprisonment for life. Other offences committed by means of criminal negligence are also serious. For example, causing death by criminal negligence is an indictable offence under s. 203 [now s. 220] of the *Criminal Code*, carrying with it a liability to life imprisonment. Causing bodily harm by criminal negligence is an indictable offence under s. 204 [now s. 221] of the *Code*, carrying a liability to ten years' imprisonment. Criminal negligence in the operation of a motor vehicle could be prosecuted under s. 233 [now s. 249] of the *Code* then in force as an indictable offence, with a liability to five years' imprisonment. Taking the above considerations into account, can it be said that s. 202 of the *Criminal Code* creates an absolute liability offence for which conviction will follow on proof of the proscribed act without reference to the accused's state of mind?

My colleague McIntyre J. has concluded that upon the wording of s. 202 it is an inescapable conclusion that Parliament intended liability to follow upon proof of the act or conduct described in the section. In particular, he stresses the reference to conduct which *shows* wanton or reckless disregard for the lives and safety of others and the fact that what is prohibited is criminal *negligence*.

. . . .

Section 202 of the *Criminal Code* is, in my view, notorious in its ambiguity. Since its enactment in its present form in the 1955 amendments to the

Criminal Code it has bedevilled both Courts and commentators who have sought out its meaning. The interpretation put upon it usually depends upon which words are emphasized. On the one hand, my colleague's judgment demonstrates that emphasizing the use of the words "shows" and "negligence" can lead to the conclusion that an objective standard of liability was intended and that proof of unreasonable conduct alone will suffice. On the other hand, if the words "wanton or reckless disregard for the lives or safety of other persons" are stressed along with the fact that what is prohibited is not negligence simpliciter but "criminal" negligence, one might conclude that Parliament intended some degree of advertence to the risk to the lives or safety of others to be an essential element of the offence. When faced with such fundamental ambiguity, it would be my view that the Court should give the provision the interpretation most consonant not only with the text and purpose of the provision but also, where possible, with the broader concepts and principles of the law: see also *R. v. Paré*, [1987] 2 S.C.R. 618, 60 C.R. (3d) 346, 38 C.C.C. (3d) 97.

. . . .

Despite the sometimes confusing characterization of the distinct crime of dangerous driving (which I note is not in issue on this appeal), the *O'Grady v. Sparling* view of criminal negligence was affirmed by various members of the Court in *obiter* comments in *Mann v. R.*, [1966] S.C.R. 238 at 243, 47 C.R. 400, [1966] 2 C.C.C. 273 [Ont.]; *Binus v. R.*, [1967] S.C.R. 594 at 598 and 600, 2 C.R.N.S. 118, [1968] 1 C.C.C. 227 [Ont.]; and *Peda v. R.*, [1969] S.C.R. 905 at 911-12, 917-18 and 919-20, 7 C.R.N.S. 243, [1969] 4 C.C.C. 245 [Ont.]. These cases are, in my respectful view, very relevant to the question that the Court faces on this appeal. They indicate that on previous occasions the Court considered s. 202 susceptible of an interpretation in keeping with the general principle that some degree of guilty knowledge is an element of all serious criminal offences. It is true that the offence of criminal negligence was not directly in issue in these cases, but at no time did any member of the Court suggest that the subjective approach to the interpretation of the offence of criminal negligence in *O'Grady v. Sparling* was incorrect or inconsistent with the statutory language or purpose.

. . . .

It is my view that the phrase "reckless disregard for the lives or safety of other persons" found in s. 202, when read in the context of Canadian criminal law jurisprudence, requires the Crown to prove advertence or awareness of the risk that the prohibited consequences will come to pass. This Court has adopted a subjective approach to recklessness in *Pappajohn, supra*, and has reaffirmed this in the recent case of *Sansregret, supra*. In doing so the Court has, I believe, implicitly rejected the view that failure to give any thought to whether or not there is a risk can be substituted for the mental state of recklessness as that view is articulated in the majority decisions in *Metro. Police Commr. v. Caldwell*, [1982] A.C. 341 (H.L.), and *R. v. Lawrence*, [1982] A.C. 510 (H.L.).

The expression *wanton* disregard for the lives and safety of others is perhaps less clear. The word *wanton* taken in its acontextual sense could signal an element of randomness or arbitrariness more akin to an objective standard but, given the context in which it appears, coupled with the adjective "reckless", and its clear use to accentuate and make more heinous the already serious matter of disregard for the lives or safety of others, I would think that the preferable interpretation is that the word "wanton" was intended to connote wilful blindness to the prohibited risk: see P.J.T. O Hearn, "Criminal Negligence: An Analysis in Depth — Part II" (1965), 7 Cr. L.Q. 407, at p. 411.

In short, the phrase "wanton or reckless disregard for the lives or safety of other persons" signifies more than gross negligence in the objective sense. It requires some degree of awareness or advertence to the threat to the lives or safety of others or alternatively a wilful blindness to that threat which is culpable in light of the gravity of the risk that is prohibited.

In recent years Courts and commentators have sought to deal with those aspects of s. 202 which seem to be in tension with a subjective standard. In his valuable treatise *Principles of Criminal Law* (1986), Professor Eric Colvin has written at p. 120:

> The reference to *showing* wanton or reckless disregard in s. 202 can be used to support the objective test. It is submitted, however, that it is wrong to interpret s. 202 as a complete definition of criminal negligence which includes its *mens rea*. The better interpretation is that the section does no more than define the *conduct* which is involved in criminal negligence. *Mens rea* then remains to be implied in accordance with general principle and this is in effect what the Supreme Court did in *O'Grady*. This construction is supported by the statement in another Supreme Court case that "conduct disclosing wanton or reckless disregard for the lives or safety of others constitutes *prima facie* evidence of criminal negligence".

. . . .

It is my view that the jurisprudence of this Court to date establishes that the criminal negligence prohibited under s. 202 is advertent negligence. I would not hesitate to depart from these precedents for solid reasons but I cannot, with due respect to those who think otherwise, agree that the case for the adoption of an objective standard of liability has been made out to the extent required to justify a departure from this Court's previous decisions. On the standard required to justify a departure from the practice of stare decisis, I find the comments of the Chief Justice in his dissent in *R. v. Bernard*, [1988] 2 S.C.R. 833 at 849-61, 67 C.R. (3d) 113, 45 C.C.C. (3d) 1, instructive. In *Bernard* the Chief Justice suggests that before overruling one of its prior decisions the Court consider the introduction of the *Canadian Charter of Rights and Freedoms*, the attenuation of a precedent in later authorities, the creation of uncertainty by the continued existence of the precedent and whether the overturning of the precedent will expand the range of criminal liability and work to the detriment of the accused. Considering these factors in the case at bar, the burden to justify such a departure would, in my view, be especially high, given that *O'Grady v. Sparling* has not been attenuated by the subsequent jurisprudence of this Court and the effect of the change proposed here is to expand criminal liability beyond its normal limits and to the detriment of the accused. The adoption of an objective standard also creates, in my view, both the possibility of a *Charter* violation and uncertainty as to the relevance of factors subjective to the accused under the new objective standard.

As I have suggested above, the words of the section can reasonably bear an interpretation which leaves room for the mental element of awareness or advertence to a risk to the lives or safety of others or wilful blindness to such risk. Conduct which shows a wanton or reckless disregard for the lives and safety of others will by its nature constitute *prima facie* evidence of the mental element, and in the absence of some evidence that casts doubt on the normal degree of mental awareness, proof of the act and reference to what a reasonable person in the circumstances must have realized will lead to a conclusion that the accused was aware of the risk or wilfully blind to the risk.

. . . .

I would add that the importance of what the reasonable person would have foreseen to the determination of whether a particular accused would have become aware or wilfully blind to the prohibited risk will vary with the context. For example, in the case of a licensed driver engaging in high-risk motoring, I am in general agreement with Morden J.A. in *R. v. Sharp* (1984), 39 C.R. (3d) 367, 12 C.C.C. (3d) 428 at 434-35 (C.A.), that it is open to the jury to find the accused's blameworthy state of mind from driving which shows wanton or reckless disregard for the lives or safety of others, subject to an explanation in the evidence which would account for the deviant conduct, such as a sudden mechanical malfunction or a bee sting or other accident beyond the accused's control. I would think that in the driving context, where risks to the lives and safety of others present themselves in a habitual and obvious fashion, the accused's claim that he or she gave no thought to the risk or had simply a negative state of mind would in most, if not all, cases amount to the culpable positive mental state of wilful blindness to the prohibited risk.

The minimal nature of the requirement of a blameworthy state of mind and the relevance of the objective standard as a rebuttable mode of proof suggests to me that a holding that s. 202 requires proof of the mental element of advertence to the risk or wilful blindness to the risk will not undermine the policy objectives of the provision. The loss in terms of deterrence and social protection would seem to be negligible when the retention of a subjective standard would at most offer protection for those who due to some peculiarity or unexpected accident commit conduct which, although it shows a reckless or wanton disregard for the lives or safety of others, can be explained as inconsistent with any degree of awareness of or wilful blindness to such a risk. Should social protection require the adoption of an objective standard it is open to Parliament to enact a law which clearly adopts such a standard. In my respectful view this Court should not do it for them.

I do not think that a subjective interpretation of s. 202 renders the role of manslaughter committed by means of criminal negligence superfluous within the scheme of the homicide provisions of the *Criminal Code*. The murder provisions will in general be available only if a higher degree of intent is proven than awareness of or wilful blindness to a risk to the lives and safety of others. For example, s. 212(*a*) and (*b*) [now s. 229(*a*) and (*b*)] involves the higher degree of *mens rea* of either meaning to cause death or meaning to cause bodily harm with the knowledge that it is likely to cause death and being reckless as to whether death ensues or not. There may be some overlap between the offence of committing culpable homicide by criminal negligence and the murder offences found in s. 212(*c*) [now s. 229(*c*)] and s. 213 [now s. 230], but these murder provisions seem to be a distinct part of the statutory scheme in that they are addressed to the specific issue of killings which result from either the pursuit of an unlawful object or the commission of specified indictable offences. Manslaughter by means of advertent criminal negligence would still, in my view, have a role to play in prohibiting killings done with a more minimal intent than required under s. 212(*a*) and (*b*) and in contexts which would not be covered by s. 212(*c*) and 213.

In recognition of the harshness of a uniform application of an objective standard of criminal liability, much of the recent work in criminal jurisprudence has canvassed the possibility of introducing a subjective dimension into the objective standard in order to relieve the harshness of imposing an objective standard on those who, because of their peculiar characteristics, could not fairly be expected to live up to the standard set by the reasonable person. H.L.A. Hart was perhaps the first to explore this possibility, in his essay "Negligence, *Mens Rea* and Criminal Responsibility" in Oxford Essays in Jurisprudence (1961), c. 2. He recognized the dangers of the use of an objective standard at p. 47:

> If our conditions of liability are invariant and not flexible *i.e.* if they are not adjusted to the capacities of the accused, then some individuals will be held liable for negligence though they could not have helped their failure to comply with the standard. In *such* cases, indeed, criminal responsibility will be made independent of any "subjective element": since the accused could not have conformed to the required standard.

In response to this most legitimate fear, Professor Hart proposed the following two-pronged test for criminal negligence:

> (i)   Did the accused fail to keep those precautions which any reasonable man with normal capacities would in the circumstances have taken?
>
> (ii) Could the accused, given his mental and physical capacities, have taken those precautions?

A similar approach has been taken by the criminal law theorist George Fletcher. Professor Fletcher also proposed that criminal liability for negligent conduct be determined in a two-step process, the first being the determination of wrongdoing, which in the case of the prohibition of negligence would proceed on the basis of breach of an objective standard, and the second being the process by which the Court determines whether it would be fair to hold a particular accused responsible for the act of wrongdoing. Professor Fletcher notes in *Rethinking Criminal Law* (1978), at p. 511:

> If the law ignored the question of attribution, namely, the question whether individuals were properly held accountable for their wrongful acts, the criminal law undoubtedly would generate some unjust decisions. If it were true that the only relevant norms of the legal system were those of wrongdoing, injustice would be inescapable in cases in which individuals could not but violate the law.

See also G. Fletcher, "The Theory of Criminal Negligence: A Comparative Analysis" (1971), 119 Univ. of Pa. L. Rev. 401; A. Stalker, "Can George Fletcher Help Solve The Problem of Criminal Negligence?" (1981), 7 Queen's L.J. 274. Professor Toni Pickard has also adopted an approach to this issue similar to that of Professors Hart and Fletcher. She proposes in "Culpable Mistakes and Rape? Relating *Mens Rea* to the Crime" (1980), 30 Univ. of Toronto L.J. 75, at p. 79, to modify an objective standard of unreasonableness so that "the relevant characteristics of the particular actor, rather than those of the ordinary person" will be "the background against which to measure the reasonableness of certain conduct or beliefs". Professor Pickard elaborates:

> This individualized standard is neither "subjective" nor "objective". It partakes of the subjective position because the inquiry the fact finder must conduct is about the defendant himself, not about some hypothetical ordinary person. It partakes of the objective position because the inquiry is not limited to what was, in fact, in the actor's mind, but includes an inquiry into what could have been in it, and a judgment about what ought to have been in it.

In their judgments in this case my colleagues McIntyre and Lamer JJ. seem to have adopted variations of the above developments. McIntyre J., for example, states [pp. 302-303]:

> The application of an objective test under s. 202 of the *Criminal Code*, however, may not be made in a vacuum. Events occur within the framework of other events and actions and, when deciding on the nature of the questioned conduct, surrounding circumstances must be considered. The decision must be made on a consideration of the facts existing at the time and in relation to the accused's perception of those facts. Since the test is objective, the accused's perception of the facts is not to be considered for the purpose of assessing malice or intention on the accused's part but only to form a basis for a conclusion as to whether or not the accused's conduct, in view of his perception of the facts, was reasonable.

My colleague then, however, goes on to suggest that the factual perceptions of the accused must be not only honest but reasonable in order to be factored into the assessment of the objective standard. For example, he suggests that the appellants in this case should not be held to the standard of honest but mistaken belief in circumstances which would render their conduct not culpable, as set out in *Pappajohn, supra*, but rather that their beliefs and perceptions in order to be considered must not be negligently or unreasonably held. To my mind, when the offence charged is criminal negligence the distinction from *Pappajohn* lies not in the introduction of an overriding standard of reasonableness, as this in effect holds the accused simply to the standards of what would be expected from the reasonable person, but rather in the degree of guilty knowledge that must be proven. Although a person may have an honest yet unreasonable view of the circumstances which would render him or her in the large sense blameless, this would not necessarily decide the relevant question of whether he or she had any awareness of the prohibited risk or at some time during the relevant transaction wilfully blinded him or herself to an otherwise obvious risk. To require, as does my colleague, that all misperceptions be reasonable will, in my view, not excuse many of those who through no fault of their own cannot fairly be expected to live up to the standard of the reasonable person.

My colleague Justice Lamer takes a somewhat different approach. He suggests [at p. 304] that Courts when applying the objective standard in s. 202 should make " 'a generous allowance' for factors which are particular to the accused, such as youth, mental development and education". I do not doubt that an expansive application of this approach could relieve some of the harshness of applying an objective standard to those who could not fairly be expected to meet the standard and I am cautiously sympathetic to attempts to integrate elements of subjective perception into criminal law standards that are clearly objective: see *R. v. Vasil*, [1981] 1 S.C.R. 469, 20 C.R. (3d) 193, 58 C.C.C. (2d) 97 [Ont.]; *R. v. Hill*, [1986] 1 S.C.R. 313, 51 C.R. (3d) 97, 25 C.C.C. (3d) 322. Despite this, the test proposed by my colleague suffers, in my respectful view, from the various degrees of over- and underinclusiveness that would be expected from a test which is only a rough substitute for a finding of a blameworthy state of mind in each case. For example, an instruction to the trier of fact that they are to hold a young accused with modest intelligence and little education to a standard of conduct that one would expect from the reasonable person of tender years, modest intelligence and little education sets out a fluctuating standard which in my view undermines the principles of equality and individual responsibility which should pervade the criminal law. It tells the jury simply to lower the standard of conduct expected from such people regardless of whether in the particular case the accused attained the degree of guilty knowledge that I have set out above. Professor Fletcher in "The Theory of Criminal Negligence: A Comparative Analysis" has termed the decision whether to make the standard of liability more or less objective by including or excluding specific personal characteristics a "policy question", "a low visibility device for adjusting the interests of competing classes of litigants", and I respectfully agree with the following criticism he makes of this process at pp. 407-408:

> The question in the criminal context is not one of adjusting the interests of competing classes of litigants, but of justifying the state's depriving an individual of his liberty.

Professor Fletcher's solution to this problem, the introduction of a comprehensive range of individualized excuses, is in my view far from realization in Canadian criminal law jurisprudence and, as such, the concern he identifies of the culpability of the individual is still, in my view, best served by continued adherence to subjective standards of liability.

One problem with attempts to individualize an objective standard is that regard for the disabilities of the particular accused can only be applied in a general fashion to alter the objective standard. It seems preferable to me to continue to address the question of whether a subjective standard (a standard, I might add, that in its form is applied equally to all and consistent with individual responsibility) has been breached in each case than to introduce varying standards of conduct which will be only roughly related to the presence or absence of culpability in the individual case. Varying the level of conduct by factoring in some personal characteristics may be unavoidable if the Court is faced with a clearly objective standard but it should, in my opinion, be avoided if the more exacting subjective test is available as a matter of statutory interpretation. I have no doubt that factors such as the accused's age and mental development will often be relevant to determining culpability, but under a subjective test they will be relevant only as they relate to the question of whether the accused was aware of or wilfully blind to the prohibited risk and will not have to be factored in wholesale in order to adjust the standard of conduct that is expected from citizens.

Attempts to introduce subjective elements into objective standards not only risk being overinclusive in the sense that they mandate a lowering of the objective standard of liability on a characteristic by characteristic basis, they also risk the danger of being underinclusive for those accused who have idiosyncracies that cannot be articulated ex ante into the necessarily limited list of personal characteristics which can be grafted on to an objective standard. For example, the characteristics listed by my colleague Lamer J. would not relieve the harshness of the application of an objective standard for a driver who, because of a sudden injury or ailment, drove a motor vehicle in a fashion which showed a reckless or wanton disregard for the lives and safety of others. It would not matter that the particular accused was not capable of adverting or wilfully closing his or her eyes to the prohibited risk; the conduct in itself would have breached the objective standard.

The limited range of personal characteristics which can be imported into a modified objective standard is often justified by the notion that a thoroughly subjective approach will allow those who deprive themselves of normal awareness through voluntary intoxication or fits of temper to be exempted from criminal liability. My answer to this (it was also my answer in the cases of *Bernard, supra,* and *R. v. Quin,* [1988] 2 S.C.R. 825, 67 C.R. (3d) 162, 44 C.C.C. (3d) 570) is that greater attention must be paid to the minimal levels of guilty knowledge that are required for conviction of many offences of violence under the *Criminal Code.* It is, in my respectful view, perfectly permissible for the trier of fact to reason from an objective standard and ask the question: must not the accused have had the minimal awareness of what he or she was doing? The important point is that this question is rebuttable and leaves room for acquitting an accused who, for whatever reason, lacked the minimal awareness that would normally accompany the commission of high-risk or violent acts.

I am in complete agreement with what my colleague Justice Lamer has to say concerning the issue of constitutionality.

WAITE v. R.

[1989] 1 S.C.R. 1436, 69 C.R. (3d) 323, 48 C.C.C. (3d) 1

The accused, who had been drinking, struck and killed four young people taking part in a hayride and injured a fifth. The hayride involved three tractors each towing a wagon with bales of hay along a public road. Four or five of the young people had been running alongside the wagons or had been running from one wagon to another when the accused came upon the hayride. The accused drove behind the hayride, passed it, turned around and deliberately approached the hayride at high speed on the wrong side of the road. The accused testified that he had said to his companions, "Let's see how close we can get". Estimates of the speed varied from 50 to 90 m.p.h. He was driving without headlights.

Following trial before a Judge and jury, the accused was found not guilty of four counts of causing death by criminal negligence and one count of causing bodily harm by criminal negligence, but guilty of five counts of the included offence of dangerous driving. The charge to the jury did not specifically mention the objective test for criminal negligence but did convey that the *mens rea* required for proof of the commission of the offence could be found in the accused's conduct. While the jury were deliberating, they returned to ask the Judge the difference between dangerous driving and criminal negligence. The Judge advised them that in dangerous driving they should look objectively at the manner of driving but that in the case of criminal negligence they had to look at a subjective element and find a "deliberate and wilful assumption of the risk involved in driving in the manner in which he was driving". The Ontario Court of Appeal allowed the Crown's appeal. It held that where allegations of criminal negligence are based upon the manner of driving or some other act of commission, the test is the objective one of whether the driving or the act of commission constitutes a marked and substantial departure from the conduct expected of a reasonable man in the same circumstances. A new trial was directed on the criminal negligence charges. The accused appealed.

The accused's appeal to the Supreme Court was heard at the same time as *Tutton*. The Court unanimously dismissed the accused's appeal. The objective McIntyre wing repeated their views in *Tutton* justifying an objective test of a marked and substantial departure from the standard of behaviour expected of reasonably prudent persons in the circumstances. In agreeing to dismiss the appeal, the subjective wing reasoned as follows:

WILSON J.: —

In my view the trial Judge's final instruction to the jury was in error as to the degree of *mens rea* required under s. 202 [now s. 219] of the *Criminal Code*, R.S.C. 1970, c. C-34 [now R.S.C. 1985, c. C-46]. When the jury asked the trial Judge to explain the moral difference between dangerous driving and causing death by criminal negligence, the trial Judge instructed the jury that the subjective element in criminal negligence was "a deliberate and wilful assumption of the risk involved in driving in the manner in which he was driving". Later in his reply to the jury he repeated that the subjective element in criminal negligence was "assumption and deliberate assumption of the risk". Although I believe there is a subjective element to criminal negligence, the

Judge in this case placed much too high an onus on the Crown to prove elements of deliberation and wilfulness. For the reasons I gave in *Tutton* I am of the view that the mental element in criminal negligence is the minimal intent of awareness of the prohibited risk or wilful blindness to the risk.

The trial Judge's erroneous instructions to the jury were given near the close of the trial and they were crucial because they were in response to a question from the jury. The facts of the case also suggest that, had the jury been instructed as to the minimal intent requirements of awareness or wilful blindness to the prohibited risk, they would not necessarily have returned the verdict of acquittal on the charges of causing death by criminal negligence: see *Vézeau v. R.*, [1977] 2 S.C.R. 277, 34 C.R.N.S. 309, 28 C.C.C. (2d) 81 [Que.].

Is this a proper application of the subjective test? Compare Stuart, "Criminal Negligence: Deadlock and Confusion in the Supreme Court" (1989), 69 C.R. (3d) 331.

R. v. ANDERSON

(1990), 75 C.R. (3d) 50 (S.C.C.)

The accused was charged with criminal negligence causing death. He had been thinking of something else, ran a red light and a passenger in the car he hit died as a result of injuries suffered in the accident. There was no evidence of any erratic driving apart from driving through the red traffic light. The accused, although legally impaired, showed little sign of impairment. The trial Judge found that the Crown had failed to prove the charge beyond a reasonable doubt. During the course of his reasons the trial Judge stated that neither the *mens rea* nor the consequences of the manner of driving were material in making a decision as to guilt or innocence. An appeal was allowed by the Court of Appeal. The accused appealed. The sole issue was whether the trial Judge's comments relating to the relevance of consequences and intention affected the outcome.

The judgment of the seven-person Court was delivered by SOPINKA J.: —

. . . .

In approaching the critique of a trial judgment dealing with a charge of criminal negligence, one can only have profound sympathy for the plight of the trial Judge. This area of the law, both here and in other common law countries, has proved to be one of the most difficult and uncertain in the whole of the criminal field. The sections of the *Criminal Code*, R.S.C. 1970, c. C-34, under consideration here are relatively simple.

The use of the word "negligence" suggests that the impugned conduct must depart from a standard objectively determined. On the other hand, the use of the words "wanton and reckless disregard" suggests that an ingredient of the offence includes a state of mind or some moral quality to the conduct which attracts the sanctions of the criminal law. The section makes it clear that the conclusion that there is a wanton or reckless disregard is to be drawn from the conduct which falls below the standard. The major disagreement in the cases centers around the manner in which this conclusion is to be drawn.

On the one hand, there are the cases that hold that it is to be done on an objective basis. If the conduct is a marked departure from the norm, then, based on the standard of an ordinary prudent individual, the accused ought to have known that his actions could endanger the lives or safety of others. On the other hand, there are cases that apply a subjective standard and require some degree of advertence to the risk to be proved. This may be done by inferring advertence from the nature of the conduct in the context of the surrounding circumstances. A refinement on the latter view is that a marked departure constitutes a *prima facie* case of negligence. The trier of fact may but it is not obliged to infer the necessary mental element from the conduct which is found to depart substantially from the norm.

In both the objective and subjective approaches, the Court is determining foreseeability of consequences. In a civil negligence case concerned with adjustment of losses, the connection between conduct and consequences is often quite tenuous. The mythical reasonable man has been equipped with a great deal of clairvoyance in order to compensate the innocent victim. Often the defendant will not, in fact, have foreseen the consequences of his negligent acts for which he is held accountable on an objective basis. In a criminal case the connection must be more substantial. To establish recklessness, the consequences must be more obvious. That is the rationale for the requirement of a marked departure from the norm. The greater the risk created, the easier it is to conclude that a reasonably prudent person would have foreseen the consequences. Equally, it is easier to conclude that the accused must have foreseen the consequences. It is apparent, therefore, that as the risk of harm increases, the significance of the distinction between the objective and subjective approaches decreases. The ultimate in this process of reasoning is reached when the risk is so high that the consequences are the natural result of the conduct creating the risk. The conduct in such circumstances can be characterized as intentional.

A finding that the impugned conduct is a marked departure from the standard is, accordingly, central to both the objective and subjective approaches. In *R. v. Tutton*, [1989] 1 S.C.R. 1392, this Court was divided as to which approach is correct.

. . . .

Criminal Negligence — Application to This Case

In this case as in most of these cases there is no direct evidence of the state of mind of the appellant. The conclusion that he had a wanton or reckless disregard for the lives and safety of others must be drawn from the conduct which is alleged to be a marked departure from the norm. If an objective standard is employed, this will be determined on the basis of the state of mind of an ordinary prudent person in the circumstances. If the subjective standard or its refinement are applied, then the conclusion, if drawn, must be drawn from the conduct of the appellant.

The conduct relied on in this case is (a) the combination of drinking and driving, and (b) the breach of a traffic light regulation. Clearly the trial Judge considered both. He concluded that the conduct was not a marked departure from the norm. That being the case, a conclusion that the appellant had a wanton or reckless disregard for the lives and safety of others could not be drawn on either a subjective or objective basis.

The trial Judge specifically addressed the question of the drinking and driving. The Court of Appeal agreed that this was so. Nevertheless he was not prepared to find that this, together with the traffic violation, was sufficient. It left him in a state of doubt. No doubt setting out to drive after drinking in some circumstances may be sufficient to conclude either objectively or subjectively that there is a wanton or reckless disregard for the lives and safety of others. It will not be so, however, in every case. The contrary conclusion would render redundant subss. (2) and (3) of s. 237 [now s. 255] of the *Criminal Code* which provides specific penalties for causing death or bodily harm through the operation of a motor vehicle while impaired. The decision, however, in each case is one of fact, and in this case the trial Judge was not prepared to so conclude.

Was this finding affected by the reference to intention? The statement in context is as follows: "nor is *mens rea*, or the intention required to be proved by the Crown. It matters not what the man's intention was when he entered the automobile to put it into use." I do not read this statement to mean that the evidence that the appellant chose to drive his car knowing he had been drinking was not relevant. Such an interpretation would constitute too microscopic an approach to the trial Judge's reasons. Clearly, the trial Judge went on to consider the relevance of this evidence. What the trial Judge was dealing with here was the Crown's obligation. Intention need not be proved by the Crown. From the Crown's point of view, it did not matter that the appellant intended to drive safely when he entered the automobile. The sentence following the above-quoted passage emphasizes that this is the context in which the statement is made: "Nevertheless, of course, the Crown must carry its burden. . . ."

The trial Judge's statement that the consequences are not relevant must also be dealt with in the context in which it was made. This reference is undoubtedly one to the tragic death of the passenger in the other vehicle involved in the collision. The death of the passenger was a necessary ingredient of the *actus reus*. It was not otherwise relevant unless a conclusion could be drawn from it with respect to whether there was a wanton and reckless disregard for the lives and safety of other persons. It was not suggested by the Crown that it was a circumstance from which such a conclusion could be drawn either on an objective or subjective basis.

In the circumstances of this case, the unfortunate fact that a person was killed added nothing to the conduct of the appellant. The degree of negligence proved against the appellant by means of the evidence that he drove after drinking and went through a red light was not increased by the fact that a collision occurred and death resulted. If driving and drinking and running a red light was not a marked departure from the standard, it did not become so because a collision occurred. In some circumstances, perhaps, the actions of the accused and the consequences flowing from them may be so interwoven that the consequences may be relevant in characterizing the conduct of the accused. That is not the case here.

In my opinion, the trial Judge came to the conclusion on the evidence that there was a reasonable doubt that the conduct of the accused constituted criminal negligence. He was entitled to do so on the facts. Although he made some general remarks that perhaps should not have been made without elaboration, I am satisfied that no error of law resulted. In any event, the statements to which I have alluded did not affect the outcome. The respondent has not satisfied me that the verdict would not necessarily have been the same. The Court of Appeal ought not to have set aside the acquittal.

In view of this conclusion, it is unnecessary to deal with the appellant's submissions with respect to *R. v. Caldwell*, [1981] All E.R. 961, nor the appellant's submissions that the judgment of the Manitoba Court of Appeal is inconsistent with the principle in *R. v. Vaillancourt* (1987), 39 C.C.C. (3d) 118.

Disposition

In the result, the appeal is allowed, the judgment of the Court of Appeal set aside and the acquittal restored.

See comment by Patrick Healy, "Anderson: Marking Time or a Step Back on Criminal Negligence?" (1990), 75 C.R. (3d) 58.

Marked Departure Test

The Supreme Court in *Creighton* and its companion cases adopted a new approach to the interpretation of objective crimes. The Court was unanimous in requiring a marked departure from the standard of care of a reasonable person. The Court however divided 5:4 over the question whether personal factors could be considered in applying an objective standard. McLachlin J. for the majority decided that no individual factors short of incapacity could be considered. Which opinion do you prefer?

R. v. CREIGHTON

[1993] 3 S.C.R. 3, 23 C.R. (4th) 189, 83 C.C.C. (3d) 346

On a charge of manslaughter, defence counsel conceded at trial that the injection into the deceased's body of cocaine constituted trafficking within the definition set out in s. 4(1) of the *Narcotic Control Act*. The Crown argued that the accused was guilty of manslaughter as the death was the direct consequence of that unlawful act, contrary to s. 222(5)(a) of the *Criminal Code*. The accused was convicted, and the Court of Appeal upheld the conviction. The common law had decided that where the accused had committed an unlawful act, objective foreseeability of the risk of bodily harm which is neither trivial nor transitory was sufficient and foreseeability of the risk of death was not required. The Supreme Court was called on to determine whether the common law definition of unlawful act manslaughter contravened s. 7 of the *Charter*. In deciding that it did not the Court expressed some thoughts on the meaning of negligence in the criminal law.

MCLACHLIN J. (L'HEUREUX-DUBÉ GONTHIER, and CORY JJ., concurring): —

The Nature of the Objective Test

I respectfully differ from the Chief Justice on the nature of the objective test used to determine the *mens rea* for crimes of negligence. In my view, the approach advocated by the Chief Justice personalizes the objective test to the point where it devolves into a subjective test, thus eroding the minimum standard of care which Parliament has laid down by the enactment of offences of manslaughter and penal negligence.

By way of background, it may be useful to restate what I understand the jurisprudence to date to have established regarding crimes of negligence and the objective test. The *mens rea* of a criminal offence may be either subjective or objective, subject to the principle of fundamental justice that the moral fault of the offence must be proportionate to its gravity and penalty. Subjective *mens rea* requires that the accused has intended the consequences of his or her acts, or that knowing of the probable consequences of those acts, the accused has proceeded recklessly in the face of the risk. The requisite intent or knowledge may be inferred directly from what the accused said or says about his or her mental state, or indirectly from the act and its circumstances. Even in the latter case, however, it is concerned with "what was actually going on in the mind of this particular accused at the time in question": L'Heureux-Dubé J. in *R. v. Martineau, supra*, at p. 655, quoting Stuart, *Canadian Criminal Law* (2nd ed. 1987), at p. 121.

Objective *mens rea*, on the other hand, is not concerned with what the accused intended or knew. Rather, the mental fault lies in failure to direct the mind to a risk which the reasonable person would have appreciated. Objective *mens rea* is not concerned with what was actually in the accused's mind, but with what should have been there, had the accused proceeded reasonably.

It is now established that a person may be held criminally responsible for negligent conduct on the objective test, and that this alone does not violate the principle of fundamental justice that the moral fault of the accused must be commensurate with the gravity of the offence and its penalty: *R. v. Hundal*, [1993] 1 S.C.R. 867.

However, as stated in *Martineau*, it is appropriate that those who cause harm intentionally should be punished more severely than those who cause harm inadvertently. Moreover, the constitutionality of crimes of negligence is also subject to the caveat that acts of ordinary negligence may not suffice to justify imprisonment: *R. v. City of Sault Ste. Marie*, [1978], 2 S.C.R. 1299; *R. v. Sansregret*, [1985] 1 S.C.R. 570. To put it in the terms used in *Hundal*: The negligence must constitute a "marked departure" from the standard of the reasonable person. The law does not lightly brand a person as a criminal. For this reason, I am in agreement with the Chief Justice in *R. v. Finlay, supra*, that the word "careless" in an underlying firearms offence must be read as requiring a marked departure from the constitutional norm.

It follows from this requirement, affirmed in *Hundal*, that in an offence based on unlawful conduct, a predicate offence involving carelessness or negligence must also be read as requiring a "marked departure" from the standard of the reasonable person. As pointed out in *DeSousa*, the underlying offence must be constitutionally sound.

To this point, the Chief Justice and I are not, as I perceive it, in disagreement. The difference between our approaches turns on the extent to which personal characteristics of the accused may affect liability under the objective test. Here we enter territory in large part uncharted. To date, debate has focused on whether an objective test for *mens rea* is ever available in the criminal law; little has been said about how, assuming it is applicable, it is to be applied. In *R. v. Hundal, supra*, it was said that the *mens rea* of dangerous driving should be assessed objectively in the context of all the events surrounding the incident. But the extent to which those circumstances include personal mental or psychological frailties of the accused was not explored in depth. In these circumstances, we must begin with the fundamental principles of criminal law.

1. Underlying Principles

The debate about the degree to which personal characteristics should be reflected in the objective test for fault in offences of penal negligence engages two fundamental concepts of criminal law.

The first concept is the notion that the criminal law may properly hold people who engage in risky activities to a minimum standard of care, judged by what a reasonable person in all the circumstances would have done. This notion posits a uniform standard for all persons engaging in the activity, regardless of their background, education or psychological disposition.

The second concept is the principle that the morally innocent not be punished (*Re B.C. Motor Vehicle Act*, [1985] 2 S.C.R. 486, at p. 513; *R. v. Gosset*, S.C.C., No.22523, reasons of Lamer C.J. at p. 20). This principle is the foundation of the requirement of criminal law that the accused must have a guilty mind, or *mens rea*.

I agree with the Chief Justice that the rule that the morally innocent not be punished in the context of the objective test requires that the law refrain from holding a person criminally responsible if he or she is not capable of appreciating the risk. Where I differ from the Chief Justice is in his designation of the sort of educational, experiential and so-called "habitual" factors personal to the accused which can be taken into account. The Chief Justice, while in principle advocating a uniform standard of care for all, in the result seems to contemplate a standard of care which varies with the background and predisposition of each accused. Thus an inexperienced, uneducated, young person, like the accused in *R. v. Naglik*, S.C.C., Nos. 22490 and 22636, September 9, 1993, could be acquitted, even though she does not meet the standard of the reasonable person (reasons of the Chief Justice, at p. 24). On the other hand, a person with special experience, like Mr. Creighton in this case, or the appellant police officer in *R. v. Gosset*, S.C.C., No. 22523 (reasons released concurrently), will be held to a higher standard than the ordinary reasonable person.

I must respectfully dissent from this extension of the objective test for criminal fault. In my view, considerations of principle and policy dictate the maintenance of a single, uniform legal standard of care for such offences, subject to one exception: incapacity to appreciate the nature of the risk which the activity in question entails.

This principle that the criminal law will not convict the morally innocent does not, in my view, require consideration of personal factors short of incapacity. The criminal law, while requiring mental fault as an element of a conviction, has steadfastly rejected the idea that a person's personal characteristics can (short of incapacity) excuse the person from meeting the standard of conduct imposed by the law.

. . . .

The Chief Justice relies on Professor H.L.A. Hart in support of importing what Wilson J. calls "individualized excusing conditions" into the objective test for offences of manslaughter and penal negligence. In fact, Professor Hart sees the principle of preventing the punishment of the morally innocent as dictating only that people should not be punished when they lacked the capacity to appreciate the consequences of their conduct. He reasons that no one should be held blameworthy and punished for criminal conduct if he or she acted without free will (H. Hart, *Punishment and Responsibility* (1968), at pp. 35-40). He states that "the need to inquire into the 'inner facts' is dictated . . . by the moral principle that no one should be punished who could not help doing what he did" (p. 39) (emphasis added).

In summary, I can find no support in criminal theory for the conclusion that protection of the morally innocent requires a general consideration of individual excusing conditions. The principle comes into play only at the point where the person is shown to lack the capacity to appreciate the nature and quality or the consequences of his or her acts. Apart from this, we are all, rich and poor, wise and naive, held to the minimum standards of conduct prescribed by the criminal law. This conclusion is dictated by a fundamental proposition of social organization. As Justice Oliver Wendell Holmes wrote in *The Common Law*

(1881), at p. 108: "when men live in society, a certain average of conduct, a sacrifice of individual peculiarities going beyond a certain point, is necessary to the general welfare."

This is not to say that the question of guilt is determined in a factual vacuum. While the legal duty of the accused is not particularized by his or her personal characteristics short of incapacity, it is particularized in application by the nature of the activity and the circumstances surrounding the accused's failure to take the requisite care. As McIntyre J. pointed out in *R. v. Tutton*, [1989] 1 S.C.R. 1392, the answer to the question of whether the accused took reasonable care must be founded on a consideration of all the circumstances of the case. The question is what the reasonably prudent person would have done in all the circumstances. Thus a welder who lights a torch causing an explosion may be excused if he has made an enquiry and been given advice upon which he was reasonably entitled to rely, that there was no explosive gas in the area. The necessity of taking into account all of the circumstances in applying the objective test in offences of penal negligence was affirmed in *R. v. Hundal*, *supra*.

. . . .

LAMER C.J. (SOPINKA, IACOBUCCI and MAJOR JJ. concurring): — The Crown bears the burden of proving beyond a reasonable doubt that a reasonable person in the context of the offence would have foreseen the risk of death created by his or her conduct. As I explain in more detail in *R. v. Gosset*, S.C.C., No. 22523, released this same day, the reasonable person will be invested with any enhanced foresight the accused may have enjoyed by virtue of his or her membership in a group with special experience or knowledge related to the conduct giving rise to the offence. For example, in *Gosset* the accused police officer's experience and training in the handling of firearms is relevant to the standard of care under s. 86(2) of the *Criminal Code* concerning the careless use of firearms. In the present case, the reasonable person should be deemed to possess Mr. Creighton's considerable experience in drug use. Once the Crown has established beyond a reasonable doubt that this reasonable person in the context of the offence would have foreseen the risk of death created by his or her conduct, the focus of the investigation must shift to the question of whether a reasonable person in the position of the accused would have been capable of foreseeing such a risk. The objective test cannot, to reiterate, relieve the accused of criminal liability simply because he or she did not, in fact, foresee creating the risk of death. I wish to reiterate that the standard of care remains uniform and unchanging irrespective of the particular accused — the prosecution must demonstrate a marked departure from the standard of a reasonable person; rather, it is in the determination of what is reasonable that the skill and expertise of the accused may be considered.

The objective test can be best understood when stated as a "checklist" for the trier of fact to apply to the accused's conduct in a particular case. Where the accused is charged with the offence of unlawful act manslaughter, the trier of fact must ask:

(1) Would a reasonable person in the same circumstances have been aware that the likely consequences of his or her unlawful conduct would create the risk of death?

This question provides the threshold to the objective test. If the answer to this question is No, then the accused must be acquitted. If the answer is Yes, however, the trier must then ask:

(2) Was the accused unaware

(a) because he or she did not turn his or her mind to the consequences of the conduct and thus to the risk of death likely to result; or

(b) because he or she lacked the capacity to turn his or her mind to the consequences of the conduct and thus to the risk of death likely to result, due to human frailties?

If the answer is (a), the accused must be convicted, since the criminal law cannot allow the absence of actual awareness to be an excuse to criminal liability. An important distinction must be maintained within the objective test between the capacity to decide to turn one's mind to a risk, and the decision not to turn one's mind to it. As Colvin, *Principles of Criminal Law* (2nd ed. 1991), notes, at p. 155:

> As long as attention is directed to the individual's own capabilities, a judgment of fault can be made on the ground that there was a fair opportunity to have recognized the risks and harm of conduct.

A key element of the objective test is that of the control an accused could have exercised over the frailty which rendered him or her incapable of acting as the reasonable person would in the same circumstances. The notion of control is related to that of moral responsibility; if one is able to act prudently and not endanger the life of others, one will be held liable for failing to do so. One must be morally — and criminally — responsible to act according to his or her capacities not to inflict harm, even unintentional harm. By contrast, the inability to control a particular frailty which resulted in the creation of the risk may offer a moral excuse for having brought about that risk. Therefore, if the answer to the second branch of the objective test is (b), the third and final stage of the inquiry is required:

(3) In the context of the particular offence, would the reasonable person with the capacities of the accused have made him or herself aware of the likely consequences of the unlawful conduct and the resulting risk of death?

In this inquiry, the accused's behaviour is still measured against the standard of the reasonable person, but the reasonable person is constructed to account for the accused's particular capacities and resulting inability to perceive and address certain risks. This test is similar to that advocated by Hart, in "Negligence, *Mens Rea* and Criminal Responsibility", *supra*, at p. 154:

(i) Did the accused fail to take those precautions which any reasonable man with normal capacities would in the circumstances have taken?

(ii) Could the accused, given his mental and physical capacities, have taken those precautions?

It must be emphasized that this is not a subjective test: if a reasonable person with the frailties of the accused would nevertheless have appreciated the risk, and the accused did not in fact appreciate the risk, the accused must be convicted.

The rationale of incorporating capacity into the objective determination of fault is analogous to the rationale underlying the defence of mistake of fact in criminal law, where an accused who has an honest and reasonably held belief in an incorrect set of facts, and acts on the basis of those facts, is excused from punishment for the resulting harm. Human frailties which may affect the capacity of an accused to recognize the risks of unlawful conduct must be considered, however, not because they result in the accused believing in an incorrect set of facts, but rather because they render the accused incapable of perceiving the correct set of facts. It is, however, only those human frailties which relate to an accused's capacity to appreciate the risk in question that may be considered in this inquiry.

I shall now turn to elaborating what "human frailties" may factor into the objective test. It is perhaps best to begin by stating clearly what is not included. Intoxication or impairment through drug use which occurs as a result of voluntary consumption cannot serve to vitiate liability for the risks created by the negligent conduct of an accused. Additionally, a sudden and temporary incapacity to appreciate risk due to exigent circumstances (an emergency which diverts one's attention from an activity, for example) is not properly considered under the third part of the test, but may well result in an acquittal under the first part of the test, that is, would a reasonable person's attention in the same circumstances of the accused have been diverted from that activity.

Human frailties encompass personal characteristics habitually affecting an accused's awareness of the circumstances which create risk. Such characteristics must be relevant to the ability to perceive the particular risk. For example, while illiteracy may excuse the failure to take care with a hazardous substance identifiable only by a label, as the accused may be unable, in this case, to apprehend the relevant facts, illiteracy may not be relevant to the failure to take care with a firearm. This attention to the context of the offence and the nature of the activity is explored in greater detail below.

It should be emphasized that the relevant characteristics must be traits which the accused could not control or otherwise manage in the circumstances. For example, while a person with cataracts cannot be faulted for having reduced vision, he or she may be expected to avoid activity in which that limitation will either create risk or render him or her unable to manage risk which is inherent in an activity (driving, for example). The reasonable person is expected to compensate for his or her frailties, to the extent he or she is conscious of them and able to do so.

This general discussion is not intended to set out an exhaustive definition, but rather to lay the groundwork for examining the different factual contexts which may arise. Two central criteria in this regard are (1) the gravity of the offence, and (2) the inherent purposefulness of the conduct involved. With respect to the gravity of the offence, there may be a significant gulf between neglecting to safely store a bottle containing a prescription drug, and neglecting to unload a firearm and return it to its cabinet. In these different contexts, the behaviour of the reasonable person who possesses all of the accused's limitations may be very different, and therefore the answer to the third question regarding the ability of an accused to control or compensate for his or her frailties may be different as well.

LaFOREST J.: —

. . . .

There are important educative and psychological differences between the two approaches that have led me to prefer the subjective view of *mens rea*. That view underlines that no one will be punished for anything he or she did not intend or at least advert to, and its use supports one's feeling that a morally innocent person will not be punished.

The objective view, however qualified, does not fully serve these ends. It is true that the qualified objective view would theoretically protect some of the individuals the subjective view would protect, but by no means all; see *Tutton*, *supra*, per Wilson J., at p. 1419. And it does not respond to the educative and psychological ends sought to be attained by those advocating subjective *mens rea*. Indeed, it introduces a differentiation between individuals in criminal proceedings that, however well-meant, seems foreign to our law. What is more, the qualified objective approach loses most of the practical advantages sought to be attained by the objective approach. Indeed, some of the difficulties that have been perceived to result from the adoption of the subjective view would be exacerbated. I think, in particular, of the difficulties of instructing a jury. On this question, too, I find McLachlin J.'s reasons more persuasive.

Creighton stands firmly against any development of a cultural defence: see Charmaine M. Wong, "Good Intentions, Troublesome Applications: The Cultural Defence and Other Uses of Cultural Evidence in Canada" (1999), 42 Crim. L.Q. 367. The author fully explores the possibilities and drawbacks to such a defence but, surprisingly, makes no mention of *Creighton*. See, too, Stephen Coughlan, "The Omission of Provocation from a General Part" in Stuart, Delisle and Manson (eds.), *Towards a Clear and Just Criminal Law* (1999), 243 at 244-245, who argues against the defence and suggests debate seems to exist only in the United States.

Prior to *Creighton*, the Supreme Court in *R. v. Hundal*, [1993] 1 S.C.R. 867, 19 C.R. (4th) 169, 79 C.C.C. (3d) 97, 38 W.A.C. 241 had held that the test for dangerous driving under s. 245 of the *Criminal Code* is a marked departure from the objective norm and that the objective standard is an individualised one. In *R. v. Reed*, [1998] 1 S.C.R. 753, 15 C.R. (5th) 28, 124 C.C.C. (3d) 257, the

Supreme Court recently confirmed the authority of *Hundal* for dangerous driving without mention of it being inconsistent with *Creighton* on the issue of an individualized objective standard. Reed was held rightly convicted of dangerous driving by driving at night on the wrong side of the road at more than 20 kms. over the speed limit.

As to the issue of incapacity, it has been held that severe mental retardation can be taken into account for criminal negligence, *Ubhi* (1994), 27 C.R. (4th) 332 (B.C. C.A.), leave to appeal refused (1994), 31 C.R. (4th) 405 (note) (S.C.C.), but not religious beliefs in an exorcism case involving the death of an infant, *Canhoto* (1999), 140 C.C.C. (3d) 321, 29 C.R. (5th) 170 (Ont. C.A.).

Creighton was seemingly ignored on the issue of no individual factors in *Brocklebank* (1996), 106 C.C.C. (3d) 234 (Can. Ct. Martial App. Ct.). The standard for negligent performance of military duty was adjusted to take into account accused's rank, degree of responsibility and exigencies of operation.

(3) Crimes Based on Predicate Offences

On the authority of *Creighton* and *DeSousa* there are some offences based on predicate offences where the fault requirement regarding the consequence of the underlying offence is much reduced but constitutional. The problem will be how to identify them. Thus far there are three: *DeSousa* concerns the offence of unlawful act causing harm; *Creighton* the manslaughter category of unlawful act causing death; and *R. v. Godin*, [1994] 2 S.C.R. 484, 31 C.R. (4th) 33, 89 C.C.C. (3d) 574, aggravated assault. In each case the unlawful act is interpreted to require objective foresight of harm. *DeSousa* also held that the unlawful act must be a provincial or federal offence, that the fault for the predicate offence must be proved and that this cannot be absolute liability. There is no requirement of a marked departure from the objective norm beyond proof of the underlying offence. However where the predicate, or underlying offence is one of negligence the gross departure limit must be applied to it. See *R. v. Gosset* (1993), 23 C.R. (4th) 280 (S.C.C.) at 284.

R. v. DESOUSA

[1992] 2 S.C.R. 944, 15 C.R. (4th) 66, 76 C.C.C. (3d) 124 (S.C.C.)

A fight broke out at a New Year's Eve party. The accused was involved in the fight. A bystander was injured on the arm when a bottle, allegedly thrown by the accused, broke against a wall and a glass fragment struck the bystander. The accused was charged with unlawfully causing bodily harm contrary to s. 269 of the *Criminal Code*. At the outset of the trial, before any evidence was heard, the accused brought a motion to have s. 269 declared of no force or effect on the ground that it violated s. 7 of the *Charter*. The trial Judge granted the motion and quashed the indictment. He found that s. 269 created criminal responsibility for causing bodily harm by way of an unlawful act. The unlawful act could be a violation of a federal or provincial statute, including an offence of absolute liability. Since the section also allowed the possibility of imprisonment, it contravened s. 7 of the *Charter* and was not justified under s. 1. On appeal, the Court of Appeal overturned the motion judgment and set aside the order quashing the indictment. The accused appealed. Notice that an assault is not an essential element of the offence charged in this case; if an assault caused bodily harm the accused would be culpable under s.267(1)(*b*).

SOPINKA J. (CORY, GONTHIER, MCLACHLIN, and IACOBUCCI JJ. concurring):

. . . .

B. Section 269 of the *Criminal Code* —

To be brought within the ambit of s. 269, an accused must have committed an underlying unlawful offence (otherwise referred to as the predicate offence) and have caused bodily harm to another person as a result of committing that underlying offence. For liability to be imposed for unlawfully causing bodily harm, the harm caused must have sufficient causal connection to the underlying offence committed (see *R. v. Wilmot*, (1940), 74 C.C.C. 1 (Alta. C.A.), at pp. 17 and 26-27 [C.C.C.], appeal dismissed for want of jurisdiction [1941] S.C.R. 53, 75 C.C.C. 161. The requirement of an underlying "unlawful" offence includes at its most general, and subject to the restrictions discussed below, only offences prohibited by federal or provincial legislation.

. . . .

(1) *The Mental Element Requirement of Section 269*

The major issue raised in this appeal concerns the mental element required by s. 269 of the *Code*. After delineating the statutorily required mental element, the question of the constitutional sufficiency of this element will then be addressed to determine whether it passes constitutional muster.

It is axiomatic that in criminal law there should be no responsibility without personal fault. A fault requirement was asserted to be a fundamental aspect of our common law by this Court in *R. v. Sault Ste. Marie (City)*, [1978] 2 S.C.R. 1299, 3 C.R. (3d) 30, 40 C.C.C. (2d) 353, and as a matter of constitutional law under s. 7 of the *Charter* in *Reference re s. 94(2) of the Motor Vehicle Act (British Columbia)*, [1985] 2 S.C.R. 486, 48 C.R. (3d) 289, 23 C.C.C. (3d) 289, (sub nom. *Constitutional Question Act, R.S.B.C. 1979, Chap. 63*) [1986] D.L.Q. 90 (headnote) [hereafter *Re B.C. Motor Vehicle Act.*] As a matter of statutory interpretation, a provision should not be interpreted to lack any element of personal fault unless the statutory language mandates such an interpretation in clear and unambiguous terms. Unlike most offences, the mental element of s. 269 is composed of two separate requirements. The first requirement is that the mental element of the underlying offence of s. 269 be satisfied. The second requirement is that the additional fault requirement supplied by the wording of s. 269, discussed more fully, *infra*, also be satisfied.

(a) *The mental element of the underlying offence*

To be convicted under s. 269, the prosecution must first satisfy the mental element requirement of the underlying offence. In interpreting the ambit of the underlying offences covered by s. 269 it is important to recognize the abhorrence of the criminal law for offences of absolute liability. While not all underlying offences will have a possibility of imprisonment and despite the fact that s. 269 has a fault requirement in addition to that supplied by the underlying offence, as a matter of statutory interpretation, underlying offences of absolute liability are excluded from forming the basis for a prosecution under s. 269. For the reasons given by this Court in *Sault Ste. Marie, supra*, and *Re B.C. Motor Vehicle Act, supra*, s. 269 should not be interpreted so as to bootstrap underlying offences of absolute liability into the criminal law. The criminal law is based on proof of personal fault and this concept is jealously guarded when a Court is asked to interpret criminal provisions, especially those with potentially serious penal consequences. This statutory conclusion is mandated by the general presumption in the interpretation of criminal statutes against absolute liability and the absence of clear words to the contrary to rebut this presumption. Thus, the concept of "unlawful" as it is used in s. 269 does not include any underlying offence of absolute liability. The inclusion of such offences would be contrary to the general canons of criminal interpretation quite apart from any *Charter* considerations (see particularly *R. v. Baril*, [1979] 2 S.C.R. 547, 8 C.R. (3d) 68, 46 C.C.C. (2d) 257, at p. 553 [S.C.R.], and *Beaver v. R.*, [1957] S.C.R. 531, 26 C.R. 193, 118 C.C.C. 129, at pp. 537-538 and 542-543 [S.C.R.]). Although not relying on constitutional requirements in foreclosing the possibility of absolute liability offences forming the predicate offences of s. 269, certainly principles of fundamental justice require no less.

In addition to satisfying the statutorily required mental element of the underlying offence, the mental element of the underlying offence must also be constitutionally sufficient in its own right. If the underlying offence contains a constitutionally insufficient mental element, it is of no force or effect and thus cannot form the basis for a prosecution under s. 269. The underlying offence must be valid in law on its own before it can be used to support a charge under s. 269.

(b) *The meaning of "unlawful" in section 269*

In addition to the mental element required by the underlying offence, the wording of s. 269, and particularly the case law interpreting the term "unlawfully", imports an additional aspect to the mental element of s. 269. The case law interpreting the use of this term in similar provisions has focused on the offence most commonly known as unlawful act manslaughter. While manslaughter is not the offence at issue in this appeal, the case law which seeks to interpret the term "unlawful" in that context is instructive.

The leading English authority on the issue of the meaning of "unlawful" in this area is *R. v. Larkin* (1942), 29 Cr. App. R. 18, where the Court of Criminal Appeal held that:

> Where the act which a person is engaged in performing is unlawful, then if at the same time it is a dangerous act, that is, an act which is likely to injure another person, and quite inadvertently the doer of the act causes the death of that other person by that act, then he is guilty of manslaughter. (At p. 23 [Cr. App. R.].)

English authority has consistently held that the underlying unlawful act required by its manslaughter offence requires proof that the unlawful act was "likely to injure another person" or in other words put the bodily integrity of others at risk. . . . This position has also been adopted by most Canadian Courts. [Citations omitted.]

. . . .

Despite ample authority that the underlying act must be objectively dangerous in order to sustain a conviction under what is now s. 222(5)(*a*), the law in this area is not entirely free from doubt. In *R. v. Smithers*, [1978] 1 S.C.R. 506, 40 C.R.N.S. 79, 34 C.C.C. (2d) 427, Dickson J. (as he then was) adopted certain comments made by G. Arthur Martin (later Martin J.A.) in a short case note on the English *Larkin* case. The adopted comments included the following:

> There are many unlawful acts which are not dangerous in themselves and are not likely to cause injury which, nevertheless if they cause death, render the actor guilty of culpable homicide. . .

. . . .

> In the case of so-called intentional crimes where death is an unintended consequence the actor is always guilty of manslaughter at least.

> ("Criminal Law — Voluntary and Involuntary Manslaughter — Lawful and Unlawful Acts" (1943), 21 Can. Bar. Rev. 503, at pp. 504-505; cited in *Smithers*, *supra*, at p. 519. [S.C.R.])

This passage appears to raise doubt as to whether the "unlawful act" must be inherently dangerous to sustain a manslaughter conviction. This issue was not addressed in *Smithers*, however, as the assault which occurred in that case was clearly an intentional, dangerous, act. As well, *Smithers* was a case concerned with the issue of causation and not the meaning to be given to the term "unlawful act". Finally, *Smithers* was not argued under the *Charter*. In the absence of a more definitive statement or a more extensive analysis of the issue, I am reluctant to freeze the meaning of "unlawful" for the purposes of s. 269 based on the 1943 comments of even as persuasive a source as G. Arthur Martin. More telling, and also more considered, authority was provided by Martin J.A. in *Tennant*, *supra*, which predates *Smithers* but was not discussed by Dickson J. in the latter decision. In *Tennant*, a Court of Appeal panel composed of Gale C.J.O. and Brooke and Martin JJ.A. rendered a per curiam judgment which concluded that:

When death is accidentally caused by the commission of an unlawful act which any reasonable person would inevitably realize must subject another person to, at least, the risk of some harm resulting therefrom, albeit not serious harm, that is manslaughter. (At p. 96 [C.C.C., p. 19 C.R.N.S.].)

The Court later noted that:

> ... if death was caused by the *accidental discharge* of the fire-arm in the commission of such unlawful act and if the jury were satisfied beyond a reasonable doubt that the *unlawful act* was such as any reasonable person would inevitably realize must subject another to the risk of, at least, some harm, albeit not serious harm, the death would amount to manslaughter. [Emphasis in original.] (At p. 96. [C.C.C., p. 19 C.R.N.S.].)

The Court thus substantially adopted the English position as articulated in *Larkin*.

In accordance with the English law and in furtherance of the developing Canadian case law, the most principled approach to the meaning of "unlawful" in the context of s. 269 is to require that the unlawful act be at least objectively dangerous. This conclusion is both supported by the meaning given to the word "unlawful act" by virtually all of the lower Courts and also is in accord with the emerging jurisprudence of this court in regard to personal fault.

Objective foresight of bodily harm should be required for both criminal and non-criminal unlawful acts which underlie a s. 269 prosecution. I can see no reason why there should be a difference between the two categories of acts. There is no need to differentiate between criminal and non-criminal unlawful acts when one unifying concept is available. Thus the test is one of objective foresight of bodily harm for all underlying offences. The act must be both unlawful, as described above, *and* one that is likely to subject another person to danger of harm or injury. This bodily harm must be more than merely trivial or transitory in nature and will in most cases involve an act of violence done deliberately to another person. In interpreting what constitutes an objectively dangerous act, the Courts should strive to avoid attaching penal sanctions to mere inadvertence. The contention that no dangerousness requirement is required if the unlawful act is criminal should be rejected. The premise on which this proposition is based is that most, if not all, criminal acts are inherently dangerous. This premise is an overstatement inasmuch as a large part of the criminal law is concerned with offences against property and other interests which are not inherently dangerous. But, even if this premise were accepted, the difference between the two positions would be simply one of semantics. To maintain the correct focus it is preferable to inquire whether a reasonable person would inevitably realize that the underlying unlawful act would subject another person to the risk of bodily harm rather than getting sidetracked on a question regarding the classification of the offence.

(2) *Constitutional Sufficiency*

The mental element of s. 269 has two separate aspects. The first aspect of the mental element is the requirement that an underlying offence with a constitutionally sufficient mental element has been committed. Additionally, s. 269 requires that the prosecution prove that the bodily harm caused by the underlying unlawful act was objectively foreseeable. This latter requirement insures that all prosecutions under s. 269 contain *at least* a fault requirement based on an objective standard. As this Court has not indicated that fundamental justice requires fault based on a subjective standard for all offences, the mental element required by s. 269 passes constitutional muster unless s. 269 is one of those few offences which due to its stigma and penalty require fault based on a subjective standard. I agree with the respondent and intervenors that s. 269 has neither the stigma nor criminal sanction to require a more demanding mental element than it already has. The criminal sanction is flexible and thus can be tailored to suit the circumstances of the case. The stigma associated with conviction will generally reflect the degree of opprobrium which the underlying offence attracts. The stigma attached to the underlying offence will in turn influence the minimum mental requirement for that offence.

Unless a minimum mind state of subjective intention in regard to consequences is constitutionally required, the test discussed above satisfies the dictates of s. 7 of the *Charter*. I will now consider that issue.

C. Foresight of Consequences

Although I have concluded by means of statutory interpretation that s. 269 requires objective foresight of the consequences of an accused's unlawful act, the appellant argues that s. 7 of the *Charter* requires subjective foresight of all consequences which comprise part of the *actus reus* of an offence. The appellant notes that in *R. v. Martineau*, [1990] 2 S.C.R. 633, 79 C.R. (3d) 129, 58 C.C.C. (3d) 353, Lamer C.J.C., speaking for the majority of the Court, discussed a:

> general principle that criminal liability for a particular result is not justified except where the actor possesses a culpable mental state in respect of that result: . . . At p. 645 [S.C.R.].)

The appellant also relies on *R. v. Metro News Ltd.* (1986), 53 C.R. (3d) 289, 29 C.C.C. (3d) 35 (C.A.), leave to appeal refused, [1986] 2 S.C.R. viii, 64 C.R. (3d) xxx (note), 29 C.C.C. (3d) 35n, for a similar proposition that:

> The minimum and necessary mental element required for criminal liability for most crimes is knowledge of the circumstances which make up the *actus reus* of the crime and foresight or intention with respect to any consequence required to constitute the *actus reus* of the crime. (At pp. 54-55 [C.C.C.], p. 309 C.R.].)

The appellant submits that this authority supports a requirement that the minimum mental element required by s. 7 of the *Charter* for s. 269 includes an intention to cause bodily harm. In isolation, it is true that the language used in some earlier decisions of this Court could be interpreted as suggested by the appellant. This proposition draws additional support from statements such as those of Wilson J. in *R. v. Docherty*, [1989] 2 S.C.R. 941, 72 C.R. (3d) 1, 51 C.C.C. (3d) 1, where she infers that proof of intention is required in regard to *each* of the elements of the *actus reus*. Wilson J. states:

> A full *mens rea* offence under the *Criminal Code* demands that the accused have an intent to perform the acts that constitute the *actus reus* of the offence. (At p. 958 [S.C.R.].)

As one of the elements of the *actus reus* in this appeal is that bodily harm be produced, it is arguable that the case law of this Court has implied that foresight of the consequences of an act must be proved when such consequences constitute an essential element of the offence. This argument, however, misconstrues and overgeneralizes the language used by this Court in these earlier judgments (see also *R. v. Rees*, [1956] S.C.R. 640, 24 C.R. 1, 115 C.C.C. 1, and *R. v. Pappajohn*, [1980] 2 S.C.R. 120, 14 C.R. (3d) 243, 19 C.R. (3d) 97, 52 C.C.C. (2d) 481, at p. 139 [S.C.R.]). In the circumstances of *Docherty*, the offence definition itself required intention in regard to all aspects of the *actus reus* and thus this proposition was not meant to be set down as an overriding principle of criminal law. Equally, in *Martineau* it was only as a result of the stigma and penal consequences of a murder conviction that subjective foresight of death was required. Here again, it was not meant to be stated as a general principle of criminal law. As far back as Blackstone's *Commentaries*, it was recognized that criminal guilt did not always require foresight of the consequences of an unlawful act:

> If a man be doing any thing *unlawful*, and a consequence ensues which he did not foresee or intend, as the death of a man or the like, his want of foresight shall be no excuse; for, being guilty of one offence, in doing antecedently what is in itself unlawful, he is criminally guilty of whatever consequence may follow the first misbehaviour.

(Blackstone, *Commentaries on the Laws of England* (1769), Book IV, at p. 27.)

In *R. v. Nguyen*, [1990] 2 S.C.R. 906, 79 C.R. (3d) 332, (sub nom. *R. v. Nguyen; R. v. Ness*) 59 C.C.C. (3d) 161 [hereinafter *Hess*], the Court concluded that a meaningful mental element was required in regard to a *blameworthy* element of the *actus reus*. Provided that there is a sufficiently blameworthy element in the *actus reus* to which a culpable mental state is attached, there is no additional requirement that any other element of the *actus reus* be linked to this mental state or a further culpable mental state. As inferred by Blackstone, *supra*, provided that the actor is already engaged in a culpable activity, foresight of consequences is not required in order to hold that actor responsible for the results of his or her unlawful activity. Lamer C.J.C. stated in *Martineau* that "[i]f Parliament wishes to deter persons from causing bodily harm during certain offences, then it should punish persons for causing the bodily harm" (p. 647 [S.C.R.]). This is exactly what s. 269 attempts to do. In this particular provision the mental element requirement is composed of both the mental element of the underlying unlawful act *and* the additional requirement of objective foresight of bodily harm. There is, however, no constitutional requirement that intention, either on an objective or a subjective basis, extend to the consequences of unlawful acts in general.

The absence of a constitutional requirement that intention extend to all aspects of an unlawful act was discussed by Wilson J. in *R. v. Bernard*, [1988] 2 S.C.R. 833, 67 C.R. (3d) 113, 45 C.C.C. (3d) 1, at pp. 888-889 [S.C.R.], where she concludes that the minimal element of the application of force is sufficient for a conviction for sexual assault causing bodily harm. She inferentially confirms that s. 7 of the *Charter* does not mandate intention in regard to all of the consequences required by the offence. The contrary position, that intention must extend to all of the required consequences of an offence, is not supported by the case law and should not be adopted as a constitutional requirement.

There are many provisions where one need not intend all of the consequences of an action. As was pointed out in *Hess, supra*, there must be an element of personal fault in regard to a culpable aspect of the *actus reus*, but not necessarily in regard to each and every element of the *actus reus*. The requirement of fault in regard to a meaningful aspect of the *actus reus* is necessary to prevent punishing the mentally, and morally innocent and is in keeping with a long line of cases of this court including *Rees, supra*, and *Pappajohn, supra*. In many offences, such as assault or dangerous driving, the offence is made out regardless of the consequences of the act but the consequences can be used to aggravate liability for the offence. For example, both assault and assault causing bodily harm have identical *mens rea* requirements and the element of causing bodily harm is merely used to classify the offence. No principle of fundamental justice prevents Parliament from treating crimes with certain consequences as more serious than crimes which lack those consequences.

A number of *Criminal Code* offences call for a more serious charge if certain consequences follow. To require intention in relation to each and every consequence would bring a large number of offences into question including manslaughter (s. 222(5)), criminal negligence causing bodily harm (s. 221), criminal negligence causing death (s. 220), dangerous operation causing bodily harm (s. 249(3)), dangerous operation causing death (s. 249(4)), impaired driving causing bodily harm (s. 255(2)), impaired driving causing death (s. 255(3)), assault causing bodily harm (s. 267(1)(*b*)), aggravated assault (s. 268), sexual assault causing bodily harm (s. 272(*c*)), aggravated sexual assault (s. 273), mischief causing danger to life (s. 430(2)) and arson causing bodily harm (s. 433(*b*)). As noted by Professor Colvin, "[i]t would, however, be an error to suppose that *actus reus* and *mens rea* always match in this neat way" (E. Colvin, *Principles of Criminal Law*, 2d ed. (Toronto: Carswell, 1991), at p. 55).

Conduct may fortuitously result in more or less serious consequences depending on the circumstances in which the consequences arise. The same act of assault may injure one person but not another. The implicit rationale of the law in this area is that it is acceptable to distinguish between criminal responsibility for equally reprehensible acts on the basis of the harm that is actually caused. This is reflected in the creation of higher maximum penalties for offences with more serious consequences. Courts and legislators acknowledge the harm actually caused by concluding that in otherwise equal cases a more serious consequence will dictate a more serious response.

There appears to be a general principle in Canada and elsewhere that, in the absence of an express legislative direction, the mental element of an offence attaches only to the underlying offence and not to the aggravating circumstances (Colvin, *supra*, at p. 57). This has been confirmed by this Court in a number of cases including those which have held that sexual assault requires intention simply in relation to the assault and not any aggravating circumstance (see *R. v. Chase*, [1987] 2 S.C.R. 293, 59 C.R. (3d) 193, 37 C.C.C. (3d) 97, and *R. v. Bernard*, *supra*, at pp. 888-889) [S.C.R.]. To require fault in regard to each consequence of an action in order to establish liability for causing that consequence would substantially restructure current notions of criminal responsibility. Such a result cannot be founded on the constitutional aversion to punishing the morally innocent. One is not morally innocent simply because a particular consequence of an unlawful act was unforeseen by that actor. In punishing for unforeseen consequences the law is not punishing the morally innocent but those who cause injury through avoidable unlawful action. Neither basic principles of criminal law, nor the dictates of fundamental justice require, by necessity, intention in relation to the consequences of an otherwise blameworthy act.

DISPOSITION

On a proper interpretation of s. 269 of the *Code*, the concept of an unlawful act as it is used in that section includes only federal and provincial offences. Excluded from this general category of offences are any offences which are based on absolute liability and which have constitutionally insufficient mental elements on their own. Additionally, the term "unlawfully", as it is used in this section requires an act which is at least objectively dangerous. Interpreted in this way s. 269 complies with the requirements of s. 7 of the *Charter*. In the absence of a violation of s. 7, there is no violation of s. 11(*d*).

For a critical comment on *DeSousa* see Stuart, "The Supreme Court Drastically Reduces the Constitutional Requirement of Fault: A Triumph of Pragmatism and Law Enforcement Expediency" (1992), 15 C.R. (4th) 88.

R. v. CREIGHTON

[1993] 3 S.C.R. 3, 23 C.R. (4th) 189, 83 C.C.C. (3d) 346

The Court divided 5-4 on the issue of whether the objective test for unlawful act manslaughter required reasonable foresight of death (Lamer C.J. for the minority) or merely reasonable foresight of bodily harm (McLachlin J. for the majority).

McLACHLIN J. (L'HEUREUX-DUBÉ, GONTHIER and CORY JJ. concurring): —
The *Criminal Code* defines three general types of culpable homicide. There is
murder, the intentional killing of another human being. There is infanticide, the
intentional killing of a child. All other culpable homicides fall into the residual
category of manslaughter.

Manslaughter is a crime of venerable lineage. It covers a wide variety of
circumstances. Two requirements are constant: (1) conduct causing the death of
another person; and (2) fault short of intention to kill. That fault may consist
either in committing another unlawful act which causes the death, or in criminal
negligence. The common-law classification of manslaughter is reflected in the
definition of culpable homicide in s. 222(5) of the *Criminal Code*.

. . . .

The structure of the offence of manslaughter depends on a predicate
offence of an unlawful act or criminal negligence, coupled with a homicide. It is
now settled that the fact that an offence depends upon a predicate offence does
not render it unconstitutional, provided that the predicate offence involves a
dangerous act, is not an offence of absolute liability, and is not unconstitutional:
R. v. DeSousa, [1992] 2 S.C.R. 944. But a further objection is raised in this case.
It is said that the offence of manslaughter is unconstitutional because it requires
only foreseeability of the risk of bodily harm and not foreseeability of death, and
that the trial Judge erred in requiring only foreseeability of bodily harm.

The cases establish that in addition to the *actus reus* and *mens rea*
associated with the underlying act, all that is required to support a manslaughter
conviction is reasonable foreseeability of the risk of bodily harm. While s.
222(5)(*a*) does not expressly require foreseeable bodily harm, it has been so
interpreted: see *R. v. DeSousa, supra*. The unlawful act must be objectively
dangerous, that is likely to injure another person. The law of unlawful act
manslaughter has not, however, gone so far as to require foreseeability of death.
The same is true for manslaughter predicated on criminal negligence; while
criminal negligence, *infra*, requires a marked departure from the standards of a
reasonable person in all the circumstances, it does not require foreseeability of
death.

. . . .

In more recent times, the prevailing view has been that foreseeability of
bodily harm is required for manslaughter. In England, it was said in *R. v. Larkin*,
[1943] 1 All E.R. 217 (C.A.), at p. 219, that the act must be "a dangerous act,
that is, an act which is likely to injure another person". In *R. v. Tennant* (1975),
23 C.C.C. (2d) 80, at p. 96, the Ontario Court of Appeal stated that the unlawful
act must be "such as any reasonable person would inevitably realize must
subject another to the risk of, at least, some harm, albeit not serious harm".
Similarly, in *R. v. Adkins* (1987), 39 C.C.C. (3d) 346 (B.C. C.A.), at p. 348,
Hutcheon J.A. wrote, "the unlawful act was such as any reasonable person
would inevitably realize must subject another to the risk of at least some harm."

This Court in *R. v. DeSousa, supra*, confirmed that a conviction for manslaughter requires that the risk of bodily harm have been foreseeable. After referring to the statement in *Larkin, supra*, that a "dangerous act" is required, Sopinka J. stated that English authority has consistently held that the underlying unlawful act required for manslaughter requires "proof that the unlawful act was 'likely to injure another person' or in other words put the bodily integrity of others at risk" (at p. 959). Moreover, the harm must be more than trivial or transitory. The test set out by Sopinka J. (at p. 961) for the unlawful act required by s. 269 of the *Criminal Code* is equally applicable to manslaughter:

> . . . the test is one of objective foresight of bodily harm for all underlying offences. The act must be both unlawful, as described above, *and* one that is likely to subject another person to danger of harm or injury. This bodily harm must be more than merely trivial or transitory in nature and will in most cases involve an act of violence done deliberately to another person. In interpreting what constitutes an objectively dangerous act, the Courts should strive to avoid attaching penal sanctions to mere inadvertence. The contention that no dangerousness requirement is required if the unlawful act is criminal should be rejected. [Emphasis in original.]

So the test for the *mens rea* of unlawful act manslaughter in Canada, as in the United Kingdom, is (in addition to the *mens rea* of the underlying offence) objective foreseeability of the risk of bodily harm which is neither trivial nor transitory, in the context of a dangerous act. Foreseeability of the risk of death is not required. The question is whether this test violates the principles of fundamental justice under s. 7 of the *Charter*.

. . . .

2. Constitutionality of the "Foresight of Bodily Harm" Test for Manslaughter

Before venturing on analysis, I think it appropriate to introduce a note of caution. We are here concerned with a common-law offence virtually as old as our system of criminal law. It has been applied in innumerable cases around the world. And it has been honed and refined over the centuries. Because of its residual nature, it may lack the logical symmetry of more modern statutory offences, but it has stood the practical test of time. Could all this be the case, one asks, if the law violates our fundamental notions of justice, themselves grounded in the history of the common law? Perhaps. Nevertheless, it must be with considerable caution that a 20th century court approaches the invitation which has been put before us: to strike out, or alternatively, rewrite, the offence of manslaughter on the ground that this is necessary to bring the law into conformity with the principles of fundamental justice.

As I read the reasons of the Chief Justice, his conclusion that the offence of manslaughter as it stands is unconstitutional, rests on two main concerns. First, it is his view that the gravity or seriousness of the offence of manslaughter, and in particular the stigma that attaches to it, requires a minimum *mens rea* of foreseeability of death. Second, considerations of symmetry between the element of mental fault and the consequences of the offence mandate this conclusion. I will deal with each concern in turn.

(a) *Gravity of the Offence*

A number of concepts fall under this head. Three of them figure among the four factors relevant to determining the constitutionality of a *mens rea* requirement, as set out by this Court in *R. v. Martineau*, [1990] 2 S.C.R. 633:

> 1. The stigma attached to the offence, and the available penalties requiring a *mens rea* reflecting the particular nature of the crime;
>
> 2. Whether the punishment is proportionate to the moral blameworthiness of the offender; and
>
> 3. The idea that those causing harm intentionally must be punished more severely than those causing harm unintentionally.

The Chief Justice in his reasons places considerable emphasis on the first factor of stigma. He argues that "there may well be no difference between the *actus reus* of manslaughter and murder; arguably both give rise to the stigma of being labelled by the state and the community as responsible for the wrongful death of another" (p. 11). But later in his reasons (at p. 12) he concedes that "the stigma which attaches to a conviction for unlawful act manslaughter", while "significant, . . . does not approach the opprobrium reserved in our society for those who knowingly or intentionally take the life of another" (emphasis is original). The Chief Justice goes on to observe that "[i]t is for this reason that manslaughter developed as a separate offence from murder at common law." Nevertheless, in the end the Chief Justice concludes that the "constitutional imperative", taken with other factors, requires a minimum *mens rea* of foreseeability of the risk of death, suggesting that stigma may remain an important factor in his reasoning.

To the extent that stigma is relied on as requiring foreseeability of the risk of death in the offence of manslaughter, I find it unconvincing. The most important feature of the stigma of manslaughter is the stigma which is not attached to it. The *Criminal Code* confines manslaughter to non-intentional homicide. A person convicted of manslaughter is not a murderer. He or she did not intend to kill someone. A person has been killed through the fault of another, and that is always serious. But by the very act of calling the killing manslaughter the law indicates that the killing is less blameworthy than murder. It may arise from negligence, or it may arise as the unintended result of a lesser unlawful act. The conduct is blameworthy and must be punished, but its stigma does not approach that of murder.

To put it another way, the stigma attached to manslaughter is an appropriate stigma. Manslaughter is not like constructive murder, where one could say that a person who did not in fact commit murder might be inappropriately branded with the stigma of murder. The stigma associated with manslaughter is arguably exactly what it should be for an unintentional killing in circumstances where risk of bodily harm was foreseeable.

. . . .

It would shock the public's conscience to think that a person could be convicted of manslaughter absent any moral fault based on foreseeability of harm. Conversely, it might well shock the public's conscience to convict a person who has killed another only of aggravated assault — the result of requiring foreseeability of death — on the sole basis that the risk of death was not reasonably foreseeable. The terrible consequence of death demands more. In short, the *mens rea* requirement which the common law has adopted — foreseeability of harm — is entirely appropriate to the stigma associated with the offence of manslaughter. To change the *mens rea* requirement would be to risk the very disparity between *mens rea* and stigma of which the appellant complains.

I come then to the second factor mentioned in *Martineau*, the relationship between the punishment for the offence and the *mens rea* requirement. Here again, the offence of manslaughter stands in sharp contrast to the offence of murder. Murder entails a mandatory life sentence; manslaughter carries with it no minimum sentence. This is appropriate. Because manslaughter can occur in a wide variety of circumstances, the penalties must be flexible. An unintentional killing while committing a minor offence, for example, properly attracts a much lighter sentence than an unintentional killing where the circumstances indicate an awareness of risk of death just short of what would be required to infer the intent required for murder. The point is, the sentence can be and is tailored to suit the degree of moral fault of the offender. It follows that the sentence attached to manslaughter does not require elevation of the degree of *mens rea* for the offence.

. . . .

This brings me to the third factor relating to the gravity of the offence set out in *Martineau*, the principle that those causing harm intentionally must be punished more severely than those causing harm unintentionally. As noted, this principle is strictly observed in the case of manslaughter. It is by definition an unintentional crime. Accordingly, the penalties imposed are typically less than for its intentional counterpart, murder.

I conclude that the standard of *mens rea* required for manslaughter is appropriately tailored to the seriousness of the offence.

b) *Symmetry Between the Element of Fault and the Consequences of the Offence*

The Chief Justice correctly observes that the criminal law has traditionally aimed at symmetry between the *mens rea* and the prohibited consequences of the offence. The *actus reus* generally consists of an act bringing about a prohibited consequence, *e.g.*, death. Criminal-law theory suggests that the accompanying *mens rea* must go to the prohibited consequence. The moral fault of the accused lies in the act of bringing about that consequence. The Chief Justice reasons from this proposition that since manslaughter is an offence involving the prohibited act of killing another, a *mens rea* of foreseeability of harm is insufficient; what is required is foreseeability of death.

The conclusion that the offence of manslaughter is unconstitutional because it does not require appreciation of the consequential risk of death rests on two propositions: (1) that risk of bodily harm is appreciably different from risk of death in the context of manslaughter; and (2) that the principle of absolute symmetry between *mens rea* and each consequence of a criminal offence is not only a general rule of criminal law, but a principle of fundamental justice which sets a constitutional minimum. In my view, neither of these propositions is free from doubt.

I turn first to the distinction between appreciation of the risk of bodily harm and the risk of death in the context of manslaughter. In my view, when the risk of bodily harm is combined with the established rule that a wrong-doer must take his victim as he finds him and the fact that death did in fact occur, the distinction disappears. The accused who asserts that the risk of death was not foreseeable is in effect asserting that a normal person would not have died in these circumstances, and that he could not foresee the peculiar vulnerability of the victim. Therefore, he says, he should be convicted only of assault causing bodily harm or some lesser offence. This is to abrogate the thin-skull rule that requires that the wrong-doer take his victim as he finds him. Conversely, to combine the test of reasonable foreseeability of bodily harm with the thin-skull rule is to mandate that in some cases, foreseeability of the risk of bodily harm alone will properly result in a conviction for manslaughter.

What the appellant asks us to do, then, is to abandon the "thin-skull" rule. It is this rule which, on analysis, is alleged to be unjust. Such a conclusion I cannot accept. The law has consistently set its face against such a policy. It decrees that the aggressor must take his victim as he finds him. Lord Ellenborough C.J. discussed the principle nearly two centuries ago:

> He who deals in a perilous article must be wary how he deals; otherwise, if he observe not proper caution, he will be responsible ... It is a universal principle that, when a man is charged with doing an act, of which the probable consequence may be highly injurious, the intention is an inference of law, resulting from the doing of the act. (*R. v. Dixon* (1814), 3 M. & S. 11; approved, per Blackburn J., *R. v. Hicklin* (1868), L.R. 3 Q.B. 375, and per Amphlett J., *R. v. Aspinall* (1876), 2 Q.B.D. 48, 65).

Stephen J. illustrated the principle in similar fashion in *R. v. Serné* (1887), 16 Cox 311, at p. 313:

> ... when a person began doing wicked acts for his own base purposes, he risked his own life as well as that of others. That kind of crime does not differ in any serious degree from one committed by using a deadly weapon, such as a bludgeon, a pistol, or a knife. If a man once begins attacking the human body in such a way, he must take the consequences if he goes further than he intended when he began.

The principle that if one engages in criminal behaviour, one is responsible for any unforeseen actions stemming from the unlawful act, has been a well-established tenet for most of this century in Canada, the U.S. and U.K. . . . . In *Smithers v. The Queen*, [1978] 1 S.C.R. 506 at pp. 521-22, Dickson J., writing for a unanimous Court, confirmed this principle:

> It is a well-recognized principle that one who assaults another must take his victim as he finds him. . . .
> Although causation in civil cases differs from that in a criminal case, the "thin-skulled man" may appear in the criminal law as in the civil law . . . Even if the unlawful act, alone, would not have caused the death, it was still a legal cause so long as it contributed in some way to the death.

The thin-skull rule is a good and useful principle. It requires aggressors, once embarked on their dangerous course of conduct which may foreseeably injure others, to take responsibility for all the consequences that ensue, even to death. That is not, in my view, contrary to fundamental justice. Yet the consequence of adopting the amendment proposed by the Chief Justice would be to abrogate this principle in cases of manslaughter.

In fact, when manslaughter is viewed in the context of the thin-skull principle, the disparity diminishes between the *mens rea* of the offence and its consequence. The law does not posit the average victim. It says the aggressor must take the victim as he finds him. Wherever there is a risk of harm, there is also a practical risk that some victims may die as a result of the harm. At this point, the test of harm and death merge.

The second assumption inherent in the argument based on symmetry between *mens rea* and each consequence of the offence is that this is not only a general rule of criminal law, but a principle of fundamental justice — a basic constitutional requirement. I agree that as a general rule the *mens rea* of an offence relates to the consequences prohibited by the offence. As I stated in *R. v. Théroux*, [1993] 2 S.C.R. 5, at p. 17, "[t]ypically, *mens rea* is concerned with the consequences of the prohibited *actus reus*." Yet our criminal law contains important exceptions to this ideal of perfect symmetry. The presence of these exceptions suggests that the rule of symmetry is just that — a rule — to which there are exceptions. If this is so, then the rule cannot be elevated to the status of a principle of fundamental justice which must, by definition, have universal application.

It is important to distinguish between criminal law theory, which seeks the ideal of absolute symmetry between *actus reus* and *mens rea*, and the constitutional requirements of the *Charter*. As the Chief Justice has stated several times, "the Constitution does not always guarantee the 'ideal'" (*R. v. Lippé*, [1991] 2 S.C.R. 114 at p. 142; *R. v. Wholesale Travel Group Inc.*, [1991] 3 S.C.R. 154, at p. 186; *R. v. Finlay*, S.C.C. No. 22596, released concurrently, at p. 12).

I know of no authority for the proposition that the *mens rea* of an offence must always attach to the precise consequence which is prohibited as a matter of constitutional necessity. The relevant constitutional principles have been cast more broadly. No person can be sent to prison without *mens rea*, or a guilty mind, and the seriousness of the offence must not be disproportionate to the degree of moral fault. Provided an element of mental fault or moral culpability is present, and provided that it is proportionate to the seriousness and consequences of the offence charged, the principles of fundamental justice are satisfied.

. . . .

Thus when considering the constitutionality of the requirement of foreseeability of bodily harm, the question is not whether the general rule of symmetry between *mens rea* and the consequences prohibited by the offence is met, but rather whether the fundamental principle of justice is satisfied that the gravity and blameworthiness of an offence must be commensurate with the moral fault engaged by that offence. Fundamental justice does not require absolute symmetry between moral fault and the prohibited consequences. Consequences, or the absence of consequences, can properly affect the seriousness with which Parliament treats specified conduct.

The issue of symmetry between *actus reus* and *mens rea* was in issue in the recent unsuccessful *Charter* challenge to Parliament's new criminal harassment offence in s. 264.

R. v. KRUSHEL

(2000), 31 C.R. (5th) 295, 142 C.C.C. (3d) 1 (Ont. C.A.)

CATZMAN J.A. (CARTHY and WEILER JJ.A. concurring): —

. . . .

All three appellants were convicted of criminal harassment under s. 264 of the *Criminal Code*. That section provides, in relevant part:

264.(1) No person shall, without lawful authority and knowing that another person is harassed or recklessly as to whether the other person is harassed, engage in conduct referred to in subsection (2) that causes that other person reasonably, in all the circumstances, to fear for their safety or the safety of anyone known to them.

(2) The conduct mentioned in subsection (1) consists of

(a) repeatedly following from place to place the other person or anyone known to them;

(b) repeatedly communicating with, either directly or indirectly, the other person or anyone known to them;

(c) besetting or watching the dwelling-house, or place where the other person, or anyone known to them, resides, works, carries on business or happens to be; or

(d) engaging in threatening conduct directed at the other person or any member of their family.

. . . .

The appellant Krushel was convicted of criminal harassment under s. 264 by engaging in the conduct referred to in s. 264(2)(c). The victim was his former common law spouse. He was sentenced to 90 days, to be served intermittently, and two years probation.

. . . .

(i)   Section 7

Counsel for Krushel submitted that s. 264 infringed s. 7 of the *Charter* for two reasons: first, that the section was impermissibly vague in that it fails to give sufficient notice of what conduct is prohibited; and second, that it allows the morally innocent to be punished, specifically, in its failure to require that the accused have the intention to cause the victim to fear for their safety or the safety of anyone known to them (the "constructive liability argument").

The constructive liability argument was considered by the Alberta Court of Appeal in *R. v. Sillipp* (1997), 120 C.C.C. (3d) 384 (Alta. C.A.), leave to appeal to S.C.C. refused (1998), 219 A.R. 107 (S.C.C.). In that case, as in this, the appellant argued that s. 264 allowed the morally innocent to be punished because it lacked a *mens rea* requirement attaching to the consequence of reasonable fear. That court concluded that s. 7 was not infringed by the provisions of s. 264. At pp. 397-398, Berger J.A., speaking for the court, described the operation of the section in the following terms:

> In my view, the *actus reus* of the offence of criminal harassment is constituted by volitional subsection (2) conduct which meets discernible standards of nature, cause and effect, with the *mens rea* requirement being that of an intention to engage in that conduct or, at minimum, recklessness or wilful blindness, relative to that conduct.

> That which is prohibited is a person engaging in subsection (2) conduct with knowledge (reckless or wilful blindness) that *such conduct* is causing the complainant to be harassed. The *mens rea* of the offence is the intention to engage in the prohibited conduct with the knowledge that the complainant is thereby harassed.

. . . .

A conviction under s. 264 requires that the accused have "known" that his subsection (2) conduct was causing the complainant to be harassed, or that he was aware of such risk and was reckless or wilfully blind as to whether or not the person was harassed. The Appellant's "morally innocent accused" who honestly believed that his subsection (2) behaviour was not known to the complainant, and who was not reckless or wilfully blind, would escape criminal liability.

In the result, Berger J.A. concluded, at p. 399:

> The Appellant's argument that it is a matter of constitutional necessity that the element of mental culpability be linked to the prohibited consequence of causing actual fear in the complainant is unfounded. Clearly Parliament has created a new kind of culpable activity — subsection (2) conduct which, by objective standards (as described earlier in this judgment), is of a nature and extent as to reasonably cause fear. Such conduct is deemed by s. 264 to be criminal activity. Thus, in accordance with the principle set out in *DeSousa (supra)*, given that there is in s. 264 a sufficiently blameworthy element in the *actus reus* to which the culpable mental state attaches, foresight of the prohibited consequence of causing actual fear is not required in order to hold the accused responsible for the results of his or her unlawful activity.

In reaching this conclusion, Berger J.A. noted (at pp. 396-398) that the contention that there must be symmetry between *mens rea* and each consequence of an offence had been expressly rejected by McLachlin J. in *R. v. Creighton* (1993), 83 C.C.C. (3d) 346 (S.C.C.) and (at p. 399) that there need only be a sufficiently blameworthy element in the actus reus to which the culpable mental state attaches: *R. v. DeSousa* (1992), 76 C.C.C. (3d) 124 (S.C.C.). I agree with Berger J.A., and I would reject the constructive liability argument.

The argument that s. 264 is impermissibly vague was not considered by the Alberta Court of Appeal. However, in an earlier challenge to s. 264, the Alberta Court of Queen's Bench rejected that argument: *R. v. Sillipp* (1995), 99 C.C.C. (3d) 394 (Alta. Q.B.). In that proceeding, Murray J. dismissed an application to declare s. 264 to be of no force and effect, finding, *inter alia*, that the section did not suffer from vagueness. His reasons on this point appear at p. 406:

> In my opinion, s. 264 does not suffer from vagueness. Certainly there are many facets of it that will have to be interpreted by the court. I have no doubt that as time progresses it will be given a constant and settled meaning. I have no problem interpreting s. 264 so as to understand that certain conduct is subject to legal restrictions and the area of risk is set out, namely, if you intentionally behave in certain ways knowing that by doing so you are harassing another person, then if your conduct causes that person to reasonably fear for his or her safety, you run the risk of being criminally sanctioned. I would think that anyone reading the section would receive that message loud and clear. I do not believe that it has the effect of permitting a "standardless sweep" so as to allow the police, or for that matter, the judiciary, to simply use its discretion in how they interpret it or apply its provisions which was the concern of Lamer C.J.C. in *Morales, supra*. I have listened to argument by Crown and defence counsel and I am satisfied that the legislation permits the framing of a meaningful legal debate with respect to the objectives contained in the legislation. In my view, it provides "an adequate basis for reaching a conclusion as to its meaning by reasoned analysis applying legal criteria".

I agree with Murray J., and I would reject the appellant's argument that s. 264 violates s. 7 because it is impermissibly vague.

R. v. BARRON

(1984), 39 C.R. (3d) 379 (Ont. H.C.)

EWASCHUK J. (orally): — The accused, Martin Barron, stands charged that he did unlawfully kill Roberto Fidanza, thereby committing manslaughter, contrary to s. 219 [now s. 236] of the *Criminal Code*, R.S.C. 1970, c. C-34. On this charge, he elected trial by a Supreme Court Judge without a jury.

. . . .

FACTUAL BACKGROUND

In 1980 the accused's mother died of cancer, leaving him an orphan. As a result he lived with his grandmother.

On 20th October 1983 the grandmother left Hamilton to visit friends. She left her then 16-year-old grandson in the charge of his aunt. The accused later lied to his aunt and told her that he would be staying at the home of Roberto Fidanza, a fellow classmate. Instead these two, and others, on Saturday, 22nd October 1983, met at the grandmother's home to party and have a general good time.

Initially, in fact, at about 7:00 p.m. that evening, three other male friends dropped over with a case of beer, which was eventually drunk. At about 8:00 p.m. two more male friends, among them the deceased, Roberto Fidanza, 16 years old, arrived with two girlfriends and another case of beer, also eventually consumed.

Between 10:30 and 11:00 p.m., Fidanza and another male teenager came up from downstairs, where they had been with the two girls. The two young girls remained downstairs. The accused, Barron, suggested that the boys "streak" the girls by disrobing themselves. All declined to do except Fidanza and Barron, the author of the escapade.

The deceased and the accused thereupon undressed themselves to their underwear. The deceased eventually reached the landing above the downstairs with the accused directly behind him, when the deceased apparently changed his mind. He hesitated and said, "No, I don't want to do it." The accused then stated, "Come on, Roberto, let's go," and with that statement gave the deceased a slight push on the back.

Unfortunately the push or shove was substantial enough for the deceased to lose his balance and fall down the stairs to his eventual death.

In fact, he died on 1st November 1983 of a pneumonic infection of his lungs brought on as a direct result of the head injuries suffered from the fall. The blood-alcohol reading of this rather small 120-pound boy proved to be 131 milligrams at the time of his death.

The events that followed the fall proved bizarre. Seemingly out of character, the accused panicked and acted callously. He struck a friend who tried to telephone for an ambulance. He then ordered everyone out of his grandmother's home, compelling the others to carry his unconscious classmate outside. In fact, the deceased never regained consciousness. Eventually, the other teenagers were able to get an ambulance and hail down a police car.

The accused himself fled the scene. Eventually he returned but denied pushing his friend. It was not until the police told him that one of the other boys claimed that the accused pushed the deceased that he admitted it. However, even then he falsely claimed that someone else pushed him from behind.

LEGAL ISSUES

In very able argument, counsel have submitted that the following constitute the legal issues in this case. First, did the push constitute an unlawful act, *i.e.*, an assault, which caused the deceased's death? Second, if not, was there an otherwise unlawful act which caused the deceased's death in dangerous circumstances? Third and finally, if not, was the accused criminally negligent in causing the deceased's death? Implicit in the last question is the admitted fact that the accused's push undoubtedly did cause the deceased's eventual death.

The above questions are predicated on the applicability of s. 205(5)(*a*) and (*b*) to s. 219, *i.e.* to the crime of manslaughter. In that regard, s. 205 formulates rules relating to causation in stating that:

"(5) A person commits culpable homicide [*i.e.*, murder, manslaughter or infanticide] when he *causes* the death of a human being

"(*a*) by means of an unlawful act, [or]
"(*b*) by criminal negligence". (The italics are mine.)

A secondary question has been raised whether the Crown can alternatively rely on the means specified in s. 205(5): see *R. v. Kitching* (1976), 32 C.C.C. (2d) 159 at 170 (Man. C.A.), per Matas J.A.

In my view, the Crown may rely on any and all means of causation listed in s. 205(5) [now s. 222(5)] where, as here, the Crown charges an accused with "unlawfully killing" someone. Where, however, the Crown specifies by which means the accused unlawfully killed the person, *e.g.*, by an unlawful act as in *R. v. Kitching*, the Crown may well be bound by that particular in the charge. Where the Crown, however, does not specify the means of causation, the Crown may then rely disjunctively or conjunctively on the means listed in s. 205(5) as alternative modes, although not particularized, of committing the same offence, *i.e.*, manslaughter: see by analogy *R. v. Williams* (1981), 63 C.C.C. (2d) 141 (C.A.).

(a)   *Unlawful Act (Assault) Causing Death*

The question then arises whether the accused committed an assault when he pushed the deceased, causing the latter to fall down the stairs and meet his eventual death. It is undoubted that, if the accused did assault the deceased, causing his death, the accused is thereby guilty of manslaughter: see *Smithers v. R.*, [1978] 1 S.C.R. 506, 40 C.R.N.S. 79, 34 C.C.C. (2d) 427 at 436. In other words, not only does the accused take his victim as he finds him, *i.e.*, with all his infirmities, he also takes all the results of his intentional crime, *e.g.*, the most trivial assault, where such crime, no matter how unforeseen or unintentional, causes death to the most normal of victims.

Thus the question to be resolved is whether the accused assaulted the deceased. In pushing the latter, it is clear that the accused intended to apply force to his friend within the words of s. 244(1)(*a*) [re-en. 1980-81-82-83, c. 125, s. 19] of the *Criminal Code*: see *R. v. Burden* (1982), 25 C.R. (3d) 283, 64 C.C.C. (2d) 68 (B.C.C.A.). In fact, he did so to persuade the deceased to start downstairs for the express purpose of streaking the girls.

It is also undoubted that a person can expressly or implicitly consent to a touching by another person. If so, no assault is committed. Here, there was no express consent. The question then arises whether there was implicit consent.

In this case, the two teenagers were classmates and good friends. Evidence has been led that they were in the habit of jostling each other, *i.e.*, the usual pushing and shoving indulged in by young teenagers. Thus Mr. Sherman for the accused contends that the deceased implicitly consented to the fatal, and indeed tragic, push by reason of his previous attitude and behaviour toward the accused.

I agree with that submission. Although the deceased expressed his objection to continuing the escapade, he did not by that statement in effect say "Don't push me" to the accused. Indeed, neither the accused nor the deceased reflected on the question of the need for consent to the push. Had the accused adverted to the dangerous circumstances and the grave risk of serious bodily harm involved, he may well have, because of his recklessness in pushing his friend, been guilty of murder under s. 212(*a*)(ii).

Instead, the push by the accused to his friend simply involved part of the normal give-and-take between his friend and himself. Such was their relationship.

Mr. Sherman submitted that I could not look at the attendant circumstances to determine whether there was implicit consent on the part of the deceased. I reject that submission. The deceased, however, did not advert to the risk involved, since had he done so he would have necessarily withdrawn his consent. Neither did the accused, since had he done so he probably would have committed a more serious crime by reason of his awareness of the risk involved and the likelihood or certainty of harm. The implicit consent therefore remained operative and continuing at the material time.

Mr. Sherman also submitted that an assault must be a hostile act: see *R. v. Baney* (1971), 17 C.R.N.S. 261, 6 C.C.C. (2d) 75 (C.A.). I respectfully disagree. Instead, I prefer the approach that, where there is an intentional application of force, then as assault is committed in the absence of exempting consent: see *R. v. Burden, supra*. In that way, many social acts are non-assaultive although involving intentional touching because the person touched accepts it as part of normal social conduct, *e.g.*, tapping a stranger on the shoulder to ask him or her for directions or the time of day. Even where the stranger does not accept the touching, the accused is excused because he normally would have honestly believed that he had implicit consent to act as he did: see s. 244(4) [en. 1980-81-

82-83, c. 125, s. 19] of the *Criminal Code*. In fact, only where the person lacks the capacity to consent, *e.g.*, a young child, need the act be hostile in the sense that the accused did the act for an improper purpose, *e.g.*, sexual gratification or revenge: see also s. 140 [re-en. 1980-81-82-83, c. 125, s. 5] re consent of child under 14 years of age to sexual intercourse.

I therefore find that in pushing the deceased the accused did not assault him by reason of implicit consent on the part of the deceased.

Unlawful Dangerous Act Causing Death

The next question to be answered involves the question whether the accused's act in pushing the deceased entails manslaughter by reason of his act being an unlawful act committed in dangerous circumstances.

At early common law, any unlawful act, including a civil tort, causing death constituted manslaughter. Here the accused was undoubtedly civilly negligent in causing his friend's death. The above doctrine, however, eventually evolved so as to require greater fault on the part of an accused before his unlawful nonassaultive act causing death amounts to manslaughter. It now seems that where the unlawful act is itself a criminal act, *e.g.*, pointing a firearm or possession of a weapon for a purpose dangerous to the public peace, then the accused commits manslaughter if death results where any reasonable person would have realized that the unlawful act would have subjected another person to the risk of some harm, albeit not serious harm: see *R. v. Tennant* (1975), 31 C.R.N.S. 1, 23 C.C.C. (2d) 80 at 96 (C.A.) — quaere whether the above principle is now valid, since it was based on *R. v. Church*, [1966] 1 Q.B. 59, later qualified in *D.P.P. v. Newbury*; *D.P.P. v. Jones*, [1977] A.C. 500 (H.L.).

In fact, where the unlawful act is a quasi-criminal statutory wrong, it seems clear that the unlawful act, viewed objectively, must itself be dangerous in the sense of its likelihood of subjecting another person to danger of harm or injury. Furthermore, it seems that the unlawful act must itself be intentional: see *R . v. Cole* (1981), 64 C.C.C. (2d) 119, leave to appeal to S.C.C. refused 42 N.R. 175.

In this case, since I have found the accused's act, albeit intentional, non-assaultive, his act was therefore neither *per se* criminal nor statutorily unlawful.

The next question to be answered is whether the fact that the accused's act constitutes the tort of negligence thereby converts the act into an unlawful act within the meaning of s. 205(5)(*a*). In my view, it does not. Furthermore, it is my opinion that, even if the accused's civil wrong was committed in dangerous circumstances, which it was, this factor also does not in itself transform the civil wrong into an unlawful act in the absence of criminal negligence.

Thus a non-statutory wrong cannot constitute an unlawful act within the intent of s. 205(5)(*a*) unless it was so dangerous as to constitute the criminal offence of criminal negligence causing death or bodily harm or when committed in the operation of a motor vehicle. Indeed, the criminal law knows no offence of "dangerous act" *per se*.

Criminal Negligence

(1) The Law

Section 202(1)(*a*) [now s. 219(1)(*a*)] states that:

"202.(1) Everyone is criminally negligent who
"(*a*) in doing anything . . .
"shows wanton or reckless disregard for the lives or safety of other persons."

There had long persisted in Canada a somewhat heated, albeit academic, debate, even at the Supreme Court level, whether to be criminally negligent of a crime an accused had to subjectively advert to risk of harm involved in his or her conduct. This controversy arose as a result of the constitutional difference between federal crimes, *e.g.*, criminal negligence in the operation of a motor vehicle and dangerous driving, and provincial offences, *e.g.*, careless driving. To clarify separate legislative powers, the Supreme Court attempted to formulate a rule that federal crimes required subjective fault, whereas provincial offences, being by definition non-crimes, required only objective fault, *e.g.*, mere negligence: see *O'Grady v. Sparling*, [1960] S.C.R. 804, 33 C.R. 293, 128 C.C.C. 1. The distinction thus revolved mainly about the accused's state of mind and in particular his subjective fault.

The controversy moreover centred directly around the meaning of the word "reckless". For an accused to be criminally liable, not only must the accused commit the prohibited act but he must also commit it with the appropriate subjective fault. This subjective fault generally depends on the accused's state of mind and has generally been termed "*mens rea*", or a guilty mind. The accused must generally then intend to do that which is prohibited by law in prescribed circumstances even if he be ignorant of the applicable law.

Intention may be general or specific. Where general, the appropriate intention will be attributed to the accused as long as the act in question is voluntary and non-accidental. If the accused is drunk, the act need not even be intended as long as it is non-accidental: see *R. v. George*, [1960] S.C.R. 871, 34 C.R. 1, 128 C.C.C. 289. Apart from drunkenness, the act, however, must be voluntary, in the sense of being willed and non-reflexive (see *R. v. Wolfe* (1974), 20 C.C.C. (2d) 382 (Ont. C.A.)) and must not merely be careless (see *R. v. Starratt* (1972), 5 C.C.C. (2d) 32 (C.A.)).

Where a specific intention is required, the accused must generally then intend to bring about a particular result, *e.g.*, by s. 302(*c*) of the *Criminal Code*, assaulting a person with intent to steal from him. In other words, the accused must assault the person for the purpose of stealing from that person. But why the accused wants or needs the money or item stolen is his motive. That purpose is not relevant to guilt.

The criminal law, however, superimposes the general doctrine of "recklessness" to crimes of intent. Thus intention will be attributed or imputed to an accused where he acts recklessly in the circumstances. In such a situation, "The term 'recklessly' is . . . used to denote the subjective state of mind of a person who foresees that his conduct may cause the prohibited result but, nevertheless, takes a deliberate and unjustifiable risk of bringing it about . . .": see *R. v. Buzzanga* (1979), 49 C.C.C. (2d) 369 at 379 (C.A.). Depending on the definitional elements of and terms employed in the crime, the accused may be sufficiently reckless to have imputed to him the necessary guilty intention where his foresight indicates to him that the unjustified risk will probably result in the prohibited harm, will be highly probable or, for certain crimes, substantially certain to occur: see, generally, G. Williams, *The Mental Element in Crime.*

The above general doctrine of recklessness has, however, to my mind been confused with the specific term "reckless" as used in the definition of the offence of criminal negligence. In my opinion, the general doctrine and the specific term substantially differ as to meaning and scope. Indeed, crimes are structurally ordered and differently punished depending generally whether specific intention, general intention or criminal negligence is required by the constituent elements of the particular crime.

All crimes involve some degree of subjective fault, with the highest subjective fault occurring in a crime of specific intent, *e.g.*, murder. Less subjective fault is involved in a crime of general intent, *e.g.*, assault, and still less in criminal negligence. The question then to be answered is whether it is criminally negligent *not* to advert to highly dangerous circumstances involving unjustifiable risk where a reasonable person would have recognized the risk.

In other words, is there subjective fault where an accused does not advert to unjustifiable risk of harm, *i.e.*, where he is heedless to the risk where ordinary people would have adverted to the risk?

Until recently it was unclear whether the failure to heed unjustifiable risk could constitute recklessness as applied to criminal negligence: see *Arthurs v. R.*, [1974] S.C.R. 287, 7 C.C.C. (2d) 438 at 453, and *R. v. Leblanc*, [1977] 1 S.C.R. 339, 29 C.C.C. (2d) 97 at 103.

The House of Lords has, however, recently dealt with the meaning of "recklessness" as it applies to criminal damage in *Metro. Police Commr. v. Caldwell*, [1982] A.C. 341, and reckless driving in *R. v. Lawrence*, [1982] A.C. 510. In the latter case, at p. 526, Lord Diplock states that:

> . . . the doer of the act is acting 'recklessly' if before doing the act, he either fails to give any thought to the possibility of there being any such risk [*i.e.*, an obvious and serious risk of causing physical injury to some other person who might happen to be using the road or of doing substantial damage to property], or, having recognized such risk, he nevertheless goes on to do it.

Thus the accused is morally blameworthy by his heedlessness, *i.e.*, his failure to advert to the clear risk, or, where he adverts to it, in running the risk.

Indeed, in the recent case of *R. v. Sharp*, ante, p. 367, the Ontario Court of Appeal has stated that for both criminal negligence and dangerous driving fault is required but it may be established by indifference in the sense of a negative state of mind.

(2) Application of the Law to the Facts

I must now determine whether the accused was criminally negligent when he pushed his classmate on the landing at the top of the stairs. I have already stated that the accused did not advert to the risk involved and that the circumstances were inherently dangerous, given the steepness of the stairs and the deceased's impaired condition.

The more particular question to be determined is whether the accused showed wanton or reckless disregard for the life or safety of his classmate by pushing him.

"Wanton" has been defined to mean ungoverned or undisciplined and "reckless" as heedless of consequences, headlong or irresponsible. The conduct involved also requires a very significant or marked departure from the standard of a reasonable person: see *R. v. Sharp, supra*, at p. 371.

Who then constitutes a reasonable person in relation to this accused, who at the time was a 16-year-old boy impaired by alcohol and excited by a teenage prank? In my view, the accused is to be judged by the standard of the reasonable 16-year-old who was sane and sober at the time: see, by analogy, *R. v. Hill* (1982), 32 C.R. (3d) 88, 2 C.C.C. (3d) 394, leave to appeal to S.C.C. granted 47 N.R. 240. Would the average 16-year-old have then adverted to the risk of death or serious injury to the deceased, Fidanza, in the circumstances of this case?

In my view, he would have. The stairs were very steep, the deceased was impaired, the landing was narrow and crowded with people. There was no handrail to grab onto. The circumstances were thus inherently very dangerous.

I am satisfied beyond a reasonable doubt that the accused, by failing to give thought to the obvious and serious risk of severe bodily harm to his friend, showed wanton or reckless disregard for his friend's life or safety. In not so adverting, he was criminally negligent, which conduct resulted in his friend's death. I therefore need not deal with the issue whether the accused owed a legal duty to aid his friend by bringing about the injury.

Accordingly, the accused is guilty of manslaughter.

Accused convicted.

Barron was reversed by the Ontario Court of Appeal, (1985), 48 C.R. (3d) 334. Can you find the error?

How would **Barron** be decided under **Creighton**? Are you satisfied with the present law?

On the above state of the law, do you think that the following accused, each charged with manslaughter, should be convicted?

1. The accused pointed a rifle at his friend and discharged it, killing him. The accused and the victim were friends who had been hunting the day before. The accused had, only moments before, pulled the trigger and the gun had not discharged. He thought that the gun was not loaded and that it would not discharge. There was evidence that the firing mechanism

on the gun was faulty. Note that under s. 86(1) of the *Criminal Code* it is an offence to point a firearm at another whether or not it is loaded.

Compare *R. v. Jakubowych* (1968), 66 W.W.R. 755 (Alta. S.C.).

2. The accused had intravenously injected a quantity of prescription asthma pills mixed with water into a friend's arm. That friend later bought a large quantity of pyribenzamine pills and requested the accused to crush six of them and mix them with water and inject them as before. He did not want to but she insisted, so he did so. In a short time she lapsed into unconsciousness and underwent convulsive spasms. She encountered difficulty in breathing. The accused summoned an ambulance only when she seemed to stop breathing. She was already dead. Pyribenzamine can be lawfully purchased at any drug store without a prescription.

Compare *R. v. Davis* (1978), 37 C.C.C. (2d) 114 (Sask. C.A.).

One would have expected that since *Creighton* the Supreme Court would be applying *DeSousa* with caution, especially in the case of a very serious crime such as that of aggravated assault. The crime of aggravated assault under what is now s. 268(1) is the most serious form of assault and carries a maximum penalty of 14 years' imprisonment. Under s. 268(1):

Everyone commits an aggravated assault who wounds, maims, disfigures or endangers the life of the complainant.

Prior to *DeSousa* and *Creighton* most Courts of Appeal had interpreted the offence of aggravated assault to merely require proof of an intent to assault and of an act which in fact caused the aggravated consequences complained of. See *Leclerc* (1991), 7 C.R. (4th) 282 (Ont. C.A.), *Lucas* (1987), 34 C.C.C. (3d) 28 (Que. C.A.), *Carriere* (1987), 56 C.R. (3d) 57 (Alta. C.A.) and *Scharf* (1988), 42 C.C.C. (3d) 378 (Man. C.A.). This meant a form of absolute liability respecting that consequence. Only the New Brunswick Court of Appeal in *Parish* (1990), 60 C.C.C. (3d) 350 (N.B. C.A.) had related the intent to the consequences prohibited in their determination that the Crown would have to prove not just an intent to assault but an intent to wound, maim, disfigure or endanger life.

In *Godin* (1993), 22 C.R. (4th) 265 (N.B. C.A.), Angers J.A. for the majority of the New Brunswick Court of Appeal persisted with this approach. He persuasively pointed out that the offence was distinguishable from the offence of unlawfully causing bodily harm at issue in *DeSousa* in that it was not defined as wounding, maiming, etc. in the course of assault nor expressly as an offence which caused certain consequences. It followed that there would have to be subjective foresight of the forbidden acts. The majority pointed out that a life might be endangered without the commission of an assault. When *Godin* reached the Supreme Court, [1994] 2 S.C.R. 484, 31 C.R. (4th) 33, 89 C.C.C. (3d) 574, the Court took but a few lines in an oral endorsement to reverse the New Brunswick Court of Appeal. The Court did not fully justify its position. It merely remarked that the section "pertains to an assault that has the consequence of wounding, maiming or disfiguring". Intent was not required respecting those consequences and the fault element was objective foresight of bodily harm. This was said to flow from *DeSousa* and *Creighton*. On the above analysis of *Creighton* can this be correct? The reference to "bodily harm" may have been a slip of the tongue. The express *mens rea* required for an assault under s. 265 (1) is applying force intentionally and there is no mention of bodily harm.

The Supreme Court in *Godin* did not consider *L. (S.R.)* (1992), 16 C.R. (4th) 311, 76 C.C.C. (3d) 502 (Ont. C.A.), in which there was a careful attempt by the Ontario Court of Appeal to apply *DeSousa* to aggravated assault. This necessitated a reversal of that Court's previous decision in *Leclerc*. The crime of aggravated assault was now to be interpreted, per Justice Doherty for the Court, as requiring not only proof of the *mens rea* required for assault, applying force intentionally, but also objective foresight of the risk of wounding, maiming, disfiguring or endangering life. The Ontario Court saw that the further pronouncement in *Desousa* that a fault element need not relate to the consequence was *obiter* and decided not to follow it. Compare *Reyat* (1993), 20 C.R. (4th) 149 (B.C. C.A.).

The Ontario Court of Appeal's interpretation was most welcome, and had the Supreme Court accepted it, would have done much to undo the Supreme Court's unnecessary and unprincipled attempt to separate the fault requirement from its factual context. However, especially since *Creighton*, there is even more to be said for the approach of the New Brunswick Court of Appeal which sought to keep objective tests out of the law of assault and to apply the usual principle of relating fault to the prohibited consequence. The effect of *Godin* is that the crime of aggravated assault has been added to the uncertain list of so-called predicate offences for which the fault requirement is much reduced.

At present the *Criminal Code* attempts through its maximum penalties to distinguish in seriousness between assault, assault with a weapon or causing bodily harm and aggravated assault. Not surprisingly, given the inconsistency and confusion in the Supreme Court, Courts of Appeal are in disarray as to how *DeSousa, Creighton* and *Godin* are to determine the *mens rea* required for assault causing bodily harm. The Saskatchewan Court of Appeal, *Swenson* (1994), 91 C.C.C. (3d) 541 (Sask. C.A.), merely requires the basic assault element of intent to apply force. There is no requirement of foresight of bodily harm. Criminal responsibility for the more serious offence of assault causing bodily harm will result even if bodily harm resulted in an unforeseen or unforeseeable way. This amounts to absolute liability as to the consequence. This is even less of a requirement than the objective foresight of harm *DeSousa* required for unlawfully causing bodily harm. In contrast the Ontario Court of Appeal, *Nurse* (1993), 83 C.C.C. (3d) 546 and *Emans* (2000), 35 C.R. (5th) 386, (*sub nom. R. v. E. (A.)*) 146 C.C.C. (3d) 449 (Ont. C.A.), and the Alberta Court of Appeal, *Dewey* (1998), 21 C.R. (5th) 232, 132 C.C.C. (3d) 348 (Alta. C.A.), assert for assault causing bodily harm a test of reasonable foresight of harm but not the specific type of harm.

Our law of assault is in urgent need of rethinking by the Supreme Court or Parliament. Crimes of assault should be based on actual foresight of the type of harm caused or risked and should carry higher penalties than those crimes based on a failure to reasonably foresee the risk, such as the present crime of criminal negligence causing bodily harm. It would be more workable to distinguish between only two types of assault based on the seriousness of the harm caused or risked. So too with crimes of criminal negligence.

Normative Theories

H.L.A. HART, SUBJECTIVE AND OBJECTIVE

Punishment and Responsibility (1968), 152-157

Excessive distrust of negligence and excessive confidence in the respectability of "foresight of harm" or "having the thought of harm in the mind" as a ground of responsibility have their roots in a common misunderstanding. Both oversimplify the character of the subjective element required in those whom we punish, if it is to be morally tolerable, according to common notions of justice, to punish them. The reason why, according to modern ideas, strict liability is odious, and appears as a sacrifice of a valued principle which we should make, if at all, only for some overriding social good, is not merely because it amounts, as it does, to punishing those who did not at the time of acting "have in their minds" the elements of foresight or desire for muscular movement. These psychological elements are not *in themselves* crucial though they are important as aspects of responsibility. What is crucial is that those whom we punish should have had, when they acted, the normal capacities, physical and mental, for doing what the law requires and abstaining from what it forbids, and a fair opportunity to exercise these capacities. Where these capacities and opportunities are absent, as they are in different ways in the varied cases of accident, mistake, paralysis, reflex action, coercion, insanity, etc., the moral protest is that it is morally wrong to punish because "he could not have helped it" or "he could not have done otherwise" or "he had no real choice". But, as we have seen, there is no reason (unless we are to reject the whole business of responsibility and punishment) *always* to make this protest when someone who "just didn't think" is punished for carelessness. For in some cases at least we may say "he could have thought about what he was doing" with just as much rational confidence as one can say of any intentional wrong-doing "he could have done otherwise".

Of course, the law compromises with competing values over this matter of the subjective element in responsibility as it does over other matters. All legal systems temper their respect for the principle that persons should not be punished if they could not have done otherwise, *i.e.* had neither the capacity nor a fair opportunity to act otherwise. Sometimes this is done in deference to genuine practical difficulties of proof; sometimes it represents an obstinate refusal to recognize that human beings may not be able to control their conduct though they know what they are doing. Difficulties of proof may lead one system to limit consideration of the subjective element to the question whether a person acted intentionally and had volitional control of his muscular movements; other systems may let the inquiry go further and, in relation to some offences, consider whether the accused had, owing to some external cause, lost the power of such control, or whether his capacity to control was "diminished" by mental abnormality or disease. In these last cases, exemplified in "provocation" and "diminished responsibility", if we punish at all we punish *less*, on the footing that, though the accused's capacity for self-control was not absent its exercise was a matter of abnormal difficulty. He is punished in effect for a failure to exercise control; and this is also involved when punishment for negligence is morally justifiable.

The most important compromise which legal systems make over the subjective element consists in its adoption of what has been unhappily termed the "objective standard". This may lead to an individual being treated for the purposes of conviction and punishment as if he possessed capacities for control of his conduct which he did not possess, but which an ordinary or reasonable man possesses and would have exercised. The expression "objective" and its partner "subjective" are unhappy because, as far as negligence is concerned, they obscure the real issue. We may be tempted to say with Dr. Turner that just because the negligent man does not have "the thought of harm in his mind", to hold him responsible for negligence is *necessarily* to adopt an objective standard and to abandon the "subjective" element in responsibility. It then becomes vital to distinguish this (mistaken) thesis from the position brought about by the use of objective standards in the application of laws which make negligence criminally punishable. For, when negligence is made criminally punishable, this itself leaves open the question whether, before we punish, both or only the first of the following two questions must be answered affirmatively:

(i) Did the accused fail to take those precautions which any reasonable man with normal capacities would in the circumstances have taken?
(ii) Could the accused, given his mental and physical capacities, have taken those precautions?

One use of the dangerous expressions "objective" and "subjective" is to make the distinction between these two questions; given the ambiguities of those expressions, this distinction would have been more happily expressed by the expressions "invariant" standard of care, and "individualised conditions of liability". It may well be that, even if the "standard of care" is pitched very low so that individuals are held liable only if they fail to take very elementary precautions against harm, there will still be some unfortunate individuals who, through lack of intelligence, powers of concentration or memory, or through clumsiness, could not attain even this low standard. If our conditions of liability are invariant and not flexible, *i.e.* if they are not adjusted to the capacities of the accused, then some individuals will be held liable for negligence though they could not have helped their failure to comply with the standard. In *such* cases, indeed, criminal responsibility will be made independent of any "subjective element", since the accused could not have conformed to the required standard. But this result is nothing to do with negligence being taken as a basis for criminal liability; precisely the same result will be reached if, in considering whether a person acted intentionally, we were to attribute to him foresight of consequences which a reasonable man would have foreseen but which he did not. "Absolute liability" results, not from the admission of the principle that one who has been grossly negligent is criminally responsible for the consequent harm even if "he had no idea in his mind of harm to anyone", but from the refusal in the application of this principle to consider the capacities of an individual who has fallen below the standard of care.

It is of course quite arguable that no legal system could afford to individualize the conditions of liability so far as to discover and excuse all those who could not attain the average or reasonable man's standard. It may, in practice, be impossible to do more than excuse those who suffer from gross forms of incapacity, *viz.* infants, or the insane, or those afflicted with recognizably inadequate powers of control over their movements, or who are clearly unable to detect, or extricate themselves, from situations in which their disability may work harm. Some confusion is, however, engendered by certain inappropriate ways of describing these excusable cases, which we are tempted to use in a system which, like our own, defines negligence in terms of what the reasonable man would do. We may find ourselves asking whether the infant, the insane, or those suffering from paralysis did all that a reasonable man would *in the circumstances* do, taking "circumstances" (most queerly) to include personal qualities like being an infant, insane or paralysed. This paradoxical approach leads to many difficulties. To avoid them we need to hold apart the primary question (1) What *would* the reasonable man with ordinary capacities have done in these circumstances? from the second question (2), *Could* the accused with *his* capacities have done that? Reference to such factors as lunacy or disease should be made in answering only the second of these questions. This simple, and surely realistic, approach avoids difficulties which the notion of individualizing the standard of care has presented for certain writers; for these difficulties are usually created by the mistaken assumption that the only way of allowing for individual incapacities is to treat them as part of the "circumstances" in which the reasonable man is supposed to be acting. Thus Dr. Glanville Williams said that if:

> regard must be had to the make-up and circumstances of the particular offender, one would seem on a determinist view of conduct to be pushed to the conclusion that there is no standard of conduct at all. For if every characteristic of the individual is taken into account, including his heredity the conclusion is that he could not help doing as he did.

But "determinism" presents no special difficulty here. The question is whether the individual had the capacity (inherited or not) to act otherwise than he did, and "determinism" has no relevance to the case of one who is accused of negligence which it does not have to one accused of intentionally killing. Dr. Williams supports his arguments by discussion of the case of a motorist whom a blow or illness had rendered incapable of driving properly. His conclusion, tentatively expressed, is that if the blow or illness occurred long ago or in infancy he should not be excused, but if it occurred shortly before the driving in respect of which he is charged he should. Only thus, it seems to him, can any standard of conduct be preserved. But there seems no need to make this extraordinary distinction. Again, the first question which we should ask is: What *would* a reasonable driver with normal capacities have done? The second question is whether or not the accused driver had at the time he drove the normal capacity of control (either in the actual conduct of the vehicle in driving or in the decision to engage in driving). If he was incapable, the date recent or otherwise of the causal origin of the incapacity is surely beside the point, except that if it was of long standing, this would suggest that he knew of it and was negligent in driving with that knowledge.

Equally obscure to me are the reasons given by Dr. Williams for doubting the efficacy of punishment for negligence. He asks, "Even if a person admits that he occasionally makes a negligent mistake, how, in the nature of things, can punishment for inadvertence serve to deter?" But if this question is meant as an argument, it rests on the old, mistaken identification of the "subjective element" involved in negligence with "a blank mind", whereas it is in fact a failure to exercise the capacity to advert to, and to think about and control, conduct and its risks. Surely we have plenty of empirical evidence to show that, as Professor Wechsler has said, "punishment supplies men with an additional motive to take care before acting, to use their faculties, and to draw upon their experience." Again there is no difficulty here peculiar to negligence, though of course we can doubt the efficacy of any punishment to deter any kind of offence.

I should add (out of abundant caution) that I have not been concerned here to advocate punishing negligence, though perhaps better acquaintance with motoring offences would convert me into a passionate advocate. My concern has been to show only that the belief that criminal responsibility for negligence is a form of strict or absolute liability, rests on a confused conception of the "subjective element" and its relation to responsibility.

G.P. FLETCHER, RE-THINKING CRIMINAL LAW

(1978), 367

When used normatively, "criminal" refers to the type of person who by virtue of his deeds deserves to be branded and punished as a criminal. When used descriptively, as in the phrase "criminal act" it may refer simply to any act that the legislature has declared to be "criminal".

G.P. FLETCHER, THE THEORY OF CRIMINAL NEGLIGENCE: A COMPARATIVE ANALYSIS

(1970-71), 119 U. of Penn. L. Rev. 401 at 414-415

We require *mens rea* as an essential condition for criminal liability, not because we suppose that mental states are essential to criminality, but because we realize intuitively that the condemnatory sanctions should apply only to those who are justly condemned for their conduct. And men are not justly condemned and deprived of their liberty unless they are personally culpable in violating the law. That is the point of Coke's saying: the act is not culpable under the law (*actus non facit reum*) unless the actor is culpable for acting as he did (*nisi mens sit rea*).

The proper construction of Coke's embezzlement case is that if the actor lacks the intent required by the law as it existed in the 17th century, he is not culpable for violating the law: there is neither an act prohibited by the law nor personal culpability for engaging in the prohibited act. It does not follow, inversely, that if the actor intended to steal at the time he received possession of the goods that the maxim *actus facit reum nisi mens sit rea* would be satisfied. The actor might be *non compos mentis*, and Coke demonstrably would say that he lacked *mens rea* even though he intentionally took the goods of another. Similarly, the actor might have performed the act under duress or necessity, and in these situations, his conduct should be treated the same as the conduct of an actor *non compos mentis*. In all of these cases, the actor acts with the subjective state prohibited by law, namely, the intention to take the goods of another. But he is not personally culpable — he lacks *mens rea* — if he is insane, or if his conduct is rendered involuntary by duress or necessity.

. . . .

Once the normative status of *mens rea* comes into focus, the problem of negligence as a form of *mens rea* is tractable. If *mens rea* refers not to a specific subjective state, but to the actor's moral culpability in acting as he does, then there might logically be a way to establish personal culpability without referring to a state of mind. In the normal case of intentional conduct, where the actor is sane and his conduct is not excused by duress or necessity, it might be sufficient in establishing *mens rea* to show that the actor acted intentionally. But surely it does not follow that intentional conduct, or something like it, is a necessary condition for criminal culpability. Structural differences between negligence and intentional conduct do not preclude treating negligence as a form of *mens rea*. Nor is the issue settled by the characteristic externality of negligent conduct. Whether negligence constitutes *mens rea* depends on whether negligent conduct is a ground for justly blaming another.

ANNE STALKER, CAN GEORGE FLETCHER HELP SOLVE THE PROBLEM OF CRIMINAL NEGLIGENCE?

(1982), 7 Queen's L.J. 274 at 291-292

A normative test is one that applies directly to the underlying policy, without translating it into measurable and consistent components. A descriptive test, on the other hand, would specify identifiable elements that are consistent from case to case. The problem with a normative test is that it is discretionary and can change from Judge to Judge and day to day. The problem with a descriptive test is that it is rigid and may not accurately reflect the underlying principle or policy in every situation.

J.M. WEILER, R. V. KUNDEUS: THE SAGA OF TWO SHIPS PASSING IN THE NIGHT

(1976), 14 Osgoode Hall L.J. 457 at 470

[Brett] asks whether there is any reason for holding the accused free from blame, rather than whether the prosecution has proved the mental element of the crime. He rejects the latter approach since he does not believe that it is possible to identify in advance all of the possible excuses that might serve to absolve the accused from blame. In his judgment, the search for the conditions of imputability which requires a precise *a priori* analysis of *mens rea* is never successful.

Something is always left out. We cannot anticipate and enumerate all of the conditions of blameworthiness in advance: better not to try. Instead we can recognize blame when we see it, and should have no need for an *a priori* definition.

ROSEMARY CAIRNS WAY, THE CHARTER, THE SUPREME COURT AND THE INVISIBLE POLITICS OF FAULT: A CRITICAL ANALYSIS OF THE CONSTITUTIONALIZATION OF FAULT

LL.M. thesis for the Faculty of Law, Queen's University, October 1992.

The political nature of subjectivism however, remains largely unexamined in the Court's judgments. Although I am concerned about the implications of subjectivism, this thesis is not an argument for objectivism. It is a plea for a multidimensional, contextualized approach to fault, and it questions whether such an approach is possible or likely within a constitutionalized discourse of rights. A great deal of energy in criminal law theory is devoted to the objective/subjective debate, which is understood as one of the fundamental conundrums of the criminal law. In my view, the current construction of the objective/subjective debate as irreconcilable polarities submerges the complexity of the question of blame. The risk of unidimensional, decontextualized approaches to law is magnified when complex concepts like fault are elevated to constitutional status. The implications of a decision to view constitutional culpability through the lens of objectivism, although different in kind from those which flow from a commitment to subjectivism would be equally grave.

. . . .

Decisions about responsibility should invoke a rich and multifaceted debate about the nature and appropriate allocation of blame, the assumption of free will and the efficacy of the criminal law as a mechanism of social control. To act without engaging in this debate is at once to impoverish our jurisprudence about the criminal law and to limit the possibilities for change.

TONI PICKARD AND PHIL GOLDMAN, DIMENSIONS OF CRIMINAL LAW

(1992), 402-405.

The basis in fairness for an objective standard. An "objective" standard presupposes the possibility of agreeing on what is reasonable or natural in any given situation. That possibility, in turn, presupposes both shared understandings, perceptions, and values among the fact finders, and shared understandings between those who are finding facts and the population subject to the law. (Remember that, in law, whether a belief is reasonable or not is conceived to be a question of fact, not a choice of values or perspectives.)

. . . .

Loss of centre and the problem of fairness. Whatever may be true of distant cultures, people in Canada, though differently situated and subject to marked disparities in power, do seem to share at least some understandings across the divisions. Indeed, if we did not think people in our culture shared some understandings, we would hardly be able to use phrases like "our culture" meaningfully. There is, however, a growing acknowledgment that people of different classes, races, ages, genders, religions, sexual orientations, ethnic backgrounds, physical abilities, political visions, and so on, not only have different and sometimes conflicting values, but that their perceptions of facts, of cause and effect, of what is natural, and of what is meant by certain words and gestures are significantly shaped by those differing and sometimes conflicting values.

Increasingly, people believe that facts (even scientific facts) and (more obviously) meanings are not out there in the world in any absolute sense, independent of the observer (that is, objectively), but that, on the contrary, a fact or a meaning — even whether something is perceived as a fact, or heard as a meaning — is in large part a function of the observer's beliefs (and hence, of social place). This insight seriously undermines our ability to believe that the way a decision maker or fact finder sees things is in fact "how things are" or "objectively true". Still more radically affected is our sense that it is fair to impose some people's judgments of what is reasonable on others.

General Review Questions

1. Emotions are running high outside a courthouse. A crowd of student protestors is awaiting the outcome of a controversial trial of acquaintance rape charges alleged to have occurred on campus.

The group is chanting "Justice for women". One member of the group, Andrew, is challenged by another student, Bob, a supporter of the accused. Bob shouts "Vigilantes go home". At this point Andrew shakes a clenched fist at Bob and says "Let's sort it out". Bob promptly lands a blow on Andrew's jaw. The punch is hard enough to knock Andrew off balance. He falls over, hits his forehead on a granite pillar of the courthouse steps

and loses consciousness. He quickly comes to and is unharmed. A nearby police officer asks Bob for his name and address. Bob gives his name but is so flustered he can't remember the number of his temporary apartment. He gives it as No. 314 Portsmouth House. It is in fact No. 217. The officer indicates Bob will be charged with assault.

At this point, Andrew's friends take him to an ambulance stationed in the courthouse parking lot. The ambulance driver, Chris, aged 60, agrees to take Andrew to be checked at the Hotel Dieu. Chris has been an ambulance driver for 30 years. This is his very last shift and he is tired. He drives down West Street with his emergency lights and siren activated. It is cold but roads are dry and visibility is fine. As he approaches an intersection the traffic signal turns red. He slows to about 5 k.p.h. but proceeds through the intersection. He collides with a Pyke milk truck which enters the intersection on a green light at about 30 k.p.h. Neither driver saw the other vehicle until it was too late. Both vehicles were damaged. Furthermore, Andrew was jolted from the stretcher and broke his leg. He was attended to in the hospital where he was pronounced fit except for the broken bone. It healed satisfactorily within six weeks.

You are serving your articles with a 65-year-old Judge who is to preside over the upcoming trial arising from these events. She asks you for a legal memorandum identifying viable legal issues and their possible resolution. She requests careful reference to appropriate case and statutory authority.

There are three charges to consider.

Bob is charged with:

1. assault causing bodily harm to Andrew (to wit, a broken leg) contrary to s. 267(1)(*b*) of the *Criminal Code*, and
2. wilful obstruction of a police officer, by giving a false address contrary to s. 129(*a*) of the *Criminal Code*.

Chris is charged with:

3. failing to stop at a red light contrary to s. 124(16) of the *Highway Traffic Act* of Ontario.

Respecting this third charge note that under s. 124:

(16) Every driver approaching a traffic control signal showing a circular red indicator and facing the indication shall stop his vehicle and shall not proceed until a green indication is shown.

(18) Notwithstanding subsection (16), a driver of an emergency vehicle, after stopping the vehicle, may proceed without a green indication being shown if it is safe to do so.

Pursuant to s. 188(1) of the Act, anyone convicted of an offence under s. 124 is subject to a minimum fine of $60 and a maximum fine of $500.

2. Hemophilia is a hereditary disorder that interferes with blood clotting in about one male in 5,000. Until the early 70's the accepted treatment was blood transfusions. The development of blood-factor concentrates allowed patients to receive treatment quickly at home by simple injection. In Canada, it has always been necessary to import a large quantity of such concentrates from the United States. Each sample injected will come from a number of separate donors.

In 1982, following the death of four hemophiliacs from AIDS in the United States, the Canadian Blood Committee, a committee of civil servants appointed from each province to implement the policy of blood distribution, were warned of the "theoretical risk" that an unknown transmissible agent present in blood-factor concentrates might cause AIDS. The Committee decided that this was too speculative a risk to cause them to change their policy and such concentrates were continued to be used. In 1984, it was widely reported that a United States agency had confirmed that there was an AIDS risk from contaminated blood and that it could be eliminated by a high-heat treatment of the blood product. The Canadian Blood Committee decided, after consultation with doctors, users and manufacturers, to use up existing inventory and phase in heat-treated blood over an eight-month period ending in July 1984.

In October 1992, Alex, a hemophiliac, dies after a debilitating illness. His wife of 20 years, Barbara, only learned that he died from AIDS from the coroner, who asked her whether the cause was contaminated blood. Barbara is devastated. Doctor Cain has been the family physician for both Alex and Barbara since 1975. Neither Doctor Cain nor Alex ever told her that Alex had the HIV virus. Doctor Cain says he was bound by a professional oath of confidentiality and, anyhow, Alex insisted that he did not trouble his wife with the bad news. Alex and Barbara never used a condom. Barbara now has her blood tested and is found to have the HIV virus herself. The HIV virus will usually lead to full-blown AIDS within six to seven years. Thereafter death will occur within three years. Barbara is 100 percent sure that Alex got the virus from contaminated blood he started to inject in January of 1984 and that the only way she could have got the virus herself is from Alex.

She consults a Crown Attorney who lays four charges.

Each member of the Blood Committee is charged, based on the Committee's delay in stopping the distribution of contaminated blood in 1984, with criminal negligence causing death of Alex and criminal negligence causing bodily harm to Barbara contrary, respectively, to ss. 220 and 221 of the *Criminal Code*. Dr. Cane is charged, based on his failure to warn Barbara of Alex's AIDS, of criminal negligence causing her bodily harm contrary to s. 221 of the *Criminal Code* and of wilful obstruction to justice contrary to s. 139(2) of the *Criminal Code*.

The Crown Attorney asks you for a legal memorandum in which you discuss, with reference to appropriate authority, possible defences to each charge assessing the chances of her obtaining convictions. Indicate what further evidence, if any, may be useful in the upcoming trials.

3. The accused, Cain, is charged, pursuant to s. 221 of the *Criminal Code*, with causing bodily harm by criminal negligence. Cain is also charged with a violation of s. 8 of the *Explosives Act* of Ontario. That section provides:

> 8. Every one who allows explosives to be stored in a manner which endangers the lives or safety of others is guilty of an offence punishable by a fine of up to $25,000 or imprisonment of six months or both.

Cain, aged 40, has just been promoted to foreman for a construction company charged with the task of excavating for a new library being erected by the University. The construction site is immediately opposite the building housing the law faculty. The task has proved more difficult than expected and Cain is finding his new job quite stressful. On the evening of December 1, 1992, the accused placed a case of explosives in a storage container on the construction site. For the last several weeks of blasting he had assumed the container was one of the type that automatically locks when the lid is closed. That was the sort of container in use at his former job. Unfortunately the container was not of that type and the explosives were left accessible to anyone who cared to lift the lid. Cain had previously delegated the storage of explosives to a particular worker. On the day in question that worker had caused trouble and Cain had told him to leave the site. Cain remembers being angry and preoccupied with that altercation. He did not notice a padlock on the container.

Arthur Able, a young law student, was disappointed with the quality of instruction in his criminal law class and also with the underground classrooms where he gained such instruction. On the evening of December 1 he decided to bury the classrooms. He climbed the fence and found the explosives left by the accused. He fashioned a crude demolition device and set the time for the beginning of the Criminal Law class. The blast destroyed the premises and the learned law professor was injured as a result.

Write a legal memorandum advising, with reference to appropriate authority, as to all the possible defences to the two charges against Cain.

Chapter 4

RAPE AND SEXUAL ASSAULT

Rape Laws in Context

The gender dimension of power and powerlessness, crucial to the understanding of all sexual assault, has been obliterated to the benefit of men and to the disadvantage of women.[1]

It is submitted that sexual assault is an equality issue. Children are singled out for sexual assault because of their age and sex, that is, because of their vulnerability, accessibility, powerlessness, and lack of credibility. Women are singled out for sexual assault and their accusations of sexual assault are systematically disbelieved because of their gender, that is, because they are relegated to an inferior social status as female, including being socially defined as appropriate targets for forced sex. As a result of these perceptions, women are made vulnerable to sexual assault.[2]

Sexual assault is endemic. According to the Badgley Committee's Report,[3] about one in two females and one in three males have been the victims of unwanted sexual acts. About four in five of these incidents first happened when these persons were children. The Committee points out that while the principal victims of first sexual offences are children and youth, females are twice as often victims as males. This is especially true in adulthood.[4]

With respect to women as victims, it has been estimated that one in four women will be sexually assaulted in Canada during her lifetime. Only 39 percent of rapes conform to the stereotype of the accused being a stranger in an alleyway, while 30 percent are committed by former husbands or lovers, and 31 percent are committed by acquaintances.[5]

The myth, that the "worst rapes" are committed by strangers, should also be dispelled. The danger is that only these types of sexual assault will be taken seriously by the police and eventually the courts. The reality is that a brutal

---

1 Pat Marshall and Maryellen Symons, "Shifting the Balance Towards Equality: A Comment on the Impact of Sexual Assault Codification on Women's Equality Rights in Canada", Conference on *Criminal Code* Reform, Washington, January, 1990, at p. 11.

2 Affidavit filed to gain intervenor status in the Supreme Court of Canada for the Legal Education and Action Fund (LEAF) in the case of *Seaboyer v. R.*, *infra*, on appeal from the Ontario Court of Appeal.

3 *Sexual Offences Against Children*, (Ottawa: Minister of Supply and Services, 1984) Volume 1 at pp. 175 and 186.

4 A thorough discussion of child sexual abuse is beyond the scope of this chapter. However, for further comment, see Nicholas Bala, "Double Victims: Child Sexual Abuse and the Canadian Criminal Justice System" (1980), 15 Queen's L.J. 3 and Institute for the Prevention of Child Abuse, Update Child Sex Abuse and the Law (1992).

5 *The Daily Telegraph*, Feb. 22, 1989, London, England. For views in both the Canadian and United States contexts that recent research as to the extent of violence against women and children has been based on faulty methodologies and has exaggerated the problem, see respectively, John Fekete, *Moral Panic. Biopolitics Rising* (1994) and Christina Hoff Sommers, *Who Stole Feminism? How Women Have Betrayed Women* (1994).

violation by a stranger may be less devastating than a brutal violation by one who the victim loved and trusted. Again, LEAF points out the very real harm that women who have been sexually violated suffer. They submit that the victims suffer "the dissolution of the foundations, values and pleasures which previously gave their life meaning and stability . . . and can include trust in relationships, a sense of security in one's home and one's bedroom, . . . control over one's physical and emotional functions, self-confidence,"[6] etc. The previous distinction was probably based on the notion that once consent has been given it cannot be withdrawn. This is clearly offensive. The devastation of victims of sexual assault is real.

Notwithstanding the frequency of this crime, the majority of sexual assault survivors never report the assault because of mistrust of the system that is trying them, not their attackers:

> Our files are filled with poignant examples of women who are twice punished. They have lived through the violation of a sexual assault and then the violation of the courtroom experience, where often they — the victims — are put on trial. These women undergo the humiliating and painful process of relating the story of their assault to a room full of strangers, of reliving the trauma, their responses directed by questions over which they have no control. Their reward often is to see their assaulter acquitted.[7]

The crime of sexual assault is unique in that the victims have traditionally been women and children. The law has responded to these victims in a particular way due to their unique role in society. Women were considered chattels and the law responded to crimes against women from this viewpoint. Consider the following roots of our sexual assault laws, as they formed part of the Laws from Alfred, King of the West Saxons, 871-900:

> If anyone seizes by the breast a young woman belonging to the commons, he shall pay her 5 shillings compensation.
>   s. 1. If he throws her down but does not lie with her, he shall pay [her] 10 shillings compensation.
>   s. 2. If he lies with her, he shall pay [her] 60 shillings compensation.
>   s. 3. If another man has previously lain with her, then the compensation shall be half this [amount].
>   s. 4. If she is accused [of having previously lain with a man], she shall clear herself by [an oath of] 60 hides, or lose half the compensation due to her.
>   s. 5. If this [outrage] is done to a woman of higher birth, the compensation to be paid shall increase according to the wergeld.[8]

The underlying rationale behind such laws is clearly rooted in viewing women as possessions.

> Rape was originally seen as a crime of theft of sexual property. A rapist would often have to pay money in damages to the woman's husband or father, because the woman was seen as having lost the value of a marriageable daughter or of a pure wife.[9]

---

6 *Supra*, n. 2, at p. 13.

7 Pat Marshall, "Sexual Assault, The Charter and Sentencing Reform", 63 C.R. (3d) 216 at 217.

8 The Laws of the Earliest English Kings, 71 (F.L. Altenborough trans. & ed., 1922).

9 Megan Ellis, *Surviving Procedures After a Sexual Assault*, (Vancouver: Press Gang Publishers, 1985) p. 4. See, too, Constance Backhouse, "Nineteenth Century Canadian Rape Law: 1800-1892" in David Flaherty, *Essays in the History of the Criminal Law* (1983, Osgoode Soc.), vol. II, 200.

Attitudes toward the crime of rape developed from these roots and produced pernicious myths:

> Many people believed that if a woman got raped it was her own fault. They thought that only certain kinds of women got raped. These attitudes meant that women who were raped did not want to tell people because they were afraid of being blamed. Because women did not tell, many people thought that rape did not happen very often.[10]

Another myth concerned women who did report their rape. Often they were not believed. They were often suspected of having provoked the attack. Again, the attitude was that women were at fault. These propositions were not held in isolation, but were also reflected in many powerful segments of society:

> These attitudes were also common among people who worked in the criminal justice system. A study done in Vancouver[11] found that of the 378 rapes reported to the police from 1970-1974, only 54 cases went to trial, and only 27 of these resulted in the attacker being found guilty. The authors of this study estimated that only one in four rapes was reported to the police and that therefore only 1.8% of all rapes resulted in a conviction. They found that how the police dealt with the case had more to do with the character of the victims that with the rape or the rapist.[12]

Such attitudes were also reflected in the way Courts treated rape cases and the clearly discriminatory evidentiary rules which were fashioned regarding rape victims. Women were often questioned about their past sexual history, for two reasons. There was the belief that sexual history or reputation was clearly relevant to the issue of consent, as well as being related to whether or not the victims were telling the truth. Also, if the woman had not reported the rape immediately, it was suggested that in the interim she had fabricated the charge of rape. In rape prosecutions the jury was warned that it was dangerous to convict on the evidence of the victim alone if there was no other corroborating evidence, independent of her, implicating the accused. In other instances the statute provided that no conviction could be had without corroboration even if the jury was satisfied of guilt beyond reasonable doubt.

(i) Prior Sexual History

Courts have long focused on the previous sexual history of the primary witness in a sexual assault case as relevant to the outcome of the trial. Unchastity was considered relevant both to the issue of consent and to the credibility of the testimony of the witness. It was not uncommon to read judicial expressions such as that "no impartial mind can resist the conclusion that a female who had been in the recent habit of illicit intercourse with others will not be so likely to resist as one spotless and pure."[13] Even Wigmore believed that such information was relevant. A sexually active victim was suspect since "[t]he unchaste . . . mentality finds incidental but direct expression in the narration of imaginary sex incidents of which the narrator is the heroine or the victim."[14] An

---

10 *Ibid.*, at 5.
11 Lorenne Clark and Debra Lewis, "Study of Rape in Canada: Phases 'C' and 'D'", *Report to the Donner Foundation*, (1976), unpublished).
12 *Supra*, n. 10, at p. 5.
13 *Lee v. State* (1915), 132 Tenn. 655 at 658, 179 S.W. 145.
14 John Henry Wigmore, *Evidence in Trials at Common Law*, rev. ed. James H. Chadbourn (Boston: Little, Brown, 1970), vol. 3A, sec. 924a, p. 736 (originally published in 1904).

unrestricted right to cross-examine a rape victim as to her previous sexual history with others was perhaps the practice that was most responsible for trials being seen as trials of the victim rather than trials of the accused.

(ii) Doctrine of Recent Complaint

The doctrine of recent complaint was embodied in the common law. It meant that a complaint by a victim of a sexual assault had to be made at the first reasonable opportunity and it had to be made spontaneously.[15] This was an exception to the general common-law rule that a witness' previous statements are inadmissible since they constitute self-confirmation of one's own version of the event.[16]

The justification for the fresh-complaint rule was clearly due to the distrust of women. As was stated in the Model Penal Code, the "requirement of prompt complaint springs in part from a fear that unwanted pregnancy or bitterness at a relationship gone sour might convert a willing participant in sexual relations into a vindictive complainant."[17] This was the "logic" behind the doctrine of recent complaint.

Such views were integral in the judicial consideration of sexual assault charges, and resulted in the establishment of certain presumptions. As was held by one Court, it "is so natural as to be almost inevitable that a female upon whom the crime has been committed will make immediate complaint."[18] Since the presumption existed that a sexual assault would lead immediately to a complaint, Judges often commented on the absence of a complaint at the first reasonable opportunity, inviting juries to draw an adverse or negative inference about the victim's credibility.[19]

(iii) Corroboration

The requirement for corroboration of a woman's evidence in sexual matters, was established by early authorities and "justified" by writers. As Wigmore stated:

> Modern psychiatrists have amply studied the behaviour of errant young girls and women coming before the Courts in all sorts of cases. Their psychic complexes are multifarious, distorted partly by inherent defects, partly by diseased derangements or abnormal instincts, partly by bad social environment, partly by temporary physiological or emotional conditions. One form taken by these complexes is that of contriving false charges of sexual offences by men. . . . The real victim, however, too often in such cases is the innocent man . . . (and) a plausible tale by an attractive, innocent-looking girl may lead to a life-sentence for the accused, because the rules of Evidence (and the Judge's unacquaintance with modern psychiatry) permit no adequate probing of the witness' veracity. . . . No Judge should ever let a sex-offence charge go to the jury unless the female complainant's social history and mental make-up have been examined and testified to by a qualified physician.[20]

---

15 R. v. Lillyman (1896), 2 L.R. 167; R. v. Osbourne, [1905] 1 K.B. 551 (C.C.R.); Thomas v. The Queen, [1952] 2 S.C.R. 344; R. v. Kulak (1979), 46 C.C.C. (2d) 30 (Ont. C.A.).

16 Cross on Evidence, (6th ed., 1979) p. 258.

17 Model Penal Code and Commentaries, (The American Law Institute, 1985) s. 213.6, Comment 5, p. 421.

18 State v. Connelly (1894), 57 Minn. 482, 59 N.W. 479, at 481.

19 See R. v. Kistendey (1975), 29 C.C.C. (2d) 382 (Ont. C.A.); R. v. Boyce (1974), 28 C.R.N.S. 336 (Ont. C.A.).

20 Supra, n. 14 at sec. 924a, p. 736-7.

The justification for this rule was very explicitly laid out in the *Columbia Law Review*:

> Surely the simplest, and perhaps the most important reason not to permit conviction for rape on the uncorroborated word of the prosecutrix is that that word is very often false ... Since stories of rape are frequently lies or fantasies, it is reasonable to provide that such a story, in itself, should not be enough to convict a man of a crime.[21]

This view was also reflected in Court decisions. Without a corroboration requirement, "every man is in danger of being prosecuted and convicted on the testimony of a base woman, in whose testimony there is no truth".[22] And as a Court quoting Glanville Williams found, "sexual cases are particularly subject to the danger of deliberately false charges, resulting from sexual neurosis, fantasy, jealousy, spite, or simply a girl's refusal to admit that she consented to an act of which she is now ashamed".[23] This reflects the state the common laws was in.

While in this day and age, the propositions Wigmore espoused seem patently unreasonable, no one can doubt the influence that Wigmore had and does have in law. For this reason, it seems important to examine his assumptions:

> Wigmore ... omitted material from ... case histories which might undermine or contradict his hypothesis that young girls who report sexual assault or abuse are lying about the charge. ....
>
> Wigmore's unequivocal assertion that young girls who complain of sexual assault are likely to be lying is not supported by recent clinical experience or by survey research data. Surveys conducted during the period of the 1950's through the 1970's suggest that a significant portion of the female population has had some type of childhood sexual encounter with an adult male, many with relatives. ....
>
> Historically, the Wigmore doctrine has survived because it appealed to society's traditional distrust and general hostility towards women, which was embodied in the law .... When Wigmore passionately expressed his view about the threatening nature of complaints of sexual assault made by female children, he articulated and memorialized an attitude which was apparently widely shared. By documenting his case, however, he has allowed later readers to discover the inherent flaw — or call it a 'blind spot' — which lay behind his ostensibly objective presentation of scientific evidence.[24]

ALAN N. YOUNG, WHEN TITANS CLASH: THE LIMITS OF CONSTITUTIONAL ADJUDICATION

(1995) 44 C.R. (4th) 152 at 153-155

In a comment on the Supreme Court's controversial decision in *R. v. O'Connor* (1995), 44 C.R. (4th) 1, 103 C.C.C. (3d) 1, [1995] 4 S.C.R. 411, which set out a two-part procedure for determining defence access to therapeutic and medical records of sexual assault complainants, Professor Alan Young described the following "battlefield":

In the last five years we have seen an ever-increasing defence strategy of requesting production of psychiatric and therapeutic records relating to sexual

---

21 "Corroborating Charges of Rape" (1967), 67 Colum. L. Rev. 1137-1138.

22 *Davis v. State* (1904), 120 Ga. 433, 48 S.E. 180, at 181.

23 *State v. Anderson* (1965), 272 Minn. 384, 137 N.W. 2d 781, at 783, quoting Glanville Williams, "Corroboration — Sexual Cases" October 1962, Crim. L. Rev. 662-671.

24 L.B. Bienen, "A Question of Credibility: John Henry Wigmore's Use of Scientific Authority" (1983), 19 Cal. Western L. Rev. 235 at 253.

assault complainants. Stripped of its ideological and political context, this phenomena is no different than the flurry of breathalyzer production requests which followed upon the *Bourget* decision in 1987. Ultimately, the breathalyzer production strategy faded into oblivion as the courts imposed an "air of reality" restriction on the applications and indicated that they would not be inclined to order stays of proceedings for failure to produce alcohol standard solutions, representative ampoules and breathalyzer mouthpieces.

Unlike the breathalyzer experience, the issue of producing sensitive and confidential records of complainants is animated by deeply held ideological and political beliefs, and, as such, this issue would not fade into oblivion notwithstanding the "likely to be relevant" threshold restriction which the courts placed upon these applications for production. In this context, battle lines appeared to be carved in stone with little incentive to adopt a compromise settlement. In fact, complainants and custodians of sensitive records have appeared willing to disregard court orders. Beyond the unprofessional conduct of the Crown in *R. v. O'Connor*, reported ante, p. 1, in failing to properly comply with an order of production, we have seen cases in which the records have been destroyed and shredded in an attempt to thwart the request for production. To date, the courts have turned a blind eye to this extra-legal obstruction and have concluded that a stay of proceeding is not warranted upon proof of an intent to obstruct but is only warranted if the obstruction truly impaired full answer and defence in a material way. [Since Professor Young wrote this piece the Supreme Court of Canada has ordered a stay when documents were shredded on the basis that they might have been helpful to the accused. See *R. v. Carosella*, (1997), 112 C.C.C. (3d) 289 (S.C.C.).]

To understand the intensity of this battle one must recognize that, historically, sexual assault victims have been re-victimized by an insensitive and patriarchal criminal justice system. Fuelled by Freud's assertion that women and children are hysterical by nature, we find countless examples of statutory and common law evidentiary rules which treated the evidence of sexual assault victims with great suspicion and skepticism. In *Wigmore's Treatise on Evidence*, the eminent commentator noted that "no judge should ever let a sexual offence charge go to the jury unless the female complainant's social history and mental makeup have been examined and testified to by a qualified physician."

The ghosts of the past still haunt the criminal justice system, and, as Madam Justice L'Heureux-Dubé, noted, "uninhibited disclosure of complainants' private lives indulges the discriminatory suspicion that women and children's reports of sexual victimization are uniquely likely to be fabricated." Therefore, it is not surprising that complainants and custodians of sensitive records would view almost all production requests as a form of character assassination which is premised upon the dangerous Freudian and Wigmorian stereotype of half the population being prone to fabrication.

On the other hand, we have a defence lawyer poised for battle because his/her client has denied the accusation. In most cases of sexual assault, there is an absence of confirmatory evidence and independent witnesses, and this raises the spectre of false accusations. This fear of false accusation is somewhat supported by a recent study by the Canadian Centre for Justice Statistics which revealed that the "unfounded"[1] rate for sexual assault was 14 per cent, 9 per cent and 14 per cent for sexual assault level I (s. 271), level II (s. 272) and level III (s. 273) respectively. These figures were compared to the unfounded rate for non-sexual assault which varied from 8 per cent with respect to assault level I (s. 266) to 3 per cent with respect to assault level II and III (ss. 267 and 268).[2] Furthermore, a recent study by an American sociologist demonstrated that 40 per cent of all rape charges investigated by city police turned out to be false as determined by recantation by the accuser and supported by other evidence.[3] Although it is conceded that further study must be given in order to explain this high unfounded rate, it is not surprising that defence counsel will search for whatever effective tools may be available to fully explore an accusation of sexual assault in order to ensure that his or her client is in the category of the unfounded complaint.

There are other offences which have higher unfounded rates than sexual assault (arson — 23.8 per cent; trespass at night — 14.3 per cent; abduction of person under 14 - 42.3 per cent),[4] yet we do not see the mad rush to impeach the credibility of Crown witnesses in these cases by resort to psychiatric and therapeutic records. This apparent inconsistency in defence strategy may suggest that defence lawyers still cling to and believe in the Wigmorian assessment of sexual assault complaints. However, it is equally plausible that the reliance on production requests in sexual assault trials is more a reflection of the nature of these trials, which turn largely on credibility battles without the luxury of independent evidence of a confirmatory nature. Regardless of which explanation is correct, it is apparent that both sides to this battle view the other with much suspicion and some disdain.

NICHOLAS BALA, FALSE MEMORY SYNDROME: BACKLASH OR BONA FIDE DEFENCE

(1996) 21 Queen's L.J. 423 at 454-455

After a lengthy review of the controversial literature and case law respecting "false memory syndrome" Professor Bala's conclusion is guarded:

The issues surrounding recovered and false memories are highly contentious, and difficult for everyone involved: survivors, abusers, complainants, therapists, researchers, lawyers, and judges. It is not uncommon

1 "Unfounded" does not necessarily mean frivolous or false. It is defined as follows: "if the preliminary enquiry conducted by the police reveals that a reported crime has not been committed, this incident is to be classified as unfounded."

2 *Juristat*, "Canadian Justice Processing of Sexual Assault Cases" (Ottawa: Centre for Justice Statistics, March 1994), vol. 14, no. 7 at p. 10.

3 E. Kanin, *False Rape Accusations (1994) Archives of Sexual Behavior* (New York: Plenum Press, 1994), at pp. 81-92.

4 Statistics Canada, *Canadian Crime Statistics 1993* (Ottawa: Centre for Justice Statistics, 1993).

for victims of childhood abuse to have no conscious memories of these experiences. For many troubled adult survivors who are manifesting symptoms of abuse but without memories, therapy can be a very important means for recovering memories, gaining awareness of the etiology of their condition, and becoming a healthier adult.

It is, however, clear that individuals who have not been abused can, in the course of therapy, develop false memories of abuse. Therapists need to have appropriate education and training to be aware of this problem. More psychological research into the processes by which memories of abuse are lost and recovered, as well as research into suggestibility and the development of false memories, would certainly be desirable. It is, however, difficult to carry out reliable, valid research in this area.

Definition of the Crime of Rape

Until it was replaced by the crime of sexual assault in 1982 [S.C. 1980-81-82, c. 125, s. 19], the offence of rape was defined by what was then s. 143 of the *Criminal Code* as follows:

A male person commits rape when he has sexual intercourse with a female person who is not his wife,

(a) without her consent, or
(b) with her consent if the consent
   (i)   is extorted by threats or fear of bodily harm,
   (ii) is obtained by personating her husband, or
   (iii) is obtained by false and fraudulent representations as to the nature and quality of the act.

Note the absolute immunity for the man who raped his wife. Note also the requirement of proof of sexual intercourse, defined elsewhere to be "penetration to even the slightest degree". This aspect often became the focal point of the trial and the reason why a prosecution might fail despite it being clear that a forced sexual encounter had occurred.

Section 143 contained no express *mens rea* requirement. That requirement and the possibility of a defence of mistaken belief was the issue in the controversial cases of *Pappajohn* and *Sansregret* which follow.

PAPPAJOHN v. R.

[1980] 2 S.C.R. 120, 14 C.R. (3d) 243, C.C.C. (2d) 481

McIntyre J. (Pigeon, Beetz and Chouinard JJ. concurring): — The appellant appeals his rape conviction, which was affirmed in the Court of Appeal for British Columbia [5 C.R. (3d) 193, 45 C.C.C. (2d) 67] with one dissent, upon the ground that the trial Judge failed to put to the jury the defence of mistake of fact. That ground is expressed in the appellant's factum in these words:

Did the learned trial Judge err in failing to instruct the jury on the question of honest belief by the accused that the Complainant consented to intercourse and thus on the facts of this case, failed to put properly before the jury a defence, such failure being a non-direction amounting to mis-direction?

A consideration of the facts of the case is vital to a resolution of the problem it poses. The complainant was a real estate saleswoman employed by a well-known and well-established real estate firm in Vancouver. She was successful in her work. The appellant is a businessman who was anxious to sell his home in Vancouver, and he had listed it for sale with the real estate firm with which the complainant was associated. She was to be responsible for the matter on her firm's behalf. On 4th August 1976 at about 1:00 p.m. she met the appellant by appointment at a downtown restaurant for lunch. The purpose of the meeting was to discuss the house sale. The lunch lasted until about 4:00 or 4:30 p.m. During this time a good deal of liquor was consumed by both parties. The occasion became convivial, the proprietor of the restaurant and his wife joined the party and estimates of the amount of alcohol consumed varied in retrospect, as one would expect. It does seem clear, however, that, while each of the parties concerned had a substantial amount to drink, each seemed capable of functioning normally.

At about 4:00 p.m. or shortly thereafter they left the restaurant. The appellant drove the complainant's car while she sat in the front passenger seat. They went to the appellant's house, the one which was listed for sale, to further consider questions arising in that connection. Up to the time of arrival at the home, at about 4:30 or 5:00 p.m., there is no significant variation in their accounts of events. From the moment of arrival, however, there is a complete divergence. She related a story of rape completely against her will and over her protests and struggles. He spoke of an amorous interlude involving no more than a bit of coy objection on her part and several acts of intercourse with her consent. Whatever occurred in the house, there is no doubt that at about 7:30 p.m. the complainant ran out of the house naked with a man's bow tie around her neck and her hands tightly tied behind her back with a bathrobe sash. She arrived at the door of a house nearby and demanded entry and protection. The occupant of the house, a priest, admitted her. She was in an upset state and exhibited great fear and emotional stress. The police were called, and these proceedings followed. More detailed reference to the facts will be made later.

When the defence closed its case, and before the trial Judge commenced his charge, the jury was excluded while counsel for the appellant argued that, on the facts of the case as it appeared from the evidence, the trial Judge should have put the defence of mistake of fact to the jury. He contended that the appellant was entitled to have the Judge tell the jury that, if the appellant entertained an honest though mistaken belief that the complainant was consenting to the acts of intercourse as they occurred, the necessary *mens rea* would not be present and the appellant would be entitled to an acquittal. Reliance for this proposition was placed upon *D.P.P. v. Morgan*; *D.P.P. v. McDonald*; *D.P.P. v. McLarty*; *D.P.P. v. Parker*, [1976] A.C. 182 (H.L.), and *R. v. Plummer* (1975), 31 C.R.N.S. 220,

24 C.C.C. (2d) 497 (Ont. C.A.). The trial Judge refused to accede to defence counsel's request and, in disposing of the motion, had this to say:

> In this case, the complainant has testified that the accused had intercourse with her during a three-hour period some five times without her consent. The accused has testified that the acts of intercourse that he had with the complainant were all with her consent and that the only resistance to his amorous advances was of a token variety, and that orally, along the lines of"; "Oh George, what are you doing?"
>
> There are many conflicts in the evidence during the critical period of time when the acts of sexual intercourse took place, and the jury will have to be directed to accept either the complainant's or the accused's version of the facts.
>
> The essence of the case, as I see it, is essentially: Has the Crown negatived the complainant's consent?

Later, he said after referring to the *Morgan* case and the case of *Plummer*, both supra:

> Although the concept of *mens rea* underlies all criminal prosecutions, I know of no obligation to instruct a jury in connection with this concept. I acknowledge and am in agreement with counsel's statements that in appropriate circumstances defences arise in favour of accused persons even where no intent is apparent from the statute creating an offence, and these defences, at a minimum, are accident and mistake of fact. Although the reasoning in *D.P.P. v. Morgan* [*supra*] may have limited application to Canadian criminal law, I am wholly in accord with the attempt made by the learned trial Judge in placing before the jury in that case what I conceive to be an alternative defence, namely, a mistaken view of the facts. That defence was justified in that case because three of the four accused persons pledged their oaths to the assertion that the victim's husband, also a co-accused, had told them before attending at the victim's residence that his wife was prone to put on a show of struggling but that this would only be a charade stimulating her sexual excitement.
>
> In answer to my questions during argument, defence counsel has suggested that acts of familiarity prior to the time of intercourse, independently testified to by disinterested persons, and the accused's evidence, where he alluded to only oral and token resistance to his advances, constituted evidence upon which I could conclude that the defence of mistake of fact should be left to the jury.
>
> In addition to that evidence I have reviewed the evidence of the accused, and, I regret to say, notwithstanding the forceful submission of defence counsel, I do not recognize in the evidence any sufficient basis of fact to leave the defence of mistake of fact to this jury.

In the Court of Appeal this ruling found support in the majority judgment of Farris C.J.B.C., with whom Craig J.A. agreed. The majority adopted the view that the issue emerging from the evidence was a simple one of consent or no consent. In a dissenting judgment, Lambert J.A. was of the opinion that there was sufficient evidence to put the defence to the jury. He would have directed the jury that the accused was entitled to an acquittal if the jury found that he entertained an honest and *reasonably held* mistaken belief in the existence of consent. This is a view which I cannot share, in view of the pronouncement in this court in *Beaver v. R..*, [1957] S.C.R. 531 at 538, 118 C.C.C. 129.

It is well-established that it is the duty of a trial Judge, in giving directions to a jury, to draw to their attention and to put before them fairly and completely the theory of the defence. In performing this task, it is also clear that the trial Judge must put before the jury any defences which may be open to the accused upon the evidence, whether raised by the accused's counsel or not. He must give all necessary instructions on the law relating to such defences, review the relevant evidence and relate it to the law applicable. This, however, does not mean that the trial Judge becomes bound to put every defence suggested to him by counsel. Before any obligation arises to put defences, there must be in the evidence some basis upon which the defence can rest, and it is only where such an evidentiary basis is present that a trial Judge must put a defence. Indeed, where it is not present he should not put a defence, for to do so would only be to confuse.

What is the standard which the Judge must apply in considering this question? Ordinarily, when there is any evidence of a matter of fact the proof of which may be relevant to the guilt or innocence of an accused, the trial Judge must leave that evidence to the jury so that they may reach their own conclusion upon it. Where, however, the trial Judge is asked to put a specific defence to the jury, he is not concerned only with the existence or non-existence of evidence of fact. He must consider, assuming that the evidence relied upon by the accused to support a defence is true, whether that evidence is sufficient to justify the putting of the defence. This question has been considered frequently in the Courts: see *Wu (Wu Chuck) v. R.*, [1934] S.C.R. 609, 62 C.C.C. 90; and *Kelsey v. R.*, [1953] 1 S.C.R. 220, 16 C.R. 119, 105 C.C.C. 97. The test to be applied has, in my opinion, been set down by Fauteux J., as he then was, in *Kelsey v. R.* [p. 125]:

> The allotment of any substance to an argument or of any value to a grievance resting on the omission of the trial Judge from mentioning such argument must be conditioned on the existence in the record of some evidence or matter apt to convey a sense of reality in the argument and in the grievance.

. . . .

McIntyre J. then reviewed the evidence in greater detail and continued:

In summary, then, this was the state of evidence when the trial Judge was called upon to make his ruling. It became his task to apply the rule enunciated above. In assessing his resolution of the matter, we must consider the situation as it presented itself to him at the time. Speculation as to what the jury did, or would have done after being charged, is not relevant here.

With that thought in mind, and bearing in mind that the object of the judicial search must be evidence of a mistaken but honest belief in the consent of the complainant, one must first ask the question "Where is this evidence to be found?" It cannot be found in the evidence of the complainant. She denies actual consent, and her evidence cannot provide any support for a mistaken belief in consent. Her conduct, according to her description, is that of a terrified, hysterical, non-consenting woman who resisted the appellant's advances, albeit unsuccessfully, and when able fled from his house in search of assistance. Turning then to the evidence of the appellant, it immediately becomes apparent that his evidence speaks of actual consent, even co-operation, and leaves little, if any, room for the suggestion that she may not have been consenting but he thought she was. The two stories are, as has been noted before, diametrically opposed on this vital issue. It is not for the trial Judge to weigh them and prefer one to the other. It is for him in this situation, however, to recognize the issue which arises on the evidence for the purpose of deciding what defences are open. In this situation the only realistic issue which can arise is the simple issue of consent or no consent. In my opinion, the trial Judge was correct in concluding that there simply was not sufficient evidence to justify the putting of the defence of mistake of fact to the jury. He left the issue of consent, and that was the only one arising on the evidence.

In reaching this conclusion, I am not unmindful of the evidence of surrounding circumstances which were said to support the appellant's contention. I refer to the absence of serious injury suffered by the complainant and the absence of damage to clothing, as well as to the long period of time during which the parties remained in the bedroom. These matters may indeed be cogent on the issue of actual consent but, in my view, they cannot by themselves advance a suggestion of a mistaken belief. The finding of the clothes at the foot of the bed and the necklace and the keys in the living room are equally relevant on the issue of actual consent and, in my view, cannot affect the issue, which was clearly framed by the opposing assertions of consent and non-consent.

It would seem to me that, if it is considered necessary in this case to charge the jury on the defence of mistake of fact, it would be necessary to do so in all cases where the complainant denies consent and an accused asserts it. To require the putting of the alternative defence of mistaken belief in consent, there must be, in my opinion, some evidence beyond the mere assertion by counsel for the appellant of belief in consent. This evidence must appear from or be supported by sources other than the appellant in order to give it any air of reality. In *R. v. Plummer, supra*, Evans J.A. (as he then was), speaking for the Ontario Court of Appeal, considered that there was such evidence as far as Brown was concerned, and directed a new trial because the defence had not been put. In that case, the complainant had gone to Plummer's "pad", where she had been raped by Plummer. Brown entered the room where the rape occurred after Plummer had gone. Apparently he had arrived at the house separately from Plummer. It was open on the evidence to find that he was unaware then that Plummer had threatened the complainant and terrorized her into submission. He had intercourse with her, and she said that because of continuing fear from Plummer's threats, she submitted without protest. In these special circumstances the defence was required. The facts clearly established at least an air of reality to Brown's defence. In *Morgan, supra*, there was evidence of an invitation by the complainant's husband to have intercourse with his wife and his assurance that her show of resistance would be a sham. In other words, there was evidence explaining, however preposterous the explanation might be, a basis for the mistaken belief. In the case at bar, there is no such evidence.

Where the complainant says rape and the accused says consent, and where on the whole of the evidence, including that of the complainant, the accused and the surrounding circumstances, there is a clear issue on this point, and where, as here, the accused makes no assertion of a belief in consent, as opposed to an actual consent, it is unrealistic, in the absence of some other circumstance or circumstances, such as are found in the *Plummer* and *Morgan* cases, *supra*, to consider the Judge bound to put the mistake of fact defence. In my opinion, the trial Judge was correct in refusing to put the defence on the evidence before him.

I might add that I have had the advantage of reading the reasons of my brother Dickson and, while it is apparent that I am unable to accept his view on the evidentiary question, I am in agreement with that part of his judgment dealing with the availability as a defence to a charge of rape in Canada of what is generally termed the defence of mistake of fact. I would dismiss the appeal.

MARTLAND J.: — I agree with the opinion expressed by my brother McIntyre that the trial judge was correct in concluding that there was not sufficient evidence to justify putting the defence of mistake of fact to the jury, and with his proposed disposition of this appeal.

I would, however, like to make a comment in respect of one passage in his reasons which refers to the dissenting opinion of Lambert J.A. in the Court of Appeal [5 C.R. (3d) 193 at 201, 45 C.C.C. (2d) 67]. Lambert J.A. was of the opinion that there was sufficient evidence to put the defence of mistake of fact to the jury, and that the trial Judge should have directed the jury that the accused was entitled to an acquittal if the jury found that he entertained an honest and *reasonably held* belief in the existence of consent. Dealing with the words underlined, my brother McIntyre says that he cannot share his view because of the pronouncement of this Court in *Beaver v. R.*, [1957] S.C.R. 531 at 538, 118 C.C.C. 129, reversing [1956] O.W.N. 798, 25 C.R. 53, 116 C.C.C. 231. The passage to which he refers is contained in the judgment of Cartwright J. (as he then was), and reads as follows:

> In *R. v. Tolson* (1889), 23 Q.B.D. 168 (C.C.R.), Stephen J. says at p. 188:
> ". . . I think it may be laid down as a general rule that an alleged offender is deemed to have acted under that state of facts which he in good faith and on reasonable grounds believed to exist when he did the act alleged to be an offence.
> "I am unable to suggest any real exception to this rule, nor has one ever been suggested to me."
> and adds at p. 189:
> "Of course, it would be competent to the Legislature to define a crime in such a way as to make the existence of any state of mind immaterial. The question is solely whether it has actually done so in this case."
> I adhere to the opinion which, with the concurrence of my brother Nolan, I expressed in *R. v. Rees*, [1956] S.C.R. 640 at 651, 24 C.R. 1, 115 C.C.C. 1, that the first of the statements of Stephen J. quoted above should now be read in the light of the judgment of Lord Goddard C.J., concurred in by Lynskey and Devlin JJ., in *Wilson v. Inyang*, [1951] 2 K.B. 799 (D.C.), which, in my opinion, rightly decides that the essential question is whether the belief entertained by the accused is an honest one and that the existence or non-existence of reasonable grounds for such belief is merely relevant evidence to be weighed by the tribunal of fact in determining that essential question.

The paragraph which follows the quotation from Stephen J. in *R. v. Tolson* is an obiter dictum. The Court which determined the *Beaver* case was a five-man Court, and two of the Judges dissented on the disposition of the case. It involved a charge of being in possession of a drug. The accused was in physical possession of a package which contained drugs, but he said he never knew that the package contained drugs. The Courts below had held that this furnished no defence to the charge, under s. 4(1)(*d*) of the *Opium and Narcotic Drug Act*, R.S.C. 1952, c. 201. The issue before the Court, and on which it divided, was whether the statute created an absolute prohibition or whether the want of knowledge as to the nature of the substance found in the possession of the accused furnished a defence. The dissenting minority held the view that *mens rea* was not an essential element of the offence charged. The reasonableness of the belief of the accused was not in issue.

Cartwright J., in the passage cited, relies on a statement of Lord Goddard C.J. in *Wilson v. Inyang, supra*. That was a case in which the charge was that of wilfully and falsely using the title of "physician", contrary to s. 407 of the *Medical Act, 1858* (21 & 22 Vict.), c. 90. The offence, as defined, included a specific mental ingredient.

Speaking of that case, Bridge J., who delivered the judgment of the Court of Appeal in *R. v. Morgan*, [1976] A.C. at 185, [1975] 1 All E.R. 8, affirmed (sub nom. *D.P.P. v. Morgan*; *D.P.P. v. McDonald*; *D.P.P. v. McLarty*; *D.P.P. v. Parker*), [1976] A.C. 182, 61 Cr. App. R. 136, [1975] 2 All E.R. 347, (H.L.), said at p.14:

> Wherever the definition of a crime includes as one of its express ingredients a specific mental element both the evidential and the probative burden lie upon the Crown with respect to that element. Typical examples are dishonesty in theft and knowledge or belief in handling. In seeking to rebut the Crown's case against him in reference to his state of mind the accused may and frequently does assert his mistaken belief in non-existent facts. Of course it is right that in this context the question whether there were reasonable grounds for the belief is only a factor for the jury's consideration in deciding whether the Crown has established the necessary mental element of the crime. This is because the issue is already before the jury and no evidential burden rests upon the accused.
>
> The decision of the Divisional Court in *Wilson v. Inyang* [*supra*] is to be understood in the light of this principle. The Court there rejected the argument that an acquittal by a Magistrate of a defendant charged with an offence under s. 40 of the *Medical Act 1858* should be reversed on appeal by case stated on the ground that the defendant had no reasonable ground for his belief that he was entitled to call himself a "physician". Lord Goddard C.J. said [at p. 803]:
>
> "'If' he has acted without any reasonable ground and says: 'I had not properly inquired, and did not think this or that,' that may be (and generally is) very good evidence that he is not acting honestly. But it is only evidence."
>
> The Act, however, under which that prosecution was brought required the prosecution to prove that the defendant acted "wilfully and falsely". Inevitably, therefore, if this subjective mental element was not proved the prosecution failed.

The remarks of Lord Goddard C.J. in *Wilson v. Inyang, supra*, were made with reference to an offence under the section of the *Medical Act, 1858*, and do not purport to be a general definition of the requisites of a defence of mistake of fact in all criminal cases.

For these reasons, it is my opinion that, if a case arises which raises the issue as to whether, on a charge of rape, an accused person who seeks to rely upon a defence of mistake of fact must, in order to succeed, establish that his mistake was reasonable as well as honest, it is open to this Court to determine that issue, and that it is not precluded from so doing by the judgment in the

Beaver case, *supra*. On the reasoning of my brother McIntyre in this case, with which I have agreed, that issue does not arise in the present appeal.

DICKSON J. (dissenting) (ESTEY J. concurring): — . . . .

It will be convenient to identify the pivotal issues on which the appellant's case turns:

(1) What is the *mens rea* of rape?

(2) Is a mistaken belief in consent available in defence to the charge of rape?

(3) If so, does mistake afford a defence only where the mistake is one which is held both honestly *and on reasonable grounds?*

(4) Did the trial Judge err in the case at bar in ruling that there was not sufficient basis of fact to justify leaving the defence of mistake of fact to the jury?

I

Mens Rea

There rests now, at the foundation of our system of criminal justice, the precept that a man cannot be adjudged guilty and subjected to punishment unless the commission of the crime was voluntarily directed by a willing mind. Blackstone spoke of a "vicious act" consequent upon a "vicious will" (Commentaries on the Laws of England (1765), vol. 4, p. 21). Proof of the mental element is an essential and constituent step in establishing criminal responsibility. Parliament can, of course, by express words, create criminal offences for which a guilty intention is not an essential ingredient. Equally, *mens rea* is not requisite in a wide category of statutory offences which are concerned with public welfare, health and safety. Subject to these exceptions, *mens rea*, consisting of some positive state of mind, such as evil intention or knowledge of the wrongfulness of the act or reckless disregard of consequences, must be proved by the prosecution. The mental element may be established by inference from the nature of the act committed, or by additional evidence.

The *mens rea* which is required, and its nature and extent, will vary with the particular crime; it can be determined only by detailed examination of the *actus reus* of the offence. Speaking generally, at least where the circumstance is not "morally indifferent", the mental element must be proved with respect to all circumstances and consequences that form part of the *actus reus*. It follows that, in a case of alleged rape, where a fact or circumstance is not known to, or is misapprehended by, the accused, leading to a mistaken but honest belief in the consent of the woman, his act is not culpable in relation to that element of the offence: Glanville Williams, *Criminal Law, The General Part*, 2nd ed. (1961), p. 52:

> For if the *actus reus* includes surrounding circumstances, it cannot be said to be intentional unless *all its elements*, including those circumstances, are known. (The italics are mine.)

Taking these principles, then, what is the mental element required under s. 143 of the *Criminal Code*, R.S.C. 1970, c. C-34, on a charge of rape? This crime was historically regarded as an offence of physical violence. Blackstone defined rape as "the carnal knowledge of a woman forcibly and against her will" (Commentaries, p. 210). A more comprehensive definition of rape at common law is found in Archbold, *Pleading, Evidence and Practice in Criminal Cases*, 38th ed. (1973), para. 2871:

> Rape consists in having unlawful sexual intercourse with a woman without her consent by force, fear or fraud [citing East's Pleas of the Crown (1803), vol. 1, p. 434, and Hale's Pleas of the Crown (1736), vol. 1, p. 627].

Section 143 of our *Code*, in brief, defines rape as an act of sexual intercourse with a female person without her consent, or with consent if that consent is extorted by threats or fear of bodily harm. It will be seen that the statutory definition does not depart in any significant way from the common law definition. For all practical purposes, the *Criminal Code* merely codifies the common law. The essence of the crime consists in the commission of an act of sexual intercourse where a woman's consent, or genuine consent, has been withheld.

AR

The *actus reus* of rape is complete upon (a) an act of sexual intercourse, (b) without consent. An affirmative finding as to each of these elements does not finish the inquiry, however, for, as I have indicated, the requirement that there be a guilty intention must also be satisfied. The important question then arises as to whether, at common law and under s. 143 of the *Code*, the guilty intention of rape extends to the element of consent. In principle it would seem that it should, as intention as to consent is central to responsibility; a man should be punished only where he proceeds with an act of violation in the knowledge that consent is withheld, or in a state of recklessness as to whether willingness is present. The intention to commit the act of intercourse, and to commit that act in the absence of consent, are two separate and distinct elements of the offence.

Is the accused's perception of consent relevant to a charge under s. 143 of the *Criminal Code*? The argument against the application of *D.P.P. v. Morgan*; *D.P.P. v. McDonald*; *D.P.P. v. McLarty*; *D.P.P. v. Parker*, [1975] 2 All E.R. 347 (H.L.), in Canada, is that the *Code* creates a statutory offence of rape which does not expressly advert to or require that there be a state of mind or intent to proceed in the absence of consent. The issue of consent as an aspect of *mens rea* for rape does not appear to have been raised directly in English authorities previous to the *Morgan* decision, although Denman J. in *R. v. Flattery* (1877), 13 Cox C.C. 388 (C.C.R.), had occasion to say (p. 392):

> There is one case where a woman does not consent to the act of connection and yet the man may not be guilty of rape, that is where the resistance is so slight and her behaviour such that the man may *bona fide* believe that she is consenting.

The question has been topical in the Australian Courts for some time, and we have the benefit of a body of case law which deals with the mental element and honest belief as a defence of mistake.

. . . .

In *Morgan, supra,* each of the law lords accepted the element of knowledge or recklessness as to consent as a feature of the guilty intention in the crime of rape. In particular, Lord Hailsham of St. Marylebone endorsed at p. 357 the test formulated by the trial Judge, that the prosecution must prove that "each defendant intended to have sexual intercourse without her consent. Not merely that he intended to have intercourse with her but that he intended to have intercourse without her consent . . ." Lord Hailsham added the qualification that, if an accused is reckless as to consent, that is equivalent, on ordinary principles, to an intent to do the prohibited act without consent. Lord Simon of Glaisdale, though dissenting on the issue of whether a belief must be reasonably held, was succinct (p. 365):

> The *actus reus* is sexual intercourse with a woman who is not in fact consenting to such intercourse. The *mens rea* is knowledge that the woman is not consenting or recklessness as to whether she is consenting or not.

In the view of Lord Edmund-Davies, also in dissent, it is incorrect to regard rape as involving no mental element save the intention to have intercourse; knowledge by the accused of the woman's unwillingness to have intercourse is essential to the crime (p. 372). (See also Lord Fraser of Tullybelton at p. 381.)

Following the *Morgan* decision, the Home Secretary commissioned an inquiry, and the Report of the Advisory Group on the Law of Rape ("The Heilbron Report") (1975) was soon published. The mandate of the group was to consider whether the *Morgan* decision necessitated immediate statutory reform. In the course of its report, which approved the principles elucidated in *Morgan*, the following is stated, at para. 23:

> The mental element, which the prosecution must additionally establish (*i.e.* to the *actus reus*) is an intention by the defendant to have sexual intercourse either knowing that she does not consent, or recklessly not caring whether she consents or not.

Moreover, the Group agreed that a mistaken though genuine belief is inconsistent with, and negatives, the requisite mental element. Such a belief need not be reasonably held, although the reasonableness of it is a relevant consideration for the jury. It is no longer disputed that, in England, perception of the woman's consent is an aspect of the mental element in crimes of rape.

Turning to Canada . . .

. . . .

The law of rape was considered by this Court in *Leary v. R.,* [1978] 1 S.C.R. 29, 37 C.R.N.S. 60, 33 C.C.C. (2d) 473. The appeal turned on the availability of intoxication as a defence to the charge. Pigeon J., although disagreeing with the contention that specific intent was required, cited the following passage from the speech of Lord Simon [p. 365] in the course of his review of what had been said in *Morgan, supra* (pp. 71-72):

This brings me to the fourth question, namely whether rape is a crime of basic or ulterior intent. Does it involve an intent going beyond the *actus reus*? Smith and Hogan [Criminal Law, 3rd ed. (1973), p. 47] say No. I respectfully agree, The *actus reus* is sexual intercourse with a woman who is not in fact consenting to such intercourse. *The mens rea is knowledge that the woman is not consenting or recklessness as to whether she is consenting or not.* (The italics are mine.)

The dissenting judgment in *Leary* contained this definition of the mental element (pp. 76-77):

> the Crown must prove, beyond reasonable doubt, intercourse without consent, together with (a) an intention to force intercourse notwithstanding absence of consent, or (b) a realization that the conduct may lead to non-consensual intercourse and a recklessness or indifference to that consequence ensuing. It will not do simply to say that because the accused committed the physical act and the woman did not consent, he must be taken to have intended to have intercourse without consent.

. . . .

It will thus be seen that the great weight of authority is in support of the view that the accused's perception of the woman's consent is an important aspect of any prosecution for the crime of rape. Counsel for the Crown in the instant appeal reviewed and compared s. 143 of the *Code* with other Pt. IV Code offences, to make the point that the subjective belief of an accused is no part of the case to be proved by the Crown. It was contended that, since reference to intention to proceed in the absence of consent is lacking in s. 143, the statutory wording prevails over case authorities which consider the mental element in terms of the common law definition. Section 148 of the *Code* was cited in comparison. This section specifies, as an ingredient of the offence, knowledge or reason for belief that the female person is, by reason of her mental condition, incapable of giving a reasonable consent. Knowledge of the existence of a blood relationship is a constituent element of the crime of incest, spelled out in s. 150 [am. 1972, c. 13, s. 10] of the *Code*.

One cannot assume on the strength of these two sections that there is no *mens rea* element relating to consent for crimes of rape. Parliament does not consistently employ wording which indicates express levels of intention (such as "knowingly", "intentionally", "wilfully") for all offences which undoubtedly import a mental element. Even within Pt. IV there is no consistency in the wording of the offences. I do not think the determination of the mental element for rape turns in any way on a comparative analysis on the wording for Pt. IV offences.

I refer to the statement by Lord Reid in *Sweet v. Parsley*, [1969] 1 All E.R. 347 at 350 (H.L.):

> for it is firmly established by a host of authorities that *mens rea* is an essential ingredient of every offence unless some reason can be found for holding that that is not necessary. It is also firmly established that the fact that other sections of the Act expressly require *mens rea*, for example because they contain the word "knowingly", is not in itself sufficient to justify a decision that a section which is silent as to *mens rea* creates an absolute offence.

In summary, intention or recklessness must be proved in relation to all elements of the offence, including absence of consent. This simply extends to rape the same general order of intention as in other crimes.

II

Mistake of Fact

Belief by an accused in a mistaken set of facts has not always afforded an answer to a criminal charge. By the early criminal law, the only real defence that could be raised was that an act had not been voluntary and therefore could not be imputed to the accused. Thus it was possible in some cases to excuse a man who had acted under a mistake by the argument that his conduct was not truly voluntary: Russell On Crime, 12th ed. (1964), vol. 1, p. 71. In the 17th century, Hale wrote: "But in some cases *ignorantia facti* doth excuse, for such an ignorance many times makes the act itself morally involuntary." (Pleas of the Crown (1736), vol. 1, p.42).

The leading English cases on mistake of fact are, of course, *R. v. Prince* (1875), 13 Cox C.C. 138 (C.C.R.), and *R. v. Tolson* (1889), 23 Q.B.D. 168 (C.C.R.). In the *Prince* decision (p. 152), Brett J. cited from Blackstone's Commentaries, p. 27:

> *Ignorance* or *mistake* is another defect of will, when a man, intending to do a lawful act, does that which is unlawful. For here, the deed and the will acting separately, there is not that conjunction between them which is necessary to form a criminal act.

Brett J. held that mistake as a defence applies whenever facts are present, in which an accused believes and has reasonable ground to believe, which if true would render his act innocent and not a crime. The *Tolson* case, following *Prince*, considered the extent to which a mistaken, though honest and reasonable, belief that the first spouse was dead could afford a defence to a charge of bigamy. The classic statement is that of Cave J. (p. 181):

> At common law an honest and reasonable belief in the existence of circumstances, which, if true, would make the act for which the prisoner is indicted an innocent act has always been held to be a good defence.

An honest and reasonable mistake of fact is on the same footing as the absence of a reasoning faculty, as with infants, or impairment of the faculty, as in lunacy (*Tolson*, p. 181). Culpability rests upon commission of the offence with knowledge of the facts and circumstances comprising the crime. If, according to an accused's belief concerning the facts, his act is criminal, then he intended the offence and can be punished. If, on the other hand, his act would be innocent, according to facts as he believed them to be, he does not have the criminal mind and ought not to be punished for his act. (See E.R. Keedy, "Ignorance and Mistake in the Criminal Law" (1908), 22 Harvard L. Rev. 75, p. 82).

As stated by Dixon J., as he then was, in *Thomas v. R.*, 59 C.L.R. 279 at 299-300 (H.C.):

> States of volition are necessarily dependant upon states of fact, and a mistaken belief in the existence of circumstances cannot be separated from the manifestation of the will which it prompts . . . the nature of an act of volition may be of an entirely different description if it is based on mistake of fact. The state of facts assumed must often enter into the determination of the will. It would be strange if our criminal law did not contain this principle and treat it as fundamental.

Mistake is a defence, then, where it prevents an accused from having the *mens rea* which the law requires for the very crime with which he is charged. Mistake of fact is more accurately seen as a negation of guilty intention than as the affirmation of a positive defence. It avails an accused who acts innocently, pursuant to a flawed perception of the facts, and nonetheless commits the *actus reus* of an offence. Mistake is a defence, though, in the sense that it is raised as an issue by an accused. The Crown is rarely possessed of knowledge of the subjective factors which may have caused an accused to entertain a belief in a fallacious set of facts.

If I am correct that: (i) s. 143 of the *Criminal Code* imports a *mens rea* requirement; and (ii) the *mens rea* of rape includes intention, or recklessness as to non-consent of the complainant, a mistake that negatives intention or recklessness entitles the accused to an acquittal. Glanville Williams notes in *Criminal Law, The General Part*, para. 65, p. 173:

> It is impossible to assert that a crime requiring intention or recklessness can be committed although the accused laboured under a mistake negativing the requisite intention or recklessness. Such an assertion carries its own refutation.

Howard (Criminal Law, 3rd ed. (1977)), points out that rape is aimed at the protection of women from forcible subjection to non-marital sexual intercourse, but that the facts of life not infrequently impede the drawing of a clean line between consensual and non-consensual intercourse (p. 149):

> it is easy for a man intent upon his own desires to mistake the intentions of a woman or girl who may herself be in two minds about what to do. Even if he makes no mistake it is not unknown for a woman afterwards either to take fright or for some other reason to regret what has happened and seek to justify herself retrospectively by accusing the man of rape.

I do not think the defence of mistaken belief can be restricted to those situations in which the belief has been induced by information received from a third party. That was the situation in the *Morgan* case, *supra*. In *Morgan*, the belief in consent was induced by information related by the complainant's husband, who spoke of his wife's sexual propensities. The foundation for the defence, incredible as it turned out to be, in view of the violence, was the misinformation of the husband. Had the defendants believed that information and had the wife's overt conduct been relatively consistent with it, the defendants would have had a defence. That is the effect of the dicta of the House of Lords in the *Morgan* case.

In principle, the defence should avail when there is an honest belief in consent or an absence of knowledge that consent has been withheld. Whether the mistake is rooted in an accused's mistaken perception or is based upon objective but incorrect facts confided to him by another should be of no consequence. The kind of mistaken fact pleaded by the *Morgan* defendants, however, is more likely to be believed than a bald assertion of mistaken belief during a face-to-face encounter. In any event, it is clear that the defence is available only where there is sufficient evidence presented by an accused, by his testimony or by the circumstances in which the act occurred, to found the plea.

III

Honest and Reasonable Mistake

The next question which must be broached is whether a defence of honest, though mistaken, belief in consent must be based on reasonable grounds. A majority of the House of Lords in *Morgan, supra,* answered the question in the negative, and that view was affirmed by the Heilbron Committee. There can be no doubt that this answer is consonant with principle. As Professor Keedy has written (p. 88), an act is reasonable in law when it is such as a man of ordinary care would do under similar circumstances: to require that the mistake be reasonable means that, if the accused is to have a defence, he must have acted up to the standard of an average man, whether the accused is himself such a man or not; this is the application of an outer standard to the individual; if the accused is to be punished because his mistake is one which an average man would not make, punishment will sometimes be inflicted when the criminal mind does not exist.

In other jurisdictions, there are divergent decisions and dicta on the question whether mistaken belief must be based on reasonable grounds to exculpate. In the affirmative are such bigamy cases as: *Tolson, supra; Thomas, supra; R. v. King,* [1964] 1 Q.B. 443; and *R. v. Gould,* [1968] 2 Q.B. 65. Non-bigamy cases are *Prince, supra; Bank of New South Wales v. Piper,* [1897] A.C. 383 (P.C.); *Warner v. Metro. Police Commr.,* [1969] 2 A.C. 256, 52 Cr. App. R. 373, [1968] 2 All E.R. 356 (H.L.); and *Sweet v. Parsley, supra.* In the majority of cases in which the Courts view the mistake as a defence only if made on reasonable grounds, such as in *Tolson,* that view is not a necessary part of the *ratio decidendi.*

Among the cases in which mistaken belief was considered and a test of reasonableness applied, are: *Flannery, supra; R. v. Bourke* (1970), 91 W.N. (N.S.W.) 793 (C.A.); and *Sperotto, supra.* Cases to the contrary are: *Thorne v. Motor Trade Assn.,* [1937] A.C. 797 (H.L.); *Wilson v. Inyang,* [1951] 2 K.B. 799 (D.C.); *R. v. Smith,* [1974] Q.B. 354; and *R. v. Brown* (1975), 10 S.A.S.R. 139. Virtually unanimous rejection of the added requirement of "reasonableness" is to be found in the scholarly writings: Glanville Williams, *Criminal Law, The General Part,* para. 70, p. 201: "The idea that a mistake, to be a defence, must be reasonable, though lurking in some of the cases, is certainly not true as a general proposition"; Glanville Williams, *Textbook of Criminal Law* (1978), p. 100; Howard, pp. 153-54; Smith and Hogan, *Criminal Law, 4th ed.* (1978), p. 182; *Russell on Crime, 12th ed.* (1964), vol. 1, p. 76; J.C. Smith annotation, [1975] Crim. L. Rev. 42; Morris and Turner, "Two Problems in the Law of Rape" (1956), 2 University of Queensland L.J. 247.

In Canada, the *Tolson* rule has already been rejected by this Court in favour of the honest belief standard. Unless this court wishes to overrule *Beaver v. R.*, [1957] S.C.R. 531, 118 C.C.C. 129, it is difficult to see how the minority in *Morgan* can decide this appeal.

In *R. v. Rees*, [1956] S.C.R. 640, 24 C.R. 1, 115 C.C.C. 1, the issue was whether there is *mens rea* for the offence of knowingly or wilfully contributing to juvenile delinquency. Cartwright J. set out the *Tolson* test and then held as follows (p. 11 C.R.):

> The first of the statements of Stephen J. quoted above should now be read in the light of the judgment of Lord Goddard C.J., concurred in by Lynskey and Devlin JJ. in *Wilson v. Inyang* [*supra*], which, in my opinion, rightly decides that the essential question is whether the belief entertained by the accused is an honest one and that the existence or non-existence of reasonable grounds for such belief is merely relevant evidence to be weighed by the tribunal of fact in determining such essential question.

One year later, in *Beaver v. R.*, *supra*, a narcotics case, the opinion of Cartwright J. was accepted by a majority of the Court. He adopted the paragraph quoted above from *Rees*. *Beaver* has since been regarded as an authoritative contribution to the law as to mental element, and mistaken belief, in true crimes.

It is not clear how one can properly relate reasonableness (an element in offences of negligence) to rape (a "true crime" and not an offence of negligence). To do so, one must, I think, take the view that the *mens rea* goes only to the physical act of intercourse and not to non-consent, and acquittal comes only if the mistake is reasonable. This, upon the authorities, is not a correct view, the intent in rape being not merely to have intercourse but to have it with a non-consenting woman. If the jury finds that mistake, whether reasonable or unreasonable, there should be no conviction. If, upon the entire record, there is evidence of mistake to cast a reasonable doubt upon the existence of a criminal mind, then the prosecution has failed to make its case. In an article by Professor Colin Howard, "The Reasonableness of Mistake in the Criminal Law" (1961), 4 University of Queensland L.J. 45, the following is offered (p. 47):

> To crimes of *mens rea*, or elements of a crime which requires *mens rea*, mistake of fact *simpliciter* is a defence; to crimes of negligence, or elements of an offence which requires only negligence, mistake of fact is a defense only if the mistake was in all the circumstances a reasonable one to make.

The same analysis is expressed by Glanville Williams, *Criminal Law, The General Part*, para. 71, p. 202.

In *D.P.P. v. Morgan*, *supra*, four law lords agreed that, having accepted the mental element of knowledge as to consent, it is inconsistent to attach a standard of reasonableness to a defence of honest belief. As Lord Hailsham pointed out, the following two propositions are totally irreconcilable:

(i) Each defendant must have intended to have sexual intercourse without her consent — not merely that he intended to have intercourse but that he intended to have intercourse without her consent; and

(ii) It is necessary for any belief in the woman's consent to be a "reasonable belief" before the defendant is entitled to be acquitted.

The difference between the majority and minority decisions in *Morgan* turned upon the way in which each law lord perceived the *Tolson* precedent, as being a wide-ranging and well-established principle or as expressing a narrow rule limited in effect to bigamy and the facts at hand.

Lambert J.A. in his dissenting judgment in the instant case reasoned, on his reading of *Leary*, supra, and *Morgan*, that a defence of honest belief in consent must be based on reasonable grounds. In his view, two law lords in *Morgan*, following *Tolson*, clearly required an honest belief to be held on reasonable grounds (Lord Simon and Lord Edmund-Davies). Two others, Lord Fraser and Lord Hailsham, invoked general principles to conclude that an honest belief in consent need not be reasonably held. The decision of the fifth Judge, Lord Cross, turned on a distinction drawn between statutory and common-law offences. Bigamy, the offence in question in *Tolson*, was a statutory offence. Rape is not. Therefore, the *Tolson* requirement that the mistake be reasonable does not apply to rape, a crime defined by common law. Were rape to be defined by statute, the defence would be available only if supported by reasonable grounds. Lambert J.A. held that, if one adapted the decision of Lord Cross to s. 143 of the *Code*, the tables would be turned, and a majority of the lords would, for purposes of the *Criminal Code*, endorse the honest and reasonable test. If the distinction Lord Cross thought might be possible between statutory and common-law offences would have the effect of giving a defence of unreasonable mistake to a person accused of a crime which, in express terms, imported *mens rea*, but would limit the defence to one of reasonable mistake to a person accused of a crime which imported *mens rea* only by implication, the justification for the distinction is not apparent. I am unable to see why the defence should be so limited. Rape is not a crime of strict or absolute liability. With respect, there is no compelling reason for extending to rape the misapprehension, having its genesis in *Tolson* and now endemic in English law, that makes bigamy a crime of negligence and would have a like effect if applied to statutory rape.

Lambert J.A. recognized that, while his conclusion was directed by precedent rather than logic, he also found it to be supported, in relation to rape, by policy and practical sense [p. 212]:

> Why should a woman who is sexually violated by such a man have to defend herself by screams or blows in order to indicate her lack of consent, or have to consent through fear, for a charge of rape to be sustained? Surely a firm oral protest, sufficient to deny any reasonable grounds for belief in consent, should be a sufficient foundation in these circumstances for a charge of rape.

I am not unaware of the policy considerations advanced in support of the view that if mistake is to afford a defence to a charge of rape it should, at the very least, be one of a reasonable man might make in the circumstances. There is justifiable concern over the position of the woman who alleges that she has been subjected to a non-consensual sexual act; fear is expressed that subjective orthodoxy should not enable her alleged assailant to escape accountability by advancing some cock-and-bull story. The usual response of persons accused of rape is: "She consented." Are such persons now to be acquitted simply by saying: "Even if she did not consent, I believed she consented"? The concern is legitimate and real. It must, however, be placed in the balance with other relevant considerations. First, cases in which mistake can be advanced in answer to a charge of rape must be few in number. People do not normally commit rape per incuriam. An evidential case must exist to support the plea. Second, if the woman in her own mind withholds consent but her conduct and other circumstances lend credence to belief on the part of the accused that she was consenting, it may be that it is unjust to convict. I do not think it will do to say that in those circumstances she in fact consented. In fact, she did not, and it would be open to a jury to so find. Third, it is unfair to the jury and to the accused to speak in terms of two beliefs, one entertained by the accused, the other by a reasonable man, and to ask the jury to ignore an actual belief in favour of an attributed belief. The mind with which the jury is concerned is that of the accused. By importing a standard external to the accused, there is created an incompatible mix of subjective and objective factors. If an honest lack of knowledge is shown, then the subjective element of the offence is not proved. The following passage from the Heilbron Report is, however, apposite:

> 66. *Morgan's* case did not decide, as some critics seem to have thought, than an accused person was entitled to be acquitted, however ridiculous his story might be, nor did it decide that the reasonableness or unreasonableness of his belief was irrelevant. Furthermore it is a mistaken assumption that a man is entitled to be acquitted simply because he asserts this belief, without more.

Perpetuation of fictions does little for the jury system or the integrity of criminal justice. The ongoing debate in the Courts and learned journals as to whether mistake must be reasonable is conceptually important in the orderly development of the criminal law, but, in my view, practically unimportant, because the accused's statement that he was mistaken is not likely to be believed unless the mistake is, to the jury, reasonable. The jury will be concerned to consider the reasonableness of any grounds found, or asserted to be available, to support the defence of mistake. Although "reasonable grounds" is not a precondition to the availability of a plea of honest belief in consent, those grounds determine the weight to be given the defence. The reasonableness or otherwise of the accused's belief is only evidence for or against the view that the belief was actually held and the intent was therefore lacking.

Canadian juries, in my experience, display a high degree of common sense and an uncanny ability to distinguish between the genuine and the specious.

The words of Dixon J. in *Thomas, supra,* at p. 309, bear repeating:

a lack of confidence in the ability of a tribunal correctly to estimate evidence of states of mind and the like can never be sufficient ground for excluding from inquiry the most fundamental element in a rational and humane criminal code.

In *Textbook Of Criminal Law* (1978), p. 102, Professor Glanville Williams states the view, with which I am in agreement, that it is proper for the trial Judge to tell the jury "that if they think the alleged belief was unreasonable, that may be one factor leading them to conclude that it was not really held; but they must look at the facts as a whole". It will be a rare day when a jury is satisfied as to the existence of an unreasonable belief. If the claim of mistake does not raise a reasonable doubt as to guilt and all other elements of the crime have been proved, then the trier of fact will not give effect to the defence. But if there is any evidence that there was such an honest belief, regardless of whether it is reasonable, the jury must be entrusted with the task of assessing the credibility of the plea.

To apply the reasonable standard in this appeal, the Court, in my view, would have to: (a) accept the minority decision in *Morgan, supra*; (b) overrule *Beaver, supra*, or find a means of distinguishing the offence of rape; and (c) defy accepted and sound principles of criminal law.

IV

The Plea and the Evidence

I come now to what is perhaps the most difficult part of this case, namely, whether there was an evidential base sufficient to require the trial Judge to place before the jury the defence of mistaken belief in consent.

. . . .

Leaving aside the possibility of post-bondage intercourse, the jury could have reached any one of three alternative conclusions: (1) the appellant was telling the truth and the complainant did consent; (2) he was not telling the truth, she did not consent and he was aware of that fact or reckless to it; or (3) though he did not plead mistake, he believed she was consenting, notwithstanding token resistance. His defence of consent is rejected and that of honest belief accepted, I think there was sufficient evidence to put that third alternative to the jury.

Because the case turns on evidential matters, detailed reference thereto is unavoidable.

. . . .

There is circumstantial evidence supportive of a plea of belief in consent: (1) Her necklace and car keys were found in the living room. (2) She confirmed his testimony that her blouse was neatly hung in the clothes closet. (3) Other items of folded clothing were found at the foot of the bed. (4) None of her clothes were damaged in the slightest way. (5) She was in the house for a number of hours. (6) By her version, when she entered the house the appellant said he was going to break her. She made no attempt to leave. (7) She did not leave while he undressed. (8) There was no evidence of struggle. (9) She suffered no physical injuries, aside from three scratches.

The Heilbron Report contains the following observations which seem pertinent to the case at bar. The crime of rape involves an act— sexual intercourse — which is not in itself either criminal or unlawful and can indeed be both desirable and pleasurable; whether it is criminal depends on complex considerations, since the mental states of both parties and the influence of each upon the other, as well as their physical interaction, have to be considered and are sometimes difficult to interpret — all the more so since normally the act takes place in private; there can be many ambiguous situations in sexual relationships; hence, however precisely the law may be stated it cannot always adequately resolve these problems; in the first place, there may well be circumstances where each party interprets the situation differently, and it may be quite impossible to determine with any confidence which interpretation is right.

Toy J. gave a full, fair and accurate summary of the testimony by the complainant and appellant. There can be no criticism of the instructions in this respect. He did not, however, charge the jury on the defence of mistaken belief, as he earlier ruled that there was not "in the evidence any sufficient basis of fact to leave the defence of mistake of fact to this jury".

In my view, with respect, the Judge erred in failing to instruct the jury: (a) that, as to pre-bondage intercourse, the issues were consent and belief in consent; and (b) that, as to post-bondage intercourse, the issue was whether an act of intercourse occurred or not. If the answer to (b) was negative, a conviction could not be founded upon the post-bondage period. If the answer was in the affirmative, a conviction would almost of necessity follow, because there was admittedly no consent or belief in consent after the "bondage".

That the case gave the jury difficulty is clear from the fact that the charge was delivered about noon on a Friday and the verdict was not rendered until about 5:00 p.m. on Saturday.

I am mindful of the comment of Pigeon J. in *Leary*, supra, that consideration should be given to the plight of a complainant, who should not be subjected to the humiliation of having to testify again unless justice makes it imperative. The possibility of a mistaken belief in consent in the pre-bondage phase was an issue that should have been placed before the jury; the Judge's failure to do so makes it imperative, in my opinion, in the interests of justice, that there be a new trial. It was open to the jury to find only token resistance prior to the "bondage" incident, which the appellant may not have perceived as withholding of consent. The accused was convicted of that which, perhaps, he did not intend to do had he known of no consent. It does not follow that, by simply disbelieving the appellant on consent, in fact, the jury thereby found that there was no belief in consent and that the appellant could not reasonably have believed in consent.

I would allow the appeal, set aside the judgment of the British Columbia Court of Appeal and direct a new trial.

Appeal dismissed.

For a view that mistaken beliefs in consent are mistakes of law rather than fact, see Lucinda Vandervoort, "Mistake of Law and Sexual Assault: Consent and *Mens Rea*" (1987-88), 2 C.J.W.L. 233.

T. PICKARD, CULPABLE MISTAKES AND RAPE: HARSH WORDS ON PAPPAJOHN

(1980) 30 U. of T. L. J. 415

I offer these comments by way of postscript to an article published a few months ago in this journal.[1] In that article, I suggested that we could move beyond the objective/subjective stalemate in criminal theory by putting aside generalities to test particular propositions in the context of specific offences. By way of doing that, I argued that the subjectivist proposition that mistakes need only be honest to exonerate is overbroad; that honest but unreasonable factual mistakes are culpable in the context of some offences (like rape), but not necessarily culpable in the context of other offences (like possession). The Supreme Court has since decided *R. v. Pappajohn*,[2] an appeal of a rape conviction in which the major substantive issue was whether or not a mistake about consent had to be reasonable in order to exonerate. Although the Court did not hold that an honest but unreasonable mistake about consent must exonerate,[3] the judgments taken together indicate that it likely will do so when an appropriate case presents itself.[4]

I do not want in this postscript to restate my arguments against the result reached by Dickson J. in his dissenting judgment (which presents the Court's apparent position on the mistake issue) or against the way both he and the majority make *R. v. Beaver* into a dispositive precedent.[5] I want, rather, to focus on the

---

1 Pickard, T., "Culpable Mistakes and Rape: Relating *Mens Rea* to the Crime" (1980), 30 U.T.L.J. 75

2 *Pappajohn v. The Queen*, unreported judgment, 20 May 1980 (S.C.C.). All page references are to the Supreme Court copy.

3 McIntyre J., writing for the majority, made a particular point of agreeing with the dissent on the mistake issue even though the majority view was that the issue did not arise on the facts of the case. It is surely strange, and to my mind unfortunate, that both the House of Lords (in *Morgan*) and the Supreme Court of Canada should choose to expound the law of this conceptually intractable and politically sensitive issue while deciding cases in which some resolution of the substantive problem was not germane to disposition.

4 I am assuming there what is perhaps not entirely clear, *i.e.*, that in the last paragraph of his judgment McIntyre J. means to express agreement with the dissent's final position on mistake, not merely with that part of the judgment which argues that a mistaken belief in consent is available in some form as a defence to rape. The ambiguity in the majority position derives from the juxtaposition of their view of *Beaver* with the last sentence in the judgment, where McIntyre J. says, "I am in agreement with that part of [Dickson J.'s] judgment dealing with the availability as a defence to a charge of rape in Canada of what is generally termed the defence of mistake of fact," which would seem to limit the points of agreement to points 1 and 2 of Dickson J.'s four points. But McIntyre J. also says, that, with Dickson, he believes *Beaver* decided for all purposes that mistakes need only be honest to exonerate; that no direction that a mistake need be based on reasonable grounds to negative *mens rea* can ever be approved (at p. 5 of the majority judgment). If that is the majority view, then despite the limited language of the last paragraph of the opinion, six of the seven justices take a position that corresponds exactly to that of Dickson J. on the mistake issue, although they do not all necessarily agree with his reasons.

5 For development of those arguments, see Pickard, *supra* note 1.

concept of recklessness in order to elucidate the relationship I see between it and the role of factual mistake in assessing culpability. I want to explore this relationship because I do not think its nature is generally appreciated, and because I think inattention to it renders Dickson J.'s judgment superficial.

i) We can take as agreed that when knowledge of inculpatory circumstances is a required element of a crime, any mistake, no matter how unreasonable, inconsistent with proof of that knowledge must exonerate.[6] But, as Dickson J. accepts in his opinion, rape is not such a crime; rape can be committed recklessly.[7] It becomes important to understand how different concepts of recklessness relate to the question of mistakes about consent.[8]

Dickson J.'s judgment rests on the idea that recklessness means conscious risk-taking.[9] For him, a defendant is reckless with respect to non-consent only if he consciously adverts to the possibility of non-consent and penetrates anyway.[10] Once this view is taken, of course an honest mistake about consent must exonerate. Just as belief in consent is necessarily inconsistent with knowledge of non-consent, so must it be inconsistent with consciously risking non-consent. By the time Dickson J. asks in the latter part of his judgment whether a mistake need be based on reasonable grounds, the question is no longer, for him, a real one. It has already been answered, even if unwittingly, by definition.[11]

6 We are here concerned with *mens rea* with respect to circumstances as distinguished from *mens rea* with respect to proscribed consequences such as injury or death. When circumstances are in issue, recklessness sets itself off from knowledge rather than from intention.

7 "In summary, intention or recklessness must be proved in relation to all elements of the offence, including absence of consent" (at p. 12 of the dissenting judgment).

8 Neither the majority nor the concurring judgment speaks to recklessness at all. Dickson J. quotes various descriptive phrases, no one of which he explicitly approves, perhaps because he views them as interchangeable. They are truly interchangeable, however, only if recklessness is given the meaning of conscious risk-taking in each passage. If recklessness is read with a broader meaning, the passages cited are susceptible of quite different applications:
   "...that the accused ... realized she might not be [consenting] and determined to have intercourse with her whether she was consenting or not" (at p. 6, citing *R. v. Daly*, [1968] V.R. 257 and *R. v. Hornbuckle*, [1945] V.L.R. 281);
   "...the mental element ... is an intention ... to have intercourse either knowing she does not consent, or recklessly not caring whether she consents or not" (at. p. 8, citing the Heilbron Report);
   " ... the Crown must prove ... (a) ... or (b) a realization that the conduct may lead to non-consensual intercourse and a recklessness or indifference to that consequence ensuing" (at p. 9, citing the dissenting judgment in *Leary v. The Queen*, [1978] S.C.R. 29, at 35).

9 That this is so is clear not only from his general use of Williams throughout, but also from his use of the following passage from Williams: "It is impossible to assert that a crime requiring intention or recklessness can be committed although the accused laboured under a mistake negativing the requisite intention or recklessness. Such an assertion carries its own refutation" (at p. 14). Dickson J. uses the passage to support his argument that mistake in some form must be available as a defence. But it supports that argument only if one takes for granted, as Dickson J. does, Williams' definition of recklessness. If one took recklessness to mean, for example, a gross deviation from the standard of care of which the defendant is capable, the passage from Williams would be nonsensical, and the question would be whether or not the making of a certain mistake constituted recklessness, never whether or not it negatived it.

10 This is, of course, an application to rape of the definition of recklessness offered by Glanville Williams in *Criminal Law: The General Part* (1961), at 31.

11 It seems unwitting because of the very structure of the opinion which suggests both that the reasonableness question is still an open one after *mens rea* is defined and that it is to be resolved by reference to precedent and what Dickson J. calls "policy considerations" rather than by reference to an analysis of *mens rea*.

ii) Now I think it undeniable that the relationship of mistakes to culpability is one of the central conundrums of criminal law. Working it through, in all its complexity, forces us to attend to the reasons for the ultimate stand-off between objective and subjective theorists. Conundrums of this nature should not — cannot — be resolved by mere definitional preference. Yet Dickson J. does nothing to anchor his preference in theory or authority.[12] Nowhere in the judgment does he either give reasons or refer us to reasons which justify his definition of recklessness by relating it to a coherent theory of culpability.[13] Nor does he acknowledge or in any way attend to our large experience with other meanings of 'recklessness' in ethical discourse, in lay language, in other areas of law, and in criminal law itself.[14] In fact he proceeds quite blithely, as if there were no opposing tradition of statute.

The strongest claim of those who would argue that some mistakes must be based on reasonable grounds is that making an unreasonable mistake can sometimes be reckless in the sense of unacceptably careless with respect to the well-being of others."[15] Consideration of this claim in the specific context of mistakes about consent to intercourse led me, in the article to which this postscript relates, to isolate some factors which may be useful generally to distinguish situations in which unreasonable mistakes are blameworthy from those in which they are not.[16] Where those, or perhaps other, factors exist, the argument is that the making of the mistake is blameworthy to an extent which warrants criminal

---

12 Whatever may be their intent, statements like "There can be no doubt this answer is consonant with principles," or "Two others . . . invoked general principles to conclude that an honest belief in consent need not be reasonably held," or "In principle, the defence should avail when there is an honest belief in consent" do not do the job of justification. Dickson J.'s use of aggrandizing references to unstated principles is capped by the third point in the conclusion of his discussion of the mistake issue: "to apply the reasonable standard in this appeal, the Court, in my view, would have to: . . . (c) defy accepted and sound principles of criminal law." As far as can be seen, when he makes these references to unspecified principles, Dickson J. has nothing more in mind than the definitions he asserted at the beginning of his discussion of *mens rea*. While the subjective definition of *mens rea* is widely known and heartily endorsed by certain Judges and academics, both its soundness and its stature as a principle need to be demonstrated by more than assertion. Until those who seek to apply the definition in particular contexts are willing to be explicit about how the resulting disposition relates to the basic issue of culpability rather than to the definitions themselves, their reasoning will remain unsatisfactory.

13 It is clear that the definition was, for Williams, a preference rather than the outcome of a coherent, fully developed position about either the minimum level of culpability in all serious criminal contexts or the appropriate way to treat mistaken harmdoers. See Pickard, *supra* note 1, 96-7. Dickson J. refers to no compelling authority for the definition because there is none.

14 Even in the current rape cases there is talk of "indifference to consent" or "not caring about consent." See *supra*, note 9. These phrases leave ample room for discussion of the possibility that the formulation of an unreasonable belief about consent to intercourse is reckless, even though inconsistent with conscious risk-taking.

15 See Pickard, *supra*, note 1, 75-83 for a development of this argument.

16 *E.g.*, whether or not he actor's mind must necessarily be focused on the legally relevant transaction at the relevant fact(s) is simple, etc. See Pickard, *supra* note 1, *passim*.

sanctions; that far from negativing recklessness and therefore liability, the making of such a mistake is itself the culpable behaviour which grounds both.[17]

iii) But Dickson J., even while making a major decision about mistakes, never pays them serious attention because he has paid no analytic attention to recklessness at all. He says, for instance, that rape can be committed recklessly, yet he entirely obscures any distinction between recklessness and knowledge about consent.[18] The act of penetration cannot be done other than intentionally. Recklessness can speak then only to the defendant's relationship to the inculpatory circumstances. The only way to ascribe any meaning to Dickson J.'s idea of reckless rape is to posit a defendant who proceeds, not on a mistaken belief in consent, but conscious of the fact that he does not know whether or not the woman is consenting. But such a state of mind in the context of intercourse is a straightforward example of wilful blindness — the actor remains ignorant deliberately because he does not want to know. Given the opportunity for, and simplicity of, inquiry into consent, there is no other realistic way to view the defendant who proceeds in conscious ignorance. The wilfully blind defendant would, of course, be liable even if liability for rape required knowledge. If this is right, Dickson J.'s position that recklessness (in his sense) is sufficient to ground liability for rape and that an honest mistake about consent must necessarily exonerate is not only tautological; it is meaningless as well.

It would, of course, be coherent to argue that rape should require knowledge of non-consent; that liability should never be grounded in recklessness. That position has not, so far as I know, been clearly embraced anywhere. Although it is apparently the position entailed by his views, Dickson J. does not seem to want to embrace it. Yet he has defined away the possibility that recklessness could ever truly operate as the basis for liability. This is the kind of obscurity and ambivalence which characterize his stance on recklessness throughout the judgment.

---

17 Dickson J. never confronts this claim. The only opposing claim he acknowledges is that the honest mistake rule is susceptible of abuse because juries will be too credulous. Although he calls this objection "legitimate and real," his basic stance is that it is no problem at all since a defendant is not likely to be believed "unless the mistake is, to the jury, reasonable" and ii/"Canadian juries . . . display a high degree of common sense, and an uncanny ability to distinguish the genuine from the specious." This section of Dickson J.'s opinion, in which he purports to deal with the 'policy considerations' which argue against his position, is, to my mind, full of startling views and peculiar reasoning.

18 *E.g.*, contrast his many statements to the effect that rape can be committed by a defendant who is reckless with respect to consent with the following: "In principle, the defence [mistake of fact] should avail when there is an honest belief in consent, or an absence of knowledge that consent has been withheld" (at p. 15). This statement excludes the possibility of liability for proceeding recklessly. In truth, it is extremely difficult to understand what Dickson has in mind when he speaks of recklessness with respect to consent.

iv) Recklessness is the term we are currently using to describe the minimum threshold of liability for serious crimes.[19] Within the analytic framework we use, arguments about whether or not certain mistakes are culpable fit neatly into an inquiry about the appropriate scope for the concept of recklessness. If we are to preserve an ability to engage in serious debate about our central conundrum, we have to keep that inquiry alive. To do so, we must challenge the justification for each reduction of the concept to its narrowest scope.

In the end, Dickson J.'s judgment cannot meet the challenge. His position lacks clarity and coherence because he neither states, commits himself to, nor appreciates the implications of the concept of recklessness which underlies his decision; it lacks seriousness because he never justifies his use of that concept with respect either to the particular decision he is making or to a general theory of culpability; it lacks perspective because he does not credit the opposing view with theoretical stature. These defects are the defects of orthodoxy: taking tenets to be self-evident and self-justifying, dissenting arguments to be superficial or non-existent.[20] As a declaration of orthodoxy, *Pappajohn* will undoubtedly comfort the faithful. The rest of us must remain unpersuaded.

For a response to Toni Pickard, see Stuart, *Canadian Criminal Law: A Treatise* (4th ed., 2001) Chapter 4.

ROBIN WEINER, SHIFTING THE COMMUNICATION BURDEN: A MEANINGFUL CONSENT STANDARD IN RAPE

(1983), 6 Harv. Women's L.J. 143 at 147, 149

Robin Weiner has commented on the potential difficulties of applying an objective approach.

> If women and men always communicated their sexual interests and desires in the same manner, or if they understood each other's communications, they could, in fact, be represented by the same hypothetical person. . . . Behavior is not so accurately perceived, however; a gender gap in sexual communications exists.

---

19 I accept that terminology. I do not think, and am not trying to argue, that negligence should be accepted as a basis for liability in rape. Dickson J. suggests that any reasonableness requirement would make negligence the basis of liability when he says, "It is not clear how one can properly relate reasonableness (an element in offences of negligence) to rape (a 'true crime' and not an offence of negligence)." This comment disregards two things: a long history of distinction between negligence and recklessness in the sense of gross deviation from a standard of care proved beyond a reasonable doubt; and the possibility of individualizing the standard used and avoiding thereby the application of an "outer standard to the individual." See Pickard, *supra* note 1, 78-80. In my view, it is folly to allow what is a proper concern for the occasional defendant who is not capable of meeting ordinary standards of care to skew our entire view of culpability. Those who can meet ordinary standards should, in appropriate circumstances, be held to them. The others should be held to that standard of which they are capable.

20 Interestingly, Dickson himself characterizes his stance as "subjective orthodoxy" (at p. 20), ignoring as he does so the negative connotations usually associated with the term *orthodoxy* by people engaged in analytic work, and disregarding the critical intention of the writer who coined the phrase. See Sellers, "*Mens rea* and the Judicial Approach to 'Bad Excuses' in the Criminal Law" (1978), 41 Mod. L.R. 246.

. . . .

Courts do not clarify the perspective from which the 'reasonableness' standard should be applied. They vary dramatically in what must be reasonable — the perpetrator's behavior, the victim's fear, or the perpetrator's perception of the victim's behavior as an indication of lack of consent.

SANSREGRET v. R.

45 C.R. (3d) 193, [1985] 1 S.C.R. 570, 18 C.C.C. (3d) 223

McINTYRE J.: — This appeal [from (1984), 37 C.R. (3d) 45, 10 C.C.C. (3d) 164] raises once more the issue of the application of the defence of mistake of fact in a rape case. On this occasion its relevance on a charge laid under s. 143(b)(i) of the *Criminal Code*, now repealed but in force when this case arose, is questioned. In view of the significant changes made in this branch of the law by the amendments in 1980-81-82-83 (Can.), c. 125, it may be thought that this question has become of minor importance, but it would appear that similar cases involving similar defence claims may well arise under the new *Code* provisions and the applicable principles will still require consideration.

The appellant, a man in his early 20s, and the complainant, a woman of 31 years, had lived together in the complainant's house for about a year before the events of 15th October 1982. Their relationship had been one of contention and discord with violence on the part of the appellant: "slappings" or "roughing up" in his description, "blows" in hers. The appellant had left the house for short periods and in September 1982 the complainant decided to end the affair. She told the appellant to leave and he did.

On 23rd September 1982, some days after his dismissal, the appellant broke into the house at about 4:30 a.m. He was "raging" at her and furious because of his expulsion. He terrorized her with a file-like instrument with which he was armed. She was fearful of what might occur, and in order to calm him down she held out some hope of a reconciliation and they had intercourse. A report was made to the police of this incident, the complainant asserting she had been raped, but no proceedings were taken. The appellant's probation officer became involved and there was evidence than he had asked the complainant not to press the matter, presumably because it would interfere with the appellant's probation.

On 15th October 1982, again at about 4:30 a.m., the appellant broke into the complainant's house through a basement window. She was alone, and awakened by the entry she seized the bedroom telephone in an effort to call the police. The appellant picked up a butcher knife in the kitchen and came into the bedroom. He was furious and violent. He accused her of having another boyfriend; pulled the cord of the telephone out of the jack and threw it into the living room; threatened her with the knife and ordered her to take off her nightdress and made her stand in the kitchen doorway, naked save for a jacket over her shoulders, so he could be sure where she was while he repaired the window to conceal his entry from the police, should they arrive. He struck her on the mouth with sufficient force to draw blood, and on three occasions rammed the knife blade into the wall with great force, once very close to her. He told her that if the police came he would put the knife through her, and added that if he had found her with a boyfriend he would have killed them both. At one point he tied her hands behind her back with a scarf. The complainant said she was in fear for her life and sanity.

By about 5:30 a.m., after an hour of such behaviour by the appellant, she tried to calm him down. She pretended again that there was some hope of a reconciliation if the appellant would settle down and get a job. This had the desired effect. He calmed down and after some conversation he joined her on the bed and they had intercourse. The complainant swore that her consent to the intercourse was solely for the purpose of calming him down, to protect herself from further violence. This, she said, was something she had learned from earlier experience with him. In her evidence she said:

> I didn't consent at any time.
> I was very afraid. My whole body was trembling. I was sure I would have a nervous breakdown. I came very, very close to losing my mind. All I knew was I had to keep this man calm or he would kill me.

At about 6:45 a.m., after further conversation with the appellant, she got dressed and prepared to leave for work. She had a business appointment at 8:00 a.m. She drove the appellant to a location which he chose, and in the course of the journey he returned her keys and some money that he had taken from her purse upon his arrival in the early morning. Upon dropping him off she drove immediately to her mother's home, where she made a complaint of rape. The police were called and the appellant was arrested that evening.

The appellant was charged with rape, unlawful confinement, robbery, breaking and entering with intent to commit an indictable offence, and possession of a weapon. At trial, before Krindle Co. Ct. J. in the County Court of Winnipeg without a jury, he was acquitted on the charge of rape but was convicted of breaking and entering and unlawful confinement [34 C.R. (3d) 162]. The Court of Appeal (Matas, Huband and Philp JJ.A., Philp J.A. dissenting) allowed the Crown's appeal on the charge of rape and entered a conviction as well as imposing a sentence of five years' imprisonment. The unlawful confinement count was held to be subsumed in the rape. The appellant appealed to this Court asserting that the defence of mistake of fact, in this case a belief by the appellant that the complainant consented to intercourse, is open to an accused under s. 143(b)(i) of the *Criminal Code* as well as under subs. (a), and that it is the honesty of such belief that is determinative in considering the defence, not its reasonableness. Reliance was placed on *Pappajohn v. R.*, [1980] 2 S.C.R. 120, 14 C.R. (3d) 243, 19 C.R. (3d) 97, 52 C.C.C. (2d) 481.

The indictment set out the rape count in these terms:

> 1. THAT he, the said John Henry Sansregret, a male person, on or about the fifteenth day of October, in the year of our Lord one thousand nine hundred and eighty-two, at the City of Winnipeg in the Eastern Judicial District in the Province of Manitoba, did unlawfully have sexual intercourse with [T.W.], a female person who was not his wife, with her consent, which consent was extorted by threats or fear of bodily harm.

It clearly falls within s. 143(*b*)(i) of the *Criminal Code*. On the facts of this case, briefly summarized above, at first glance it may appear strange indeed that a defence of mistake of fact could be suggested, let alone made out. To appreciate how the issue arises, reference must be made to the findings of fact made at trial and to the judgments given in the Court of Appeal.

The trial Judge described the complainant as a bright, sophisticated woman, articulate, capable, and well-employed. She considered that the appellant was neither particularly intelligent nor "verbal" and expressed surprise that any intimate relationship had ever arisen between them. She described the events of 23rd September 1982, a month before the events in question, and she considered that there was no evidence that the appellant knew she had complained of rape as a result of that incident. Comment will be made on this question later. She then referred to the defence of mistake of fact, and said [at p. 164]:

> If there were any evidence before me that the accused was aware on 15th October that the complainant had considered the sexual relations of 23rd September 1982 to have been non-consensual, I would have rejected this defence out of hand. There is no such evidence. I can speculate, but that is not proof.

She described in detail the events of 15th October and said that she accepted the complainant's version insofar as it differed from the appellant's, but she observed that in many respects his evidence confirmed hers. She continued [at p. 166):

> I am satisfied beyond any doubt that the accused broke and entered the complainant's residence on 15th October motivated primarily by jealousy and I do not doubt for a moment that, had the complainant had a man there, the knife would have been used aggressively. Having not found another man, he was bound and determined to make the complainant hear what he had to say to her by confining her unlawfully. He certainly broke and entered the dwelling-house with the intent to commit an indictable offence therein, and he certainly took possession of the butcher knife for purposes dangerous to the public peace.
>
> Having entered the house and discovering that the complainant was on the telephone, being unsure about whether or not she had called the police, two things became paramount. One was to cover up the evidence of his break-in so that it would not be visible from the street, and to cover up his presence in the house by reducing it to darkness. The second was to prevent the escape of the complainant, or her use of the telephone, particularly probable events while he was outside putting the basement window back on the house. What better way to confine her than to take her car keys, her house keys and her money, to strip her naked, to bind her hands and to force her to stand by the back door and whistle so he could hear where she was.
>
> I find that the accused forced the complainant to strip and tied her hands, not by way of preliminaries to an intended rape, but by way of confining the complainant. I similarly find the forced taking of her keys and money to part of the unlawful confinement.

She said that once the appellant became satisfied that the police would not come he set out to convince the complainant to reconcile. She accepted the evidence of the complainant that she was absolutely terrified, and that her consent was given solely to protect herself from further violence or death. She told him the things he wanted to hear regarding reconciliation, and she assured him that no other man was of interest to her. Then the trial Judge continued [at pp. 167-68]:

As I said, no rational person could have been under any honest mistake of fact. However, people have an uncanny ability to blind themselves to much that they do not want to see, and to believe in the existence of facts as they would wish them to be. The accused says that, notwithstanding the reign of terror which preceded their chat, notwithstanding that he held a knife while they talked, notwithstanding that he did most of the talking and that the complainant's answers were clearly equivocal, he presumed and believed that everything between them was peachy, this notwithstanding that three weeks earlier, on a replay of the same sort of evening, his probation officer became involved and the complainant moved out of her house. Very honestly, despite my confidence in the ability of people to blind themselves to reality, and even if the accused had not lied about other parts of his testimony, I would have been hard pressed to credit the honesty of his belief.

However, his honest belief finds support in the testimony of the complainant. She knows him and, in her opinion, notwithstanding all the objective facts to the contrary, he did believe that everything was back to normal between them by the time of the sexual encounter. His subsequent behaviour as well attests to that fact.

I do not like the conclusion which this leads me to. There was no real consent. There was submission as a result of a very real and justifiable fear. No one in his right mind could have believed that the complainant's dramatic about-face stemmed from anything other than fear. But the accused did. He saw what he wanted to see, heard what he wanted to hear, believed what he wanted to believe.

The facts in *R. v. Pappajohn*, [1980] 2 S.C.R. 120, 14 C.R. (3d) 243, 19 C.R. (3d) 97, 52 C.C.C.(2d) 481, are quite dissimilar to those in this case. The dictum of the Supreme Court of Canada, however, is clear and broad and in no way seems to limit itself to the peculiar circumstances of that case. Perhaps the Crown will appeal this decision to obtain some direction from the Supreme Court on whether it was that Court's intention to cover situations where an accused who demonstrates the clarity and shrewdness this accused showed in securing his own safety at the outset can turn around and, because it does not suit his wishes, can go wilfully blind to the obvious shortly thereafter. In any event, the ratio of *Pappajohn* is clear and it leaves me no alternative but to acquit.

To summarize, the trial Judge found that the appellant did not enter the house with intent to make a sexual assault on the complainant; that the complainant consented to intercourse only because of the fear engendered by the threats of the appellant and to save herself, and that the appellant honestly believed that the complainant was giving a free and genuine consent to intercourse. She found as well that the complainant, who knew the appellant, also believed in the honesty of his belief.

. . . .

Rape, as defined in s. 143(*a*) of the *Criminal Code*, is of course the act of having sexual intercourse without consent. The issue with which we are concerned arises directly in a charge under subs. (*a*). The question will be: Did the accused have an honest belief that the woman gave her consent? It is in this form that the issue arose in *Pappajohn*, in *Morgan, supra*, and in *R. v. Plummer* (1975), 31 C.R.N.S. 220, 24 C.C.C. (2d) 497 (Ont. C.A.). While those cases provide authority for the existence of the defence and for its application where the consent is in issue, in my view they do not cover a charge under s. 143(*b*)(i) where consent is assumed from the outset. In other words, the existence of the consent is established and only its nature, that is, whether it was freely given or procured by threats, is in issue. Where the accused in a case arising under s. 143(*b*)(i) asserts an honest belief in consent, the honest belief must encompass more than the fact of consent. It must include a belief that it has been freely given and not procured by threats. I agree in this respect with Huband J.A. The defence would apply then, subject to what is said later about wilful blindness, in favour of an accused who had an honest belief that the consent was not the result of threats but one freely given.

. . . .

I would conclude then that the *mens rea* for rape under s. 143(*a*) of the *Code* must involve knowledge that the woman is not consenting, or recklessness as to whether she is consenting or not, and, for s. 143(*b*)(i), knowledge that the consent was given because of threats or fear of bodily harm, or recklessness as to its nature. It would follow, as has been held by the majority of this Court in *Pappajohn*, that an honest belief on the part of the accused, even though unreasonably held, that the woman was consenting to intercourse freely and voluntarily and not because of threats would negate the *mens rea* under s. 143(*b*)(i) of the *Code* and entitle the accused to an acquittal.

The concept of recklessness as a basis for criminal liability has been the subject of much discussions. Negligence, the failure to take reasonable care, is a creature of the civil law and is not generally a concept having a place in determining criminal liability. Nevertheless, it is frequently confused with recklessness in the criminal sense and care should be taken to separate the two concepts. Negligence is tested by the objective standard of the reasonable man. A departure from his accustomed sober behaviour by an act or omission which reveals less than reasonable care will involve liability at civil law but forms no basis for the imposition of criminal penalties. In accordance with well-established principles for the determination of criminal liability, recklessness, to form a part of the criminal *mens rea*, must have an element of the subjective. It is found in the attitude of one who, aware that there is danger that his conduct could bring about the result prohibited by the criminal law, nevertheless persists, despite the risk. It is, in other words, the conduct of one who sees the risk and who takes the chance. It is in this sense that the term "recklessness" is used in the criminal law and it is clearly distinct from the concept of civil negligence.

On the face of it, one would have thought that a man who intimidates and threatens a woman and thereafter obtains her consent to intercourse would know that the consent was obtained as a result of the threats. If specific knowledge of the nature of the consent was not attributable to him in such circumstances, then one would think that at the very least recklessness would be. It might be said then that this case could have been disposed of on the basis of recklessness. The trial Judge, however, did not do so because of her application of the "mistake of fact" defence.

There was indeed an abundance of evidence before the trial Judge upon which a finding of recklessness could have been made. After a stormy period of cohabitation, the complainant dismissed the appellant from her house in September 1982, thus demonstrating her rejection of him. He broke into the house on 23rd September and there went through a performance which led to an act of intercourse with a consent given by the complainant out of fear for her life. This incident led to a report to the police and the involvement of the appellant's probation officer. In the early morning hours of 15th October he again broke into the house and repeated his earlier performance, which provided the basis for the present charges.

There was also evidence from which the clear inference can be drawn that the appellant knew a complaint of rape had been made in respect of the first incident. Though the complainant complained to the police about that incident, no charges were laid. She was persuaded not to pursue the matter by the appellant's probation officer, who had approached her and told her that he would find a job for Sansregret if she did not press the charges. A police officer testified as to a conversation which occurred between himself and Sansregret after the latter's arrest. In response to a question as to why he ran from the police when they approached him on the evening of 16th October, the appellant replied: "From before, that time she phoned the police on me before." This reply was confirmed by Sansregret on direct examination but then denied on cross-examination. Sansregret admitted that he knew his probation officer had called the complainant with respect to the September incident and that he knew that he was not welcome in her house. There was then evidence that the appellant knew of her attitude towards him; knew that she had complained to the police with respect to the 23rd September incident; and knew that it was only the intervention of his parole officer which prevented charges from being laid after that incident. I therefore disagree with the trial Judge, who, in my opinion, was in error in not drawing the inference that the appellant knew that the complainant had complained of rape as a result of the incident on 23rd September.

It is evident that the trial Judge would have convicted the appellant of rape had it not been for the defence of mistake of fact. She considered that the belief in the consent expressed by the appellant was an honest one and therefore on the basis of *Pappajohn, supra*, even if it were unreasonably held, as it is clear she thought it was, he was entitled to his acquittal. This application of the defence of mistake of fact would be supportable were it not for the fact that the trial Judge found in addition that the appellant had been wilfully blind to reality in his behaviour on 15th October. Such a finding would preclude the application of the defence and lead to a different result. It is my opinion then that the trial Judge erred in this matter in that, though she made the requisite findings of fact that the appellant was wilfully blind to the consequences of his acts, she did not apply them according to law.

The idea of wilful blindness in circumstances such as this has been said to be an aspect of recklessness. While this may well be true, it is wise to keep the two concepts separate because they result from different mental attitudes and lead to different legal results. A finding of recklessness in this case could not override the defence of mistake of fact. The appellant asserts an honest belief that the consent of the complainant was not caused by fear and threats. The trial Judge found that such an honest belief existed. In the facts of this case, because of the reckless conduct of the appellant, it could not be said that such a belief was reasonable but, as held in *Pappajohn*, the mere honesty of the belief will support the "mistake of fact" defence, even where it is unreasonable. On the other hand, a finding of wilful blindness as to the very facts about which the honest belief is now asserted would leave no room for the application of the defence because, where wilful blindness is shown, the law presumes knowledge on the part of the accused, in this case knowledge that the consent had been induced by threats.

Wilful blindness is distinct from recklessness because, while recklessness involves knowledge of a danger or risk and persistence in a course of conduct which creates a risk that the prohibited result will occur, wilful blindness arises where a person who has become aware of the need for some inquiry declines to make the inquiry because he does not wish to know the truth. He would prefer to remain ignorant. The culpability in recklessness is justified by consciousness of the risk and by proceeding in the face of it, while in wilful blindness it is justified by the accused's fault in deliberately failing to inquire when he knows there is reason for inquiry. Cases such as *Wretham v. R.* (1971), 16 C.R.N.S. 124 (Ont. C.A.); *R. v. Blondin*, 2 C.C.C. (2d) 118, affirmed [1971] S.C.R. v, 4 C.C.C. (2d) 566; *R. v. Currie* (1976), 24 C.C.C. (2d) 292 (Ont. C.A.); *R. v. McFall* (1976), 26 C.C.C. (2d) 181 (B.C.C.A.); *R. v. Aiello* (1978), 38 C.C.C. (2d) 485 (Ont. C.A.); *Taylor's Central Garages (Exeter) Ltd. v. Roper*, [1951] 2 T.L.R. 284 (Div. Ct.), among others, illustrate these principles. The textwriters have also dealt with the subject, particularly Glanville Williams, *Criminal Law: The General Part*, 2nd ed. (1961), at pp. 157-60. He says, at p. 157:

> Knowledge, then, means either personal knowledge or (in the licence cases) imputed knowledge. In either event there is someone with actual knowledge. To the requirement of actual knowledge there is one strictly limited exception. Men readily regard their suspicions as unworthy of them when it is to their advantage to do so. To meet this, the rule is that if a party has his suspicion aroused but then deliberately omits to make further enquiries, because he wishes to remain in ignorance, he is deemed to have knowledge.

He then referred to the words of Lord Sumner in *Re The Zamora*, [1921] 1 A.C. 801 at 811-12 (P.C.), which was a case wherein a ship and cargo were condemned in the Prize Court as contraband. The managing director of the shipping company denied knowledge of the contraband carried by the ship, and on this subject Lord Sumner said, at pp. 811-12:

> Lord Sterndale [the president of the Prize Court] thus expressed his final conclusion: "I think the true inference is that, if Mr. Banck did not know this was a transaction in contraband, it was because he did not want to know, and that he has not rebutted the presumption arising from the fact of the whole cargo being contraband."
>
> Their Lordships have been invited to read this as saying that Mr. Banck is not proved to have known the contraband character of the adventure; that if he did not know, because he did not want to know, he was within his rights and owed no duty to the belligerents to inform himself; and that the *Zamora* is condemned contrary to the passage above cited from *The Hakan* upon a legal presumption arising solely and arbitrarily from the fact that the whole cargo was contraband. It may be that in his anxiety not to state more than he found against Mr. Banck, the learned President appeared to state something less, but there are two senses in which a man is said not to know something because he does not want to know it. A thing may be troublesome to learn, and the knowledge of it, when acquired, may be uninteresting or distasteful. To refuse to know any more about the subject or any, thing at all is then a wilful but a real ignorance. On the other hand, a man is said not to know because he does not want to know, where the substance of the thing is borne in upon his mind with a conviction that full details or precise proofs may be dangerous, because they may embarrass his denials or compromise his protests. In such a case he flatters himself that where ignorance is safe, 'tis

folly to be wise, but there he is wrong, for he has been put upon notice and his further ignorance, even though actual and complete, is a mere affectation and disguise.

Glanville Williams, however, warns that the rule of deliberate blindness has its dangers and is of narrow application. He says, at p. 159:

> The rule that wilful blindness is equivalent to knowledge is essential, and is found throughout the criminal law. It is, at the same time, an unstable rule, because judges are apt to forget its very limited scope. A Court can properly find wilful blindness only where it can almost be said that the defendant actually knew. He suspected the fact; he realised its probability; but he refrained from obtaining the final confirmation because he wanted in the event to be able to deny knowledge. This, and this alone, is wilful blindness. It requires in effect a finding that the defendant intended to cheat the administration of justice. Any wider definition would make the doctrine of wilful blindness indistinguishable from the civil doctrine of negligence in not obtaining knowledge.

This subject is also dealt with by Professor Stuart in *Canadian Criminal Law* (1982), at p. 130 et seq., where its relationship to recklessness is discussed.

This case reveals, in my view, an appropriate set of circumstances for the application of the "wilful blindness" rule. I have outlined the circumstances which form the background. I have referred to the findings of the trial Judge that the appellant blinded himself to the obvious and made no inquiry as to the nature of the consent which was given. If the evidence before the Court was limited to the events of 15th October, it would be difficult indeed to infer wilful blindness. To attribute criminal liability on the basis of this one incident would come close to applying a constructive test to the effect that he should have known she was consenting out of fear. The position, however, is changed when the evidence reveals the earlier episode and the complaint of rape which it caused, knowledge of which, as I have said, had clearly reached the accused. Considering the whole of the evidence, then, no constructive test of knowledge is required. The appellant was aware of the likelihood of the complainant's reaction to his threats. To proceed with intercourse in such circumstances constitutes, in my view, self-deception to the point of wilful blindness.

In my view, it was error on the part of the trial Judge to give effect to the "mistake of fact" defence in these circumstances where she had found that the complainant consented out of fear and the appellant was wilfully blind to the existing circumstances, seeing only what he wished to see. Where the accused is deliberately ignorant as a result of blinding himself to reality the law presumes knowledge, in this case knowledge of the nature of the consent. There was therefore no room for the operation of this defence.

This is not to be taken as a retreat from the position taken in *Pappajohn*, *supra*, that the honest belief need not be reasonable. It is not to be thought that any time an accused forms an honest though unreasonable belief he will be deprived of the defence of mistake of fact. This case rests on a different proposition. Having wilfully blinded himself to the facts before him, the fact that an accused may be enabled to preserve what could be called an honest belief, in the sense that he has no specific knowledge to the contrary, will not afford a defence because, where the accused becomes deliberately blind to the existing facts, he is fixed by law with actual knowledge and his belief in another state of facts is irrelevant.

I would dismiss this appeal.

A. MANSON, ANNOTATION

45 C.R. (3d) 194

McIntyre J. clarifies much of the confusion apparent in the lower Court judgments by accurately characterizing the issue as whether the accused believed, not just in the existence of consent, but that the consent had been freely given and not procured by threats. The trial Judge found as a fact that "the appellant honestly believed that the complainant was giving a free and genuine consent to intercourse" (p. 200). McIntyre J. states at p. 206 that a "finding of recklessness in this case could not override the defence of mistake of fact". However, he ultimately concludes (p. 208) that the accused's mistaken honest belief cannot exonerate him, since he "was wilfully blind to the existing circumstances, seeing only what he wished to see". In so doing, McIntyre J. seems to misunderstand the relationship between recklessness, wilful blindness and mistaken honest belief when knowledge of some factual element is an essential issue. In the result, he effectively reverses the finding of fact made by the trial Judge.

Let us assume that a case involves as an essential element the issue of whether the accused knew that a thing was black or white. The accused would be guilty if he knew that the thing was black. If the offence can be committed recklessly, then the accused would be reckless as to this essential element if he recognized that it was a question whether the thing was black or white but acted in the face of this issue without resolving it. The accused would be wilfully blind if he had a strong suspicion that the thing was black and had steps available which would confirm the suspicion, but deliberately chose not to take the steps. In other words, where knowledge is an element, wilful blindness is tantamount to knowledge, in that the accused virtually knows but insulates himself from perfect knowledge. By comparison, an accused could be said to have an honest but mistaken belief only if he in fact believed that the thing was white. A finding of recklessness as to the colour, or wilful blindness about blackness cannot coexist with a finding that the accused had an honest belief in whiteness. Regardless of the reasonableness of the conclusion, a finding of honest belief can arise only if the accused has resolved the question of colour, albeit erroneously. Of course, the question is not answered simply by listening to the accused's version of what he knew or believed, but by examining and weighing all of the evidence. At the end of the day, however, if the trial Judge finds that the accused honestly believed that the thing was white, then there is no room any longer for a question of wilful blindness or recklessness.

Rape is committed when the accused intentionally acts without the free consent of the complainant or is reckless as to the issue of consent. Thus, both knowledge of non-consent and recklessness as to this element would result in a conviction. Because knowledge is incorporated into the calculus, then wilful blindness is necessarily also applicable, since it is tantamount to knowledge. McIntyre J. may be correct when he assesses the evidence and indicates that there was substantial support for a finding of wilful blindness given the antecedent relations between the accused and the complainant. Nonetheless, as a matter of fact, the trial Judge found an honest belief in freely given consent. An exculpatory mistake of fact requires a finding of honest belief, which cannot coexist with a concomitant conclusion that the accused was wilfully blind as to the element in issue. The former is an honest but mistaken belief in whiteness, while the latter is a strong suspicion — deliberately unconfirmed — of blackness.

McIntyre J. obviously doubts whether the accused in fact had an honest belief in freely given consent. That, however, was the trial Judge's finding (p. 168): "No one in his right mind could have believed that the complainant's dramatic about-face stemmed from anything other than fear. *But the accused did.*" (The italics are mine.) The question of the accused's belief in the impact of the threats was clearly within the trial Judge's contemplation. In the circumstances, the finding certainly appears dubious. However, the Crown did not dispute it, nor did the Manitoba Court of Appeal reverse it: see 36 C.R. (3d) 45.

The jurisdiction of the Supreme Court of Canada is limited to questions of law alone: see *R. v. Warner*, [1960] S.C.R. 144, 34 C.R. 246, 128 C.C.C. 366; *Hobbins v. R.*, [1982] 1 S.C.R. 553, 27 C.R. (3d) 289, 66 C.C.C. (2d) 289 at 291. In the absence of a power to reverse the finding of fact, the appeal should have been allowed.

Crimes of Sexual Assault

In 1983 the crime of rape was replaced by a three-tier structure of sexual assault offences, now ss. 271, 272 and 273. The aim was to reflect the violent rather than the sexual nature of the offence. Heavy reliance was placed on the study by L. Clark and D. Lewis, *Rape: The Price of Coercive Sexuality.*[1] The House of Commons Debates reflect the impetus and the result of ten years of protest from rape crisis centres, women's groups and many others:

> [T]he current laws relating to rape and indecent assault are being changed to emphasize the violence as opposed to the sexual aspects to these crimes. In other words, we will no longer have the term 'rape' in law.
> This legislation has a long history. Individual women and groups of women all across the country have been pushing for years to change the rape laws. It was apparent that this section of the *Criminal Code* cried out for reform. The number of reported rape cases was far below the actual number of offences. It has been estimated that only one in ten cases of rape was reported. That was due largely to the stigma which surrounded the rape victim — the idea that nice girls do not get raped and the belief that she must have asked for it. . . . The conviction rate for rape has traditionally been much lower than the conviction rate for other serious crimes — only 52 percent conviction rate for rape, compared with an 82 percent conviction rate in the case of other indictable offences. As a result, women's groups such as the National Action Committee on the Status of Women and the National Council of Women began calling for a complete removal of

---

1 (Toronto: The Women's Press, 1977).

the existing rape sections from the *Criminal Code*. They wanted, instead, the enactment of a new offence dealing with rape as a type of assault.

The government responded with Bill C-52 some four years ago, and that had one major beneficial effect. It brought together all women's groups calling for four basic principles which they wanted to see embodied in the law: treatment of rape as a type of assault, creating tiers of sexual assault to parallel existing assault offences, abolishing spousal immunity, and limiting admissibility of past sexual history . . . .

We now have a bill which provides that the assault and sexual assault structure of the *Criminal Code* will have three tiers. The Minister has outlined those three tiers. The women's groups which appeared before the committee were unanimous in their desire that the new law would be modeled on existing assault provisions in the *Criminal Code*, so that there would be a firm foundation for the new sexual assault provisions. This was the reason our party insisted in committee on three tiers of assault and sexual assault. . . .

I know the bill before us is not perfect, but indeed it is a great step forward and it is of particular significance to women. I believe this piece of legislation will mark a new beginning in the way society views coercive sexual acts.[2]

Along with this new, gender neutral definition of the offence came the abolition of spousal immunity, restrictions on the cross-examination of the primary witness as to her previous sexual history, ss. 276-277, the abrogation of the doctrine of recent complaint, s. 275, (see *R. v. Page* (1984), 40 C.R. (3d) 85, 12 C.C.C. (3d) 250 (Ont. H.C.) and accompanying Annotation criticizing the same) and the repeal of corroboration requirements and warnings, s. 274. It is clear that these legislative changes have answered some of the complaints of legal bias against victims of sexual assault. To what extent *attitudes* have changed remains to be seen.

––––––––––––

Since 'rape' was replaced with the term 'sexual assault', there has been some confusion over the definition of the crime since Parliament did not define the term in the *Criminal Code*. The Supreme Court of Canada had to grapple with the issue in the following case.

R. v. CHASE

[1987] 2 S.C.R. 293, 59 C.R. (3d) 193, 37 C.C.C. (3d) 97

McIntyre J.: — This appeal concerns the meaning of the term 'sexual assault', as it is used in ss. 244 and 246.1 of the *Criminal Code*.

. . .

The facts may be briefly described. The respondent, Chase, was a neighbour of the complainant, a 15-year-old girl. They lived in a small hamlet near Fredericton, New Brunswick. On October 22, 1983, Chase entered the home of the complainant without invitation. The complainant and her 11-year-old brother were in the downstairs portion of the house, playing pool. Their 83-year-old grandfather was upstairs sleeping. Their parents were absent. The

––––––––––––

2 Hon. Flora MacDonald, reported in *House of Commons Debates*, Official Reporter Vol. XVII, First Session, *Thirty-Second Parliament.*(Quebec: Supply and Services Canada) p. 20041. (4 August, 1982)

respondent seized the complainant around the shoulders and arms and grabbed her breasts. When she fought back, he said: "Come on dear, don't hit me, I know you want it." The complainant said at trial that: "He tried to grab for my private, but he didn't succeed because my hands were too fast." Eventually, the complainant and her brother were able to make a telephone call to a neighbour and the respondent left. Prior to leaving, he said that he was going to tell everybody that she had raped him. The whole episode lasted little more than half an hour. The respondent was charged with the offence of sexual assault and was found guilty after trial in the Provincial Court. He appealed to the Court of Appeal for New Brunswick where his appeal was dismissed, a verdict of guilty of the included offence of common assault under s. 245(1) of the *Criminal Code* was substituted, and a sentence of six months' imprisonment was imposed.

. . .

In the Court of Appeal, Angers J.A., speaking for a unanimous Court (Stratton C.J.N.B., Ryan and Angers JJ.A.), expressed the view that the principles developed with respect to rape and indecent assault were of little assistance in approaching the question of sexual assault. In his view, the modifier "sexual" should be taken to refer to parts of the body, particularly the genitalia. He considered that a broader definition of the term could lead to absurd realities if it encompassed other portions of the human anatomy described as having "secondary sexual characteristics". He also expressed the view that sexual assault did not require or involve a specific intent. Because there was no contact with the complainant's genitals, the conviction at trial was set aside and a conviction for common assault substituted. It becomes evident from the recital of these facts that the only question arising on the appeal is that of the definition of the offence of sexual assault.

The new sexual assault provisions of the *Criminal Code* were enacted in the Act to amend the *Criminal Code* in relation to sexual offences and other offences against the person and to amend certain other Acts in relation thereto or in consequence thereof, S.C. 1980-81-82-83, c. 125. They replace the previous offences of rape, attempted rape, sexual intercourse with the feeble-minded, and indecent assault on a female or male. It is now for the Courts to endeavour to develop a realistic and workable approach to the construction of the new sections. The key sections are 244 and 246.1 [now ss. 265 and 271], *supra*. Section 246.1 creates the offence of sexual assault, an expression nowhere defined in the *Criminal Code*. To determine its nature, we must first turn to the assault section 244 (1), where an assault is defined in terms similar, if not identical, to the concept of assault at common law. Section 244 (2) provides that the section applies to sexual assaults. It was suggested in argument by the respondent that paras. (a), (b) and (c) of s. 244 (1) are to be read disjunctively so that only para. (a) could be applicable to the offence of sexual assault. This, it was said, must have been the position taken by the New Brunswick Court of Appeal because, in its consideration of s. 244, it dealt only with para. (a), apparently considering that contact was necessary to complete a sexual assault. I would dispose of this argument by simply referring to the specific words of s. 244 (2) which make the section applicable to sexual assaults. In my view, however sexual assault may be defined, its definition cannot be limited to the provisions of s. 244 (1) (a).

Since judgment was given in this case in the New Brunswick Court of Appeal, other appellate Courts have dealt with the problem. As far as I am able to determine, none has followed the approach of the Court of Appeal in this case. In *R. v. Alderton* (1985), 49 O.R. (2d) 257, the matter was presented to the Ontario Court of Appeal. In that case, the accused gained entry to an apartment building at night, wearing a face mask. He entered the apartment of the complainant who was alone and asleep in her bedroom. He seized her and forced her back upon the pillows but after a struggle she managed to escape. The Court of Appeal dismissed an appeal from a conviction of sexual assault made at trial. Martin J.A., speaking for a unanimous Court (Martin, Lacourcière and Finlayson JJ.A.), said at p. 263:

> We are, with the greatest deference, unable to accept the views of the Court expressed in that case [*Chase*]. Without in any way attempting to give a comprehensive definition of a "sexual assault" we are all satisfied that it includes an assault with the intention of having sexual intercourse with the victim without her consent, or an assault made upon a victim for the purpose of sexual gratification.

> We are all of the view that in the circumstances of the present case, there was ample evidence upon which the jury could find that the appellant committed a sexual assault upon the complainant and, indeed, we think the evidence did not permit of any other conclusion.

As he said, in these words, Martin J.A. was not attempting a comprehensive definition of sexual assault, nor was he saying that the concept of sexual assault was limited to an assault with the intention of having sexual intercourse or for the purposes of sexual gratification. His view was that, where these elements were present, it would be sufficient to categorize the assault as sexual. They do not constitute the sole basis for a finding of sexual assault, nor may this reference to them be taken as a finding that a specific intent is required for the completion of the offence.

In *R. v. Taylor* (1985), 44 C.R. (3d) 263, the matter was considered in the Alberta Court of Appeal. The accused, in seeking to discipline a teenage girl placed in his care, tied the girl's wrists to an overhead metal support and made her stand naked for periods of ten to fifteen minutes and, on one occasion, administered several blows with a wooden paddle on the buttocks. There were no other acts which could have been described as sexual in nature. The accused was acquitted at trial. The Crown's appeal was allowed and a new trial was ordered. Laycraft C.J.A., for a unanimous Court (Laycraft C.J.A., Haddad and Belzil JJ.A.), said, at p. 268:

> The new provisions do not define "sexual assault". However, "assault" is defined and this the new offences are an assault with some additional meaning required by the modifier "sexual". In the offences which were replaced this was also true of "indecent assault", a term which gave no difficulty in judicial interpretation. For decades, juries were charged that indecent assault was an assault in circumstances of indecency (*R. v. Louie Chong* (1914), 32

O.L.R. 66, 23 C.C.C. 250 (C.A.); *R. v. Quinton*, [1947] S.C.R. 234, 3 C.R. 6, 88 C.C.C. 231). Though this approach was susceptible to the comment that it was simply an assertion that an assault is indecent if it is indecent, it was nevertheless an approach perfectly understandable by generations of juries, and eminently practicable in the administration of the criminal law.

He then went on to discuss various authorities and rejected the Chase approach with its reliance on the specific involvement of areas of body and the dictionary definitions of the term "sexual". He noted that all the decisions he discussed rejected the Chase approach and he spoke approvingly of the position of Martin J.A. in the Ontario Court of Appeal in *Alderton, supra*, saying, at p. 269:

> Without joining a battle of dictionaries, it is my view that these words were intended to comprehend a wide range of forcible acts within the definition of "assault" to which, in the circumstances disclosed by the evidence, there is a carnal aspect. "Sexual assault" is therefore an act of force in circumstances of sexuality as that can be seen in the circumstances. Like Martin J.A. I would not attempt a comprehensive definition of "sexual assault". The term includes, however, an act which is intended to degrade or demean another person for sexual gratification. Nothing in the new sections of the *Code* in my view restricts the carnal or sexual aspect only to acts of force involving the sexual organs and I respectfully disagree with the restricted meaning expressed in *R. v. Chase, supra*.

It was his view that the carnal aspect was to be judged objectively: "Viewed in the light of all the circumstances, is the sexual or carnal context of the assault visible to a reasonable observer?"

In the British Columbia Court of Appeal, the matter was considered in *R. v. Cook* (1985), 20 C.C.C. (3d) 18. In this case, on facts which clearly revealed conduct which would qualify as sexual assaults, the Chase approach was again rejected. Lambert J.A. did not attempt to give a precise definition of sexual assault where Parliament had declined to do so, but he did consider that the characteristic which made a simple assault into a sexual assault was not solely a matter of anatomy. He considered that a real affront to sexual integrity and sexual dignity may be sufficient.

It will be seen from this brief review of the cases that the approach taken by the New Brunswick Court of Appeal in the case at bar has found little, if any, support. All the cases cited have recognized the need for a broader approach and all have recognized the difficulty in formulating one. While I would agree that it is difficult and probably unwise to attempt to develop a precise and all-inclusive definition of the new offence of sexual assault at this stage in its development, it seems to me to be necessary to attempt to settle upon certain considerations which may be of assistance to the courts in developing on a case-to-case basis a workable definition of the offence.

To begin with, I agree, as I have indicated, that the test for the recognition of sexual assault does not depend solely on contact with specific areas of the human anatomy. I am also of the view that sexual assault need not involve an attack by a member of one sex upon a member of the other; it could be perpetrated upon one of the same sex. I agree as well with those who say that the new offence is truly new and does not merely duplicate the offences it replaces. Accordingly, the definition of the term "sexual assault" and the reach of the offence it describes is not necessarily limited to the scope of its predecessors. I would consider as well that the test for its recognition should be objective.

While it is clear that the concept of a sexual assault differs from that of the former indecent assault, it is nevertheless equally clear that the terms overlap in many respects and sexual assault in many cases will involve the same sort of conduct that formerly would have justified a conviction for an indecent assault. The definitional approach to indecent assault also an offence not defined in the *Criminal Code*, therefore offers a guide in our approach to the new offence, as recognized by Laycraft C.J.A. After many years of dealing with the concept of indecent assault, the courts developed the definition, "an assault in circumstances of indecency". This, of course, was in imprecise definition but everyone knew what an indecent assault was. The law in that respect was reasonably clear and there was little difficulty with its enforcement. In my view then, a similar approach may be adopted in formulating a definition of sexual assault.

Applying these principles and the authorities cited, I would make the following observations. Sexual assault is an assault within any one of the definitions of that concept in s. 244 (1) of the *Criminal Code* which is committed in circumstances of a sexual nature, such that the sexual integrity of the victim is violated. The test to be applied in determining whether the impugned conduct has the requisite sexual nature is an objective one: "Viewed in the light of all the circumstances, is the sexual or carnal context of the assault visible to a reasonable observer" (*Taylor, supra,* per Laycraft C.J.A., at p. 269). The part of the body touched, the nature of the contact, the situation in which it occurred, the words and gestures accompanying the act, and all other circumstances surrounding the conduct, including threats which may or may not be accompanied by force will be relevant (see S.J. Usprich, "A New Crime in Old Battles: Definitional Problems with Sexual Assault" (1987), 29 Crim. L. Q. 200, at p. 204) The intent or purpose of the person committing the act, to the extent that this may appear from the evidence, may also be a factor in considering whether the conduct is sexual. If the motive of the accused is sexual gratification, to the extent that this may appear from the evidence, it may be a factor in determining whether the conduct is sexual. It must be emphasized, however, that the existence of such a motive is simply one of many factors to be considered, the importance of which will vary depending on the circumstances.

Implicit in this view of sexual assault is the notion that the offence is one requiring a general intent only. This is consistent with the approach adopted by this Court in cases such as *Leary v. The Queen*, [1978] 1 S.C.R. 29, and *Swietlinski v. The Queen*, [1980] 2 S.C.R. 956, where it was held that rape and indecent assault were offences of general intent. I am unable to see any reason why the same approach should not be taken with respect to sexual assault. The factors which could motivate sexual assault are said to be many and varied (see C. Boyle, *Sexual Assault* (1984), at p. 74). To put upon the Crown the burden of proving a specific intent would go a long way toward defeating the obvious purpose of the enactment. Moreover, there are strong reasons in social policy which would support this view. To import an added element of specific intent in such offences, would be to hamper unreasonably the enforcement process. It would open the question of the defence of drunkenness, one which has always been related to the capacity to form a specific intent and which has generally been excluded by law and policy from offences requiring only the minimal intent to apply force (see *R. v. Bernard* (1985), 18 C.C.C. (3d) 574 (Ont. C.A., per Dubin J.A.)) For these reasons, I would say that the offence will be one of general rather than specific intent.

Turning to the case at bar I have no difficulty in concluding, on the basis of the principles I have discussed above, that there was ample evidence before the trial Judge upon which he could find that sexual assault was committed. Viewed objectively in the light of all the circumstances, it is clear that the conduct of the respondent in grabbing the complainant's breasts constituted an assault of a sexual nature. I would therefore allow the appeal, set aside the conviction of common assault recorded by the Court of Appeal and restore the conviction of sexual assault made at trial. The sentence of six months should stand.

Appeal allowed.

Problem

The accused is charged with sexually assaulting his three-year-old son. He admits that he grabbed his son's testicles on three occasions as a disciplinary response to the child having engaged in similar activity with others, including the accused. He wanted to show him how much it hurt. There is evidence of bruising. Has the accused committed a sexual assault?

Compare *R. v. V. (K.B.)* (1993), 22 C.R. (4th) 86, 82 C.C.C. (3d) 382, [1993] 2 S.C.R. 857.

In the 1983 amendments, Parliament changed the provisions concerning coerced consent (s. 265(3), considered earlier in Chapter 2). It also codified for the first time a defence of mistake as to consent applicable to all assaults, including sexual assaults. See s. 265(4). **Does the section continue the *Pappajohn* interpretation?**

R. v. BULMER

[1987] 1 S.C.R. 782, 58 C.R. (3d) 48, 33 C.C.C. (3d) 385

On the trial of the accused on charges of rape, attempted rape and indecent assault, the evidence indicated that the complainant, a prostitute, agreed to provide her services to the accused L. for a certain price. She testified that they went to a hotel room and, on entering, she discovered the two other accused, B. and I., and objected to their presence. I. sought to engage her services. She quoted her price and told him to come back in 20 minutes. B. and I. then left, but returned shortly after. A discussion followed, and I. told the complainant that she would have to provide her services without payment. Frightened, she performed various sexual acts with all three. She denied giving consent and receiving payment. There was no physical violence other than the various sexual acts. B. did not give evidence. L. and I. testified that price was discussed with the complainant after B. and I. returned to the room and that she finally agreed to have sex with them for $20 each. No threats were made. The occupant of an adjoining room testified that he heard two persons leave and return. He also heard a woman complaining about their presence. Her voice seemed normal at first, but as time passed it took on a whining, wheedling tone. There was also discussion about price.

In defence, the accused took the position that the complainant had consented to the acts. Counsel made the alternative submission that L. had held an honest but mistaken belief in consent. The trial Judge left the defence to the jury and told them that all three could rely upon the defence. The jury returned verdicts of guilty of rape against both L. and I. B. was acquitted of rape, but convicted of indecent assault. The majority of the British Columbia Court of Appeal having dismissed their appeals, the accused appealed further.

The Supreme Court agreed that there was evidence of the mistake defence fit to go to the jury but ordered a new trial on the basis that the trial Judge had wrongly instructed, in his supplementary charge, that the belief had to be both honest and reasonable.

MCINTYRE J. (DICKSON C.J., WILSON, LEDAIN, and LAFOREST JJ. concurring): —

In discussing the application of the "air of reality" test in the *Pappajohn* case, I said, at p. 133:

> To require the putting of the alternative defence of mistaken belief in consent, there must be, in my opinion some evidence beyond the mere assertion of belief in consent by counsel for the appellant. This evidence must appear from or be supported by sources other than the appellant in order to give it any air of reality.

These words appear, on occasion, to have been misunderstood, but I do not withdraw them. There will not be an air of reality about a mere statement that "I thought she was consenting" not supported to some degree by other evidence or circumstances arising in the case. If that mere assertion were sufficient to require a trial Judge to put the "mistake of fact" defence, it would be a simple matter in any rape case to make such an assertion and, regardless of all other circumstances, require the defence to be put. It must be remembered that at this stage of the proceedings the trial Judge is not in any way concerned with the question of guilt or innocence. He is not concerned with the weight of evidence or with the credibility of evidence. The question he must answer is this. In all the circumstances of this case, is there any reality in the defence? To answer this question, he must consider all the evidence, all the circumstances. The statement of the accused alleging a mistaken belief will be a factor but will not by itself be decisive, and even in its total absence, other circumstances might dictate the putting of the defence. This view finds support in the passage from the Heilbron Report (Great Britain, Report of the Advisory Group on the Law of Rape (1975)) referred to by Dickson J., at p. 155 in *Pappajohn*, in these terms:

66. *Morgan's* case did not decide, as some critics seem to have thought, that an accused person was entitled to be acquitted, however ridiculous his story might be, nor did it decide that the reasonableness or unreasonableness of his belief was irrelevant. *Furthermore it is a mistaken assumption that a man is entitled to be acquitted simply because he asserts his belief, without more.* [Emphasis added.]

When the defence of mistake of fact — or for that matter any other defence — is raised, two distinct steps are involved. The first step for the trial Judge is to decide if the defence should be put to the jury. It is on this question, as I have said, that the "air of reality" test is applied. It has nothing to do with the jury and is not a factor for its consideration. If it is decided to put the defence, the second step requires the trial judge to explain the law to the jury, review the relevant evidence, and leave the jury with the issue of guilt or innocence. The jury must consider all the evidence, and they must be satisfied beyond a reasonable doubt in the case of a rape charge that there was no consent before they may convict. Where they find there was consent or honest belief in consent or if they have a doubt on either issue, they must acquit. They should be told as well that the belief, if honestly held, need not be based on reasonable grounds. Before going further, it should be observed that since the decision of this Court in *Pappajohn*, the *Criminal Code* has been amended by the addition of s. 244(4) [now s. 265(4)], which provides:

> (4) Where an accused alleges that he believed that the complainant consented to the conduct that is the subject-matter of the charge, a Judge, if satisfied that there is sufficient evidence and that, if believed by the jury, the evidence would constitute a defence, shall instruct the jury, when reviewing all the evidence relating to the determination of the honesty of the accused's belief, to consider the presence or absence of reasonable grounds for that belief.

This section, in my view, does not change the law as applied in *Pappajohn*. It does not require that the mistaken belief be reasonable or reasonably held. It simply makes it clear than in determining the issue of the honest of the asserted belief, the presence or absence of reasonable grounds for the belief are relevant factors for the jury's consideration. This approach was, I suggest, foreshadowed in *Pappajohn* by Dickson J., at pp. 155-56, where he said:

> Perpetuation of fictions does little for the jury system or the integrity of criminal justice. The ongoing debate in the Courts and learned journals as to whether mistake must be reasonable is conceptually important in the orderly development of the criminal law, but in my view, practically unimportant because the accused's statement that he was mistaken is not likely to be believed unless the mistake is, to the jury, reasonable. The jury will be concerned to consider the reasonableness of any grounds found, or asserted to be available, to support the defence of mistake. Although "reasonable grounds" is not a precondition to the availability of a plea of honest belief in consent, those grounds determine the weight to be given the defence. The reasonableness, or otherwise, of the accused's belief is only evidence for, or against, the view that the belief was actually held and the intent was, therefore, lacking.

The jury should then be instructed, in accordance with s. 244 (4) of the *Code*, that when considering all the evidence relating to the question of the honesty of the accused's asserted belief in consent they must consider the presence or absence of reasonable grounds for that belief.

. . .

LAMER J. — I have read the reasons for judgment of my colleague Justice McIntyre and, for the reasons he sets out, I agree that this appeal should succeed. I wish to add, however, the following qualifications to certain statements made in his reasons.

I agree with McIntyre J. that "a trial Judge is not bound to put every defence suggested by counsel in the absence of some evidentiary base" (at p. 789), and that "to put a wholly unsupported defence would only cause confusion" (at p. 790) amongst the jurors. In addition I do not take issue with the "air of reality" test referred to in *Pappajohn v. The Queen*, [1980] 2 S.C.R. 120 by McIntyre J.

With respect, however, I have difficulties with his application of the "air of reality" test. In *Pappajohn*, he said, at p. 133:

> To require the putting of the alternative defence of mistaken belief in consent, there must be, in my opinion, some evidence beyond the mere assertion of belief in consent by counsel for the appellant. This evidence must appear from or be supported by sources other than the appellant in order to give it any air of reality.

In his reasons in this case, he says (at p. 790):

> These words [air of reality] appear, on occasion, to have been misunderstood, but I do not withdraw them. There will not be an air of reality about a mere statement that "I thought she was consenting" not supported to some degree by other evidence or circumstances arising in the case. If that mere assertion were sufficient to require a trial Judge to put the mistake of fact defence, it would be a simple matter in any rape case to make such an assertion and, regardless of all other circumstances, require the defence to be put.

If this means that the trial Judge is not required to put the defence to the jury merely because the accused's lawyer has referred to the defence in argument, then I agree. There must be some evidence supporting the defence before it is to be put to the jury. However, I must respectfully take issue with the "air of reality" norm if it is to be understood as going so far as enabling the trial Judge to choose not to leave the defence of honest belief with the jury even in a case where the accused has taken the stand and asserted under oath that he or she honestly believed in consent. An accused's oath to the effect that he or she honestly believed in consent is always some evidence, and its probative value in any given case belongs to the jury and not to the trial Judge. It is, of course, open to the trial Judge to comment on the probative value of the evidence, but the jury remains the master of the facts. The trial Judge must not usurp the role of the jury by removing the evidence from the jury's consideration on the ground that, in his or her view, the defence lacks and "air of reality".

. . .

The old common-law rule in sexual assault cases that the trial Judge must instruct the jury that it is unsafe to convict in the absence of corroboration of the complainant's testimony (which was abolished by s. 246.4 of the *Criminal Code*) would in effect be replaced by a rule requiring corroboration of the accused's testimony. Such a requirement will often work an injustice to the accused. Clearly the best, and quite often the only, evidence of the accused's subjective belief will be his or her testimony, and there is no basis in law or in principle for requiring corroboration. In addition, this Court decided in *Pappajohn* that the accused's belief must be honest but need not be reasonable. As a result, there clearly cannot be a requirement that the accused's belief be supported by the circumstances before it can be submitted to the jury. As Dickson J., as he then was, wrote, at p. 156:

> It will be a rare day when a jury is satisfied as to the existence of an unreasonable belief. If the claim of mistake does not raise a reasonable doubt as to guilt, and all other elements of the crime have been proved, then the trier of fact will not give effect to the defence. But, it there is any evidence that there was such an honest belief, regardless of whether it is reasonable, the jury must be entrusted with the task of assessing the credibility of the plea.

I should, in passing, add that in my view the issue of mistaken belief in consent should also be submitted to the jury in all cases where the accused testifies at trial that the complainant consented. The accused's testimony that the complainant consented must be taken to mean that he believed that the complainant consented. As a result, if the jury believes the complainant and concludes that the complainant did not consent, that does not end the matter, for the accused's assertion cannot be disposed of completely unless consideration is then given to his or her being honestly mistaken in believing that the complainant consented.

Finally, I wish to add that I do not believe that this view of the "air of reality" test will open the floodgates to claims of honest mistake as to consent in sexual assault cases. An accused who wishes to raise the defence in the absence of any other evidence supporting an honest mistake will be required to take the stand and will run the risks of cross-examination. In addition, I do not think that the jury will be fooled by false claims of the defence. Juries are constantly assessing and then discarding defences because they lack an air of reality and do not raise a reasonable doubt. Sexual offence cases are no different.

Subject to these reservations, I agree with McIntyre J.'s reasons and would accordingly allow the appeal and direct a new trial.

Appeal allowed and new trial ordered.

In *R. v. Reddick*, [1991] 1 S.C.R. 1086, 5 C.R. (4th) 389, 64 C.C.C. (3d) 257, the majority adopted and applied the *Pappajohn* requirement of sources other than the accused. It seems clear that this special "air of reality" ruling in *Pappajohn* accounted for the reality that the mistaken belief defence has rarely been put to juries. Since *Pappajohn* there have been very few decisions with written reasons where an acquittal has been based on a mistaken belief defence and only one such acquittal confirmed by a Court of Appeal; see *R. v. Weaver* (1990), 80 C.R. (3d) 396 (Alta. C.A.).

The pattern seemed likely to change with the decision in *R. v. Osolin*, [1993] 4 S.C.R. 595, 26 C.R.(4th) 1, 86 C.C.C. (3d) 481. The Court in *Osolin* unanimously decided that the air of reality test declared in s. 265(4) did not violate the presumption of innocence of s. 11(*d*) of the *Charter* nor the right to trial by jury under s. 11(*f*). Mr. Justice Cory reached this conclusion by changing or reading down. He expressly rejected the McIntyre view that there must be a source of evidence other than the accused:

> In my view, this proposition cannot be correct. There is no requirement that there be evidence independent of the accused in order to have the defence put to the jury. However, the mere assertion by the accused that "I believed she was consenting" will not be sufficient. What is required is that the defence of mistaken belief be supported by evidence beyond the mere assertion of a mistaken belief

The Court was unanimous on this point. McLachlin J. expressly adopted Cory J.'s "resolution of the confusion which existed in the earlier cases". This is as close as Her Ladyship gets to acknowledging that her previous position for the Court in *Reddick* has changed.

The Court in *Osolin* did not accept all of the Lamer position in *Bulmer*. The mistaken belief defence need not always be put where the accused testifies as to mistaken belief. Like any other defence, the trial Judge must assess whether there is an evidentiary basis for the defence to be considered by the jury.

In a complex series of split opinions the Supreme Court has now reached further agreement on this issue of air of reality. This was summarized by Chief Justice Lamer for a unanimous Court in *Davis*.

R. v. DAVIS

[1999] 3 S.C.R. 759, 29 C.R. (5th) 1, 139 C.C.C. (3d) 193

LAMER C.J.C. (L'HEUREUX-DUBÉ, GONTHIER, CORY, McLACHLIN, MAJOR and BINNIE JJ. concurring): —

. . . .

The defence of honest but mistaken belief in consent is simply a denial of the *mens rea* of sexual assault: *R. v. Ewanchuk*, [1999] 1 S.C.R. 330 (S.C.C.) at para. 43; *R. v. Pappajohn*, [1980] 2 S.C.R. 120 (S.C.C.) at p. 148. The *actus reus* of sexual assault requires a touching, of a sexual nature, without the consent of the complainant. The *mens rea* requires the accused to intend the touching and to know of, or to be reckless or wilfully blind as to the complainant's lack of consent: *Ewanchuk, supra*, at paras. 25 and 42. In some circumstances, it is possible for the complainant not to consent to the sexual touching but for the accused to honestly but mistakenly believe that the complainant consented. In these circumstances, the *actus reus* of the offence is established, but the *mens rea* is not.

Before the defence can be considered, there must be sufficient evidence for a reasonable trier of fact to conclude that (1) the complainant did not consent to the sexual touching, and (2) the accused nevertheless honestly but mistakenly believed that the complainant consented: see *R. v. Osolin*, [1993] 4 S.C.R. 595 (S.C.C.) at p. 648, per McLachlin J. In other words, given the evidence, it must be *possible* for a reasonable trier of fact to conclude that the *actus reus* is made out but the *mens rea* is not. In these circumstances, the defence is said to have an "air of reality", and the trier of fact, whether a judge or jury, must consider it. Conversely, where [page795] there is no air of reality to the defence, it should not be considered, as no reasonable trier of fact could acquit on that basis: see *R. v. Park*, [1995] 2 S.C.R. 836 (S.C.C.) at para. 11.

In determining whether there is an air of reality to the defence, the trial judge should consider the totality of the evidence: see *Osolin, supra*, at p. 683, per Cory J.; *Park, supra*, at para. 16. The role of the judge in making this determination was set out by Major J. in *Ewanchuk, supra*, at para. 57. He held that the judge should make "no attempt to weigh the evidence". The sole concern is "with the facial plausibility of the defence", and the judge should "avoid the risk of turning the air of reality test into a substantive evaluation of the merits of the defence". Care should be taken not to usurp the role of the trier of fact. Whenever there is a possibility that a reasonable trier of fact could acquit on the basis of the defence, it must be considered.

It is not necessary for the accused to specifically assert a belief that the complainant consented. By simply asserting that the complainant consented, either directly under oath or through counsel, the accused is also asserting a *belief* that the complainant consented: see *Park, supra*, at para. 17. However, the accused's mere assertion will not give the defence an air of reality: see *R. v. Bulmer, (sub nom. R. v. B.)* [1987] 1 S.C.R. 782 (S.C.C.) at p. 790.

While this is evidence of a belief in consent, it is not sufficient evidence of an *honest but mistaken* belief in consent. Sexual assault is not a crime that is generally committed by accident: see *Pappajohn*, at p. 155, per Dickson J.; *Osolin*, at pp. 685-86, per Cory J. In most cases, the issue will be simply one of "consent or no consent", and there will be only one of two possibilities. The first is that the complainant consented, in which case there is no *actus reus*. The second is that the complainant did not consent, and the accused had subjective knowledge of this fact. Here, the *actus reus* [page796] is made out, and the *mens rea* follows straightforwardly.

For example, suppose the complainant and the accused relay diametrically opposed stories. The complainant alleges a brutal sexual assault and vigorous resistance, whereas the accused claims consensual intercourse. Suppose further that it is impossible to splice together the evidence to create a third version of events in which the accused honestly but mistakenly believed the complainant consented. In such circumstances, the trial becomes, essentially, a pure question of credibility. If the complainant is believed, the *actus reus* is made out and the *mens rea* follows straightforwardly. If the accused is believed, or if there is a reasonable doubt as to the complainant's version of events, there is no *actus reus*. There is no third possibility of an honest but mistaken belief in consent, notwithstanding the accused's assertion that the complainant consented: *Park, supra*, at paras. 25-26.

Although the accused's mere assertion that the complainant consented will not be sufficient evidence to raise the defence, the requisite evidence may nevertheless come from the accused: see *Park, supra*, at pp. 852-53, paras. 19-

20, per L'Heureux-Dubé J.; *Osolin, supra,* at pp. 686-87, *per* Cory J., and pp. 649-50, *per* McLachlin J. It may also come from the complainant, other sources, or a combination thereof. In *R. v. Esau,* [1997] 2 S.C.R. 777 (S.C.C.). McLachlin J., dissenting in the result, accurately conveyed the nature of this evidence at para. 63:

> There must be evidence not only of non-consent and belief in consent, but in addition evidence capable of explaining how the accused could honestly have mistaken the complainant's lack of consent as consent. Otherwise, the defence cannot reasonably arise. There must, in short, be evidence of a situation of ambiguity in which the accused could honestly have misapprehended that the complainant was consenting to the sexual activity in question.

Finally, the Court has held that there will be no air of reality where the evidence shows that the accused was reckless or wilfully blind as to whether the complainant consented. In those circumstances, the accused has subjectively adverted to the absence of consent, and therefore cannot have an *honest* but mistaken belief that the complainant consented.

I note that the appellant was charged with offences allegedly committed prior to the introduction of s. 273.2 in August of 1992. Consequently, the statutory amendments to the defence of honest but mistaken belief in consent do not apply to this appeal.

Problem

The accused was charged with the sexual assault of V, a 15-year-old girl. V and her young friend, T, had willingly gone with the accused and another man, both aged 28. The men had picked them up in the accused's car at 1:30 a.m. The accused drove to a parking lot where the four consumed some beer. The other man kissed V in the back seat. They then went to a second parking lot, where the two girls exchanged seats at the request of the other man. They drove to a third lot, where the accused had sexual intercourse with V. The accused then drove the two girls to T's home. V testified that she resisted the accused throughout. She said she told him no during intercourse and tried to push him away. She testified that, although the accused was not violent and the windows were open and the doors unlocked, she was afraid to scream. V stated that when they arrived at T's apartment, Livermore hugged her. V said that it was possible that she had hugged him back, before saying "bye". When asked by counsel for the accused why, on returning to T's apartment building, she didn't run into the apartment with T to escape, she stated that she didn't because she didn't want the men "to know that anything was wrong". The accused testified that V had been a willing partner while they mutually kissed and touched each other and that he climbed over the gear shift onto her side of the car after she touched his leg and penis. He stated that V hugged him before she left the car. The accused stated that he gave a slip of paper to T on which he had written his name and telephone number before she and V switched places in the car. He also argued that, in light of V's denial that she had consented, circumstances were such that he had entertained an honest but mistaken belief in consent. The trial judge put both defences to the jury. The accused was acquitted.

Was there an air of reality to the mistaken belief defence? Compare *Livermore*, [1995] 4 S.C.R. 123, 43 C.R. (4th) 1, 102 C.C.C. (3d) 212 (S.C.C.) and *Esau*, [1997] 2 S.C.R. 777, 7 C.R. (5th) 357, 116 C.C.C. (3d) 289 (S.C.C.).

In *Livermore* a new trial was ordered on the basis of misdirections on the issue of consent. In sole dissent on this point, Major J. concluded as follows:

> The circumstances giving rise to the complaint were decisive in this case. The alleged sexual assault took place in the bucket seat of a sports car. The cramped quarters were such that on the facts of this case some co-operation, if not the consent, of the complainant was necessary for the alleged offence to have occurred. This was consistent with the accused's testimony and inconsistent with that of the complainant. The errors of the trial judge such as they were would not have changed the result.

What do you think of Major J's reasoning?

SUSAN ESTRICH, TEACHING RAPE LAW

(1992), 102 Yale L.J. 509

I know many students, and even a few professors, who believe that the women are always right and the men are always wrong; that if she didn't consent fully and voluntarily, it is rape, no matter what she said or did, or what he did or did not realize. Everything about his past should be admitted, and nothing about hers. And that's what they want to hear in class.

This kind of orthodoxy is not only bad educationally but, in the case of rape, it also misses the point. Society is not so orthodox in its views. There is a debate going on in courthouses and prosecutors' offices, and around coffee machines and dinner tables, about whether Mike Tyson was guilty or not, and whether William Kennedy Smith ever should have been prosecuted; about when women should be believed, and what counts as consent. There's a debate going on in America as to what is reasonable when it comes to sex. Turn on the radio and you will hear it. To silence that debate in the classroom is to remove the classroom from reality, and to make ourselves irrelevant. It may be hard for some students, but ultimately the only way to change things — and that's usually the goal of those who find the discussions most difficult — is to confront the issues squarely, not to pretend that they don't exist. Besides, the purpose of education, in my classes anyway, is to prepare our students to participate in the controversies that animate the law, not to provide them with a shelter from reality.

. . . .

When I first started teaching rape, the hard questions were whether and when "no means yes," whether nonconsent meant more than saying no, and whether force required more than a push onto the bed and a heavy caress. In those days, it was possible to argue that both the man and the woman in a typical acquaintance rape case were telling the truth: that she said no and did not consent, and that he thought he was engaging in consensual intercourse. The question was not just who to believe, but what standard to apply — male or female, objective or subjective — and how to define it. Is the reasonable man the average man, or the man most reasonable women would like to date? And who is the reasonable woman?

Today, the old questions seem a little easier, but there is a new set that is, in many respects, even more difficult. In the William Kennedy Smith trial, for example, the defense lawyers took pains to point out that they were not arguing that no means yes, or that necking constitutes presumptive consent or even that going to a man's house in the middle of the night entitles him to make any assumptions. Rather, they argued that the complainant said yes.

The Smith defence strategy, I think, reflects an accurate assumption that judges and juries these days are less inclined to accept male conduct that only a few years ago was tolerted as understandably macho. I don't find as many students in my classes these days who believe that a man has the right to ignore the fact that a woman is saying no. And I don't think the reason for this change is that feminists have defined what is "politically correct" in the classroom; I think instead that most of my students, male and female, actually believe that a man should listen to a woman's words, and take her at her word.

This shift in our thinking about the elements of culpability leaves credibility as the only defense game in town. After all, rapes rarely take place in front of witnesses. If no doesn't mean yes, if bruises aren't necessary, and if no unusual force is required, then in many cases there's not going to be much physical evidence to rely on. She gives her version and he gives his. If you are the defense attorney, your job is to convince the jury not to believe what she says — which means that the only way to defend may be to destroy the credibility of the victim.

The key question in many acquaintance rape cases today thus becomes not what counts as rape but rather what we need to know about the victim, and the defendant, in order to decide who is telling the truth.

. . . .

It is one thing to exclude evidence of a woman's sexual past or of psychiatric treatment when she has been beaten and burned; it is easy to argue there that admitting such evidence does almost nothing except to deter legitimate prosecutions and to victimize the victim. But is surely a harder case when there have been no weapons and no bruises, and when the man's liberty depends on convincing a jury not to believe a woman who appears at least superficially credible.

Many of the traditional rules of rape liability were premised on the notion that women lie; Wigmore went so far as to view rape complainants as fundamentally deranged. I don't buy that for a moment nor, I expect, do most of my students. Yet even if only one of a hundred men, or one of a thousand, is falsely accused, the question is still how we can protect that man's right to disprove his guilt. Assume for a moment, I tell my students, that it was you, or your brother, or your boyfriend or your son, who was accused of rape by a casual date with a history of psychiatric problems, or by a woman he met in a bar who had a history of one-night stands. Would you exclude that evidence? What else can the man do to avoid a felony conviction and a ruined life? Where do you draw the line? But if you don't exclude the evidence, will some women as a result become unrapable, at least as a matter of law? That is, will women who have histories of mental instability or of "promiscuity" ever be able to convince juries who know those histories that they really were raped?

Similar issues arise with respect to the man's credibility. The first question many people asked when Anita Hill charged that Clarence Thomas had harassed her was whether there were other women who had been similarly mistreated. The first significant ruling in the Smith case, indeed the decisive ruling, was the Judge's pretrial decision to exclude the testimony of three other women who claimed that they had been sexually abused by the defendant. If the testimony of only one woman cannot be believed — unless she is a Sunday school teacher, camera in hand, as Desiree Washington was, and the defendant is a black man who has made a host of inconsistent statements, as Mike Tyson did — is it fair to exclude the testimony of the other women? And if the testimony is not excluded, do we risk convicting a defendant for being a bad man, indeed being a rapist, rather than committing the particular act charged?

One answer is to say that we need symmetry: exclude all the evidence about both of them. That's the approach the Judge followed in the William Kennedy Smith case. On the surface, it is neat and appealing. The only problem is that it's a false symmetry that is being enforced. After all, evidence that a man has abused other women is much more probative of rape than evidence that a woman has had consensual sex with other men is probative of consent. Most women have had sexual experiences, and unless those experiences fall into some kind of unusual pattern, the mere fact that a woman has had lovers tells us almost nothing about whether she consented on the particular occasion that she is charging as rape. But won't we all look at a defendant differently if three other women have also come forward to say they were abused? The danger with such evidence is not that it proves so little, but that it may prove too much. Symmetry won't get you out of this hole, at least not in my classroom.

Thus, even if most students can agree these days that no means no, and that force can be established if you push a woman down, there's very little agreement about what we need to know about her or him before deciding whether she in fact said yes or no, and whether he actually pushed her down or just lay down with her. The consensus on what counts as rape is more apparent than real. These days, society's continued ambivalence towards acquaintance rape is increasingly being expressed in evidentiary rules and standards of credibility rather than in the definitions of force and consent. The questions have shifted; answering them is no easier.

R. v. SEABOYER; R. v. GAYME

[1991] 2 S.C.R. 577, 7 C.R. (4th) 117, 66 C.C.C. (3d) 321

The rape shield provisions inserted into the *Criminal Code* in 1983 were ss. 276 and 277. The former section dealt with evidence of the complainant's sexual activity as referable to the issue of consent and the latter as referable to the credibility of the complainant. The Court, by a majority of 7:2, decided s. 277 was constitutional but not s. 276.

McLACHLIN J. (LAMER C.J.C., LAFOREST, SOPINKA, CORY, STEVENSON and IACOBUCCI JJ. concurring): — These cases raise the issue of the constitutionality of ss. 276 and 277 of the *Criminal Code*, R.S.C. 1985, c. C-46 (formerly ss. 246.6 and 246.7), commonly known as the "rape-shield" provisions. The provisions restrict the right of the defence on a trial for a sexual offence to cross-examine and lead evidence of a complainant's sexual conduct on other occasions. The question is whether these restrictions offend the guarantees accorded to an accused person by the *Canadian Charter of Rights and Freedoms*.

My conclusion is that one of the sections in issue, s. 276, offends the *Charter.* While its purpose — the abolition of outmoded, sexist-based use of sexual conduct evidence — is laudable, its effect goes beyond what is required or justified by that purpose. At the same time, striking down s. 276 does not imply reversion to the old common law rules, which permitted evidence of the complainant's sexual conduct even though it might have no probative value to the issues on the case and, on the contrary, might mislead the jury. Instead, relying on the basic principles that actuate our law of evidence, the courts must seek a middle way that offers the maximum protection to the complainant compatible with the maintenance of the accused's fundamental right to a fair trial.

. . . .

I deal first with *Seaboyer*. The accused was charged with sexual assault of a woman with whom he had been drinking in a bar. On the preliminary inquiry the Judge refused to allow the accused to cross-examine the complainant on her sexual conduct on other occasions. The appellant contends that he should have been permitted to cross-examine as to other acts of sexual intercourse which may have caused bruises, and other aspects of the complainant's condition which the Crown had put in evidence. While the theory of the defence has not been detailed at this early stage, such evidence might arguably be relevant to consent, since it might provide other explanations for the physical evidence tendered by the Crown in support of the use of force against the complainant.

The *Gayme* case arose in different circumstances. The complainant was 15, the appellant 18. They were friends. The Crown alleges that the appellant sexually assaulted her at his school. The defence, relying on the defences of consent and honest belief in consent, contends that there was no assault and that the complainant was the sexual aggressor. In pursuance of this defence, the appellant at the preliminary inquiry sought to cross-examine and present evidence of prior and subsequent sexual conduct of the complainant.

. . . .

It should be noted that the admissibility of the evidence sought to be tendered in the two cases is not at issue. In neither case did the preliminary inquiry Judge consider whether the evidence would have been relevant or admissible in the absence of ss. 276 or 277 of the *Criminal Code*.

RELEVANT LEGISLATION

Criminal Code, s. 276:

276. (1) In proceedings in respect of an offence under section 271, 272 or 273, no evidence shall be adduced by or on behalf of the accused concerning the sexual activity of the complainant with any person other than the accused unless
  (*a*) it is evidence that rebuts evidence of the complainant's sexual activity or absence thereof that was previously adduced by the prosecution;
  (*b*) it is evidence of specific instances of the complainant's sexual activity tending to establish the identity of the person who had sexual contact with the complainant on the occasion set out in the charge; or
  (*c*) it is evidence of sexual activity that took place on the same occasion as the sexual activity that forms the subject-matter of the charge, where that evidence relates to the consent that the accused alleges he believed was given by the complainant.

(2) No evidence is admissible under paragraph (1)(*c*) unless
  (*a*) reasonable notice in writing has been given to the prosecutor by or on behalf of the accused of his intention to adduce the evidence together with particulars of the evidence sought to be adduced; and
  (*b*) a copy of the notice has been filed with the clerk of the court.

(3) No evidence is admissible under subsection (1) unless the Judge, provincial Court Judge or justice, after holding a hearing in which the jury and the members of the public are excluded and in which the complainant is not a compellable witness, is satisfied that the requirements of this section are met.

Criminal Code, s. 277:

277. In proceedings in respect of an offence under section 271, 272 or 273, evidence of sexual reputation, whether general or specific, is not admissible for the purpose of challenging or supporting the credibility of the complainant.

. . . .

Everyone, under s. 7 of the *Charter*, has the right to life, liberty and security of person and the right not to be deprived thereof except in accordance with the principles of fundamental justice.

. . . .

The real issue under s. 7 is whether the potential for deprivation of liberty flowing from ss. 276 and 277 takes place in a manner that conforms to the principles of fundamental justice.

. . . .

All the parties agree that the right to a fair trial — one which permits the trier of fact to get at the truth and properly and fairly dispose of the case — is a principle of fundamental justice. Nor is there any dispute that encouraging reporting of sexual offences and protection of the complainant's privacy are legitimate goals, provided they do not interfere with the primary objective of a fair trial. Where the parties part company is on the issue of whether ss. 276 and 277 of the *Criminal Code* in fact infringe the right to a fair trial. The supporters of the legislation urge that it furthers the right to a fair trial by eliminating evidence of little or no worth and considerable prejudice. The appellants, on the other hand, say that the legislation goes too far and in fact eliminates relevant evidence which should be admitted notwithstanding the possibility of prejudice.

. . . .

This Court has affirmed the trial Judges' power to exclude Crown evidence the prejudicial effect of which outweighs its probative value in a criminal case, but a narrower formula than that articulated by McCormick has emerged. In *Wray, supra*, at p. 293, [[1971] S.C.R.] the Court stated that the Judge may exclude only "evidence gravely prejudicial to the accused, the admissibility of which is tenuous, and whose probative force in relation to the main issue before the Court is trifling". More recently, in *R. v. Sweitzer*, [1982] 1 S.C.R. 949, at p. 953, an appeal involving a particularly difficult brand of circumstantial evidence offered by the Crown, the Court said that "admissibility will depend upon the probative effect of the evidence balanced against the prejudice caused to the accused by its admission." In *Morris, supra*, at p. 193 [[1983] 2 S.C.R.], the Court without mentioning *Sweitzer* cited the narrower *Wray* formula. But in *R. c. Potvin*, [1989] 1 S.C.R. 525, 68 C.R. (3d) 193, 47 C.C.C. (3d) 289, La Forest J. (Dickson C.J.C. concurring) affirmed in general terms "the rule that the trial Judge may exclude admissible evidence if its prejudicial effect substantially outweighs its probative value" (p. 531 [S.C.R.]).

I am of the view that the more appropriate description of the general power of a Judge to exclude relevant evidence on the ground of prejudice is that articulated in *Sweitzer* and generally accepted throughout the common law world.

. . . .

The Canadian cases cited above all pertain to evidence tendered by the Crown against the accused. The question arises whether the same power to exclude exists with respect to defence evidence. Canadian Courts, like Courts in most common-law jurisdictions, have been extremely cautious in restricting the power of the accused to call evidence in his or her defence, a reluctance founded in the fundamental tenet of our judicial system that an innocent person must not be convicted. It follows from this that the prejudice must substantially outweigh the value of the evidence before a Judge can exclude evidence relevant to a defence allowed by law.

. . . .

Section 277 excludes evidence of sexual reputation for the purpose of challenging or supporting the credibility of the plaintiff. The idea that a complainant's credibility might be affected by whether she has had other sexual experience is today universally discredited. There is no logical or practical link between a woman's sexual reputation and whether she is a truthful witness. It follows that the evidence excluded by s. 277 can serve no legitimate purpose in the trial. Section 277, by limiting the exclusion to a purpose which is clearly illegitimate, does not touch evidence which may be tendered for valid purposes, and hence does not infringe the right to a fair trial.

I turn then to s. 276. Section 276, unlike s. 277, does not condition exclusion on use of the evidence for an illegitimate purpose. Rather, it constitutes a blanket exclusion, subject to three exceptions — rebuttal evidence, evidence going to identity, and evidence relating to consent to sexual activity on the same occasion as the trial incident. The question is whether this may exclude evidence which is relevant to the defence and the probative value of which is not substantially outweighed by the potential prejudice to the trial process. To put the matter another way, can it be said a priori, as the Attorney-General for Ontario contends, that any and all evidence excluded by s. 276 will necessarily be of such trifling weight in relation to the prejudicial effect of the evidence that it may fairly be excluded?

In my view, the answer to this question must be negative. The Canadian and American jurisprudence affords numerous examples of evidence of sexual conduct which would be excluded by s. 276 but which clearly should be received in the interests of a fair trial, notwithstanding the possibility that it may divert a jury by tempting it to improperly infer consent or lack of credibility in the complainant.

Consider the defence of honest belief. It rests on the concept that the accused may honestly but mistakenly (and not necessarily reasonably) have believed that the complainant was consenting to the sexual act. If the accused can raise a reasonable doubt as to his intention on the basis that he honestly held such a belief, he is not guilty under our law and is entitled to an acquittal. The basis of the accused's honest belief in the complainant's consent may be sexual acts performed by the complainant at some other time or place. Yet s. 276 would preclude the accused leading such evidence.

. Another category of evidence eliminated by s. 276 relates to the right of the defence to attack the credibility of the complainant on the ground that the complainant was biased or had motive to fabricate the evidence. In *State v. Jalo*, 27 Or. App. 845, 557 P.2d 1359 (1976), a father accused of sexual acts with his young daughter sought to present evidence that the source of the accusation was his earlier discovery of the fact that the girl and her brother were engaged in intimate relations. The defence contended that when the father stopped the relationship, the daughter, out of animus toward him, accused him of the act. The father sought to lead this evidence in support of his defence that the charges were a concoction motivated by animus. Notwithstanding its clear relevance, this evidence would be excluded by s. 276. The respondent submits that the damage caused by its exclusion would not be great, because all that would be forbidden would be evidence of the sexual activities of the children, and the father could still testify that his daughter was angry with him. But surely the father's chance of convincing the jury of the validity of his defence would be greatly diminished if he were reduced to saying, in effect, "My daughter was angry with me, but I can't say why or produce any corroborating evidence." As noted above, to deny a defendant the building blocks of his defence is often to deny him the defence itself.

Other examples abound. Evidence of sexual activity excluded by s. 276 may be relevant to explain the physical conditions on which the Crown relies to establish intercourse or the use of force, such as semen, pregnancy, injury or disease — evidence which may go to consent. . . . In the case of young complainants, where there may be a tendency to believe their story on the ground that the detail of their account must have come from the alleged encounter, it may be relevant to show other activity which provides an explanation for the knowledge.

. . . .

Even evidence as to pattern of conduct may on occasion be relevant. Since this use of evidence of prior sexual conduct draws upon the inference that prior conduct infers similar subsequent conduct, it closely resembles the prohibited use of the evidence and must be carefully scrutinized. . . . Yet such evidence might be admissible in non-sexual cases under the similar fact rule. Is it fair, then, to deny it to an accused, merely because the trial relates to a sexual offence?

. . . .

These examples leave little doubt that s. 276 has the potential to exclude evidence of critical relevance to the defence. Can it honestly be said, as the Attorney-General for Ontario contends, that the value of such evidence will always be trifling when compared with its potential to mislead the jury? I think not. The examples show that the evidence may well be of great importance to getting at the truth and determining whether the accused is guilty or innocent under the law — the ultimate aim of the trial process. They demonstrate that s. 276, enacted for the purpose of helping Judges and juries arrive at the proper and just verdict in the particular case, overshoots the mark, with the result that it may have the opposite effect of impeding them in discovering the truth.

. . . .

2. Is s. 276 Saved by s. 1 of the *Charter?*

Is s. 276 of the *Criminal Code* justified in a free and democratic society, notwithstanding the fact that it may lead to infringements of the *Charter?*

The first step under s. 1 is to consider whether the legislation addresses a pressing and substantial objective.

. . . .

The second requirement under s. 1 is that the infringement of rights be proportionate to the pressing objective. . . . In creating exceptions to the exclusion of evidence of the sexual activity of the complainant on other occasions, Parliament correctly recognized that justice requires a measured approach, one which admits evidence which is truly relevant to the defence notwithstanding potential prejudicial effect. Yet Parliament at the same time excluded other evidence of sexual conduct which might be equally relevant to a legitimate defence and which appears to pose no greater danger of prejudice than the exceptions it recognizes. To the extent the section excludes relevant defence evidence whose value is not clearly outweighed by the danger it presents, the section is overbroad.

I turn finally to the third aspect of the proportionality requirement — the balance between the importance of the objective and the injurious effect of the legislation. The objective of the legislation, as discussed above, is to eradicate the erroneous inferences from evidence of other sexual encounters that the complainant is more likely to have consented to the sexual act in issue or less likely to be telling the truth. The subsidiary aims are to promote fairer trials and increased reporting of sexual offences and to minimize the invasion of the complainant's privacy. In this way the personal security of women and their right to equal benefit and protection of the law are enhanced. The effect of the legislation, on the other hand, is to exclude relevant defence evidence, the value of which outweighs its potential prejudice. As indicated in the discussion of s. 7, all parties agree that a provision which rules out probative defence evidence which is not clearly outweighed by the prejudice it may cause to the trial strikes the wrong balance between the rights of complainants and the rights of the accused. The line must be drawn short of the point where it results in an unfair trial and the possible conviction of an innocent person. Section 276 fails this test.

I conclude that s. 276 is not saved by s. 1 of the *Charter*.

. . . .

4. What Follows From Striking Down s. 276?

The first question is whether the striking down of s. 276 revives the old common-law rules of evidence permitting liberal and often inappropriate reception of evidence of the complainant's sexual conduct.

. . . .

The answer to this question is no. The rules in question are common-law rules. Like other common-law rules of evidence, they must be adapted to conform to current reality. As all counsel on these appeals accepted, the reality in 1991 is that evidence of sexual conduct and reputation in itself cannot be regarded as logically probative of either the complainant's credibility or consent.

Although they still may inform the thinking of many, the twin myths which s. 276 sought to eradicate are just that — myths — and have no place in a rational and just system of law. It follows that the old rules which permitted evidence of sexual conduct and condoned invalid inferences from it solely for these purposes have no place in our law.

The inquiry as to what the law is in the absence of s. 276 of the *Code* is thus remitted to consideration of the fundamental principles governing the trial process and the reception of evidence. Harking back to Thayer's maxim, relevant evidence should be admitted, and irrelevant evidence excluded, subject to the qualification that the value of the evidence must outweigh its potential prejudice to the conduct of a fair trial. Moreover, the focus must be not on the evidence itself, but on the use to which it is put. As Professor Galvin puts it, our aim is "to abolish the outmoded, sexist-based use of sexual conduct evidence while permitting other uses of such evidence to remain": at p. 809 [70 Minn. L. Rev.].

This definition of the problem suggests an approach which abolishes illegitimate uses and inferences, while preserving legitimate uses. There is wide agreement that the approach of a general exclusion supplemented by categories of exceptions is bound to fail because of the impossibility of predicting in advance what evidence may be relevant in a particular case: see Galvin, Doherty, and Elliott. On the other hand, Judges are not free to act on whim. As Professor Vivian Berger puts it in her article "Man's Trial, Woman's Tribulation: Rape Cases in the Courtroom" (1977), 77 Colum. L. Rev. 1, at p. 69:

> The problem is to chart a course between inflexible legislative rules and wholly untrammelled judicial discretion: The former threatens the rights of defendants; the latter may ignore the needs of complainants.

Professor Galvin, after a comprehensive review of the various approaches to rape-shield legislation which have been adopted in different jurisdictions, proposes a prohibition on illegitimate uses of the evidence, combined with case-by-case judgment exercised with the aid of guidelines.

. . . .

Galvin's proposal, with some modification, reflects an appropriate response to the problem of avoiding illegitimate inferences from evidence of the complainant's sexual conduct, while preserving the general right to a fair trial. It is, moreover, a response which is open to trial Judges in the absence of legislation. It reflects, in essence, an application of the fundamental common-law notions which govern the reception of evidence on trials. The general prohibition on improper use of evidence of sexual conduct reflects the fact that it is always open to a Judge to warn against using a particular piece of evidence for an inference on an issue for which that evidence has no probative force. Similarly, the mandate to the Judge to determine when the evidence may be properly receivable is a reflection of the basic function of the trial Judge of determining the relevance of evidence and whether it should be received, bearing in mind the balance between its probative value and its potential prejudice.

As for the procedures which should govern the determination of whether the sexual conduct evidence should be admitted, Galvin proposes a written motion followed by an in camera hearing (p. 904). The devices of a preliminary affidavit and an in camera hearing are designed to minimize the invasion of the complainant's privacy. If the affidavit does not show the evidence to be relevant, it will not be heard at all. Where this threshold is met, the evidence will be heard in camera so that, in the event the Judge finds its value is outweighed by its potential prejudice, it will not enter the public domain. Such procedures do not require legislation. It has always been open to the Courts to devise such procedures as may be necessary to ensure a fair trial. The requirements of a *voir dire* before a confession can be admitted, for example, is Judge-made law.

While accepting the premise and the general thrust of Galvin's proposal, I suggest certain modifications. There seems little purpose in having separate rules for the use of sexual conduct evidence for illegitimate inferences of consent and credibility in the Canadian context. Again, I question whether evidence of other sexual conduct with the accused should automatically be admissible in all cases; sometimes the value of such evidence might be little or none. The word "complainant" is more compatible with the presumption of innocence of the accused than the word "victim". Professor Galvin's reference to the defence of reasonable belief in consent must be adapted to meet Canadian law, which does not require reasonableness. And the need to warn the jury clearly against improper uses of the evidence should be emphasized, in my view.

In the absence of legislation, it is open to this Court to suggest guidelines for the reception and use of sexual conduct evidence. Such guidelines should be seen for what they are — an attempt to describe the consequences of the application of the general rules of evidence governing relevance and the reception of evidence — and not as judicial legislation cast in stone.

In my view, the trial Judge under this new regime, shoulders a dual responsibility. First, the Judge must assess with a high degree of sensitivity whether the evidence proffered by the defence meets the test of demonstrating a degree of relevance which outweighs the damages and disadvantages presented by the admission of such evidence. The examples presented earlier suggest that while cases where such evidence will carry sufficient probative value will exist, they will be exceptional. The trial Judge must ensure that evidence is tendered for a legitimate purpose, and that it logically supports a defence. The fishing expeditions which unfortunately did occur in the past should not be permitted. The trial Judge's discretion must be exercised to ensure that neither the in camera procedure nor the trial become forums for demeaning and abusive conduct by defence counsel.

The trial Judge's second responsibility will be to take special care to ensure that, in the exceptional case where circumstances demand that such evidence be permitted, the jury is fully and properly instructed as to its appropriate use. The jurors must be cautioned that they should not draw impermissible inferences from evidence of previous sexual activity. While such evidence may be tendered for a purpose logically probative of the defence to be presented, it may be important to remind jurors that they not allow the allegations of past sexual activity to lead them to the view that the complainant is less worthy of belief, or was more likely to have consented for that reason. It is hoped that a sensitive and responsive exercise of discretion by the judiciary will reduce and even eliminate the concerns which provoked legislation such as s. 276, while at the same time preserving the right of an accused to a fair trial.

I would summarize the applicable principles as follows:

1. On a trial for a sexual offence, evidence that the complainant has engaged in consensual sexual conduct on other occasions (including past sexual conduct with the accused) is not admissible solely to support the inference that the complainant is by reason of such conduct:
   (a) more likely to have consented to the sexual conduct at issue in the trial;
   (b) less worthy of belief as a witness.

2. Evidence of consensual sexual conduct on the part of the complainant may be admissible for purposes other than an inference relating to the consent or credibility of the complainant, where it possesses probative value on an issue in the trial and where that probative value is not substantially outweighed by the danger of unfair prejudice flowing from the evidence.

   By way of illustration only, and not by way of limitation, the following are examples of admissible evidence:

   (A) Evidence of specific instances of sexual conduct tending to prove that a person other than the accused caused the physical consequences of the rape alleged by the prosecution;
   (B) Evidence of sexual conduct tending to prove bias or motive to fabricate on the part of the complainant;
   (C) Evidence of prior sexual conduct, known to the accused at the time of the act charged, tending to prove that the accused believed that the complainant was consenting to the act charged (without laying down absolute rules, normally one would expect some proximity in time between the conduct that is alleged to have given rise to an honest belief and the conduct charged);
   (D) Evidence of prior sexual conduct which meets the requirements for the reception of similar act evidence, bearing in mind that such evidence cannot be used illegitimately merely to show that the complainant consented or is an unreliable witness.
   (E) Evidence tending to rebut proof introduced by the prosecution regarding the complainant's sexual conduct;

3. Before evidence of consensual sexual conduct on the part of a victim is received, it must be established on a *voir dire* (which may be held in camera) by affidavit or the testimony of the accused or third parties, that the proposed use of the evidence of other sexual conduct is legitimate.

4. Where evidence that the complainant has engaged in sexual conduct on other occasions is admitted on a jury trial, the Judge should warn the jury against inferring from the evidence of the conduct itself, either that the complainant might have consented to the act alleged, or that the complainant is less worthy of credit.

. . . .

L'HEUREUX-DUBÉ J. (GONTHIER J. concurring) (dissenting in part): — [She agreed to allow the appeal on jurisdictional grounds but held that, in any event, there had been no *Charter* violation and that any violation could have been justified under section 1.]

. . . .

Sexual assault is not like any other crime. In the vast majority of cases the target is a woman and the perpetrator is a man. . . . Unlike other crimes of a violent nature, it is for the most part unreported. Yet, by all accounts, women are victimized at an alarming rate, and there is some evidence that an already frighteningly high rate of sexual assault is on the increase. The prosecution and conviction rates for sexual assault are among the lowest for all violent crimes. Perhaps more than any other crime, the fear and constant reality of sexual assault affects how women conduct their lives and how they define their relationship with the larger society. Sexual assault is not like any other crime.

. . . .

There are a number of reasons why women may not report their victimization: fear of reprisal, fear of a continuation of their trauma at the hands of the police and the criminal justice system, fear of a perceived loss of status and lack of desire to report due to the typical effects of sexual assault such as depression, self-blame or loss of self-esteem. Although all of the reasons for failing to report are significant and important, more relevant to the present inquiry are the numbers of victims who choose not to bring their victimization to the attention of the authorities due to their perception that the institutions, with which they would have to become involved, will view their victimization in a stereotypical and biased fashion.

The woman who comes to the attention of the authorities has her victimization measured against the current rape mythologies, *i.e.*, who she should be in order to be recognized as having been, in the eyes of the law, raped; who her attacker must be in order to be recognized, in the eyes of the law, as a potential rapist; and how injured she must be in order to be believed. If her victimization does not fit the myths, it is unlikely that an arrest will be made or a conviction obtained. As prosecutors and police often suggest, in an attempt to excuse their application of stereotype, there is no point in directing cases toward the justice system if juries and Judges will acquit on the basis of their stereotypical perceptions of the "supposed victim" and her "supposed" victimization.

. . . .

More specifically, police rely in large measure upon popular conceptions of sexual assault in order to classify incoming cases as "founded" or "unfounded". It would appear as though most forces have developed a convenient shorthand regarding their decisions to proceed in any given case. This shorthand is composed of popular myth regarding rapists (distinguishing them from men as a whole), and stereotype about women's character and sexuality. Holmstrom and Burgess, at pp. 174-199, conveniently set out and explain the most common of these myths and stereotypes:

1. *Struggle and Force: Woman As Defender of Her Honour.* There is a myth that a woman cannot be raped against her will, that if she really wants to prevent a rape she can.

The prosecution attempts to show that she did struggle, or had no opportunity to do so, while the defence attempts to show that she did not.

Women know that there is no response on their part that will assure their safety. The experience and knowledge of women is borne out by the *Canadian Urban Victimization Survey: Female Victims of Crime* (1985). At p. 7 of the report, the authors note:

> Sixty percent of those who tried reasoning with their attackers, and 60 percent of those who resisted actively by fighting or using weapon [sic] were injured. Every sexual assault incident is unique and so many factors are unknown (physical size of victims and offenders, verbal or physical threats, etc.) that no single course of action can be recommended unqualifiedly.

2. *Knowing the Defendant: The Rapist As a Stranger.* There is a myth that rapists are strangers who leap out of bushes to attack their victims. . . . [T]he view that interaction between friends or between relatives does not result in rape is prevalent.

The defence uses the existence of a relationship between the parties to blame the victim. . . .

3. *Sexual Reputation: The Madonna-Whore Complex.* . . . [W]omen . . . are categorized into one-dimensional types. They are maternal or they are sexy. They are good or they are bad. They are madonnas or they are whores.

The legal rules use these distinctions.

4. *General Character: Anything Not 100 Percent Proper and Respectable.* . . . Being on welfare or drinking or drug use could be used to discredit anyone, but where women are involved, these issues are used to imply that the woman consented to sex with the defendant or that she contracted to have sex for money.

5. *Emotionality of Females.* Females are assumed to be "more emotional" than males. The expectation is that if a woman is raped, she will get hysterical during the event and she will be visibly upset afterward. If she is able to "retain her cool," then people assume that "nothing happened".

6. *Reporting Rape.* Two conflicting expectations exist concerning the reporting of rape. One is that if a woman is raped she will be too upset and ashamed to report it, and hence most of the time this crime goes unreported. The other is that if a woman is raped, she will be so upset that she will report it. Both expectations exist simultaneously.

7. *Woman as Fickle and Full of Spite.* Another stereotype is that the feminine character is especially filled with malice. Woman is seen as fickle and as seeking revenge on past lovers.

8. *The Female Under Surveillance: Is the Victim Trying to Escape Punishment?* . . . It is assumed that the female's sexual behaviour, depending on her age, is under the surveillance of her parents or her husband, and also more generally of the community. Thus, the defense argues, if a woman says she was raped, it must be because she consented to sex that she was not supposed to have. She got caught, and now she wants to get back in the good graces of whomever's surveillance she is under.

9. *Disputing That Sex Occurred.* That females fantasize rape is another common stereotype. Females are assumed to make up stories that sex occurred when in fact nothing happened. . . . Similarly, women are thought to fabricate the sexual activity not as part of a fantasy life, but out of spite.

10. *Stereotype of the Rapist.* One stereotype of the rapist is that of a stranger who leaps out of the bushes to attack his victim and later abruptly leaves her. . . . [S]tereotypes of the rapist can be used to blame the victim. She tells what he did. And because it often does not match what jurors *think* rapists do, his behaviour is held against her.

· · · ·

This list of stereotypical conceptions about women and sexual assault is by no means exhaustive. Like most stereotypes, they operate as a way, however flawed, of understanding the world and, like most such constructs, operate at a level of consciousness that makes it difficult to root them out and confront them directly. This mythology finds its way into the decisions of the police regarding their "founded"/"unfounded" categorization, operates in the mind of the Crown when deciding whether or not to prosecute, influences a judge's or juror's perception of guilt or innocence of the accused and the "goodness" or "badness" of the victim, and finally, has carved out a niche in both the evidentiary and substantive law governing the trial of the matter.

· · · ·

Absolutely pivotal to an understanding of the nature and purpose of the provisions and constitutional questions at issue in this case is the realization of how widespread the stereotypes and myths about rape are, notwithstanding their inaccuracy.

The appellants argue that we, as a society, have become more enlightened, that prosecutors, police, Judges and jurors can be trusted to perform their tasks without recourse to discriminatory views about women manifested through rape myth. Unfortunately, social science evidence suggests otherwise. Rape myths still present formidable obstacles for complainants in their dealings with the very system charged with discovering the truth. Their experience in this regard is illustrated by the following remarks of surprisingly recent vintage:

> Women who say no do not always mean no. It is not just a question of saying no, it is a question of how she says it, how she shows and makes it clear. If she doesn't want it she has

only to keep her legs shut and she would not get it without force and there would be marks of force being used.

(Judge David Wild, Cambridge Crown Court, 1982, quoted in Elizabeth Sheehy, "Canadian Judges and the Law of Rape: Should the *Charter* Insulate Bias?" (1989) 21 Ottawa L. Rev. 741, at p. 741.)

Unless you have no worldly experience at all, you'll agree that women occasionally resist at first but later give in to either persuasion or their own instincts.

(Judge Frank Allen, Manitoba Provincial Court, 1984, quoted in Sheehy at p. 741.)

[I]t is easy for a man intent upon his own desires to mistake the intentions of a woman or girl who may herself be in two minds about what to do. Even if he makes no mistake it is not unknown for a woman afterwards either to take fright or for some other reason to regret what has happened and seek to justify herself retrospectively by accusing the man of rape.

(Colin Howard, *Criminal Law*, 3d ed. (Sydney: Law Book Co., 1977), at p. 149.)

Modern psychiatrists have amply studied the behaviour of errant young girls and women coming before the courts in all sorts of cases. Their psychic complexes are multifarious, distorted partly by inherent defects, partly by diseased derangements or abnormal instincts, partly by bad social environment, partly by temporary physiological or emotional conditions. One form taken by these complexes is that of contriving false charges of sexual offenses by men.

(J.H. Wigmore, *Evidence in Trials at Common Law*, Vol. 3A, rev. J.H. Chadbourn (Boston: Little, Brown, 1970), at p. 736.)

Regrettably, these remarks demonstrate that many in society hold inappropriate stereotypical beliefs, and apply them when the opportunity presents itself.

. . . .

It is thus clear that, from the making of the initial complaint down to the determination of the issue at trial, stereotype and mythology are at work, lowering the number of reported cases, influencing police decisions to pursue the case, thereby decreasing the rates of arrest, and, finally, distorting the issues at trial and necessarily, the results. Professor Catharine MacKinnon asserts that in the United States:

It is not only that women are the principal targets of rape, which by conservative definition happens to almost half of all women at least once in their lives. It is not only that over one-third of all women are sexually molested by older trusted male family members or friends or authority figures as an early, perhaps initiatory, interpersonal sexual encounter. . . . All this documents the extent and terrain of abuse and the effectively unrestrained and systematic sexual aggression by less than one-half of the population against the other more than half. It suggests that it is basically allowed.

(Catherine MacKinnon, *Toward a Feminist Theory of the State* (Cambridge, Mass.: Harvard, University Press, 1989), at pp. 142-143.)

. . . .

Under the guise of a principled application of the legal concept of relevance, the common law allowed the accused to delve at great length into the moral character of the complainant by adducing "relevant" sexual history. The prejudicial impact of such an inquiry has already been discussed at length. The true nature and purpose of the inquiry into sexual history is revealed by the resulting prejudice and by the fact that these concepts were only applicable in respect of sexual offences and, in addition, were not deemed relevant to the credibility of the male accused.

Application of the relevance concept was not the only way in which the common law integrated stereotype and myth into trials of sexual offences. Also part of the unique body of evidentiary law surrounding sexual offences were, among other things, the doctrine of recent complaint and corroboration rules. These evidentiary concepts were also based upon stereotypes of the female complainant requiring independent evidence to support her evidence and, in addition, evidence that she raised a "hue and cry" after her assault. It is noteworthy that both recent complaint and corroboration rules formed exceptions to general rules of evidence.

. . . .

Relevance and Admissibility at Common Law and Under the Legislative Provisions

Like many of the other legal rules and principles that are brought to bear in trials of persons charged with sexual offences, the concept of relevance has been imbued with stereotypical notions of female complainants and sexual assault. That this is so is plain from the common law, which held that evidence of "unchasteness" was relevant to both consent and credibility. Any connection between the evidence sought to be adduced and the fact or matter of which it was supposedly probative must be bridged by stereotype (that "unchaste" women lie and "unchaste" women consent indiscriminately), otherwise the propositions make no sense. While some may think that these represent egregious examples of the use of stereotype, it is well to remember that relevancy determinations such as this are still being made, though the myth which drives the particular determination may be better obscured or, due to the entrenchment of these beliefs, more automatically made.

Traditional definitions of what is relevant include "whatever accords with common sense" (Peter K. McWilliams, *Canadian Criminal Evidence*, 3d ed. (Aurora, Ont.: Canada Law Book, 1990), at p. 35); "'relevant' means that any two facts to which it is applied are so related to each other that according to the common course of events one either taken by itself or in connection with other facts proves or renders probable the past, present or future existence or non-existence of the other" (Sir James Fitzjames Stephen's *Digest of the Law of Evidence* 12th ed. (London: Macmillan, 1936), art. 1), and finally Thayer's "logically probative" test with relevance as an affair of logic and not of law, a test adopted by this Court in Morris.

. . . .

Whatever the test, be it one of experience, common sense or logic, it is a decision particularly vulnerable to the application of private beliefs. Regardless of the definition used, the content of any relevancy decision will be filled by the particular Judge's experience, common sense and/or logic. For the most part there will be general agreement as to that which is relevant, and the determination will not be problematic. However, there are certain areas of inquiry where experience, common sense and logic are informed by stereotype and myth. As I have made clear, this area of the law has been particularly prone to the utilization of stereotype in determinations of relevance and, again, as was demonstrated earlier, this appears to be the unfortunate concomitant of a society which, to a large measure, holds these beliefs. It would also appear that recognition of the large role that stereotype may play in such determinations has had surprisingly little impact in this area of the law.

. . . .

Once the mythical bases of relevancy determinations in this area of the law are revealed (discussed at greater length later in these reasons), the irrelevance of most evidence of prior sexual history is clear. Nevertheless, Parliament has provided broad avenues for its admissibility in the setting out of the exceptions to the general rule in s. 246.6 (now s. 276). Moreover, *all* evidence of the complainant's previous sexual history with the accused is *prima facie* admissible under those provisions. Evidence that is excluded by these provisions is simply, in a myth- and stereotype-free decision-making context, irrelevant.

For comments on *Seaboyer* see Christine Boyle and Marilyn MacCrimmon, "*R. v. Seaboyer*: A Lost Cause?" (1992), 7 C.R. (4th) 225 and a reply by Anthony Allman in (1992), 10 C.R. (4th) 153.

Most would agree that receiving evidence of the complainant's previous sexual history on a trial of sexual assault will so prejudice the trial that the same should rarely be admitted. Has the Court drawn the proper line?

While striking down the complainant's statutory protection, the Court recognized the possibility that the then existing common-law rules could permit the inappropriate reception of evidence of the complainant's sexual conduct and the majority therefore changed the common law. The majority said it was suggesting "guidelines for the reception of sexual conduct evidence" and these were not to be seen as "judicial legislation cast in stone". Rather they were "an attempt to describe the consequences of the application of the general rules of evidence governing relevance and the reception of evidence". While the majority wrote that it was not legislating but only offering "guidelines", if the "guidelines" are the Supreme Court of Canada's thoughts on the common law of today, their expression differs little from the exercise of legislating. There will surely be no different result waiting for the trial Judge who decides not to follow the guidelines.

The new regime announced in *Seaboyer* offers greater protection to the complainant than did the legislative provision that was struck down. The old s. 276 forbade the introduction of evidence "concerning the sexual activity of the complainant with *any person other than the accused*". The common law had always recognized that previous sexual conduct with the accused was relevant to the issue of whether the complainant consented on the occasion under review. The majority's opinion "question(ed) whether evidence of other sexual conduct with the accused should automatically be admissible in all cases; sometimes the value of such evidence might be little or none". While sometimes the value of such evidence will be little or none the majority decided to exclude it in all cases: "evidence that the complainant has engaged in consensual sexual conduct on other occasions (*including past sexual conduct with the accused*) is not admissible solely to support the inference that (she) was more likely to have consented".

Suppose A and B have been living together for a year. The evidence is clear and undisputed that the parties regularly engaged in consensual sexual intercourse. On the evening brought into question before the Court sexual intercourse occurred. A says it was consensual and B says it was not. The Court in *Seaboyer* says that evidence of the previous consensual activity is not admissible. Such evidence cannot come in if the sole purpose is to show consent. No one, of course, would suggest that such previous conduct would be determinative of the issue, but is it relevant and at least worth considering along with the other evidence?

The commonly accepted meaning of relevance, we noted earlier, bespeaks a very low threshold: does the evidence offered render the desired inference more probable than it would be without the evidence? Consider the absolute nature of the prohibition which operates regardless of whether the probative value of the evidence outweighs the potential prejudice to the proper outcome of the trial. There is no discretion in the trial Judge to receive the evidence if, in her opinion, the probative value outweighs the prejudice.

The majority in *Seaboyer* cited frequently and quoted heavily from Professor Galvin's article, "Shielding Rape Victims in the State and Federal Courts: A Proposal for the Second Decade".[1] Galvin's proposed rape shield law, however, was confined to the exclusion of evidence of sexual conduct with persons other than the accused. The majority in *Seaboyer* wrote "Galvin's proposal, with some modification, reflects an appropriate response to the problem."[2] One "modification" eliminates the distinction regarding sexual conduct with the accused. This is a major modification. Professor Galvin wrote:

> Even the most ardent reformers acknowledged the high probative value of past sexual conduct in at least two instances. The first is when the defendant claims consent and establishes prior consensual relations between himself and the complainant. . . . Although the evidence is offered to prove consent, its probative value rests on the nature of the complainant's specific mindset toward the accused rather than on her general unchaste character. . . . All 25 statutes adopting the Michigan approach (to rape shield laws) allow the accused to introduce evidence of prior sexual conduct between himself and the complainant. The high probative value and minimal prejudicial effect of this evidence have been discussed.[3]

---

1 (1986), 70 Minn. L. Rev. 763.
2 *Ibid.*, at 156.
3 *Supra*, n. 8 at 807-880.

Another article quoted by the majority in *Seaboyer* is Professor Vivian Berger's *"Man's Trial, Woman's Tribulation"*.[4] Professor Berger justified the reception of evidence of sexual conduct with the accused in this way:

> The inference from past to present behaviour does not, as in cases of third party acts, rest on highly dubious beliefs about "women who do 'and' women who don't" but rather relies on common sense and practical psychology. Admission of the proof supplies the accused with a circumstance making it probable that he did not obtain by violence what he might have secured by persuasion.[5]

Another *major* modification to Galvin's proposal is with respect to so-called similar fact evidence. Galvin proposed that "evidence of a pattern of sexual conduct so distinctive and so closely resembling the accused's version of the alleged encounter with the victim as to tend to prove that the victim consented to the act charged" could be received. The majority in *Seaboyer* wrote that "similar fact evidence . . . cannot be used illegitimately merely to show that the complainant consented" and where evidence of sexual conduct on other occasions is admitted, the trial Judge should warn the jury against this prohibited use. Why? This major modification of Galvin's proposal is not explained unless we are to take it as a given that previous sexual conduct of the complainant can never be indicative of a propensity, a disposition, a willingness, to have sexual intercourse, from which a trier could infer that she acted in conformity with that character.

Suppose the evidence is that the accused and complainant met in Sam's Bar one Saturday night and left to go to her apartment. It's agreed that sexual intercourse occurred but the parties disagree on the issue of consent. The accused's evidence is that he was sitting at the bar when complainant approached him, offered him a drink and propositioned him. Should the accused be able to call Sam to testify that every Saturday night for the previous four weeks the complainant came into his bar, offered a stranger a drink, propositioned him and left in his company?

On the issue of receiving similar fact evidence tendered by the accused, Professor Berger wrote:

> What if the accused were offering to show that the victim habitually goes to bars on Saturday nights, picks up strangers and takes them home to bed with her, and that over the past 12 months she has done so on more than 20 occasions. Now could one assert with assurance that this particular sexual record does not substantially reinforce the defendant's version of the night's events? And if it does, should he not be permitted as a matter of constitutional right to place this evidence before the jury?[6]

---

4 (1977), 77 Colum. L. Rev. 1.
5 *Ibid.*, at 58-59.
6 *Ibid.*

New Legislation — Bill C-49

Seaboyer produced an immediate outcry on the basis that it would mean that women and children would be even less likely to pursue charges of sexual assault given that there would be unrestricted cross-examination of their prior sexual history. Such comments were quite unfair to the majority of the Supreme Court of Canada. For the majority, Madam Justice McLachlin had been quite alive to the dangers of leaving this crucial issue to unfettered judicial discretion and had crafted what she considered to be careful guidelines as to the admissibility of such evidence. She had also extended the protection to prior sexual conduct *with the accused*. One of the sources of the vehement reaction was that the majority took but a line to hold that, although victims might have equality rights, these had to give way to the accused's right to make full answer and defence.

The response from the Minister of Justice, the Honourable Kim Campbell, was swift. She announced that Parliament would better respond to protect women and children. She called a meeting of national and regional women's groups and thereafter worked very closely with them in drafting and revising a Bill.[7] The coalition of some 60 women's groups reached unanimity at each point and agreed to oppose any attempt to water down the Bill.

Bill C-49 was tabled on December 12, 1991. It was referred to committee after second reading on April 16, 1992. It quickly passed through the House of Commons and Senate and received Royal Assent on June 23, 1992. Bill C-49 was proclaimed to be in force on August 15, 1992.

The new s. 276, regarding the admissibility of evidence of the complainant's sexual activity, provides:

> **276.** (1) In proceedings in respect of an offence under section 151, 152, 153, 155 or 159, subsection 160(2) or (3) or section 170, 171, 172, 173, 271, 272 or 273, evidence that the complainant has engaged in sexual activity, whether with the accused or with any other person, is not admissible to support an inference that, by reason of the sexual nature of that activity, the complainant
>> (a) is more likely to have consented to the sexual activity that forms the subject-matter of the charge; or
>> (b) is less worthy of belief.
>
> (2) In proceedings in respect of an offence referred to in subsection (1), no evidence shall be adduced by or on behalf of the accused that the complainant has engaged in sexual activity other than the sexual activity that forms the subject-matter of the charge, whether with the accused or with any other person, unless the Judge, provincial Court Judge or justice determines, in accordance with the procedures set out in sections 276.1 and 276.2, that the evidence
>> (a) is of specific instances of sexual activity;
>> (b) is relevant to an issue to be proved at trial; and
>> (c) has significant probative value that is not substantially outweighed by the danger of prejudice to the proper administration of justice.
>
> (3) In determining whether evidence is admissible under subsection (2), the Judge, provincial Court Judge or justice shall take into account
>> (a) the interests of justice including the right of the accused to make a full answer and defence;

---

7 *Proceedings of the Standing Senate Committee on legal and Constitutional Affairs*, 3rd Sess., 34 Parl. 1991-92 (June 22, 1992): 29-31. See, too, Sheila McIntyre, "Redefining Reformism: The Consultations that Shaped Bill C-49" in J. Roberts and R. Mohr, eds., *Confronting Sexual Assault. A Decade of Legal and Social Change* (1994), chapter 12.

(b) society's interest in encouraging the reporting of sexual assault offences;

(c) whether there is a reasonable prospect that the evidence will assist in arriving at a just determination in the case;

(d) the need to remove from the fact-finding process any discriminatory belief or bias;

(e) the risk that the evidence may unduly arouse sentiments of prejudice, sympathy or hostility in the jury;

(f) the potential prejudice to the complainant's personal dignity and right of privacy;

(g) the right of the complainant and of every individual to personal security and to the full protection and benefit of the law; and

(h) any other factor that the Judge, provincial Court Judge or justice considers relevant.

The new s. 276.1 imposes a requirement of written notice for a hearing to determine admissibility under s. 276(2). Section 276.2 provides for the exclusion of the public at the hearing and the non-compellability of the complainant. The new s. 276.4 requires the trial Judge to instruct the jury as to the proper use of the evidence received.

Does the new legislation give more or less discretion to Judges than did *Seaboyer*? What are the differences?

Section 276(1) seems to contain an express blanket prohibition on what is commonly referred to as the "twin myths" reasoning. It prohibits the use of prior sexual history of the complainant on the issue of consent or to show that the complainant was less worthy of belief. This seemed to make it unconstitutional because *Seaboyer* had called for discretion (see Delisle, "Potential Charter Challenges to the New Rape Shield Law" (1992), 13 C.R. (4th) 309).

However, Professor David Paciocco, "The New Rape Shield Provision Should Survive Charter Challenge" (1993), 21 C.R. (4th) 223, suggested that the legislation could be read down. Section 276(1) only prohibited general stereotypical inferences. Evidence of prior sexual history with the accused could be admitted under s. 276(2) where the defence could establish that a specific inference can be drawn from such evidence to an issue relevant in the trial. In *Charter* challenges in lower courts the Paciocco position carried the day and was increasingly relied on as the proper interpretation.

When the Supreme Court finally considered the constitutionality of the "new" statutory scheme in *Darrach* a unanimous Court had little difficulty in declaring the "new" rape shield provisions constitutional.

R. v. DARRACH

[2000] 2 S.C.R. 443, 36 C.R. (5th) 223, 148 C.C.C. (3d) 97

The accused was charged with sexual assault and, at his trial, attempted to introduce evidence of the complainant's sexual history. He unsuccessfully challenged the constitutionality of s. 276.1(2)(a) of the *Criminal Code* (which requires that the affidavit contain "detailed particulars" about the evidence), ss. 276(1) and 276(2)(c) (which govern the admissibility of sexual conduct evidence generally), and s. 276.2(2) (which provides that the complainant is not a compellable witness at the hearing determining the admissibility of evidence of prior sexual activity). After a *voir dire*, the trial judge refused to allow the accused to adduce the evidence of the complainant's sexual history. The accused was convicted and the Court of Appeal dismissed the accused's appeal, concluding that the impugned provisions did not violate the accused's right to make full answer and defence, his right not to be compelled to testify against himself or his right to a fair trial as protected by ss. 7, 11(*c*) and 11(*d*) of the *Canadian Charter of Rights and Freedoms*. Here we consider the accused's argument that s. 276 (1) was unconstitutional.

GONTHIER J. (McLACHLIN C.J.C., L'HEUREUX-DUBÉ, IACOBUCCI, MAJOR, BASTARACHE, BINNIE, ARBOUR, LeBEL J.J. concurring): —

. . . .

The current s. 276 categorically prohibits evidence of a complainant's sexual history only when it is used to support one of two general inferences. These are that a person is more likely to have consented to the alleged assault and that she is less credible as a witness by virtue of her prior sexual experience. Evidence of sexual activity may be admissible, however, to substantiate other inferences.

. . . .

The current version of s. 276 is carefully crafted to comport with the principles of fundamental justice. It protects the integrity of the judicial process while at the same time respecting the rights of the people involved. The complainant's privacy and dignity are protected by a procedure that also vindicates the accused's right to make full answer and defence. The procedure does not violate the accused's s. 7 *Charter* right to a fair trial nor his s. 11(*c*) right not to testify against himself or his s. 11(*d*) right to a fair hearing.

. . . .

[T]he Court's jurisprudence . . . has consistently held that the principles of fundamental justice enshrined in s. 7 protect more than the rights of the accused.

. . . .

One of the implications of this analysis is that while the right to make full answer and defence and the principle against self-incrimination are certainly core principles of fundamental justice, they can be respected without the accused being entitled to "the most favourable procedures that could possibly be imagined" (*R. v. Lyons*, [1987] 2 S.C.R. 309 (S.C.C.) at p. 362; cited in *Mills*, *supra*, at para. 72). Nor is the accused entitled to have procedures crafted that take only his interests into account. Still less is he entitled to procedures that would distort the truth-seeking function of a trial by permitting irrelevant and prejudicial material at trial.

In *Seaboyer*, the Court found that the principles of fundamental justice include the three purposes of s. 276 identified above: protecting the integrity of the trial by excluding evidence that is misleading, protecting the rights of the accused, as well as encouraging the reporting of sexual violence and protecting "the security and privacy of the witnesses" (p. 606). This was affirmed in *Mills*, *supra*, at para. 72. The Court crafted its guidelines in *Seaboyer* in accordance with these principles, and it is in relation to these principles that the effects of s. 276 on the accused must be evaluated.

The Court in *Mills* upheld the constitutionality of the provisions in the *Criminal Code* that control the use of personal and in therapeutic records in trials of sexual offences. The use of these records in evidence is analogous many ways to the use of evidence of prior sexual activity, and the protections in the *Criminal Code* surrounding the use of records at trial are motivated by similar policy considerations. L'Heureux-Dubé J. has warned that therapeutic records should not become a tool for circumventing s. 276: "[w]e must not allow the defence to do indirectly what it cannot do directly" (*R. v. O'Connor*, [1995] 4 S.C.R. 411 (S.C.C.), at para. 122, and *R. v. Osolin*, [1993] 4 S.C.R. 595, at p. 624). Academic commentators have observed that the use of therapeutic records increased with the enactment of s. 276 nonetheless (see K. Kelly, "'You must be crazy if you think you were raped': Reflections on the Use of Complainants' Personal and Therapy Records in Sexual Assault Trials" (1997), 9 *C.J.W.L.* 178, at p. 181).

. . . .

[T]he test for admissibility in s. 276(2) requires not only that the evidence be relevant but also that it be more probative than prejudicial. *Mills* dealt with a conflict among the same three *Charter* principles that are in issue in the case at bar: full answer and defence, privacy and equality (at para. 61). The Court defined these rights relationally: "the scope of the right to make full answer and defence must be determined in light of privacy and equality rights of complainants and witnesses" (paras. 62-66 and 94). The exclusionary rule was upheld. The privacy and equality concerns involved in protecting the records justified interpreting the right to make full answer and defence in a way that did not include a right to all relevant evidence.

. . . .

In the case at bar, I affirm the reasons in *Seaboyer* and find that none of the accused's rights are infringed by s. 276 as he alleges. *Seaboyer* provides a basic justification for the legislative scheme in s. 276, including the determination of relevance as well as the prejudicial and probative value of the evidence. *Mills* and *White* show how the impact of s. 276 on the principles of fundamental justice relied on by the accused should be assessed in light of the other principles of fundamental justice that s. 276 was designed to protect. The reasons in *Mills* are apposite because they demonstrate how the same principles of equality, privacy and fairness can be reconciled. I shall show below how the procedure created by s. 276 to protect the trial process from distortion and to protect complainants is consistent with the principles of fundamental justice. It is fair to the accused and properly reconciles the divergent interests at play, as the Court suggested in *Seaboyer*.

. . . .

Section 276(1) — The Exclusionary Rule

The accused objects to the exclusionary rule itself in s. 276(1) on the grounds that it is a "blanket exclusion" that prevents him from adducing evidence necessary to make full answer and defence, as guaranteed by ss. 7 and 11(*d*) of the *Charter*. He is mistaken in his characterization of the rule. Far from being a "blanket exclusion", s. 276(1) only prohibits the use of evidence of past sexual activity when it is offered to support two specific, illegitimate inferences. These are known as the "twin myths", namely that a complainant is more likely to have consented or that she is less worthy of belief "by reason of the sexual nature of the activity" she once engaged in.

This section gives effect to McLachlin J.'s finding in *Seaboyer* that the "twin myths" are simply not relevant at trial. They are not probative of consent or credibility and can severely distort the trial process. Section 276(1) also clarifies *Seaboyer* in several respects. Section 276 applies to all sexual activity, whether with the accused or with someone else. It also applies to non-consensual as well as consensual sexual activity, as this Court found implicitly in *R. v. Crosby*, [1995] 2 S.C.R. 912 (S.C.C.), at p. 924. Although the *Seaboyer* guidelines referred to "consensual sexual conduct" (pp. 634-35), Parliament enacted the new version of s. 276 without the word "consensual". Evidence of non-consensual sexual acts can equally defeat the purposes of s. 276 by distorting the trial process when it is used to evoke stereotypes such as that women who have been assaulted must have deserved it and that they are unreliable witnesses, as well as by deterring people from reporting assault by humiliating them in court. The admissibility of evidence of non-consensual sexual activity is determined by the procedures in s. 276. Section 276 also settles any ambiguity about whether the "twin myths" are limited to inferences about "unchaste" women in particular; they are not (as discussed by C. Boyle and M. MacCrimmon, "The Constitutionality of Bill C-49: Analyzing Sexual Assault As If Equality Really Mattered" (1998), 41 *Crim. L.Q.* 198, at pp. 231-32).

The *Criminal Code* excludes all discriminatory generalizations about a complainant's disposition to consent or about her credibility based on the *sexual nature* of her past sexual activity on the grounds that these are improper lines of reasoning. This was the import of the Court's findings in *Seaboyer* about how sexist beliefs about women distort the trial process. The text of the exclusionary rule in s. 276(1) diverges very little from the guidelines in *Seaboyer*. The mere fact that the wording differs between the Court's guidelines and Parliament's enactment is itself immaterial. In *Mills, supra*, the Court affirmed that "[t]o insist on slavish conformity" by Parliament to judicial pronouncements "would belie the mutual respect that underpins the relationship" between the two institutions (para. 55). In this case, the legislation follows the Court's suggestions very closely.

The phrase "by reason of the sexual nature of the activity" in s. 276 is a clarification by Parliament that it is inferences from the *sexual nature* of the activity, as opposed to inferences from other potentially relevant features of the activity, that are prohibited. If evidence of sexual activity is proffered for its non-sexual features, such as to show a pattern of conduct or a prior inconsistent statement, it may be permitted. The phrase "by reason of the sexual nature of the activity" has the same effect as the qualification "solely to support the inference" in *Seaboyer* in that it limits the exclusion of evidence to that used to invoke the "twin myths" (p. 635).

. . . .

An accused has never had a right to adduce irrelevant evidence. Nor does he have the right to adduce misleading evidence to support illegitimate inferences: "the accused is not permitted to distort the truth-seeking function of the trial process" (*Mills, supra*, at para. 74). Because s. 276(1) is an evidentiary rule that only excludes material that is not relevant, it cannot infringe the accused's right to make full answer and defence. Section 276(2) is more complicated, and I turn to it now.

Section 276(2) — "Significant Probative Value"

If evidence is not barred by s. 276(1) because it is tendered to support a permitted inference, the judge must still weigh its probative value against its prejudicial effect to determine its admissibility. This essentially mirrors the common law guidelines in *Seaboyer* which contained this balancing test (at p. 635). The accused takes issue with the fact that s. 276(2)(c) specifically requires that the evidence have "significant probative value". The word "significant" was added by Parliament but it does not render the provision unconstitutional by raising the threshold for the admissibility of evidence to the point that it is unfair to the accused.

. . . .

The context of the word "significant" in the provision in which it occurs substantiates this interpretation. Section 276(2)(c) allows a judge to admit evidence of "*significant* probative value that is not *substantially* outweighed by the danger of prejudice to the proper administration of justice" (emphasis added). The adverb "substantially" serves to protect the accused by raising the standard for the judge to exclude evidence once the accused has shown it to have significant probative value. In a sense, both sides of the equation are heightened in this test, which serves to direct judges to the serious ramifications of the use of evidence of prior sexual activity all parties in these cases.

In light of the purposes of s. 276, the use of the word "significant" is consistent with both the majority and the minority reasons in *Seaboyer*. Section 276 is designed to prevent the use of evidence of prior sexual activity for improper purposes. The requirement of "significant probative value" serves to exclude evidence of trifling relevance that, even though not used to support the two forbidden inferences, would still endanger the "proper administration of justice". The Court has recognized that there are inherent "damages and disadvantages presented by the admission of such evidence" (*Seaboyer, supra*, at p. 634). As Morden A.C.J.O. puts it, evidence of sexual activity must be significantly probative if it is to overcome its prejudicial effect. The *Criminal Code* codifies this reality.

By excluding misleading evidence while allowing the accused to adduce evidence that meets the criteria of s. 276(2), s. 276 enhances the fairness of trials of sexual offences. Section 11(*d*) guarantees a fair trial. Fairness under s. 11(d) is determined in the context of the trial process as a whole (*R. v. Stoddart* (1987), 37 C.C.C. (3d) 351 (Ont. C.A.), at pp. 365-66). As L'Heureux-Dubé J. wrote in *Crosby*, *supra*, at para. 11, "[s]ection 276 cannot be interpreted so as to deprive a person of a fair defence." At the same time, the accused's right to make full answer and defence, as was held in *Mills*, *supra*, at para. 75, is not "automatically breached where he or she is deprived of relevant information." Nor is it necessarily breached when the accused is not permitted to adduce relevant information that is not "significantly" probative, under a rule of evidence that protects the trial from the distorting effects of evidence of prior sexual activity.

. . . .

Thus the threshold criteria that evidence be of "significant" probative value does not prevent an accused from making full answer and defence to the charges against him. Consequently his *Charter* rights under ss. 7 and 11(*d*) are not infringed by s. 276(2)(*c*).

The Procedural Sections to Determine Relevance: The Affidavit and *Voir Dire*

The constitutionality of the procedure that must be followed to introduce evidence of prior sexual activity has also been challenged. It requires that whoever seeks to introduce it "by or on behalf of the accused" must present an affidavit and establish on a *voir dire* that the evidence is admissible in accordance with the criteria in the *Criminal Code*.

[The Court determined that the procedural provisions were not violative of the accused's constitutional rights. In the course of its analysis the Court later commented on relevance and probative value of evidence of previous sexual activity.]

Although the Supreme Court has determined the issue of constitutionality, it seems very likely that *Darrach* has not resolved the question of the proper application of ss. 276 (1) and (2), especially in the context of prior sexual history with the accused where the issue is consent. We have seen that the Court in *Darrach* at one point says that such evidence is not relevant, then in the next breath it says it may be admitted. Towards the end of the judgment this is put in yet another way:

> Evidence of prior sexual activity will rarely be relevant to support a denial that sexual activity took place or to establish consent (C.R., para. 58).

That judges have different views on the issue of the relevance and probative value of evidence of prior sexual history with the accused on the issue of consent is reflected in the views of the Ontario Court of Appeal in the Court below in *Darrach*, which were not addressed in the Supreme Court. According to Morden

A.C.J.O. for the Court, (1998), 13 C.R. (5th) 283, 122 C.C.C. (3d) 225 (Ont. C.A.), (Osborne and Doherty JJ.A. concurring):

> It will likely be that evidence of previous sexual activity with the accused will satisfy the requirements of admissibility in s. 276(2) more often than that relating to sexual activity with others. This does not mean that this evidence should always be admitted (C.R. at 299).

Trial judges appear to regularly admit evidence of a prior or ongoing relationship where there is a viable issue of consent. That is not to say that such evidence is determinative. Otherwise the trial would be devoid of context and potentially unfair to accused.

The new s. 273.1 seeks to define consent in the case of sexual assault but, consistent with *R. v. Jobidon*, is expressly not exhaustive:

> **273.1**(1) Subject to subsection (2) and subsection 265(3), "consent" means, for the purposes of sections 271, 272 and 273, the voluntary agreement of the complainant to engage in the sexual activity in question.
>
> (2) No consent is obtained, for the purposes of sections 271, 272 and 273, where
>> (a) the agreement is expressed by the words or conduct of a person other than the complainant;
>> (b) the complainant is incapable of consenting to the activity;
>> (c) the accused induces the complainant to engage in the activity by abusing a position of trust, power or authority;
>> (d) the complainant, expresses, by words or conduct, a lack of agreement to engage in the activity; or
>> (e) the complainant, having consented to engage in sexual activity, expresses, by words or conduct, a lack of agreement to continue to engage in the activity.
>
> (3) Nothing in subsection (2) shall be construed as limiting the circumstances in which no consent is obtained.

These provisions clearly set out to give Courts better guidance as to situations in which consent can be held to have been not genuine and therefore not consent in law. Subsections (b), (c) and (e) were amended as the bill passed through committee. The amendments were largely inconsequential, merely clarifying rather than changing the original intent. Subsection (b) had read that the complainant was incapable of consenting to the activity "by reason of intoxication or other condition". The provision was criticized as being vague, especially in its reference to "other condition". Parliament clearly decided to leave the matter to the discretion of trial Judges while preserving the common-law principle that one incapable of giving consent cannot be considered to have consented.

These new consent provisions seem adequately drafted and a welcome assertion of the "No Means No" philosophy. With the exception of subs. (c), which will require judicial interpretation, the provisions appear to merely restate existing legal principles.

Some interpreted subs. (d) as preserving the existing common law that consent can be express or implied. A suggestion by the women's coalition that consent should be limited to unequivocal expressions[8] was rejected. Critics of

---

8 The Coalition's rejected proposal of November 27, 1991, had the following definition: "For the purposes of sections 271, 272 and 273 consent shall be sought and obtained and shall mean words or gestures which unequivocally express or manifest voluntary agreement to the sexual activity": see, further, Sheila McIntyre, "Redefining Reformism: The Consultations that Shaped Bill C-49" in J. Roberts and R. Mohr (eds.), *Sexual Assault. A Decade of Legal and Social Change* (1994), Chapter 12.

Bill C-49 suggested that in future written consent will be needed in advance for any sexual conduct, that there is an onus of proof on the accused[9] or that Bill C-49 criminalizes seduction.[10]

While Bill C-49 does not remove a belief in consent defence to a charge of sexual assault it substantially restricts it. Under s. 273.2 belief in consent is not a defence to any sexual assault charge where

    (a) the accused's belief arose from the accused's
        (i)   self-induced intoxication, or
        (ii) recklessness or wilful blindness; or

    (b) the accused did not take reasonable steps, in the circumstances known to the accused at the time, to ascertain that the complainant was consenting.

Sections 273.1 and 273.2 were recently authoritatively interpreted by the Supreme Court.

R. v. EWANCHUK

[1999] 1 S.C.R. 330, 22 C.R. (5th) 1, 131 C.C.C. (3d) 481

The accused initiated a number of touching incidents, each progressively more intimate although the complainant clearly said "no" on each occasion. He stopped each time she said "no" but persisted shortly afterwards. The accused was charged with sexual assault.

At a trial before a judge of the Alberta Court of Queen's Bench the accused did not testify, leaving only the complainant's evidence as to what took place between them. The accused was acquitted. The trial judge found that the complainant was a credible witness. He found that in her mind she had not consented to any of the sexual touching which took place, that she had been fearful throughout the encounter, that she didn't want the accused to know she was afraid and that she had actively projected a relaxed and unafraid visage. He concluded that the failure of the complainant to communicate her fear, including her active efforts to the contrary, rendered her subjective feelings irrelevant. He characterized the defence as one of "implied consent". On the totality of the evidence, provided solely by the Crown's witnesses, the trial judge concluded that the Crown had not proven the absence of consent beyond a reasonable doubt and acquitted the accused.

A majority of the Alberta Court of Appeal dismissed the Crown appeal. Each of the three justices of the Court of Appeal issued separate reasons. McClung and Foisy JJ.A. both dismissed the appeal on the basis that it was a fact-driven acquittal from which the Crown could not properly appeal. In addition, McClung J.A. concluded that the Crown had failed to prove beyond a reasonable doubt that the accused had intended to commit an assault upon the complainant. Fraser C.J. delivered a lengthy dissent.

---

9 This was the position of an editorial in *The Globe and Mail*, May 19, 1992: "An assault on the law, not to say common sense", effectively rebutted by the Minister of Justice in a letter published in *The Globe and Mail*, May 27, 1992.

10 *Ibid.*

The Supreme Court allowed the Crown appeal, substituting a conviction and remitting the matter for sentence.

MAJOR J. (LAMER C.J., CORY, IACOBUCCI, BASTARACHE and BINNIE JJ. concurring): —

. . . The trial judge relied on the defence of implied consent. This was a mistake of law as no such defence is available in assault cases in Canada. This mistake of law is reviewable by appellate courts . . .

1. Facts

The complainant was a 17-year-old woman living in the city of Edmonton. She met the accused respondent Ewanchuk on the afternoon of June 2, 1994, while walking through the parking lot of the Heritage Shopping Mall with her roommate. The accused, driving a red van towing a trailer, approached the two young women. He struck up a conversation with them. He related that he was in the custom wood-working business and explained that he displayed his work at retail booths in several shopping malls. He said that he was looking for staff to attend his displays, and asked whether the young women were looking for work. The complainant's friend answered that they were, at which point the accused asked to interview her friend privately. She declined, but spoke with the accused beside his van for some period of time about the sort of work he required, and eventually exchanged telephone numbers with the accused.

The following morning the accused telephoned the apartment where the complainant and her friend resided with their boyfriends. The complainant answered the phone. She told the accused that her friend was still asleep. When he learned this, the accused asked the complainant if she was interested in a job. She indicated that she was, and they met a short time later, again in the Heritage Mall parking lot. At the accused's suggestion, the interview took place in his van. In the words of the complainant, a "very business-like, polite" conversation took place. Some time later, the complainant asked if she could smoke a cigarette, and the accused suggested that they move outside since he was allergic to cigarette smoke. Once outside the van, he asked the complainant if she would like to see some of his work, which was kept inside the trailer attached to his van, and she indicated that she would.

The complainant entered the trailer, purposely leaving the door open behind her. The accused followed her in, and closed the door in a way which made the complainant think that he had locked it. There is no evidence whether the door was actually locked, but the complainant stated that she became frightened at this point. Once inside the trailer, the complainant and the accused sat down side-by-side on the floor of the trailer. They spoke and looked through a portfolio of his work. This lasted 10 to 15 minutes, after which the conversation turned to more personal matters.

During the time in the trailer the accused was quite tactile with the complainant, touching her hand, arms and shoulder as he spoke. At some point the accused said that he was feeling tense and asked the complainant to give him a massage. The complainant complied, massaging the accused's shoulders for a few minutes. After she stopped, he asked her to move in front of him so that he could massage her, which she did. The accused then massaged the complainant's shoulders and arms while they continued talking. During this mutual massaging the accused repeatedly told the complainant to relax, and that she should not be afraid. As the massage progressed, the accused attempted to initiate more intimate contact. The complainant stated that, "he started to try to massage around my stomach, and he brought his hands up around — or underneath my breasts, and he started to get quite close up there, so I used my elbows to push in between, and I said, "No".

The accused stopped immediately, but shortly thereafter resumed non-sexual massaging, to which the complainant also said, "No". The accused again stopped, and said, "See, I'm a nice guy. It's okay."

The accused then asked the complainant to turn and face him. She did so, and he began massaging her feet. His touching progressed from her feet up to her inner thigh and pelvic area. The complainant did not want the accused to touch her in this way, but said nothing as she said she was afraid that any resistance would prompt the accused to become violent. Although the accused never used or threatened any force, the complainant testified that she did not want to "egg [him] on". As the contact progressed, the accused laid himself heavily on top of the complainant and began grinding his pelvic area against hers. The complainant testified that the accused asserted, "that he could get me so horny so that I would want it so bad, and he wouldn't give it to me because he had self-control".

The complainant did not move or reciprocate the contact. The accused asked her to put her hands across his back, but she did not; instead she lay "bone straight". After less than a minute of this the complainant asked the accused to stop. "I said, Just please stop. And so he stopped". The accused again told the complainant not to be afraid, and asked her if she trusted that he wouldn't hurt her. In her words, the complainant said, "Yes, I trust that you won't hurt me." On the stand she stated that she was afraid throughout, and only responded to the accused in this way because she was fearful that a negative answer would provoke him to use force.

After this brief exchange, the accused went to hug the complainant and, as he did so, he laid on top of her again, continuing the pelvic grinding. He also began moving his hands on the complainant's inner thigh, inside her shorts, for a short time. While still on top of her the accused began to fumble with his shorts and took out his penis. At this point the complainant again asked the accused to desist, saying, "No, stop."

Again, the accused stopped immediately, got off the complainant, smiled at her and said something to the effect of, "It's okay. See, I'm a nice guy, I stopped." At this point the accused again hugged the complainant lightly before opening up his wallet and removing a $100 bill, which he gave to the complainant. She testified that the accused said that the $100 was for the massage and that he told her not to tell anyone about it. He made some reference to another female employee with whom he also had a very close and friendly relationship, and said that he hoped to get together with the complainant again.

Shortly after the exchange of the money the complainant said that she had to go. The accused opened the door and the complainant stepped out. Some further conversation ensued outside the trailer before the complainant finally left and walked home. On her return home the complainant was emotionally distraught and contacted the police.

At some point during the encounter the accused provided the complainant with a brochure describing his woodwork and gave her his name and address, which she wrote on the brochure. The investigating officer used this information to locate the accused at his home, where he was arrested.

B. The Components of sexual assault

A conviction for sexual assault requires proof beyond reasonable doubt of two basic elements, that the accused committed the *actus reus* and that he had the necessary *mens rea*. The *actus reus* of assault is unwanted sexual touching. The *mens rea* is the intention to touch, knowing of, or being reckless of or wilfully blind to, a lack of consent, either by words or actions, from the person being touched.

(1) Actus Reus

The crime of sexual assault is only indirectly defined in the *Criminal Code*, R.S.C., 1985, c. C-46. The offence is comprised of an assault within any one of the definitions in s. 265(1) of the *Code*, which is committed in circumstances of a sexual nature, such that the sexual integrity of the victim is violated: see *R. v. S. (P.L.)*, [1991] 1 S.C.R. 909.

. . . .

The *actus reus* of sexual assault is established by the proof of three elements: (i) touching, (ii) the sexual nature of the contact, and (iii) the absence of consent. The first two of these elements are objective. It is sufficient for the Crown to prove that the accused's actions were voluntary. The sexual nature of the assault is determined objectively; the Crown need not prove that the accused had any *mens rea* with respect to the sexual nature of his or her behaviour: see *R. v. Litchfield*, [1993] 4 S.C.R. 333, and *R. v. Chase*, [1987] 2 S.C.R. 293.

The absence of consent, however, is subjective and determined by reference to the complainant's subjective internal state of mind towards the touching, at the time it occurred: see *R. v. Jensen* (1996), 106 C.C.C. (3d) 430 (Ont. C.A.), at pp. 437-38, aff'd [1997] 1 S.C.R. 304, *R. v. Park*, [1995] 2 S.C.R. 836, at p. 850, per L'Heureux-Dubé J., and D. Stuart, Canadian Criminal Law (3rd ed. 1995), at p. 513.

. . . .

While the complainant's testimony is the only source of direct evidence as to her state of mind, credibility must still be assessed by the trial judge, or jury, in light of all the evidence. It is open to the accused to claim that the complainant's words and actions, before and during the incident, raise a reasonable doubt against her assertion that she, in her mind, did not want the sexual touching to take place. If, however, as occurred in this case, the trial judge believes the complainant that she subjectively did not consent, the Crown has discharged its obligation to prove the absence of consent.

. . . .

(a) "Implied Consent"

Counsel for the respondent submitted that the trier of fact may believe the complainant when she says she did not consent, but still acquit the accused on the basis that her conduct raised a reasonable doubt. Both he and the trial judge refer to this as "implied consent". It follows from the foregoing, however, that the trier of fact may only come to one of two conclusions: the complainant either consented or not. There is no third option. If the trier of fact accepts the complainant's testimony that she did not consent, no matter how strongly her conduct may contradict that claim, the absence of consent is established and the third component of the *actus reus* of sexual assault is proven. The doctrine of implied consent has been recognized in our common law jurisprudence in a variety of contexts but sexual assault is not one of them. There is no defence of implied consent to sexual assault in Canadian law.

(b) Application to the Present Case

In this case, the trial judge accepted the evidence of the complainant that she did not consent. That being so, he then misdirected himself when he considered the actions of the complainant, and not her subjective mental state, in determining the question of consent. As a result, he disregarded his previous finding that all the accused's sexual touching was unwanted. Instead he treated what he perceived as her ambiguous conduct as a failure by the Crown to prove the absence of consent.

As previously mentioned, the trial judge accepted the complainant's testimony that she did not want the accused to touch her, but then treated her conduct as raising a reasonable doubt about consent, described by him as "implied consent". This conclusion was an error. See D. Stuart, Annotation on *R. v. Ewanchuk* (1998), 13 C.R. (5th) 330, where the author points out that consent is a matter of the state of mind of the complainant while belief in consent is, subject to s. 273.2 of the *Code*, a matter of the state of mind of the accused and may raise the defence of honest but mistaken belief in consent.

The finding that the complainant did not want or consent to the sexual touching cannot co-exist with a finding that reasonable doubt exists on the question of consent. The trial judge's acceptance of the complainant's testimony regarding her own state of mind was the end of the matter on this point.

. . . .

(c) Effect of the Complainant's Fear

To be legally effective, consent must be freely given. Therefore, even if the complainant consented, or her conduct raises a reasonable doubt about her non-consent, circumstances may arise which call into question what factors prompted her apparent consent. The *Code* defines a series of conditions under which the law will deem an absence of consent in cases of assault, notwithstanding the complainant's ostensible consent or participation. As enumerated in s. 265(3), these include submission by reason of force, fear, threats, fraud or the exercise of authority, and codify the longstanding common law rule that consent given under fear or duress is ineffective: see G. Williams, *Textbook of Criminal Law* (2nd ed. 1983), at pp. 551-61.

. . . . .

The words of Fish J.A. in *Saint-Laurent v. Hétu*, [1994] R.J.Q. 69 (C.A.), at p. 82, aptly describe the concern which the trier of fact must bear in mind when evaluating the actions of a complainant who claims to have been under fear, fraud or duress:

> "Consent" is . . . stripped of its defining characteristics when it is applied to the submission, non-resistance, non-objection, or even the apparent agreement, of a deceived, unconscious or compelled will.

In these instances the law is interested in a complainant's reasons for choosing to participate in, or ostensibly consent to, the touching in question. In practice, this translates into an examination of the choice the complainant believed she faced. The courts' concern is whether she freely made up her mind about the conduct in question. The relevant section of the *Code* is s. 265(3)(b), which states that there is no consent as a matter of law where the complainant believed that she was choosing between permitting herself to be touched sexually or risking being subject to the application of force.

. . . The trier of fact has to find that the complainant did not want to be touched sexually and made her decision to permit or participate in sexual activity as a result of an honestly held fear. The complainant's fear need not be reasonable, nor must it be communicated to the accused in order for consent to be vitiated. While the plausibility of the alleged fear, and any overt expressions of it, are obviously relevant to assessing the credibility of the complainant's claim that she consented out of fear, the approach is subjective.

Section 265(3) identifies an additional set of circumstances in which the accused's conduct will be culpable. The trial judge only has to consult s. 265(3) in those cases where the complainant has actually chosen to participate in sexual activity, or her ambiguous conduct or submission has given rise to doubt as to the absence of consent. If, as in this case, the complainant's testimony establishes the absence of consent beyond a reasonable doubt, the *actus reus* analysis is complete, and the trial judge should have turned his attention to the accused's perception of the encounter and the question of whether the accused possessed the requisite *mens rea*.

(2) Mens Rea

Sexual assault is a crime of general intent. Therefore, the Crown need only prove that the accused intended to touch the complainant in order to satisfy the basic *mens rea* requirement. See *R. v. Daviault*, [1994] 3 S.C.R. 63.

However, since sexual assault only becomes a crime in the absence of the complainant's consent, the common law recognizes a defence of mistake of fact which removes culpability for those who honestly but mistakenly believed that they had consent to touch the complainant. To do otherwise would result in the injustice of convicting individuals who are morally innocent: see *R. v. Creighton*, [1993] 3 S.C.R. 3. As such, the *mens rea* of sexual assault contains two elements: intention to touch and knowing of, or being reckless of or wilfully blind to, a lack of consent on the part of the person touched. See *Park*, supra, at para. 39.

The accused may challenge the Crown's evidence of *mens rea* by asserting an honest but mistaken belief in consent. The nature of this defence was described in *Pappajohn v. The Queen*, [1980] 2 S.C.R. 120, at p. 148, by Dickson J. (as he then was) (dissenting in the result):

> Mistake is a defence . . . where it prevents an accused from having the mens rea which the law requires for the very crime with which he is charged. Mistake of fact is more accurately seen as a negation of guilty intention than as the affirmation of a positive defence. It avails an accused who acts innocently, pursuant to a flawed perception of the facts, and nonetheless commits the actus reus of the offence. Mistake is a defence though, in the sense that it is raised as an issue by an accused. The Crown is rarely possessed of knowledge of the subjective factors which may have caused an accused to entertain a belief in a fallacious set of facts.

The defence of mistake is simply a denial of *mens rea*. It does not impose any burden of proof upon the accused (see *R. v. Robertson*, [1987] 1 S.C.R. 918, at p. 936) and it is not necessary for the accused to testify in order to raise the issue. Support for the defence may stem from any of the evidence before the court, including, the Crown's case-in-chief and the testimony of the complainant. However, as a practical matter, this defence will usually arise in the evidence called by the accused.

(a) Meaning of "Consent" in the Context of an Honest but Mistaken Belief in Consent

As with the *actus reus* of the offence, consent is an integral component of the *mens rea*, only this time it is considered from the perspective of the accused. Speaking of the *mens rea* of sexual assault in *Park*, supra, at para. 30, L'Heureux-Dubé J. (in her concurring reasons) stated that:

> . . . the mens rea of sexual assault is not only satisfied when it is shown that the accused knew that the complainant was essentially saying "no", but is also satisfied when it is shown that the accused knew that the complainant was essentially not saying "yes".

In order to cloak the accused's actions in moral innocence, the evidence must show that he believed that the complainant communicated consent to engage in the sexual activity in question. A belief by the accused that the complainant, in her own mind wanted him to touch her but did not express that desire, is not a defence. The accused's speculation as to what was going on in the complainant's mind provides no defence.

For the purposes of the *mens rea* analysis, the question is whether the accused believed that he had obtained consent. What matters is whether the accused believed that the complainant effectively said "yes" through her words and/or actions. The statutory definition added to the *Code* by Parliament in 1992 is consistent with the common law:

> 273.1 (1) Subject to subsection (2) and subsection 265(3), "consent" means, for the purposes of sections 271, 272 and 273, the voluntary agreement of the complainant to engage in the sexual activity in question.

There is a difference in the concept of "consent" as it relates to the state of mind of the complainant vis-à-vis the *actus reus* of the offence and the state of mind of the accused in respect of the *mens rea*. For the purposes of the *actus reus*, "consent" means that the complainant in her mind wanted the sexual touching to take place.

In the context of *mens rea* — specifically for the purposes of the honest but mistaken belief in consent — "consent" means that the complainant had affirmatively communicated by words or conduct her agreement to engage in sexual activity with the accused. This distinction should always be borne in mind and the two parts of the analysis kept separate.

(b) Limits on Honest but Mistaken Belief in Consent

Not all beliefs upon which an accused might rely will exculpate him. Consent in relation to the *mens rea* of the accused is limited by both the common law and the provisions of ss. 273.1(2) and 273.2 of the *Code*.

. . . .

For instance, a belief that silence, passivity or ambiguous conduct constitutes consent is a mistake of law, and provides no defence: see *R. v. M. (M.L.)*, [1994] 2 S.C.R. 3. Similarly, an accused cannot rely upon his purported belief that the complainant's expressed lack of agreement to sexual touching in fact constituted an invitation to more persistent or aggressive contact. An accused cannot say that he thought "no meant yes". As Fraser C.J. stated at p. 272 of her dissenting reasons below:

> One "No" will do to put the other person on notice that there is then a problem with "consent". *Once a woman says "No" during the course of sexual activity, the person intent on continued sexual activity with her must then obtain a clear and unequivocal "Yes" before he again touches her in a sexual manner.* [Emphasis in original.]

I take the reasons of Fraser C.J. to mean that an unequivocal "yes" may be given by either the spoken word or by conduct.

Common sense should dictate that, once the complainant has expressed her unwillingness to engage in sexual contact, the accused should make certain that she has truly changed her mind before proceeding with further intimacies. The accused cannot rely on the mere lapse of time or the complainant's silence or equivocal conduct to indicate that there has been a change of heart and that consent now exists, nor can he engage in further sexual touching to "test the waters". Continuing sexual contact after someone has said "No" is, at a minimum, reckless conduct which is not excusable. In *R. v. Esau*, [1997] 2 S.C.R. 777, at para. 79, the Court stated:

> An accused who, due to wilful blindness or recklessness, believes that a complainant . . . in fact consented to the sexual activity at issue is precluded from relying on a defence of honest but mistaken belief in consent, a fact that Parliament has codified: Criminal Code, s. 273.2(a)(ii).

(c) Application to the Facts

In this appeal the accused does not submit that the complainant's clearly articulated "No's" were ambiguous or carried some other meaning. In fact, the accused places great reliance on his having stopped immediately each time the complainant said "no" in order to show that he had no intention to force himself upon her. He therefore knew that the complainant was not consenting on four separate occasions during their encounter.

.   .   .   .

As the accused did not testify, the only evidence before the Court was that of the complainant. She stated that she immediately said "NO" every time the accused touched her sexually, and that she did nothing to encourage him. Her evidence was accepted by the trial judge as credible and sincere. Indeed, the accused relies on the fact that he momentarily stopped his advances each time the complainant said "NO" as evidence of his good intentions. This demonstrates that he understood the complainant's "NO's" to mean precisely that. Therefore, there is nothing on the record to support the accused's claim that he continued to believe her to be consenting, or that he re-established consent before resuming physical contact. The accused did not raise nor does the evidence disclose an air of reality to the defence of honest but mistaken belief in consent to this sexual touching.

The trial record conclusively establishes that the accused's persistent and increasingly serious advances constituted a sexual assault for which he had no defence. But for his errors of law, the trial judge would necessarily have found the accused guilty. In this case, a new trial would not be in the interests of justice.

In her reasons, Justice L'Heureux-Dubé makes reference to s. 273.2(b) of the *Code*. Whether the accused took reasonable steps is a question of fact to be determined by the trier of fact only after the air of reality test has been met. In view of the way the trial and appeal were argued, s. 273.2 (b) did not have to be considered.

. . . .

Cases involving a true misunderstanding between parties to a sexual encounter infrequently arise but are of profound importance to the community's sense of safety and justice. The law must afford women and men alike the peace of mind of knowing that their bodily integrity and autonomy in deciding when and whether to participate in sexual activity will be respected. At the same time, it must protect those who have not been proven guilty from the social stigma attached to sexual offenders.

L'HEUREUX-DUBÉ (GONTHIER J. concurring): —

. . . So pervasive is violence against women throughout the world that the international community adopted in December 18, 1979 (Res. 34/180), in addition to all other human rights instruments, the Convention on the Elimination of All Forms of Discrimination Against Women, Can. T.S. 1982 No. 31, entered into force on September 3, 1981, to which Canada is a party, which has been described as "the definitive international legal instrument requiring respect for and observance of the human rights of women." (R. Cook, "Reservations to the Convention on the Elimination of All Forms of Discrimination Against Women" (1990), 30 Va. J. Int'l L. 643, at p. 643).

. . . .

Our *Charter* is the primary vehicle through which international human rights achieve a domestic effect (see *Slaight Communications Inc. v. Davidson*, [1989] 1 S.C.R. 1038; *R. v. Keegstra*, [1990] 3 S.C.R. 697). In particular, s. 15 (the equality provision) and s. 7 (which guarantees the right to life, security and liberty of the person) embody the notion of respect of human dignity and integrity.

. . . .

I have had the benefit of the reasons of Justice Major in this appeal and I agree generally with his reasons on most issues and with the result that he reaches. However, I wish to add some comments and discuss some of the reasoning of the trial judge and of the majority of the Court of Appeal.

. . . .

This case is not about consent, since none was given. It is about myths and stereotypes . . .

The trial judge believed the complainant and accepted her testimony that she was afraid and he acknowledged her unwillingness to engage in any sexual activity. In addition, there is no doubt that the respondent was aware that the complainant was afraid since he told her repeatedly not to be afraid. The complainant clearly articulated her absence of consent: she said no. Not only did the accused not stop, but after a brief pause, as Fraser C.J. puts it, he went on to an "increased level of sexual activity" to which twice the complainant said no. What could be clearer?

. . . .

In the circumstances of this case, it is difficult to understand how the question of implied consent even arose. Although he found the complainant credible, and accepted her evidence that she said "no" on three occasions and was afraid, the trial judge nonetheless did not take "no" to mean that the complainant did not consent. Rather, he concluded that she implicitly consented and that the Crown had failed to prove lack of consent. This was a fundamental error. As noted by Professor Stuart in Annotation on *R. v. Ewanchuk* (1998), 13 C.R. (5th) 330, at p. 330:

> Both the trial judgment and that of Justice McClung do not make the basic distinction that consent is a matter of the state of mind of the complainant and belief in consent is, subject to s. 273.2 of the Criminal Code, a matter of the state of mind of the accused.

This error does not derive from the findings of fact but from mythical assumptions that when a woman says "no" she is really saying "yes," "try again," or "persuade me." To paraphrase Fraser C.J. at p. 263, it denies women's sexual autonomy and implies that women are "walking around this country in a state of constant consent to sexual activity".

In the Court of Appeal, McClung J.A. compounded the error made by the trial judge. At the outset of his opinion, he stated at p. 245 that "it must be pointed out that the complainant did not present herself to Ewanchuk or enter his trailer in a bonnet and crinolines." He noted, at pp. 245-46, that "she was the mother of a six-month-old baby and that, along with her boyfriend, she shared an apartment with another couple".

Even though McClung J.A. asserted that he had no intention of denigrating the complainant, one might wonder why he felt necessary to point out these aspects of the trial record. Could it be to express that the complainant is not a virgin? Or that she is a person of questionable moral character because she is not married and lives with her boyfriend and another couple? These comments made by an appellate judge help reinforce the myth that under such circumstances, either the complainant is less worthy of belief, she invited the sexual assault, or her sexual experience signals probable consent to further sexual activity. Based on those attributed assumptions, the implication is that if the complainant articulates her lack of consent by saying "no," she really does not mean it and even if she does, her refusal cannot be taken as seriously as if she were a girl of "good" moral character. "Inviting" sexual assault, according to those myths, lessens the guilt of the accused . . .

McClung J.A. writes, at p. 247:

> There is no room to suggest that Ewanchuk knew, yet disregarded, her underlying state of mind as he furthered his <u>romantic intentions</u>. He was not aware of her true state of mind. Indeed, his ignorance about that was what she wanted. The facts, set forth by the trial judge, provide support for the overriding trial finding, couched in terms of consent by implication, that the accused had no proven preparedness to assault the complainant to get what he wanted. [Emphasis added.]

On the contrary, both the fact that Ewanchuk was aware of the complainant's state of mind, as he did indeed stop each time she expressly stated "no," and the trial judge's findings reinforce the obvious conclusion that the accused knew there was no consent. These were two strangers, a young 17-year-old woman attracted by a job offer who found herself trapped in a trailer and a man approximately twice her age and size. This is hardly a scenario one would characterize as reflective of "romantic intentions." It was nothing more than an effort by Ewanchuk to engage the complainant sexually, not romantically.

The expressions used by McClung J.A. to describe the accused's sexual assault, such as "clumsy passes" (p. 246) or "would hardly raise Ewanchuk's stature in the pantheon of chivalric behaviour" (p. 248), are plainly inappropriate in that context as they minimize the importance of the accused's conduct and the reality of sexual aggression against women.

McClung J.A. also concluded that "the sum of the evidence indicates that Ewanchuk's advances to the complainant were far less criminal than hormonal" (p. 250) having found earlier that "every advance he made to her stopped when she spoke against it" and that "[t]here was no evidence of an assault or even its threat" (p. 249). According to this analysis, a man would be free from criminal responsibility for having non-consensual sexual activity whenever he cannot control his hormonal urges. Furthermore, the fact that the accused ignored the complainant's verbal objections to any sexual activity and persisted in escalated sexual contact, grinding his pelvis against hers repeatedly, is more evidence than needed to determine that there was an assault.

Finally, McClung J.A. made this point: "In a less litigious age going too far in the boyfriend's car was better dealt with on site — a well-chosen expletive, a slap in the face or, if necessary, a well directed knee" (p. 250). According to this stereotype, women should use physical force, not resort to courts to "deal with" sexual assaults and it is not the perpetrator's responsibility to ascertain consent, as required by s. 273.2(b), but the women's not only to express an unequivocal "no," but also to fight her way out of such a situation. In that sense, Susan Estrich has noted that "rape is most assuredly not the only crime in which consent is a defense; but it is the only crime that has required the victim to resist physically in order to establish nonconsent" ("Rape" (1986), Yale L.J. 1087, at p. 1090).

.   .   .   .

This case has not dispelled any of the fears I expressed in *Seaboyer*, supra, about the use of myths and stereotypes in dealing with sexual assault complaints (see also Bertha Wilson, "Will Women Judges Really Make a Difference?" (1990), 28 Osgoode Hall L.J. 507). Complainants should be able to rely on a system free from myths and stereotypes, and on a judiciary whose impartiality is not compromised by these biased assumptions. The *Code* was amended in 1983 and in 1992 to eradicate reliance on those assumptions; they should not be permitted to resurface through the stereotypes reflected in the reasons of the majority of the Court of Appeal. It is part of the role of this Court to denounce this kind of language, unfortunately still used today, which not only perpetuates archaic myths and stereotypes about the nature of sexual assaults but also ignores the law.

. . . .

I agree entirely with Chief Justice Fraser that, unless and until an accused first takes reasonable steps to assure that there is consent, the defence of honest but mistaken belief does not arise (see *R. v. Daigle*, [1998] 1 S.C.R. 1220; *Esau*, supra, per McLachlin J. dissenting; and J. McInnes and C. Boyle, "Judging Sexual Assault Law against a Standard of Equality" (1995), 25 U.B.C. L. Rev. 341). In this case, the accused proceeded from massaging to sexual contact without making any inquiry as to whether the complainant consented. Obviously, interpreting the fact that the complainant did not refuse the massage to mean that the accused could further his sexual intentions is not a reasonable step. The accused cannot rely on the complainant's silence or ambiguous conduct to initiate sexual contact. Moreover, where a complainant expresses non-consent, the accused has a corresponding escalating obligation to take additional steps to ascertain consent. Here, despite the complainant's repeated verbal objections, the accused did not take any step to ascertain consent, let alone reasonable ones. Instead, he increased the level of his sexual activity. Therefore, pursuant to s. 273.2(b) Ewanchuk was barred from relying on a belief in consent.

. . . .

McLACHLIN J.: — I agree with the reasons of Justice Major. I also agree with Justice L'Heureux-Dubé that stereotypical assumptions lie be at the heart of what went wrong in this case. The specious defence of implied consent (consent implied by law), as applied in this case, rests on the assumption that unless a woman protests or resists, she should be "deemed" to consent (see L'Heureux-Dubé J.). On appeal, the idea also surfaced that if a woman is not modestly dressed, she is deemed to consent. Such stereotypical assumptions find their roots in many cultures, including our own. They no longer, however, find a place in Canadian law.

Heureux-Dubé J.'s rebuke to McLung J. lead him to protest in press statements. These in turn were the subject of a formal complaint to the Canadian Judicial Council. On May 9, 1999, a panel chaired by Constance Glube, Chief Justice of Nova Scotia, issued a report expressing strong disapproval of the judge's conduct. It did not recommend his removal from office.

What do you think of each of the new limits the Court imposes on the mistaken belief defence? For a critical review see Stuart, *Canadian Criminal Law. A Treatise* (4th ed., 2001) Chapter 4.

The acid test of the new *Ewanchuk* tests will be in borderline cases. A rapist does not have consent and makes no mistake. So, too, with any other sexual predator. But the key question is how the assault doctrines of consent and mistake work out when the situation between the two parties was ambiguous and there is a real issue of whether a sexual assault occurred.

In *Ewanchuk*, Major J. expressed the opinion that ambiguous situations are rare in sexual assault cases:

Cases involving a true misunderstanding between parties to a sexual encounter infrequently arise but are of profound importance to the community's sense of safety and justice (para. 66).

This assessment may be contrasted with that of Justice Casey Hill of the Ontario Court of Justice, General Division, who wrote in a recent unreported judgment in *T.S.*, [1999] O.J. No. 268, (January 25, 1999), Doc. Brampton 2084/98 (Ont. Gen. Div.) as follows:

Ordinarily, people communicate things like consent or no-consent simply and effectively: *The Queen v. Esau*, *per* McLachlin J. Be that as it may, however, we have also acknowledged "the complex and diverse nature of consent" (*The Queen v. Currier*, *per* McLachlin J.) and that the dynamics of a sexual encounter are not infrequently far from simple. In *Regina v. Welch* (1995), 25 O.R. (3d) 665 (C.A.) at 674, Griffiths J.A. referred to "the varying and private nature of sexual relations". As Dickson J. stated in dissent in *Pappajohn v. The Queen* (1980), 52 C.C.C. (2d) 481 (S.C.C.) at 505, there can be many "ambiguous situations" in sexual relationships and there may well be circumstances where each party interprets the situation differently. It has been said that it is difficult to draw clear bright lines in defining human relations particularly those of a consenting sexual nature: *The Queen v. Currier*, *per* Cory J. at para. 102.

It has always seemed obvious that extending the reach of sexual assault laws to include such conduct as unwanted touching would inevitably embroil trial courts in deciding whether to criminalize conduct where the parties actually miscommunicated. This is especially likely in situations where there was first consensual conduct and later, according to the complainant, a withdrawal of consent. The acquittal rates for sexual assault are unknown but widely believed to be relatively high. This also suggests triers of fact are finding ambiguity.

To assess whether the Supreme Court has got the balance right consider the *Ewanchuk* tests in the following problems:

Problem

1. Two teenagers, Jack and Jill, have their first date at the movies. After the movies they go to Jack's apartment for coffee. They talk. Jill tells Jack that she has a boyfriend but also that she is an open, friendly, and affectionate person; and that she often likes to touch people. Jack tells her that he is an open, friendly, and affectionate person; and that he often likes to touch people. They talk more. They touch each other; they hug. At some point Jack kisses Jill. Jack thinks she has responded positively to his sexual advance although nothing was said. Jill did not welcome the kiss and felt she did nothing to encourage Jack. She was not scared of him. She admits that at that point she opened two buttons of her blouse but this was because she felt claustrophobic and nothing else. Jack felt he was being encouraged by her action and touched her breasts. Jill slaps him.

Problem

2. The same as problem 1, except that it was Jill who kissed Jack.

Problem

3. The accused is charged with sexual assault. The accounts of the complainant and the accused varied significantly. The complainant was 15 years old, a ward of the Children's Aid Society and living in a group home. The accused was 23 years old, and lived in a bachelor apartment. They met at a bus stop, chatted briefly and then agreed to walk to the accused's apartment and drink beer together. On the way from the beer store the accused made flirtatious and sexually suggestive remarks. When the two returned to the apartment, they sat and drank beer for some time. The complainant testified that she became increasingly withdrawn and uncomfortable as the evening progressed and that this frustrated the accused. The accused denied this.

At one point, the complainant got up to go to the bathroom, and when she returned she found the accused lying on the bed. At his urging she joined him on the bed, although she said she felt awkward. The accused testified that the complainant had gone to get massage oil and then allowed him to massage her, which the complainant denied. The accused then began to play with the complainant's hair, and used his hand to lay her down on the bed. They then began to have intercourse and, at some time during that intercourse, he asked her whether he should use a condom, and, according to the accused, the complainant said that that would be a good idea. He then went into the bathroom to put on a condom and returned. However, on his account, he had difficulty sustaining an erection and no further intercourse took place. He then manually stimulated himself and he and the complainant went to sleep. The complainant testified that there was an initial brief period of intercourse, followed by her becoming quiet and withdrawn, followed by a second encounter. On cross-examination, the accused acknowledged that at some time the complainant had said "No", but he took that as meaning "No" without a condom. The accused also testified that he told the complainant, at some point, that he knew when a woman said no, she meant no. The complainant testified that she said "No" on the earlier occasion as the accused was trying to take her pants off, but the accused testified that she took off her own pants. The trial judge found that "it is common ground that she did say 'No' at one stage, although, on the evidence, it is not clear to me just when that was said and under what circumstances". The trial judge found that the complainant was not an active participant in the sexual activity and that in her mind, she had decided she didn't want to have sexual relations with the accused that night. Compare *O. (M.)* (2000), 36 C.R. (5th) 258 (S.C.C.).

Problem

4. The accused is charged with sexual assault. The accused and the complainant went to a birthday party at a private residence.

The complainant arrived at the party at about 12:30 a.m. with a male friend. At around 4 a.m. she felt she was intoxicated and unable to drive. She decided to stay the night and lay down on a couch in the living-room. She testified she later "woke up to intercourse". The person with whom she was having intercourse was behind her. At first she thought it was the friend with whom she had come to the party and with whom she had a relationship. When she turned round and saw it was the accused, she was in shock. She got up and left. She testified that when she awoke her pants and underwear had been pulled down. She was unable to provide an explanation as to how this had occurred or whether she had assisted.

The accused testified that he too tried to go to sleep on the couch at about 4 a.m. He testified that the complainant, some time after daylight, started to rub herself against him. He asked her if she wanted to have sex and she said "yes". According to the accused she pulled down her clothes and consented to intercourse. He was surprised she got up and left the house without saying anything.

Is there an air of reality to the accused's alternative defences of consent and mistaken belief? If so, should the defence or defences succeed? Are you satisfied with result?

Compare *R. v. Osvath* (1996), 46 C.R. (4th) 124 (Ont. C.A.), appeal quashed by the majority of the Supreme Court on the basis that the decision did not involve an error of law: (1997) 4 C.R. (5th) (S.C.C.).

Would it have been preferable for Parliament to have created a separate offence of negligent sexual assault penalizing unreasonable behaviour in a sexual context with a maximum penalty of five years' imprisonment? Would the possibility of guilty pleas to this lesser offence be an advantage? Should the distinction between deliberate and negligent conduct be left to sentencing? Should it make a difference?

For the case for a separate negligent sexual assault offence see Stuart, "Sexual Assault Substantive Issues Before and After Bill C-49" (1993), 35 Crim. L.Q. 1.

After *Creighton*, challenges based on assertion of a constitutional requirement of fault now seem far less likely to succeed. There would nevertheless appear to be at least four possible *Charter* challenges to Bill C-49's substantive regime. Of course, given the seriousness of the problem of sexual violence, if any of these challenges were accepted the Court might well wish to consider saving Parliament's scheme as a demonstrably justified reasonable limit under s. 1.

(1) Section 273.2's exclusion of any intoxication defence imposes absolute liability which threatens the liberty interest.

It is quite clear that any penal law that imposes absolute liability will violate s. 7 of the *Charter* and be declared of no force and effect where there is a potential deprivation of the liberty interest. Absolute liability occurs where a conviction can be based on mere proof of the act without any necessity to prove any form of fault on the part of the accused. Absolute liability seems to occur where the extreme drunkenness of the accused is said to be irrelevant but that of the victim determinative. Such a challenge succeeded in the contoversial decision of the Supreme Court in *Daviault*, considered later under the defence of intoxication.

(2) Sexual assault is one of those few offences requiring a minimum degree of *mens rea* in the form of subjective foresight.

The Supreme Court has identified a few offences which have a constitutional requirement of subjective foresight. It placed considerable emphasis on the special nature of the stigma attached and the penalties available. Thus far the list of offences is short. The criterion of stigma has been often criticized as an inadequate and unreliable test but if it remains the discriminating factor, is sexual assault an offence calling for such special treatment?

(3) The duty to take reasonable steps in s. 273.2 is an objective standard which is unconstitutional because the legislation does not require a marked departure from the objective norm.

This argument flows from *Creighton*. Of course, the offence could be read down as requiring the marked departure standard. There could also be a strong argument that one engaging in sexual conduct without taking reasonable steps to ascertain whether there was consent has necessarily markedly departed from the expected norm. Furthermore, the section refers to "in the circumstances known to the accused at the time" and this would appear to allow for some individual factors and thus be a less severe objective standard than that imposed by the majority in *Creighton*.

(4) Section 273.2 is unconstitutional because it violates the constitutional principle that those causing harm intentionally must be punished more severely than those causing harm unintentionally.

This principle, ackowledged and applied in *Creighton*, is sound and should be boldly asserted by all Judges. In *Creighton*, the flexible penalty for manslaughter was held to satisfy the *Charter* requirement. This suggests that the new sexual assault scheme will also survive. However, there may be a difference. While the maximum penalty for sexual assault remains the same, Parliament has criminalized, in the same prohibition carrying the same penalty, one who is deliberately aware of a risk and one who was acting unreasonably. The new sexual assault scheme could be struck down or at least read down to ensure that these fundamental principles are respected. The key determination of whether the actor was deliberate or negligent should be made at trial and not left to the uncertain exercise of sentencing.

Do you think that any of these *Charter* arguments should succeed?

Prior to *Ewanchuk*, the Ontario Court of Appeal interpreted s. 273.2(*b*) and held it to be constitutional:

R. v. DARRACH

(1998), 122 C.C.C. (3d) 225, 13 C.R. (5th) 283 (Ont. C.A.), affirmed [2000] 2
S.C.R. 443, 36 C.R. (5th) 223, 148 C.C.C. (3d) 97

MORDEN A.C.J.O. (OSBORNE and DOHERTY JJ.A. concurring): —

With respect to the challenge [to s. 273.2(b)] based on s. 7, I am far from satisfied that sexual assault is one of those "very few" offences (*R. v. Vaillancourt*, [1987] 2 S.C.R. 636 (S.C.C.), at 653) which carries such a stigma that its *mens rea* component must be one of subjectivity. See Hogg, *Constitutional Law of Canada* (1992), loose-leaf ed., Vol. 2 at pp. 44-34 to 44-35. I say this because: it is an offence of general intent; it can be prosecuted by way of summary conviction; it is a generic offence which covers a broad range of conduct, some of which may be very minor compared to other offences; there is no minimum penalty, the maximum penalty is 10 years, and within this range the sentence can be tailored to reflect the moral opprobrium of both the offence and the offender. See *R. v. Creighton*, [1993] 3 S.C.R. 3 (S.C.C.), particularly at pp. 48-49, with respect to the offence of manslaughter. Further, I accept that the stigma characterization has been fairly criticized as being a most unstable one for making important constitutional decisions on the applicability of s. 7 of the *Charter* to the substantive elements of offences. See, for example, Hogg, *Constitutional Law of Canada* (1992) loose-leaf ed., at p. 44-35 and Stuart, *Charter Justice in Canadian Criminal Law*, 2nd ed. (1996) at p. 74.

Notwithstanding the foregoing reservations, I am prepared to decide this issue on the basis that the offence of sexual assault carries with it a sufficient social stigma as to require a subjective fault requirement on the part of the accused person. In my view, notwithstanding s. 273.2(b), the offence is still largely one based on subjective fault — at least to a level that would satisfy constitutional requirements.

No doubt, the provision can be regarded as introducing an objective component into the mental element of the offence but it is one which, in itself, is a modified one. It is personalized according to the subjective awareness of the accused at the time. The accused is to "take reasonable steps, *in the circumstances known to the accused at the time*, to ascertain that the complainant was consenting". In other words, the accused is not under an obligation to determine all the relevant circumstances — the issue is what he actually knew, not what he ought to have known.

In addition, while the provision requires reasonable steps, it does not require that *all* reasonable steps be taken, as it did in the first version of the bill (Bill C-49, s. 1) that resulted in s. 273.2 and as does s. 150.1(4) of the *Criminal Code*, which is referred to in the judgment of the Supreme Court of Canada in *R. v. Nguyen*, [1990] 2 S.C.R. 906 (S.C.C.) at 922 and 925. Clearly, "all reasonable steps" imposes a more onerous burden than that in s. 273.2(b). I, of course, do not intend to express any view on the constitutionality of s. 150.1(4).

The subjective *mens rea* component of the offence remains largely intact. The provision does not require that a mistaken belief in consent must be reasonable in order to exculpate. The provision merely requires that a person about to engage in sexual activity take "reasonable steps . . . to ascertain that the complainant was consenting." Were a person to take reasonable steps, and nonetheless make an unreasonable mistake about the presence of consent, he or she would be entitled to ask the trier of fact to acquit on this basis.

The extent to which the provision alters principles of liability underlying the offence of sexual assault is indicated in the reasons of McLachlin J. in *R. v. Esau* (1997), 116 C.C.C. (3d) 289 (S.C.C.) at 314. Although the statement is in a dissenting judgment I do not think that there is any proposition in the majority judgment of Major J. at variance with it. McLachlin J. said:

> A person is not entitled to take ambiguity as the equivalent of consent. If a person, acting honestly and without wilful blindness, perceives his companion's conduct as ambiguous or unclear, his duty is to abstain or obtain clarification on the issue of consent. This appears to be the rule at common law. In this situation, to use the words of Lord Cross of Chelsea in *Morgan, supra*, [[1976] A.C. 182] at p. 203, "it is only fair to the woman and not in the least unfair to the man that he should be under a duty to take reasonable care to ascertain that she is consenting to the intercourse and be at risk of a prosecution if he fails to take such care". As Glanville Williams, *Textbook of Criminal Law* (London: Stevens & Sons, 1978), at p. 101, put it: "the defendant is guilty if he realized the woman might not be consenting and took no steps to find out".

Following this quotation, she said at pp. 314-15:

> I note that Parliament has affirmed this common sense proposition in enacting s. 273.2 of the *Criminal Code* of Canada which states that "[i]t is not a defence to a charge [of sexual assault] that the accused believed that the complainant consented to the activity that forms the subject-matter of the charge, where . . . the accused did not take reasonable steps, in the circumstances known to the accused at the time, to ascertain that the complainant was consenting". See also *R. v. Darrach* (1994), 17 O.R. (3d) 481 (Prov. Div.) [the judgment under appeal before this court]. The question is whether the defendant at bar, properly attentive to the issue of consent (i.e., not wilfully blind), could have, in light of the ambiguity, honestly concluded that the complainant had the capacity and was consenting to the sexual activity.

Finally, having regard to the basic rationale underlying constitutionally mandated fault requirements that it is wrong to punish a person who is "morally innocent" (*Reference re s. 94(2) of the Motor Vehicle Act (British Columbia)* (1985), 23 C.C.C. (3d) 289 (S.C.C.) at 311), it is difficult to contemplate that a man who has sexual intercourse with a woman who has not consented is morally innocent if he has not taken reasonable steps to ascertain that she was consenting.

. . . .

It is strange that the duty to take reasonable steps in s. 273.2(*b*) was not considered when *Darrach* reached the Supreme Court or by the majority in *Ewanchuk*. There are undoubted difficulties in interpreting s. 273.2(*b*), which clearly has subjective and objective elements and was drafted to demand that reasonable steps be taken but not necessarily all steps that could be imagined. In *Malcolm* (2000), 35 C.R. (5th) 365, 147 C.C.C. (3d) 34 (Man. C.A.), Madam Justice Helper, speaking for the Manitoba Court of Appeal, recently carefully reviewed case law and writings on s. 273.2(*b*) and arrived at a commendably clear test:

> Section 273.2(b) requires the court to apply a quasi-objective test to the situation. First, the circumstances known to the accused must be ascertained. Then, the issue which arises is, if a reasonable man was aware of the same circumstances, would he take further steps before proceeding with the sexual activity? If the answer is yes, and the accused has not taken further steps, then the accused is not entitled to the defence of honest belief in consent. If the answer is no, or even maybe, then the accused would not be required to take further steps and the defence will apply. (C.R. at 373, para. 24.)

The Court held that a new trial had to be ordered where a trial judge had acquitted on the basis of mistaken belief defence without considering the reasonable steps requirement. After a night of partying and drinking, without any invitation to so do, the accused entered the complainant's bedroom while she was sleeping, knowing that she was married to a close friend. He did not engage in any conversation with her. He stated that by her conduct, he believed she wanted to have sexual intercourse with him. Surely in such a situation, the Court had to be satisfied that the accused took reasonable steps to ascertain that the complainant was consenting to that sexual activity.

Some commentators express concern that placing rape in the same category as sexual touching, including an unwanted kiss, has trivialized rape. Some view rape as more than a crime of violence:

CATHERINE MCKINNON, FEMINISM, MARXISM AND THE STATE: TOWARDS FEMINIST JURISPRUDENCE

(1983), 8 Signs: Journal of Women in Culture and Society 635 at 646-647

Feminists have reconceived rape as central to women's condition in two ways. Some see rape as an act of violence, not sexuality, the threat of which intimidates all women. Others see rape, including its violence, as an expression of male sexuality, the social imperatives of which define all women. . . . The more feminist view to me, one which derives from victims' experiences, sees sexuality as a social sphere of male power of which forced sex is paradigmatic. Rape is not less sexual for being violent: to the extent that coercion has become integral to male sexuality, rape may be sexual to the degree that, and because, it is violent.

The point of defining rape as "violence not sex" or "violence against women" has been to separate sexuality from gender in order to affirm sex (heterosexuality) while rejecting violence (rape). The problem remains what it has always been: telling the difference. The convergence of sexuality with violence, long used at law to deny the reality of women's violation, is recognized by rape survivors, with a difference: where the legal system has seen the intercourse in rape, victims see the rape in intercourse. The uncoerced context for sexual expression becomes as elusive as the physical acts come to feel indistinguishable. Instead of asking, what is the violation of rape, what if we ask, what is the nonviolation of intercourse? To tell what is wrong with rape, explain what is right about sex. If this, in turn, is difficult, the difficulty is as instructive as the difficulty men have in telling the difference when women see one. Perhaps the wrong of rape has proven so difficult to articulate because the unquestionable starting point has been that rape is definable as distinct from intercourse, when for women it is difficult to distinguish them under conditions of male domination.

KATIE ROIPHE, RAPE HYPE BETRAYS FEMINISM

New York Times Magazine, June 13, 1993

People have asked me if I have ever been date-raped. And thinking back on complicated nights, on too many glasses of wine, on strange and familiar beds, I would have to say yes. With such a sweeping definition of rape, I wonder how many people there are, male or female, who haven't been date-raped at one point or another. People pressure and manipulate and cajole each other into all sorts of things all of the time.

With their expansive version of rape, rape-crisis feminists are inventing a kinder, gentler sexuality. Beneath the broad definition of rape, these feminists are endorsing their own utopian vision of sexual relations: sex without struggle, sex without power, sex without persuasion, sex without pursuit. If verbal coercion constitutes rape, then the word rape itself expands to include any kind of sex a woman experiences as negative.

Experience since 1983 suggests that rape prosecutions are now routinely prosecuted at the lowest level of sexual assault, as sexual assault *simpliciter*. The problem is that the second category under s. 272 requires proof of bodily harm, a threat or the use of a weapon. This may be difficult to prove in many acquaintance-rape situations where there may be no physical injury such as bruises.

In *B. (W.P.)* (1992), 13 C.R. (4th) 281 (Ont. Prov. Ct.), Judge Cole decided on his own motion to commit an accused charged with sexual assault *simpliciter* to trial on the more serious offence of sexual assault causing bodily harm. He utilized the recent ruling in *R. v. McCraw*, [1991] 3 S.C.R. 72, where the Supreme Court of Canada interpreted bodily harm to include psychological injury. Judge Cole recognizes that *McCraw* was reached in the different context of s. 264.1(1)(*a*), involving the crime of threatening serious bodily harm, but holds that the Supreme Court clearly intended to make a general pronouncement.

There would appear to be dangers in the approach of Judge Cole. He holds that Judges at preliminary inquiries and at trial must be satisfied that there is evidence of psychological harm and that it is non-trivial. This may well have the indirect effect of compelling victims to testify as to the consequences of the assault and to be submitted to cross-examination as to the extent of injury. In this sense, the victim will be back on trial once again. Another problem is that it is difficult to see how any form of sexual assault will not involve at least some psychological harm. If this is true, sexual assault *simpliciter* will have ceased to exist by judicial fiat.

Should any form of attempted penetration of any orifice become a new category placed in the second level of sexual assault, where the maximum penalty is raised from 10 to 14 years. What shall the offence be called?

The amendment would emphasize the seriousness of all rapes and make it unnecessary and indeed irrelevant to hear evidence as to the consequences for the victim. If rapists were again singled out for special legal treatment it would be much easier to track and assess responses to rape. At present rape statistics are not separated from those for other types of sexual assault.

In its controversial decision in *R. v. O'Connor* (1995), 44 C.R. (4th) 1, 103 C.C.C. (3d) 1, [1995] 4 S.C.R. 411, respecting defence access to medical records of sexual assault complaints, the Court unanimously decided that the right of the accused to full answer and defence should be weighed against the privacy rights of complainants which were constitutionally protected under ss. 7 and 8 of the *Charter*. However a 5-4 majority refused to recognize s. 15 equality rights for such complainants. Parliament, in Bill C-49, and in Bill C-72 in response to *Daviault*, see later, and in its proposed Bill in response to *O'Connor*, invokes in aid in preambles, equality rights of women and children. Recently feminist commentators have voiced increasing frustration at the courts for not recognizing equality rights for victims.

Recognition of equality rights for sexual assault complainants came with a revised composition of the Court in *Mills*, [1999] 3 S.C.R. 668, 28 C.R. (5th) 207, 139 C.C.C. (3d) 321 (S.C.C.). When it came to establish a s. 15 right to equality, the Court proceeded by mere assertion. Particularly stunning is the lack of any reference to the ten-part test for judging s. 15 claims established in *Law v. Canada (Minister of Human Resources Development)*, [1999] 1 S.C.R. 497 (S.C.C.), by Justice Iacobucci J. for a unanimous Court, as recently as March, 1999. The Court in *Law* set out to describe basic principles under which courts are to analyze claims of discrimination under s. 15. The essence of the *Law* test is that there is in fact no *Charter* guarantee of equality per se. The guarantee is against discrimination within the meaning of s. 15. This is set out in part 3 of *Law* as follows:

(3) Accordingly, a court that is called upon to determine a discrimination claim under s. 15(1) should make the following three broad inquiries:

A. Does the impugned law (a) draw a formal distinction between the claimant and others on the basis of one or more personal characteristics, or (b) fail to take into account the claimant's already disadvantaged position within Canadian society resulting in substantively differential treatment between the claimant and others on the basis of one or more personal characteristics?

B. Is the claimant subject to differential treatment based on one or more enumerated and analogous grounds?

and

C. Does the differential treatment discriminate, by imposing a burden upon or withholding a benefit from the claimant in a manner which reflects the stereotypical application of presumed group or personal characteristics, or which otherwise has the effect of perpetuating or promoting the view that the individual is less capable or worthy of recognition or value as a human being or as a member of Canadian society, equally deserving of concern, respect, and consideration? (para 88).

The Court in *Law* also requires careful identification of "one or more relevant comparators", discrimination on an enumerated or analogous ground and a consideration of context. Why then did the Court in *Mills* not apply any of this careful analysis? In *Law*, Iacobucci J. did indicate that they were guidelines for analysis and not to be interpreted as a rigid test. He certainly didn't suggest they could be ignored. It would clearly be an error of law for lower courts to do so. Is the comparator group in *Mills* all other victims of crime or is it male victims of sexual assault? It surely couldn't be the accused given that the context is a criminal trial where the issue is punishment rather than compensation. Is the violation discrimination by gender or age or is it an analogous ground because complainants in sexual assault cases have been discriminated against through myths and stereotypical views?

The implications of an enforceable s. 15 claim for complainants in sexual assault cases is left unexplored. The policy issues are far wider than establishing rights for protection of therapeutic and other records of complainants. Can complainants now seek status to be represented throughout a sexual assault trial? How about rights to cross-examine the accused, to challenge the similar fact evidence rule or to reverse the presumption of innocence?

See, further, Stuart, *Charter Justice in Canadian Criminal Law* (3rd. ed., 2001) Chapters 1 and 10.

Chapter 5

MISTAKE

Mistake of Fact

On the issue of whether a mistake of fact is a defence, *Pappajohn v. R.* (see previous chapter) is still the leading decision. Chief Justice Dickson there decided for the majority that a mistake of fact defence constitutes a denial that the Crown has proved the fault element. It follows that, in the absence of statutory wording to the contrary:

1. Where there is a subjective *mens rea* requirement the mistake need merely be honestly held with reasonableness only relevant to assessment of credibility;
2. Where the fault element requires objective negligence, the mistake must be both honest and reasonable;
3. Where there is a due diligence defence, the mistake must be both honest and reasonable, with an onus of proof on the accused in the case of regulatory offences; and
4. Where the offence is one of absolute liability, mistake of fact is not a defence.

The fourth situation may raise a constitutional challenge.

Until repealed in 1988 it was an offence, often known as statutory rape, to have sexual intercourse with a girl under 14 even if she consented or, indeed, even if she was the initiating partner. The provision was as follows:

> 146. (1) Every male person who has sexual intercourse with a female person who
> (a) is not his wife, and
> (b) is under the age of 14 years,
> whether or not he believes that she is 14 years of age or more, is guilty of an indictable offence and is liable to imprisonment for life. [am. 1972, c. 13, s. 70]

The express exclusion of the defence of mistake as to age of the victim was challenged under s. 7 of the *Charter*.

R. v. HESS; R. v. NGUYEN

[1990] 2 S.C.R. 906, 79 C.R. (3d) 332, 59 C.C.C. (3d) 161

H and N were both charged with sexual intercourse with a female person under the age of 14 under what was then s. 146(1) of the *Criminal Code* (since repealed). In the case of H, the trial Judge quashed the indictment on the ground that s. 146(1) violated s. 15 of the *Charter*. The Ontario Court of Appeal reversed the decision and ordered a new trial. In the case of N, the trial Judge convicted. The conviction was upheld by the Manitoba Court of Appeal which found that there had been no violation of s. 15 and that although s. 146(1) breached s. 7 of the *Charter*, that breach was saved by s. 1. The accused appealed and the appeals were heard together.

WILSON J. (LAMER C.J.C., LA FOREST and L'HEUREUX-DUBÉ JJ. concurring): — I have had the advantage of reading the reasons of my colleague Justice McLachlin. While I agree that s. 146(1) of the *Criminal Code of Canada* (as it read in May 1985) infringes s. 7 of the *Canadian Charter of Rights and Freedoms*, in my view the impugned provision is not saved by s. 1 of the *Charter*. I am also of the view that s. 146(1) does not trigger s. 15(1) of the *Charter*.

. . . .

Section 146(1) of the *Code* makes it an indictable offence punishable by a maximum of life imprisonment for a man to have sexual intercourse with a female under the age of 14 who is not his wife. The provision expressly removes the defence that the accused bona fide believed that the female was 14 years of age or older. An accused may not resort to the defence of mistake of fact, a defence which the principles set out in *R. v. Sault Ste. Marie (City)* . . . and *Pappajohn v. R.* . . ., make clear would normally be available. These cases provide that absent a legislative decision to eliminate the *mens rea* requirement, where one is dealing with a "true" criminal offence as opposed to a "public welfare" offence of the kind seen in *Sault Ste. Marie*, the Crown must prove *mens rea* (*i.e.*, "some positive state of mind such as intent, knowledge or recklessness") either by an inference from the nature of the act committed or by additional evidence (per Dickson J. (as he then was) in *Sault Ste. Marie*, at p. 1325).

. . . .

[I]t seems to me particularly important to reiterate that long before the *Charter* was enacted our system of law had a profound commitment to the principle that the innocent should not be punished.

Even the most cursory review of the history of the doctrine of *mens rea* confirms this observation and reveals that the doctrine is an integral and indispensable feature of our criminal law.

. . . .

The doctrine of *mens rea* reflects the conviction that a person should not be punished unless that person knew that he was committing the prohibited act or would have known that he was committing the prohibited act if, as Stroud put it, "he had given to his conduct, and to the circumstances, that degree of attention which the law requires, and which he is capable of giving".

Our commitment to the principle that those who did not intend to commit harm and who took all reasonable precautions to ensure that they did not commit an offence should not be imprisoned stems from an acute awareness that to imprison a "mentally innocent" person is to inflict a grave injury on that person's dignity and sense of worth. Where that person's beliefs and his actions leading up to the commission of the prohibited act are treated as completely irrelevant in the face of the state's pronouncement that he must automatically be incarcerated for having done the prohibited act, that person is treated as little more than a means to an end. That person is in essence told that because of an overriding social or moral objective he must lose his freedom even although he took all reasonable precautions to ensure that no offence was committed.

Prior to the *Charter*, Parliament had to use express statutory language in order to displace the requirement that the prosecutor prove *mens rea*. With the advent of the *Charter*, Parliament must now be prepared to show that a provision that purports to make it unnecessary for the Crown to prove *mens rea* and that does not provide an accused, at a minimum, with a due diligence defence is a reasonable limit that can be demonstrably justified in a free and democratic society. I therefore turn to s. 1 of the *Charter*.

. . . .

(iii) *Minimal Impairment and Proportionality*

When the respondents turn to the question whether the impugned provision impairs the right as little as possible, they assert that the defence of due diligence or reasonable belief would not provide as effective a deterrent to men who might wish to engage in sexual intercourse with a female under 14 as the removal of all defences based on the accused's lack of knowledge of the victim's age. They also submit that the fact that Parliament has chosen to replace s. 146(1) with a provision that allows for a due diligence defence does not mean that one cannot justify s. 146(1) as a reasonable limit on s. 7 of the *Charter*. I note that Justice McLachlin not only accepts these submissions but that she is also of the view that in those instances where an accused is truly mentally innocent this factor may be taken into account in the sentence [p. 327]: "if . . . persuaded that the accused was truly morally blameless, he may be set free: see s. 663 (now s. 737) of the *Criminal Code*".

I think it useful to consider these arguments under three separate headings.

(a) The Deterrence Argument

The respondents place a great deal of weight on arguments about deterrence in their analysis of whether the impugned provision is rationally connected to the legislative objective and in their submissions with respect to the proportionality test set out in *Oakes*. . . .[T]he premise on which the deterrence arguments are based is not a strong one since it assumes that before having sexual intercourse with a young girl the accused, including a teen-aged accused, will in fact address his mind to a fairly obscure provision of the *Code*.

But if I am wrong in this, it seems to me that any deterrence value that s. 146(1) might have would only protect a narrow sub-set of the group that s. 146(1) addresses. Whatever deterrence value the fear of making a mistake might have would only protect that group of young females close enough to the age of 14 that a mistake as to whether they were under or over 14 was a realistic possibility.

. . . .

More importantly, the deterrent effect of the rule cannot readily be documented and the respondents have not submitted *any* evidence to support their deterrence argument. Where one is dealing with the potential for life imprisonment it is not good enough, in my view, to rely on intuition and speculation about the potential deterrent effect of an absolute liability offence. We need concrete and persuasive evidence to support the argument.

. . . .

The respondents contend that all that a person need do to avoid the risk of conviction is to refrain from having sex with a young girl unless he is sure that she is over fourteen. But this begs the question: what if he is sure that she is over 14 but turns out to be wrong? This argument boils down to the proposition that all that a person who has made a mistake of fact needs to do to avoid the risk of conviction is to make sure that he is not making a mistake of fact. The argument would appear to be somewhat circular.

This point leads me to another, more fundamental, problem with the deterrence argument, one that Dickson J. identified in *Sault Ste. Marie*. I noted in connection with my s. 7 analysis that the criminal law has come to recognize that punishing the mentally innocent with a view to advancing particular objectives is fundamentally unfair. It is to use the innocent as a means to an end. While utilitarian reasoning may at one time have been acceptable, it is my view that when we are dealing with the potential for life imprisonment it has no place in a free and democratic society. Thus, even if there were some substance to the premise on which the deterrence argument is based, the argument would still, in my opinion, lead to a fundamentally unfair state of affairs.

(b) Sentencing

Justice McLachlin recognizes that there *is* something troubling about subjecting someone who has made a genuine mistake of fact to life imprisonment. She feels that mental innocence may be taken into account when sentencing the accused. It seems to me that her discomfort with the idea of incarcerating the mentally innocent for as extended a period as the mentally guilty is entirely natural. But in my view, rather than work in favour of s. 146(1), this serves to highlight the weaknesses of arguments upholding the linking of life imprisonment to an absolute liability offence. Indeed, it seems to me that my colleague implicitly accepts that there *should* be some correlation between moral blame and punishment.

But one cannot leave questions of mental innocence to the sentencing process. The legislature must take into account the implications of the distinction between the mentally innocent and the mentally guilty when drafting legislation. Any flaws in the provision cannot be justified by arguments that ask us to have faith that the prosecutor and judge will take these flaws into account when deciding how the accused will be punished. Reliance on prosecutorial or judicial discretion to mitigate the harshness of an unjust law will provide little comfort to the mentally innocent and cannot, in my view, serve to justify a fundamentally unsound provision.

(c) Section 150.1(4) of the *Criminal Code*, R.S.C., 1985, c. C-46

In 1987, Parliament repealed s. 146(1) and put in place a series of measures that include a provision that allows a person who would previously have been charged under s. 146(1) the defence of due diligence [An Act to amend the *Criminal Code* and the *Canada Evidence Act*, R.S.C. 1985, c. 19 (3rd Supp.)]. Sections 151 and 152 of the current *Code* create the new substantive offences of sexual interference and invitation to sexual touching. Both of these provisions apply to sexual conduct with a person under the age of 14. Section 150.1(4) limits the range of defences available to an accused charged under these sections, removing the defence of consent but allowing a due diligence defence:

150.1 . . .

> (4) It is not a defence to a charge under section 151 or 152, subsection 160(3) or 173(2), or section 271, 272 or 273 that the accused believed that the complainant was fourteen years of age or more at the time the offence is alleged to have been committed *unless the accused took all reasonable steps to ascertain the age of the complainant.* [Emphasis added.]

. . . .

Sections 151 and 152 seek to protect young people from a broad range of sexual activity. These provisions continue to protect young females from the physical and emotional trauma of premature sexual intercourse. . . . Parliament has concluded that it can effect its objective of protecting young females from the undesirable consequences of premature sexual intercourse in a manner that does not restrict an accused's right as much as s. 146(1).

I am therefore of the view that s. 146(1) does not satisfy the proportionality test set out in *Oakes*. The potential benefits flowing from the retention of absolute liability are far too speculative to be able to justify a provision that envisages the possibility of life imprisonment for one who is mentally innocent. At a minimum the provision must provide for a defence of due diligence.

. . . .

While it is not, strictly speaking, necessary for me to consider s. 15(1) of the *Charter*, it may be useful to address the question whether in addition to a s. 7 violation there is also a s. 15(1) violation, particularly since I cannot agree with Justice McLachlin's conclusion that s. 146(1) of the *Code* infringes s. 15(1) of the *Charter*.

The appellants Hess and Nguyen submit that s. 146(1) of the *Code* creates a distinction that violates s. 15(1) of the *Charter*. They say that s. 146(1) distinguishes between potential accused on the basis of a ground enumerated in s. 15(1) of the *Charter* in that only men may be charged under the provision. They point out, moreover, that the provision clearly envisages that only females may be complainants. The question arises therefore whether it is open to the Legislature to create an offence that applies only to accused of one sex and to victims of one sex.

. . . .

In these appeals we are asked to consider when a distinction drawn on the basis of sex may legitimately be made and when it may not. In the context of the criminal law it seems to me that the answer to this question will depend on the nature of the offence in issue. If the impugned provision creates an offence that can, as a matter of fact, be committed by either sex but goes on to specify that it is only an offence when committed by one sex, then there may well be an infringement of s. 15(1) that would have to be justified under s. 1 of the *Charter*.

. . . .

It seems to me that the first question that we face in these appeals is whether s.146(1) addresses an offence that as a matter of biological fact can only be committed by males.

I note that s. 3(6) of the *Code* states:

> (6) For the purposes of this Act, sexual intercourse is complete upon penetration to even the slightest degree, notwithstanding that seed is not emitted.

In addition, s. 147 states that only males over 14 may commit the offence envisaged in s. 146, a provision that reflects the common law's rather artificial assumption that boys under 14 are not physically capable of sexual intercourse. . . . When s. 146(1) is read in light of ss. 147 and 3(6), it becomes clear that the legislature was of the opinion that, because only males over a certain age were physically capable of penetrating another person, only they needed to be listed as potential accused. . . . In my view, we are therefore dealing with an offence that involves an act that as a matter of biological fact only men over a certain age are capable of committing. And given that only men may be the penetrators, it is as absurd to suggest that the provision discriminates against males because it does not include women in the category of potential offenders as it is to suggest that a provision that prohibits self-induced abortion is discriminatory because it does not include men among the potential class of offenders.

. . . .

[I]t is appropriate to issue a declaration to the effect that the words in s. 146(1) "whether or not he believes that she is 14 years of age or more" are of no force and effect. The section shorn of its offensive words therefore reads:

146. (1) Every male person who has sexual intercourse with a female person who

(*a*) is not his wife, and
(*b*) is under the age of 14 years,

is guilty of an indictable offence and is liable to imprisonment for life.

MᴄLᴀᴄʜʟɪɴ J. (dissenting) (Gᴏɴᴛʜɪᴇʀ J. concurring): —

. . . .

An accused can be convicted under s. 146(1) although he lacks a guilty mind. He clearly must intend to have intercourse. But that is not an offence. Without wishing to commit the crime or intending to commit the crime of having intercourse with a girl of less than 14 years, an accused may stand convicted. It follows from the principles laid down by this Court in *Re B.C. Motor Vehicle Act* and *Vaillancourt* that s. 146(1) violates s. 7 of the *Charter*.

2. *Does s. 146(1) of the Criminal Code violate s. 15 of the Charter?*

It is argued that s. 146(1) violates s. 15 of the *Charter* in two ways.

The first is that only men can be convicted under s. 146(1). Men are thus deprived of a benefit or advantage enjoyed by women. The second is that only young women are protected by s. 146(1). Thus males of 14 years or less are not given the same benefit as females.

Two requirements must be met to establish infringement of s. 15 of the *Charter*. First, an inequality or distinction in the treatment of members of groups must be established. Second, this distinction must constitute discrimination: *Andrews v. Law Soc. of B.C.*, [1989] 1 S.C.R. 143.

The alleged violations of s. 15 raised in this case both involve distinctions on the basis of sex, one of the categories enumerated in s. 15. Thus the first condition for a violation of s. 15 is met. The question is whether the second requirement, discrimination, is established.

. . . .

In my view, the essential requirements for discrimination under s. 15 remain as set forth in *Andrews*.

Applying that test, I find that s. 146(1) constitutes discrimination under s. 15 of the *Charter*. It makes distinctions on the enumerated ground of sex. It burdens men as it does not burden women. It offers protection to young females which it does not offer to young males. It is discriminatory.

. . . .

3. *Are the violations of ss. 7 and 15 saved under s. 1 of the Charter?*

   (a) Is the Breach of s. 7 Saved by s. 1 of the *Charter*?

   (i) *The objective of the proposed limit*

. . . .

Section 146(1) represents the Canadian equivalent of a provision which is known throughout the western democratic world. The offence has long been part of the criminal law of England which we in Canada inherited. It has survived innumerable constitutional challenges in the United States. . . . It is not an exaggeration to say that the offence of "statutory rape", as it is commonly referred to, is embedded in our social consciousness.

These facts attest to the importance of the objective served by the offence.

. . . .

What then is the objective of s. 146(1)? It has two aspects. The first is the protection of female children from the harms which may result from premature sexual intercourse and pregnancy. The second is the protection of society from the impact of the social problems which sexual intercourse with children may produce.

. . . .

[T]he protection of children from the evils of intercourse is multi-faceted and so obvious as not to require formal demonstration. Children merit this protection for three primary reasons. The first is the need to protect them from the consequences of pregnancies with which they are ill-equipped to deal from the physical, emotional and economic point of view. The second is the need to protect them from the grave physical and emotional harm which may result from sexual intercourse at such an early age. The third is the need to protect them from exploitation by those who might seek to use them for prostitution and related nefarious purposes.

. . . .

I conclude that the objectives of s. 146(1) of the *Criminal Code* are of great importance — sufficient importance to justify overriding a constitutionally protected right.

   (ii) *Are the means chosen to effect the objective reasonable and demonstrably justified in a free and democratic society?*

A. Rational Connection

Is there a rational connection between the imposition of strict liability and deterrence of men from intercourse with young girls? In my view, there is. Were the defence of reasonable belief available, a man could escape conviction simply by saying that he believed the girl to be older than 14. The defence of due diligence would require him to make inquiries to avoid conviction, but still leaves open the possibility that the girl may lie as to her age or even produce false identification, not an uncommon practice in the world of juvenile prostitution.

The imposition of strict liability eliminates these defences. In doing so, it effectively puts men who are contemplating intercourse with a girl who might be under 14 years of age on guard. They know that if they have intercourse without being certain of the girl's age, they run the risk of conviction, and many conclude that they will not take the chance. That wisdom forms part of the substratum of consciousness with which young men grow up, as exemplified by terms such as "jailbait". There can be no question but that the imposition of absolute liability in s. 146(1) has an additional deterrent effect.

B. Degree of Impairment

The limit should impair the right or freedom "as little as possible" . . . The infringement would not extend beyond what is reasonably necessary to achieve the legislative objective. This is because a measure which infringes more than necessary is to that extent infringing a right without justification. That is inconsistent with s. 1 of the *Charter*.

In dealing with this point, I find it useful to ask whether there is another way the same objective could be achieved without infringement of the right or with a lesser infringement of the right. In the case of s. 146(1), the answer to this question must be negative for the reasons I discussed under A. Rational Connection.

. . . .

I cannot leave this aspect of the analysis without adverting to the fact that Parliament has repealed s. 146(1) and adopted a provision allowing the defence of due diligence. In my opinion, the fact that Parliament has chosen to do this does not establish that the objectives of s. 146(1) can be accomplished with a lesser infringement of the accuseds rights. An equally viable explanation is that Parliament has chosen, for whatever reasons, to reduce its objective.

. . . .

C. Proportionality Between the Effect of the Limit and the Objective

We arrive at the point where we must weigh the impact of the infringement of the accused's constitutional right against the importance of what is achieved by the legislation. In the case at bar, what hangs in the balance is the public and private interest in protecting very young girls from intercourse on the one hand, and on the other the right of a person charged with an offence not to be convicted if he did not intend to commit the offence.

In the abstract, both considerations are of high importance.

. . . .

The question in the case at bar is whether deviation from the principle which requires *mens rea* can *ever* be tolerated in our society. The submission put before us was essentially that in no case could a measure which violated the requirement for *mens rea* be justified under s. 1 of the *Charter*.

. . . .

I cannot accept this submission.

As a matter of construction, to hold that s. 1 can never as a matter of law be applicable to *Charter* rights falling within certain categories is to rewrite the *Charter*. The framers of the *Charter* expressly subjected all the rights and freedoms which it guarantees to the override of s. 1.

. . . .

I therefore proceed on the premise that important as the right not to be convicted in the absence of *mens rea* is, one must nevertheless proceed to s. 1 of the *Charter* to determine if s. 146(1) can be saved as a reasonable measure justified in a free and democratic society.

The first point is that many societies which we would regard as free and democratic, such as England and the United States, consider the offence of statutory rape to be both reasonable and justifiable notwithstanding its elimination of *mens rea*.

. . . .

The second is that the elimination of *mens rea* from s. 146(1) of the *Criminal Code* may be viewed as less offensive than, for example, the elimination of *mens rea* from the offence of murder.

. . . .

Although one may postulate the case of a "morally blameless" person being convicted under s. 146(1), however rare that case may be, one must also remember that all that a person need do to avoid the risk of this happening is to refrain from having sex with girls of less than adult age unless he knows for certain that they are over 14. Viewed thus, the infringement on the freedom imposed by s. 146(1) of the *Criminal Code* does not appear unduly Draconian, considering the great harms to which the section is directed.

. . . .

The actual effect of the absence of *mens rea* in s. 146(1) is much less serious than it may be in other cases.

. . . .

These considerations, coupled with the fact that the lack of *mens rea* in s. 146(1) is less intrusive of the accused's rights than is the case in other absolute liability offences, lead me to conclude that the intrusion on the accused's right not to be convicted in the absence of a guilty mind represented by s. 146(1) is reasonable and demonstrably justifiable in a free and democratic society.

(b) Is the breach of s. 15 saved by s. 1 of the *Charter*?

. . . .

I need not expatiate further on the objective of s. 146(1); it is clearly capable of overriding other *Charter* rights, provided the means used are appropriate and proportionate. The rational link between the objective and the measure and impairment to a minimum degree are likewise established. The only question is whether the infringement of s. 15 is justified, given the objectives of s. 146(1).

I am satisfied that the means represented by s. 146(1) are proportionate and justified when weighed against the seriousness of the infringement of the rights of equality of accused persons and victims under s. 15 of the *Charter*. The singling out of males as the only offenders is justified given the fact that only males can cause pregnancies, one of the chief evils addressed by s. 146(1). The protection of female children to the exclusion of male children may be justified on the same ground; only females are likely to become pregnant.

Justice Sopinka agreed with the majority that the section contravened s. 7 and could not be saved by s. 1. He also agreed with the minority that the section infringed s. 15 of the *Charter* but he believed it was saved by s. 1.

For commentary, see William Black and Isabel Grant, "Equality and Biological Differences" (1990), 79 C.R. (3d) 372.

The remainder of this chapter addresses the issue of how courts determine whether a mistake of fact exonerates. Normally this will not be a difficult determination. For example, if the accused believed the gun was not loaded that is clearly relevant to the fault required for murder or manslaughter. There are, however, more difficult cases particularly where on the accused's view of the facts he is committing a particular offence but had he not been mistaken he would be guilty of another, usually more serious offence. May fault for the lesser offence be transferred?

The traditional approach is from the old English case of *Tolson* (1889), 23 Q.B.D., which only allows the defence if, on the accused's view, he was innocent of any offence. The other less often used test is that in *Beaver,* [1957] S.C.R. 531, which asks whether the mistake relates to the essence of the offence. The Supreme Court in *Beaver* were deciding what the *mens rea* should be for drugs offences. What if the accused thought she was possessing sugar rather than a drug? The majority established that the principle that one cannot knowingly possess something without knowledge of the character of the substance possessed.

Problem

A plainclothes police officer intervenes to stop a fight between two youths. An onlooker, not knowing that he was a police officer, tries to pull him away telling him to mind his own business. The officer punched the onlooker in the nose and the onlooker punched him back. The officer then drew his revolver and gained control of the situation. The onlooker is charged with assault on a police officer contrary to s. 270 of the *Criminal Code*. This offence carries a maximum penalty on indictment of 5 years imprisonment. The maximum penalty for assault under s. 266 is the same although in practice the offence of assault on a police officer is considered more serious and attracts a higher penalty. Consider whether the mistake defence should succeed on the *Tolson* and *Beaver* tests. Which result do you prefer and why?

Compare *R. v. McLeod* (1954), 20 C.R. 281 (B.C. C.A.) and *R. v. Collins* (1989), 69 C.R. (3d) 235, 48 C.C.C. (3d) 343 (Ont. C.A.).

What test was applied in the following two decisions. Do you agree with the results?

R. v. LADUE

[1965] 4 C.C.C. 264, 45 C.R. 287 (Y.T. C.A.)

DAVEY J.A.: — Ladue either copulated or attempted to copulate with a dead woman and was convicted under s. 167(*b*) [now s. 182(*b*)] of the *Criminal Code* of indecently interfering with a dead human body. The material part of the section reads as follows:

167. Every one who
(*b*) improperly or indecently interferes with or offers any indignity to a dead human body or human remains, whether buried or not,
is guilty of an indictable offence and is liable to imprisonment for five years.

The only point of substance in Ladue's appeal against his conviction is whether the learned trial Judge was right in holding that it was not open to the appellant to contend that he was not guilty because he did not know the woman was dead. There was considerable evidence upon which the learned Judge might have held, if he had not considered the defence untenable in law, that while

Ladue knew what he was doing physically, he was so intoxicated that he did not realize the woman was dead. Subject to what I have to say later that would have been a good defence.

In his oral reasons the learned trial Judge, in dealing with the effect of intoxication upon the appellant's understanding, said this:

> What does the argument amount to? The only way you can make it, the only way in which you could make this argument — certainly I don't know. She was dead. He thought she was unconscious. Because she was dead? No. That is about it. At the time of the incident can a person be heard to say "that it didn't occur to me she was dead, and I am therefore innocent." I will tell you, I will not listen to such an argument. That would be an admission he was having intercourse with a person.

It is a fundamental principle of criminal law that, unless excluded by statute, *mens rea*, that is guilty intention, is necessary to constitute a crime, and that a person doing an act is not guilty of a crime if his mind be innocent: *R. v. Prince* (1875), L.R. 2 C.C.R. 154; *R. v. Tolson* (1889), 23 Q.B.D. 168, *per* Willis J., at pp. 171-2. I see nothing in s. 167(*b*) to exclude that principle. Accordingly it was open to the appellant to attempt to rebut the inference of *mens rea* flowing from what he deliberately did to the body by proving that he did not know the woman was dead.

But in attempting to defend himself in that way the appellant runs into the insuperable difficulty alluded to by the learned trial Judge. The appellant could not have failed, even in his drunken state, to perceive that the woman was unconscious, and incapable of giving her consent to copulation. Indeed the appellant does not suggest that he thought he had her consent to the act. So if the woman was alive he was raping her. Therefore it is impossible for him to argue that, not knowing her to be dead, he was acting innocently. An intention to commit a crime, although not the precise crime charged, will provide the necessary *mens rea* under a statute in the form of s. 167(*b*): *R. v. Tolson per* Willis J., at p. 172, Stephen J., at pp. 189-90; *R. v. Prince, per* Brett J., at pp. 169-170, because in those circumstances an accused cannot contend he was acting lawfully or innocently.

It follows that in my respectful opinion the learned trial Judge was right in the particular circumstances of this case in saying that he would not entertain an argument that appellant was innocent because he did not know the woman was dead.

. . . .

The nature of the offence under s. 167(*b*) and the language of that section would not seem to require knowledge that the body is dead as a specific ingredient of an offence under that section, because in most cases that fact would be clear, and proof of a deliberate act improperly or indecently interfering with a body that was in fact dead would be sufficient proof of a criminal intention or *mens rea*. It would be only in the most exceptional case where the offender might have any doubt whether a body was quick or dead, and in such a case he might defend himself by showing that he did not know the body was dead and that according to his understanding he was acting lawfully and innocently. That is what the appellant cannot show in this case, because if the woman was alive he was raping her.

I would dismiss the appeal.

Appeal dismissed.

R. v. KUNDEUS

[1976] 2 S.C.R. 272, 32 C.R.N.S. 129 at 135, 24 C.C.C. (2d) 276

26th June 1975. DE GRANDPRÉ J. (MARTLAND, JUDSON, RITCHIE, PIGEON, DICKSON and BEETZ JJ. concurring): — With leave of this Court, the Crown appeals the unanimous judgment of the British Columbia Court of Appeal, ante p. 133, setting aside the conviction of respondent. In the words of the indictment, Kundeus was charged that he did:

> on the 24th day of August A.D. 1972, unlawfully traffic in a restricted drug, to wit: Lysergic Acid Diethylamide (LSD), contrary to the provisions of the *Food and Drugs Act.*

The facts are stated in the reasons for judgment of the trial Judge [p. 132]:

> Police Constable MacKay-Dunn testified that on 24th August 1972 at about 10:15 p.m., the constable, acting undercover in the Gastown area, and the accused were at a table in the Travellers Hotel, 57 West Cordova in the City of Vancouver. The police constable testified the accused was calling out, "Speed, acid, MDA or hash" to passers-by in the beer parlor. The police constable asked for hash or acid. The accused said they were all sold out. The accused offered mescaline at $2. The police constable accepted the offer, requested two "hits" and paid $4 to the accused for same. The accused left, returned in about five minutes, and handed two capsules, Ex. 1, to the police constable. Exhibit 1 was, in fact, two capsules of L.S.D. (see Ex. 2).

The trial Judge adds that [p. 132]: "The accused elected not to adduce any evidence in defence."

After having stated that the sole issue was *mens rea*, the trial Judge examined the relevant parts of the *Food and Drugs Act*, R.S.C. 1970, c. F-27, and the regulations thereunder, as well as the cases of *Regina v. Blondin* (1971), 2 C.C.C. (2d) 118, affirmed (1972), 4 C.C.C. (2d) 566n (Can.); *Regina v. Burgess*, [1970] 3 C.C.C. 268 (Ont. C.A.); and *Regina v. Custeau*, 17 C.R.N.S 124, 6 C.C.C. (2d) 179 (Ont. C.A.), and concluded:

> The Court has considered the evidence in this trial and the able submissions of respective counsel.
> The Court concludes that the prosecution has proved, beyond a reasonable doubt, the guilt of the accused.

Respondent inscribed an appeal alleging an error involving a question of law upon the following ground:

> The learned trial Judge misdirected himself in law in holding that if he was satisfied beyond a reasonable doubt that the accused knew it was illegal to sell the drug mescaline,

although said drug is not a restricted drug as defined in the *Food and Drugs Act*, and in fact intended to sell the drug mescaline, he should convict the accused of trafficking in L.S.D., a restricted drug under the Food and Drugs Act, when the substance sold as mescaline was analyzed to be L.S.D., even if the accused did not know that the substance was in fact the restricted drug L.S.D.

The Court of Appeal disagreed with the conclusion reached by the trial Judge and specifically refused to follow *Regina v. Custeau*. The conviction was consequently set aside.

Mens rea cannot, of course, be examined without reference to *Beaver v. The Queen*, 26 C.R. 193, [1957] S.C.R. 531, 118 C.C.C. 129.

. . . .

Our facts are different. They are very simple and uncontradicted. One reading of them is that Kundeus was offering L.S.D. for sale, actually sold L.S.D. and received payment therefor. On that reading, it is obvious that the conviction should have been affirmed.

Another reading is that adopted by the Court of Appeal and expressed by McFarlane J.A., speaking for the Court (*ante* p. 133):

> The evidence disclosed, and the trial Judge found, that the appellant offered to sell mescaline at $2 to a police constable acting undercover. The constable accepted the offer and paid the appellant $4 for two "hits". The appellant left, returned in about five minutes and handed the constable two capsules which were found, on analysis, to contain L.S.D.
>
> I think I must interpret the reasons for judgment of the trial Judge as a finding that although the appellant did in fact sell L.S.D. he thought he was selling, and intended to sell, mescaline and that the constable also thought he was purchasing mescaline.

Assuming that this reading of the trial judgment is the proper one, was the Court of Appeal right in holding that the necessary *mens rea* had not been proved? I do not believe so.

In *Regina v. Blondin, supra*, a case dealing with the importation of narcotics, the Crown succeeded on the following ground of its appeal [p. 6]:

> (e) THAT the learned trial Judge misdirected the jury in instructing it that the Crown was obliged to prove beyond a reasonable doubt that the accused knew that the contents of the scuba diving tank (Exhibit 1) was a narcotic drug as alleged in the Indictment herein, namely, Cannabis Resin.

After a full review of the authorities, Robertson J.A. concluded (pp. 13-14):

> Basing my opinion upon what I understand to be the principle enunciated in the several passages I have quoted, I am of the respectful opinion that the learned trial Judge erred when he instructed the jury that, in order to find Blondin guilty, they must find that he knew that the substance in the tank was cannabis resin. It would be sufficient to find, in relation to a narcotic, *mens rea* in its widest sense.

An appeal to this Court by the accused was dismissed by the full bench in the following terms: "We agree that the Court of Appeal rightly allowed the appeal and directed a new trial on ground (e) of the notice of appeal to that Court."

That judgment must be read with another decision of this Court, namely, *Regina v. King*, 38 C.R. 52, [1962] S.C.R. 746, 133 C.C.C. 1, where the facts, the question submitted to this Court and the holding are expressed in the [S.C.R.] headnote:

> The accused went to his dentist by appointment to have two teeth extracted. He was injected with a drug known as sodium pentothal, a quick-acting anaesthetic. Earlier, he had been required to sign a printed form containing a warning not to drive after the anaesthetic until his head had cleared. After he regained consciousness, the nurse in attendance, to whom he appeared to be normal, warned him not to drive until his head was "perfectly clear". He replied that he intended to walk. The accused said that he heard no such warning and did not remember signing any form containing a warning. He remembered getting into his car and that while driving he became unconscious. His car ran into the rear of a parked vehicle. Medical evidence was given that his mental and physical condition (he was staggering and his co-ordination was poor) was consistent with the after-effects of the drug in question which may induce a state of amnesia accompanied by a period during which the subject may feel competent to drive a car and in the next second be in a condition in which he would not know what was happening. The accused stated that he did not know anything about this drug.
>
> He was charged and convicted of the offence of driving a motor vehicle while his ability to do so was impaired by a drug, contrary to s. 223 of the *Criminal Code*. After a trial *de novo* before a County Court judge under s. 720 of the *Code*, his conviction was affirmed. The Court of Appeal granted him leave to appeal and quashed the conviction. The Crown was granted leave to appeal to this Court on the question as to whether *mens rea* relating to both the act of driving and to the state of being impaired was an essential element of the offence.

I refer particularly to a paragraph of the reasons of Ritchie J., speaking also for the Chief Justice and for Martland J., at p. 763:

> The existence of *mens rea* as an essential ingredient of an offence and the method of proving the existence of that ingredient are two different things, and I am of the opinion that when it has been proved that a driver was driving a motor vehicle while his ability to do so was impaired by alcohol or a drug, then a rebuttable presumption arises that his condition was voluntarily induced and that he is guilty of the offence created by s. 223 and must be convicted unless other evidence is adduced which raises a reasonable doubt as to whether he was, through no fault of his own, disabled when he undertook to drive and drove, from being able to appreciate and know that he was or might become impaired.

In the case at bar, such a rebuttable presumption has arisen. No evidence having been tendered by the accused, it is not possible to find that he had an honest belief amounting to a non-existence of *mens rea* and the Court of Appeal was in error in its conclusion.

The quality of respondent's conduct is not to be determined by the existence or non-existence of a binding civil agreement as to the purchase of L.S.D. between him and the constable. That is not the test. In *Poitras v. The Queen* (1973), 12 C.C.C. (2d) 337 (Can.), where the question was to determine the exact meaning of "trafficking" under the *Narcotic Control Act*, R.S.C. 1970, c. N-1, Dickson J., speaking for the majority, wrote at pp. 416-17:

> It was argued on behalf of the appellant that the words "to buy" do not appear in the definition of "trafficking" under the *Narcotic Control Act*; therefore, a mere purchaser does not traffic and an agent for the purchaser comes under the same protective umbrella. I do not

agree. One cannot apply the civil law of "agency" in this context. "Agency" does not serve to make non-criminal an act which would otherwise be attended by criminal consequences. Even if the appellant could be said to be the "agent" of Constable Arsenault for the purposes of civil responsibility, his acts may, none the less, amount to trafficking in narcotics or aiding in such trafficking. If, as the trial Judge would seem to have found, the evidence was consistent with the accused delivering or selling or trading in drugs or offering to do so, the fact that he may have been acting as an agent for Arsenault would not exculpate him.

In my view, the result in *Regina v. Custeau* was the proper one and this notwithstanding the error committed by the Court of Appeal of Ontario and underlined by the Court of Appeal of British Columbia in the case at bar, mescaline having been described as a controlled drug when it is a drug mentioned in the regulations under the Act which cannot be sold without a prescription.

I would allow the appeal, set aside the order of the Court of Appeal of British Columbia and restore the judgment at trial together with the sentence imposed thereat.

LASKIN C.J.C. (SPENCE J. concurring) (dissenting): —

. . . .

The scheme of the *Food and Drugs Act* is of considerable relevance in this case. Sections 40 and 42, on which the prosecution was based, are in Pt. IV of the Act dealing with "restricted drugs", which are those included in Sched. H, and L.S.D. is one of those mentioned. Part III of the Act deals with "controlled drugs" which are those included in Sched. G, and among them are amphetamine and methamphetamine. Sections 33 and 34 are provisions in Pt. III (relating to controlled drugs) which are to the same effect as ss. 40 and 42 relating to restricted drugs under Pt. IV. Sections 40 and 42 read as follows:

> 40. In this Part,
> "possession" means possession as defined in the *Criminal Code*;
> "regulations" means regulations made as provided for by or under section 45;
> "restricted drug" means any drug or other substance included in Schedule H;
> "traffic" means to manufacture, sell, export from or import into Canada, transport or deliver, otherwise than under the authority of this Part or the regulations . . .
> 42. (1) No person shall traffic in a restricted drug or any substance represented or held out by him to be a restricted drug.
> (2) No person shall have in his possession any restricted drug for the purpose of trafficking.
> (3) Every person who violates subsection (1) or (2) is guilty of an offence and is liable
> (*a*) upon summary conviction, to imprisonment for eighteen months; or
> (*b*) upon conviction on indictment, to imprisonment for ten years.

Mescaline is neither a controlled drug nor a restricted drug, but is a drug within Sched. F, included thereunder by virtue of s. 15 of the Act ("no person shall sell any drug described in Schedule F") and governed by regulations made pursuant to s. 25 of the Act. Section 15 of the Act is in Pt. I which deals with adulterated food, drugs and cosmetics, with deceptive advertising and labelling, with control of standards of manufacturing and with the sanitary condition of premises. Part II of the Act deals with administration and enforcement of the Act by inspectors and includes very wide regulation-making powers as set out in s. 25. Penalties for violation of the Act or of the regulations are prescribed by s. 26 which reads as follows:

> 26. Every person who violates any of the provisions of this Act or the regulations is guilty of an offence and is liable
>
> (a) on summary conviction for a first offence to a fine not exceeding five hundred dollars or to imprisonment for a term not exceeding three months, or to both, and for a subsequent offence to a fine not exceeding one thousand dollars or to imprisonment for a term not exceeding six months, or to both; and
>
> (b) on conviction upon indictment to a fine not exceeding five thousand dollars or to imprisonment for a term not exceeding three years, or to both.

It is common ground that any offence under the Act or regulations relating to the sale of mescaline would be punishable under s. 26. On the other hand, this provision would have no application to controlled or restricted drugs in the face of the penalty provisions of ss. 34 and 42 which alone govern illegal dealing in them. A comparison of the respective penalty provisions governing mescaline and L.S.D. shows how much heavier the penalty is in respect of illegal dealing in the latter than in the former, both where the prosecution is on summary conviction and on indictment.

The regulation respecting mescaline is Reg. C.01.041 which prohibits the sale of any substance containing a drug listed or described in Sched. F unless on written or verbal prescription, and the regulation goes on to elaborate on these types of prescriptions. I may observe here that it is not an offence to possess mescaline but it is an offence to possess a controlled or a restricted drug for the purpose of "trafficking", defined (as already noted) to include, inter alia, selling, transporting and delivering.

Mescaline has been a Sched. F drug since 1958: see SOR/58-115 (P.C. 1958-450); SOR/59-274 (P.C. 1959-956). The statutory history of its position in Sched. F is somewhat involved, as witness the fact that by SOR/63-269 (P.C. 1963-1119) mescaline was included in Sched. F which was added to the regulations under the *Food and Drugs Act*, operating apparently as supplementary to Sched. F to the Act proper (SOR/63-269 was replaced by SOR/65-548). In view of this history, I may note that there was error in the judgment of the Ontario Court of Appeal in *Regina v. Custeau* (1972), 17 C.R.N.S. 124, 6 C.C.C. (2d) 179, in the statement therein that mescaline was a controlled drug. In that case, the accused was charged and convicted on appeal of trafficking in L.S.D. although he thought he was selling mescaline. The Court of Appeal in entering the conviction gave as one of its reasons that it is an offence to traffic in either a controlled drug or a restricted drug, and, although there were separate penalties prescribed, the maximum penalty was the same in either case. In fact, however, mescaline was not then nor ever was a controlled drug or a restricted drug.

It was the contention of the appellant Crown that the required proof of *mens rea* was furnished by evidence showing what Crown counsel called a general intention to traffic in drugs; and, this being shown, it was immaterial that the accused did not intend to traffic in the specific drug which was named in the charge but thought (as did his purchaser) that he was trafficking in another drug. Crown counsel thus takes the position to which I referred earlier in these reasons, and he stated in this connection that the accused could meet the case against him only by relying on mistake of fact which must be an honest mistake on reasonable grounds that the facts believed by him to be true would not attract culpability of any drug offence. That, according to Crown counsel, was not this case.

There are, in my opinion, three issues that stem from this submission. The first is whether mistake of fact arises at all as a separate defence for the accused in the face of the burden on the Crown to prove *mens rea* as an element of the offence charged. The offence charged was trafficking in a restricted drug, namely, L.S.D.; and although I would agree that proof of knowledge by the accused that he was trafficking in a drug of that class might be enough, even if it be not L.S.D., the question that must be faced is whether it is enough for the Crown to offer proof of trafficking in any drug or, as here, in a drug that is in a lower scale of prohibition and regulation.

Having regard to the evidence adduced at the trial and to the findings of fact on that evidence, I do not think it necessary in the present case to consider the relationship between the Crown's burden of proof, where *mens rea* is an element of the offence charged, and mistake of fact as an affirmative defence. Clearly enough, mistake of fact in that sense does not arise where proof of *mens rea* is an element of proof of the offence charged and the evidence adduced by the Crown does not establish it. If mistake is put forward in this context by evidence offered by or on behalf of the accused, it is only by way of meeting an evidentiary burden and raising a reasonable doubt that the Crown has met the persuasive burden of proof resting upon it. What we are concerned with here, on the record, is whether evidence by the Crown going to show that the accused intended to commit a lesser offence than that charged is enough to support the conviction entered after trial.

The second issue which arises on the Crown's submissions is whether the mistake of fact must be objectively reasonable or whether it is enough that it be based upon an honest belief. Leaving to one side cases of strict criminal liability (on which the judgment of Dixon J. in *Proudman v. Dayman* (1941), 67 C.L.R. 536 at 539-41, is specially instructive), where serious criminal charges are involved, this Court put the matter as follows in *Beaver v. The Queen, supra*, where Cartwright J. said this (at p. 538):

> the essential question is whether the belief entertained by the accused is an honest one and
> . . . the existence or non-existence of reasonable grounds for such belief is merely relevant
> evidence to be weighed by the tribunal of fact in determining that essential question.

See also *D.P.P. v. Morgan*, [1975] 2 All E.R. 347.

The third issue, which is tied in with the first, is whether mistake of fact is shown on proof that, on the facts as the accused honestly believed them to be, he was innocent of the offence charged, albeit guilty of another offence, or whether he must show that he was innocent of any offence. This last matter invites consideration of a proposition advanced in *Regina v. Prince* (1875), L.R. 2 C.C.R. 154, by the one dissenting Judge of the 16 who heard the case in the Court of Crown Cases Reserved. The majority of that Court held that *mens rea* was not an essential ingredient of the offence charged, which was unlawfully taking any unmarried girl under age 16 out of the possession and against the will of her father or mother. (The word "knowingly" was not in the charge.) The accused reasonably believed that the girl he had abducted was over age 16. One of the points made by Brett J., who dissented on the ground that *mens rea* was an ingredient of the offence as it related to age, was that where *mens rea* must be proved it would suffice to show, if the facts were as the accused believed them to be, that he would still be guilty of a crime, albeit one of a lesser degree than that charged as a result of the *actus reus*.

I do not think that this view is any longer sustainable. The requirement that where the *actus reus* of an offence is proved there must also be proof of the *mens rea* of the same crime is now basic in our criminal law. Williams, *Criminal Law: The General Part*, 2nd ed. (1961), at p. 129, makes the point when dealing with the question of "transferred malice" as follows:

> The accused can be convicted where he both has the *mens rea* and commits the *actus reus* specified in the rule of law creating the crime, though they exist in respect of different objects. He cannot be convicted if his *mens rea* relates to one crime and his *actus reus* to a different crime, because that would be to disregard the requirement of an appropriate *mens rea*.

And again at p. 131:

> What are different crimes for the purpose of the rule depends primarily upon the arrangement of the statute; each section presumptively creates a different crime or group of crimes. It is possible for a single sentence of a section to create a number of different crimes, as is shown by the decisions on duplicity in pleading. If a section is thus held to create different crimes, it would not he possible to transfer the malice from one crime to another even within the same section.

See also Smith and Hogan, *Criminal Law*, 3rd ed. (1973), at pp. 49-51.

This is apt for the statutory situation which exists here and to which I have referred earlier in these reasons. Even if it be proper to describe trafficking in controlled drugs, whatever be the drug, or trafficking in restricted drugs, whatever be the drug, as being, in each case, a description of the same crime, I think it is impossible to bring mescaline within either category when it stands entirely outside the group of controlled or restricted drugs and is governed by other statutory provisions than those governing controlled or restricted drugs. I am unable to agree that where *mens rea* is an element of an offence, as it is here, it can be satisfied by proof of its existence in relation to another offence unless, of course, the situation involves an included offence of which the accused may be found guilty on his trial of the offence charged. A number of authors who have examined this problem in depth and, particularly in relation to the "lesser crime" doctrine, have come to this very conclusion: see Williams, at pp. 185 ff.; Howard, *Australian Criminal Law*, 2nd ed. (1970), at pp. 375 ff.; and Smith, "The Guilty Mind in the Criminal Law" (1960), 76 L.Q.R. 78 at 91 ff. If judges are to be faced with a choice of policy in this area, it should be one consonant with fundamental principle, namely, that the *actus reus* and the *mens rea* must relate to the same crime: see Smith.

This view has been the subject of consideration and some application in a number of decisions of appellate Courts in Canada, some of which were considered and distinguished by the British Columbia Court of Appeal in the present case. I begin my reference to them by taking up first those cases that dealt with drug offences. The *Custeau* case, already mentioned, and *Regina v. Burgess*, [1970] 3 C.C.C. 268 (Ont. C.A.), may be considered together as being cases where (on the assumption in *Custeau* that mescaline was a controlled drug) offences of the same quality were involved if the facts had been as the accused believed them to be. In *Custeau*, the offence charged was trafficking in a restricted drug; the accused would have it that there was trafficking in a controlled drug. Although it may well be proper to treat trafficking in a restricted drug as being essentially the same offence as trafficking in a controlled drug, the conviction is not sustainable on a wider principle of liability that the honest belief of the accused is of no avail unless it would result in his act being entirely innocent. In *Burgess*, the charge was unlawful possession of a narcotic, to wit, opium, and the defence was that the accused believed he had hashish which was a narcotic whose possession was similarly prohibited. This was simply a case of the actual and intended act constituting the same crime, both drugs being in the class of narcotics and caught by the same penal provision, namely, s. 3 of the *Narcotic Control Act*, R.S.C. 1970, c. N-1.

Regina v. Blondin (1971), 2 C.C.C. (2d) 118, a judgment of the British Columbia Court of Appeal (of which McFarlane J.A., who delivered the reasons in the present case, was a member), also concerned an offence involving a narcotic which proved to be cannabis resin or hashish. The charge was unlawfully importing a narcotic, namely, cannabis resin. The trial Judge had charged the jury that the Crown was obliged to prove that the accused knew that the narcotic was that alleged in the indictment. This was held to be misdirection, the Appellate Court being of the opinion, in the light of *Burgess* and other cases cited, that it was a proper direction to the jury that it was enough if the accused knew that some kind of narcotic was involved. This view of the matter was affirmed by this Court on appeal: see [1972] 1 W.W.R. 479, 4 C.C.C. (2d) 566n. I may note here that under the *Narcotic Control Act* the importation of all narcotics is caught by a single proscription, namely, s. 4 of the Act, so that the same offence is involved regardless of the narcotic. The British Columbia Court of Appeal also held that it was not a proper instruction that the accused might be found guilty of unlawfully importing a narcotic if he knew that it was illegal to import the substance that was found although he did not know it was a narcotic. In short, there was a marked difference between the offence of importing a narcotic and that of smuggling goods in breach of the *Customs Act*, R.S.C. 1970,

c. C-40; *mens rea* in the latter respect was not enough to support a conviction of the former. This point was not passed upon by this Court, but it was referred to by McFarlane J.A., in delivering the judgment of the British Columbia Court of Appeal in the present case, to distinguish *Blondin*.

A second group of cases which considered "the lesser crime" doctrine is illustrated by *Regina v. McLeod* (1954), 20 C.R. 281, 111 C.C.C. 106 (B.C. C.A.), which involved a charge of assaulting a peace officer in the execution of his duty, contrary to what is now s. 246(2)(*a*) of the *Criminal Code*, R.S.C. 1970, c. C-34. The question at issue was whether proof must be made that the accused knew that the victim was a peace officer. The British Columbia Court of Appeal held that this was an essential element of the offence charged and, notwithstanding that there was an assault, the requirement of *mens rea* was not satisfied by proof of a lesser crime, that is, common assault. A different view in the same situation was taken by the High Court of Australia in a majority judgment in *Regina v. Reynhoudt* (1962), 107 C.L.R. 381, which held that it was enough for the Crown to establish the intentional assault without being required to prove that the accused knew that the person assaulted was a peace officer acting in the execution of his duty. The dissenting judgment of Dixon C.J. was to the effect that intent must go to all the elements of the whole offence, an opinion shared by Kitto J. The South African Supreme Court, Appellate Division, in *Rex v. Wallendorf*, [1920] S.A.L.R. 383, took a similar majority view to that in the *Reynhoudt* case in holding that it was not essential to prove that the accused knew that the victim of the assault was a constable.

A different class of case, raising the question of *mens rea* referable to a more serious crime than that charged, is *Regina v. Ladue*, 45 C.R. 287, [1965] 4 C.C.C. 264, a judgment of the Yukon Territory Court of Appeal which is staffed by members of the British Columbia Court of Appeal. The charge was indecently interfering with a dead human body, and the evidence showed copulation or attempted copulation with a woman who was then dead, albeit the accused testified that by reason of his intoxication he did not know that she was dead. The Court held that knowledge that the woman was dead was not an ingredient of the offence and hence, I take it, not an element requiring proof by the Crown. The Court also appears to have held, somewhat inconsistently, that proof that he did not know the woman was dead could be offered in defence by the accused, but it added that here he would be in the dilemma of admitting to rape (there being no question of consent), a more serious offence than that charged. It does occur to me, however, that the facts being what they were, the proper charge ought to have been attempted rape.

Is any general principle deducible from the foregoing catalogue of instances? Certainly, it cannot be said that, in general, where *mens rea* is an ingredient of an offence and the *actus reus* is proved it is enough if an intent is shown that would support a conviction of another crime, whether more or less serious than the offence actually committed. Coming to the particular, to the case before this Court, where proof is made of an *actus reus* that, in a general sense, is common to a range or variety of offences which require *mens rea* but those offences differ as to gravity by reason of different classifications and different penalties, is a charge of a more serious offence established by proof only that the accused intended to commit and could have been found guilty of a less serious, a lesser offence? The matter, in terms of principle, depends on how strict an observance there should be of the requirement of *mens rea*. If there is to be a relaxation of the requirement, should it not come from Parliament, which could provide for the substitution of a conviction of the lesser offence, in the same way as provision now exists in our criminal law for entering a conviction on an included offence?

This position is the one taken by the Model Penal Code of the American Law Institute (1962) which provides as follows in s. 2.04(2):

> Although ignorance or mistake would otherwise afford a defense to the offense charged, the defense is not available if the defendant would be guilty of another offense had the situation been as he supposed. In such case, however, the ignorance or mistake of the defendant shall reduce the grade and degree of the offense of which he may be convicted to those of the offense of which he would be guilty had the situation been as he supposed.

In the present case, and under present Canadian law, this sensible solution to a difficult problem is not open to this Court.

There may be some regret on the part of a Court to free a person who appears to be guilty of an offence with which he has not been charged. That regret, if any there be, cannot be a vehicle for making a particular charge which cannot be proved serve as a foundation for imposing culpability of another, which is not an included offence. If there is to be a modification of principle in a situation like the present one, it must come from Parliament.

I return in this connection to the judgment of this Court in *Beaver v. The Queen, supra*, which also involved a conviction of selling a narcotic drug as well as a conviction of possession. In respect of both charges the appellant's position was that he believed that a harmless substance, sugar of milk, was contained in the package sold to an undercover policeman and did not know that the package contained a narcotic. There was this difference in the formulation of the two offences: the possession offence was one simply of forbidden possession of a narcotic without lawful authority, while the selling offence related to sale of any substance represented or held out to be a drug. Because there was evidence of such a representation or holding out, the conviction of selling was affirmed. Parliament, in short, had made a distinction in the applicability of *mens rea* to each of the two offences.

There is another consideration which should be brought into account in this case. The Crown's case was built on evidence of an undercover policeman which must have been as well known to the prosecuting authorities before the trial as it was as a result of the trial. I can appreciate that there could have been some difficulty in determining what charge should be laid on the facts disclosed by the chief Crown witness. Although the Crown may have felt that it could support the charge actually laid, it could also, as a matter of precaution, have laid a charge of attempting to traffic in mescaline. Such a charge is supportable under s. 24 of the *Criminal Code* which makes it immaterial whether it was possible or not to commit the intended offence: see 10 Hals. (3d) 306; *Regina v. Scott,*

[1964] 2 C.C.C. 257 (Alta. C.A.). I have already indicated the view of the facts that the record compels. If there should be any doubt on the evidence whether the accused offered and intended to sell mescaline, that doubt cannot be translated into an affirmative finding, certainly not in this Court, that he offered and intended to sell L.S.D. At the worst, it would require a new trial.

I see no such doubt and, on the considerations I have canvassed, I would dismiss the appeal.

Mistake of Law

Section 19 of the *Criminal Code* declares:

> Ignorance of the law by a person who commits an offence is not an excuse for committing that offence.

O.W. HOLMES, THE COMMON LAW

Howe, ed., (1963), 40-41

Ignorance of the law is no excuse for breaking it. This substantive principle is sometimes put in the form of a rule of evidence, that every one is presumed to know the law. It has accordingly been defended by Austin and others, on the ground of difficulty of proof. If justice requires the fact to be ascertained, the difficulty of doing so is no ground for refusing to try. But every one must feel that ignorance of the law could never be admitted as an excuse, even if the fact could be proved by sight and hearing in every case. Furthermore, now that parties can testify, it may be doubted whether a man's knowledge of the law is any harder to investigate than many questions which are gone into. The difficulty, such as it is, would be met by throwing the burden of proving ignorance on the law-breaker.

The principle cannot be explained by saying that we are not only commanded to abstain from certain acts, but also to find out that we are commanded. For if there were such a second command, it is very clear that the guilt of failing to obey it would bear no proportion to that of disobeying the principal command if known, yet the failure to know would receive the same punishment as the failure to obey the principal law.

The true explanation of the rule is the same as that which accounts for the law's indifference to a man's particular temperament, faculties, and so forth. Public policy sacrifices the individual to the general good. It is desirable that the burden of all should be equal, but it is still more desirable to put an end to robbery and murder. It is no doubt true that there are many cases in which the criminal could not have known that he was breaking the law, but to admit the excuse at all would be to encourage ignorance where the law-maker has determined to make men know and obey, and justice to the individual is rightly outweighed by the larger interests on the other side of the scales.

P.K. RYU, H. SILVING, ERROR JURIS: A COMPARATIVE STUDY

(1957), 24 U. of Chic. L. Rev. 421 at 466-471

There is a noticeable trend toward increasing recognition of error of law as a defense in several legal systems.

. . . .

Within the concept of responsibility, conceived to imply a basic freedom of choice, knowledge of the law is essential for there can be no choice without knowledge. In answering the crucial question — For what is man responsible? — Binding, the most ardent advocate of the defense of legal error, stated that criminality was defiance of the legal prohibition, a contempt of the law or a rebellion against its commands. The idea that the essence of law violation is "rebellion against the law," however, implies that every lawbreaker is a revolutionary. We believe that in a free society the sanction of the community is imposed neither for "rebellion" nor for "disobedience" but simply for violation of a duty toward the community — the actor's duty, as a member of the community, to abide by its rules. To be subject to a sanction thus conceived, the actor, as a free agent, must know the rule which he violates.

The duty of free men, however, is not exhausted merely by compliance with known law. They must also exert their conscience to ascertain what the law is.

. . . .

Lastly, the difficulty of proving legal knowledge is not in itself greater than is the difficulty of showing the presence of any other mental element. When a man shoots another in broad daylight from a distance of five feet, he will not, in the absence of special circumstances, be heard to say that he believed the target to be a hare. Nor would any man — in legal systems which admit error of law as a defense — be heard to say that he did not know the killing of a human being to be unlawful. The problem of proof changes with circumstances. A man who shoots another might well be heard to say he thought the target a hare if he had shot, in a place reserved for hunting, at great distance and under unfavorable light conditions. So might a man be heard to say that he believed he did no wrong in abbreviating the life of a friend who had but a short time to live, in order to save him from extreme suffering. As in the case of the hunter it might be deemed significant that his companions shared his optical illusion, so in the case of the mercy killer it might be considered relevant that many other persons of his environment shared his legal illusion. Thus a significant question in judging a claim of legal error is: "Is he alone ignorant of that which everybody in the State knows?"

. . . .

The policy suggested in this article may be summarized thus: Any restraint imposed upon man is, in a sense, offensive to human dignity. The aim of free society is hence to reduce legal restraint to the minimum required in a given situation. Restraint is less undignified when imposed upon conscious nonconformance with law. Subjection of man to sanctions under a law which is unknown and unknowable to him and which he has no opportunity to accept or to reject expresses the view that he is a mere object of the law. We believe, however, that in a democratic society man is the ultimate end of the law.

R. v. ESOP

(1836), 173 E.R. 203

The prisoner was indicted for an unnatural offence, committed on board of an East India ship, lying in St. Katherine's Docks. It appeared that he was a native of Bagdad.

Chambers, for the prisoner. — In the country from which the prisoner comes, it is not considered an offence; and a person who comes into this country and does an act, believing that it is a perfectly innocent one, cannot be convicted according to the law of England. A party must know that what he does is a crime. This is the principle upon which infants, idiots, and lunatics are held not to be answerable. If a person is unconscious that he is doing a wrong act, or believes that it is a right or innocent act, he is exonerated. Where one man kills another under the persuasion that he is doing a good action, he is not liable to punishment, for he knows not the distinction between right and wrong, and upon that point is insane.

Bosanquet, J. — I am clearly of opinion that this is no legal defence.

Vaughan, J. — Where is the evidence that it is not a crime in the prisoner's own country? But if it is not a crime there, that does not amount to a defence here. Numbers have been most improperly executed if it is a defence.

The prisoner, after the examination of some witnesses on his behalf, from whose statements it appeared that the witnesses for the prosecution acted under the influence of spite and ill will, was found

Not guilty.

Chambers, for the prisoner.

R. v. CAMPBELL AND MLYNARCHUK

21 C.R.N.S. 273, 10 C.C.C. (2d) 26 (Alta. Dist. Ct.)

KERANS D.C.J. (orally): — This is an appeal by Darlene Agatha Campbell from conviction and sentence.

. . . .

On a charge before the summary conviction Court that she did, between February 9, 1972, and February 21, 1972, at the City of Edmonton, in the Province of Alberta, unlawfully take part as a performer in an immoral performance at Chez Pierre's situated at 10615 Jasper Ave., Edmonton, contrary to s. 163(2) [now s. 167(2)] of the *Criminal Code.*

This matter, therefore, comes before me by way of a trial *de novo*. That section provides, in s-s. (2):

> (2) Everyone commits an offence who takes part or appears as an actor, performer, or assistant in any capacity, in an immoral, indecent or obscene performance, entertainment or representation in a theatre.

The facts before me are relatively straightforward. On the dates in question, at the place in question, the appellant danced on stage, before an audience. At the start of her performance, she was wearing some clothes. By the end of her performance, she was not wearing any clothes. The dance was described to me as a "go-go dance" which, I understand, is a violent movement of almost all parts of the body, more or less in time to strongly rhythmic music.

I have no doubt in coming to the conclusion that this is a performance within the meaning of the section, and that, in doing what she did, the appellant took part as a performer in that performance. On the question of whether or not the performance was immoral, both counsel have agreed that I am bound to follow the recent decision of the Appellate Division of the Supreme Court of Alberta in *R. v. Johnson (No. 1)*, 8 C.C.C. (2d) 1. This was a stated case before the learned Riley J. [(1972), 6 C.C.C. (2d) 462], and appealed from him to the Appellate Division.

In that case, McDermid J.A., speaking for the Court, said, after drawing attention to the fact that s. 170 of the *Criminal Code* makes it a crime for anyone to appear nude in a public place, that he understood the enactment of that offence, by the Parliament of Canada, and, I quote, "declared that it is a breach of a moral standard in Canada". And he goes on,

> We know of no better way of establishing a moral standard than a declaration by the Parliament of Canada, and so the Provincial Judge was justified in accepting this as his standard in finding that the dance by the respondent in the nude was an immoral performance.

I understand, therefore, that since, to be nude in a public place is itself an offence; to perform in the nude, therefore, is an immoral performance within the meaning of the charging section. Therefore, I must conclude that the performance here was immoral within the meaning of that section.

. . . .

The next argument raised on behalf of the appellant is that the appellant lacked the necessary *mens rea* for this offence. The facts in this respect were these: she engaged to do this performance, where, earlier, she had refused to engage to do this performance, because she relied upon the statement made to her, by Pierre Couchard, that he, in turn, had been informed that a Supreme Court Judge had, to use his words because he also gave evidence, "Ruled that we could go ahead with bottomless dancing." That decision arose out of a charge in the City of Calgary, of a business acquaintance of Couchard, who was the manager of the place where this performance took place. Ironically, the decision to which Couchard and the appellant referred is the decision at the Trial Division level in *R. v. Johnson (No. 1)*, to which I earlier referred, and which, the witnesses tell me, obtained some newspaper publicity. It was a decision then, that subsequently was reversed on appeal.

Mistake of fact is a defence to a criminal charge, where it can be said that the facts believed by the accused, if true, would have afforded him a defence. It is also said that a mistake of mixed fact and law is a defence. I understand that proposition to be correct, simply because, if there is a mistake of mixed fact and law, then there is a mistake of fact. In my view, there was no mistake of fact by the appellant here. What she was told had happened, in fact, did happen.

Her mistake, if she made any mistake, was in concluding that a statement of law, expressed by the learned Riley J., was the law. That is not a mistake of fact, that is a mistake of law. It is a mistake of law to misunderstand the significance of the decision of a Judge, or of his reasons. It is also a mistake of law to conclude that the decision of any particular Judge correctly states the law, unless that Judge speaks on behalf of the ultimate Court of Appeal.

This is not a situation like others, where a mistake of law can be a defence, not because a mistake of law is a defence, but because a mistake of law can negative a malicious intent required for that crime. Thus, for example, where the law requires that a person wilfully, or maliciously, or knowingly, does something wrong, it could conceivably be a defence as negativing intention, to show that, because of the mistake in the understanding of the law, there was no wilful intent or malice. This is not one of those situations, as no such special intention is required for this offence. The only *mens rea* required here is that the appellant intended to do that which she did. And there is no suggestion, for a moment, that she lacked that *mens rea*.

This statement, that mistake of law is no defence, is contained in the *Criminal Code*, in s. 19, under the old numbering, which says:

> 19. Ignorance of the law by a person who commits an offence is not an excuse for committing that offence.

Excuse, or legal justification, is a defence at law, and I understand that defence to mean that it is a defence to a criminal charge to show that the act complained of was authorized by some other law. Section 19 says that defence is not available, in effect, when a person has made a mistake as to whether or not this act is excused by another law or authorized by another law.

Properly understood, in my view, the section removing ignorance of the law as a defence, in criminal matters, is not a matter of justice, but a matter of policy. There will always be cases, not so complicated as this, where honest and reasonable mistakes as to the state of the law will be the explanation of the conduct of an accused. In such a circumstance, one cannot help but have sympathy for the accused. But that situation, traditionally, is not a defence. It is not a defence, I think, because the first requirement of any system of justice, is that it work efficiently and effectively. If the state of understanding of the law of an accused person is ever to be relevant in criminal proceedings, we would have an absurd proceeding. The issue in a criminal trial would then not be what the accused did, but whether or not the accused had a sufficiently sophisticated understanding of the law to appreciate that what he did offended against the law. There would be a premium, therefore, placed upon ignorance of the law.

Our Courts, following the traditions of English jurisprudence, have closed that avenue from consideration in the criminal court-room. I respectfully disagree with the learned American Judges in those cases cited by the counsel for the appellant.

The defence should not be allowed as a matter of public policy, contrary to the statement of those learned Judges. Indeed, it cannot be allowed because of public policy. This is the case, notwithstanding the sympathy evoked by the situation of an accused person.

Kenny, in his book, *Outlines of Criminal Law*, and I am quoting from the first edition, said at p. 69:

> although mistakes of law, unreasonable or even reasonable, thus leave the offender punishable for the crime which he has blundered into, they may of course afford good grounds for inflicting on him a milder punishment.

That is the only relevance, in my view, of the situation in which the appellant finds herself.

I have given some consideration as to whether or not this position varies at all, because of the unique circumstances here, where the appellant relied upon a specific judgment of a Court very immediate in terms of time and place, as opposed to a solicitor's opinion or some understanding as to the law. There is no question that there is something of an anomaly here. Reliance on a specific order, of a specific Judge, granted at a specific time and place, seems, at first sight, not to be ignorance of the law, but knowledge of the law. If it turns out that that Judge is mistaken, then, of course, the reliance on that Judge's judgment is mistaken. The irony is this: people in society are expected to have a more profound knowledge of the law than are the Judges. I am not the first person to have made that comment about the law, and while it is all very amusing, it is really to no point.

The principle that ignorance of the law should not be a defence in criminal matters is not justified because it is fair, it is justified because it is necessary, even though it will, sometimes produce an anomalous result.

When this appellant relied on the decision of the learned trial Judge, she relied on his authority for the law. As it turns out, that reliance was misplaced, as misplaced as reliance on any statement as to the law I might make. Less so, I am sure.

Like counsel, I have had difficulty finding any authorities on this point. I was referred to *Conway v. The King* (1943), 81 C.C.C. 189, by counsel for the appellant. I have read that case. This issue, in my view, is not discussed in that case.

I have also read *R. v. Brinkley* (1907), 12 C.C.C. 454, in which the matter is discussed, although not this specific situation. In that case, a man had received advice from his counsel that a decree of divorce, made by a foreign Court, validly dissolved his marriage in the eyes of the Courts of Canada, and that he was, therefore, free to remarry without fear of bigamy. That opinion was mistaken. He was charged with bigamy, and he was convicted, notwithstanding his reliance on that opinion.

I have also read *Kokoliades v. Kennedy* (1911), 18 C.C.C. 495, which, to me, comes as close as can be to the situation here. This was a case in the Quebec Supreme Court, and arose in 1911. In that case, the accused was charged in the City of Montreal, with selling candy on a Sunday, contrary to a provision in a federal statute. His defence was that he relied on a municipal by-law licensing him to sell candy on a Sunday.

It would appear that this strange situation arose because there was some doubt as to the validity of the federal legislation which had been removed from the revised statutes, although not repealed. Subsequently, the Province of Quebec and the City of Montreal passed regulatory legislation purporting to permit in certain cases sales on the Lord's Day forbidden in the federal statute. The Magistrate hearing the trial heard argument from the Crown that the federal legislation was constitutionally valid, and the Montreal City by-law was constitutionally invalid, and therefore an excuse was not available to the accused because the law authorizing him to do what he did, and upon which he relied, although enacted by a Legislature, or under the authority of the Legislature, was *ultra vires*.

The learned Magistrate in that case, found that the Montreal by-law was *ultra vires*, and the federal statute *intra vires*; a decision which, in another case, was subsequently confirmed by the Privy Council, as we all know.

The learned Magistrate went on to say that, because the law upon which the accused relied was unconstitutional, it was no law at all. He had nothing to rely upon, and he was guilty. This matter was appealed to Quebec Supreme Court. The Supreme Court Judge said that a statute authorizing an act should give rise to the defence of excuse, even though that statute may be *ultra vires*, and that the defence of excuse should be available in such a situation until there has been a judgment declaring the statute to be *ultra vires* spoken by a Court of high jurisdiction "after the gravest consideration". That is a strange remark. I would have thought that Courts of high or low jurisdiction give every case grave consideration.

The situation there is not unlike the situation here. The accused there, saw a city by-law, seemingly authorizing him to do what he did, and relied upon it. It turned out the by-law had no validity. But it would take sophistication in the law to appreciate that.

Similarly, here, the appellant relied upon a statement of law, by a Supreme Court Judge in Alberta. It would take the greatest of sophistication of knowledge of the law to conclude that he was or might be mistaken. In the first case, a Judge, on appeal, held that the defence of excuse ought to be allowed.

I respectfully disagree with the Judge in that case, for the reasons I have mentioned.

. . . .

I, therefore, conclude that the mistake of law of the appellant affords no defence to her on this charge. There being no other defences, and the facts necessary having been made out, the conviction of the Court below, in my opinion, was correct. The appeal as to conviction is dismissed.

. . . .

I should have been more careful in my language a moment ago, when I said the appeal as to conviction was dismissed. Under the new law, I should have more properly said that I find the appellant guilty of the charge, and will hear argument as to whether or not to allow or dismiss the appeal as to conviction.

. . . .

Well, I have already indicated, in a quotation from Kenny, that, in this awkward situation, the matter does not afford a defence, but should certainly be considered in mitigation of sentence. Indeed, there are several cases, not as awkward as this, in the law reports, involving a person who had an honest and reasonable mistake in belief as to the law, and for whom the Courts expressed sympathy, and, in respect of whom, sentence was mitigated.

It is at this stage where the scales of justice are balanced. Clothed with very recent power to refuse to enter a conviction, I can now balance the scales of justice even more delicately. I have read a note in vol. 14 of the English and Empire Digest, at p. 51 of an old case, *R. v. Bailey* (1800), Russ & Ry. 1. It goes back to 1800. In that case, the Government of England had passed a statute, making something a crime which was not previously a crime. Subsequently, the accused did the forbidden act. The Courts found that, in fact, in the district in which this crime was committed, no news had yet reached anyone of the passage of this Act. Nor could any news have reached this district of the passage of this Act. And that the accused, therefore, had to be convicted of an offence which he did not and could not have known was an offence. And they said there that the proper way of dealing with the matter was to give a pardon, which I understand to be a conviction followed immediately by the wiping out of a conviction.

I have no power to give a pardon, but I do have power to give an absolute discharge. In my view, this is the proper case.

Ironically, the decision of Riley J. in *Johnson*, relied on by Campbell to her detriment, was later upheld on final appeal: *Johnson v. R.* (1974), 23 C.R.N.S. 273, 13 C.C.C. (2d) 402 (S.C.C.).

Given the rigid s. 19 rule, the characterization of the mistake as one of fact or law will be crucial. **Do you agree with the following classifications?**

R. v. ARYEH

(1972), 6 C.C.C. (2d) 171 (Ont. C.A.)

MacKay J.A. (Kelly J.A. concurring) (orally): — The appellant appeals from the decision of a County Court Judge on a trial *de novo* dismissing an appeal to that Court from a conviction by a Provincial Court Judge on a charge that the appellant did, without lawful excuse have in his possession certain goods unlawfully imported into Canada, namely, a quantity of gem stones, rings, vases, jewellery boxes, the value for duty of the said goods being $200 or over, contrary to s. 203 of the *Customs Act*, R.S.C. 1952, c. 58 [now s. 205, R.S.C. 1970, c. C-40].

It is not disputed that these goods were brought in by the appellant as household goods under his wife's name and it is also not disputed that the Crown proved the goods were brought into this country and that they were dutiable goods.

His defence was that he believed he was entitled to bring the goods into Canada as household goods under his wife's name.

My brother Kelly and myself are of the view that the appeal must be dismissed. The learned trial Judge in his reasons for judgment in the Court below said:

> It appears to me that the accused very foolishly included these items with his wife's household effects in the mistaken belief that they could be brought to Canada under the cloak of the exemption. I doubt that he realized that he was committing a deliberate act of smuggling. I, therefore, dismiss the appeal as to the conviction.

Section 19 of the *Criminal Code* is as follows:

> 19. Ignorance of the law by a person who commits an offence is not an excuse for committing that offence.

It is clear in the view of the majority of the Court that his defence was based on ignorance of the law and that defence therefore fails by reason of s. 19 and my brother Kelly and myself would dismiss the appeal.

Brooke J.A. (dissenting orally): — My brother has accurately set out the facts and I do not wish to add anything in that respect.

The trial Judge found what happened here was the result of an error that was made by the appellant. His findings are clear that he believed the appellant's evidence in this respect and they show that he was free of any blameworthy state of mind or any intention to break the law. He was charged with a crime here. His defence was no *mens rea* and in my view that defence should have succeeded on the findings of the trial Judge and I would have acquitted him.

Appeal dismissed.

In *R. v. Jorgensen* (1996), 43 C.R. (4th) 137, 102 C.C.C. (3d) 97, [1995] 4 S.C.R. 55, the Supreme Court held that for a conviction of "knowingly" selling obscene material contrary to s. 163(2)(*a*) of the *Criminal Code*, the Crown must prove that the accused was aware that the subject-matter had as its dominant characteristic the exploitation of sex and knew of the presence of ingredients of the subject-matter which as a matter of law rendered the exploitation of sex undue. Approval by a provincial censor board could not constitute a justification or excuse but might be relevant to the determination of community standards of tolerance. It not relevant to the issue of the accused's knowledge. The Crown need not prove that the accused knew that the subject-matter exceeded community standards.

Where the mistake or ignorance relates to law, s. 19 must be applied. There are, however, two major exceptions — colour of right, which is a statutory exception applying to certain property offences, and that of officially induced error of law, which is emerging as a common law defence.

R. v. HOWSON

47 C.R. 322, [1966] 3 C.C.C. 348 (Ont. C.A.)

LASKIN J.A.: — This is an appeal from a conviction of theft in a "law school" case. The owner of a car parked it on a private parking lot without having any authority to do so. The superintendent of the property of which the lot was a part, telephoned the Ace Towing Service with which he had a standing arrangement for removal by that firm of cars unlawfully parked on the lot. The accused, an employee of the firm, towed the car to a compound maintained by the firm for cars taken in such circumstances or repossessed on behalf of conditional sellers or assignees for contractual default. The car owner in the present case traced his car to the compound, but his demand for its return was met by a refusal unless he paid a towing charge of $10 and a storage charge of $2 per day. There was evidence that such charges were in ordinary circumstances reasonable charges. The trespassing car owner later paid $14 under protest, but before reclaiming his car he laid a charge of theft against the accused under s. 269 of the *Criminal Code*. J.L. Addison, Magistrate, before whom the charge was tried, convicted the accused on the ground that he wrongfully withheld the car from its owner after demand for its return. The neat question is whether it is theft to hold a trespasser to reasonable ransom of his goods, placed by him on another's land, after they are removed, at the behest of the occupier of the land, by a third person who refuses on demand to return them unless the ransom is paid.

There was evidence in this case that there were large signs on the parking lot stating that it was for private parking only and that cars unlawfully parked there would be towed away at the owner's expense. The informant in the case at bar had parked his car on the lot on a cold wintry night and his evidence was that he did not see the signs. He knew, however, that he was trespassing on private property.

Section 269 [now s. 322], so far as relevant to the instant case, reads as follows:

> 269(1) Every one commits theft who fraudulently and without colour of right takes, or fraudulently and without colour of right converts to his use or to the use of another person, anything whether animate or inanimate, with intent,
>> (a) to deprive, temporarily or absolutely, the owner of it or a person who has a special property or interest in it, of the thing or of his property or interest in it . . .
>> (3) A taking or conversion of anything may be fraudulent notwithstanding that it is effected without secrecy or attempt at concealment.
>> (4) For the purposes of this Act the question whether anything that is converted is taken for the purpose of conversion, or whether it is, at the time it is converted, in the lawful possession of the person who converts it is not material.

These provisions cover not only an originally wrongful taking but also a wrongful detention by the way of refusal to return, where this is done "fraudulently and without colour of right", with intent to deprive the owner of his goods even temporarily. This last-mentioned element must be reasonably construed to exonerate an accused who, for example, refuses to get up in the middle of the night to return goods to an owner. No exoneration on this ground arises in this case because the evidence is clear that the accused and his firm claimed the right to retain the informant's car until such time as he paid towing and storage charges, and the latter would multiply on a daily basis.

. . . .

There remains for consideration the accused's contentions that he was not shown to have removed and detained the informant's car fraudulently and without colour of right as required by s. 269. Although it may be doubtful (as is pointed out by Glanville Williams, *Criminal Law: General Part*, 2nd ed. (1961), p. 322) whether, apart from special situations, the term "fraudulent" adds anything to the phrase "without colour of right", it is enough to say that it merely emphasizes the intentional character of the offence; an intention to take or keep that involves knowledge of what is being done and that the property of another is the subject of the intention and of the appropriation or detention: See *R. v. Williams and Williams*, [1953] 1 Q.B. 660; *R. v. Shymkowich*, [1954] S.C.R. 606, 110 C.C.C. 97, 19 C.R. 401.

It is unnecessary to find deceit: that is not an element of the offence of theft under s. 269, but its presence may be a factor in the evidence offered to prove guilty intent to steal. See *R. v. Wolfe* (1961), 132 C.C.C. 130. It must be remembered that the technicalities of common law larceny have been overcome by legislative formulations of theft designed to cover such situations as theft by bailees or agents or trustees in which fraud plays a stronger role than in straight theft under s. 269. The accused in the present case is not charged under those provisions of the *Criminal Code* dealing with such special aspects of theft.

A strong contention was made by the accused on the issue of "colour of right". The phrase is not defined in the *Criminal Code*. There may be, as is suggested by *R. v. Shymkowich*, at least this difference in the application of the terms "fraudulently" and "without colour of right", that whereas in respect of the former a mistaken belief as to legal rights will not avail the accused if he none the less intends to take or keep another's goods, it may be a shield on the basis of colour of right. Accepting that colour of right embraces belief in either matters of law or of fact justifying the challenged taking or detention, the authorities are clear that it must be an honest belief even though a mistaken one; see *R. v. Shymkowich, supra*; *R. v. Lyon* (1898), 2 C.C.C. 242; *R. v. Johnson* (1904), 8 C.C.C. 123; *R. v. Bernhard*, [1938] 2 K.B. 264; and *cf. R. v. Laroche*, [1964] S.C.R. 667, [1965] 1 C.C.C. 261, 43 C.R. 228; reversing [1963] 3 C.C.C. 5, 40 C.R. 144. Thus, an honest belief of a repairer that he is entitled to retake the repaired goods by way of lien or security for his unpaid charges will warrant an acquittal of theft: See *R. v. Wade* (1869), 11 Cox C.C. 549; *R. v. Clay* (1909), 3 Cr. App. R. 92.

Although the unreasonableness of a belief, when objectively considered, does not necessarily destroy the honesty of the belief, it may be considered, along with other evidence in determining whether the Crown has established that a taking or a conversion was without colour of right. Certainly, it cannot alone be a ground for establishing that there was no colour of right. The issue requires, however, some evidence from the accused although the ultimate burden is on the Crown. What then does the record in this case disclose on the matter?

The accused knew he was taking and detaining property that was not his own and he knew also that the property did not belong to the parking lot operator. Nor did either of them have any interest in it unless the taking and detention could be founded on a claim of lien or right of distress. I have already stated that no right of lien arose in the circumstances, nor any right to distrain for the towing and storage charges. But the critical question is whether the accused can be said to have had no honest belief in his right to take and detain the informant's car at the time that he did so.

The convicting Magistrate did not address himself expressly to this point but it cannot be assumed that he was oblivious to it; and, certainly, if the record supports an absence of colour of right the conviction cannot be disturbed. The accused's evidence goes no farther than to say that he acted on the authority of the parking lot operator and believed he could detain the car until his firm's charges were paid. There was nothing in his cross-examination to suggest that this was other than an honest belief. The owner of Ace Towing Service also gave evidence but the questions put to him on cross-examination fell short of establishing that there was an absence of honest belief in his right to operate as he did. He admitted to previous criminal convictions but what they were for was not in evidence. Again, questions were put as to his belief at the time of trial but the Magistrate, quite properly, refused to permit him to answer. No questions were put as to any like experiences that Ace Towing Service may have had before the present incident. If there were like experiences, in the Courts, whether the proceedings were civil or criminal, they would have a decided bearing on colour of right. This "defence" (it is, strictly speaking, part of the Crown's case on the issue of *mens rea*) is not one on which an accused can rely more than once in the same kind of transaction. An acquittal on the ground only of want of proof that there was no colour of right removes the basis for any subsequent claim of colour of right on a similar charge where neither in law or in fact does the accused have the right claimed.

I have read and reread the record in this matter and have considered very carefully whether on the record I should conclude as Judson J. did, speaking for the majority in *R. v. Laroche, supra,* that "there could be no honesty or honest opinion of right in [this transaction]". The situation here differs considerably from that in the *Laroche* case, and I have a doubt that I must resolve in favour of the accused. The conviction will, therefore, be set aside and a verdict of acquittal entered, but since there is no basis on which the accused in the circumstances herein could lawfully assert a lien or a right to distrain, the accused is put on notice as is the firm which employs him that "colour of right" can no longer be invoked to avoid a conviction for theft if another's car should be taken and detained as was that of the informant in this case.

PORTER C.J.O.: —

. . . .

The *Criminal Code* and the *Larceny Act,* 1916 (U.K.), c. 50, are similar in so far as they apply to facts corresponding to those in issue here. If upon all the facts, the only inference which may reasonably be drawn points to an intent to steal, a conviction must follow. If the evidence shows, as in this case, that there was no legal right to withhold the vehicle and unlike this case, that there was no other evidence, there would I should think, be an irresistible inference of theft. If, however, upon consideration of all the evidence before them, a jury, properly instructed, were satisfied that the accused honestly but mistakenly believed that he had a right in law or in fact, they should acquit. The question is whether upon all the evidence the proper inference to be drawn would be that the accused did have an honest belief. This is a question for the tribunal of first instance. The weight of authority would indicate, I think, that the test for the determination of the presence of an honest belief is a subjective rather than an objective one.

. . . .

Thus there is considerable authority in the English cases culminating in the decision of the Court of Criminal Appeal in *R. v. Bernhard, supra,* to establish that colour of right applies equally to fact and law. I think that in England, honest mistake of either fact or law would be a defence to a charge of theft. The Canadian authorities are less clear. In *R. v. Lyon, supra,* a Divisional Court dealt with a situation where the defendant had a right to demand payment. In *R. v. Laroche, supra,* it is doubtful whether the Supreme Court intended to overrule the judgment of McLennan J.A., which was consistent with *R. v. Bernhard.* In *R. v. Shymkowich,* Rand J. adopted a statement from Kenny to the effect that mistake of law is not an excuse, and in this Taschereau J. concurred. Estey J., Fauteux J. concurring, considered a mistake of law as well as of fact to be a defence. Locke J. in his judgment said [p. 624 S.C.R., p. 114 C.C.C.]:

Other than to construe the language of the Code defining theft, I see no question of law in this matter other than as to whether there was any evidence upon which the learned County Court Judge could find that the respondent took possession of the logs believing that he was entitled to do so with the intention not of stealing them but of profiting by obtaining salvage from the owners it they were found, or which left him in such doubt as to require him to acquit him. I respectfully agree with the Chief Justice of British Columbia that there was evidence upon which the trial Judge could so find.

Thus the judgments of Estey and Locke JJ. turned mainly upon the facts.

Rand J. did not deal with the question of colour of right. He relied upon s. 19 of the *Criminal Code* which states:

19. Ignorance of the law by a person who commits an offence is not an excuse for committing that offence.

In my view the word "right" should be construed broadly. The use of the word cannot be said to exclude a legal right. The word is in its ordinary sense charged with legal implications. I do not think that s. 19 affects s. 269. Section 19 only applies when there is an offence. There is no offence if there is colour of right. If upon all the evidence it may fairly be inferred that the accused acted under a genuine misconception of fact or law, there would be no offence of theft committed. The trial tribunal must satisfy itself that the accused has acted upon an honest, but mistaken belief that the right is based upon either fact or law, or mixed fact and law.

The following are extracts from the evidence:

A. No. The car was picked up and taken up to our pound. To Ace Towing compound.

Q. Why to your pound? Why do you have to take it to your pound, that's what I want to know. Who gave you permission to take the car to your pound? That's what I'm asking you.

A. The superintendent of the building.

Q. To take it to your pound? A. Yes.

Q. All right. Now, on whose consent did you hold the car there? On whose authority and who gave you consent to hold the car at your pound? A. Whose consent?

Q. Yes. To hold the car there. A. Well, the car was being held there for the towing and storage charges of it.

Q. To be charged to who? A. To the owner of the car.

Q. To the owner of the car. Now, so you are holding. . . . Am I right in saying that you held the car in your possession and that you held it there on the authority of exhibit three, and you feel you believed this, did you? That you had authority to hold the car? A. This letter right there?

Q. Yes. A. Yes.

. . . .

Q. How long did you feel that you could keep this car without the consent of the owner of the car? A. Until he retrieved the car, sir.

Q. Until he retrieved it on whose terms? A. On the terms of the company, sir.

Q. On the terms of the towing company? A. To pay the towing charges.

The learned trial Judge held that the removal of the vehicle to Merton St. was not an unreasonable thing to do. Under the circumstances, I would agree with this finding. The real question here is whether the accused had, under the circumstances, a colour of right sufficient to justify his refusal to release the vehicle. If not, upon the facts of this case, he would be guilty of theft.

The accused was an employee of his brother, Walter Howson, who was the owner of the towing company. The evidence indicates that the accused acted upon instructions from his brother. He stated that he believed he had a right to retain the car until the towing charges were paid. He produced a letter from the building superintendent which ostensibly gave him the right to retain the car. Because the accused was asked to give up the car and refused to do so without payment, the Magistrate said that he was wrongfully withholding the car, the company having no lien upon it. He thereupon convicted the accused. However, the Magistrate then proceeded to make certain comments. He said that the accused was not trying to steal a car or intending to steal one. He then said that the type of business was not one that he would encourage.

I think that it is clear from this evidence that the Magistrate misdirected himself by failing to consider the question of colour of right. From what he said after the conviction, it was obvious that he did not believe that the accused was trying or intending to steal the car. Under these circumstances he should, I think, have acquitted the accused. There were other points raised in the argument, but since, upon the grounds stated, I would acquit, I do not think it necessary to deal with them.

EVANS J.A. concurs with PORTER C.J.O.

Appeal allowed; accused acquitted.

R. v. DRAINVILLE

(1991), 5 C.R. (4th) 38 (Ont. Prov. Div.)

The accused, a priest and elected member of the provincial Legislature, was charged with mischief contrary to s. 430(1)(c) of the *Criminal Code*. With others he had blocked a parcel of land to protest the construction of a road. Although the province had title to the land, the protestors believed that the aboriginal rights to the lands should prevail. The Ontario Supreme Court and the Court of Appeal had ruled that the aboriginal rights were extinguished by an 1850 treaty. The accused and other protestors had to be taken away from the land by the police. The incident resulted in a delay of approximately one hour.

FOURNIER Prov. Div. J.: —

. . . .

On Civil Disobedience & The Rule of Law

Another line of defence advanced on behalf of the accused, is that his actions constitute at best passive resistance, a type of civil disobedience which ought not result in his conviction. It is said that his involvement was indeed minimal, that his motives and intentions were noble and good, and that in fact, he has contributed in his own small way to a just and honourable political solution. In referring to a "political solution", counsel is no doubt alluding to the memorandum of agreement dated April 23, 1990, entered into by the representatives of the Teme-Augama Anishnabai Nation and those of the Ontario Government. Though the issue of title is now before the Supreme Court of Canada, though the actual title is still with the Ontario Government, it seems that this agreement provides for a stewardship arrangement covering some four Townships; over the next 10 to 25 years, it seems that this "stewardship management" approach could be expanded gradually so that, ultimately, all of the contested lands known to the Teme-Augama Anishnabai Nation as N'Daki Mena will be so governed. It seems that indeed a viable political solution may be been found after a long period of hardship and legal complications. It seems that the protestors and the accused in this case may have had a valid point; and what can we make of that within the context of this case?

As I pointed out in my decision *R. v. Gary Potts* (unreported) this Court is certainly mindful, that civil disobedience is a time-honoured method of drawing public attention to claims of fundamental freedoms and human rights. I mentioned such notable examples as Rev. Martin Luther King and Mahatma Ghandhi.

Ironically enough Father Drainville, during the course of his examination in chief, cited a passage from a book entitled "The Words of Ghandhi" a selection of Richard Attenborough, released by Newmarket Press, 1982. At p. 57 thereof he quotes:

> Civil disobedience is the inherent right of a citizen. He dare not give it up without ceasing to be a man. Civil disobedience is never followed by anarchy. Criminal disobedience can lead to it. Every state puts down criminal disobedience by force. It perishes, if it does not. But to put down civil disobedience is to attempt to imprison conscience.

Father Drainville would no doubt qualify his actions in obstructing the roadway as "civil disobedience", which presumably should be condoned by this Court. In order to gain a better insight as to what Ghandhi had in mind when he wrote these words, I took the liberty of referring to a book entitled *The Life of Mahatma Ghandhi* by Louis Fischer (New York: Harper & Row, 1st Harper Paperback ed., 1983). It seems that Ghandhi was significantly influenced by the writings of Henry David Thoreau, a poet and essayist, born in 1817, and referred to as a "New England rebel" who hated Negro slavery, the individual's slavery to the Church, the State, property, customs and traditions (see p. 88). At one point, Thoreau allegedly refused to pay his taxes and was sent to jail until a friend of his bailed him out. That experience apparently evoked his most provoking political essay entitled "Civil Disobedience". In this essay he wrote:

> The only obligation which I have a right to assume, is to do at any time what I think right. To be right, is more honourable than to be *law-abiding*. [Emphasis added.]

It is said that Mahatma Ghandhi referred to this essay as a "masterly treatise" and that "it left a deep impression on me".

In that light, it is clear that Mahatma Ghandhi was more concerned with doing what he felt in his conscience to be right, rather than observe the legislated provisions of a government. One cannot assume that what he meant by "civil disobedience" was lawful activity as we know it in our judicial system, and that "criminal disobedience" was unlawful. It is clear that he had his own standards, that he was a self-appointed judge of what was acceptable and not acceptable, that he arrogated himself with the power and ability to determine what was criminal and what was not!

Surely, this approach is not exactly consistent with what we commonly refer to as the "rule of law"; and anyone relying on such ideology, conceivably does so at his peril. This also illustrates the great wisdom behind the expression: "don't believe everything you read"!

In an unreported decision of the Provincial Court of Saskatchewan, *R. v. Pratt*, Judge Nutting is quoted as follows [p. 126, [1990] 3 C.N.L.R. 120]:

> The adoption of civil disobedience methods in the promotion of a just cause does not transform illegal actions into legal ones. Certainly, the motives and idealism of those who commit an act of civil disobedience are to be weighed in the balance in regard to any penal sanctions; however, no honourable or just cause justifies the breaking of an acceptable and reasonable law.

In the unreported case of *R. v. Potts*, this Court made its views known with respect to civil disobedience. I had occasion to quote Mr. Chief Justice Howland, as he then was, when he addressed the government at the opening of Courts ceremony, in Toronto, in January 1990. He said:

> It is one of the fundamental principles of our democratic society that no one is above the law, and everyone is equal before the law. The rule of law is based on the fact that our current laws represent the will of the majority of the people. If a law no longer represents the will of the majority, then it should be changed but until it is changed by lawful means, it must be obeyed. Defiance of the law is not the answer.

Finally, let me reiterate this Court's position. Is "civil disobedience" or even "passive resistance" such a small infraction, or such a minimal use of force, that the "*actus reus*" ought to be overlooked? Should such activity as obstructing a road be justified by some sort of approval by the Courts on the grounds that the motives are good and noble, or that the situation is really a "political" one? In light of the existing circumstances of this case, where it seems a just and appropriate political solution appears to have been found, this might be a tempting proposition. But certainly that would be tantamount to a declaration that, in some instances, at the discretion of some judge, and irrespective of the "rule of law", there are times when "the ends justify the means". Even in this case, where it appears that the government of Ontario may be about to change its policies and perhaps admit to a previous error in judgment, where it appears that a memorandum of agreement termed a viable "political solution" is now in place and that those protestors may have been morally right, surely, the process of legitimizing previously unlawful acts, after the fact is an inherently dangerous concept which is simply not acceptable as an alternative to the "rule of law".

To permit this process to replace the "rule of law" would be to grant permission to anyone to arrogate himself with the powers of a Judge and determine for himself or herself, and from time to time, what is acceptable or just, and what is not, on behalf of the majority. As such anyone could adjudicate himself or herself above the law, and no one would be equal before the law. Such a situation would surely lead to anarchy, and very quickly so.

For these reasons, this Court is of the view that an apparently insignificant or harmless step taken without respect for the "rule of law" is indeed one which is made of the very same substance that disrespect, insult, mischief, filibuster, insurrection, mutiny and ultimately, outright war, are all made of. For these reasons "civil disobedience" cannot be condoned. Those who wish to resort to it as a means of expression are able to do so in our free and democratic society, but they must also suffer the consequences of their actions. They must be made to suffer the sanctions which are provided for as Mr. Chief Justice Howland stated: "defiance of the law is not the answer!"

Accordingly, and for the reasons just given, that line of defence cannot succeed.

Colour of Right:

The defence places most of its emphasis on this line of defence. In determining whether Father Drainville might benefit from this approach, a quick review of the law and pertinent cases is useful.

Firstly, s. 429(2) of the *Code* provides that:

> No person shall be convicted of an offence under sections 430 to 446 where he proves that he acted with legal justification or excuse and with colour of right.

A correct interpretation of this section provides a successful defence to anyone able to demonstrate "legal justification or excuse" or "colour of right". See *R. v. Creaghan* (1982), 31 C.R. (3d) 277, 1 C.C.C. (3d) 449 (Ont. C.A.). Furthermore, "colour of right" is defined as:

> an honest belief in the existence of a state of facts which, if it actually existed, would at law justify or excuse the act done."

It is also a fair statement of the law that a successful defence can arise from a mistake of fact or law, or mixed law and fact, and that the test to be used by the presiding judge in the determination of the presence of an honest belief, is a "subjective test". See *R. v. Howson*, [1966] 2 O.R. 63, 47 C.R. 322, [1966] 3 C.C.C. 348 (C.A.).

There is further direction in the *Howson* decision, to the effect that the word "right" should be construed broadly, and that it is in its ordinary sense, charged with legal implications. Finally, it seems that "reasonableness" is not a necessary element in these considerations. (See *Howson, supra*)

In *R. v. Nundah* (1916), 16 N.S.W. R. 482 referred to by Mr. Justice Porter in the *Howson* decision, at p. 482, Cullen C.J.C. in dealing with the questions of honesty on the part of the accused in his belief in his ownership said:

> The question whether he honestly believed the property to be his is that which is material. Possibly some of the stronger beliefs held by human beings might be found by other minds to be completely destitute of reasonable grounds. . . . A man may be ever so much mistaken in his reasoning processes and yet be honest, though you would not accept his mere statement of opinion unless there was some colour in the circumstances for his entertaining the opinion he claims to have had.

And still on the subject of "reasonableness" Mr. Justice Laskin in *R. v. Howson* goes on to say at p. 79 [O.R.]:

> Although the unreasonableness of a belief, when objectively considered, does not necessarily destroy the honesty of the belief, it may be considered, along with other evidence in determining whether the Crown has established that a taking or a conversion was without colour of right. Certainly, it cannot alone be a ground for establishing that there was no colour of right. The issue requires, however, some evidence from the accused although the ultimate burden is on the Crown.

In this case, as I ruled in *R. v. Potts* recently, using an "objective" test, it could not be said that Mr. Drainville harboured an honest belief that the Teme-Augama Anishnabai Nation had title to the lands, where the road blockade and obstruction took place. In the absence of an explanation of some sort, the Court would certainly draw a very adverse inference in the circumstances at hand. In the case of *R. v. Potts*, the Court ruled in favour of the accused, as it was left with a reasonable doubt as to Mr. Potts' state of mind, relating to colour of right. It could be said that Chief Gary Potts had a point of view as to the ownership of the contested lands, which was based in part on certain very strong moral convictions, but also based on a belief in a state of mixed law and fact, which if it actually had existed, would at law have justified or excused his actions. In fact he would have been obstructing a roadway which belonged to him and his people, a clear defence to allegations pursuant to s. 430(1)(*c*) of the *Criminal Code*.

This brings us to another consideration, not brought up in the *Gary Potts* trial, and that is the distinction between an honest belief in a "moral" as opposed to a "legal or lawful" right. It is clear that in Ontario, at least, an honest belief in a moral as opposed to legal right cannot constitute a colour of right defence. See *R. v. Hemmerly* (1976), 30 C.C.C. (2d) 141 (Ont. C.A.). Martin J.A. at p. 145 writes:

> Even if the appellant believed that he had a moral claim to the money (which I am far from holding), a belief in a moral claim could not constitute a colour of right: see Glanville Williams' *Criminal Law* (*the General Part*, 2nd ed. (1961), p. 322, Harris v. Harrison [1963] Crim. L.R. 497, and commentary.)

> Glanville Williams in his well-known work, referred to above, expresses the view that while belief in a moral right as distinct from a legal right is irrelevant to the question of a claim of right, belief in a moral right in exceptional circumstances may show that the act is not done fraudulently.

It is true that the *Canadian Charter of Rights and Freedoms* starts off as follows:

> Whereas Canada is founded upon principles that recognize the supremacy of God and the rule of law:

But one must recognize that this is perhaps an ideal which we as a nation would like to achieve, but without being successful necessarily all the time. This great declaration seems to assume that both the supremacy of God and the rule of law are consistent with each other, without there being any conflicts between the two. One need only consider for a moment our great struggles with the law as it pertains to contentious issues such as "abortion" to realize that we have, at times, great conflicts between what we accept as "legal" and what we accept as "moral". Perhaps in an imperfect world such as ours, such conflicts are inevitable.

However one thing is certain; when there have been conflicts between our "legal" rules, and our "moral" rules, the courts invariably have ruled in favour of change along the lines provided by the "rule of law".

Though we strive as much as we can towards as near perfect a legal system as is possible, one which hopefully might be in perfect harmony with our "moral values", our real life experience is full of instances where from time to time there are difficult conflicts for us to accept between the "legal" and the "moral". Judging from developments enunciated in *R. v. Hemmerly, supra,* the "rule of law" must prevail.

Accordingly, this has been an area of grave concern for Father Drainville, the accused in these proceedings. A brief review of his evidence before this Court convinces us that certainly he has a great and deep moral conviction as the basis for his belief that the Teme-Augama Anishnabai Nation has a good claim to the lands — subject of these proceedings.

As noble and honourable his motives might be, they are really irrelevant in our considerations pertaining to "colour of right". Unless it can be demonstrated to this Court that his honest belief in the existence of a state of facts, in this case title to the subject lands, is based on a mistake of fact or law, his defence cannot succeed on moral conviction alone. Moral convictions though deeply and honestly held cannot transform illegal actions into legal ones; only the "rule of law" must prevail.

. . . .

Father Drainville did not find himself inextricably caught in a conflict as such between "moral rules of God" and the "rule of law"; his moral convictions, or his devotion to God did not entail his obstructing of a roadway, but only that he stand in solidarity perhaps with his brothers and sisters of the Teme-Augama Anishnabai Nation. That could have been done "lawfully" without offence pursuant to the *Criminal Code* of Canada, and certainly without offence to God! On the contrary he purposely and deliberately placed himself at peril, perhaps indeed for the sake of emphasis or additional media coverage of his "message" in support of a cause which could be termed "noble". However, having chosen that path, he must now walk it to its very end!

This of course places this Court in a somewhat difficult position as enunciated by my brother Judge Michel in his unreported decision in this Court on July 16, 1990 of *R. v. Smith*. However, the Court cannot and must not become emotionally or politically involved in such disputes. The Court must apply the law of the land as it existed at the relevant time according to the principles of the "rule of law".

Accordingly, by virtue of the principles enunciated in *R. v. Hemmerly*, a belief in a moral claim of right such as demonstrated by Father Drainville in these proceedings cannot constitute a defence of "colour of right". His defence must fail. There will be a finding of guilt.

So, too, the defence did not avail an environmental protester against a mischief charge resulting from the throwing of acid at a ship to stop it fishing: *Watson* (1999), 27 C.R. (5th) 139, 137 C.C.C. (3d) 422 (Nfld. C.A.). Three reasons were given for holding a mistaken belief that Canadian law did not apply beyond a 200-mile limit did not constitute a colour of right defence. There were no cases in which colour of right had been an answer to ignorance of the jurisdiction of the *Criminal Code*. It is no part of the *mens rea* of the offence of mischief that one intend to commit the crime within the jurisdiction of the *Criminal Code* of Canada. Thirdly, the basis of the defence of colour of right as it relates to law is the misunderstanding of the law respecting private rights. **Are these reasons convincing?**

Officially induced error of law has emerged as a new exception in a series of decisions:

R. v. MacLEAN
(1974), 27 C.R.N.S. 31, 17 C.C.C. (2d) 84 (N.S. Co. Ct.)

7th March 1974. O'HEARN Co. Ct. J.: — The Attorney General of Nova Scotia has appealed the defendant's acquittal on a charge under the *Criminal Code*, R.S.C. 1970, c. C-34, s. 238 (3) [now s. 259(4)]. In October 1972 the defendant was convicted under *Code* s. 235(2), refusing to take a breathalyzer test, and this resulted in the automatic revocation of his driver's licence in Nova Scotia under The *Motor Vehicle Act*, R.S.N.S. 1967, c. 191, s. 250(2). It is clear that the defendant was aware of this revocation.

The defendant is employed in radar maintenance by the telecommunications branch of the Department of Transport at the Halifax International Airport, at Kelly Lake, Halifax County. On 10th January 1973 he was driving a telecommunications vehicle on the driveway at the airport on his way to a radar site, when he became involved in a rear-end collision with another vehicle. He did not have a driver's licence at the time. The collision led to an investigation and the investigation brought about the charge in question.

The driveway where the collision took place describes an almost rectangular circuit in front of the airport terminal building in order to give access to the building and a parking lot on the other side of the circuit. The driveway is much in use by the public for these purposes, and the facts about its location and use are so notorious that they are subject to judicial notice. Any jury of this county would be aware of them. There is some evidence of the layout of the road but hardly enough to form a complete picture of it. Corporal H.L. Wilson, a member of the R.C.M.P., airport detachment, testified that the road in question was "federal property" and, accordingly, it was not governed by The Motor Vehicle Act although certain sections of that Act were incorporated by ss. 21 and 25 of the Regulations, *i.e.*, the sections requiring licences. He did not, to the best of my recollection, identify the Regulations, nor were they proved in any of the usual ways, and the only copy of them that I have seen is one supplied subsequent to the trial by defence counsel. This is a xerox copy of an extract from the Canada Gazette, Pt. II, vol. 98, pp. 948-55, 9th September 1964, purporting to contain the Airport Vehicle Control Regulations, P.C. 1964-1326. Sections 21 and 25 of these Regulations deal with parking meters and illegal parking and are not germane to this inquiry. Section 4 provides (in part):

> 4. No person shall operate a vehicle on an airport unless
> (*a*) He holds all licences and permits that he is by the laws of the province and municipality in which the airport is situated, required to hold in order to operate the vehicle in that province and municipality.

The defendant explained that since the revocation of his licence he did not drive on the highways, but he had permission from his superiors and the R.C.M.P. to drive on the airport property. He says that on 8th January 1973 it came to the attention of his superiors that he did not have a licence. He told them what he had done before but they suggested that he should not drive until the question was cleared up. Accordingly, the defendant telephoned the office of the Registrar of Motor Vehicles and talked to one Laporte (who did not testify) and was told on this occasion that it was not necessary to have a licence to drive on government property, all he needed was permission of his boss.

. . . .

4. *Is ignorance of the Regulations an excuse?*

. . . .

In the instant case, the defendant was, of course, aware that his licence had been revoked. His ignorance was of the existence of Regulations that, I must confess, are rather difficult to track down. The Regulations themselves purport to be made under two federal statutes rather than the usual one (*Department of Transport Act*, s. 25 and *Government Property Traffic Act*, s. 2), possibly because both are so general in the way they are expressed that there might be some doubt that the Regulations fell squarely within the ambit of either. Thus, under the former Act, there might be a question whether airports fall under the phrase "canals or other works under the management or control of the Minister", keeping in mind the possible impact of the *ejusdem generis* rule, while in the latter case there is no specific mention of licensing, although other elements of traffic control are specified.

More to the point, however, is the ignorance not only of the defendant but of his superiors in the telecommunications branch of that same Department of Transport concerning these Regulations. The defendant made a conscientious effort to find out what the legal situation was: he applied for information to the Motor Vehicle Department and was told that there was no need of a licence in the circumstance. He could, of course, have applied to the R.C.M.P. detachment at the airport, but I can well understand that that might not have occurred to him. Moreover, the evidence indicated that Corporal Wilson, the R.C.M.P. officer in question, was not fully conversant with the Regulations, as he cited the wrong sections for his authority.

This, I think, is a very different situation from that of the defendant in *Villeneuve* as far as the justness of holding him to a knowledge of the law is concerned. Of course, the maxim "hard cases make bad law" must be kept in mind, but this is the kind of case that could be of such general occurrence as to warrant making an exception if that is possible under the jurisprudence. What is the state of the law?

As noted, I am proceeding here on the basis I worked out in *Villeneuve*. I think some distinction can be made between statutes, especially those of general application, and Regulations such as are incidentally yet essentially in issue here; that is, the defendant's guilt turns not on his ignorance of the *Code* but of these Regulations. There is a distinction between statutes and Regulations of a general nature, in that the public is generally more aware of statutory law than of Regulations, statutory law is easier to find than Regulations (especially so with respect to amendments), and promulgation is generally more effective with respect to statutes than with respect to Regulations.

I discern some governmental and parliamentary consciousness of this in the provisions of the Statutory Instruments Act and in its predecessor the *Regulations Act*, R.S.C. 1970, c. R-5. (I had some difficulty in ascertaining that the former Act was actually in force, as I had forgotten where notes of proclamations could be found in the annual Statutes of Canada.) The *Statutory Instruments Act* s. 11(2) expresses a concern with proper publication of Regulations to those governed by them. This, I think, is all part of a movement of late years towards more care in all aspects of legal process to make sure that our procedures are just, *i.e.*, that they are "due process": see for example, Canadian Bill of Rights R.S.C. 1970, App. III, s. 1(*a*). That is, our legislative sources are trying to avoid, at least to some extent, the "Through the Looking-Glass" situation that arose in the noted case of *Rex v. Bailey* (1800), Russ. & Ry. 1, 168 E.R. 651, where the accused was on the high seas when the statute was passed that enacted the offence he committed while still at sea. It is hardly a sufficient consolation in such a case to pardon the offender after he has undergone a trial and conviction, a course that most commentators suggest would be followed today. The situation strikes the ordinary individual as radically unjust.

In fact, legal philosophers from the earliest times have noted that adequate promulgation is an essential element of any law that deserves the name. Williams (p. 295 s. 104) remarks:

> Although a statute takes effect without promulgation, there is authority for saying that "before a continuous act or proceeding, not originally unlawful, can be treated as unlawful by reason of the passing of an Act of Parliament by which it is in terms made so, a reasonable time must be allowed for its discontinuance."

It might be better to put it that the royal assent given in Parliament to an Act is deemed to be its promulgation: In English legal theory nothing more is requisite to give the Act the force of law as distinct from the theory in some continental countries that a decree of the head of state is necessary to bring legislation into force: see The Encyclopaedia Britannica (1941), vol. 6, p. 317c, under "Constitution and Constitutional Law". But with respect to subordinate legislation a decision of Bailhache J. in 1918, anticipated Statutory Instruments Act, s. 11(2) and probably led to its enactment indirectly by inspiring a corresponding provision in the English Statutory Instruments Act, 1946: see *Johnson v. Sargant & Sons*, [1918] 1 K.B. 101; followed by *Rex v. Ross* (1945), 84 C.C.C. 107 (B.C.), Harrison Co. Ct. J. (There is an interesting note by G.S. Rutherford on these two cases in 24 Can. Bar Rev. 151.)

One further consideration suggests that the provisions of Code s. 19 cannot be applied absolutely to everything that happens to be law. The section itself derives from a maxim that is the common property of European as well as English law makers — *ignorantia facti excusat — ignorantia juris non excusat.* It is true that on occasion the word *legis* has been substituted for *juris* and the maxim does apply to that kind of law, but only when the lex, *i.e.*, the positive command of the prince or legislature, has entered into the realm of jus, *i.e.*, the realm of legal right and obligation generally. This distinction, so familiar in European law, is also the common inheritance of our own legal predecessors but has become obscured in common-law countries by the lack of appropriate legal terminology and the consequent use of "law" for the entire field. Lex becomes part of jus by promulgation and assimilation. For if an enactment is notably at odds with general notions of justice it usually suffers considerable attrition in judicial and other legal interpretation until its rough edges have been smoothed down enough to fit into the general plan. The point of noting this, however, is that it again accentuates the need in justice to give publicity to an enactment as distinct from the common law, including other enactments of long standing, if the subject is to be required to conform himself to it.

This, no doubt, inspired the approach of the Supreme Court of Delaware in *Long v. State* (1949), 65 A. 2d 489 at 490, where one of the headnotes accurately gives the ruling:

> Mistake of law will be allowed as defense to defendant engaged in criminal conduct where defendant made *bona fide* diligent effort to ascertain and abide by law by adopting course and resorting to sources and means as appropriate as any afforded under our legal system and acted in good faith reliance on results of such effort.

The editors of Corpus Juris Secundum have used this case in 22 C.J.S., s. 48 p. 184 as authority for the proposition given. Williams characterizes the decision of the Court, given by Pearson J. as "a persuasively reasoned judgment" (p. 304). It was a case where a man was prosecuted for bigamy where he had remarried after diligently seeking legal advice as to the validity of a divorce he secured in a state which was not his domicile. The Supreme Court of Delaware, after noting ignorance of law could effectively negate a specific intent such as is required in theft or larceny (*Regina v. DeMarco, supra*), held that the statute did not exclude as a defence the absence of a general criminal intent, that is, mens rea as we commonly understand it: see for example, the definition given by Stephen J. in *Regina v. Tolson* (1889), 23 Q.B.D. 168. The Court then went on to make the holding noted above in the following argument:

[17, 18] We turn now to the ground that this is a case to which ignorance of law maxim applies. In many crimes involving a *specific* criminal intent, an honest mistake of law constitutes a defense if it negatives the specific intent. *State v. Pullen*, 3 Pennewill 184, 50 A. 538 (larceny); *State v. Collins*, 1 Marv. 536, 41 A. 144 (embezzlement); see list of cases in the Keedy article, supra, at p. 89; also Perkins: Ignorance and Mistake in Criminal Law, 88 Univ. of Pa. Law Rev. 35, 45, 46. As to crimes not involving a specific intent, an honest mistake of law is usually, though not invariably, held not to excuse conduct otherwise criminal. (Perkins article, pp. 41-45 and cases cited.) A mistake of law, where not a defense, may nevertheless negative a general criminal intent as effectively as would an exculpatory mistake of fact. Thus, mistake of law is disallowed as a defense in spite of the fact that it may show an absence of the criminal mind. The reasons for disallowing it are practical considerations dictated by deterrent effects upon the administration and enforcement of the criminal law, which are deemed likely to result if it were allowed as a general defense. As stated in the Perkins article, supra, p. 41: "But if such ignorance were available as a defense in every criminal case, this would be a constant source of confusion to juries, and it would tend to encourage ignorance at a point where it is peculiarly important to the state that knowledge should be as widespread as is reasonably possible. In the language of one of the giants of the profession, this is a point at which 'justice to the individual is rightly outweighed by the larger interests on the other side of the scale.' " (Quoting from Holmes: The Common Law, p. 48.)

[19] Similar considerations are involved when we disallow ignorance or mistake of law as a defense to a defendant who engages in criminal conduct (even though not obviously immoral or anti-social) where his ignorance or mistake consists merely in (1) unawareness that such conduct is or might be within the ambit of any crime; or (2) although aware of the existence of criminal law relating to the subject of such conduct, or to some of its aspects, the defendant erroneously concludes (in good faith) that his particular conduct is for some reason not subject to the operation of any criminal law. But it seems to us significantly different to disallow mistake of law where (3) together with the circumstances of the second classification, it appears that before engaging in the conduct, the defendant made a bona fide, diligent effort, adopting a course and resorting to sources and means at least as appropriate as any afforded under our legal system, to ascertain and abide by the law, and where he acted in good faith reliance upon the results of such effort. It is inherent in the way our legal system functions that the criminal law consequences of any particular contemplated conduct cannot be determined in advance with certainty. Not until after the event, by final court decision, may the consequences be definitely ascertained. Prior to the event, the ultimate that can be ascertained about the legal consequences consists of predictions of varying degrees of probability of eventuations. Hence, in the sense in which we are concerned with the expression, a "mistake of law" of the second or third classification refers to the failure of predictions of legal consequences to come to pass. No matter how logical, plausible and persuasive may be the bases for a prediction (assumptions, abstract legal rules, reasoning, etc.)

a mistake of law arises if the prediction does not eventuate; and there is no mistake of law if the prediction eventuates.

With these thoughts in mind, let us examine how the considerations which justify the rejection of a mistake of the first and second classifications operate with respect to a mistake of the third classification. The objection of tending to "encourage ignorance" of the law would hardly seem applicable. The very conditions of the third classification include a diligent effort, in good faith, by means as appropriate as any available under our legal system, to acquire knowledge of the relevant law. The objection of difficulties of proof, including facilitation of subterfuge, is applicable, if at all, in a far less degree than in the case of mistakes of the first and second classifications. For them, the facts are essentially confined to the defendant's subjective state of mind. The conditions of the third classification are not so limited. They include an affirmative showing of effort to abide by the law, tested by objective standards rather than the defendant's subjective state of mind.

Any deterrent effects upon the administration of the criminal law which might result from allowing a mistake of the third classification as a defense seem greatly outweighed by considerations which favor allowing it. To hold a person punishable as a criminal transgressor where the conditions of the third classification are present would be palpably unjust and arbitrary. Most of the important reasons which support the prohibition of *ex post facto* legislation are opposed to such a holding. It is difficult to conceive what more could be reasonably expected of a "model citizen" than that he guide his conduct by "the law" ascertained in good faith, not merely by efforts which might seem adequate to a person in his situation, but by efforts as well designed to accomplish ascertainment as any available under our system. We are not impressed with the suggestion that a mistake under such circumstances should aid the defendant only in inducing more lenient punishment by a Court, or executive clemency after conviction. The circumstances seem so directly related to the defendant's behavior upon which the criminal charge is based as to constitute an integral part of that behaviour, for purposes of evaluating it. No excuse appears for dealing with it piecemeal. We think such circumstances should entitle a defendant to full exoneration as a matter of right, rather than to something less, as a matter of grace. Unless there be aspects of the particular crime involved which give rise to considerations impelling a contrary holding, — some special, cogent reasons why "justice to the individual is rightly outweighted by the larger interests on the other side of the scales" — a mistake of the third classification should be recognized as a defense.

I have given this rather long excerpt from the decision in *Long v. State* not because it would apply in Canada to the crime in question, bigamy, or to any other statutory offence because of the present state of our jurisprudence, which I have outlined in *Villeneuve*, but because of the persuasive weight of the judgment with respect to the field of delegated legislation where there has been an English precedent since 1918 for making such a distinction and a precedent accepting that distinction in Canada since 1945. These cases all reinforce the impression of common sense and common experience that there is a distinction between the discoverability and availability of statutes on the one hand and subordinate legislation on the other. Every Judge and lawyer knows the difficulty in discovering the exact text of some non-statutory enactments, in particular municipal by-laws, and while federal government Regulations and other statutory instruments are kept in much better shape and in much or more adequate supply, they offer the additional challenge of vast bulk and frequent amendment. Moreover, it is almost 20 years since they were issued in consolidated form.

Accordingly, I hold that the principle enunciated in *Long v. State* is applicable to the case at bar, is supported by the analogy of *Rex v. Ross* and *Johnson v. Sargant & Sons*, *supra*, and that justice and correct legal principle require that it constitute a possible defence in this case. That leaves the remaining question to be considered.

5. Has the defendant established the defence to the required degree?

I am satisfied that the defendant made the kind of inquiry required by the rule in the circumstances. That is to say, while there were other sources of information open to him, he went to the source that people ordinarily use to secure information about drivers' licences and the requirements of licensing and in that sense the source was appropriate. In an objective sense it was not appropriate of course, but subjective ignorance of that fact is merely part of the communal ignorance of the law and things legal.

. . . .

Accordingly, the appeal is dismissed with the usual order as to costs, including in this case a brief fee because of the legal points involved.

R. v. POTTER

(1978), 3 C.R. (3d) 154, 39 C.C.C. (2d) 538 (P.E.I. S.C.)

17th February 1978. C.R. McQUAID J.: — Stephen Reid Potter stood charged at the January sittings of the jury assize that:

> He did on or about the 16th day of March, A.D. 1977, at Cornwall, in the said County and Province, did knowingly allow to be kept in a place under his control, to wit, 41 Brookside Drive, Cornwall, a devise for gambling, or betting, contrary to Section 186(1)(*b*) [now s. 202(1)(*b*)] of the *Criminal Code* of Canada and amendments thereto.

. . . .

The defences argued are essentially three: (a) mistake of law; (b) mistake of fact; and (c) absence of *mens rea*, all on the part of the accused Potter. Basically, it was argued that Potter believed, and had reason to believe, that his operation was not an illegal one and that, therefore, he lacked any guilty intent.

Before examining the case law relating to these defences, it is useful to examine the evidence which, it was suggested, gives rise to those defences.

As noted earlier, all the materials seized, and which are the subject of this charge, were manufactured by, and originated in, Peerless, or, in effect, Maltz. Referring to the commission evidence taken in Chicago.

. . . .

> Q. When the customs official was in your office, can you recall the conversation dealing with the importation of these products, for the record? A. I asked, "Is it legal to ship into

Canada?" And he didn't answer me. And he requested that I send in the samples, as I did. They returned them, and that was all that I ever heard. . . .

The charge before the Court is, of course, not against Maltz, nor does it relate directly to the importation of punchboards. The significance of the evidence above referred to, however, is that Maltz was concerned about the legality of shipping punchboards into Canada and directed his inquiry to those Crown officers — the customs officials directly concerned with their importation — who would be the natural and logical Canadian officials to whom such an inquiry would be directed by a foreign national. If the law assumes, as it does, that the ordinary citizen is deemed to know the law, it can be fairly assumed that officers of the Crown charged with the administration of the law can be deemed to know that same law which they are directly and specifically charged with administering.

In my opinion, when such a question is put to a Crown officer: Is it illegal to import punchboards into Canada?, it is incumbent upon, and the duty of, that Crown officer either to give a direct answer if he knows it, which he should, and which the law assumes that he does, or if he does not know it, to find out. This information is readily available to him, but not to a foreign national. By not so advising Maltz, as he should have done, he lulled him into a false sense of security.

It is interesting to note that the *Customs Tariff*, R.S.C. 1970, c. C-41, s. 14, provides that: "The importation into Canada of any goods enumerated, described or referred to in Schedule C is prohibited". Schedule C makes no reference to any goods described in s. 186 [am. 1974-75-76, c. 93, s. 11] of the *Code*, which provides that it is an offence to import such items into Canada. The fact that the goods did pass customs on a regular basis, subject to the payment of duty, suggests that they are presumably to be found in Sched. A or Sched. B, though I have been unable to identify them in a cursory perusal of either schedule.

I think it can be logically assumed that if one, after making appropriate inquiry as to the legality or otherwise of the importation of a certain genre of goods into Canada, is not advised or informed by those Crown officers to whom the inquiry is directed that it is, in fact, illegal, he might, not without reason, conclude that such was not illegal, hence legal, and if it were as a result legal, then it would in consequence be legal to have them in his possession in Canada.

This conclusion would be further fortified if that person, subsequent to his inquiry, continued to ship, *over a period of years*, on each occasion having the goods pass customs and on each occasion paying a customs tariff.

The only conclusion at which I can arrive, therefore, is that Maltz was acting throughout under a mistake of law, law which he took reasonable precautions to ascertain from officials whom he had every reason to believe would be in a position to advise him, officers of the Crown itself. His mistake in law was that it was legal to import punchboards into Canada and, in consequence, that once having legally imported them, their possession in Canada would not be illegal. It must be remembered that they were being imported, and taken into possession, by E.M. and B.M. Sales which was, in effect, Maltz himself. By logical extension, Maltz had every reason to believe that when the sales arm of E.M. and B.M. Sales — Regent (in effect, Potter) — took charge of the goods, his, Potter's, possession would not be illegal.

. . . .

Potter, being in a very subordinate position to either Maltz or Gendron, would have no reasonable reason to question further, and I would, in consequence, hold that he, Potter, thereby became impressed with the same mistake of law.

If indeed Potter was operating under a mistake of law, and I hold he was, the local customs officials did nothing to dispel his error, notwithstanding the fact that under the Code the importation of punchboards is strictly prohibited. George MacDonald, chief customs officer of some 31 years' experience, stated that he regularly cleared the boards through customs, not only to E.M. and B.M. Sales but others as well, so long as the appropriate duty was paid. His only directive was that whenever a shipment was cleared he was to notify the R.C.M.P. by letter, which he states he did regularly. He stated that he had never mentioned this to either any representative of E.M. and B.M. Sales or St. John, their customs broker with whom he dealt regularly. Until 16th March 1977 there is no evidence that the R.C.M.P. acted on this information, despite the fact that, in the two years prior to that date, he, MacDonald, described the importation of punchboards as "booming" and that Potter estimated that during this period he had received approximately 30 shipments and his estimate of duty paid ran at about $5,000 per month. If the officers of the Crown, be they either customs or R.C.M.P., were, in effect, condoning the commission of the offence, and if customs, as they were, were continuously over the period during which Potter was engaged in the operation releasing the goods on the payment of the stipulated levy, it is unreasonable to hold that Potter was to be put to inquiry as to the legality, not only to import, but as well to have in his possession or custody when imported. I hold, then, that Potter was operating under mistake of law, not only with respect to the importation of the punchboards, but, in consequence and specifically, with respect to the custody and possession thereof, for which he is charged, and that this was not culpable mistake on his part.

To what extent, then, does this constitute a defence? Counsel have been good enough to provide me with numerous authorities on the point, which I will consider in chronological order.

The first of these is *R. v. Prairie Schooner News Ltd.* (1971), 1 C.C.C. (2d) 251, a judgment of the Manitoba Court of Appeal. This dealt with the importation into Canada of allegedly obscene books which were allowed into Canada by the customs department. The defence raised was, as here, that since the books were not prohibited under Sched. C, the accused had accordingly been led to believe that they were not obscene, and that he should be acquitted. The Court did not accept this argument. This case, however, I think, must be distinguished in that the ratio decidendi of the Court was that whether or not a book was obscene was a question to be determined by the Court and not by the customs officials.

However, at p. 271 Dickson J.A. makes the following observation:

> It was argued that there was an absence of *mens rea* in that Mr. Powers had an honest and reasonable belief that the admission to Canada of the material impugned herein without demur on the part of the Customs Department negatived a finding of obscenity.
>
> The Judge rejected this submission and I am of the opinion that he was correct in so doing. One does not escape accountability for criminal acts by saying that someone led him to believe the acts were not criminal.

The case of *R. v. Campbell*, 21 C.R.N.S. 273, 10 C.C.C. (2d) 26 (Alta.), is directly on the point of mistake of law.

· · · ·

Any decision of Judge O'Hearn of the County Court of Nova Scotia warrants serious consideration, and in this instance I refer to *R. v. MacLean* (1974), 27 C.R.N.S. 31, 17 C.C.C. (2d) 84. In the instant case, Potter heard his employer, Gendron, inquire of Maltz respecting the legal status of punchboards in Canada and heard Maltz describe his own inquiries from customs and the results of those inquiries. Understandably, Potter could not be reasonably expected to make personal inquiries with the local customs, who were regularly clearing his assignments, much less with the R.C.M.P. to whom, unbeknowst to Potter, customs were reporting regularly, and who, themselves, were totally quiescent.

The following pungent observation appears at pp. 54-55:

> I am satisfied that the defendant made the kind of inquiry required by the rule in the circumstances. That is to say, while there were other sources of information open to him, he went to the source that people ordinarily use to secure information open to him, he went to the source that people ordinarily use to secure information about drivers' licences and the requirements of licensing and in that sense the source was appropriate. In an objective sense it was not appropriate of course, but subjective ignorance of that fact is merely part of the communal ignorance of the law and things legal.

That comment can, I think, mutatis mutandis, be applied to Potter.

R. v. MacPhee (1975), 24 C.C.C. (2d) 229 (N.S.), follows in principle the *MacLean* case, *supra*, and, in addition, with reference to the *mens rea* aspect, cites the leading Nova Scotia case of *R. v. Jollimore* (1961), 36 C.R. 300, 131 C.C.C. 319, which, in turn, relies on *Beaver v. R.*, [1957] S.C.R. 531, 26 C.R. 193, 118 C.C.C. 129 at 140:

> The essence of the crime is the possession of the forbidden substance and in a criminal case there is in law no possession without knowledge of the character of the forbidden substance.

As I see the situation, then, there is the "traditional" body of law which enunciates the principle that ignorance of the law is no excuse; indeed, such is clearly spelled out in s. 19 of the *Code*. It would further appear to be the law that such ignorance, if inculpable and existing despite reasonable efforts to ascertain the law in a sincere effort to conform to and comply with it, or at least not to infringe upon it, is a factor to be taken into consideration in mitigation.

There would, in addition, appear to be a developing trend away from this rigidity by a more reasoned and reasonable approach, of which the *MacLean* case may well be the forerunner and which Courts of Appeal may well, in the future, endorse. As yet, it remains the decision of a lower Court, not tested in the crucible of higher scrutiny and acceptance. With some reluctance, therefore, I feel that I cannot follow the learned O'Hearn Co. Ct. J.

I find the accused, Stephen Reid Potter, guilty as charged.

As to disposition, I think that in view of all of the circumstances above referred to, an absolute discharge would be appropriate and I so order.

Accused guilty but absolute discharge granted.

R. v. CANCOIL THERMAL CORP.

(1986), 52 C.R. (3d) 188, 27 C.C.C. (3d) 295 (Ont. C.A.)

The Court ordered a new trial on the basis that, since the *Charter*, the accused, charged for safety violations, was entitled to the defence if due diligence could be proved. It further considered whether there was also a defence of "officially induced error of law":

LACOURCIÈRE J.A. (MARTIN and GOODMAN JJ.A. concurring): —

The inspector from the Ministry of Labour (Occupational Health and Safety Division), Mr. J.J. Ogoniek, had inspected the factory on January 16, 1984, more than two months before the accident. At the time of the inspection, the guard installed by the manufacturers had been removed. Although the machine had not been put into production, it was run while the inspector was present so that he could observe the cycle of operation. The absence of the manufacturer's guard was pointed out by the respondent Parkinson. According to the evidence of the respondent Parkinson, the inspector commented that it was "safe to remove the particular piece of metal in question and that with the machine being operated according to instructions that it was safe to do so". Mr Pare who had not then operated the machine, stated that he had "no unresolved health and safety concerns". In any event, the inspector was satisfied apparently that no provision of the Act or regulations was being contravened and he made no order pursuant to his powers under s. 29 of the Act. However, on March 21st, the day after the accident, the inspector issued an order that the metal shear was not to be used until access to the blade area had been blocked. This order was complied with on the following day "by welding 1/4 inch x 1 inch steel bars across the openings in the hold down".

On the record, it is clear that the inspector was an official of the Occupational Health and Safety Division of the Ministry of Labour, appointed for the purpose of inspection and examination of the work place and that he was clothed with wide powers to enforce compliance with the Act and its regulations.

The defence of "officially induced error", exists where the accused, having adverted to the possibility of illegality, is led to believe, by the erroneous advice of an official, that he is not acting illegally. In *R. v. Walker and Somma* (1980), 51 C.C.C. (2d) 423, Martin J.A., in an *obiter dictum*, left open the possibility of this defence, and stated at p. 429:

> I would not wish to be taken to assent to the proposition that if a public official charged with responsibility in the matter led a defendant to believe that the act intended to be done was lawful, the defendant would not have a defence if he were subsequently charged under a regulatory statute with unlawfully doing that act: see "Excusable Mistake of Law", [1974] Crim. L.R. 652 at p. 660, by A.J. Ashworth. I leave aside that difficult question until it is necessary to decide it. Suffice it to say that no suggestion arises in this case that the respondents were misled by Customs officials.

An article by Professor P.G. Barton, "Officially Induced Error as a Criminal Defence: A Preliminary Look", 22 Crim. L.Q. 314, contains a helpful consideration of this defence.

In *R. v. MacDougall* (1981), 60 C.C.C. (2d) 137, the Nova Scotia Court of Appeal, per MacDonald J.A., recognized the defence in the following words:

> The defence of officially induced error has not been sanctioned, to my knowledge, by any appellate Court in this country. The law, however, is ever-changing and ideally adapts to meet the changing mores and needs of society. In this day of intense involvement in a complex society by all levels of Government with a corresponding reliance by people on officials of such Government, there is, in my opinion, a place and need for the defence of officially induced error, at least so long as a mistake of law, regardless how reasonable, cannot be raised as a defence to a criminal charge.

On further appeal to the Supreme Court of Canada, Ritchie J. appeared to give approval to the defence:

> It is not difficult to envisage a situation in which an offence could be committed under mistake of law arising because of, and therefore induced by, "officially induced error" and if there was evidence in the present case to support such a situation existing it might well be an appropriate vehicle for applying the reasoning adopted by MacDonald J.A. In the present case, however, there is no evidence that the accused was misled by an error on the part of the registrar.

The defence of "officially induced error" is available as a defence to an alleged violation of a regulatory statute where an accused has reasonably relied upon the erroneous legal opinion or advice of an official who is responsible for the administration or enforcement of the particular law. In order for the accused to successfully raise this defence, he must show that he relied on the erroneous legal opinion of the official and that his reliance was reasonable. The reasonableness will depend upon several factors including the efforts he made to ascertain the proper law, the complexity or obscurity of the law, the position of the official who gave the advice, and the clarity, definitiveness and reasonableness of the advice given.

I agree with the following statement made by Professor Barton in the article referred to supra at p. 331:

> Where the advice is given by an official who has the job of administering the particular statute, and where the actor relies on this advice and commits what is in fact an offence, even if the agency cannot be estopped does it follow that the actor should not be excused? To do so is not to condone an illegality or say that the agency is estopped into a position of illegality, but to recognize that the advice was illegal but excuse the actor because he acted reasonably and does not deserve punishment.

It may well be that the individual respondent and the respondent corporation in the s. 14(1)(c) count (either count against the corporation would probably fall under the Kineapple principle if a conviction were entered against it under the other count) need not rely on this novel defence if they can satisfy the trier of fact that they acted with due diligence. But, although it may at times overlap with the defence of due diligence, the defence of "officially induced error of law" is separate and distinct and can be asserted, in the same way as other defences.

In the present case, it will be for the trier of fact to decide whether the accused has proved, by a preponderance of evidence, that he was misled by the inspector into thinking that the removal of the manufacturer's guard would not be in contravention of the law. The record makes it clear that the inspector was an official involved in the administration of the relevant law, presumably familiar with the Act and regulations and having the expertise to determine whether a machine was equipped with the prescribed safety devices. Ordinarily, mistake of law cannot be successfully raised as a defence to a criminal or quasi-criminal charge or regulatory offence, but an officially induced error of law may, in some circumstances, constitute a valid defence. This will, of course, depend on whether the opinion of the official was reasonable in the circumstances and whether it was reasonable for the accused to follow it.

The evidence in the present case is too sparse and inconsistent to allow an appellate court to determine the availability of the defence. Officially induced error was not relied on at trial and was only raised by the Court, *proprio motu*, during the argument of the appeal. However, I should, in fairness, point out that the respondent relied on the defence of estoppel which would encompass the other defence. If a new trial is directed, the prosecution as well as the defence may adduce further evidence. I note that the inspector of the ministry, J.J. Ogoniek, was present at the trial but was not called by either party although his reports were filed.

VIII. CONCLUSION

For these reasons, I would allow the appeal, set aside the acquittals of both respondents and direct a new trial.

According to Chief Justice Lamer in *R. v. Jorgensen* (1996), 43 C.R. (4th) 137, 102 C.C.C. (3d) 97, [1995] 4 S.C.R. 55, the defence of officially induced error of law should be recognized as an excuse for both criminal and regulatory offences. The accused should prove on a balance of probabilities reasonable reliance on appropriate advice and the remedy should be a stay rather than an acquittal. The other justices preferred to leave the issue open as it had not been argued. **Do you think that the defence should be recognized in this form? Discuss the pros and cons of the Chief Justice's views.**

For an argument that a rigid division of legally significant error into ignorance of law and mistake of fact is contrary to s. 7 of the *Charter*, see Hamish Stewart, "Mistake of Law Under The Charter" (1998), 3&4 Crim. L.Q. 476.

1. A motorist is stopped by the police and requested to provide a breathalyzer sample at the police station. At the police station he refuses to provide a sample and is charged with failing to provide a breath sample without reasonable excuse contrary to the *Criminal Code*. Consider whether he has a defence

> **(1) If he refused because he had heard of a Provincial Court ruling that the breathalyzer provisions are unconstitutional. That decision was reversed by the Court of Appeal before the accused's trial on the refusal charge.**

In *R. v. MacIntyre* (1983), 24 M.V.R. 67, leave to appeal to S.C.C. refused 2 O.A.C. 400, the Ontario Court of Appeal dismissed the defence without reasons being given.

> **(2) If the situation is the same but before the refusal a lawyer advised the accused, in error, that the provincial Judge's decision was still valid law.**

Compare *R. v. Dunn* (1977), 21 N.S.R. (2d) 334 (C.A.).

> **(3) Would your answer to (2) differ if the advice had been that of the Registrar of Motor Vehicles?**

2. The accused were operating a laboratory in which they were manufacturing various chemicals. Unknown to the accused a police investigation discovered that one of these drugs was M.D.M.A., which was not an illegal drug under any of the schedules of the *Food and Drugs Act*, R.S.C. 1970, c. F-27. However the police suspected it could be used in combination with others to produce illegal drugs. The police managed to have M.D.M.A. added to the schedule of restricted drugs under the *Food and Drugs Act*. This amendment was published in the *Canada Gazette*. The accused continued to produce M.D.M.A. and, two months later, were charged with trafficking in that drug. Can the accused rely on ignorance of the law?

Compare *Mollis v. R.*, [1980] 2 S.C.R. 356, 55 C.C.C. (2d) 558.

3. The accused is charged with possession of a prohibited weapon contrary to s. 90(1) of the *Criminal Code*. When stopped by the police he was wearing a knife sheath attached to his belt. The officer examined the knife and, with a forceful downward motion of his arm and wrist, while holding the handle of the knife, was able to open its blade. The accused immediately indicated that he was unaware that the knife could be opened in this manner. Section 84(1)(b) of the *Criminal Code* defines a prohibited weapon in part as "any knife that has a blade that opens automatically by gravity or centrifugal force or by hand pressure applied to a button, spring or other device in or attached to the handle of the knife". Has the accused made a mistake of law or fact?

Compare *R. v. Archer* (1983), 6 C.C.C. (3d) 129 (Ont. C.A.).

4. The accused were charged with unlawfully conducting a bingo contrary to s. 206(1)(*d*) of the *Criminal Code*. The charges arose out of gaming operations on a reserve. The accused maintained that they were entitled to be acquitted by reason of a defence of colour of right. That right was the belief that s. 206 did not apply to their activities since they were carried out on a reserve which they thought was not subject to the laws of Canada relating to gaming. Is this a mistake of fact or law? Is there a colour of right defence?

Compare *R. v. Jones* (1991), 8 C.R. (4th) 137 (S.C.C.).

5. The accused relied on the information of a firearms officer that a permit was not required for a garage sale. He was charged with the *Criminal Code* offence of selling firearms without a permit.

Compare *R. v. Dubeau* (1993), 80 C.C.C. (3d) 54 (Ont. Gen. Div.).

6. The accused is charged with contravening a municipal bylaw by using a family dwelling as a professional office. On first conviction the penalty is a fine of not more that $25,000. The accused, a registered denture therapist, and the co-accused, her husband, opened an office for some of her work at their place of residence. Before doing so the husband purchased a copy of the relevant bylaw at the city offices and asked a city planner whether he could open a business in his place. The planner advised that his wife could open the office as she qualified as a drugless practitioner. Should there be a defence of officially induced error of law? Would it matter if the offence was one of absolute liability? Compare *R. v. Bauman* (1994) 32 C.R. (4th) 176 (Ont. Prov. Ct.).

General Review Questions

1. Al Capone is charged with speeding contrary to s. 109 of the *Highway Traffic Act*, R.S.O. 1980, c. 198, in that he drove a motor vehicle in excess of 50 k.p.h. in a 50 k.p.h. zone. If he is convicted the penalty is mandatory: a fine of $18.75.

The uncontested evidence is that the accused was driving at 65 k.p.h. in a 50 k.p.h. zone and that he was knowingly exceeding that speed limit as he genuinely believed he was in a 70 k.p.h. zone. The source of the mistake was a sign reading "70 k.p.h. limit ahead" which Al interpreted to immediately raise the speed limit, whereas this was in reality only achieved 300 metres further along the street, by a sign reading "70 k.p.h. limit". Al, a school principal, had been troubled about this ambiguity before and had telephoned the local police detachment. A sergeant had unambiguously informed him (in error) that the speed limit was raised by the first sign.

You are articled to the defence lawyer. She requests a memorandum discussing all possible defences and the authorities on which they would be based. In each case assess the likelihood of success.

2. Kevin owns a bar. A customer, Susan, comes into the bar and orders a double whisky. Kevin asks her how old she is, to which she answers in unambiguous terms that he should mind his own business. Kevin is pretty confident that she is about 16 years of age. The problem is that he is not sure whether the recent raising of the drinking age from 16 to 18 is in effect. He asks a lawyer in the bar who advises, "The Act comes into effect next week". Kevin serves Susan. Susan's seemingly younger companion, Gordon, then also orders whisky. Kevin, suspecting Gordon is underage, asks him for his driver's licence. Gordon produces the driver's licence of one Ross, whose age is shown as 18, Kevin is surprised but gives no thought to whether the licence is really that of the customer. He serves Gordon.

In fact the new provincial *Liquor Act* is already in force. Section 10 reads:

> Every one who supplies liquor to a person under the age of 18 is guilty of an offence and liable to a fine of not less than $300.

Kevin is facing two charges under s. 10 since Susan is 17 and Gordon 15. Write a legal memorandum on his possible defences, discussing appropriate authorities and assessing his chances of acquittal.

Chapter 6

INCAPACITY

Age

Until 1982 the age of absolute exemption from criminal responsibility was set by the *Criminal Code* at seven. That a child under seven committed the *actus reus* with the requisite *mens rea* made no difference. Furthermore children over seven and under 14 were likewise exempt unless the prosecutor could show that the child was "competent to know the nature and consequence of his conduct and to appreciate that it was wrong". In 1982 this latter so-called *doli incapax* presumption was abolished and the age of criminal responsibility was raised from seven to twelve years in a new s. 13 [en. 1980-81-82, c. 110, s. 72] of the *Criminal Code*. The *Young Offenders Act*, S.C. 1980-81-82, c. 110, replaced the *Juvenile Delinquents Act*. It governs the trials of all children over the age of 12 but under the age of 18. Consideration of the special procedural and dispositional alternatives dealt with in this new Act are beyond the scope of this book. For our purposes it is sufficient to observe that the substantive law principles that we are exploring apply equally in Youth Court. The passage of the *Young Offenders Act* was the culmination of years of controversial debate. See, generally, Corrado, Bala, Linden and LeBlanc, *Juvenile Justice in Canada* (Butterworths, 1992) and Nicholas Bala, *Young Offenders Law* (Irwin Law, 1997).

Insanity (Mental Disorder)

N.D. WALKER, CRIME AND PUNISHMENT IN BRITAIN

Rev. ed. (1968), 61-67 (revised by the author)

Mental illnesses can be broadly subdivided into those which are clearly associated with an identifiable cerebral normality, and those which are not. These groups are sometimes distinguished by the labels "organic" and "functional".

Some organic illnesses are distinguishable from others in being more frequently associated with anti-social behaviour. Among these is epilepsy. It is possible for the innumerable minute transfers of electric potential which constitute the everyday activity of the brain to be suddenly overwhelmed by what has been likened to an electrical storm. This produces the unconsciousness, convulsions, and cries which are characteristic of the full epileptic fit; but the effects may be milder, so that consciousness is hardly disturbed and convulsion are confined to a few muscles. . . .

Epileptics are of special interest from the criminological point of view. Even at normal times their brains reveal, under the electroencephalograph, a characteristic type of rhythmical electric activity known as the "spike and wave". Similar rhythms can sometimes be observed in the brains of other members of their family, either in their normal resting state or under some physiological stress, although those members may never show any of the other symptoms of epilepsy. Men who have committed assaults are sometimes found to have electroencephalograms with this abnormality, or epileptic relatives, or both; and if so are strongly suspected of having committed their crimes in an "epileptiform" state, although they have never been known to have an overt seizure.

Examples of other organic abnormalities of the brain which are sometimes discovered in offenders are tumours or advanced syphilitic infection. Encephalitis infections in children quite often result in permanent damage to the brain of a kind which seems to deprive them of self-control or regard for others, so that they commit thefts, assaults, acts of cruelty, or sexual misdemeanours.

Acts of aggression are sometimes committed by people who are in temporary states of cerebral abnormality as a result of some kind of poisoning. The commonest example is drunkenness, but there are more inadvertent types, such as oxygen deficiency or hypoglycaemia, a condition which can occur in careless or badly doctored diabetics.

Brain injuries. On the other hand, brain injuries are probably blamed for criminal behaviour more often than the facts justify, and more often by defence counsel than by psychiatrists or neurologists. Cases are described in which wounds in the head, concussion, or the multitude of tiny injuries in the brain of the punch-drunk boxer, are probably responsible for anti-social behaviour. But where there are no symptoms of damage other than the offence itself, neurologists are sceptical.

Some disorders are attributed to degenerative changes which are common in old age and may begin in middle age. Hypertension and arteriosclerosis may affect the cerebral blood vessels, or the cells of the brain itself may atrophy or degenerate. Certain disorders of this kind — for example Huntington's chorea and Pick's disease — are genetically transmitted by single genes, although unlike most characteristics inherited in this way they do not usually manifest themselves until early middle age or even later. Sometimes the clinical symptoms of the disease are preceded by a phase in which the sufferer begins to behave in grossly anti-social ways for the first time in his life, with the result that he is mistakenly held responsible for his conduct until the clinical symptoms appear.

Psychoses. Of special importance, however, are the disorders which are sometimes called the "functional psychoses". These are the disturbances of thought for which no unmistakable physiological cause has yet been demonstrated, and which are still regarded by a minority of psychiatrists as the result of a highly abnormal upbringing.

Schizophrenia. One of the most frequent diagnoses in mental hospitals is "schizophrenia", although the symptoms and course of this disorder vary so widely that several sub-species are recognised, and it is quite possible that, like "psychopathy" this category will eventually be broken up into two, three, or more quite distinct disorders. Thus Mayer-Gross *et alii* distinguish four types of schizophrenia. Commonest among young adults is hebephrenic schizophrenia, which seems to consist of a disorder of thought. This is insidious in its onset, so that it may at first be dismissed as neurosis. A promising student may find it harder and harder to concentrate and think logically; he drifts off into vague metaphysical interests. Or he may degenerate into a ceaseless joker: mild hebephrenics have become successful clowns or stage humorists through their ability to exploit their spontaneous silliness. Occasionally, in the early stages of the disorder, there is a sudden flare-up of sexual impulses, or of rage or terror, which may lead to anti-social behaviour. The progress of the disorder sometimes halts spontaneously, more often under treatment, If it is not halted, symptoms such as hallucinations and withdrawal from reality manifest themselves.

In contrast is the catatonic, whose chief symptom is stupor and a resistant, negative attitude to attempts to induce purposive activity. Advanced catatonics will assume bizarre poses and maintain them for long periods. They may occasionally commit impulsive and brutal attacks, for example on doctors or nurses, but since the disorder is so easily recognised and leads so surely to hospital the public is usually protected from them.

Paranoia is the most frequent form among the middle-aged or elderly, and especially among elderly women. The distinguishing symptom is a delusion of persecution which may drive the sufferer to flee into various parts of the country, and eventually to retaliate against his fancied persecutors, as M'Naghten did when he fled to London and then shot the man whom he mistook for the Prime Minister. Often the delusions take a sexual form. A husband or wife will suspect the other spouse of infidelities of the most improbable kind or frequency, and will eventually commit an assault upon the spouse; or an elderly woman may imagine that indecent suggestions are being made to her, often by mysterious means. "Poison pen" letters are sometimes the work of paranoiacs.

Fourthly, Mayer-Gross distinguishes the "simple" schizophrenia, without catatonia, hallucinations or delusions, but consisting apparently of a rapidly developing shallowness of emotion, irresponsibility and lack of willpower. He cites the

> solitary solicitor who fell out with all his former friends because of his seclusiveness and aggressiveness. For a long time he spent his nights in a brothel with a low prostitute, giving away large sums and munificent presents. He procured the money by fraudulent receipts which he presented to the authorities. At the same time he continued his law practice with relative success.

. . . More spectacular, of course, is the solitary, quiet schizophrenic who suddenly commits a crime of violence, often involving sexually motivated mutilations, and not infrequently against his wife, mother, father or other relative with whom he is living at the time.

Depression. Another type of psychosis which seems to be associated with offences is depression. This can be a temporary result of the administration of some therapeutic drugs — such as the sulphonamides — or of an illness such as influenza. It may be "reactive": that is, the response to an occurrence such as a bereavement or a failure in one's career, although we can usually distinguish between grief or disappointment which is normal and that which is excessive in duration and intensity — there is a point at which "mourning becomes melancholia". Thirdly, there is the endogenous depression, which seems, as its name implies, to develop from within, unprovoked by any but the slightest changes in the external environnment. Some psychiatrists would say that an apparently reactive depression which is more severe or protracted than seems appropriate to the outward occasion for it is really an endogenous depression which has simply been "triggered off'. The depression may be periodic, improving and relapsing independently of treatment or changes in the patient's environment. The state seems to be most acute in the early part of the day. Women seem to be somewhat more prone than men to endogenous depression, and the older the patient the longer the state seems to last.

Suicidal behaviour is, of course, a frequent accompaniment of depression, and a depressed mother or father, in a state of unrealistic despair over the future of their families, will often kill spouse and children as well as himself. A depressed lover may persuade his beloved into a suicide pact. Some investigators have also found an association between shoplifting and depression among women. The condition is usually treated by drugs or in severe cases by electro-convulsion.

Mania. The contrasting condition of abnormal elation, known as "mania", is sometimes associated with violence and occasionally other forms of anti-social behaviour. It is less often encountered, perhaps because its milder forms (the "hypomanic state") are less easily recognised as pathological than are the milder depressions. Stallworthy writes:

> What in one person could be his normal state could in another be a definite hypomania. The friends . . . of the man in hypomania will say that his talkativeness and exuberance are quite out of keeping with what for him is normal: sometimes the patient will admit the same. His exuberance and chatter soon make him a nuisance to those about him. He is too excited and elated to go to bed at a normal hour. . . . He wakes up his neighbours at 3 a.m. to tell them a wonderful scheme for altering their garden; he puts through a person-to-person call to the Prime Minister to tell him how to run the country. . . . One very capable solicitor . . . drew all his trust funds to found a grandiose scheme in France without thought of his responsibility to his clients. . . . The hypomanic man with a full bladder may, wherever he is, see no reason for not emptying it. If he sees a comely girl, he may feel it is an honour for her to see his virility. . . . If he is thwarted or disagreed with he may be consumed by brief anger, in which . . . he may be viciously abusive or physically violent. In acute mania the patient is so noisy, destructive, often obscene . . . that his insanity is obvious to the most unskilled eye.

Manic "episodes" may begin with slight depressions, or may alternate with more acute depressions, in which case they are known as "manic-depressive" conditions. They often disappear and reappear spontaneously. Treatment usually consists of the administration of lithium.

Psychosis and Violence. Like the crimes of the ordinary offender or the subnormnal, those of the mentally ill are usually "property offences". . . . But whereas sexual offences are over-represented among the subnormal, it is personal violence that is obviously the special risk in the case of the psychoses, and especially the schizophrenias and depressions.

Neuroses. All or most of the mental illnesses I have been describing would be classified by most psychiatrists as psychoses, although some would be doubtful whether depression should be. Those which I am about to discuss are usually classified as neuroses. Their symptoms never include hallucinations or delusions; their onset is less sudden and definite than that of the usual psychosis; they are usually attributed to faulty upbringing rather than to some physiological cause, although it is usually recognized that inborn susceptibility to neurosis-inducing influences varies from one individual to another. They usually respond better to psychotherapeutic methods of treatment than to drugs, although of course tranquillisers are often prescribed by baffled general practitioners in order to relieve the symptoms.

Anxiety. The most frequent type of neurosis is the anxiety state, in which the apprehension and worry which are normal human reactions to certain situations become chronic and severe. In some individuals the anxiety is chiefly focused on their health, and the slightest *malaise* is taken for signs of cancer or heart disease. In others it centres on their work, their relations with their acquaintances, or their children's health or conduct. In the most severe cases the sufferer has to be admitted to hospital. It is only rarely, however, that this kind of disorder leads to a criminal offence; usually the sufferer is his own victim.

Compulsive Behaviour. People whose behaviour is otherwise more or less normal may suffer from recurrent impulses or longings to perform irrational acts; and although this is sometimes associated with a diagnosable psychosis it is often the only detectable abnormality. Sometimes the compulsion is trivial and harmless, such as the desire to touch walls as one walks beside them, or to make sure again and again that all the doors and windows are locked. Sometimes it takes an anti-social form — for instance, compulsive stealing of more or less useless objects by people who could easily afford to pay for them. Often deviant sexual desires become compulsive, and force the sufferer to expose himself, or make physical advances to small boys. The sufferer seems to be able to resist the compulsive desire at first, but gradually to be worn down until he performs the action; thereupon he feels a feeling of almost physical relief, but often with remorse, self-digust or fear of the consequences if the act was anti-social.

Hysteria. "Hysteria", like "schizophrenia" and "psychopathy", is a diagnostic category which used to be overloaded by psychiatrists with cases which were difficult to classify in any other way, and it is very difficult to offer a definition which would not be regarded as inadequate by a substantial minority. . . . .

Diagnostic Difficulties. The disorders which have been briefly described so far are those which are not only associated to an appreciable extent with anti-social behaviour but are also diagnosed with a certain degree of confidence by orthodox psychiatrists. For several reasons, diagnosis is more difficult in psychiatry than in other branches of medicine. Symptoms fluctuate more in their severity, and may even disappear completely for a time; this is said to be especially likely after some act which satisfies a compulsive urge or after an outburst of psychotic violence. Even mildly subnormal patients may appear more intelligent when they are in situations with which they are familiar. If the patient is very subnormal or psychotic, it is not easy to obtain useful information from him about his history, his background or the introspectible aspect of his symptoms. Thirdly, just as more than one physical disorder — for instance, tuberculosis and peptic ulcer — can be present in the same individual, so the same patient may be suffering both from a psychosis and from subnormality of intelligence; and either subnormality or a psychosis may very well be associated with a neurosis. (Indeed, in some cases the neurosis is said to be attributable to the abnomal difficulties which subnormality or incipient psychosis impose on the sufferer.) Finally, the borderline between disorder and normality is even more indefinite than in the case of physical ailments. Apart from disorders with a demonstrable genetic or physiological origin — such as Huntington's chorea or epilepsy — almost all mental abnormalities have their "sub-clinical" fringe of cases in which the symptoms are too mild to justify a definite clinical label. This is most obvious where the principal symptom — depression, anxiety, elation — is merely an exaggeration of normal emotional states. But even in the cause of schizophrenia many psychiatrists recognise what is called "the schizoid personality" — withdrawn, unemotional, day-dreaming — as a sub-clinical form.

The Limited Truths of Psychiatry

There are problems inherent in any classifications that make expertise in diagnosis elusive in all but the most obvious cases. In particular, each psychiatric label is a shorthand expression of relative rather than absolute conditions which are difficult to define; any one individual can present the conditions more strongly at some times rather than others, and each individual can present symptoms of more than one psychiatric label at any one time.

These limits are recognized in the influential DSM-111 classification announced by the American Psychiatric Association in 1980. The classification is now known as DSM-IV to reflect changes made up until 1994.[1] This divides "mental disorder" into, *inter alia*, "mental retardation", psychoses,[2] "anxiety disorders" and "personality disorders". It is, for example, stated at the outset:

> In DMS-IV there is no assumption that each category of mental disorder is a completely discrete entity with absolute boundaries dividing it from other mental disorders or from no mental disorder.[3]

Clinicians are encouraged to assign more than one label whenever appropriate. The DSM-IV "personality disorder" label includes "Anti-social Personality

---

1 *Diagnostic and Statistical Manual of Mental Disorders*, 4th ed. (1994) (DSM-IV).
2 The classification avoids the umbrella "psychosis" label but has a category of "psychotic disorders not elsewhere specified".
3 At xxii.

Disorder"[4] as a form of mental disorder. This has also been known as the concept of "psychopathy" or "sociopathy". The label appears frequently in the criminal law and is highly controversial.

The classic description of "psychopathic syndrome" is provided by the McCords[5] in their exhaustive study:

> The psychopath is asocial. His conduct often brings him into conflict with society. The psychopath is driven by primitive desires and an exaggerated craving for excitement. In his self-centred search for pleasure, he ignores restrictions of his culture. The psychopath is highly impulsive. He is a man for whom the moment is a segment of time detached from all others. His actions are unplanned and guided by his whims. The psychopath is aggressive. He has learned few socialized ways of coping with frustration. The psychopath feels little, if any, guilt. He can commit the most appalling acts, yet view them without remorse. The psychopath has a warped capacity for love. His emotional relationships, when they exist, are meager, fleeting, and designed to satisfy his own desires. These last two traits, guiltlessness and lovelessness, conspicuously mark the psychopath as different from other men.[6]

The World Health Organization's 1978 International Classification of Diseases[7] similarly describes a "personality disorder with predominantly sociopathic or asocial manifestation" as a:

> Personality disorder characterized by disregard for social obligations, lack of feeling for others, and impetuous violence or callous unconcern. There is a gross disparity between behaviour and the prevailing social norms. Behaviour is not readily modifiable by experience, including punishment. People with this personality are often affectively cold and may be abnormally aggressive or irresponsible. Their tolerance to frustration is low; they blame others or offer plausible rationalizations for the behaviour which brings them into conflict with society.

The DSM-IV classification avoids abstraction and instead identifies[8] a host of "diagnostic criteria":

> Diagnostic criteria for 301.7 Anti-social Personality Disorder
>
> A. There is a pervasive pattern of disregard for and violation of the rights of others occurring since age 15 years, as indicated by three (or more) of the following:
>
> (1) failure to conform to social norms with respect to lawful behaviours as indicated by repeatedly performing acts that are grounds for arrest
> (2) deceitfulness, as indicated by repeated lying, use of aliases, or conning others for personal profit or pleasure
> (3) impulsivity or failure to plan ahead
> (4) irritability and aggressiveness, as indicated by repeated physical fights or assaults
> (5) reckless disregard for safety of self or others
> (6) consistent irresponsibility, as indicated by repeated failure to sustain consistent work behaviour or honor financial obligations
> (7) lack of remorse, as indicated by being indifferent to or rationalizing having hurt, mistreated, or stolen from another
>
> B. The individual is at least age 18 years.

---

4 At 649-650.
5 W. and J. McCord, *The Psychopath: An Essay on the Criminal Mind*, (1964).
6 Above note 5, 16-17.
7 W.H.O., *Mental Disorders: Glossary and Guide to Their Classifiction in Accordance with the Ninth Revision of the International Classification of Diseases*, (1978), point 301.7.
8 At 649-650. Reproduced by permission of the American Psychiatric Association.

C. There is evidence of Conduct Disorder . . . with onset before age 15 years.

D. The occurrence of anti-social behaviour is not exclusively during the course of Schizophrenia or a Manic Episode.

Conduct disorders are defined[9] as involving repetitive and persistent patterns of violations of social norms falling into four categories: aggression to people and animals, destruction of property, deceitfulness or theft and serious violation of rules.

The DSM guide highlights the glaring deficiencies of the label "psychopathic syndrome". Surely the criteria, based on consensus, rather than being verified by research, are arbitrary, extremely ambiguous, over inclusive and, above all, circular. A startling example of the process occurred in 1973 where it took a vote of the trustees and a 60 percent vote of the membership by ballot to remove homosexuality from the Manual's list of mental disorders.[10] The criteria were even vaguer in the 1980 classification. In 1987 they were changed because in constructing questions for use by clinicians "it was found that many of those criteria were imprecise and in need of further specification". This label seems to be a ragbag description of a persistent recidivist who carries on committing crimes for no apparent reason. There is a strong body of opinion in England[11] but less so in Canada[12] that the label "obliterates more information than it conveys".[13] It tells us nothing about causation, prognosis or treatment. Changing the label to "sociopath", "personality disorder", "character disorder" or the like will not address these criticisms.[14] With any psychiatric label, and this one in particular, lawyers should request that psychiatrists be as precise as possible in their descriptions of the actual behaviour of the individual before the court rather than hide behind imperfect abstractions. Clearly they are too imprecise for use as legal criteria of responsibility.

Some psychiatrists accept this perspective. Professor Orchard[15], for example, recognizes that the issue of legal insanity,

ultimately must be decided by the Judge and jury. This conclusion is consistent with the important legal principle that expert opinion, including medical and psychiatric opinion, should be used to assist the court in arriving at a finding, but that the responsibility of making this finding is, and must remain, in the hands of the triers of fact. Doctors may not enjoy the obvious questioning of the validity of their diagnosis and opinions which this entails. However, as no one, not even a doctor, sad to say, is infallible, it is most important that any Judge or jury look at all the evidence, including the psychiatric opinion and the data upon which it is based, with the

---

9 At 85, 646.

10 See Eric H. Marcus, "Unbiased Medical Testimony: Reality or Myth?" (1985), 6 Am. J. For. Psych. 3.

11 See especially Walker, *Crime and Punishment in Britain*, rev. ed. (1968), 82-8 and (with S. McCabe) *Crime and Insanity in England*, (1973), vol. 2, chapter 10.

12 J. Nemeth, "Psychopathic Personality. Its Relevance in the Correctional Afer-Care Agency" (1961), 3 Can. J. Corr. 128, but compare H.H.A. Cooper, "The Inadequate Psychopath: Some Medico-Legal Problems and a Clinical Profile" (1973), 21 Chitty's L.J. 325, R.D. Hare, Manual for the Revised Checklist (1991) and G.T. Harris, M.E. Rice and C.A. Cormier, "Psychopathy and Violent Recidivism" (1991), 15 *Law and Human Behaviour* at 625-637.

13 Walker, above note 11.

14 Walker, above, note 11, but see *contra* the *Report of the Butler Committee on Mentally Abnormal Offenders*, (1975) (Cmnd. 6244), which recommends the term "personality disorder".

15 B.C.L. Orchard, "Insanity — A Psychiatrist's View of the Recent Rulings of the Supreme Court of Canada" (1981), 2 Sup. Crt. L. Rev. 405.

utmost of careful scrutiny. In the light of the serious consequences that may ensue, this means vigorous examination and cross-examination are necessary.

Defence of Mental Disorder under Criminal Code

In February, 1992, Bill C-30 came into force. It enacted a new Part XXI of the *Criminal Code*, which declares a comprehensive legal regime to deal with accused who suffer from mental disorder. The law is sometimes concerned with the accused's state of mind at the time of his trial. The accused must be both mentally and physically present. There are detailed provisions in Part XXI relating to remands for observation and for determinations whether an accused is fit to stand his trial. Our concern here, however, is with an accused who is fit to stand trial and who seeks a verdict under s. 672.45 of not criminally responsible on account of mental disorder. Such an inquiry relates to the accused's state of mind at the time of the alleged act.

Until Bill C-30, such a verdict had been called an acquittal on account of insanity. The key provisions were as follows:

THE CRIMINAL CODE

R.S.C. 1985, c. C-46

16. (1) No person shall be convicted of an offence in respect of an act or omission on his part while he was insane.

(2) For the purposes of this section a person is insane when he is in a state of natural imbecility or has disease of the mind to an extent that renders him incapable of appreciating the nature and quality of an act or omission or of knowing that an act or omission is wrong.

(3) A person who has specific delusions, but is in other respects sane, shall not be acquitted on the ground of insanity unless the delusions caused him to believe in the existence of a state of things that, if it existed, would have justified or excused his act or omission.

(4) Every one shall, until the contrary is proved, be presumed to be and to have been sane.

. . . .

614. (1) Where, upon the trial of an accused who is charged with an indictable offence, evidence is given that the accused was insane at the time the offence was committed and the accused is acquitted,

(*a*) the jury, or

(*b*) the Judge or Magistrate, where there is no jury, shall find whether the accused was insane at the time the offence was committed and shall declare whether he is acquitted on account of insanity.

(2) Where the accused is found to have been insane at the time the offence was committed, the Court, Judge or Magistrate before whom the trial is held shall order that he be kept in strict custody in the place and in the manner that

the Court, Judge or Magistrate directs, until the pleasure of the lieutenant governor of the province is known.

Section 16 was a Canadian version of the famous *M'Naghten* rules, whose history is described in the following decision.

U.S. v. FREEMAN

(1966), 357 F. (2d) 606 (2nd. Circ.)

Kaufman J.: —

. . . .

M'Naghten and its antecedents can, in many respects, be seen as examples of the law's conscientious efforts to place in a separate category, people who cannot be justly held "responsible" for their acts. As far back as 1582, William Lambard of Lincolns' Inn set forth what can be viewed as the forerunner of the M'Naghten test as we know it: "If a man or a natural fool, or a lunatic in the time of his lunacy, or a child who apparently has no knowledge of good or evil do kill a man, this is no felonious act . . . for they cannot be said to have any understanding will." By 1724, the language had shifted from "good or evil" to the more familiar emphasis on the word "know." Thus, in *Rex v. Arnold*, 16 How. St. Tr. 695, 764 the "Wild Beast" test was enunciated. It provided for exculpation if the defendant "doth not *know* what he is doing, no more than . . . a wild beast." (Emphasis added.)

By modern scientific standards the language of these early tests is primitive. In the 18th century, psychiatry had hardly become a profession, let alone a science. Thus, these tests and their progeny were evolved at a time when psychiatry was literally in the Dark Ages.

In the pre-M'Naghten period, the concepts of phrenology and monomania were being developed and had significant influence on the right and wrong test. Phrenologists believed that the human brain was divided into 35 separate areas, each with its own peculiar mental function. The sixth area, for example, was designated "destructiveness." It was located, we are told, above the ear because this was the widest part of the skull of carnivorous animals. Monomania, on the other hand, was a state of mind in which one insane idea predominated while the rest of the thinking processes remained normal.

Of course, both phrenology and monomania are rejected today as meaningless medical concepts since the human personality is viewed as a fully integrated system. But, by an accident of history, the rule of M'Naghten's case froze these concepts into the common law just at a time when they were becoming obsolete. A discussion of M'Naghten's case will demonstrate how this came about. Daniel M'Naghten suffered from what now would be described as delusions of persecution. Apparently, he considered his major persecutor to be Robert Peel, then Prime Minister of England, for M'Naghten came to London with the intention of assassinating the chief of the Queen's government. His plan would have succeeded but for the fact that Peel chose to ride in Queen Victoria's carriage because of her absence from the city, while Drummond, his secretary, rode in the vehicle which normally would have been occupied by Peel. M'Naghten, believing that the Prime Minister was riding in his own carriage, shot and killed Drummond in error.

After a lengthy trial in 1843, M'Naghten was found "not guilty by reason of insanity." M'Naghten's exculpation from criminal responsibility was most significant for several reasons. His defense counsel had relied in part upon Dr. Isaac Ray's historic work, Medical Jurisprudence of Insanity which had been published in 1838. This book, which was used and referred to extensively at the trial, contained many enlightened views on the subject of criminal responsibility in general and on the weaknesses of the right and wrong test in particular. Thus, for example, the jury was told that the human mind is not compartmentalized and that a defect in one aspect of the personality could spill over and affect other areas. As Chief Judge Biggs tells us in his Isaac Ray lectures compiled in The Guilty Mind, the court was so impressed with this and other medical evidence of M'Naghten's incompetency that Lord Chief Justice Tindal practically directed a verdict for the accused.

For these reasons, M'Naghten's case could have been the turning point for a new approach to more modern methods of determining criminal responsibility. But the Queen's ire was raised by the acquittal and she was prompted to intervene. Mid-19th century England was in a state of social upheaval and there had been three attempts on the life of the Queen and one on the Prince Consort. Indeed, Queen Victoria was so concerned about M'Naghten's acquittal that she summoned the House of Lords to "take the opinion of the Judges on the law governing such cases." Consequently, the 15 Judges of the common-law Courts were called in a somewhat extraordinary session under a not too subtle atmosphere of pressure to answer five prolix and obtuse questions on the status of criminal responsibility in England. Significantly, it was Lord Chief Justice Tindal who responded for 14 of the 15 Judges, and thus articulated what has come to be known as the M'Naghten Rules or M'Naghten test. Rather than relying on Dr. Ray's monumental work which had apparently impressed him at M'Naghten's trial, Tindal, with the Queen's breath upon him, reaffirmed the old restricted right-wrong test despite its 16th century roots and the fact that it, in effect, echoed such uninformed concepts as phrenology and monomania.

Under s. 614(2) where an accused was acquitted on account of insanity, the trial Judge had to order that the accused be kept in strict custody "until the pleasure of the lieutenant governor of the province is known". The trial Judge had no discretion or power in this matter. In practice, it was up to provincial Mental Health Review Boards to decide if, when and how the accused should be detained. This amounted to indeterminant detention at the discretion of the mental health authorities .

In *R. v. Swain* (1991), 5 C.R. (4th) 253 (S.C.C.), the Supreme Court held that the mandatory detention of an insane acquittee under s. 614(2) without any chance of a hearing offended s. 7 of the *Charter* and also that detention without criteria constituted arbitrary detention under s. 9. Neither violation could be saved by s. 1. The Court ordered a six-month period of temporary validity for s. 614(2). The Minister of Justice obtained one extension. Finally, Bill C-30 was passed as a general reform package and also to respond to *Swain*.

The 1991 amendments abandoned the legalistic terminology of "insanity" in favour of "mental disorder" now used by most psychologists and psychiatrists. However, the change is not as significant as first appears given that s. 2 defines "mental disorder" as "a disease of the mind" and that the tests remain tests of legal irresponsibility derived from the M'Naghten rules. There is thus a descriptive advantage in continuing to refer to the defence of insanity at trial. It is still clear that the issue is still not determined by modern psychology and psychiatry. The revised s. 16 reads as follows:

16.(1) No person is criminally responsible for an act committed or an omission made while suffering from a mental disorder that rendered the person incapable of appreciating the nature and quality of the act or omission or of knowing that it was wrong.

(2) Every person is presumed not to suffer from a mental disorder so as to be exempt from criminal responsibility by virtue of subsection (1), until the contrary is proved on the balance of probabilities.

(3) The burden of proof that an accused was suffering from a mental disorder so as to be exempt from criminal responsibility is on the party that raises the issue.

Parliament has made it clear that the accused has the burden of proving the exemption on a balance of probabilities. It will be recalled that in *Chaulk* (1991), 2 C.R. (4th) 1 (S.C.C.), the Supreme Court of Canada, over the sole dissent of Wilson J., held that this was the effect of the former presumption of sanity. The majority further ruled that the onus of proof on the accused could be demonstrably justified as a reasonable limit under s. 1.

The verdict is now "not criminally responsible on account of mental disorder" (s. 672.34). Following such a verdict the trial Judge now has a discretion, and an obligation on application by the accused or the Crown, to hold a disposition hearing (s. 672.45). Such disposition may be an absolute or conditional discharge or detention in custody in a hospital (s. 672.54). See Laura Burt, "The Mental Disorder Provisions: Community Residence and Dispositions Under Section 672.54 (*c*)" (1993), 36 Crim. L. Q. 40. Subject to such a Court order, detention or release is in the jurisdiction of Provincial Review Boards, which are now mandatory and subject to detailed procedural requirements. See ss. 672.38-672.94 and see, generally, A.J.C. O'Marra, "Hadfield To Swain: The *Criminal Code* Amendments Dealing With the Mentally Disordered Accused" (1993), 36 Crim. L. Q. 49. This includes a right of appeal to a Court of Appeal. See *R. v. Peckham* (1994), 33 C.R. (4th) (C.A.), where the Court held that in applying the test of reasonableness the Court "must be cognizant of the Board's expertise and show that expertise appropriate curial deference". Parliament also enacted caps on detention such as life for first or second degree murder and ten years for certain designated offences and two years for other offences, see s. 672.64. However the capping provision has not been proclaimed. Unless and until such proclamation there would appear to have been little change to the former reality of indeterminate detention especially as trial Judges may wish to defer to mental health authorities.

The new legal regime survived *Charter* review in *Winko v. Forensic Psychiatric Institute*, [1999] 2 S.C.R. 625. For a Court unanimous on the issues of constitutionality, McLachlin J. held that the provisions did not violate s. 7 protections. The scheme was premised on treatment and assessment, and balanced the rights of the offender and society. The offender found not criminally responsible by reason of mental disorder had to be discharged absolutely unless the board or the Court found that the offender was a significant threat to public safety. This meant a real risk of physical or psychological harm beyond the trivial or annoying. The provisions were not vague or overbroad and did not impose a burden on the offender. The regime did not violate the equality guarantee under s. 15. Although there was differential treatment based on the personal characteristic of medical illness it was not discriminatory. At every stage of Part XX.1 the assessment was based on the individual's situation and needs and was subject to the overriding rule of the least restrictive avenue and annual review.

Regrettably, the Court in *Winko* did not address the significance of the non-proclamation of the capping provisions. This had prompted the Manitoba Court of Appeal to declare that ss. 672.54 and 672.81(1) violated s. 7 and were of no force or effect: *Hoeppner* (1999), 25 C.R. (5th) 91 (Man. C.A.), reconsideration refused (1999), 145 Man. R. (2d) 160 (note) (S.C.C.). In *Winko*, McLachlin J., in the course of deciding that the new scheme was not overbroad, indicated baldly that "I cannot agree with the contrary decision" in *Hoeppner* (at para. 71, C.R.).

Where the defence of lack of responsibility through mental disorder has not been raised or has been rejected, upon conviction the trial Judge has the normal range of sentencing options. These powers do not include the jurisdiction to order the place and type of imprisonment although the prison regime can be determined by setting the length at two years or more, federal, or less than two years, provincial. The Judge has no power to order psychiatric treatment in a prison or that the accused be transferred from a prison to a psychiatric facility; see *R. v. Deans* (1977), 37 C.C.C. (2d) 221 (Ont. C.A.); *R. v. Trecroce* (1980), 55 C.C.C.(2d) 202 (Ont. C.A.) at 218. Judicial recommendations do not have to be followed by prison authorities. There is no sentence alternative in Canada, as there is in England, of a hospital order where a Judge may sentence directly to a mental institution. A power to order detention in a psychiatric facility for up to 60 days in acute cases was contained in the 1992 amendments, s. 736.11, but this provision has not been proclaimed. Provincial psychiatric hospitals appear reluctant to accept more mentally-disordered persons sent from the criminal justice system.

It would appear that even under the new *Criminal Code* regime there are limited dispositional options. A defence based on mental disorder will still likely result in indeterminate detention at the discretion of health authorities. The defence is therefore likely to be rare except in those cases where the accused faces the option of a long prison sentence and would prefer secure custody in a mental facility.

COOPER v. R.

(1979), [1980] 1 S.C.R. 1149, 13 C.R. (3d) 97, 51 C.C.C. (2d) 129

The accused was charged with the murder of a patient at a psychiatric hospital (the detailed facts and the accused's psychiatric history are considered below). At the trial the defence of insanity was not raised by the accused but the trial Judge nevertheless put it to the jury. The accused's appeal to the Ontario Court of Appeal was dismissed. Only the dissenting Judge, Dubin J.A., would have ordered a new trial on the ground of misdirection as to defence of insanity.

DICKSON J. (LASKIN C.J.C., BEETZ, ESTEY and MCINTYRE JJ. concurring): — Issues fundamental to the design and range of the "insanity defence" and to notions of responsibility in our criminal justice system are before the Court in this appeal.

The case opens up the broad and difficult question of the obligation of a trial Judge to charge on insanity in circumstances where an accused has a lengthy psychiatric history but the medical evidence is that he does not suffer from "disease of the mind".

The appellant, Gary Albert Cooper, was charged with the murder of one Denise Hobbs, at the time an in-patient at the Hamilton Psychiatric Hospital. The appellant was an out-patient at the same institution. There was evidence that the appellant had been drinking during the day of 8th October 1975. That evening he arrived at a regularly scheduled dance held at a nearby church for patients of the hospital, and there met Denise Hobbs, with whom he was acquainted. At his invitation, the two left the dance to seek a bottle of pop and cigarettes. Ultimately, after an unsuccessful attempt at sexual intercourse the appellant choked the deceased. The cause of death was asphyxiation by strangulation.

At trial, counsel for the defence directed argument to raising a doubt on the issue of intent, and did not plead the "defence" of insanity. Nonetheless, the trial Judge, Van Camp J., charged the jury on insanity, though in a manner vigorously challenged in this appeal. The jury found the appellant guilty of non-capital murder, and an appeal was dismissed without written reasons, Dubin J.A. dissenting. At a later date Dubin J.A. delivered lengthy reasons in dissent [40 C.C.C. (2d) 145].

. . . .

The question raised by this appeal is whether there was evidence from which a properly charged jury could conclude, on a balance of probabilities, that the appellant had disease of the mind to an extent that rendered him incapable of appreciating the nature and quality of the act of which he was charged or of knowing that it was wrong. "Wrong" means legally wrong: *Schwartz v. R.*, [1977] 1 S.C.R. 673, 34 C.R.N.S. 138, 29 C.C.C. (2d) 1. Before turning to the evidence adduced at trial, it will be convenient to consider this question at some length, for it raises two distinct legal issues fundamental to our defence of insanity under s. 16(2). First, the meaning to be ascribed to the phrase "disease of the mind" and, second, the interpretation to be given the words "incapable of appreciating the nature and quality of an act".

I
DISEASE OF THE MIND

Let me say by way of commencement that, to date, the phrase "disease of the mind" has proven intractable and has eluded satisfactory definition by both medical and legal disciplines. It is not a term of art in either law or psychiatry. Indeed, Glanville Williams (*Textbook of Criminal Law* (1978), p. 592) says that the phrase is no longer in medical use. "It is a mere working concept, a mere abstraction, like sin" (Wily and Stallworthy, Mental Abnormality and the Law (1962), p. 20). Although the term expresses a legal concept, and a finding is made according to a legal test, psychiatric knowledge is directly linked to the legal conclusion, for medical testimony forms part of the evidence on which the trier of fact must reach its decision. But medical and legal perspectives differ.

. . . .

In *R. v. Kemp*, [1957] 1 Q.B. 339, an oft-cited decision, the primary issue was whether arteriosclerosis came within the meaning of "disease of the mind". Devlin J. agreed that there was an absence of medical opinion as to the categories of malfunction properly to be termed "diseases of the mind", and rejected the idea that, for legal purposes, a distinction should be made between diseases physical and mental in origin. In his view, arteriosclerosis is a disease of the mind and can provide a defence to a criminal charge. He reviewed the relationship between medical evidence and the legal conclusions to be drawn therefrom (p. 406):

> Doctors' personal views, of course, are not binding on me. I have to interpret the rules according to the ordinary principles of interpretation, but I derive help from their interpretations inasmuch as they illustrate the nature of the disease and the matters which from the medical point of view have to be considered in determining whether or not it is a disease of the mind.

In *Bratty v. A.G. for Northern Ireland*, [1963] A.C. 386, [1961] 3 All E.R. 523 (H.L.), Lord Denning agreed that the question of whether an accused suffers from a disease of the mind is properly resolved by the Judge. He acknowledged that "The major mental diseases, which the doctors call psychoses . . . are clearly diseases of the mind" and that "any mental disorder which has manifested itself in violence and is prone to recur is a disease of the mind" (p. 534).

. . . .

Support for a broad and liberal legal construction of the words, "disease of the mind" will be found in the writings of the renowned jurist Sir Owen Dixon, formerly Chief Justice of Australia, who wrote in "A Legacy of Hadfield, M'Naghten and Maclean" (1957), 31 A.L.J. 225 at 260:

> The reason why it is required that the defect of reason should be "from disease of the mind", in the classic phrase used by Sir *Nicholas Tindal*, seems to me no more than to exclude drunkenness, conditions of intense passion and other transient states attributable either to the fault or to the nature of man. In the advice delivered by Sir *Nicholas Tindal* no doubt *the words "disease of the mind" were chosen because it was considered that they had the widest possible meaning. He would hardly have supposed it possible that the expression would be treated as one containing words of the law to be weighed like diamonds. I have taken it to include, as well as all forms of physical or material change or deterioration, every recognizable disorder or derangement of the understanding whether or not its nature, in our present state of knowledge, is capable of explanation or determination.* (The italics are mine.)

To the learned authors of Smith and Hogan, *Criminal Law*, 4th ed. (1978), p. 164: "It seems that any disease which produces a malfunction is a disease of the mind."

Recently, in Canada, the Ontario Court of Appeal contributed judicial direction in this area of the law in the cases of *R. v. Rabey* (1977), 40 C.R.N.S. 46, 37 C.C.C. (2d) 461, and *R. v. Simpson* (1977), 35 C.C.C. (2d) 337, both of which were decided subsequent to the trial of the appellant. Judgment in *Rabey* postdates the decision of the Court of Appeal in the case at bar, and is presently on appeal to this Court on an issue unrelated to those raised herein. Martin J.A., who wrote for the Court in both *Rabey* and *Simpson*, was not among the members of the Court who heard the Cooper appeal.

Simpson has greater significance for the present appeal. There, the accused appealed the finding of not guilty by reason of insanity on two charges of attempted murder. The facts, which indicate two incidents of stabbing, are not remarkable. As framed by Martin J.A., the issue was whether a personality disorder is a disease of the mind within the meaning of s. 16 of the *Code*. He held that, notwithstanding the psychiatric evidence, the question raised must be resolved as a question of law. But the legal position, as I understand it, is properly expressed in the following passage (pp. 349-50):

> The term "disease of the mind" is a legal concept, although it includes a medical component, and what is meant by that term is a question of law for the Judge. . . . It is the function of the psychiatrist to describe the accused's mental condition and how it is considered from the medical point of view. It is for the Judge to decide whether the condition described is comprehended by the term "disease of the mind."

As a matter of practice, the trial Judge can permit the psychiatrist to be asked directly whether or not the condition in question constitutes a disease of the mind. Concerning the controversy over the classification of a "psychopathic personality", Martin J.A. found implicit recognition in Canadian and British authorities for the proposition that such a disorder can constitute a disease.

The general principles, not in issue on the further appeal to this Court, were reiterated by Marin J.A. in *R. v. Rabey*. Disease of the mind is a legal term. It is within the province of the Judge to determine what mental conditions are within the meaning of that phrase and whether there is any evidence that an accused suffers from an abnormal mental condition comprehended by that term. More importantly, he held that, if there is any evidence that the accused did suffer from such a disease, in legal terms, the question of fact must be left with the jury.

I think Dubin J.A. correctly characterizes the decision in *Simpson* as holding that "personality disorder" has been recognized as "being capable of constituting a 'disease of the mind' ". I share his view that "there is no reason to give a narrow or limited interpretation to the term 'disease of the mind' ". Admittedly, in *Simpson* both of the psychiatrists stated that the personality disorder there in question did or could constitute a disease of the mind. While Martin J.A. in that case had little difficulty finding evidence that the appellant suffered from a "disease of the mind", the case foundered upon the second segment of s. 16(2). It should also be kept in mind that *Simpson* presented an odd situation, in which the Crown successfully raised the insanity defence against the wishes of the accused, who appealed the verdict of not guilty by reason of insanity.

What is interesting in these two cases, for our purposes, is the maintenance of a clear distinction between the weight to be given medical opinions expressed in evidence, however relevant, and the task of the trial Judge to form an independent conclusion as to whether the mental condition falls within the legal concept.

In summary, one might say that, in a legal sense, "disease of the mind" embraces any illness, disorder or abnormal condition which impairs the human mind and its functioning, excluding, however, self-induced states caused by alcohol or drugs, as well as transitory mental states such as hysteria or concussion. In order to support a defence of insanity, the disease must, of course, be of such intensity as to render the accused incapable of appreciating the nature and quality of the violent act or of knowing that it is wrong.

Underlying all of this discussion is the concept of responsibility and the notion that an accused is not legally responsible for acts resulting from mental disease or mental defect.

. . . .

With great respect, in the case at bar, the trial Judge, in her charge to the jury, which I will discuss shortly, fell into error, in that she confused the legal issue of whether the appellant's disorder could constitute disease of the mind with the factual issue of whether the appellant was suffering from disease of the mind at the relevant time. Once the evidence is sufficient to indicate that an accused suffers from a condition which could, in law, constitute disease of the mind, the Judge must leave it open to the jury to find, as a matter of fact, whether the accused had disease of the mind at the time the criminal act was committed. The more troublesome issue, where a defence of insanity has been pleaded, concerns the second criterion to be applied in determining criminal responsibility. As Martin J.A. pointed out in *Rabey* (p. 474):

> In many, if not most cases involving the defence of insanity, the question whether the accused suffered from a disease of the mind is not the critical issue; the pivotal issue is whether a condition which, admittedly, constitutes a disease of the mind rendered the accused incapable of appreciating the nature and quality of the act or of knowing that it was wrong.

The real question in this case, in my view, is not whether the accused was suffering from a disease of the mind but whether he was capable of appreciating the nature and quality of the act. That second question ought to have been left to the jury in clear terms.

II
APPRECIATE

In contrast to the position in England under the M'Naghten Rules, where the words used are "knows the nature and quality of his act", s. 16 of the *Code* uses the phrase "appreciating the nature and quality of an act or omission". The two are not synonymous. The draftsman of the *Code*, as originally enacted, made a deliberate change in language from the common-law rule in order to broaden the legal and medical considerations bearing upon the mental state of the accused and to make it clear that cognition was not to be the sole criterion. Emotional as well as intellectual awareness of the significance of the conduct is in issue. The Report of the Royal Commission on the law of Insanity as a Defence in Criminal Cases (McRuer Report) (1956), contains a useful discussion on the point (p. 12):

> The word "appreciating", not being a word that is synonymous with "knowing", requires far-reaching legal and medical consideration when discussing Canadian law. It had its origin in the Stephen Draft Code. Not infrequently judicial reference is made to the New Oxford Dictionary for the definition of words used in Canadian statutes. The New Oxford Dictionary gives five different uses of the word 'appreciate", depending on the context. The one applicable to this statute is:
>
> "2. To estimate aright, to perceive the full force of.
> "b. esp. to be sensitive to, or sensible of, any delicate impression or distinction.
> " 'Until the truth of any thing . . . be appreciated, its error, if any, cannot be detected.' "
>
> An examination of the civil law of England and Canada shows that there is an important difference between "know" or "knowledge" on the one hand and "appreciate" or "appreciation" on the other when used and applied to a given set of circumstances. This is best illustrated by the principles of law underlying those cases in which the maxim *volenti non fit injuria* is involved. There is a clear distinction between mere knowledge of the risk and appreciation of both the risk and the danger.

To "know" the nature and quality of an act may mean merely to be aware of the physical act, while to "appreciate" may involve estimation and understanding of the consequences of that act. In the case of the appellant, as an example, in using his hands to choke the deceased he may well have known the nature and quality of that physical act of choking. It is entirely different to suggest, however, that in performing the physical act of choking he was able to appreciate its nature and quality, in the sense of being aware that it could lead to or result in her death. In the opinion of the medical expert who testified at the trial, the appellant could have been capable of intending bodily harm and of choking the girl, but not of having intended her death.

Our *Code* postulates an independent test, requiring a level of understanding of the act, which is more than mere knowledge that it is taking place; in short, a capacity to apprehend the nature of the act, and its consequences. The position in law is well expressed in the McRuer Report at p. 12:

> Under the Canadian statute law a disease of the mind that renders the accused person incapable of an appreciation of the nature and quality of the act must necessarily involve more than mere knowledge that the act is being committed; there must be an appreciation of the factors involved in the act and a mental capacity to measure and foresee the consequences of the violent conduct.

It should be noted that the issue of appreciation of the nature and quality of the act was not before this court in *Schwartz v. R.*, *supra*. The sole issue was the meaning of the word "wrong". The decision in *Schwartz* should not be taken as authority for the proposition that "appreciating" the nature and quality of an act is synonymous with "knowing" the physical character of that act.

The test proposed in the McRuer Report, which I would adopt (save for deletion of the "fully" in the fourth line) is this (p. 13):

> The true test necessarily is, was the accused person at the very time of the offence — not before or after, but at the moment of the offence — by reason of disease of the mind, unable fully to appreciate not only the nature of the act but the natural consequences that would flow from it? In other words, was the accused person, by reason of disease of the mind, deprived of the mental capacity to foresee and measure the consequences of the act?

The legally relevant time is the time when the act was committed.

In *R. v. O'Brien*, supra, Ritchie J.A. referred to the McRuer Report and stated at pp. 301-302:

> If an accused person is to be deprived of the protection of s. 16, he must, at the time of committing the offence, have had an *appreciation of the factors involved in his act and the mental capacity to measure and foresee the consequences of it.*

In the *Simpson* decision, *supra*, Martin J.A. offered the view that s. 16(2) exempts from liability an accused who, due to a disease of the mind, has no real understanding of the nature, character and consequences of the act at the time of its commission. I agree. With respect, I accept the view that the first branch of the test, in employing the word "appreciates", imports an additional requirement to mere knowledge of the physical quality of the act. The requirement, unique to Canada, is that of perception, an ability to perceive the consequences, impact and results of a physical act. An accused may be aware of the physical character of his action (*i.e.*, in choking) without neccessarily having the capacity to appreciate that, in nature and quality, that act will result in the death of a human being. This is simply a restatement, specific to the defence of insanity, of the principle that *mens rea*, or intention as to the consequences of an act, is a requisite element in the commission of a crime.

III
EVIDENCE — NON-MEDICAL

It will now be convenient to turn to the evidence, because, as I understand him, counsel for the Crown concedes that, if there was sufficient evidence to go to the jury on the question of insanity, the trial Judge failed to deal adequately with insanity in her charge and effectively withdrew the insanity defence from the jury.

It is important to observe at the outset that the trial Judge did charge the jury on insanity, although, as I have stated, the defence was not raised by the appellant's counsel. The Judge felt the evidence sufficient to warrant an instruction to the jury on the issue, whatever the posture of defence counsel. In my opinion, she was correct in doing so, having regard to the evidence upon this issue, which I will now endeavour to summarize.

The Crown adduced evidence that before 7:00 p.m. on the night in question a resident nursing assistant, present at the church where the dance was being held, addressed the appellant upon his arrival. The appellant had a "faraway", "dazed", "blank" look in his eyes, and appeared unresponsive. The appellant's father testified that he received a telephone call at approximately 8:15 p.m. from his son, who seemed excited and out of breath. The appellant, trying to speak quickly, was having difficulty "getting his words out". He told his father, "Hello dad, how are you doing? Dad I just killed somebody . . . on James Street Mountain steps . . . I was coming down the steps and thought somebody was following me . . . I jumped over the railing . . . I jumped out and grabbed hold of them." In response to the question "Is he dead'." the appellant said: "Yes. I felt for a heartbeat and a pulse. I dragged her out in the bushes."

Constable Slote of the Hamilton police force testified that he received a call at 8:39 p.m. from the appellant, who attested to having "just seen a murder". The conversation was recorded on the police dispatcher:

> I seen somebody kill a girl. I don't know if he dragged her in the bushes or not . . . I was just coming down the James Street stairs and I heard a screams [sic); I don't know, I'd just turned around and seen somebody grab some girl and drag her into the bushes . . . I don't know, you know, if she's dead or alive or what.

Constable Slote considered it a crank call, as there was a lack of emotion in the caller's voice. A police cruiser dispatched to the telephone booth, and thereafter to Cooper's apartment, was unable to locate the appellant.

The deceased was discovered the following morning, 9th October, in the bushes near the James Street steps. Her upper body and part of her face were covered by her jacket, and her brassiere, unfastened, was in place. Her slacks, also unfastened, were about her hips. Soil and leaves adhered to her back. There was no evidence of sexual intercourse. However, she had been undressed and an attempt made to redress her. There was no evidence of struggle, and the deceased was neither battered nor badly bruised. Her strangulation was by hand, without the use of a rope or weapon.

At 11:35 a.m. that morning the appellant was apprehended and detained by police officers until 12:10 p.m., at which time an interrogation commenced. At the time he was true to his story of having seen a murder committed by another person. To both officers in attendance, the appellant appeared mentally slow and spoke slowly.

The officers left the appellant to continue the investigation and returned to the interview at 7:25 p.m. Upon their confronting him with additional facts and indicating that he would be charged with murder, the appellant said, "Hold it. Hold it. I didn't mean to kill her." The appellant offered to give a full statement (which I have paraphrased, except where in quotes):

> I went to the church and bumped into Denise Hobbs. . . . we went for a walk down the James Street stairs then I kissed her then she wanted to go back up then I grabbed her around the throat and choked her [with] my hands. Then I got scared and tried to feel for pulse or something and got none so I ran downstairs for a phone booth.
> ". . . we were in the bushes standing up, I kissed her and I grabbed her around the throat and choked her *I was afraid she would go back and tell them I was kissing her.*"(The italics are mine.)

The appellant did testify at trial. Defence counsel attempted to establish a lack of intention to commit the murder, supported by the evidence of the appellant's intoxication and susceptibility to abnormal behaviour.

The appellant was 31 years of age. His father, Albert Cooper, testified that, as a young boy, the appellant was subject to seizures, convulsions and sudden mood changes — he would quickly become very excited for no apparent reason and then quickly calm down. Often the appellant would seem to be "far away" and his "mind was elsewhere". Sometimes he would have blackouts and fall down. He heard things which were not there to be heard. His condition worsened as he got older. The appellant was first seen by psychiatrists at age 7. At age 10 or 12 he was treated for auditory hallucinations. He experienced a great deal of difficulty at school, and at age 16 had progressed only as far as Grade V at a trade school. He held a series of menial jobs, from which he was discharged after short periods of time. In his testimony the appellant stated that he had been admitted to the Hamilton Psychiatric Hospital in 1965 (it was in fact in 1962) and remained until 1971, after which time he was an out-patient and still had contact with the doctors at the hospital. He married in April 1972 (he had met his wife at the psychiatric hospital) and had two children. He returned to the hospital for a period of 15 days in 1974.

IV
EVIDENCE — MEDICAL

Medical evidence relating to the appellant's mental and behavioural problems is offered in testimony of Dr. Sim. I think it useful to break down his evidence, reorganized slightly from the sequence in which it was given at trial, as follows:

(a) *General history*

The hospital records indicated that the appellant was first seen at age 7, as he was failing at school and exhibited disturbing behaviour. A condition of borderline mental deficiency was diagnosed at that time. He was re-examined at age 8 and described as being wild and hyperactive and having a poor sense of reality. At 10, an abnormal E.E.G. reading was discovered upon examination for his problem of narcolepsy (sleep seizures). At 11, further I.Q. testing disclosed borderline deficiency, and at age 12 the appellant was treated by a psychiatrist for mental confusion and auditory hallucinations. He was admitted to the Hamilton Psychiatric Hospital as a young man and diagnosed as "without psychosis — borderline intelligence". In 1965 his condition was described as "psychosis with mental deficiency". Dr. Sim described "psychosis" in this way:

> Psychosis, basically, involves a break with reality in which the person may or may not be confused, and have other symptoms like hallucinations of his hearing, seeing, tasting, or smelling, feeling things that are not actually around, or can have such symptoms as delusions. And delusion is usually described as a false belief which cannot be changed by persuasion and/or reason.

In 1965 there was a bizarre episode wherein the appellant was reported to have swallowed part of a lighter, his belt buckle, buttons from his clothing and a zipper from his trousers. In 1967 he swallowed part of a disassembled cigarette lighter. In 1967 he was re-diagnosed as "mental deficiency without psychosis". Since, he has also been described medically as having "personality disorder, anti-social type with borderline mental retardation". Other evidence indicated that the appellant was released from the hospital in 1971 and returned subsequently in 1974 for a period of 15 days.

(b) *Electroencephalogram*

Dr. Sim reviewed the medical history of abnormal brainwave patterns (electrical discharges from the brain). All such tests (from March 1962 to June 1974) showed generalized abnormality, and in one or two of the E.E.G. tests there was abnormality in brainwaves from the temporal lobe. However, the E.E.G. tests were suggestive, at most, of an "epileptic diathesis" (tendency or propensity to epilepsy, without necessarily resulting in seizures). Dr. Sim could say only that it is possible that Cooper could experience epileptic seizures.

(c) *Intelligence*

The appellant's intellectual ability was measured on a number of occasions according to the full-scale intelligence quotient. His I.Q. ranged from 69 to 79 and was usually between 71 and 79. The normal I.Q. reading is in the region of 90 to 110. In Dr. Sim's opinion, the appellant is of borderline intelligence (*i.e.*, bordering on retardation or classification as an "outright mentally defective person"). The changeover is at an I.Q. of 70. To quote the doctor:

In summary we are dealing with a male who has shown evidence of breaking with reality in the past. He has a long history of unstable, aggressive and inadequate behaviour. He was unable to adjust at school, academically, socially, economically, in his marriage. He has some brainwave abnormalities which could more readily make this man more irritable and aggresive by alcohol than a person without these abnormalities. He is also of limited intelligence, having a borderline to high-grade defective level of I.Q. Putting all this together, and bringing the stress — the fact that he was under stress financially and so forth, plus the alcohol and under the circumstances which are described as having occurred at the time, it would be my opinion that he would be in such a state of clouded consciousness that he would not be able to form the intent to kill.

Dr. Sim agreed with the diagnosis of other psychiatrists of 26th March 1976 that the appellant had "personality disorder, mixed type, showing schizoid, anti-social explosive and inadequate features, borderline mental retardation". However, on direct examination Dr. Sim was of the view that at the time of the offence the appellant was *not* suffering from a disease of the mind.

(d) *Intention*

Dr. Sim expressed the opinion that, although the appellant probably knew he was causing bodily harm, he was incapable of forming an intent to kill and he could not have known that any harm he was causing might result in death.

. . . .

V
THE CHARGE

The charge on insanity was sketchy in the extreme. It was introduced with these words:

However, I do have to consider one further defence with you, I would prefer not to, but, as I look at it, it seems to me that the question will be in your minds, and so I must discuss with you the question of insanity.

And concluded with these words:

With that evidence before you, again it would seem to be impossible for you to bring in a finding of not guilty by reason of insanity, but the evidence is yours to consider, and it is your finding.

In the course of the charge on insanity, the following was said:

The reason I have been reluctant to put this before you but have considered I should is that the evidence of Dr. Sim was that this man did not have a disease of the mind. However, if there is other evidence before you, you are entitled to weigh the evidence of Dr. Sim with the other evidence. The other evidence that you had was the evidence of his father as to the nature of thc convulsions, the mood changes, the faraway looks, the low I.Q., the rapid speech, the blackouts, the falls, the hearing of things throughout his early life.

Crown counsel, commenting upon the charge, objected that it was unnecessary to put the insanity defence to the jury, as that defence was not available to the accused. The Judge replied:

> I do agree that the charge on insanity was sparse: little attention was drawn to the evidence. I considered that it had to be put before the jury. I had hoped that by indicating that the evidence was so weak that [sic] it would not form a major part of their concern.

At the time of sentencing, counsel for the accused said:

> In light of that, my Lady, I think his problem is more a psychiatric one than a penal system is geared to handle, and I ask your Ladyship not to make a recommendation, or, I should say, an order, beyond the minimum period of ten years.

The Judge replied:

> I would agree that this is a matter in which, if there is any provision for psychiatric help, it should be obtained, and I will endeavour to make such a recommendation.

VI
CONCLUSIONS

In my opinion, there was evidence sufficient to require the Judge to fully instruct the jury on the issue of insanity. The Judge was of the opinion that that issue should go to the jury. With respect, the trial Judge erred:

(1) In treating Dr. Sim's reply to the Judge's isolated question as virtually determinative of the issue of whether the appellant had a "disease of the mind". Although in practice it is often convenient to do so, in strictness a medical witness is not entitled to state that a particular condition is or is not a disease of the mind, since this is a legal question. Mental disease is not purely a matter of psychiatric definition. It is for the jury, and not for medical men, of whatever eminence, to determine the issue: *R. v. Rivett* (1950), 34 Cr. App. R. 87 at 94 (C.A.). The entire psychiatric history, if accepted by the jury, was such as would have entitled the jury to hold that the accused suffered from a disease of the mind, within its legal meaning, regardless of whether one isolates the personality disorder. Personality disorders such as the appellant displayed at various stages in his life can constitute a disease of the mind. The real question before the jury was the extent to which the accused's appreciation of the nature and quality of his act was impaired. Included in the evidence on this point was the evidence of Dr. Sim that the appellant lacked the capacity to form the intent to cause death.

(2) In failing to review adequately the evidence bearing upon the insanity issue and in failing to relate the evidence of the accused's capacity to intend certain acts to the issue of insanity. The Judge did not analyze the evidence of Dr. Sim or the other evidence as it may have related to the defence of insanity on the issue of whether the appellant appreciated the nature and quality of his act. Failure before the jury on the issues of intent and intoxication did not preclude success on the issue of insanity. The insanity question should have

been put to the jury in such a way as to ensure their due appreciation of the value of the evidence: *R. v. Laycock*, [1952] O.R. 908, 15 C.R. 292, 104 C.C.C. 274 (C.A.).

(3) In concluding this portion of the charge in language which, to all intents, withdrew from the jury the essential determination of fact which it was its province to decide. If the issue was to go to the jury, then, in fairness to the accused, a much more careful charge was warranted. The issue should have been clearly left with the jury to decide. On a matter of such importance, and having regard to the strong evidence of personality disorder, s. 613 [am. 1974-75-76, c. 93, s. 75] of the *Code* should not be applied in this case.

Before concluding, I should state that Dubin J.A. discussed at some length "natural imbecility". I have refrained from doing so, as I believe the present appeal can be decided without broaching that aspect of the case.

I would allow the appeal and order a new trial.

The dissenting judgment of Martland J., Pratte J. concurring, is omitted.

Appeal allowed; new trial ordered.

KJELDSON v. R.

24 C.R. (3d) 289, [1981] 2 S.C.R. 617, 64 C.C.C. (2d) 161

McIntyre J., on behalf of the Court, held that psychopathy was a disease of the mind within the meaning of *Criminal Code*, s. 16, and also adopted the further analysis of Martin J.A. in *R. v. Simpson* (1977), 35 C.C.C. (2d) 337 at 355 (Ont. C.A.):

Emotional disturbance caused by disease of the mind may be so severe as to deprive the accused of the use of his understanding at the time of the act, rendering him incapable of appreciating the nature and quality of the act or of knowing that it was wrong, and thus exempting him from liability under s. 16(2) of the *Code*: see *R. v. Gorecki* (1976), 32 C.C.C. (2d) 135, a judgment of this Court . . . I do not, however, read the psychiatric evidence to be that the accused was by reason of emotional turmoil produced by disease of the mind incapable of understanding or realizing what he was doing, but rather that he lacked normal emotions and was therefore incapable of experiencing normal feelings concerning the acts assuming he committed them.

While I am of the view that s. 16(2) exempts from liability an accused who by reason of disease of the mind has no real understanding of the nature, character and consequences of the act at the time of its commission, I do not think the exemption provided by the section extends to one who has the necessary understanding of the nature, character and consequences of the act, but merely lacks appropriate feelings for the victim or lacks feelings of remorse or guilt for what he has done, even though such lack of feeling stems from "disease of the mind". Appreciation of the nature and quality of the act does not import a requirement that the act be accompanied by appropriate feeling about the effect of the act on other people: see *Willgoss v. R.* (1960), 105 C.L.R. 295 (Aust. H.C.); *R. v. Leech*, 21 C.R.N.S. 1, 10 C.C.C. (2d) 149 (Alta. T.D.); *R. v. Craig* (1975), 22 C.C.C. (2d) 212, affirmed 28 C.C.C. (2d) 311 (Alta. C.A.). No doubt the absence of such feelings is a common characteristic of many persons who engage in repeated and serious criminal conduct.

R. v. ABBEY

29 C.R. (3d) 193, [1982] 2 S.C.R. 24, 68 C.C.C. (2d) 394

The accused was charged with importing cocaine and unlawfully possessing cocaine for the purpose of trafficking. Upon his arrival at Vancouver International Airport from Lima, Peru, the accused's shoulder bag was searched and found to contain two plastic bags with 5.5 ounces of 50 percent pure cocaine. When asked what was in the bags, the accused answered, "Naturally, cocaine", and advised the police in a written statement about the events leading to his arrest. In his defence the accused raised insanity. The psychiatric evidence suggested that he suffered a disease of the mind which, although not rendering him incapable of appreciating the nature and quality of his act, involved a delusional belief that he was committed to a course of action, no harm would come to him and he would not be punished. The trial Judge acquitted the accused by reason of insanity, ruling that he was insane within the meaning of *Code*, s. 16(2) because he failed to appreciate the penal consequences of his act. When the matter reached the Supreme Court it was held that this was one of the errors necessitating a new trial.

DICKSON J.: —

. . . .

. . . . As the Court observed in *Cooper, supra*, the requirement that the accused be able to perceive the consequences of a physical act is a restatement, specific to the defence of insanity, of the principle of *mens rea*, or intention as to the consequences of an act, as a requisite element in the commission of a crime. The mental element must be proved with respect to all circumstances, and consequences, that form part of the *actus reus*. As the Crown in this case correctly points out, "while punishment may be a *result* of the commission of a criminal act it is not an *element* of the crime itself". A delusion which renders an accused "incapable of appreciating the nature and quality of his act" goes to the *mens rea* of the offence and brings into operation the "first arm" of s. 16(2): he is not guilty by reason of insanity. A delusion which renders an accused incapable of appreciating that the penal sanctions attaching to the commission of the crime are applicable to him does not go to the *mens rea* of the offence, does not render him incapable of appreciating the nature and quality of the act, and does not bring into operation the "first arm" of the insanity defence.

Abbey was charged with importing and trafficking in cocaine. There is no dispute as to the fact that he carried cocaine into the country. In his statement to police, it was his admitted intention to import cocaine for the purposes of trafficking. In other words, Abbey appreciated that the *actus reus* of each of the offences charged was being committed. Both the psychiatrist called for the defence and the psychiatrist who testified on behalf of the Crown stated that Abbey appreciated the nature and quality of his act. The Judge erred, in my view, in going on to say that a failure to appreciate the penal sanctions ("consequences of punishment") brought the accused within the ambit of the "first arm" of the insanity defence of s. 16(2).

The second arm of s. 16(2)

Should the question of "personal penal consequences" be relevant at all, it is more appropriately discussed within the context of the second arm of s. 16(2), *i.e.*, "knowing that an act is wrong". Glanville Williams in his *Criminal Law, The General Part*, at p. 478 says:

> "It has been determined that this phrase ['nature and quality'] refers to the physical character of the act, not its legal quality: legal right and wrong are cared for by the second question [citing *R. v. Codere, supra*, at p. 27]."

This Court having decided in *Schwartz v. R.*, *supra*, that "wrong" means wrong according to law, and it being established that Abbey knew his act was "wrong", his inability to "appreciate" the penal consequences is really irrelevant to the question of legal insanity. There seems to be no doubt on the evidence, and on the Judge's findings, that Abbey knew that he was doing an act forbidden by law.

With respect, the trial Judge homogenized the first and second arms of s. 16(2), collapsing the one into the other in, for example, the following passage from his judgment:

> "As I understand the evidence and the submissions of counsel, the accused had the capacity to appreciate the nature of the act of importing and of possessing the cocaine. He also had the capacity to appreciate the immediate consequences of those acts, that is to say, that they were illegal, that he should not commit them overtly . . ."

In *Schwartz v. R.*, [1977] I S.C.R. 673, 34 C.R.N.S. 138, 29 C.C.C. (2d) 1, Mr. Justice Martland, for a 5:4 majority of the Court, adopted the interpretation of the English Court of Criminal Appeal in *R. v. Windle*, [1952] 2 Q.B. 826, that "wrong" in s. 16(2) of the *Criminal Code* means "contrary to law". In fact the majority specified criminal law. The four dissenting Judges, through Dickson J., would have adopted the opinion of the Australian High Court in *Stapleton v. R.* (1952), 86 C.L.R. 358, that "wrong" means morally wrong. In determining which interpretation of the word "wrong" should be adopted, the Court relied more on traditional legal sources than on assessment of the social policy considerations. Mr. Justice Martland was unwilling to acquit an insane person who knew that his act was illegal but considered it morally justifiable, pointing out that this would not acquit a sane person. He was also of the view that the interpretation of morally wrong required a subjective test of insanity which would be dangerous. Mr. Justice Dickson in dissent held that "moral wrong" was "not to be judged by the personal standards of the offender but by his awareness that society regards the act as wrong". Mr. Justice Dickson used an historical and contextual approach to statutory construction in reasoning that, if a wrong meant contrary to law, Parliament would have used the word "unlawful" as it had done elsewhere in the *Code*, that the law in 1843 dealt with insanity in terms of rightness and wrongness, and that the McRuer Report concluded that "wrong" means "something that would be condemned in the eyes of mankind".

R. v. CHAULK

[1990] 3 S.C.R. 1303, 2 C.R. (4th) 1, 62 C.C.C. (3d) 193

The Supreme Court overruled *Schwartz*.

LAMER C.J.C. (DICKSON C.J.C. and WILSON, LA FOREST, GONTHIER and CORY JJ.): —

[I]t is plain to me that the term "wrong" as used in s. 16(2) must mean more than simply legally wrong. In considering the capacity of a person to know whether an act is one that he ought or ought not to do, the inquiry cannot terminate with the discovery that the accused knew that the act was contrary to the formal law. A person may well be aware that an act is contrary to law but, by reason of "natural imbecility" or disease of the mind, is at the same time incapable of knowing that the act is morally wrong in the circumstances according to the moral standards of society. This would be the case, for example, if the person suffered from a disease of the mind to such a degree as to know that it is legally wrong to kill but, as described by Dickson J. in *Schwartz*, kills "in the belief that it is in response to a divine order and therefore not morally wrong" (p. 678).

. . . .

[T]he insanity defence should not be made unavailable simply on the basis that an accused knows that a particular act is contrary to law and that he knows, generally, that he should not commit an act that is a crime. It is possible that a person may be aware that it is ordinarily wrong to commit a crime but, by reason of a disease of the mind, believes that it would be "right" according to the ordinary morals of his society to commit the crime in a particular context. In this situation, the accused would be entitled to be acquitted by reason of insanity.

McLACHLIN J. (L'HEUREUX-DUBÉ and SOPINKA JJ. concurring): —

Lamer C.J.C. has accepted the appellants' invitation to reconsider this Court's earlier conclusion that the capacity to know the act or omission was *legally* wrong suffices. In his view, an accused who is capable of knowing an act or omission is legally wrong is not subject to the criminal process, if mental illness rendered him or her incapable of knowing the act or omission was morally wrong. I, on the other hand, take the view that it does not matter whether the capacity relates to legal wrongness or moral wrongness — all that is required is that the accused be capable of knowing that the act was in some sense "wrong". If the accused has this capacity, then it is neither unfair nor unjust to submit the accused to criminal responsibility and penal sanction.

. . . .

[W]hat is essential is that the accused know that he or she ought not to do the act in question. This condition is met if the accused knows that the act is legally wrong.

. . . .

To hold that absence of moral discernment due to mental illness should exempt a person who knows that legally he or she ought not to do a certain act is, moreover, to introduce a lack of parallelism into the criminal law; generally absence of moral appreciation is no excuse for criminal conduct. When the moral mechanism breaks down in the case of an individual who is sane, we do not treat that as an excuse for disobeying the law; for example, in the case of a psychopath. The rationale is that an individual either knows or is presumed to know the law, and the fact that his or her moral standards are at variance with those of society is not an excuse. Why, if the moral mechanism breaks down because of disease of the mind, should it exempt the accused from criminal responsibility where he or she knows, or was capable of knowing, that the act was illegal and hence one which he or she "ought not to do"? Why should deficiency of moral appreciation due to mental illness have a different consequence than deficiency of moral appreciation due to a morally-impoverished upbringing, for example? I see no reason why the policy of the law should differ in the two cases.

. . . .

The problem with making capacity to appreciate moral wrong the test for criminal responsibility where the incapacity is caused by mental illness, is that of determining what society's moral judgment will be in every situation. What result is to obtain on those occasions where an accused claims an incapacity to know that his or her unlawful act was morally wrong and, objectively, the act was one for which the moral wrongfulness can be disputed? Certainly a Court is in no position to make determinations on questions of morality, nor is it fair to expect a jury to be able to agree on what is morally right or morally wrong. The prospect of greater certainty, and the avoidance of metaphysical arguments on right and wrong is the chief advantage of adhering to the traditional *M'Naghten* test for criminal responsibility where causative disease of the mind exists — whether the accused, for whatever reason, was capable of appreciating that his or her act is wrong.

The importance of certainty in the criminal law cannot be over-estimated. It should be relatively clear when criminal responsibility attaches and when it does not if the criminal law is to have the requisite deterrent effect, and if it is to be seen to function fairly and equitably to all. A person's criminal responsibility should not hinge on questions of whether an act would be generally perceived as immoral.

In *R. v. Oommen*, [1994] 2 S.C.R. 507, 30 C.R. (4th) 195, 91 C.C.C. (3d) 8, the Court applied the new *Chaulk* test in holding that an insanity defence had been wrongly rejected by the trial Judge in a murder case. Late one night the accused shot and killed, without apparent motive, a young female friend at his apartment. He had long suffered from a mental disorder described as "a psychosis of a paranoid delusional type". His specific belief at the time of the shooting was that members of a local union had conspired to "destroy" him and that they had given a commission to the victim to kill him.

At his murder trial before Judge alone the accused raised the defence of insanity. The trial Judge rejected it. Although the accused had had a compulsive fear that the young girl would kill him, it was more probable than not that at the time of the killing the accused was capable of knowing that he was doing wrong according to moral standards of society. The evidence of medical witnesses was that his delusion would not prevent him from being aware of what he was doing in the sense that he knew his discharge of the firearm was a death-threatening act. His subjective belief that the act was not wrong would not, according to the trial Judge, assist him.

The Supreme Court unanimously confirmed the Alberta Court of Appeal's order of a new trial. The Court confirmed that under s. 16(1) of the *Criminal Code* a person who lacks capacity to know that the act he is committing is wrong is exempt from criminal responsibility. The inquiry is to focus not on general capacity to know right from wrong but rather on the ability to know that a particular act was wrong in the circumstances. The question is whether the accused lacks the capacity to rationally decide whether the act is right or wrong and hence to make a rational choice about whether to do it or not. Does the accused possess the capacity present in the ordinary person to know that the act was wrong having regard to the everyday standards of the ordinary person? Since s. 16 is an independent condition of criminal responsibility the Supreme Court decided that it was not necessary to show that a defence such as self-defence would apply; this rejected the view of the Alberta Court of Appeal in the Court below (1993), 21 C.R. (4th) 117 (Alta. C.A.). The findings of the trial Judge were consistent with the conclusion that the accused's mental disorder deprived him of the capacity to know his act was wrong by the standards of the ordinary person.

Evidence of Mental Disorder Negativing **Mens Rea**

In *R. v. Swain*, [1991] 1 S.C.R. 933, Mr. Justice Lamer, for the majority, held that the common-law rule allowing the Crown to adduce evidence of insanity over and above the accused's wishes was not in accordance with principles of fundamental justice under s. 7 and could not be saved by s. 1. His Lordship referred to the relaxation of the *Oakes* test to require merely that the violation infringed rights as "little as is reasonably possible" but however determined, that consideration of judicial deference had no place respecting common-law violations for which only the "least intrusive" alternative would do. The majority went on to fashion a new common-law rule which would only allow the Crown to independently raise the issue of insanity after the trier of fact had concluded that the accused was otherwise guilty. The issue of insanity would be tried after a finding of guilt, but before a conviction was entered. The Court also recognized that the Crown could adduce evidence of insanity during the trial, if the accused had put his or her mental state in issue.

The Court in *Swain* refers to evidence of mental impairment short of insanity negativing the requisite mental element, for example, planning and deliberation in the case of first degree murder or the specific intent required for murder. This ruling was obiter but was accepted as the law in *Jacquard* (1997), 113 C.C.C. (3d) 1 (S.C.C.), the Court dividing only on whether the judge's direction had been sufficiently clear. Thus the Supreme Court has recognized that evidence of mental disorder short of a full-blown defence under s.16 may be admitted on the issue of *mens rea*.

In *R. v. Wade* (1995), 41 C.R. (4th) 100, 98 C.C.C. (3d) 97, [1995] 2 S.C.R. 737, the majority of the Supreme Court rejected the view of the Ontario Court of Appeal that a trial judge should have put the possibility of manslaughter to a jury in a case where the husband killed his wife in extreme rage. The Ontario Court of Appeal had accepted that the jury had rejected the defence of automatism in their verdict of second degree murder but had pointed to evidence that he was in some form of altered mental state when he attacked his wife.

Reform Options

U.S. v. FREEMAN

(1966), 357 F. (2d) 606 (2nd. Circ.)

KAUFMAN J.: —

. . . .

After consideration reflection on the issues presented, we therefore conclude that we cannot escape our duty to consider whether the M'Naghten Rules or the M'Naghten Rules augmented by the "irresistible impulse" test should continue to remain the test of criminal responsibility in this federal jurisdiction.

. . . .

Because M'Naghten focuses only on the cognitive aspect of the personality, *i.e.*, the ability to know right from wrong, we are told by eminent medical scholars that it does not permit the jury to identify those who can distinguish between good and evil but who cannot control their behavior. The result is that instead of being treated at appropriate mental institutions for a sufficiently long period to bring about a cure or sufficient improvement so that the accused may return with relative safety to himself and the community, he is ordinarily sentenced to a prison term as if criminally responsible and then released as a potential recidivist with society at his mercy. To the extent that these individuals continue to be released from prison because of the narrow scope of M'Naghten, that test poses a serious danger to society's welfare.

Similarly, M'Naghten's single track emphasis on the cognitive aspect of the personality recognizes no degrees of incapacity. Either the defendant knows right from wrong or he does not and that is the only choice the jury is given. But such a test is grossly unrealistic; our mental institutions, as any qualified psychiatrist will attest, are filled with people who to some extent can differentiate between right and wrong, but lack the capacity to control their acts to a substantial degree. As the commentary to the American Law Institute's Model Penal Code observes, "The law must recognize that when there is no black and white it must content itself with different shades of gray."

A further fatal defect of the M'Naghten Rules stems from the unrealistically tight shackles which they place upon expert psychiatric testimony. When the law limits a testifying psychiatrist to stating his opinion whether the accused is capable of knowing right from wrong, the expert is thereby compelled to test guilt or innocence by a concept which bears little relationship to reality. He is required thus to consider one aspect of the mind as a "logic-tight compartment in which the delusion holds sway leaving the balance of the mind intact. . . ."

Prominent psychiatrists have expressed their frustration when confronted with such requirements. Echoing such complaints, Edward de Grazia has asked,

> How [does one] translate "psychosis" or "psychopathy" or "dementia praecox" or even "sociopathy" or "mental disorder" or "neurotic character disorder" or "mental illness" into a psychiatric judgment of whether the accused knew "right" from "wrong."

In stronger and more vivid terms, Dr. Lawrence Kolb, Director of the New York Psychiatric Institute, Professor and Chairman of the Department of Psychiatry at Columbia University and Director of the Psychiatric Service at Presbyterian Hospital, expressed a similar viewpoint when he declared that "answers supplied by a psychiatrist in regard to questions of rightness or wrongness of an act or 'knowing' its nature constitute a professional perjury."

Psychiatrists are not alone in their recognition of the unreality of M'Naghten. As long ago as 1930, Mr. Justice Cardozo observed that "everyone contends that the present definition, of insanity has little relation to the truths of mental life." And Mr. Justice Frankfurter, as a witness before the Royal Commission on Capital Punishment, declared with his usual fervor:

> I do not see why the rules of law should be arrested at the state of psychological knowledge of the time when they were formulated. . . . I think the M'Naghten Rules are in large measure shams. That is a very strong word, but I think the M'Naghten Rules are very difficult for conscientious people and not difficult enough for people who say, "We'll just juggle them."

The tremendous growth of psychiatric knowledge since the Victorian origins of M'Naghten and even the near-universal disdain in which it is held by present-day psychiatrists are not by themselves sufficient reasons for abandoning the test. At bottom, the determination whether a man is or is not held responsible for his conduct is not a medical but a legal, social or moral judgment. . . .

The true vice of M'Naghten is not, therefore, that psychiatrists will feel constricted in artifically structuring their testimony but rather that the ultimate deciders — the Judge or the jury — will be deprived of information vital to their final judgment. For whatever the social climate of Victorian England, today's complex and sophisticated society will not be satisfied with simplistic decisions, based solely upon a man's ability to "know" right from wrong. . . .

Efforts to supplement or replace the M'Naghten Rules with a more meaningful and workable test have persisted for generations, with varying degrees of success. Perhaps the first to receive judicial approval, however, was more an added fillip to M'Naghten than a true substitute: the doctrine which permits acquittal on grounds of lack of responsibility when a defendant is found to have been driven by an "irresistible impulse" to commit his offense. In one form or another, the "irresistible impulse:" test has become encrusted on the law of several jurisdictions, including the District Courts of this Circuit, and is now a familiar part of the vocabulary of millions since it was successfully invoked by the defendant of Robert Travers' celebrated novel and motion picture, "Anatomy of a Murder."

As it has commonly been employed, however, we find the "irresistible impulse" test to be inherently inadequate and unsatisfactory. Psychiatrists have long questioned whether "irresistible impulses" actually exist; the more basic legal objection to the term "irresistible impulse" is that it is too narrow and carries the misleading implication that a crime impulsively committed must have been perpetrated in a sudden and explosive fit. Thus, the "irresistible impulse" test is unduly restrictive because it excludes the far more numerous instances of crimes committed after excessive brooding and melancholy by one who is unable to resist sustained psychic compulsion or to make any real attempt to control his conduct. In seeking one isolated and indefinite cause for every act, moreover, the test is unhappily evocative of the notions which underlay M'Naghten — unfortunate assumptions that the problem can be viewed in black and white absolutes and in crystal-clear causative terms.

In so many instances the criminal act may be the reverse of impulsive; it may be coolly and carefully prepared yet nevertheless the result of a diseased mind. The "irresistible impulse" test is therefore little more than a gloss on M'Naghten, rather than a fundamentally new approach to the problem of criminal responsibility. It is, as one professor explained, "a relatively unobnoxious attempt to improve upon M'Naghten."

With the exception of New Hampshire, American Courts waited until 1954 and Judge Bazelon's opinion for the District of Columbia Circuit in *Durham v. United States*, for legal recognition that disease or defect of the mind may impair the whole mind and not a subdivided portion of it. The *Durham* Court swept away the intellectual debris of a century and articulated a test which was as simple in its formulation as its sources were complex. A defendant is not criminally responsible, wrote Judge Bazelon, "if his unlawful act was the product of mental disease or mental defect."

The advantages of *Durham* were apparent and its arrival was widely hailed. The new test entirely eliminated the "right-wrong" dichotomy, and hence interred the overriding emphasis on the cognitive element of the personality which had for so long plagued M'Naghten. The fetters upon expert testimony were removed and psychiatrists were permitted and indeed encouraged to provide all relevant medical information for the common sense application of Judge or jury.

Finally, *Durham* ended to a large degree the "professional perjury" decried by psychiatrists — the "juggling" of legal standards made inevitable by M'Naghten and rightly deplored by Justice Frankfurter. Too often, the unrealistic dogma of M'Naghten had compelled expert witnesses to "stretch" its requirements to "hard cases"; sympathetic to the plight of a defendant who was not, in fairness, responsible for his conduct, psychiatrists had found it necessary to testify that the accused did not know his act was "wrong" even when the defendant's words belied this conclusion. In its frank and express recognition that criminality resulting from mental disease or defect should not bring forth penal sanctions, *Durham* brought an end to this all too-frequent practice of "winking" at legal requirements, a practice which had contributed little to the self-respect and integrity of either medicine or the law.

In the aftermath of *Durham*, however, many students of the law recognized that the new rule, despite its many advantages, also possessed serious deficiencies. It has been suggested, for example, that *Durham's* insistence that an offense be the "product" of a mental disease or defect raised near-impossible problems of causation, closely resembling those encountered by the M'Naghten and irresistible impulse tests.

The most significant criticism of *Durham*, however, is that it fails to give the fact-finder any standard by which to measure the competency of the accused. As a result, psychiatrists when testifying that a defendant suffered from a "mental disease or defect" in effect usurped the jury's function. This problem was strikingly illustrated in 1957, when a staff conference at Washington's St. Elizabeth's Hospital reversed its previous determination and reclassified "psychopathic personality" as a "mental disease." Because this single hospital provides most of the psychiatric witnesses in the District of Columbia Courts, juries were abruptly informed that certain defendants who had previously been considered responsible were now to be acquitted. *Blocker v. United States*, 110 U.S. App. D.C. 41, 288 F.2d 853, 860 (1961) (Burger J. concurring). It seems clear that a test which permits all to stand or fall upon the labels or classifications employed by testifying psychiatrists hardly affords the Court the opportunity to perform its function of rendering an independent legal and social judgment.

In 1953, a year before *Durham*, the American Law Institute commenced an exhaustive study of criminal conduct including the problem of criminal responsibility. In the ensuing months and years, under the scholarly direction of Professors Herbert Wechsler of Columbia University, its Chief Reporter, and

Louis B. Schwartz of the University of Pennsylvania, Co-Reporter, the leading legal and medical minds of the country applied themselves to the task. Gradually and painstakingly a new definition of criminal responsibility began taking shape as Section 4.01 of the "Model Penal Code was evolved. Before its penultimate articulation, drafts and redrafts of the section were submitted to and revised by an advisory committee comprised of distinguished judges, lawyers, psychiatrists, and penologists. After committee approval was obtained, successive drafts were debated and considered by the Council, and later by the full membership, of the Institute. Nine long years of research, exploration and consideration culminated in the definitive version of Section 4.01, which was finally adopted by the Institute in 1962.

Section 4.01 provides that "A person is not responsible for criminal conduct if at the time of such conduct as a result of mental disease or defect he lacks substantial capacity either to appreciate the wrongfulness of his conduct or to conform his conduct to the requirements of law." For reasons which will be more fully set forth, we believe this test to be the soundest yet formulated and we accordingly adopt it as the standard of criminal responsibility in the Courts of this Circuit.

The gravamen of the objections to the M'Naghten Rules is that they are not in harmony with modern medical science which, as we have said, is opposed to any concept which divides the mind into separate compartments — the intellect, the emotions and the will. The Model Penal Code formulation views the mind as a unified entity and recognizes that mental disease or defect may impair its functioning in numerous ways. The rule, moreover, reflects awareness that from the perspective of psychiatry absolutes are ephemeral and gradations are inevitable. By employing the telling word "substantial" to modify "incapacity," the rule emphasizes that "any" incapacity is not sufficient to justify avoidance of criminal responsibility but that "total" incapacity is also unnecessary. The choice of the word "appreciate," rather than "know" in the first branch of the test also is significant; mere intellectual awareness that conduct is wrongful, when divorced from appreciation or understanding of the moral or legal import of behavior, can have little significance.

While permitting the utilization of meaningful psychiatric testimony, the American Law Institute formulation, we believe, is free of many of the defects which accompanied *Durham*. Although it eschews rigid classification, the Section is couched in sufficiently precise terms to provide the jury with a workable standard when the Judge charges in terms comprehensible to laymen. Expert testimony, in short, will be admissible whenever relevant but always *as* expert testimony — and not as moral or legal pronouncement. Relieved of their burden of divining precise causal relationships, the Judge or jury can concentrate upon the ultimate decisions which are properly theirs, fully informed as to the facts.

Under the American Law Institute formulation, an inquiry based on meaningful psychological concepts can be pursued. The most modern psychiatric insights will be available, but, even more importantly, the legal focus will be sharper and clearer. The twin branches of the test, significantly phrased in the alternative, will remove from the pale of criminal sanctions precisely those who are in no meaningful sense responsible for their actions.

We do not delude ourselves in the belief that the American Law Institute test is perfect. Perfection is unattainable when we are dealing with a fluid and evolving science. Furthermore, we are aware that the Courts of Appeal for the District of Columbia, Third and Tenth Circuits have not adopted the American Law Institute test *haec verba*, but have employed their own language approaching the objectives of the Model Penal Code formulation. . . .

We believe, in sum, that the American Law Institute test — which makes no pretension at being the ultimate in faultless definition — is an infinite improvement over the M'Naghten Rules, even when, as had been the practice in the Courts of this Circuit, those Rules are supplemented by the "irresistible impulse" doctrine. All legal definitions involve elements of abstraction and approximation which are difficult to apply in marginal cases. The impossibility of guaranteeing that a new rule will always be infallible cannot justify continued adherence to an outmoded standard, sorely at variance with enlightened medical and legal scholarship.

The concurring judgment of Waterman J. is omitted.

T.S. SZASZ, PSYCHIATRY, ETHICS AND THE CRIMINAL LAW

(1958), 58 Col. L. Rev. 183 at 190

The controversial sceptic of psychology and author of *The Manufacture of Madness* and *The Myth of Mental Illness*, displays his usual boisterous style in condemning the *Durham* rule:

According to the *Durham* decision, if the defence of insanity has been raised in a criminal trial, it is considered to be a "matter of fact" for the jury to decide whether the offender suffered from a "mental illness" at the time of the commission of the act with which he is charged.

This is unadulterated nonsense. It could come about only as a result of the great prestige which the medical profession commands in our present-day society, and is, in fact, an expression of that prestige. Disregarding even the most obvious doubt concerning exactly what the expression "mental illness" is supposed to denote, it denotes a *theory* (if it denotes anything) and not a fact. This would be true, of course, for any disease, and especially for a bodily disease, after which the notion of "mental disease" is fashioned. Thus, it may be a fact that a patient is jaundiced, that is, that his skin appears to be yellow to the average observer. But being jaundiced is not the same as having a "disease". And whether this hypothetical patient with yellow skin has a gall stone, infectious hepatitis, or whatever, his "disease" is a *theory* which physicians (or others) form in order to explain his yellow skin. Accordingly, it would be a perversion of our language and thought to refer to a "disease" (or "illness", which I use as a synonym) as if it were a "fact".

To speak of "mental illness" is, epistemologically, very much worse than it is to speak of diseases of the body. Yet the jury is supposed to determine, as a matter of *fact*, whether the accused has or has not a "mental illness". Of course, it is quite possible for a group of people (a jury) to decide that someone is "crazy" or "mentally ill". But this is then *their theory* of why he has acted the way he did. It is no more — or less — a fact than it would be to assert that the accused is possessed by the devil; that is another "theory", now discarded. To believe that one's own theories are facts is considered by many contemporary psychiatrists as a "symptom" of schizophrenia. Yet this is what the language of the *Durham* decision does. It rectifies some of the shakiest and most controversial aspects of contemporary psychiatry (*i.e.*, those pertaining to what is "mental disease" and the classification of such alleged diseases) and by legal fiat seeks to transform inadequate theory into "judicial fact".

Further, *Durham* takes the notion of "mental illness" and requires the psychiatrist and the jury to determine whether the criminal act in question was committed as a result of such "illness". This, too, is supposed to be a "fact". Unfortunately, this not only cannot be a fact, but it cannot even be a theory. For, if the notion of "mental illness" means anything, it means that it is the theory by means of which we "explain" how the events in question might have occurred.

S.N. VERDUN-JONES, THE INSANITY DEFENCE SINCE SCHWARTZ V. R.

(1979), 6 C.R. (3d) 300 at 319-325

POSTSCRIPT: THE FUTURE OF THE INSANITY DEFENCE

Although the conspicuous flurry of reported decisions relating to insanity in recent years may be a function of the interests of the editors of the various law report series, it does appear that the *Schwartz* case has at least forced Canadian Courts to consider some of the issues left unanswered for so many years. However, while those who were "acquitted" on the ground of insanity continue to be incarcerated at the Lieutenant-Governor's pleasure, it is unlikely that a great number of defendants will choose to pursue the insanity route. The only accused persons who might be tempted to take greater advantage of the defence are those charged with first or second degree murder who, upon conviction, will inevitably face seemingly interminable minimum periods of imprisonment under recent *Criminal Code* amendments: see s. 669.

In *R. v. Barnier*, [1978] 1 W.W.R. 137, 37 C.C.C. (2d) 508 (B.C. C.A.), Farris C.J.B.C. strenuously contended that major reform is vital if the insanity provisions of the *Criminal Code* are to maintain any relevance to modern Canadian society (p. 139):

> It seems to me the tests laid down in the *Criminal Code* as to whether a person is insane are unrealistic in today's context. These tests are essentially based on the accused's capacity to distinguish between right and wrong. In my view, the real question is, should the accused be confined in a mental institution, and this will depend on how dangerous he is, irrespective of legal guilt. The test should be whether the accused is suffering from a disease or disorder of the mind to such an extent that he is a menace to society. In the first instance there is a medical problem. It should be resolved under judicial supervision but on the basis of modern medical knowledge and not on the basis of antiquated legal definitions.

It is not clear precisely which type of procedure the learned chief justice would recommend as an alternative to the present system. However, it is clear that he would endorse radical — rather than minor — reform in this area.

Some analysts have urged that the insanity defence should be totally abolished. As J. Goldstein and J. Katz in "Abolish the 'Insanity Defense' — Why Not?" (1963), 72 Yale L.J. 853 at 864, have pointed out, the insanity defence is a misnomer in that:

> its real function is to authorize the state to hold those "who must be found not to possess the guilty mind *mens rea*," even though the criminal law demands that no person be held criminally responsible if doubt is cast on any material element of the offense charged.

These authors advocate that where insanity negatives the *mens rea* required for any specific criminal offence the defendant should be absolutely acquitted. If there is a question of danger to the public then the defendant may be committed to hospital as the result of a post-trial hearing; however, he would be treated in exactly the same manner as any other patient committed through civil (rather than criminal justice) processes. This proposal has been strongly criticized by some commentators, who suggest that many defendants may suffer from serious mental disorders which nevertheless do not negative the legalistic concept of "intention". A further practical problem associated with the Goldstein and Katz position is the refusal of many hospitals to admit persons who have engaged in certain types of dangerous behaviour. Ironically, the insanity defence may be the only method by means of which such persons may be detained within the confines of present medical practice.

In recent years, the abolitionist position has taken a decidedly different twist. For example, a report submitted to the governor of New York State in February 1978 has advocated that insanity should no longer serve as an *absolute* defence to a criminal charge. In place of the present insanity defence, the report advocates the adoption of a rule of "diminished capacity":

> Under a rule of diminished capacity, evidence of abnormal mental condition would be admissible to affect the degree of crime for which an accused could be convicted. Specifically, those offenses requiring intent or knowledge could be reduced to lesser included offenses requiring only reckless or criminal negligence.
>
> While abolishing mental disease or defect as a complete defence, recognition would still be given to higher degrees of culpability affected by the presence of abnormal mental condition. The result would entail conviction and processing in the correctional system for serious offenders; and, acquittal — perhaps civil commitment — for minor offenders. Convictions would be for lesser included criminal offenses not requiring an accused to have

acted either intentionally or knowingly. The Sentencing court would then take the present mental condition of the offender into account in determining an appropriate disposition.

The most striking aspect of the New York proposal is the explicit assumption that the correctional system is the appropriate place in which to treat the mentally ill person who commits a serious offence. Such an assumption may not be warranted in Canada. On the other hand, it is significant to note that Canadian Courts already recognize a limited doctrine of diminished capacity, but such a doctrine exists *alongside* (rather than in place of) the traditional insanity defence. The Canadian approach recognizes that there may be a number of mental disorders which fall short of meeting the requirements of s. 16(2) but which nevertheless may operate to negative the defendant's capacity to form the "specific intent" required for such offences as murder, robbery or theft.

A less drastic alternative to the Goldstein and Katz and New York proposals is the retention of the insanity defence while still providing for total acquittal of the defendant who asserts it successfully. As with the Goldstein-Katz option, there would be a post-acquittal hearing but, under this proposal, there would be a distinctive test of insanity rather than an application of the general principles of *mens rea*. In what Must surely rank as one of the briefest justifications for major legal reform in recent years, the Law Reform Commission of Canada recommends such a proposal in a two-page consideration of the insanity defence in its report entitled Mental Disorder in the Criminal Process (1976). It is significant that this proposal has already been adopted by a number of American states.

If the insanity defence is to be retained, the critical issue to be considered is whether the test of insanity specified by s. 16(2) should be modified. In recent years, a number of American jurisdictions have abandoned the time-honoured formulation in the M'Naghten Rules and have adopted the test of insanity contained in the American Law Institute's Model Penal Code:

> (1) A person is not responsible for criminal conduct if at the time of such conduct as a result of mental disease or defect he lacks substantial capacity either to appreciate the criminality [wrongfulness] of his conduct or to conform his conduct to the requirements of law.
> (2) As used in this Article, the terms "mental disease or defect" do not include an abnormality manifested only by repeated criminal or otherwise anti-social conduct.

The American Law Institute test diverges from the Canadian approach primarily in its extension of the insanity defence to those mental conditions which, while they clearly impair the defendant's ability to control his conduct, nevertheless do not prevent him from appreciating the physical nature of his act or from knowing that it is contrary to law. The particular virtues of the test were forcefully presented by the judgment of the United States Court of Appeals, Second Circuit, in *U.S. v. Freeman* (1966), 357 F. 2d 606.

. . . .

Detractors of the American Law Institute test, on the other hand, contend that critical terms such as "substantial" and "appreciate" are inherently vague or confusing and particular attention has been paid to the alleged impracticality of para. (2) which purports to exclude psychopathic personality disorders from the operation of the insanity defence. Furthermore, some commentators have expressed the view that the quest for a specific test of insanity will — at least for the foreseeable future — inevitably amount to little more than a futile attempt to realize what is, in the view of many, a costly chimera. The New York Report, for example, strenuously contends that the very belief that psychiatry can answer the type of question posed by a legal test of criminal responsibility is fundamentally misguided:

> Psychiatric participation in the determination of legal guilt or innocence is premised upon false assumptions of psychiatric expertise in what are essentially legal, moral and social judgements.

Similarly, in the dissenting judgment in *U.S. v. Brawner* (1972), 471 F. 2d 969, Bazelon C.J. of the United States Court of Appeals, District Court Circuit, has argued that it is time to demystify the insanity defence and to frankly recognize that the determination of this issue is anything but scientific [pp. 1012 and 1032]:

> Since we have no simple, scientific formula that will provide a clear-cut answer to every case, we have no choice, in my opinion, but to tell the truth: that the jury, not the experts, must judge the defendant's blameworthines; that a calibrated, easily-applied standard is not yet available to guide that decision; and that the jury must resolve the question with reference to its own understanding of community concepts of blameworthiness. . . .
>
> Our instruction to the jury should provide that a defendant is not responsible *if at the time of his unlawful conduct his mental or emotional processes or behaviour controls were impaired to such an extent that he cannot justly be held responsible for his act.*

In any event, it remains to be seen whether legislative change will take place in Canada and, if so, whether an attempt will be made only to alter the *consequences* of an insanity verdict, whether changes will be effected in the nature of the defence itself or whether the defence will be totally abolished.

Perhaps the reason for the failure of Parliament to address itself to the insanity defence up to this point in time may well be that we have harboured deep-seated doubts as to what the basic philosophy underlying our criminal law *should* be. As Abraham S. Goldstein has stated most eloquently:

> The insanity defence is caught in a cross-current of conflicting philosophies. Its roots are deep in a time when people spoke confidently of individual responsibility and of "blame", of the choice to do wrong. The emphasis was on the individual offender and the defence was seen as an instrument for separating the sick from the bad. It was not long, however, before ideas drawn from social utilitarianism took over the insanity defence. It was now feared that treating an offender as " sick" might weaken the deterrent effect of the criminal law.

Automatism

R. v. RABEY

[1980] 2 S.C.R. 513, 15 C.R. (3d) 225, 54 C.C.C. (2d) 1

The accused was charged with causing bodily harm with intent to wound and possessing a weapon for the purpose of committing an offence. The trial Judge acquitted. On appeal the Ontario Court of Appeal ordered a new trial on the charge of wounding on the basis that the defence of sane automatism was not available. Any defence would be that of insanity or lack of *mens rea*. The acquittal on the weapons charge was confirmed on the basis of lack of proof of *mens rea*. On further appeal the majority of the Supreme Court adopted the approach of Martin J.A. in the Court of Appeal. Reproduced first is the review of the evidence in the Court of Appeal:

MARTIN J.A.: —

Factual background

On 1st March 1974 the respondent, Wayne Kenneth Rabey, then aged 20, was a third-year student at the University of Toronto at Erindale College where he was enrolled in the honours science course, majoring in geology. Miss X was also a third-year student at Erindale College.

An association between Miss X and the respondent began in September 1973 when, in their third year, they commenced to have most of their classes together. Along with two classmates, John Lund and Rick Hampel, they studied together in their spare periods, lunched together and went to the "pub" together.

Miss X and the respondent had also gone for walks together and visited each other's homes. During the Christmas holidays in 1973, along with John Lund they had gone with a group of students to Quebec to ski.

It is clear that respondent was emotionally attached to Miss X, but his feelings were not reciprocated, and she described her relationship with the respondent as "just a friend". On Miss X's initiative, her association with the respondent lessened after their return from the trip to Quebec.

Miss X on 28th February 1974, during a lecture, wrote a letter to a girlfriend. She put the letter in her notebook which she placed in her locker. The letter referred to another student, a young man by whose sexual experience Miss X was impressed and in whom she expressed a sexual interest. The letter also stated that even though she insulted Wayne and Rick they still "bugged" her in class, and she implied that they were "nothings".

The respondent, whose evidence was accepted by the trial Judge, testified that he was sitting outside the library on the afternoon of 28th February when Miss X came out of the library and asked him to help her with some problems. He said that they went inside the library to work on the problems, and when flipping through Miss X's notebook to find some equations, during her absence for a few minutes, he came across the letter mentioned above. He read part of the letter, was interested in its contents, and put it in his pocket. The respondent read the letter that evening at home and underlined certain passages. He said that he was upset, confused and angry at the time.

The following day, 1st March 1974, the respondent went to the geology lab to review some problems posted on the board, and while there he took a piece of Galena rock, wrapped it in paper towelling and put it in his pocket. He testified that he intended to take the rock home to study it, as he had previously done with other samples of rock with the consent of his professor.

There was a class starting at 11:00 a.m. but the respondent decided not to take it as he wanted to study for an examination that he had in the afternoon. He testified that later that morning he met another student who said that he was going to be playing squash at 12:00 o'clock, and the respondent said he would go and watch him play. The respondent said that, quite by chance, while on the way to the squash courts, he met Miss X in the locker area. He said that when he first saw her he felt strange for a second but that this feeling passed. He invited Miss X to go with him to watch the game, and she accepted the invitation.

When they reached the observation gallery no one was playing in any of the squash courts. Miss X said the respondent seemed surprised to find the courts empty. They then returned downstairs; the respondent seemed his normal self, When they had reached the foot of the stairs he asked Miss X what she thought of "Gord", a mutual friend, and she replied that he was "just a friend". The respondent then asked her what she thought of him, referring to himself. She said he was a friend too. They then started to go through a set of fire doors located near the bottom of the stairs, which, being heavy, were hard to push open. Before Miss X could get the door on her side open she heard a crash and a "crumbling sound", and she thought something was falling down from the roof. She turned around to see what was happening, and the respondent grabbed her around the arms and struck her on the head twice. She then became unconscious, and when she recovered consciousness the respondent was on his knees, leaning forward and choking her. She asked him why he was doing this, and he yelled, "You bitch, you bitch", after which she again lost consciousness.

Kenneth Turner, a student at Erindale College, was walking down the stairs on his way to the gymnasium when he noticed the respondent crouched at the bottom of the stairs near some books and a red puddle. As Turner continued down the stairs, the respondent apparently noticed him and came up the stairs towards him. The respondent said there had been a terrible accident. Turner noticed the respondent was very pale, sweating, glassy-eyed and had a frightened expression, and Turner endeavoured to reassure him. Turner also noticed that there was a trail which led under the stairwell from the pool of blood which he had first noticed. He looked over the railing and saw Miss X's head, her body being under the stairs.

At this time the respondent said, "I've killed her and I am going to kill you too." The respondent then seized Turner, who freed himself and then went for assistance. Turner met Professor Houston in the hall and requested Professor Houston to accompany him. On the way to the area where Turner had seen Miss

X they encountered the respondent, whom Professor Houston sought to restrain momentarily by placing his hand on the respondent's wrist. The respondent said he had to get a nurse, and continued on his way. Professor Houston noticed that the respondent was very pale and seemed bewildered.

The respondent appeared in the office of Mrs. Degutis, a nurse employed at the college health centre, and asked her to come quickly to help him; that he thought he had killed someone. Mrs. Degutis said he looked very upset and seemed filled with fear and anxiety. His pulse was very fast and was not strong; he had a limp, "clammy" appearance. As a result of her observation of the respondent she placed him in a room by himself. In subsequent contacts with the respondent after Miss X had been found, Mrs. Degutis was unable to convince him that Miss X was not dead.

In the meantime, Professor Houston had found Miss X in an unconscious condition "under" the stairwell. She soon recovered consciousness and was taken to the college health centre and then to a hospital. She was found to have three puncture wounds in her head in which fragments of rock were embedded and which required 20 stitches to close. She also had a reddish mark on her throat. She, however, made a complete recovery within a short time.

Two quantities of black rock, which fragmented easily, were found at two different sites in the area of the bottom of the stairwell. The largest piece of rock, some school books and a purse were found in the vicinity of a pool of blood near the foot of the stairwell. There was a smear of blood, some 14 feet long, leading from the pool of blood at the bottom of the stairwell to another pool of blood beside the stairwell. The physical findings support the inference that Miss X was struck near the foot of the stairs and then dragged to the position, partly underneath the stairs, where she was found.

William Huggett, Associate Dean of Erindale College, shortly after 12:00 o'clock on 1st March 1974, was requested to go to the nursing station, and on arriving there he found the respondent in an inner room. The respondent appeared depressed or dazed; he recognized Dean Huggett and said, "I don't know why I started or why I stopped", and also said that he "liked her better than anyone he had ever known".

Constable Pollitt arrived at the college shortly after 1:00 o'clock and went to the nursing station where he arrested the respondent at about 1:25 p.m. After being cautioned by Constable Pollitt the respondent said: "I did it, I know I did it, I just couldn't stop hitting her."

The letter written by Miss X the day before was found in the pocket of the respondent's jacket. Detective Price took a statement from the respondent between 4:30 and 4:45 p.m. The statement reads, in part, as follows:

> I was asking her about the ballet, then I asked her if she liked this guy Gord. She said something about just as a friend. Then I guess I hit her right then on the head. She was bleeding from the head and the next thing I remember it all happened so fast she was on the floor and I was sitting on top of her and choking her. I thought she was dead, there was blood everywhere. I just don't know what happened.

The respondent, of whom a number of character witnesses spoke highly, recounted how he obtained Miss X's letter, his chance meeting with her in the locker area and their fruitless visit to the squash courts, as previously outlined. He testified that he remembered asking Miss X what she thought of a mutual friend, and her replying that he was just a friend. The next thing he remembered was choking her; that her face was a "funny" colour. He remembered seeing a lot of blood and stopped choking her. The next thing he remembered was being on the bottom of the steps and seeing Turner coming down. He thought he remembered asking Turner to go for help, but he did not remember Turner answering. He remembered grabbing Turner but did not remember Turner running away; he was "just gone". He remembered seeing Turner's face and a lady's face; the next thing he remembered was being at the nurse's office and telling her that he had killed someone, or he thought that he had killed someone. He recalled talking to Dean Huggett and the nurse, calling his mother on the telephone and being arrested.

The psychiatric evidence

The respondent was admitted, on 5th March 1974, to the Lakeshore Psychiatric Hospital for psychiatric assessment on a warrant of remand by the Provincial Court, and was discharged on 1st April 1974. A detailed neurological examination of the respondent disclosed no neurological disease. Dr. Slyfield's report to the Provincial Court stated that if the respondent was telling the truth about his amnesia for most of the incident, then it was probable that his consciousness was dissociated at the time but that such a psychological mechanism need not indicate mental illness.

The medical reports of the Lakeshore Psychiatric Hospital with respect to the psychiatric assessment of the respondent were admitted in evidence by the consent of both counsel.

Dr. Orchard, assistant professor of psychiatry at the University of Toronto, examined the respondent on 18th May 1974.

Dr. Orchard testified that, in his opinion, the respondent entered into a complete dissociative state at the foot of the stairs. The dissociative state is a recognized diagnosis and is a disorder of consciousness which occurs as a result of part of the nervous system shutting off. Dr. Orchard said that a person in a severe dissociative state may be capable of performing physical actions without consciousness of such actions. In Dr. Orchard's opinion, when the respondent entered the dissociative state near the foot of the stairs his mind "shut off", and the return of consciousness was gradual; he returned to some awareness when he found his hands around Miss X's neck. The clouding of consciousness did not completely lift, however, until later when he spoke to his mother and the police.

Dr. Orchard said that the dissociative state which occurred was caused by a powerful emotional shock which resulted from the shattering of the respondent's image of Miss X; he was unable to tolerate seeing her as she revealed herself in the letter, and because the reality was not tolerable for him the dissociative state occurred as a psychological defence mechanism. The conversation at the foot of the stairs as to how she regarded "Gord" and himself, against the background of the letter, "triggered" the dissociative state. In Dr. Orchard's opinion the dissociative state which occurred was comparable to that produced by a physical blow; it was caused by a "psychological blow" which produced certain physical effects as observed by Turner, Professor Houston, Mrs. Degutis and Dean Huggett. Dr. Orchard did not consider that the subsequent statements made by the respondent, indicating that he was aware that he had struck Miss X, were inconsistent with the respondent being in a dissociative state that was total at the time he struck Miss X with the rock and, by a process of reconstruction, realizing what he had done when some awareness returned to him and he found himself choking Miss X while she was lying on the floor with blood around her.

Dr. Orchard said that the respondent was a young man of average health, or better than average health, with no pre-disposition to dissociate. Dr. Orchard distinguished between the dissociative state and dissociation which may occur as a result of a major pathological condition, such as schizophrenia, manic-depressive psychosis or injury to the brain. The severe dissociative state, such as the respondent suffered, usually occurs in persons within the category of normal people where the mind is unable to cope with stress in an area that is important to that individual, and it is more severe than the dissociation which occurs as a symptom of other conditions. He said that it is rare for the severe dissociative state not caused by some underlying pathology to recur, and that there was only a very slight possibility that the respondent would suffer from a recurrence of this disorder of consciousness.

Dr. Orchard said that he could find no evidence that the respondent suffered from any pathological condition which he defined as a "diseased condition or abnormally sick condition". He testified that the dissociative state itself is an occurrence, is not a mental illness and is not a "disease of the mind". There are three main groups of mental disorders, which he categorized as follows:

(1) The psychoses which are the major mental illnesses involving a loss of contact with reality.

(2) The neuroses which are the minor mental illnesses which do not involve loss of contact with reality.

(3) The personality or character disorders which are neither psychoses nor neuroses but are a "maladaptive pattern or life-style".

Dr. Orchard agreed that in the medical literature the dissociative state is included as one of the neuroses in the subdivision of hysteria. Although, in cross-examination, Dr. Orchard rejected as authoritative a number of textbooks on psychiatry to which he was referred, he acknowledged that in a textbook, which he accepted as generally authoritative, the dissociative state is classified as a neurosis. It was Dr. Orchard's view that the dissociative state is not "fully categorizable"; it is not a psychosis because there is no ongoing pathological condition, and it occurs without a pre-disposing personality; it is not a neurosis, which by definition is a minor mental illness without loss of contact with reality, since in the dissociative state there is a loss of contact with reality.

Dr. Rowsell, who, like Dr. Orchard, is a psychiatrist of eminence, examined the respondent on 16th May 1975. He had available to him, as Dr. Orchard had, the reports of the Lakeshore Psychiatric Hospital.

It was the opinion of Dr. Rowsell that the respondent did not go into a dissociative state; that he is a controlled young man who went into an extreme state of rage at that moment and while in that state, struck Miss X on the head and choked her; he had good reason to think from the amount of blood that he had killed her. Dr. Rowsell testified that, in his opinion, the respondent was aware that he was hitting Miss X, being then in a state of rage. Dr. Rowsell testified that if, contrary to his opinion, the respondent was in a dissociative state, he suffered from "disease of the mind". Dr. Rowsell said that consciousness is the distinguishing feature of mental life; the dissociative state is, by definition, a subdivision of hysterical neurosis, which is a definite mental illness. It is, by definition, a disorder of the mind.

Dr. Rowsell was of the opinion that the "blotting out" of parts of the incident by the respondent occurred after the event. Dr. Rowsell, unlike Dr. Orchard, was of the opinion that the respondent still had a psychiatric problem for which he required treatment to help him face up to what had occurred. He considered that the treatment would take six months to a year and could be undertaken on an out-patient basis. The prognosis was excellent.

RABEY v. R.

[1980] 2 S.C.R. 513, 15 C.R. (3d) 225, 54 C.C.C. (2d) 1

RITCHIE J. (MARTLAND, PIGEON and BEETZ JJ. concurring): —

. . . .

It should be observed also that the appellant was subjected to a number of interviews with psychiatrists, with the result that the courts have found themselves involved in the shadowy area of mental disorders, concerning which it is not surprising to find that there are wide differences in opinion amongst the "experts". The meaning of the word "automatism" — in any event so far as it is employed in the defence of non-insane automatism — has in my opinion been satisfactorily defined by Lacourcière J. (as he then was) of the Ontario High Court of Justice in the case of *R. v. K.* (1971), 3 C.C.C. (3d) 84 at 84:

> Automatism is a term used to describe unconscious, involuntary behaviour, the state of a person who, though capable of action, is not conscious of what he is doing. It means an unconscious, involuntary act, where the mind does not go with what is being done.

The defence of automatism, as used in the present case, of course involves a consideration of the provisions of s. 16.

. . . .

What is said here is that at the relevant time the appellant was in a state where, though capable of action, he was not conscious of what he was doing, and more particularly that he was not suffering from a disease of the mind and was therefore not insane. The central question in deciding any case involving the defence of automatism is whether or not the accused was suffering from a disease of the mind. The opinions of psychiatrists go no further than characterizing the condition in which the appellant was found as being "a dissociative state", but it is clear, at least since the case of *Bratty v. A.G. Northern Ireland*, [1963] A.C. 386, 46 Cr. App. R. 1, [1961] 3 All E.R. 523 (H.L.), that the question of whether or not such a state amounts to "a disease of the mind" is a question of law for the Judge to determine. The general rule is that it is for the Judge as a question of law to decide what constitutes a "disease of the mind", but that the question of whether or not the facts in a given case disclose the existence of such a disease is a question to be determined by the trier of fact. I think it would be superfluous for me to retrace the line of authorities in this area, as they have been so exhaustively discussed by my brother Dickson and also by Martin J.A. of the Court of Appeal and by the learned trial Judge. I am satisfied in this regard to adopt the following passages from the reasons for judgment of Martin J.A. at pp. 62-63:

> In general, the distinction to be drawn is between a malfunctioning of the mind arising front some cause that is primarily internal to the accused, having its source in his psychological or emotional makeup, or in some organic pathology, as opposed to a malfunctioning of the mind, which is the transient effect produced by some specific external factor such as, for example, concussion. Any malfunctioning of the mind or mental disorder having its source primarily in some subjective condition or weakness internal to the accused (whether fully understood or not) may be a "disease of the mind" if it prevents the accused from knowing what he is doing, but transient disturbances of consciousness due to certain specific external factors do not fall within the concept of disease of the mind. (For an interesting and helpful discussion see "The Concept of Mental Disease In Criminal Law Insanity Tests" 33 University of Chicago L. Rev. 229, by Herbert Fingarette.) Particular transient mental disturbances may not, however, be capable of being properly categorized in relation to whether they constitute "disease of the mind" on the basis of a generalized statement and must be decided on a case-by-case basis.

The same learned Judge later stated in the same judgment at p. 68:

> In my view, the ordinary stresses and disappointments of life which are the common lot of mankind do not constitute an external cause constituting an explanation for a malfunctioning of the mind which takes it out of the category of a "disease of the mind". To hold otherwise would deprive the concept of an external factor of any real meaning. In my view, the emotional stress suffered by the respondent as a result of his disappointment with respect to Miss X cannot be said to be an external factor producing the automatism within the authorities, and the dissociative state must be considered as having its source primarily in the respondent's psychological or emotional makeup. I conclude, therefore, that, in the circumstances of this case, the dissociative state in which the respondent was said to be constituted a "disease of the mind". I leave aside, until it becomes necessary to decide them, cases where a dissociative state has resulted from emotional shock without physical injury, resulting from such causes, for example, as being involved in a serious accident although no physical injury has resulted; being the victim of a murderous attack with an uplifted knife, notwithstanding that the victim has managed to escape physical injury; seeing a loved one

murdered or seriously assaulted, and like situations. Such extraordinary external events might reasonably be presumed to affect the average normal person without reference to the makeup of the person exposed to such experience.

For the above reasons I am of the opinion, with deference, that the learned trial Judge erred in holding that the so-called "psychological blow", which was said to have caused the dissociative state, was, in the circumstances of this case, an externally originating cause, and she should have held that if the respondent was in a dissociative state at the time he struck Miss X he suffered from "disease of the mind". A new trial must, accordingly, be had on count 2.

In my view a possible key to the cause of the malfunctioning of the appellant's mind at the time of the alleged assault is to be found in para. 5 of the agreed statement of facts, to which I have already referred, and where it is said of him:

> 5. The Appellant had never dated any other girl for any length of time, and had only a minimal amount of sexual experience. An introvert, he was infatuated with the attractive, outgoing. . . .

It seems to me that his infatuation with this young woman had created an abnormal condition in his mind, under the influence of which he acted unnaturally and violently to an imagined slight to which a normal person would not have reacted in the same manner.

It was contended on behalf of the appellant that a finding of disease of the mind and consequently of insanity in the present case would involve gross unfairess to the appellant, who could be subject to the provisions of s. 545 [re-en. 1972, c. 13, s. 45; am. 1974-75-76, c. 93, s. 69] of the *Criminal Code* and thus detained at the pleasure of the Lieutenant-Governor of the province. That such a result does not carry with it the hardship contended for is illustrated by the following passage from the reasons for judgment of Martin J.A. at p. 69:

> It would, of course, be unthinkable that a person found not guilty on account of insanity because of a transient mental disorder constituting a disease of the mind, who was not dangerous and who required no further treatment, should continue to be confined. The present provisions of s. 545(l)(b) [re-en. 1972, c. 13, s. 45], however, authorize the Lieutenant-Governor to make an order if, in his opinion, it would be in the best interest of the accused and not contrary to the interest of the public for the discharge of a person found not guilty on account of insanity, either absolutely or subject to such conditions as he prescribes. In addition to the periodic reviews required to be made by a board of review appointed pursuant to s. 547(1) of the *Code*, the Lieutenant-Governor under s. 547(6) of the *Code* may request the board of review to review the case of any person found not guilty on account of insanity, in which case the board of review is required to report forthwith whether such person has recovered and, if so, whether in its opinion it is in the interest of the public and of that person for the Lieutenant-Governor to order that he be discharged absolutely or subject to such conditions as the Lieutenant-Governor may prescribe.

For all these reasons, as well as for those expressed by Martin J.A. in the Court of Appeal for Ontario, I would dismiss the appeal and dispose of the matter in the manner proposed by him.

DICKSON J. (dissenting, ESTEY and MCINTYRE JJ. concurring): — The automatism "defence" has come into considerable prominence in recent years.

Although the word "automatism" made its way but lately to the legal state, it is basic principle that absence of volition in respect of the act involved is always a defence to a crime. A defence that the act is involuntary entitles the accused to a complete and unqualified acquittal. That the defence of automatism exists as a middle ground between criminal responsibility and legal insanity is beyond question. Although spoken of as a defence, in the sense that it is raised by the accused, the Crown always bears the burden of proving a voluntary act.

The issue in this appeal is whether automatism resulting from a "psychological blow" is available to an accused in answer to a charge of causing bodily harm with intent to wound. The appellant, Wayne Kenneth Rabey, suddenly and without warning assaulted a fellow student and friend, causing her injury. The theory of the defence was that his behaviour was caused by a psychological blow, an intense emotional shock which induced a "dissociative state", during which, for a time, the appellant was neither conscious of nor able to control his conduct, so that it was involuntary. This is sometimes spoken of as non-insane automatism, to distinguish it from cases in which the state of automatism is attributable to disease of the mind.

At common law a person who engaged in what would otherwise have been criminal conduct was not guilty of a crime if he did so in a state of unconsciousness or semi-consciousness. Nor was he responsible if he was, by reason of disease of the mind or defect of reason, unable to appreciate the nature and quality of an act or that its commission was wrong. The fundamental precept of our criminal law is that a man is responsible only for his conscious, intentional acts. Devlin J. summed up the position in *R. v. Kemp*, [1956] 3 All E.R. 249 at 251:

> In the eyes of the common law if a man is not responsible for his actions he is entitled to be acquitted by the ordinary form of acquittal, and it matters not whether his lack of responsibility was due to insanity or to any other cause.

In order to protect the public from the dangerous criminally insane the common law was changed by statute, long ago. By the *Criminal Lunatics Act*, 1800 (39 & 40 Geo. 3), c. 94, and the *Trial of Lunatics Act*, 1883 (46 & 47 Vict.), c. 38, and in Canada by the *Criminal Code*, [now] R.S.C. 1970, c. C-34, a verdict of not guilty by reason of insanity results in committal to an institution. The purpose of the qualified verdict of acquittal is, of course, to ensure custody and treatment for those who might pose a continuing threat to society by reason of mental illness. In Canada, an accused who is acquitted on the ground of insanity is kept in strict custody in the place and in the manner that the Court directs, until the pleasure of the Lieutenant-Governor of the province is known [s. 542(2) of the *Code*].

The term "automatism" first appeared in the cases and in the periodical literature about 30 years ago. It is seen with increasing frequency. The defence of automatism is successfully invoked in circumstances of a criminal act committed unconsciously, and, in the past, has generally covered acts done while sleepwalking or under concussional states following head injuries.

The defence of automatism is, in some respects, akin to that of insanity. In both instances, the issue is whether an accused had sufficient control over or knowledge of his criminal act to be held culpable. The two defences are, however, separate and distinct. As Professor J. Ll. J. Edwards observed in "Automatism and Criminal Responsibility" (1958), 21 Mod. L. Rev. 375 at 384:

> Both circumstances are concerned to prove mental irresponsibility, the essential difference . . . being that in the case of insanity the defect of the understanding must originate in a disease of the mind, whereas in the defence of automatism *simpliciter* the criminal law is not concerned with any question of the disease of the mind.

Although separate, the relationship between the two defences cannot be discounted. Automatism may be subsumed in the defence of insanity in cases in which the unconscious action of an accused can be traced to, or rooted in, a disease of the mind. Where that is so, the defence of insanity prevails. This is all felicitously expressed by Gresson P. in *R. v. Cottle*, [1958] N.Z.L.R. 999 at 1007 (C.A.):

> It would appear that automatism raised as a defence to a criminal charge may be something quite different and distinct from insanity. In a partcular case, it may be that the automatism relied on is due to some "disease of the mind" but is not necessarily so. Automatism, which strictly means action without conscious volition, has been adopted in criminal law as a term to denote conduct of which the doer is not conscious — in short doing something without knowledge of it, and without memory afterwards of having done it — a temporary eclipse of consciousness that nevertheless leaves the person so affected able to exercise bodily movements. In such a case, the action is one which the mind in its normal functioning does not control. This may be due to some "disease of the mind" or it may not; it may happen with a perfectly healthy mind (*e.g.* in somnambulism which may be unaccompanied by an abnormality of mind), or it may occur where the mind is temporarily affected as the result of a blow, or by the influence of a drug or other intoxication. It may on the other hand be caused by an abnormal condition of the mind capable of being designated a mental disease. What are known as the M'Naghten Rules can have no application unless there is some form of "disease of the mind", which is not necessarily present in all cases of automatism.

. . . .

This case raises interesting issues, and the judicial conclusion, in my view, should be guided by general principles of criminal responsibility. Before alluding to those principles, it is useful to recall s. 16(4) of the *Criminal Code*, which reads:

> (4) Every one shall, until the contrary is proved, be presumed to be and to have been sane.

In the usual case in which an accused pleads insanity, he has the burden of overcoming the presumption of sanity. In the present case the appellant is not seeking to establish that he was insane on 1st March 1974. The Crown is asserting the insanity in answer to the defence of automatism raised by the appellant. The presumption of sanity runs in the appellant's favour.

We turn to s. 16(2): a person is insane when he is in a state of natural imbecility or has a disease of the mind to an extent that renders him incapable of appreciating the nature and quality of an act or omission or of knowing that an act or omission is wrong. The important words, for present purposes, are "disease of the mind".

The first principle, fundamental to our criminal law, which governs this appeal is that no act can be a criminal offence unless it is done voluntarily. Consciousness is a sine qua non to criminal liability.

The prosecution must prove every element of the crime charged. One such element is the state of mind of the accused, in the sense that the act was voluntary. The circumstances are normally such as to permit a presumption of volition and mental capacity. That is not so when the accused, as here, has placed before the Court, by cross-examination of Crown witnesses or by evidence called on his own behalf, or both, evidence sufficient to raise an issue that he was unconscious of his actions at the time of the alleged offence. No burden of proof is imposed upon an accused raising such defence beyond pointing to facts which indicate the existence of such a condition: *R. v. Berger* (1975), 27 C.C.C. (2d) 357 at 379, leave to appeal to the Supreme Court of Canada refused 27 C.C.C. (2d) 357n. Whether lack of consciousness relates to *mens rea* or to *actus reus* or both may be important in a case in which the offence charged is one of absolute liability, but the conceptual distinction does not concern us in the case at bar.

The second principle is that no person should be committed to a hospital for the criminally insane unless he suffers from disease of the mind in need of treatment or likely to recur.

The Ontario Court of Appeal held that the excusing factor was insanity. This finding was reached though the appellant exhibited no pathological symptoms indicative of a previously existing, or ongoing, psychiatric disorder. On medical evidence accepted by the trial Judge, the prospect of a recurrence of dissociation is extremely remote. There was no finding that the appellant suffered from psychosis, neurosis or personality disorder. He does not have an organic disease of the brain. This was an isolated event. The appellant has already spent several weeks in a mental institution undergoing psychiatric, neurological and psychological assessment, the result of which did not indicate need for treatment.

There are undoubtedly policy considerations to be considered. Automatism as a defence is easily feigned. It is said the credibility of our criminal justice system will be severely strained if a person who has committed a violent act is allowed an absolute acquittal on a plea of automatism arising from a psychological blow. The argument is made that the success of the defence depends upon the semantic ability of psychiatrists, tracing a narrow path between the twin shoals of criminal responsibility and an insanity verdict. Added to these concerns is the in terrorem argument that the floodgates will be raised if psychological blow automatism is recognized in law.

There are competing policy interests. Where the condition is transient rather than persistent, unlikely to recur, not in need of treatment and not the result of self-induced intoxication, the policy objectives in finding such a person insane are not served. Such a person is not a danger to himself or to society generally.

The Ontario Court of Appeal in the present case focused upon "external cause". The "ordinary stresses and disappointments of life" were held not to constitute an external cause. The Court considered that the "emotional stress" suffered by the appellant could not be said to be an external factor producing the automatism; the dissociative state had its source primarily in the psychological or emotional makeup of the appellant.

There is no evidence to support Martin J.A.'s statement attributing the dissociated state to the psychological or emotional makeup of the appellant. To exclude the defence of automatism it lay upon the Crown to establish that the appellant suffered from a disease of the mind at the time of the attack. The existence of the mental disease must be demonstrated in evidence. Here there is no such evidence from any of the expert or other witnesses with reference to the crucial period of the assault. Moreover, as earlier noted, s. 16(4) presumes sanity. The Court of Appeal's conclusion was directly contrary to the testimony of Dr. Orchard, accepted by the trial Judge, and finds no support in the testimony of Dr. Rowsell.

Martin J.A. left open the question whether it is possible to dissociate as a result of emotional shock rather than physical injury. The effect of the appellate Court judgment was to differ from the trial Judge's finding that the dissociation was brought about by an externally operating cause. In the circumstances, I do not think it is open to this Court to disturb the findings of fact at trial.

If the effect of the appellate Court judgment is that, as a matter of law, emotional stress can never constitute an external factor then, with respect, I disagree. Indeed, in the passage quoted below the court seems to concede as much. If the controlling factor is one of degree of emotional stress, and the application of some form of quantitative test, then the question becomes one of fact for the trier of fact and not one of law for an appellate Court.

It is not clear to me why, as a matter of law, an emotional blow — which can be devastating — should be regarded as an external cause of automatism in some circumstances and an internal cause in others, as the Court of Appeal would seem to propose in this passage [p. 68]:

> I leave aside, until it becomes necessary to decide them, cases where a dissociative state has resulted from emotional shock without physical injury, resulting from such causes, for example, as being involved in a serious accident although no physical injury has resulted; being the victim of a murderous attack with an uplifted knife, notwithstanding that the victim has managed to escape physical injury; seeing a loved one murdered or seriously assaulted, and the like stiuations. Such extraordinary external events might reasonably be presumed to affect the average normal person without reference to the subjective makeup of the person exposed to such experience.

I cannot accept the notion that an extraordinary external event, *i.e.*, an intense emotional shock, can cause a state of dissociation or automatism if and only if all normal persons subjeccted to that sort of shock would react in that way. If I understood the quoted passage correctly, an objective standard is contemplated for one of the possible causes of automatism, namely, psychological blow, leaving intact the subjective standard for other causes of automatism, such as physical blow or reaction to drugs.

As in all other aspects of the criminal law (except negligence offences) the inquiry is directed to the accused's actual state of mind. It is his subjective mental condition with which the law is concerned. If he has a brittle skull and sustains a concussion which causes him to run amok, he has a valid defence of automatism. If he has an irregular metabolism which induced an unanticipated and violent reaction to a drug, he will not be responsible for his acts. If he is driven into shock and unconsciousness by an emotional blow, and was susceptible to that reaction but has no disease, there is no reason in principle why a plea of automatism should not be available. The fact that other people would not have reacted as he did should not obscure the reality that the external psychological blow did cause a loss of consciousness. A person's subjective reaction, in the absence of any other medical or factual evidence supportive of insanity, should not put him into the category of persons legally insane. Nor am I prepared to accept the proposition, which seems implicit in the passage quoted, that whether an automatic state is an insane reaction or a sane reaction may depend upon the intensity of the shock.

M.E. Schiffer, in his text *Mental Disorder and the Criminal Trial Process* (1978), states that psychological blow automatism is described as a reaction to a shock (p. 101):

> However, in cases where the psychological stress has taken the form of a sudden jolt or blow to the accused, the Court may be more willing to treat a short-lived bout of automatism as sane. Because the automatism, in order to be a defence in itself, must be an "on the sudden" reaction to psychological stress, the defence of "psychological blow automatism" may be seen as somewhat analogous to the defence of provocation.

I agree with the requirement that there be a shock precipitating the state of automatism. Dissociation caused by a low stress threshold and surrender to anxiety cannot fairly be said to result from a psychological blow. In a recent decision of the British Columbia Court of Appeal, *R. v. MacLeod* (1980), 52 C.C.C. (2d) 193, Craig J.A. adopted the judgment of Martin J.A. in *Rabey*. The facts of *MacLeod* cannot be compared with those in the instant appeal. There, the accused absorbed four double drinks of liquor prior to entering the alleged state of dissociation. His loss of consciousness cannot be traced to an immediate emotional shock. He had been subject to ongoing stress for some time, which was heightened by his wife's recent departure. "Though unwilling to classify it a disease of the mind, the accused's medical witness described it as a "neurotic disorder" which could be induced by an "anxiety reaction". The Court of Appeal held that non-insane automatism was not available.

Dr. Glanville Williams' new book, *Textbook of Criminal Law* (1978), is helpful in this discussion, in particular c. 27. The author cites, as the main instances of automatism, "sleepwalking, concussion, some cases of epilepsy, hypoglycaemia and dissociative states". Williams says (pp. 608-609) that "automatism" has come to express "any abnormal state of consciousness (whether confusion, delusion or dissociation) that is regarded as incompatible with the existence of *mens rea*, while not amounting to insanity", adding:

> It would better be called "impaired consciousness", but the orthodox expression can be used if we bear in mind that it does not mean what it says.

And in a footnote [on p. 609]:

> Because automatism is a legal concept, a psychiatrist should be asked to testify to the mental condition as psychiatrically recognized, not to "automatism". It is for the Judge to make the translation. In most of the conditions referred to legally as automatism the psychiatrist would speak of an altered state of consciousness.

The *Parnerkar* case is discussed at some length and the following observations made with respect thereto [p. 613]:

> The decision illustrates the difficulty that can be caused to the courts by over-enthusiastic psychiatrists. If such evidence were regularly given and accepted a considerable breach would be made in the law of homicide. A medical witness who proclaims that the defendant, though awake, did not know that he was stabbing a person because of his dissociated state invites incredulity, particularly where it is shown that the defendant immediately afterwards telephoned for an ambulance and the police. Further, to assert that this medical condition amounts to insanity ignores the distinction that has been developed between sane and non-sane automatism. *If Parnerkar was in a state of automatism at all it was of the non-insane variety, since there was no evidence of psychosis or brain damage or continuing danger.* (The italics are mine.)

At the conclusion of the discussion on *Parnerkar*, Williams makes the following comment, particularly apt in the present case [p. 613]:

> It may also be remarked that commitment to hospital is inappropriate in a case of hysterical dissociation, since once the episode is over the patient does not need to be detained.

Under the heading "Insanity versus Automatism" Williams states that before the decision in *Quick*, *supra*, Lord Denning's view in *Bratty*, *supra*, was generally accepted. The test of insanity was the likelihood of recurrence of danger. In *Quick* the Court of Appeal adopted what might seem at first sight to be a different test for insane versus non-insane automatism. But the real question is whether the violence is likely to be repeated. Williams concludes that "on the whole, it would be much better if the Courts kept to Lord Denning's plain rule; the rule in *Quick* adds nothing to it" (p. 615).

This view, which the Ontario Court of Appeal appears to have rejected, finds ample support in the legal literature. See S.M. Beck, "Voluntary Conduct: Automatism, Insanity and Drunkenness" (1966-67), 9 Cr. L.Q. 315 at 321: "The cause of the automatic conduct, and the threat of recurrence, are plainly factors that determine the line between sane and insane automatism"; F.A. Whitlock, *Criminal Responsibility and Mental Illness* (1963), p. 120: "The test of whether or not an episode of automatism is to be judged as sane or insane action seems to rest on the likelihood of its repetition"; Professor J. Ll J. Edwards, "Automatism and Criminal Responsibility", at p. 385: "Where evidence is available of recurrent attacks of automatisrn during which the accused resorts to violence . . . . [this] inevitably leads to consideration of the imposition of some restraint"; S. Prevezer, "Automatism and Involuntary Conduct", [1958] Crim. L.R. 440 at 441: "If . . . it can safely be predicted that his conduct is not likely to recur, having regard to the cause of the automatism, there can be no point in finding him insane and detaining him in Broadmoor"; G.A. Martin, "Insanity as a Defence" (1965-66), 8 Cr. L.Q. 240 at 253: "Perhaps the distinction lies in the likelihood of recurrence and whether the person suffering from it is prone to acts of violence when in that state."

In principle, the defence of automatism should be available whenever there is evidence of unconsciousness throughout the commission of the crime that cannot be attributed to fault or negligence on his part. Such evidence should be supported by expert medical opinion that the accused did not feign memory loss and that there is no underlying pathological condition which points to a disease requiring detention and treatment.

I would add only that s. 16 determines the consequences of the finding of "no consciousness" on the basis of a legal conclusion guided by the medical evidence of the day. What is disease of the mind in the medical science of today may not be so tomorrow. The Court will establish the meaning of disease of the mind on the basis of scientific evidence as it unfolds from day to day. The Court will find as a matter of fact in each case whether a disease of the mind, so defined, is present.

The circumstances in this case are highly unusual, uncomplicated by alcohol or psychiatric history. The real question in the case is whether the appellant should be confined in an institution for the criminally insane. The trial Judge negated an act of passion, lack of self-control or impulsiveness. The medical evidence negated a state of disease or disorder or mental disturbance arising from infirmity. Save what was said by Dr. Rowsell, whose evidence as to *ex post facto* hysterical amnesia was rejected by the trial Judge, the medical experts gave the appellant a clean mental bill of health. I can see no possible justification for sending the case back for a new trial.

I would allow the appeal, set aside the judgment of the Ontario Court of Appeal and restore the verdict of acquittal.

Appeal dismissed.

R. v. PARKS

[1992] 2 S.C.R. 871, 15 C.R. (4th) 289, 75 C.C.C. (3d) 287

The accused was experiencing serious personal problems, including the loss of his job, which made it difficult for him to sleep. One night he fell asleep in the living room, but a few hours later he got up, put on a jacket and running shoes, grabbed his car keys and the keys to his in-laws' home and drove 23 kilometres to their home. Some of this distance is a multi-lane high-speed highway, and the trip takes 20 minutes in moderate traffic. He then parked in a somewhat confined underground parking area, took a tire iron from his car and entered the home. He got a knife from the kitchen and went to his in-laws' bedroom, where they were sleeping. He strangled his father-in-law until he was unconscious and at some stage inflicted cuts to his head and chest. The father-in-law was hospitalized but recovered. The accused repeatedly stabbed his mother-in-law and brutally beat her with a blunt instrument. She died. The accused then drove to a nearby police station, taking the knife with him. He arrived at the police station with badly-cut hands. He was agitated and in great distress. He made various exclamations to the effect that he had just killed two people with his bare hands. He indicated that these people were his mother and father-in-law. The accused had previously had a good relationship with both of his wife's parents. He was charged with murder and attempted murder.

At his murder trial, he raised the defence of sleepwalking and was acquitted by a jury. The trial Judge ruled that his defence should be left to the jury as non-insane automatism, entitling him to an acquittal, rather than as a form of the defence of insanity which, if accepted, would result in the special verdict of not guilty by reason of insanity. At the subsequent trial for attempted murder, the trial Judge acquitted the accused on the basis that the doctrine of issue estoppel required him to accept the previous jury's determination that the defence of sleepwalking had been made out.

The Crown appealed these acquittals. The Ontario Court of Appeal [(1990) 78 C.R. (3d) 1] dismissed the appeals on the basis that there was no evidence of a disease of the mind and that, while the facts of the case stretched credulity, an appellate Court had to guard against the temptation to usurp the jury's function. The Crown appealed further. The Supreme Court dismissed the appeal. The Court was in agreement that, on this evidence, the trial Judge had not erred in leaving the jury the defence of automatism rather than that of insanity.

Chief Justice Lamer (for the Court on this point): —

This Court has only ruled on sleepwalking in an *obiter dictum* in *R. v. Rabey*, [1980] 2 S.C.R. 513, 15 C.R. (3d) 225. The Court found that sleepwalking was not a "disease of the mind" in the legal sense of the term and gave rise to a defence of automatism. Should the Court maintain this position?

In *Black's Law Dictionary*, 5th ed. (St. Paul, Minn.: West Publishing Co., 1979) automatism is defined as follows:

> Behaviour performed in a state of mental unconsciousness or dissociation without full awareness, *i.e.*, somnambulism, fugues. Term is applied to actions or conduct of an individual apparently occurring without will, purpose, or reasoned intention on his part; a condition sometimes observed in persons who, without being actually insane, suffer from an obscuration of the mental faculties, loss of volition or of memory, or kindred affections. . . .

In *Rabey* this Court affirmed the judgment of the Ontario Court of Appeal (1977), 40 C.R.N.S. 46, 37 C.C.C. (2d) 461, in which Martin J.A. defined the expression "disease of the mind" at pp. 472-473 [C.C.C., p. 57 C.R.N.S.]:

> "Disease of the mind" is a legal term, not a medical term of art; although a legal concept, it contains a substantial medical component as well as a legal or policy component.

The legal or policy component relates to (a) the scope of the exemption from criminal responsibility to be afforded by mental disorder or disturbance, and (b) the protection of the public by the control and treatment of persons who have caused serious harms while in a mentally disordered or disturbed state. The medical component of the term, generally, is medical opinion as to how the mental condition in question is viewed or characterized medically. Since the medical component of the term reflects or should reflect the state of medical knowledge at a given time, the concept of "disease of the mind" is capable of evolving with increased medical knowledge with respect to mental disorder or disturbance.

As Martin J.A. pointed out at p. 477 [C.C.C., p. 62 C.R.N.S.], Canadian and foreign courts and authors have recognized that sleepwalking is not a disease of the mind:

Sleepwalking appears to fall into a separate category. Unconscious behaviour in a state of somnambulism is non-insane automatism . . . .

In Canada, see also *R. v. Hartridge* (1966), 48 C.R. 389, [1967] 1 C.C.C. 346 (Sask. C.A.).

In Britain, Lord Denning in *Bratty v. Attorney General for Northern Ireland*, [1963] A.C. 386 (H.L.), at p. 409, recognized that sleepwalking gave rise to a defence of automatism:

No act is punishable if it is done involuntarily: and an involuntary act in this context — some people nowadays prefer to speak of it as "automatism" — means an act which is done by the muscles without any control by the mind, such as a spasm, a reflex action or a convulsion; or an act done by a person who is not conscious of what he is doing, such as an act done whilst suffering from concussion or whilst sleepwalking.

Other foreign decisions have recognized the same principle: *Ryan v. R.*, [1967] A.L.R. 577; *R. v. Cottle*, [1958] N.Z.L.R. 999; *R. v. Ngang*, [1960] 3 S.A.L.R. 363; *R. v. Tolson* (1889), 23 Q.B.D. 168 (C.C.R.); *H.M. Advocate v. Fraser* (1878), 4 Couper 70.

However, two British decisions seem to go against this line of authority: *R. v. Sullivan*, [1984] A.C. 156, [1983] 2 All E.R. 673 (H.L.), and *R. v. Burgess*, [1991] 2 Q.B. 92 (C.A.). The comment in Sullivan at p. 677 [All E.R.] was *obiter*, since the case concerned epilepsy:

If the effect of a disease is to impair these faculties so severely as to have either of the consequences referred to in the latter part of the [*M'Naghten*] rules, it matters not whether the aetiology of the impairment is organic, as in epilepsy, or functional, or whether the impairment itself is permanent or is transient and intermittent, provided that it subsisted at the time of commission of the act.

Some writers have interpreted this *obiter* as an indication that future cases of sleepwalking would only lead to a defence of insanity:

Although sleepwalkers have always received an absolute acquittal for what they do, no social inconvenience has hitherto resulted. There seems to be no recorded instance of a sleepwalker doing injury a further time after being acquitted. However, since the decision in *Sullivan*, to be discussed in the next section, it seems very likely that sleepwalkers will in future find themselves saddled with an insanity verdict. [Williams, *supra*, at p. 666.]

However, the evidence in the case at bar does not indicate the presence of an illness. Accordingly, I do not believe that this *obiter* can be applied to sleepwalking cases such as that of Mr. Parks. *Burgess* cannot be applied here for the same reason, but we will return to it later.

. . . .

In the case at bar the trial Judge first reviewed the case law and scholarly analysis and said he did not intend to go against it:

> In *Rabey*, *supra*, Martin J.A. considered somnambulism or sleepwalking to be a special category or case of non-insane automatism, one that perhaps could not be justified in accordance with a strict application of principles invoked to determine whether a condition from which an accused suffers amounts to "a disease of the mind" within s-s. 16(2) of the *Criminal Code*. Quite simply put, and notwithstanding that the observations concerning the legal characterization of sleepwalking as a separate category of non-insane automatism would not appear to have been necessary to a decision of the issue on appeal in *Rabey*, *supra*, I am not prepared to depart from the pronouncement of such an eminent authority as Martin J.A. on matters concerning the scope of criminal responsibility. The statement there made is, as one might expect, amply supported by the jurisprudence and academic writings upon the issue.

He then considered the facts of the instant case:

> In the circumstances of the present case, it is doubtful whether the sleep disorder from which the accused suffers would constitute a disease of the mind under s-s. 16(2) in accordance with general principle.

I therefore propose to review the evidence in this matter. A large part of the defence evidence in this case was medical evidence. Five physicians were heard: Dr. Roger James Broughton, a neurophysiologist and specialist in sleep and sleep disorders, Dr. John Gordon Edmeads, a neurologist, Dr. Ronald Frederick Billings, a psychiatrist, Dr. Robert Wood Hill, a forensic psychiatrist, and finally, Dr. Frank Raymond Ervin, a neurologist and psychiatrist.

The medical evidence in the case at bar showed that the respondent was in fact sleepwalking when he committed the acts with which he is charged. All the expert witnesses called by the defence said that in their opinion Parks was sleepwalking when the events occurred. This is what Dr. Broughton said:

> Q. . . . assuming for a moment that Mr. Parks caused the death of Barbara Woods, did you, sir, reach an opinion as to his condition at the time he caused that death?
>
> A. Yes. My opinion is that he did it during a sleepwalking episode.

Though sceptical at the outset, the expert witnesses unanimously stated that at the time of the incidents the respondent was not suffering from any mental illness and that, medically speaking, sleepwalking is not regarded as an illness, whether physical, mental or neurological.

. . . .

They also unanimously stated that a person who is sleepwalking cannot think, reflect or perform voluntary acts.

. . . .

The evidence also disclosed that sleepwalking was very common, almost universal, among children, and that 2 to 2.5 percent of "normal" adults had sleepwalked at least once. Dr. Hill further noted that he found it significant that there were several sleepwalkers in the respondent's family:

> Thirdly, I think, as I indicated, it turns out, as enquiries are made more and more, that there is a significant history in the background family of Mr. Parks of difficulties, of bedwetting difficulties, of sleeptalking and sleepwalking, that is in keeping with what we know about the phenomena of sleepwalking. We know that there are often family members so affected and that was present.

Dr. Broughton, for his part, indicated that he had never known of sleepwalkers who had acted violently who had repeated this kind of behaviour:

> Q. Yes. Now, with respect to Mr. Parks, do you have any opinion, sir, as to the probability of a recurrence of an event of sleepwalking with serious aggression involving physical harm to others?
>
> A. I think the risk of that is infinitesimal, I don't think it would exceed the risk of the general population almost. He has the family predisposition to sleepwalk, but it would only be in the likelihood of all precipitating and extenuating and so forth factors that built up to this crisis that would theoretically have to almost reappear.
>
> Q. And even if they were to reappear, would there be any probability of another homicidal event?
>
> A. It would still — As I say, there are no reported cases in the literature, so there is essentially — The probability of it occurring is not statistically significant. It is just absolutely improbable.

In cross-examination he also added that sleepwalking episodes in which violent acts are committed are not common:

> Q. And does that, in fact, agree with your own experience with respect to people that you have dealt with at the sleep lab and have seen over the years, that the majority of sleepwalking episodes generally involve what you call trivial behaviour?
>
> A. It is well known that aggression during sleepwalking is quite rare.
>
> Q. How many cases of aggression during sleepwalking have you personally deal[t] with or been involved with at your sleep lab?
>
> A. In the last — Perhaps a total of five or six. In the last five years we have seen three.

Further, on being questioned about a cure or treatment, Dr. Broughton answered that the solution was sleep hygiene, which involved eliminating factors that precipitated sleepwalking such as stress, lack of sleep and violent physical exercise.

. . . .

Three very important points emerge from this testimony: (1) the respondent was sleepwalking at the time of the incident; (2) sleepwalking is not a neurological, psychiatric or other illness — it is a sleep disorder very common in children and also found in adults; (3) there is no medical treatment as such, apart from good health practices, especially as regards sleep. It is important to note that this expert evidence was not in any way contradicted by the prosecution, which as the trial Judge observed, did have the advice of experts who were present during the testimony given by the defence experts and whom it chose not to call.

The Crown, for its part, relied on a decision of the English Court of Appeal, *R. v. Burgess*, *supra*, in which the Court held that sleepwalking was a mental illness. It is worth noting here, however, that the evidence in *Burgess* was completely different from or even contradictory to that presented in the case at bar.

The facts in *Burgess* are more or less similar to those at issue here. Burgess and a friend fell asleep watching a video. The friend woke up when she felt a blow on the head. Burgess was facing her, holding the video recorder in the air, about to strike her on the head with it, and he did so. Burgess, who woke up immediately after the incident, testified that he did not remember having hit her. He presented a defence of automatism, which the Judge rejected. He was acquitted on grounds of insanity and appealed this judgment. Nevertheless, while the facts are similar the medical evidence was very different. Expert witnesses were called. The first witness, a Dr. D'Orban, agreed that Burgess was sleepwalking, but regarded this as a pathological condition. Another expert, called by the Crown, Dr. Fenwick, said that in his opinion this was not sleepwalking but a "hysterical dissociative state". The following is a passage from this judgment at pp. 775-776 [All E.R.], which states the situation very clearly:

> One turns then to examine the evidence upon which the Judge had to base his decision and for this purpose the two medical experts called by the defence are the obvious principal sources. Dr. d'Orban in examination-in-chief said:
>
>> "On the evidence available to me, and subject to the results of the tests when they became available, I came to the same conclusion as Dr. Nicholas and Dr. Eames, whose reports I had read, and that was that (the appellant's) actions had occurred during the course of a sleep disorder."
>
> He was asked . . . in cross-examination:
>
>> "Q. Would you go so far as to say that it was liable to recur? A. It is possible for it to recur, yes.
>
> *Judge Lewis.* Is this a case of automatism associated with a pathological condition or not?
>
>> A. I think the answer would have to be Yes, because it is an abnormality of the brain function, so it would be regarded as a pathological condition."

. . . .

The prosecution, as already indicated, called Dr Fenwick, whose opinion was that this was not a sleepwalking episode at all. If it was a case where the appellant was unconscious of what he was doing, the most likely explanation was that he was in what is described as a hysterical dissociative state. . . .

He then went on to describe features of sleepwalking. This is what he said:

. . . .

> "Finally, should a person be detained in hospital? The answer to that is: Yes, because sleepwalking is treatable. Violent night terrors are treatable. There is a lot which can be done for the sleepwalker, so sending them to hospital after a violent act to have their sleepwalking sorted out, makes good sense."

In my view, therefore, that case is clearly distinguishable from the one at bar. I am of the view that in the instant case, based on the evidence and the testimony of the expert witnesses heard, the trial Judge did not err in leaving the defence of automatism rather than that of insanity with the jury, and that the instant appeal should be dismissed. For a defence of insanity to have been put to the jury, together with or instead of a defence of automatism, as the case may be, there would have had to have been in the record evidence tending to show that sleepwalking was the cause of the respondent's state of mind. As we have just seen, that is not the case here. This is not to say that sleepwalking could never be a disease of the mind, in another case on different evidence.

LA FOREST J. (five justices concurring): — I have had the advantage of reading the reasons of the Chief Justice. I agree with him that the trial Judge was correct in leaving only the defence of non-insane automatism with the jury. I am also in agreement with what the Chief Justice has to say on that issue, but I wish to add the following comments concerning the distinction in law between insane and non-insane automatism, particularly as it relates to somnambulism.

In his reasons, the Chief Justice finds that the evidence and expert testimony from the trial of the accused support the trial Judge's decision to instruct the jury on non-insane automatism. I agree with this finding, but in my view that is not the end of the matter. In distinguishing between automatism and insanity the trial Judge must consider more than the evidence; there are overarching policy considerations as well. Of course, the evidence in each case will be highly relevant to this policy inquiry.

Automatism occupies a unique place in our criminal law system. Although spoken of as a "defence", it is conceptually a subset of the voluntariness requirement, which in turn is part of the *actus reus* component of criminal liability. A useful introduction is found in the dissenting reasons of Dickson J. (as he then was) in *R. v. Rabey*, [1980] 2 S.C.R. 513, 15 C.R. (3d) 225, at p. 522 [S.C.R.]:

> Although the word "automatism" made its way but lately to the legal stage, it is basic principle that absence of volition in respect of the act involved is always a defence to a crime. A defence that the act is involuntary entitles the accused to a complete and unqualified acquittal. That the defence of automatism exists as a middle ground between criminal responsibility and legal insanity is beyond question. Although spoken as a defence, in the sense that it is raised by the accused, the Crown always bears the burden of proving a voluntary act.

One qualification to this statement should be noted. When the automatistic condition stems from a disease of the mind that has rendered the accused insane, then the accused is not entitled to a full acquittal, but to a verdict of insanity; see *Bratty v. Attorney General for Northern Ireland*, [1963] A.C. 386 (H.L.), at pp. 403-404 and 414 [A.C.]. The condition in that instance is referred to as insane automatism, and the distinction between it and non-insane automatism is the crucial issue in this appeal.

Step 1:
laying
the proper
foundation
for the Defence?
evidence
Defendant

When a defence of non-insane automatism is raised by the accused, the trial Judge must determine whether the defence should be left with the trier of fact. This will involve two discrete tasks. First, he or she must determine whether there is some evidence on the record to support leaving the defence with the jury. This is sometimes referred to as laying the proper foundation for the defence; see *Bratty, supra*, at pp. 405 and 413 [A.C.]. Thus an evidential burden rests with the accused, and the mere assertion of the defence will not suffice; see *Bratty*, at p. 414 [A.C.]. Dickson J. summarized the point in comprehensive fashion in the following passage in *Rabey*, at p. 545 [S.C.R.]:

> The prosecution must prove every element of the crime charged. One such element is the state of mind of the accused, in the sense that the act was voluntary. The circumstances are normally such as to permit a presumption of volition and mental capacity. That is not so when the accused, as here, has placed before the court, by cross-examination of Crown witnesses or by evidence called on his own behalf, or both, evidence sufficient to raise an issue that he was unconscious of his actions at the time of the alleged offence. No burden of proof is imposed upon an accused raising such defence beyond pointing to facts which indicate the existence of such a condition.

Step 2:
Source?
TJ

If the proper foundation is present the Judge moves to the second task: he or she must consider whether the condition alleged by the accused is, in law, non-insane automatism. If the trial Judge is satisfied that there is some evidence pointing to a condition that is in law non-insane automatism, then the defence can be left with the jury; see *Rabey*, per Ritchie J., at p. 519 [S.C.R.]. The issue for the jury is one of fact: did the accused suffer from or experience the alleged condition at the relevant time? Because the Crown must always prove that an accused has acted voluntarily, the onus rests on the prosecution at this stage to prove the absence of automatism beyond a reasonable doubt.

In the present case, there is no question that the accused has laid the proper foundation for the defence of automatism. The expert testimony reviewed by the Chief Justice is more than adequate on that score. At issue here is the question of law: is sleepwalking properly classified as non-insane automatism, or does it stem from a disease of the mind, thereby leaving only the defence of insanity for the accused? When considering this question, s. 16(4) of the *Criminal Code*, R.S.C., 1985, c. C-46, should be recalled: "Every one shall, until the contrary is proved, be presumed to be and to have been sane." If the accused pleads automatism, the Crown is then entitled to raise the issue of insanity, but the prosecution then bears the burden of proving that the condition in question stems from a disease of the mind; see *Rabey, supra*, at pp. 544-545 [S.C.R.].

In Canada, the approach to distinguishing between insane and non-insane automatism was settled by this Court's judgment in *Rabey*.

. . . .

In part because of the imprecision of medical science in this area, the legal community reserves for itself the final determination of what constitutes a "disease of the mind". This is accomplished by adding the "legal or policy component" to the inquiry.

A review of the cases on automatism reveals two distinct approaches to the policy component of the disease of the mind inquiry. These may be labelled the "continuing danger" and "internal cause" theories; see E. Colvin, *Principles of Criminal Law,* 2d ed. (Toronto: Carswell, 1991), at p. 293. At first glance these approaches may appear to be divergent, but in fact they stem from a common concern for public safety. This was recognized by Martin J.A. who referred to "protection of the public" as a focus of the policy inquiry. More recently, the Chief Justice had occasion to comment on this aspect of the insanity provisions of the *Criminal Code*, albeit in a division of powers context, in *R. v. Swain*, [1991] 1 S.C.R. 933, 5 C.R. (4th) 253, 63 C.C.C. (3d) 481, at p. 998 [S.C.R.]:

> It is true that the dominant characteristic of these provisions is not punishment; however, neither is it treatment. The "pith and substance" of the legislative scheme dealing with individuals acquitted by reason of insanity is the protection of society from dangerous people who have engaged in conduct proscribed by the *Criminal Code* through the prevention of such acts in the future. While treatment may be incidentally involved in the process, it is not the dominant objective of the legislation.

The continuing danger theory holds that any condition likely to present a recurring danger to the public should be treated as insanity. The internal cause theory suggests that a condition stemming from the psychological or emotional makeup of the accused, rather than some external factor, should lead to a finding of insanity. The two theories share a common concern for recurrence, the latter holding that an internal weakness is more likely to lead to recurrent violence than automatism brought on by some intervening external cause.

It would appear that the internal cause approach has gained a certain ascendancy in both Canadian and English jurisprudence. The theory was the basis for deciding *Rabey*.

. . . .

The theory has also been adopted in England, first in *R. v. Quick*; *R. v. Paddison*, [1973] 3 All E.R. 347 (C.A.) [hereafter *R. v. Quick*], at p. 356 [All E.R.], and most recently in *R. v. Hennessy*, [1989] 2 All E.R. 9 (C.A.), where Lord Lane C.J. stated the approach as follows, at p. 13 [All E.R.]:

> The question in many cases, and this is one such case, is whether the function of the mind was disturbed on the one hand by disease or on the other hand by some external factor.

The judgments in both *Rabey* and *Hennessy* are careful to state that the internal cause theory is not a universal approach to the disease of the mind inquiry. Indeed Martin J.A., at p. 477 [C.C.C., p. 62 C.R.N.S.], appears to suggest that sleepwalking is one of those conditions that is not usefully assessed on this basis.

The internal cause approach has been criticized as an unfounded development of the law, and for the odd results the external/internal dichotomy can produce; see G. Williams, *Textbook of Criminal Law* 2d ed. (London: Sweet & Maxwell, 1983), at pp. 671-676; D. Stuart, *Canadian Criminal Law* 2d ed. (Toronto: Carswell, 1987), at pp. 92-94; Colvin, *supra*, at p. 291. These criticisms have particular validity if the internal cause theory is held out as the definitive answer to the disease of the mind inquiry. However, it is apparent from the cases that the theory is really meant to be used only as an analytical tool, and not as an all-encompassing methodology. As Watt J. commented in his reasons in support of his charge to the jury in this case, the dichotomy "constitutes a general, but not an unremitting or universal, classificatory scheme for 'disease of the mind'".

As Martin J.A. suggested in *Rabey*, somnambulism is an example of a condition that is not well suited to analysis under the internal cause theory. The poor fit arises because certain factors can legitimately be characterized as either internal or external sources of automatistic behaviour. For example, the Crown in this case argues that the causes of the respondent's violent sleepwalking were entirely internal, a combination of genetic susceptibility and the ordinary stresses of everyday life (lack of sleep, excessive afternoon exercise, and a high stress level due to personal problems). These "ordinary stresses" were ruled out as external factors by this Court in *Rabey* (although by a narrow majority). However, the factors that for a waking individual are mere ordinary stresses can be differently characterized for a person who is asleep, unable to counter with his conscious mind the onslaught of the admittedly ordinary strains of life. One could argue that the particular amalgam of stress, excessive exercise, sleep deprivation and sudden noises in the night that causes an incident of somnambulism is, for the sleeping person, analogous to the effect of a concussion upon a waking person, which is generally accepted as an external cause of non-insane automatism; see Williams, *supra*, at p. 666. In the end, the dichotomy between internal and external causes becomes blurred in this context, and is not helpful in resolving the inquiry.

The continuing danger approach stems from an *obiter* comment of Lord Denning in *Bratty*, *supra*, where he proposes the following test for distinguishing between insane and non-insane automatism, at p. 412 [A.C.]:

> It seems to me that any mental disorder which has manifested itself in violence and is prone to recur is a disease of the mind. At any rate it is the sort of disease for which a person should be detained in hospital rather than be given an unqualified acquittal.

Lord Denning's casual proposition has not been universally accepted, although some elements of the theory remain today. It was questioned in *R. v. Quick*, *supra*, at pp. 351-352 [All E.R.], and legal academics have questioned the utility of the test; see Stuart, *supra*, at pp. 94-95; Colvin, *supra*, at p. 294. As well, medical authorities have doubted the ability of their profession to predict recurrent dangerousness; see Roth, "Modern Psychiatry and Neurology and the Problem of Responsibility", in S.J. Hucker, C. Webster and M. Ben-Aron, eds., *Mental Disorder and Criminal Responsibility* (Toronto: Butterworths, 1981), at pp. 104-109. In *Rabey*, Martin J.A. doubted the merit of Lord Denning's test, noting, at p. 476 [C.C.C., p. 60 C.R.N.S.], that the converse of Denning's proposition was surely not good law. He stated:

> It would be quite unreasonable to hold that a serious mental disorder did not constitute a disease of the mind because it was unlikely to recur. To so hold would be to exclude from the exemption from responsibility afforded by insanity, persons, who by reason of a severe mental disorder were incapable of appreciating the nature and quality of the act or of knowing that it was wrong, if such mental disorder was unlikely to recur.

The majority of this Court approved these comments, and Dickson J. in dissent conceded the point, at p. 533 [S.C.R.]:

> A test of proneness to recur does not entail the converse conclusion, that if the mental malady is not prone to recur it cannot be a disease of the mind. A condition, organic in nature, which causes an isolated act of unconscious violence could well be regarded as a case of temporary insanity.

Nonetheless, Dickson J. sought to revive Lord Denning's basic formulation. . .

. . . .

While Dickson J.'s views did not carry the day in *Rabey*, nothing in the majority judgment precludes the consideration of a continuing danger as a factor at the policy stage of the inquiry.

Since *Rabey*, the House of Lords has revisited the question of disease of the mind, in *R. v. Sullivan*, [1984] A.C. 156, Lord Diplock, speaking for a unanimous Court, commented, at p. 172 [A.C.], as follows:

> The nomenclature adopted by the medical profession may change from time to time; Bratty was tried in 1961. But the meaning of the expression "disease of the mind" as the cause of "a defect of reason", remains unchanged for the purposes of the application of the M'Naghten Rules. I agree with what was said by Devlin J. in *Reg. v. Kemp* [1957] 1 Q.B. 399, 407, that "mind" in the M'Naghten Rules is used in the ordinary sense of the mental faculties of reason, memory and understanding. If the effect of a disease is to impair these faculties so severely as to have either of the consequences referred to in the latter part of the rules, it matters not whether the aetiology of the impairment is organic, as in epilepsy, or functional, or whether the impairment itself is permanent or is transient and intermittent, provided that it subsisted at the time of commission of the act. *The purpose of the legislation relating to the defence of insanity, ever since its origin in 1800, has been to protect society against recurrence of the dangerous conduct. The duration of a temporary suspension of the mental faculties of reason, memory and understanding, particularly if, as in Mr. Sullivan's case, it is recurrent, cannot on any rational ground be relevant to the application by the courts of the M'Naghten Rules*, though it may be relevant to the course adopted by the Secretary of State, to whom the responsibility for how the defendant is to be dealt with passes after the return of the special verdict of "not guilty by reason of insanity." [My emphasis.]

This passage, while not entirely clear, appears to endorse the consideration of recurrence as a non-determinative factor in the insanity inquiry. Lord Diplock states that the *duration* of the condition in question is not a relevant consideration: a disease of the mind can be temporary or permanent. He also suggests that the relative impermanence of a condition is particularly inconsequential *if the condition is prone to recur*. A necessary corollary of these statements is the more general proposition that recurrence suggests insanity, but the absence of recurrence does not preclude it. This view of the law was stated explicitly in *R. v. Burgess*, [1991] 2 All E.R. 769 (C.A.), at p. 774 [All E.R.]:

> It seems to us that if there is a danger of recurrence that may be an added reason for categorising the condition as a disease of the mind. On the other hand, the absence of the danger of recurrence is not a reason for saying that it cannot be a disease of the mind. Subject to that possible qualification, we respectfully adopt Lord Denning's suggested definition.

In my view, the Court of Appeal has properly stated the law on this point. Recurrence is but one of a number of factors to be considered in the policy phase of the disease of the mind inquiry. Moreover, the absence of a danger of recurrence will not automatically exclude the possibility of a finding of insanity.

In this case, then, neither of the two leading policy approaches determines an obvious result. It is clear from the evidence that there is almost no likelihood of recurrent violent somnambulism. A finding of insanity is therefore less likely, but the absence of a continuing danger does not mean that the respondent must be granted an absolute acquittal. At the same time, the internal cause theory is not readily applicable in this case. It is therefore necessary to look further afield.

In his dissenting reasons in *Rabey*, at p. 546, [S.C.R.] Dickson J. enumerates certain additional policy considerations that are relevant to the distinction between insanity and automatism:

> There are undoubtedly policy considerations to be considered. Automatism as a defence is easily feigned. It is said the credibility of our criminal justice system will be severely strained if a person who has committed a violent act is allowed an absolute acquittal on a plea of automatism arising from a psychological blow. The argument is made that the success of the defence depends upon the semantic ability of psychiatrists, tracing a narrow path between the twin shoals of criminal responsibility and an insanity verdict. Added to these concerns is the *in terrorem* argument that the floodgates will be raised if psychological blow automatism is recognized in law.

These factors are raised by Dickson J. as arguments against a finding of non-insane automatism. In the present case, however, none of these arguments is persuasive. It seems unlikely that the recognition of somnambulism as non-insane automatism will open the floodgates to a cascade of sleepwalking defence claims. First of all, the defence of somnambulism has been recognized, albeit in *obiter* discussion, in an unbroken line of cases stretching back at least a century, yet I am unaware of any current problem with specious defence claims of somnambulistic automatism. Indeed, this case and *Burgess* are among the few appellate decisions in which the status of somnambulism was a question to be decided. Moreover, it is very difficult to feign sleepwalking — precise symptoms and medical histories beyond the control of the accused must be presented to the trier of fact, and as in this case the accused will be subjected to a battery of medical tests. Finally, a comprehensive listing of the indicia of sleepwalking can be consulted by both the court and the medical experts; see P. Fenwick, "Somnambulism and the Law: A Review" (1987), 5 Behavioral Sciences and the Law 343, at p. 354.

It may be that some will regard the exoneration of an accused through a defence of somnambulism as an impairment of the credibility of our justice system. Those who hold this view would also reject insane automatism as an excuse from criminal responsibility. However, these views are contrary to certain fundamental precepts of our criminal law: only those who act voluntarily with the requisite intent to commit an offence should be punished by criminal sanction. The concerns of those who reject these underlying values of our system of criminal justice must accordingly be discounted.

In the end, there are no compelling policy factors that preclude a finding that the accused's condition was one of non-insane automatism. I noted earlier that it is for the Crown to prove that somnambulism stems from a disease of the mind; neither the evidence nor the policy considerations in this case overcome the Crown's burden in that regard. Committal under s. 614(2) of the *Criminal Code* is therefore precluded, and the accused should be acquitted.

As I noted at the outset, it is apparent that the medical evidence in this case is not only significant in its own right, but also has an impact at several stages of the policy inquiry. As such, I agree with the Chief Justice that in another case, on different evidence, sleepwalking might be found to be a disease of the mind. As Dickson J. commented in *Rabey*, at p. 552 [S.C.R.]:

> What is disease of the mind in the medical science of today may not be so tomorrow. The court will establish the meaning of disease of the mind on the basis of scientific evidence as it unfolds from day to day. The court will find as a matter of fact in each case whether a disease of the mind, so defined, is present.

The Supreme Court split over whether, notwithstanding the confirmation of the acquittal, the matter should be referred to the trial Judge to consider a common-law peace bond. This issue had been raised by Chief Justice Lamer when the case was argued in the Supreme Court. The Chief Justice (Cory J. concurring) held that the matter should be remitted for a consideration of such an order. However, the other six justices rejected such a possibility, each expressing agreement with three separate opinions given by Sopinka, McLachlin and LaForest JJ.

LAMER C.J.C. (dissenting on this point): —

As I see it, however, that does not end the matter. Although the expert witnesses were unanimous in saying that sleepwalkers are very rarely violent, I am still concerned by the fact that as the result of an acquittal in a situation like this (and I am relieved that such cases are quite rare), the accused is simply set free without any consideration of measures to protect the public, or indeed the accused himself, from the possibility of a repetition of such unfortunate occurrences. In the case of an outright acquittal, should there not be some control? And if so, how should this be done? I am of the view that such control could be exercised by means of the common-law power to make an order to keep the peace vested in any Judge or Magistrate. This power of "preventive justice" has been recognized in England for centuries and has its origin in one or more sources:

> The cases do, however, in tracing the history of the law, suggest that it is derived from one or more sources:
>
> (i) The common law;
>
> (ii) The statute law, being the Justices of the Peace Act, 1361 (Imp.), c. 1 (hereinafter the "Statute of Edward III"); and/or
>
> (iii) The form of commission which the justice of the peace is required to take in England.

In Canada this power has already been used in Ontario and British Columbia and was recognized by this Court in 1954 in *Mackenzie v. Martin*, [1954] S.C.R. 361, 108 C.C.C. 305, at pp. 368-369 [S.C.R.]:

> In my view the common-law preventive justice was in force in Ontario; s-s. [(2)] of s. 748, or any other provision of the *Criminal Code* to which our attention was directed, does not interfere with the use of that jurisdiction, and the respondent was intending to exercise it. He, therefore, had jurisdiction over the subject-matter of the complaint, and did not exceed it.

In exercising this power, the rules of natural justice must be observed and in this regard the more recent decision of the Ontario Court of Appeal, *Broomes v. R.* (1984), 12 C.C.C. (3d) 220, is of particular interest for these purposes. A Judge who acquitted an accused of assault decided, however, to exercise this "preventive justice" and made an order binding over the accused to keep the peace on certain conditions. On appeal, the accused argued that he had been denied the rules of natural justice because he was not told in advance that such an order would be made. Steele J. of the Ontario High Court of Justice dismissed the appeal, relying on an English decision (at p. 221):

> I accept the decision in *R. v. Woking Justices, Ex p. Gossage*, [1973] 2 All E.R. 621 at p. 623 (Eng. C.A.), where Lord Widgery C.J. stated as follows:
>
>> It seems to me that a very clear distinction is drawn between, on the one part, persons who come before the justices as witnesses, and on the other, persons who come before the justices as defendants. Not only do the witnesses come with no expected prospect of being subjected to any kind of penalty, but also the witnesses as such, although they may speak in evidence, cannot represent themselves through counsel and cannot call evidence on their own behalf. *By contrast*, the defendant comes before the Court knowing that allegations are to be made against him, knowing that he can be represented if appropriate, and knowing that he can call evidence if he wishes. It seems to me that a rule which requires a witness to be warned of the possibility of a binding-over should not necessarily apply to a defendant in that different position.

I think from the extracts from Lord Parker C.J.'s judgment that I have read, Lord Parker C.J. would have taken the same view; but, be that as it may, it seems to me to be putting it far too high in the case of an acquitted defendant to say that it is a breach of the rules of natural justice not to give him an indication of the prospective binding-over before the binding-over is imposed. That is not to say that it would not be wise, and indeed courteous in these cases for justices to give such a warning; there certainly would be absolutely no harm in a case like the present if the justices, returning to Court, had announced they were going to acquit, but had immediately said "We are however contemplating a binding-over; what have you got to say?" *I think it would be at least courteous and perhaps wise that that should be done, but I am unable to elevate the principle to the height at which it can be said that a failure to give such a warning is a breach of the rules of natural justice.* [Emphasis added.]

Accordingly, such a power exists. The question remains whether it should be exercised in the case of the respondent Parks, or at least whether its exercise should be considered. I am of the view that this approach should be considered. As I have already said, despite the unanimous and uncontradicted evidence that the chances of such an occurrence taking place again are for all practical purposes nil, I feel that all necessary measures should be taken to ensure that such an event does not recur. After all, before this tragic incident occurred, the probability of Mr. Parks killing someone while in a somnambulistic state was infinitesimal. Yet this is precisely what took place. Furthermore, the evidence at trial was not adduced with a view to determining whether an order would be justifed and to determine the appropriate conditions of such an order. Thus, for example, an order might be made requiring Parks to do certain things suggested by a specialist in sleep disorders, for example to report to him periodically. In appropriate cases of outright acquittals on grounds of automatism measures that would reinforce sleep hygiene and thereby provide greater safety for others should always be considered. If the trial judge considers that making such an order would be in the interest of the public, he should so advise the parties and consider whatever evidence and submissions are tendered. In those situations where an order is made, it should be complied with in the same way as any other order of the Court.

If conditions should be imposed on Mr. Parks they will restrict his liberty. It follows that the decision to impose such conditions and the terms of those conditions should not violate the rights guaranteed under s. 7 of the *Canadian Charter of Rights and Freedoms*. However, such a hearing is justified, as the sleepwalker has, although innocently, committed an act of violence which resulted in the death of his mother-in-law. Members of the community may quite reasonably be apprehensive for their safety. In those circumstances it cannot be said that the Court has unduly intruded upon the liberty of the accused by exploring, on notice to the accused, the possibility of imposing some minimally intrusive conditions which seek to assure the safety of the community. If conditions are imposed, then they obviously must be rationally connected to the apprehended danger posed by the person and go no further than necessary to protect the public from this danger.

I would therefore refer this matter back to the trial Judge so that he can hear the parties on this point and decide, upon the evidence before him, whether such an order is appropriate. If this proves to be the case, it will be up to the trial Judge to determine the content of the order.

I would accordingly dismiss this appeal and uphold the acquittal of the respondent but refer the matter back to the trial Judge for him to decide on the making of an order to keep the peace on certain conditions, pursuant to the "preventive justice" power which he possesses.

SOPINKA J.: —

. . . .

This Court has recognized the existence of a common-law preventative justice power in addition to the specific statutory power to make an order to keep the peace pursuant to an information laid under what is now s. 810 of the *Criminal Code*, R.S.C., 1985, c. C-46: *Mackenzie v. Martin*, [1954] S.C.R. 361, 108 C.C.C. 305. However even at common law this power has significant limits. In *Mackenzie*, Kerwin J. quoted from Blackstone on the nature of the power:

> This preventative justice consists in obliging those *persons, whom there is probable ground to suspect of future misbehaviour*, to stipulate with and to give full assurance to the public, that *such offence as is apprehended* shall not happen; by finding pledges or securities for keeping the peace, or for their good behaviour. [At p. 368 [S.C.R.], emphasis added.]

Several lower Court decisions have similarly recognized that this common-law power cannot be exercised on the basis of mere speculation, but requires a proven factual foundation which raises a probable ground to suspect of future misbehaviour. See: *R. v. Chohan* (1968), 5 C.R.N.S. 30, (sub nom. *R. v. White*) [1969] 1 C.C.C. 19 (B.C. S.C.); *R. v. Shaben* (1972), 19 C.R.N.S. 35, 8 C.C.C. (2d) 422 (H.C.); *Stevenson v. Saskatchewan (Minister of Justice)*, (June 8, 1987), (Q.B.), unreported [now reported (1987), 61 Sask. R. 91 (Q.B.)].

The uncontroverted expert evidence in this case is wholly inconsistent with such a conclusion. The Chief Justice characterizes that evidence as indicating that "the chances of such an occurrence taking place again are for all practical purposes nil" (at p. 322, poste).

Moreover the extent and continued validity of this common-law power has yet to be considered in light of the *Canadian Charter of Rights and Freedoms*. Restrictions on an individual's liberty can only be effected in accordance with principles of fundamental justice or must be justified under s. 1. This applies to deprivations of liberty following a criminal conviction as well as those effected in other circumstances.

Our criminal justice system is premised on the requirement that the Crown must prove all the elements of an offence in accordance with legal principles. Leaving aside the question of a lack of criminal responsibility on account of mental disorder, the failure to prove the guilt of the accused beyond a reasonable doubt in accordance with such principles will result in an acquittal. That is exactly what has happened in this case. The respondent has been acquitted in accordance with ordinary criminal law principles.

Turning to the common law power relied upon by the Chief Justice, I have grave doubts as to whether a power that can be exercised on the basis of "probable ground[s] to suspect future misbehaviour" without limits as to the type of "misbehaviour" or potential victims, would survive *Charter* scrutiny. If such a power allowed the imposition of restrictive conditions following an acquittal on the basis of a remote possibility of recurrence, it may well be contrary to s. 7.

Furthermore the potential implications of the course of action contemplated by the Chief Justice are significant not only for the respondent, but also in other cases. Consider an individual who is convicted of a violent crime at trial, but on appeal a stay is entered on the basis that his right to be tried within a reasonable time has been violated. Would the Court nonetheless impose restrictions on his liberty in an attempt to ensure that such an event does not recur? Such restrictions would be a significant departure from fundamental principles of criminal law, yet there is nothing in the authorities relied upon by the Chief Justice which limits the consideration of an order to keep the peace to cases such as the one at bar.

I note that there still exists the possibility of an information being laid pursuant to s. 810 of the *Criminal Code*. This, of course, is subject to the evidentiary basis required under that section, "that the informant has reasonable grounds for his fears" (s. 810(3)), and to constitutional challenge. If such a proceeding is to be initiated, it should not be done so by this Court acting *proprio motu*.

Finally I observe that the respondent cross-appealed on the ground that if this court were inclined to interfere with the decision of the Court of Appeal, a stay should be entered by reason of the violation of his rights under s. 11(*b*) of the *Charter*. If the respondent remains subject to the criminal justice system and potential restraints on his liberty, it would be necessary to deal with this cross-appeal.

McLACHLIN J.: —

. . . .

I share the Chief Justice's concern that notwithstanding the justice of an acquittal in this case and the evidence that a recurrence is highly unlikely, great care should be taken to avoid the possibility of a similar episode in the future. However, I also have concerns about the appropriateness of referring the matter back at this stage for a supervisory order in the circumstances of this case.

In addition to the difficult issues raised by an order restricting a person's liberty on account of an act for which he has been acquitted, I have concerns whether further proceedings are appropriate in the circumstances before us. Mr. Parks has been living in the shadow of these charges since May 24, 1987, over five years. His acquittal is now confirmed. We are told he has been making courageous efforts to re-establish his life. Should he now be embroiled in a further set of proceedings concerned, not with his guilt or innocence, but with the maintenance of his liberty?

Generally, the Courts do not grant remedies affecting the liberty of the subject unless they are asked to do so by the Crown, which is charged with instituting such legal processes as it deems appropriate having regard to the public interest and fairness to the individual involved. In the absence of an application by the Crown, I hesitate to remit the case for consideration of further measures against the accused.

I add that the possibility of supervisory orders in this situation may be a matter which Parliament would wish to consider in the near future.

LaForest J.: —

. . . .

To be effective, any order to keep the peace would have to be permanent. This would violate established practice (if not the law) regarding peace orders, which requires a defined period for the order; see *R. v. Edgar* (1913), 9 Cr. App. R. 13 (C.C.A.). Of course, the Courts could impose a succession of limited-term orders that would amount to a permanent injunction governing the respondent. However, even this course of action may not be feasible in light of concerns over enforcement of the orders, to which I now turn.

Generally, there are two mechanisms for the enforcement of a traditional order to keep the peace. First, any complainant who seeks an order will return to Court to complain of any breach of the peace. Thus the complainant acts as a watchdog much like the plaintiff in a civil injunction action. In the instant case, however, there is no "complainant" as such. Only the respondent's immediate family would have a vested interest in the order and an ability to monitor compliance with it, and it would be unrealistic to expect them to complain of any breach of the peace.

A second enforcement mechanism is the imposition of a bond with a guarantee from some third person. This is the standard procedure under the *Magistrate's Courts Act* 1952, c. 55, in England, where the Courts require a surety to guarantee the recognizance; see *Halsbury's Laws of England* 4th ed., vol. 29 (London: Butterworths, 1979, para. 444). The surety is entitled to complain to the Court if the principal has been or is about to be in breach of the conditions of the recognizance, and as such the surety becomes the Court's watchdog. Such an arrangement is feasible over a short term, as the cost of the surety can reasonably be imposed upon the accused. But with a permanent order, the costs of a life-long surety would be onerous, and it would be unreasonable to require the respondent to bear this cost.

It appears, then, that the judiciary is not practically equipped to administer a "keep the peace order" in the circumstances of this case. For this reason, along with the reasons of my colleagues, I would not remit this case back to the trial Judge for the consideration of such an order. I would accordingly dismiss the appeal and uphold the acquittal of the respondent.

R. v. STONE

[1999] 2 S.C.R. 290, 24 C.R. (5th) 1, 134 C.C.C. (3d) 353

The accused decided to visit his sons from a previous marriage. His current wife insisted on accompanying him and expressed her objections to the visit before and after the accused saw his sons for some 15 minutes. According to the accused his wife raised the issue of divorce, told him she had falsely reported to the police that he was abusing her and that they were ready to arrest him, that she would stay in the house and have him support her and their children, and that "she couldn't stand to listen to me whistle, that every time I touched her, she felt sick, that I was a lousy fuck and that I had a small penis and that she's never going to fuck me again". He testified he felt a "whoosh" sensation washing over him from his feet to his head. When his eyes focused again, he was staring straight ahead and felt something in his hand. He was holding a six-inch hunting knife. He looked over and saw his wife slumped over on the seat. She was dead. It was later established she had been stabbed 47 times. He put the body in his truck tool box, cleaned up, drove home, prepared a note for his stepdaughter, packed, checked into a hotel for a shower and shave, collected a debt, sold a car and flew to Mexico. While in Mexico, he awoke one morning to the sensation of having his throat cut. In trying to recall his dream, he remembered stabbing his wife twice in the chest before experiencing a "whooshing" sensation. On his return to Canada he surrendered to police and was charged with murder.

At his trial before judge and jury the accused admitted stabbing his wife. His defences were insane automatism, non-insane automatism, lack of intent, and alternatively, provocation. The trial judge found that there was evidence of unconsciousness throughout the commission of the crime but ruled the defence had laid a proper evidentiary foundation for insane but not non-insane automatism. Accordingly, he instructed the jury on insane automatism, intention in relation to second degree murder and provocation.

The accused was found guilty of manslaughter and sentenced to four years imprisonment. In imposing this sentence, the trial judge took into account the 18 month pre-trial period as the equivalent of three years imprisonment.

The Supreme Court accepted that this was a proper case for provocation to go to the jury and also dismissed the Crown Appeal against sentence. The 5-4 division in the Court came on the issue of whether sane automatism should have been left with the jury. Justice Bastarache determined that the judge had been correct in not putting the defence to the jury. The majority also decided to reverse the onus of proof. Bastarache J. also offered detailed guidance on how this burden can be discharged and how to distinguish cases of sane automatism from those of insanity which are subsumed by the defence of mental disorder under s. 16.

BINNIE J., dissenting (LAMER C.J., IACOBUCCI and MAJOR JJ. concurring): — A fundamental principle of the criminal law is that no act can be a criminal offence unless it is performed or omitted voluntarily. In this case the appellant acknowledges that he killed his wife. He stabbed her 47 times with his knife in a frenzy. His defence was that he lost consciousness when his mind snapped under the weight of verbal abuse which the defence psychiatrist characterized as "exceptionally cruel" and "psychologically sadistic". The trial judge ruled in favour of the appellant that "there is evidence of unconsciousness throughout the commission of the crime", and the British Columbia Court of Appeal agreed ((1997), 86 B.C.A.C. 169, at p. 173) that "a properly instructed jury, acting reasonably, could find some form of automatism".

The appellant had elected trial by jury. He says he was entitled to have the issue of voluntariness, thus properly raised, determined by the jury. He says that there was no proper legal basis for the courts in British Columbia to deprive him of the benefit of an evidentiary ruling which put in issue the Crown's ability to prove the *actus reus* of the offence.

The trial judge ruled that the evidence of involuntariness was only relevant (if at all) to a defence of not criminally responsible by reason of mental disorder (NCRMD). This was upheld by the Court of Appeal. When it is appreciated that all of the experts agreed the appellant did not suffer from any condition that medicine would classify as a disease of the mind, it is perhaps not surprising that the jury found the accused to be sane. He was convicted of manslaughter. The contention of the appellant that the act of killing, while not the product of a mentally disordered mind, was nevertheless involuntary, was never put to the jury.

The appellant argues that the judicial reasoning that effectively took the issue of voluntariness away from the jury violates the presumption of his innocence and his entitlement to the benefit of a jury trial guaranteed by s. 11(*d*) and (*f*) and is not saved by s. 1 of the Canadian *Charter of Rights and Freedoms*.

. . . .

In my view, it follows from the concurrent findings in the courts below (that the appellant successfully put in issue his consciousness at the time of the offence) that he was entitled to the jury's verdict on whether or not his conduct, though sane, was involuntary. That issue having been withdrawn from the jury, and the Crown thereby having been relieved of the one real challenge to its proof, the appellant is entitled to a new trial.

. . . .

(5) Conclusion on the Automatism Issue

In the result, I believe the appellant was entitled to have the plea of non-mental disorder automatism left to the jury in this case in light of the trial judge's evidentiary ruling that there was evidence the appellant was unconscious throughout the commission of the offence, for the following reasons.

Firstly, I do not accept the Crown's argument that a judge-made classification of situations into mental disorder automatism and non-mental disorder automatism can relieve the Crown of the obligation to prove all of the elements of the offence, including voluntariness. As stated, such an interpretation encounters strong objections under s. 7 and s. 11(*d*) of the *Charter*, and there has been no attempt in this case to provide a s. 1 justification.

Secondly, imposition of a persuasive burden of proof on the appellant to establish "involuntariness" on a balance of probabilities, in substitution for the present evidential burden, runs into the same *Charter* problems, and no attempt has been made in the record to justify it.

Thirdly, the "internal cause" theory, on which the Crown rested its argument, cannot be used to deprive the appellant of the benefit of the jury's consideration of the voluntariness of his action, once he had met the evidential onus, without risking a violation of s. 11(*f*) of the *Charter*. *Rabey*'s treatment of the internal cause theory has to be looked at in light of the decision of this Court in *Parks*, *supra*, which signalled some serious reservations about the usefulness of the "internal cause" theory, except as an "analytical tool". *Rabey*, as clarified in *Parks*, does not impose a presumption that a lack of voluntariness must be attributed to the existence of a mental disorder any time there is no identification of a convincing external cause. Once the appellant in this case had discharged his evidential onus, he was entitled to have the issue of voluntariness go to the jury.

Fourthly, it was wrong of the courts to require the appellant to substitute for his chosen defence of involuntariness the conceptually quite different plea of insanity. One of the few points of agreement between the defence and Crown experts at trial was that the appellant did not suffer from anything that could be described medically as a disease of the mind. He was either unconscious at the time of the killing or he was not telling the truth at the time of the trial. This was a question for the jury. The statutory inquiry into whether he was "suffering from a mental disorder" that rendered him "incapable of appreciating the nature and quality of the act or omission or of knowing that it was wrong" are qualitative questions that are not really responsive to his allegation that he was not conscious of having acted at all.

Finally, the evidence established that there *are* states of automatism where perfectly sane people lose conscious control over their actions. At that point, it was up to the jury, not the judge, to decide if the appellant had brought himself within the physical and mental condition thus identified. As Dickson C.J. observed in *Bernard, supra,* at p. 848, the jurors were "perfectly capable of sizing the matter up".

BASTARACHE J. (L'HEUREUX-DUBÉ, GONTHIER, CORY, and MCLACHLIN JJ. concurring): — The present case involves automatism, and more specifically, "psychological blow" automatism. The appellant claims that nothing more than his wife's words caused him to enter an automatistic state in which his actions, which include stabbing his wife 47 times, were involuntary. How can an accused demonstrate that mere words caused him to enter an automatistic state such that his actions were involuntary and thus do not attract criminal law sanction? This is the issue raised in this appeal.

. . . .

*Nature and Origin of the Burdens Applied in Cases Involving Claims of
Automatism*

This Court has stated on many occasions that it is a fundamental principle
of criminal law that only voluntary actions will attract findings of guilt.
[Citations omitted.]

In *Parks*, *supra*, La Forest J. classified automatism as a sub-set of the
voluntariness requirement, which he too recognized as part of the *actus reus*
component of criminal responsibility. I agree and would add that voluntariness,
rather than consciousness, is the key legal element of automatistic behaviour
since a defence of automatism amounts to a denial of the voluntariness
component of the *actus reus*.

The law presumes that people act voluntarily. Accordingly, since a defence
of automatism amounts to a claim that one's actions were not voluntary, the
accused must rebut the presumption of voluntariness. An evidentiary burden is
thereby imposed on the accused. The nature of this evidentiary burden stems
from the legal burden imposed in cases involving claims of automatism.
Generally, the legal burden in such cases has been on the Crown to prove
voluntariness, a component of the *actus reus*, beyond a reasonable doubt —
hence Dickson J.'s contention in *Rabey* that an accused claiming automatism
need only raise evidence sufficient to permit a properly instructed jury to find a
reasonable doubt as to voluntariness in order to rebut the presumption of
voluntariness. The Crown then has the legal burden of proving voluntariness
beyond a reasonable doubt to the trier of fact. If the Crown fails to satisfy this
burden, the accused will be acquitted.

. . . .

In her 1993 *Proposals to amend the Criminal Code (general principles)*,
the Minister of Justice recommended that the legal burden of proof in all cases
of automatism be on the party that raises the issue on a balance of probabilities.
This is the same legal burden that this Court applied to a claim of extreme
intoxication akin to a state of automatism in *Daviault, supra*. It is also the legal
burden Parliament assigned to the defence of mental disorder in s. 16 of the
Code, which, as mentioned above, is equally applicable to voluntary and
involuntary actions stemming from a disease of the mind and therefore applies
to mental disorder automatism. As I explained above, different legal approaches
to claims of automatism, whether based on the context in which the alleged
automatism arose or on the distinction between mental disorder and non-mental
disorder automatism, is problematic and should be avoided.

. . . .

An appropriate legal burden applicable to all cases involving claims of
automatism must reflect the policy concerns which surround claims of
automatism.

. . . .

The foregoing leads me to the conclusion that the legal burden in cases
involving claims of automatism must be on the defence to prove involuntariness

on a balance of probabilities to the trier of fact. This is the same burden supported by Lord Goddard, dissenting in *Hill v. Baxter*, [1958] 1 Q.B. 277, at pp. 282-83, and imposed in some American jurisdictions; see for example *State v. Caddell*, 215 S.E.2d 348 (N.C. 1975); *Fulcher v. State*, 633 P.2d 142 (Wyo. 1981); *Polston v. State*, 685 P.2d 1 (Wyo. 1984); *State v. Fields*, 376 S.E.2d 740 (N.C. 1989).

In *Chaulk* and *Daviault* this Court recognized that although placing a balance of probabilities burden on the defence with respect to an element of the offence constitutes a limitation of an accused person's rights under s. 11(*d*) of the *Charter*, it can be justified under s. 1. In my opinion, the burden is also justified in the present case. The law presumes that people act voluntarily in order to avoid placing the onerous burden of proving voluntariness beyond a reasonable doubt on the Crown. Like extreme drunkenness akin to automatism, genuine cases of automatism will be extremely rare. However, because automatism is easily feigned and all knowledge of its occurrence rests with the accused, putting a legal burden on the accused to prove involuntariness on a balance of probabilities is necessary to further the objective behind the presumption of voluntariness. In contrast, saddling the Crown with the legal burden of proving voluntariness beyond a reasonable doubt actually defeats the purpose of the presumption of voluntariness. Thus, requiring that an accused bear the legal burden of proving involuntariness on a balance of probabilities is justified under s. 1. There is therefore no violation of the Constitution.

. . . .

To sum up, in order to satisfy the evidentiary or proper foundation burden in cases involving claims of automatism, the defence must make an assertion of involuntariness and call expert psychiatric or psychological evidence confirming that assertion. However, it is an error of law to conclude that this defence burden has been satisfied simply because the defence has met these two requirements. The burden will only be met where the trial judge concludes that there is evidence upon which a properly instructed jury could find that the accused acted involuntarily on a balance of probabilities. In reaching this conclusion, the trial judge will first examine the psychiatric or psychological evidence and inquire into the foundation and nature of the expert opinion. The trial judge will also examine all other available evidence, if any. Relevant factors are not a closed category and may, by way of example, include: the severity of the triggering stimulus, corroborating evidence of bystanders, corroborating medical history of automatistic-like dissociative states, whether there is evidence of a motive for the crime, and whether the alleged trigger of the automatism is also the victim of the automatistic violence. I point out that no single factor is meant to be determinative. Indeed, there may be cases in which the psychiatric or psychological evidence goes beyond simply corroborating the accused's version of events, for example, where it establishes a documented history of automatistic-like dissociative states. Furthermore, the ever advancing state of medical knowledge may lead to a finding that other types of evidence are also indicative of involuntariness. I leave it to the discretion and experience of trial judges to weigh all of the evidence available on a case-by-case basis and to determine whether a properly instructed jury could find that the accused acted involuntarily on a balance of probabilities.

Step 2: Determining Whether to Leave Mental Disorder or Non-Mental Disorder Automatism with the Trier of Fact

. . . .

The determination of whether mental disorder or non-mental disorder automatism should be left with the trier of fact must be undertaken very carefully since it will have serious ramifications for both the individual accused and society in general. As mentioned above, mental disorder automatism is subsumed by the defence of mental disorder as set out in the *Code*. Accordingly, a successful defence of mental disorder automatism will result in a verdict of not criminally responsible on account of mental disorder as dictated by s. 672.34 of the *Code*. Under s. 672.54, an accused who receives this qualified acquittal may be discharged absolutely, discharged conditionally or detained in a hospital. In contrast, a successful defence of non-mental disorder automatism will always result in an absolute acquittal.

. . . .

Taken alone, the question of what mental conditions are included in the term disease of the mind is a question of law. However, the trial judge must also determine whether the condition the accused claims to have suffered from satisfies the legal test for disease of the mind. This involves an assessment of the particular evidence in the case rather than a general principle of law and is thus a question of mixed law and fact. See *Southam, supra*, at paras. 35 and 36. The question of whether the accused actually suffered from a disease of the mind is a question of fact to be determined by the trier of fact. See *Rabey* (S.C.C.), *supra*, at p. 519, *per* Ritchie J.; *Parks, supra*, at p. 897, *per* La Forest J.; and *Bratty, supra*, at p. 412, *per* Lord Denning.

In response to the above-mentioned proposed revisions to the *Code* regarding automatism, the Canadian Psychiatric Association submitted a Brief to the House of Commons Standing Committee on Justice and the Solicitor General. In this brief, the Association, on behalf of its 2,400 members nationwide, suggested that from a medical perspective, all automatism necessarily stems from mental disorder. Accordingly, the Association recommended that non-mental disorder automatism be eliminated and all claims of automatism be classified as mental disorders.

Since mental disorder is a legal term, the opinion of the Canadian Psychiatric Association, while relevant, is not determinative of whether two distinct forms of automatism, mental disorder and non-mental disorder, should continue to be recognized at law. In my opinion, this Court should not go so far as to eliminate the defence of non-mental disorder automatism as the Association suggests. However, I take judicial notice that it will only be in rare cases that automatism is not caused by mental disorder. Indeed, since the trial judge will have already concluded that there is evidence upon which a properly instructed jury could find that the accused acted involuntarily on a balance of probabilities, there is a serious question as to the existence of an operating mind by the time the disease of the mind issue is considered. The foregoing lends itself to a rule that trial judges start from the proposition that the condition the accused claims to have suffered from is a disease of the mind. They must then determine whether the evidence in the particular case takes the condition out of the disease of the mind category. This approach is consistent with this Court's decision in *Rabey, supra.*

Determining Whether the Conditions the Accused Claims to Have Suffered from is a Disease of the Mind

In *Parks*, La Forest J. recognized that there are two distinct approaches to the disease of the mind inquiry: the internal cause theory and the continuing danger theory. He recognized the internal cause theory as the dominant approach in Canadian jurisprudence but concluded, at p. 902, that this theory "is really meant to be used only as an analytical tool, and not as an all-encompassing methodology". This conclusion stemmed from a finding that somnambulism, the alleged trigger of the automatism in *Parks*, raises unique problems which are not well-suited to analysis under the internal cause theory. I agree that the internal cause theory cannot be regarded as a universal classificatory scheme for "disease of the mind". There will be cases in which the approach is not helpful because, in the words of La Forest J., at p. 903, "the dichotomy between internal and external causes becomes blurred". Accordingly, a new approach to the disease of the mind inquiry is in order. As I will explain below, a more holistic approach, like that developed by La Forest J. in *Parks*, must be available to trial judges in dealing with the disease of the mind question. This approach must be informed by the internal cause theory, the continuing danger theory and the policy concerns raised in this Court's decisions in *Rabey* and *Parks*.

[The Court then described the jurisprudence surrounding the Internal Cause Theory and the Continuing Danger Theory and concluded.]

(3) Other Policy Factors

There may be cases in which consideration of the internal cause and continuing danger factors alone does not permit a conclusive answer to the disease of the mind question. Such will be the case, for example, where the internal cause factor is not helpful because it is impossible to classify the alleged cause of the automatism as internal or external, and the continuing danger factor is inconclusive because there is no continuing danger of violence. Accordingly, a holistic approach to disease of the mind must also permit trial judges to consider other policy concerns which underlie this inquiry. As mentioned above, in *Rabey* and *Parks*, this Court outlined some of the policy concerns which surround automatism. I have already referred to those specific policy concerns earlier in these reasons. I repeat that I do not view those policy concerns as a closed category. In any given automatism case, a trial judge may identify a policy factor which this Court has not expressly recognized. Any such valid policy concern can be considered by the trial judge in order to determine whether the condition the accused claims to have suffered from is a disease of the mind. In determining this issue, policy concerns assist trial judges in answering the fundamental question of mixed law and fact which is at the centre of the disease of the mind inquiry: whether society requires protection from the accused and, consequently, whether the accused should be subject to evaluation under the regime contained in Part XX.1 of the *Code*.

Application to the Present Case

                    . . . .

Turning to the disease of the mind stage of the automatism analysis, I note that the evidence in this case raised *only one alleged cause* of automatism, Donna Stone's words. Based on this evidence, the trial judge found that only mental disorder automatism should be left with the jury. This conclusion was based primarily on a finding that the present case is indistinguishable from *MacLeod*, *supra*. Such reliance on precedent fails to reveal what effect, if any, the internal cause factor, the continuing danger factor and other policy factors had on the decision to leave only mental disorder automatism with the jury. This is not in accordance with the holistic approach to the disease of the mind question set out in these reasons. However, the internal cause factor and the continuing danger factor, as well as the other policy factors set out in this Court's decisions in *Rabey* and *Parks* all support the trial judge's finding that the condition the appellant alleges to have suffered from is a disease of the mind in the legal sense. In particular, the trigger in this case was not, in the words of Martin J.A. quoted in this Court's decision in *Rabey*, at p. 520, "extraordinary external events" that would amount to an extreme shock or psychological blow that would cause a normal person, in the circumstances of the accused, to suffer a dissociation in the absence of a disease of the mind. Accordingly, I find that the trial judge nevertheless reached the correct result on the disease of the mind question. As previously noted, in such a case, only mental disorder automatism must be put to the jury. There is no reason to go beyond the facts of this case in applying the rules discussed above.

In the end, I must conclude that no substantial wrong or miscarriage of justice occurred in the present case.

It is usually regarded as a wise proposition that a judge should not pronounce on matters that were not in issue between the parties and accordingly were not argued. Should the Court have considered reversing the onus of proof although the Crown and no intervenor addressed the issue? Are you satisfied with the majority's authority and justification of a presumption of voluntariness and requiring the accused to prove sane automatism on a balance of probabilities? What are the onus implications

for other defences such as intoxication and self-defence? Wasn't the presumption of innocence under s. 11(*d*) implicated? What of *Laba* concerning s. 1 justification? The Court in *Laba* held that an evidentiary burden should be considered before justifying a persuasive burden for an accused. See critical comments by Delisle, "Stone: Judicial Activism Gone Awry to Presume Guilt" (1999), 24 C.R. (5th) 91; David Paciocco, "Death by Stone-ing: The Demise of the Defence of Simple Automatism" (1999), 24 C.R. (5th) 273 and "Editorial, Rewriting Automatism" (1999), 4 Can. Crim. L.R. 119.

Premenstrual Syndrome

On December 16, 1980, a 36 year-old English woman ended a love affair by deliberately running down her lover with her car and killing him. At trial she pled guilty to manslaughter because of diminished responsibility. She was discharged from custody and had her driver's licence revoked for one year. In a separate decision decided one day earlier, Sandie Smith, an East London barmaid, was placed on probation for carrying a knife and threatening to kill a policeman, though she was already on probation for having stabbed a fellow barmaid to death. In both of these cases the English Courts found that the defendants were suffering from premenstrual syndrome (PMS), and as a result recognized PMS as a mitigating factor in sentencing these women. "Criminal Law: Premenstrual Syndrome in the Courts?" (1984), 24 Washburn Law Journal 54-77.

PMS can be defined as "The recurrence of symptoms in the premenstruum with complete absence of symptoms in the postmenstruum". Symptoms of PMS occur in the same phase of the cycle each month: Irritability, anxiety, tension, depression, hostility, decreased self-esteem, indecision, mood swings, impulsive behaviour, difficulty concentrating, social isolation, etc. The symptoms range from mild inconvenience to complete, although temporary, debilitation.

In most instances a woman with PMS understands her actions and the consequences but is simply powerless to control those actions.

Could PMS be a defence under existing Canadian law? Should it be a defence?

See, further, E. Meehan and K. MacRae, "Legal Implications of Premenstrual Syndrome: A Canadian Perspective" (1986), 133 C.M.A.J. 601 and a reply by Dr. Robinson in (1986), 135 C.M.A.J. 1340 ("the association between PMS and violent, impulsive or criminal acts is by no means firmly established").

R. v. REVELLE

(1979), 48 C.C.C. (2d) 267 (Ont. C.A.)

MARTIN J.A.: — The Attorney-General of Ontario, pursuant to s. 605(l)(*a*) of the *Code*, appeals from the acquittal of the respondent following a trial by jury on an indictment containing three counts as follows:

COUNT #1: that he the said Cameron Frederick REVELLE on or about the 17th day of February, in the year 1978, at the City of Kingston, in the County of Frontenac, unlawfully did attempt to rob Stephen Amey of a sum of money, his property, and did thereby commit an indictable offence, contrary to s. 42(a) of the *Criminal Code*.

COUNT #2: AND FURTHER THAT at the time and place aforesaid he the said Cameron Frederick REVELLE unlawfully did use a firearm while attempting to commit an indictable offence and did thereby commit an indictable offence, contrary to s. 83(l)(a) of the *Criminal Code*.

COUNT #3: AND FURTHER THAT at the time and place aforesaid he the said Cameron Frederick REVELLE did without lawful excuse point a firearm at one Samuel Smith and did thereby commit an indictable offence, contrary to s. 84(1)(a) of the *Criminal Code*.

The principal defence advanced on behalf of the respondent was non-insane automatism, although the defences of drunkenness and insanity arose from the evidence, and the trial Judge left all three defences with the jury.

The Attorney-General appeals from the acquittal on the ground of law that the learned trial Judge erred in leaving the defence of non-insane automatism to the jury and, alternatively, on the ground that if there was evidence proper to be submitted to the jury on the defence of non-insane automatism, the learned trial Judge erred in his charge to the jury.

In view of the conclusion which we have reached that there was no evidence of non-insane automatism proper to be left with the jury, it is unnecessary to consider separately the second ground of appeal. Since we have concluded that there must be a new trial, we will refer to the facts only in sufficient detail to enable the grounds of our decision to be understood.

Briefly stated the facts are these. Shortly after two o'clock on the afternoon of February 17, 1978, the respondent wearing a nylon balaclava, a yellow construction "hard hat", and carrying a sawed-off shot-gun entered the home of Mr. and Mrs. Stephen Amey and demanded that Mr. Amey give him $10,000. Mrs. Amey, when she saw the respondent downstairs, locked herself in the bathroom, broke a window and attracted the attention of a neighbour who summoned the police. Four police officers arrived. Two of the officers entered the front door; they saw the respondent coming down the staircase carrying a shot-gun. The officers requested the respondent to drop the gun and the respondent pointed the gun at the officers. Both officers fired shots which struck the respondent. He was also struck by bullets fired by the other two officers who had entered through the rear portion of the house.

The shot-gun did not have a shell in the firing chamber, although there were two shells in the magazine. The respondent subsequently asked why the police had shot him because he had not intended to hurt anyone. He was taken to the hospital where a blood sample was taken shortly after three o'clock in the afternoon. The sample showed that his blood-alcohol level was 260 mg. of alcohol in 100 ml. of blood, a very high concentration. The medical evidence was that at that level a person is moving toward unconsciousness.

The respondent gave evidence on his own behalf. His wife had died of leukaemia on December 7, 1977. After her death, the respondent went on a protracted drinking bout which culminated in his contracting pneumonia and being removed to the hospital. He was subsequently transferred to the psychiatric ward of the hospital suffering from a depressive neurosis. Doctor Jarrett who attended the respondent treated him for alcoholism and the depressive neurosis. He also found objective evidence of a memory disturbance that he considered to be a result of a disease of the brain.

The respondent discharged himself from the psychiatric ward of the hospital on February 16th, and thereafter commenced to drink again. He testified that he was able to remember very little of what occurred after he began to drink on February 16th and remembered nothing of the events which gave rise to the charge. He had no recollection of going to the home of Mr. and Mrs, Amey nor of being shot and taken to the hospital. He testified that he could neither identify nor recall anything about the shot-gun and the nylon balaclava or the yellow construction hard hat. The respondent testified that when he was nine years old, he had fallen from a height to the ground and fractured his skull. He was discharged from the army for medical reasons related to episodes of loss of memory.

Doctor Stevens, a psychiatrist of eminent qualifications, examined the respondent on four occasions during a period of two and one-half weeks immediately prior to the trial. In answer to a hypothetical question, Dr. Stevens expressed the opinion that the respondent was in a state of automatism during the events which gave rise to the charge. It was also the opinion of Dr. Stevens that the respondent suffered from brain damage.

Doctor Stevens was of the view that the dissociative state in which the respondent was at the time of the events in question was the result of a combination of the following factors:

1) the predisposiition in the Respondent to automatic behaviour resulting from brain damage;
2) the consumption of alcohol which tends to release automatic behavior in brain damaged people;
3) the grief reaction that he was experiencing as a result of his wife's death;
4) his poor state of physical health, and
5) his deep-seated hostility and anger.

It is clear from the evidence of Dr. Stevens that the dissociative state would not have occurred but for the brain damage. It is also clear from his evidence that no one of the five enumerated facts would have produced the dissociative state, but that it resulted from a combination of all five factors.

The evidence in this case presented a question of great difficulty. The learned trial Judge quite properly left with the jury the defence of insanity and the defence of drunkenness. We are, however, with deference, of the view that he erred in leaving with the jury the defence of non-insane automatism. There was in this case evidence upon which it was open to the jury to find that the respondent at the time of the conduct in question was in a dissociative state in which his acts were unconscious and involuntary due to a combination of the five factors mentioned by Dr. Stevens. It is also clear on the evidence, that the dissociative state would not have been produced by the other factors but for the brain damage from which the respondent suffered.

In our view, in the circumstances, the dissociative state, if found to exist, was a disease of the mind, and the defence of non-insane automatism was not open to the respondent. We take it to be established that a malfunctioning of the mind produced solely by brain damage of a pathological nature as distinct, for example, from a transient state caused by a blow on the head resulting in concussion is a disease of the mind. We are of the view that if the brain damage as described by Dr. Stevens contributed to the dissociated state said to exist, the resulting automatism was insane automatism, notwithstanding that other factors, including drunkenness, contributed to the respondent's condition. It is well established that if automatism is produced solely by drunkenness only the defence of drunkenness, which is limited to crimes of specific intent, need be left to the jury. It would be surprising if automatism produced solely by pathological brain damage leads to a verdict of not guilty by reason of insanity, and a state of automatism resulting solely from intoxication leads only to the limited defence of drunkenness but that a combination of the two factors could lead to a complete defence of non-insane automatism. Such a result would be illogical. The other contributing factors present here do not alter the situation; the defence of non-insane automatism was not open to the respondent on the facts of this case.

We do not wish to be taken, however, as holding that where an accused is suffering from a disease of the mind that the defence of non-insane automatism can never arise. By way of example only, a person suffering from a disease of the mind might as a result of a blow on the head resulting in concussion go into an automatic state. If the jury were left in a state of doubt whether the blow on the head, as distinct from the disease of the mind, resulted in the automatism, the jury would be entitled to return a verdict of acquittal based on non-insane automatism. That is not this case. Whether there is; any evidence of an external factor of a kind capable of producing non-insane automatism is a question for the Judge, but there was no evidence in this case of such an external factor. If there had been evidence of such an external factor, the trial Judge should have specified it for the jury and not as in this case have left it to them to see if there was such an external factor.

Consequently, we are of the view that the trial Judge should have instructed the jury that if they were satisfied on a balance of probabilities that the respondent was in a dissociative state as a result of the factors enumerated by Dr. Stevens, this was a disease of the mind and if it rendered the respondent incapable of appreciating the nature and quality of his act or of knowing that it was wrong, they should return a verdict of not guilty on account of insanity in respect of all three counts.

On the other hand, if they were not so satisfied they should consider the defence of drunkenness and if they entertained a reasonable doubt whether the accused by reason of drunkenness and the other facts, including the accused's vulnerability to alcohol by reason of brain damage, lacked the specific intent required to constitute the offences charged in counts 1 and 2, they should find him not guilty on those counts, but that drunkenness, as the trial Judge pointed out in his charge to the jury, was not a defence to count 3 which does not require a specific intent.

. . . .

For these reasons, the appeal must be allowed. The verdict of acquittal set aside and a new trial ordered.

Appeal allowed; new trial ordered.

This judgment was adopted on further appeal: (1981), 21 C.R. (3d) 161 (S.C.C.). *Revelle* was, however, reversed by a majority of the Supreme Court in *Daviault*, considered in the next section on Intoxication, on the basis that it did not meet fundamental *Charter* standards of voluntariness. Ignoring the *Charter* issue, what principle did *Revelle* stand for and do you agree with the result?

R. v. McDOWELL

(1980), 52 C.C.C. (2d) 298 (Ont. C.A.)

MARTIN J.A.: — This is an appeal by the Crown from the acquittal of the respondent on a charge of dangerous driving after a trial at Ottawa, before His Honour Judge Smith, sitting without a jury.

It was conceded by defence counsel at the trial, and also by counsel for the respondent on the appeal that, objectively viewed, the driving in question constituted dangerous driving and the only element in dispute is the requisite mental element. The facts are not in dispute.

The circumstances out of which the charge arose are, to say the least, unusual. At the time of the occurrence giving rise to the charge, the respondent was a member of the Ottawa police force with eight years of service. He was a married man, said to be a quiet person and well respected by his fellow officers.

In 1974, he had, while on duty, sustained a serious injury to his right elbow, permanently damaging a nerve. He had been under the care of several physicians and at the time of the occurrence in question, he was under medication.

On August 12, 1978, he was on duty on the midnight shift commencing at 11:15 p.m. He was observed in the constable's lounge during his lunch hour at approximately 3:30 a.m. on August 13th, sleeping as was normal practice on one of the couches. At approximately 4:00 a.m., while on duty in a police cruiser, the respondent picked up two young girls and drove them to the Bayshore Apartment in the west end of the City of Ottawa where a friend of one of the girls, Chris Small, lived. He asked the girls to get him a "beer". One of the girls went to Small's apartment, got a bottle of beer and brought it down to the respondent, who drank it in the cruiser. The respondent, accompanied by the two girls and Small, drove around in the cruiser, returned and went up to the apartment where he had another bottle of beer. The respondent consumed altogether four bottles of beer in the cruiser and had another bottle of beer in the apartment. He entered his cruiser again and drove at a high rate of speed to a service station. At approximately 6:25 a.m., as the respondent approached the Bayshore Apartments he noticed several police officers and a security guard. Upon seeing the police, the respondent did not stop his car but drove away at a high rate of speed. He was followed by a number of police cruisers. During the course of the chase the respondent drove at speeds as high as a 100 m.p.h. or more, failing to stop at stop signs and on occasion momentarily losing control of the vehicle. The respondent finally stopped when his car crashed into two police cruisers, which had been set up as a road-block. When the respondent emerged from his cruiser he was dishevelled, angry and behaving in an irrational manner. He appeared disoriented and did not recognize constables whom he had known for a considerable period of time. He appeared upset that cars had been following him. He was unsteady and reluctant to get into the police cruiser. At the police station he moved from periods of excitement to periods of calm. His fellow officers testified that his behaviour was completely out of character. There was an odour of alcohol on the respondent's breath. He ultimately submitted to a breathalyzer test which disclosed a blood alcohol level of 100 mg. of alcohol in a 100 ml. of blood. He was also submitted to certain physical tests, and the officer conducting the tests concluded that the effect of alcohol on the respondent was slight. No charge relating to the consumption of alcohol was laid because of a general policy not to lay such a charge where the blood-alcohol level was less than 110 mg. of alcohol to 100 ml. of blood and the physical tests were good.

The respondent testified in his own defence. He stated, as previously indicated, that he had sustained an injury in March, 1974, to the ulnar nerve in his right elbow. He suffered considerable pain as a result of the injury; he had seen a number of physicians with respect to the pain, and medication was prescribed. In August of 1978, he was taking 30 mg. of Daimane or sleeping tablets, 10 mg. of Valium for his arm, and 222's which contain codeine. After July, the pain was such that it was affecting the respondent's sleep and he was only getting approximately two hours of sleep each day. The respondent testified that on August 12th, he took one Dalmane tablet of 30 mg. at 8:30 a.m. At approximately 1:00 p.m. he took another 30 mg. tablet of Dalmane. Later that day the respondent took three Valium tablets between 7:00 and 8:00 p.m., explaining at trial that his normal Valium dosage would be two tablets, but he had injured his arm the day before. He said that between 5:00 and 8:00 p.m. he had three drinks of vodka and "coke" at his brother's home. Each drink was approximately one and one-half ounces and he noticed no effects from the consumption of alcohol. At approximately 8:30 in the evening he visited an acquaintance and had some coffee. He said that he remembered playing bridge until approximately 9:30 p.m. and had no memory of events after 9:30 on the evening of August 12th. His next recollection was being at the Civic Hospital in Ottawa on August 13, 1978, the day on which these events occurred. The respondent also testified that he had previously never experienced a loss of memory and that he had never had any problems with alcohol. He also said that he had mixed alcohol and medication prior to this date without any problems occurring. There was also evidence that at this time the respondent was suffering from emotional distress because a friend had recently died of cancer.

Doctor Selwyn Smith, the psychiatrist in chief at the Royal Ottawa Hospital, was called as a witness for the defence. He testified that Valium is a mild tranquillizer and muscle relaxant and can relieve tension and agitation associated with pain. Dalmane is a hypnotic. The respondent's usual dosage was one or two Valium tablets with one or two Dalmane tablets. Dr. Smith examined the respondent on August 24, 1978. The doctor testified that the respondent's abnormal mental state, on the morning of August 13, 1978, was caused by the following factors:

(1) the traumatic injury several years before to the right elbow, which had recently become exacerbated by blows;
(2) the medication in addition to the alcohol which in his opinion was not excessive, and
(3) the distress associated with the friend's death.

He testified that these factors were a unique combination never before experienced by the respondent. He was of the opinion that these factors, superimposed upon the exhaustion which had been building up in the respondent, accounted for his abnormal behaviour on the morning of August 13, 1978. He was also of the opinion that the respondent was psychiatrically normal and did not suffer from any organic injury which could have caused him to be in the abnormal state, other than the above factors in combination. Dr. Smith was of the opinion that the respondent at the time of the occurrence was incapable of being aware or attentive except for fleeting seconds. His perception would be diminished. He would be indifferent to any factor that required intelligent or rational thought. Dr. Smith also testified that if any one of the enumerated factors were removed, the state of mind or condition would not likely have occurred. The doctor testified that the respondent, at the time these events occurred, was in a "toxic confusional state". He testified, however, that the respondent was not in a state of automatism and that his actions in driving the car would be voluntary. He further testified that the organic effect of the respondent's consumption of alcohol and drugs was to precipitate his confusional state.

Thus, while the respondent was in a state akin to automatism during the chase by the police, the alcohol and drugs which the respondent had consumed between 5:00 p.m. and 8:00 p.m. was a factor contributing to the toxic confusional state.

The learned trial Judge after, if I may be permitted to say so, a most able analysis of the law and the facts, held that dangerous driving was a crime of general intent and self-induced intoxication was not a defence. He further held, that the respondent, at the time of the consumption of the beer around 4:00 a.m., did not know what he was doing, or the trial Judge entertained a reasonable doubt on that issue. In other words, the consumption of the beer in the early hours of the morning of August 13th, occurred at a time when the accused was not conscious of his acts. However, the learned trial Judge quite rightly, in our view, held that the crucial question was whether the voluntary consumption of alcohol and drugs by the respondent between 5:00 p.m. and 8:00 p.m. on the evening of August 12th, in the circumstances supplied the necessary fault essential to constitute the offence of dangerous driving. The learned trial Judge, after concluding that the respondent was not in his normal mental state when he picked up the girls and drank the beer, said:

> Even that does not end the matter. We are dealing in this instance with an individual accused, on medication for a considerable period of time, of a very significant or strong dosage, freely indulging in the consumption of alcohol albeit holding it to a definite limit when about to go on duty, and an obviously tense individual unable to sleep and suffering great pain. He certainly should not have been driving a car, any car, let alone a police cruiser and on duty and unaccompanied by another officer at that. To do so was to invite foreseeable trouble of some nature although not necessarily the tragic version now known to us.
>
> I have really agonized over this question of whether this realization and foresight during the hours that preceded his start of duty on August 12, 1978, at 11:15 p.m., this kind of realization and foresight, as I say, which I attribute to the accused qualifies as criminal intent in the absence of any previous symptoms or signs over many months and years even of mixing medical drugs with alcohol. Can it be said that the accused showed the kind of indifference or recklessness sufficient to fasten criminal liability upon him? I do think his actions were careless, foolish, but I am unable to bring myself to characterizing these actions as reckless within the meaning of the second basis that I have already referred to for attracting the consequence of criminal sanctions. They surely come dangerously close. The circumstances here were serious and tragic, and on the surface appear to cry out for a finding of fault on the part of the accused, but it is precisely in those cases or in that kind of case, I think, that ultimate care must be taken to apply the criminal law dispassionately in accordance with recognized principles. Justice surely demands nothing less.

We are, with the greatest deference to the learned trial Judge, of the view that he erred in holding that notwithstanding the respondent should have foreseen that the consumption of alcohol and drugs in combination might cause trouble, the necessary fault was not present. It is clear from the learned trial Judge's reasons that he was of the view that unless the respondent was reckless in his consumption of alcohol and drugs the necessary fault was lacking. In our view, if the respondent either foresaw or *should have foreseen* that the combination of alcohol and drugs consumed prior to 8:00 p.m. might impair his ability to drive a motor vehicle, the fault required to constitute the offence was present.

In the case of *R. v. King* (1962), 133 C.C.C. 1, [1962] S.C.R. 746, the accused had been injected with sodium pentothal, a quick acting anesthetic, when having some teeth extracted. Although there was evidence that the accused had been warned not to drive his motor vehicle until his head cleared, he testified that he did not hear this warning. He drove his car, became unconscious and was involved in an accident. He was charged with impaired driving under s. 223 (now s. 234) of the *Code*. The Supreme Court of Canada affirmed the majority judgment of the Ontario Court of Appeal (129 C.C.C. 391) holding that the accused in those circumstances was free from fault. Ritchie J., delivering the judgment of himself and Martland J., said at p. 763:

The existence of *mens rea* as an essential ingredient of an offence and the method of proving the existence of that ingredient are two different things, and I am of opinion that when it has been proved that a driver was driving a motor vehicle while his ability to do so was impaired by alcohol or a drug, then a rebuttable presumption arises that his condition was voluntarily induced and that he is guilty of the offence created by s. 223 and must be convicted unless other evidence is adduced which raises a reasonable doubt as to whether he was, through no fault of his own, disabled when he undertook to drive and drove, from being able to appreciate and know that he was or might become impaired.

If the driver's lack of appreciation when he undertook to drive was induced by voluntary consumption of alcohol or of a drug *which he knew or had any reasonable ground for believing* might cause him to be impaired, then he cannot, of course, avoid the consequences of the impairment which results by saying that he did not intend to get into such a condition, but if the impairment has been brought about without any act of his own will, then, in my view, the offence created by s. 223 cannot be said to have been committed. (Emphasis supplied.)

He further said at p. 764:

It seems to me that it can be taken as a matter of "common experience" that the consumption of alcohol may produce intoxication and, therefore, "impairment" in the sense in which that word is used in s. 223, and I think it is also to be similarly taken to be known that the use of narcotics may have the same effect, but if it appears that the impairment was produced as a result of using a drug in the form of medicine on a doctor's order or recommendation and that its effect was unknown to the patient, then the presumption is, in my view, rebutted.

In *R. v. Saxon*, 22 C.C.C. (2d) 370 at p. 375, Prowse J.A., delivering the judgment of the Alberta Supreme Court, Appellate Division, quoted with approval, the following passage from Professor Colin Howard's well-known work *Strict Responsibility* (1963), in which the author states (p. 203):

"Intoxication may perfectly well be regarded as voluntary even if it is not strictly intentional, as if a man over-estimates his own capacity for withstanding the effects of alcohol. All that is required for a case of voluntary intoxication to arise is that through drinking D place himself in a position where his faculties are materially, although not necessarily drastically, affected by alcohol. Since this is likely to happen at an early stage, the only practical case of involuntary intoxication is if a harmless drink is surreptitiously replaced by an intoxicant which the unsuspecting defendant takes."

Mr. Justice Prowse further said at pp. 375-6:

In my view, the learned trial Judge misconstrued the law as set out in the *King* case and consequently failed to view the evidence of the accused's knowledge before he commenced drinking in the light of what a reasonable person would have appreciated might occur if he consumed tranquillizers and alcohol. In my view, had he done so, he would have reached the conclusion that the accused was guilty as there is no evidence upon which, when the proper test is applied, he could have based a reasonable doubt.

On the facts not in dispute and the findings implicit in the reasons of the trial Judge, the voluntary cconsumption of alcohol and drugs on the early evening of August 12th contributed to the abnormal state in which the respondent was when the events occurred which gave rise to the charge. The necessary fault is to be found in the consumption of alcohol and drugs under circumstances in which he knew or ought to have known that his ability might thereby be impaired. We think, with deference, that the learned trial Judge applied the wrong test in holding that recklessness was necessary in order to provide the necessary element of fault.

For these reasons the appeal is allowed, the acquittal is set aside, and a verdict of guilty is entered. In the highly unusual circumstances of this case we are satisfied that it is in the best interests of the respondent and not contrary to the public interest to direct that the respondent be discharged absolutely. This, therefore, is the disposition which we direct, a disposition which counsel for the Attorney-General does not oppose.

Appeal allowed.

Problem

1. The accused is charged with second degree murder. The victim, who was known to be gay, died from 79 knife wounds, including a cut throat. The accused stated to the police that he had had a few drinks with the victim, felt sick and laid down on a bed. He woke up suddenly and saw the victim naked, standing near him. He ran to the kitchen, grabbed the knife, killed the victim and simulated a theft. The accused's defence was that he was in a state of automatism caused by psychological shock. As a trial Judge, rule as to the whether the defence of automatism should be left with the jury. Compare *Fournier v. R.* (1982), 30 C.R. (3d) 346, 70 C.C.C. (2d) 351 (Que. C.A.).

Problem

2. The accused is charged with the attempted murder of a police officer. He sat astride the officer who was lying on the sidewalk, and choked him with his hands. The police officer was rescued by a bystander, who struck the accused three times on the head before rendering him unconscious. The altercation between the accused and the officer had occurred when a car driven by the accused's brother, in which the accused was the passenger, had been stopped and the accused's brother arrested for impaired driving. The police evidence was that the accused had started the fight by karate-kicking the police officer in the chest. The defence was that, after some verbal abuse and physical resistance by the accused, the police officer had struck him in the face and the accused had no further recollection until he woke up in the hospital. An independent eye-witness testified that the police officer had struck the accused forcefully in the face. Should the defence of automatism succeed? Compare *R. v. Bartlett* (1983), 33 C.R. (3d) 247, 5 C.C.C. (3d) 321 (Ont. H.C.).

Problem

3. The accused was charged with aggravated assault upon her 7-year-old child. The defence introduced expert evidence to suggest that the accused may, as a result of depression, have suffered from intermittent explosive disorder, which may result in a dissociative state. The Crown expert testified to the contrary, citing the fact that the accused had some memory of the incident and the attack had purposive elements. Should the defence of sane automatism succeed? Compare *R. v. Bergamin* (1996), 3 C.R. (5th) 140, 111 C.C.C. (3d) 550 (Alta. C.A.).

Problem

4. The accused is charged with attempted murder of H contrary to s. 239 of the *Criminal Code* and assaulting H with a weapon contrary to s. 267(a). The accused visited H, a friend, one morning. He pulled a knife out of a drawer and stabbed H repeatedly. In the struggle he also stabbed H with a screwdriver. The testimony of the victim was that the accused was not intoxicated but was not himself, looked totally blank and was in a robotic state. After the stabbing the accused stole a vehicle and was involved in an accident. A defence forensic psychiatrist testified that the accused was in a dissociated state. The accused is a heroin addict. There was no apparent motive for the attack. He testified that he was suffering from depression and acute pain from heroin withdrawal. On the day in question the accused consumed approximately 52 Clonidine pills and 20 Imovane pills, mind altering drugs which in sufficient quantity may produce disorders together with hallucinations. There was no evidence that the accused received any warnings about this medication, either via the containers or the doctor. The drugs had been prescribed for his addiction. As trial judge you are not satisfied the accused consumed any heroin that day. The defence was automatism. Give judgment. Compare *R. v. Vickberg* (1998), 16 C.R. (5th) 164 (B.C. S.C.).

Intoxication

S.M. BECK AND G.E. PARKER, THE INTOXICATED OFFENDER —
A PROBLEM OF RESPONSIBILITY

(1966), 44 Can. Bar Rev. 563 at 570-573

What happens when an individual becomes intoxicated? The rather surprising answer, in view of the social and scientific interest in the problem, is that, in behavioural terms, we do not yet know with any degree of precision. An analysis of the experimental literature in 1940 evoked the following comment:

> In view of the psychiatric as well as lay interest in the effect of alcohol on these aspects [changes in volition, emotion and personality] of the individual, it is surprising how little attention they have received from experimental psychologists.

Another review in 1962 indicated little change:

> A review of the psychological literature since 1940 suggests that little progress has been made in developing a knowledge of how and in what way alcohol affects behaviour. It appears that a reformulation of the concepts that guide thinking about the action of alcohol in all areas is needed. Except in a few areas . . . , little creative effort appears to have been spent in research on the effect of alcohol on human behaviour. The exploratory experiment to find out what alcohol does, rather than to confirm some hypothesis, is rare.

It would be easy to conclude that because experimental psychology has so far told us little about the effects of alcohol on behaviour, the criminal law would not be justified in altering the criteria of responsibility. Medical science does know, in broad terms, what effects alcohol has on the individual, and this knowledge might well justify a change in the degree of responsibility attributed to the intoxicated offender.

It is certain that intoxication impairs perception, judgment and muscular coordination. Along with this impairment goes an increase in self-confidence, a lessening of inhibitions, and a release of sexual and aggressive impulses. The fact that an individual's repressed instincts may break through and manifest themselves in overt acts during intoxication has led some commentators to the incorrect conclusion that drunken offenders intend their acts in the same manner as do sober men. Their argument is as follows: all men have repressed desires — repressed intents — which they usally manage to control. The drunk is freed from his inhibitions and acts out these desires. His intent while drunk is thus his real intent and his acts are as purposive, or end-directed, as those of a sober man.

Psychoanalysts tell us, however, that people have repressed instincts, sexual and aggressive, not intents. Intents refer to cognitive functions. Alcohol brings about a diminution of the repressive mechanisms, allowing the instinctual to occur in behaviour. These repressive mechanisms are of emotional, not intellectual, origin. In simple terms, the emotional brakes which act as the restraint in all of us are released, and inhibited or self-controlled desires are converted into action. Striking confirmation of this effect of alcohol is provided by a recently published study of the sex offender by the Institute for Sex

Research at Indiana University. The study, the most extensive of its kind ever undertaken, is a statistical analysis of interviews with 1,356 men convicted of rape, homosexuality, offences against children and a variety of other sexual crimes. The report shows that 67 percent of the men who threatened or used force on little girls were intoxicated at the time of their offences, as were 40 percent of the rapists whose victims were over 15. The report states that ". . . in very few cases does intoxication seem to do more than simply release pre-existing desires".

The same argument about "real" intent can be made in regard to the actions of a psychotic. Suppose the case of a person who, acting under the delusion that he has been commanded by God to make a sacrifice, kills his child. Certainly it could not be said that such a person's action was not purposive. In fact such a person might realize that ordinary people regard his act as wrong. Consequently he could be held responsible on a strict application of the M'Naghten rules. He would probably be declared insane, however, as most juries are not hindered by the rigidity of the rules when evidence of disease of the mind is so great. Few, if any, would object to that verdict as it would be clear that the offender had lost his power of self-control; that he was incapable of appreciating the moral quality of his act; and that he was incapable of exercising any, rational judgment in the matter.

But an acutely intoxicated person has also lost his power of self-control; his ability to make judgments is impaired, and he might be quite incapable of foreseeing the consequences of his acts.

> This effect of alcohol in depressing the inhibitory centres of the brain is of considerable medico-legal importance. It may lead to a failure to realize that a contemplated act is fraught with danger to oneself or others, or even if the possibility of danger be realized it may result in recklessness, that is, disregard of risk.

Indeed, the language of the report of the Royal Commission on the Law of Insanity in delineating the important differences between the wording of the M'Naghten rules and s. 16 of the *Canadian Criminal Code*, points up the similarity between the state of mind of a person who falls within the ambit of s. 16 and that of one who is acutely intoxicated.

Section 16 speaks of being "incapable of appreciating the nature and quality of an act". The M'Nalghten rules say "as not to know the nature and quality of the act he was doing". The Commissioners concluded that:

> there is an important distinction to be drawn under Canadian law between a mental capacity, whether caused by drunkenness or disease of the mind, to "know" what is being done and a mental capacity to "foresee and measure the consequences of the act".
>
> The true test necessarily is, was the accused person at the very time of the offence . . . by reason of disease of the mind, unable fully to appreciate not only the nature of the act but the natural consequences that would flow from it? In other words, was the accused person, by reason of disease of the mind, deprived of the mental capacity to foresee and measure the consequences of the act?

Medical science clearly indicates that one who is acutely intoxicated might also fit within the above test, with the exception, of course, that his incapacity is not due to a disease of the mind (unless the individual is suffering from delirium tremens which is an alcoholic psychosis). The issue then comes back to voluntariness, for the truth is that the acutely intoxicated offender may have no more appreciation of the nature of an act and its consequences than the psychotic offender who may be excused from responsibility under s. 16(2) of the *Criminal Code*. Society, however, refuses to accept the plea of lack of responsibility from one who commits a crime in an intoxicated state. The act of becoming acutely intoxicated is itself judged as irresponsible and the consequences must be paid for. The result is a compromise between the requirement of the criminal law for a responsible or voluntary act, and the judgment of society that a wrongdoer not be exonerated simply because he was drunk. It is that compromise that we shall next examine.

R. v. BERNARD

[1988] 2 S.C.R. 833, 67 C.R. (3d) 113, 45 C.C.C. (3d) 1

The accused was charged with sexual assault causing bodily harm, contrary to s. 246.2(*c*) [now s. 272(c)] of the *Criminal Code*. The complainant testified that she had been forced to have sexual intercourse in her apartment without her consent and had then been subjected to serious bodily injury by the accused. There was evidence that the accused had punched the complainant twice with a closed fist, once above the eye, causing the eyelid to bleed profusely, and that he had threatened to kill her. The complainant testified that the accused had been drinking but was able to walk, to see everything, to talk clearly and to put albums on the record player. One of the accused's friends testified that he had been drinking on the night in question and, though he became rowdy, he was walking straight and talking. When the police arrived at the apartment he was awakened from a deep sleep and seemed to be suffering somewhat from his drinking. The accused stated that his drunkenness caused the attack on the complainant.

At trial before Judge and jury, the accused did not testify. However, the Crown read evidence of a statement made to the police in which the accused admitted forcing the complainant to have sexual intercourse with him. He stated that he did know why he had done it, because he was drunk, and that "When I realized what I was doing, I got off." The trial Judge directed the jury that there was no evidence of drunkenness except the accused's statement and, even if they found that he was drunk, drunkenness would be no defence to the charge alleged. The jury returned a verdict of guilty. The Ontario Court of Appeal dismissed an appeal from conviction, holding that the offence of sexual assault causing bodily harm was an offence of general intent, to which the defence of drunkenness did not apply. The accused appealed.

McINTYRE J. (BEETZ J. concurring): —

. . . .

There are two issues which arise in this appeal. The first is whether sexual assault causing bodily harm (*Criminal Code* s. 246.2(c)) is an offence requiring proof of specific or of general intent, and the second is whether evidence of self-induced drunkenness is relevant to the issue of guilt or innocence in an offence of general intent. Before dealing in detail with these questions, it will be helpful to make certain observations.

A distinction has long been recognized in the criminal law between offences which require the proof of a specific intent and those which require only the proof of a general intent. This distinction forms the basis of the defence of drunkenness and it must be understood and kept in mind in approaching this case. In *R. v. George*, [1960] S.C.R. 871, Fauteux J. said, at p. 877:

> In considering the question of *mens rea*, a distinction is to be made between (i) intention as applied to acts considered in relation to their purposes and (ii) intention as applied to acts considered apart from their purposes. A general intent attending the commission of an act is, in some cases, the only intent required to constitute the crime while, in others, there must be, in addition to that general intent, a specific intent attending the purpose for the commission of the act.

This statement makes the distinction clear. The general intent offence is one in which the only intent involved relates solely to the performance of the act in question with no further ulterior intent or purpose. The minimal intent to apply force in the offence of common assault affords an example. A specific intent offence is one which involves the performance of the *actus reus*, coupled with an intent or purpose going beyond the mere performance of the questioned act. Striking a blow or administering poison with the intent to kill, or assault with intent to maim or wound, are examples of such offences.

This distinction is not an artificial one nor does it rest upon any legal fiction. There is a world of difference between the man who in frustration or anger strikes out at his neighbour in a public house with no particular purpose or intent in mind, other than to perform the act of striking, and the man who strikes a similar blow with intent to cause death or injury. This difference is best illustrated by a consideration of the relationship between murder and manslaughter. He who kills intending to kill or cause bodily harm is guilty of murder, whereas he who has killed by the same act without such intent is convicted of manslaughter. The proof of the specific intent, that is, to kill or to cause bodily harm, is necessary in murder because the crime of murder is incomplete without it. No such intent is required, however, for the offence of manslaughter because it forms no part of the offence, manslaughter simply being an unlawful killing without the intent required for murder. The relevance of intoxication which could deprive an accused of the capacity to form the necesary specific intent in murder and its irrelevance in the crime of manslaughter can readily be seen.

The present law relating to the drunkenness defence has developed in this Court from the application of principles set out in *Director of Public*

Prosecutions v. Beard, [1920] A.C. 479 (H.L.), discussed and adapted in other United Kingdom cases, including *Attorney General for Northern Ireland v. Gallagher*, [1961] 3 All E.R. 299 (H.L.), *Bratty v. Attorney General for Northern Ireland*, [1961] 3 All E.R. 523 (H.L.), and *Director of Public Prosecutions v. Majewski*, [1977] A.C. 443 (H.L.). In this Court, the matter has been dealt with in *R. v. George, supra*, and other cases, but particularly in *Leary v. The Queen* (1978), 1 S.C.R. 29. where Pigeon J., speaking for the majority of the Court, said, at p. 57, that rape is a crime of general intention as distinguished from specific intention, a crime therefore "in which the defence of drunkenness can have no application". This may be said to have confirmed the law as it stands in Canada on this question and the appellant's principal attack in this Court is upon that decision. It is not necessary for the purposes of this judgment to review in detail the authorities in this Court on the question. It will be sufficient to summarize their effect in the following terms. Drunkenness in a general sense is not a true defence to a criminal act. Where, however, in a case which involves a crime of specific intent, the accused is so affected by intoxication that he lacks the capacity to form the specific intent required to commit the crime charged it may apply. The defence, however, has no application in offences of general intent.

The criticism of the law with respect to the defence of drunkenness is based on two propositions. It is said, firstly, that the distinction between the general intent and specific intent offences is artificial and is little more than a legal fiction. Secondly, it is said that it is illogical, because it envisages a defence of drunkenness in certain situations and not in others; it is merely a policy decision made by Judges and not based on principle or logic. It will be evident from what I have said that I reject the first ground of criticism. As to the second criticism that it is based upon grounds of policy, I would say that there can be no doubt that considerations of policy are involved in this distinction. Indeed, in some cases, principally *Majewski, supra*, the distinction has been defended on the basis that it is sound social policy. The fact, however, that considerations of policy have influenced the development of the law in this field cannot, in my view, be condemned. In the final analysis all law should be based upon and consistent with sound social policy. No good law can be inconsistent with or depart from sound policy.

If the policy behind the present law is that society condemns those who, by the voluntary consumption of alcohol, render themselves incapable of self-control so that they will commit acts of violence causing injury to their neighbours, then in my view no apology for such policy is needed, and the resulting law affords no affront to the well established principles of the law or to the freedom of the individual. Furthermore, the existing law is not divorced from logical underpinnings as suggested in some academic writings. Not all the academic literature has been critical. A strong statement in support of the law on utilitarian or policy grounds made shortly after *Majewski* is by Sir Rupert Cross in *"Blackstone v. Bentham"* (1976), 92 L.Q.R. 516, where he said, at pp. 525-6:

In reply to Bentham and the academics I would ask why it is "hard and unthinking" to refuse to allow people to exempt themselves from criminal responsibility for harm done by their bodies by incapacitating their minds from controlling them. Why should the requirement that intention or recklessness must be proved in order to establish liability for an assaullt not be subject to what appears to be the wholly reasonable retributive principle that it is unjust to those who remain sober to allow those who become drunk to allege that they were unaware of consequences of their bodily movements of which all sober people would have been aware? This is what Blackstone meant when he said that the law would not suffer any man "to privilege one crime by another." . . . Punishment is an evil and the less of it the better. But the evil of inflicting punishment is justified if the harm which is thus avoided is greater than that caused by the punishment. It may be asceticism to blame people for simply getting drunk, but it is sound utilitarianism to seek to prevent people from doing certain kinds of harm while they are drunk. In so far as this object can be achieved by punishment, it is achieved most economically by singling out for punishment those who commit the kind of harm which the law seeks to prevent while they are drunk.

A.J. Ashworth ("Reason, Logic and Criminal Liability" ((1975), 91 L.Q.R. 102) says, at p. 130:

> Moreover, it is hardly appropriate to regard a defence of acute intoxciation as a simple denial of mens rea; it has been suggested that defences should not be classified solely according to the effect of the accused's condition, without reference to their cause. The criminal law permits reason to override the logical application of the traditional doctrines in cases of deliberately self-induced incapacities; to do otherwise would be tantamount to allowing a fraud on the law. It is submitted that, if the law provides no other means of imposing criminal liability in the cases of "voluntarily-induced" incapacities discussed in this article, then there are sufficient reasons for restricting the scope of the defences as the English Judges have done.

. . . .

In my view, the common law rules on the defence of drunkenness, though frequently the subject of criticism, have a rationality which not only accords with criminal law theory, but has also served society well. It is not questioned in this case that the defence of drunkenness, as it applies to specific intent offences, is supportable. It is submitted, however, that it should be extended to include all criminal charges. It is my view that this proposition is not sustainable.

Turning now to the issues raised, the first one is to consider whether the offence of sexual assault causing bodily harm is an offence requiring a general or specific intent. In *Swietlinski v. The Queen*, [1980] 2 S.C.R. 956, this Court held that indecent assault, then an offence under the *Criminal Code*, was an offence of general intent. The indecent character of the assault was to be judged upon an objective view of the facts and not upon the mental state of the accused. It was said, at p. 968:

> What acts are indecent and what circumstances will have that character are questions of fact that will have to be decided in each case, but the determination of those questions will depend upon an objective view of the facts and circumstances in relation to the actual assault, and not upon the mental state of the accused.

and later at pp. 970-71:

Because indecent assault is an offence of general or basic intent, the defence of drunkenness cannot apply where a person is charged with that offence.

This Court dealt with the question of sexual assault *simpliciter* under s. 246(1)(*a*) in *R. v. Chase*, [1987] 2 S.C.R. 293.

. . . .

It would therefore be my view that the mental element of the offence in s. 246.2(*c*) is only the intention to commit the assault. The surrounding circumstances must be considered for evidence of its sexual nature and of the resulting bodily harm. The Crown need not show any further mental element (see J.D. Watt, *The New Offences Against the Person* (1984), at p. 113).

In my view, the comments in *Chase*, *supra*, are equally applicable to an offence under s. 246.2(*c*) which merely adds to the sexual assault *simpliciter* the requirement of bodily harm to the complainant. The resulting interference with the physical integrity of the complainant aggravates the seriousness of a sexual assault but the mental element remains the same. I would conclude that s. 246.2(*c*) creates an offence of general rather than specific intent.

The second issue, whether the defence of drunkenness applies to an offence of general intent includes the question of whether the Court should overrule its earlier decision in *Leary*. The attack on *Leary* was based on its rejection of the defence for crimes of general intent. As already mentioned, nobody has suggested that it should not apply in cases of specific intent. The Chief Justice has expressed the view that evidence of self-induced intoxication should be a relevant consideration in determining whether the *mens rea* of any particular offence has been proved by the Crown. As I have indicated, I am unable to agree with this conclusion. The effect of such a conclusion would be that the more drunk a person becomes by his own voluntary consumption of alcohol or drugs, the more extended will be his opportunity for a successful defence against conviction for the offences caused by such drinking, regardless of the nature of the intent required for those offences.

The appellant made two principal arguments in seeking the reversal of the *Leary* rule. He contended that it relieves the Crown from the burden of proving *mens rea* in cases of general intent and, in effect, imposes strict liability upon proof of the *actus reus*. He also contended that the *Leary* rule violates s. 7 and s. 11(*d*) of the *Canadian Charter of Rights and Freedoms*.

In my opinion, both of these submissions must be rejected. I would say at the outset that in crimes of general intent the Crown is not relieved from proving any element of the offence. The effect of excluding the drunkenness defence from such offences is merely to prevent the accused from relying on his self-imposed drunkenness as a factor showing an absence of any necessary intent. While this Court has consistently recognized the basic proposition that an accused person should not be subject to criminal sanction unless the Crown shows the existence of a blameworthy or criminal mental state associated with the *actus reus* of the crime, it does not follow that a person who so deprives himself by the voluntary consumption of alcohol or a drug of the normal power of self-restraint that a crime results, should be entitled to an acquittal. Compelling reasons grounded in logic, common sense, and sound social policy dictate otherwise.

As I indicated earlier, it is not necessary to review all of the authorities which have dealt with this issue. It is clear from a review of the cases, however, that until the early years of the nineteenth century drunkenness was considered "rather an aggravation than a defence": see Lord Birkenhead in *D.P.P. v. Beard, supra*, at p. 494. The early principle of the common law was that a voluntary destruction of will power would entitle a person to no more favourable treatment with regard to criminal conduct than a sober person. By the latter part of the 19th century this earlier rule was "mercifully relaxed" (see Lawton LJ. in *Majewski*, [1975] 2 All E.R. 296 (C.A.), at p. 305) in respect of crimes of specific intent where the capacity to form the required specific intent was not present because of intoxication: see the early cases such as *R. v. Doherty* (1887), 16 Cox. C.C. 306, per Stephen J., at p. 308. This new approach was given approval in *Beard's* case and the more mordern authorities have been based upon it. This relaxation stems no doubt from a recognition of the severity of the penal consequence of most of the specific intent offences, as compared with the generally lesser penalties associated with the general intent offences. Therefore, the exclusion of the defence from general intent offences was not an exception to the general rule. The exception was the allowance of the defence in specific intent cases adopted to recognize the more complicated mental processes required for the crimes of special intent and the greater penalties involved. Some measure of relief for such cases was therefore provided. Otherwise, the common law preserved the general rule that a person may not by voluntary intoxication render himself immune from the consequences of his conduct.

. . . .

In *Leary*, this Court followed the approach taken in the House of Lords in *Majewski*, where the House of Lords unanimously approved the distinction between general and specific intent on the basis that the rule had evolved to protect the community and that voluntary intoxication was a sufficient substitute for the fault element in crimes of general intent.

. . . .

This Court in *Leary* approved the *Majewski* approach which has long been accepted in the law of Canada and, for the reasons which I have set out, it is my opinion that this Court's judgment in *Leary* ought not to be overruled. I must re-emphasize that the *Leary* rule does not relieve the Crown from its obligation to prove the *mens rea* in a general intent offence. The fact that an accused may not rely on voluntary intoxication in such offences does not have that effect because of the nature of the offence and the mental elements which must be shown. The requisite state of mind may be proved in two ways. Firstly, there is the general proposition that triers of fact may infer *mens rea* from the *actus reus* itself: a person is presumed to have intended the natural and probable consequences of his actions. For example, in an offence involving the mere application of force, the minimal intent to apply that force will suffice to constitute the necessary *mens rea* and can be reasonably inferred from the act itself and the other evidence. Secondly, in cases where the accused was so intoxicated as to raise doubt as to the voluntary nature of his conduct, the Crown may meet its evidentiary obligation respecting the necessary blameworthy mental state of the accused by proving the fact of voluntary self-induced intoxication by drugs or alcohol. This was the approach suggested in *Majewski*. In most cases involving intoxication in general intent offences, the trier of fact will be able to apply the first proposition, namely, that the intent is inferable from the *actus reus* itself. As Fauteux J. observed in *George, supra*, at p. 879, it is almost metaphysically inconceivable for a person to be so drunk as to be incapble of forming the minimal intent to apply force. Hence, only in cases of the most extreme self-intoxication does the trier of fact need to use the second proposition, that is, that evidence of self-induced intoxication is evidence of the guilty mind, the blameworthy mental state.

The result of this two-fold approach is that for these crimes accused persons cannot hold up voluntary drunkenness as a defence. They cannot be heard to say: "I was so drunk that I did not know what I was doing". If they managed to get themselves so drunk tht they did not know what they were doing, the reckless behaviour in attaining that level of intoxication affords the necessary evidence of the culpable mental condition. Hence, it is logically impossible for an accused person to throw up his voluntary drunkenness as a defence to a charge of general intent. Proof of his voluntary drunkenness can be proof of his guilty mind.

As I have endeavoured to show, the exclusion of the drunkenness defence in general intent cases is not without logical underpinnings but, whatever the logical weaknesses may be, an overwhelming justification for the exclusion may rest on policy, policy so compelling that it possesses its own logic. Intoxication, whether by alcohol or drugs, lies at the root of many if not most violent assaults: intoxication is clearly a major cause of violent crime. What then is preferable, a recognition of this fact and the adoption of a policy aimed at curbing the problem, or the application of what is said to be logic by providing in law that he who voluntarily partakes of that which is the cause of the crime should for that reason be excused from the consequences of his crime? If that is logic, I prefer policy.

It was argued by the appellant that the *Leary* rule converts the offence of sexual assault causing bodily harm into a crime of absolute liability in that the Crown need not prove the requisite intention for the completion of the offence. Therefore, it is said that *Leary* violates s. 7 and s. 11(*d*) of the *Charter*. In *Re Motor Vehicle Act Reference*, [1985] 2 S.C.R. 486 and in *R. v. Vaillancourt*, [1987] 2 S.C.R. 636, it was held that the requirement for a minimum mental state before the attachment of criminal liability is a principle of fundamental justice. Criminal offences, as a general rule, must have as one of their elements the requirement of a blameworthy mental state. The morally innocent ought not to be convicted. It is said that the *Leary* rule violates this fundamental premise. In my opinion, the *Leary* rule clearly does not offend this essential principle of criminal law but rather upholds it. The *Leary* rule recognizes that accused persons who have voluntarily consumed drugs or alcohol, thereby depriving themselves of self-control leading to the commission of a crime, are not morally innocent and are, indeed, criminally blameworthy. While the rule excludes consideration of voluntary intoxication in the approach to general intent offences, it nonetheless recognizes that it may be a relevant factor in those generally more serious offences where the *mens rea* must involve not only the intentional performance of the *actus reus* but, as well, the formation of further ulterior motives and purposes. It therefore intrudes upon the security of the person only in accordance with sound principle and within the established boundaries of the legal process. For these reasons, I would say that the *Charter* is not violated.

. . . .

I would therefore conclude that the Courts below made no error and I would dismiss the appeal.

In any event, should it be considered that I am wrong in my approach to the *Leary* case, this is nonetheless a case in which the provisions of s. 613(1)(*b*)(iii) of the *Criminal Code* should be applied. . . . It is my view that there is no sufficient evidence of drunkeness to form any basis whatever for the defence of drunkenness.

WILSON J. (L'HEUREUX-DUBÉ J. concurring): — I have had the benefit of the reasons of the Chief Justice and of my colleagues McIntyre and La Forest JJ. I agree with McIntyre JJ. for the reasons given by him that sexual assault causing bodily harm is an offence of general intent requiring only the minimal intent to apply force. I agree with him also that in most cases involving general intent offences and intoxication the Crown will be able to establish the accused's blameworthy mental state by inference from his or her acts. I think that is the case here. The evidence of intoxication withheld from the trier of fact in this case could not possibly have raised a reasonable doubt as to the existence of the minimal intent to apply force. It is accordingly not necessary in this case to resort to self-induced intoxication as a substituted form of *mens rea*. And, indeed, I have some real concerns as to whether the imposition of criminal liability on that basis would survive a challenge under the *Canadian Charter of Rights and Freedoms*.

The facts are fully set out in the reasons of the Chief Justice and I refer to them only to underline why I agree with my colleague, McIntyre J., that the rule in *Leary v. The Queen*, [1978] 1 S.C.R. 29, should be preserved and applied in this case.

Sexual assault is a crime of violence. There is no requirement of an intent or purpose beyond the intentional application of force. It is first and foremost an assault. It is sexual in nature only because, objectively viewed, it is related to sex either on account of the area of the body to which the violence is applied or on account of words accompanying the violence. Indeed, the whole purpose, as I understand it, of the replacement of the offence of rape by the offence of sexual assault was to emphasize the aspect of violence and put paid to the benign concept that rape was simply the act of a man who was "carried away" by his emotions.

The appellant in his statement to the police admitted that he had forced the complainant to have sexual intercourse with him but claimed that because of his drunkenness he did not know why he had done this and that when he realized what he was doing he "got off" the complainant. There was evidence that the appellant had punched the complainant twice with his closed fist and had threatened to kill her. The doctor who examined the complainant testified that the complainant's right eye was swollen shut and that three stitches were required to close the wound. It is clear from this that there was intentional and voluntary, as opposed to accidental or involuntary, application of force.

The evidence of the appellant's intoxication consisted of his own statements to the police that he was drunk; the complainant's testimony that, while the appellant was acting out of character in making advances to her, he was able to walk, talk and put albums on the record player; a friend's testimony that prior to the incident the appellant had been drinking at a bar and had become "very rowdy" although still capable of talking and walking straight. By his own admission the appellant had sufficient wits about him after the violent assault to hide a bloodied towel and pillowcase from the police. There is no evidence that we are dealing here with extreme intoxication, verging on insanity or automatism, and as such capable of negating the inference that the minimal intent to apply force was present: see *R. v. Swietlinski*, (1978) 44 C.C.C. (2d) 267 (Ont. C.A.), at p. 294, aff'd [1980] 2 S.C.R. 956. The evidence of intoxication in this case was simply not capable of raising a reasonable doubt as to the existence of the minimal intent required. In this I agree with McIntyre J.

I am less confident about the proposition accepted by my colleague that self-induced intoxication may substitute for the mental element required to be present at the time the offence was committed although I realize that there are statements in judgments of this Court to that effect. I do not believe, however, that the Court has clearly adopted that proposition. The decision of the House of Lords in *Director of Public Prosecutions v. Majewski*, [1977] A.C. 443, may stand for the rather harsh proposition that even self-induced intoxication producing a state of automatism cannot constitute a defence to an offence of general intent such as assault but I doubt that our Canadian jurisprudence goes that far.

. . . .

I believe that the *Leary* rule is perfectly consistent with an onus resting on the Crown to prove the minimal intent which should accompany the doing of the prohibited act in general intent offences. I view it as preferable to preserve the *Leary* rule in its more flexible form as Pigeon J. applied it, *i.e.*, so as to allow evidence of intoxication to go to the trier of fact in general intent offences only if it is evidence of extreme intoxication involving an absence of awareness akin to a state of insanity or automatism. Only in such a case is the evidence capable of raising a reasonable doubt as to the existence of the minimal intent required for the offence. I would not overrule *Leary*, as the Chief Justice would, and allow evidence of intoxication to go to the trier of fact in every case regardless of its possible relevance to the issue of the existence of the minimal intent required for the offence.

It was argued by the appellant and indeed accepted by the Chief Justice in his reasons that the *Leary* rule converts the offence of sexual assault causing bodily harm into a crime of absolute liability in that the Crown need not prove any mental element. This is said to offend s. 7 of the *Charter* as interpreted in *Re B.C. Motor Vehicle Act*, [1985] 2 S.C.R. 486 and in *R. v. Vaillancourt*, [1987] 2 S.C.R. 636. With all due respect to those who think differently I do not believe that the Crown is relieved from proving the existence of the required minimal intent by the operation of *Leary*. In *R. v. Sault Ste. Marie*, [1978] 2 S.C.R. 1299, Dickson J., as he then was, stated at p. 1310:

> In sharp contrast, "absolute liability" entails conviction on proof merely that the defendant committed the prohibited act constituting the *actus reus* of the offence. There is no relevant mental element. It is no defence that the accused was entirely without fault. He may be morally innocent in every sense, yet be branded as a malefactor and punished as such.

When the *Leary* rule is applied in this case the Crown must still prove beyond a reasonable doubt the existence of the required mental element of the intentional application of force. The offence cannot be said to be one of absolute liability in the sense that no mental element has to be proved in order to obtain a conviction. As Alan Mewett and Morris Manning write in *Criminal Law* (2nd ed. (1985)), at p. 210:

> The Courts are not saying that crimes of general or basic intent do not require *mens rea*. Rather they are saying that those crimes have a *mens rea* of a type directed solely to the present and that drunkenness is not sufficient to negate that type of thought process.

Similarly, Glanville Williams argues in his *Textbook of Criminal Law* (2nd ed. (1983)), at pp. 475-76, that it is a misunderstanding to read even *Majewski, supra*, as transforming general intent offences into absolute liability offences because "even on a charge of a crime of basic intent the jury must have regard to all the evidence except the evidence of intoxication in determining the defendant's intention." In short, when evidence of intoxication is withheld from the jury the Crown still bears the burden of proving a blameworthy state of mind.

It was also argued by the appellant and accepted by the Chief Justice that the application of the Leary rule violates s. 11(*d*) of the *Charter* by allowing an accused to be convicted even although the trier of fact might well have a reasonable doubt as to the existence of the essential mental element of the offence or as to the availability of a defence which could raise a reasonable doubt as to the guilty of the accused: see *Vaillancourt, supra; R. v. Whyte*, [1988] 2 S.C.R. 3. Again I find myself in respectful disagreement with the Chief Justice and the appellant on this issue. To my mind, the operation of the *Leary* rule in this case does not have that result because the Crown still must prove that the accused applied force intentionally and the evidence of intoxication is withheld from the jury only because it is incapable of raising a reasonable doubt as to the accused's guilt. This is not a case in which self-induced intoxication is being resorted to as a substituted *mens rea* for the intentional application of force.

It is, my view, not strictly necessary in this case to address the constitutionality of substituting self-induced intoxication of general intent offences. The issue would, in my view, only arise in those rare cases in which the intoxication is extreme enough to raise doubts as to the existence of the minimal intent which characterizes conscious and volitional conduct. However, as both the Chief Justice and McIntyre J. have addressed the issue, I will express my own somewhat tentative views upon it.

This Court has affirmed as fundamental the proposition that a person should not be exposed to a deprivation of liberty unless the Crown proves the existence of a blameworthy or culpable state of mind: see *Re B.C. Motor Vehicle Act, supra*, at pp. 513-20. It does not follow from this, however, that those who, through the voluntary consumption of alcohol or drugs incapacitate themselves from knowing what they are doing, fall within the category of the "morally innocent" deserving of such protection. This is not to say that such persons do not have a right under s. 7n or s. 12 of the *Charter* to be protected against punishment that is disproportionate to their crime and degree of culpability: see *Re B.C. Motor Vehicle Act, supra*, at pp. 532-34; *R. v. Smith*, [1987] 1 S.C.R. 1045. They do, especially if the consequences of their becoming intoxicated were not intended or foreseen.

The real concern over the substituted form of *mens rea* arises, it seems to me, under s. 11(*d*) of the *Charter*. While this Court has recognized that in some cases proof of an essential element of a criminal offence can be replaced by proof of a different element, it has placed stringent limitations on when this can happen.

. . . .

In my tentative view, it is unlikely that in those cases in which it is necessary to resort to self-induced intoxication as the substituted element for the minimal intent, proof of the substituted element will "inexorably" lead to the conclusion that the essential element of the minimal intent existed at the time the criminal act was committed. But I prefer to leave this question open as it is unnecessary to decide it in order to dispose of this appeal.

I agree with my colleagues McIntyre and La Forest JJ. that, had there been error in the Court below, no substantial wrong or miscarriage of justice resulted from it and that it would accordingly be appropriate to apply s. 613(1)(*b*)(iii) of the *Criminal Code*. I would dismiss the appeal.

DICKSON C.J. (LAMER J. concurring) (dissenting): —

. . . .

DRUNKENNESS AND *MENS REA*

In my view, the only issue the Court needs to address may be put as follows: should evidence of self-induced intoxication be considered by the trier of fact, along with all other relevant evidence, in determining whether the prosecution has proved beyond a reasonable doubt the *mens rea* required to constitute the offence? I am of the opinion that the Court should answer that question in the affirmative.

I wish to make clear at the outset, however, that nothing in these reasons is intended to apply with respect to the quite distinct issues raised by offences, such as driving while impaired, where intoxication or the consumption of alcohol is itself an ingredient of the offence. The *mens rea* of such offences can be left for consideration another day.

In *Leary v. The Queen*, [1978] 1 S.C.R. 29, Pigeon J. for the majority of the Court, held that rape was an offence requiring proof of only "basic" or "general" intent rather than "specific" intent. Under that categorization, the Court held, the jury should be instructed that evidence that drunkenness may have deprived the accused of the capacity to form the requisite intent should not be taken into account when considering whether the Crown had satisfied the burden of proving beyond a reasonable doubt that the accused had acted with the requisite intent. (See also *Swietlinski v. The Queen*, [1980] 2 S.C.R. 956, dealing with the offence of indecent assault). The offence of rape has now been removed from the *Criminal Code* and in its place are the sexual assault provisions. More recently, in *R. v. Chase*, [1987] 2 S.C.R. 293, the Court held that sexual assault was a crime of "basic" or "general" intent. In *Chase*, however, drunkenness was not in issue and the propriety of maintaining the distinction between general and specific intent for purposes of evidence regarding intoxication was not considered. The present case raises that much more basis issue which, in my view, the Court should reconsider.

In my dissent in *Leary*, I sought to advance the view that respect for basic criminal law principles required that the legal ficiton, the artificial "specific" intent threshold requirement, be abandoned. I do not intend in these reasons to repeat what I said in *Leary*. With due regard for *stare decisis*, as to which I will have more to say in a moment, and with the greatest of respect for those of a contrary view, I would only add that nothing I have heard or read since the judgment in *Leary* has caused me to abandon or modify in the slightest degree the views of dissent which I there expressed. Analysis of the *Leary* dissent may be summarized as follows.

First of all, one must recognize the fundamental nature of the *mens rea* requirement. To warrant the condemnation of a conviction and the infliction of punishment, one who has caused harm must have done so with a blameworthy state of mind. It is always for the Crown to prove the existence of a guilty mind beyond a reasonable doubt. Intoxication affects one's mental state, one's ability to perceive the circumstances in which one acts, and to appreciate possible consequences. In principle, therefore, intoxication is relevant to the mental element in crime, and should be considered, together with all other evidence, in determining whether the Crown has proved the requisite mental state beyond a reasonable doubt.

It is quite wrong, I think, to characterize the issue as whether the "defence of drunkeness" should apply to this or that offence. While this expression is commonly used, it is misleading and perhaps even unduly emotive. It suggests that those who would otherwise be liable for their criminal conduct will escape because they were drunk at the time the offence was committed. But, of course, no one suggests that special concessions should be made to drunken offenders. The issue is really whether the Crown should be relieved of the usual burden of proving the requisite mental element for the offence, because the accused was intoxicated. Should the jury be entitled to assess all of the evidence relevant to intent and be entitled to decide on the basis of all of the evidence whether the Crown has satisfied that burden?

The categories of "specific" intent on the one hand and "basic" or "general" intent on the other have evolved as an artificial device whereby evidence, otherwise relevant, is excluded from the jury's consideration. This Court, in *Swietlinski*, has recognized that intoxication may as a matter of fact deprive an accused of "basic" or "general" intent. It is said, however, by those who support the classifiction that as a matter of policy, consideration of evidence of intoxication must be excluded. Indeed, a notable feature to be found in the analysis of many of those who support restricting the jury's use of evidence relating to drunkenness is the concession that while principle and logic lead in an opposite direction, the policy of protection of the public requires that principle and logic should yield: see, *e.g. Director of Public Prosecutions v. Majewski*, [1976] 2 All E.R. 142, at pp. 167-8 per Lord Edmund-Davies, quoted by Pigeon J. in *Leary, supra*, at pp. 52-3.

In my view, there are two fundamental problems with this approach. First, if the law is to be altered in the name of policy over principle, that is surely a task for Parliament rather than the Courts. As Barwick C.J. of the High Court of Australia concluded in *O'Connor* (1980), 4 A. Crim. R. 348, at pp. 363-64:

> It seems to me to be completely inconsistent with the principles of the common law that a man should be conclusively presumed to have an intent which, in fact, he does not have, or to have done an act which, in truth, he did not do.
>
> I can readily understand that a person who has taken alcohol or another drug to such an extent that he is intoxicated thereby to the point where he has no will to act or no capacity to form an intent to do an act is blameworthy and that his act of having ingested or administered the alcohol or other drug ought to be visited with severe consequences. The offence of being drunk and disorderly is not maintained these days in all systems of the common law. In any case it has not carried a sufficient penalty properly to express the public opprobrium which should attach to one who, by the taking of alcohol or the use of drugs, has become intoxicated to the point where he is the vehicle for unsocial or violent behaviour. But, though blameworthy for becoming intoxicated, I can see no ground for presuming his acts to be voluntary and relevantly intentional. For what is blameworthy there should be an appropriate criminal offence. But it is not for the Judges to create an offence appropriate in the circumstances: cf. *Knuller (Publishing, Printing & Promotions) Ltd. v. D.P.P.*, [1973] A.C. 435, at pp. 457-458, 464-465 and 490). It must be for the Parliament.

Secondly, even if it were appropriate for the Courts to bend principle in the name of policy, so far as I am aware, there is no evidence that the artificiality of the specific intent requirement is actually required for social protection.

An unrestrained application of basic *mens rea* doctrine would not, in my opinion, open a gaping hole in the criminal law inimical to social protection.

There are several reasons for this. To the extent that intoxication merely lowers inhibitions, removes self-restraint or induces unusal self-confidence or aggressiveness, it would be of no avail to an accused, as such effects do not relate to the *mens rea* requirement for volitional and intentional or reckless conduct. Similarly, intoxication would be of no avail to an accused who got drunk in order to gain the courage to commit a crime or to aid in his defence. Thirdly, one can trust in the good sense of the jury and that of our trial Judges to weigh all the evidence in a fair and responsbile manner, and they are unlikely to acquit too readily those who have committed offences while intoxicated.

The High Court of Australia held in *O'Connor, supra*, that the distinction between specific and general intent should not be followed and that in all cases, evidence of drunkenness should be left with the jury along with all other evidence relative to the issue of intent. The New Zealand Court of Appeal also rejected the artificial specific intent distinction: *R. v. Kamipeli*, [1975] 2 N.Z.L.R. 610.

· · · ·

The experience in New Zealand and Australia, where the specific intent has been abandoned, suggests that the public will be adequately protected if the issue is left to the good sense of the jury. *O'Connor* was preceded in the State of Victoria by *R. v. Keogh*, [1964] V.R. 400. In *O'Connor*, Stephen J. explained as follows, at 358:

> A distrust of jurors and an anxiety that they may too readily be persuaded to an acquittal if evidence of the result of self-induced intoxication, particularly by drugs other than alcohol, were allowed, may have formed some part of the public policy on which the decision rests. I may say at once that I have, of course, no experience of English juries: but I have of juries in New South Wales. Starke J., a most experienced Judge in the hearing of criminal charges in Victoria, having had as well a long and distinguished career as an advocate, expressed himself in the present case in relation to the impact of evidence of intoxication upon Victoria jurors. He said:
>
>> "I, of course, have no knowledge of how English juries react. But over nearly 40 years' experience in this State I have found juries to be very slow to accept a defence based on intoxication. I do not share the fear held by many in England that if intoxication is accepted as a defence as far as general intent is concerned the floodgates will open and hordes of guilty men will descend on the community."
>
> I share his views, as if they had been expressed about jurors in New South Wales. In my opinion, properly instructed jurors would be scrupulous and not indulgent in deciding an issue of voluntariness or of intention. Indeed, I am inclined to think that they may tend to think that an accused who had taken alchohol and particularly other drugs to the point of extreme intoxication had brought on himself what flowed from that state of intoxication.

The empirical evidence is to the same effect: see George Smith J., "Footnote to O'Connor's Case" (1981), 5 Crim. L.J. 270, reviewing the effects of the *O'Connor* decision in Australia, and concluding, after review of over 500 trials held in the District Court of New South Wales, that the actual impact on the acquittal rate was minimal (at p. 277):

Certainly my inquiries would indicate that the decision in *O'Connor's* case, far from opening any floodgates has at most permitted an occasional drip to escape from the tap.

. . . .

III

STARE DECISIS

The real issue in this appeal, it seems to me, is whether the Court should now overrule *Leary*. Let me say immediately that, even if a case were wrongly decided, certainty in the law remains an important consideration. There must be compelling circumstances to justify departure from a prior decision. On the other hand, it is clear that this Court may overrule its own decisions and indeed, it has exercised that discretion on a number of occasions. . . .

There are at least four separate factors which find support in the jurisprudence of the Court which in my submission lead to the conclusion that *Leary* should be overruled.

A. *Canadian Charter of Rights and Freedoms*

Since *Leary* was decided, the *Canadian Charter of Rights and Freedoms* has come into force. This Court has held that legislation which imposes the sanction of imprisonment without proof of a blameworthy state of mind violates the guarantee of fundamental justice contained in s. 7 of the *Charter* and must be struck down unless it can meet the exacting test of s. 1 (see *Re B.C. Motor Vehicle Act*, [1985] 2 S.C.R. 486, *R. v. Vaillancourt*, [1987] 2 S.C.R. 636).

The appellant submits that *Leary* runs counter to s. 7 by providing that intoxication is no defence to a crime of general intent. In circumstances where the requisite mental intent is lacking due to an intoxicated condition, a general intent offence is converted into one of absolute liability in which proof of the commission of the actus reus by itself mandates conviction. It is also submitted that *Leary* runs counter to the presumption of innocence and the right to a fair hearing as guaranteed by s. 11(*d*) of the *Charter*, in so far as wrongful intent is irrebuttably presumed upon the showing of intoxication.

. . . .

In *Leary*, I expressed the opinion that the fundamental rationale for the *mens rea* presumption could be framed in the following terms, at p. 34:

> The notion that a Court should not find a person guilty of an offence against the criminal law unless he has a blameworthy state of mind is common to all civilized penal systems. It is founded upon respect for the person and for the freedom of human will. A person is accountable for what he wills. When, in the exercise of the power of free choice, a member of society chooses to engage in harmful or otherwise undesirable conduct proscribed by the criminal law, he must accept the sanctions which that law has provided for the purpose of discouraging such conduct. Justice demands no less. But, to be criminal, the wrongdoing must

have been consciously committed. To subject the offender to punishment, a mental element as well as a physical element is an essential concomitant of the crime. The mental state basic to criminal liability consists in most crimes in either (a) an intention to cause the *actus reus* of the crime, *i.e.* an intention to do the act which constitutes the crime in question, or (b) foresight or realization on the part of the person that his conduct will probably cause or may cause the *actus reus*, together with assumption of or indifference to a risk, which in all of the circumstances is substantial or unjustifiable. This latter mental element is sometimes characterized as recklessness.

In my view, that same principle is now given constitutional force in *Re B.C. Motor Vehicle Act, supra, Vaillancourt, supra*. In *Re B.C. Motor Vehicle Act, supra*, the Court held, at p. 514, that "absolute liability in penal law offends the principles of fundamental justice." In *Vaillancourt*, Justice Lamer stated that the *B.C. Motor Vehicle Act Reference* "elevated *mens rea* from a presumed element in *Sault Ste. Marie, supra* to a constitutionally required element" (p. 652). While the Court has not yet dealt directly with the extent to which objective foreseeability may suffice for the imposition of criminal liability (*Vaillancourt* at pp. 653-54), that issue is not raised in the present context.

The effect of the majority holding in *Leary* is to impose a form of absolute liability on intoxicated offenders, which is entirely inconsistent with the basic requirement for a blameworthy state of mind as a prerequisite to the imposition of the penalty of imprisonment mandated by the above-cited authorities. I agree with the observation of Professor Stuart in *Canadian Criminal Law* (2nd ed. 1987) that s. 7 of the *Charter* mandates the reversal of *Leary* and the assertion of "the fundamental principles of voluntariness and fault" in relation to intoxication and the criminal law (at p. 378). If the constitutional guarantee empowers the Court to strike down legislation as in the two cases cited above, surely it provides a sufficient basis for overruling a prior decision of the Court which fails to respect constitutionally entrenched values.

The majority holding in *Leary* also runs counter to the s. 11(*d*) right to be presumed innocent until proven guilty. With respect to crimes of general intent, guilty intent is in effect presumed upon proof of the fact of intoxication. Moreover, the presumption of guilt created by the *Leary* rule is irrebuttable.

The same argument made in the context of s. 7 can be made in relation to s. 11(*d*). By providing that intoxication is no defence to a crime of general intent, *Leary* renders the offence one of absolute liability and runs counter to the presumption of innocence by presuming an essential element required by s. 7 upon the proof of the fact of intoxication.

In my view, the *Leary* rule cannot be upheld by reference to s. 1, as it cannot survive the "proportionality" inquiry. While the protection of the public, said to underlie the *Leary* rule, could serve as an important objective, in my view the *Leary* rule does not achieve that objective in a manner consistent with the proportionality test of *Oakes, supra. Oakes* requires that "the measures adopted must be carefully designed to achieve the objective in question." As I have noted, there is no agreement in the case law as to how to distinguish between crimes of "general intent" and crimes of "specific intent". This distinction was plainly not in the minds of the *Code* drafters, and the mental elements of many crimes are not readily classified into one category or the other. There is no rational reason for protecting the public against some drunken offenders but not against others, particularly where the distinction is not based upon the gravity of the offence or the availability of included offences. If the public protection does require special measures, that should be accomplished through comprehensive legislation rather than ad hoc judicial recasting of some offences. For a recent review of possible legislative schemes, see Quigley, "Reform of the Intoxication Defence" (1987), 33 McGill L.J. 1.

The *Leary* rule in effect treats the deliberate act of becoming intoxicated as culpable in itself, but inflicts punishment measured by the unintended consequences of becoming intoxicated. Punishment acts as a deterrent where the conduct is intended or foreseen. There is no evidence to support the assertion that the *Leary* rule deters the commission of unintended crimes. Hence, there is no warrant for violating fundamental principles and convicting those who would otherwise escape criminal liability.

The *Leary* rule fails to satisfy the second branch of the proportionality test as well, namely, that the means chosen should impair as little as possible the right or freedom in question. In general intent offences, the jury is to be instructed to excise from their minds any evidence of drunkenness with the result that the Crown, because the accused is intoxicated, is relieved of proving *mens rea*, thereby placing the intoxicated person in a worse position than a sober person. Alternatively, the jury is required to examine the mental state of the accused, without reference to the alcohol ingested, and consequently find a fictional intent. In my view, imposition of this form of absolute liability goes well beyond what is required to protect the public from drunken offenders. As I have already indicated, striking down the artificial rule which precludes the trier of fact from considering evidence of intoxication in relation to *mens rea* has not produced an increase in the threat to public safety from drunken offenders in Australia, and there is no evidence to suggest that it would do so in Canada.

Finally, it is my view that there is a disproportionality between the effects of *Leary* on rights protected by the *Charter* and the objective of public safety. To paraphrase Lamer J. in *Re B.C. Motor Vehicle Act, supra*, at p. 521, it has not been demonstrated that risk of imprisonment of a few innocent persons is required to attain the goal of protecting the public from drunken offenders.

As stated in *R. v. Holmes*, [1988] 1 S.C.R. 914, at p. 940: "This effect, given the range of alternative legislative devices available to Parliament, is too deleterious to be justified as a reasonable limit under s. 1 of the *Charter*. Simply put, the provision exacts too high a price to be justified in a free and democratic society."

B. *Leary* Attenuated by Subsequent Cases

Since *Leary* there have been developments in the jurisprudence of the Court which, in my submission, seriously undermine the view taken by the majority in *Leary*. The Court has held that where the holding of a case has been "attenuated" by subsequent decisions, it may be appropriate to overrule that earlier decision: *Reference re the Agricultural Products Marketing Act*, [1978] 2 S.C.R. 1198.

In my view, *Leary* has also been undermined quite independently of the *Charter*. The Court has consistently held that an honest but unreasonable mistaken belief in consent will negate the *mens rea* required for rape, indecent assault or sexual assault: see *Pappajohn v. The Queen* [1980] 2 S.C.R. 120; *Sansregret v. The Queen*, [1985] 1 S.C.R. 570; *R. v. Bulmer*, [1987] 1 S.C.R. 782, and *R. v. Robertson*, [1987] 1 S.C.R. 918 at pp. 939-40. While the reasonableness of the accused's belief is a factor for the jury to consider in determining whether or not the belief was honestly held, a mistaken belief in consent need not be reasonable.

The *Leary* rule fits most awkwardly with that enunciated in *Pappajohn*. Lower courts have held that in the light of *Leary*, where intoxication is a factor in inducing a mistaken belief in consent, the jury must be instructed that while an honest but unreasonable belief will negate *mens rea* (*Pappajohn*) they are to disregard the effect that intoxication might have had in inducing that mistake (*Leary*). In *R. v. Moreau* (1986), 26 C.C.C. (3d) 359 (Ont. C.A.), at pp. 386-7, Martin J.A. described the task of the jury as follows:

> It does not follow that the defence of honest belief in consent is unavailable on a charge of sexual assault to an accused who is voluntarily intoxicated. Where an issue arises on the evidence as to the accused's honest belief in consent, the defence of honest belief in consent must be put to the jury, notwithstanding the accused's self-induced intoxication. There may be a basis in the evidence for the accused's honest belief in consent apart altogether from his intoxication; there may even be reasonable grounds for that belief even though he was intoxicated. The intoxication may not be the cause of the mistaken belief. However, the accused cannot rely on his self-induced intoxication as the basis for his belief that the complainant consented. As Mayrand J.A. said in *R. v. Bresse, Vallieres and Theberge* (1978), 48 C.C.C. (2d) 78 at p. 87, 7 C.R. (3d) 50 (Que. C.A.):

> > One must distinguish the case in which, because of one's voluntary inebriation, a man takes no account of the refusal manifested by a woman from the case in which a man, because of the ambiguous conduct of the woman, believes sincerely that she consented to sexual relations. This *error of fact committed for reasons other than one's voluntary inebriation* is, in my opinion, a valid ground of defence. (Emphasis added.)

> In those circumstances the jury is required to engage in the difficult, and perhaps somewhat artificial task, of putting out of their minds the evidence of intoxcation on the issue whether the accused honestly believed that the complainant consented. The test is not whether a reasonable and sober person would have made the same mistake but whether the accused would have made the same mistake if he had been sober; see Glanville Williams, *Textbook on Criminal Law*, 2nd ed. (1983) at pp. 481-2. However, to hold that evidence of self-induced intoxication is relevant to the honesty of the accused's belief in consent where his belief is founded on his mistaken appreciation, due to intoxication, of the facts relating to the complainant's consent is, in my view, incompatible with the rule laid down in *Leary*, and would completely negate the policy rule that self-induced intoxication is not a defence in crimes of general intent.

In my view, the *Leary* qualification on the criminal law principle of general application with respect to mistake of fact unnecessarily and unduly complicates the jury's task. Indeed, I find it difficult to imagine how it is humanly possible to follow the jury instruction apparently mandated by the combination of *Leary* and *Pappajohn*. This confusing and anomalous result is entirely the product of the deviation from basic criminal-law principles which occurred in *Leary* and accordingly there is much to support the view that it should be overruled.

The inconsistency between *Leary* and *Pappajohn* has not gone unnoticed in the literature. In *Canadian Criminal Law* (2nd ed. 1987), at p. 378, Professor Stuart describes the collision between *Leary* and *Pappajohn* as a "glaring inconsistency". In "Regina v. O'Connor: *Mens Rea* Survives in Australia" (1981), 19 U.W.O. L. Rev. 281, at pp. 300-301, David H. Doherty observes:

> The two judgments are clearly inconsistent. *Pappajohn* confirms the essential requirement of a subjective mental culpability as a prerequisite to criminal liability. *Leary* creates a fundamental exception to that requirement. The facts of *Pappajohn* show that the judgments will inevitably come into conflict. The Supreme Court of Canada chose to avoid dealing with the conflict in *Pappajohn* by ignoring the evidence of drinking by the accused. It is to be hoped that in a later case the Court will seek a more positive resolution to the problem. In seeking that resolution the majority position in *O'Connor* deserves emulation. After reading the opinions expressed in *O'Connor*, one concludes as did the minority in *Leary*, that the position taken in *Majewski* and adopted by the majority in *Leary* constitutes an illogical, unwarranted, and detrimental departure from the contemporary trend in criminal law which recognizes subjective mental blameworthiness at the time of the doing of the prohibited act as the sine qua non of criminal liability. The creation of exceptions to the principle compelled by considerations of public policy must be left to Parliament.

See also Peter J. Connelly, "Drunkenness and Mistake of Fact: Pappajohn v. The Queen; Swietlinski v. The Queen" (1981), 24 Crim. L. Q. 49; Christine Boyle, *Sexual Assault* (1984), at pp. 89-90.

C. *Leary* Creates Uncertainty

The third general consideration justifying the Court in overruling *Leary* is the principle established in *Minister of Indian Affairs and Northern Development v. Ranville, supra*, where the Court overruled its previous decision in *Commonwealth of Puerto Rico v. Hernandez*, [1975] 1 S.C.R. 228, on the ground that continued recognition of the *persona designata* category could only have the effect of creating doubt as to which procedure a party should follow. The prior decision itself was a cause of uncertainty, and therefore following the prior decision because of *stare decisis* would be contrary to the underlying value behind that doctrine, namely, clarity and certainty in the law. Similarly, in *Vetrovec, supra*, the Court overruled previous decisions relating to corroboration and stated, "The law of corroboration is unduly and unnecessarily complex and technical".

I have already indicated the confusion created by the combination of *Leary* and *Pappajohn*. I suggest that the distinction between "general" and "specific" intent which *Leary* mandates and the notorious difficulty in articulating a clear and workable definition of specific intent falls squarely within the principle enunciated in *Ranville* and *Vetrovec*. Because that category is based on policy rather than principle, classification of offences as falling within or without the specific intent category is necessarily an ad hoc, unpredictable exercise.

The situation with respect to the offence of break and enter, raised by the companion case, *R. v. Quin* (reasons being delivered contemporaneously) provides an example. In *R. v. Campbell* (1974), 17 C.C.C. (2d) 320 (Ont. C.A.), the accused was charged with breaking and entering with intent pursuant to s. 306(1)(*a*). The Ontario Court of Appeal held that offence to be a crime of specific intent and hence drunkenness was relevant to the issue of intention. In *Quin*, the accused was charged with breaking and entering and committing an indictable offence pursuant to s. 306(1)(*b*). The same Court held that under that subsection, the break and enter offence was one requiring only proof of general intent and hence evidence of intoxication could not be considered. A legal category which creates distinctions of this king, in my view, complicates and confuses the law to an unacceptable degree and, absent some compelling need for its retention, should be abandoned.

Another example of the complexity and uncertainty caused by the specific/general intent dichotomy is provided by *Swietlinski, supra*. In that case, the accused was charged with murder pursuant to s. 213(*d*) of the *Criminal Code*. The enumerated offence the accused was alleged to have committed was indecent assault. *Leary* had held that rape was an offence of general intent and in *Swietlinski*, the Court applied *Leary* to the offence of indecent assault. However, because of the constructive murder provision, this would have led to a situation where the accused would be convicted of murder without any criminal intent. To avoid that result, the Court held that where indecent assault formed the ingredient of constructive murder pursuant to s. 213, evidence of drunkenness could be taken into account in determining whether in fact the accused had the requisite intent for the offence of indecent assault. In other words, the Court held quite explicitly that intoxication did logically bear upon the issue of intent to commit indecent assault, and that the only issue was whether, as a matter of policy, the jury should be told to put that evidence out of mind. In the light of *Vaillancourt, Swietlinski* is no longer significant for its result. Indeed, *Vaillancourt* and *Swietlinski* have this in common: both cases demonstrate the Court's aversion to the imposition of liability without *mens rea*. In my view, to hold that evidence of intoxication can be taken into account with reference to an offence for certain purposes but not for other purposes is further reflection of the confusion, uncertainty, and lack of principle which motivates the specific/general intent dichotomy.

D. *Leary* Unfavourable to Accused

The fourth factor which bears directly upon whether or not the Court should overrule *Leary* in my view, is that the *Leary* rule is one which operates against the accused by expanding the scope of criminal liability beyond normal limits. Respect for the principle of certainty and the institutional limits imposed upon the law-making function of the Courts should constrain the Court from overruling a prior decision where the effect would be to expand criminal liability. It is not for the Courts to create new offences, or to broaden the net of liability, particularly as changes in the law through judicial decision operate retrospectively. The same argument does not apply, however, where the result of overruling a prior decision is to establish a rule favourable to the accused. In my submission, this principle underlies the decision of the Court in *Paquette v. The Queen, supra,* at p. 197, where the Court overruled its previous decision in *Dunbar v. The King, supra,* which had held that an accused who was a party to murder, but who had not himself committed the act, could not rely upon the defence of duresss. (See also *R. v. Santeramo* (1976), 32 C.C.C. (2d) 35 (Ont. C.A.), at p. 46 per Brooke J.A. "I do not feel bound by a judgment of this Court where the liberty of the subject is in issue if I am convinced that that judgment is wrong.")

IV

DISPOSITION

The trial Judge made no reference in his charge to the jury to the requirement that the Crown prove that the accused acted with the requisite intent. In my view, this is fatal to the conviction. Although the Crown presented a strong case against the accused at trial, no request was made by the respondent that this Court apply the provision of s. 613(1)(*b*)(iii) of the *Criminal Code,* and in any event, it is not for this Court to speculate as to the likely result had the jury been properly instructed.

It follows that the appeal should be allowed, the conviction set aside, and a new trial ordered.

La Forest J. (concurring in the result only): — I have had the advantage of reading the opinions prepared by the Chief Justice and Mr. Justice McIntyre. The requirement of *mens rea* in truly criminal offences is, as the Chief Justice had demonstrated, so fundamental that it cannot, since the *Charter,* be removed on the basis of judicially developed policy. It would be anomalous if the Courts could infringe such a fundamental right on the basis of such policies when not demonstrated to be essential, while any attempt by Parliament to do so would be subjected to searching scrutiny under s. 1 as established by this Court.

In my dissenting reasons in *R. v. Landry,* [1986] 1 S.C.R. 145, at p. 187, I set forth my views regarding the general issue posed here. I there observed that in the changed constitutional environment brought about by the *Charter,* if incursions are to be made upon fundamental legal values, it is for Parliament to do so, not the Courts. It is the duty of Parliament to respond to the challenge of criminal activities. While the Courts must sensitively consider actions taken by Parliament for the protection of the public generally, they must be forever diligent to prevent undue intrusions on our liberty. The courts are the protectors of our rights. It does not sit well for them to make rules intruding on fundamental rights even when this may appear to them to be desirable in a properly balanced system of criminal justice. That is Parliament's work. I added, at p. 189 of *Landry*:

> If Parliament in its wisdom finds it necessary to adjust the balance, it can do so. It is in a better position to provide for the precise balance and has a far better access to the knowledge required to achieve that balance than the Courts. The Courts can then perform their duty of scrutinizing Parliament's laws both in their general tenor and in their particular application to safeguard our traditional values.

Established common-law rules should not, it is true, lightly be assumed to violate the *Charter*. As a repository of our traditional values they may, in fact, assist in defining its norms. But when a common-law rule is found to infringe upon a right or freedom guaranteed by the *Charter*, it must be justified in the same way as legislative rules. No adequate justification was made here.

Accordingly, I am in general agreement with the law as stated by the Chief Justice. However, I agree with McIntyre J. that on the particular facts of this case no substantial wrong or miscarriage of justice has occurred and it is, therefore, a proper case to apply s. 613(1)(*b*)(iii) of the *Criminal Code*. For this reason, I would dispose of the case in the manner proposed by McIntyre J.

For comments on *Bernard*, see T. Quigley and A. Manson in 67 C.R. (3d) 168-182 and K. Campbell, "Intoxicated Mistakes" (1989), 32 Crim. L.Q. 110.

In *Daviault* a 6:3 majority of the Supreme Court adopted the Wilson compromise that extreme intoxication akin to automatism or insanity had, under the *Charter*, to be a defence to general intent crimes such as sexual assault. The majority, however, likening the defence to insanity, reversed the onus of proof.

R. v. DAVIAULT

[1994] 3 S.C.R. 63, 33 C.R. (4th) 165, 93 C.C.C. (3d) 21

The accused was charged with sexual assault. The complainant was a 65-year-old woman who was partially paralyzed and thus confined to a wheel chair. She knew the accused through his wife. At approximately 6 p.m. the accused, at her request, went to her home. He brought a 40-ounce bottle of brandy. The accused, aged 69, was a chronic alcoholic. He would later testify that he had already consumed seven or eight bottles of beer in a bar. The complainant drank part of a bottle of brandy and then fell asleep in her wheelchair. When she awoke during the night to go to the bathroom, the accused appeared, grabbed her chair, wheeled her into the bedroom, threw her on the bed and sexually assaulted her. The accused left the apartment at about 4 a.m. The trial Judge found that he had drunk the rest of the bottle of brandy between 6 p.m. and 3 a.m. The accused testified he had no recollection of the events until he awoke nude in the complainant's bed. He denied sexually assaulting her. A pharmacologist called as an expert witness for the accused testified that the accused's alcoholic history made him less susceptible to the effects of alcohol. He estimated that if the accused had consumed seven or eight beers and 35 ounces of brandy his blood alcohol level would be between 400 and 600 milligrams per 100 millilitres of blood. That ratio would cause death or a coma in an ordinary person. According to the expert an individual with this level of alcohol in his blood might suffer an episode of amnesia-automatism or "blackout". In such a state the individual loses contact with reality and the brain is temporarily dissociated from normal functioning. The individual has no awareness of his actions and likely no memory of them the next day. According to the witness it is difficult to distinguish between a person in a blackout and one simply acting while intoxicated. The latter state is more likely if the person has departed from his normal behaviour to act in a gratuitous or violent manner.

The trial Judge found that the accused had committed the offence described by the complainant. However, he acquitted because he had a reasonable doubt about whether the accused, by virtue of extreme intoxication to the point of automatism within the meaning of the judgment of Wilson J. in *Bernard*, had possessed the minimal intent necessary to commit the offence. The Quebec Court of Appeal allowed the Crown appeal and substituted a conviction. The Quebec Court of Appeal decided the majority of the Supreme Court in *Bernard* had not held that self-induced intoxication resulting in a state of akin to automatism or insanity was available as a defence to sexual assault. The accused appealed.

The majority of the Supreme Court allowed the appeal and ordered a new trial.

CORY J. (L'HEUREUX-DUBÉ, MCLACHLIN and IACOBUCCI JJ. concurring): —

Can a state of drunkenness which is so extreme that an accused is in a condition that closely resembles automatism or a disease of the mind as defined in s. 16 of the *Criminal Code*, R.S.C., 1985, c. C-46, constitute a basis for defending a crime which requires not a specific but only a general intent? That is the troubling question that is raised on this appeal.

. . . .

Categorization of Crimes as Requiring Either a Specific Intent or a General Intent

The distinction between crimes of specific and general intent has been acknowledged and approved by this Court on numerous occasions. . . . On this issue, I am in general agreement with Sopinka J.'s presentation. The categorization of crimes as being either specific or general intent offences and the consequences that flow from that categorization are now well-established in this Court. However, as he observes, we are not dealing here with ordinary cases of intoxication but with the limited situation of very extreme intoxication and the need, under the *Charter*, to create an exception in situations where intoxication is such that the mental element is negated. Sopinka J. sees no need for such an exception. This is where I must disagree with my colleague.

. . . .

The passage of the *Charter* makes it necessary to consider whether the decision in *Leary* contravenes s. 7 or 11(*d*) of the *Charter*. There have been some statements by this Court which indicate that one aspect of the decision in *Leary* does infringe these provisions of the *Charter*. The first occurred in *R. v. Bernard*. . . . Wilson J. (L'Heureux-Dubé J. concurring), agreed with the conclusion reached by McIntyre and Beetz JJ. However, she advocated a modification of the rule set out in *Leary*. Her reasoning proceeds in this way. Sexual assault causing bodily harm is an offence of general intent which requires only a minimal intent to apply force. Ordinarily the Crown can establish the requisite mental state by means of the inferences to be drawn from the actions of the accused. Wilson J. found that the *Leary* rule was perfectly consistent with an onus resting upon the Crown to prove the minimal intent which should accompany the doing of the prohibited act in general intent offences, but she would have applied it in a more flexible form. In her view, evidence of intoxication could properly go before a jury in general intent offences if it demonstrated such extreme intoxication that there was an absence of awareness which was akin to a state of insanity or automatism. Only in such cases would she find that the evidence was capable of raising a reasonable doubt as to the existence of the minimal intent required for a general intent offence.

. . . .

The Alternative Options

What options are available with regard to the admissibility and significance of evidence of drunkenness as it may pertain to the mental element in general intent offences? One choice would be to continue to apply the *Leary* rule. Yet, as I will attempt to demonstrate in the next section, the rule violates the *Charter* and cannot be justified. Thus this choice is unacceptable.

Another route would be to follow *O'Connor* [(1980), 4 A. Crim. R. 348.] Evidence relating to drunkenness would then go to the jury along with all other relevant evidence in determining whether the mental element requirement had been met. It is this path that is enthusiastically recommended by the majority of writers in the field. Yet it cannot be followed. It is now well-established by this Court that there are two categories of offences. Those requiring a specific intent and others which call for nothing more than a general intent. To follow *O'Connor* would mean that all evidence of intoxication of any degree would always go to the jury in general intent offences. This, in my view, is unnecessary. Further, in *Bernard, supra*, the majority of this Court rejected this approach.

A third alternative, which I find compelling, is that proposed by Wilson J. in *Bernard*. I will examine the justifications for adopting this position in more detail shortly, but before doing that it may be helpful to review the nature of the *Charter* violations occasioned by a rigid application of the *Leary* rule.

How the Leary Rule Violates Sections 7 and 11(d) of the Charter

What then is the rule of law established by the decision in *Leary*? The conclusion of the majority in that case establishes that, even in a situation where the level of intoxication reached by the accused is sufficient to raise a reasonable doubt as to his capacity to form the minimal mental element required for a general intent offence for which he is being tried, he still cannot be acquitted. In such a situation, self-induced intoxication is substituted for the mental element of the crime. The result of the decision in *Leary*, applied to this case, is that the intentional act of the accused to voluntarily become intoxicated is substituted for the intention to commit the sexual assault or for the recklessness of the accused with regard to the assault. This is a true substitution of *mens rea*. First, it would be rare that the events transpiring from the consumption of alcohol through to the commission of the crime could be seen as one continuous series of events or as a single transaction. Secondly, the requisite mental element or *mens rea* cannot necessarily be inferred from the physical act or *actus reus* when the very voluntariness or consciousness of that act may be put in question by the extreme intoxication of the accused.

It has not been established that there is such a connection between the consumption of alcohol and the crime of assault that it can be said that drinking leads inevitably to the assault. Experience may suggest that alcohol makes it easier for violence to occur by diminishing the sense of what is acceptable behaviour. However, studies indicate that it is not in itself a cause of violence.

. . . .

In my view, the strict application of the *Leary* rule offends both ss. 7 and 11(*d*) of the *Charter* for a number of reasons. The mental aspect of an offence, or *mens rea*, has long been recognized as an integral part of crime. The concept is fundamental to our criminal law. That element may be minimal in general intent offences; nonetheless, it exists. In this case, the requisite mental element is simply an intention to commit the sexual assault or recklessness as to whether the actions will constitute an assault. The necessary mental element can ordinarily be inferred from the proof that the assault was committed by the accused. However, the substituted *mens rea* of an intention to become drunk cannot establish the *mens rea* to commit the assault.

R. v. Whyte, [1988] 2 S.C.R. 3, dealt with the substitution of proof of one element for proof of an essential element of an offence and emphasized the strict limitations that must be imposed on such substitutions. The position is put in this way at pp. 18-19:

In the passage from *Vaillancourt* quoted earlier, Lamer J. recognized that in some cases substituting proof of one element for proof of an essential element will not infringe the presumption of innocence if, upon proof of the substituted element, it would be unreasonable for the trier of fact not to be satisfied beyond a reasonable doubt of the existence of the essential element. This is another way of saying that a statutory presumption infringes the presumption of innocence if it requires the trier of fact to convict in spite of a reasonable doubt. *Only if the existence of the substituted fact leads inexorably to the conclusion that the essential element exists, with no other reasonable possibilities, will the statutory presumption be constitutionally valid.* [Emphasis added.]

The substituted *mens rea* set out in *Leary* does not meet this test. The consumption of alcohol simply cannot lead inexorably to the conclusion that the accused possessed the requisite mental element to commit a sexual assault, or any other crime. Rather, the substituted *mens rea* rule has the effect of eliminating the minimal mental element required for sexual assault. Furthermore, *mens rea* for a crime is so well-recognized that to eliminate that mental element, an integral part of the crime, would be to deprive an accused of fundamental justice. See *R. v. Vaillancourt*, [1987] 2 S.C.R. 636.

. . . .

Sopinka J. refers to the common law rules of automatism in order to support his position that voluntariness is not a requirement of fundamental justice. With respect I cannot agree. The decision of this Court in *Revelle v. The Queen*, [1981] 1 S.C.R. 576, predates the *Charter*. The rule that self-induced automatism cannot be a defence has never been subjected to a *Charter* analysis. In my view, automatism raises the same concerns as those presented in this case. Thus, to state that the rule in *Leary*, which precludes the accused from negating the mental element of voluntariness on the basis of an extreme state of intoxication, does not violate the *Charter* because the same principle has been developed in the context of the defence of automatism begs the very question which is now before this Court. The presumption of innocence requires that the Crown bear the burden of establishing all elements of a crime. These elements include the mental element of voluntariness. That element cannot be eliminated without violating s. 11(*d*) and s. 7 of the *Charter*.

It was argued by the respondent that the "blameworthy" nature of voluntary intoxication is such that it should be determined that there can be no violation of the *Charter* if the *Leary* approach is adopted. I cannot accept that contention. Voluntary intoxication is not yet a crime. Further, it is difficult to conclude that such behaviour should always constitute a fault to which criminal sanctions should apply. However, assuming that voluntary intoxication is reprehensible, it does not follow that its consequences in any given situation are either voluntary or predictable. Studies demonstrate that the consumption of alcohol is not the cause of the crime. A person intending to drink cannot be said to be intending to commit a sexual assault.

Further, self-induced intoxication cannot supply the necessary link between the minimal mental element or *mens rea* required for the offence and the *actus reus*. This must follow from reasoning in *R. v. DeSousa*, [1992] 2 S.C.R. 944, and *R. v. Theroux*, *supra*. Here, the question is not whether there is some symmetry between the physical act and the mental element but whether the necessary link exists between the minimal mental element and the prohibited act; that is to say that the mental element is one of intention with respect to the *actus reus* of the crime charged. As well, as Sopinka J. observes, the minimum *mens rea* for an offence should reflect the particular nature of the crime. See *R. v. Creighton*, [1993] 3 S.C.R. 3. I doubt that self-induced intoxication can, in all circumstances, meet this requirement for all crimes of general intent.

In summary, I am of the view that to deny that even a very minimal mental element is required for sexual assault offends the *Charter* in a manner that is so drastic and so contrary to the principles of fundamental justice that it cannot be justified under s. 1 of the *Charter*. The experience of other jurisdictions which have completely abandoned the *Leary* rule, coupled with the fact that under the proposed approach, the defence would be available only in the rarest of cases, demonstrate that there is no urgent policy or pressing objective which need to be addressed. Studies on the relationship between intoxication and crime do not establish any rational link. Finally, as the *Leary* rule applies to all crimes of general intent, it cannot be said to be well-tailored to address a particular objective and it would not meet either the proportionality or the minimum impairment requirements.

. . . .

Far more writers have supported the approach advocated by Dickson J. in *Leary*, and adopted in *O'Connor*. In my view, the most vehement and cogent criticism of both *Majewski* and *Leary* is that they substitute proof of drunkenness for proof of the requisite mental element. The authors deplore the division of crimes into those requiring a specific intent and those which mandate no more than a general intent. They are also critical of the resulting presumption of recklessness, and of the loss of a requirement of a true *mens rea* for the offence. They would prefer an approach that would permit evidence of drunkenness to go to the jury together with all the other relevant evidence in determining whether the requisite *mens rea* had been established.

. . . .

I find further support for adopting the approach suggested by Wilson J. in studies pertaining to the effect of the *O'Connor* and *Kamipeli* decisions which have been undertaken in Australia and New Zealand. (Reference to these studies can be found in the English Law Commission's *Intoxication and Criminal Liability*, *supra*, at pp. 60-63.) One of these studies was conducted in New South Wales, by means of a survey of approximately 510 trials (see Judge G. Smith, "Footnote to O'Connor's Case", *supra*. The author, Judge George Smith, concluded, at p. 277, that:

> Those figures disclose that a "defence" of intoxication which could not have been relied upon pre-*O'Connor* was raised in 11 cases or 2.16 percent of the total. Acquittals followed in three cases or 0.59 percent of the total, but only in one case or 0.2 percent of the total could

it be said with any certainty that the issue of intoxication was the factor which brought about the acquittal.

. . . .

It seems to me that no one with any experience of the criminal Courts should be greatly surprised at this result for the simple practical reason that any "defence" of drunkenness poses enormous difficulties in the conduct of a case. To name but one, if the accused has sufficient recollection to describe relevant events, juries will be reluctant to believe that he acted involuntarily or without intent whereas, if he claims to have no recollection, he will be unable to make any effective denial of facts alleged by the Crown.

. . . .

Certainly my inquiries would indicate that the decision in *O'Connor*'s case, far from opening any floodgates has at most permitted an occasional drip to escape from the tap.

That study clearly indicates that the *O'Connor* decision has not had an effect of any significance on trials or on the numbers of acquittals arising from evidence of severe intoxication.

. . . .

It is obvious that it will only be on rare occasions that evidence of such an extreme state of intoxication can be advanced and perhaps only on still rarer occasions is it likely to be successful. Nonetheless, the adoption of this alternative would avoid infringement of the *Charter*.

I would add that it is always open to Parliament to fashion a remedy which would make it a crime to commit a prohibited act while drunk.

. . . .

It should not be forgotten that if the flexible "Wilson" approach is taken, the defence will only be put forward in those rare circumstances of extreme intoxication. Since that state must be shown to be akin to automatism or insanity, I would suggest that the accused should be called upon to establish it on the balance of probabilities. This Court has recognized, in *R. v. Chaulk*, [1990] 3 S.C.R. 1303, that although it constituted a violation of the accused's rights under s. 11(*d*) of the *Charter*, such a burden could be justified under s. 1. In this case, I feel that the burden can be justified. Drunkenness of the extreme degree required in order for it to become relevant will only occur on rare occasions. It is only the accused who can give evidence as to the amount of alcohol consumed and its effect upon him. Expert evidence would be required to confirm that the accused was probably in a state akin to automatism or insanity as a result of his drinking.

. . . .

Should it be thought that the mental element involved relates to the *actus reus* rather than the *mens rea* then the result must be the same. The *actus reus* requires that the prohibited criminal act be performed voluntarily as a willed act. A person in a state of automatism cannot perform a voluntary willed act since the automatism has deprived the person of the ability to carry out such an act. It follows that someone in an extreme state of intoxication akin to automatism must also be deprived of that ability. Thus a fundamental aspect of the *actus reus* of the criminal act is absent. It would equally infringe s. 7 of the *Charter* if an accused who was not acting voluntarily could be convicted of a criminal offence. Here again the voluntary act of becoming intoxicated cannot be substituted for the voluntary action involved in sexual assault. To do so would violate the principle set out in *Vaillancourt, supra*. Once again to convict in the face of such a fundamental denial of natural justice could not be justified under s. 1 of the *Charter*.

Summary of Proposed Remedy

In my view, the *Charter* could be complied with, in crimes requiring only a general intent, if the accused were permitted to establish that, at the time of the offence, he was in a state of extreme intoxication akin to automatism or insanity. Just as in a situation where it is sought to establish a state of insanity, the accused must bear the burden of establishing, on the balance of probabilities, that he was in that extreme state of intoxication. This will undoubtedly require the testimony of an expert. Obviously, it will be a rare situation where an accused is able to establish such an extreme degree of intoxication. Yet, permitting such a procedure would mean that a defence would remain open that, due to the extreme degree of intoxication, the minimal mental element required by a general intent offence had not been established. To permit this rare and limited defence in general intent offences is required so that the common law principles of intoxication can comply with the *Charter*.

In light of the experience in Australia or New Zealand, it cannot be said that to permit such a defence would open the floodgates to allow every accused who had a drink before committing the prohibited act to raise the defence of drunkenness. As observed earlier, studies made in Australia and New Zealand indicate that there has not been any significant increase in the number of acquittals following the *O'Connor* and *Kamipelli* decisions.

Disposition

In the result, I would allow the appeal, set aside the order of the Court of Appeal and direct a new trial.

LAMER C.J.: — I have read the reasons of my colleagues, Justice Sopinka and Justice Cory. My views of the matter were enunciated through my concurrence in the reasons of Dickson C.J. in *R. v. Bernard*, [1988] 2 S.C.R. 833. While I now prefer characterizing the mental element involved as relating more to the *actus reus* than the *mens rea*, so that the defence clearly be available in strict liability offences, my views have not changed. I agree with my colleague Cory J.'s position on the law and, given my position in *Bernard*, which goes much further, I would of course support carving out, as he does, an exception to the rule laid down in *Leary v. The Queen*, [1978] 1 S.C.R. 29. I would accordingly allow the appeal and direct a new trial.

LA FOREST J.: — In *R. v. Bernard*, [1988] 2 S.C.R. 833, as well as in *R. v. Quin*, [1988] 2 S.C.R. 825, I, along with the Chief Justice, shared the view of then Chief Justice Dickson which strongly challenged the rule in *Leary v. The Queen*, [1978] 1 S.C.R. 29. While the majority of the Court differed as to the specific interpretation of *Leary*, what is clear is that they rejected the view espoused by Dickson C.J. I am, therefore, left to choose between the approach set forth in McIntyre J.'s reasons in that case, developed here by Justice Sopinka, and those of Wilson J., developed here by Justice Cory. Of the two, I prefer the latter and accordingly (though I would be inclined to attribute the mental element he describes as going to the *actus reus*) I concur in the reasons of Cory J. and would dispose of this appeal in the manner proposed by him.

SOPINKA J. (GONTHIER and MAJOR JJ. concurring) (dissenting): —

. . . .

Central to [the *Charter*'s] values are the integrity and dignity of the human person. These serve to define the principles of fundamental justice. They encompass as an essential attribute and are predicated upon the moral responsibility of every person of sound mind for his or her acts. The requirement of *mens rea* is an application of this principle. To allow generally an accused who is not afflicted by a disease of the mind to plead absence of *mens rea* where he has voluntarily caused himself to be incapable of *mens rea* would be to undermine, indeed negate, that very principle of moral responsibility which the requirement of *mens rea* is intended to give effect to.

The second requirement of the principles of fundamental justice is that punishment must be proportionate to the moral blameworthiness of the offender. This was held to be a principle of fundamental justice in *R. v. Martineau*, [1990] 2 S.C.R. 633, and *R. v. Creighton*, *supra*. There are a few crimes in respect of which a special level of *mens rea* is constitutionally required by reason of the stigma attaching to a conviction and by reason of the severity of the penalty imposed by law. Accordingly, murder and attempted murder require a *mens rea* based on a subjective standard. No exception from the principle of fundamental justice should be made with respect to these offences and, as specific intent offences, drunkenness is a defence.

By contrast, sexual assault does not fall into the category of offences for which either the stigma or the available penalties demand as a constitutional requirement subjective intent to commit the *actus reus*. Sexual assault is a heinous crime of violence. Those found guilty of committing the offence are rightfully submitted to a significant degree of moral opprobrium. That opprobrium is not misplaced in the case of the intoxicated offender. Such individuals deserve to be stigmatized. Their moral blameworthiness is similar to that of anyone else who commits the offence of sexual assault and the effects of their conduct upon both their victims and society as a whole are the same as in any other case of sexual assault. Furthermore, the sentence for sexual assault is not fixed. To the extent that it bears upon his or her level of moral blameworthiness, an offender's degree of intoxication at the time of the offence may be considered during sentencing. Taking all of these factors into account, I cannot see how the stigma and punishment associated with the offence of sexual assault are disproportionate to the moral blameworthiness of a person like the appellant who commits the offence after voluntarily becoming so intoxicated as to be incapable of knowing what he was doing. The fact that the *Leary* rule permits an individual to be convicted despite the absence of symmetry between the *actus reus* and the mental element of blameworthiness does not violate a principle of fundamental justice.

It is further contended that the *Leary* rule violates the presumption of innocence because it permits an individual to be convicted despite the existence of a reasonable doubt as to whether or not that individual performed the *actus reus* of his or her own volition. This argument is premised upon the assumption that voluntariness is a constitutionally required element of the *actus reus* of an offence of universal application. Again, I do not think that this assumption is warranted.

. . . .

It is true that as a general rule, an act must be the voluntary act of an accused in order for the *actus reus* to exist. See *R. v. Parks*, [1992] 2 S.C.R. 871, at p. 896, per La Forest J., and *R. v. Theroux*, [1993] 2 S.C.R. 5, at p. 17, per McLachlin J. This, as in the case of *mens rea*, is a general rule of the criminal law, but when elevated to a principle of fundamental justice it too, exceptionally, is not absolute. One well-recognized exception is made relating to the defence of non-insane automatism. As I explain below, automatism does not apply to excuse an offence if the accused's state is brought on by his or her own fault. The condition of automatism deprives the accused of volition to commit the offence but the general rule gives way to the policy that, in the circumstances, the perpetrator who by his or her own fault brings about the condition should not escape punishment. An accused person who voluntarily drinks alcohol or ingests a drug to the extent that he or she becomes an automaton is in the same position. The rules of fundamental justice are satisfied by a showing that the drunken state was attained through the accused's own blameworthy conduct.

Another criticism of the current rules governing the availability of the intoxication defence is that the distinction between offences of specific and general intent is illogical. Critics of the rule contend that there is no principled basis for distinguishing between offences of general and specific intent and thus there is no logical reason why intoxication should be a defence to offences of specific intent but not to offences of general intent.

The appellant does not, however, take issue with the proposition that in general the distinction between offences of specific and general intent is a valid one. His submission is that when drunkenness reaches the stage of automatism, the distinction should no longer apply. This essentially was the tentative view of Wilson J. as expressed in her *obiter* statement in *R. v. Bernard* to which I referred above.

Notwithstanding the position of the appellant, I propose to briefly address the criticism of the rule that it is illogical. In my view, the concept has strong policy underpinnings which, despite the fact that its definition and application may have produced some illogical results, have permitted it to survive for over 150 years in England and to be adopted in Canada and most states of the United States.

. . . .

The principles that emerge from the cases which serve as guidelines in classifying offences as specific or general intent offences are as follows. General intent offences as a rule are those which require the minimal intent to do the act which constitutes the *actus reus*. Proof of intent is usually inferred from the commission of the act on the basis of the principle that a person intends the natural consequences of his or her act. Without attempting to exhaust the policy reasons for excluding the defence of drunkenness from this category of offences, I would observe that it is seldom, even in cases of extreme drunkenness, that a person will lack this minimal degree of consciousness. Moreover, these are generally offences that persons who are drunk are apt to commit and it would defeat the policy behind them to make drunkenness a defence.

Specific intent offences are as a rule those that require a mental element beyond that of general intent offences and include "those generally more serious offences where the *mens rea* must involve not only the intentional performance of the *actus reus* but, as well, the formation of further ulterior motives and purposes" (per McIntyre J. in *R. v. Bernard, supra*, at p. 880). These are often referred to as "ulterior intent" offences. See *Majewski, supra*. Professor Colvin, in "A Theory of the Intoxication Defence" (1981), 59 Can. Bar Rev. 750, correctly points out that it is the further intent in addition to the basic intent that is the hallmark of ulterior intent offences. The policy behind this classification is in part the importance of the mental element over and above the minimal intent required for general intent offences. This distinction demands that the accused not be convicted if the added important mental state is negated by the drunken condition of the accused. Failure to prove the added element will often result in conviction of a lesser offence for which the added element is not required. One example is the offence of assault to resist or prevent arrest which is a specific intent offence. Absent the intent to resist arrest, the accused would be convicted of assault *simpliciter*, a general intent offence.

In addition to the ulterior intent offences there are certain offences which by reason of their serious nature and the importance of the mental element are classed as specific intent offences notwithstanding that they do not fit the criteria usually associated with ulterior intent offences. The outstanding example is murder. This is the most serious of criminal offences which carries a fixed penalty. By reason of the importance of the required mental element and the fixed penalty, this offence is classified as a specific intent offence. The defence of drunkenness is allowed so as to reduce the crime to manslaughter tempering the harshness of the law which precludes drunkenness as a consideration as to sentence. The classification of murder as a specific intent offence illustrates the proper application of policy in a case in which the application of the normal criteria might lead to a different result.

I accept that the application of the terms "specific" and "general" may lead to some illogical results. This is not surprising in light of the circumstances outlined above. Moreover, even the clearest unifying principle will in its application not produce perfect harmony. I am, however, convinced that the underlying policy of the *Leary* rule is sound. I am of the opinion that the criticism of the rule on the grounds of illogicality has been overdone. Applying criteria similar to the above, Professor Colvin has been able to explain "the broad pattern of the decisions emanating from the Courts". See Colvin, *supra*, at p. 768.

. . . .

Conclusion

For all of these reasons, in my opinion the best course is for the Court to reaffirm the traditional rule that voluntary intoxication does not constitute a defence to an offence of general intent, subject to the comments I have made with respect to improvements in the definition and application of the distinction between offences of specific and general intent. If a different approach is considered desirable because the *Leary* approach does not comport with social policy, Parliament is free to intervene. I note that this observation was made by McIntyre J. in *R. v. Bernard* but Parliament has not intervened. It has been suggested that Parliament should create a new offence of dangerous intoxication. Such a recommendation was made by the Butler Committee in England and by the Law Reform Commission in Canada. (See Butler Committee Report on Mentally Abnormal Offenders (1975) (Cmnd. 6244, paras. 18.51-18.59) and Law Reform Commission of Canada, Recodifying Criminal Law, Report 30, vol. 1 (1986), at pp. 27-28.) Such legislation could be coupled with amendments to the *Criminal Code* to extend the defence of drunkenness to some or all offences to which it does not apply. Such changes, however, are for Parliament and not for this Court to make.

In *Majewski*, Lord Elwyn-Jones L.C. summed up the situation in words with which I fully agree. He stated, at p. 475:

> It may well be that Parliament will at some future time consider, as I think it should, the recommendation in the Butler Committee Report on Mentally Abnormal Offenders (Cmnd. 6244, 1975) that a new offence of "dangerous intoxication" should be created. But in the meantime it would be irresponsible to abandon the common-law rule, as "mercifully relaxed," which the Courts have followed for a century and a half.

Disposition

The trial Judge stated that but for his opinion that the appellant's extreme state of drunkenness constituted a defence, he would have convicted the appellant. I agree with the Court of Appeal that the trial Judge erred in law in this regard. The Court of Appeal was right, therefore, to substitute a conviction. I would dismiss the appeal.

The only description of the facts provided by the Supreme Court appears in the judgment of Sopinka J., who indicates that they were "not in dispute". The record appears incomplete. For further details gathered from the Crown factum and from communications with both counsel, see Patrick Healy, "Another Round on Intoxication", published in the Criminal Reports Forum issue on *Daviault*:

> He threw her from the chair onto the bed, began to fondle her under her dressing-gown, and then attempted to rape her. The victim struggled and demanded twice to go to the toilet. The accused insisted that they have sex. He said several times "We are going to make love". He spoke of going to Florida with the victim and more than once he called the victim by a name that was neither hers nor his wife's. He prevented her from going to the toilet and she urinated on him in the bed. When she attempted to call 911 for assistance, he struck her several times in the face with full force. He also struck the telephone from her hand. He pulled her up by her hair and demanded that she perform *fellatio*, at which point she squeezed and twisted his testicles. She testified that he showed no reaction to this. He then fell onto the bed. She dragged herself along the floor and pulled herself into the wheelchair. All this occurred over a period of about an hour. At about 4 a.m. he searched about to find the shirt that he had been wearing when he arrived. He found it, dressed himself and went home.

> The victim testified that during the assault the accused did not appear to be drunk but she did state that the bottle of brandy and the glass from which she had been drinking were empty. The wife of the accused testified that Daviault came home at about 4:20 and did not appear to be drunk. He let himself into the house with his key, walked entirely straight, undressed and went to bed. She said that when he came home very drunk he was usually unable to open the door and slept fully dressed after passing out. On this occasion he also appeared quite calm and not "agitated or tormented" as he normally was after drinking strong liquor. She later noticed that his testicles had turned black.

On *Daviault*, see also, in the Criminal Reports, comments by Isabel Grant, Tim Quigley and Don Stuart. See also Martha Shaffer, "Criminal Responsibility and the Charter: The Case of *R. v. Daviault*" in Cameron (ed.), *The Charter's Impact on the Criminal Justice System* (1996) pp. 313-325.

The new trial ordered in *Daviault* resulted in a judicial stay of proceedings: (1995), 39 C.R. (4th) 269 (C.Q.). The complainant by then was deceased and disclosure of statements made originally to the police revealed inconsistencies such that the cross-examination would have been quite different. It was held that to proceed would be a denial of natural justice. See comment by Patrick Healy in (1995), 39 C.R. (4th) 272.

Public reaction to *Daviault* was swift. The Minister of Justice, Allan Rock, was reported to be "deeply troubled" by the ruling because of its "tremendous ramifications in sexual assault cases". It was widely condemned as giving the wrong message to those who drink and harm. Commentators used extravagant hypotheticals of rapists getting off on the basis of having had a few drinks. That such views were misreadings of the majority opinion is quite clear.

The number of acquittals that followed *Daviault* was wildly exaggerated.

Later, Martha Drassinower and Don Stuart, "Nine Months of Judicial Application of the *Daviault* Defence" (1995), 39 C.R. (4th) 280, surveyed reported and unreported judgments in the nine months following the Supreme Court's ruling. Eleven *Daviault* defences were considered at trial. Five were successful but two were subsequently reversed on appeal. Given what must have been thousands of criminal cases involving intoxicated accused over that period, the survey provides some validation of Justice Cory's prediction that the defence would be rarely used and would rarely succeed.

On February 24, 1995, the Minister of Justice, Allan Rock, tabled Bill C-72 in the House of Commons, purporting to provide that "extreme intoxication is not a defence to crimes of violence". **Is this amendment wise? Is it constitutional?**

Bill C-72

An Act to amend the *Criminal Code* (self-induced intoxication)

Preamble

WHEREAS the Parliament of Canada is gravely concerned about the incidence of violence in Canadian society;

WHEREAS the Parliament of Canada recognizes that violence has a particularly disadvantaging impact on the equal participation of women and children in society and on the rights of women and children to security of the person and to the equal protection and benefit of the law as guaranteed by sections 7, 15 and 28 of the *Canadian Charter of Rights and Freedoms*;

WHEREAS the Parliament of Canada recognizes that there is a close association between violence and intoxication and is concerned that self-induced intoxication may be used socially and legally to excuse violence, particularly violence against women and children;

WHEREAS the Parliament of Canada recognizes that the potential effects of alcohol and certain drugs on human behaviour are well-known to Canadians and is aware of scientific evidence that many intoxicants, including alcohol, may not cause a person to act involuntarily;

WHEREAS the Parliament of Canada shares with Canadians the moral view that people who, while in a state of self-induced intoxication, violate the physical integrity of others are blameworthy in relation to their harmful conduct and should be held criminally accountable for it;

WHEREAS the Parliament of Canada desires to promote and help to ensure the full protection of the rights guaranteed under sections 7, 11, 15 and 28 of the

Canadian Charter of Rights and Freedoms for all Canadians, including those who are or may be victims of violence;

WHEREAS the Parliament of Canada considers it necessary to legislate a basis of criminal fault in relation to self-induced intoxication and general intent offences involving violence;

WHEREAS the Parliament of Canada recognizes the continuing existence of a common-law principle that intoxication to an extent that is less than that which would cause a person to lack the ability to form the basic intent or to have the voluntariness required to commit a criminal offence of general intent is never a defence at law;

AND WHEREAS the Parliament of Canada considers it necessary and desirable to legislate a standard of care, in order to make it clear that a person who, while in a state of incapacity by reason of self-induced intoxication, commits an offence involving violence against another person, departs markedly from the standard of reasonable care that Canadians owe to each other and is thereby criminally at fault;

NOW, THEREFORE, Her Majesty, by and with the advice and consent of the Senate and House of Commons of Canada, enacts as follows:

Self-induced Intoxication

When defence not available

33.1 (1) It is not a defence to an offence referred to in subsection (3) that the accused, by reason of self-induced intoxication, lacked the basic intent or the voluntariness required to commit the offence, where the accused departed markedly from the standard of care as described in subsection (2).

Criminal fault by reason of intoxication

(2) For the purposes of this section, a person departs markedly from the standard of reasonable care generally recognized in Canadian society and is thereby criminally at fault where the person, while in a state of self-induced intoxication that renders the person unaware of, or incapable of consciously controlling, their behaviour, voluntarily or involuntarily interferes or threatens to interfere with the bodily integrity of another person.

Application

(3) This section applies in respect of an offence under this Act or any other Act of Parliament that includes as an element an assault or any other

interference or threat of interference by a person with the bodily integrity of another person.

The effect of this most complex provision is to use a deemed fault provision to remove the *Daviault* defence to most general intent offences. Most such offences involve at least threats to bodily integrity so as to come within the ambit of subs. (3). However, s. 33.1 does not affect the common law defence of drunkenness available to specific intent crimes such as murder and robbery.

Whether s. 33.1 will survive *Charter* review remains to be seen. Lower courts have accepted that s. 33.1 flies in the face of the determination in *Daviault* that principles of fundamental justice require a defence of intoxication where this is akin to automatism. But they are equally divided on the further question of whether the s. 7 violation can be saved under s. 1 as a demonstrably justified reasonable limit. Rulings of constitutionality were reached in *Vickberg* (1998), 16 C.R. (5th) 164 (B.C. S.C.) and *Decaire* (September 11, 1998), (Ont. Gen. Div.). Section 33.1 was ruled unconstitutional in *Dunn* (1999), 28 C.R. (5th) 295 (Ont. Gen. Div.) and *Brenton* (1999), 28 C.R. (5th) 308 (N.W.T. S.C.). These rulings are fully discussed by Kelly Smith, "Section 33.1: Denial of *Daviault* Defence Should Be Held Constitutional" (2000), 28 C.R. (5th) 350. The Supreme Court is not yet on record as justifying a s. 7 violation. On the other hand, in *Mills* (2000), 28 C.R. (5th) 207 (S.C.C.), the Court spoke of a need for dialogue with Parliament which should allow for deference to legislative schemes. Furthermore, *Mills* also recognized that complainants in sexual assault cases have enforceable s. 15 rights which must be balanced not just as a matter of principles of fundamental justice. Isabel Grant, "Second Chances: Bill C-72 and the *Charter*" (1995), 33 Osgoode Hall L.J. 381, argues sex equality considerations should determine that s. 33.1 does not offend s. 7. The clear subtext to the negative reaction and Parliamentary response to *Daviault* was clearly grounded in that context. Another complication is that evidence was tendered at the Parliamentary committee hearings leading to Bill C-72 refuting the *Daviault* view that intoxication can lead to a state of automatism. See review by Smith, above, at 362-364. See, too, Joseph Wilkinson, "The Possibility of Alcoholic Automatism: Some Empirical Evidence" (1997), 2 Can. Crim. L. Rev. 217. Even if s. 33.1 survives *Charter* review in the Supreme Court, fundamental questions will remain as to the wisdom of the current legal regime for intoxication, rooted, as it still is, in the untenable distinction between specific and general intent.

R. v. ROBINSON

46 C.R. (4th) 1, 105 C.C.C. (3d) 97, [1996] 1 S.C.R. 683

The accused was charged with second degree murder. He had struck the victim with a rock after the victim had said something to him. He then fatally stabbed him. The accused was convicted following trial before judge and jury. The majority of the British Columbia Court of Appeal allowed the appeal on the basis of misdirection as to the defence of intoxication. The Crown appealed. The appeal was dismissed.

LAMER C.J.C. (LA FOREST, SOPINKA, GONTHIER, CORY, MCLACHLIN, IACOBUCCI and MAJOR JJ. concurring): —

In March of 1920, Britain's House of Lords handed down judgment in the now famous *Beard* case (*Director of Public Prosecutions v. Beard*, [1920] A.C. 479). The issue before the court concerned the manner in which a jury should be instructed on the relationship between intoxication and intent. Lord Birkenhead, in speaking for the court, formulated rules that evidence of intoxication is to be considered by a jury only in those cases where its effect was to render the accused incapable of forming the requisite intent. In *MacAskill v. The King*, [1931] S.C.R. 330, the Beard rules were incorporated into our law and they have been, for the most part, applied by this Court ever since.

. . . .

In delivering his speech in *Beard*, Lord Birkenhead reviewed the developments over the last century and formulated the following famous rules of intoxication which he believed properly reflected the current state of the English law:

> That evidence of drunkenness which renders the accused incapable of forming the specific intent essential to constitute the crime should be taken into consideration with the other facts proved in order to determine whether or not he had this intent.

> That evidence of drunkenness falling short of a proved incapacity in the accused to form the intent necessary to constitute the crime, and merely establishing that his mind was affected by drink so that he more readily gave way to some violent passion, does not rebut the presumption that a man intends the natural consequences of his acts.

Under these rules, intoxication is not a relevant factor for triers of fact to consider except in those cases where the alcohol or drugs has removed the accused's capacity to form the requisite intent.

Some eleven years after the decision in *Beard*, this Court was given an opportunity to consider the manner in which juries should be instructed on the circumstances under which intoxication could reduce a charge of murder to manslaughter in *MacAskill*. *MacAskill* had been convicted of murder and sentenced to death. In ruling on the propriety of the trial judge's charge to the jury, this Court held that the *Beard* "propositions embody the rules governing us on this appeal".

. . . .

The only modification to the *Beard* rules came in *Malanik v. The Queen*, [1952] 2 S.C.R. 335, at p. 341, where this Court held that the word "proved" should be removed from its rules. In other words, intoxication should be treated like any other defence where there is simply an evidentiary burden on the accused to adduce some evidence capable of raising a reasonable doubt . . . . I wish to take the opportunity in this case to hold that the presumption of intent, to which *Beard* refers, should only be interpreted and referred to as a common

sense and logical inference that the jury can but is not compelled to make . . . .
Since *MacAskill*, the *Beard* rules and "capacity" language have been approved
of and relied on in many decisions of this Court . . . . The important issue raised
by this appeal is whether the Court should now overrule the *Beard* rules of
intoxication incorporated in *MacAskill* and its progeny.

. . . .

In deciding that the time has come to overrule *MacAskill*, I am cognizant of
the fact that the *Beard* rules are no longer followed by any provincial appellate
court in this country that has considered the issue. In place of the *Beard* rules,
two different approaches have developed over the years. The Ontario Court of
Appeal was the first provincial appellate court to develop an alternative
approach. The Ontario approach culminated in Martin J.A.'s decision in *R. v.
MacKinlay* (1986), 28 C.C.C. (3d) 306 (C.A.). Under *MacKinlay* a jury is to be
instructed as follows:

> Where intoxication is in issue, I think it would be helpful for the trial judge to draw the
> jury's attention to the common knowledge of the effects of the consumption of alcohol. He
> should first instruct the jury that intoxication causing a person to cast off restraint and act in
> a manner in which he would not have acted if sober affords no excuse for the commission of
> a crime while in that state if he had the intent required to constitute the crime. He should then
> instruct the jury that where a specific intent is necessary to constitute the crime, the crime is
> not committed if the accused lacked the specific intent essential to constitute the crime. In
> considering whether the Crown has proved beyond a reasonable doubt that the accused had
> the specific intent required to constitute the crime charged, they should take into account the
> accused's consumption of alcohol or drugs along with the other facts which throw light on the
> accused's intent. It would, as a general rule, be desirable for the judge to refer to the evidence
> as to the consumption of alcohol or drugs and to the other facts which throw light on the
> accused's intention. If the accused by reason of intoxication was incapable of forming the
> required intent, then obviously he could not have it. If the jury entertain a reasonable doubt
> whether the accused by reason of intoxication had the capacity to form the necessary intent,
> then the necessary intent has not been proved. If they are satisfied beyond a reasonable doubt
> that the accused had the capacity to form the necessary intent, they must then go on to consider
> whether, taking into account the consumption of liquor and the other facts, the prosecution has
> satisfied them beyond a reasonable doubt that the accused in fact had the required intent.

. . . .

In *R. v. Korzepa* (1991), 64 C.C.C. (3d) 489, the British Columbia Court of
Appeal rejected *MacKinlay* as unfaithful to *Beard* and other cases in this Court.
However, some two years later in *R. v. Canute* (1993), 80 C.C.C. (3d) 403, that
Court, faced with a constitutional challenge directed at *Beard* and *MacAskill*,
agreed that the *Beard* rules were unconstitutional because they created a form of
constructive liability that violated ss. 7 and 11(*d*) of the *Charter* and did not
constitute a reasonable limit under s. 1. In deciding on the appropriate charge
that should replace *Beard*, the Court in that case went further than *MacKinlay*
and recommended that all references to capacity be removed. Wood J.A., for the
Court, held: ·

In fact, as was pointed out in *Korzepa*, the two-step test in *MacKinlay* is inherently confusing. What reason could there be for requiring a jury to struggle with the elusive concept of "capacity to form an intent", when at the end of that exercise they will only be required to turn their consideration to the real legal issue, namely, the actual intent of the accused? The issue of actual intent necessarily renders the question of capacity to form that intent redundant. With respect, it seems that the only likely result of retaining the two-step approach in *MacKinlay*, with its reference to "capacity", would be to confuse the jury into considering something other than the actual intent of the accused, with potentially unconstitutional consequences.

. . . .

Having reached the conclusion that the *Beard* rules are constitutionally infirm and that therefore *MacAskill* should now be overruled, we need to determine what new common law rule should be put in its place. How then should juries be instructed on the use they can make of evidence of intoxication? I am of the view that before a trial judge is required by law to charge the jury on intoxication, he or she must be satisfied that the effect of the intoxication was such that its effect might have impaired the accused's foresight of consequences sufficiently to raise a reasonable doubt. Once a judge is satisfied that this threshold is met, he or she must then make it clear to the jury that the issue before them is whether the Crown has satisfied them beyond a reasonable doubt that the accused had the requisite intent. In the case of murder the issue is whether the accused intended to kill or cause bodily harm with the foresight that the likely consequence was death.

Therefore, a *Canute*-type charge is a useful model for trial judges to follow as it omits any reference to "capacity" or "capability" and focuses the jury on the question of "intent in fact". In most murder cases, the focus for the trier of fact will be on the foreseeability prong of s. 229(*a*)(ii) of the *Criminal Code*, that is, on determining whether the accused foresaw that his or her actions were likely to cause the death of the victim. For example, consider the case where an accused and another individual engage in a fight outside a bar. During the fight, the accused pins the other individual to the ground and delivers a kick to the head, which kills that person. In that type of a case, the jury will likely struggle, assuming they reject any self-defence or provocation claim, with the question of whether that accused foresaw that his or her actions would likely cause the death of the other individual. At this level of inquiry, the need for the jury to consider issues of capacity will rarely arise since a level of impairment falling short of incapacity will often be sufficient to raise a reasonable doubt on the question of foreseeability. In these types of murder prosecutions, the evidence of intoxication usually consists of witnesses testifying as to the quantity of alcohol consumed by the accused, his or her appearance (*i.e.*, slurred speech or bloodshot eyes), and sometimes evidence of the accused as to his or her mental state. This evidence is usually offered by the defence not in isolation but along with other relevant evidence to be considered in relation to the question of whether the accused knew the likely consequences of his or her acts.

Those who would favour a two-stage charge even in these types of cases argue that such a charge is necessary in order to put in context for the jury the evidence of experts who often testify in "capacity" terms. While it is true that experts will testify in terms of the effect of alcohol or other intoxicants on capacity if so questioned, this need not always be the case. We could simply have experts only testify about such things as the effects of alcohol on the functioning of the brain. Experts could also testify by way of a hypothetical and be asked whether in their opinion, taking into consideration all of the relevant facts, the hypothetical person would have foreseen that his or her actions would likely cause death. I should not want to be taken as suggesting that reference to "capacity" as part of a two-step procedure will never be appropriate in a charge to the jury. Indeed, in cases where the only question is whether the accused intended to kill the victim (s. 229(*a*)(i) of the *Code*), while the accused is entitled to rely on any evidence of intoxication to argue that he or she lacked the requisite intent and is entitled to receive such an instruction from the trial judge (assuming of course that there is an "air of reality" to the defence), it is my opinion that intoxication short of incapacity will in most cases rarely raise a reasonable doubt in the minds of jurors. For example, in a case where an accused points a shotgun within a few inches of someone's head and pulls the trigger, it is difficult to conceive of a successful intoxication defence unless the jury is satisfied that the accused was so drunk that he or she was not capable of forming an intent to kill. It is in these types of cases where it may be appropriate for trial judges to use a two-step *MacKinlay*-type charge. In addition, I suspect that most accused will want the trial judge to refer to capacity since his or her defence will likely be one of incapacity.

Furthermore, there may well be some other cases where a two-step charge will be helpful to the jury, for example, where there has been expert evidence concerning issues of capacity, where the evidence reveals that the accused consumed a considerable amount of alcohol or where the accused specifically requests a "capacity" charge as part of his or her defence. If a two-step charge is used and the charge is later challenged on appeal, the role of an appellate court will be to review the charge and determine whether there is a reasonable possibility that the jury may have been misled into believing that a determination of capacity was the only relevant inquiry.

It may be of some assistance to summarize my conclusions in the following manner:

1. A *MacAskill* charge which only refers to capacity is constitutionally infirm and constitutes reversible error.
2. A *Canute*-type charge which only asks the jury to consider whether the evidence of intoxication, along with all of the other evidence in the case, impacted on whether the accused possessed the requisite specific intent is to be preferred for the reasons set out above.
3. In certain cases, in light of the particular facts of the case and/or in light of the expert evidence called, it may be appropriate to charge both with regard to the capacity to form the requisite intent and with regard to the need to determine in all the circumstances whether the requisite intent was in fact formed by the accused. In these circumstances a jury might be instructed that their overall duty

is to determine whether or not the accused possessed the requisite intent for the crime. If on the basis of the expert evidence the jury is left with a reasonable doubt as to whether, as a result of the consumption of alcohol, the accused had the capacity to form the requisite intent then that ends the inquiry and the accused must be acquitted of the offence and consideration must then be given to any included lesser offences. However, if the jury is not left in a reasonable doubt as a result of the expert evidence as to the capacity to form the intent then of course they must consider and take into account all the surrounding circumstances and the evidence pertaining to those circumstances in determining whether or not the accused possessed the requisite intent for the offence.

4. If a two-step charge is used with "capacity" and "capability" type language and the charge is the subject of an appeal, then a determination will have to be made by appellate courts on a case by case basis of whether there is a reasonable possibility that the jury may have been misled into believing that a determination of capacity was the only relevant inquiry. The following factors, not intended to be exhaustive, should be considered:

(a) the number of times that reference to capacity is used;

(b) the number of times that reference to the real inquiry of actual intent is used;

(c) whether there is an additional "incapacity" defence;

(d) the nature of the expert evidence (*i.e.*, whether the expert's evidence relates to the issue of capacity rather than on the effect of alcohol on the brain);

(e) the extent of the intoxication evidence;

(f) whether the defence requested that references to "capacity" be used in the charge to the jury;

(g) whether during a two-step charge it was made clear that the primary function of the jury was to determine whether they were satisfied beyond a reasonable doubt that the accused possessed the requisite intent to commit the crime. If this is emphasized during the course of the two- step charge, that will often be sufficient to make the charge acceptable and appropriate in this respect.

See comment on *Robinson* by Patrick Healy, "Beard Still Not Cut Off" (1996), 46 C.R. (4th) 65.

Chapter 7

JUSTIFICATIONS AND EXCUSES

The reason for preserving common-law defences in s. 8(3) in 1955 seems to lie in the acceptance of the pragmatic rationale of the English Royal Commission of 1880 which considered it "if not absolutely impossible, at least not practicable" to anticipate with acceptable precision every future defence. In the following extract Stephen raises another pragmatic consideration with considerable force.

J.F. STEPHEN, THE NINETEENTH CENTURY . . .

Quoted in G.L. Williams, "Necessity" (1978), Crim. L. Rev. 128 at 129-130

It appears to me that the two proposed enactments stand on entirely different principles. After the experience of centuries, and with a Parliament sitting every year, and keenly alive to all matters likely to endanger the public interests, we are surely in a position to say the power of declaring new offences shall henceforth be vested in Parliament only. The power which has at times been claimed for the Judges of declaring new offences cannot be useful now, whatever may have been its value in earlier times.

On the other hand it is hardly possible to foresee all the circumstances which might possibly justify or excuse acts which might otherwise be crimes. A long series of authorities have settled certain rules which can be put into a distinct and convenient form, and it is of course desirable to take the opportunity of deciding by the way minor points which an examination of the authorities shows to be still open. In this manner rules can be laid down as to the effect of infancy, insanity, compulsion, and ignorance of law, and also as to the cases in which force may lawfully be employed against the person of another; but is it therefore wise or safe to go so far as to say that no other circumstances than those expressly enumerated shall operate by way of excuse or justification for what would otherwise be a crime? To do so would be to run a risk, the extent of which it is difficult to estimate, of producing a conflict between the *Code* and the moral feelings of the public. Such a conflict is upon all possible grounds to be avoided. It would, if it occurred, do more to discredit codification than anything which would possibly happen, and it might cause serious evils of another kind. Cases sometimes occur in which public opinion is at once violently excited and greatly divided, so that conduct is regarded as criminal or praiseworthy according to the sympathies of excited partisans. If the *Code* provided that nothing should amount to an excuse or justification which was not within the express words of the *Code*, it would, in such a case, be vain to allege that the conduct of the accused person was normally justifiable; that, but for the *Code*, it would have been legally justifiable; that every legal analogy was in its favour; and that the omission of an express provision about it was probably an oversight. I think such a result would be eminently unsatisfactory. I think the public would feel that the allegations referred to ought to have been carefully examined and duly decided upon.

To put the whole matter very shortly, the reason why the common-law definitions of offences should be taken away, whilst the common-law principles as to justification and excuse are kept alive, is like the reason why the benefit of a doubt should be given to a prisoner. The worst result that could arise from the abolition of the common-law offences would be the occasional escape of a person morally guilty. The only result which can follow from preserving the common law as to justification and excuse is, that a man morally innocent, not otherwise protected, may avoid punishment. In the one case you remove rusty spring-guns and man-traps from unfrequented plantations, in the other you decline to issue an order for the destruction of every old-fashioned drag or life-buoy which may be found on the banks of a dangerous river, but is not in the inventory of the Royal Humane Society.

This indeed does not put the matter strongly enough. The continued existence of the undefined common-law offences is not only dangerous to individuals, but may be dangerous to the administration of justice itself. By allowing them to remain, we run the risk of tempting the Judges to express their disapproval of conduct which, upon political, moral, or social grounds, they consider deserving of punishment, by declaring upon slender authority that it constitutes an offence at common law; nothing, I think, could place the bench in a more invidious position, or go further to shake its authority.

. . . .

Besides the well-known matters dealt with by the *Code*, there are a variety of speculative questions which have been discussed by ingenious persons for centuries, but which could be raised only by such rare occurrences that it may be thought pedantic to legislate for them expressly beforehand, and rash to do so without materials which the course of events has not provided. Such cases are the case of necessity (two shipwrecked men on one plank), the case of a choice of evils (my horses are running away, and I can avoid running over A only by running over B), and some others which might be suggested.

. . . .

Any ingenious person may divert himself, as Hecato did, by playing with such questions. The Commission acted on the view that in practice the wisest answer to all of them is to say, "When the case actually happens it shall be decided;" and this is effected by the preservation of such parts of the common law as to justification and excuse as are not embodied in the *Code*. Fiction apart, there is at present no law at all upon the subject, but the Judges will make one under the fiction of declaring it, if the occasion for doing so should ever arise.

Necessity

R. v. DUDLEY AND STEPHENS

(1884), 14 Q.B.D. 273 (C.C.R.)

INDICTMENT for the murder of Richard Parker on the high seas within the jurisdiction of the Admiralty.

At the trial before Huddleston B., at the Devon and Cornwall Winter Assizes, November 7, 1884, the jury, at the suggestion of the learned Judge, found the facts of the case in a special verdict which stated:

that on July 5, 1884, the prisoners, Thomas Dudley and Edward Stephens, with one Brooks, all able-bodied English seamen, and the deceased also an English boy, between 17 and 18 years of age, the crew of an English yacht, a registered English vessel, were cast away in a storm on the high seas 1600 miles from the Cape of Good Hope, and were compelled to put into an open boat belonging to the said yacht. That in this boat they had no supply of water and no supply of food, except two 1 lb. tins of turnips, and for three days they had nothing else to subsist upon. That on the fourth day they caught a small turtle, upon which they subsisted for a few days, and this was the only food they had up to the 20th day when the act now in question was committed. That on the 12th day the remains of the turtle were entirely consumed, and for the next eight days they had nothing to eat. That they had no fresh water, except such rain as they from time to time caught in their oilskin capes. That the boat was drifting on the ocean, and was probably more than 1000 miles away from land. That on the 18th day, when they had been seven days without food and five without water, the prisoners spoke to Brooks as to what should be done if no succour came, and suggested that some one should be sacrificed to save the rest, but Brooks dissented, and the boy, to whom they were understood to refer, was not consulted. That on the 24th of July, the day before the act now in question, the prisoner Dudley proposed to Stephens and Brooks that lots should be cast who should be put to death to save the rest, but Brooks refused to consent, and it was not put to the boy, and in point of fact there was no drawing of lots. That on that day the prisoners spoke of their having families, and suggested it would be better to kill the boy that their lives should be saved, and Dudley proposed that if there was no vessel in sight by the morrow morning the boy should be killed. The next day, the 25th of July, no vessel appearing, Dudley told Brooks that he had better go and have a sleep, and made signs to Stephens and Brooks that the boy had better be killed. The prisoner Stephens agreed to the act, but Brooks dissented from it. That the boy was then lying at the bottom of the boat quite helpless, and extremely weakened by famine and by drinking sea water, and unable to make any resistance, nor did he ever assent to his being killed. The prisoner Dudley offered a prayer asking forgiveness for them all if either of them should be tempted to commit a rash act, and that their souls might be saved. That Dudley, with the assent of Stephens, went to the boy, and telling him that his time was come, put a knife into his throat and killed him then and there; that the three men fed upon the body and blood of the boy for four days; that on the fourth day after the act had been committed the boat was picked up by a passing vessel, and the prisoners were rescued, still alive, but in the lowest state of prostration. That they were carried to the port of Falmouth, and committed for trial at Exeter. That if the men had not fed upon the body of the boy they would probably not have survived to be so picked up and rescued, but would within the four days have died of famine. That the boy, being in a much weaker condition, was likely to have died before them. That at the time of the act in question there was no sail in sight, nor any reasonable prospect of relief. That under these circumstances there appeared to the prisoners every probability that unless they then fed or very soon fed upon the boy or one of themselves they would die of starvation. That there was no appreciable chance of saving life except by killing some one for the others to eat. That assuming any necessity to kill anybody, there was no greater necessity for killing the boy than any of the other three men.

But whether upon the whole matter by the jurors found the killing of Richard Parker by Dudley and Stephens be felony and murder the jurors are ignorant, and pray the advice of the Court thereupon, and if upon the whole matter the Court shall be of opinion that the killing of Richard Parker be felony and murder, then the jurors say that Dudley and Stephens were each guilty of felony and murder as alleged in the indictment.

. . . .

Dec. 9. The judgment of the Court (LORD COLERIDGE C.J., GROVE and DENMAN J.J., POLLOCK and HUDDLESTON BB.) was delivered by LORD COLERIDGE C.J.: —

. . . .

There remains to be considered the real question in the case — whether killing under the circumstances set forth in the verdict be or be not murder. The contention that it could be anything else was, to the minds of us all, both new and strange, and we stopped the Attorney-General in his negative argument in order that we might hear what could be said in support of a proposition which appeared to us to be at once dangerous, immoral, and opposed to all legal principle and analogy. All, no doubt, that can be said has been urged before us, and we are now to consider and determine what it amounts to. First it is said that it follows from various definitions of murder in books of authority, which definitions imply, if they do not state, the doctrine, that in order to save your own life you may lawfully take away the life of another, when that other is neither attempting nor threatening yours, nor is guilty of any illegal act whatever towards you or any one else. But if these definitions be looked at they will not be found to sustain this contention. . . .

Is there, then, any authority for the proposition which has been presented to us? Decided cases there are none. . . .

The American case cited by my Brother Stephen in his Digest, from Wharton on Homicide, in which it was decided, correctly indeed, that sailors had no right to throw passengers overboard to save themselves, but on the somewhat strange ground that the proper mode of determining who was to be sacrificed was to vote upon the subject by ballot, can hardly, as my Brother Stephen says, be an authority satisfactory to a Court in this country.

. . . .

Now, except for the purpose of testing how far the conservation of a man's own life is in all cases and under all circumstances, an absolute, unqualified, and paramount duty, we exclude from our consideration all the incidents of war. We are dealing with a case of private homicide, not one imposed upon men in the service of their Sovereign and in the defence of their country. Now it is admitted that the deliberate killing of this unoffending and unresisting boy was clearly murder, unless the killing can be justified by some well-recognized excuse admitted by the law. It is further admitted that there was in this case no such excuse, unless the killing was justified by what has been called "necessity." But the temptation to the act which existed here was not what the law has ever called necessity. Nor is this to be regretted. Though law and morality are not the same, and many things may be immoral which are not necessarily illegal, yet the absolute divorce of law from morality would be of fatal consequence; and such divorce would follow if the temptation to murder in this case were to be held by law an absolute defence of it. It is not so. To preserve one's life is generally speaking a duty, but it may be the plainest and the highest duty to sacrifice it. War is full of instances in which it is a man's duty not to live, but to die. The duty in case of shipwreck, of a captain to his crew, of the crew to the passengers, of soldiers to women and children, as in the noble case of the *Birkenhead*; these duties impose on men the moral necessity, not of the preservation, but of the sacrifice of their lives for others, from which in no country, least of all, it is to be hoped, in England, will men ever shrink, as indeed, they have not shrunk. It is not correct, therefore, to say that there is any absolute or unqualified necessity to preserve one's life. "Necesse est ut eam, non ut vivam," is a saying of a Roman officer quoted by Lord Bacon himself with high eulogy in the very chapter on necessity to which so much reference has been made. It would be a very easy and cheap display of commonplace learning to quote from Greek and Latin authors, from Horace, from Juvenal, from Cicero, from Euripides, passage after passage, in which the duty of dying for others has been laid down in glowing and emphatic language as resulting from the principles of heathen ethics; it is enough in a Christian country to remind ourselves of the Great Example whom we profess to follow. It is not needful to point out the awful danger of admitting the principle which has been contended for. Who is to be the Judge of this sort of necessity? By what measure is the comparative value of lives to be measured? Is it to be strength, or intellect, or what? It is plain that the principle leaves to him who is to profit by it to determine the necessity which will justify him in deliberately taking another's life to save his own. In this case the weakest, the youngest, the most unresisting, was chosen. Was it more necessary to kill him than one of the grown men? The answer must be "No"—

> So spake the Fiend, and with necessity,
> The tyrant's plea, excused his devilish deeds.

It is not suggested that in this particular case the deeds were "devilish," but it is quite plain that such a principle once admitted might be made the legal cloak for unbridled passion and atrocious crime. There is no safe path for Judges to tread but to ascertain the law to the best of their ability and to declare it according to their judgment; and if in any case the law appears to be too severe on individuals, to leave it to the Sovereign to exercise that prerogative of mercy which the Constitution has intrusted to the hands fittest to dispense it.

It must not be supposed that in refusing to admit temptation to be an excuse for crime it is forgotten how terrible the temptation was; how awful the suffering; how hard in such trials to keep the judgment straight and the conduct pure. We are often compelled to set up standards we cannot reach ourselves, and to lay down rules which we could not ourselves satisfy. But a man has no right to declare temptation to be an excuse, though he might himself have yielded to it, nor allow compulsion for the criminal to change or weaken in any manner the legal definition of the crime. It is therefore our duty to declare that the prisoners' act in this case was wilful murder, that the facts as stated in the verdict are no legal justification of the homicide; and to say that in our unanimous opinion the prisoners are upon this special verdict guilty of murder.[1]

THE COURT then proceeded to pass sentence of death upon the prisoners.[2]

1. My brother Grove has furnished me with the following suggestion, too late to be embodied in the judgment but well worth preserving: "If the two accused men were justified in killing Parker, then if not rescued in time, two of the three survivors would be justified in killing the third, and of the two who remained the stronger would be justified in killing the weaker, so that three men might be justifiably killed to give the fourth a chance of surviving."—C.
2. This sentence was afterwards commuted by the Crown to six months' imprisoment.

PERKA v. R.

42 C.R. (3d) 113, [1984] 2 S.C.R. 233, 14 C.C.C. (3d) 385

DICKSON J . (RITCHIE, COUINDARD and LAMER JJ. concurring): — . . . .

I FACTS

The appellants are drug smugglers. At trial, they led evidence that in early 1979 three of the appellants were employed, with 16 crew members, to deliver, by ship (the Samarkanda), a load of cannabis (marijuana) worth $6,000,000 or $7,000,000 from a point in international waters off the coast of Colombia, South America, to a drop point in international waters 200 miles off the coast of Alaska. The ship left Tumaco, Colombia, empty with a port clearance document stating the destination to be Juneau, Alaska. For three weeks the ship remained in international waters off the coast of Colombia. While there, a DC-6 aircraft made four trips, dropping into the water shrimp nets with a total of 634 bales of cannabis which were retrieved by the ship's longboats.

A "communications" package was also dropped from a light aircraft, giving instructions for a rendezvous with another vessel, the Julia B., which was to pick up the cargo of cannabis from the Samarkanda in international waters off the coast of Alaska. En route, according to the defence evidence, the vessel began to encounter a series of problems; engine break-downs, overheating generators and malfunctioning navigation devices, aggravated by deteriorating weather. In the meantime the fourth appellant, Nelson, part-owner of the illicit cargo, and three other persons left Seattle in a small boat, the Whitecap, intending to rendezvous with the Samarkanda at the drop point in Alaska. The problems of the Samarkanda intensified as fuel was consumed. The vessel became lighter, the intakes in the hull for sea water, used as a coolant, lost suction and took in air instead, causing the generators to overheat. At this point the vessel was 180 miles from the Canadian coastline. The weather worsened. There were 8-to-10-foot swells and a rising wind. It was finally decided for the safety of ship and crew to seek refuge on the Canadian shoreline for the purpose of making temporary repairs. The Whitecap found a sheltered cove on the west coast of Vancouver Island, No Name Bay. The Samarkanda followed the Whitecap into the bay but later grounded amidships on a rock because the depth sounder was not working. The tide ran out. The vessel listed severely to starboard, to the extent that the Captain, fearing the vessel was going to capsize, ordered the men to offload the cargo. That is a brief summary of the defence evidence.

Early on the morning of 22nd May 1979 police officers entered No Name Bay in a marked police boat with siren sounding. The Samarkanda and the Whitecap were arrested, as were all the appellants except Perka and Nelson, the same morning. The vessels and 33.49 tons of cannabis marijuana were seized by the police officers.

Charged with importing cannabis into Canada and with possession for the purpose of trafficking, the appellants claimed that they did not plan to import into Canada or to leave thieir cargo of cannabis in Canada. They had planned to make repairs and leave. Expert witnesses on marine matters called by the defence testified that the decision to come ashore was, in the opinion of one witness, expedient and prudent and, in the opinion of another, essential. At trial, counsel for the Crown alleged that the evidence of the ship's distress was a recent fabrication. Crown counsel relied on the circumstances under which the appellants were arrested to belie the "necessity" defence; when the police arrived on the scene most of the marijuana was already onshore, along with plastic ground sheets, battery-operated lights, liquor, food, clothing, camp stoves, and sleeping bags. Nevertheless, the jury believed the appellants and acquitted them.

. . . .

II THE NECESSITY DEFENCE

(a) *History and Background*

From earliest times it has been maintained that in some situations the force of circumstances makes it unrealistic and unjust to attach criminal liability to actions which, on their face, violate the law. Aristotle, Nicomachean Ethics, translated by Sir David Ross, Book III, p. 49, 1110a, discusses the jettisoning of cargo from a ship in distress and remarks that "any sensible man does so" to secure the safety of himself and his crew. Pollard, arguing for the defendant in the case of *Renniger v. Fogossa* (1551), 1 Plowden 1 at 18, 75 E.R. 1, maintained:

> . . . in every law there are some things which when they happen a man may break the words of the law, and yet not break the law itself; and such things are exempted out of the penalty

of the law, and the law privileges them although they are done against the letter of it, for breaking the words of the law is not breaking the law, so as the intent of the law is not broken. And therefore the words of the law of nature, of the law of this realm, and of other realms, and of the law of God also will yield and give way to some acts and things done against the words of the same laws, and that is, where the words of them are broken to avoid greater inconveniences, or through necessity, or by compulsion.

In Leviathan, Pelican ed. (1968), c. 27, at p. 157, Hobbes writes:

If a man by the terrour of present death, be compelled to doe a fact against the law, he is totally excused; because no law can oblige a man to abandon his own preservation. And supposing such a law were obligatory: yet a man would reason thus, If I doe it not, I die presently; if I doe it I die afterwards; therefore by doing it there is time of life gained; Nature therefore compells him to the fact.

To much the same purpose Kant, in Metaphysical Elements of Justice, translated by Ladd (1965), discussing the actions of a person who, to save his own life, sacrifices that of another, says at p. 41:

A penal law applying to such a situation could never have the effect intended, for the threat of an evil that is still uncertain (being condemned to death by a Judge) cannot outweigh the fear of an evil that is certain (being drowned). Hence, we must judge that, although an act of self-preservation through violence is not inculpable, it still is unpunishable.

In those jurisdictions in which such a general principle has been recognized or codified it is most often referred to by the term "necessity". Classic and harrowing instances which have been cited to illustrate the arguments both for and against this principle include the mother who steals food for her starving child, the shipwrecked mariners who resort to cannibalism (*R. v. Dudley*, (1884), 14 Q.B.D. 273 (C.C.R.)) or throw passengers overboard to lighten a sinking lifeboat (*U.S. v. Holmes*, 26 F. Cas. 360 (1842)), and the more mundane case of the motorist who exceeds the speed limit taking an injured person to the hospital.

. . . .

In Canada the existence and the extent of a general defence of necessity was discussed by this Court in *Morgentaler v. R.*, [1976] 1 S.C.R. 616, 30 C.R.N.S. 209, 20 C.C.C. (2d) 449. As to whether or not the defence exists at all I had occasion to say at p. 678:

On the authorities it is manifestly difficult to be categorical and state that there is a law of necessity, paramount over other laws, relieving obedience from the letter of the law. If [such a principle exists] it can go no further than to justify non-compliance in urgent situations of clear and imminent peril when compliance with the law is demonstrably impossible.

. . . .

In the present appeal the Crown does not challenge the appellants' claim that necessity is a common law defence preserved by the *Criminal Code*, R.S.C. 1970, c. C-34, s. 7(3). Rather, the Crown claims, the trial Judge erred in: (1) instructing the jury on the defence in light of the facts; and (2) imposing the burden of disproof of the defence upon the Crown, rather than imposing the burden of proof on the appellants.

(b) *The Conceptual Foundation of the Defence*

In *Morgentaler v. R., supra.* I characterized necessity as an "ill-defined and elusive concept". Despite the apparently growing consensus as to the existence of a defence of necessity, that statement is equally true today.

This is no doubt in part because, though apparently laying down a singe rule as to criminal liability, the "defence" of necessity in fact is capable of embracing two different and distinct notions. As Macdonald J.A. observed succinctly but accurately in the *Salvador* case [*R. v. Salvador* (1981), 21 C.R. (3d) 1, 59 C.C.C. (2d) 521 (N.S.C.A.)], at p. 542:

> Generally speaking, the defence of necessity covers all cases where non-compliance with law is excused by an emergency or justified by the pursuit of some greater good.

Working Paper 29, Criminal Law — The General Part: Liability and Defences (1982), of the Law Reform Commission of Canada at p. 93 makes this same point in somewhat more detail:

> The rationale of necessity, however, is clear. Essentially it involves two factors. One is the avoidance of greater harm or the pursuit of some greater good, the other is the difficulty of compliance with law in emergencies. From these two factors emerge two different but related principles. The first is a utilitarian principle to the effect that, within certain limits, it is justifiable in an emergency to break the letter of the law if breaking the law will avoid a greater harm than obeying it. The second is a humanitarian principle to the effect that, again within limits, it is excusable in an emergency to break the law if compliance would impose an intolerable burden on the accused.

Despite any superficial similarities, these two principles are in fact quite distinct and many of the confusions and difficulties in the cases (and, with respect, in academic discussions) arise from a failure to distinguish between them.

Criminal theory recognizes a distinction between "justifications" and "excuses". A "justification" challenges the wrongfulness of an action which technically constitutes a crime. The police officer who shoots the hostage-taker, the innocent object of an assault who uses force to defend himself against his assailant, the Good Samaritan who commandeers a car and breaks the speed laws to rush an accident victim to the hospital, these are all actors whose actions we consider *rightful*, not wrongful. For such actions people are often praised, as motivated by some great or noble object. The concept of punishment often seems incompatible with the social approval bestowed on the doer.

In contrast, an "excuse" concedes the wrongfulness of the action but asserts that the circumstances under which it was done are such that it ought not to be attributed to the actor. The perpetrator who is incapable, owing to a disease of the mind, of appreciating the nature and consequences of his acts, the person who labours under a mistake of fact, the drunkard, the sleepwalker: these are all actors of whose "criminal" actions we disapprove intensely, but whom, in appropriate circumstances, our law will not punish.

Packer, *The Limits of the Criminal Sanction*, expresses the distinction thus at p. 113:

> Conduct that we choose not to treat as criminal is "justifiable" if our reason for treating it as noncriminal is predominantly that it is conduct that we applaud, or at least do not actively seek to discourage: conduct is "excusable" if we deplore it but for some extrinsic reason conclude that it is not politic to punish it.

It will be seen that the two different approaches to the "defence" of necessity from Blackstone forward correspond, the one to a justification, the other to an excuse. As the examples cited above illustrate, the criminal law recognizes and our *Criminal Code* codifies a number of specific categories of justification and of excuse. The remainder, those instances that conform to the general principle but do not fall within any specific category such as self-defence on the one hand or insanity on the other, purportedly fall within the "residual defence" of necessity.

As a "justification" this residual defence can be related to Blackstone's concept of a "choice of evils". It would exculpate actors whose conduct could reasonably have been viewed as "necessary" in order to prevent a greater evil than that resulting from the violation of the law. As articulated, especially in some of the American cases, it involves a utilitarian balancing of the benefits of obeying the law as opposed to disobeying it, and, when the balance is clearly in favour of disobeying, exculpates an actor who contravenes a criminal statute. This is the "greater good" formulation of the necessity defence: in some circumstances, it is alleged, the values of society, indeed of the criminal law itself, are better promoted by disobeying a given statute than by observing it.

With regard to this conceptualization of a residual defence of necessity, I retain the scepticism I expressed in *Morgentaler v. R.*, *supra*, at p. 678. It is still my opinion that "No system of positive law can recognize any principle which would entitle a person to violate the law because on his view the law conflicted with some higher social value." The *Criminal Code* has specified a number of identifiable situations in which an actor is justified in committing what would otherwise be a criminal offence. To go beyond that and hold that ostensibly illegal acts can be validated on the basis of their expediency would import an undue subjectivity into the criminal law. It would invite the courts to second-guess the Legislature and to assess the relative merits of social policies underlying criminal prohibitions. Neither is a role which fits well with the judicial function. Such a doctrine could well become the last resort of scoundrels and, in the words of Edmund Davies L.J. in *Southwark London Borough Council v. Williams*, [1971] Ch. 734 at 746 (C.A.), it could "very easily become simply a mask for anarchy".

Conceptualized as an "excuse", however, the residual defence of necessity is, in my view, much less open to criticism. It rests on a realistic assessment of human weakness, recognizing that a liberal and humane criminal law cannot hold people to the strict obedience of law in emergency situations where normal human instincts, whether of self-preservation or of altruism, overwhelmingly impel disobedience. The objectivity of the criminal law is preserved; such acts are still wrongful, but in the circumstances they are excusable. Praise is indeed not bestowed, but pardon is, when one does a wrongful act underpressure which, in the words of Aristotle in the Nicomachean Ethics p. 49, ll10a10, "overstrains human nature and which no one could withstand".

George Fletcher, *Rethinking Criminal Law* (1978), describes this view of necessity as "compulsion of circumstance", which description points to the conceptual link between necessity as an excuse and the familiar criminal law requirement that in order to engage criminal liability the actions constituting the *actus reus* of an offence must be voluntary. Literally this voluntariness requirement simply refers to the need that the prohibited physical acts must have been under the conscious control of the actor. Without such control, there is, for purposes of the criminal law, no act. The excuse of necessity does not go to voluntariness in this sense. The lost alpinist who on the point of freezing to death breaks open an isolated mountain cabin is not literally behaving in an involuntary fashion. He has control over his actions to the extent of being physically capable of abstaining from the act. Realistically, however, his act is not a "voluntary" one. His "choice" to break the law is no true choice at all; it is remorselessly compelled by normal human instincts. This sort of involuntariness is often described as "moral or normative involuntariness". Its place in criminal theory is described by Fletcher at pp. 804-805 as follows:

> The notion of voluntariness adds a valuable dimension to the theory of excuses. That conduct is involuntary — even in the normative sense — explains why it cannot fairly be punished. Indeed, H.L.A. Hart builds his theory of excuses on the principle that the distribution of punishment should be reserved for those who voluntarily break the law. Of the arguments he advances for this principle of justice, the most explicit is that it is preferable to live in a society where we have the maximum opportunity to choose whether we shall become the subject of criminal liability. In addition, Hart intimates that it is ideologically dcsirable for the government to treat its citizens as self-actuating, choosing agents. This principle of respect for individual autonomy is implicitly confirmed whenever those who lack an adequate choice are excused for their offences.

I agree with this formulation of the rationale for excuses in the criminal law. In my view this rationale extends beyond specific codified excuses and embraces the residual excuse known as the defence of necessity. At the heart of this defence is the perceived injustice of punishing violations of the law in circumstances in which the person had no other viable or reasonable choice available; the act was wrong but it is excused because it was realistically unavoidable.

Punishment of such acts, as Fletcher notes at p. 813, can be seen as purposeless as well as unjust:

> . . . involuntary conduct cannot be deterred and therefore it is pointless and wasteful to punish involuntary actors. This theory . . . of pointless punishment, carries considerable weight in currcnt Anglo-American legal thought.

Relating necessity to the principle that the law ought not to punish involuntary acts leads to a conceptualization of the defence that integrates it into the normal rules for criminal liability rather than constituting it as a *sui generis* exception and threatening to engulf large portions of the criminal law. Such a conceptualization accords with our traditional legal, moral and philosophic views as to what sorts of acts and what sorts of actors ought to be punished. In this formulation it is a defence which I do not hesitate to acknowledge and would not hesitate to apply to relevant facts capable of satisfying its necessary prerequisites.

(c) *Limitations on the Defence*

If the defence of necessity is to form a valid and consistent part of our criminal law it must, as has been universally recognized, be strictly controlled and scrupulously limited to situations that correspond to its underlying rationale. That rationale, as I have indicated, is the recognition that it is inappropriate to punish actions which are normatively "involuntary". The appropriate controls and limitations on the defence of necessity are therefore addressed to ensuring that the acts for which the benefit of the excuse of necessity is sought are truly "involuntary" in the requisite sense.

In *Morgentaler v. R.*, *supra*, I was of the view that any defence of necessity was restricted to instances of non-compliance "in urgent situations of clear and imminent peril when compliance with the law is demonstrably impossible". In my opinion this restriction focuses directly on the "involuntariness" of the purportedly necessitous behaviour by providing a number of tests for determining whether the wrongful act was truly the only realistic reaction open to the actor or whether he was in fact making what in fairness could be called a choice. If he was making a choice, then the wrongful act cannot have been involuntary in the relevant sense.

The requirement that the situation be urgent and the peril be imminent tests whether it was indeed unavoidable for the actor to act at all. In Lafave and Scott, *Criminal Law*, at p. 388, one reads:

> It is sometimes said that the defence of necessity does not apply except in an emergency — when the threatened harm is immediate, the threatened disaster imminent. Perhaps this is but a way of saying that, until the time comes when the threatened harm is immediate, there are generally options open to the defendant to avoid the harm, other than the option of disobeying the literal terms of the law — the rescue ship may appear, the storm may pass; and so the defendant must wait until that hope of survival disappears.

At a minimum the situation must be so emergent and the peril must be so pressing that normal human instincts cry out for action and make a counsel of patience unreasonable.

The requirement that compliance with the law be "demonstrably impossible" takes this assessment one step further. Given that the accused had to act, could he nevertheless realistically have acted to avoid the peril or prevent the harm, without breaking the law? *Was there a legal way out?* I think this is what Bracton means when he lists "necessity" as a defence, providing the wrongful act was not "avoidable". The question to be asked is whether the agent had any real choice: could he have done otherwise? If there is a reasonable legal alternative to disobeying the law, then the decision to disobey becomes a voluntary one, impelled by some consideration beyond the dictates of "necessity" and human instincts.

The importance of this requirement that there be no reasonable legal alternative cannot be overstressed.

Even if the requirements for urgency and "no legal way out" are met, there is clearly a further consideration. There must be some way of assuring proportionality. No rational criminal justice system, no matter how humane or liberal, could excuse the infliction of a greater harm to allow the actor to avert a lesser evil. In such circumstances we expect the individual to bear the harm and refrain from acting illegally. If he cannot control himself we will not excuse him. According to Fletcher, this requirement is also related to the notion of voluntariness:

> . . . if the gap between the harm done and the benefit accrued becomes too great, the act is more likely to appear voluntary and therefore inexcusable. For example, if the actor has to blow up a whole city in order to avoid the breaking of his finger, we might appropriately expect him to endure the harm to himself. His surrendering to the threat in this case violates our expectations of appropriate and normal resistance and pressure. Yet as we lower the degree of harm to others and increase the threatened harm to the person under duress we will reach a threshold at which, in the language of the Model Penal Code, "a person of reasonable firmness" would be "unable to resist". Determining this threshold is patently a matter of moral judgment about what we expect people to be able to resist in trying situations. A valuable aid in making that judgment is comparing the competing interests at stake and assessing the degree to which the actor inflicts harm beyond the benefit that accrues from his action.

I would therefore add to the preceding requirements a stipulation of proportionality expressable, as it was in *Morgentaler v. R.*, *supra*, by the proviso that the harm inflicted must be less than the harm sought to be avoided.

(d) *Illegality or Contributory Fault*

The Crown submits that there is an additional limitation on the availability of the defence of necessity. Citing *R. v. Salvador*, *supra*, it argues that because the appellants were committing a crime when their necessitous circumstances arose they should be denied the defence of necessity as a matter of law".

. . . .

In any event, I have considerable doubt as to the cogency of such a limitation. If the conduct in which an accused was engaging at the time the peril arose was illegal, then it should clearly be punished, but I fail to see the relevance of its illegal character to the question of whether the accused's subsequent conduct in dealing with this emergent peril ought to be excused on the basis of necessity. At most the illegality — or, if one adopts Jones J.A.'s approach, the immorality — of the preceding conduct will colour the subsequent conduct in response to the emergency as also wrongful. But that wrongfulness is never in any doubt. Necessity goes to *excuse* conduct, not to *justify* it. Where it is found to apply it carries with it no implicit vindication of the deed to which it attaches. That cannot be over-emphasized. Were the defence of necessity to succeed in the present case, it would not in any way amount to a vindication of importing controlled substances or to a critique of the law prohibiting such importation. It would also have nothing to say about the comparative social utility of breaking the law against importing as compared to obeying the law. The question, as I have said, is never whether what the accused has done is wrongful. It is always and by definition wrongful. The question is whether what he has done is voluntary. Except in the limited sense I intend to discuss below, I do not see the relevance of the legality or even the morality of what the accused was doing at the time the emergency arose to this question of the voluntariness of the subsequent conduct.

. . . .

In my view the better approach to the relationship of fault to the availability of necessity as a defence is based once again on the question of whether the actions sought to be excused were truly "involuntary". If the necessitous situation was clearly foreseeable to a reasonable observer, if the actor contemplated or ought to have contemplated that his actions would likely give rise to an emergency requiring the breaking of the law, then I doubt whether what confronted the accused was in the relevant sense an emergency. His response was in that sense not "involuntary". "Contributory fault" of this nature, but only of this nature, is a relevant consideration to the availability of the defence.

. . . .

(e) *Onus of Proof*

Although necessity is spoken of as a defence, in the sense that it is raised by the accused, the Crown always bears the burden of proving a voluntary act. The prosecution must prove every element of the crime charged. One such element is the voluntariness of the act. Normally, voluntariness can be presumed, but if the accused places before the Court, through his own witnesses or through cross-examination of Crown witnesses, evidence sufficient to raise an issue that the situation created by external forces was so emergent that failure to act could endanger life or health and upon any reasonable view of the facts, compliance with the law was impossible, then the Crown must be prepared to meet that issue. There is no onus of proof on the accused.

. . . .

(f) *Preliminary Conclusions as to the Defence of Necessity*

It is now possible to summarize a number of conclusions as to the defence of necessity in terms of its nature, basis and limitations: (1) the defence of necessity could be conceptualized as either a justification or an excuse; (2) it should be recognized in Canada as an excuse, operating by virtue of s. 7(3) of the *Criminal Code*; (3) necessity as an excuse implies no vindication of the deeds of the actor; (4) the criterion is the moral involuntariness of the wrongful action; (5) this involuntariness is measured on the basis of society's expectation of appropriate and normal resistance to pressure; (6) negligence or involvement in criminal or immoral activity does not disentitle the actor to the excuse of necessity; (7) actions or circumstances which indicate that the wrongful deed was not truly involuntary do disentitle, (8) the existence of a reasonable legal alternative similarly disentitles; to be involuntary the act must be inevitable, unavoidable and afford no reasonable opportunity for an alternative course of action that does not involve a breach of the law; (9) the defence applies only in circumstances of imminent risk where the action was taken to avoid a direct and immediate peril; and (10) where the accused places before the Court sufficient evidence to raise the issue, the onus is on the Crown to meet it beyond a reasonable doubt.

(g) *The Judge's Charge*

The trial Judge concluded that there was before him an adequate body of evidence to raise the issue of necessity and proceeded to direct the jury with respect to the defence. As I have earlier indicated, the Crown disputes whether the defence was open to the accused in the circumstances of the case and submits further that if it was in fact available the trial Judge erred in his direction.

In my view the trial Judge was correct in concluding that on the evidence before him he should instruct the jury with regard to necessity. There was evidence before him from which a jury might conclude that the accused's actions in coming ashore with their cargo of cannabis were aimed at self-preservation in response to an overwhelming emergency. I have already indicated that in my view they were not engaged in conduct that was illegal under Canadian criminal law at the time the emergency arose, and that, even if they were, that fact alone would not disentitle them to raise the defence. The question then becomes whether the trial Judge erred in charging the jury in the terms that he did.

The summary of conclusions with regard to necessity in the forgoing section indicates that for the defence to succeed an accused's actions must be, in the relevant sense, an "involuntary" response to an imminent and overwhelming peril. The defence cannot succeed if the response was disproportionate to the peril or if it was not "involuntary" in the sense that the emergency was not "real" or not imminent or that there was a reasonable alternative response that was not illegal.

In the course of his charge on the issue of necessity the trial Judge instructed the jury, using the specific words that appear in *Morgentaler*, to the effect that they must find facts which amount to "an urgent situation of clear and imminent peril when compliance with the law is demonstrably impossible" in order for the appellants' non-compliance with the law against importation and possession of cannabis to be excused. That is the correct test. It is, with respect, however, my view that in explaining the meaning and application of this test the trial Judge fell into error.

The trial Judge was obliged, in my opinion, to direct the jury's attention to a number of issues pertinent to the test for necessity. Was the emergency a real one? Did it constitute an immediate threat of the harm purportedly feared? Was the response proportionate? In comparing this response to the danger that motivated it, was the danger one that society would reasonably expect the average person to withstand? Was there any reasonable legal alternative to the illegal response open to the accused? Although the trial Judge did not explicitly pose each and every one of these questions, in my view his charge was adequate to bring the considerations underlying them to the jury's attention on every issue except the last one, the question of a reasonable alternative.

This issue was the determining obstacle to the success of the defence of necessity in a number of the cases referred to earlier, including *Gilkes, Doud, Byng* and, for the present case most notably, because of the similarity of its factual basis, *Salvador*. Indeed, in most cases where the defence is raised, this consideration will almost certainly be the most important one.

In his charge, the trial Judge did not advert to this requirement. He did tell the jury that they must find facts capable of showing that "compliance with the law was demonstrably impossible" but on his recharge he put before the jury a significantly different test. The test, he said, is:

> . . . can you find facts from this evidence, and that means all the evidence, of course, that the situation of the Samarkanda at sea was so appallingly dire and dangerous to life that a reasonable doubt arises as to whether or not their decision was justified?

And again, at the conclusion of the recharge:

> There is no need for the evidence to show you that a certainty of death would result unless the action complained of by the Crown was taken. It doesn't go so far as that. You have to look at it as reasonable people and decide on any reasonable view of the matter, would these people have been justified in doing what they did? That is all that necessity means.

Both of these passages imply that the crucial consideration was whether the accused acted reasonably in coming into shore with their load of cannabis rather than facing death at sea. That is not sufficient as a test. Even if it does deal with the reality of the peril, its imminence and the proportionality of putting into shore, it does not deal at all with the question of whether there existed any other reasonable responses to the peril that were not illegal. Indeed, aside from the initial repetition of the *Morgentaler* formula, the trial Judge did not advert to this consideration at all, nor did he direct the jury's attention to the relevance of evidence indicating the possibility of such alternative courses of action. In these respects I believe he erred in law. He did not properly put the question of a "legal way out" before the jury.

In my view, this was a serious error and omission going to the heart of the defence of necessity. The error justifies a new trial.

. . . .

V CONCLUSION

On the basis of all the above, it is my conclusion that the Court of Appeal was correct in the result in ordering a new trial and was correct in sustaining the trial Judge's decision to withhold the botanical defence from the jury.

I would dismiss the appeals.

WILSON J.: — The factual background of this case, the history of the litigation in the Courts below and the grounds on which the appeal [from 69 C.C.C. (2d) 405] was taken in this Court are very fully set out in the reasons for judgment of the Chief Justice (Dickson J. at the date of the hearing) and it is not necessary for me to repeat them. Indeed, inasmuch as the Chief Justice's conclusion as to the defence of necessity seems clearly correct on the facts of this case and his disposition of the appeal manifestly just in the circumstances, I am dealing in these reasons only with the proposition very forcefully advanced by the Chief Justice in his reasons that the appropriate jurisprudential basis on which to premise the defence of necessity is exclusively that of excuse. My concern is that the learned Chief Justice appears to be closing the door on justification as an appropriate jurisprudential basis in some cases and I am firmly of the view that this is a door which should be left open by the court.

As the Chief Justice points out, criminal-law theory recognizes a distinction between justification and excuse. In the case of justification of the wrongfulness of the alleged offensive act is challenged; in the case of excuse the wrongfulness is acknowledged but a ground for the exercise of judicial compassion for the actor is asserted. By way of illustration, an act may be said to be justified when an essential element of the offence is absent, so that the defence effectively converts the accused's act from wrongful to rightful. Accordingly, those defences which serve to establish a lack of culpable intent on the part of the accused, or which demonstrate that, although the accused intended to commit the act, the act was one which the accused was within his rights to commit, may be labeled justification insofar as they elucidate the innocent nature of the act giving rise to the charge. Such doctrines as mistake of fact, automatism, etc., which, in the words of Lord Hailsham in *D.D.P. v. Morgan*; *D.P.P. v. McDonald*; *D.P.P. v. McLarty*, [1976] A.C. 182 (H. L.), are raised in order to "negative" *mens rea*, may be appropriately placed in this category, as they are invoked in order to undermine the very ingredient of culpability. Similarly, the accused who claims to have acted out of self-defence or provocation in utilizing aggressive force against another individual raises a justificatory defence in that he asserts the essential rightfulness of his aggressive act.

On the other hand, an excuse requires the Court to evaluate the presence or absence of the accused's will. In contemporary jurisprudence the most forceful champion of excuse in criminal law has been Professor George Fletcher, who has advocated a trend toward individualizing the conceptual basis for culpability, so that all circumstances subjectively relevant to the accused be considered by the Court. As such, the jury is requested to exercise compassion for the accused's predicament in its evaluation of his claim "I couldn't help myself": Fletcher, "The Individualization of Excusing Conditions" (1974), 47 Southern California L. Rev. 1264, at p. 1269. This type of analysis is reflected in the dissent of Seiler J. of the Supreme Court of Missouri in *State v. Green*, 470 S.W. 2d 565 (1971), in which the accused's prison escape was seen as excusable due to the intolerability of his confinement with aggressive homosexual inmates by whom he had been repeatedly victimized. The basis of the defence could not have been that of justification based on an objective balance of evils, since numerous United States courts had already established that the evil of prison escape outweighed the evil of intolerable prison conditions: see, *e.g.*, *People v. Whipple*, C.A. California, 279 P. 1008 (1929); *People v. Noble*, C.A. Michigan, 170 N.W. 2d 916 (1969). Rather, the issue for Seiler J. was the blamelessness of an accused in committing an act which, although admittedly wrong, was one for which any juror might have compassion. Thus the nature of an excuse is to personalize the plea so that, while justification looks to the rightness of the act, excuse speaks to the compassion of the Court for the actor.

As Dickson C.J.C. points out, although the necessity defence has engendered a significant amount of judicial and scholarly debate, it remains a somewhat elusive concept. It is, however, clear that justification and excuse are conceptually quite distinct and that any elucidation of a principled basis for the defence of necessity must be grounded in one or the other.

Turning first to the category of excuse, the concept of "normative involuntariness" stressed in the reasons of the Chief Justice may, on one reading, be said to fit squarely within the framework of an individualized plea which Professor Fletcher indicates characterizes all claims of excusability. The notional involuntariness of the action is assessed in the context of the accused's particular situation. The Court must ask not only whether the offensive act accompanied by the requisite culpable mental state (*i.e.*, intention, recklessness, etc.) has been established by the prosecution, but whether or not the accused acted so as to attract society's moral outrage. In some Unitied States jurisdictions this type of evaluation has been utilized to excuse from criminal liability individuals who commit intentional offensive acts but who operate under mental or sociological impairments with which one can sympathize (see *State v. St. Clair*, S.C. Missouri, 262 S.W. 2d 25 (1953)), or to form the theoretical basis for a defence where the accused confronted a desperate situation for which society might well be expected to express its compassion (see *U.S. v. Holmes*, 26 F. Cas. 360 (1842)). In evaluating a claim of "normative involuntariness" we seem to be told that the individual's criminally wrongful act was nevertheless blameless in the circumstances.

The position in English law, by contrast, was most accurately stated in the well-known case of *R. v. Dudley* (1884), 14 Q.B.D. 273 at 288 (C.C.R.), in which Lord Coleridge C.J. warned against allowing "compassion for the criminal to change or weaken in any manner the legal definition of the crime". The underlying principle here is the universality of rights, that all individuals whose actions are subjected to legal evaluation must be considered equal in standing. Indeed, it may be said that this concept of equal assessment of every actor, regardless of his particular motives or the particular pressures operating upon his will, is so fundamental to the criminal law as rarely to receive explicit articulation. However, the entire premise expressed by such thinkers as Kant and Hegel that man is by nature a rational being, and that this rationality finds expression both in the human capacity to overcome the impulses of one's own will and in the universal right to be free from the imposition of the impulses and will of others (see Hegel, *Philosophy of Right*, translated by Knox (1952), at pp. 226-27) supports the view that an individualized assessment of offensive conduct is simply not possible. If the obligation to refrain from criminal behaviour is preceived as a reflection of the fundamental duty to be rationally cognizant of the equal freedom of all individuals, then the focus of an analysis of *culpability* must be on the act itself (including its physical and mental elements) and not on the actor. The universality of such obligations precludes the relevance of what Fletcher refers to as "an individualized excusing condition".

On the other hand, the necessity of an act may be said to exempt an actor from *punishment*, since the person who acts in a state of what the Chief Justice calls "normative involuntariness" may be viewed as having been moved to act by the instinct for self-preservation. If so, the defence does not invoke the Court's compassion but rather embodies an implicit statement that the sanction threatened by the law (*i.e.*, future punishment in one form or another) could never overcome the fear of immediate death which the accused faced. Accordingly, in such a case the law is incapable of controlling the accused's conduct and responding to it with any punishment at all. Although such an act dictated by the necessity of self-preservation is a voluntary one (in the normal sense of the word), its "normative involuntariness" (in the sense that the actor faced no realistic choice) may form the basis of a defence if this is conceived as based on the pointlessness of punishment rather than on a view of the act itself as one the accused was entitled to commit. Indeed, one finds an explicit warning to this effect in Kant, *The Metaphysical Elements of Justice*, translated by Ladd (1965), at pp. 41-42, where it is asserted that "through a strange confusion among jurists" the analysis of the wrongfulness of an act is often interwined with the unquestionable futility of inflicting punishment on a person who has acted in despair or in circumstances of dire necessity.

It may be opportune at this point to comment briefly on the need to avoid slipping into what may be labeled an "instrumentalist analysis" of the purposes of punishment. For example, an analytic focus on excusing conditions is often premised on the fact that punishment in such situations will not serve the further goals of deterrence, rehabilitation, etc.: see, *e.g.*, Williams, Criminal Law: *The*

General Part, 2nd ed. (1961), especially at pp. 738-39. Such considerations, however, cannot form the basis of an acceptable defence, since they seem to view criminal culpability merely as a phenomenon in a chain of cause and effect. From an instrumentalist point of view the question is not whether liability is demanded in and of itself (as Lord Coleridge C.J. insisted must be the case in *Dudley, supra*), but rather whether the infliction of punishment will have some positive consequential effect: see, *e.g.*, J. Bentham, *An Introduction to the Principles of Morals and Legislation*, 2nd ed. (1823), vol. 2, p. 1.

The view of criminal liability as purposive only when it serves as a means to a further end is inherently problematic, since the further goals of punishment are by their very nature one step removed from the determination of guilt or innocence. Just as we do not inquire into the socio-economic effects of a particular remedy for determining parties' respective rights in civil litigation (see, *e.g.*, *Shelfer v. City of London Elec. Lighting Co.*; *Meux's Brewery Co. v. City of London Elec. Lighting Co.*, [1895] 1 Ch. 287 (C.A.)), it does not seem possible to evaluate criminality with regard to the end results which punishment will or will not achieve. Accordingly, if the basis for the accused's defence is reducible to compassion for his individual attributes or predicament, or the ineffectiveness of punishment in rehabilitating him or deterring future acts, the question raised is the type of remedy and the fashioning of an appropriate sentence. The concerns embodied in such a defence are legitimately addressed to the sentencing process but cannot, in my view, be the basis of a successful defence leading to an acquittal.

This, however, is distinguishable from the situation in which punishment cannot on any grounds be justified, such as the situation where a person has acted in order to save his own life. As Kant indicates, although the law must refrain from asserting that conduct which otherwise constitutes an offence is rightful if done for the sake of self-preservation, there is no punishment which could conceivably be appropriate to the accused's act. As such, the actor falling within the Chief Justice's category of "normative involuntariness" is excused, not because there is no instrumental ground on which to justify his punishment, but because no purpose inherent to criminal liability and punishment — *i.e.*, the setting right of a wrongful act — can be accomplished for an act which no rational person would avoid.

Returning to the defence of necessity as a justification, it may generally be said that an act is justified on grounds of necessity if the Court can say not only that was the act a necessary one but that it was rightful rather than wrongful. When grounded on the fundamental principle that a successful defence must characterize an act as one which the accused was within his rights to commit, it becomes immediately apparent that the defence does not depend on the immediacy or "normative involuntariness" of the accused's act unless, of course, the involuntariness is such as to be pertinent to the ordinary analysis of *mens rea*. The fact that one act is done out of a sense of immediacy or urgency and another after some contemplation cannot, in my view, serve to distinguish the quality of the act in terms of right or wrong. Rather, the justification must be premised on the need to fulfil a duty conflicting with the one which the accused is charged with having breached.

In discussing justification based on a conflict of duties one must be mindful of the viewpoint expressed by Dickson J. (as he then was) in *Morgentaler v. R.*, [1976] 1 S.C.R. 616 at 678, 30 C.R.N.S. 209, 20 C.C.C. (2d) 449, to the effect that: "No system of positive law can recognize any principle which would entitle a person to violate the law because on his view the law conflicted with some higher social value." This statement, in my view, is clearly correct if the "higher social value" to which the accused points is one which is not reflected in the legal system in the form of a duty. That is to say, pursuit of a purely ethical "duty", such as, for example, the duty to give to charity, may represent an ethically good or virtuous act but is not within the realm of legal obligations and cannot therefore validly be invoked as a basis on which to violate the positive criminal law. This illustration exemplifies the essential proposition that, although "a morally motivated act contrary to law may be ethically justified . . . the actor must accept the (legal) penalty for his action": *U.S. v. Moylan*, U.S.C.A., 4th Circ., 417 F. 2d 1002 (1969), certiorari denied 397 U.S. 910, 25 L. Ed. 2d 91, 90 S. Ct. 908.

Similarly, the Chief Justice in his reasons for judgment in the present case correctly underlines the tract that a utilitarian balancing of the benefits of obeying the law as opposed to disobeying it cannot possibly represent a legitimate principle against which to measure the legality of an action, since any violation of right permitted to be justified on such a utilitarian calculus does not, in the Chief Justice's words, "[fit] well with the judicial function" [p. 304]. The maximization of social utility may well be a goal of legislative policy but it is not part of the judicial task of delineating right and wrong. The case of *Southwark London Borough Council v. Williams*, [1971] 2 All E.R. 175 (C.A.), affords an appropriate illustration. In raising a defence of necessity to a charge of trespass the defendants implicitly argued that a violation of the rights of the property owner was justified because of the maximized social utility achieved by their using the property, in that otherwise the defendants would remain homeless and the property unused. Megaw L.J. recognized that it was no part of the adjudicator's task either to maximize utility or to distribute scarce resources on some criterion of merit as demanded by the defendants, since the distribution of society's resources is a political process that must be accomplished by a distributive mechanism encompassing the entire polity. Lord Denning M.R. pointed out that if such claims became a matter of right for an adjudicative body to determine and enforce the very notion of right would be undermined. He said at p. 179: "If homelessness were once admitted as a defence to trespass, no one's house could be safe."

Accordingly, not only can the system of positive law not tolerate an individual opting to act in accordance with the dictates of his conscience in the event of a conflict with legal duties, but it cannot permit acts in violation of legal obligations to be justified on the grounds that social utility is thereby increased. In both situations the conflicting "duty" to which the defence arguments point is one which the Court cannot take into account, as it invokes considerations external to a judicial analysis of the rightness or wrongness of the impugned act. As Lord Coleridge C.J. succinctly put it in *Dudley, supra*, at p. 287: "Who is to be the Judge of this sort of necessity?"

On the other hand, in some circumstances defence counsel may be able to point to a conflicting duty which Courts can and do recognize. For example, one may break the law in circumstances where it is necessary to rescue someone to whom one owes a positive duty of rescue (see *R. v. Walker* (1979), 48 C.C.C. (2d) 126 (Ont. Co. Ct.)), since failure to act in such a situation may itself constitute a culpable act or omission: see *R. v. Instan*, [1893] 1 Q.B. 450, 17 Cox C.C. 602 (C.C.R.). Similarly, if one subscribes to the viewpoint articulated by Laskin C.J.C. in *Morgentaler, supra*, and perceives a doctor's defence to an abortion charge as his legal obligation to treat the mother rather than his alleged ethical duty to perform an unauthorized abortion, then the defence may be invoked without violating the prohibition enunciated by Dickson J. in *Morgentaler* against choosing a non-legal duty over a legal one.

It must be acknowledged, however, that on the existing state of the law the defence of necessity as justification would not be available to the person who rescues a stranger, since the absence of a legal duty to rescue strangers reduces such a case to a conflict of a legal with a purely ethical duty. Such an act of rescue may be one deserving of no punishment and, indeed, deserving of praise, but it is nevertheless a culpable act if the law is violated in the process of the rescue.

. . . .

In summary, it seems to me that the category of "normative involuntariness" into which an act done in the interests of self-preservation falls is characterized not by the literal voluntariness of the act but by its unpunishable nature. As such, the act may be exempted from culpability if it arose in a life-threatening situation of necessity. Where, however, a defence by way of excuse is premised on compassion for the accused or on a perceived failure to achieve a desired instrumental end of punishment, the judicial response must be to fashion an appropriate sentence but to reject the defence as such. The only conceptual premise on which necessity as an excuse could rest is the inherent impossibility of a Court's responding in any way to an act which, although wrongful, was the one act which any rational person would commit.

Where the defence of necessity is invoked as a justification, the issue is simply whether the accused was right in pursuing the course of behaviour giving rise to the charge. Thus, where the act otherwise constitutes a criminal offence (*i.e.*, it embodies both *mens rea* and the *actus reus*) the accused must show that he operated under a conflicting legal duty which made his seemingly wrongful act right. But such justification must be premised on a right or duty recognized by law. This excludes conduct attempted to be justified on the ground of an ethical duty internal to the conscience of the accused as well as conduct sought to be justified on the basis of a perceived maximization of social utility resulting from it. Rather, the conduct must stem from the accused's duty to satisfy his legal obligations and to respect the principle of the universality of rights.

I would dismiss the appeals.

Appeals dismissed.

Is it necessary to distinguish justification from excuse? What legal consequences flow from the distinction? How does one determine whether the situation should be labelled a justification or an excuse? Should consequences flow from labels?

R. v. MORGENTALER, SMOLING and SCOTT

(1985), 48 C.R. (3d) 1, 22 C.C.C. (3d) 353 (Ont. C.A.)

Per Curiam

This appeal revolves around an issue which engages the deepest of human emotions, an issue which, understandably, brings into conflict sincerely and strongly held opposing views. However, we wish to emphasize at the outset that our task is not to express an opinion on the merits or demerits of abortion, but rather to determine whether Parliament has the jurisdiction to enact s. 251 of the *Criminal Code* now under attack and, if so, whether this case was properly put to the jury. We would adopt the statement of Dickson J. in *Morgentaler v. R.*, [1976] I S.C.R. 616, 30 C.R.N.S. 209, 20 C.C.C. (2d) 449 at 491 [Que.], where he said:

> It seems to me to be of importance, at the outset, to indicate what the Court is called upon to decide in this appeal and, equally important, what it has not been called upon to decide. It has not been called upon to decide, or even to enter, the loud and continuous public debate on abortion which has been going on in this country between, at the two extremes, (i) those who would have abortion regarded in law as an act purely personal and private of concern only to the woman and her physician in which the state has no legitimate right to interfere, and (ii) those who speak in terms of moral absolutes and, for religious or other reasons, regard an induced abortion and destruction of a foetus, viable or not, as destruction of a human life and tantamount to murder. The values we must accept for the purposes of this appeal are those expressed by Parliament which holds the view that the desire of a woman to be relieved of her pregnancy is not, of itself, justification for performing an abortion.

THE APPEAL

The respondents were charged on an indictment which reads as follows:

> Henry Morgentaler and Leslie Frank Smoling and Robert Scott stand charged that they during the period commencing in the month of November, 1982 and ending on the 5th day of July, 1983 at the Municipality of Metropolitan Toronto in the Judicial District of York, did conspire with each other, with intent to procure the miscarriage of female persons, to use an induced suction method for the purpose of carrying out that intent, thereby committing an indictable offence contrary to sections 251(1) and 423(1)(d) of the *Criminal Code of Canada*.

Upon their arraignment and before plea, their counsel moved to quash the indictment on the basis that s. 251 of the *Criminal Code* was unconstitutional.

After very lengthy proceedings the learned trial Judge rejected the defence plea and held the section to be constitutionally valid.

Following the ruling of the trial Judge, the trial then proceeded on the premise that the charge laid against the accused was valid in law. At the conclusion of the trial, the jury acquitted the respondents, and it is from that acquittal that this appeal is taken by the Crown.

. . .

Having rejected the attack on the constitutionality of s. 251 and the submissions in support of the motion to quash, it is now necessary to turn to the appeal by the Crown.

The Crown's right of appeal is limited to questions of law. Crown counsel urged that the learned trial Judge erred in law in leaving the defence of necessity to the jury. In the alternative, Crown counsel submitted that, even if it might be said that there was some evidence upon which the defence of necessity could have been placed before the jury, the learned trial Judge erred in instructing the jury that evidence was relevant to that defence when as a matter of law it was not and in failing to instruct the jury on other matters which were relevant to their proper consideration of that defence.

. . .

THE "DEFENCE" OF NECESSITY

The "defence" of necessity was thoroughly reviewed in the recent judgment of the Supreme Court of Canada in *Perka v. R.*, [1984] 2 S.C.R. 233.

. . .

This issue had earlier been considered by the Supreme Court of Canada in *Morgentaler* (1975), *supra*. In that case Dr. Morgentaler had been charged with the substantive offence of unlawfully procuring the miscarriage of a female person contrary to s. 251 of the *Criminal Code*. The facts of the case were set forth in the dissenting judgment of Laskin C.J.C. at pp. 465-66 as follows:

> The appellant was charged with performing an illegal abortion on August 15, 1973, upon a 26-year old unmarried female who had come to Canada from a foreign country in 1972 on a student visa. She was without family or close friends in Canada, ineligible to take employment and also ineligible for Medicare benefits, on becoming apprehensive of possible pregnancy in July, 1973, she consulted a physician in general practice who referred her to a gynecologist. He confirmed that she was pregnant, but refused assistance to procure an abortion. On her own initiative she canvassed five Montreal hospitals by telephone and learned that if an abortion was to be performed she would have to bear the fees of a surgeon and an anaesthetist, and could envisage two or three days' hospitalization at $140 per day. This was far beyond her means.
>
> Throughout the period following her apprehension and confirmation of her pregnancy and until the abortion performed by the appellant, she was anxious, unable to eat or sleep properly, prone to vomiting and quite depressed. Her condition had an adverse effect upon her studies and it was aggravated by her being told that the longer she delayed in having an

abortion the more dangerous it would be. One hospital offered her an appointment (which would result in her case coming before the therapeutic abortion committee) at the end of August, 1973, when she would be eight to 10 weeks' pregnant. She got in touch with the appellant at the suggestion of a hospital or hospitals that she had contacted. There is some discrepancy between her evidence and that of the appellant as to the scope and nature of the conversation between them when she visited his clinic where the abortion was performed. In this appeal I think it proper to accept the evidence of the appellant who testified that his discussion with her went beyond asking whether she had previously had an abortion, when she realized she was pregnant and what his fee would be. He asserted that the conversation also encompassed reference to her country of origin, her vocation, her marital status and why an abortion was necessary. During the conversation the appellant said that he assessed the necessity of an abortion by reference to her state of anxiety, her inability to eat or sleep properly and the consequent adverse effect of her physical health. He also considered that her determination to have an abortion might lead her to do something foolish. The appellant was aware that his patient had approached a number of hospitals without success, but did not know that she had been offered an appointment at the end of August, 1973.

The majority of the Supreme Court of Canada in that case agreed with the conclusion of the Quebec Court of Appeal that the defence of necessity was not open to the accused on those facts. Pigeon J., in commenting on the reasons for judgment of the Quebec Court of Appeal, stated in part as follows at p. 482:

> The views expressed by the other Judges were not significantly different on this question. As I read them they were all of the view that there was no evidence of the urgent necessity which, as the Crown conceded may, in very exceptional circumstances, justify a violation of the criminal law, this being a common law defence preserved by s. 7(3) of the *Criminal Code*. Before this Court, nothing was said that would tend to show that there was any evidence of an urgent necessity for effecting the abortion in disregard of s. 251, *Criminal Code*.

In more extended reasons on this issue, Dickson J. stated at pp. 499-500:

> It is, therefore, clear that a medical practitioner who wishes to procure a miscarriage because continued pregnancy may endanger the life or health of his patient may legally do so if he secures the certificate mentioned in s. 251(4)(*c*). *The defence of necessity, whatever that vague phrase may import, does not entitle a medical practitioner, in circumstances of time and place such as those under consideration, to procure an abortion on his own opinion of the danger to life and health.*
>
> ⋅   Assuming the theoretical possibility of such a defence in the present case, it remains to be seen whether there is evidence to support it. Amid the general imprecision and philosophic uncertainty discernible among the authors as to reach and effect of a defence of necessity, the most definite assertion would seem to be that found in Kenny's *Outlines of Criminal Law*, 19th ed. (1966), where the author says, p 73:
>
> "Probably no such defence can be accepted in any case (1) where the evil averted was a lesser evil than the offence committed to avert it, or (2) where the evil could have been averted by anything short of the commission of that offence, or (3) where more harm was done than was necessary for avering the evil. Hence it is scarcely safe to lay down any more definite rule trail than suggested by Sir James Stephen, viz. that 'it is just possible to imagine cases in which the expediency of breaking the law is so overwhelmingly great that people may be justified in breaking it; but these cases cannot be defined beforehand'."
>
> Kenny says, p. 72:
>
> "Yet, though theoretical writers have been willing to accept this ground of defence, there is no English case in which the defence has been actually raised with success;"

Turning our attention to Kenny's (2), we must ask whether the evil averted could have been averted by anything short of the commission of the offence. This raises the question of the urgency of the operation performed by the appellant and whether the appellant could have complied with the law. *A defence of necessity at the very least must rest upon evidence from which a jury could find (i) that the accused in good faith considered the situation so emergent that failure to terminate the pregnancy immediately could endanger life or health and (ii) that upon any reasonable view of the facts compliance with the law was impossible.* [The italics are mine.]

And at pp. 502-503:

The appellant conceded that from 10:00 a.m. until noon on the day in question he had completed six abortions. The evidence also disclosed that at the time of the operation Verona Parkinson was six to eight weeks' pregnant, leaving some four to six weeks before completion of the first trimester of pregnancy, and that she had an appointment with the Montreal General Hospital for August 28, 1973, 13 days after the appellant performed the abortion. The risk attendant upon abortion would have become greater the longer Verona Parkinson waited. Perhaps that is some evidence of urgency, but it does not go to establish impossibility.

Upon this evidence I think it perfectly clear the Court of Appeal did not err in concluding there was on the record little evidence of real and urgent medical need. More important, in answer to the question: "Was there any legal way out?" I think one must say that evidence from which a jury could conclude it was impossible for appellant to comply with the law is wholly wanting. The plain fact is that appellant made no attempt to bring himself within the bounds of legality in deciding to perform this abortion. Appellant failed to establish the second condition which Kenny says must be satisfied before the defence of necessity can be accepted in any case. I would hold, therefore, that the defence of necessity was not open to the appellant.

This is not a case where a physician is attended upon by a patient whose condition is such that the physician in good faith considers the situation so emergent that failure to terminate the pregnancy immediately could endanger the life or health of the patient and upon any reasonable view of the facts compliance with the law was impossible. That was the issue in the earlier cases involving Dr. Morgentaler, reference to which played such an important part in this trial and yet which really were quite irrelevant to the charge of conspiracy which the respondents faced.

Taking the most favourable view of the evidence for the defence in this case, the respondents were dissatisfied with the present law relating to abortions in Canada. They believed that every pregnant woman should have the freedom of choice as to whether to have an abortion or not. They thus agreed to establish a free-standing clinic. They agreed to procure miscarriages for female persons who had been rejected by a therapeutic abortion clinic on the basis that the continuation of their pregnancies would not endanger their life or health. They also agreed to preform miscarriages for pregnant women in Metropolitan Toronto who certified that they could not get a therapeutic abortion within a reasonable time. The statements to that effect were taken at face value. For those outside Metropolitan Toronto the fact that they had travelled some distance to attend the clinic was considered evidence in itself that they could not obtain a therapeutic abortion within a reasonable time, whether they were eligible for such abortion or not. They further agreed to procure miscarriages for female persons who did not desire to attend a therapeutic clinic because they found the procedures at such clinics to be distasteful. Evidence was tendered to show that many women in Ontario left the province to obtain abortions elsewhere, including Dr. Morgentaler's free-standing clinic in Montreal. They also agreed to procure miscarriages for all pregnant women in their second trimester on the theory that the procedures at the Morgentaler Clinic were safer for such women than the procedures carried out in a hospital.

It was their further contention that, notwithstanding the requirements of the *Criminal Code*, hospitals were unnecessary for the procuring of a miscarriage.

Dr. Morgentaler testified that any delay in carrying out the medical procedures increased the risk to life or health, although there was no evidence to suggest that the procedures adopted in hospitals in Ontario for procuring miscarriages exposed the patients to any serious risk to their life or health.

In short, the respondents admitted entering into an agreement of a global nature to procure miscarriages of all female persons who had made the decision to terminate their pregnancies. The medical procedure was to be carried out in a clinic which was not a hospital accredited by the Canadian Council on Hospital Accreditation or approved by the provincial Minister of Health, and there was to be no therapeutic abortion committee. Thus, the evidence for the defence supported the allegation of the Crown that the respondents had agreed to procure miscarriages of female persons contrary to s. 25 of the *Criminal Code*.

. . . .

With respect, we think that the defence of necessity was misconceived. As has previously been noted, before a defence of necessity is available the conduct of the accused must be truly involuntary, in the sense ascribed to that term in the precedents cited. There was nothing involuntary in the agreement entered into in this case by the respondents. As stated by Fletcher, *Rethinking Criminal Law* (1978), pp. 811-12:

> Planning, deliberating, relying on legal precedents — all of these are incompatible with the uncalculating response essential to "involuntary" conduct.

Furthermore, there must be evidence that compliance with the law was demonstrably impossible, and that there was no legal way out.

Not only did the defendants fail to make every reasonable effort to comply with the law, but they consciously agreed to violate it. Their dissatisfaction with the state of the law, although perhaps relevant to the issue of motive, afforded no basis for the defence of necessity.

The constitutional validity of s. 251 having been upheld by the trial Judge, it was not an issue for the jury to weigh the merits of the law enacted by Parliament and to be invited to resolve the public debate on abortion. Yet, it was on the basis of the dissatisfaction with the law that the defence sought to rely on the legal defence of necessity. On this issue the trial Judge accurately placed before the jury the theory of the defence as follows:

I am dealing now with the next objection. The next objection, in dealing with the theory of the defence, I said, and I better read it to you: It is the theory of the defence that women in Ontario who find themselves with an unwanted pregnancy and who desire an abortion often discover that this medical service is unavailable to them due to the present state of the law and because of the service necessity of having to obtain an abortion at a hospital with the approval of a therapeutic abortion committee, and that, even when the service is available, women who have qualified for an abortion are required to suffer delay which increases the risk to them, and I said to their "health". I should have said "health or life".

The theory of the defence is that this situation was an emergency so pressing and so perilous that it was involuntary and that the accused had no other choice than to agree to open a clinic, in effect.

With respect, the defence of necessity is not premised on dissatisfaction with the law. The defence of necessity recognizes that the law must be followed, but there are certain factual situations which arise which may excuse a person for failure to comply with the law. It is not the law which can create an emergency giving rise to a defence of necessity, but it is the facts of a given situation which may do so.

This was not a case where two or more doctors agreed to procure the miscarriage of a female person who was in immediate need of medical services in order to avoid danger to her life or health, and in which case the defence of necessity would be a live issue. The defence of necessity cannot be resorted to as an excuse for medical practitioners in Canada to agree in the circumstances of this case to procure abortions on their own opinion of the danger to life or health and at a place of their own choosing in complete disregard of the provisions of s. 251 of the *Criminal Code*.

Although it was for the jury to weigh the evidence, it is the function of an appellate court to examine the record with a view to ascertaining whether there is any evidence to support a defence. On the record before us, including the evidence tendered by the Crown as well as for the defence, the defence of necessity was not open to the respondents, and the trial Judge erred in leaving that defence to the jury.

This substantive issue of the relevance of the defence of necessity was not directly considered by the Supreme Court of Canada in its subsequent decision to declare the abortion provisions of the *Criminal Code* unconstitutional: (1988), 62 C.R. (3d) 1 (S.C.C.).

R. v. LATIMER

(2001), 39 C.R. (5th) 1, 150 C.C.C. (3d) 129 (S.C.C.)

The defence of necessity received another high profile test in this heartwrenching case. A father was on trial for the first degree murder of Tracy, his 12-year-old daughter, who had a severe form of cerebral palsy. Tracy was quadriplegic and her physical condition rendered her immobile. Her condition was permanent, caused by neurological damage at the time of her birth. She was said to have the mental capacity of a four-month-old baby, and could communicate only by means of facial expressions, laughter and crying. She was completely dependent on others for her care. She suffered five to six seizures daily. It was thought that she experienced a great deal of pain. This could not be reduced by medication since this would conflict with her anti-epileptic medication and her difficulty in swallowing. She had to be spoon-fed, and her lack of nutrients caused weight loss. There was evidence that Tracy could have been fed with a feeding tube into her stomach, an option that would have improved her nutrition and health, and that might also have allowed for more effective pain medication to be administered. The accused and his wife rejected this option as intrusive and the first step to artificially preserving her life. Tracy had a serious disability but was not terminally ill. She had undergone numerous surgeries including the implanting of metal rods to support her spine. The Latimers learned that the doctors wished to perform additional surgery on a dislocated hip which involved removing her upper thigh bone. According to the accused's wife they perceived this as mutilation.[1]

The accused decided to take his daughter's life. While his wife and Tracy's siblings were at church, he carried Tracy to his pickup truck, seated her in the cab, and inserted a hose from the truck's exhaust pipe into the cab. She died from the carbon monoxide. The accused at first maintained that she had simply passed away in her sleep, but later confessed to having taken her life. Charged with first degree murder, the jury found him guilty of second degree murder. The trial judge had withdrawn the defence of necessity from the jury by the following instruction:

---

1 The above facts are taken from the Supreme Court's review of the record. The tragic context has been further described by Professor Barney Sneiderman, "The Latimer Mercy-Killing Case: A Rumination on Crime and Punishment", (1997), 5 Health L.J. 1 at 1-2 as follows:

Gravely affected since birth by cerebral palsy, Tracy Latimer was a "totally body-involved spastic quadriplegic", whose constant muscle spasms and seizures had wrenched her body into a twisted frozen position. She had the mental age of a two- or three-month-old baby, weighed 38 pounds, wore diapers, often needed suppositories to unplug her bowels, had impaired vision, and could not sit up, talk, or feed herself. Her parents kept a bucket at hand when feeding her as she had difficulty in swallowing and would constantly vomit. She spent her days either in bed or propped in a wheelchair, tightly fitted to prevent her thrashing about during her daily seizure episodes.

Tracy had undergone a number of surgical procedures to relieve the painful muscular tension afflicting her grossly contorted body; muscles had been cut at the top of her legs, her toes, her heel cords, and knees. There was also surgery on her spine; stainless steel rods were inserted on each side to relieve the cramping of her stomach and lungs. Because Tracy was on anticonvulsant medication to control her seizures, her parents were fearful that using narcotics to control her pain could prove fatal by depressing her respiration (a concern shared by Tracy's orthopaedic surgeon). She was in constant pain from a dislocated hip, and Latimer was appalled at the prospect of impending surgery that would involve the removal of part of her hip and thigh bone. And there would be more surgery to come.

Sneiderman's sources are the reported decision in (1995), 41 C.R. (4th) 1 (Sask. C.A.), the trial transcript and newspaper accounts. The notion Tracy was in constant pain has been disputed: see Ruth Enns, A Voice Unheard. The Latimer Case and People with Disabilities (1999). An appendix at pp.166-170 shows that Tracy's mother's communication books had multiple entries as to her happiness and smiles.

[W]hile the doctrine of necessity can sometimes operate to excuse criminal misconduct, I must tell you as a matter of law that the doctrine does not apply in this case. The defence of necessity exists only where the perpetrator's decision to break the law is inescapable and unavoidable and necessary to avert some imminent risk of peril. It arises only in cases where there is no option, no other choice. That was not the situation here. There was an option, albeit not a particularly happy one. The option was to persevere in the attempts to make Tracy comfortable in her life, however, disagreeable and heartwrenching those attempts may have been. (41 C.R. (4th) at 38)

The jury returned a verdict of second degree murder. The sentence was life imprisonment with no parole eligibility for ten years.

In dismissing Latimer's appeal the Saskatchewan Court of Appeal held that the trial judge had properly withdrawn the defence of necessity from the jury given the *Perka* criteria. A majority, over the dissent of Chief Justice Bayda, rejected the argument for a constitutional exemption from the mandatory sentence.

At the second trial, ordered by the Supreme Court for other reasons, the charge was second degree murder. The trial proceeded on the basis the accused had been motivated by concern for his daughter's present and future pain. For very similar reasons to those offered in the first trial, the trial judge, Noble J., withdrew the defence of necessity but only after the addresses by counsel. The jury again convicted but were visibly upset when asked to make a recommendation whether parole eligibility should be set at more than ten years. They recommended one year! This reality was a factor Noble J. took into account in opting for a constitutional exemption and imposing a sentence of one year followed by probation for one year less one day. During the second trial, defence counsel asked the trial judge for a ruling, in advance of his closing submissions, on whether the jury could consider the defence of necessity. The trial judge told counsel that he would rule on necessity after the closing submissions. Some of the defence counsel's address referred to the defence of necessity. The judge later ruled that the defence was not available.

The Saskatchewan Court of Appeal affirmed the conviction but reversed the sentence. It imposed the mandatory minimum sentence of life imprisonment without parole eligibility for ten years. The Supreme Court in a short unanimous judgment dismissed the accused's further appeals against conviction and sentence.

Per curiam:

. . . .

(1) The Availability of the Defence of Necessity
(a) The Three Requirements for the Defence of Necessity

We propose to set out the requirements for the defence of necessity first, before applying them to the facts of this appeal. The leading case on the defence of necessity is *Perka v. The Queen* . . . .

. . . .

Dickson J. insisted that the defence of necessity be restricted to those rare cases in which true "involuntariness" is present. The defence, he held, must be "strictly controlled and scrupulously limited" (p. 250). It is well-established that the defence of necessity must be of limited application. Were the criteria for the defence loosened or approached purely subjectively, some fear, as did Edmund Davies L.J., that necessity would "very easily become simply a mask for anarchy": *Southwark London Borough Council v. Williams*, [1971] Ch. 734 (C.A.), at p. 746.

Perka outlined three elements that must be present for the defence of necessity. First, there is the requirement of imminent peril or danger. Second, the accused must have had no reasonable legal alternative to the course of action he or she undertook. Third, there must be proportionality between the harm inflicted and the harm avoided.

To begin, there must be an urgent situation of "clear and imminent peril": *Morgentaler v. The Queen*, [1976] 1 S.C.R. 616, at p. 678. In short, disaster must be imminent, or harm unavoidable and near. It is not enough that the peril is foreseeable or likely; it must be on the verge of transpiring and virtually certain to occur. In *Perka*, Dickson J. expressed the requirement of imminent peril at p. 251: "At a minimum the situation must be so emergent and the peril must be so pressing that normal human instincts cry out for action and make a counsel of patience unreasonable". The *Perka* case, at p. 251, also offers the rationale for this requirement of immediate peril: "The requirement . . . tests whether it was indeed unavoidable for the actor to act at all". Where the situation of peril clearly should have been foreseen and avoided, an accused person cannot reasonably claim any immediate peril.

The second requirement for necessity is that there must be no reasonable legal alternative to disobeying the law. *Perka* proposed these questions, at pp. 251-52: "Given that the accused had to act, could he nevertheless realistically have acted to avoid the peril or prevent the harm, without breaking the law? *Was there a legal way out?*" (emphasis in original). If there was a reasonable legal alternative to breaking the law, there is no necessity. It may be noted that the requirement involves a realistic appreciation of the alternatives open to a person; the accused need not be placed in the last resort imaginable, but he must have no reasonable legal alternative. If an alternative to breaking the law exists, the defence of necessity on this aspect fails.

The third requirement is that there be proportionality between the harm inflicted and the harm avoided. The harm inflicted must not be disproportionate to the harm the accused sought to avoid.

. . . .

Evaluating proportionality can be difficult. It may be easy to conclude that there is no proportionality in some cases, like the example given in *Perka* of the person who blows up a city to avoid breaking a finger. Where proportionality can quickly be dismissed, it makes sense for a trial judge to do so and rule out the defence of necessity before considering the other requirements for necessity. But most situations fall into a grey area that requires a difficult balancing of harms. In this regard, it should be noted that the requirement is not that one harm (the harm avoided) must always clearly outweigh the other (the harm inflicted). Rather, the two harms must, at a minimum, be of a comparable gravity. That is, the harm avoided must be either comparable to, or clearly greater than, the harm inflicted. As the Supreme Court of Victoria in Australia has put it, the harm inflicted "must not be out of proportion to the peril to be avoided": *R. v. Loughnan*, [1981] V.R. 443, at p. 448.

Before applying the three requirements of the necessity defence to the facts of this case, we need to determine what test governs necessity. Is the standard objective or subjective? A subjective test would be met if the person believed he or she was in imminent peril with no reasonable legal alternative to committing the offence. Conversely, an objective test would not assess what the accused believed; it would consider whether in fact the person *was* in peril with no reasonable legal alternative. A modified objective test falls somewhere between the two. It involves an objective evaluation, but one that takes into account the situation and characteristics of the particular accused person. We conclude that, for two of the three requirements for the necessity defence, the test should be the modified objective test.

The first and second requirements — imminent peril and no reasonable legal alternative — must be evaluated on the modified objective standard described above. As expressed in *Perka*, necessity is rooted in an objective standard: "involuntariness is measured on the basis of society's expectation of appropriate and normal resistance to pressure" (p. 259). We would add that it is appropriate, in evaluating the accused's conduct, to take into account personal characteristics that legitimately affect what may be expected of that person. The approach taken in *R. v. Hibbert*, [1995] 2 S.C.R. 973, is instructive. Speaking for the Court, Lamer C.J. held, at para. 59, that:

> it is appropriate to employ an objective standard that takes into account the particular circumstances of the accused, including his or her ability to perceive the existence of alternative courses of action.

While an accused's perceptions of the surrounding facts may be highly relevant in determining whether his conduct should be excused, those perceptions remain relevant only so long as they are reasonable. The accused person must, at the time of the act, honestly believe, on reasonable grounds, that he faces a situation of imminent peril that leaves no reasonable legal alternative open. There must be a reasonable basis for the accused's beliefs and actions, but it would be proper to take into account circumstances that legitimately affect the accused person's ability to evaluate his situation. The test cannot be a subjective one, and the accused who argues that *he* perceived imminent peril without an alternative would only succeed with the defence of necessity if his belief was reasonable given his circumstances and attributes. We leave aside for a case in which it arises the possibility that an honestly held but mistaken belief could ground a "mistake of fact" argument on the separate inquiry into *mens rea*.

The third requirement for the defence of necessity, proportionality, must be measured on an objective standard, as it would violate fundamental principles of the criminal law to do otherwise. Evaluating the nature of an act is fundamentally a determination reflecting society's values as to what is appropriate and what represents a transgression. Some insight into this requirement is provided by George Fletcher, in a passage from *Rethinking Criminal Law* (1978), at p. 804. Fletcher spoke of the comparison between the harm inflicted and the harm avoided, and suggested that there was a threshold at which a person must be expected to suffer the harm rather than break the law. He continued:

> Determining this threshold is patently a matter of moral judgment about what we expect people to be able to resist in trying situations. A valuable aid in making that judgment is comparing the competing interests at stake and assessing the degree to which the actor inflicts harm beyond the benefit that accrues from his action.

The evaluation of the seriousness of the harms must be objective. A subjective evaluation of the competing harms would, by definition, look at the matter from the perspective of the accused person who seeks to avoid harm, usually to himself. The proper perspective, however, is an objective one, since evaluating the gravity of the act is a matter of community standards infused with constitutional considerations (such as, in this case, the s. 15(1) equality rights of the disabled). We conclude that the proportionality requirement must be determined on a purely objective standard.

(b) The Application of the Requirements for Necessity in This Case

The inquiry here is not whether the defence of necessity should in fact *excuse* Mr. Latimer's actions, but whether the jury should have been left to consider this defence. The correct test on that point is whether there is an air of reality to the defence.

. . . .

The question is whether there is sufficient evidence that, if believed, would allow a reasonable jury — properly charged and acting judicially — to conclude that the defence applied and acquit the accused.

For the necessity defence, the trial judge must be satisfied that there is evidence sufficient to give an air of reality to each of the three requirements. If the trial judge concludes that there is no air of reality to any one of the three requirements, the defence of necessity should not be left to the jury.

In this case, there was no air of reality to the three requirements of necessity.

The first requirement is imminent peril. It is not met in this case. The appellant does not suggest he himself faced any peril; instead he identifies a peril to his daughter, stemming from her upcoming surgery which he perceived as a form of mutilation. Acute suffering can constitute imminent peril, but in this case there was nothing to her medical condition that placed Tracy in a dangerous situation where death was an alternative. Tracy was thought to be in pain before the surgery, and that pain was expected to continue, or increase, following the surgery. But that ongoing pain did not constitute an emergency in this case. To borrow the language of Edmund Davies L.J. in *Southwark London Borough Council*, *supra*, at p. 746, we are dealing not with an emergency but with "an obstinate and long-standing state of affairs". Tracy's proposed surgery did not pose an imminent threat to her life, nor did her medical condition. In fact, Tracy's health might have improved had the Latimers not rejected the option of relying on a feeding tube. Tracy's situation was not an emergency. The appellant can be reasonably expected to have understood that reality. There was no evidence of a legitimate psychological condition that rendered him unable to perceive that there was no imminent peril. The appellant argued that, for him, further surgery *did* amount to imminent peril. It was not reasonable for the appellant to form this belief, particularly when better pain management was available.

The second requirement for the necessity defence is that the accused had no reasonable legal alternative to breaking the law. In this case, there is no air of reality to the proposition that the appellant had no reasonable legal alternative to killing his daughter. He had at least one reasonable legal alternative: he could have struggled on, with what was unquestionably a difficult situation, by helping Tracy to live and by minimizing her pain as much as possible. The appellant might have done so by using a feeding tube to improve her health and allow her to take more effective pain medication, or he might have relied on the group home that Tracy stayed at just before her death. The appellant may well have thought the prospect of struggling on unbearably sad and demanding. It was a human response that this alternative was unappealing. But it was a reasonable legal alternative that the law requires a person to pursue before he can claim the defence of necessity. The appellant was aware of this alternative but rejected it.

The third requirement for the necessity defence is proportionality; it requires the trial judge to consider, as a question of law rather than fact, whether the harm avoided was proportionate to the harm inflicted. It is difficult, at the conceptual level, to imagine a circumstance in which the proportionality requirement could be met for a homicide. We leave open, if and until it arises, the question of whether the proportionality requirement could be met in a homicide situation. In England, the defence of necessity is probably not available for homicide: *R. v. Howe*, [1987] 1 A.C. 417 (H.L.), at pp. 453 and 429; Smith and Hogan, *Criminal Law* (9th ed. 1999), at pp. 249-51. The famous case of *R. v. Dudley and Stephens* (1884), 14 Q.B.D. 273, involving cannibalism on the high seas, is often cited as establishing the unavailability of the defence of necessity for homicide, although the case is not conclusive: see Card, Cross and Jones, *Criminal Law* (12th ed. 1992), at p. 352; Smith and Hogan, *supra*, at pp. 249 and 251. The Law Reform Commission of Canada has suggested the defence should not be available for a person who intentionally kills or seriously harms another person: *Report on Recodifying Criminal Law* (1987), at p. 36. American jurisdictions are divided on this question, with a number of them denying the necessity defence for murder: P.H. Robinson, *Criminal Law Defenses* (1984), vol. 2, at pp. 63-65; see also *United States v. Holmes*, 26 F. Cas. 360 (C.C.E.D. Pa. 1842) (No. 15,383). The American *Model Penal Code* proposes that the defence of necessity *would* be available for homicide: American Law Institute, *Model Penal Code and Commentaries* (1985), at para.

3.02, pp. 14-15; see also W.R. LaFave and A.W. Scott, *Substantive Criminal Law* (1986), vol. 1, at p. 634.

Assuming for the sake of analysis only that necessity could provide a defence to homicide, there would have to be a harm that was seriously comparable in gravity to death (the harm inflicted). In this case, there was no risk of such harm. The "harm avoided" in the appellant's situation was, compared to death, completely disproportionate. The harm inflicted in this case was ending a life; that harm was immeasurably more serious than the pain resulting from Tracy's operation which Mr. Latimer sought to avoid. Killing a person — in order to relieve the suffering produced by a medically manageable physical or mental condition — is not a proportionate response to the harm represented by the non-life-threatening suffering resulting from that condition.

We conclude that there was no air of reality to *any* of the three requirements for necessity. As noted earlier, if the trial judge concludes that even one of the requirements had no air of reality, the defence should not be left to the jury. Here, the trial judge was correct to remove the defence from the jury. In considering the defence of necessity, we must remain aware of the need to respect the life, dignity and equality of all the individuals affected by the act in question. The fact that the victim in this case was disabled rather than able-bodied does not affect our conclusion that the three requirements for the defence of necessity had no air of reality here.

The decision in *Latimer* that there was no evidentiary foundation for the defence of necessity to be put to the jury is in stark contrast to the three *Morgentaler* trials in Quebec where the necessity defence was weak but nevertheless left with the jury. **Should the defence of necessity have been put in *Latimer*?**

Latimer is clearly a hard case. It engages the emotions of disabled persons who understandably feel vulnerable if the accused was not to be punished for deliberately taking an innocent life without consent. There is also understandable fear that a lenient sentence would encourage other similar actions and moves to decriminalize assisted suicide and euthanasia.

There is, however, the issue of Parliament's inaction. It has refused to consider legislation to deal with mercy killings and euthanasia and assisted suicide, despite a common "do not resuscitate" practice in many Canadian hospitals. **Given this reality, should the Supreme Court have granted Latimer a constitutional exemption?** Chief Justice Bayda carefully considered public outrage expressed against the sentence and four other mercy killing cases, two involving consent, where the charges were reduced from murder and the sentences were probation. This is a powerful judgment: see, too, Tim Quigley, "*R. v. Latimer*: Hard Cases Make Interesting Law" (1995), 41 C.R. (4th) 89 at 96-98. At its heart the concern is for equal justice. Unfortunately, it was not even referred to by the Supreme Court. See, too, Barney Sneiderman, "The Latimer Mercy-Killing Case: A Rumination of Crime and Punishment" (1997), 5 Health L.J. 1 and "The Case of Robert Latimer. A Commentary on Crime and Punishment" (1999), 37 Alta. L. Rev. 1017. The latter article was relied on by defence counsel in the Supreme Court but is not even acknowledged by the

Court. For a wide rang of views on the Supreme Court's decision see comments by Barney Sneiderman, Archibald Kaiser, Allan Manson and Stuart in the C.R.'s. For general discussion of cruel and unusual punishment and constitutional exemptions see Stuart, *Charter Justice in Canadian Criminal Law* (3rd. ed., 2001) chapts. 7 and 11.

In the United Kingdom the authority of *Dudley and Stephens* has been weakened by a ruling of the Court of Appeal: *A (Children), Re (Siamese Twins Decision)*, (September 22, 2000) (C.A.). The Court ruled that necessity would legalize an operation to separate conjoined twins against the wishes of their Catholic parents. The operation would result in the instant death of one of the twins but would likely save the other from death for a normal life. The defence of necessity is fully reviewed by Brooke L.J. and also relied on by Ward L.J. Walker L.J. somehow rests on the view that death was not intended. Brooke L.J. refers to a real life example:

> At the coroner's inquest conducted in October 1987 into the Zeebrugge [ferry] disaster, an army corporal gave evidence that he and dozens of other people were near the foot of a rope ladder. They were all in the water and in danger of drowning. Their route to safety, however, was blocked for at least ten minutes by a young man who was petrified by cold or fear (or both) and was unable to move up or down. Eventually the corporal gave instructions that the man should be pushed off the ladder, and he was never seen again (at para. 311).

---

1. The accused is charged with speeding and dangerous driving. He was clocked on radar at l20 k.p.h. in a 50 k.p.h. zone. He was operating his vehicle in a heavily built-up residential area and was observed maintaining this speed over a distance of several city blocks. During this time he was being closely followed by another automobile. The automobile alternately slowed and accelerated with the second vehicle always maintaining a distance of seven to eight feet from the lead vehicle. The accused testified that each time he speeded up he did so to ensure maintenance of interval between himself and the car behind him to avoid the hazard presented by the other driver's tailgating. The driver of the other vehicle admitted that he was crowding the accused intentionally as he was "out for thrills". The accused relies on necessity. What do you, as Crown counsel, argue?

Compare *R. v. Fry* (1977), 36 C.C.C. (2d) 396 (Sask. Prov. Ct.), *R. v. Kennedy* (1972), 18 C.R.N.S. 80, 7 C.C.C. (2d) 42 (N.S. Co. Ct.) and *R. v. Morris* (1994), 32 C.R. (4th) 191 (B.C. S.C.).

2. The accused is charged with fishing in a place where, at that time, fishing was prohibited by law. The waters had been closed to fishing from 1400 hours that day. The basis of his defence is that, owing to the very inclement weather the day before, his punts, used for collecting the herring from the gillnets, were beached. The accused was therefore unable to retrieve all his nets before 1400 hours although he worked all morning and did manage to retrieve some. Give judgment.

Compare *R. v. Pootlass* (1978), 1 C.R. (3d) 378 (B.C. Prov. Ct.).

3. The accused is a police constable and at the material time was driving a police cruiser. He received a radio call that a bank alarm had gone off at the Bank of Montreal a few blocks away. He was advised that the

robbers were armed and still on the premises. He turned on the siren and roof lights and headed for the bank. As he approached the bank he was aware of a stop sign which required him to stop at the intersection. Because of the emergency and his concern for the safety of the people in the bank, he decided not to stop. He slowed to 20 k.p.h., looked both ways, and entered the intersection without stopping. He collided with a car coming from his right. He was aware of his exemption under the circumstances from the speed provisions of the *Highway Traffic Act*, but realized there was no other exemption. The accused is charged with failing to stop and advances the defence of necessity. Result?

Compare *R. v. Walker* (1979), 48 C.C.C. (2d) 126 (Ont. Co. Ct.).

4. The accused is charged with having committed an assault on his wife. The assault allegedly occurred in the accused's truck as they were returning from an evening at the tavern. The accused was driving. He was sober but his wife was drunk. His wife became agitated about an occurrence earlier that evening and demanded that they return to town. The accused refused to turn around and his wife threatened to jump. She reached for the door handle and he grabbed her and pulled her back. She grabbed at the steering wheel and the truck nearly went into the ditch. The accused grabbed her around the neck and held her in that fashion all the way home. Grounds of necessity?

Compare *R. v. Morris* (1981), 23 C.R. (3d) 175, 61 C.C.C. (2d) 163 (Alta. Q.B.).

5. The accused was charged with trespassing contrary to a provincial statute. The trespass occurred on the grounds of Litton Industries. The accused testified that she believed Litton Industries to manufacture component systems for the Cruise missile and that the Cruise missile was aimed at targets in other countries which could trigger a nuclear conflict. She believed Litton Industries was commiting a serious offence and she was prepared to commit the offence of trespass to avert this evil. She testified she was involved in the protest because "I have to!". The defence relied on necessity.

Compare *R. v. Young* (1984), 39 C.R. (3d) 290 (Ont. Prov. Ct.).

6. The accused, a 33-year old mother of five young children, was charged with defrauding the Ministry of Community and Social Services of more than $1,000. It was alleged that during a common law relationship over a ten year period she had misrepresented that her partner and the father of four of the children had not been living with her. It was further alleged that as a result she had obtained family benefits to which she was not entitled. Over the ten years until final separation she had received benefits of some $130,000. On the final separation the accused went to a women's shelter.

The trial judge found that the accused had failed to disclose that the parties were from time to time living together and that as a result she had received family benefits to which she was not entitled. However, there was evidence that he was abusive and spent any money he had on alcohol. She testified she was afraid to tell General Welfare that he was living with her in case the welfare cheque was made out to him. She feared he would drink away the money and they would be without food or shelter or both. Should the defence of necessity succeed?

Compare *R. v. LaLonde* (1995), 37 C.R. (4th) 97 (Ont. Gen. Div.) and see comment by Sheila Noonan, "LaLonde: Evaluating The Relevance of BWS Evidence" (1995), 37 C.R. (4th) 110.

Duress

See sections 17 and 18 of the *Criminal Code*.

R. v. CARKER (NO. 2)

[1967] S.C.R. 114, 2 C.R.N.S. 16, [1967] 2 C.C.C. 190

RITCHIE J.: — This is an appeal by the Attorney-General of British Columbia from a judgment of the Court of Appeal of that Province, from which Mr. Justice MacLean dissented, and by which it was ordered that the respondent's conviction for unlawfully and wilfully damaging public property and thereby committing mischief, should be set aside and that a new trial should be had.

At the trial the respondent admitted having damaged the plumbing fixtures in the cell where he was incarcerated at Oakalla Prison Farm in British Columbia but, through his counsel, he sought to introduce evidence to show that he had committed this offence under the compulsion of threats and was therefore entitled to be excused for committing it by virtue of the provisions of s. 17 of the *Criminal Code* and that he was also entitled to avail himself of the common-law defence of "duress" having regard to the provision of s. 7 of the *Criminal Code*.

. . . .

I agree with the learned trial Judge and with MacLean J.A. that in respect of proceedings for an offfence under the *Criminal Code* the common-law rules and principles respecting "duress" as an excuse or defence have been codified and exhaustively defined in s. 17.

. . . .

At the outset of the proceedings at the trial in the present case and in the absence of the jury, Mr, Greenfield, who acted on behalf of the accused, informed the Court that he intended to call evidence of compulsion and duress and he elected to outline the nature of this evidence which was that the offence had been committed during a disturbance, apparently organized by way of protest, to damage property at the Prison Farm in the course of which a substantial body of prisoners, shouting in unison from their separate cells, threatened the respondent, who was not joining in the disturbance, that if he did not break the plumbing fixtures in his cell he would be kicked in the head, his arm would be broken and he would get a knife in the back at the first opportunity.

. . . .

There can be little doubt that the evidence outlined by Mr. Greenfield, which was subsequently confirmed by the evidence given by the ringleaders of the disturbance in mitigation of sentence, disclosed that the respondent committed the offence under the compulsion of threats of death and grievous bodily harm, but although these threats were "immediate" in the sense that they were continuous until the time that the offence was committed, they were not threats of "immediate death" or "immediate grievous bodily harm" and none of the persons who delivered them was present in the cell with the respondent when the offence was committed. I am accordingly of opinion that the learned trial Judge was right in deciding that the proposed evidence did not afford an excuse within the meaning of s. 17 of the *Criminal Code*.

. . . .

In support of the suggestion that the threat in the present case was "immediate and continuous" Mr. Justice Norris relied on the case of *Subramaniam v. Public Prosecutor*, in which the Privy Council decided that the trial Judge was wrong in excluding evidence of threats to which the appellant was subjected by Chinese terrorists in Malaya. In that case it was found that the threats were a continuous menace up to the moment when the appellant was captured because the terrorists might have come back at any time and carried them into effect. Section 94 of the Penal Code of the Federated Malay States, which the appellant sought to invoke in that case provided:

> 94. Except murder and offences included in Chapter VI punishable with death, nothing is an offence which is done by a person who is compelled to do it by threats, which, at the time of doing it, reasonably cause the apprehension that instant death to that person will otherwise be the consequence.

The distinctions between the *Subramaniam* case and the present one lie in the fact that Subramaniam might well have had reasonable cause for apprehension that instant death would result from his disobeying the terrorists who might have come back at any moment, whereas it is virtually inconceivable that "immediate death" or "grievous bodily harm" could have come to Carker from those who were uttering the threats against him as they were locked up in separate cells, and it is also to be noted that the provisions of s. 17 of the *Criminal Code* are by no means the same as those of s. 94 of the Penal Code of the Federated Malay States; amongst other distinctions the latter section contains no provision that the person who utters the threats must be present when the offence is committed in order to afford an excuse for committing it.

. . . .

The evidence outlined to the learned trial Judge discloses that the criminal act was committed to preserve the respondent from future harm coming to him, but there is no suggestion in the evidence tendered for the defence that the accused did not know that what he was doing would "probably cause" damage. Accepting the outline made by defence counsel as being an accurate account of the evidence which was available, there was in my view nothing in it to support the defence that the act was not done "wilfully" within the meaning of s. 371(1) and 372(1) of the *Criminal Code* and there was accordingly no ground to justify the learned trial Judge in permitting the proposed evidence to be called in support of such a defence.

In view of all the above, I would allow this appeal, set aside the judgment of the Court of Appeal and restore the conviction.

Appeal allowed and conviction restored.

R. v. PAQUETTE

[1977] 2 S.C.R. 189, 39 C.R.N.S. 257, 30 C.C.C. (2d) 417

MARTLAND J.: — The facts which give rise to this appeal are as follows:

During the course of a robbery at the Pop Shoppe, in the City of Ottawa, on March 18, 1973, an innocent bystander was killed by a bullet from a rifle fired by one Simard. The robbery was committed by Simard and one Clermont, both of whom, together with the appellant, were jointly charged with non-capital murder. Simard and Clermont pleaded guilty to this charge.

The appellant was not present when the robbery was committed or when the shooting occurred. The charge against him was founded upon s. 21(2) of the *Criminal Code*. Section 21 provides as follows:

> 21(1) Every one is a party to an offence who
>   (a) actually commits it,
>   (b) does or omits to do anything for the purpose of aiding any person to commit it, or
>   (c) abets any person in commiting it.
>   (2) Where two or more persons form an intention in common to carry out an unlawful purpose and to assist each other therein and any one of them, in carrying out the common purpose, commits an offence, each of them who knew or ought to have known that the commission of the offence would be a probable consequence of carrying out the common purpose is a party to that offence.

The appellant made a statement to the police, which was admitted in evidence at the trial and which described his involvement in the matter as follows: On the day of the robbery Clermont telephoned the appellant for a ride as his own car was broken. Clermont asked the appellant where he used to work and was told at the Pop Shoppe. Clermont told him to drive to the Pop Shoppe because Clermont wanted to rob it, and, when the appellant refused, Clermont pulled his gun and threatened to kill him. Simard was picked up later and also a rifle. The appellant drove them to the Pop Shoppe. The appellant had been threatened with revenge if he did not wait for Clermont and Simard. The appellant, in his statement, stated he was afraid and drove around the block. After the robbery and homicide Clermont and Simard attempted twice, unsuccessfully, to get into the appellant's car. Three of the Crown's witnesses supported this latter statement.

The appellant did not testify at trial but relied on the above statement and two other statements also introduced at the trial by the Crown to support his argument that he had no intention in common with Simard and Clermont to carry out the robbery; *i.e.*:

(1) an oral statement to a police officer on his arrest that he had been threatened with death "if he squealed";
(2) the written statement to the police outlined above in which he stated that he had only participated in the robbery by driving because he was threatened with death;
(3) a statement to his girlfriend the day after the robbery that he was forced to do it. The trial Judge charged the jury as follows:

> Now, the defence are asserting that Paquette participated in this robbery because he was compelled to do so, and in that connection I charge you that if Paquette joined in the common plot to rob the Pop Shoppe under threats of death or grievous bodily harm, that would negative his having a common intention with Simard to rob the Pop Shoppe, and you must find Paquette not guilty.

The appellant was acquitted. The Crown appealed to the Court of Appeal for Ontario [19 C.C.C. (2d) 154, 5 O.R. (2d) 1]. The reasons delivered by that Court make it clear that the appeal would have been dismissed had it not been for the decision of this Court in *Dunbar v. The King*, 67 C.C.C. 20, [1936] 4 D.L.R. 737.

The relevant portions of the majority judgment in that case are as follows [at pp. 27-8 C.C.C., pp. 743-4 D.L.R.]:

> On January 15, 1936, three men entered and robbed a branch of the Canadian Bank of Commerce in Vancouver and in the course of the robbery the teller was fatally shot. The appellant Dunbar was not among those who entered the bank but he had brought the robbers to the bank in an automobile and after the robery was over drove back for them and took them away to the house where they had all been living together. He subsequently shared with them in the proceeds of the robbery. He had a criminal record, had met one or other of the robbers in the penitentiary and had been living with them in the same house for some days prior to the robbery. He knew when driving the car to the bank that his associates were going there with the purpose of robbing the bank, that these men were armed and that in the course of such robbery it was not improbable that someone might be killed. His sole excuse for his conduct was that he had acted under compulsion as one of his associates had threatened his life unless he accompanied them and had further threatened that if he did anything to betray them that he would be killed. The point of alleged misdirection most stressed by counsel for the prisoner before us was a statement as follows:—
> "If you accept Dunbar's evidence that he was so bereft of reason that his reasoning faculties were suspended and that he was really in the position of having his hand held by somebody, that he had two men standing over him — you had this story of the thing put to you in the way that he would have you believe — well, then it seems to me there should be some evidence to show his mental condition."

Section 20 of the *Criminal Code*, dealing with compulsion, excludes murder and robbery, and therefore is inapplicable to this case, but it was argued that if compulsion were shown it might be sufficient to negative any common intention under the provision of s. 69(2) of the *Code*. It seems to me that this argument fails to recoginze the distinction between intention and the motive giving rise to intention.

If Dunbar's story of the threat to him was true then he was faced with a choice between endangering his own life or assisting those about to commit a robbery which might, as he knew, be accompanied by murder of an innocent person. The motive giving rise to his choice between these two courses is irrelevant. This being so, in my opinion the issue was not unfairly put before the jury in the learned trial Judge's charge. I would, therefore, dismiss the appeal.

Counsel for the Crown submits that the principles of law applicable to the excuse or defence of duress or compulsion are exhaustively codified in s . 17 [am. 1974-75-76, c. 105, s. 29] of the *Criminal Code*, and that the appellant is precluded from relying upon this provision because of the exception contained at the end of it. Section 17 provides:

> 17. A person who commits an offence under compulsion hy threats of immediate death or grievous bodily harm from a person who is present when the offence is committed is excused for committing the offence if he believes that the threats will be carried out and if he is not a party to a conspiracy or association whereby he is subject to compulsion, but this section does not apply where the offence that is committed is treason, murder, piracy, attempted murder, assisting in rape, forcible abduction, robbery, causing bodily harm or arson.

In my opinion, the application of s. 17 is limited to cases in which the person seeking to rely upon it has himself committed an offence. If a person who actually commits the offence does so in the presence of another party who has compelled him to do the act by threats of immediate death or grievous bodily harm, then, if he believes the threats would be carried out, and is not a party to a conspiracy whereby he is subject to such compulsion, he is excused for committing the offence. The protection afforded by this section is not given in respect of the offences listed at the end of the section, which include murder and robbery.

The section uses the specific words "a person who commits an offence". It does not use the words "a person who is a party to an offence". This is significant in the light of the wording of s. 21(1) which, in para. (*a*), makes a person a party to an offence who "actually commits it". Paragraphs (*b*) and (*c*) deal with a person who aids or abets a person committing the offence. In my opinion, s. 17 codifies the law as to duress as an excuse for the actual commission of a crime, but it does not, by its terms, go beyond that. *R. v. Carker (No. 2)*, [1967] 2 C.C.C. 190, [1967] S.C.R. 114, 2 C.R.N.S. 16, in which reference was made to s. 17 having codified the defence or excuse of duress, dealt with a situation in which the accused had actually committed the offence.

The appellant, in the present case, did not himself commit the offence of robbery or of murder. He was not present when the murder occurred, as was the case in *R. v. Farduto* (1912), 21 C.C.C. 144, and *R. v. Warren* (1973), 14 C.C.C. (2d) 188, 24 C.R.N.S. 349, to which counsel for the Crown referred. In the former case the accused provided the razor with which the murderer cut the throat of the victim in his presence. The Court was of the view that the trial Judge could conclude that there was no case of such compulsion as would constitute an excuse. In the latter case the accused, the brother of the actual murderer was present with him over a period of time after the robbery occurred and before the deceased was killed in his presence. The report does not indicate the nature of the compulsion alleged. The emphasis appears to have been on the subnormal intelligence of the accused making him willing to go along with what was suggested to him.

The appellant could only be considered to be a party to the murder on the basis of the application of s. 21(2). Section 21(1) is not applicable because the offence to which he is alleged to be a party is murder, and it is clear that he did not commit murder, nor did he aid or abet in its commission.

Subsection (2) is only applicable if it is established that the appellant, in common with Simard and Clermont, formed an intention to commit robbery. The question in issue is as to whether the trial Judge erred in law in telling the jury that if the appellant joined in the plot to rob under threats of death or of grievous bodily harm, this would negative such common intention.

I have already stated my reasons for considering s. 17 to be inapplicable. That being so, the appellant is entitled, by virtue of s. 7(3) of the *Code* to rely upon any excuse or defence available to him at common law. The defence of duress to a charge of murder against a person who did not commit the murder, but who was alleged to have aided and abetted, was recently considered by the House of Lords in *Director of Public Prosecutions for Northern Ireland v. Lynch*, [1975] A.C. 653, in which the decided cases were fully reviewed. The facts in that case were as follows [headnote]:

> The defendant drove a motor car containing a group of the I.R.A. in Northern Ireland on an expedition in which they shot and killed a police officer. On his trial for aiding and abetting the murder there was evidence that he was not a member of the I.R.A. and that he acted unwillingly under the orders of the leader of the group, being convinced that, if he disobeyed, he would himself be shot. The trial Judge held that the defence of duress was not available to him and the jury found him guilty. The Court of Criminal Appeal in Northern Ireland upheld the conviction.

The House of Lords, by a three to two majority, held that on a charge of murder the defence of duress was open to a person accused as a principal in the second degree (aider and abettor) and ordered a new trial.

The conclusion of Lord Morris of Borth-y-Gest is stated at p. 677, as follows:

> Having regard to the authorities to which I have referred it seems to me to have been firmly held by our Courts in this country that duress can afford a defence in criminal cases. A recent pronouncement was that in the Court of Appeal in 1971 in the case above referred to (*Reg. v. Hudson*, [1971] 2 Q.B. 202). The Court stated that they had been referred to a large number of authorities and to the views of writers of textbooks. In the judgment of the Court delivered by Lord Parker C.J. and prepared by Widgery L.J. the conclusion was expressed, at p. 206, that "it is clearly established that duress provides a defence in all offences including perjury (except possibly treason or murder as a principal)."

We are only concerned in this case to say whether duress could be a possible defence open to Lynch who was charged with being an aider and abettor. Relying on the help given in the authorities we must decide this as a matter of principle. I consider that duress in such a case can be open as a possible defence. Both general reasoning and the requirements of justice lead me to this conclusion.

Lord Wilberforce, at pp. 682-3, cited with approval a passage from the dissenting reasons of Bray C.J., in *R. v. Brown and Morley*, [1968] S.A.S.R. 467 at 494:

"The reasoning generally used to support the proposition that duress is no defence to a charge of murder is, to use the words of Blackstone cited above, that 'he ought rather to die himself, than escape by the murder of an innocent.' Generally speaking I am prepared to accept this proposition. Its force is obviously, considerably less where the act of the threatened man is not the direct act of killing but only the rendering of some minor form of assistance, particularly when it is by no means certain that if he refuses the death of the victim will he averted, or conversely when it is by no means certain that if he complies the death will be a necessary consequence. It would seem hard, for example, if an innocent passer-by seized in the street by a gang of criminals visibly engaged in robbery and murder in a shop and compelled at the point of a gun to issue misleading comments to the public, or *an innocent driver compelled at the point of a gun to convey the murderer to the victim*, were to have no defence. Are there any authorities which compel us to hold that he would not?"

I am in agreement with the conclusion reached by the majority that it was open to Lynch, in the circumstances of that case, to rely on the defence of duress, which had not been put to the jury. If the defence of duress can be available to a person who has aided and abetted in the commission of murder, then clearly it should be available to a person who is sought to be made a party to the offence by virtue of s. 21(2). A person whose actions have been dictated by fear of death or of grievous bodily injury cannot be said to have formed a genuine common intention to carry out an unlawful purpose with the person who has threatened him with those consequences if he fails to co-operate.

The *Dunbar* case could be distinguished from the present case on its facts. The accused, in that case, had been living with the persons who committed the robbery in which the shooting occurred. He drove them to and from the scene of the crime and shared with them in the proceeds of the robbery. However, the decision is based upon the proposition that on a charge of murder founded on the operation of what is now s. 21(2) of the *Code*, duress does not negative the intention of the accused to carry out an unlawful purpose in common with others, but only relates to his motive for joining in that common purpose, which is irrelevant to the issue of his guilt. I am not in agreement with this view and I am of the opinion that it should not be followed.

I would allow the appeal, set aside the judgment of the Court of Appeal, and restore the verdict of acquittal.

Appeal allowed.

R. v. HIBBERT

40 C.R. (4th) 141, 99 C.C.C. (3d) 193, [1995] 2 S.C.R. 973

The accused was charged with attempted murder, based on the allegation that he was a party to the shooting of C by B. The accused had gone with B to C's apartment and arranged for C to come to the lobby. When C entered the lobby, he was shot four times by B. The accused testified that B had threatened to shoot him if he did not cooperate and that he was terrified throughout the event. The accused believed that he had no opportunity to run away or warn C without being shot. The trial judge charged the jury that if the accused acted under fear of death or grievous bodily harm, he could not form a common intention with the person who had threatened him. The trial judge also said that if there was a safe avenue of escape, then the defence of duress was not available. The jury acquitted the accused of attempted murder but convicted him of the included offence of aggravated assault. His conviction appeal was dismissed and he appealed to the Supreme Court of Canada.

LAMER C.J. (LA FOREST, L'HEUREUX-DUBÉ, SOPINKA, GONTHIER, CORY, MCLACHLIN, IACOBUCCI and MAJOR JJ. concurring): —

. . . .

The Relationship Between Mens Rea and the Defence of Duress

The holding in *Paquette* that the common law defence of duress is available to persons liable as parties is clear and unambiguous, and has stood as the law in Canada for almost twenty years. The case has a second aspect, however, that is less firmly established, having given rise to differing interpretations, and having been the subject of considerable debate in the legal community. The controversy stems from certain comments made by Martland J. on the issue of the relationship between duress and the *mens rea* for party liability under s. 21(2) of the *Code*. . . . As noted above, the main holding of the Court was that s. 17 applied only to principals and not to parties, from which it followed that *Paquette* could rely on the common law defence of duress, to which the restrictions set out in s. 17 did not apply. Martland J. went on, however, to make an observation regarding duress and the mental element of party liability under s. 21(2) of the *Code*, stating:

> A person whose actions have been dictated by fear of death or of grievous bodily injury cannot be said to have formed a genuine common intention to carry out an unlawful purpose with the person who has threatened him with those consequences if he fails to co-operate.

The significance of this comment in terms of the judgment as a whole is rather difficult to determine. Martland J. had earlier endorsed the decision of the House of Lords in *Director of Public Prosecutions for Northern Ireland v. Lynch*, [1975] A.C. 653, in which a majority of the House of Lords had clearly taken the view that the common law defence of duress provided an excuse, rather than operating by negating *mens rea*. Thus, Martland J. evidently did not intend to suggest that duress provides a defence at common law only when the accused's culpable mental state can be said to have been "negated". Instead, he appears to have been holding out an alternative route by which a person charged as a party under s. 21(2) could escape criminal liability, distinct from the "defence of duress" per se — that is, a "defence" founded not on concepts of excuse or justification, but based instead on the absence of an essential element of the offence.

. . . .

That threats of death or serious bodily harm can have an effect on a person's state of mind is indisputable. However, it is also readily apparent that a person who carries out the *actus reus* of a criminal offence in response to such threats will not necessarily lack the *mens rea* for that offence. Whether he or she does or not will depend both on what the mental element of the offence in question happens to be, and on the facts of the particular case. As a practical matter, though, situations where duress will operate to "negate" *mens rea* will be exceptional, for the simple reason that the types of mental states that are capable of being "negated" by duress are not often found in the definitions of criminal offences.

. . . .

As Professor D. Stuart observes (*Canadian Criminal Law: A Treatise* (3rd ed. 1995)), introducing the notion of duress "negating" *mens rea* into the analysis serves only to muddy the conceptual waters. As he points out (at p. 420):

> The advantages [of viewing the operation of duress solely in terms of an excuse] are more than linguistic. If the defence of duress is viewed like any other justification or excuse as based squarely on policy considerations allowing one who has committed an actus reus with mens rea to escape in certain circumstances, the policy issues are focussed without confusing the matter as one of mens rea.

For these reasons, I conclude that the expression "for the purpose of aiding" in s. 21(1)(*b*), properly understood, does not require that the accused actively view the commission of the offence he or she is aiding as desirable in and of itself. As a result, the *mens rea* for aiding under s. 21(1)(*b*) is not susceptible of being "negated" by duress. The trial judge's charge to the jury in the present case was thus incorrect in two respects. First, the reference to the relevant mental state in the present case as being a "common intention to carry out an unlawful purpose" was erroneous since, unlike *Paquette*, what was at issue in the present case was s. 21(1)(*b*), as opposed to s. 21(2). Second, in light of the mental element for commission of an offence under s. 21(1)(*b*), the suggestion that duress might "negate" the accused's *mens rea* was also incorrect.

. . . .

As noted earlier, in *Paquette, supra,* Martland J. took the position that "intention in common" meant something more than "intention to commit or aid in the same offence", arguing that:

> A person whose actions have been dictated by fear of death or of grievous bodily injury cannot be said to have formed a genuine common intention to carry out an unlawful purpose with the person who has threatened him with those consequences if he fails to co-operate.

The phrase "intention in common" is certainly open to being interpreted in this manner. However, notwithstanding the considerable weight I place on and the respect I have for the opinion of Martland J., I have come to the conclusion that, in the context of s. 21(2), the first interpretation discussed above is more consistent both with Parliament's intention and with the interpretation of s. 21(1)(*b*) I have adopted in these reasons.

. . . .

The "Safe Avenue of Escape" Requirement in the Common Law of Duress

The second and third issues raised by the appellant have to do with the so-called "safe avenue of escape" rule. The Court must decide whether such a rule in fact exists, and, if it does, whether the availability of a "safe avenue" is to be determined on an objective or subjective basis. In my opinion, it is best to start the analysis by examining the juristic nature of the defence of duress and its relationship to other common law defences, since I am of the view that by so doing the answers to the questions posed in the present appeal will become clear.

(1) The Relation Between Duress and Other Excuses

As I have explained, the common law defence of duress, properly understood, is not based on the idea that coercion negates *mens rea*. Rather, it is one of a number of defences that operate by justifying or excusing what would otherwise be criminal conduct. Once duress is recognized as providing a defence of this type, it becomes apparent that much can be learned about its juristic nature by examining other existing legal excuses or justifications, such as the defences of necessity, self-defence and provocation, and by considering the extent to which analogies between these defences and the defence of duress can be drawn and sustained.

. . . .

The similarities between defences of duress and necessity have been noted on previous occasions by other commentators. . . . . In *Perka* the status of the defence of necessity in the common law of Canada was firmly established. In his majority reasons, Dickson J. summarized the considerable debate in the academic literature over the question of whether the defence of necessity should be conceptualized as a "justification" or an "excuse". Dickson J. described the justification-based approach to the defence of necessity .... He went on to reject this basis for the defence. Instead, he adopted an understanding of the defence of necessity based on the alternative concept of an "excuse" .... The common law defences of necessity and duress apply to essentially similar factual situations. Indeed, to repeat Lord Simon of Glaisdale's observation, "[d]uress is ... merely a particular application of the doctrine of "necessity"". In my view, the similarities between the two defences are so great that consistency and logic requires that they be understood as based on the same juristic principles. Indeed, to do otherwise would be to promote incoherence and anomaly in the criminal law. In the case of necessity, the Court has already considered the various alternative theoretical positions available, in *Perka, supra*, and has expounded a conceptualization of the defence of necessity as an excuse, based on the idea of normative involuntariness. In my opinion, the need for consistency and coherence in the law dictates that the common law defence of duress also be based on this juridical foundation. If the defence is viewed in this light, the answers to the questions posed in the present appeal can be seen to follow readily from the reasons of Dickson J. in *Perka*.

(a) The Safe Avenue of Escape Requirement

The so-called "safe avenue of escape" requirement in the law of duress is, in my view, simply a specific example of a more general requirement, analogous to that in the defence of necessity identified by Dickson J. — the requirement that compliance with the law be "demonstrably impossible". As Dickson J. explained, this requirement can be derived directly from the underlying concept of normative involuntariness upon which the defence of necessity is based. As I am of the view that the defence of duress must be seen as being based upon this same theoretical foundation, it follows that the defence of duress includes a similar requirement — namely, a requirement that it can only be invoked if, to adopt Dickson J.'s phrase, there is "no legal way out" of the situation of duress the accused faces. The rule that the defence of duress is unavailable if a "safe avenue of escape" was open to the accused is simply a specific instance of this general requirement — if the accused could have escaped without undue danger, the decision to commit an offence becomes, as Dickson J. observed in the context of necessity, "a voluntary one, impelled by some consideration beyond the dictates of 'necessity' and human instincts".

(b) Is the Existence of a Safe Avenue of Escape to Be Determined Subjectively or Objectively?

How this question is answered depends, in my view, on how one conceives of the notion of "normative involuntariness" upon which the defence of duress is based. That is, is an action "normatively involuntary" when the actor believes that he has no real choice, or is this the case only when there is in fact no reasonable alternative course of action available?

Cogent arguments can be made in support of each of these positions. The issue can be framed in slightly different terms. The question of when a person "could not help doing what he did", and thus performs a normatively involuntary act can, however, be understood in two different ways. On the one hand, it can be argued that actors who perform acts that appear reasonable in relation to their knowledge of their surrounding circumstances "cannot help" what they did, even if their understanding of their situation is objectively unreasonable. Put another way, it can be argued that a person's acts are normatively involuntary if he or she honestly believes there are no reasonable alternatives, even if he or she has overlooked an alternative that a reasonable person would have been aware of. On the other hand, it can also be argued that an actor's failure to take steps to inform himself or herself of the true state of affairs is itself a choice, and that a decision based on the resulting erroneous view of the circumstances is thus not normatively involuntary, since it could have been avoided. In my opinion, the latter argument accords most closely with the view of normative involuntariness adopted by the Court in *Perka*, which, as I have explained, should be seen as the theoretical foundation of both the defences of duress and necessity. As Dickson J.'s reasons in *Perka* suggest, a degree of objectivity is inherent to excuses that are based on the notion of normative involuntariness, to the extent that this concept turns on the objective availability, or lack of availability, of true choice. Indeed, Dickson J. clearly indicates that the operative standard for the defence of necessity is to be an objective one, based on whether "there is a reasonable legal alternative to disobeying the law".

However, simply adopting the second of the two arguments set out above does not fully resolve the issue of the standard to be applied in assessing whether a safe avenue of escape existed. Even if it is accepted that an actor's failure to take steps to acquire reasonable knowledge of his or her full range of options can, in itself, constitute a form of choice, it can still be argued that this only holds true when the actor is able to acquire and process additional information. That is, a person does not "choose" inaction when he or she is incapable in the first place of acting, or of knowing when to act. Thus, an argument can be made for framing the objective standard used in determining the availability of alternative options, such as "safe avenues of escape", in terms of the particular actor's capacities and abilities. This argument reflects a more general concern about the application of the negligence standard in criminal law, which Hart, *supra*, has summarized in the following terms:

> If our conditions of liability are invariant and not flexible, i.e. if they are not adjusted to the capacities of the accused, then some individuals will be held liable for negligence though they could not have helped their failure to comply with the standard.

This Court has previously indicated that when assessing the reasonableness of an accused's conduct for the purposes of determining whether he or she should be excused from criminal responsibility, it is appropriate to employ an objective standard that takes into account the particular circumstances of the accused, including his or her ability to perceive the existence of alternative courses of action. For instance, in *R. v. Lavallee*, [1990] 1 S.C.R. 852, a self-defence case, Wilson J., writing for a majority of the Court, declared (at p. 889):

> I think the question the jury must ask itself [in a case of self-defence] is whether, given the history, circumstances and perceptions of the appellant, her belief that she could not preserve herself from being killed by [her "common-law" spouse] that night except by killing him first was reasonable.

The defences of self-defence, duress and necessity are essentially similar, so much so that consistency demands that each defence's "reasonableness" requirement be assessed on the same basis. Accordingly, I am of the view that while the question of whether a "safe avenue of escape" was open to an accused who pleads duress should be assessed on an objective basis, the appropriate objective standard to be employed is one that takes into account the particular circumstances and human frailties of the accused.

It should be noted that the question of what sort of objective standard is to be used when assessing the "reasonableness" of the conduct of persons raising an excuse-based defence is different in several key respects from the issue that was before the Court in *R. v. Creighton*, [1993] 3 S.C.R. 3. In that case, in the course of considering the *mens rea* for "unlawful act manslaughter" under s. 222(5)(*a*) of the *Criminal Code*, a majority of the Court was of the view that (at p. 61, per McLachlin J.):

> [C]onsiderations of principle and policy dictate the maintenance of a single, uniform legal standard of care for [offences with a mens rea of negligence], subject to one exception: incapacity to appreciate the nature of the risk which the activity in question entails.

Although I dissented on this point in *Creighton* (while concurring in the result), I now consider myself bound by the majority judgment. However, I do not believe that *Creighton* is applicable when what is at issue is the standard of reasonableness to be used in establishing the availability of an excuse-based defence, as opposed to the determination of liability under an offence that is defined in terms of a mental state of negligence. In my view, the relevant "considerations of policy and principle" in such cases are quite different from those identifiable in the context of negligence-based offences. Offences defined in terms of negligence typically impose criminal liability on an accused person for the consequences that flowed from his or her inherently hazardous activities — activities that he or she voluntarily and willingly chose to engage in. In *Creighton*, *supra*, the majority was of the view that people "may properly be held to [a strict objective standard] as a condition of choosing to engage in activities which may maim or kill other innocent people" (p. 66). Even if a person fails to foresee the probable consequences of their freely chosen actions, these actions remain the product of genuine choice. In contrast, excuse-based defences, such as duress, are predicated precisely on the view that the conduct of the accused is involuntary, in a normative sense — that is, that he or she had no realistic alternative course of action available. In my view, in determining whether an accused person was operating under such constrained options, his or her perceptions of the surrounding facts can be highly relevant to the determination of whether his or her conduct was reasonable under the circumstances, and thus whether his or her conduct is properly excusable.

. . . .

D. Assessing the Charge to the Jury

. . . .

It is quite possible that the jury determined that the appellant aided the assault "intentionally", in the sense that he performed acts that he knew would probably assist Bailey to commit the assault because he believed that if he did not Bailey would kill him. The jurors might have thus concluded that the appellant's *mens rea* was not "negated" by duress, under circumstances in which they might well have concluded that his conduct could be excused if they had been aware of the existence of the common law defence of duress, properly conceptualized.

Appeal allowed; new trial is ordered.

R. v. RUZIC

(April 20, 2001), 2001 SCC 24, 2001 CarswellOnt 1238 (S.C.C.)

The accused was charged with importing two kilograms of heroin into Canada. The accused admitted having imported the narcotics but claimed that she was then acting under duress. She conceded that her claim of duress did not meet the immediacy and presence requirements of s. 17 of the *Criminal Code* but challenged the constitutionality of s. 17 under s. 7 of the *Charter* and raised the common law defence of duress. She was acquitted at trial and the Crown's appeal was dismissed. The Crown appealed further. The Supreme Court was unanimous in dismissing the appeal and holding that s. 7 was in part unconstitutional.

LeBel J.: —

. . . .

An expert witness testified at trial that, in 1994, large paramilitary groups roamed Belgrade and engaged in criminal and mafia-like activities. The same expert maintained that people living in Belgrade during that period did not feel safe. They believed the police could not be trusted. There was a real sense that the rule of law had broken down. There was a series of encounters between Mirkovic and the respondent while she was walking her dog. Each time he approached her, he knew more about her, although she had shared no details of her life with him. He phoned her at home. He told her he knew her every move. Ms. Ruzic alleged that his behaviour became more and more intimidating, escalating to threats and acts of physical violence. On one occasion, he burned her arm with a lighter. On another, he stuck a syringe into her arm and injected her with a substance that smelled like heroin and made her nauseous. She indicated that these physical assaults were coupled with sexual harassment and finally threats against her mother.

On April 25, 1994, Mirkovic phoned the respondent and instructed her to pack a bag and meet him at a hotel in central Belgrade. Once there, he allegedly strapped three packages of heroin to her body and indicated that she was to take them to a restaurant in Toronto. He gave her a false passport, a bus ticket from Belgrade to Budapest and some money. He told her to fly from Budapest to Athens, and then from Athens to Toronto. When she protested, he warned her that, if she failed to comply, he would harm her mother.

. . . .

A. Are Statutory Defences Owed Special Deference by Reviewing Courts?

. . . .

The appellant now appeared to concede that the scope of s. 17 is susceptible to *Charter* review, but maintained that the courts should assume a posture of deference when undertaking such an assessment. The prosecution contends it belongs to Parliament to decide when otherwise criminal conduct should be excused, because determining who can rely on the statutory defence of duress and in what circumstances is an inherently policy-driven exercise. The appellant asserts that the legislature is best placed to determine what constitutes "morally involuntary" conduct for the purpose of invoking s. 17, given the difficult value judgments involved in defining duress. The appellant submits that the appropriate standard of review would restrict courts to consider simply whether the restrictions on the defence are irrational or arbitrary. As a corollary of its approach, the Crown did not seek to justify s. 17 under s. 1 of the *Charter*. Before the Court, it argued rather that, if properly construed, s. 17 would not even infringe the *Charter*.

. . . .

Soon after the *Charter* came into force, Lamer J. pointed out in *Re B.C. Motor Vehicle Act*, that courts have not only the power but the duty to evaluate the substantive content of legislation for *Charter* compliance. In the realm of criminal law, the courts routinely review the definition of criminal offences to ensure conformity with *Charter* rights. This has included the *mens rea* element of an offence: *e.g., R. v. Vaillancourt* and *R. v. Wholesale Travel Group*. These powers and responsibilities extend equally to statutory defences. Courts would be abdicating their constitutional duty by abstaining from such a review. Defences and excuses belong to the legislative corpus that the *Charter* submits to constitutional review by the courts.

. . . .

[S]tatutory defences do not warrant more deference simply because they are the product of difficult moral judgments. The entire body of criminal law expresses a myriad of policy choices. Statutory offences are every bit as concerned with social values as statutory defences.

. . . .

B. Is it a Principle of Fundamental Justice That Only Morally Voluntary Conduct Can Attract Criminal Liability?

. . . .

The notion of moral voluntariness was first introduced in *Perka v. The Queen*, for the purpose of explaining the defence of necessity and classifying it as an excuse. It was borrowed from the American legal theorist George Fletcher's discussion of excuses in *Rethinking Criminal Law* (1978). A person acts in a morally involuntary fashion when, faced with perilous circumstances, she is deprived of a realistic choice whether to break the law. By way of illustration in *Perka*, Dickson J. evoked the situation of a lost alpinist who, on the point of freezing to death, breaks into a remote mountain cabin. The alpinist confronts a painful dilemma: freeze to death or commit a criminal offence. Yet as Dickson J. pointed out, the alpinist's choice to break the law "is no true choice at all; it is remorselessly compelled by normal human instincts", here of self-preservation. The Court in *Perka* thus conceptualized the defence of necessity as an excuse. An excuse, Dickson J. maintained, concedes that the act was wrongful, but withholds criminal attribution to the actor because of the dire circumstances surrounding its commission.

Extending its reasoning in *Perka* to the defence of duress, the Court found in *R. v. Hibbert* that it too rests on the notion of moral voluntariness. In the case of the defences of necessity and duress, the accused contends that he should avoid conviction because he acted in response to a threat of impending harm. The Court also confirmed in *Hibbert* that duress does not ordinarily negate the *mens rea* element of an offence. Like the defence of necessity, the Court classified the defence of duress as an excuse, like that of necessity. As such, duress operates to relieve a person of criminal liability only after he has been found to have committed the prohibited act with the relevant *mens rea*. Thus duress, like necessity, involves the concern that morally involuntary conduct not be subject to criminal liability. Can this notion of "moral voluntariness" be recognized as a principle of fundamental justice under s. 7 of the *Charter*? Let us examine possible avenues which have been put forward by the respondent towards such recognition.

1. Moral Voluntariness and Moral Blameworthiness

As we will see below, this Court has recognized on a number of occasions that "moral blameworthiness" is an essential component of criminal liability which is protected under s. 7 as a "principle of fundamental justice". The respondent in the case at bar attempts to link the principles of "moral blameworthiness" and "moral voluntariness" as a means of securing the constitutional status of the defence of duress. Laskin J.A. in the Court below has followed this line of reasoning. However, the appellant argues that "moral blamelessness" only arises in the absence of either the *actus reus* or the *mens rea* of an offence. One who acts under duress, he contends, remains a morally responsible agent whose behaviour is not blame-free. Further, the appellant submits that moral involuntariness is too vague and amorphous a concept to constitute a principle of fundamental justice. This controversy about the concepts of moral blamelessness and moral involuntariness brings us back to the foundations of criminal responsibility. In the analysis of duress and of its relationship with the tenets of the criminal justice system, is it appropriate to equate moral blamelessness with moral involuntariness?

. . . .

It should be emphasized that this Court, in cases like *Sault Ste. Marie* and *Re B.C. Motor Vehicle Act*, has referred to moral innocence in the context of the discussion of the mental element of an offence. *Hibbert*, on the other hand, held that the defence of duress does not normally negate *mens rea*. Rather, it operates to excuse a wrongful act once the *actus reus* and *mens rea* components of the offence have been made out. Laskin J.A. conceded this point, but countered that moral blameworthiness is a broader concept, extending beyond the traditional elements of an offence. Both Laskin J.A. and the respondent rely heavily, in this respect, on Professor Martha Shaffer's article "Scrutinizing Duress: The Constitutional Validity of Section 17 of the Criminal Code" (1998), 40 C.L.Q. 444, in making this argument.

Professor Shaffer acknowledges in her article that moral blameworthiness is an ambiguous concept, the meaning of which this Court has not had occasion to discuss in any significant way. I am reluctant to do so here, particularly since, in my opinion, conduct that is morally involuntary is not always intrinsically free of blame. Moral involuntariness is also related to the notion that the defence of duress is an excuse. Dickson J. maintained in *Perka* that an excuse acknowledges the wrongfulness of the accused's conduct. Nevertheless, the law refuses to attach penal consequences to it because an "excuse" has been made out. In using the expression "moral involuntariness", we mean that the accused had no "real" choice but to commit the offence. This recognizes that there was indeed an alternative to breaking the law, although in the case of duress that choice may be even more unpalatable — to be killed or physically harmed.

Let us consider again the situation of the lost alpinist: can we really say he is blameless for breaking into somebody else's cabin? The State refrains from punishing him not because his actions were innocent, but because the circumstances did not leave him with any other realistic choice than to commit the offence. As Fletcher puts it, excuses absolve the accused of personal accountability by focussing, not on the wrongful act, but on the circumstances of the act and the accused's personal capacity to avoid it. Necessity and duress are characterized as concessions to human frailty in this sense. The law is designed for the common man, not for a community of saints or heroes.

To equate moral involuntariness with moral innocence would amount to a significant departure from the reasoning in *Perka* and *Hibbert*. It would be contrary to the Court's conceptualization of duress as an excuse. Morally involuntary conduct is not always inherently blameless. Once the elements of the offence have been established, the accused can no longer be considered blameless. This Court has never taken the concept of blamelessness any further than this initial finding of guilt, nor should it in this case. The undefinable and potentially far-reaching nature of the concept of moral blamelessness prevents us from recognizing its relevance beyond an initial finding of guilt in the context of s. 7 of the *Charter*. Holding otherwise would inject an unacceptable degree of uncertainty into the law. It would not be consistent with our duty to consider as "principles of fundamental justice" only those concepts which are constrained and capable of being defined with reasonable precision. I would therefore reject this basis for finding that it is a principle of fundamental justice that morally involuntary acts should not be punished.

2. Moral Voluntariness and Voluntariness in the Physical Sense

The respondent's second approach, which relates moral voluntariness back to voluntariness in the physical sense, rests on firmer ground. It draws upon the fundamental principle of criminal law that, in order to attract criminal liability, an act must be voluntary. Voluntariness in this sense has ordinarily referred to the *actus reus* element of an offence. It queries whether the actor had control over the movement of her body or whether the wrongful act was the product of a conscious will. Although duress does not negate ordinarily *actus reus per se* (just as it does not ordinarily negate *mens rea* as we have just seen), the principle of voluntariness, unlike that of "moral blamelessness", can remain relevant in the context of s. 7 even after the basic elements of the offence have been established. Unlike the concept of "moral blamelessness", duress in its "voluntariness" perspective can more easily be constrained and can therefore more justifiably fall within the "principles of fundamental justice", even after the basic elements of the offence have been established.

Let us examine the notion of "voluntariness" and its interplay with duress more closely. As Dickson J. stated in *Rabey v. The Queen*, "it is a basic principle that absence of volition in respect of the act involved is always a defence to a crime. A defence that the act is involuntary entitles the accused to a complete and unqualified acquittal." Dickson J.'s pronouncement was endorsed by the Court in *R. v. Parks*. The principle of voluntariness was given constitutional status in *Daviault*, where Cory J. held for the majority that it would infringe s. 7 of the *Charter* to convict an accused who was not acting voluntarily, as a fundamental aspect of the *actus reus* would be absent. More recently, in *R. v. Stone*, [1999] 2 S.C.R. 290, the crucial role of voluntariness as a condition of the attribution of criminal liability was again confirmed in an appeal concerning the defence of automatism.

In introducing the concept of moral voluntariness in *Perka*, the Court specifically linked it to the more familiar notion of physical voluntariness discussed above. Dickson J. acknowledged that the two concepts are not identical. The lost alpinist, for instance, does not act in a literally involuntary fashion; he is physically capable of avoiding the criminal act. Fletcher puts forth another example, more pertinent to the defence of duress. Suppose someone puts a knife in the accused's hand and forces it into the victim's chest. The accused's body is literally overpowered, as is her will. Consider next the situation of someone who gives the accused a knife and orders her to stab the victim or else be killed herself. Unlike the first scenario, moral voluntariness is not a matter of physical dimension. The accused here retains conscious control over her bodily movements. Yet, like the first actor, her will is overborne, this time by the threats of another. Her conduct is not, in a realistic way, freely chosen.

What underpins both of these conceptions of voluntariness is the critical importance of autonomy in the attribution of criminal liability. The treatment of criminal offenders as rational, autonomous and choosing agents is a fundamental organizing principle of our criminal law. Its importance is reflected not only in the requirement that an act must be voluntary, but also in the condition that a wrongful act must be intentional to ground a conviction. *Sault Ste. Marie, Re B.C. Motor Vehicle Act*, and *Vaillancourt* all stand for the proposition that a guilty verdict requires intentional conduct or conduct equated to it like recklessness or gross negligence. Like voluntariness, the requirement of a guilty mind is rooted in respect for individual autonomy and free will and acknowledges the importance of those values to a free and democratic society: *Martineau*. Criminal liability also depends on the capacity to choose — the ability to reason right from wrong. As McLachlin J. observed in *Chaulk* in the context of the insanity provisions of the *Criminal Code*, this assumption of the rationality and autonomy of human beings forms part of the essential premises of Canadian criminal law.

Punishing a person whose actions are involuntary in the physical sense is unjust because it conflicts with the assumption in criminal law that individuals are autonomous and freely choosing agents: see Shaffer, *supra*, at pp. 449-50. It is similarly unjust to penalize an individual who acted in a morally involuntary fashion. This is so because his acts cannot realistically be attributed to him, as his will was constrained by some external force. . . .

Although moral involuntariness does not negate the *actus reus* or *mens rea* of an offence, it is a principle which, similarly to physical involuntariness, deserves protection under s. 7 of the *Charter*. It is a principle of fundamental justice that only voluntary conduct — behaviour that is the product of a free will and controlled body, unhindered by external constraints — should attract the penalty and stigma of criminal liability. Depriving a person of liberty and branding her with the stigma of criminal liability would infringe the principles of fundamental justice if the accused did not have any realistic choice. The ensuing deprivation of liberty and stigma would have been imposed in violation of the tenets of fundamental justice and would thus infringe s. 7 of the *Charter*.

B. Do the Immediacy and Presence Requirements in Section 17 Infringe the Principle of Involuntariness in the Attribution of Criminal Responsibility?

. . . .

The appellant argues that the immediacy and presence requirements do not dictate that the threatener be physically present at the scene of the crime. Rather, they require a temporal connection between the commission of the offence and the threatener's presence, in the sense that the threatener must be able to execute the threat immediately should the accused fail to comply. The respondent replies that the appellant's proposed interpretation would stretch the language of s. 17 beyond recognition. As counsel for one of the interveners put it during the hearing of this appeal, it would amount to construing presence as absence and immediate as sometime later.

The plain meaning of s. 17 is quite restrictive in scope. Indeed, the section seems tailor-made for the situation in which a person is compelled to commit an offence at gun point. The phrase "present when the offence is committed", coupled with the immediacy criterion, indicates that the person issuing the threat must be either at the scene of the crime or at whatever other location is necessary to make good on the threat without delay should the accused resist. Practically speaking, a threat of harm will seldom qualify as immediate if the threatener is not physically present at the scene of the crime.

The Court has in the past construed s. 17 in a narrow fashion. *R. v. Carker* and *Paquette v. The Queen*, are the two leading cases on the interpretation of s. 17. . . .

. . . .

I agree with the respondent that a threat will seldom meet the immediacy criterion if the threatener is not physically present at or near the scene of the offence. The immediacy and presence requirements, taken together, clearly preclude threats of future harm.

Neither the words of s. 17 nor the Court's reasons in *Carker* and *Paquette* dictate that the target of the threatened harm must be the accused. They simply require that the threat must be made to the accused. Section 17 may thus include threats against third parties. However, the language of s. 17 does not appear capable of supporting a more flexible interpretation of the immediacy and presence requirements. Even if the threatened person, for example, is a family member, and not the accused person, the threatener or his accomplice must be at or near the scene of the crime in order to effect the harm immediately if the accused resists. Thus, while s. 17 may capture threats against third parties, the immediacy and presence criteria continue to impose considerable obstacles to relying on the defence in hostage or other third party situations.

Thus, by the strictness of its conditions, s. 17 breaches s. 7 of the *Charter* because it allows individuals who acted involuntarily to be declared criminally liable. Having said that, it will be interesting to see how the common law addresses the problem of duress, especially with respect to the immediacy component. In that regard, we will have the opportunity to see how the common law on duress in Canada, Great Britain, Australia, and even in some U.S. jurisdictions is often more liberal than what s. 17 provides and takes better account of the principle of voluntariness. This will confirm the view that s. 17 is overly restrictive and therefore breaches s. 7 of the *Charter*. We recall that the principles of fundamental justice may be distilled from the "legal principles which have historically been reflected in the law of this and other similar states" (*Seaboyer*). Examining the common law of other states like Great Britain and Australia to confirm our interpretation of s. 7 will therefore be relevant. The analysis of duress in common law will also be useful as it will shed some light on the appropriate rules which had to be applied to the defence of the accused in the case at bar and which will now be applied in all other cases, once s. 17 of the *Criminal Code* is partially struck down.

D. The Common Law of Duress

. . . .

[The Court then examined the Canadian common law of duress as illustrated in *Paquette*, *Hibbert* and *Langlois*. It then reviewed the English common law of duress which was seen as generally similar to its Canadian counterpart. The Court found that in the Australian common law of duress there were some differences from state to state but that overall, the state courts appear to have followed quite closely the English courts' approach. Examining the American common law of duress, LeBel J. concluded that while in some states the defence is subject to quite strict constraints, several American cases have displayed a flexible view of the temporal criterion in the context of duress. While the common law was not unanimous in the United States, a substantial consensus had thus grown in Canada, England and Australia to the effect that the strict criterion of immediacy is no longer a generally accepted component of the defence.]

E. The Breach of Section 7 of the *Charter*: Conclusion in the Case at Bar

At the heart of Laskin J.A.'s decision is a concern that the immediacy and presence requirements are poor substitutes for the safe avenue of escape test at common law. In his view, their focus on an instantaneous connection between the threat and the commission of the offence misses the point in a number of special cases. He highlights two situations in particular. The first is the battered woman who is coerced by her abusive partner to break the law. Even though her partner is not present when she commits the offence and is therefore unable to execute it immediately, a battered woman may believe nonetheless that she has no safe avenue of escape. Her behaviour is morally involuntary, yet the immediacy and presence criteria, strictly construed, would preclude her from resorting to s. 17. There may also be other situations in which a person is so psychologically traumatized by the threatener that he complies with the threat, even though it was not immediate and to the objective observer, there was a legal way out. The second scenario described by Laskin J.A. is the case of a person like Ms. Ruzic, for whom effective police protection was unavailable. Do the immediacy and presence requirements demand that a person go to the authorities if he has the opportunity to do so, even when he believes it would be useless or even dangerous to do so? It should be noted that in this second scenario, a court might face a delicate task in assessing the validity of a claim that, in a foreign land, no police protection was available. It illustrates some of the difficulties in the practical implementation of a defence of duress which involves a risk of abuse through unverifiable assertions of danger and harm.

Nevertheless, s. 17's reliance on proximity as opposed to reasonable options as the measure of moral choice is problematic. It would be contrary to the principles of fundamental justice to punish an accused who is psychologically tortured to the point of seeing no reasonable alternative, or who cannot rely on the authorities for assistance. That individual is not behaving as an autonomous agent acting out of his own free will when he commits an offence under duress.

The appellant's attempts at reading down s. 17, in order to save it, would amount to amending it to bring it in line with the common law rules. This interpretation badly strains the text of the provision and may become one more argument against upholding its validity. The underinclusiveness of s. 17 infringes s. 7 of the *Charter*, because the immediacy and presence requirements exclude threats of future harm to the accused or to third parties. It risks jeopardizing the liberty and security interests protected by the *Charter*, in violation of the basic principles of fundamental justice. It has the potential of convicting persons who have not acted voluntarily.

F. Can the Infringement Be Justified Under Section 1?

Having found that the immediacy and presence requirements infringe s. 7 of the *Charter*, I turn now to consider whether the violation is a demonstrably justifiable limit under s. 1. The government, of course, bears the burden of justifying a *Charter* infringement. Consistent with its strategy in the courts below, the appellant made no attempt before this Court to justify the immediacy and presence criteria according to the s. 1 analysis. I therefore conclude at the outset that the appellant has failed to satisfy its onus under s. 1.

Moreover, it is well established that violations of s. 7 are not easily saved by s. 1. Indeed, the Court has indicated that exceptional circumstances, such as the outbreak of war or a national emergency, are necessary before such an infringement may be justified: *R. v. Heywood, Re B.C. Motor Vehicle Act.* No such extraordinary conditions exist in this case. Furthermore, I am inclined to agree with Laskin J.A. that the immediacy and presence criteria would not meet the proportionality branch of the s. 1 analysis. In particular, it seems to me these requirements do not minimally impair the respondent's s. 7 rights. Given the appellant's failure to make any submissions on the issue, the higher standard of justification for a violation of s. 7, and my doubts concerning proportionality, I conclude that the immediacy and presence conditions cannot be saved by s. 1.

. . . .

H. The Jury Charge

. . . .

Viewed in its entirety, the trial judge's charge explained adequately the elements of the defence of duress at common law to the members of the jury.

The charge contained all the elements required by the common law rules on duress. The criterion of the safe avenue of escape was well explained as was the objective component of this test. Notwithstanding the argument of the appellant, the law does not require an accused to seek the official protection of police in all cases. The requirement of objectivity must itself take into consideration the special circumstances where the accused found herself as well as her perception of them. Herold J. drew the attention of the jury both to that objective component and to the subjective elements of the defence. This argument must thus fail.

As to the immediacy of the threat, as Laskin J.A.'s reasons point out, Herold J. brought home to the jury the fact that the threat had to be a real threat affecting the accused at the time of the offence. This instruction at least implied that the jury had to consider the temporal connection between the threat and the harm threatened, although it would have been preferable to say so in so many express words.

There was no misdirection either on the burden of proof. The accused must certainly raise the defence and introduce some evidence about it. Once this is done, the burden of proof shifts to the Crown under the general rule of criminal evidence. It must be shown, beyond a reasonable doubt, that the accused did not act under duress. . . .

Disposition

The appellant's submissions cannot be accepted. The immediacy and presence requirements of s. 17 of the *Criminal Code* infringe s. 7 of the *Charter*. As the infringement has not been justified under s. 1, the requirements of immediacy and presence must be struck down as unconstitutional. The Court of Appeal and the trial judge were right in allowing the common law defence of duress go to the jury, and the trial judge adequately instructed the jury on the defence.

Is *Ruzic* consistent with *Stone*? Is *Ruzic* consistent with *Latimer*?

Professor Martha Shaffer has recently persuasively argued that a revised law of duress must be broad to deal fairly with the experiences of battered women coerced into crime: see "Coerced into Crime: Battered Women and the Defence of Duress" (1999), 4 Can. Crim. L. Rev. 272 and "Scrutinizing Duress: The Constitutional Validity of Section 17 of the Criminal Code" (1998), 3 & 4 Crim. L.Q. 444.

The Law Reform Commission of Canada's Draft *Criminal Code* of 1986, s. 3(8) would codify the defence of duress as follows:

No one is liable for committing a crime in reasonable response to threats of immediate serious harm to himself or another person unless he himself purposely causes the death of, or seriously harms, another person.

Would this reform be wise? Consider whether the defence of duress would succeed under the present law and under that proposed by the Commission in the following situations:

1. The accused is charged with impaired driving. She admits that she was very drunk when she drove, but her defence is that she was compelled to do so to escape a sure beating at the hands of her enraged husband.

She had been celebrating with fellow workers and her husband had discovered her with another male when he had gone to look for her four hours after he had expected her to return. In a state of rage he had smashed the window of the car in which she was seated and had also rammed the car when she drove off.

Compare *R. v. Smith* (1977), 40 C.R.N.S. 390 (B.C. Prov. Ct).

2. The accused is charged with kidnapping contrary to s. 247(l)(*c*) of the *Criminal Code*. At the instigation of her husband she had lured a 20 year-old woman, whom she had previously known, into her husband's automobile on the pretext that she was going to a fashion show. The husband then grabbed the victim and tied her up while the accused drove her to a place where they were going to hold her. A ransom demand was made of the victim's father but the ransom was not paid and eventually the victim was released. Two weeks after the kidnapping and the failed extortion attempt, the accused confessed her participation to the police. Her defence was that she had acted entirely out of fear of her husband, who had previously assaulted her and had warned her that, if she did not do what he said, she would never see her daughter again, as the daughter would be kidnapped and taken to the United States.

Compare *R. v. Robins* (1982), 66 C.C.C. (2d) 550 (Que. C.A.).

3. The accused was charged with possession of stolen property and weapons offences arising from an exchange, with an undercover police officer, of handguns for an automatic rifle. A third party, G., had earlier approached the police with a scheme to get stolen handguns off the street. Over the course of several meetings G. had persuaded the accused that he was working for the C.I.A. to recruit mercenaries to fight in Nicaragua. He later began to terrorize the accused with threats that he would blow off his head. He also threatened the accused with a gun and said that he had contacts and had agents who were watching the accused. He said that these agents would gun down the accused if his requests were ignored and that he personally would shoot the accused if he did not provide the requested handguns.

Compare *R. v. Gardiner* (1983), 34 C.R. (3d) 237 (B.C. Co. Ct.), discussed by D. Galloway, "Gardiner: Defining Duress. Must the Threats be Sudden?" (1983), 34 C.R. (3d) 245.

4. An accused refuses to testify at the first degree murder trial of a fellow inmate in respect of a killing in a penitentiary. The accused indicates that he has been threatened by fellow prisoners that he will be killed if he testifies. He is now cited for contempt of Court for not testifying.

Compare *R. v. Ayres* (1984), 42 C.R. (3d) 33 (C.A.).

Defence of Person

See sections 34-37 of the *Criminal Code*.

R. v. PINTAR

(1996), 2 C.R. (5th) 151, 110 C.C.C. (3d) 402 (Ont. C.A.)

The accused was charged with two counts of second degree murder. One of the deceased, R, blamed the accused for the break-up of his marriage, and threatened on many occasions to kill him. G, the other deceased was a stranger to the accused. He had been working for R for a brief time prior to the offence.

On the day of the shooting, R and the other deceased, G, were drinking at a dance and were overheard agreeing to attack the accused. The accused was awakened at daybreak by noises outside his bedroom. He went to investigate and found R standing in the hallway and told him to leave. R refused, saying that he was there to "finish this off" and took a swing at the accused. The accused knocked R out onto the front porch and went back into the house to get dressed. R screamed that he had killed the accused's dog and the accused was next. R continued to yell threats at him and G, who had been waiting in R's truck, got out of the vehicle. The accused got his rifle and went outside with it held across his chest. G and R advanced towards the accused, while R said that he would kill the accused and other members of his family. R grabbed the gun, a struggle ensued and the two deceased were shot by the accused during the struggle. The jury found the accused guilty of two counts of manslaughter. The accused appealed, raising several objections to the trial judge's charge to the jury on the issue of self-defence, including whether the charge on this issue was unnecessarily confusing and complex. The trial judge instructed the jury on ss. 34(1), 34(2), 35 and 37.

MOLDAVER J.A.: — This is yet another case where the court is faced with difficult issues arising out of the complex and confusing self-defence regime in the *Criminal Code*.

. . . .

It is no secret that many trial judges consider their instructions on the law of self-defence to be little more than a source of bewilderment and confusion to the jury. Regardless of their efforts to be clear, trial judges often report glazed eyes and blank stares on the faces of the jury in the course of their instructions on self-defence. Disheartening as this may be, most judges tend to believe that juries are extremely adept at assessing legitimate cases of self-defence and are therefore likely to come to the right result in spite of the confusion created by the charge. While this may be true, it provides little comfort to an accused who has been convicted in the face of legal instruction so complex and confusing that it may well have diverted the jury's attention away from the real basis upon which the claim to self-defence rests.

. . . .

Unquestionably, trial judges do encounter difficulties in explaining the self-defence provisions to juries for the reasons expressed by the Chief Justice. In my opinion, these difficulties are compounded by the standards which appellate courts have imposed, or are perceived to have imposed, when assessing the adequacy of self-defence instructions. Trial judges are often heard to say that 90 per cent of their legal instruction on self-defence is for the Court of Appeal and 10 per cent for the jury. Expressed somewhat differently, fear of under-charging has led to over-charging.

. . . .

To give effect to the functional approach, I would urge trial judges to consider the following guidelines when faced with the prospect of charging a jury on the law of self-defence:

(1) Consider the evidence carefully with a view to determining the essence of the claim to self-defence and the *Code* provision(s) realistically available to that claim.

(2) To the extent that the evidence fails the air of reality test in respect of one or more of the constituent elements of a particular provision, that provision should not be left with the jury.

(3) To the extent that the evidence clearly establishes one or more of the constituent elements of a particular provision, Crown counsel should be encouraged to admit the underlying facts and thereby avoid unnecessary legal instruction.

(4) Where a particular provision affords the accused a wider scope of justification than a companion provision, the narrower provision should only be put to the jury if the evidence lends an air of reality to the factual underpinnings of that provision, and the provision somehow fills a gap unaccounted for in the justification afforded by the wider provision.

. . . .

Experience reveals that it is not uncommon, particularly in murder cases, that even though the primary claim to self-defence rests upon s. 34(2), s. 34(1) remains marginally relevant and theoretically available. This type of situation generally arises when, despite evidence to the contrary, the Crown has made out a strong case that the accused either provoked the initial assault, or intended to kill or cause grievous bodily harm, or both. Nonetheless, since provocation and intent are matters of fact for the jury, s. 34(1) cannot be ruled out, even though the scope of its justification is much narrower than that provided by s. 34(2).

On a practical level, in those cases where s. 34(1) remains theoretically available, it is often difficult, if not impossible, to imagine a scenario wherein the jury would reject the wider justification afforded by s. 34(2) and apply s. 34(1) to acquit. The question then becomes whether the risk of confusing the jury and complicating the charge justifies the inclusion of instruction on s. 34(1), when its application is at best tenuous and its scope of justification narrower than that available under s. 34(2).

For my part, I am of the view that when trial judges are faced with situations like this, they should call upon counsel to justify instruction on the narrower provision. If the results of that exercise reveal either the lack of an evidentiary base for putting the narrower provision, or an inability to demonstrate how the narrower provision might be available to fill a gap not provided for by the broader one, the narrower provision should be discarded. Once again, let me be clear that the underlying purpose of this exercise is not to remove self-defence from the jury's consideration. Rather it is designed to focus the jury's attention on the essence of the claim to self-defence and the available *Code* provision(s) most relevant to it.

New trial ordered.

———————————

For at least the last ten years successive Ministers of Ministers of Justice have been very active in amending a *Criminal Code* that is growing increasingly unwieldy. The strong trend is to only move to widen the net of the criminal sanction. Reforms that might make it easier for those accused of crime are resisted. This may explain but not justify why calls by the Law Reform Commission of Canada to clarify the law of self-defence in 1987 (*Report No. 31: Recodify Criminal Law* (rev. ed., 1987) p. 36) and by Chief Justice Lamer in *R. v. McIntosh* (1995), 36 C.R. (4th) 171, 95 C.C.C. (3d) 481, [1995] 1 S.C.R. 686 at 180, have been ignored. For discussion of law reform proposals see Stuart, *Canadian Criminal Law: A Treatise* (3rd ed., 1995) pp. 451-452. It is time for a flexible defence that abandons the *Criminal Code's* present arbitrary and complex distinctions between situations of fatal and non-fatal self-defence, defence of those under protection and defence of strangers, and self-defence by an aggressor and simple self-defence. See, now, "Final Report: Self Defence Review" (Ratushny Report) (1997) and Department of Justice Consultation Paper, "Reforming Criminal Code Defences: Provocation, Self-defence and Defence of Property" (1998).

In the meantime the courts must soldier on trying to make sense out of ss. 34(1), 34(2), 35 and 37. In *R. v. McIntosh*, above, the majority of the Supreme Court decided that s. 34(2) is also available to an initial aggressor. The words "without having provoked" were not to be read in so as to trigger the more restrictive s. 35. The decision of the Ontario Court of Appeal in *Pintar* provides further welcome relief against boilerplate directions dealing at length with all these conflicting sections at great risk of being incomprehensible to jurors. The major pronouncement of Mr. Justice Moldaver is that a narrower provision must not be put where there is an air of reality in the evidence for a wider provision. That is a very sensible pronouncement. The particular message of *Pintar* is that s. 34(2) and not s. 34(1) should be put in all murder cases whether or not the accused intended to kill or cause grievous bodily harm. The Court relies on the analysis that s. 34(2) is wider than s. 34(1) as it applies on present interpretations even if the accused provoked the assault, even if the accused intended to kill or cause grievous bodily harm and the question is not whether more force was used than was necessary but whether the accused believed on reasonable grounds that he could not otherwise preserve himself from death or grievous bodily harm.

It is certainly debatable whether s. 34(2) is indeed wider as the proportionality test for s. 34(1) has always been interpreted not as a strict mechanical test but one under which a person defending against an attack need not weigh to a nicety the exact measure of necessary defence. Mr. Justice Martin for the Ontario Court of Appeal in *R. v. Baxter* (1975), 27 C.C.C. (2d) 96 (Ont. C.A.), viewed ss. 34(1) and (2) as *not* mutually exclusive. The words in s. 34(2) "who causes death or grievous bodily harm" had to mean "even though he intentionally causes death or grievous bodily harm". The Court reasoned that any other interpretation would leave unprotected one who, using no more force than was necessary to defend himself against an unprovoked assault, accidentally killed or caused bodily harm to his attacker but did not meet the requirements of s. 34(2). That Justices Martin and Moldaver differ again points to the need for legislative reform. For criticism of both *McIntosh* and *Pintar* see Gerry Ferguson, "Self-Defence: Selecting the Applicable Provisions" (2000), 5 Can. Crim. L.R. 179.

See, now, Gary Trotter, "*R. v. Pawliuck*: Further Efforts to Clarify Self-Defence" (2001), 40 C.R. (5th) 55.

R. v. CADWALLADER

[1966] 1 C.C.C. 380 (Sask. Q.B.)

SIROIS J.: — John Kenneth Marcella Cadwallader of Kyle, Saskatchewan, a 14-year-old boy, was charged that he was on or about October 24, 1964, at the White Bear District, in the Province of Saskatchewan, a juvenile, and that he did unlawfully kill and slay one John Cadwallader, thereby committing manslaughter and thus violating a provision of the *Criminal Code* of Canada, and did thereby commit a delinquency contrary to the provisions of the *Juvenile Delinquents Act*, R.S.C. 1952, c. 160.

The trial was held at Swift Current, Saskatchewan, before His Honour Judge J.H. Sunstrum, Judge of the Juvenile Court for Saskatchewan, commencing on January 27th, and ending on February 1, 1965. At the close of the hearing the learned Juvenile Court Judge gave an oral judgment as follows:

> Now you can just stand up, Mr. Cadwallader. You are charged on the 24th day of October, 1964, at the White Bear district, a juvenile, did unlawfully kill and slay one, John Cadwallader, thereby committing manslaughter, and thus violating a provision of the *Criminal Code* of Canada, and thereby commit a delinquency, contrary to the provisions of the *Juvenile Delinquents Act*.
>
> Now we have heard evidence over the last few days as to the circumstances under which the body of your father was found, and the explanation you gave this morning. The explanation is that your father was coming up the stairs with a loaded 30-30 and apparently with the intention of carrying out a threat to kill you. Now your evidence is that you took your .22 and put a loaded magazine in it and then swung around and, without aiming, shot at your father, who then apparently fell down the stairs, and a total of five wounds were found in the body of your father. Now I feel that the last shot, particularly the one that was fired from a

very close distance to the body of your father, and possibly any that were fired after the first one or two. You stated that the third one you were on the stairs at the time you fired the third shot, the fourth shot that you were possibly three-quarters of the way up the stairs, and then the fifth shot fired when the gun was only a few inches away. Now I feel that the extent of force used here was far more than was reasonable under the circumstances. I don't feel that you had any concern at that time that your father was in any condition to — able to carry out any threat to kill you, and therefore I find you guilty of the charge, and you will be found guilty of committing a delinquency contrary to the provisions of the *Juvenile Delinquents Act*.

. . . .

The appellant, an only child, reached his 14th birthday a few months before the tragedy. His mother had passed away on July 19, 1956, before the boy was six years of age. The child was cared for by an uncle and aunt for approximately one school year after his mother died. Thereafter the father hired a housekeeper who reared the child in a fashion until the end of 1963, and from that time on the appellant and his father lived alone together. From the evidence it would seem that the father was reserved and quiet; his social contacts were very limited; he had a strange sense of humour and was inclined to be moody. While the father and son relationship seemed normal and healthy to outsiders, it in fact according to the boy's evidence left much to be desired. They lived in the father's house in Kyle during the week so the boy could attend school. But on week-ends and during the summer holidays they would go to the farm and indulge in their favorite pastime — firing guns of various descriptions. The appellant in his evidence related over twenty incidents prior to the tragedy — these occurring with increasing frequency in the years 1962 to 1964 — wherein the father seemed to want to do away with him or to kill him. The appellant, who is possessed of above average intelligence and who had always done well in school previously, began to slip badly academically in June and again in September and October of 1964. Something obviously was worrying and troubling him but he refused to tell anyone about his personal problems. During the week of October 18, 1964, remains of a mammoth were located in the Kyle district and specialists from the University came down to unearth the discovery. The appellant and his father drove down from Kyle, as did many others, to see the men at work on Wednesday, October 21st. The appellant found out that they would be busy on the project until the coming Saturday or Monday of the following week. The appellant and his father talked about the discovery on their return to Kyle, at which time the father told the boy, "You will be in the ground before the mammoth is out of the ground." The father was serious when he spoke these words and the boy's apprehension increased.

On Friday, October 23rd, the boy and his father went to the mammoth site again and continued on to the farm for the weekend as was the custom. On Saturday morning, the 25th, father and son had breakfast together but the boy did not go out to work as he had just recovered from a cold and was not feeling his normal self. About 1:30 p.m. father and son had a light dinner together, after which the father went outside to repair the fence. The boy went upstairs to lay down on his bed again as he was not feeling well. About 3:30 p.m. the boy heard his father make a lot of noise on the doorstep, he mumbled as he entered the house, slammed the door, and he was heard to say: "I'm going to kill that God Damned little bastard." The father walked noisily to his room (situated roughly beneath the boy's room), started loading a 30-30, pumped a shell into the barrel, and walked noisily again across the kitchen towards the stairway. The boy arose from his bed and peeked over the edge of the stairway; he saw his angry and determined father start up the stairs with the 30-30 rifle in his hand. The boy figured this was it — that his father was coming up to get him. The boy returned to his bed, quickly grabbed the magazine on the nail keg as well as his semi-automatic Cooey rifle leaning against the east wall, and slipped the magazines into the gun. The boy swung around and saw his father up the steps aiming at him with his 30-30 rifle. The boy took a quick shot without aiming; there followed four other shots, according to the evidence, but the accused at the time did not remember. He was "a little scared and excited" and "it all happened so quickly." The evidence of the pathologist as well as the photographs and the boy's recollection of the rapid series of events at the crucial moment seem to indicate that two shots followed quickly after the first one before or as the father and his gun started to fall back down the stairs. The fourth shot was fired with the boy standing near the top or about three quarters of the [way] up the stairs, the father was still partly on the stairs and the bullet struck him in the back. The father was still moving around and the boy says he was still scared of his ability to shoot. The accused followed down the stairs and fired the fifth and last shot in the neck of the deceased from a distance of about three inches. Either the fourth or fifth shot could have been fatal whereas the first three shots were not.

The boy, under rigorous cross-examination, staunchly maintained that he did not want to kill his father but that up until the final or fifth shot he figured his father was still able to shoot him. The boy's feelings and reactions at the tragic moment were, I believe, adequately summarized in his answers to the following questions:

> Q. 4616. Well why did you hold the gun up to his head and shoot three inches away? Why did you do that? A. Well there is so much strain and everything.

And again later on:

> Q. 4813. Why did you move the 30-30 rifle at all? A. I apparently didn't I hadn't had sleep for a long time — and I didn't think at the time.

. . . .

The appellant's defence was self-defence. The Crown agrees with this but submits that the force used by the appellant was excessive and that the conviction for manslaughter should be upheld.

The evidence establishes that the events immediately prior to the actual shooting constituted an unprovoked assault by the deceased upon the appellant.

Section 34 of the *Cr. Code* provides as follows:

34(1) Every one who is unlawfully assaulted without having provoked the assault is justified in repelling force by force if the force he uses is not intended to cause death or grievous bodily harm and is no more than is necessary to enable him to defend himself.

(2) Every one who is unlawfully assaulted and who causes death or grievous bodily harm in repelling the assault is justified if

(a) he causes it under reasonable apprehension of death or grievous bodily harm from the violence with which the assault was originally made or with which the assailant pursues his purposes, and

(b) he believes, on reasonable and probable grounds, that he cannot otherwise preserve himself from death or grievous bodily harm.

Section 37 deals with the extent of justification:

37(1) Every one is justified in using force to defend himself or any one under his protection from assault, if he uses no more force than is necessary to prevent the assault or the repetition of it.

(2) Nothing in this section shall be deemed to justify the wilful infliction of any hurt or mischief that is excessive, having regard to the nature of the assault that the force used was intended to prevent.

While a person is not justified in killing another because of fear, there are many cases where killing in self-defence has been condoned on the ground of the necessity to preserve life.

There are numerous cases dealing with the defence of self-defence. . . .

Self-defence proceeds from necessity and each case must therefore be determined upon its own facts. The force used can only be justified when it is necessary for the avoidence or prevention of an offered injury, and again it must be no more than is necessary under the circumstances. To use an extreme example, you could not use a tank against a chariot. But if one believes he is in danger of life or limb he is entitled to use such force as would effectually put his assailant out of action. Where the means of defence used is not disproportionate to the severity of the assault, the plea is valid although the defender fails to measure with nicety the degree of force necessary to ward off the attack and inflicts serious injury. The test as to the extent of justification is whether the accused used more force *than he on reasonable grounds believed necessary*. It is not an objective test: the determination must be made according to the accused's state of mind at the time. The question is: Did he use more force than he on reasonable grounds believed to be necessary?

To establish the defence there should be evidence — (a) that the facts amount to self-defence, and (b) that the mode of defence used was justifiable under the circumstances.

When the defence of self-defence is raised it does not affect the burden upon the Crown of establishing its case — that is of proving the accused guilty of the offence beyond a reasonable doubt. All that the accused has to do to establish this defence is introduce evidence raising at least a reasonable doubt as to his guilt; the burden rests on the prosecution of negativing that defence. If, on consideration of the whole of the evidence, the jury are either convinced of the innocence of the prisoner or are left, in doubt whether he was acting in necessary self-defence they should acquit.

The appellant in this instance is a 14-year-old boy, who barely remembers his mother — he was five years old when she died. For most of the time thereafter he lived a closed life with a father who was a strange man in many ways. Incidents punctured this boy's life with his father, especially in the two years prior to the tragedy and particularly in the summer and fall of 1964 which worried and frightened this boy. [The appellant in his evidence related over twenty incidents prior to the tragedy — these occurring with increasing frequency in the years 1962 to 1964 — wherein the father seemed to want to do away with him or to kill him.] Such an incident, previously referred to, occurred in the course of a conversation with his father a few days only before the tragedy. On the afternoon of the fateful day the boy was lying down on his bed, he was not well and was worried. His angry father was coming up the stairs with a 30-30 to kill him. The boy was trapped and he reacted in the only way it seems to me that an ordinary person would under the circumstances. Can one adequately visualize the fear, terror and confusion which would grip any man, let alone a 14-year-old boy in a situation such as this.

It is clear that he acted in self-defence. On his uncontradicted evidence he used only sufficient force as he reasonably thought necessary under the circumstances to put his assailant out of action. You cannot put a higher test on a 14-year-old boy than that known to our law.

In my respectful opinion the case against the appellant was not proved with that certainty, in the light of all the evidence, which is necessary in order to justify a verdict of guilty. Therefore upon that ground the appeal is allowed and it is directed that this conviction be quashed.

Appeal allowed; conviction quashed.

R. v. BOGUE

(1976), 30 C.C.C. (2d) 403 (Ont. C.A.)

HOWLAND J.A.: — The appellant was found guilty of manslaughter on December 9, 1974, following her trial in the Court of General Sessions of the Peace for the Judicial District of Hamilton-Wentworth, before His Honour Judge Scime and a jury and was sentenced to a term of imprisonment for five years. The indictment was as follows:

> The Jurors for Her Majesty the Queen present that at the Judicial District of Hamilton Wentworth on or about the 22nd June 1974, DOREEN FRANCIS BOGUE unlawfully did kill John Moran, and thereby did commit manslaughter, contrary to the provisions of the *Criminal Code*.

Several weeks before the killing the appellant had rented an apartment in the City of Hamilton in the name of the deceased, John Moran. There was evidence that the appellant and Moran had consumed a considerable quantity of intoxicating liquor on June 21, 1974. Neighbours, Mr. and Mrs. Avalis, gave evidence of hearing noises, like someone fighting, coming from the apartment in the late evening of that day followed by a thud on the floor, and a woman screaming for help. The neighbours went to the apartment and found the appellant in a defensive position on the floor at Moran's feet. The appellant had a black eye and part of her face was discoloured. Moran who was 5' 10" and weighed 210 pounds, had a gash over his left eye which was bleeding. Mrs. Avalis returned to her own apartment on a lower floor twice to call the police. Mr. Avalis attempted to separate the appellant and the deceased. In the scuffle, Moran was hit over the head with an iron by the appellant. Mr. Avalis then returned to his own apartment to call the police again.

Returning to the scene of the argument, Mr. Avalis found the deceased lying on a bed with stab wounds. The appellant later stated to a police officer that she had stabbed Moran with a knife. According to the evidence of the pathologist, Moran's death resulted from the stab wounds which the appellant admitted she had inflicted.

The investigating officer swore that the appellant had been drinking, but did not think that she was intoxicated. Moran's blood was analyzed and found to contain 220 mg. of alcohol per 100 ml. of blood, a high blood-alcohol level.

The appellant did not testify at her trial but in her written statement, ex. 44, she said: "It was self-defence, I did not mean to kill him. . .". She described the drinking bout and her argument with Moran.

> With this he pushed me over the electric fan that was on the floor. I then said "I am now really leaving". He started to choke me and I told him to leave me alone. He grabbed the electric iron and hit me with the side of it. I grabbed the electric iron off him and hit him in the face. He turned around and he had blood on his face. I began crying and said I am sorry I did not mean to hurt you. He picked up a knife off the floor near the chesterfield and said "I'll Kill You", but he had blood dripping in his eyes. He came at me with the knife grabbed me by my hair pulling my head back, saying "I'll Kill You", I said why don't you wait till I turn my back and you can kill me like Pete Hodgins killed Bev George. But he had blood in his eyes and he fell back. I grabbed the knife off him as he fell back onto the bed and said you wont kill me I'll kill you, why don't you fight a man. I then put the knife in his side, and told him you killed Bernice and took all her money, I also said you won't kill me, I'll kill myself after I see my father. Then the police came in.

. . . .

In my opinion the learned trial Judge misdirected the jury when dealing with the extent to which self-defence is justified under s. 34(2) of the *Criminal Code* Section 34 provides:

> 34(1) Every one who is unlawfully assaulted without having provoked the assault is justified in repelling force by force if the force he uses is not intended to cause death or grievous bodily harm and is no more than is necessary to enable him to defend himself.
>
> (2) Every one who is unlawfully assaulted and who causes death or grievous bodily harm in repelling the assault is justified if
>
> (a) he causes it under reasonable apprehension of death or grievous bodily harm from the violence with which the assault was originally made or with which the assailant pursues his purpose, and
>
> (b) he believes, on reasonable and probable grounds, that he cannot otherwise preserve himself from death or grievous bodily harm.

There is a basic distinction between s. 34(1) and s. 34(2). Section 34(1) deals with a situation where the accused repels an unprovoked assault, but does not intend the force that he uses to cause death or grievous bodily harm. Section 34(2) applies where the accused intentionally kills or intentionally causes grievous bodily harm to his assailant. As Martin J.A., pointed out in delivering the judgment of this Court in *R. v. Baxter* (unreported, October 29, 1975) at p. 22 [since reported 27 C.C.C. (2d) 96 at p. 110, 33 C.R.N.S. 22]:

> In my opinion, the words in s. 34(2) "who causes death or grievous bodily harm" mean "even though he intentionally causes death or grievous bodily harm."

Section 34(1) also specifically provides that in repelling force by force, the force which is used must be no more than is necessary for self-defence. Under s. 34(2) there is no specific requirement that the repelling force used by the accused shall be proportionate to the unlawful assault, if the other conditions of the subsection are satisfied.

As Martin J.A., stated in *R. v. Baxter, supra,* at p. 17 [p. 107]:

> Under s. 34(2) of the *Code* the ultimate question for the jury is not whether the accused was *actually* in danger of death or grievous bodily harm, and whether the causing of death or grievous bodily harm by him was *in fact* necessary to preserve himself from death or grievous bodily harm, but whether:
> (1) He caused death or grievous bodily harm under a *reasonable apprehension* of death or grievous bodily harm, and
> (2) He *believed on reasonable and probable grounds* that he could not otherwise preserve himself from death or grievous bodily harm.

He is entitled to be acquitted, if upon all the evidence, there was reasonable doubt whether or not the blow was delivered under reasonable apprehension of death or grievous bodily harm, and if he believed on reasonable grounds that he could not otherwise preserve himself from death or grievous bodily harm. He does not have to prove that it was so delivered: *R. v. Philbrook*, 77 C.C.C. 26 at p. 30.

There are two criteria to be satisfied under s. 34(2). The reasonable apprehension of death or grievous bodily harm in s. 34(2)(*a*) must satisfy an objective standard. In addition, s. 34(2)(*b*) imports a subjective element, the belief of the accused that he cannot otherwise preserve himself from death or grievous bodily harm. However, this belief must meet an objective standard that it is based "on reasonable and probable grounds". As Martin J.A. stated in *R. v. Baxter, supra,* at p. 19 [pp. 108-9]:

> In deciding whether the accused's belief was based upon reasonable grounds the jury would of necessity draw comparisons with what a reasonable person in the accused's situation might believe with respect to the extent and the imminence of the danger by which he was threatened, and the force necessary to defend himself against the apprehended danger.

In considering whether the degree of force used by the accused was justified, the difference between the criteria under s. 34(1) and (2) must be carefully borne in mind. In neither case is a person defending himself against a reasonably apprehended attack expected to weigh to a nicety the exact measure of necessary defensive action. *R. v. Baxter, supra*, at p. 24 [p. 111]; *Palmer v. The Queen* (1971), 55 Cr. App. R. 223 at p. 242; *R. v. Preston* (1953), 106 C.C.C. 135 at p. 140, 17 C.R. 20,; *R. v. Ogal* (1928), 50 C.C.C. 71 at pp. 73-4; *R. v. Antley*, [1964] 2 C.C.C. 142 at p. 147, 42 C.R. 384 at p. 389.

There is, however, a real difference between the test under s. 34(1) that the force be no more than is necessary to enable the accused to defend himself, and that under s. 34(2)(*b*) that the accused believe on reasonable grounds that he cannot otherwise preserve himself from death or grievous bodily harm. The belief of the accused may be a reasonable one, but it may be mistaken: *R. v. Chisam* (1963), 47 Cr. App. R. 130. If as a result of threats or an assault a person believes that he may momentarily be shot or stabbed, and he in turn instinctively shoots or stabs his assailant, it may properly be concluded that only reasonable defensive action had been taken to save his life. If on the other hand, the test is an objective one requiring that the force be proportionate to the attack, then the accused may not be justified if he shoots or stabs his assailant, when knocking him unconscious would have been all that was required to preserve his life or save him from grievous bodily harm.

Section 34(2)(*b*) recognizes the fact that when a man's life is in the balance he cannot be expected to make the same decision as he would on sober reflection. As Holmes J. stated in *Brown v. United States* (1921), 256 U.S. 335 at p. 343: "Detached reflection cannot be demanded in the presence of an uplifted knife." The essential question to be determined under s. 34(2)(*b*) in considering whether the force is excessive, is the state of mind of the accused at the time the force is applied. *R. v. Preston, supra*, is in point. In that case Preston was convicted of manslaughter for having caused the death of Stevenson by striking him in the head with a partly full whiskey bottle during a struggle in which Stevenson was the aggressor. The trial Judge read verbatim to the jury s. 53 of the *Criminal Code*, which was the predecessor of s. 34. He continued:

> You will remember of course the defence of the accused when he went in the box. He said "I struck this blow, and I struck it in self-defence. I was trying to get away" — and he said he just received a severe blow from the deceased, and saw the deceased coming at him again and that he raised his hands, and as the deceased came at him he brought down the whiskey bottle on the head of the deceased with his hand grasping the bottle. As I say, it is for you to decide whether the accused used more force than was reasonably necessary in his own self-defence. If he used no more force than was necessary in defending himself, then he is entitled to be acquitted, but if you find that he used more force than was necessary in defending himself, then you must convict him.

Bird J.A., in delivering the judgment of the majority of the Court of Appeal of British Columbia stated at pp. 139-40:

> In my view the effect of the charge, read as a whole, was to withdraw from the minds of the jury the issue relative to the state of mind of the prisoner when the blow was struck. The concluding direction quoted above, I think could have conveyed to the minds of the jury that the issue as to whether excessive force had been used was to be determined solely by the severity of the blow and the type of weapon used, whereas in my opinion the proper direction in the circumstances was that the jury must determine whether, when the blow was struck, the prisoner had reasonable apprehension of grievous bodily harm from the violence of the deceased's attack, and then believed on reasonable grounds that he could not preserve himself

from such harm otherwise than by striking the deceased with the bottle, in which last mentioned circumstances the weight to be attached to the amount of force used is of less consequence than if these factors were absent.

The question as to whether or not excessive force is used, I think must be determined pursuant to s. 53(2) with regard to the state of mind of the person at the time the force is applied by him.

In the present case, there was evidence on which the jury, if properly directed, could have concluded that s. 34(2) was applicable. The trial Judge stated the theory of the defence at pp. 613-5 in part as follows:

The theory for the defence is that Mr. Moran pushed the accused over the fan; that he choked her; that he hit her with the side of the iron that this constituted an unlawful assault; that she began to cry and expressed the apology over the assault with which she retaliated; that she intended to withdraw from the fighting at this point; that Mr. Moran picked up the knife and renewed his assault. He expressed his intention to kill her. This was either a new unprovoked assault or a continuation of the earlier unprovoked assault; then, when he came at her with the knife, grabbing her by the hair and pulling her back saying, "I'll kill you", she had reasonable and probable grounds for believing that he intended to kill her; that she was justified in repelling the murderous assault from a man in a drunken rage by repelling force by force; that she was justified, when the facts and situation are examined in using such force as she thought was necessary to defend herself from death or grievous bodily harm. Self-defence arose from necessity. . . . That when she stated, "You won't kill me, I'll kill you", that the situation reached such a dangerous point that either she would be killed by him or she would have to act to preserve her life, which she did.

The important question is whether the trial Judge properly directed the jury with respect to s. 34(2). There were three passages in particular where the trial Judge dealt with self-defence within the meaning of s. 34(2).

At pp. 600-1 he stated:

Subsection (2) of Section 34, which I have already read to you, is not dependent on the intention of the accused. In this situation the accused is justified in repelling an unlawful assault if:

she was under a reasonable apprehension herself of death or grievous bodily harm from the violent nature of the original assault and in addition, she believed on reasonable and probable grounds that there was no other way she could protect herself from death or grievous bodily harm.

This subsection is basically self-explanatory. In the first instance you must ask yourselves did the accused have a reasonable apprehension of death or grievous bodily harm as a result of the initial unlawful assault by the deceased or the way the deceased person pursued his purpose. Now, with the second situation, the question is, did the accused have a reasonable belief that there was no other way that she could protect herself, *always bearing in mind that the force employed must be not out of proportion to the original assault by the deceased, Moran*. As has been mentioned to you before, the onus is on the Crown to prove the constituent elements of the offence charged. Therefore, if you are satisfied the accused acted in self-defence or are left in doubt whether the accused acted in self-defence, you must acquit. In considering this issue, including the reasonableness of the force used, you may take into account all the surrounding circumstances and the state of mind of the accused at the time of the assault. (Emphasis added.)

At p. 607:

> A section that is relevant and that is applicable to the evidence is Section 34(2). If you find that the assault by Mr. Moran on Mrs. Bogue was unprovoked by Mrs. Bogue, it provides, as you will recall, that person who kills in meeting force by force, is justified it she acts under the reasonable apprehension of death or grievous bodily harm from the violence with which the assault was originally made or with which the victim pursues his purpose, and also, that she believes on reasonable and probable grounds that she cannot otherwise preserve herself from death or grievous bodily harm *and the amount of the force used must not be out of proportion to the original assaullt by the deceased.* (Emphasis added.)

Finally at p. 637:

> Is that an act of self-defence? Did she have an opportunity to leave, to retreat? Was it necessary for her to inflict the stab wound to protect herself to preserve her own safety? It is for you the members of the jury to consider. . . .
> Was this an act of self-defence? If you find it was self-defence; was it necessary for her to stab him twice to protect herself in those circumstances? *Is the force applied by her out of proportion to the circumstances?* Was she under a reasonable apprehension of death or grievous bodily harm at the time she inflicted the wounds? These are matters for you the jury to decide. (Emphasis added.)

In each of these three statements the trial Judge has clearly indicated that in addition to the criteria in s. 34(2)(*a*) and (*b*) the force must be proportionate to the original assault by the deceased. Whether the amount of force used against the accused was disproportionate to the nature of the force used by her was proper to be considered by the jury as a circumstance, or an item of evidence, in deciding whether she had a *reasonable* apprehension of death or grievous bodily harm and whether she had *reasonable and probable* grounds to believe that she could not otherwise preserve herself from death or grievous bodily harm. If, however, the jury was either satisfied that the accused had such apprehension and belief, or entertained a reasonable doubt with respect to it, she was entitled to be acquitted. No further requirement existed that the force used by the accused be proportionate to the nature of the attack upon her.

The jury might, however, reasonably have understood from the above passages in the charge that, in addition to the requirements specified in s. 34(2), there was, as a matter of law, a further requirement that the force used by the accused must be proportionate to the assault made upon her by the deceased in order for the defence of self-defence to be available. The addition of the criterion of the force being proportionate to the assault led the trial Judge to concentrate on the reasonableness of the force, rather than on the reasonableness of the accused's belief. The state of mind of the accused at the time when the force is applied has to be considered, and not merely the type of weapon and the severity of the blow. At p. 637 of his charge he asked: "Was it necessary for her to inflict the stab wound to protect herself to preserve her own safety? . . . Was it necessary for her to stab him twice to protect herself in these circumstances?" He should have asked whether she believed on reasonable and probable grounds that it was necessary to stab him as she did.

In my opinion there was a serious misdirection with respect to s. 34(2). It cannot be said that this misdirection did not result in any substantial wrong or miscarriage of justice. One can only speculate whether the jury if properly directed, would have been satisfied beyond a reasonable doubt that the acts of the accused were not justified as self-defence within s. 34(2) of the *Code*.

In my opinion the appeal should be allowed, the verdict of guilty set aside, and a new trial should be directed.

Appeal allowed: new trial ordered.

Kelly J.A. concurred. The concurring judgment of Lacourcière J.A. is omitted.

Is there an absolute duty to retreat?

R. v. DEEGAN

(1979), 49 C.C.C. (2d) 417 at 440-1 (Alta. C.A.)

HARRADENCE J.A.: —

. . . .

In *R. v. Stanley*, [(1977), 36 C.C.C. (2d) 216] Branca J.A. said at p. 226:

> Ever since *Semaynes Case* (1605), 5 Co. Rep. 91a, at p. 91b, 77 E.R. 194, it was said: "That the house of every one is to him as his (*a*) castle and fortress, as well for his defence against injury and violence as for his repose . . .".
>
> That is something that people who live in our country have been told to understand is the law of our land. The precept that a man's home is his castle is as true today as it was then.

I am in complete agreement with this statement.

In *R. v. Hussey* (1924), 18 Cr. App. R. 160, Lord Hewart said at p. 161:

> No sufficient notice had been given to appellant to quit his room, and therefore he was in the position of a man who was defending his house. In Archbold's *Criminal Pleading, Evidence and Practice*, 26th ed. p. 887, it appears that: "In defence of a man's house, the owner or his family may kill a trespasser who would forcibly dispossess him of it, in the same manner as he might, by law, kill in self-defence a man who attacks him personally; with this distinction, however, that in defending his home he need not retreat, as in other cases of self-defence, for that would be giving up his house to his adversary." That is still the law, but not one word was said about that distinction in the summing-up, which proceeded on the foundation that the defence was the ordinary one of self-defence.

Even if the appellant were not in his home, I do not accept that retreat is imperative if a defence of self-defence is to be relied on; rather, I adopt the statement of Dixon C.J. in *R. v. Howe* (1958), 100 C.L.R. 448 at pp. 462-3:

> The view of the Supreme Court appears also to be correct as to the position which the modern law governing a plea of self-defence gives to the propriety of a person retreating in face of an assault or apprehended assault before resorting to violence to defend himself. The view which the Supreme Court has accepted is that to retreat before employing force is no

longer to be treated as an independent and imperative condition if a plea of self-defence is to be made out.

Dixon C.J. then referred to the judgment of Holmes J. in *Brown v. United States of America* (1920), 256 U.S. 335 at p. 343;

Holmes J. pronounced upon the question in a way which one may well be content to adopt: "Rationally, the failure to retreat is a circumstance to be considered with all the others in order to determine whether the defendant went farther than he was justified in doing; not a categorical proof of guilt. The law has grown, and even if historical mistakes have contributed to its growth, it has tended in the direction of rules consistent with human nature. Many respectable writers agree that if a man reasonably believes that he is in immediate danger of death or grievous bodily harm from his assailant, he may stand his ground, and that if he kills him, he has not exceeded the bounds of lawful self-defence. That has been the decision of this Court. *Beard v. United States.* Detached reflection cannot be demanded in the presence of an uplifted knife. Therefore, in this Court, at least, it is not a condition of immunity that one in that situation should pause to consider whether a reasonable man might not think it possible to fly with safety, or to disable his assailant rather than to kill him": *Brown v. United States of America.*

I am quite content to adopt the pronouncement of Holmes J.

R. v. LAVALLEE

[1990] 1 S.C.R. 852, 76 C.R. (3d) 329, 55 C.C.C. (3d) 97

The accused was a a battered woman in a volatile common-law relationship who killed her partner late one night by shooting him in the back of the head as he left her room. A psychiatrist with extensive professional experience in the treatment of battered wives, Dr. Shane, prepared a psychiatric assessment of the appellant which was used in support of her defence of self-defence. The accused was acquitted at trial but the Manitoba Court of Appeal ordered a new trial. On the accused's appeal the Supreme Court of Canada was faced with the decision of the Nova Scotia Court of Appeal in *R. v. Whynot*. That Court followed what was then considered to be the law, that it was inherently unreasonable to apprehend death or grievous bodily harm unless and until the physical assault was actually in progress. The Supreme Court of Canada announced a change in the law. It was informed by the expert opinion led at the trial and by books and articles which it read for itself. Notice how the Court reasons; how it judicially notices legislative facts; how it decides the case; how it creates law.

Wilson J. (Dickson C.J.C. and Lamer, L'Heureux-Dubé, Sopinka, Gonthier and McLachlin JJ. concurring): —

The appellant did not testify but her statement made to police on the night of the shooting was put in evidence. Portions of it read as follows:

Me and Wendy argued as usual and I ran in the house after Kevin pushed me. I was scared, I was really scared. I locked the door. Herb was downstairs with Joanne and I called for Herb but I was crying when I called him. I said, "Herb come up here please." Herb came up to the top of the stairs and I told him that Kevin was going to hit me actually beat on me again. Herb said he knew and that if I was his old lady things would be different, he gave me a hug. OK, we're friends, there's nothing between us. He said "Yeah, I know" and he went outside to talk to Kevin leaving the door unlocked. I went upstairs and hid in my closet from Kevin. I was so scared. . . My window was open and I could hear Kevin asking questions about what I was doing and what I was saying. Next thing I know he was coming up the stairs for me. He came into my bedroom and said "Wench, where are you?" And he turned on my light and he said "Your purse is on the floor" and he kicked it. OK then he turned and he saw me in the closet. He wanted me to come out but I didn't want to come out because I was scared. I was so scared. [The officer who took the statement then testified that the appellant started to cry at this point and stopped after a minute or two.] He grabbed me by the arm right there. There's a bruise on my face also where he slapped me. He didn't slap me right then, first he yelled at me then he pushed me and I pushed him back and he hit me twice on the right hand side of my head. I was scared. All I thought about was all the other times he used to beat me, I was scared, I was shaking as usual. The rest is a blank, all I remember is he gave me the gun and a shot was fired through my screen. This is all so fast. And then the guns were in another room and he loaded it the second shot and gave it to me. And I was going to shoot myself. I pointed it to myself, I was so upset. OK and then he went and I was sitting on the bed and he started going like this with his finger [the appellant made a shaking motion with an index finger] and said something like "You're my old lady and you do as you're told" or something like that. He said "wait till everybody leaves, you'll get it then" and he said something to the effect of "either you kill me or I'll get you" that was what it was. He kind of smiled and then he turned around. I shot him but I aimed out. I thought I aimed above him and a piece of his head went that way.

. . . .

Expert evidence on the psychological effect of battering on wives and common-law partners must, it seems to me, be both relevant and necessary in the context of the present case. How can the mental state of the appellant be appreciated without it? The average member of the public (or of the jury) can be forgiven for asking: Why would a woman put up with this kind of treatment? Why should she continue to live with such a man? How could she love a partner who beat her to the point of requiring hospitalization? We would expect the woman to pack her bags and go. Where is her self-respect? Why does she not cut loose and make a new life for herself? Such is the reaction of the average person confronted with the so-called "battered wife syndrome". We need help to understand it and help is available from trained professionals.

The gravity, indeed, the tragedy of domestic violence can hardly be overstated. Greater media attention to this phenomenon in recent years has revealed both its prevalence and its horrific impact on women from all walks of life. Far from protecting women from it, the law historically sanctioned the abuse of women within marriage as an aspect of the husband's ownership of his wife and his "right" to chastise her. One need only recall the centuries old law that a man is entitled to beat his wife with a stick "no thicker than his thumb".

Laws do not spring out of a social vacuum. The notion that a man has a right to "discipline" his wife is deeply rooted in the history of our society. The woman's duty was to serve her husband and to stay in the marriage at all costs "till death do us part" and to accept as her due any "punishment" that was meted out for failing to please her husband. One consequence of this attitude was that "wife battering" was rarely spoken of, rarely reported, rarely prosecuted, and even more rarely punished. Long after society abandoned its formal approval of spousal abuse, tolerance of it continued and continues in some circles to this day.

Fortunately, there has been a growing awareness in recent years that no man has a right to abuse any woman under any circumstances. Legislative initiatives designed to educate police, judicial officers and the public, as well as more aggressive investigation and charging policies, all signal a concerted effort by the criminal justice system to take spousal abuse seriously. However, a woman who comes before a Judge or jury with the claim that she has been battered and suggests that this may be a relevant factor in evaluating her subsequent actions still faces the prospect of being condemned by popular mythology about domestic violence. Either she was not as badly beaten as she claims or she would have left the man long ago. Or, if she was battered that severely, she must have stayed out of some masochistic enjoyment of it.

. . . .

In my view, there are two elements of the defence under s. 34(2) of the *Code* which merit scrutiny for present purposes. The first is the temporal connection in s. 34(2)(*a*) between the apprehension of death or grievous bodily harm and the act allegedly taken in self-defence. Was the appellant "under reasonable apprehension of death or grievous bodily harm" from Rust as he was walking out of the room? The second is the assessment in s. 34(2)(*b*) of the magnitude of the force used by the accused. Was the accused's belief that she could not "otherwise preserve herself from death or grievous bodily harm" except by shooting the deceased based "on reasonable grounds"?

The feature common to both s. 34(2)(*a*) and s. 34(2)(*b*) is the imposition of an objective standard of reasonableness on the apprehension of death and the need to repel the assault with deadly force. . . .

If it strains credulity to imagine what the "ordinary man" would do in the position of a battered spouse, it is probably because men do not typically find themselves in that situation.

. . . .

It will be observed that subsection 34(2)(*a*) does not actually stipulate that the accused apprehend *imminent* danger when he or she acts. Case law has, however, read that requirement into the defence. . . . The sense in which "imminent" is used conjures up the image of "an uplifted knife" or a pointed gun. The rationale for the imminence rule seems obvious. The law of self-defence is designed to ensure that the use of defensive force is really necessary. It justifies the act because the defender reasonably believed that he or she had no alternative but to take the attacker's life. If there is a significant time interval between the original unlawful assault and the accused's response, one tends to suspect that the accused was motivated by revenge rather than self-defence. In the paradigmatic case of a one-time barroom brawl between two men of equal size and strength, this inference makes sense. How can one feel endangered to the point of firing a gun at an unarmed man who utters a death threat, then turns his back and walks out of the room? One cannot be certain of the gravity of the threat or his capacity to carry it out. Besides, one can always take the opportunity to flee or to call the police. If he comes back and raises his fist, one can respond in kind if need be. These are the tacit assumptions that underlie the imminence rule.

All of these assumptions were brought to bear on the respondent in *R. v. Whynot* (1983), 37 C.R. (3d) 198, 9 C.C.C. 449 (N.S.C.A.). The respondent, Jane Stafford, shot her sleeping common-law husband as he lay passed out in his truck. The evidence at trial indicated that the deceased "dominated the household and exerted his authority by striking and slapping the various members and from time to time administering beatings to Jane Stafford and the others" (at p. 452). The respondent testified that the deceased threatened to kill all of the members of her family, one by one, if she tried to leave him. On the night in question he threatened to kill her son. After he passed out, the respondent got one of the many shotguns kept by her husband and shot him. The Nova Scotia Court of Appeal held that the trial Judge erred in leaving s. 37 (preventing assault against oneself or anyone under one's protection) with the jury. The Court stated at p. 464:

> I do not believe that the trial Judge was justified in placing s. 37 of the *Code* before the jury any more than he would have been justified in giving them s. 34. Under s. 34 the assault must have been underway and unprovoked, and under s. 37 the assault must be such that it is necessary to defend the person assaulted by the use of force. No more force may be used than necessary to prevent the assault or the repetition of it. In my opinion, no person has the right in anticipation of an assault that may or may not happen, to apply force to prevent the imaginary assault.

The implication of the Court's reasoning is that it is inherently unreasonable to apprehend death or grievous bodily harm unless and until the physical assault is actually in progress, at which point the victim can presumably gauge the requisite amount of force needed to repel the attack and act accordingly. In my view, expert testimony can cast doubt on these assumptions as they are applied in the context of a battered wife's efforts to repel an assault.

The situation of the appellant was not unlike that of Jane Stafford in the sense that she too was routinely beaten over the course of her relationship with the man she ultimately killed. According to the testimony of Dr. Shane these assaults were not entirely random in their occurrence.

. . . .

The cycle described by Dr. Shane conforms to the Walker Cycle Theory of Violence named for clinical psychologist, Dr. Lenore Walker, the pioneer researcher in the field of the battered wife syndrome. Dr. Shane acknowledged his debt to Dr. Walker in the course of establishing his credentials as an expert at trial. Dr. Walker first describes the cycle in the book The Battered Woman (1979). In her 1984 book, The Battered Woman Syndrome, Dr. Walker reports the results of a study involving 400 battered women. Her research was designed to test empirically the theories expounded in her earlier book. At pp. 95-96 of The Battered Woman Syndrome she summarizes the Cycle Theory as follows:

A second major theory that was tested in this project is the Walker Cycle Theory of Violence (Walker, 1979). This tension reduction theory states that there are three distinct phases associated in a recurring battering cycle: (1) tension building, (2) the acute battering incident, and (3) loving contrition. During the first phase, there is a gradual escalation of tension displayed by discrete acts causing increased friction such as name-calling, other mean intentional behaviours, and/or physical abuse. The batterer expresses dissatisfaction and hostility but not in an extreme or maximally explosive form. The woman attempts to placate the batterer, doing what she thinks might please him, calm him down, or at least, what will not further aggravate him. She tries not to respond to his hostile actions and uses general anger reduction techniques. Often she succeeds for a little while which reinforces her unrealistic belief that she can control this man . . .

The tension continues to escalate and eventually she is unable to continue controlling his angry response pattern. "Exhausted from the constant stress, she usually withdraws from the batterer, fearing she will inadvertently set off an explosion. He begins to move more oppressively toward her as he observes her withdrawal. . . . Tension between the two becomes unbearable" (Walker, 1979, p. 59). The second phase, the acute battering incident, becomes inevitable without intervention. Sometimes, she precipitates the inevitable explosion so as to control where and when it occurs, allowing her to take better precautions to minimize her injuries and pain.

"Phase two is characterized by the uncontrollable discharge of the tensions that have built up during phase one" (p. 59). The batterer typically unleashes a barrage of verbal and physical aggression that can leave the woman severely shaken and injured. In fact, when injuries do occur it usually happens during this second phase. It is also the time police become involved, if they are called at all. The acute battering phase is concluded when the batterer stops, usually bringing with its cessation a sharp physiological reduction in tension. This in itself is naturally reinforcing. Violence often succeeds because it does work.

In phase three which follows, the batterer may apologize profusely, try to assist his victim, show kindness and remorse, and shower her with gifts and/or promises. The batterer himself may believe at this point that he will never allow himself to be violent again. The woman wants to believe the batterer and, early in the relationship at least, may renew her hope in his ability to change. This third phase provides the positive reinforcement for remaining in the relationship, for the woman. In fact, our results showed that phase three could also be characterized by an absence of tension or violence, and no observable loving-contrition behaviour, and still be reinforcing for the woman.

Dr. Walker defines a battered woman as a woman who has gone through the battering cycle at least twice. As she explains in her introduction to The Battered Woman at p. xv, "Any woman may find herself in an abusive relationship with a man once. If it occurs a second time, and she remains in the situation, she is defined as a battered woman".

Given the relational context in which the violence occurs, the mental state of an accused at the critical moment she pulls the trigger cannot be understood except in terms of the cumulative effect of months or years of brutality.

. . . .

Another aspect of the cyclical nature of the abuse is that it begets a degree of predictability to the violence that is absent in an isolated violent encounter between two strangers. This also means that it may in fact be possible for a battered spouse to accurately predict the onset of violence before the first blow is struck, even if an outsider to the relationship cannot. Indeed, it has been suggested that a battered woman's knowledge of her partner's violence is so heightened that she is able to anticipate the nature and extent (though not the onset) of the violence by his conduct beforehand. In her article "Potential Uses for Expert Testimony: Ideas Toward the Representation of Battered Women Who Kill" (1986), 9 Women's Rights Law Reporter 227, psychologist Julie Blackman describes this characteristic at p. 229:

> Repeated instances of violence enable battered women to develop a continuum along which they can "rate" the tolerability or survivability of episodes of their partner's violence. Thus, signs of unusual violence are detected. For battered women, this response to the ongoing violence of their situations is a survival skill. Research shows that battered women who kill experience remarkably severe and frequent violence relative to battered women who do not kill. They know what sorts of danger are familiar and which are novel. They have had myriad opportunities to develop and hone their perceptions of their partner's violence. And, importantly, they can say what made the final episode of violence different from the others: they can name the features of the last battering that enabled them to know that this episode would result in life-threatening action by the abuser.

. . . .

Where evidence exists that an accused is in a battering relationship, expert testimony can assist the jury in determining whether the accused had a "reasonable" apprehension of death when she acted by explaining the heightened sensitivity of a battered woman to her partner's acts. Without such testimony I am skeptical that the average fact-finder would be capable of appreciating why her subjective fear may have been reasonable in the context of the relationship. After all, the hypothetical "reasonable man" observing only the final incident may have been unlikely to recognize the batterer's threat as potentially lethal. Using the case at bar as an example the "reasonable man" might have thought, as the majority of the Court of Appeal seemed to, that it was unlikely that Rust would make good on his threat to kill the appellant that night because they had guests staying overnight.

The issue is not, however, what an outsider would have reasonably perceived but what the accused reasonably perceived, given her situation and her experience.

Even accepting that a battered woman may be uniquely sensitized to danger from her batterer, it may yet be contended that the law ought to require her to wait until the knife is uplifted, the gun pointed or the fist clenched before her apprehension is deemed reasonable. This would allegedly reduce the risk that the woman is mistaken in her fear, although the law does not require her fear to be correct, only reasonable. In response to this contention, I need only point to the observation made by Huband J.A. that the evidence showed that when the appellant and Rust physically fought the appellant "invariably got the worst of it". I do not think it is an unwarranted generalization to say that due to their size, strength, socialization and lack of training, women are typically no match for men in hand-to-hand combat. The requirement imposed in *Whynot* that a battered woman wait until the physical assault is "underway" before her apprehensions can be validated in law would, in the words of an American Court, be tantamount to sentencing her to "murder by installment". . . . I share the view expressed by M.J. Willoughby in "Rendering Each Woman Her Due: Can a Battered Woman Claim Self-Defense When She Kills Her Sleeping Batterer" (1989), 38 Kan. L. Rev. 169, at p. 184, that "society gains nothing, except perhaps the additional risk that the battered woman will herself be killed, because she must wait until her abusive husband instigates another battering episode before she can justifiably act".

. . . .

Subsection 34(2) requires an accused who pleads self-defence to believe "on reasonable grounds" that it is not possible to otherwise preserve him or herself from death or grievous bodily harm. The obvious question is if the violence was so intolerable, why did the appellant not leave her abuser long ago? This question does not really go to whether she had an alternative to killing the deceased at the critical moment. Rather, it plays on the popular myth already referred to that a woman who says she was battered yet stayed with her batterer was either not as badly beaten as she claimed or else she liked it. Nevertheless, to the extent that her failure to leave the abusive relationship earlier may be used in support of the proposition that she was free to leave at the final moment, expert testimony can provide useful insights. Dr. Shane attempted to explain in his testimony how and why, in the case at bar, the appellant remained with Rust:

> She had stayed in this relationship, I think, because of the strange, almost unbelievable, but yet it happens, relationship that sometimes develops between people who develop this very disturbed, I think, very disturbed quality of a relationship. Trying to understand it, I think, isn't always easy and there's been a lot written about it recently, in the recent years, in psychiatric literature. But basically it involves two people who are involved in what appears to be an attachment which may have sexual or romantic or affectionate overtones.

> And the one individual, and it's usually the women in our society, but there have been occasions where it's been reversed, but what happens is the spouse who becomes battered, if you will, stays in the relationship probably because of a number of reasons.

> One is that the spouse gets beaten so badly — so badly — that he or she loses the motivation to react and becomes helpless and becomes powerless. And it's also been shown sometimes, you know, in — not that you can compare animals to human beings, but in laboratories, what you do if you shock an animal, after a while it can't respond to a threat of its life. It becomes just helpless and lies there in an amotivational state, if you will, where it feels there's no power and there's no energy to do anything.

> So in a sense it happens in human beings as well. It's almost like a concentration camp, if you will. You get paralyzed with fear.

> The other thing that happens often in these types of relationships with human beings is that the person who beats or assaults, who batters, often tries — he makes up and begs for forgiveness. And this individual, who basically has a very disturbed or damaged self-esteem, all of a sudden feels that he or she — we'll use women in this case because it's so much more common — the spouse feels that she again can do the spouse a favour and it can make her feel

needed and boost her self-esteem for a while and make her feel worthwhile and the spouse says he'll forgive her and whatnot.

Apparently, another manifestation of this victimization is a reluctance to disclose to others the fact or extent of the beatings. For example, the hospital records indicate that on each occasion the appellant attended the emergency department to be treated for various injuries she explained the cause of those injuries as accidental. Both in its address to the jury and in its written submissions before this Court the Crown insisted that the appellant's injuries were as consistent with her explanations as with being battered and, therefore, in the words of Crown counsel at trial, "the myth is, in this particular case, that Miss Lavallee was a battered spouse". In his testimony Dr. Shane testified that the appellant admitted to him that she lied to hospital staff and others about the cause of her injuries. In Dr. Shane's opinion this was consistent with her overall feeling of being trapped and helpless.

. . . .

The account given by Dr. Shane comports with that documented in the literature. Reference is often made to it as a condition of "learned helplessness", a phrase coined by Dr. Charles Seligman, the psychologist who first developed the theory by experimenting on animals in the manner described by Dr. Shane in his testimony. A related theory used to explain the failure of women to leave battering relationships is described by psychologist and lawyer Charles Patrick Ewing in his book, Battered Women Who Kill (1987). Ewing describes a phenomenon labelled "traumatic bonding" that has been observed between hostages and captors, battered children and their parents, concentration camp prisoners and guards, and batterers and their spouses.

. . . .

I emphasize at this juncture that it is not for the jury to pass judgment on the fact that an accused battered woman stayed in the relationship. Still less is it entitled to conclude that she forfeited her right to self-defence for having done so. I would also point out that traditional self-defence doctrine does not require a person to retreat from her home instead of defending herself: R. v. Antley, (1964), 42 C.R. 384, [1964] 2 C.C.C. 142 (C.A.). A man's home may be his castle but it is also the woman's home even if it seems to her more like a prison in the circumstances.

If, after hearing the evidence (including the expert testimony), the jury is satisfied that the accused had a reasonable apprehension of death or grievous bodily harm and felt incapable of escape, it must ask itself what the "reasonable person" would do in such a situation. The situation of the battered woman as described by Dr. Shane strikes me as somewhat analogous to that of a hostage. If the captor tells her that he will kill her in three days time, is it potentially reasonable for her to seize an opportunity presented on the first day to kill the captor or must she wait until he makes the attempt on the third day? I think the question the jury must ask itself is whether, given the history, circumstances and perceptions of the appellant, her belief that she could not preserve herself from being killed by Rust that night except by killing him first was reasonable. To the extent that expert evidence can assist the jury in making that determination, I would find such testimony to be both relevant and necessary.

. . . .

I would accordingly allow the appeal, set aside the order of the Court of Appeal, and restore the acquittal.

For comments by Donna Martinson, Marilyn MacCrimmon, Isabel Grant and Christine Boyle see "A Forum on *Lavallee v. R.*: Women and Self-Defence" (1991), 25 U.B.C. Law Rev. 23-68.

Although *Lavallee* has been widely-heralded there have been some concerns expressed. Some question the reliability of the opinion of the expert given that it was based on so much hearsay evidence and that the trial Crown expected to have an opportunity to cross-examine the accused, but she was not called. The heavy reliance on the expert testimony as to the "cycle of learned helplessness" has produced the criticism that the particular research relied upon is suspect and unduly restrictive: see Neil Vidmar, "One or Many Words for a Camel? An Overview on Judicial Evaluation of Social Science Evidence", a paper presented to a Canadian Institute for the Administration of Justice conference, October 13-16, 1993. There is also the perspective that resting on expert medical opinion potentially medicalizes the problem and discounts the voice of the particular woman. This is very well-expressed by Professor Isabel Grant:

> A fundamental problem with developing a category like the "battered woman syndrome" is that we risk transforming the reality of this form of gender oppression into a psychiatric disorder. The victim of spousal violence becomes the abnormal actor, the one whose conduct must be explained by the expert. When a woman uses force to defend herself, it is evaluated with reference to a male standard of reasonableness or to an exceptional standard for certain women, *i.e.*, those who are "battered women". The focus is on the irrationality of a woman's response and on the need for medical terminology to transform that irrational response into a reasonable one for a "battered woman". She must either be reasonable "like a man" or reasonable "like a battered woman". Trapped in this dichotomy, the "reasonable" woman may disappear.

The research of Dr. Lenore Walker, relied on by the Court in Lavallee, has been scathingly denounced:

> The battered woman syndrome illustrates all that is wrong with the law's use of science. The working hypothesis of the battered woman syndrome was first introduced in Lenore Walker's 1979 book, The Battered Woman. When it made its debut, this hypothesis had little more to support it beyond the clinical impressions of a single researcher. Five years later, Walker published a second book that promised a more thorough investigation of the hypothesis. However, this book contains little more than a patchwork of pseudo-scientific methods employed to confirm a hypothesis that its author and participating researchers never seriously doubted.

(Faigman and Wright, "The Battered Woman Syndrome in the Age of Science" (1997), 39 Arizona L. Rev. 67. See, further, Alan Gold's Netletter (ADGN/97-253 and ADGN/97-038). See, too, David Paciocco, *Getting Away with Murder; the Canadian Criminal Justice System* (Irwin Law, 1999), who dismisses the battered women's syndrome theory as "junk science" and little more than public interest advocacy dressed in the imposing garb of "study, experimentation and psychobabble" that imperils justice (p. 306).

R. v. PETEL

[1994] 1 S.C.R. 3, 26 C.R. (4th) 145, 87 C.C.C. (3d) 97

The accused was charged with the second degree murder of R. R and E were involved in drug-trafficking. E's girlfriend was the accused's daughter. The accused testified as to the terrible existence caused by E moving into her house and engaging in drug-trafficking from the house. She said he was always angry, threatened her frequently and beat her daughter. The accused moved to put an end to E's presence in her house but this was unsuccessful as E continued to go to her home to conduct his drug-trafficking operations. On the day in question E went to the accused's home with a revolver, cocaine and scales. He asked her to hide the weapon. He forced her to weigh some cocaine and suggested he would kill her, together with her daughter and granddaughter. Shortly after the daughter arrived with R. On the accused's testimony she consumed a small amount of drugs, got the weapon she had hidden in the bathroom, and fired at E who fell. Seeing that R was lunging at her she also fired at him. E survived but R died of his injuries. The accused admitted to police that she had fired at both E and R and that she wished both of them dead.

In his charge to the jury on self-defence the trial Judge identified the elements of the defence under s. 34(2) of the *Criminal Code*, emphasized that the jury had to base its decision on the accused's assessment of the situation and summarized the evidence. After the jury had begun its deliberations they returned with a question of whether self-defence concerned threats or acts over several months or only that evening. The trial Judge answered that the threat or act giving rise to self-defence had to occur on the evening of the crime and that the previous threats or acts were only relevant to assessing the assault that evening. The accused was convicted of second degree murder.

The Quebec Court of Appeal allowed the appeal and ordered a new trial. On further appeal the majority of the Supreme Court dismissed the appeal holding that the trial Judge had erred in answering the jury's question.

LAMER C.J. (SOPINKA, CORY, McLACHLIN and IACOBUCCI JJ. concurring):

. . . .

Issue

As this is an appeal as of right, the only issue before this Court is the one on which there was a dissent, namely whether the trial Judge erred in his answer to the jury's question in differentiating the threats made on the evening of the incident from the previous threats and in relating the latter only to whether there had been an assault.

. . . .

In a case involving self-defence, it is the accused's state of mind that must be examined, and it is the accused (and not the victim) who must be given the benefit of a reasonable doubt. The question that the jury must ask itself is therefore not "was the accused unlawfully assaulted?" but rather "did the accused reasonably believe, in the circumstances, that she was being unlawfully assaulted?".

Moreover, *Lavallee*, *supra*, rejected the rule requiring that the apprehended danger be imminent. This alleged rule, which does not appear anywhere in the text of the *Criminal Code*, is in fact only a mere assumption based on common sense. As Wilson J. noted in *Lavallee*, this assumption undoubtedly derives from the paradigmatic case of self-defence, which is an altercation between two persons of equal strength. However, evidence may be presented (in particular expert evidence) to rebut this presumption of fact. There is thus no formal requirement that the danger be imminent. Imminence is only one of the factors which the jury should weigh in determining whether the accused had a reasonable apprehension of danger and a reasonable belief that she could not extricate herself otherwise than by killing the attacker.

. . . .

The question asked by the jury was specific, as the jury had identified its concern: the threats made by the victim in the months preceding the incident and those made on the day itself and, it can be assumed, the distinction that should be made between the two types of threat or act. The question was general, however, in the sense that the jury did not indicate whether its concern related only to one element of self-defence. The question concerned the "definition of self-defence", without more detail. The Judge nonetheless limited his answer to only one of the elements, the existence of an assault and the assailant's ability to carry it out. This led him to make two errors.

First, the Judge's answer suggested that the only relevance of the threats prior to July 21 was in enabling the jury to determine whether there had actually been an assault on the evening of July 21, that is, in the present case, death threats, and whether the assailant was in a position to carry out those threats. In a way the Judge treated the earlier threats like similar fact evidence of the present threats. Their only use would then be to make it more plausible that Edsell also made threats in the minutes preceding the shots fired by the accused. This in my view diverted the jury from the question it really should have been considering, namely the reasonable belief of the accused in the existence of an assault. Emphasizing the victim's acts rather than the accused's state of mind has the effect of depriving the latter of the benefit of any error, however reasonable. The jury's attention should not be diverted from its proper concern, the guilt of the accused, by an inquiry into the guilt of the victim.

Secondly, and this is the crucial point, the Judge's answer might have led the jury to believe that the threats made before July 21 could serve no other purpose than to determine the existence of the assault and the assailant's ability, thus denying their relevance to reasonable apprehension of a danger of death or grievous bodily harm and to the belief that there was no solution but to kill the attacker. The Judge said that the previous threats served to [Translation] "assess the assault on the evening of July 21". He then explained what "assess the assault" meant:

> [Translation] . . . these previous acts or threats help you to determine whether Alain Raymond and Serge Edsell attempted or threatened . . . to apply force to Mrs. Pétel . . . whether the assailant had or caused . . . *the alleged victim to believe on reasonable grounds that he had present ability to effect his purpose.* [Emphasis added.]

The Judge was in fact here repeating almost exactly the wording of s. 265(1)(*b*) of the *Criminal Code*. Although it is true that the previous threats can help the jury to decide whether threats were made immediately before the respondent shot Edsell and Raymond, they are also very relevant in determining what the respondent believed, not only concerning the existence of the threats, but also concerning her apprehension of the risk of death and her belief in the need to use deadly force. By failing to mention these two elements in his answer, the trial Judge seriously limited the relevance of the earlier threats. In explaining how these threats could be used he should actually have referred not only to s. 265(1)(*b*) but also, most importantly, to s. 34(2) of the *Code*.

The importance of failing to relate the earlier threats to the elements of self-defence cannot be underestimated. The threats made by Edsell throughout his cohabitation with the respondent are very relevant in determining whether the respondent had a reasonable apprehension of danger and a reasonable belief in the need to kill Edsell and Raymond. The threats prior to July 21 form an integral part of the circumstances on which the perception of the accused might have been based. The Judge's answer to this question might thus have led the jury to disregard the entire atmosphere of terror which the respondent said pervaded her house. It is clear that the way in which a reasonable person would have acted cannot be assessed without taking into account these crucial circumstances. As Wilson J. noted in *Lavallee*, at p. 883:

> The issue is not, however, what an outsider would have reasonably perceived but what the accused reasonably perceived, given her situation and her experience.

By unduly limiting the relevance of the previous threats the Judge in a sense invited the jury to determine what an outsider would have done in the same situation as the respondent.

VI. Conclusion

The undisputed evidence that Edsell, her alleged attacker, handed over his weapon and asked his future victim to hide it, conduct that is odd to say the least for someone intending to kill, must have had a clear effect on the jury, indeed on any jury composed of reasonable individuals. In the Court of Appeal and in this Court, however, counsel for the Crown did not argue that, given the evidence in this case, no substantial wrong or miscarriage of justice occurred, and that s. 686(1)(*b*)(iii) of the *Criminal Code* should thus be applied. The Crown has the burden of showing that this provision is applicable: *Colpitts v. The Queen*, [1965] S.C.R. 739. This Court cannot apply it *proprio motu*. Having found an error of law in the Judge's answer to the question by the jury, I must accordingly dismiss the appeal and affirm the order for a new trial.

GONTHIER, J. (LA FOREST, L'HEUREUX-DUBÉ, and MAJOR JJ. concurring): — I have had the benefit of reading the reasons of the Chief Justice. I agree with his statement of the applicable principles of law and his explanation of those principles. However, I cannot concur in his reading of the answer given by the trial Judge to the question asked by the jury regarding previous threats or acts and the threats of the evening of July 21, 1989 as they affect the definition of self-defence. In my view the Judge's answer did not overlook the very important element of the accused's belief. In his answer to the jury the Judge clearly said:

> In other words, these previous acts or threats help you to determine whether Alain Raymond and Serge Edsell attempted or threatened . . . on the evening of July 21, by an act or a gesture, to apply force to Mrs. Pétel, to her daughter or to her granddaughter, whether the assailant had or caused the alleged victim to believe on reasonable grounds that he had present ability to effect his purpose.

It is true that the Judge did not elaborate on the accused's belief, nor did he elaborate on the elements of the definition of self-defence other than the relative importance of the previous threats and the threats at the time of the crime, which was all that the question asked by the jury dealt with.

However, he emphasized and pointed to each of the elements of this defence by three times re-reading s. 265(1)(*b*) of the *Criminal Code*, R.S.C., 1985, c. C-46. He could not have done this any better or any more succinctly and clearly. This re-reading, which he characterized as such, repeated his reading of the paragraph in his general charge the day before, which was immediately followed by clear and complete explanations of the essential criterion of the accused's state of mind at the time she caused the death, including her apprehension of death or grievous bodily harm from which she could not preserve herself except by the force she used.

There could be no doubt as to the "purpose" in question. Only one thing was discussed, the purpose to kill on the part of the victim. The belief on reasonable grounds that the victim had present ability to effect this purpose could mean nothing other than the accused's belief that the victim was capable of killing the accused, thus leaving her no alternative but to act first. With all due respect, I cannot conclude that the Judge's answer could have been understood by the jury or could have led it to make a finding other than on the basis of a reasonable belief by the accused in a danger of death which she could not avoid except by killing her attacker. In my opinion, the Judge's answer contained no error and was adequate.

I would therefore allow the appeal. I would set aside the Court of Appeal's judgment and restore the guilty verdict.

Is *Petel* inconsistent with *Creighton*?

R. v. MALOTT

[1998] 1 S.C.R. 123, 121 C.C.C. (3d) 456

The accused was charged with murder. The accused and the deceased had lived as common law spouses for almost 20 years. The deceased abused the accused physically, sexually, psychologically and emotionally. On the day of the shooting the accused was scheduled to go to a medical centre with the deceased to get prescription drugs for use in his illegal drug trade. She took a pistol from the deceased's gun cabinet. After driving to the medical centre she shot him to death. She then took a taxi to the deceased's girlfriend's home, shot her and stabbed her with a knife.

At trial, the accused testified to the extensive abuse which she had suffered and led expert evidence to show that she suffered from battered woman syndrome.

The jury found her guilty of second degree murder in the death of the deceased and of attempted murder of his girlfriend. The majority of the Court of Appeal affirmed the convictions. There was no air of reality to the defence of self-defence as it related to the charge of attempted murder. With respect to the deceased, the jury was clearly instructed that the perception of the accused developed against the background of her abuse, was required to be assessed in determining if her actions were reasonable self-defence. The accused appealed, complaining about the adequacy of the trial judge's charge to the jury on the murder charge on the issue of battered woman syndrome as a defence.

The Supreme Court was unanimous in dismissing the appeal on the basis that the trial judge's charge on self-defence and the evidence of abuse while not perfect was adequate. There was a noteworthy *obiter* by the two female members of the Court.

L'HEUREUX-DUBÉ J. (McLACHLIN J. concurring): —

. . . [G]iven that this Court has not had the opportunity to discuss the value of evidence of "battered woman syndrome" since *R. v. Lavallee*, [1990] 1 S.C.R. 852 (S.C.C.), and given the evolving discourse on "battered woman syndrome" in the legal community, I will make a few comments on the importance of this kind of evidence to the just adjudication of charges involving battered women.

First, the significance of this Court's decision in *Lavallee*, which first accepted the need for expert evidence on the effects of abusive relationships in order to properly understand the context in which an accused woman had killed her abusive spouse in self-defence, reaches beyond its particular impact on the law of self-defence. A crucial implication of the admissibility of expert evidence in *Lavallee* is the legal recognition that historically both the law and society may have treated women in general, and battered women in particular, unfairly. *Lavallee* accepted that the myths and stereotypes which are the products and the tools of this unfair treatment interfere with the capacity of judges and juries to justly determine a battered woman's claim of self-defence, and can only be dispelled by expert evidence designed to overcome the stereotypical thinking.

The expert evidence is admissible, and necessary, in order to understand the reasonableness of a battered woman's perceptions, which in *Lavallee* were the accused's perceptions that she had to act with deadly force in order to preserve herself from death or grievous bodily harm. Accordingly, the utility of such evidence in criminal cases is not limited to instances where a battered woman is pleading self-defence, but is potentially relevant to other situations where the reasonableness of a battered woman's actions or perceptions is at issue (e.g. provocation, duress or necessity). See *R. v. Hibbert*, [1995] 2 S.C.R. 973 (S.C.C.), at p. 1021.

It is clear from the foregoing that "battered woman syndrome" is not a legal defence in itself such that an accused woman need only establish that she is suffering from the syndrome in order to gain an acquittal. As Wilson J. commented in *Lavallee*, at p. 890: "Obviously the fact that the appellant was a battered woman does not entitle her to an acquittal. Battered women may well kill their partners other than in self-defence." Rather, "battered woman syndrome" is a psychiatric explanation of the mental state of women who have been subjected to continuous battering by their male intimate partners, which can be relevant to the legal inquiry into a battered woman's state of mind. Second, the majority of the Court in *Lavallee* also implicitly accepted that women's experiences and perspectives may be different from the experiences and perspectives of men. It accepted that a woman's perception of what is reasonable is influenced by her gender, as well as by her individual experience, and both are relevant to the legal inquiry. This legal development was significant, because it demonstrated a willingness to look at the whole context of a woman's experience in order to inform the analysis of the particular events. But it is wrong to think of this development of the law as merely an example where an objective test — the requirement that an accused claiming self-defence must *reasonably* apprehend death or grievous bodily harm — has been modified to admit evidence of the subjective perceptions of a battered woman. More important, a majority of the Court accepted that the perspectives of women, which have historically been ignored, must now equally inform the "objective" standard of the reasonable person in relation to self-defence.

When interpreting and applying *Lavallee*, these broader principles should be kept in mind. In particular, they should be kept in mind in order to avoid a too rigid and restrictive approach to the admissibility and legal value of evidence of a battered woman's experiences. Concerns have been expressed that the treatment of expert evidence on battered women syndrome, which is itself admissible in order to combat the myths and stereotypes which society has about battered women, has led to a new stereotype of the "battered woman": see, e.g., Martha Shaffer, "The battered woman syndrome revisited: Some complicating thoughts five years after *R. v. Lavallee*" (1997), 47 U.T.L.J. 1, at p. 9; Sheila Noonan, "Strategies of Survival: Moving Beyond the Battered Woman Syndrome", in Ellen Adelberg and Claudia Currie, eds., *In Conflict with the Law: Women and the Canadian Justice System* (1993), 247, at p. 254; Isabel Grant, "The 'syndromization' of women's experience", in Donna Martinson, et al., "A Forum on *Lavallee v. R.*: Women and Self-Defence" (1991), 25 U.B.C.L. Rev. 23, at pp. 53-54; and Martha R. Mahoney, "Legal Images of Battered

Women: Redefining the Issue of Separation" (1991), 90 Mich. L. Rev. 1, at p. 42.

It is possible that those women who are unable to fit themselves within the stereotype of a victimized, passive, helpless, dependent, battered woman will not have their claims to self-defence fairly decided. For instance, women who have demonstrated too much strength or initiative, women of colour, women who are professionals, or women who might have fought back against their abusers on previous occasions, should not be penalized for failing to accord with the stereotypical image of the archetypal battered woman. See, e.g., Julie Stubbs and Julia Tolmie, "Race, Gender, and the Battered Woman Syndrome: An Australia Case Study" (1995), 8 C.J.W.L. 122. Needless to say, women with these characteristics are still entitled to have their claims of self-defence fairly adjudicated, and they are also still entitled to have their experiences as battered women inform the analysis. Professor Grant, *supra*, at p. 52, warns against allowing the law to develop such that a woman accused of killing her abuser must either have been "reasonable 'like a man' or reasonable 'like a battered woman'". I agree that this must be avoided. The "reasonable woman" must not be forgotten in the analysis, and deserves to be as much a part of the objective standard of the reasonable person as does the "reasonable man".

How should the courts combat the "syndromization", as Professor Grant refers to it, of battered women who act in self-defence? The legal inquiry into the moral culpability of a woman who is, for instance, claiming self-defence must focus on the *reasonableness* of her actions in the context of her personal experiences, and her experiences as a woman, not on her status as a battered woman and her entitlement to claim that she is suffering from "battered woman syndrome". This point has been made convincingly by many academics reviewing the relevant cases: see, e.g., Wendy Chan, "A Feminist Critique of Self-Defense and Provocation in Battered Women's Cases in England and Wales" (1994), 6 Women & Crim. Just. 39, at pp. 56-57; Elizabeth M. Schneider, "Describing and Changing: Women's Self-Defense Work and the Problem of Expert Testimony on Battering" (1992), 14 Women's Rts. L. Rep. 213, at pp. 216-17; and Marilyn MacCrimmon, "The social construction of reality and the rules of evidence", in Donna Martinson et al., *supra*, at pp. 48-49. By emphasizing a woman's "learned helplessness", her dependence, her victimization, and her low self-esteem, in order to establish that she suffers from "battered woman syndrome", the legal debate shifts from the objective rationality of her actions to preserve her own life to those personal inadequacies which apparently explain her failure to flee from her abuser. Such an emphasis comports too well with society's stereotypes about women. Therefore, it should be scrupulously avoided because it only serves to undermine the important advancements achieved by the decision in *Lavallee*.

There are other elements of a woman's social context which help to explain her inability to leave her abuser, and which do not focus on those characteristics most consistent with traditional stereotypes. As Wilson J. herself recognized in *Lavallee*, at p. 887, "environmental factors may also impair the woman's ability to leave — lack of job skills, the presence of children to care for, fear of retaliation by the man, etc. may each have a role to play in some cases." To this list of factors I would add a woman's need to protect her children from abuse, a fear of losing custody of her children, pressures to keep the family together, weaknesses of social and financial support for battered women, and no guarantee that the violence would cease simply because she left. These considerations necessarily inform the reasonableness of a woman's beliefs or perceptions of, for instance, her lack of an alternative to the use of deadly force to preserve herself from death or grievous bodily harm.

How should these principles be given practical effect in the context of a jury trial of a woman accused of murdering her abuser? To fully accord with the spirit of *Lavallee*, where the reasonableness of a battered woman's belief is at issue in a criminal case, a judge and jury should be made to appreciate that a battered woman's experiences are both individualized, based on her own history and relationships, as well as shared with other women, within the context of a society and a legal system which has historically undervalued women's experiences. A judge and jury should be told that a battered woman's experiences are generally outside the common understanding of the average judge and juror, and that they should seek to understand the evidence being presented to them in order to overcome the myths and stereotypes which we all share. Finally, all of this should be presented in such a way as to focus on the reasonableness of the woman's actions, without relying on old or new stereotypes about battered women.

My focus on women as the victims of battering and as the subjects of "battered woman syndrome" is not intended to exclude from consideration those men who find themselves in abusive relationships. However, the reality of our society is that typically, it is women who are the victims of domestic violence, at the hands of their male intimate partners. To assume that men who are victims of spousal abuse are affected by the abuse in the same way, without benefit of the research and expert opinion evidence which has informed the courts of the existence and details of "battered woman syndrome", would be imprudent.

For strong criticism of the concepts of battered woman syndrome and learned helplessness see Paciocco, *Getting Away With Murder; the Canadian Criminal Justice System* (1999), pp. 297-312.

The accused and his co-accused were inmates in a penitentiary. There had been considerable tension between the accused and a group of other inmates. The group had made threats that the accused took seriously. Fearing for his safety and anticipating an attack, the accused armed himself with knuckledusters and a stick. The co-accused got a knife. When one of the group members walked by, the accused hit him on the head repeatedly with the knuckledusters, while the co-accused stabbed him in the stomach. The injuries were fatal. The accused and co-accused were charged with first degree murder. In his charge to the jury the trial judge stated that the accused and the co-accused could not claim the defence of self-defence under s. 34(2) unless they believed that they were in imminent danger of death or serious bodily harm from the victim at the time they attacked him. The jury convicted the accused of manslaughter and the co-accused of second degree murder. On appeal the accused argued that the trial judge erred in his direction on s. 34(2). They argued they suffered from "prison environment syndrome" which was analogous to battered wife

syndrome in that they lived in an environment in which inmates had to "kill or be killed". Should there be a new trial to consider such a defence? Should it succeed?

Compare *R. v. McConnell* (1996), 48 C.R. (4th) 199, [1996] 1 S.C.R. 1075 and see annotation by Christine Boyle (1996), 48 C.R. (4th) 200.

Defence of Property

See sections 38-42 of the *Criminal Code.*

R. v. TAYLOR

(1970), 73 W.W.R. 636 (Y.T. Mag. Ct.)

VARCOE P.M. (orally): — The accused Frederick Allison Taylor is charged that on or about December 25, 1969, at or near Whitehorse in the Yukon Territory, without lawful excuse he did unlawfully use a firearm in a manner that was dangerous to the safety of other persons contrary to sec. 86(*b*) (substituted 1968-69, ch. 38) of the *Criminal Code*, 1953-54, ch. 51.

On December 26, 1969, Cst. Mosicki arrived at the Taylor residence at about 2:52 a.m. Upon entering the small one-roomed house, 15 feet, three inches by eight feet, seven inches, he saw Joseph John Jack sitting in an awkward position with one hand on his leg. The accused came to the officer and gave him a rifle and one empty cartridge, saying he just used it to defend himself as he had had three breakings and enterings in his house in the last month. In the room were located two beds, one used by the accused, the other used by his common-law wife and child. The accused had been drinking but was not intoxicated and was co-operative with the police officers. The Taylor residence is located at the north end of the Indian village area. The police officer stated the police received quite a number of complaints from the area.

Joseph John Jack stated that he and Joseph Paul Jack left the Edith Kane house and went next door to the Taylor residence about 2:30 a.m. to get two chairs lent by Kane to Taylor, and states he knocked on the door, it opened and someone then said, "Come in." He further states that the lights went on just before the door opened and he went inside. Accordingly to Jack, Taylor was sitting on the bed in the house and immediately reached for his rifle located near the end of the bed. He says Taylor pointed the gun at him and Jack reached out and pushed the gun down towards the floor and at the same time it went off, hitting him in the right leg below the right knee on the inside of the leg. Jack claims before he was shot he asked Taylor for the chairs "borrowed from Edith". After he shot Jack, Taylor told him to get out.

Joseph Paul Jack gave evidence how he followed Joseph John Jack into the house after knocking on the door approximately five times. His evidence is similar to the other witness except he says he heard no conversation except Taylor saying, "Get out" after the shot. He said Taylor was told about the purpose of the visit after the shot.

The accused gave evidence and confirmed that he borrowed a chair, but only one, from his neighbour Edith Kane. He said he went to bed about 12:30 a.m. on the date in question with his rifle at the head of the bed and a cartridge nearby. His common-law wife and young son were in the other bed. When he went to bed the door was not locked. He states he next recalls the door opening and he hollered, "Get out," and he then switched the lights on in the house. He claims to be a light sleeper and heard no knock prior to the door opening. At this point of time he saw a man whom he did not recognize coming through the door and another behind him. He said, "Get out," again and reached over, grabbed the rifle and loaded it. The person he saw coming through the door kept coming and made no reply. He pointed the gun to the floor, at which time Jack made a movement towards him, either to grab Taylor or his rifle. At this moment Taylor shot into the floor as a warning shot but Jack was too close and the bullet went into his leg. He states that at this time Jack was one-and-a-half feet from his bed. He emphasized that his intention in shooting was just a warning to Jack to get out of his house. In evidence he said, "I didn't know for sure what was going to happen." After the shot he states two women from the neighbouring residence came over and told him he had shot their uncle and he only wanted the chair. Taylor stated this was the first time he ever heard any mention of a chair. Taylor stated further he had met Jack on only one previous occasion, at a time when he and Jack had been in an argument. He describes the area in which he lives as a rough district. The police officer stated in his evidence that when he returned to the Taylor residence after taking the injured Jack to hospital and Taylor and his common-law wife to the detachment it was evident the house had been broken into. The officer also stated that Jack, the injured person, appeared to have been drinking.

Under sec. 86 of the *Criminal Code* the charge includes the ingredient, "without lawful excuse". The provisions of s. 41 of the *Criminal Code* appear to suggest that it is the use being made of the weapon at the time of the event that has to be considered in determining whether it was unlawful. Section 41 reads as follows:

> 41. (1) Every one who is in peaceable possession of a dwelling house or real property and every one lawfully assisting him or acting under his authority is justified in using force to prevent any person from trespassing on the dwelling house or real property, or to remove a trespasser therefrom, if he uses no more force than is necessary.

In the case at bar, in my opinion, I should now consider whether the use being made of the rifle at the time was lawful. If I come to the conclusion that the accused was justified, in self defence or defence of his property, in firing the rifle into the floor and pointing it at Jack to keep him from attacking him or removing him from the premises, or that the shot that injured Jack was accidental, then may I acquit the accused. The accused is not bound to put forth an explanation. There does not appear to be a general rule of law that when facts are peculiarly within the knowledge of the accused, the burden is on him to establish a defence based on these facts: See *Reg. v. Spurge*, [1961] 2 Q.B. 205, at 212-213. The Crown must establish absence of consent in charges of rape or assault and in my opinion the burden of proving lack of lawful excuse in the case at bar also is borne by the Crown: *Abrath v. N. East. Ry.* (1883), 11 Q.B.D. 440, at 457, 458. See also *Attygalle v. Reg.*, [1936] A.C. 338, and *Seneviratne v. Reg.*, [1936] 3 AII E.R. 36. At no time, during the trial is the onus on the accused to establish lawful excuse. This onus does not shift but is continually on the Crown. In the case before us the accused did come forth and in evidence give an explanation. If the explanation given by him might be true in the light of all the evidence, and thereby, raise a reasonable doubt, as to the question of lawful excuse, then the accused is entitled to the benefit of this doubt and the charge should then be dismissed.

In *Rex v. Yuman* (1910), 22 O.L.R, 500, at 504, 17 C.C.C. 474 (C.A.) Moss C.J.O. said:

> The question of lawful excuse is to be determined upon all the facts and circumstances, the onus being upon the Crown.

The evidence indicates the accused was on his bed when Joseph John Jack entered his home. I accept the evidence of Joseph Paul Jack that Taylor at this time did not say "Come in", and that Joseph John Jack, followed by Joseph Paul Jack, entered the home uninvited and were in fact trespassers.

In *Reg. v. Antley*, [1964] 2 C.C.C. 142, 42 C.R. 384 (C.A.), it was stated that a person need not wait until he has first been struck by an attacker before he strikes, and when a person is on his own property he is entitled to use as much force as is necessary to eject a trespasser. The property owner may not use more force than is reasonably necessary but if he fails to measure with nicety the degree of force necessary he will not be convicted: See *Rex v. Ogal* (1928), 50 C.C.C. 71 (App. Div.).

In *Reg. v. Preston* (1953), 17 C.R. 20, 106 C.C.C. 135 (B.C. C.A.), Bird J.A. says at p. 24:

> The question as to whether or not excessive force is used, I think, must be determined pursuant to s. 53(2) with regard to the state of mind of the person at the time the force is applied by him.
>
> In *Rex v. Ogal* [*supra*], it was held that where the means of defence is not disproportionate to the severity of the assault, the plea (of self-defence) is valid, though the prisoner fails to measure with nicety the degree of force necessary to ward off the attack. At p. 467 Hyndman J.A., speaking for the Court, said:
>
> "If defendant reasonably believed he was in danger . . . then he was justified in using such force as he thought necessary to defend himself and ward off such danger."
>
> Again in *Rex v. Philbrook*, [1941] O.R. 352, at 359, 77 C.C.C. 26, Robertson C.J.O. discussed the elements which will justify the use of force in self-defence in these terms:
>
> "The prisoner was entitled to acquittal if, upon all the evidence, there was reasonable doubt whether or not the blow was delivered under reasonable apprehension of death or grievous bodily harm, and if he believed on reasonable grounds that he could not otherwise preserve himself from death or grievous bodily harm."
>
> In *Latour v. Reg.*, [1951] S.C.R. 19, at 27, 11 C.R 19, at 11, 98 C.C.C. 258, Fauteux J., speaking for the Supreme Court of Canada, said on the same subject:

"Once properly instructed as to what the law recognizes as ingredients of self-defence . . .
the accurate question for the jury is . . . *whether the evidence indicates them*. And they, then,
must be directed that, should they find affirmatively or be left in doubt on the question put to
them, the accused is entitled, in the case of self-defence, to a complete acquittal."

The question of whether excess force beyond what was required was used
is not to be considered objectively, but must be determined according to the state
of mind of the accused at the time. Under such circumstances the issue is not,
did he use more force than in fact was necessary, but did he use more force than
he on reasonable ground believed necessary. The accused lived in a very small
house with his common-law wife and child located in an area described as a
"rough" locality. Two persons entered his home at an early hour of the morning
unannounced and uninvited. They were told to leave but continued to approach
the accused while he was on his bed. In his evidence the accused stated he shot
the rifle, pointing it at the floor for the purpose of encouraging Jack to leave the
premises. He stated how Jack made a motion towards him either to grab him or
the gun, and finally stated, "I didn't know for sure what was going to happen."
There is nothing in the evidence of Taylor or his demeanour on the stand to
indicate his evidence should not be accepted. Undoubtedly the event occurred
suddenly and quickly in the early hours of the morning. I therefore find that on
the basis of the evidence there is a reasonable doubt as to the guilt of the accused
and I therefore dismiss the charge.

R. v. BAXTER

(1975), 33 C.R.N.S. 22 at 40-3, 27 C.C.C. (2d) 96 (Ont. C.A.)

MARTIN J.A.: —

. . . .

The grounds of appeal based upon the Judge's charge with respect to the use of
force to remove a trespasser may be conveniently dealt with together.

Counsel for the appellant contended that the trial Judge erred in instructing
the jury that killing or causing grievous bodily harm to a trespasser was not
justifiable unless the circumstances were such as to give rise to the defence of
self-defence under s. 34(2) of the *Code*, and should have left with the jury, as a
separate defence, the provisions of s. 4.1(1) of the *Code* authorizing the use of
force to prevent any person from trespassing on a dwelling house or real
property if he uses no more force than is necessary.

. . . .

Complaint is also made with respect to the following instruction to the jury
by the trial Judge. The learned trial Judge, after reading s. 41 of the *Code* to the
jury, said:

So that in the circumstances here, one, if you are satisfied that either generally or on this occasion the people who were hurt had been ordered from the property then, and were still on it, not getting off it, then they were trespassers if they did not get off when they were asked to get off; if you find that in the evidence, then that was an assault, but the difficulty about that assault under s. 34(2) that I have read to you is that it is very hard to say that; that assault deemed to be such under s. 41(2) of the *Criminal Code* is a violent assault.

The sections of the *Code* authorizing the use of force in defence of a person or property, to prevent crime, and to apprehend offenders, in general, express in greater detail the great principle of the common-law that the use of force in such circumstances is subject to the restriction that the force used is necessary; that is, that the harm sought to be prevented could not be prevented by less violent means and that the injury or harm done by, or which might reasonably be anticipated from the force used, is not disproportioned to the injury or harm it is intended to prevent: see Report of Criminal Code Bill Commission, 1879, referred to in Russell, at p. 432.

Mr. Cooper referred the Court to authorities holding that the use of firearms is justified, even though death ensues, in order to prevent burglary or arson: see 1 Hale P.C. 487. The common law cast a special protection around the dwelling. In such cases there is, of course, an element of personal danger which may justify the use even of extreme force in self-defence. Moreover, s. 27 of the *Criminal Code* authorizes the use of as much force as is reasonably necessary to prevent the commission of any offence, for which the offender may be arrested without warrant, and that would be likely to cause immediate and serious injury to the person or property of anyone or to prevent anything being done that, on reasonable and probable grounds, the person using such force believes would, if it were done, constitute such an offence.

The sections of the *Code* authorizing the use of force in defence of a person or property or to prevent the commission of certain serious crimes overlap, and the use of force in particular circumstances may be justified under more than one section. There was, however, in this case no evidence of a reasonable apprehension on the part of the appellant of serious injury to the property of anyone, and his right to use force to prevent reasonably apprehended serious injury to himself was dealt with under self-defence. I should also add that the trial Judge was not requested to charge the jury with respect to s. 27.

. . . .

Firing at a mere trespasser is, of course, not justifiable, and the trial Judge in the circumstances of this case correctly charged the jury that killing or causing grievous bodily harm to a trespasser could only be justified in self-defence: *Rex v. Meade and Belt* (1823), 1 Lew. C.C. 184; *Rex v. Scully* (1824), 1 Car & P. 319; *Regina v. McKay*, [1957] V.R. 560; Lanham, supra.

I now turn to the ground of appeal relating to the Judge's charge with respect to s. 41(2). Under s. 41(2) a trespasser who resists an attempt by a person in peaceable possession of a dwelling house or real property to prevent his entry or to remove him is deemed to commit an assault without justification or provocation.

The meaning of this subsection is not entirely clear. I am disposed to think that its effect is not to convert mere passive resistance into an assault but merely to provide that if any *force* is used by the wrongdoer in resisting an attempt to prevent his entry or to remove him, such force is unlawful, and hence an assault. The amount of force that may be used to prevent or defend against any assault actually committed by the wrongdoer depends upon the ordinary principles of self-defence as set out in s. 34 of the *Code*. So regarded, s. 41(2) does not alter the common law as stated by Stephen H.C.L., vol. III, p. 15, who says:

> For instance, he may put a trespasser out of his house, or out of his field by force, but he may not strike him, still less may he shoot or stab him. If the wrongdoer resists, the person who is on the defensive may overcome his resistance, and may proportion his efforts to the violence which the wrongdoer uses. If the wrongdoer assaults the person who is defending his property, that person is in the position of a man wrongfully assaulted, and may use whatever violence may become necessary for the protection of his person.

In *Pockett v. Pool* (1896), 11 Man. R. 275 (C.A.), after referring to s. 53 of the then *Code* (now s. 41), Killam J. said at p. 286:

> The latter part of the section does not, in my opinion, apply until there is an overt act in the direction of prevention or removal and an overt act in resistance. . . . Similarly, in the present case, if the defendant had used force to remove the plaintiff and the latter had merely remained passive and allowed himself to be pushed or dragged out of the field, there would have been no assault.

R. v. SPENCER

(1977), 38 C.C.C. (2d) 303 (B.C. S.C.)

BERGER J.: — This is an appeal by way of stated case from a conviction for assault under s. 41 of the *Criminal Code*.

Section 41 of the *Criminal Code* provides:

> 4(1) Every one who is in peaceable possession of a dwelling-house or real property and every one lawfully assisting him or acting under his authority is justified in using force to prevent any person from trespassing on the dwelling-house or real property, or to remove a trespasser therefrom, if he uses no more force than is necessary.
> (2) A trespasser who resists an attempt by a person who is in peaceable possession of a dwelling-house or real property or a person lawfully assisting him or acting under his authority to prevent his entry or to remove him, shall be deemed to commit an assault without justification or provocation.

Wagenaar, a tenant in an apartment building, sought to remove the accused Spencer from the common hallway of the building. She resisted. The Judge found her guilty of assault under s. 41(2). The question that arises on this appeal is whether a tenant in an apartment building can be said to be in peaceable possession of the common hallway of the building. If Wagenaar was not in peaceable possession of the hallway, the accused's resistance did not make her guilty of assault.

There is no question that the tenant is entitled to possession of his own suite. He has the right to remove a trespasser from his suite. But does he have the right to remove a trespasser from the building who is found in one of the common hallways?

The stated case says Spencer was a trespasser. So no issue arises as to whether she had any right to be there. She did not. No argument that the common hallway was a public place can be advanced here. But if the hallway is a private place, that is not the end of the matter. The question still remains, who is in possession?

The landlord would have the right to possession of the hallway. The building manager would have the right to possession because he would be acting under the authority, express or implied, of the landlord. But in the case at bar, Wagenaar was not acting under the authority of the landlord or the building manager. So the question is, did he, as a tenant, have a right to peaceable possession of the hallway?

The point does not appear to have come up before. But it can, I think, be answered simply: the landlord did not lease the common hallway to his tenant. The landlord did not grant possession of the common hallway to his tenant. No authority has been advanced to support the notion that the tenant can be said to be in possession of premises that were not rented to him. The authorities tend to be inconsistent with such a proposition.

The tenant of an apartment building has a right to use the common hallway, as a right appurtenant to his occupation: *Wallich v. Great West Construction Co.* (1914), 20 D.L.R. 553 (Man. K.B.). But this is not possession. The assumption is made in Halsbury that the landlord retains the common part of the building in his possession and control: 23 Hals., 3rd ed., p. 488. Williams on *Landlord and Tenant*, 4th ed., dealing with a landlord's duty to repair, makes the same assumption (see pp. 384-5).

In *R. v. Peters* (1971), 2 C.C.C. (2d) 336, the case turned on the question whether demonstrators in a shopping plaza became trespassers in law when the owner withdrew from them the invitation extended to the public to enter the plaza. Gale C.J.O., speaking for the Ontario Court of Appeal, said, at p. 338:

> In addition, it is also our view with respect to trespass that possession [by the owner] does not cease to be exclusive so long as there is the right to control entry of the general public, and here the owner had not relinquished that right of control.

The Supreme Court of Canada upheld *R. v. Peters* in *Harrison v. Carswell*, 25 C.C.C. (2d) 186, [1976] 2 S.C.R. 200. They held that the owner of a shopping centre has sufficient possession or control to invoke the remedy of trespass.

It is useful to examine the provisions of the *Strata Titles Act*, 1974 (B.C.), c. 89. It is in conformity with similar statutes in other provinces. Section 8 of the Act provides that the common property shall be held by the owners of apartments as tenants-in-common. It seems to me in such a case each of the owners would be in peaceable possession (though not exclusive possession) of the common hallway of an apartment block. But this is provided for by statute. If an owner of an apartment cannot assert such a right apart from the statute, then

I do not see how a tenant can. Thus the removal of trespassers is a matter for the landlord or the police.

I hold that a tenant of a suite in an apartment building is not, by virtue of his tenancy, in peaceable possession of the common hallway. Wagenaar had no right to seek to evict the accused. So her resistance did not constitute an assault on Wagenaar.

This Court has the power, under s. 768(i)(*a*), to reverse the conviction made below. The conviction is reversed.

Appeal allowed.

Partial Defence to Murder

Under section 232 of the *Criminal Code*, provocation as there defined is a partial defence to a murder charge in that it reduces it to a conviction of manslaughter.

R. v. HILL

(1985), [1986] 1 S.C.R. 313, 51 C.R. (3d) 97, 25 C.C.C. (3d) 322

DICKSON C.J.C. (BEETZ, ESTEY, CHOUINARD and LA FOREST JJ. concurring): — Gordon James Elmer Hill was charged with committing first degree murder at the city of Belleville, county of Hastings, on the person of Verne Pegg, contrary to s. 218(1) [now s. 235] of the *Criminal Code*, R.S.C. 1970, c. C-34. He was found by the jury not guilty of first degree murder but guilty of second degree murder. He was sentenced to imprisonment for life without eligiblity for parole until ten years of his sentence had been served.

Hill appealed his conviction to the Court of Appeal of Ontario [32 C.R. (3d) 88, 2 C.C.C. (3d) 394]. He raised many grounds of appeal, but the Court of Appeal called upon the Crown with respect to one ground only, relating to the charge on the issue of provoction. The ground of appeal was that the trial Judge failed to instruct the jury properly as to the "ordinary person" in s. 215(2) of the *Criminal Code*. Section 215 of the *Code* reads in part:

> 215.(1) Culpable homicide that otherwise would be murder may be reduced to manslaughter if the person who committed it did so in the heat of passion caused by sudden provoction.

> (2) A wrongful act or insult that is of such a nature as to be sufficient to deprive an ordinary person of the power of self-control is provocation for the purposes of this section if the accused acted upon it on the sudden and before there was time for his passion to cool.

These two subsections, given their plain meaning, produce three sequential questions for answer by the tribunal:

1. Would an ordinary person be deprived of self-control by the act or insult?

2. Did the accused in fact act in response to those "provocative" acts; in short, was he or she provoked by them whether or not an ordinary person would have been?

3. Was the accused's response sudden and before there was time for his or her passion to cool?

At this stage it is important to recall the presence of subs. (3) of s. 215, which provides:

> (3) For the purposes of this section the questions
>
> (a) whether a particular wrongful act or insult amounted to provocation, and
>
> (b) whether the accused was deprived of the power of self-control by the provocation that he alleges he received.
>
> are questions of fact . . .

In the answering of these successive questions, the first, or "ordinary person", test is clearly determined by objective standards. The second, *de facto*, test, as to the loss of self-control by the accused, is determined, like any other question of fact as revealed by the evidence, from the surrounding facts. The third test, as to whether the response was sudden and before passions cooled, is again a question of fact.

At the time of the killing. Hill was a male 16 years of age. The narrow question in this appeal is whether the trial Judge erred in law in failing to instruct the jury that if they found a wrongful act or insult they should consider whether it was sufficient to deprive an ordinary person "of the age and sex of the appellant" of his power of self-control. Was it incumbent in law on the trial Judge to add that gloss to the section? That is the issue.

I. THE FACTS

At trial both parties agreed that it was the acts of Hill which caused the death of Pegg, but disagreed otherwise. The position of the Crown at trial was that Hill and Pegg were homosexual lovers and that Hill had decided to murder Pegg after a falling out between them. The Crown argued that Hill deliberately struck Pegg in the head while Pegg lay in bed. This did not kill Pegg, who immediately ran from the bedroom into the bathroom to try and stop the flow of blood from his head. Realizing that he had been unsuccessful, Hill took two knives from the kitchen and stabbed Pegg to death.

Hill's version of the events was very different. He admitted to causing the death of Pegg, but put forward two defences: self-defence and provocation. Hill testified that he had known Pegg for about a year through the latter's involvement with the "Big Brother" organization. Hill stated that on the night in question he had been the subject of unexpected and unwelcome homosexual advances by Pegg while asleep on the couch in Pegg's apartment. Pegg pursued Hill to the bathroom and grabbed him, at which time Hill picked up a nearby hatchet and swung it at Pegg in an attempt to scare him. The hatchet struck Pegg in the head. Hill then ran from the apartment but returned shortly afterward. Upon re-entering the apartment, he was confronted by Pegg, who threatened to kill him. At this point. Hill obtained two knives from the kitchen and stabbed Pegg to death.

Hill was arrested, after a car chase with the police, at the wheel of a Pontiac automobile owned by Pegg. At the scene of arrest Hill denied knowing Pegg, but later he made a statement to the police which was substantially similar to his oral testimony at trial.

II. THE CHARGE

The trial Judge instructed the jury on the defence of provocation in the following terms:

> The *Criminal Code* provides that culpable homicide that would otherwise be murder shall be reduced to manslaughter if the person who committed it did so in the heat of passion caused by sudden provocation.

> Under the *Code*, a wrongful act or insult that is of such a nature as to be sufficient to deprive an ordinary person of the power of self-control is provocation, if the accused acted upon it on the sudden and before there was time for his passion to cool.

The foregoing paragraphs are simply a recital of the *Code*. The Judge continued [quoted at p. 90]:

> Provocation may come from actual words or a series of each or a combination of both, and it must be looked at in the light of all the surrounding circumstances.

> First, the actual words must be such as would deprive an ordinary person of self-control. In considering this part of the defence you are not to consider the particular mental make-up of the accused; rather the standard is that of the ordinary person. You will ask yourselves: Would the words or acts in this case have caused an ordinary person to lose his self-control?

After reviewing the evidence in support of the defence of provocation, the Judge continued [quoted in part at p. 90]:

> You will consider that evidence and you will decide whether the words and acts were sufficient to cause an ordinary person to lose his self-control.

> The acts were rubbing the accused's legs and chest, grabbing him by the shoulder and spinning him around, and later Pegg grabbing his right wrist before the second stab. The words were: "I am going to kill you, you little bastard."

> If you find that they were, you will then secondly consider whether the accused acted on the provocation on the sudden before there was time for his passion to cool. In deciding this

question you are not restricted to the standard of the ordnary person. You will take into account the mental, the emotional the physical characteristics and the age of the accused.

The incidents or the words upon which the provocation is based must be contemporaneous words or closely related to the tragedy. The killing must take place immediately after the acts or words constituting the provocation or so soon thereafter that the accused's passion had not time to cool.

You will also ask yourselves: Was the provocation such that it would have led a person with the mental and physical condition and the age of the accused to respond in this way?

At trial, counsel for Hill objected to the instruction of the trial Judge as to the objective requirement of the defence of provocation, submitting that the "ordinary person" referred to in s. 215(2) ought to have been defined as an ordinary person of the age and sex of the accused. Counsel submitted that the objective requirement would be satisfied if the Judge were to recharge the jury by defining "ordinary person" as an "ordinary person in the circumstances of the accused". The Judge refused to recharge the jury in those terms.

III. THE COURT OF APPEAL

In oral reasons Brooke J.A. (Martin and Morden JJ.A. concurring) noted that counsel for the defence, relying on *R. v. Camplin* (1978), 67 Cr. App. R. 14 (H.L.), submitted that the Judge should have instructed the jury to consider whether the wrongful act or insult was sufficient to deprive an "ordinary person" of the age and sex of the accused of his power of self-control. The Court of Appeal held that because the trial Judge declined to do so he erred. In reaching this conclusion, Brooke J.A. stated [at p. 90]:

The age and sex of the appellant are not "peculiar characteristics" excluded from consideration of the "ordinary person" in the objective test in s. 215(2): see Fauteux J. (as he then was) in *Wright v. R.*, [1969] S.C.R. 335, [1969] 3 C.C.C. 258 at 264-65, discussing *Bedder v. D.P.P.*, [1954] 1 W.L.R. 1119 (H.L.).

He also added [at pp. 90-91]:

In our respectful opinion, there is nothing in that judgment which precludes charging the jury as the defence requested. As the matter was left to the jury, the age of the appellant was a consideration only if and when the jury turned to the question of whether the wrongful act or insult deprived him of his power of self-control. The effect of the charge was that an ordinary person did not include a 16-year-old youth. If this is so, the jury may have rejected the defence judging the objective test on that basis.

In the result, the Court of Appeal held that the Judge was in error and there may well have been misdirection which seriously prejudiced Hill and so the conviction could not stand. The appeal was allowed, the conviction set aside and a new trial on the charge of second degree murder ordered.

IV. The Issue

The issue in this appeal is whether the Ontario Court of Appeal erred in law in holding that the trial Judge erred in law with respect to the elements of the objective test relevant to the defence of provocation in failing to direct the jury that the "ordinary person" within the meaning of that term in s. 215(2) of the *Criminal Code* was an "ordinary person of the same age and sex as the accused".

V. The Defence of Provocation

The defence of provocation appears to have first developed in the early 1800s. Tindal C.J. in *R. v. Hayward* (1833), 6 C. & P. 157 at 159, told the jury that the defence of provocation was derived from the law's "compassion to human infirmity". It acknowledged that all human beings are subject to uncontrollable outbursts of passion and anger which may lead them to do violent acts. In such instances, the law would lessen the severity of criminal liability.

Nevertheless, not all acts done in the heat of passion were to be subject to the doctrine of provocation. By the middle of the 19th Century, it became clear that the provoking act had to be sufficient to excite an ordinary or reasonable person under the circumstances. As Keating J. stated in *R. v. Welsh* (1869), 11 Cox C.C. 336 at 338:

> The law is, that there must exist such an amount of provocation as would be excited by the circumstances in the mind of a reasonable man, and so as to lead the jury to ascribe the act to the influence of that passion.

The *Criminal Code* codified this approach to provocation by including under s. 215 three general requirements for the defence of provocation. First, the provoking wrongful act or insult must be of such a nature that it would deprive an ordinary person of the power of self-control. That is the initial threshold which must be surmounted. Secondly, the accused must actually have been provoked. As I have earlier indicated, these two elements are often referred to as the objective and subjective test of provocation respectively. Thirdly, the accused must have acted on the provocation on the suddenn and before there was time for his or her passion to cool.

(a) *The Objective Test of Provocation and the Ordinary Person Standard*

In considering the precise meaning and application of the ordinary person standard or objective test, it is important to identify its underlying rationale. Lord Simon of Glaisdale has perhaps stated it most succinctly when he suggested in *Camplin, supra,* at p. 726, that:

> ... the reason for importing into this branch of the law the concept of the reasonable man [was] ... to avoid the injustice of a man being entitled to rely on his exceptional excitablity or pugnacity or ill-temper or on his drunkenness.

If there were no objective test to the defence of provocation, anomalous results could occur. A well-tempered, reasonable person would not be entitled to benefit from the provocation defence and would be guilty of culpable homicide amounting to murder, while an ill-tempered or exceptionally excitable person would find his or her culpability mitigated by provocation and would be guilty only of manslaughter. It is society's concern that reasonable and non-violent behaviour be encouraged that prompts the law to endorse the objective standard. The criminal law is concerned, among other things, with fixing standards for human behaviour. We seek to encourage conduct thtat complies with certain societal standards of reasonableness and responsibility. In doing this, the law quite logically employs the objective standard of the reasonable person.

With this general purpose in mind, we must ascertain the meaning of the ordinary person standard. What are the characteristics of the "ordinary person"? To what extent should the attributes and circumstances of the accused be ascribed to the ordinary person? To answer these question, it is helpful to review the English developments, I shall begin with the English cases.

(i) English Law of Provocation and the Ordinary Person Standard

In *R. v. Lesbini*, [1914] 3 K.B. 1116, the English Court of Criminal Appeal refused to take into account the mental deficiency of the accused in assessing the availability of the provocation defence. It confirmed the threshold objective test for provocation, whereby there must be sufficient provocation to excite a reasonable person. A reasonable or ordinary person was not one with mental deficiencies. In *Mancini v. Pub. Prosecutions Dir.*, [1942] A.C. 1, the House of Lords endorsed the *Lesbini* case and further elaborated the objective test of provocation. Viscount Simon L.C. stated, at p. 9:

> The test to be applied is that of the effect of the provocation on a reasonable man, as was laid down by the Court of Criminal Appeal in *Rex v. Lesbini*, so that an unusually excitable or pugnacious individual is not entitled to rely on provocation which would not have led an ordinary person to act as he did.

The ordinary or reasonable person, therefore, was one of normal temperament and average mental capacity.

In 1954, the House of Lords was faced with the question of whether, in applying the objective test of provocation, it should take into account certain physical characteristics of the accused. In *Bedder v. D.P.P.*, [1954] 1 W.L.R. 1119, a sexually impotent man killed a prostitute after she taunted him about his physical condition. The House of Lords had to determine whether, in applying the objective test of provocation, the sexual impotence of the accused should be taken into account. The test would then have been whether an ordinary person who was sexually impotent would have been provoked. The Court rejected this approach and held that the peculiar physical characteristics of the accused were not to be ascribed to the ordinary person for the purposes of the objective test.

Despite the House of Lords' conclusion that the physical characteristics of the accused were irrelevant to the determination of whether a reasonable person would have been provoked, it appears that the Court was primarily concerned with the difficulty of distinguishing "temperament" from "physical defects". As Lord Simonds L.C. stated, at p. 1121:

> It appears to that Court, as it appears to me, that "no distinction is to be made in the case of a person who, though it may not be a matter of termperament, is physically impotent, is conscious of that impotence, and therefore mentally liable to be more excited unduly if he is 'twitted' or attacked on the subject of that particular infirmity". The court thereupon approved and reiterated the proposition that the question for the jury was whether on the facts . . . from the evidence the provocation was in fact enough to lead a reasonable person to do what the accused did.

The *Bedder* approach to the ordinary person standard is no longer the law in England. In *Camplin, supra*, the House of Lords expressly rejected the narrow objective test articulated in *Bedder*. The *Camplin* case involved a youth of 15 years of age who maintained that he had been provoked by a homosexual assault. The House of Lords unanimously concluded that the ordinary person, for the purposes of the objective test of provocation, was to be an ordinary person of the same age and sex as the accused. It should be noted that in *Camplin* the trial Judge had specifically directed the jury to take age and sex into account and the appeal sought to establish that this was wrong. In the present case, there was no such instruction.

In justifying its shift away from the *Bedder* approach, the House of Lords relied in part on legislative changes in the law of provocation introduced after the *Bedder* opinion. Specifically, in 1957, s. 3 of the *Homicide Act, 1957* (5 & 6 Eliz. 2, c. 11), was passed; it provides:

> 3. Where on a charge of murder there is evidence on which the jury can find that the person charged was provoked (whether by things done or by things said or by both together) to lose his self-control, the question whether the provocation was enough to make a reasonable man do as he did shall be left to be determined by the jury: and in determining that question the jury shall take into account everything both done and said according to the effect which, in their opinion, it would have on a reasonable man.

The phrase "the jury shall take into account everything" was interpreted to allow a consideration of relevant characteristics in connection with the objective test.

Lord Diplock clarified the underlying rationale for expanding the notion of the ordinary person when he wrote, at p. 717:

> To taunt a person because of his race, his physical infirmities or some shameful incident in his past may well be considered by the jury to be more offensive to the person addressed, however equable his temperament, if the facts on which the taunt is founded are true than it would be if they were not.

On a similar note, Lord Morris of Borth-y-Gest held, at p. 721:

> If the accused is of particular colour or particular ethnic origin and things are said which to him are grossly insulting it would be utterly unreal if the jury had to consider whether the words would have provoked a man of a different colour or ethnic origin — or to consider how such a man would have acted or reacted.

Taking these considerations into account, Lord Simon of Glaisdale formulated the objective test as follows, at p. 727:

> I think that the standard of self-control which the law requires before provocation is held to reduce murder to manslaughter is still that of the reasonable person ... but that, in determining whether a person of reasonable self-control would lose it in the circumstances, the entire factual situation, which includes the characteristics of the accused, must be considered.

One conceptual difficulty was acknowledged by Lord Diplock. He recognized at p. 717 that:

> ... in strict logic there is a transition between treating age as a characteristic that may be taken into account in assessing the gravity of the provocation addressed to the accused and treating it as a characteristic to be taken into account in determining what is the degree of self-control to be expected of the ordinary person.

In most cases, it is appropriate to assume that the level of self-control or degree of reasonableness is the same regardless of certain physical differences. Age, however, in Lord Diplock's view posed a more difficult problem. He resolved this problem with respect to age by appealing to the acknowledged importance of the law's compassion to human infirmity. On a more general level, he rejected the solution of separating out the inquiry into two phases as overly complicated for the jury.

(ii) Canadian Case Law

The Supreme Court of Canada has also had occasion to provide guidance on the ordinary person standard for provocation. In *Taylor v. R.*, [1947] S.C.R. 462, 3 C.R. 475, 89 C.C.C. 209 [Ont.], a case in which the accused was drunk at the time of his alleged provocation, Kerwin J. at p. 471 made clear that for the purposes of the objective test of provocation the "criterion is the effect on the ordinary person ... the jury is not entitled to take into consideration any alleged drunkenness on the part of the accused".

This Court again rejected a consideration of the drunkenness of the accused in connection with the objective test in *Salamon v. R.*, [1959] S.C.R. 404, 30 C.R. 1, 123 C.C.C. 1 [Ont.]. Fauteux endorsed the trial Judge's instruction to the jury [quoted at p. 410] not to consider "the character, background, temperament, or condition of the accused" in relation to the objective test of provocation. Similarly, Cartwright J. (dissenting on another issue) wrote, at p. 415, that the trial Judge correctly "made it plain that on this [objective] branch of the inquiry no account should be taken of the idiosyncrasies of the appellant and that the standard was that of an ordinary person".

Finally, in *Wright v. R.*, [1969] S.C.R. 335, [1969] 3 C.C.C. 258 [Sask.], a son was charged with the shooting death of his father. The evidence suggested that there had been some difficulties in their relationship. The father was said to have been a bad-tempered and violent man who had mistreated his son on a number of occasions. The accused had not seen his father for a period of about five years until a few days prior to the fatal incident. On the evening of the shooting, the accused had spent most of the day drinking with his friends. In considering the objective test of provocation, the Court rejected the relevance of the quality of the accused's relationship with his father, the mentality of the accused or his possible drunkenness. Fauteux J. quoted, at p. 340, the words of Lord Simmonds L.C. in *Bedder*, *supra*, that the purpose of the objective test is:

> ... to invite the jury to consider the act of the accused by reference to a certain standard or norm of conduct and with this object the "reasonable" or the "average" or the "normal" man is invoked.

The Court went on to state, at p. 340:

> While the character, background, temperament, idiosyncrasies, or the drunkenness of the accused are matters to be considered in the second branch of the enquiry, they are excluded from consideration in the first branch. A contrary view would denude of any sense the objective test.

Appellate Courts at the provincial level have also considered the nature of the ordinary person standard or provocation. In *R. v. Clark* (1975), 22 C.C.C. (2d) 1 (Alta. C.A.), the "morbid jealousy" and "slight mental degeneration" [p. 15] suffered by the accused was held not to be relevant to the objective test. According to Clement J.A., at p. 16:

> In the first branch of the inquiry, the objective test, which in essence has to be determined as a standard of comparison is the reaction that might be expected from ordinary human nature to the wrongful act, or to the alleged insult in the present case.

In *R. v. Parnerkar* (1972), 16 C.R.N.S. 347, 5 C.C.C. (2d) 11, affirmed [1974] S.C.R. 449, 21 C.R.N.S. 129, 10 C.C.C. (2d) 253, the Saskatchewan Court of Appeal held that the cultural and religious background of the accused was not relevant to the determination of the objective test. The accused, born in India, was alleged to have been provoked by, *inter alia*, the deceased's statement: "I am not going to marry you because you are a black man." The Court's ruling seems to narrow unduly the conception of the ordinary person and rigidly prohibit a consideration of the physical characteristics of the accused along the lines of the *Bedder* case. I should note that *Parnerkar* was affirmed by this Court on appeal; however, this particular question was not addressed.

In more recent decisions, appellate Courts at the provincial level appear to be moving towards the *Camplin*, *supra*, approach. The Ontario Court of Appeal's decision in the present appeal, and *Daniels v. R.* (1983), 7 C.C.C. (3d) 542 (C.A.), reflect this trend. In *Daniels* case, Laycraft J.A. held that in instructing the jury on the objective test of provocation the trial Judge should tell the jury to take into account all of the external events putting pressure on the accused. He stated at p. 554:

> The purpose of the objective test prescribed by s. 215 is to consider the actions of the accused in a specific case against the standard of the ordinary person. Hypothetically, the ordinary person is subjected to the same external pressures of insult by acts or words as was the accused. Only if those pressures would cause an ordinary person to lose self-control does

the next question arise whether the accused did, in fact, lose self-control. In my view, the objective test lacks validity if the reaction of the hypothetical ordinary person is not tested against all of the events which put pressure on the accused.

(iii) The Appropriate Content of the Ordinary Person Standard

What lessons are to be drawn from this review of the case law? I think it is clear that there is widespread agreement that the ordinary or reasonable person has a normal temperament and level of self-control. It follows that the ordinary person is not exceptionally excitable, pugnacious or in a state of drunkenness.

In terms of other characteristics of the ordinary person, it seems to me that the "collective good sense" of the jury will naturally lead it to ascribe to the ordinary person any general characteristics relevant to the provocation in question. For example, if the provocation is a racial slur, the jury will think of an ordinary person with the racial background that forms the substance of the insult. To this extent, particular characteristics will be ascribed to the ordinary person. Indeed, it would be impossible to conceptualize a sexless or ageless ordinary person. Features such as sex, age, or race do not detract for a person's characterization as ordinary. Thus particular characteristics that are not peculiar or idiosyncratic can be ascribed to an ordinary person without subverting the logic of the objective test of provocation. As Lord Diplock wrote in *Camplin, supra*, at pp. 716-17:

> . . . the "reasonable man" man has never been confined to the adult male. It means an ordinary person of either sex, not exceptionally excitable or pugnacious, but possessed of such powers of self-control as everyone is entitled to expect that his fellow citizens will exercise in society as it is today.

It is important to note that in some instances certain characteristics will be irrelevant. For example, the race of a person will be irrelevant if the provocation involves an insult regarding a physical disability. Similarly, the sex of an accused will be irrelevant if the provocation relates to a racial insult. Thus the central criterion is the relevance of the particular feature to the provocation in question. With this in mind, I think it is fair to conclude that age will be a relevant consideration when we are dealing with a young accused person. For a jury to assess what an ordinary person would have done if subjected to the same circumstances as the accused, the young age of an accused will be an important contextual consideration.

I should also add that my conclusion that certain attributes can be ascribed to the ordinary person is not meant to suggest that a trial Judge must in each case tell the jury what specific attributes it is to ascribe to the ordinary person. The point I wish to emphasize is simply that, in applying their common sense to the factual determination of the objective test, jury members will quite naturally and properly ascribe certain characteristics to the "ordinary person".

(b) *The Subjective Test and Actual Provocation*

Once a jury has established that the provocation in question was sufficient to deprive an ordinary person of the power of self-control, it must still determine whether the accused was so deprived. It may well be that an ordinary person would have been provoked but in fact the accused was not. This second test of provocation is called "subjective" because it involves an assessment of what actually occurred in the mind of the accused. At this stage, the jury must also consider whether the accused reacted to the provocation on the sudden and before there was time for his passion to cool.

In instructing the jury with the respect to the subjective test of provocation, the trial Judge must make clear to the jury that its task at this point is to ascertain whether the accused was *in fact* acting as a result of provocation. In this regard, a trial Judge may wish to remind the jury members that, in determining whether an accused was actually provoked, they are entitled to take into account his or her mental state and psychological temperament.

VI. THE VALIDITY OF THE JUDGE'S CHARGE

To apply this statement of the law to the present appeal, we must return to the actual words of the trial Judge. When instructing the jury on the objective test of provocation, he began by stating [quoted at p. 90]:

> First, the actual words must be such as would deprive an ordinary person of self-control. In considering this part of the defence you are not to consider the particular mental make-up of the accused: rather the standard is that of the ordinary person. You will ask yourselves: Would the words or acts in this case have caused an ordinary person to lose his self-control?

He later added:

> You will consider that evidence and you will decide whether the words and acts were sufficient to cause an ordinary person to lose his self-control.

In my view, this part of the charge was well-stated and correct in law. The trial Judge did not err in failing to specify that the ordinary person, for the purpose of the objective test of provocation, is to be deemed to be of the same age and sex as the accused. Although this type of instruction may be helpful in clarifying the application of the ordinary person standard. I do not think it wise or necessary to make this a mandatory component of all jury charges or provocation. Whenever possible, we should retain simplicity in charges to the jury and have confidence that the words of the *Criminal Code* will provide sufficient guidance to the jury. Indeed, in this area of the law I take heed of the words of Lord Goddard C.J. in *R. v. McCarthy*, [1954] 2 Q.B. 105 at 112:

> No court has ever given, nor do we think ever can give, a definition of what constitutes a reasonable or average man. That must be left to the collective good sense of the jury . . .

It has been suggested that the instruction of the trial Judge on the subjective prong of the provocation defence had the effect of misleading the jury on the appropriate content of the ordinary person standard. The charge stated [quoted in part at p. 90]:

> ... you will then secondly consider whether the accused acted on the provocation on the sudden before there was time for his passion to cool. In deciding this question you are not restricted to the standard of the ordinary person. You will take into account the mental, the emotional, the physical characteristics and the age of this accused . . .

In my opinion, these words would not have misled the average juror with respect to the objective test, particularly when viewed in the context of the charge as a whole.

I have the greatest of confidence in the level of intelligence and plain common sense of the average Canadian jury sitting on a criminal case. Juries are perfectly capable of sizing the matter up. In my experience as a trial Judge I cannot recall a single instance in which a jury returned to the courtroom to ask for further instructions on the provocation portion of a murder charge. A jury frequently seeks further guidance on the distinction between first degree murder, second degree murder and manslaughter, but rarely, if ever, on provocation. It sems to be common ground that the trial Judge would not have been in error if he had simply read s. 215 of the *Code* and left it at that, without embellishment. I am loath to complicate the task of the trial Judge, in cases such as the case at bar, by requiring him or her as a matter of law to point out to the members of the jury that in applying the objective test they must conceptualize an "ordinary person" who is male and young. The accused is before them. He is male and young. I cannot conceive of a Canadian jury conjuring up the concept of an "ordinary person" who would be either female or elderly, or banishing from their minds the possibility that an "ordinary person" might be both young and male. I do not think anything said by the Judge in the case at bar would have lead the jury to such an absurdity.

VII. Conclusion

I find that the trial Judge's charge to the jury on the ordinary person standard in the defence of provocation was consistent with the requirements of the *Criminal Code* and correct in law. It was not necessary to direct the jury that the ordinary person means an ordinary person of the same age and sex as the accused. I would therefore allow the appeal and restore the conviction

McIntyre J. gave a concurring judgment. Three separate dissenting judgments were delivered by Lamer, Wilson and LeDain JJ. None of the dissenters unequivocally favoured a mandatory direction to the jury as had the House of Lords in *Camplin*. In general, the dissenting justices were of the view that this trial Judge's direction had excluded age from consideration under the "ordinary person" test and that this had in the circumstances been unfairly prejudicial to the accused.

Should the Supreme Court have adopted the full *Camplin* approach?

In *R. v. Jackson* (1991), 68 C.C.C. (3d) 385 at 410, the Ontario Court of Appeal applied the "modified objective test" of *Hill* to consider "whether a reasonable young adult would have been deprived of self-control by an assault committed by a long-time friend, lover, provider and protector in the course of an argument which signalled the end of this long-standing relationship". This issue was not addressed when the Supreme Court dismissed the further appeal: [1993] 4 S.C.R. 573, 26 C.R. (4th) 178, 86 C.C.C. (3d) 385.

For a view that the present provocation defence contributes to homophobia and violence against gay men and lesbians see N. Kathleen (Sam) Banks, "The 'Homosexual Panic' Defence in Canadian Criminal Law" (1997), 1 C.R. (5th) 371.

R. v. THIBERT

45 C.R. (4th) 1, 104 C.C.C. (3d) 1, [1996] 1 S.C.R. 37

The accused was charged with first degree murder for the killing of his wife's lover. While he was attempting to persuade his wife to go somewhere to talk, the victim came out of the building and began to lead her back into the office. The accused removed a rifle from his car. The victim was then told by the accused's wife that the rifle was not loaded and he may have believed her. He began walking towards the accused, with his hands on the wife's shoulders swinging her back and forth, saying, "Come on big fellow, shoot me? You want to shoot me? Go ahead and shoot me." At some point, she was moved aside and the victim kept coming towards the accused, ignoring his instructions to stay back. The accused testified that his eyes were closed as he tried to retreat inward and the gun discharged. The trial judge left the defence of provocation with the jury, but in his charge did not instruct the jury that the Crown had the onus of disproving provocation beyond a reasonable doubt. The accused was found guilty of second degree murder. The Court of Appeal in a majority decision dismissed the accused's appeal, holding that the trial judge erred in leaving the defence of provocation with the jury but that this error did not prejudice the accused. The accused appealed.

CORY J. (SOPINKA and McLACHLIN JJ. concurring): — The sole question to be considered on this appeal is whether the trial judge was correct in leaving the defence of provocation with the jury. Put another way, the issue is whether there was any evidence upon which a reasonable jury acting judicially and properly instructed could find that there had been provocation. If the trial judge was correct in leaving provocation with the jury, then it is conceded that there must be a new trial. This is the result of the failure to instruct the jury that there was no onus resting upon the appellant to establish the defence but rather that it rested upon the Crown to establish beyond a reasonable doubt that there had not been provocation.

. . . .

The section, s. 232, specifies that there is both an objective and a subjective element to the defence. Both must be satisfied if the defence is to be invoked. First, there must be a wrongful act or insult of such a nature that it is sufficient to deprive an ordinary person of the power of self-control as the objective element. Second, the subjective element requires that the accused act upon that insult on the sudden and before there was time for his passion to cool. The objective aspect would at first reading appear to be contradictory for, as legal writers have noted, the "ordinary" person does not kill. Yet, I think the objective element should be taken as an attempt to weigh in the balance those very human frailties which sometimes lead people to act irrationally and impulsively against the need to protect society by discouraging acts of homicidal violence.

The Objective Element of the Test: How Ordinary Is the "Ordinary Person" and Would That Person Have Been Provoked by the Wrongful Act or Insult?

The provincial courts of appeal have widened I believe correctly the approach to the objective element in order to consider the background relationship between the deceased and the accused . . . . In my view, so long as the provocation section remains in the *Criminal Code* in its present form certain characteristics will have to be assigned to the "ordinary person" in assessing the objective element. The "ordinary person" must be of the same age, and sex, and share with the accused such other factors as would give the act or insult in question a special significance and have experienced the same series of acts or insults as those experienced by the accused. In summary then, the wrongful act or insult must be one which could, in light of the past history of the relationship between the accused and the deceased, deprive an ordinary person, of the same age and sex, and sharing with the accused such other factors as would give the act or insult in question a special significance, of the power of self-control.

. . . .

In this case, there is no doubt that the relationship of the wife of the accused with the deceased was the dominating factor in the tragic killing. Obviously, events leading to the break-up of the marriage can never warrant taking the life of another. Affairs cannot justify murder. Yet the provocation defence section has always been and is presently a part of the *Criminal Code*. Any recognition of human frailties must take into account that these very situations may lead to insults that could give rise to provocation. Some European penal codes recognize "crimes of passion" as falling within a special category. Indeed many of the Canadian cases which have considered the applicability of the defence arise from such situations. The defence of provocation does no more than recognize human frailties. Reality and the past experience of the ages recognize that this sort of situation may lead to acts of provocation. Each case must be considered in the context of its particular facts to determine if the evidence meets the requisite threshold test necessary to establish provocation . . . . Taking into account the past history between the deceased and the accused, a jury could find the actions of the deceased to be taunting and insulting. It might be found that, under the same circumstances, an ordinary person who was a married man, faced with the break-up of his marriage, would have been provoked by the actions of the deceased so as to cause him to lose his power of self-control. There was some evidence, therefore, that would satisfy the objective element of the test. Next it remains to be seen whether there was evidence that could fulfil the subjective element of the test.

The Subjective Element of the Test

It must be determined whether there was evidence that the appellant was actually provoked. Once again it is necessary to take into account the past history involving the accused, the deceased and his wife. Further, it cannot be forgotten that the accused hadn't slept for some 34 hours and that he described himself as being devastated, stressed out and suicidal. He emphasized how important it was to him to talk to his wife in private, away from the deceased. It was in this manner that he successfully persuaded his wife to stay with him on the earlier occasion. When his wife returned to her employer's parking lot and the deceased came out of the building, he testified that his thoughts were "here is the man that won't give me a half hour alone with my wife after 21 years and he has had her for 24 hours the night before". It was when the deceased put his arm around his wife's waist and started leading her back towards the building that the appellant removed the rifle from the car. He testified that he did so as a bluff. He hoped it would make them take him more seriously and succeed in convincing his wife to accompany him so that they could talk privately. From this point, the deceased's actions could be construed as a conscious attempt to test the appellant's limits. When he saw that the appellant had a gun, he advanced towards him. The appellant's wife was in front of the deceased and the deceased had his hands on her shoulders. The appellant recalled that the deceased was swinging Mrs. Thibert from side to side like a moving target. While doing this, the deceased was laughing and grinning at the appellant. He also dared the appellant to fire and taunted him by saying "Come on big fellow, shoot me. You want to shoot me? Go ahead and shoot me." The deceased continued to approach the appellant, proceeding as fast as he could. In turn, the appellant kept backing up and told the deceased to "stay back", but the deceased continued to approach him. The appellant testified that he remembered wanting to scream because the deceased would not stop coming towards him. The appellant's eyes were tightly closed when he fired the gun. The time the appellant held the gun until he fired was not long. The events unfolded very quickly, in a matter of moments, seconds, not minutes . . . . In my view there was evidence upon which a reasonable jury acting judicially and properly instructed could have concluded that the defence of provocation was applicable.

. . . .

In the result, I would allow the appeal, set aside the decision of the Court of Appeal and direct a new trial on the charge of second degree murder.

MAJOR J. (IACOBUCCI J. concurring) (dissenting): —

. . . .

In my opinion, in this case there is no evidence of a wrongful act or insult sufficient to deprive an ordinary person of the power of self-control. That the deceased may have positioned Mrs. Thibert between himself and the appellant cannot constitute a wrongful act or insult. Nor can the statements "You want to shoot me? Go ahead and shoot me" and "Come on big fellow, shoot me" be considered a wrongful act or insult. Those actions are not contemptuous or scornful; they are legitimate reactions to a dangerous situation. It would be improper to require victims to respond in a certain way when faced with armed, threatening individuals. The defence claim that the wrongful act or insult came from the appellant's evidence that the deceased used Joan Thibert as a shield while taunting him to shoot is ironic. The appellant had control of the only true weapon involved in this situation, the rifle.

Further, that the deceased had a personal relationship with Mrs. Thibert is not a wrongful act or insult sufficient to cause an ordinary person to lose the power of self-control. The break-up of a marriage due to an extramarital affair cannot constitute such a wrongful act or insult. I agree with the statement of Freeman J.A. in *R. v. Young* (1993), 78 C.C.C. (3d) 538 at 542, that:

> It would set a dangerous precedent to characterize terminating a relationship as an insult or wrong act capable of constituting provocation to kill. The appellant may have been feeling anger, frustration and a sense of loss, particularly if he was in a position of emotional dependency on the victim as his counsel asserts, but that is not provocation of a kind to reduce murder to manslaughter.

Similarly, it would be a dangerous precedent to characterize involvement in an extramarital affair as conduct capable of grounding provocation, even when coupled with the deceased's reactions to the dangerous situation he faced. At law, no one has either an emotional or proprietary right or interest in a spouse that would justify the loss of self-control that the appellant exhibited.

In that connection, Cory J. states that the events leading to the break-up of a relationship are not factors going to provocation but I wonder whether the effect of his reasons is such that these factors have been taken into account in the context of provocation. My colleague emphasizes that the accused still wished to see his wife alone after the end of the relationship. However, in my view, she had made it clear on a number of occasions that she did not wish to be alone with him. This was a choice that Joan Thibert was free to make. The accused had no right or entitlement to speak with his wife in private. The fact that the accused believed that the deceased was preventing him from doing so is not, with respect, a fact that ought to be taken into account when considering the defence of provocation.

If I am wrong and the objective threshold test for provocation is met, the appeal would fail on the subjective element of the test. The appellant had known of his wife's involvement with the deceased for some time. He knew his wife wanted to leave him, and had seen the deceased with his wife earlier that day. It cannot be said that the appellant's mind was unprepared for the sight of his wife with the deceased such that he was taken by surprise and his passions were set aflame. There was no element of suddenness on the facts of this case.

For these reasons, I am of the opinion that neither the objective branch nor the subjective branch of the threshold test for leaving the defence of provocation with the jury has been met. There is no evidence on which a reasonable jury, acting judicially could find a wrongful act or insult sufficient to deprive the ordinary person of the power of self-control. Neither is there any evidence that the appellant acted on the sudden. The defence should not have been left with the jury. This was an error that did not prejudice the appellant.

The partial defence of provocation is presently extremely controversial and has been under review by the Department of Justice for several years: see, now, *Reforming Criminal Code Defences: Provocation, Self-defence and Defence of Property* (Department of Justice, 1998) pp.1-20. There is no legislative resolution in sight, no doubt because of a lack of consensus on reform options. A study by a Federal-Provincial-Territorial working group, reported in the Justice study at pp. 5-6, of 115 reported cases in which the defence of provocation was raised, warns against generalizations or special interest solutions. Sixty-two cases involved domestic homicides. In 55 cases men killed women and in 7 women killed men. The remaining 53 cases involving men killing men. Sixteen of these cases involved alleged homosexual advances. In all types of cases the study revealed that the defence of provocation was more often than not unsuccessful.

Some see the solution as being the abolition of the mandatory life sentence for murder. See Peter MacKinnon, "Two Views of Murder" (1985), 53 Can. Bar Rev. 130; "Annotation to Latimer" (1996), 41 C.R. (4th) 6; and Tim Quigley, "*R. v. Latimer* : Hard Cases Make Interesting Law" (1995), 41 C.R. (4th) 89 at 98). The law and order mood of the times makes this change unlikely.

The Supreme Court has recently spoken to the issue of sentencing in provoked murder cases. In *Stone* (1999), 24 C.R. (5th) 1 (S.C.C.), the accused stabbed his wife 47 times after she verbally insulted him and a "whoosh" came over him. The defence of provocation was left with the jury and they returned a verdict of manslaughter. The trial judge imposed a sentence of four years, taking into account 18 months pre-trial custody as equivalent to three years. On the sentence appeal, Justice Bastarache for a Court unanimous on this point rejected the Crown's position that an accused should not gain a "double benefit" of considering provocation in reducing a verdict from murder to manslaughter under s. 232 of the *Code* and then again on sentencing. Rather, s. 232 provided an accused with a single benefit of a reduction of a verdict of murder to one of manslaughter to allow for consideration of the provoked nature of the killing in the determination of the appropriate penalty. A spousal connection between offender and victim was recognized as an aggravating factor in sentencing under s. 718.2(*a*)(ii) and previously under the common law, which applied to this case (the sentencing had been before the new section came into effect). However, the Crown had failed to establish that the sentencing judge did not properly consider the domestic nature of this offence in reaching his decision on sentence.

R. v. CAMERON

(1992), 12 C.R. (4th) 396, 71 C.C.C. (3d) 272 (Ont. C.A.)

The accused was convicted of second degree murder. He appealed, arguing that the statutory defence of provocation set out in s. 232 of the *Criminal Code* contravened ss. 7 and 11(*d*) of the *Charter* in that it is premised in part on an objective standard. The Ontario Court of Appeal dismissed the constitutional challenge.

DOHERTY J.A. (DUBIN C.J.O. and GRIFFITHS J. concurring): —

. . . .

The appellant contends that the "defence of provocation operates by negativing an essential element of the *mens rea* for murder". He goes on to argue that as provocation is premised in part on an objective standard, the statutory definition of provocation cannot stand in light of the authorities which hold that liability for murder cannot be determined by reference to an objective fault standard: see *R. v. Martineau*, [1990] 2 S.C.R. 633, 79 C.R. (3d) 129, 58 C.C.C. (3d) 353.

The argument misconceives the effect of s. 232. The section does not detract from or negative the fault requirement for murder, but serves as a partial excuse for those who commit what would be murder but for the existence of the partial defence created by s. 232. As the opening words of s. 232 plainly indicate, the defence only need be considered where the Crown has proved beyond a reasonable doubt that the accused committed murder: see *R. v. Campbell* (1977), 38 C.C.C. (2d) 6 (C.A.), at p. 15; *R. v. Oickle* (1984), 11 C.C.C. (3d) 180 (C.A.) at p. 190.

The statutory defence of provocation does not detract from the *mens rea* required to establish murder, but rather, where applicable, serves to reduce homicides committed with the *mens rea* necessary to establish murder to manslaughter.

The appellant also argues that, even if the statutory defence of provocation stands apart from the *mens rea* required for murder, ss. 7 and 11(*d*) of the *Charter* render the section inoperative insofar as it imposes an objective standard on the availability of the defence. He argues that for constitutional purposes there could be no distinction between a statutory provision which imposes liability for murder on an objective basis (*e.g.*, s. 230(*d*)) and a statutory provision like s. 232 which limits the availability of a defence to murder according to an objective criterion.

I disagree. The former imposes liability in the absence of a constitutionally mandated minimum level of fault. The latter provides a partial excuse despite the existence of the constitutionally required level of fault. Section 232 does not impose liability where subjective fault does not exist, but reduces the liability even when that fault exists.

The objective component of the statutory defence of provocation serves a valid societal purpose (see *R. v. Hill*, [1986] 1 S.C.R. 313, 51 C.R. (3d) 97, 25 C.C.C. (3d) 322, at pp. 330-331 [C.C.C., pp. 108-109 C.R.] and cannot be said to be contrary to the principles of fundamental justice.

Resort to s. 11(*d*) of the *Charter* does not assist the appellant. Section 232 does not place any burden of proof on an accused to disprove anything essential to the establishing of his culpability. Indeed, the onus is on the Crown to negate provocation beyond a reasonable doubt: *Linney v. R.*, [1978] 1 S.C.R. 646, 32 C.C.C. (2d) 294. Nor, for the reasons set out above, does s. 232 modify the statutory definition of murder so as to eliminate an element of the offence required by s. 7 of the *Charter*.

The constitutional argument fails.

At common law there are two partial defences to murder. We earlier saw that voluntary intoxication may reduce a murder charge to manslaughter since murder is considered to be a specific intent crime. There is also the possibility, especially under Ontario case law, of a what has become known as the "rolled up" charge which asks the jury to consider the cumulative effect of all the factors on whether the Crown has proved the intent required for murder.

R. v. NEALY

(1986), 54 C.R. (3d) 158 (Ont. C.A.)

CORY J.A.: —

. . . .

A brief history of the facts will suffice for the purposes of this appeal.

During the early morning hours of 20th August 1982 the appellant, Patrick Nealy, stabbed and killed Larry Casimiri. At the time, Nealy was 23 years old and Casimiri was 33 years old, married, with three children.

Earlier, during the afternoon of 19th August, Nealy injected into his arm a drug known as "stovetop". He thought that the plateau from that injection occurred late in the afternoon. In the evening, he and his girlfriend, Alison McKinley, drank together at the St. Charles Tavern. This is a bar which was frequented by members of the gay community and was well known to Nealy. While at this tavern, Nealy and his girlfriend met the deceased and two friends of the deceased. Some time around 11:00 p.m., Nealy and his girlfriend, together with the deceased and his two friends, proceeded to the Albany Tavern. This tavern as well was often frequented by members of the gay community.

Both the appellant and the deceased continued to drink at the Albany Tavern. The deceased danced with Nealy's girlfriend. According to Nealy, after dancing with her, Casimiri repeatedly said that Nealy's girlfriend "had nice tits and that he was going to fuck her". Nealy told Casimiri to keep quiet. Eventually, the two men began pushing and then punching each other. Nealy suggested to Casimiri that they continue their fight outside. Casimir left the Albany Tavern and Nealy followed him.

Before Nealy left the tavern, he removed a knife from his girlfriend's purse and placed it in his belt with the handle exposed. Once out on the street, the men continued to fight. To many of the witnesses, it appeared that Nealy was the aggressor and better-co-ordinated. Casimiri, although heavier-set, appeared drunk and unco-ordinated. It was Nealy's evidence that he was upset by what Casimiri had said about his girlfriend and that he was afraid of Casimiri, who came at him, as he said, "like a grizzly bear".

Nealy stated that he had the knife only to frighten Casimiri and he warned Casimiri to "back off". In any event, he stabbed Casimiri several times — on his evidence, three times. With the last stroke of the knife, Casimiri collapsed in front of a van parked on King Street and Nealy fled. Nealy testified that he had not intended to kill Casimiri and that he was angry with himself for what had happened and sorry for what he had done.

At the opening of the trial, Nealy entered a plea of not guilty to the charge of murder but guilty of manslaughter. This plea was not accepted by the Crown and the trial proceeded. Despite the plea, Nealy raised the issue of self-defence at trial.

At the conclusion of the evidence it was clear that the jury would have to consider: first, the issue of drunkenness and the effect upon the accused of the alcohol consumed; second, the question of self-defence; third, the question of provocation; and fourth, the effect that the alcohol he had consumed, coupled with the fear and anger experienced by the accused, would have upon the issue of whether he ever formed the requisite intent to murder Casimiri.

. . . .

The trial Judge, early in his charge, read to the jury s. 212(a)(iii) and advised them of the intent that was required in order to find the accused guilty of murder.

Later he told the jury that he was going to deal specifically with self-defence, provocation and drunkenness. He dealt first, in an exemplary manner, with self-defence. He then said that the second defence was drunkenness, and gave instructions with regard to it, and lastly dealt with what he termed the "third defence" of provocation. Each of these aspects of the charge was, to a certain extent, "compartmentalized". It is conceded that he did not at any time instruct the jury as to the cumulative effect that the consumption of alcohol and the fear and anger that were experienced by Nealy as a result of his dispute with the deceased might have had upon Nealy's ability to form the requisite intent to commit murder.

It would, I think, have been better if the trial Judge, at the conclusion of his reference to these three specific elements, had advised the jury as to the possible cumulative effect of the evidence.

In this case, it would have been preferable if the jury had been instructed along these lines: first, that, in considering whether the accused formed the requisite intent, they were to take into account the alcohol that had been consumed by Nealy; further, that they were to consider the evidence which Nealy had given as to his fear and anger as a result of the words uttered by Casimiri in the Albany Tavern and the punching and shoving which followed both inside the tavern and on the street. The jury should have been told that, even if the words spoken by Casimiri, coupled with his actions, did not raise in their minds a reasonable doubt as to whether or not Nealy had been "provoked" as that term is defined in s. 215 of the *Code*, or that Nealy was incapable of forming the required intent by reason of the consumption of alcohol, the jury was still to consider all these surrounding circumstances in coming to a conclusion as to whether Nealy possessed the requisite intent needed to commit murder pursuant to s. 212 (*a*) of the *Code*.

That, I believe, is the position that has been adopted by this Court. In *R. v. Clow* (1985), 44 C.R. (3d) 228 at 231 (Ont. C.A.), there appears a statement of this Court which is applicable to the facts of this case:

> "It is respectfully submitted that the learned trial Judge erred in failing to instruct the jury as to the cumulative effects of consumption of alcohol or drugs, provocation and excessive force in self-defence as it might relate to the requisite specific intent 'to mean to cause death or to mean to cause bodily harm which she knew was likely to cause death and was reckless as to whether death ensued'."

We agree.

In *R. v. Trecroce* (1980), 55 C.C.C. (2d) 202 (Ont. C.A.), Martin J.A. stated at p. 211:

> "That is not to say, of course, that a jury, if they consider that the accused was honestly defending himself, may not entertain a reasonable doubt whether acting instinctively in the excitement of the moment he really contemplated the consequences of his actions and actually had the requisite intent for murder even though that inference might normally be drawn from his acts apart from the circumstances that he was defending himself."

And in *R. v. Campbell* (1977), 17 O.R. (2d) 673, 1 C.R. (3d) 309, S-49, 38 C.C.C. (2d) 6 (C.A.), Martin J.A. again stated at p. 683:

> "Provocation may, of course, inspire the intent required to constitute murder. There may, however, be cases where the conduct of the victim amounting to provocation produces in the accused a state of excitement, anger or disturbance, as a result of which he might not contemplate the consequences of his acts and might not, in fact, intend to bring about those consequences. The accused's intent must usually be inferred from his conduct and the surrounding circumstances, and in some cases the provocation afforded by the victim, when considered in relation to the totality of the evidence, might create a reasonable doubt in the mind of the jury whether the accused had the requisite intent. Thus, in some cases, the provocative conduct of the victim might be a relevant item of evidence of the issue of intent

whether the charge be murder or attempted murder. This, I take it, was the view of Eveleigh, J., in *R. v. Bruzas, supra,* at p. 369. Provocation in that aspect, however, does not operate as a 'defence' but rather as a relevant item of evidence on the issue of intent."

The case referred to, *R. v. Campbell, supra,* was one of attempted murder. The argument there advanced on behalf of the accused was that provocation within the meaning of the *Code* would reduce the offence to attempted manslaughter. That argument was rejected because provocation is applicable only to reduce an act which would otherwise be murder to manslaughter. Nevertheless it was held in that case that acts of provocation, whether in murder or attempted murder, and by implication whether or not sufficient to satisfy the *Code* definition, might be relevant to the issue of intent.

R. v. Clow, supra, was relied upon and followed by this Court in *R. v. Desveaux* (1986), 51 C.R. (3d) 173, 26 C.C.C. (3d) 88. In that case as well the statement of principle contained in *R. v. Clow* was a fundamental element in the decision of the Court.

Although the question has not been specifically considered by the Supreme Court of Canada, there are some statements in various reasons of that Court that lend support to the position set forth in *R. v. Clow* and *R. v. Desveaux*. In *R. v. Faid,* [1983] 1 S.C.R. 265, 33 C.R. (3d) 1, 2 C.C.C. (3d) 513 at 517-18, Dickson J. was considering the question as to whether or not excessive force in self-defence could result in a conviction of manslaughter. He stated:

> ... though the facts on which the defence of self-defence was unsuccessfully sought to be based may in some cases go to show that the defendant acted under provocation or that, although acting unlawfully, he lacked the intent to kill or cause grievous bodily harm. In such cases a verdict of manslaughter would be proper.

In *Brisson v. R.*, [1982] 2 S.C.R. 227, 29 C.R. (3d) 289, 69 C.C.C. (2d) 97 [Que.], the Court was once again considering whether excessive force in self-defence could reduce a charge of murder to manslaughter. Dickson J., speaking on behalf of the Court, stated at p. 258-59:

> To summarize, I would reject the notion that excessive force in self-defence, *unless related to intent under s. 212 of the Code* or to provocation, reduces what would otherwise be murder to manslaughter. [The italics are mine.]

In *R. v. Gee,* [1982] 2 S.C.R. 286, 29 C.R. (3d) 347, 68 C.C.C. (2d) 516, 43 N.R. 128 at 137, Dickson J., speaking for the majority, stated:

> In my view, it cannot be said that force can be partially justified. Success under s. 27 leads to acquittal. If the defence under s. 27 does not succeed, the jury should render the verdict which would have been rendered, absent s. 27. This may be a verdict of manslaughter, not because of partial justification under s. 27 but because the special mental element required for guilt of murder has not been proven. In other words, the half-way house is not to be found in s. 27 but, if at all, in s. 212.

These authorities emphasize the importance of the issue of intent. Further, they indicate that all the circumstances surrounding the act of killing must be taken into account in determining whether or not the accused had the intent required for the commission of murder. It may well be that the evidence does not give rise to a reasonable doubt as to whether there was provocation or whether the accused lacked the ability to form that intent as a result of consuming alcohol or durgs. Nevertheless, the evidence adduced on these issues, viewed cumulatively, may be of great importance in determining the crucial issue of intent.

Not every case where the consumption of alcohol and some form of provocation is involved will require a specific direction as to the cumulative effect of these factors. Still, it will be preferable in most cases and essential in some that such a direction be given. In the circumstances of this case, fairness required no less than the addition to the charge of two or three sentences which would be sufficient to bring to the jury's mind the necessity of considering all the pertinent facts in resolving the issue of intent.

The omission of the trial Judge to give such a direction coupled with the improper aspects of the cross-examination of the accused, are sufficient to require a direction for a new trial. In the result, I would, with some regret, allow the appeal and direct a new trial.

General Review Questions

1. Jack and Jill have had a tempestuous love affair for over a year. Jack had always been highly strung. He had also endured periods of acute depression for which he had received several weeks of psychiatric counselling. He always seemed to fear the worst. Actually his often expressed suspicions that Jill was dating another man were well-grounded. Her other boyfriend, Bill, with whom she was much more emotionally involved, demanded that she "ditch"Jack. She decided on the strategy of first calming him with alcohol and then playing him a pre-recorded message on a cassette, during which she would leave his apartment. She carried her unloaded pistol in her purse for "protection". They had about five whiskys each at a local pub in less than two hours. As Jack was driving Jill to his apartment, Jill for some unknown reason — probably as a result of her intoxication — departed from her plan and started to play her cassette tape in the car. The message began brutally: "Jack, I've had enough. You are physically repulsive and a mental wreck. I love Bill and have done so passionately for two months . . .". It is not clear what happened next. All that is known is that Jack's car suddenly veered off the road, somersaulted and struck a fence. Miraculously Jack and Jill were unhurt. According to Jack, he was devastated by the message and he might well have lunged at Jill while he was still driving. In any event his mind was blank until he realized he had been in an accident, that Jill was pointing a gun at him and that he then stabbed her repeatedly with a screwdriver, which had been on the dashboard. A third party on the scene says Jack had a dull glazed look about him, was shouting "You bitch! You bitch!" hysterically and that it was extremely difficult to stop Jack's convulsive-like assault. Jill later died of the multiple wounds. Her pistol was found on the front seat of the car.

Jack stands charged with second degree murder. His defence counsel asks you for a brief as to his viable total or partial defences. Discuss relevant authorities and comment on the strength or weakness of each defence.

2. Jamie has had a tortured adolesence struggling with his sexual identity. At the age of 16 he recently came to terms with the fact that he was gay. Until his arrest he was living with his lover, Fred, a chartered accountant, aged 28. One of Jamie's former girlfriends, Bettie, realized Jamie's preference had changed. She became partly jealous and partly plain vicious. Whenever she saw Jamie she taunted him with anti-gay remarks. One night Jamie and Fred had been at a bar for several hours. Each had consumed about ten beers. Bettie came up to them. Just the sight of her made his blood boil. She again taunted him with several anti-gay remarks before moving off. Jamie told Fred he'd had enough. "The next time", said Jamie, "I'll thrash her to teach her a lesson she'll never forget." Fred said, "She deserves it." Jamie found a stick used to prop up a window and put it on the bar table. An hour and two beers later — during which time Jamie was morose — Bettie again arrived. She went up to Jamie and said "You all deserve AIDS. It's God's way of disapproving." Jamie would testifiy, "This was the last straw. I saw red again, picked up the stick and hit, hit, hit." In fact Bettie was knocked unconscious with about six very heavy blows. She died in hospital several days later. The fatal assault took less than a minute. Fred just watched, only intervening after the sixth blow, saying "That's enough".

You are an articled clerk to the prosecutor. She has charged both Jamie and Fred with first degree murder on the basis that they commited murder contrary to s. 229(*a*) that was planned and deliberate under s. 231(2). She is incensed by the wanton violence and will press hard for a conviction of first degree murder. She asks you for a legal memorandum assessing the strengths and weaknesses of all possible full and partial defences and the likely verdict. She notes there is no possibility of the defence of insanity.

Entrapment

R. v. MACK

[1988] 2 S.C.R. 903, 67 C.R. (3d) 1, 44 C.C.C. (3d) 513

Lamer J. —

INTRODUCTION

The central issue in this appeal concerns the doctrine of entrapment. The parties, in essence, ask this Court to outline its position on the conceptual basis for the application of the doctrine and the manner in which an entrapment claim should be dealt with by the Courts. Given the length of these reasons due to the complexity of the subject, I have summarized my findings on pages 964 to 966 of these reasons.

The Facts

The appellant was charged with unlawful possession of a narcotic for the purpose of trafficking. He testified at trial and, at the close of the case for the defence, brought an application for a stay of proceedings on the basis of entrapment. The application was refused and a conviction entered by Wetmore Co. Ct. J., sitting without a jury, in written reasons reported in (1983), 34 C.R. (3d) 228. A notice of appeal from that decision was filed with the British Columbia Court of Appeal but the appeal books were not filed within the time prescribed. Counsel for the appellant sought and obtained, with the consent of Crown Counsel, an order dispensing with the requirement that transcripts of evidence be filed and permitting counsel to base their arguments solely on the reasons for judgment of Wetmore Co. Ct. J. The Chief Justice of British Columbia directed that a panel of five judges hear the appeal. For the reasons given by Craig J.A., on behalf of the Court, the appeal was dismissed. This decision is now reported at (1985), 49 C.R. (3d) 169. Leave to appeal was garnted by this Court.

It is necessary to describe in some detail the relevant facts. In view of the particular procedural history of this appeal, I think it is appropriate to reproduce in its entirety the summary of the evidence provided for in the reasons for judgment of Wetmore Co. Ct. J. (at pp. 234-37):

> Through information obtained from an officer of the Ontario Provincial Police, one Momotiuk was brought to British Columbia. This man had apparently been dealing in narcotics in Kenora, Ontario. He was placed under police "handlers" in Vancouver, he visited the accused on a number of occasions, and eventually a transaction was set up whereby the accused would deliver cocaine to Momotiuk.
>
> The accused testified. He first met Momotiuk in 1979 in Montreal where the accused was visiting one Franks. The accused understood Franks and Momotiuk to be associated in some clothing franchise.
>
> The accused at this time was attempting to develop some property for sale near De Roche, British Columbia, and told Franks and Momotiuk of this and both expressed some interest in buying. Both arrived in British Columbia in October 1979. In the course of this visit the accused says that Momotiuk told him he was a drug trafficker in Kenora and wanted some "Thai pot". The accused says he had no interest.
>
> Momotiuk, according to the accused, called later still wanting to make drug deals, and the accused told him he was interested only in real estate deals.
>
> The accused again went to a yoga retreat near Montreal in December 1979. Franks and Momotiuk visited him there. Momotiuk produced some cocaine, which he and Franks used, and again asked the accused to become a supplier. A few days later they met again. At this time conversation was directed to show Momotiuk as an importer of drugs on a large scale, and again the accused was invited to join in and refused.
>
> In January and February there were approximately seven telephone calls from Momotiuk to the accused soliciting his involvement. The accused says he refused.
>
> In mid-February 1980 Momotiuk visited the accused again, asking him to supply drugs. The accused says he told Momotiuk he was not interested and asked to be left alone. Momotiuk continued to visit two or three times and also telephoned.

In March the accused says Momotiuk arrived again. They went for a walk in the woods. Momotiuk produced a pistol and was going to show the accused his marksmanship. He was dissuaded because of the probability of startling the horses nearby. The accused says that at this remote area Momotiuk said, "A person could get lost." This the accused says was a threat. He says the matter of drugs was again raised and the accused says he was adamant that he had no knowledge of drugs sources.

The accused was asked to phone him twice and did not. One Matheson attended at the accused's residence on 13th March with a message that Momotiuk was very excited and wanted to see him at the Biltmore Hotel. The accused says he wanted nothing to do with Momotiuk but was terrified of him and agreed to go into town to the Biltmore. He also says that Matheson told him Momotiuk had some friends with him. This the accused took to be other members of this illegal syndicate.

While en route to the city he twice noted a car which seemed to be following him. This was probably so, because undercover police officers were doing a surveillance at the time.

On arrival at the hotel he met Momotiuk. Again he was informed of the syndicate. He was asked then if he wished to see the buying power. The accused agreed. He was directed to a car outside the hotel. In this car was an open briefcase with $50,000 exposed. The custodian, unknown to the accused, was an undercover policeman.

The accused returned to the hotel, Momitiuk asked him to get a sample and gave him $50 for this purpose.

The accused left and went to a supplier he had known of from years back. This supplier, one Goldsmith, now dead, heard the accused's story and agreed to supply "in order to get Doug (Momotiuk) off me". He obtained the sample and delivered it to Momotiuk, who tested it and said to get as much as he could. He returned to the supplier and offered $35,000 to $40,000 for a pound.

At the meeting the following day the accused had still not acquired the drugs and he says that at this point he was told to get his act together, in a threatening way.

I need not detail the accused's evidence of the following two days. He obtained 12 ounces of cocaine, and was to pay $27,000 for it. This credit, he says, was extended to him by Goldsmith on the basis of payment when delivered to Momotiuk. It was in the course of this delivery that he was arrested.

It is on the basis of this testimony that the accused says he was entrapped. Momotiuk, Matheson and Franks did not testify. Neither did "Bonnie", the accused's former wife, who was apparently present at one of the Montreal meetings, where cocaine was produced and some discussion took place.

The accused has drug convictions in 1972 and 1976, two in 1978 and one in 1979. Those in 1976, one in 1978 and one in 1979 involved cocaine. He says his former use of drugs arose to relieve back pain, but in 1978 he discovered relief from yoga and gave up the use of narcotics. The offence in 1979 was a fall from grace when he met up with old friends.

Decisions of the Courts Below

Wetmore Co. Ct. J. held that the judgment of Estey J. in *Amato v. The Queen*, [1982] 2 S.C.R. 418, and of the British Columbia Court of Appeal in *R. v. Jewitt* (1983), 34 C.R. (3d) 193 (rev'd on other grounds, [1985] 2 S.C.R. 128), established that entrapment is recognized as part of the abuse of process doctrine and a stay of proceedings arising from a finding of entrapment is not a "defence" in the traditional sense of that word. This distinction between a "stay" and a "defence" was important in terms of the burden and standard of proof. Wetmore Co. Ct. J. decided the evidential burden rested on the party seeking the stay to satisfy a Court on a balance of probabilities that there had been entrapment which would constitute an abuse of the Courts' processes. He stated at p. 232:

> To ask the Court to preclude either side — the state, represented by the prosecution, or the defence — from the adjudication of their differences must involve satisfying the Court that its processes cannot result in the attainment of jusitce through the traditional avenue of a full and open trial. To make that finding, it seems fundamental to a system of justice in a free and democratic society that the Court must be satisfied that its processes have been so abused that those very processes are precluded from attaining justice. Satisfaction in such a state of affairs existing must be more than a reasonable suspicion.

In Wetmore Co. Ct. J.'s view, the presumption of innocence until proven guilty beyond a reasonable doubt was not violated. He stated that this presumption applied at trial while a motion for a stay was to really determine whether the appellant would have a trial. It was not significant that in this case the motion came at the end of the proceeding: "What counsel is asking is that I stop the proceedings before a verdict. This amounts to aborting the trial" (p. 234). Wetmore Co. Ct. J.'s view of the nature of the entrapment claim may be discerned in the following passage, at p. 234:

> This evidentiary burden is of great importance in the matter of entrapment because fundamental to any such finding is the conclusion that the accused had no disposition to commit the crime but succumbed to improper enticement by authorities of the state. As in all matters of the mental element in criminal matters, the state of mind usually comes from inferences from established facts. I must test those facts to say then which is more probable as to the accused's predisposition, not merely if something is rationally possible.

After reviewing the evidence, Wetmore Co. Ct. J. noted, at p. 237, that the appellant's evidence found support in the testimony of the police officers to some extent: "They agree that Momotiuk was difficult to 'handle' ". The stay was refused, however, because the appellant had not met the burden of proof. Wetmore Co. Ct. J. concluded, at p. 237:

> In fairness to the accused, I should say that, if I were to decide this issue on the basis of the Crown having to negate entrapment beyond a reasonable doubt, I would have such a doubt.
>
> I find, however, that it is far more probable that the accused became involved in this transaction for profit, rather than through persistent inducement and fear. Given his record and the alacrity with which he produced on seeing the $50,000 in March 1980, I find it much more probable that he then saw a situation of profit and acted upon it. There is no doubt in my mind that the opportunity was made available through the tactics of the police and their agent, but that falls short of entrapping a person into the commission of an act that he had no intention of doing.

The British Columbia Court of Appeal held that having regard to this Court's decision in *Jewitt, supra,* and the opinion of several of the Justices in *Amato, supra,* entrapment is available in response to a criminal charge as an aspect of abuse of process but not as a substantive defence. It was further held that the determination of the existence of entrapment is a question of law to be decided by the trial Judge. The appellant bore the onus of proof on a balance of probabilities, since an accused claiming entrapment is seeking to have the case disposed of on the basis of police misconduct as opposed to the merits.

Having decided the applicable legal issues, the Court of Appeal referred to the trial Judge's conclusion that the appellant acted out of a desire for profit.

Craig J.A. then stated at p. 183: "I think that the Judge was right in concluding that there was no entrapment in this case." The appeal was therefore dismissed.

Justice Lamer then thoroughly reviewed the American and Canadian jurisprudence and summarized his conclusions.

. . . .

Summary

In conclusion, and to summarize, the proper approach to the doctrine of entrapment is that which was articulated by Estey J. in *Amato, supra,* and elaborated upon in these reasons. As mentioned and explained earlier there is entrapment when,

(a) the authorities provide a person with an opportunity to commit an offence without acting on a reasonable suspicion that this person is already engaged in criminal activity or pursuant to a *bona fide* inquiry;

(b) although having such a reasonable suspicion or acting in the course of a *bona fide* inquiry, they go beyond providing an opportunity and induce the commission of an offence.

It is neither useful nor wise to state in the abstract what elements are necessary to prove an entrapment allegation. It is, however, essential that the factors relied on by a Court relate to the underlying reasons for the recognition of the doctrine in the first place.

Since I am of the view that the doctrine of entrapment is not dependant upon culpability, the focus should not be on the effect of the police conduct on the accused's state of mind. Instead, it is my opinion that as far as possible an objective assessment of the conduct of the police and their agents is required. The predisposition, or the past, present or suspected criminal activity of the accused, is relevant only as a part of the determination of whether the provision of an opportunity by the authorities to the accused to commit the offence was justifiable. Further, there must be sufficient connection between the past conduct of the accused and the provision of an opportunity, since otherwise the police suspicion will not be reasonable. While predisposition of the accused is, though not conclusive, of some relevance in assessing the initial approach by the police of a person with the offer of an opportunity to commit an offencem it is never relevant as regards whether they went beyond an offer, since that is to be assessed with regard to what the average non-predisposed person would have done.

The absence of a reasonable suspicion or a *bona fide* inquiry is significant in assessing the police conduct because of the risk that the police will attract people who would not otherwise have any involvement in a crime and because it is not a proper use of the police power to simply go out and test the virtue of people on a random basis. The presence of reasonable suspicion or the mere existence of a *bona fide* inquiry will, however, never justify entrapment techniques: the police may not go beyond providing an opportunity regardles of their perception of the accused's character and regardless of the existence of an honest inquiry. To determine whether the police have employed means which go further than providing an opportunity, it is useful to consider any or all of the following factors:

— the type of crime being investigated and the availability of other techniques for the police detection of its commission;
— whether an average person, with both strengths and weaknesses, in the position of the accused would be induced into the commission of a crime;
— the persistence and number of attempts made by the police before the accused agreed to committing the offence;
— the type of inducement used by the police including: deceit, fraud, trickery or reward;
— the timing of the police conduct, in particular whether the police have instigated the offence or became involved in ongoing criminal activity;
— whether the police conduct involves an exploitation of human characteristics such as the emotions of compassion, sympathy and friendship;
— whether the police appear to have exploited a particular vulnerability of a person such as a mental handicap or a substance addiction;
— the proportionality between the police involvement, as compared to the accused, including an assessment of the degree of harm caused or risked by the police, as compared to the accused, and the commission of any illegal acts by the police themselves;
— the existence of any threats, implied or express, made to the accused by the police or their agents;
— whether the police conduct is directed at undermining other constitutional values.

This list is not exhaustive, but I hope it contributes to the elaboration of a structure for the application of the entrapment doctrine. Thus far, I have not referred to the requirement in *Amato, supra*, per Estey J., that the conduct must, in all the circumstances, be shocking or outrageous. I am of the view that this is a factor which is best considered under the procedural issues to which I will now turn.

Procedural Issues

The resolution of the issues surrounding the manner in which an entrapment claim should be considered at trial is, in my view, entirely dependant upon the conceptual basis for the defence, outlined earlier. If I were of the opinion that there was a substantive or culpability-based defence of entrapment, I would readily come to the conclusion that the defence raised a question of fact, which should be decided by a jury when there is a sufficient evidentiary basis on which to raise the defence, and I would hold that the onus would rest on the Crown to disprove the existence of entrapment beyond a reasonable doubt. Having come to the opposite viewpoint on the rationale for recognizing the doctrine of entrapment, I am not persuaded that the adoption of rules which historically, and by virtue of the *Charter*, conform to most substantive defences is either necessary or correct. It seems to me, however, that this Court must be clear on how an entrapment claim is to be handled, as a brief review of some lower Court decisions suggests that there is, at present, and understandably so, a great deal of confusion on the matter.

A: Who Decides: Judge or Jury?

Both the appellant and respondent agree that objective entrapment, involving police misconduct and not the accused's state of mind, is a question to be decided by the trial Judge, and that the proper remedy is a stay of proceedings. I too am of this view. The question of unlawful involvement by the state in the instigation of criminal conduct is one of law, or mixed law and fact.

. . . .

Supporting the view that a Judge should decide is the decision of the Court of Appeal in the present case, referred to earlier. Further, Tallis J.A. (Cameron J.A. concurring) in *R. v. Mistra* (1986), 32 C.C.C. (3d) 97 (Sask. C.A.), at p. 122, appears to have approved the decision of the British Columbia Court of Appeal in the present case and in *R. v Showman*, (unreported). In *Jewitt, supra*, at the level of the Court of Appeal, Anderson J.A. gave four reasons for his conclusion that the issue of entrapment is one to be decided by a trail Judge (*supra*, at pp. 219-20). I am in complete agreement with the first and the fourth of these reasons. Anderson J.A. began by observing, at p. 219:

> . . . the Courts have always been the masters of their own process and it is for the Courts alone to determine whether there has been an abuse of process. All issues relating to abuse of process require a factual determination but it does not follow that such a determination should be made by a jury.

And he concluded at p. 220:

> . . . as a matter of policy, the issue of entrapment should be left to the courts so that standards and guidelines may be established by case law. Such a development will be impossible if issues of entrapment are left to juries.

Anderson J.A. made reference to potential prejudice arising should the issue go to the jury, for the jury may find the accused guilty because of the accused's crimial record or bad reputation (citing Frankfurter J. in *Sherman, supra*, at p. 382). I am not concerned by this for two reasons: firstly, as I noted earlier, in most cases the accused will have committed the offence and his or her guilt is not in issue; secondly, in my view the past criminal conduct of the accused is not relevant to the analysis, except where it relates to the reasonable suspicions of the police. The last point made by Anderson J.A. was that an accused could ask for evidence to be excluded by a trial Judge under s. 24(2) of the *Charter* because of entrapment, and be denied that request and yet, in the same case, a jury may find that the police conduct brought the administration of justice into disrepute. He felt that such a result should be avoided. I prefer to express no opinion in this case on the propriety of a s. 24(2) application to exclude evidence because of entrapment. I am, however, of the view that the reasons which support a judicial determination of applications under s. 24(2) for the exclusion of evidence are equally relevant to the present discussion.

This Court has held that the determination of whether the admission of evidence obtained in violation of a *Charter* right would bring the administration of justice into disrepute is one which should be made by a trial Judge (*R. v. Therens*, [1985] 1 S.C.R. 613, per Le Dain J., at p. 653). In articulating how a trial Judge should engage him or herself in that analysis, I stated in *Collins, supra*, that a Judge should consider the question from the perspective of a reasonable person, "dispassionate and fully apprised of all the circumstances", and I commented that "The reasonable person is usually the average person in the community but only when that community's current mood is reasonable" (*supra*, at p. 282). The issue there, as here, is maintaining respect for the values which, over the long term, hold the community together. One of those very fundamental values is the preservation of the purity of the administration of justice. In my opinion a Judge is particularly well suited to make this determination and this finding should be guided by the above quoted comments from *Collins, supra*. Further, as noted by Anderson J.A. in *Jewitt, supra*, and commented on by Vallerand J.A. in *Baxter, supra*, if one of the advantages of allowing claims of entrapment is the development of standards of conduct on the part of the state, it is essential that decisions on entrapment, and those allowing the claim especially, be carefully explained so as to provide future guidance; this is not something the jury process lends itself to. Accordingly, I am of the firm opinion that the issue of entrapment should be resolved by the trial Judge for policy reasons.

Finally, I am of the view that before a Judge considers whether a stay of proceedings lies because of entrapment, it must be absolutely clear that the Crown had discharged its burden of proving beyond a reasonable doubt that the accused had committed all the essential elements of the offence. If this is not clear and there is a jury, the guilt or innocence of the accused must be determined apart from evidence which is relevant only to the issue of entrapment. This protects the right of an accused to an acquittal where the circumstances so warrant. If the jury decides the accused has committed all of the elements of the crime, it is then open to the Judge to stay the proceedings because of entrapment by refusing to register a conviction. It is not necessary nor advisable in this case to expand on the details of procedure. Because the guilt or innocence of the accused is not in issue at the time an entrapment claim is to be decided, the right of an accused to the benefit of a jury trial in s. 11(*f*) of the *Charter* is in no way infringed.

B. Who Bears the Burden of Proof and on What Standard?

. . . .

I have come to the conclusion that it is not inconsistent with the requirement that the Crown prove the guilt of the accused beyond a reasonable doubt to place the onus on the accused to prove on a balance of probabilities that the conduct of the state is an abuse of process because of entrapment. I repeat: the guilt or innocence of the accused is not in issue. The accused has done nothing that entitles him or her to an acquittal; the Crown has engaged in conduct, however, that disentitles it to a conviction. This point was made by Dickson C.J. in *Jewitt, supra,* in a passage cited earlier. This Court in *Jewitt,* and more recently in *R. v. Keyowski,* [1988] 1 S.C.R. 657, affirmed that a Court may only enter a stay for an abuse of process in the "clearest of cases" (*Jewitt, supra,* at p. 137; *Keyowski, supra,* at p. 659). It is obvious to me that requiring an accused to raise only a reasonable doubt is entirely inconsistent with a rule which permits a stay in only the "clearest of cases". More fundamentally, the claim of entrapment is a very serious allegation against the state. The state must be given substantial room to develop techniques which assist it in its fight against crime in society. It is only when the police and their agents engage in a conduct which offends basic values of the community that the doctrine of entrapment can apply. To place a lighter onus on the accused would have the result of unnecessarily hampering state action against crime. In my opinion the best way to achieve a balance between the interests of the Court as guardian of the administration of justice, and the interests of society in the prevention and detection of crime, is to require an accused to demonstrate by a preponderance of evidence that the prosecution is an abuse of process because of entrapment. I would also note that this is consistent with the rules governing s. 24(2) applications (*Collins, supra,* at p. 277), where the general issue is similar to that raised in entrapment cases: would the administration of justice be brought into disrepute?

Before turning to the particular case at bar I would like to comment on the requirement in *Amato, supra,* that "In the result, the scheme so perpetrated must in all the circumstances be so shocking and outrageous as to bring the administration of justice into disrepute" (at p. 446, emphasis in original). I would, upon reconsideration, prefer to use the language adopted by Dickson C.J. in *Jewitt, supra,* and hold that the defence of entrapment be recognized in only the "clearest of cases". The approach set out in these reasons should provide a court with the necessary standard by which to judge the particular scheme. Once the accused has demonstrated that the strategy used by the police goes beyond the limits described earlier, a judicial condonation of the prosecution would by definition offend the community. It is not necessary to go further and ask whether the demonstrated entrapment would "shock" the community, since the accused has already shown that the administration of justice has been brought into disrepute.

In conclusion, the onus lies on the accused to demonstrate that the police conduct has gone beyond permissible limits to the extent that allowing the prosecution or the entry of a conviction would amount to an abuse of the judicial process by the state. The question is one of mixed law and fact and should be resolved by the trial Judge. A stay should be entered in the "clearest of cases" only.

Disposition

In determining whether the doctrine of entrapmemt applies to the present appeal, this Court is restricted to the summary of evidence provided by Wetmore Co. Ct. J. in his reasons. I am of the view that a stay of proceedings should be entered in this case. While the trial Judge had the advantage of hearing the testimony of the appellant, and normally findings on entrapment cases should not be disturbed because of this, I am concerned that in this case too much emphasis was placed on the appellant's state of mind. Earlier in my summary of the decisions below I cited a passage from the trial Judge's reasons wherein he stated that the fundamental issue was the appellant's state of mind and his predisposition to crime. This, perhaps, explains why in his conclusion the trial Judge stated the appellant was not entrapped because he acted out of a desire to profit from the transaction. If the trial Judge had been permitted only to evaluate the conduct of the police objectively, I think he might well have, and in any event, ought ot have come to the conclusion the police conduct amounted to entrapment.

From the facts it appears that the police had reasonable suspicion that the appellant was involved in criminal conduct. The issue is whether the police went too far in their efforts to attract the appellant into the commission of the offence.

Returning to the list of factors I outlined earlier, this crime is obviously one for which the state must be given substantial leeway. The drug-trafficking business is not one which lends itself to the traditional devices of police investigation. It is absolutely essential, therefore, for police or their agents to get involved and gain the trust and confidence of the people who do the trafficking or who supply the drugs. It is also a crime of enormous social consequence which causes a great deal of harm in society generally. This factor alone is very critical and makes this case somewhat difficult.

The police do not appear, however, to have been interrupting an ongoing criminal enterprise, and the offence was clearly brought about by their conduct and would not have occurred absent their involvement. The police do not appear to have exploited a narcotics addiction of the appellant since he testified that he had already given up his use of narcotics. Therefore, he was not, at the time, trying to recover from an addiction. Nonetheless, he also testified that he was no longer involved in drugs and, if this is ture, it suggests that the police were indeed trying to make the appellant take up his former lifestyle. The persistence of the police requests, as a result of the equally persistent refusals by the appellant, supports the appellant's version of events on this point. The length of time, approximately six months, and the repetition of requests it took before the appellant agreed to commit the offence also demonstrate that the police had to go further than merely providing the appellant with the opportunity once it became evident that he was unwilling to join the alleged drug syndicate.

Perhaps the most important and determinative factor in my opinion is the appellant's testimony that the informer acted in a threatening manner when they went for a walk in the woods, and the further testimony that he was told to get his act together after he did not provide the supply of drugs he was asked for. I believe this conduct was unacceptable. If the police must go this far, they have gone beyond providing the appellant with an opportunity. I do not, therefore, place much significance on the fact that the appellant eventually committed the offence when shown the money. Obviously the appellant knew much earlier that he could make a profit by getting involved in the drug enterprise and he still refused. I have come to the conclusion that the average person in the position of the appellant might also have committed the offence, if only to finally satisfy this threatening informer and end all further contact. As a result I would, on the evidence, have to find that the police conduct in this case was unacceptable. Thus, the doctrine of entrapment applies to preclude the prosecution of the appellant. In my opinion, the appellant has met the burden of proof and the trial Judge should have entered a stay of proceedings for abuse of process.

I would accordingly allow the appeal, set aside the conviction of the appellant and enter a stay of proceedings.

Appeal allowed.

For a comment, see Stuart, "*Mack:* Resolving Many But Not All Questions of Entrapment" (1989), 67 C.R. (3d) 68.

Chapter 8

PARTIES TO A CRIME

See sections 21-23 of the *Criminal Code*.

R. v. KULBACKI

[1966] 1 C.C.C. 167 (Man. C.A.)

MILLER C.J.M.: — APPEAL from a conviction by B.P. McDonald P.M., for dangerous driving contrary to s. 221(4) [now s. 249(4)], *Criminal Code*.

The accused, a young man 20 years of age, was not actually driving the motor vehicle himself but was the owner of it and had permitted a female infant, 16 years of age, although duly licensed to drive, to take the wheel of the car and drive the motor vehicle over an unimproved municipal highway in excess of 90 m.p.h. The accused, who was sitting in the front seat beside the driver, was charged with the substantive offence. According to the stated case, the accused did or said nothing to stop, prevent, or attempt to stop or prevent the driver of the car from driving in the manner in which she did.

The Crown contended that the conviction was proper in that the accused had aided and abetted the commission of the offence and, as such, under s. 21(1) of the *Code*, was liable to the same extent as if he had been driving the vehicle.

The defence was strictly one of law that the accused, although present, did nothing to encourage the commission of the offence and did not omit to do anything that [would have] contributed to its commission. The defence maintained that, although the accused was present, he did not participate in the commission of the crime but was merely a passive observer, and, at the most, guilty of mere passive acquiescence. Accused argued that he did not have any duty and was not under any liability to do anything as long as he did not in some way encourage the commission of the offence. Defence counsel cited *R. v. Dutchak*, 43 C.C.C. 74; *R. v. Hendrie* (1905), 10 C.C.C. 298; *R. v. Dumont* (1921), 37 C.C.C. 166; and *R. v. Dick*, 87 C.C.C. 101, 2 C.R. 417.

Each of the above-cited cases was decided on its own special facts and the only principles of application to the instant case are that the accused, in order to have been convicted, must have done something to encourage the commission of the offence or omitted to do something which assisted in its commission. It appears to me that when the accused, the owner of car, sat in the front seat on the passenger's side and permitted this young lady to increase the speed to such a dangerous rate, he did, by his lack of action, encourage her to violate the law.

Certainly it would not have been wise for him to have grabbed the wheel at this dangerous speed, nor at any time when the car was being driven in excess of 60 m.p.h., as to do so would probably have been catastrophic. To turn off the ignition, as was suggested to us by the Crown, might not have been the best course either. In no uncertain terms he should have told this young lady, the minute she started to speed on this municipal road, to desist and slow down. In my opinion, the failure to even protest is equivalent to encouragement and is fatal to his defence.

The Crown cited to us two very pertinent cases with which I will deal briefly.

The first was *Du Cros v. Lambourne* (1907), 21 Cox C.C. 311. The facts of that case are very similar to the facts in the instant case. There, the accused, who had permitted a young lady to drive his car, was charged with the substantive offence when she drove it in an improper manner, and was convicted on the ground that he was an aider and abettor. In 21 Cox C.C. at p. 315, Lord Alverstone C.J. said:

> "If Miss Godwin was then driving, she was doing so with consent and approval of the appellant, who was the owner and in control of the car, and was sitting by her side, and he could and ought to have prevented her driving at such excessive and dangerous speed, but instead thereof he allowed her to do so, and did not interfere in any way."

The Court of Appeal held that on that finding of fact it was justified in convicting the accused as if he were the driver, as he was an aider, abettor, etc.

The other case in *R. v. Halmo* (1941), 76 C.C.C. 116, a decision of the Ontario Court of Appeal. In that case the owner of the vehicle was found guilty of the offence of reckless driving committed by his chauffeur.

It is true that in the *Halmo* case, *supra*, the accused, owner of the car, had full knowledge that his chauffeur was intoxicated; in fact, they became intoxicated together. Perhaps in the *Halmo* case circumstances are stronger than in the instant case but, nevertheless, it is an authority in support of the Crown's position. The *Halmo* and the *Du Cros* cases were discussed with apparent approval by the Manitoba Court of Appeal in *R. v. Harder* (1947), 88 C.C.C. 21, 3 C.R. 49. The *Halmo* case was referred to by the Supreme Court of Canada in another *R. v. Harder* case reported (1956), 114 C.C.C. 129, 23 C.R. 295, and apparently approved. The following quotation from the *Halmo* case has some application to the instant case (At p. 127 [C.C.C.]):

> Three facts combine to make the accused a person who had in his charge and under his control the motor vehicle in question: (a) He was the owner of the motor vehicle; (b) He was the master of Mayville, his hired servant, who was driving the car; (c) He was personally present at all material times both before and at the time when the motor vehicle was being driven in a manner dangerous to the public.
>
> Being personally present and having in his charge and under his control the motor vehicle, he is a principle party to the offence of a breach of s. 285(6)(*a*) of the *Code*. *Reg. v. Brown* (1878), 14 Cox C.C. 144. He was guilty of negligence in that being so in charge and control of a dangerous machine he failed and omitted to control his drunken chauffeur and to prevent him from driving the car to the danger of the public.

Every passenger in an unlawfully driven motor vehicle is not necessarily subject to conviction as an aider and abettor, as it is conceivable that a passenger might not have any authority over the car or any right to control the driver, but that is not the situation in the instant case. As above stated, he failed to make any effort to stop or prevent the commission of the offence when he was in a position to do so and when he had the authority to do so.

Therefore, as intimated, I am of the opinion that the learned Magistrate was right in convicting the accused of the substantive offence on the ground that he was an aider and abettor and liable to conviction by virtue of s. 21(1).

Appeal dismissed.

DUNLOP AND SYLVESTER v. R.

[1979] 2 S.C.R. 881, 8 C.R. (3d) 349, 47 C.C.C. (2d) 93

DICKSON J. (LASKIN C.J.C., ESTEY and SPENCE JJ. concurring): — The appellants were twice tried and convicted on a charge of rape. The indictment alleges that on June 26, 1975, they did unlawfully have sexual intercourse with B.R. without her consent. They were sentenced to serve six years in penitentiary. In an appeal taken following the second trial, the Manitoba Court of Appeal found error on the part of the trial Judge, but by a three to two majority sustained the conviction by applying s. 613(1)(*b*)(iii) of the *Code* [37 C.C.C. (2d) 90]. It is from that judgment that the present appeal is taken.

The facts

A rather detailed recital of the facts is essential to an understanding of the issues. In June, 1975, B.R. was 16 years of age. On the night of the alleged offence, accompanied by a friend, A.M., she went to the Waldorf Hotel in the City of Winnipeg to listen to a band and drink beer.

A number of members of a motorcycle club known as the Spartans were present at the hotel. The two girls were joined at their table by two members of the club, one Hawryluk and the appellant Dunlop, and by a prospective member, one Douglas. During the evening the complainant consumed five or six glasses of beer. At about 11:30 p.m. she, riding on the back of Douglas' motorcycle, and A.M., riding on the back of Hawryluk's motorcycle, went briefly to the Balmoral Hotel. Leaving there, they proceeded on the motorcycles to an isolated area, the site of a former dump, located in Elmwood on the outskirts of Winnipeg. The Elmwood dump was favoured as a *rendezvous* by motorcyclists because of the hillocks. After arrival, the four sat on the grass and talked for about five minutes, following which A.M. and Hawryluk went for a walk. The complainant and Douglas remained for three or four minutes, then Douglas left to repair his bike, leaving the complainant alone.

Lonely, she arose and went looking for A.M. and Hawryluk. At this moment, four men in black leather jackets bearing the Spartan emblem arrived on motorcycles. They approached the complainant, picked her up by the arms and legs, carried her to a nearby area bordering a creek and threw her on the ground. By this time, quite a few other men, similarly dressed, arrived. The complainant's clothes were torn from her, and each of the men, about 18 in number, had intercourse with her while she was being held by two of the others. On direct examination the complainant was asked whether she was able to recognize any of the men who had had intercourse, to which she replied, "Yes, those two right there", looking at the appellants Dunlop and Sylvester. The night was very dark, but the complainant explained that after the men had laid her down a bonfire had been lighted, and she could see by the light of the fire. At one point she was threatened with a knife. There are more unpleasant details, but they need not be here recounted.

The following day the complainant picked Dunlop from a police line-up as one of the men who had attacked her. Sylvester was identified in a second line-up later the same day. Asked by Crown counsel what it was about them that made it possible for her to recall the two men so clearly, the complainant answered: "Well, not really that much, but I seen their faces as they were getting on top of me." Later, she testified that she remembered very clearly the two accused, and that she was positive in her identification. She conceded on cross-examination that neither of the two accused was among the four men who first approached her, nor had either of them pinned her arms or produced a knife. Her sole testimony implicating the two accused was to the effect that each of them had performed the physical act of intercourse with her during the course of the sexual attack. The case for the Crown was put forward on that footing.

Each of the accused gave evidence. Dunlop testified that he had attended a meeting of the Spartan Motorcycle Club at the Elmwood dump early in the evening in question, at which time Douglas had been introduced as a prospective member. Later, according to his evidence, Dunlop went to the Waldorf Hotel, joined the two girls at a table for a while, and then played pool until he left the hotel at about 1:00 a.m. He explained that Sylvester had been asked to bring beer to the dump for a party. He, Dunlop, accompanied Sylvester in the latter's car to the Vibrations discotheque, where they remained about half-an-hour and then proceeded to the dump, arriving at 2:15 a.m. Upon arrival, he said, he and Sylvester "grabbed the beer which was four cases", walked over to the top of a knoll and set down the beer. Douglas was there. He told Sylvester that everyone was angry over the delay in delivering the beer. Dunlop walked to the other side of the knoll and noticed a few people down near the creek bed about 25 yd. distant. Some of them displayed their ire at the delay in fetching the beer, by yelling at Dunlop and Sylvester. Dunlop saw a female having intercourse; with whom, he could not say, but he believed the person to be a Spartan. After three minutes he and Sylvester left. Dunlop denied having intercourse with B.R., or in any way assisting anyone else to have intercourse with her. Sylvester's evidence was to the same effect as that of Dunlop.

The issue for the jury was a simple one — did the two accused have intercourse with B.R.? She said that they had, and they denied it. The issue was well-formulated by the trial Judge just before the conclusion of his summing up, in these words:

> If you accept the evidence of B.R., and if after weighing all the evidence you come to the conclusion that you are satisfied beyond a reasonable doubt that the two accused did have sexual intercourse with B.R. without her consent, then you may find them both guilty as charged.
>
> If, on the other hand you have a reasonable doubt that either one or both accused participated in this way, then you must give that particular accused the benefit of that reasonable doubt and acquit the accused on the charge.

That is all the case was about. The Judge chose, however, to instruct the jury upon parties to an offence under s. 21 of the *Code*, and it is in this respect that the convictions are challenged. The general effect of s. 21 is to make equally culpable (i) the person who actually commits the offence; (ii) any person who aids or abets in committing the offence, and (iii) persons who form an intention in common to carry out an unlawful purpose leading to the commission of the offence.

Section 21(2) of the Criminal Code

The first ground of appeal is that the trial Judge erred in charging the jury on s. 21(2) of the *Code*, common intention, when there was no evidence that the appellants Dunlop and Sylvester had formed any common intention with those involved in the gang rape to commit rape upon B.R. It is common ground that the trial Judge erred in this respect. Crown counsel concedes as much. There was no evidence that the appellants participated in a plan or scheme to lure the complainant to the dump as part of the initiation proceeding. In the Court of Appeal for Manitoba, Mr. Justice Matas, writing for the majority of the Court, considered that there was "merit in the appellants' argument that the comments were inappropriate in the circumstances of the case". Mr. Justice Hall, writing the minority opinion, said [at p. 96]:

> In my respectful opinion, there was no evidence upon which a jury, properly instructed, could find or infer that the accused were parties to an offence under that subsection. In my view, it was a pure invitation to the jury to resort to surmise, speculation and conjecture, as opposed to proper legal inference, against which they were cautioned not to do in the general charge.

Section 21(1) of the Criminal Code

The second ground of appeal was set out in the formal judgment of the Court of Appeal in this manner:

> 2. That the Learned Trial Judge erred in charging the Jury with respect to Section 21(1) of the *Criminal Code*, as there was insufficient evidence in law to make the Appellant . . . a party to the offence.

In ascertaining the real ground upon which dissent is based, if the formal judgment fails to make that clear, this Court may look to the written reasons of the dissenting Judges: *Roy v. The King*, 69 C.C.C. 177 at pp. 188-9, [1938] S.C.R. 32 at p. 43, *per* Crocket J., and *Savard and Lizotte v. The King*, 85 C.C.C. 254 at pp. 255-6, [1946] S.C.R. 20 at p. 23, *per* Taschereau J.

Mr. Justice Hall in his dissenting judgment left no doubt that the "insufficient evidence in law", of which he spoke, was insufficient in the sense that the trial Judge ought not to have charged the jury at all with respect to s. 21(1) [at p. 98]:

> The presence of the accused at the dump, and their passive observation of a girl having sexual intercourse is not sufficient in law to make them parties to an offence under s. 21(1) of the *Code*.
>
> The case for the Crown should have been allowed to stand or fall on the issue of whether the Crown had proved beyond a reasonable doubt that the accused were two of the Spartans who had sexual intercourse with B.R. against her will. She said they did, and identified them as two of the attackers. They denied any involvement and pointed to her uncorroborated testimony and to the unreliability of her identification of them. The trial Judge fully and clearly exposed that issue. The charge should have stopped there.

As I read this passage, there is no suggestion that the evidence was insufficient to support a conviction, which is a question of fact or, at best, a question of mixed fact and law. That was the situation in *R. v. Warner*, 128 C.C.C. 366, [1961] S.C.R. 144, 34 C.R. 246. The error alleged in the dissent here is that there was insufficient evidence to go to the jury under s. 21(1), as opposed to insufficient evidence to support the jury's verdict. The question of whether there is sufficient evidence to go to the jury, *i.e.*, any evidence upon which a jury, properly instructed, could find the appellants guilty as parties to the offence under s. 21(1), is a question of law, which can found an appeal to this Court under s. 618(1)(*a*) [am. 1974-75-76, c. 105, s. 18]: *R. v. Decary*, 77 C.C.C. 191 at pp. 194-5, [1942] S.C.R. 80 at p. 83, and *Calder v. The Queen*, 129 C.C.C. 202 at pp. 202-3, [1960] S.C.R. 892 at pp. 896-7, *per* Cartwright J.

On s. 21(1) of the *Code*, the jury was instructed as follows:

> Secondly, I should also instruct you on the law relating to parties to an offence. Section 21(1) of the *Criminal Code*, reads as follows:
> "Everyone is a party to an offence who:
> (*a*) actually commits it,
> (*b*) does or omits to do anything for the purpose of aiding any person to commit it, or
> (*c*) abets any person in committing it."
> Abets, that word abets means encourages, supports, upholds. It is another way of expressing a person giving assistance to someone committing the offence. Everyone who aids and encourages the person in the commission of the offence is as guilty as the person who commits the actual criminal act.
>
> To find that the accused is guilty of aiding or abetting the commission of an offence by another person, it is only necessary to show that he understood what was being done and by some act on his part assisted or encouraged the attainment of that act.

Mere presence at the scene of a crime is not sufficient to ground culpability. Something more is needed: encouragement of the principal offender; an act which facilitates the commission of the offence, such as keeping watch or enticing the victim away, or an act which tends to prevent or hinder interference with accomplishment of the criminal act, such as preventing the intended victim from escaping or being ready to assist the prime culprit. Thus, in an early work, *Foster's Crown Law*, p. 350, we read:

> in order to render a person an accomplice and a principal in felony, he must be aiding and abetting at the fact, or ready to afford assistance if necessary, and therefore if A. happeneth to be present at a murder, for instance, and taketh no part in it, nor endeavoureth to prevent it, nor apprehendeth the murderer, nor levyeth hue and cry after him, this strange behaviour of his, though highly criminal, will not of itself render him either principal or accessory.

The leading case of *R. v. Coney* (1882), 8 Q.B.D. 534, decided that non-accidental presence at the scene of the crime was not conclusive of aiding and abetting. The accused were present at a prize fight, then illegal, though taking no part in the management of the fight, It did not appear that the accused said or did anything. The Chairman of the Quarter Sessions directed the jury that, prize fights being illegal, all persons who went to a fight to see the combatants strike each other, and being present when they did so, were guilty of assault unless they were casually passing by. If they stayed at the place, they encouraged it by their presence although they did not say or do anything. Eight of the 11 Judges hearing the case reserved were of the opinion that the direction was not correct. Two passages from the judgment of Cave J. at p. 539 bear repeating:

> Now it is a general rule in the case of principals in the second degree that there must be participation in the act, and that, although a man is present whilst a felony is being committed, if he takes no part in it, and does not act in concert with those who commit it, he will not be a principal in the second degree merely because he does not endeavour to prevent the felony, or apprehend the felon.

and [at p. 540]:

> Where presence may be entirely accidental, it is not even evidence of aiding and abetting. Where presence is *prima facie* not accidental it is evidence, but no more than evidence, for the jury.

Hawkins J., in a well-known passage had this to say, pp. 557-8:

> In my opinion, to constitute an aider and abettor some active steps must be taken by word, or action, with the intent to instigate the principal, or principals. Encouragement does not of necessity amount to aiding and abetting, it may be intentional or unintentional, a man may unwittingly encourage another in fact by his presence, by misinterpreted words, or gestures, or by his silence, on non-interference, or he may, encourage intentionally by expressions, gestures, or actions intended to signify approval. In the latter case he aids and abets, in the former he does not. It is no criminal offence to stand by, a mere passive spectator of a crime, even of a murder. Non-interference to prevent a crime is not itself a crime. But the fact that a person was voluntarily and purposely present witnessing the commission of a crime, and offered no opposition to it, though he might reasonably be expected to prevent and had the power to do so, or at least to express his dissent, might under some circumstances, afford cogent evidence upon which a jury would be justified in finding that he wilfuliy encouraged and so aided and abetted. But it would be purely a question for the jury whether he did so or not. So if any number of persons arrange that a criminal offence shall take place,

and it takes place accordingly, the mere presence of any of those who so arranged it would afford abundant evidence for the consideration of a jury of an aiding and abetting.

In this Court the question of aiding and abetting was canvassed in *Preston v. The King*, 93 C.C.C. 81, [1949] S.C.R. 156, 7 C.R. 72. The appellant and another were accused of having set fire to a school. Mr. Justice Estey delivered the majority judgment in this Court, in the course of which he stated (p. 159) that in order to find the appellant guilty of aiding, abetting, counselling or procuring, it was only necessary to show that he understood what was taking place and by some act on his part encouraged or assisted in the attainment thereof. Later he said (p. 160) that mere presence does not constitute aiding and abetting, but presence under certain circumstances may itself be evidence thereof. He proceeded to review the evidence and concluded, p. 85 C.C.C., p. 161 S.C.R.:

> If appellant's explanation was not believed by the jury there was *evidence in addition to his mere presence* upon which they might well conclude that he was guilty of aiding, abetting, counselling or procuring. (Emphasis added.)

Two Canadian cases make the distinction between presence with prior knowledge, and accidental presence. In *R. v. Dick* (1947), 87 C.C.C. 101, 2 C.R. 417 (Ont. C.A.), the accused was charged with the murder of her husband. According to her own statement, she met her husband and Bohozuk, a friend, and they went with her in a borrowed car, her husband in the front seat and Bohozuk in the back. The two men began to quarrel, both were drinking; Bohozuk pulled a gun and shot Mr. Dick. It was not a happy marriage, nor were Mr. Dick and Bohozuk on best of terms. There was some surrounding evidence casting doubt upon the non-involvement of the accused. As Chief Justice Robertson noted, she did not admit that there was any design, nor that she knew Bohozuk intended to shoot Dick, nor even that she knew Bohozuk had a weapon with him. Yet the trial Judge gave only general directions on aiding and abetting to the jury. Robertson C.J.O. concluded at p. 116 C.C.C., pp. 432-3 C.R.:

> Now, while it may be that a jury might infer from the evidence a good deal that is not expressly admitted, it is not at all certain that this jury did infer that the appellant knew more than she admits knowing of Bohozuk's then present purpose. This jury should have been instructed that if they found that the appellant was no more than passively acquiescent at the time of the shooting, and that she had no reason to expect that there would be any shooting until it actually occurred, then s. 69 did not apply:

In the result, a new trial was ordered.

In *R. v. Hoggan*, [1966] 3 C.C.C. 1, 47 C.R. 256 (Alta. C.A.), the charge was that the accused aided and abetted in wilfully attempting to defeat the course of justice by attempting to dissuade a witness from giving evidence. Johnson J.A. concluded at p. 5 C.C.C., p. 260 C.R.:

> There are two things that must be proved before an accused can be convicted of being a party by aiding and abetting. It must first be proved that he had knowledge that the principal intended to commit the offence and that the accused aided and abetted him. Where there is no knowledge that an offence is to be committed, the presence of an accused at the scene of the crime cannot be a circumstance which would be evidence of aiding and abetting.

The basis for Johnson J.A.'s approach to aiding and abetting is found in *Preston* and *Coney*, both of which he cites.

The case of *R. v. Salajko*, [1970] 1 C.C.C. 352, 9 C.R.N.S. 145 (Ont. C.A.), is like the instant case in many respects. A girl was raped by 15 young men in a lonely field. Three were charged. Two of these were identified as having had intercourse with the girl. She admitted, however, that the third accused, Salajko, though seen to be near the girl with his pants down while she was being raped by others, did not have intercourse with her. The Crown placed its case against him on s. 21 (1)(*b*) and (*c*) of the *Criminal Code*. One might be forgiven for thinking that it was open to the jury to infer encouragement by conduct, but the Ontario Court of Appeal thought otherwise. Chief Justice Gale, delivering the judgment of the Court, stated that in the absence of evidence to suggest something in the way of aiding, or counselling, or encouraging on the part of the accused with respect to that which was being done by the others, there was simply no evidence upon which a jury could properly arrive at a verdict of guilty against the particular accused. The learned Chief Justice also found error in the trial Judge's charge which seemed to indicate that a person could abet another in the commission of an offence if, knowingly, he stood by while the offence was being committed.

Finally, there are the cases of *R. v. Black*, [1970] 4 C.C.C. 251, 10 C.R.N.S. 17, and *R. v. Clarkson*, [1971] 3 All E.R. 344. The victim in *Black's* case was conveyed to a clubhouse where he was subjected to various sordid indignities. Many of the accused took an active part in torturing the victim while others stood around laughing and yelling. The British Columbia Court of Appeal confirmed the convictions, being of the view that the spectators furnished encouragement to the perpetrators of the outrages and their mere presence in the circumstances of the case ensured against the escape of the victim. There was thus something more than "mere presence", as in *R. v. Coney, supra*. Most important, the trial Judge directed the jury in language drawn from the judgment of Hawkins J. in *Coney* and reviewed the evidence relating to the presence of the accused in clear terms.

In contrast to *R. v. Black* is the case of *R. v. Clarkson*, a decision of the Court Martial Appeal Court. A girl was raped in a room in a barracks in Germany by a number of soldiers. Another group of soldiers clustered outside the door and later "piled in" to the room. They remained there for a considerable time while the girl was raped. There was no evidence that the appellants had done any physical act, or uttered any word, which involved direct physical participation or verbal encouragement. There was no evidence that they touched the girl, or did anything to prevent others from assisting her or to prevent her from escaping. The Appeal Court held that it was not enough that the presence of the accused, in fact, gave encouragement, "It must be proved that the accused intended to give encouragement; that he *wilfully* encouraged" (p. 347). There must be, the Court held, an intention to encourage and encouragement in fact. The convictions were quashed.

The case at bar

In the case at bar I have great difficulty in finding any evidence of anything more than mere presence and passive acquiescence. Presence at the commission of an offence can be evidence of aiding and abetting if accompanied by other factors, such as prior knowledge of the principal offender's intention to commit the offence or attendance for the purpose of encouragment. There was no evidence that while the crime was being committed either of the accused rendered aid, assistance or encouragement to the rape of B.R. There was no evidence of any positive act or omission to facilitate the unlawful purpose. One can infer that the two accused knew that a party was to be held, and that their presence at the dump was not accidental or in the nature of casual passers-by, but that is not sufficient. A person cannot properly be convicted of aiding or abetting in the commission of acts which he does not know may be or are intended: *per* Viscount Dilhorne in *Director of Public Prosecutions for Northern Ireland v. Maxwell*, [1978] 3 All E.R. 1140 at p. 1144 (H.L.). One must be able to infer that the accused had prior knowledge that an offence of the type committed was planned, *i.e.*, that their presence was with knowledge of the intended rape. On this issue, the Crown elicited no evidence.

In concluding that there was evidence of a nature which would permit the jury to draw an inference that the accused were more than merely present at a crime and had done nothing to prevent it, Mr. Justice Matas referred to the earlier meeting of the Spartans at the dump (with Sylvester and Dunlop present) when Douglas was introduced as a prospect, the presence of members of the group at the Waldorf beverage room where the complainant and her friend were spending some time, the bringing of the complainant by Douglas to the dump, the reappearance of a group of Spartans at the same location (where the gang rape took place), the arrival of the accused with a substantial quantity of beer, and the observation by both accused of intercourse taking place by the complainant and one male, but with other men nearby.

The activities of Douglas are twice mentioned by Mr. Justice Matas, but it must be recalled that Douglas was not one of the accused. Dunlop and Sylvester bear no responsibility for what he may or may not have done. Apart from presence earlier in the evening at the dump and at the Waldorf beverage room, the evidence Mr. Justice Matas marshalls against Dunlop and Sylvester is (i) their arrival at the dump with a substantial quantity of beer, and (ii) their observation of intercourse. In my view, for the reasons I have earlier sought to express, neither of these facts is capable in law of affording evidence that the appellants aided and the commission of the crime of rape. They go only to mere presence and not to complicity.

With great respect, I am unable to find in the evidence to which Mr. Justice Matas alludes, or elsewhere, any facts as distinguished from surmise or suspicion, upon which any jury could conclude beyond reasonable doubt that the accused had assumed a role which would qualify them as aiders and abettors under s. 21(1) of the *Code*.

In these circumstances, in my view, the trial Judge erred in charging the jury on the alternative bases of (i) principal offender, and (ii) aider and abettor.

Question by the jury

The error, unfortunately, was compounded when the jury, which had retired at 3:15 p.m., returned at 5:40 with the following question:

> If the accused were aware of a rape taking place in their presence and did nothing to prevent or persuade the discontinuance of the act, are they considered as an accomplice to the act under law?

That question should have been answered in one word — "No".

A person is not guilty merely because he is present at the scene of a crime and does nothing to prevent it: Smith & Hogan, *Criminal Law*, 4th ed. (1978), p. 117. If there is no evidence of encouragement by him, a man's presence at the scene of the crime will not suffice to render him liable as aider and abettor. A person who, aware of a rape taking place in his presence, looks on and does nothing is not, as a matter of law, an accomplice. The classic case is the hardened urbanite who stands around in a subway station when an individual is murdered.

The Judge here initially intended to respond to the jury's question with a "No" answer, but during argument, he was persuaded to the point of view, advanced for the first time on behalf of the Crown, that the accused might be guilty as parties to the offence under s. 21 of the *Code*. As a result, the Judge recharged in these words:

> Now, I have decided that the best way to reply to your query is to refer again to a portion of the law that I gave you in respect to parties to an offence, and to make one or two further comments on it.
>
> Under Section 21(1) of the *Criminal Code*, everyone is a party to an offence who; (a) actually commits it, (b) does or omits to do anything for the purpose of aiding any person to commit it — and I will come back to that, or (c) abets any person in committing it. And abets, I told you before means encourages, supports, upholds, is another form of giving assistance to a person committing the offence.
>
> Everyone who aids and encourages another person in the commission of a criminal offence is as guilty as the person who actually commits the criminal act. To find that an accused is guilty of aiding or abetting in the commission of an offence by another person, it is only necessary to show that he understood what was being done, and by some act on his part, assisted or encouraged in the attainment of what was being done.
>
> But when you are considering what I have said, going back to that middle section of the definition I read, everyone is a party to an offence who does or omits to do anything for the purpose of aiding another person to commit it, I should say the phrase omitting to do anything, that phrase, omitting to do anything means intentionally omitting to do something for the purpose of aiding another to commit an offence, that if it had been done, would have been prevented or hindered the person from committing an offence. Intentionally omitting to do something for the purpose of aiding another to commit an offence, that if it had been done, would have prevented or hindered the person front committing the offence.
>
> So that if you find an accused person knew that an offence was being committed and intentionally omitted to do something, for the purpose of aiding another to commit the offence, that if he had done it might have hindered or actually prevented the offence, then

presumably you can find that the person was a party to the offence. But unless it reaches that level, then you cannot find him a party.

I think, with respect, that this recharge is in error in three respects: (i) it is not responsive to the question asked; (ii) on the facts of the case, it might leave the jury with the impression that the accused could be parties to the offence if they knew that an offence was being committed and failed to do anything to hinder or prevent it, and (iii) the jury received no help in applying the instruction given; no act or omission is identified as providing a possible factual underpinning to the operation of s. 21.

Conclusion

If the trial Judge was in error in charging upon s. 21(2), which is admitted and, as I believe, in error in his recharge on s. 21(1), what disposition is to be made of the case? The majority view in the Manitoba Court of Appeal was that the trial Judge had not erred in his answer to the jury's question. As to the admitted error in charging as to common intention under s. 21(2), Mr. Justice Matas said [at p. 101]:

> But it is apparent from the juror's question that the members were not troubled by the concept of common intention. In any event, in light of all the evidence and the whole charge, I am satisfied that no substantial wrong or miscarriage of justice occurred.

The difficulty one faces is that we do not know, and will never know, whether the jury found the appellants guilty because they had had intercourse with the complainant, or by reason of the operation of s-ss. (1) or (2) of s. 21 of the *Code*. We do know from the question of the jury, and its timing, that after two hours and 25 minutes of deliberation the jury had not accepted the evidence of the complainant as to direct participation by the appellants. Fifteen minutes after resuming deliberation, following the recharge, the guilty verdict was returned.

I do not think this is an appropriate case for the application of s. 613(1)(*b*)(iii). I am unable to say that the verdict would have been the same in the absence of error. For the following reasons given by Mr. Justice Hall, I would direct a verdict of acquittal, rather than have the applicants undergo a third trial [at p. 98]:

> The accused have been subjected to two trials and a like number of appeals. They have been in custody over a year. The doubt raised on their innocence or guilt should be resolved now. The substance of the case is their denial against the testimony of B.R., without much more. In the circumstances, the needs of justice would be met by directing a verdict of acquittal, rather than having the accused submit to a trial for the third time.

I would allow the appeals, set aside the judgment of the Manitoba Court of Appeal, and direct a verdict of acquittal in respect of each appellant.

MARTLAND J. (dissenting) (RITCHIE and PIGEON JJ. concurring): — The appellants were convicted by a jury on a charge of rape. The facts giving rise to this charge are stated in the reasons of my brother Dickson.

It is not disputed that mere presence at the scene of a crime is not, in itself, sufficient to establish aiding or abetting the commission of an offence, but the trial Judge did not instruct the jury that it was. He charged the jury that "it is only necessary to show that he understood what was being done and by some act on his part assisted or encouraged the attainment of that act".

. . . .

In my opinion, there was evidence on which the jury could conclude that the appellants had aided and abetted the commission of the offence. The jury had been properly instructed as to what was necessary in order to establish aiding and abetting. The sufficiency of that evidence was solely a matter for the determination of the jury and was not a matter to be decided by the Court of Appeal.

Martland J. regarded the response of the trial Judge to the jury in question as not offensive when read in the context of the evidence of that evening's events. The minority accordingly would have dismissed the appeal. Pratte J. (Beetz J. concurring) agreed that the appeal should be disposed of in the manner proposed by Dickson J. but on the narrower ground relating to the response of the trial Judge to the jury's question.

Appeals allowed; acquittals entered.

R. v. F.W. WOOLWORTH CO.

(1974), 18 C.C.C. (2d) 23 (Ont. C.A.)

KELLY J.A.: — On the application made on behalf of F.W. Woolworth Co. Limited (Woolworth) pursuant to s. 762 of the *Criminal Code* the summary conviction Court started a case in the following terms:

> STATED CASE by His Honour Judge R.B. Dnieper, Provincial Court Judge (Criminal Division) Judicial District of York, under the provisions of Section 734 of the *Criminal Code* of Canada.

> I On the 29th day of March, 1971, an Information was laid under oath by Mr. Jules Arvay for that the above-named F.W. Woolworth Co. Limited:

> "Between the 3rd day of February, 1971, and the 10th day of February, 1971, at the Municipality of Metropolitan Toronto in the Judicial District of York, unlawfully did for the purpose of promoting the sale of 'Ball Point' Pens, named — Auto Magic — make a misleading representation to the public concerning the price at which such articles have been, are, or will be ordinarily sold, contrary to Section 33C (1) of the *Combines Invesigation Act*, R.S.C., 314, and its amendments."

> II On the 17th day of May, 1971, the said charge was duly heard before me in the presence of the accused and after hearing the evidence adduced and the submissions made by counsel on behalf of the Crown and the accused, I found the said F.W. Woolworth Co. Limited guilty of the said offence and convicted it thereof, but at the request of counsel for the said F.W.

Woolworth Co. Limited, I state the following case for the consideration of this Honourable Court:

It was shown before me and I found as a fact:

1. The accused, F.W. Woolworth Co. Limited, the Appellant herein ("Woolworth") is a corporation carrying on the business of a retail department store at the corner of Yonge Street and Queen Street in the Municipality of Metropolitan Toronto in the Judicial District of York (the "store premises").

2. The said store premises were managed at the material times hereinafter set out by one Peter Fawcett ("Fawcett"), a full-time store manager employed by the accused Woolworth. Fawcett, as store manager, had authority to enter into agreements on behalf of Woolworth with persons for the purpose of allowing such persons to demonstrate, display, and sell or give away wares owned by the said persons in the said store premises.

3. On or about January 15, 1971, Fawcett was approached by one James Healey ("Healey") who requested that Fawcett agree to allow Healey to demonstrate and sell certain pens hereinafter more particularly described in the said store premises. Fawcett on behalf of the accused Woolworth in consideration for Healey's agreement to pay Woolworth 30 percent of the sales of the said pens agreed to rent Healey a store counter and an area of floor space in front thereof in the said store premises for the purpose of demonstrating and selling the said pens during Woolworth's normal store hours. There was no discussion with respect to Healey being an employee of Woolworth and the parties understood that Healey was in business for himself. There was no discussion of Healey being a representative or agent of the accused Woolworth. The agreement was oral and there was no document or other written evidence of same admitted in evidence.

4. Healey employed one John McPhee ("McPhee") on a day-to-day basis in consideration for 25 percent of the sales of the said pens. McPhee demonstrated and sold the pens to the public in the manner hereinafter more particularly set out.

5. For a period of approximately five weeks in January and February of 1971, including the dates hereinafter referred to, Healey and McPhee were on the said store premises under the terms of the said agreement referred to in paragraph 3 hereof.

6. The property, fixtures, equipment and wares used in connection with the demonstration and sale of the said pens were as follows:

   (i)   a store counter, floor space and cash register, being part of the said store premises and equipment owned by the accused Woolworth;

   (ii) a display booth which was placed on top of the said store counter and a sign affixed thereto with the wording "free sample" or similar words written on a sign attached thereto, and a small microphone and public address speaker, both of which were brought onto the premises and owned by Healey, and removed by him at the end of the said five week period;

   (iii) an inventory of the following types of pens and pen refills:
         (a) a pen and pencil set consisting of a ball point pen named — "Auto Magic" ball point pen and a pencil said to be a liquid lead pencil also named — "Auto Magic",
         (b) a ball point pen and pen stand with a clip called a "telephone clip-on" pen, and
         (c) ball point pen refills.

Healey owned the inventory of "Auto Magic" ball point pen and pencil sets, telephone clip-on pens and ball point pen refills which he brought onto the said store premises at the commencement of the said five week period. Healey purchased further inventory of pens and pen refills in his own name which was ordered from a U.S. supplier, described as Speedy Sales, and picked up by Healey at the Toronto International Airport from time to time to replace pens and pen refills sold out of inventory. Healey removed the remainder of the inventory of pens and pen refills on the termination of the said five week period.

7. Any refunds requested by purchasers from time to time were the responsibility of Healey.

8. On February, 4 of 1971 McPhee at the said counter and booth in the said store premises represented to a group of people in the course of a demonstration and sales speech in effect that he represented a large manufacturing company, that the said pen set which he called "Auto Magic" by Packard was made to retail for $7.95, that his company was giving the pens away free to persons who purchased the said telephone clip-on pen which was made to retail at $3.95, but which was being sold for $2.98, and that there were also further bonuses being refills for ball point pens.

9. On February 5 at the said store premises, McPhee made the following representations to a group of people in the course of demonstrating the said Auto Magic ball point pens and making a sales speech said to be for the purpose of launching a brand new product not yet on sale:

"Now, remember the name, that's Auto Magic by Packard, the dual pen set, as you see. Designed to retail at $7.95," and
"Now, remember the name, that is telephone clip-on pen by Packard. Goes on sale and designed to retail at $3.98."

10. On February 5 at the said store premises, McPhee made the following representions to a group of people in the course of demonstrating the said Auto Magic ball point pens and making a sales speech said to be for the purpose of launching a brand new product not yet on sale:

"It's Packard Auto Magic, the dual pen set. The two, designed to retail at $7.95, get one, they're really worth it.", and
"Now remember the name. It's telephone clip-on pen by Packard. Designed to retail at $3.98", and
"One of our Packard Auto Magic dual pen sets which you see here is $7.95", and
"One of our new telephone clip-on pens at the nationally advertised price of $3.98."

11. On completion of each of the said sales speeches, McPhee sold a number of telephone clip-on pens for $2.98 and subsequently delivered to each purchaser one "Auto Magic" ball point pen set, and a number of ball point pen refills which were represented to be as bonuses to the purchasers. No receipts were given to persons making purchases.

12. I found that the aforesaid representations were made for the purpose of promoting the sale of the ball point pens named "Auto Magic".

13. I also found as a fact that McPhee made the following statement as part of his sales speech:

"How many of you same people would take this set from me now, absolutely free? Now take it home and show it to your friends and help us to advertise our new product and take along with you one of our new telephone clip-on pens at the nationally advertised price of $3.98. Would you like to raise your hands? Thank you sir, thank you sir, thank you ladies."

14. I found that the aforesaid representations were false representations of the ordinary selling price of the ball point pens named "Auto Magic" since testimony from the several witnesses which I accepted placed the maximum selling price between $2.00 and $6.95 and not $7.95 as was stated by McPhee.

15. The said sales speeches including the representations aforesaid were prepared in writing by Healey. They were not considered or approved by Fawcett. There was no evidence of consideration or approval of the said representations by any other person on behalf of the accused Woolworth.

16. McPhee in his sales speeches represented that he was associated with a large manufacturing company, the Packard Pen Company. At no time during the said sales speeches did McPhee represent that he was an employee, agent, servant or representative of Woolworth or hold himself out as being associated with Woolworth.

17. Fawcett made no express arrangement directly with McPhee permitting him to be on the premises but understood that he was employed by Healey. Fawcett had no knowledge of the terms of the agreement between McPhee and Healey or of what they did with the proceeds gained from sales.

18. Fawcett had no control over the manner in which Healey or McPhee demonstrated and sold the said pens except to terminate their permission to be on the said store premises.

19. I found that the accused Woolworth:

 (i)   knew or should have known by informing itself as to what was said by Mr. McPhee;
 (ii) was a participant;
 (iii) was a partner with Healey in this venture;
 (iv) provided the facilities without charge for the selling of the ball point pens named "Auto Magic";
 (v)   received a commission from the accused Healey of 30 percent of the gross sales of the ball point pens named "Auto Magic".

· · · ·

The said F.W. Woolworth Co. Limited desires to question the validity of the said conviction on the grounds that it is erroneous in point of law.

· · · ·

Before this Court it was conceded that Healey and his employee McPhee had violated s. 33c(1) of the Act (as enacted by 1960, c. 45, s. 13 [now s. 36]) and that Fawcett came within the class of employees whose acts were those of his corporate employer in relation to the arrangement made with Healey.

I am of the opinion that there was evidence to support the conviction of Healey and McPhee on the charge as particularized in the information.

Since the offence is the making of a misleading representation, to fix Woolworth with criminal responsibility for the making of it, the Crown was required to connect Woolworth with the "making" in some manner which would in law constitute Woolworth criminally liable for such representation. This could have been done only:

1. By fixing Woolworth with the vicarious liability for the acts of Healey and McPhee.

2. By establishing that Woolworth was a party to the offence by reason of s. 21 of the *Criminal Code*.

· · · ·

It is sought to make Woolworth a party as having done or omitted to do something for the purpose of aiding Healey and McPhee to commit the substantive offence.

There are two principal reasons for holding that Woolworth was not a party to the offence charged:

1. Even with respect to offences of strict liability the alleged aider must know that he is aiding. Although it is not necessary that it be proven that he know that the conduct he is aiding constitutes an offence it is necessary that the accused be proven at least to have known the circumstances necessary to constitute the offence he is accused of aiding.

Counsel before Houlden J. informed him that diligent search had not disclosed any authority in point. He was left to rely upon the following dictum in *R. v. Jacobs et. al.*, [1944] K.B. 417 at p. 420:

> We desire, however, to guard ourselves against being supposed to assent to the proposition that a person who aids and abets another in the commission of an offence not involving any *mens rea* in the principal cannot be convicted in the absence of proof of *mens rea* on his own part.

This dictum formed no essential part of the decision of the issue before the Court. The Court was dealing with the sufficiency of a direction given to a jury in the trial of charges of conspiracy as to what constituted aiding and abetting. After approving as correct the instructions given by the trial Judge the judgment went on to make, due perhaps to over-caution, a reservation as to what the Court was not deciding. It is sufficient to say that when a Court indicates the exact limits it wishes to be put upon its pronouncements no inference may be drawn as to what would have been its decision on the points it has disclaimed as part of its decision.

Subsequent cases appear to have more relevancy to the point at issue than has the case quoted. In *National Coal Board v. Gamble*, [1959] 1 Q.B. 11, the Board as the operator of a mine, through its employee, a weighmaster, gave to the driver of an independent haulage contractor a delivery ticket which indicated that the vehicle was overweight. The driver of the vehicle, who chose to risk driving as he had loaded, was apprehended and convicted. The Board which had no control over the driver, but whose ticket was necessary for the driver to leave the Board's premises, was charged as an aider and abettor. On the review of the conviction by the Queen's Bench Division, Lord Goddard C.J. stated at p. 18:

> In *Ackroyds Air Travel, Ltd. v. Director of Public Prosecutions*, [1950] 1 All E.R. 933, 936, I stated the law with regard to aiding and abetting in this way: ". . . a person could only be convicted . . . as an aider and abettor if he knew all the circumstances which constituted the offence. Whether he realized that those circumstances constituted an offence was immaterial. If he knew all the circumstances and those circumstances constituted the offence . . . that was enough to convict him of being an aider and abettor." Humphreys J. in the same case said: ". . . it must he shown that the unlawful act has been committed, and, therefore, that the offence has been committed, and, further, that the person charged as an aider and abettor was aware of the facts sufficiently to enable him to know that the act was unlawful."

It may be noted that the judgment of Lord Goddard C.J., in *Ackroyds Air Travel, Ltd. v. Director of Public Prosecutions*, [1950] 1 All E.R. 933, was delivered in 1950 and refers to an earlier statement to the same effect, in *Carter Patersons & Pickford Carriers Ltd. v. Wessel*, [1947] 1 K.B. 849.

The statement of Lord Goddard C.J. above quoted was applied in *John Henshall (Quarries) Ltd. v. Harvey*, [1965] 2 W.L.R. 758.

In *Sweet v. Parsley, supra*, the attention of the Court was directed principally to another point: but there seems to have been no challenge to the Court's assumption that, even in offences of strict liability, to hold one guilty as an aider and abettor, the Crown had the onus of proving knowledge on the part of the alleged aider of the circumstances necessary to constitute the offence which he is alleged to have aided, although it is not required that it be proven the alleged aider knew that those circumstances constituted an offence.

In the light of the foregoing authorities I am of the view that, it not having been shown that Woolworth had knowledge of the facts which constituted the offence, it could not be convicted as an aider by the application of s. 21. I use knowledge in this connection as actual knowledge as defined by Devlin J., that is, actual knowledge or deliberate ignorance which is the equivalent of actual knowledge.

2. There is another reason why I am of the opinion that the convictions cannot stand. Section 21 requires that an alleged party must do or omit to do something for the purpose of aiding the principal to commit the offence. That purpose must be the purpose of the one sought to be made a party to the offence (*Sweet v. Parsley, supra*) but if what is done incidentally and innocently assists in the commission of an offence that is not enough to involve the alleged party whose purpose was not that of furthering the perpetration of the offence.

If the owner of a car rents or loans it to one he knows contemplates using it for the purpose of committing a robbery, he would thereby render himself liable as a party, or if an owner of a house rents the house knowing it is to be used for recording bets, he similarly would be a party to the offence. But one does not render himself liable by renting or loaning a car for some legitimate business or recreational activity merely because the person to whom it is loaned or rented chooses in the course of his use to transport some stolen goods, or by renting a house for residential purposes to a tenant who surreptitiously uses it to store drugs.

Hence where, as here, the arrangement between Woolworth and the actual offender was for the purpose of merchandising in the normal conduct of which there would be no infraction of s. 33, the departure of Healey and McPhee from the legitimate course of business by making statements constituting an infraction of s. 33 was outside the purpose of the arrangement. There is no evidence that Woolworth's purpose in providing space and facilities in its store was for the purpose of aiding and abetting Healey in the commission of this offence. Woolworth, having no actual knowledge of the illegal conduct or of Healey's intention to commit it, cannot be held to have provided the facilities and premises for the purpose of aiding and abetting in the commission of an offence.

Appeal allowed: conviction quashed.

GAMBLE AND NICHOLS v. R.

(1978), 40 C.C.C. (2d) 415 (Alta. C.A.)

SINCLAIR J.A.: — The appellants are each charged that on March 12, 1976, they unlawfully killed Allan Keith Harrison, a police officer acting in the course of his duty, and did thereby commit first degree murder, contrary to the *Criminal Code*.

Tried by Judge and jury, each was found guilty as charged. Each appeals.

Before turning to consider the grounds, it will be helpful to give a brief summary of the events that occurred.

William Nichols and Janice Gamble had come to Calgary from Vancouver in a rented car with two other people: John' Gamble, husband of Mrs. Gamble, and Tracie Perry, a young girl. John Gamble eventually took his life from an overdose of drugs during the events that followed the shooting of Detective Sergeant Harrison.

The foursome was headed for Toronto. Its members were in a car rented by Nichols. They changed to another rented car in Penticton, and arrived in Calgary later that day. They spent the night in a motel.

The next day, after some shopping, they drove to the rear of the Inglewood Credit Union in south-east Calgary. Nichols was the driver. They parked behind the building. The two men got out, and went into the Credit Union, using a hold-up note written on a large envelope. Hand guns were displayed to the teller; $1,631 was taken. It was about 3:00 p.m.

The two girls did not go into the Credit Union. There was evidence that Janice Gamble was seen walking back and forth in front of the building.

The four people then left in the car with Janice Gamble at the wheel, and the other girl beside her. The two men were in the back. Nichols was on the driver's side, Gamble on the passenger's. When the vehicle reached Memorial Dr., it headed west towards downtown Calgary. When it was about 8/10 of a mile from the scene of the robbery, the car stopped so that Nichols could replace Mrs. Gamble as driver. Soon thereafter at least four other cars, which had been following not far behind, also stopped.

The vehicle immediately to the rear of the hold-up car was an unmarked police car, equipped with a radio. The radio was partially defective because while messages could be heard, no transmissions could be made. The sole occupant of the police car was the victim, Detective Sergeant Harrison. Although in plain clothes, he was clearly acting in the course of his duties.

An exchange of shots then took place between the two male occupants of the getaway vehicle, on the one hand, and the detective, on the other. All were outside their vehicles when the shots were fired. The policeman was hit, by a shot from Nichols' gun, and died a few hours later.

Numerous witnesses testified as to the manner in which the so-called "shoot-out" occurred.

It seems that Detective Sergeant Harrison got out of his car with his gun drawn, and ordered the occupants of the getaway car to get out of theirs. The two men got out first, Nichols on the driver's side, and Gamble on the passenger's side.

Following the exchange of shots, the getaway car took off at high speed, with Nichols driving.

The first stop was at a restaurant, where a married couple were taken as hostages, and money was stolen from the cash register. The group then got into a taxi, and continued to a service station. The taxi-driver stopped to get gas, since he had become suspicious. When he refused to return to the taxi, Nichols relieved him of the keys.

Nichols then drove the taxi, and, some distance further, a lady, Mrs. Diane Perry (not to be confused with Tracie Perry, Nichols' companion from Vancouver), was tricked into stopping her car. Mrs. Perry was taken hostage, and the four Vancouver people and the three hostages continued to a house not far away. There the occupants fled the house upon the arrival of the robbers and their hostages.

Nichols and Gamble entered into negotiations with the police by telephone shortly after their arrival at the house about 4:10 p.m. That evening, the male restaurant keeper, Mr. Jivraj, was released in return for some demerol.

The next day, Saturday, at around 7:00 p.m., Mrs. Jivraj and Mrs. Diane Perry, the remaining hostages, were released, and left the house. They were followed shortly thereafter by Tracie Perry and Janice Gamble.

The next day, Sunday, the police entered the home to find John Gamble dead and William Nichols unconscious.

That is a very brief outline of the events that occurred. Some of the events will be dealt with more fully later on.

.   .   .   .

I will now consider the appeal of Janice Gamble. Before dealing further with the arguments advanced on behalf of this appellant I would refer generally to the trial Judge's charge to the jury relating to her involvement in the affair.

He first read s. 21 in its entirety. The meaning of the words "aiding" and , "abets" found in s-s. (1)(b) and (c) was discussed.

The presiding Judge then turned to consider the effect of s . 21 (2). He said this to the jury:

> In order to bring her under s-s. (2) of s. 21, the Crown must prove to your satisfaction beyond a reasonable doubt:
> (1) that the two accused formed an intention in common to resist lawful arrest and assist each other in doing it,
> (2) that it was in fact a probable consequence of that common purpose that William John Nichols would, to facilitate the offence of resisting lawful arrest, intentionally cause bodily harm to someone,
> (3) that it was known or ought to have been known to Janice Marie Gamble that such a consequence was probable,
> (4) that in fact the death of Sergeant Allan Keith Harrison ensued from such bodily harm.

Two things should be said at once in connection with those instructions: First, no mention is made of the use of the gun by Nichols. Secondly, the offence of robbery is not referred to.

In my opinion, the learned trial Judge might well have charged the jury as to the combined effect of ss. 21(2) and 213 along the following lines:

1. that Janice Gamble, her husband John Gamble and William Nichols formed an intention in common to carry out the robbery of the Credit Union and assist each other therein;

2. that it was a probable consequence of the prosecution of the robbery that Nichols would intentionally cause bodily harm to someone to facilitate the robbery or the subsequent flight;
3. that it was known or ought to have been known by Janice Gamble that such a consequence was probable;
4. in the alternative, that it was known or ought to have been known by Janice Gamble that Nichols had upon his person a gun and would use it if needed (*per* Fauteux C.J.C. in *R. v. Caouette*, 9 C.C.C. (2d) 449, [1973] S.C.R. 859), and
5. that the death of Sergeant Allan Keith Harrison ensued from such bodily harm.

Those words are based upon a passage from the judgment of Lacourcière J.A. of the Ontario Court of Appeal in *R. v. Riezebos* (1975), 26 C.C.C. (2d) 1 at p. 20, and to which reference was made by Mr. Justice Moir of this Division in his dissenting judgment in *R. v. Augustus, Rivett and Sartor*, [1977] 6 W.W.R. 36.

Counsel for Mrs. Gamble then drew our attention to the following passages in the charge:

> Now, with respect to the accused Janice Marie Gamble and the Crown's contention that she was a party to the murder committed by William John Nichols, that is the Crown's position is that he committed the murder and that she was a party to it. With respect to her position as a party, I suggest that you consider the following items of evidence.

The presiding Judge then referred to:

1. Mrs. Homan's evidence that she saw Janice Gamble pacing back and forth in front of the Credit Union when Gamble and Nichols were inside robbing it.
2. Evidence that Mrs. Gamble's fingerprint was on the hold-up note.
3. The finding of a fully-loaded .38 special pearl-handled revolver at the scene of the shoot-out, near where Mrs. Gamble was knocked or fell down.
4. The conversation in the house regarding a lost gun.
5. The counting of the money.
6. The theft of money from the Thunderbird Motel.
7. The tying-up of the hostages.
8. The holding of knives to the hostages' throats.

I should add, in passing, that in my view the Judge summarized the evidence touching on these points in a manner that was favourable to the accused.

The charge continued with these words:

> The testimony of William Nichols, the accused William Nichols, tended to exonerate her from criminal activities. You will recall that his testimony on that subject, he said that she knew nothing of the plan to rob the Credit Union and that he never saw her carrying a gun. Indeed, he said the men took steps to conceal the weapons from her and Tracie Perry.

Now those are some of the items that you can consider in determining whether or not Janice Gamble was a party. I'm sure that there are others that I have not mentioned. The decision as to her role is for you to make.

Based upon these references, counsel for Mrs. Gamble says that nowhere in this critical portion of the charge did the presiding Judge instruct the jury that if they believed that evidence, they might draw the inference that there was a common intention to resist arrest. Counsel submits that the Judge did not make it clear that it was for the jury to draw any inferences, and that the matters to which the Judge referred did not, of themselves, constitute proof of the formation of an intent to resist arrest.

Counsel says that failure to make such a distinction is fatal. He referred us to *R. v. Riezebos, supra.*

In my opinion the charge, read as a whole, does not support the contention that the jury would be under the impression that these matters would constitute proof of an intention to resist arrest, rather than being merely evidence from which it could make such an inference if it chose to do so. In the first place, in the standard part of the charge the jury members were instructed that they were to be the sole Judges of the facts. They were, moreover, told how they could draw inferences from the proven facts.

Then, just before the section of the charge to which complaint is made, the learned Judge explained to the jury that common intention is found from the conduct of the parties. In the very important part of his review of the evidence dealing with the Crown's contention that Mrs. Gamble was a look-out, the Judge said: "The Crown's suggestion there is that you should draw the inference that she was acting as a lookout."

In my view, there was no misdirection by the learned trial Judge.

The next ground of appeal made on behalf of Mrs. Gamble was expressed in these terms by Taschereau J. in *Henderson v. The King*, 91 C.C.C. 97 at p. 108, [1948] S.C.R. 226 at p. 237:

> Unfortunately, all these aspects of the case were not dealt with, and these omissions were, I believe, highly prejudicial to the accused. The defence was not presented so as to give it all its force and effect. It is true that no witnesses were called on behalf of the appellant, but it is nevertheless the duty of the trial Judge, in his charge to the jury, to explain the exculpatory effect of the evidence, whether it is given by the witnesses for the Crown or for the accused: *Wu v. The King*, 92 C.C.C. 90, [1934] S.C.R. 609. It was the fundamental right of the appellant, who has been charged of murder, purely by construction of the law, which in this particular case creates a presumptive guilt, to have all the features of his defence adequately put to the jury.

Counsel for Mrs. Gamble submits that the trial Judge did not refer to critical portions of the evidence which the defence relied upon as evidence from which no common intent could be inferred. In essence, counsel says that evidence of William Nichols and Tracie Perry favourable to Mrs. Gamble was not mentioned. The items of which he complains are:

(1) that no eyewitness to the shooting saw this appellant do any act which could be considered as resisting arrest;

(3) that she fell to the ground and was screaming during the incident;

(4) that the shooting started as she and Tracie Perry were in the process of getting out of the car;

(5) that the appellant was screaming and saying "What is going on" as they left the scene;

(6) the appellant's conduct in the car behind the Credit Union before and after the robbery;

(7) the evidence that the loaded pearl-handled gun was placed on the passenger side by John Gamble, and was found near his glasses on the road;

(8) the evidence as to how the appellant treated the hostages in consoling them and untying them, and

(9) the situation in general at the house where the hostages were taken.

I do not think a trial Judge is obliged to refer to *every* piece of evidence in favour of an accused. Moreover, he could have mentioned, but did not, some other evidence which, if accepted by the jury, was damaging to Mrs. Gamble:

(a) that she had, on the morning of the robbery, bought the large envelope on which the holdup note was written;

(b) the evidence of the hostage, Mrs. Perry, that Janice Gamble said a spent bullet shell fell out when she took her coat off in the restaurant, and

(c) that the only time Mrs. Gamble drove the car was just after the robbery of the Credit Union.

It may be appropriate at this stage to refer to the words of Anglin J. in *Picariello et al. v. The King* (1923), 39 C.C.C. 229 at p. 245 (S.C.C.):

> No doubt there may be found some sentences in the charge that might have been better expressed; some passages, if isolated, may be open to criticism. But taken as a whole, as it should be, and having regard to the evidence with which the trial Judge was dealing, I do not find any substantial misdirection.

I do not think there is any need to deal with the defence of duress, if it can be called that in the circumstances of this case. I am of the opinion that when the jury was recalled the learned Judge put Mrs. Gamble's position on this score to the jury as fairly as it could be put. Nor do I believe it necessary to consider the argument that the jury might have been led to believe that all the evidence of the unlawful acts that occurred following the shoot-out was admissible to prove unlawful purpose or common intent.

Finally, before leaving the arguments which turn around the effect of ss. 21 and 213, there can be no doubt, in my view, that the manner in which the jury was directed, based upon the aspect of resisting arrest, was favourable to Mrs. Gamble.

There was, in my opinion, powerful evidence which, if accepted by the jury, could have established her guilt through the combination of ss. 21(1)(*b*) and 213. I am referring here to such matters as the purchase of the envelope, her presence outside the Credit Union and her driving of the getaway car. These are things which a jury might well have found to have been done by Mrs. Gamble for the purpose of aiding Nichols to commit the robbery.

I am of the opinion that it would have been better had the jury been instructed along the lines I have just mentioned, or by using words, as earlier indicated, based upon the passage from *R. v. Reizebos*. Had the jury been so charged, I am of the view that it must inevitably have convicted Mrs. Gamble. No miscarriage of justice having occurred, I would apply s. 613(1)(*b*)(iii).

. ·. . .

Appeals dismissed.

Janice Gamble was sentenced to life imprisonment without eligibility for parole until 25 years of her sentence had expired. While the offence was committed prior to the enactment of the current murder provisions, she was tried, convicted and punished in accordance with those provisions. On December 8th, 1988, the majority of the Supreme Court of Canada (1989), 66 C.R. (3d) 193, accepted her claim that fundamental justice under s. 7 of the *Charter* entitled her to be punished to no greater extent than the law in effect at the time of the commission of her offence. The Court declared her immediately eligible for parole. She was subsequently released on parole, having served 13 years' imprisonment. She was killed in a motor vehicle accident shortly thereafter.

In *R. v. Simpson* (1988), 62 C.R. (3d) 137 (S.C.C.), the Supreme Court unanimously held that the unlawful purpose in s. 21(2) must be different from the offence actually charged. The "unlawful purpose" and the "offence" committed in the course of the pursuit of the unlawful purpose were different. This settled a long-standing conflict of opinion in lower Courts.

R. v. LOGAN

[1990] 2 S.C.R. 731, 79 C.R. (3d) 169, 58 C.C.C. (3d) 391

The accused were convicted of attempted murder. During a robbery a person was shot and severely injured. Neither accused did the shooting. Johnson admitted to being one of the robbers but stated that he had no intention to shoot and that there had been no discussion concerning the use of guns. Logan had boasted of being involved in planning the robberies. The trial Judge instructed the jury that there could be convictions, under s. 21(2), if the Crown established beyond a reasonable doubt that the accused knew or ought to have known that someone would probably shoot with the intention of killing. The Court of Appeal allowed appeals with respect to the convictions for attempted murder and substituted convictions for robbery. The Crown appealed.

LAMER C.J.C. (DICKSON C.J.C. and WILSON, GONTHIER and CORY JJ. concurring): —

. . . .

The appellant is challenging the constitutionality of s. 21(2) in general and, in particular, of the objective component of the section ("ought to have known"). However, the Court of Appeal, quite correctly, did not declare the objective component of s. 21(2) inoperative for all offences. They dealt specifically with the operation of the provision in relation to the offence of attempted murder and the possibility that a party to an attempted murder could be convicted upon proof of objective intent, whereas a conviction of the principal would require proof of subjective intent. More generally, as a basis for their decision, the Court determined that it is a principle of fundamental justice that a party to *any* offence cannot be found guilty of the offence based on a lower standard of requisite *mens rea* than that required for convicting the principal.

For this proposition, the Court relied on our judgment in *Vaillancourt*. In that case, this Court held that for a few offences the principles of fundamental justice require that a conviction cannot stand unless there is proof beyond a reasonable doubt of a minimum degree of *mens rea*, and that legislation providing for any lesser degree violates the *Charter* and is inoperative. Murder was one of those offences.

With respect, I cannot construe *Vaillancourt* as saying that, as a general proposition, Parliament cannot ever enact provisions requiring different levels of guilt for principal offenders and parties. Although I readily admit that, as a matter of policy, the proposition seems more equitable than not, I am not ready to characterize it as a principle of fundamental justice. It must be remembered that within many offences there are varying degrees of guilt, and it remains the function of the sentencing process to adjust the punishment for each individual offender accordingly. The argument that the principles of fundamental justice prohibit the conviction of a party to an offence on the basis of a lesser degree of *mens rea* than that required to convict the principal could be supported only, if at all, in a situation where the sentence for a particular offence is fixed. However, currently in Canada the sentencing scheme is flexible enough to accommodate the varying degrees of culpability resulting from the operation of ss. 21 and 22.

That said, however, there are a few offences with respect to which the operation of the objective component of s. 21(2) will restrict the rights of an accused under s. 7. If an offence is one of the few for which s. 7 requires a minimum degree of *mens rea*, *Vaillancourt* does preclude Parliament from providing for the conviction of a party to that offence on the basis of a degree of *mens rea* below the constitutionally-required minimum.

Requisite mens rea for conviction pursuant to s. 21(2)

Therefore, the question whether a party to an offence had the requisite *mens rea* to found a conviction pursuant to s. 21(2) must be answered in two steps. Firstly, is there a minimum degree of *mens rea* which is required as a principle of fundamental justice before one can be convicted as a principal for this particular offence? This is an important initial step because if there is no such constitutional requirement for the offence, the objective component of s. 21(2) can operate without restricting the constitutional rights of the party to the offence. Secondly, if the principles of fundamental justice do require a certain minimum degree of *mens rea* in order to convict for this offence, then that minimum degree of *mens rea* is constitutionally required to convict a party to that offence as well.

Step 1: Section 7 and Attempted Murder

With respect to the case at bar, then, the first question which must be answered is whether the principles of fundamental justice require a minimum degree of *mens rea* in order to convict an accused of attempted murder. *Ancio* established that a specific intent to kill is the *mens rea* required for a principal on the charge of attempted murder. However, as the constitutional question was not raised or argued in that case, it did not decide whether that requisite *mens rea* was a *constitutional* requirement. The case simply interpreted the offence as currently legislated.

In *R. v. Martineau*, a judgment handed down this day, this Court has decided, as a constitutional requirement, that no one can be convicted of murder unless the Crown proves beyond a reasonable doubt that the person had *subjective* foresight of the fact that the death of the victim was likely to ensue. Because of both the stigma and the severe penal consequences which result from a conviction for murder, the Constitution requires at least that degree of intent.

As defined in *Ancio*, the elements of *mens rea* for attempted murder are identical to those for the most severe form of murder, murder under s. 212(*a*)(i) [now s. 229 (*a*)(i)]. For each, the accused must have had the specific intent to kill. All that differs is the "consequences" component of the *actus reus*. Quite simply, an attempted murderer is, if caught and convicted, a "lucky murderer". Therefore, it would seem logical that the requisite *mens rea* for a murder conviction, as described in *Martineau*, must be the same for a conviction of attempted murder. However, logic is not sufficient reason to label something a "constitutional requirement". As I have stated in *Vaillancourt*, the principles of fundamental justice require a minimum degree of *mens rea* for only a very few offences. The criteria by which these offences can be identified are, primarily, the stigma associated with a conviction and, as a secondary consideration, the penalties available.

The stigma associated with a conviction for attempted murder is the same as it is for murder. Such a conviction reveals that, although no death ensued from the actions of the accused, the intent to kill was still present in his or her mind. The attempted murderer is no less a killer than a murderer: he may be lucky — the ambulance arrived early, or some other fortuitous circumstance — but he still has the same killer instinct. Secondly, while a conviction for attempted murder does not automatically result in a life sentence, the offence is punishable by life and the usual penalty is very severe.

It should be noted that, as a basis for a constitutionally-required minimum degree of *mens rea*, the social stigma associated with a conviction is the most important consideration, not the sentence. Few offences have a high minimum sentence such as that for murder. For some offences there is a high maximum and a low minimum penalty available; for other offences the maximum penalty is much reduced and there is no minimum imposed whatsoever. In either situation, the fact that a lesser sentence is available or imposed, by statute or through the exercise of judicial discretion, in no way ends the inquiry. The sentencing range available to the Judge is not conclusive of the level of *mens rea* constitutionally required. Instead, the crucial consideration is whether there is a continuing serious social stigma which will be imposed on the accused upon conviction.

For example, the offence of theft in the most serious circumstances is punishable by a maximum of ten years or, in less serious circumstances, a maximum of two years if the Crown proceeds by indictment; if the Crown proceeds summarily, the maximum is six months. The constitutional *mens rea* requirement would not, under s. 7, be triggered by any punishment within these ranges which the sentencing Judge decided to impose. Whether the actual or available punishment is severe or not, the social stigma associated with being labelled dishonest will be automatically and unavoidably imposed upon conviction. It is because of this stigma that the principles of fundamental justice will require a minimum degree of *mens rea*, that is, as I said in *Vaillancourt*, at p. 653, "proof of some dishonesty".

For these reasons, the *mens rea* for attempted murder cannot, without restricting s. 7 of the *Charter*, require of the accused less of a mental element than that required of a murderer under s. 212(*a*)(i), that is, subjective foresight of the consequences. While Parliament, as I have already implied, could well extend our definition of attempted murder in *Ancio* to include the unsuccessful murderers of s. 212(*a*)(ii), it cannot go further and include objective foresight as being sufficient for a conviction without restricting s. 7 of the *Charter*.

Step 2: *Mens Rea* for Attempted Murder Pursuant to S. 21(2)

Having completed the initial step of the inquiry, one can proceed to the second step in determining the requisite *mens rea* for the conviction of a party pursuant to s. 21(2) on a charge of attempted murder. When the principles of fundamental justice require *subjective* foresight in order to convict a principal of attempted murder, that same minimum degree of *mens rea* is constitutionally required to convict a party to the offence of attempted murder. Any conviction for attempted murder, whether of the principal directly or of a party pursuant to s. 21(2), will carry enough stigma to trigger the constitutional requirement. To the extent that s. 21(2) would allow for the conviction of a party to the offence of attempted murder on the basis of objective foresight, its operation restricts s. 7 of the *Charter*.

Section 1 Analysis

Given the finding that s. 7 is restricted in the present case, can that restriction be found to be a reasonable limit demonstrably justified in a free and democratic society? The s. 1 analysis to be followed in answering this question has been set out in the decision of this Court in *R. v. Oakes*, [1986] 1 S.C.R. 103, 50 C.R. (3d) 1, 24 C.C.C. (3d) 321.

. . . .

However, even though Parliament has sought to achieve an important legislative objective by enacting the restriction in issue in this appeal and even though such restriction is rationally connected to that objective, I am of the view that it does not satisfy the proportionality test because it unduly impairs an accused's rights under s. 7 of the *Charter*: see *Vaillancourt, supra*, at p. 651.

The objective component of s. 21(2) unduly impairs rights under s. 7 of the *Charter* when it operates with respect to an offence for which a conviction carries severe stigma and for which, therefore, there is a constitutionally-required minimum degree of *mens rea*. The words "ought to know" allow for the possibility that while a party may not have considered and accepted the risk that an accomplice may do something with the intent to kill in furtherance of the common purpose, the party, through this negligence, could still be found guilty of attempted murder. In other words, parties could be held to be criminally negligent with respect to the behaviour of someone else. For most offences under the *Criminal Code*, a person is convicted for criminal negligence only if consequences have ensued from their actions. While a person may be convicted, absent consequences, for criminal negligence (*e.g.*, dangerous operation of a motor vehicle), none of these forms of criminal negligence carry with them the stigma of being labelled a "killer". In a situation where s. 21(2) is operating in relation to the offence of attempted murder, no consequences have resulted from the actions of the party, and yet the party could be convicted of this offence and suffer severe accompanying stigma and penalty.

Because of the importance of the legislative purpose, the objective component of s. 21(2) can be justified with respect to most offences. However, with respect to the few offences for which the Constitution requires subjective intent, the stigma renders the infringement too serious and outweighs the legislative objective, which therefore cannot be justified under s. 1.

Conclusion

I would, therefore, as did the Court of Appeal, declare inoperative the words "or ought to have known" when considering under s. 21(2) whether a person is a party to any offence where it is a constitutional requirement for a conviction that foresight of the consequences be subjective, which is the case for attempted murder. Once these words are deleted, the remaining section requires, in the context of attempted murder, that the party to the common venture know that it is probable that his accomplice would do something with the intent to kill in carrying out the common purpose.

I would dismiss the appeal. I would restrict my answers to the constitutional questions as follows:

1. Does s. 21(2) of the *Criminal Code* contravene the rights and freedoms guaranteed by section 7 and/or section 11(*d*) of the *Canadian Charter of Rights and Freedoms*?

Yes, on charges where subjective foresight is a constitutional requirement, to the extent that a party may be convicted if that person objectively "ought to have known" that the commission of the offence would be a probable consequence of carrying out the common purpose.

2. If the answer to question 1 is in the affirmative, is section 21(2) of the *Criminal Code* justified under section 1 of the *Canadian Charter of Rights and Freedoms*, and therefore not inconsistent with the *Constitution Act, 1982*?
No.

L'Heureux-Dubé and Sopinka JJ. delivered separate concurring opinions.

CANADIAN DREDGE AND DOCK CO. v. R.

[1985] 1 S.C.R. 662, 45 C.R. (4th) 289, 19 C.C.C. (3d) 1, 59 N.R. 241

This is the leading decision on the difficult issue of the "identification doctrine" under which Canadian Courts impute fault, including *mens rea*, to corporations. The case concerned appeals of several corporate accused against their *Criminal Code* convictions for conspiracy to defraud. The charges stemmed from bids for dredging contracts found to have been collusive. The Supreme Court rejected arguments that the companies were not guilty as the bids had been conducted by managers acting in fraud of the companies or contrary to corporate instructions.

The Supreme Court confirmed the convictions and took the opportunity to assert and justify the identification doctrine for holding corporations responsible for *mens rea* offences.

ESTEY J.: —

The position of the corporation in criminal law must first be examined. Inasmuch as all criminal and quasi-criminal offences are creatures of statute the amenability of the corporation to prosecution necessarily depends in part upon the terminology employed in the statute. In recent years there has developed a system of classification which segregates the offences according to the degree of intent, if any, required to create culpability.

(a) *Absolute Liability Offences*

Where the Legislature by the clearest intendment establishes an offence where liability arises instantly upon the breach of the statutory prohibition, no particular state of mind is a prerequisite to guilt. Corporations and individual persons stand on the same footing in the face of such a statutory offence. It is a case of automatic primary responsibility. Accordingly, there is no need to establish a rule for corporate liability nor a rationale therefore. The corporation is treated as a natural person.

(b) *Offences of Strict Liability*

Where the terminology employed by the Legislature is such as to reveal an intent that guilt shall not be predicated upon the automatic breach of the statute — but rather upon the establishment of the *actus reus*, subject to the defence of due diligence, an offence of strict liability arises. See *R. v. City of Sault Ste. Marie*, [1978] 2 S.C.R. 1299. As in the case of an absolute liability offence, it matters not whether the accused is corporate or unincorporate, because the liability is primary and arises in the accused according to the terms of the statute in the same way as in the case of absolute offences. It is not dependent upon the attribution to the accused of the misconduct of others. This is so when the statute, properly construed, shows a clear contemplation by the Legislature that a breach of the statute itself leads to guilt, subject to the limited defence above noted. In this category, the corporation and the natural defendant are in the same position. In both cases liability is not vicarious but primary.

(c) *Offences Requiring Mens Rea*

These are the traditional criminal offences for which an accused may be convicted only if the requisite *mens rea* is demonstrated by the prosecution. At common law a corporate entity could not generally be convicted of a criminal offence. Corporate criminal immunity stemmed from the abhorrence of the common law for vicarious liability in criminal law, and from the doctrine of *ultra vires*, which regarded criminal activities by corporate agents as beyond their authority and beyond corporate capacity. At the other extreme in the spectrum of criminal offences there are certain crimes which cannot in any real sense be committed by a corporation as a principal, such as perjury and bigamy, whatever the doctrine of corporate criminal liability may be. As a corporation may only act through agents, there are basically only three approaches whereby criminal intent could be said to reside or not reside in the corporate entity:

(i) a total vicarious liability for the conduct of any of its agents whatever their level of employment or responsibility so long as they are acting within the scope of their employment;

(ii) no criminal liability unless the criminal acts in question have been committed on the direction or at the request, express or clearly implied of the corporation as expressed through its board of directors;

(iii) a median rule whereby the criminal conduct, including the state of mind, of employees and agents of the corporation is attributed to the corporation so as to render the corporation criminally liable so long as the employee or agent in question is of such a position in the organization and activity of the corporation that he or she represents its *de facto* directing mind, will, centre, brain area or ego so that the corporation is identified with the act of that individual. There is said to be on this theory no responsibility through vicarious liability or any other form of agency, but rather a liability arising in criminal law by reason of the single identity wherein is combined the legal entity and the natural person; in short, a primary liability. This rule stands in the middle of the range or spectrum. It is but a legal fiction invented for pragmatic reasons.

. . . .

This [median] rule of law was seen as a result of the removal of the officer or managerial level employee from the general class of "inferior servants or agents" for whose acts the corporate employer continued (as in the case of the human employer) to be immune from vicarious liability in criminal law. This result is generally referred to as the "identification" theory. It produces the element of *mens rea* in the corporate entity, otherwise absent from the legal entity but present in the natural person, the directing mind. This establishes the "identity" between the directing mind and the corporation which results in the corporation being found guilty for the act of the natural person, the employee. . . . The essence of the test is that the identity of the directing mind and the company coincide so long as the actions of the former are performed by the manager within the sector of corporation operation assigned to him by the corporation. The sector may be functional, or geographic, or may embrace the entire undertaking of the corporation. The requirement is better stated when it is said that the act in question must be done by the directing force of the company when carrying out his assigned function in the corporation. It is no defence to the application of this doctrine that a criminal act by a corporate employee cannot be within the scope of his authority unless expressly ordered to do the act in question. Such a condition would reduce the rule to virtually nothing. Acts of the ego of a corporation taken within the assigned managerial area may give rise to corporate criminal responsibility, whether or not there be formal delegation; whether or not there be awareness of the activity in the board of directors or the officers of the company; and, as discussed below, whether or not there be express prohibition.

. . . .

Generally the directing mind is also guilty of the criminal offence in question. Glanville Williams, in *Textbook of Criminal Law* (1978), states, at p. 947:

> . . . the director or other controlling officer will almost always be a co-perpetrator of or accessory in the offence . . . .

. . . .

The corporation is but a creature of statute, general or special, and none of the provincial corporation statutes and business corporations statutes, or the federal equivalents, contain any discussion of criminal liability or liability in the common law generally by reason of the doctrine of identification. It is a court-adopted principle put in place for the purpose of including the corporation in the pattern of criminal law in a rational relationship to that of the natural person. The identity doctrine merges the board of directors, the managing director, the superintendent, the manager or anyone else delegated by the board of directors to whom is delegated the governing executive authority of the corporation, and the conduct of any of the merged entities is thereby attributed to the corporation.

... A corporation may, by this means, have more than one directing mind. This must be particularly so in a country such as Canada where corporate operations are frequently geographically widespread. The transportation companies, for example, must of necessity operate by the delegation and subdelegation of authority from the corporate centre; by the division and subdivision of the corporate brain; and by decentralizing by delegation the guiding forces in the corporate undertaking.

The Court in *Dredge and Dock* decided that there could be corporate responsibility on the identification doctrine whether or not there had been formal delegation, awareness of the activity in the board of directors or offices of the company, or express authorization or prohibition. However, the Court also noted that the identification doctrine could not be used where the criminal act of the directing mind had been totally in fraud of the corporation or where the act was intended to, or did result in, benefit exclusively to the directing mind.

For some 15 years the Australian scholar, Professor Brent Fisse, see, for example, "Corporate Criminal Responsibility" (1991), 15 Crim. L.J. 166 and "Criminal Law: The Attribution of Criminal Liability to Corporations: A Statutory Model" (1991), 13 Sydney L. Rev. 277, and others, have called for a new approach for holding corporations responsible for intentional crimes. The argument is that under the identification doctrine the imputing of intent of employees to the corporate entity misses the point. Corporate behaviour is not just the sum of individual employee behaviour but must be considered in the context of the organizational structure and culture.

Professor Pamela Bucy, "Corporate Ethos: A Standard for Imposing Corporate Criminal Liability" (1991), 75 Minnesota L. Rev. 1095, has recently proposed a standard of corporate criminal liability which turns on whether there was a corporate ethos which encouraged the commission of crime. The inquiry is not only into whether the actors were sufficiently high in the hierarchy but also looks at such aspects as company goals and practices, the reaction to past offences and the existence and sufficiency of compliance programs.

General Review Question

A group of five youths, aged 17 to 19 and including A and B, are in a Kingston bar watching the televising of a National Hockey League play-off game between the Montreal Canadiens and Quebec Nordiques, won by Quebec 4-1. During this game each consumes only about three beers. During the second period a Quebec supporter, Pierre, is discovered in the bar. He is sitting alone. His actions are limited to smiling a lot and applauding Quebec goals. After the game the group of five corner Pierre outside the bar and begin deriding him and elbowing him. B shouts "Let's beat up the Frog". A leaves the group momentarily, goes to the back of the bar premises, picks up a four-foot-long loose fence picket, returns and proceeds to savagely beat Pierre, who has fallen to the ground. B removes his leather belt from his jeans and is about to join the attack when Pierre lapses into unconsciousness. The group runs off. C, a passing pedestrian who is a doctor, turns Pierre over, starts to examine him but then departs.

Later C explains "Ontario doctors were on work-stoppage". An ambulance is summoned by another passer-by. It only arrives 35 minutes later as the ambulance service is involved in a rash of hospital transfers due to the doctors' work-stoppage. Pierre dies in transit. The autopsy assigns the death to a combination of the beating, the delay and Pierre's previously undiagnosed heart aneurism.

The responsible Crown Attorney is appalled by the incident. He asks you for a memorandum of law and advice as to the maximum viable charges (discussing possible defences) against A (the attacker), B (the bystander) and C (the doctor).

Chapter 9

INCHOATE CRIMES

Attempts

See sections 24 and 463 of the *Criminal Code*.

R. v. ANCIO

39 C.R. (3d) 1, [1984] 1 S.C.R. 225, 10 C.C.C. (3d) 385

MCINTYRE J. (DICKSON, BEETZ, ESTEY, CHOUINARD, LAMER and WILSON JJ. concurring): — This appeal [from 63 C.C.C. (2d) 309] involves consideration of the mental element required for proof of the crime of attempted murder, the subject of this Court's earlier judgment in *Lajoie v. R.*, [1974] S.C.R. 399, 20 C.R.N.S. 360, [1974] 10 C.C.C. (2d) 313, affirming 16 C.R.N.S. 180, 4 C.C.C. (2d) 402.

At the date of the events which give rise to this appeal the respondent had been married some 25 years. His wife had left the matrimonial home and was living with one Kurely. The responent was depressed and had been drinking to excess on the date in question. He telephoned his wife at Kurely's residence and told her he was afraid that their 23-year-old son was about to commit suicide and asked her to meet him. She refused to co-operate. Later the same evening the respondent broke into a friend's home while its owners were absent and took away three shotguns. He sawed off the barrel of one, loaded it and, taking some extra ammunition with him, went to Kurely's apartment building and gained entry by breaking the glass in the front door. On hearing the noise caused by the breaking glass, Kurely came from his bedroom to investigate, carrying a chair with a jacket hanging on it. He saw the respondent, carrying the shotgun, ascending the stairs to the second floor. He threw the chair and jacket, hitting the respondent. The gun went off. The blast missed Kurely by some three feet but put a hole in the jacket, which had been on the chair. A struggle followed, in which Kurely appears to have wrestled the gun from the respondent. When the police arrived, having been called during the course of the fight between the two men, Kurely was on the floor with his head partly under a bed and with the respondent upon him striking him weakly.

Shortly after his arrest the respondent stated to the police:

> I just went over to see my wife. I had phoned her earlier. I broke the window and went in. Then I heard what sounded like a gun go off. You are lucky you got there when you did. I had him by the throat and I would have killed him.

According to the respondent's account of events, the gun was discharged accidentally, although under tests conducted by the police the weapon was not found to be prone to accidental discharge.

The respondent was charged with a number of offences arising out of this affair but only one, that of attempted murder, is involved in this appeal. It was contained in the first count of the information and was in these terms:

> . . . did attempt to murder Michael Kurely by discharging a sawed off shotgun at him contrary to s. 222 of the *Criminal Code* of Canada [R.S.C. 1970, c. C-34].

He elected trial by Judge alone and was convicted. The conviction was quashed in the Court of Appeal and a new trial directed. This appeal is taken by leave of this Court.

. . . .

The Crown contended in this Court that the Court of Appeal was in error in holding that the *mens rea* in attempted murder was limited to an intention to cause death (s. 212(a)(i)), or an intention to cause bodily harm knowing it to be likely to cause death and being reckless whether death ensues (s. 212(a)(ii)). The Crown's position was stated in its factum in these words:

> . . . the intention for attempted murder is not restricted to an actual intention to kill or an intention to cause grievous bodily harm that one knows is likely to cause death and is reckless whether death ensues or not, but *extends to an intention to do that which constitutes the commission of the offence of murder as defined in ss. 212 and 213 am. 1974-75-76, c. 93, s. 13; c. 105, s. 29; since am. 1980-81-82-83, c. 125 s. 15 of the Criminal Code. It is the Crown's position that s. 24 and s. 213(d) in combination can form the basis for a conviction of attempted murder.* (The italics are mine)

The respondent supported the judgment of the Court of Appeal, which followed the judgment of this Court in *Lajoie v. R., supra.* In that case it was held that a conviction for attempted murder could be sustained where the Crown had shown on the part of the accused either an intent to kill the potential victim or an intent to cause bodily harm which he knows is likely to cause death and is reckless whether death ensues or not. Although reference was made in *Lajoie* to the possibility of committing attempted murder as defined in s. 213 (see the concluding sentence on p. 408), the respondent and the Court of Appeal in the case at bar adopted the view that this was merely obiter. . . . .

. . . .

The respondent submitted that the Crown's position, that s. 213(d) coupled with s. 24(1) described a further intent sufficient to warrant a conviction for attempted murder, should not be accepted because there was no authority to extend the concept of a constructive intent further than *Lajoie* had taken it. While contending on the facts of this case that he was not obliged to go further, he argued that in reason and logic a specific intent to kill should be the only intent sufficient to ground a conviction for attempted murder. It was said that the effect of the Crown's argument in extending the concept of an attempt to s. 213(d) of the *Criminal Code* would be to justify a conviction for attempted murder in the absence of any mental element with respect to the causing of death which would be to ignore the words of s. 24(1) specifically requiring an intent to commit the offence in question.

Lying at the heart of the controversy which arises in this case is the judgment of this Court in *Lajoie, supra*.

. . . .

A great deal of the confusion surrounding the nature of the intent required to found a conviction for attempted murder may well stem from an assumption that murder and attempted murder are related offences which must share the same mental elements. A brief review of the historical development of the law relating to the two offences demonstrates that the crime of attempt developed as a separate and distinct offence from the offence of murder.

In very early times murder was simply the killing of a human being. The law was concerned with the injury done to the family of the deceased and the compensation which should follow. The consequence of the killing was the important feature and the intent or *mens rea* was of little if any significance. Special mental elements were recognized in statutes as early as the 13th Century, and by the 14th Century the concept of malice aforethought had developed: see *Act of the King's Charters of Pardon, 1389* (13 Ric. 2, star. 2), c. 1. Thus two elements came to be recognized in murder: the killing, and the malice aforethought, which in modern times has come to mean the necessary intent or intents.

As the common law developed, the mental element required for the commission of murder expanded to include both constructive intent and knowledge of the likelihood of death as a result of a person's acts, with recklessness as to whether death ensued or not.

. . . .

The offence of attempts developed much later than the offence of murder. In early times an attempt to commit an offence was not itself a crime. It was considered that in the absence of a guilty act intention alone was not punishable. The modern offence of attempting the commission of a crime is said to have its origins in the Court of Star Chamber. An early venture into this field is found in the *Case of Duels* (1615), 2 State Tr. 1033, which involved proceedings against one William Priest for sending a written challenge to duel and one Richard Wright for carrying it and a stick that was to be the measure of the length of the weapons to be employed. It was asserted by Sir Francis Bacon, then Attorney General, at p. 1041, that:

> For the Capacity of this Court, I take this to be a ground infallible: that wheresoever an offence is capital, or matter of felony, though it be not acted, there the combination or practice tending to that offence is punishable in this Court as a high misdemeanor. So practice to impoison, though it took no effect; waylaying to murder, though it took no effect; and the like; have been adjudged heinous misdemeanors punishable in this Court. Nay, inceptions and preparations in inferior crimes, that are not capital, as suborning and preparing of witnesses that were never deposed, or deposed nothing material, have likewise been censured in this Court, as appeareth by the decree in *Garnon's Case*.

The Court in its decree gave effect to the Attorney General's submission saying, in part, at p. 1046:

> And the Court with one consent did declare their opinions: That by the ancient law of the land, all inceptions, preparations, and combinations to execute unlawful acts, though they never be performed, as they be not to be punished capitally, except it be in case of treason, and some other particular cases of statute law, so yet they are punishable as misdemeanors and contempts: and that this Court was proper for offences of such nature.

The practice of the Court of Star Chamber in this respect became firmly established in that Court (see Hall, *General Principles of Criminal Law*, 2nd ed. (1960), p. 565 *et seq.*) and was in time adopted in the Court of King's Bench. It has been said that the origin of the doctrine of criminal attempt as it is known in the common-law was Lord Mansfield's judgment in *R. v. Scofield* (1784), Cald. Mag. Rep. 397. Scofield was charged in an indictment with "wickedly, unlawfully and maliciously intending devising and contriving to feloniously set fire to, burn and consume a certain house".

. . . .

Whether *Scofield* was the starting point for the common-law doctrine is doubted by Hall (pp. 569-70) but the question seems to have been settled in *R. v. Higgins* (1801), 102 E.R. 269 (K.B.), where it was said, at p. 274, by Grose J.:

> First, as to the offence itself, it must be admitted that an attempt to commit a felony is in many cases at least a misdemeanor . . .

Any doubt remaining regarding the existence of the offence of attempted murder in England was set to rest by the enactment of the *Offences Against the Person Act, 1861* (24 & 25 Vict.), c. 100, ss. 11 to 15. These sections made it a felony to attempt the commission of murder in the various ways described.

In Canada the common-law offence of attempt was codified in the *1892 Criminal Code* as s. 64.

. . . .

A minor change in the 1953-54 *Code* changed the section to its present form in s. 24.

. . . .

The section has therefore covered the law of attempt in general since the codification of the law in 1892. In addition, particular provision has been made in the *Criminal Code* for the offence of attempted murder . . . .

. . . .

It is clear from the foregoing that in common law and under the criminal law of Canada criminal attempt is itself an offence separate and distict from the crime alleged to be attempted. As with any other crime, the Crown must prove a *mens rea*, that is, the intent to commit the offence in question, and the *actus reus*, that is, some step towards the commission of the offence attempted going beyond mere acts of preparation. Of the two elements the more significant is the *mens rea*. In *R. v. Ciine* [(1956), 115 C.C.C. 18], Laidlaw J.A., speaking for the Ontario Court of Appeal, said, at p. 27:

> Criminal intention alone is insufficient to establish a criminal attempt. There must be *mens rea* and also an *actus reus*. But it is to be observed that whereas in most crimes it is the *actus reus* which the law endeavours to prevent, and the *mens rea* is only a necessary element of the offence, in a criminal attempt the *mens rea* is of primary importance and the *actus reus* is the necessary element.

And in *Russell on Crime*, 12th ed. (1964), vol. 1, p. 175, it is said:

> Since the mischief contained in an attempt depends upon the nature of the crime intended, the criminality lies much more in the intention than in the acts done.

This proposition was accepted by Goddard L.C.J. in *Whybrow* [(1951), 35 Cr. App. R. 51], at p. 147, where he stated that "the intent becomes the principal ingredient of the crime".

The common-law recognition of the fundamental importance of intent in the crime of attempt is carried forward into the *Criminal Code*. A reading of s. 24 of the *Code* and all its predecessors since the enactment of the first *Code* in 1892 confirms that the intent to commit the desired offence is a basic element of the offence of attempt. Indeed, because the crime of attempt may be complete without the actual commission of any other offence and even without the performance of any act unlawful in itself, it is abundantly clear that the criminal element of the offence of attempt may lie solely in the intent. As noted by Glanville Williams, *Criminal Law: The General Part*, 2nd ed. (1961), p. 642, para. 207, in discussing attempts:

> An *actus reus* . . . need not be a crime apart from the state of mind. It need not even be a tort or a moral wrong or a social mischief.

The question now arises: What is the intent required for an attempt to commit murder? As has been indicated earlier, the Crown's position is that the intent required for a conviction on a charge of attempt to murder is the intent to do that which will, if death is caused, constitute the commission of murder as defined in ss. 212 and 213 of the *Code*, so that a combination of ss. 24 and 213(*d*) can form the basis for a conviction of attempted murder. Tbe respondent, on the other hand, argues that, although the authorities presently limit the intent to that which would constitute murder as defined in s. 212 of the *Code*, logic and principle dictate that the intent should be limited to the specific intent to kill described in s. 212(*a*)(i).

While it is clear from ss. 212 and 213 of the *Criminal Code* that an unintentional killing can be murder, it is equally clear that, whatever mental elements may be involved and whatever means may be employed, there cannot be a murder without a killing. Section 24 of the *Code* defines, in part, the offence of attempt as "having an intent to commit an offence". As Estey J. observed in *R. v. Quinton*, [1947] S.C.R. 234 at 235-36, 3 C.R. 6, 88 C.C.C. 231, in referring to the then s. 72 (now s. 24):

> This section requires that one to be guilty of an attempt must intend to commit the completed offence and to have done some act toward the accomplishment of that objective.

The completed offence of murder involves a killing. The intention to commit the complete offence of murder must therefore include an intention to kill. I find it impossible to conclude that a person may intend to commit the unintentional killings described in ss. 212 and 213 of the *Code*. I am then of the view that the *mens rea* for an attempted murder cannot be less than the specific intent to kill.

As I have said earlier, there is a division of opinion upon this point and strong arguments have been raised in favour of the Crown's position that a "lesser intent", such as that provided in s. 212(*a*)(ii), or even no intent at all relating to the causing of death, as provided in s. 213(*d*), may suffice to found a conviction for attempted murder. This view is supported in *Lajoie, supra*. In my view, with the utmost respect for those who differ, the sections of the *Criminal Code* relied on in that case do not support that position.

As noted above, Martland J.'s analysis of the intent required to found a conviction for attempted murder is based primarily on the change in wording of s. 222. In my opinion, emphasis on the amendment of this section is unwarranted, for two reasons. Firstly, s. 222 does not define or create the offence of attempted murder. The scheme of the *Criminal Code* in relation to attempts has been the same from its inception. One section defines the offence of attempts generally (s. 72 of the 1927 *Code*, now s. 24). Another sets out the penalties of attempts (s. 57 of the 1927 Code, now s. 421), and a third creates a separate penalty for attempted murder (s. 264 of the 1927 *Code*, s. 210 in *Lajoie*, now s. 222). Rather than defining or creating an offence, s. 222 merely fixes a penalty for a specific attempt. Despite the categorization of the various means of committing murder set out in the old s. 264, there is no essential difference between the old and the new sections in this respect.

Secondly, the elimination of the words "with intent to commit murder" from s. 264 is not significant. Section 24 defines an attempt as "having an intent to commit an offence". Because s. 24 is a general section it is necessary to "read in" the offence in question. The offence of attempted murder then is defined as "having an intent to commit murder". This does not differ from the old s. 264 reference to "with intent to commit murder", which Martland J. acknowledged was interpreted, in *R. v. Flannery* [[1923] 3 W.W.R. 97], to require the specific intent to kill.

Martland J. placed further emphasis on s. 222 of the *Criminal Code* by relying on the words "attempts by any means" to support his conclusion that murder may be attempted in any of the "ways" set out in ss. 212 and 213. In my view, the reference to "any means" in s. 222 refers to ways in which a murder could be accomplished, such as by poisoning, shooting, or stabbing. The earlier version of s. 222 (s. 232 in 1892, s. 264 in 1906) listed the various methods by which a killing could be effected, but the illustrations were replaced in the 1953-54 revision with a general reference to murder "by any means". In any event, ss. 212 and 213 have nothing to do with the means of killing. They are concerned solely with describing the mental elements which will suffice to make a completed killing murder. The fact that certain mental elements, other than an intent to kill, may lead to a conviction for murder where there has been a killing does not mean that anything less than an intent to kill will suffice for an attempt at murder.

It was argued, and it has been suggested in some of the cases and academic writings on the question, that it is illogical to insist upon a higher degree of *mens rea* for attempted murder, while accepting a lower degree amounting to recklessness for murder. I see no merit in this argument. The intent to kill is the highest intent in murder and there is no reason in logic why an attempt to murder, aimed at the completion of the full crime of murder, should have any lesser intent. If there is any illogic in this matter, it is in the statutory characterization of unintentional killing as murder. The *mens rea* for attempted murder is, in my view, the specific intent to kill. A mental state falling short of that level may well lead to conviction for other offences, for example, one or other of the various aggravated assaults, but not to a conviction for an attempt at murder. For these reasons, it is my view that *Lajoie, supra*, should no longer be followed.

I would accordingly dismiss the Crown's appeal and confirm the Court of Appeal's order for a new trial.

RITCHIE J.: — 1 am unable to distinguish this case from that of *Lajoie v. R.*, [*supra*], which is a unanimous judgment of this Court and by which I feel bound.

I would therefore allow this appeal.

Appeal dismissed.

R. v. SORRELL AND BONDETT

(1978), 41 C.C.C. (2d) 9 (Ont. C.A.)

Ontario Court of Appeal, DUBIN, MARTIN and BLAIR JJ.A. April 27, 1978.

BY THE COURT: — The Attorney-General of Ontario appeals against the acquittal of the respondents on a charge of attempted robbery.

The respondents were tried at Kingston before His Honour Judge Campbell, sitting without a jury, on an indictment containing three counts.

Count 1 charged the respondents jointly with, on or about March 3, 1977, attempting to rob Peter Mason of Aunt Lucy's Fried Chicken store at 240 Montreal St. in Kingston. Count 2 charged the respondent Sorrell with carrying, at the time and place aforesaid, a concealed weapon, to wit: a Smith and Wesson revolver. Count 3 charged the respondent Sorrell with having in his possession, at the time and place aforesaid, a Smith and Wesson revolver, knowing the same was obtained by an offence committed in Canada punishable on indictment. The respondent Sorrell, on arraignment, pleaded guilty to the charge of carrying a concealed weapon contained in count 2; his plea of guilty was accepted by the trial Judge after the evidence was completed, and he was sentenced to imprisonment for 18 months. The trial Judge acquitted the respondent Sorrell on count 3, on the ground that the Crown had failed to prove the necessary element of guilty knowledge. The Crown does not appeal the acquittal of Sorrell on count 3, and we are not further concerned with it.

On the evening of Thursday, March 3, 1977, Miss Dawn Arbuckle was the cashier at Aunt Lucy's Fried Chicken store at 240 Montreal St. in Kingston. The store is located at the corner of Montreal and Markland Sts., the customer entrances being on Montreal St. Mr. Peter Mason was the manager of the store. The regular closing time for the store was 11:00 p.m., but, on the evening in question, since almost all the chicken had been sold, the manager decided to close the store earlier, and locked the customer entrances at approximately 10:45 p.m. Around 10 minutes to 11:00 Miss Arbuckle noticed two men, wearing balaclavas, on the Markland St. side of the store; they then came to one of the customer entrances in Montreal St. The area outside the store was illuminated, and the lights normally on in the store, when open, were still on.

One of the men was wearing a blue ski jacket and the other was wearing a brown coat. The balaclavas worn by the two men were pulled down completely over their heads, and one man was also wearing sunglasses. Miss Arbuckle said that the balaclava worn by one man was blue and white in colour, and that worn by the other man was brown and white.

One of the men rapped on the door and on the window. The manager, who had been mopping the floor, turned around and said, "Sorry we are closed", and returned to his mopping. The two men turned toward each other, and made a gesture of surprise. At this time Miss Arbuckle noticed that one of the men had a silver-coloured gun in his hand. The two men then walked away on Montreal Street in the direction of Princess St.; whereupon Mr. Mason, the manager, telephoned the police. Two officers in a cruiser responded to the call, drove to the area and saw two men, whose clothing corresponded to the description that the officers had been given, walking on Montreal St. The officers drove past the two men, then made a U-turn and drove back towards them.

As the officers passed the two men, before making the U-turn, they saw one of the men throw "an article of material" towards a snow bank on the side of the street. The two men, who proved to be the respondents, were then arrested. The respondent Sorrell had a loaded .357 Magnum revolver concealed in his waistband. The gun was loaded with six Dominion .38 shells, and another five Dominion .38 shells were removed from the respondent Sorrell's pants' pocket.

An officer conducted a search of the immediate area where the respondents had been arrested, and found a brown balaclava on a snowbank on the side of Montreal St. The point on Montreal St. where the respondents were arrested was some 411 yards from the Aunt Lucy's store, where the attempted robbery is alleged to have occurred. The officer proceeded along Montreal St. in the direction of the Aunt Lucy's store, and found a blue balaclava in the middle of the sidewalk on Montreal St. at the intersection of Raglan St.

Neither of the respondents testified in his defence.

The Crown appeals against the acquittal of the respondents on the charge of attempted robbery on the ground that the trial Judge erred in law in holding that the acts of the respondents did not go beyond mere preparation, and hence did not constitute an attempt.

Section 24 of the *Code* defines an attempt as follows:

> 24(1) Everyone who, having an intent to commit an offence, does or omits to do anything for the purpose of carrying out his intention is guilty of an attempt to commit the offence whether or not it was possible under the circumstances to commit the offence.
>
> (2) The question whether an act or omission by a person *who has an intent to commit an offence* is or is not mere preparation to commit the offence, and too remote to constitute an attempt to commit the offence, is a question of law. (Emphasis supplied.)

In order to establish the commission of the offence of attempted robbery charged, it was necessary for the Crown to prove that the respondents:

> (i) Intended to do that which would in law amount to the robbery specified in the indictment (*mens rea*), and
> (ii) took steps in carrying out that intent which amounted to more than mere preparation (*actus reus*).

By virtue of s. 24(2) of the *Code*, the existence of element (i) is a question of fact, but whether the steps taken are sufficient to satisfy element (ii) is a question of law.

In *R. v. Cline*, 115 C.C.C. 18 at p. 29, Laidlaw J.A., in his much-quoted judgment, said:

> (1) There must be *mens rea* and also an *actus reus* to constitute a criminal attempt, but the criminality of misconduct lies mainly in the intention of the accused. . . . (5) The *actus reus* must be more than mere preparation to commit a crime. But (6) when the preparation to commit a crime is in fact fully complete and ended, the next step done by the accused for the purpose and with the intention of committing a specific crime constitutes an *actus reus* sufficient in law to establish a criminal attempt to commit that crime.

Thus, proof of the respondents' intention to commit the robbery particularized in the indictment, which is a question of fact, was the central issue in the case. Mr. Doherty for the Crown contended before us that on the facts found by the trial Judge, he erred in law in failing to draw the legal conclusion of guilt required by the facts accepted by him as proved, and, in particular, erred in law in holding that the acts of the respondents, found by him to have been proved, had not gone beyond mere preparation. Counsel for the respondents, on the other hand, contended that the trial Judge's reasons for judgment, considered in their entirety, show that he acquitted the respondents because he entertained a reasonable doubt whether they had the intent to rob the Aunt Lucy's store, the existence of which intent was essential to constitute the attempt charged.

A detailed examination of the trial Judge's reasons for judgment is necessary in order to endeavour to ascertain the basis upon which he acquitted the respondents. The trial Judge said:

> Turning to count 1, that is the count that effects both Sorrel and Bondett, namely, this attempted robbery count. There are many conclusions that I have drawn from the credible evidence, beyond a reasonable doubt, and I say that those conclusions complete substantially

the Crown's case subject only — and I say only — to the thorny question as to whether or not the events in question constitute an attempt within the meaning of the *Criminal Code*.

After referring to certain discrepancies in the evidence of the Crown witnesses, which he did not consider material, the trial Judge continued:

The Crown's case on count 1 has been proved beyond a reasonable doubt in my finding on the matters of identity of the accused, the date, the place and, subject only to what I am going to be saying on the matter of attempt, as to the allegation that the attempted robbery, if there was an attempted robbery, was committed in respect of Peter Mason of Aunt Lucy's Kentucky Fried Chicken.

He then held that Mr. Mason, as the manager of the store, had the custody of the money in the store, and said:

It brings me down then to the sole remaining question, did what took place at the time and at the place, as referred to by the witnesses Arbuckle and Mason, constitute an attempt at robbery? I may say that I found the evidence of both of those witnesses to be satisfactory, credible, and my findings are based on that evidence. I as well look to the evidence at the trial as to the manner of departure from the premises — from in front of the premises — by the two accused and the actions that they were performing when seen and practically immediately apprehended by the police. I am finding that between them they rid themselves of the balaclavas which could raise the inference of guilty mind; but that, of course, raises the question: a mind having a sense of guilt of what? They may have thought that what they did at the front of the store was criminal in some way and that they should take some steps to cover up — whether they were right in that belief or not. Was what they had actually done illegal as being an attempt to rob, whether they believed it or not, that still leaves to me the question: was what they did within the ambit of an attempt to rob? The inference is pretty plain, and I think I would be naive to conclude otherwise, that they were up to no good on that occasion, that they may well have had robbery of the store in mind. But, again, I am driven back to the provisions of the *Code* that differentiate between mere preparation and the actual commencement of steps to commit the robbery

I am obliged to counsel for their references to cases on the point, one of which endeavours to lay down tests for the assistance of the Court, and subsequent cases, but all of which have their own set of facts and circumstances with which the Court then in those cases had to deal. It is an extremely thin line, but whether thin or otherwise, if my finding is that that line had been crossed beyond mere preparation, the finding — if it were to be made — that the line had been crossed would be sufficient to bring me to a conclusion beyond a reasonable doubt. Nevertheless, the fineness of the line is a bother to me. I am conscious of the fact that the accused timed their arrival at the store such that they could expect a fund of money to be in the till, such they could expect there would likely be few if any persons there other than the store personnel, and that they had costumed themselves for the purpose of disguising their features to render subsequent identification difficult, but I am also of the view that it is important for me to consider the fact that apart from rattling the door and perhaps rattling on the window — that would be consistent with an innocent person's endeavour to get in the food store — there was no gesture of threat of violence or threat of force. The case before me is attempted robbery and not attempted break, enter and theft, or break and enter with intent, or conspiracy, or whatever. So that the endeavour to open the door would — were one of those other charges to have been before me, and I am not saying in any way that it should have been before me — what was done by way of attempt to open the door could relate more to a charge of attempted breaking rather than the charge of robbery. In brief, in my finding, the accused by virtue of I suppose good luck of not having been able to progress further in doing whatever they were going to do had not yet crossed the line between preparation and attempt. Accordingly, I am finding that count 1 as regards both accused has not been proved on that narrow ground, and I have endorsed the indictment on count 1: both accused not guilty.

It will be observed that while the trial Judge made an express finding that he was satisfied beyond a reasonable doubt that the respondents were the two men who had approached the store, and that one of them had a gun, he made no similar finding with respect to the existence of the necessary intent to rob. Mr. O'Hara, on behalf of the respondent Sorrell particularly emphasized the following passages in the trial Judge's reasons, relative to intent, which Mr. O'Hara characterized as "powerful expressions of doubt", namely: ". . . they may well have had robbery of the store in mind", and ". . . what was done by way of attempt to open the door could relate more to a charge of attempted breaking rather than the charge of robbery". In our view, the trial Judge's reasons are more consistent with a finding that the necessary intent to commit robbery was not proved beyond a reasonable doubt, than with a finding that such intent was established by the evidence. In any event, the Crown has not satisfied us that the trial Judge found the existence of an intent to rob.

The Crown's right of appeal under s. 605(l)(a) of the *Code* is confined to a ground of appeal that involves a question of law alone. The failure of the trial Judge to draw the appropriate inference of intent from the facts found by him, is an error of fact, and does not raise a question of law.

. . . .

If the trial Judge had found that the respondents intended to rob the store, the acts done by them clearly had advanced beyond mere preparation, and were sufficiently proximate to constitute an attempt: see *Henderson v. The King*, 91 C.C.C. 97, [1948] S.C.R. 226, *per* Kerwin J., at p. 98 C.C.C., p. 228 S.C.R., *per* Estey J., at pp. 114-16 C.C.C., pp. 243-6 S.C.R., *per* Locke J., at pp. 116-17 C.C.C., p. 246 S.C.R.; *R. v. Carey*, 118 C.C.C. 241, [1957] S.C.R. 266, 25 C.R. 177, *per* Kerwin C.J.C., at pp, 246-7, *per* Rand J., at p. 251. If the trial Judge had found that the respondents had the necessary intent his finding that the acts done by the respondents did not go beyond mere preparation and did not constitute attempted robbery, would constitute an error of law that would not only warrant, but require our intervention.

Because of the doubt that he entertained that the respondents had the necessary intent to commit robbery, however, his error in law in holding that the respondents' acts did not go beyond mere preparation, could not have affected the verdict of acquittal, unless, of course, his self-misdirection with respect to what constituted mere preparation, led him into error in entertaining a reasonable doubt whether the requisite intent had been proved. This question is one of considerable difficulty. The following passage (included in those previously quoted), would tend to support the conclusion that the trial Judge was led into error with respect to the existence of the necessary intent by self-misdirection that the respondents' acts had not gone beyond mere preparation:

> It is an extremely thin line, but whether thin or otherwise, if my finding is that that line had been crossed beyond mere preparation, the finding — if it were to be made — that the line had been crossed would be sufficient to bring me to a conclusion beyond a reasonable doubt. Nevertheless, the fineness of the line is a bother to me.

The trial Judge then proceeded, however, to refer to the matters in the passages previously quoted, relating to the issue of intent, which gave him difficulty in finding that the required mental element was present. The issue of intent was basic and, the trial Judge, in our view, could not logically or appropriately make a determination whether the acts of the respondents went beyond mere preparation until he had first found the intent with which those acts were done. The issue whether the acts of the respondents went beyond mere preparation could not be decided in the abstract apart from the existence of the requisite intent.

In the present case, there was no evidence of the intent to rob other than that furnished by the acts relied on as constituting the *actus reus*. There was no extrinsic evidence in the form of statements of intention, or admissions by the respondents showing what their intention was.

The prosecution in this case was forced to rely exclusively upon the acts of the accused, not only to constitute the *actus reus*, but to supply the evidence of the necessary *mens rea*. This Court in *R. v. Cline, supra*, rejected the so-called "unequivocal act" test for determining when the stage of attempt has been reached. That test excludes resort to evidence *aliunde*, such as admissions, and holds that the state of attempt has been reached only when the acts of the accused show unequivocally on their face the criminal intent with which the acts were performed. We are of the view that where the accused's intention is otherwise proved, acts which on their face are equivocal may, none the less, be sufficiently proximate to constitute an attempt. Where, however, there is no extrinsic evidence of the intent with which accused's acts were done, acts of the accused, which on their face are equivocal, may be insufficient to show that the acts were done with the intent to commit the crime that the accused is alleged to have attempted to commit, and hence insufficient to establish the offence of attempt.

Counsel for the respondents while conceding that the trial Judge's reasons are not free of ambiguity, submitted that they are reasonably open to the interpretation that he was searching for evidence that satisfied him beyond a reasonable doubt that the accused intended to rob the store in question, and at the end of his quest was not satisfied beyond a reasonable doubt, that the acts done by the accused supplied the necessary proof of intent.

We think that this submission accurately states the basis upon which the trial Judge acquitted the respondents, and the Crown has not satisfied us that, but for the self-misdirection with respect to which complaint is made, the verdict of the trial Judge would not necessarily have been the same. It is not to the point that, on the evidence, we would have reached a different conclusion with respect to the respondent's intentions.

. . . .

Appeal dismissed.

R. v. DEUTSCH

[1986] 2 S.C.R. 2, 52 C.R. (3d) 305, 27 C.C.C. (3d) 385

Le Dain J.: — This appeal, which involves a charge of attempting to procure a person to have illicit sexual intercourse with another person contrary to s. 195(1)(a) of the *Criminal Code*, raises two issues: the distinction between attempt and mere preparation, and the meaning of "illicit sexual intercourse".

The appeal is from the judgment of the Ontario Court of Appeal on March 17, 1983 setting aside the acquittal of the appellant by Graburn Co. Ct. J. on August 13, 1982 of the charge of attempting to procure a person to have illicit sexual intercourse with another person and ordering a new trial of the appellant on that charge.

During the period covered by the indictment, which is the three months ending on or about September 3, 1981, the appellant was carrying on a business known as Global Franchises Marketing, which was engaged in selling franchises of various kinds. During this period the appellant placed an advertisement in newspapers in Ottawa, Hamilton and Toronto inviting applications for the position of secretary/sales assistant and conducted interviews with three women who responded to the advertisement and with a police officer who posed as an applicant for the position and recorded the interview on a tape recorder. The advertisement read as follows:

ENJOY TRAVEL

SECRETARY — Sales Assistant to Sales Executive. $600-$800 per month to start plus commission, bonuses, company benefits and expenses. Must be free to travel extensively. Call 746-2440 ask for Mel.

In the interviews the appellant indicated that a secretary/sales assistant would be expected to have sexual intercourse with clients or potential clients of the company where that appeared to be necessary to conclude a contract. The appellant also indicated that a successful secretary/sales assistant could earn as much as $100,000 per year through commission or bonus on the sale of franchises. The appellant did not make an offer of employment to the three applicants who testified at his trial. After hearing what the position required they said they were not interested and the interviews terminated. Nor did he make an offer of employment to the police officer who posed as an applicant, but when she told him she was interested in the position, despite its requirements, he told her to think it over and let him know.

The appellant was tried upon an indictment containing two counts: attempting to procure female persons to become common prostitutes, and attempting to procure female persons to have illicit intercourse with another person. Graburn Co. Ct. J. acquitted the appellant on both counts. He found that the appellant intended that a person hired for the position should have sexual relations with clients or potential clients, but he held, as a matter of law, that the acts or statements of the appellant did not, in the absence of an offer of employment, constitute the *actus reus* of an attempt to procure. In his opinion they were mere preparation. He accordingly did not find it necessary to decide whether the sexual intercourse contemplated by the appellant would be illicit sexual intercourse within s. 195(1)(*a*) or make those who engaged in it common prostitutes within s. 195(1)(*d*), as it then read.

The Ontario Court of Appeal (Martin, Houlden and Robins JJ.A.) (1983), 5 C.C.C. (3d) 41, dismissed the appeal from the acquittal on the charge of attempting to procure female persons to become common prostitutes, but allowed the appeal from the acquittal on the charge of attempting to procure female persons to have illicit sexual intercourse with another person and directed a new trial of the appellant on that count of the indictment. The Court held that the trial Judge erred in concluding that the acts or statements of the appellant could not, in the absence of an offer of employment, constitute an attempt to procure rather than mere preparation. It held that there was evidence from which the trial Judge could have concluded that there was both the *mens rea* and the *actus reus* required for an attempt to procure. The Court also held that the sexual intercourse contemplated by the appellant would be illicit sexual intercourse within s. 195(1)(*a*). The appellant appeals from the judgment of the Court of Appeal with respect to the second count of the indictment.

The appellant, who appeared in person on the appeal, expressed his grounds of appeal in several different ways, but in my opinion there are only two issues that require consideration by the Court:

1. Whether the Court of Appeal erred in holding that the acts or statements of the appellant could, as a matter of law, constitute an attempt to procure rather than mere preparation; and
2. Whether the Court of Appeal erred in holding that the sexual intercourse contemplated by the appellant would be illicit sexual intercourse within s. 195(1)(*a*) of the *Code*.

. . . .

[The Court first considered the second issue and concluded that the Court of Appeal did not err in holding that the sexual intercourse contemplated by the appellant would be "illicit sexual intercourse" within s. 195(1)(*a*) of the *Code*.]

. . . .

I turn now to the question whether the acts or statements of the appellant could, as a matter of law, constitute the *actus reus* of an attempt to procure a person to have illicit sexual intercourse with another person, contrary to s. 195(1)(*a*) of the *Code*. The general provision of the *Code* defining the constituent elements of an attempt to commit an offence is s. 24, which provides:

> 24. (1) Every one who, having an intent to commit an offence, does or omits to do anything for the purpose of carrying out his intention is guilty of an attempt to commit the offence whether or not it was possible under the circumstances to commit the offence.
>
> (2) The question whether an act or omission by a person who has an intent to commit an offence is or is not mere preparation to commit the offence, and too remote to constitute an attempt to commit the offence, is a question of law.

The issue is whether, if there was the necessary intent, the acts of the appellant were mere preparation to commit the offence of procuring a person to have illicit sexual intercourse with another person or whether any of them was a step in the commission of the offence, and the extent to which that distinction is to turn on the relative remoteness of the act in question from what would have been the completion of the offence. This issue, as s. 24 indicates, is a question of law. The appellant contends that the Court of Appeal erred in holding that one of the acts of the appellant could, if there was the necessary intent, constitute the *actus reus* of an attempt to procure.

The trial Judge found that the appellant "intended that the women in question should have sexual relations with prospective customers and clients", but that the acts of the appellant consisting of the advertisements, the interviews and what was said during the interviews concerning the requirements of the position and the money to be earned, were mere preparation and too remote from the complete offence of procuring to constitute the *actus reus* of an attempt to procure. He said:

. . . .

> I consider that the interview and its content was an act remotely leading to the commission of the offence, and was not an act immediately connected with it, nor sufficiently proximate to it so as to constitute an attempt; the latter language being used by the Ontario Court of Appeal in the case of *Sorrell and Bondett* which was decided in 1978 and is reported in 41 C.C.C. (2d) at p. 9.

. . . .

Several different tests for determining whether there is the *actus reus* of attempt, as distinct from mere preparation to commit an offence, have been identified as reflected at one time or another in judicial decisions and legislation. All of them have been pronounced by academic commentators to be unsatisfactory in some degree. For a thorough analysis of the various tests, with suggestions for an improved test, see Meehan, *The Law of Criminal Attempt — A Treatise*, 1984, chapter 5, and Stuart, *Canadian Criminal Law*, 1982, pp. 529ff. There is a succinct appraisal of the various tests in the English Law Commission's Report No. 102 of 1980 entitled, Criminal Law: Attempt, and Impossibility in Relation to Attempt, Conspiracy and Incitement. It has been frequently observed that no satisfactory general criterion has been, or can be, formulated for drawing the line between preparation and attempt, and that the application of this distinction to the facts of a particular case must be left to common sense judgment.

. . . .

In my opinion the distinction between preparation and attempt is essentially a qualitative one, involving the relationship between the nature and quality of the act in question and the nature of the complete offence, although consideration must necessarily be given, in making that qualitative distinction, to the relative proximity of the act in question to what would have been the completed offence, in terms of time, location and acts under the control of the accused remaining to be accomplished. I find that view to be compatible with what has been said about the *actus reus* of attempt in this Court and in other Canadian decisions that should be treated as authoritative on this question.

The most recent expression of opinion in this Court on what constitutes an attempt to commit an offence is the judgment in *R. v. Ancio*, [1984] 1 S.C.R. 225, where the issue was the intent required for attempted murder. McIntyre J., in the course of a review of the development of the law of attempt, said with reference to the *mens rea* and the *actus reus* of attempt at p. 247:

> As with any other crime, the Crown must prove a *mens rea*, that is, the intent to commit the offence in question and the *actus reus*, that is, some step towards the commission of the offence attempted going beyond mere acts of preparation. Of the two elements the more significant is the *mens rea*.

McIntyre J. referred with approval to the judgment of Laidlaw J.A. in *R. v. Cline, supra*, particularly for what it said concerning the relative importance of *mens rea* in attempt, but that judgment has also been treated as helpful for what it said concerning the application of the distinction between preparation and attempt. With reference to this question Laidlaw J.A. said at p. 28:

> The consummation of a crime usually comprises a series of acts which have their genesis in an idea to do a criminal act; the idea develops to a decision to do that act; a plan may be made for putting that decision into effect; the next step may be preparation only for carrying out the intention and plan; but when that preparation is in fact fully completed, the next step in the series of acts done by the accused for the purpose and with the intention of committing the crime as planned cannot, in my opinion, be regarded as remote in its connection with that crime. The connection is in fact proximate.

Laidlaw J.A. offered six propositions by way of guidance for determination of the requisite *mens rea* and *actus reus* of attempt, the last two of which, with reference to the *actus reus*, are as follows:

> (5) The *actus reus* must be more than mere preparation to commit a crime. But (6) when the preparation to commit a crime is in fact fully complete and ended, the next step done by the accused for the purpose and with the intention of committing a specific crime constitutes an *actus reus* sufficient in law to establish a criminal attempt to commit that crime.

The extent to which some version of the proximity test, which was formulated in *R. v. Eagleton* (1854), Dears. C.C. 376 (C.C.R.), and applied in the much-criticized case of *R. v. Robinson*, [1915] 2 K.B. 342 (C.C.A.), as a "last step" or "last stage" test (*cf.* English Law Commission, op cit., pp. 335-36), is to be applied in drawing the distinction between preparation and attempt has also been the subject of commentary in this Court. In *Henderson v. The King*, [1948] S.C.R. 226, where one of the issues was whether there had been an attempt to rob a bank, Estey J., who was one of the majority holding that there had been an attempt, said at p. 244:

> Counsel for the accused referred to a number of cases in which the attempted crime was either against the person or that of obtaining by false pretences. He contended that any act not "immediately connected with" the completed crime would be too remote to constitute an attempt. Even under the cases which he cited the accused may still have one or more acts to

do, and these may be separated by an intervening period of time, in order to complete the offence and yet may be guilty of an attempt.

Among the cases referred to by Estey J. in support of this statement were *R. v. Cheeseman* (1862), 169 E.R. 1337, where Blackburn J. said at p. 1339, "But, if the actual transaction has commenced which would have ended in the crime if not interrupted, there is clearly an attempt to commit the crime", and *R. v. White*, [1910] 2 K.B. 124, where Bray J. said at p. 130: " . . . the completion or attempted completion of one of a series of acts intended by a man to result in killing is an attempt to murder even although this completed act would not, unless followed by other acts, result in killing. It might be the beginning of the attempt, but would none the less be an attempt." Taschereau J., dissenting, in *Henderson*, although he differed in the result, would not appear to have applied a different concept of proximity. He said, after referring to the authorities, including *Eagleton* and *Robinson*, at pp. 234-35:

> Although it may be said that no one could doubt the express purpose of the bandits, I do not believe that it can be held that the mere fact of going to the place where the contemplated crime is to be committed, constitutes an attempt. There must be a closer relation between the victim and the author of the crime; there must be an act done which displays not only a preparation for an attempt, but a commencement of execution, a step in the commission of the actual crime itself.

In *Detering v. The Queen*, [1982] 2 S.C.R. 583, which involved a conviction for attempted fraud, Laskin C.J. raised a question, as I read his reasons, as to the weight to be given to the proximity test in the essential task under s. 24 of the *Code* of distinguishing between preparation and attempt. With reference to the contention of counsel that "proximity was an essential requirement in the sense, to put it generally, that the actions of the accused must go beyond mere preparation and close (a question of degree) to the realization of his purpose", Laskin C.J. said at p. 586:

> This leaves for consideration the so-called proximity principle. It may well be that this is envisaged by the reference to remoteness in s. 24(2), but I do not see that it advances the essential issue in attempt which requires going beyond mere preparation. Nor do I find cogency in the appellant's submission that if there is impossibility this does not bring any act of the accused closer to realization so as to establish proximity. I read s. 24(1) as making a different distinction, one merely requiring proof of intent and of accused going beyond mere preparation by making, as in this case, a false representation even though not resulting in full realization of his objective.

In my opinion, relative proximity may give an act which might otherwise appear to be mere preparation the quality of attempt. That is reflected, I think, in the conclusion of the majority in *Henderson* and in the conclusion of the Ontario Court of Appeal with respect to *actus reus* in *R. v. Sorrell and Bondett* (1978), 41 C.C.C. (2d) 9. But an act which on its face is an act of commission does not lose its quality as the *actus reus* of attempt because further acts were required or because a significant period of time may have elapsed before the completion of the offence.

In the case at bar the Court of Appeal agreed with the trial Judge on the applicable meaning of "procure". The meaning selected by the trial Judge and approved by the Court of Appeal was "to cause, or to induce, or to have a persuasive effect upon the conduct that is alleged." Martin J.A. expressed his agreement at p. 49 with the following statement of the issue by the trial Judge: "The question for decision is did Mr. Deutsch attempt to cause or attempt to induce or attempt to have a persuasive effect upon the woman in question to have illicit sexual intercourse with another person. . . ." I agree that the sources referred to by the trial Judge and Martin J.A. support the meaning given by them to the word "procure".

The Court of Appeal differed with the trial Judge as to what would have constituted the completed offence of procuring a person to have illicit sexual intercourse with another person. The trial Judge held that the offence of procuring would have been completed, in the particular context of this case, by the acceptance of an offer of employment. The Court of Appeal held, citing *R. v. Johnson* (1963), 48 Cr. App. R. 25, and *R. v. Gruba*, [1969] 2 C.C.C. 365, that the offence of procuring a person to have illicit sexual intercourse with another person is not committed unless sexual intercourse actually takes place. In the appeal to this Court the respondent accepted this statement of the law as to what is required for the complete offence of procuring a person to have illicit sexual intercourse with another person. It was not challenged, and I accept it for purposes of deciding whether the acts of the appellant could, as a matter of law, constitute the *actus reus* of an attempt to procure.

I agree with the Court of Appeal that if the appellant had the necessary intent to induce or persuade the women to seek employment that would require them to have sexual intercourse with prospective clients then the holding out of the large financial rewards in the course of the interviews, in which the necessity of having sexual intercourse with prospective clients was disclosed, could constitute the *actus reus* of an attempt to procure. It would clearly be a step, and an important step, in the commission of the offence. Before an offer of employment could be made in such circumstances an applicant would have to seek the position, despite its special requirement. Thus such inducement or persuasion would be the decisive act in the procuring. There would be little else that the appellant would be required to do towards the completion of the offence other than to make the formal offer of employment. I am further of the opinion that the holding out ot the large financial rewards in the course of the interviews would not lose its quality as a step in the commission of the offence, and thus as an *actus reus* of attempt, because a considerable period of time might elapse before a person engaged for the position had sexual intercourse with prospective clients or because of the otherwise contingent nature of such sexual intercourse.

For these reasons I would dismiss the appeal. I agree with the Court of Appeal that because the trial Judge did not make a finding as to whether or not there was the necessary intent to procure there must be a new trial.

One of the most heated debates in Anglo-American criminal law has been as to whether courts should acquit in some cases of attempting the impossible. The embers were fanned by a complex decision of the House of Lords in *Haughton v. Smith*, [1974] 3 W.L.R. 1 (H.L.), to the effect that there were distinctions to be made. It is generally accepted by writers that a court should be able to convict of an attempt to commit a crime which, in the circumstances, was physically impossible to commit. Examples are a would-be assassin throwing a bomb that will never explode. The major difference of opinion is between those who favour criminal responsibility and those who do not for cases of attempts which would only be criminal if the acts were as the accused wrongly supposed them to be. The classic examples are stealing an umbrella that turns out to be your own or stabbing a corpse thinking it was a live person. Glanville Williams urged Canadian courts:

> to lend no ear to the arguments of those who would persuade them, notwithstanding the clear and wise words of the *Code*, to introduce questions of impossibility into the law of attempt and its associated crimes: "Attempting the Impossible — A Reply" (1979), 22 Crim. L.Q. 49 at 57.

The Supreme Court did just that in *Dynar*.

UNITED STATES v. DYNAR

[1997] 2 S.C.R. 462, 8 C.R. (5th) 79, 115 C.C.C. (3d) 481

The U.S. government requested the extradition of D, a Canadian citizen who had been the subject of a failed "sting" operation by the FBI. D had placed a telephone call from Canada to a former associate who was living in Nevada and who had become a confidential informant working for an FBI agent. The issue for the Supreme Court was whether D's conduct would have amounted to a criminal attempt under Canadian law.

Cory and Iacobucci JJ. (Lamer C.J.C., LaForest, L'Heureux-Dubé, and Gonthier JJ. concurring): —

. . . .

(2) The Law of Attempt

The *Criminal Code* creates the crime of attempt to commit an offence:

24. (1) Every one who, having an intent to commit an offence, does or omits to do anything for the purpose of carrying out the intention is guilty of an attempt to commit the offence *whether or not it was possible under the circumstances to commit the offence.* [Emphasis added.]

On its face, the statute is indifferent about whether or not the attempt might possibly have succeeded. Therefore it would seem, at first blush, not to matter that Mr. Dynar could not possibly have succeeded in laundering money known to be the proceeds of crime. So long as he attempted to do so, he is guilty of a crime.

In our view, s. 24(1) is clear: the crime of attempt consists of an intent to commit the completed offence together with some act more than merely preparatory taken in furtherance of the attempt. This proposition finds support in a long line of authority. [Citations omitted.] In this case, sufficient evidence was produced to show that Mr. Dynar intended to commit the money-laundering offences, and that he took steps more than merely preparatory in order to realize his intention. That is enough to establish that he attempted to launder money contrary to s. 24(1) of the *Criminal Code*.

However, the respondent argues that Parliament did not intend by s. 24(1) to criminalize all attempts to do the impossible, but only those attempts that the common law has classified as "factually impossible". An attempt to do the factually impossible, according to the respondent, is an attempt that runs up against some intervening obstacle and for that reason cannot be completed. The classic example involves a pickpocket who puts his hand into a man's pocket intending to remove the wallet, only to find that there is no wallet to remove.

Traditionally, this sort of impossibility has been contrasted with "legal impossibility". An attempt to do the legally impossible is, according to those who draw the distinction, an attempt that must fail because, even if it were completed, no crime would have been committed. See Eric Colvin, *Principles of Criminal Law* (2nd ed. 1991), at pp. 355-56.

According to the respondent, the *Criminal Code* criminalizes only attempts to do the factually impossible. An attempt to do the legally impossible, in the absence of an express legislative reference to that variety of impossibility, is not a crime.

As support for this interpretation, the respondent offers two arguments. The first is that Parliament based s. 24(1) on an English provision whose purpose was to overrule a decision of the House of Lords that had made factual impossibility a defence. See Barry Brown, "'Th'attempt, and not the deed, Confounds us': Section 24 and Impossible Attempts" (1981), 19 *U.W.O. L. Rev.* 225 at pp. 228-29. On the strength of this argument, the New Zealand Court of Appeal accepted that New Zealand's equivalent to s. 24(1) criminalizes attempts whose completion is factually impossible but not those whose completion is legally impossible. See *R. v. Donnelly*, [1970] N.Z.L.R. 980 (C.A.) at pp. 984 and 988.

The respondent's second argument is that Parliament, had it intended to criminalize attempts to do the legally impossible, would have used the words "whether or not it was factually or legally impossible" in s. 24(1). As examples of statutes that were intended to criminalize attempts to do the legally impossible, the respondent cites provisions of statutes from the United Kingdom and from the United States . . . .

. . . .

A third argument, which the respondent does not advance, is that the words "under the circumstances" restrict the scope of s. 24(1) to attempts to do the factually impossible. An attempt that is not possible "under the circumstances", according to this argument, is by implication possible under some other set of circumstances. Otherwise, there would be no need to mention circumstances — the mere mention of impossibility would suffice.

. . . .

In addition there is another way of turning the same language to the respondent's advantage. "Circumstances", in ordinary parlance, are facts. Laws, by contrast, are not circumstances. Accordingly, applying the rule that *expressio unius est exclusio alterius*, the mention in s. 24(1) of attempts that are circumstantially or factually impossible may be taken to exclude attempts that are legally impossible. The question, as one Canadian writer has framed it, is whether "'the circumstances' referred to in [s. 24(1)] include the legal status of the actor's conduct". Brown, *supra*, at p. 229.

Still another argument in favour of the respondent's position, though one that reflects judicial policy rather than the strict ascertainment of legislative intent, is that penal statutes, if ambiguous, should be construed narrowly, in favour of the rights of the accused. "[T]he overriding principle governing the interpretation of penal provisions is that ambiguity should be resolved in a manner most favourable to accused persons". *R. v. McIntosh*, [1995] 1 S.C.R. 686, at para. 38.

Although some of these arguments have a certain force, what force they have is greatly attenuated when it is realized that the conventional distinction between factual and legal impossibility is not tenable. The only relevant distinction for purposes of s. 24(1) of the *Criminal Code* is between imaginary crimes and attempts to do the factually impossible. The criminal law of Canada recognizes no middle category called "legal impossibility". Because Mr. Dynar attempted to do the impossible but did not attempt to commit an imaginary crime, he can only have attempted to do the "factually impossible". For this reason, Mr. Dynar's proposal that s. 24(1) criminalizes only attempts to do the factually impossible does not help him.

As we have already indicated, an attempt to do the factually impossible is considered to be one whose completion is thwarted by mere happenstance. In theory at least, an accused who attempts to do the factually impossible could succeed but for the intervention of some fortuity. A legally impossible attempt, by contrast, is considered to be one which, even if it were completed, still would not be a crime. One scholar has described impossible attempts in these terms:

> Three main forms of impossibility have set the framework for contemporary debate. First, there is impossibility due to inadequate means (Type I). For example, A tries to kill B by shooting at him from too great a distance or by administering too small a dose of poison; C tries to break into a house without the equipment which would be necessary to force the windows or doors. . . .

> The second form of impossibility arises where an actor is prevented from completing the offence because some element of its *actus reus* cannot be brought within the criminal design (Type II). For example, A tries to kill B by shooting him when he is asleep in bed, but in fact B has already died of natural causes; C tries to steal money from a safe which is empty. . . .

The third form of impossibility arises where the actor's design is completed but the offence is still not committed because some element of the *actus reus* is missing (Type III). For example, A may take possession of property believing it to have been stolen when it has not been; B may smuggle a substance for reward believing it to be a narcotic when it is sugar. (Colvin, *supra*, at pp. 355-56.)

According to Professor Colvin, factually impossible attempts are those that fall into either of the first two categories. Legally impossible attempts are those that fall into the third category.

Colvin's schema appears attractive. But in fact it draws distinctions that do not stand up on closer inspection. There is no legally relevant difference between the pickpocket who reaches into the empty pocket and the man who takes his own umbrella from a stand believing it to be some other person's umbrella. Both have the *mens rea* of a thief. The first intends to take a wallet that he believes is not his own. The second intends to take an umbrella that he believes is not his own. Each takes some steps in the direction of consummating his design. And each is thwarted by a defect in the attendant circumstances, by an objective reality over which he has no control: the first by the absence of a wallet, the second by the accident of owning the thing that he seeks to steal. It is true that the latter seems to consummate his design and still not to complete an offence; but the semblance is misleading. The truth is that the second man does not consummate his design, because his intention is not simply to take the particular umbrella that he takes, but to take an umbrella that is not his own. That this man's design is premised on a mistaken understanding of the facts does not make it any less his design. A mistaken belief cannot be eliminated from the description of a person's mental state simply because it is mistaken.

If it were otherwise, the effect would be to eliminate from our criminal law the defence of mistaken belief. If mistaken beliefs did not form part of an actor's intent — if an actor's intent were merely to do what he in fact does — then a man who honestly but mistakenly believed that a woman had consented to have sexual relations with him and who on that basis actually had sexual relations with that woman, would have no defence to the crime of sexual assault. His intention, on this limited understanding of intention, would have been to sleep with the particular woman with whom he slept; and that particular woman, by hypothesis, is one who did not consent to sleep with him. Substituting the one description ("a woman who did not consent to sleep with him") for the other ("the particular woman with whom he slept"), it would follow that his intention was to sleep with a woman who had not consented to sleep with him. But of course, and as we have already strenuously urged, intention is one thing and the truth is another. Intention has to do with how one sees the world and not necessarily with the reality of the world.

Accordingly, there is no difference between an act thwarted by a "physical impossibility" and one thwarted "following completion". Both are thwarted by an attendant circumstance, by a fact: for example, by the fact of there being no wallet to steal or by the fact of there being no umbrella to steal. The distinction between them is a distinction without a difference. Professor Colvin himself agrees that "[t]he better view is that impossibility of execution is never a defence to inchoate liability in Canada" (p. 358).

There is, however, a relevant difference between a failed attempt to do something that is a crime and an imaginary crime. [Citation omitted.] It is one thing to attempt to steal a wallet, believing such thievery to be a crime, and quite another thing to bring sugar into Canada, believing the importation of sugar to be a crime. In the former case, the would-be thief has the *mens rea* associated with thievery. In the latter case, the would-be smuggler has no *mens rea* known to law. Because s. 24(1) clearly provides that it is an element of the offence of attempt to have "an intent to commit an offence", the latter sort of attempt is not a crime.

Nor should it be. A major purpose of the law of attempt is to discourage the commission of subsequent offences. See Williams' *Textbook of Criminal Law, supra*, at pp. 404-5. [Citations omitted.] But one who attempts to do something that is not a crime or even one who actually does something that is not a crime, believing that what he has done or has attempted to do is a crime, has not displayed any propensity to commit crimes in the future, unless perhaps he has betrayed a vague willingness to break the law. Probably all he has shown is that he might be inclined to do the same sort of thing in the future; and from a societal point of view, that is not a very worrisome prospect, because by hypothesis what he attempted to do is perfectly legal.

Therefore, we conclude that s. 24(1) draws no distinction between attempts to do the possible but by inadequate means, attempts to do the physically impossible, and attempts to do something that turns out to be impossible "following completion". All are varieties of attempts to do the "factually impossible" and all are crimes. Only attempts to commit imaginary crimes fall outside the scope of the provision. Because what Mr. Dynar attempted to do falls squarely into the category of the factually impossible — he attempted to commit crimes known to law and was thwarted only by chance — it was a criminal attempt within the meaning of s. 24(1). The evidence suggests that Mr. Dynar is a criminal within the contemplation of the Canadian law and so the double criminality rule should be no bar to his extradition to the United States.

Conspiracy

See section 465 of the *Criminal Code*.

R. v. CELEBRITY ENTERPRISES LTD. (NO. 2)

(1977), 42 C.C.C. (2d) 478 (B.C. C.A.)

APPEAL by the Crown from the accused's acquittal by Trainor Co. Ct. J., [1977] 4 W.W.R. 144, on a charge of conspiracy to produce a public mischief. The indictment contained two counts: count 1, conspiracy to live on the avails of prostitution; and count 2, conspiracy to produce a public mischief. The accused were convicted on count 1 and acquitted on count 2. The accused appealed from their conviction on count 1 and the Crown appealed the acquittal on count 2. The Court dealt with the accused's appeal first, and the judgment in that appeal is reported at 41 C.C.C. (2d) 540. Following are the reasons for judgment on the Crown appeal.

ROBERTSON J.A. (orally): — The learned trial Judge held that count 2 disclosed no offence known to the law and he accordingly entered an acquittal upon it. Against that acquittal the Crown has cross-appealed. Count 2 reads in part:

> they did conspire together and with Eleanor Harrigan and Tony Pizani and other persons unknown, to effect an unlawful purpose, to wit, produce a public mischief at or in the premises located at 1019 Seymour Street, and known as the New Penthouse Cabaret, with intent thereby to corrupt public morals, contrary to the form of the Statute.

I am unable to see how one can eliminate from the count the words "produce a public mischief". If then the offence charged is conspiracy to produce a public mischief at common law, it is bad in view of the holding by the House of Lords in *Director of Public Prosecutions v. Withers*, [1975] A.C. 842, that there is no such offence. If the offence charged is conspiracy to produce a public mischief under the *Criminal Code*, it is bad because, while the *Code* makes certain defined kinds of public mischief offences, it does not provide that public mischief with intent to corrupt public morals is an offence.

As an alternative argument Mr. Jaques submits that one may treat the count as a charge of conspiracy to corrupt public morals. Assuming — contrary to my view — that one can so read the charge, the question arises whether a conspiracy to corrupt public morals is a conspiracy to effect an unlawful purpose within the meaning of s. 423(2)(*a*) of the *Criminal Code*. An unlawful purpose must be a purpose which is unlawful by the law of Canada, and it is of no significance that counsel for the accused has conceded that a conspiracy to corrupt public morals is by the common law of England an indictable offence, because s. 8 of the *Criminal Code* provides that

> 8. Notwithstanding anything in this Act or any other Act no person shall be convicted (*a*) of an offence at common law . . .

If something that someone does is not something of which he can be convicted, that something cannot, in my opinion, be "unlawful" in the sense in which the word is used in s. 423(2)(*a*).

It is consistent with this that, since s. 8 came into force in 1955, there is no reported case in Canada where there has been conviction of conspiracy to effect an unlawful purpose where there has not been a breach of either a Dominion statute or a provincial statute.

I would, therefore, dismiss the cross-appeal.

McFarlane and Taggart JJ.A. concurred.

R. v. GRALEWICZ

[1980] 2 S.C.R. 493, 54 C.C.C. (2d) 289

CHOUINARD J. (RITCHIE, DICKSON, BEETZ and ESTEY JJ. concurring): — Upon motion of the appellants the following information was quashed by order of Judge Brown of the Provincial Court (Criminal Division) of the District of York:

> That Roman Adolfe Gralewicz, John Royce, Roy Norris Willis, Roger Desjardins, Richard Thomasson, Edwin Aldon Williams, Hedley Harnum, Andre Bansept, William Lisenchuk, Walter Mercer, and George Baldo between the 1st day ot January, 1971 and the 21st day of January, 1977, in the Province of Ontario and elsewhere in the Dominion of Canada, unlawfully did conspire and agree together, the one with the other and with John Robert Lazarus, John Pearson, Glen Patrick Milley, Ian Joseph Vickers. Lawrence Carey, George Keagan, Donald Roy Swait, Arthur Hunt, Michael Dabour, John Richard Wood, Kenneth Henry McGuire, and with another person or persons unknown to effect an unlawful purpose, to wit: to prevent members of the Seafarers' International Union of Canada from participating in the lawful activities of their Union, in accordance with Section 110(1) of the *Canada Labour Code* R.S.C. 1970 Chapter L-1 as amended, by committing the following acts, to wit:
>
> (1) Threats and assaults upon members of the said Union;
> (2) Possession and use of offensive weapons;
> (3) Defrauding members of the said Union through falsifying expenses;
> (4) Violations of the articles of the said Union's Constitution as they relate to elections, trials and individual rights,
> (5) Unlawfully preventing the said Union members from obtaining employment,
>
> Thereby committing an offence contrary to Section 423(2)(a) of the *Criminal Code*, R.S.C. 1970, Chapter C-34.

. . . .

In the appellants' submission an agreement to prevent anyone from exercising his freedom under s. 110 of the *Canada Labour Code*, R.S.C. 1970, c. L-1, to participate in the lawful activities of his union does not amount to a conspiracy to effect an unlawful purpose within the meaning of s. 423(2) of the *Criminal Code*.

Section 110(l) [rep. & sub. 1972, c. 18, s. 1] of the *Canada Labour Code* reads as follows:

> 110(1) Every employee is free to join the trade union of his choice and to participate in its lawful activities.

The first submissioin advanced on behalf of the appellants is that:

> The *Canada Labour Code* is a complete and exhaustive code provided by the Parliament of Canada for the conduct of those industrial relations which come under federal jurisdiction. It was not the intention of Parliament that its provisions should be enforced by resort to the *Criminal Code* or to any other statute since it provides its own mechanisms for enforcement.

In the appellants' submission, s. 110 is merely declaratory and contains no requirement and no prohibition. It does not create an offence. Various offences are created by ss. 184 and 185 [rep. & sub. *idem*] relating to interference with the freedoms of employees and employers recognized by s. 110 but none in the nature of that alleged in the information. Section 186 [rep. & sub. *idem*] enacts a general prohibition to the effect that "no person shall seek by intimidation or coercion to compel a person to become or refrain from becoming or to cease to be a member of a trade union." This deals with membership, not with participation in the lawful activities of a union.

The only section of the Act under which a prosecution could be contemplated for preventing members of a union from participating in the lawful activities of their union would be s. 191(1) [rep. & sub. *idem*]:

> 191(1) Subject to section 190, every person other than an employer or a trade union who violates or fails to comply with any provision of this Part other than section 148, 184 or 185 is guilty of an offence and liable on summary conviction to a fine not exceeding one thousand dollars.

Counsel for the respondent conceded however, and rightly so in my opinion, that this section could not apply because the words "violates or fails to comply" imply a prohibition or a requirement and there are none in section 110.

I see little merit in the appellants' first submission and I can but conclude as suggested by the respondent that "the fact that within a code of labour relations there is no specific sanction to enforce the rights of employees to participate in the lawful activities of their union does not sanctify otherwise criminal conduct".

The appellants further submit that their conduct as charged in the information does not constitute an offence under the *Criminal Code*. In their submission:

> If a statute does not expressly provide a penalty then, the only possible offence one can commit with respect to it, is the one set out in s. 115(1) of the *Criminal Code*.
> 115(1) Every one who, without lawful excuse, contravenes an Act of the Parliament of Canada by wilfully doing anything that it forbids or by wilfully omitting to do anything that it requires to be done, is, unless some penalty or punishment is expressly provided by law, guilty of an indictable offence and is liable to imprisonment for two years.

Section 115(1) has no application here since s. 110(1) of the *Canada Labour Code* contains no prohibition and no requirement.

The only specific offences in the *Criminal Code* related to interference with union membership are those by employers under s. 382.

As regards interference with the right of a person to do something or to abstain from doing something s. 381 enacts:

> 381(1) Every one who, wrongfully and without lawful authority, for the purpose of compelling another person to abstain from doing anything that he has a lawful right to do, or to do anything that he has a lawful right to abstain from doing,
>
> > (a) uses violence or threats of violence to that person or to his wife or children, or injures his property,
> > (b) intimidates or attempts to intimidate that person or a relative of that person by threats that, in Canada or elsewhere, violence or other injury will be done to or

punishment inflicted upon him or a relative of his, or that the property of any of them will be damaged,

(c) persistently follows that person about from place to place,

(d) hides any tools, clothes or other property owned or used by that person, or deprives him of them or hinders him in the use of them,

(e) with one or more other persons follows that person, in a disorderly manner, on a highway,

(f) besets or watches the dwelling-house or place where that person resides, works, carries on business or happens to be, or

(g) blocks or obstructs a highway,

is guillty of an offence punishable on summary conviction.

(2) A person who attends at or near or approaches a dwelling-house or place, for the purpose only of obtaining or communicating information, does not watch or beset within the meaning of this section.

The appellants have not been charged under section 381. We were told by counsel that the respondent never relied on this section and that any similarity between allegations in the information and s. 381 is purely coincidental.

On the other hand, as recognized by counsel for the appellants, "it is evident that there may be interference with the rights of a person to do what he has the right to do other than by the means set out in section 381. However, those other means of interference do not attract criminal law sanctions unless, of course, they constitute crimes in themselves."

In this case what the appellants have been charged with is conspiracy "to effect an unlawful purpose, to wit: to prevent members of the Seafarers' International Union of Canada from participating in the lawful activities of their Union, in accordance with s. 110(1) of the *Canada Labour Code*".

It is, therefore, necessary to determine whether preventing members of a union from participating in the lawful activities of their union is an unlawful purpose within the meaning of s. 423(2) of the *Criminal Code*, or what is the meaning of unlawful purpose.

According to the appellants' counsel an unlawful purpose can only be one prohibited by statute either federal or provincial:

In our respectful submission, the law does not create offences consisting of conspiracies to do acts not themselves prohibited by law under the guise of a conspiracy to effect an unlawful purpose. If the act which is the subject of the conspiracy is not prohibited by statute, it cannot form an unlawful act or purpose as the subject of a conspiracy.

They rely principally on *R. v. Celebrity Enterprises Ltd. et al.*, *supra* [at p. 146], where Judge Trainor acquitted the accused of a count of conspiracy "to effect an unlawful purpose, to wit, produce a public mischief . . . with intent thereby to corrupt public morals, contrary to the form of the statute".

Analyzing the sections of the *Criminal Code* dealing with public mischief (s. 128 [rep. & sub. 1972, c. 13, s. 8]), mischief (s. 387) and offences tending to corrupt morals (ss. 159 and following) as well as other sections, Judge Trainor determined that none applied to the case and that consequently the unlawful purpose charged did not relate to an offence under the *Criminal Code*.

It would relate, however, to an offence at common law. While no such generalized offence as conspiracy to effect a public mischief was known to the law (*R. v. Withers*, [1975] A.C. 842), a conspiracy to corrupt morals was indictable (*Shaw v. Director of Public Prosecutions*, [1962] A.C. 220; *Knuller (Publishing, Printing and Promotions) v. Director of Public Prosecutions*, [1973] A.C. 435).

Judge Trainor was of the opinion that unlawful purpose does not extend to common law offences and he stated at p. 176:

> I cannot accept the Crown's invitation to follow *Shaw* and *Knuller* and either extend the meaning of "unlawful purpose" to include a purpose not authorized by law or to hold that a common law offence can be an unlawful purpose. In my view our law has developed clearly and surely to the point that the "unlawful purpose" in s. 423(2) must be one contrary to law. Although the point is not before me I would think this reasoning applies equally to "unlawful means" in s. 423(2)(*b*).
>
> By contrary to law I mean prohibited by federal or provincial legislation. Thus would be included all summary conviction offences under the *Criminal Code* and other federal legislation and offences created by provincial legislation.

That decision was upheld by the British Columbia Court of Appeal (1979), 42 C.C.C. (2d) 478, where speaking for the Court Robertson J.A. states at p. 480:

> If something that someone does is not something of which he can be convicted, that something cannot, in my opinion, be "unlawful" in the sense in which the word is used in s. 243(2)(*a*).

Leave to appeal to this Court was refused, [1978] 1 S.C.R. xi.

All the Canadian cases in which conduct was held capable of being the subject of a criminal conspiracy to effect an unlawful purpose were based on conduct prohibited by legislation: see *Wright, McDermott and Feely v. The Queen*, [1964] 2 C.C.C. 201, [1964] S.C.R. 192, *R. v. Layton, Ex p. Thodas et al.*, [1970] 5 C.C.C. 260, 10 C.R.N.S. 290; *R. v. Chapman and Grange* (1973), 11 C.C.C. (2d) 84; *R. v. Jean Talon Fashion Centre Inc.* (1975), 22 C.C.C. (2d) 223. Counsel for the respondent recognized that there are no Canadian cases where a charge of conspiracy was upheld based on conduct not prohibited by legislation.

The respondent relies, however, on the following passage by Fauteux J., as he then was, in *Wright, McDermott & Feeley, supra*, at p. 202 C.C.C., pp. 193-4 S.C.R.:

> While marginal notes in the body of an Act form no part of the Act, the marginal note appended to s. 408(2) accurately designates as "Common-law conspiracy" the offence described in this section which, as defined by Lord Denman C.J. in *R. v. Jones* (1832), 4 B. & Ad. 345 at p. 349, consists in a combination "to do an unlawful act, or a lawful act by unlawful means". Common-law conspiracy is one of the few common-law offences which, upon the 1954 revision of the *Cr. Code*, Parliament thought advisable to perpetuate by codification: *Martin's Criminal Code*, 1955, p. 35. Hence the law pertaining to this offence, its elements and the wide embracing import of the term "unlawful purpose", remains unchanged.

But all that was decided in that case was that unlawful purpose extends to a breach of a Provincial statute, in that case the Ontario Provincial *Police Act*. After the above passage, Fauteux J. continues:

> While the term, as shown in *Harrisons Law of Conspiracy*, 1924, encompasses more than criminal offences, sufficient it is to say, for the purpose of this case, that the purpose alleged in the charge, to wit, the obtention from a constable of information which it is his duty not to divulge, is an unlawful purpose. In the language of Lord Mansfield, in *R. v. Bembridge* (1783), 3 Doug, 327 at p. 332, ". . . a man accepting an office of trust concerning the public, especially if attended with profit, is answerable criminally to the King for misbehaviour in his office." The fact that the purpose or the breach of trust contemplated by the conspirators, whether as their ultimate aim or only as a means to it, be, it carried into effect, punishable either under s. 103 of the *Cr. Code (vide, R. v. McMorran* (1948), 91 C.C.C. 19 at pp. 26 *et seq.*, 5 C.R. 338 at pp. 345 *et seq.*) or under s. 60 of the *Ontario Provincial Police Act*, adequately manifests the unlawfulness of the purpose within the meaning of the law attending common-law conspiracies.

When the *Criminal Code* was revised in 1954, s. 8 was introduced:

> 8. Notwithstanding anything in this Act or any other Act no person shall be convicted
> - (*a*) of an offence at common law
> - (*b*) of an offence under an Act of the Parliament of England, or of Great Britain, or of the United Kingdom of Great Britain and Ireland, or
> - (*c*) of an offence under an Act or ordinance in force in any province, territory or place before that province, territory or place became a province of Canada,
>
> but nothing in this section affects the power, jurisdiction or authority that a Court, Judge, Justice or Magistrate had, immediately before the 1st day of April 1955, to impose punishment for contempt of Court.

It follows that common-law conspiracy would have ceased to be part of Canadian criminal law had it not been retained as a statutory offence. But to make it a statutory offence does not necessarily mean that it was embodied with all its implications and uncertainties recognized by the decisions of the English Courts when no decisions in Canada had ever gone as far as those of the English Courts. And Fauteux J. in the above cited passage clearly does not say that.

The *Withers* case, *supra*, is authority to the effect "that it is not open to the Courts nowadays either to create new offences or so to widen existing offences as to make punishable conduct of a type hitherto not subject to punishment". The more so in Canada and Cartwright J., as he then was, speaking for himself and five other members of this Court, stated in *Frey v. Fedoruk et al.* 97 C.C.C. 1 at p. 14, [1950] S.C.R. 517 at p. 530:

> To so hold would, it seems to me, be to assert the existence of what is referred to in Stephen's *History of the Criminal Law of England*, vol. 2, p. 190, as "*the power which has in some instances been claimed for the Judges of declaring anything to be an offence which is injurious to the public although it may not have been previously regarded as such*".
> The writer continues: "*The power, if it exists at common law.*"
> In my opinion, this power has not been held and should not be held to exist in Canada. I think it safer to hold that no one shall be convicted of a crime unless the offence with which he is charged is recognized as such in the provisions of the *Criminal Code*, or can be established by the authority of some reported case as an offence known to the law. I think that if any course of conduct is now to be declared criminal, which has not up to the present time

been so regarded, such declaration should be made by Parliament and not by the Courts. [Emphasis added.]

It is difficult for me to see how the mere enactment of conspiracy as a statutory offence would have the effect of extending its scope beyond what it had been held to extend to at common law by the Canadian Courts prior to its becoming a statutory offence while at the same time Parliament enacted s. 8 to exclude common-law offences from the ambit of the criminal law of Canada. I am, therefore, of the opinion, that in s. 423(2)(a) unlawful purpose means contrary to law, that is prohibited by federal or provincial legislation.

But even assuming that the meaning of unlawful purpose could be extended as far as it was at English common law prior to the 1977 amendments I do not believe that it would comprise a purpose to prevent members of a union from participating in the lawful activities of their union. (The law concerning conspiracy has been modified in England by the *Criminal Law Act*, 1977 (U.K.), c. 45, and in brief it now relates to the commission of an *offence*, meaning an offence triable in England and Wales.)

In Kenny's *Outlines of Criminal Law*, 19th ed. (1966), to which reference is made in the *Withers* case, *supra*, unlawful purpose as it then stood is described as follows at pp. 428-30:

451. The term "unlawful" is here used in a sense which, unhappily, has never yet been defined with precision. The purposes which it comprises appear to be of the following species.

(i) Agreements to commit a substantive crime; *e.g.* a conspiracy to steal, or even merely to incite someone else to steal. This extends to all cases where it would be criminal for any of the conspirators to commit the act agreed upon, even though there be in the gang other persons in whom it would be no offence to commit it; and to all "crimes", even non-indictable ones, *e.g.* non-payment of poor rates. A conspiracy to obstruct the *course of justice* can exist without there being any obstruction of the *police* (*e.g.* to fabricate evidence, or to keep witnesses away from the Court). It therefore differs from a conspiracy to *obstruct the police* in the execution of their duty, for this may not be concerned in any way with the course of public justice, but have as its object, for example, to prevent the police from maintaining public order or keeping the highway clear.

(ii) Agreements to commit any tort that is malicious or fraudulent. Some say that agreements to commit any tort, of whatever kind, are indictable as conspiracies. But the weight of authority seems to be in favour of limiting the rule to torts of fraud or malice thus excluding, for instance, a trespass committed *bona fide* by persons eager to assert their supposed right of way.

(iii) Agreements to commit a breach of contract under circumstances that are peculiarly injurious to the public.

(iv) Agreements to do certain other acts, which (unlike all those hitherto mentioned) are not breaches of law at all, but which nevertheless are outrageously immoral or else are, in some way, extremely, injurious to the public. We may quote, as instances, agreements to facilitate the seduction of a woman; or to run slackly in a race so as to enable a confederate to win his bets: or to hiss a play unfairly; or to defraud a shipowner by secretly putting stowaways on board. Similar criminality would arise in agreements to raise by false reports the price of the Funds or of any other vendible commodity; or so to carry on trade as to diminish the revenue; or to persuade a prosecutor not to appear at the trial; or to give false information to the police; or to indemnify a prisoner's bail. On the other hand, it is doubtful whether an agreement to make loud noises for the purpose of disturbing an invalid neighbour would be indictable as a conspiracy. And a thrifty combination of poor-law authorities to marry a female pauper to a pauper of another parish, in order to relieve the ratepayers of the woman's parish, is not a conspiracy. Yet some combinations for procurement of marriage will amount to conspiracy; *e.g* taking a young woman of property from the custody of her relations in order to marry her to one of the conspirators. And although some combinations "in restraint of trade" may be so far illegal as to be unenforceable, it is now settled that they do not necessarily constitute a criminal offence. As to the question whether a conspiracy formed in England to effect some unlawful purpose abroad would be indictable here, the House of Lords has laid it down that a conspiracy to commit a crime abroad is not indictable in this country unless the contemplated crime is one for which an indictment would lie here, and that a conspiracy to attain a lawful object by unlawful means, rather than to commit a crime, is not triable here when the unlawful means and the ultimate object are both outside the jurisdiction. (I have omitted the footnotes and the references thereto.)

Reviewing this extensive list I do not see one head under which would come the conduct described in the information.

This is understandable because as it appears to me, to prevent members of a union from participating in the lawful activities of their union is not necessarily unlawful nor "outrageously immoral", nor "extremely injurious to the public". It is possible to conceive of many situations where to do that would not be so. This seems to be recognized by the Court of Appeal when speaking for the Court, Brooke J.A. says [at p. 191]:

The *Canada Labour Code* is silent as to acts by others outside of the employer-employee relationship which may interfere with the exercise by the employee of the right or freedom to participate in lawful activities of the union. This is no doubt in recognition of the right or freedom of others to perhaps peacefully persuade such employee as to his participation in the lawful activities of the trade union.

But then Brooke J.A., goes on to say:

But that is quite a different matter than acts or an agreement which has the purpose of preventing or depriving an employee from exercising his right or freedom to participate in the lawful activities of his union.

The distinction that is drawn here appears to me to relate to the means rather than to the purpose. The purpose in either case is the same, namely, that there be no participation by an employee in the lawful activities of his union. Only the means differ: persuasion in the first case, intimidation or other unlawful means in the other.

But we are not here concerned with the means. This information is not laid under s. 423(2)(*b*), nor under s. 381, nor under any other section charging a specific crime. It is laid under s. 423(2)(*a*) and, in my opinion, as laid it does not set out an offence known to the law of Canada.

I would allow the appeal, set aside the judgment of the Court of Appeal and that of the Supreme Court of Ontario, and restore the order of the Provincial Court quashing the information.

McINTYRE J. (dissenting) (MARTLAND J. concurring): —

. . . .

The principal question raised in this appeal is whether the information discloses an offence known to the law. The fact that Crown counsel considered that a particular section of the *Criminal Code* was not relied upon in drafting the information does not preclude this Court from considering the effect of the section and finding that the unlawful purpose, alleged in the information, falls within the terms of s. 381 of the *Criminal Code*. While the information, to disclose an offence, must allege a conspiracy to effect an unlawful purpose, specific reference to a numbered section of the *Criminal Code* is not necessary.

Section 110 [rep. & sub. 1972, c. 18, s. 1] of the *Canadian Labour Code*, R.S.C. 1970, c. L-1, confers rights upon employees to join trade unions and participate in their lawful activities. While it may be doubtful if any effective sanction for the enforcement or protection of such rights appears in the *Canada Labour Code*, s. 381 of the *Criminal Code* makes it an offence and, therefore, an unlawful purpose to use the means therein described to compel a person to abstain from doing anything he has a lawful right to do. The information alleges a conspiracy to prevent members of the Seafarers' International Union of Canada from participating in the lawful activities of their union by committing the acts described in the infomation, thereby making the use of the described means a part of the unlawful purpose alleged. Such a conspiracy would, therefore, be a conspiracy to effect an unlawful purpose, and would be an offence within s. 423(2)(*a*) of the *Criminal Code*. I am, of course, far from saying that the Crown would be able to prove its case at trial, but I am of the view that an offence has been alleged in the information and the trial should proceed.

To the argument, which could be raised by counsel for the appellants, that reliance on s. 381 of the *Criminal Code* could take the appellants by surprise and prejudice them in their defence, there is a short answer. This argument might well have force where a previously unmentioned issue is raised after the completion of the evidence at a trial and before judgment, or even where it is produced during a trial when the defence has already adopted a position without consideration of the effect or influence such a change in the Crown position might have. However, that does not apply here where no trial has been commenced, and the appellants would have, from the outset, abundant notice of the problems they face.

. . . .

Appeal dismissed.

R. v. DUNGEY

(1979), 51 C.C.C. (2d) 86 (Ont. C.A.)

DUBIN J.A.: — Thomas Dungey is a solicitor who was charged with unlawfully conspiring with a client to defraud the Law Society of Upper Canada of money or valuable securities of a value in excess of $200. The client was not charged.

When the solicitor was originally retained, the client agreed to pay to him a sum of money, and, indeed, made partial payment.

The case asserted against the solicitor, in essence, was that he entered into an agreement with the client to have the client apply for legal aid in a manner wherein the solicitor would be paid pursuant to the Legal Aid Plan for services rendered to the client, including the services for which the client had agreed to pay him, and the fact of such payment would not be disclosed by either the solicitor or the client. In order to accomplish such purposes, it was alleged that the solicitor asked the client to seek to have the legal aid certificate "back-dated" to the date of his original retainer.

The contention of the defence was that the client had agreed to pay for services rendered prior to the effective date of the legal aid certificate, and the legal aid certificate was not to cover any services rendered prior to its effective date. Although a legal aid certificate was obtained, it was not back-dated, nor did the client seek to have the certificate back-dated. No reference was made in the documentation for the legal aid certificate of the client's agreement to pay for some of the services to be rendered.

The trial Judge was not satisfied that the client ever entered into the alleged illegal agreement. He appears to have been of the view that the solicitor requested the client to enter into the agreement, but was in doubt that the client ever intended to do that which was requested of him, and was left in a state of reasonable doubt as to whether the client intended the legal aid certificate to provide only for payment for those services to be rendered subsequent to those for which the client had agreed to pay. Being left in doubt as to the intention of the client, the trial Judge ruled that the Crown had failed to prove the necessary agreement to found the charge.

On this Crown appeal no issue was taken with the verdict of acquittal on the charge of conspiracy. It was urged, however, that the trial Judge, although not requested to do so, ought to have considered whether the Crown had made out a charge of attempt to conspire to defraud the Law Society, there being evidence that the solicitor had requested the client to join him in a conspiracy to defraud the Law Society.

The contention by counsel for the solicitor on appeal was that there was no such offence as an attempt to conspire to defraud the Law Society.

Viewing the evidence and the reasons for judgment of the trial Judge in a manner most favourable to the Crown, the gravamen of the complaint against the solicitor was that he intended to defraud the Law Society. It was clear that no such offence was committed. The evidence fell short of establishing an attempt to defraud the Law Society. The Crown resorted to the charge of conspiring to defraud the Law Society and failed. Even if a conspiracy had been established, the evidence would have fallen short of proving an attempt to defraud the Law Society.

The Crown now seeks to take a step further back and urges that the accused should be convicted of an attempt to conspire to defraud the Law Society.

What is now being urged by the Crown is that once it is shown that a request was made to the client to enter into an agreement to commit the substantive offence of fraud, such a request attaches the criminal sanction of an attempt to conspire to defraud in a case where the Crown is unable to show that the client had agreed to the request. In effect, it is an effort to attach the criminal sanction of an attempt to commit a crime to what turned out to be merely a guilty intention. In my respectful opinion, there is no such offence as an attempt to conspire to commit a substantive offence.

The definition of an attempt is set forth in s. 24 of the *Criminal Code* as follows:

> 24(1) Every one who, having an intent to commit an offence, does or omits to do anything for the purpose of carrying out his intention is guilty of an attempt to commit the offence *whether or not it was possible under the circumstances to commit the offence.*
>
> (2) The question whether an act or omission by a person who has an intent to commit an offence is or is not mere preparation to commit the offence, and too remote to constitute all attempt to commit the offence, is a question of law. (Emphasis added.)

It is to be observed that by that definition one can be guilty of an attempt to committ an offence whether or not it was possible under the circumstances to commit the offence, and regard must be had to that definition when consideration is given to English authority to which I will subsequently refer.

Of some importance, in my view, is the specific offence created for what is loosely called incitement, and which is dealt with by s. 422(*a*) of the *Code*, which provides as follows:

> 422. Except where otherwise expressly provided by law, the following provisions apply in respect of persons who counsel, procure or incite other persons to commit offences, namely,
>
> (*a*) every one who counsels, procures or incites another person to commit an indictable offence is, if the offence is not committed, guilty, of an indictable offence and is liable to the same punishment to which a person who attempts to commit that offence is liabile.
>
> . . .

I should note at once that it has been assumed in all the leading texts on criminal law that there did exist at common law the offence of attempting to conspire. In Glanville Williams, *Criminal Law; The General Part,* 2nd ed. (1961), p. 615, §197, the learned author states:

> A person may be convicted of attempting to incite, or (presumably) attempting to conspire. *There is one indictable crime of intention that cannot be attempted, and that is attempt itself.* (Emphasis added.)

In Glanville Williams, *Textbook of Criminal Law* (1978), the learned author states at p. 351:

> Isn't there a danger that the law of conspiracy may be used to punish some nebulous agreement that the schemers might never have had the courage or ability to carry out?
>
> Some presecutorial discretion may be exercised in respect of vague conspiracies. But the only limitation upon the law is that there must be a concluded agreement to commit the wrong, not just the negotiation for such an agreememt. An agreement to commit the wrong on a condition, namely, if the opportunity shall arise, is sufficient.

It seems to be possible at common law for a person to be convicted of incitement or attempt to conspire, which would push liability even further back, to a stage where there is no agreement to commit the offence. This possibility is now excluded by s. 5(7) of the *Criminal Law Act.* It would seem, however, that almost all cases of incitement to conspire could be charged as an incitement to commit the crime. (Emphasis added.)

The abolition of an offence of attempting to conspire effected by s. 5(7) of the *Criminal Law Act* 1977 (U.K.), would appear to have been the result of the recommendations made in the Law Commission, Working Paper No. 50 on Inchoate Offences — Conspiracy, Attempt and Incitement. At p. 27, para. 44, of that Working Paper, the following appears:

44. The rationale for the existence of the offence of conspiracy is, in part, as we have indicated, the opportunity which it presents for authority to intervene at an early stage in the conduct leading to the commission of the ultimate offence. *Of the three inchoate offences, it is, perhaps, the one which permits the earliest such intervention.*Nevertheless, there is authority for the existence of the offence of attempting or inciting to conspire, *R. v. De Kromme* (1892) 17 Cox C.C. 492, 494. Our provisional view is, however, that, as a matter of principle, such extensions of the law of inchoate offences in relation to conspiracy cannot be justified. *The matter presents some difficulty since conspiracy postulates an agreement and mere negotiation for an agreement is insufficient to found a conspiracy charge. Most situations which it is necessary to cover will be dealt with by a charge of incitement to commit the substantive offence,* since the concept postulates that one individual will approach another to persuade the other to join with him in a criminal enterprise. In other situations we believe that extending the law in this way takes it further back in the course of conduct to be penalized than is necessary or justifiable. (Emphasis added.)

Section 5(7) of the said enactment provides:

5(7) Incitement and attempt to commit the offence of conspiracy (whether the conspiracy incited or attempted would be an offence at common law or under section 1 above or any other enactment) shall cease to be offences.

The charge in the case of *R. v. De Kromme* (1892), 17 Cox C.C. 492, cited in the Law Commissions; Working Paper No. 50 as authority for the existence of the offence of attempting to conspire, read as follows at p. 493:

"Wickedly and designedly did solicit and incite the said Samuel Dash, then being such servant to the said John Thomas Whitley and others, trading together as Ridley, Whitley and Co. as aforesaid, a certain indictable misdemeanour unlawfully to do and commit, to wit, did then and there unlawfully solicit and incite the said Samuel Dash, unlawfully, fraudulently, and deceitfully to conspire, combine, confederate, and agree with himself the said Jacob de Kromme unlawfully to cheat and defraud and deprive the said John Thomas Whitley and others of their goods and chattels and moneys, &c."

The substance of the charge laid in the *De Kromme* case, *supra,* was a charge of inciting to defraud, although in language perhaps broad enough to include that of inciting to conspire or attempting to conspire. With respect, I do not find that case to be a satisfactory authority for holding that there was a common-law offence of attempt to conspire.

It is to be observed that the language of s. 5(7) abolishes the offence of inciting to commit the offence of conspiracy as well as the offence of attempting to commit the offence of conspiracy.

. . . .

Conspiracy — An Historical Analysis

As already noted, there can be no such offence as an attempt to attempt. An historical analysis of the offence of conspiracy discloses that in the early days of its development, it was viewed as an inchoate offence and very much like an attempt to commit the substantive offence.

. . . .

If the offence of conspiracy is an auxiliary to the law which creates the crime agreed to be committed, and if the object of making such agreements punishable is to prevent the commission of the substantive offence before it has even reached the stage of an attempt, there appears to be little justification in attaching penal sanction to an act which falls short of a conspiracy to commit the substantive offence.

In the instant case the substantive offence was fraud. To hold that there is an offence of attempting to conspire to defraud is tantamount to convicting a person of an attempt to attempt to defraud.

Attempt

In my opinion, an analysis of what constitutes an attempt also supports the proposition that what occurred in this case could not be said to be an attempt to conspire to defraud.

In the case of *Haughton v. Smith*, [1973] 3 All E.R. 1109, Lord Reid addressed himself to this matter at pp. 1120-21:

> What, then, is meant by an attempt to commit a crime? Normally, when a person commits a deliberate crime he begins by making any necessary preparations and then he sets out to take the various steps which culminate in the final act which accomplishes the crime. But he may stop or be interrupted at some stage. Then the question will be whether he has gone so far that he can be said to have attempted to commit the crime. It is well settled that mere preparation is not criminal. A few statutes have made acts preparatory criminal but otherwise the accused must have gone beyond that stage. It has often been said that to constitute an attempt the act must be proximate to and not remote from the crime itself. But that is hardly illuminating. It can be said that the accused must have begun to perpetrate the crime. But no words, unless so general as to be virtually useless, can be devised which will fit the immense variety of possible cases. Any attempted definition would, I am sure, do more harm than good. It must be left to common sense to determine in each case whether the accused has gone beyond mere preparation.
>
> But this theory attaches a very different meaning to the word "attempt". The accused has done, as he did here, everything which he intended to do. There is no question of drawing a line so that remote acts of preparation are not attempts but acts proximate to the crime are attempts. The crime is impossible in the circumstances, so no acts could be proximate to it. The theory confuses attempt with intent. If the facts had been as he believed they were the

man would have committed a crime. He intended to commit it. But he took no step towards the commission of a crime because there was no crime to commit.

I would not, however, decide the matter entirely on logical argument. The life blood of the law is not logic but common sense. So I would see where this theory takes us. A man lies dead. His enemy comes along and thinks he is asleep, so he stabs the corpse. The theory inevitably requires us to hold that the enemy has attempted to murder the dead man. The law may sometimes be an ass but it cannot be so asinine as that. And take another case. A man marries a woman believing that her husband is still alive; but in fact he died last week. The theory requires us to hold him guilty of attempted bigamy. Then suppose that the husband disappeared some time ago. The man who marries the wife may have a variety of beliefs. He may think it highly probable that the husband is still alive or he may think it quite likely or he may think the chance that the husband is still alive is small. In fact the husband is dead. I do not know how the theory would deal with those three possible cases.

The theory is really an attempt to punish people for their guilty intention. The man who stabs the corpse may be as deserving of punishment as a man who attempts to murder a living person. The accused in the present case may be as deserving of punishment as he would have been if the goods had still been stolen goods. But such a radical change in the principles of our law should not be introduced in this way even if it were desirable.

In my judgment this theory must be rejected. I think that the law was properly stated in *R. v. Percy Dalton (London) Ltd.*, [1949] L.J.R. 1626 at 1630 per Birkett J.:

> "*Steps on the way to the commission of what would be a crime, if the acts were completed, may amount to attempts to commit that crime, to which, unless interrupted, they would have led; but steps on the way to the doing of something which is thereafter done, and which is no crime, cannot be regarded as attempts to commit a crime.*" (Emphasis added.)

In the *Director of Public Prosecutions v. Nock and Alsford* case, [(1978), 67 Cr. App. R. 116 (H.L.)], Lord Scarman considered the application of what was stated in *Haughton v. Smith, supra*, to cases of conspiracy when he stated at pp. 127-8:

> It is necessary, therefore, to analyse the decision in *Haughton v. Smith (supra)* in order to determine whether it can reasonably be applied to cases of conspiracy. The Court of Appeal thought that there were difficulties. But I do not agree.
>
> It was — somewhat half-heartedly — suggested by the Crown that the House might reconsider the decision, which we were told is causing difficulties in some respects. It is, however, a very recent decision; and a unanimous one reached after full argument which brought to the attention of this House the relevant case law and exposed the difficulties. More importantly, the decision is, in my, respectful opinion, correct in principle. I would not question the decision, though its proper limits may have to be considered. The House decided the case upon two grounds, either of which would have sufficed, standing alone, to support the decision, but both of which commended themselves to the House. They may be described as the statutory (and narrower) ground and the common law principle.
>
> The statutory ground was provided by sections 22 and 24(3) of the *Theft Act 1968*. The offence being considered by the House was one of attempting to handle stolen goods. At the time of the attempted handling, the goods had been (this was conceded) restored to lawful custody. The House ruled that, in the case of a statutory offence, "The only possible attempt would be to do what Parliament has forbidden. But Parliament has not forbidden that which the accused did, *i.e.* handling goods which have ceased to be stolen goods. . . . Hence the *mens rea* was proved but there was no *actus reus* so the case is not within the scope of the section": *per* Lord Reid at p. 216 and p. 498 of the respective reports.
>
> With all respect to the Court of Appeal, there is no difficulty in applying this line of reasoning to a case in which the allegation is not an attempt but a conspiracy to commit a statutory offence. First, there is no logical difficulty in applying a rule that an agreement is a

conspiracy to commit a statutory offence only if it is an agreement to do that which Parliament has forbidden. It is no more than the application of the principle that an *actus reus* as well as *mens rea* must be established. And in the present case there was no *actus reus*, because there was no agreement upon a course of conduct forbidden by the statute. Secondly, the application of such a rule is consistent with principle. *Unless the law requires the actus reus as well as mens rea to be proved, men, whether they be accused of conspiracy or attempt, will be punished for their guilty intentions alone.* I conclude the consideration of this ground of decision with a further quotation from Lord Reid's speech (p. 219 and p. 550); "But such a radical change in the principles of our law should not be introduced in this way even if it were desirable."

The Second ground of decision — the common law principle — can be summarized in words which commended themselves to all the noble and learned Lords concerned with the case. In *Percy Dalton (London) Ltd.*, (1949) 33 Cr. App. R. 102, 110 Birkett J., giving the judgment of the Court of Criminal Apppeal, said: "Steps on the way to the commission of what would be a crime, if the acts were completed, may amount to attempts to commit that crime, to which, unless interrupted, they would have led; but steps on the way to the doing of something, which is thereafter done, and which is no crime, cannot be regarded as attempts to commit a crime." (Emphasis added.)

In light of the definition of an attempt as set forth in s. 24 of the *Criminal Code*, some of the examples set forth in *Haughton v. Smith, supra*, as instances of there being no attempt to commit an offence because of the impossibility of committing the offence itself may not be applicable in Canada: see the admirable article by Alan Gold, " 'To Dream the Impossible Dream': A Problem in Criminal Attempts (and Conspiracy) Revisited" (1979), 21 Crim. L.Q. 218. No question of the impossibility of the commission of the offence of conspiracy in the sense that it was considered in the *Haughton v. Smith* case, *supra*, arises here. However, I find helpful the analysis of the offence of attempt as set forth in *Haughton v. Smith, supra*, and *Director of Public Prosecutions v. Nock and Alsford, supra*.

In the instant case the solicitor's act was complete and uninterrupted. In the absence of an agreement, there was no offence, and a conviction for attempt to conspire to defraud would be punishment for a guilty intention alone. Notwithstanding that the charge was one of conspiracy, the conduct of the respondent should be viewed as a step preparatory to commiting the substantive offence of fraud and, in that sense, what he did would be too remote to constitute an attempt.

I have noted the specific offence in our *Criminal Code* of "incitement". It would be inappropriate here to consider whether that section could have been invoked to meet the circumstances of this case, but where the evidence warrants it, a more fitting charge would be that of inciting to commit the substantive offence of fraud. If conduct falls short of such an offence, it is neither necessary nor desirable to extend the law so that a person could be convicted of an attempt to conspire to commit the substantive offence of fraud.

Since in my view there is no such offence as attempt to conspire to commit a further substantive offence, it is unnecessary for me to consider whether, if I were of the contrary view, I would direct a new trial under all the circumstances.

I also leave for further consideration whether there could be an attempt to conspire where the conspiracy is the substantive offence, and the question of remoteness would not arise, as distinguished from a case such as this where the offence alleged was a conspiracy to commit a further substantive offence.

I conclude, therefore, that the learned trial Judge did not err in failing to consider whether the facts before him constituted an attempt to conspire to defraud the Law Society, and I would dismiss the appeal.

Appeal dismissed.

For discussion and criticism of the 1997 Criminal Code amendments dealing with organized crime, including the new offence of participation in a criminal organization in s. 467.1, and for an account of the fiasco of the Manitoba Warriors trial, see Stuart, *Canadian Criminal Law* (4th ed., 2001) Chapter 9.

Chapter 10

SENTENCING

See, generally, Allan Manson, *The Law of Sentencing* (Irwin Law, 2001), and Manson, Healy and Trotter, eds., *Sentencing and Penal Policy in Canada* (Emond Montgomery, 2000).

R. v. SWEENEY

(1992), 11 C.R. (4th) 1, 71 C.C.C. (3d) 82 (B.C. C.A.)

Sweeney was convicted of one count of criminal negligence causing death, one count of driving with a blood alcohol level in excess of .08 and one count of failing to remain at the scene of an accident. The incident took place on September 1, 1989, when Sweeney drove his motor vehicle into another while being chased by the police. The driver of the other vehicle was killed. Sweeney was 20 years old at the time of this offence. He was sentenced to four and one-half years' imprisonment on the first count, six months concurrent on the second and six months consecutive on the third. His right to drive was suspended for 15 years. The Court allowed the appeal from sentence. The majority opinion was written by Hutcheon J.A., concurred in by McEachern C.J.B.C., Lambert, and Toy JJ.A. The Court decided there was an error in principle when the trial Judge used a sentencing starting point of five years' imprisonment for all drinking and driving offences causing either death or bodily harm. The Court substituted a sentence of 18 months' imprisonment less one day for the sentence of four and one-half years imposed on the count of criminal negligence causing death, but did not interfere with the sentence of six months concurrent for impaired driving or the sentence of six months consecutive for failing to remain at the scene of the accident. The reason for deducting a single day from the 18 months was to indicate that, for this offender, provincial time would have been more appropriate than federal time. The driving prohibition of 15 years also remained. The majority judgment was relatively short. Separate and concurring reasons for judgment were delivered by Wood J.A.

WOOD J.A. (McEACHERN C.J.B.C. concurring): —

These appeals presented the Court with a rare opportunity to undertake a thorough re-examination of the principles governing the imposition of sanctions in our criminal justice system. We sat five Judges so that we could embark upon that exercise free from the constraints imposed by previous decisions. I believe that it is important, not only for the guidance of trial Judges, but also for the information of the public, that such an opportunity not be missed.

II

While the proper role of this Court on a sentence appeal is to determine the fitness of the sentence imposed in the Court below according to the application of recognized legal principles, we do not perform that function in a legal vacuum devoid of any understanding of the realities of life to which our decisions must be applied. In order to understand the approach which I have taken on these appeals, it is necessary to consider some of those realities which cannot be ignored while en route to a principled determination of the fitness of the sentences imposed below.

I start with the fact that the drinking driver is an enormous social problem. The numbers alone tell us that. Every year over 10,000 convictions are recorded in this province for drinking/driving offences. The experts agree that these numbers represent only a fraction of the number of such offences actually committed. While only a small number of those who are caught have caused death or bodily harm, it is beyond dispute that in most cases that is more the result of good luck than it is an accurate reflection of the risk or danger created by such an offender.

. . . .

Ordinary, reasonable and fair-minded people expect that any punishment meted out under our criminal law will bear some direct proportionality to the moral culpability of the offence for which it is imposed. For reasons which I will explain more fully later, the moral culpability of the offence of impaired driving *simpliciter* is the same as that of the same offence, committed by the same individual, which causes either death or bodily harm to an innocent victim, irrespective of whether the latter offence is characterized as impaired, dangerous or criminally negligent driving. That is because, apart from the personal circumstances relating to that offender, the moral culpability of both offences lies in the intention to drive a motor vehicle after having voluntarily consumed more alcohol than the law permits, together with a reckless disregard for the foreseeable consequences of such driving.

And yet the maximum penalties which Parliament has set for simple impaired driving and related offences are very much lower than those which it has mandated where an impaired driver causes either death or bodily harm. And while the tragic consequences of motor vehicle accidents caused by impaired drivers continue to shock and outrage our community, the daily parade of those convicted of simple impaired driving continues to pass with little comment. Furthermore, while the sentences imposed upon drinking/driving offenders who have caused either death or bodily harm have increased dramatically in the last decade, the average penalty imposed for the simple impaired driving or related offence, despite various Parliamentary initiatives, has not.

. . . .

Prior to 1985, at the discretion of Crown counsel, an impaired driver who caused death could face a charge of either criminal negligence causing death (s. 203), for which the maximum penalty was life imprisonment; manslaughter (s.

219), for which the maximum sentence was also life imprisonment; or criminal negligence in the operation of a motor vehicle (s. 233(1)), for which the maximum penalty was imprisonment for five years. By virtue of s. 589(5) of the *Criminal Code*, R.S.C. 1970, c. C-34, dangerous driving (which was also an offence under s. 233(4), and punishable as an indictable offence by imprisonment for up to two years) was an included offence of all three charges. For the impaired driver who caused bodily harm, the only available charge was criminal negligence causing bodily harm, for which the maximum punishment was imprisonment for 10 years.

The 1985 amendments, which did away with the offence of criminal negligence in the operation of a motor vehicle, increased the range of charges that can now be laid in a drinking/driving case resulting in either death or bodily harm:

s. 220	Criminal Negligence Causing Death	Life
s. 236	Manslaughter	Life
s. 221	Criminal Negligence Causing Bodily Harm	10 yrs.
s. 249(4)	Dangerous Driving Causing Death	14 yrs.
s. 249(3)	Dangerous Driving Causing Bodily Harm	10 yrs.
s. 255(3)	Impaired Driving Causing Death	14 yrs.
s. 255(2)	Impaired Driving Causing Bodily Harm	10 yrs.

The stated purpose of this Parliamentary initiative was to enhance the role of the criminal justice system in the war against the drinking driver. Thus it is important to note that the maximum sentences set for the offences created to address that specific problem, *i.e.*, impaired driving causing death and impaired driving causing bodily harm, were 14 years and 10 years respectively.

. . . .

In 1988, Parliament amended the *Criminal Code* by enacting subss. 735(1.1) to (1.4), which permit a Judge to consider a written statement by the victim of an offence, or by the victim's close relatives, in which the harm done by the commission of the offence is described. By this amendment Parliament sought to ensure that the Courts would not overlook the consequences to the victims of a crime when considering the seriousness of the offence committed.

Several things need to be said about these provisions. First of all, it is important to note that they are permissive, not mandatory. Thus, while they confirm the admissibility of victim impact statements in the sentencing process, they do not require that such statements be before the Court. The result is that they will be present in some cases and not in others, a circumstance which necessarily minimizes the role which they can play in a principled approach to sentencing.

Secondly, they do not purport, and I do not believe that they were ever intended, to require the sentencing Court to take a retributive approach when sentencing an offender. In *R. v. Hinch* (1967), 2 C.R.N.S. 350, [1968] 3 C.C.C. 39, Norris J.A., for a majority of this Court concluded that there is no role for revenge in a principled system of sentencing. I endorse that view. Such a system requires a balanced, objective approach, separate and detached from the subjective consideration of retribution.

This does not mean, of course, that the tragic consequences to innocent victims are to be ignored when passing sentence on the convicted drinking driver. Indeed, as already noted, with the 1985 amendments Parliament specifically made those consequences part of the *actus reus* of the crime itself. And, notwithstanding the view of some, the Courts have never been insensitive to the suffering which victims of crime must endure. The dilemma facing the sentencing Court is to balance a proper consideration of the consequences of a criminal act against the reality that the criminal justice system was never designed or intended to heal the suffering of the victims of crime.

In few cases is that dilemma more acute than it is in connection with the offences under consideration in these appeals. The terrible consequences of drinking and driving shock the sensibilities of all of us, so much so that not only the surviving victims of such crimes, but also many impartial, reasonable and fair-minded people instinctively cry out for the harshest form of punishment for the offender.

But if the tragic consequences to innocent victims were to become the standard by which appropriate sentences for such offences are determined, the courts would soon be reduced to choosing between either imposing the maximum legal term of imprisonment in all cases or embarking upon a comparative analysis of the seriousness of the consequences in individual cases. The first alternative would be an abdication of our responsibility and the second is unthinkable.

(c) The Principles of Sentencing .

Much has been written in recent years about the purpose of sentencing. In February of 1987 the Canadian Sentencing Commission, under the chair of Judge J.R. Omar Archambault, published its report entitled *Sentencing Reform: A Canadian Approach* (Ottawa: Supply and Services, 1987). That study was devoted to recommending legislative initiatives designed to correct perceived inadequacies in the existing sentencing process. While it would not be proper for the Courts to implement specific legislative proposals, particularly when Parliament has chosen not to do so, the report nonetheless contains much information and learned discussion which is of assistance when searching for a principled judicial approach to sentencing within the existing legislative framework. Although I do not accept all of the commission's conclusions, much of what I have to say in this part of my reasons borrows heavily from the theoretical content and the informational material contained in its report.

At p. 153 of that report the Commission suggested the following "Fundamental Purpose of Sentencing":

> It is recognized and declared that in a free and democratic society peace and security can only be enjoyed through the due application of the principles of fundamental justice. In furtherance of the overall purpose of the criminal law of maintaining a just, peaceful and safe society, the fundamental purpose of sentencing is to preserve the authority of and promote respect for the law through the imposition of just sanctions.

This philosophical statement, which I adopt, finds a more practical equivalent in the simple proposition that the purpose of sentencing is to enhance the protection of society. That purpose is achieved if the imposition of legal sanctions discourages both convicted offenders from re-offending and those who have yet to offend from doing so at all. Overlying and influencing the ability of the legal sanction or sentencing process to achieve this purpose, however, is the extent to which that process enjoys the acceptance and respect of the community at large.

A number of factors govern the community's acceptance of the sentencing process. There is a prevailing belief that sentences should reflect, and be proportionate to, both "the gravity of the offence and the degree of responsibility of the offender". In my view the gravity of the offence and the degree of responsibility of the offender are determined by the moral culpability of the offender's conduct.

As a society, we long ago opted for a system of criminal justice in which the moral culpability of an offence is determined by the state of mind which accompanies the offender's unlawful act. Thus the consequences of an unlawful act when either intended, or foreseen and recklessly disregarded, aggravate its moral culpability. But consequences which are neither intended nor foreseen and recklessly ignored cannot aggravate the moral culpability of an unlawful act, except and to the extent that Parliament so decrees.

As I noted earlier, for the same offence committed by the same offender, the moral culpability of the offence of impaired driving *simpliciter* is the same as that of impaired driving causing either death or bodily harm. That is because in both cases the mental element of the crime consists of the intention to drive with a reckless disregard for foreseeable consequences. The fact that death or bodily harm does or does not result when any such offence is committed is more likely to be due to chance than to any circumstance of foreseeability, for such consequences are always foreseeable whenever a person impaired by alcohol gets behind the wheel of a car and drives.

The degree of moral culpability will, of course, vary from offender to offender according to a number of factors which will be discussed later in these reasons, all of which relate in some way to that person's state of mind. But, except to the extent that Parliament has made the consequences of impaired driving part of the *actus reus* of the offences under consideration, I do not accept that the moral culpability of an impaired driver who unintentionally, albeit recklessly, causes either death or bodily harm is greater than it would otherwise have been if he had been caught before such tragic consequences occurred.

And even though Parliament has made the consequences of impaired driving part of the *actus reus* of the offences under consideration, as a civilized society we recognize that the criminal justice system alone cannot be expected to eliminate criminal wrongdoing, a circumstance which necessarily means that we must show restraint when imposing punishment. Accountability of the offender, not punishment for the sake of punishment, must be the primary focus of the sentencing process. Thus any sentence imposed should be the least onerous sanction appropriate to the circumstances of both the offence and the offender.

Another factor which enhances community acceptance of the sentencing process is the extent to which it reflects consistency in the ultimate sanctions imposed upon like offenders for similar offences. However, while consistent treatment of like cases is an important goal in a principled approach to sentencing, the principle of accountability requires that the aggravating and mitigating circumstances peculiar to each offence and each offender be taken into account. Therefore, each sentence must, to some extent, be tailor-made for the circumstances peculiar to its own case. Any adherence to the principle of consistency which denies such legitimate variation would necessarily result in the imposition of arbitrary sanctions.

The respect which the community at large has for the sentencing process will also depend on the extent to which the specific goals of any sanction imposed can be seen to serve the ultimate purpose of sentencing. Those goals have traditionally been described as (i) general deterrence, (ii) specific deterrence, (iii) isolation, and (iv) rehabilitation. In recent years some cases and literature on the subject have suggested a fifth, which has come to be known as "denunciation". The Archambault Commission suggested a sixth called "just deserts". Each of these goals must be examined more closely, with particular reference to the offences under consideration in these appeals.

(i) *General Deterrence*

The theory behind the general deterrence goal of sentencing is that the legal sanction imposed on actual offenders will discourage potential offenders. While there is little empirical evidence to support such a theory, common sense tells us that to some extent, that must be so. Indeed, there can be little doubt but that the very existence of a criminal justice system acts as a deterrent which prevents many people from engaging in criminal conduct.

The problem with the theory lies in its extension to the conclusion, which I believe has been too easily accepted in the past, that the greater the sanction imposed in any given case, the greater will be its general deterrent effect. There is an increasingly persuasive body of evidence and learned opinion to the contrary.

In its report, at p. 136, the Archambault Commission noted:

> With regard to general deterrence, the overall assessment of the deterrent effects of criminal sanctions ranges from an attitude of great caution in expressing an opinion to outright scepticism.

. . . .

The Commission concluded that it is extremely doubtful that an exemplary sentence imposed in a particular case can have any perceptible effect in deterring potential offenders.

. . . .

(ii) *Specific Deterrence*

While it is easier, from a historical vantage, to determine whether any particular sanction has been successful in persuading an individual not to re-offend, there are also reasonable limits to the specific deterrent effect which can be expected from a sentence of imprisonment in connection with the offences under discussion. In many cases, of course, imprisonment will not be necessary to ensure that the individual does not re-offend. But in those cases where the Court finds that such a sanction is necessary to meet the goal of specific deterrence, it would be unreasonable, in the absence of any cogent evidence to the contrary, to conclude that the specific deterrent value of a sentence of imprisonment will be any greater than its over-all general deterrent effect. Any person who would not likely be deterred by such a sentence falls into the category of offender for whom an isolative sentence must be considered.

(iii) *Isolation*

Isolation is achieved primarily by a sentence of imprisonment. It is justified as a "goal" of sentencing by the simple proposition that so long as an offender is separated from society, he or she cannot re-offend. In terms of the protection of society, it is the option of last resort. Even as such, it suffers from the ultimate weakness that if the fundamental requirement of proportionality is observed, the individual concerned must eventually be released from jail. Experience teaches us that most people emerge from prison a worse threat to society than when they entered. Thus care and restraint must be exercised when imposing a sentence of imprisonment even when the goal is to isolate the offender.

In relation to the offences under consideration, of course, the chronic alcohol abuser, whose inability to refrain from driving a motor vehicle while intoxicated is demonstrated by a number of previous convictions for drinking/driving-related offences, presents as a candidate for an isolative sentence unless the Court is persuaded that rehabilitative treatment can and will be undertaken with a reasonable prospect of success. Even in such cases, however, the fundamental requirement of proportionality must be observed.

(iv) *Rehabilitation*

It has long been recognized that rehabilitation, as a goal of the sentencing process, cannot be achieved through the imposition of custodial sentences. That does not mean that rehabilitation should be regarded as a less important goal of sentencing. Indeed, in my view it is self-evident that rehabilitation remains the only certain way of permanently protecting society from a specific offender.

Thus if the rehabilitation of a specific offender remains a reasonable possibility, that is a circumstance which requires the sentencing Court to consider seriously a non-custodial form of disposition. In some cases, even those involving serious criminal offences, where the chances of rehabilitation are significant, or its benefits to society substantial, the importance of imposing a rehabilitative non-custodial form of sentence may outweigh the perceived general deterrent advantages of a custodial sentence. If so, a court should not hesitate to impose the former, for in such circumstances the requirements of accountability and proportionality can be met with carefully crafted terms and conditions which both restrict the individual's freedom and enhance supervision of the rehabilitative process.

I have previously noted that while minimum penalties are provided in the *Criminal Code* for simple impaired driving and its related offences, Parliament has so far seen fit not to impose any such requirement on drinking and driving offences which result in death or bodily harm. Thus it clearly remains open to a Court to impose a non-custodial sentence upon conviction for offences of this sort where the circumstances in favour of such a disposition are sufficiently compelling to overcome the need for a sentence of imprisonment, which would otherwise be required to meet the other goals of sentencing.

(v) *Denunciation*

This Court first gave formal recognition to denunciation, as a goal of sentencing in *R. v. Oliver*, [1977] 5 W.W.R. 344, a case in which a lawyer was convicted of converting trust funds to his own benefit with the intent of defrauding his clients. Chief Justice Farris, speaking for the Court, said at p. 346 of the report:

> Courts do not impose sentences in response to public clamour, nor in a spirit of revenge. On the other hand, justice is not administered in a vacuum. Sentences imposed by Courts for criminal conduct by and large must have the support of concerned and thinking citizens. If they do not have such support, the system will fail. There are cases, as Lord Denning has said, where the punishment inflicted for grave crimes should reflect the revulsion felt by the majority of citizens for them. In his view, the objects of punishment are not simply deterrent or reformative. The ultimate justification of punishment is the emphatic denunciation by the community of a crime.

. . . .

As pointed out in the report of the Archambault Commission, the notion of denunciation as a goal of sentencing is one associated with the retributive theory of sentencing. I would affirm this Court's rejection of that theory of sentencing as declared in *R. v. Hinch*. That means that denunciation as a goal of sentencing must be strictly limited to ensuring that sentences imposed for criminal convictions are proportionate to the moral culpability of the offender's unlawful act.

. . . .

(vi) *Just Deserts*

Notwithstanding the efforts of the authors of the Archambault Commission report to distinguish this "goal" of sentencing from that of retribution, I am of the view that, from a practical as opposed to a theoretical viewpoint, they are indistinguishable. Accordingly, I am of the view that it has no place in a principled approach to sentencing.

IV

I turn then to the fitness of the sentences under appeal.

. . . .

For those who would argue that these sentences do not adequately reflect the gravity of the offences committed, I point to the 10,000 or more convictions for impaired driving-related offences, which occur annually in the Courts of this province, the majority of which result in a fine and a modest, albeit inconvenient, licence suspension. By contrast, the sentences I have set for these appellants are very much more severe, sufficiently so to reflect Parliament's mandate to treat such offences more seriously even though, in each case, the moral culpability of their crime is no greater than it would have been if they had been arrested before innocent victims had suffered.

For those to whom the call for more and longer sentences of imprisonment comes easily, I reiterate my determination not to sanction the imposition of retributive sentences. If retribution is to become a principle by which the severity of legal sanctions is to be determined in this country, then let Parliament say so in language which is clear and unequivocal and which can withstand close scrutiny under s. 12 of the *Charter of Rights and Freedoms.*

Most Canadians take pride in the belief that our criminal justice system responds in a balanced and reasonable way to the actions of the small minority of our population who offend against the law. But Canada has one of the highest per capita imprisonment rates of the so-called western industrialized world. In the last 35 years, nine separate national studies, royal commissions and parliamentary committees, which have considered in depth the question of a principled approach to sentencing, have all concluded that we jail too many people for too long. I believe that the fundamental purpose of sentencing can be achieved without contributing to that problem. Indeed, I am of the view that if the traditional principles of sentencing are applied with appropriate judicial restraint, we can reduce our resort to long terms of imprisonment in many cases without in any way reducing the protection which the public receives from the sentencing process.

For commentary, see *Code*, "Proportionate Blameworthiness and the Rule Against Constructive Sentencing" (1992), 11 C.R. (4th) 40.

R. v. C.A.M.

[1996] 1 S.C.R. 500, 46 C.R. (4th) 269, 105 C.C.C. (3d) 327

The accused pleaded guilty to a number of counts of sexual assault, incest and assault with a weapon, arising from a largely uncontested pattern of sexual, physical and emotional abuse inflicted upon his children over a number of years. The trial judge, remarking that the offences were as egregious as any he had ever had occasion to deal with, sentenced the accused to a cumulative sentence of 25 years' imprisonment, with individual sentences running both consecutively and concurrently. The Court of Appeal reduced the sentence to 18 years and 8 months.

The appeal was allowed and a sentence of 25 years' imprisonment restored. In the course of his reasons Chief Justice Lamer wrote, for the Court:

Did the Court of Appeal err in holding that retribution is not a legitimate principle of sentencing?

As a second and independent ground of appeal, the Crown argues that the Court of Appeal erred in law by relying on the proposition that "retribution is not a legitimate goal of sentencing" in reducing the sentence imposed by Filmer Prov. Ct. J. to 18 years and 8 months. In my reading of the judgment of the Court of Appeal below, I find little evidence that the passing remarks of Wood J.A. in relation to the legitimacy of retribution played a significant role in his conclusion that the respondent's sentence ought to be reduced to 18 years and 8 months' imprisonment. It should be noted that Rowles J.A., in her concurring reasons, did not even discuss retribution as a principle of sentencing. Similarly, there is no evidence that Filmer Prov. Ct. J. placed any explicit reliance on the objective of "retribution" in initially rendering his stern sentence. Accordingly, whether or not Wood J.A. erred as a strict matter of law in his discussion of the philosophical merits of retribution as a principle of sentencing, I conclude that Wood J.A.'s discussion of retribution was not a decisive element in the majority of the Court of Appeal's conclusion that the sentence of the respondent ought to be reduced to below 19 years. Therefore, I am persuaded that the remarks of Wood J.A. in relation to retribution did not constitute a reversible error.

However, given the continued judicial debate over this issue, particularly in recent judgments of the British Columbia Court of Appeal (see, e.g., *R. v. Hicks* (1995), 56 B.C.A.C. 259, at para. 14 (rejecting retribution), *R. v. Eneas*, [1994] B.C.J. No. 262, at paras. 45 and 46 (endorsing retribution); *R. v. M. (D.E.S.)* (1993), 80 C.C.C. (3d) 371, at p. 376 (rejecting retribution); *R. v. Hoyt*, [1992] B.C.J. No. 2315, at paras. 21 and 22 (rejecting retribution); *R. v. Pettigrew* (1990), 56 C.C.C. (3d) 390, at pp. 394-95 (endorsing retribution)), it would be prudent for this Court to clarify briefly the existing state of Canadian law in this important area.

It has been recognized by this Court that retribution is an accepted, and indeed important, principle of sentencing in our criminal law. As La Forest J. acknowledged in discussing the constitutionality of the dangerous offender provisions of the *Criminal Code* in *R. v. Lyons*, [1987] 2 S.C.R. 309, at p. 329:

> In a rational system of sentencing, the respective importance of prevention, deterrence, retribution and rehabilitation will vary according to the nature of the crime and the circumstances of the offender. No one would suggest that any of these functional considerations should be excluded from the legitimate purview of legislative or judicial decisions regarding sentencing.

This Court has since re-endorsed this passage on a number of occasions as a proper articulation of some of the guiding principles of sentencing in a number of subsequent cases. See *Luxton, supra*, at p. 721; *Goltz, supra*, at p. 503; and *Shropshire, supra*, at para. 23.

The Canadian Sentencing Commission in its 1987 Report on Sentencing Reform also endorsed retribution as a legitimate and relevant consideration in the sentencing process. While the Commission noted that strict retributivist theory on its own fails to provide a general justification for the imposition of criminal sanctions, the Commission argued that retribution, in conjunction with other utilitarian justifications of punishment (*i.e.*, deterrence and rehabilitation), contributes to a more coherent theory of punishment (*supra*, at pp. 141-42, 143-45). More specifically, the Commission argued that a theory of retribution centred on "just deserts" or "just sanctions" provides a helpful organizing principle for the imposition of criminal sanctions (at p. 143). Indeed, as the Commission noted, retribution frequently operates as a principle of restraint, as utilitarian principles alone may direct individualized punishments which unfairly exceed the culpability of the offender. As the Report stated at pp. 133-34:

> The ethical foundation of retributivism lies in the following principle: it is immoral to treat one person as a resource for others. From this principle it follows that the only legitimate ground for punishing a person is the blameworthiness of his or her conduct. It also follows that sanctions must be strictly proportionate to the culpability of a person and to the seriousness of the offence for which that person has been convicted. ... According to these principles, all exemplary sentences (i.e. the imposition of a harsher sanction on an individual offender so that he or she may be made an example to the community) are unjustified, because they imply that an offender's plight may be used as a means or as a resource to deter potential offenders.

See, similarly, B. P. Archibald, *Crime and Punishment: The Constitutional Requirements for Sentencing Reform in Canada* (1988) 22 R.I.T. 307, at p. 18. With these considerations in mind, the Commission explicitly defined the fundamental purpose of sentencing with reference to the normative goal of imposing "just sanctions". As the Commission cast the guiding purpose of criminal sentencing, at p. 153:

> In furtherance of the overall purpose of the criminal law of maintaining a just, peaceful and safe society, the fundamental purpose of sentencing is to preserve the authority of and promote respect for the law through the imposition of just sanctions.

A majority of this Court has since expressed approval of this passage as an accurate statement of the essential goals of sentencing. See *R. v. Jones*, [1994] 2 S.C.R. 229, at p. 291 (although I dissented on the merits of the case). Retribution, as an objective of sentencing, represents nothing less than the hallowed principle that criminal punishment, in addition to advancing utilitarian considerations related to deterrence and rehabilitation, should also be imposed to sanction the moral culpability of the offender. In my view, retribution is integrally woven into the existing principles of sentencing in Canadian law through the fundamental requirement that a sentence imposed be "just and appropriate" under the circumstances. Indeed, it is my profound belief that retribution represents an important unifying principle of our penal law by offering an essential conceptual link between the attribution of criminal liability and the imposition of criminal sanctions. With regard to the attribution of criminal liability, I have repeatedly held that it is a principle of "fundamental justice" under s. 7 of the *Charter* that criminal liability may only be imposed if an accused possesses a minimum "culpable mental state" in respect of the ingredients of the alleged offence. See *Martineau, supra*, at p. 645. See, similarly, *Re B.C. Motor Vehicle Act, supra*; *R. v. Vaillancourt*, [1987] 2 S.C.R. 636. It is this mental state which gives rise to the "moral blameworthiness" which justifies the state in imposing the stigma and punishment associated with a criminal sentence. See *Martineau*, at p. 646. I submit that it is this same element of "moral blameworthiness" which animates the determination of the appropriate quantum of punishment for a convicted offender as a "just sanction". As I noted in *Martineau* in discussing the sentencing scheme for manslaughter under the *Code*, it is a recognized principle of our justice system that "punishment be meted out with regard to the level of moral blameworthiness of the offender" (p. 647). See the similar observations of W.E.B. Code in "Proportionate Blameworthiness and the Rule Against Constructive Sentencing" (1992), 11 C.R. (4th) 40, at pp. 41-42.

However, the meaning of retribution is deserving of some clarification. The legitimacy of retribution as a principle of sentencing has often been questioned as a result of its unfortunate association with "vengeance" in common parlance. See, *e.g., R. v. Hinch and Salanski, supra*, at pp.43-44; *R. v. Calder* (1956), 114 C.C.C. 155 (Man. C.A.), at p. 161. But it should be clear from my foregoing discussion that retribution bears little relation to vengeance, and I attribute much of the criticism of retribution as a principle to this confusion. As both academic and judicial commentators have noted, vengeance has no role to play in a civilized system of sentencing. See *Ruby*, Sentencing, *supra*, at p. 13. Vengeance, as I understand it, represents an uncalibrated act of harm upon another, frequently motivated by emotion and anger, as a reprisal for harm inflicted upon oneself by that person. Retribution in a criminal context, by contrast, represents an objective, reasoned and measured determination of an appropriate punishment which properly reflects the moral culpability of the offender, having regard to the intentional risk-taking of the offender, the consequential harm caused by the offender, and the normative character of the offender's conduct. Furthermore, unlike vengeance, retribution incorporates a principle of restraint; retribution requires the imposition of a just and appropriate punishment, and nothing more. As R. Cross has noted in *The English Sentencing System* (2nd ed. 1975), at p. 121: "The retributivist insists that the punishment must not be disproportionate to the offender's deserts."

Retribution, as well, should be conceptually distinguished from its legitimate sibling, denunciation. Retribution requires that a judicial sentence properly reflect the moral blameworthiness of that particular offender. The objective of denunciation mandates that a sentence should also communicate society's condemnation of that particular offender's conduct. In short, a sentence with a denunciatory element represents a symbolic, collective statement that the offender's conduct should be punished for encroaching on our society's basic code of values as enshrined within our substantive criminal law. As Lord Justice Lawton stated in *R. v. Sargeant* (1974), 60 Cr. App. R. 74, at p. 77:

> society, through the courts, must show its abhorrence of particular types of crime, and the only way in which the courts can show this is by the sentences they pass.

The relevance of both retribution and denunciation as goals of sentencing underscores that our criminal justice system is not simply a vast system of negative penalties designed to prevent objectively harmful conduct by increasing the cost the offender must bear in committing an enumerated offence. Our criminal law is also a system of values. A sentence which expresses denunciation is simply the means by which these values are communicated. In short, in addition to attaching negative consequences to undesirable behaviour, judicial sentences should also be imposed in a manner which positively instills the basic set of communal values shared by all Canadians as expressed by the *Criminal Code*.

As a closing note to this discussion, it is important to stress that neither retribution nor denunciation alone provides an exhaustive justification for the imposition of criminal sanctions. Rather, in our system of justice, normative and utilitarian considerations operate in conjunction with one another to provide a coherent justification for criminal punishment. As Gonthier J. emphasized in *Goltz, supra*, at p. 502, the goals of the penal sanction are both "broad and varied". Accordingly, the meaning of retribution must be considered in conjunction with the other legitimate objectives of sentencing, which include (but are not limited to) deterrence, denunciation, rehabilitation and the protection of society. Indeed, it is difficult to perfectly separate these interrelated principles. And as La Forest J. emphasized in *Lyons*, the relative weight and importance of these multiple factors will frequently vary depending on the nature of the crime and the circumstances of the offender. In the final analysis, the overarching duty of a sentencing judge is to draw upon all the legitimate principles of sentencing to determine a "just and appropriate" sentence which reflects the gravity of the offence committed and the moral blameworthiness of the offender.

Major amendments to the *Criminal Code* came into force on September 3, 1996 when Bill C-41 was proclaimed in force. Mr. Justice Vancise of the Saskatchewan Court of Appeal hails the amendments as providing a framework under which there should be less custodial sentencing: "To Change or Not to Change — That is the Issue" (1996), 1 Can. Crim. L.R. 263. In addition to a number of specific amendments to sentencing powers, Bill C-41 declared the Purpose and Principles of Sentencing in ss. 718, 718.1 and 718.2. These were first considered by the Ontario Court of Appeal in *Priest*.

R. v. PRIEST

(1996), 1 C.R. (5th) 275, 110 C.C.C. (3d) 289 (Ont. C.A.)

The accused was a 19-year-old first offender. He had no prior record. He pleaded guilty to breaking and entering a convenience store and stealing computer games and accessories worth approximately $2,700. He confessed when confronted by the store owner. All of the stolen property was recovered and there were no aggravating features involved in the offence. There was no violence or vandalism. There was no breach of trust involved. All of the stolen property was recovered. At the sentencing hearing, which lasted for less than five minutes, the accused was unrepresented by counsel. There was no presentence report or other information about the accused's background, family, roots in the community, education or work history. Crown counsel suggested a sentence of 30 to 60 days. Taking judicial notice of the prevalence of the crime of breaking and entering in the community and stating that general deterrence was for that reason the primary sentencing consideration, the trial judge imposed a sentence of one year's imprisonment. The accused appealed. The sentencing of the appellant took place on July 15, 1996. On August 22, Carthy J.A. ordered the appellant released on bail pending appeal and ordered that the appeal be expedited. Thus, when the appeal came before the Court of Appeal on August 30, the accused had already served five weeks in jail. Crown counsel conceded that this sentence could not stand and suggested that it be reduced to time served and probation for one year, with conditions that the accused report to a probation officer and seek and maintain employment.

ROSENBERG J.A: —

It is obvious that the original sentence of one year imprisonment cannot stand. In imposing the sentence that he did, the trial judge ignored principles and procedural guidelines that have been laid down by this court on many occasions.

Prevalence of the Crime

In imposing the sentence, the trial judge found that general deterrence was the paramount consideration. In stressing general deterrence to the exclusion of all other objectives, he relied upon the apparent prevalence of the offence of break and enter in Hearst. It is not necessary to decide in this case whether the trial judge had sufficient information before him from which he could safely conclude that there was a serious problem of break and enter in Hearst. I note, however, that unlike some cases that have come before this court, there were no statistics placed before the trial judge and he based his opinion on the court dockets of persons accused of the crime of break and enter.

The principles to be applied where there appears to be an unusually high incidence of a particular crime in the community have been set down by this court. In 1978, Arnup J.A. in *R. v. Sears* (1978), 39 C.C.C. (2d) 199 at p. 200, (Ont. C.A.), pointed out that prevalence of a particular crime in the community can never be more than one factor to be taken into account . . . . This court has specifically spoken on this principle in relation to break and enter in *R. v. Rohr* (1978), 44 C.C.C. (2d) 353 (Ont. C.A.). In that case the youthful appellant had broken into an aquatic centre, done considerable damage, and stolen some $600 worth of goods from the snack bar. The 16-year-old appellant had no prior record but was sentenced to six months imprisonment pursuant to the trial judge's policy of imposing lengthy jail terms even on first offenders for break and enter because of the increase in the number of break-ins in the community. Martin J.A. made it clear that even where break and enter is prevalent in a particular community, it is a circumstance to be taken into consideration, but not the exclusive consideration.

The trial judge was entirely wrong to state that due to the apparent prevalence of the crime of break and enter in Hearst, general deterrence was the paramount objective in sentencing this accused. This was a serious error in principle and wholly distorted the decision as to the appropriate disposition.

This court has stressed that before imposing a sentence of imprisonment upon a first offender, the trial judge should have either a presentence report or some very clear statement with respect to the accused's background and circumstances. That principle has particular application in the case of a youthful offender like this appellant. This requirement of a presentence report or statement about the offender is not a mere formality. As discussed below, the trial judge has a duty to consider whether any disposition other than imprisonment would be appropriate. Without some understanding of the accused's background, the trial judge cannot possibly make that determination. Based on the scanty information before him, the trial judge would have no means of determining that imprisonment was the appropriate sanction for this appellant.

Youthful First Offender

The primary objectives in sentencing a first offender are individual deterrence and rehabilitation. Except for very serious offences and offences involving violence, this court has held that these objectives are not only paramount but best achieved by either a suspended sentence and probation or a very short term of imprisonment followed by a term of probation . . . . It has been an important principle of sentencing in this province that the sentence should constitute the minimum necessary intervention that is adequate in the particular circumstances. This principle implies that trial judges consider community-based dispositions first and impose more serious forms of punishment only when necessary. These principles have now been codified in the recently proclaimed ss. 718 and 718.2 of the *Criminal Code*, R.S.C. 1985, c. C-46. Section 718(*c*) instructs that separation of offenders from society is an appropriate objective of sentencing "where necessary". Section 718.2(*d*) directs that an offender should not be deprived of liberty "if less restrictive sanctions may be appropriate in the circumstances". The principle embodied in now s. 718.2(*e*) was of particular significance in this case. It provides that "all available sanctions other than imprisonment that are reasonable in the circumstances should be considered for all offenders, with particular attention to the circumstances of aboriginal offenders". Although these sections had not been proclaimed when the appellant appeared before Judge Cloutier, the provisions to a large extent codify existing practice and principles in this province, especially in relation to first offenders.

. . . .

Proportionality

In the recently proclaimed s. 718.1, Parliament sets out the fundamental principle of sentencing:

> 718.1 A sentence must be proportionate to the gravity of the offence and the degree of responsibility of the offender.

Although only now codified, this principle is well established in this country. Chief Justice Lamer in *R. v. M. (C.A.)*, [1996] 1 S.C.R. 500 at p. 530, 105 C.C.C. (3d) 327 at p. 349, noted that this principle now has a constitutional dimension:

> Within broader parameters, the principle of proportionality expresses itself as a constitutional obligation. As this court has recognized on numerous occasions, a legislative or judicial sentence that is grossly disproportionate, in the sense that it is so excessive as to outrage standards of decency, will violate the constitutional prohibition against cruel and unusual punishment under s. 12 of the Charter.

The principle of proportionality is rooted in notions of fairness and justice. For the sentencing court to do justice to the particular offender, the sentence imposed must reflect the seriousness of the offence, the degree of culpability of the offender, and the harm occasioned by the offence. The court must have regard to the aggravating and mitigating factors in the particular case. Careful adherence to the proportionality principle ensures that this offender is not unjustly dealt with for the sake of the common good.

The sentence imposed by the trial judge in this case was wholly disproportionate to what occurred. This was a break-in of non-residential premises. There were a number of mitigating factors that were completely ignored by the trial judge. The appellant had no prior record; he confessed to the offence; he returned all of the stolen goods; and he pled guilty at an early opportunity. The trial judge was required to give effect to these mitigating factors in imposing sentence on this appellant.

While I hesitate to label the sentence grossly disproportionate, it approaches that standard. It was well above the threshold of the "clearly unreasonable" or "demonstrably unfit" sentence requiring intervention by this court.

The Role of the Courts

In his reasons for sentence, the trial judge stated that the citizens of Hearst must know that the court is doing its job. He was rightly concerned with the need to protect society and that the courts be seen to be doing their part. The courts of this country must accept the fundamental purpose of sentencing that imposition of appropriate sanctions can contribute to the maintenance of a safe and peaceful society. As Parliament has stated in the recently proclaimed s. 718 of the *Criminal Code*, the purpose of sentencing is also to contribute to respect for the law and maintenance of a just society. Respect for the law is not enhanced when overly harsh sanctions are imposed and a trial court ignores well established sentencing principles. The trial court does not fulfil its duty to fashion a sanction that will contribute to the maintenance of a more just society when it imposes a sentence on the offender that is far beyond the usual penalty imposed for this offence in other parts of the province and the country. The offender and the offender's family would harbour a well-justified sense of grievance over the offender's treatment by the judicial system. Chief Justice Lamer made this crucial point in *R. v. M. (C.A.)*, *supra*, at pp. 558-59 S.C.R., p. 369 C.C.C. He was there discussing the rationale for the objectives of denunciation and retribution in a just system of punishment. His statements, however, have a broader application. He said:

> The relevance of both retribution and denunciation as goals of sentencing underscores that our criminal justice system is not simply a vast system of negative penalties designed to prevent objectively harmful conduct by increasing the cost the offender must bear in committing an enumerated offence. Our criminal law is also a system of values. A sentence which expresses denunciation is simply the means by which these values are communicated. In short, in addition to attaching negative consequences to undesirable behaviour, judicial sentences should also be imposed in a manner which positively instills the basic set of communal values shared by all Canadians as expressed in the *Criminal Code*.

This positive aspect of sentencing, reinforcing the basic values of the society, can only be achieved if the court exercises its broad discretion in sentencing in a just manner having regard to established principles. Section 717(1) (now s. 718.3) of the *Criminal Code* emphasizes that the sentence to be imposed is in the discretion of the trial judge. That discretion is, however, not unfettered. The various principles and objectives of sentencing set out by this court and in the *Criminal Code* are designed to guide the exercise of the discretion. The substantial deference that appeal courts are required to pay to the exercise of the trial judge's discretion is not unlimited. In *R. v. M. (C.A.)*, *supra*, at p. 374, Chief Justice Lamer described the imposition of sentence by the trial judge as a "delicate art" where the judge attempts to balance carefully the societal goals of sentencing against the moral blameworthiness of the offender and the circumstances of the offence, "while at all times taking into account the needs and current conditions of and in the community". Regrettably, the sentencing judge failed to exercise his discretion in this careful and measured way.

For the foregoing reasons, we allowed the appeal and reduced the sentence to time served (approximately five weeks) and one year probation on the statutory terms and on the special terms that the appellant report forthwith to a probation officer and thereafter once per month if required and that he make reasonable efforts to seek and maintain employment or education.

The Tools of Sentencing

Discharges

See section 730 of the *Criminal Code*.

In *R. v. Derkson* (1972), 20 C.R.N.S. 129, 9 C.C.C. (2d) 97 (B.C. P.C.), on a charge of possession of cannabis resin, the prosecutor asked that the Court grant an absolute or conditional discharge since it was a first offence. Ostler J. expressed concern that it could not be in the best interests of an accused and not contrary to the public interest to approach all unremarkable cases of this sort with a uniform policy of a discharge; to do so would be seen by many as condoning the offence and inviting a further breach. He concluded:

> In fine, it is my opinion that the discharge — the finding of guilt without the usual concomitant of conviction — should never be applied routinely to any criminal offence, in effect labelling the enactment violable. It should be used frugally, selectively and judiciously, as Parliament obviously intended. If it is considered that an absolute or conditional discharge is the appropriate penalty for a first offence under this section, then Parliament should so declare. The Courts should not compromise or circumvent the law.

In *R. v. Fallofield* (1973), 22 C.R.N.S. 342, 13 C.C.C. (2d) 450 (B.C. C.A.), the defendant had been convicted of possession of stolen goods of a value of less than $200; while delivering refrigerators to a new apartment building, he took some left-over pieces of carpet of a value of $33.07. Evidence at the trial showed the defendant to be a corporal in the Armed Services, married, no previous record, and that a conviction could very possible affect his future career in the Navy. The Court of Appeal reviewed the discharge cases to that date and, with the caveat that the discretion to grant a discharge should not be fettered, offered the following conclusions respecting what is now s. 730:

(1) The section may be used in respect of *any* offence other than an offence for which a minimum punishment is prescribed by law or the offence is punishable by imprisonment for 14 years or for life or by death.

(2) The section contemplates the commission of an offence. There is nothing in the language that limits it to a technical or trivial violation.

(3) Of the two conditions precedent to the exercise of the jurisdiction, the first is that the Court must consider that it is in the best interests of the accused that he should be discharged either absolutely or upon condition. If it is not in the best interests of the accused, that, of course, is the end of the matter. If it is decided that it is in the best interests of the accused, then that brings the next consideration into operation.

(4) The second condition precedent is that the Court must consider that a grant of discharge is not contrary to the public interest.

(5) Generally, the first condition would presuppose that the accused is a person of good character, without previous conviction, that it is not necessary to enter a conviction against him in order to deter him from future offences or to rehabilitate him, and that the entry of a conviction against him may have significant adverse repercussions.

(6) In the context of the second condition the public interest in the deterrence of others, while it must be given due weight, does not preclude the judicious use of the discharge provisions.

(7) The powers given by s. 662.1 [now s. 730] should not be exercised as an alternative to probation or suspended sentence.

(8) Section 662.1 should not be applied routinely to any particular offence. This may result in an apparent lack of uniformity in the application of the discharge provisions. This lack will be more apparent than real and will stem from the differences in the circumstances of cases.

The granting of a discharge does *not* mean that an accused has no criminal record. Under s. 730(3) of the *Criminal Code* a discharged accused "shall be deemed not to have been convicted of the offence". A 1972 amendment to the *Criminal Records Act* prescribed that one subject to a discharge could apply to the Parole Board, subject to a shorter waiting period, for a pardon. A pardon "vacates" a record. This amendment thwarted the aim of the discharge provisions and risked misinformation and confusion. It was only amended in 1992. Under s. 6.1, after one year following an absolute discharge and three years following a conditional discharge, no disclosure of such a record can be made without the approval of the Minister and all reference must be removed from the automated criminal conviction records retrieval system maintained by the R.C.M.P. This provides only partial relief to one discharged and there is no remedy for breach.

What, then, is the legal effect of a discharge? If the question is "Have you been convicted?" it would appear that the discharged accused can answer "No", relying on the *Criminal Code* deeming provision. If the question is "Do you have a criminal record?" it seems that the answer still has to be "Yes" unless the time period for non-disclosure has arrived. Presumably a discharged accused can still apply for a pardon. After such a pardon the answer could presumably be "No" to both questions, otherwise the application for pardon would be meaningless.

Fines

See s. 734 of the *Criminal Code*, and compare the counterpart provisions with respect to summary conviction offences in s. 787.

Probation

See section 731 of the *Criminal Code*.

In *R. v. Sangster* (1973), 21 C.R.N.S. 339 (Que. C.A.), the trial Judge had given a suspended sentence of five years' imprisonment and placed the accused on probation for three years. Kaufman J.A. dismissed the Crown's appeal but noted:

> I do, however, wish to point out that the true intent of s. 663 (1)(a) of the *Code* is to suspend "the passing of sentence", and not the sentence itself. With respect, I therefore consider it unwise to indicate to an accused the precise sentence which might be imposed on him should he fail to observe the conditions set by the Court. To do so may well put the Judge in a predicament: keep his word and sentence an accused to a term of imprisonment which might be considerably longer than the circumstances would warrant or, in the alternative, give a proper, sentence, but lose credibility. Neither situation is good — the first an injustice to the accused, the second an unnecessary embarrassment to the Court.
>
> This should not be taken to mean that an accused cannot be told that failure to abide by the conditions might entail serious consequences, indeed even imprisonment for a lengthy period. But I do think that no Court should bind itself in so absolute a fashion that all room for discretion will have vanished.

The Court may suspend the passing of sentence and place the accused on probation when there is no minimum punishment provided (cf. *R. v. Bradshaw*, [1976] 1 S.C.R. 162, 29 C.R.N.S. 221, 21 C.C.C. (2d) 69). The Court may fine the accused and place him on probation or the Court may imprison the accused and place him on probation. (The imprisonment in such a case cannot be for a period longer than two years: *R. v. Nutter, Collishaw and Dulong* (1972), 7 C.C.C. (2d) 224 (B.C. C.A.)). The Court cannot fine the accused and place him on probation and imprison him: *R. v. Smith* (1972), 7 C.C.C. (2d) 468 (N.W.T.) and *R. v. Blacquiere* (1975), 24 C.C.C. (2d) 168 (Ont. C.A.).

Section 732.1 provides that the Court may prescribe, besides the statutory conditions listed, "such other *reasonable* conditions as the Court considers desirable for securing the good conduct of the accused and for preventing a repetition by him of the same offence or the commission of other offences". The condition imposed then cannot be as additional punishment. In *R. v. Ziatas* (1973), 13 C.C.C. (2d) 287 (Ont. C.A.), the trial Judge, on an assault charge, fined the accused and placed him on probation for one year with the condition that he not operate a motor vehicle during that period. The condition was struck out on appeal because:

> we are all of the view that he proceeded upon a wrong principle, inasmuch as he imposed this term of the probation order as an additional punishment to be imposed upon the accused, whereas his only power, if he had any jurisdiction to impose the condition under s. 663(2) of the *Criminal Code*, was to impose such reasonable conditions as he considered desirable for securing the good conduct of the accused and for preventing the repetition by him of the same offence or the commission of other offences.

In *R. v. Gladstone* (1978), 2 C.R. (3d) S.-9, 40 C.C.C. (2d) 42 (B.C. Co. Ct.), the accused was convicted of breach of a regulation made under the *Fisheries Act* and the Court made it a condition of probation that he surrender his permit to fish for a period of one month. The appeal Court allowed the accused's appeal and noted:

> A condition of probation based upon s. 663(2)(*h*) [now s. 732.1] should be reasonable and it should be designed to secure the good conduct of the accused and to prevent a repetition by the accused of the same offence or the commission of other offences. The primary purpose of a condition of probation attached under 663(2)(*a*) to (*h*) inclusive, should be for the rehabilitation of the accused, not the imposition of punishment. That is particularly relevant when a condition of probation has been prescribed following the suspension of sentence, as distinct from a condition of probation being imposed following the passing of sentence, be it the imposition of a term in jail, or of a fine.
>
> In this case the comments expressed by the learned Provincial Court Judge in sentencing the accused indicate that his primary purpose in directing the accused to surrender his permit to fish was to punish the accused, because he had violated his privilege to fish under the permit, and also to deter the accused and other native people from a repetition of the offence.
>
> In my respectful view, the condition attached by the learned Provincial Court Judge to the probation order was inappropriate for several reasons. First, having suspended sentence, he in effect punished the accused by depriving him of his permit to fish for a period of 30 days. Secondly, in view of the particular circumstances of the accused — that he was a native Indian, no longer employable, in receipt of Social Assistance, and who represented that he was catching fish to smoke for winter food for himself and his family — I am not persuaded that it was a "reasonable condition" within the general purview of s. 663(2)(*h*). Thirdly, the primary purpose of the condition was not directed to the rehabilitation of tlhe accused. Fourthly, the effect of the condition was to prohibit the accused from fishing under his permit for one month, as distinct from restricting the accused from fishing under the permit for specified periods of time within the period of one month.
>
> In view of the accused's alleged lack of understanding of the precise terms of his permit to fish, including the requirement that fish be "marked" (which may have been caused by his

difficulty in hearing), a condition of probation under s. 663(2)(a), that the accused be required to report to and be under the supervision of a fisheries officer for a fixed period of time would have been more appropriate. It would have had the primary purpose of encouraging the rehabilitation of the accused. It would have enabled a fisheries officer to ensure that the accused clearly understood the terms of his permit. Alternatively, a condition of probation under s. 663(2)(h) that the accused report for several weeks to a fisheries officer on the completion of each weekly period of fishing under the permit, to demonstrate to such fisheries officer that any fish caught had been "marked" properly, would have complied with the scope and purpose of s. 663(2)(h).

In *R. v. Pawlowski*, above, the accused's probation order which provided for restitution also contained a condition that he pay costs of $1000. The Magistrate said he was assessing heavy costs to indicate to the accused disapproval of his actions and because of his lack of remorse. Dickson J.A., struck out the condition as illegal and said that s. 737(2)(h) did not authorize the imposition of punishment by means of a fine nor a requirement to pay costs.

In *R. v. DeKleric*, [1969] 2 C.C.C. 367 (B.C.C.A.), the Magistrate suspended the passing of sentence and imposed a condition of probation that the accused pay the sum of $500 in favour of the Vancouver Superannuated Police Officer's Association. Davey C.J.B.C. noted:

> However, I cannot part with this case without some remarks about condition (3), which required the respondent to pay the sum of $500 to the Vancouver Superannuated Police Officers' Association at the rate of $100 per month. It seems to me, with the greatest respect to this experienced Magistrate, that that is quite wrong. If the circumstances required a fine, it should have been imposed as a fine. If the circumstances required as a condition of suspended sentence, restitution or reparation to the injured parties within the meaning of the provisions of the *Code* which allow such a condition to be imposed as a term of the suspended sentence, then it should have been done that way. This innovation is a most dangerous one. It can lead to the greatest abuses, and for myself I hope it is the last time we see such a condition imposed as a term of any suspended sentence.
>
> I have considered whether we should impose a fine or not. If we impose a fine, then this is no longer a suspended sentence. The only consequence of breach of the recognizance will be an action to recover the amount of the recognizance. Under a suspended sentence, if the respondent is in breach of the conditions of the recognizance, he may be brought before the Court to have an appropriate sentence imposed in the light of the conditions which then exist. That is what I think should be done.

Restitution

Sections 738-741.2 now authorize orders of restitution. In *R. v. Dashner* (1974), 25 C.R.N.S. 340, 15 C.C.C. (2d) 139 (B.C. C.A.), the accused, convicted on two counts of assault causing bodily harm was fined and placed on probation. One condition of the probation order required the accused to pay each victim $500 within two months. This condition was struck out on appeal and McFarlane J.A. noted:

> I think, however, that great care should be taken to ensure that restitution or reparation will not be made a condition of a probation order unless the Court is satisfied that the convicted person is able to pay and that the circumstances come clearly within the paragraph, particularly that the amount ordered represents "actual loss or damage sustained". My reason for this view is that breach of a probation order is itself an offence under the *Criminial Code* which may involve very serious consequences.
>
> I think assistance in the task of interpretation and application of s. 737(2)(e) may be found in para. (h) which authorizes:
>
>> (h) . . . such other reasonable conditions as the Court considers desirable for securing the good conduct of the accused and for preventing a repetition by him of the same offence or the commission of other offences.

> It appears that the general purpose of probation orders is to secure the good conduct of the convicted person as opposed to compensating victims of crime. The remedies available to them by ordinary civil suit and under the *Criminal Injuries Compensation Act*, 1972 (B.C.), c. 17, should not be overlooked: nor the difference between compensation on the one hand and restitution or reparation on the other.

So, too, in *R. v. Groves* (1977), 39 C.R.N.S. 366, 37 C.C.C. (2d) 429 (Ont. H.C.), where McEwan P.C.J. had made it a condition that the accused pay to his victim, a police officer, $500 for his pain and suffering which resulted from the accused twisting and bending the officer's little finger. The officer had received workmen's compensation for his injury during his absence from duty. He was still experiencing discomfort at the date of the trial. On appeal, O'Driscoll J. noted the lack of discovery mechanisms in the criminal process for accurately determining extent of loss and concluded:

> In my view, had Parliament intended to confer upon the criminal Courts a remedial power to order an offender to compensate a victim for pain and suffering, it would have set out its intent in clear language. Indeed, it seems to me, that the word "actual" as used in the section suggests that Parliament intended to restrict its scope to those damages that are relatively concrete and easily ascertainable and as such exclude such vague, amorphous and difficult matters as "pain and suffering". Consequently, I am of the opinion that an order under s. 663(2)(*e*) should be restricted to those damages in the nature of special damages.

The amount of restitution is to be fixed by the sentencing Judge. In *R. v. Shorten* (1976), 29 C.C.C. (2d) 528 (B.C. C.A.), the accused were convicted of welfare fraud. The trial Judge fined the accused and placed them on probation with a condition requiring restitiution in such amounts and at such times as the probation officer should order. In striking out this condition McIntyre J.A. stated:

> It seems to me that the condition in question can be attacked from either of two angles: (1) Because the Judge has delegated to the probation officer the duty to form a judicial opinion of the convicted person's ability from time to time to pay. (2) Because the Judge has delegated to the probation officer the power to make an order or orders. It is apparent that the trial Judge, in what may well have been a commendable effort to make a realistic order which would offer some hope of compliance did attempt to delegate his functions in dealing with sentence. This part of his order cannot stand.
>
> In reaching this conclusion I am not overlooking the provisions of s. 738(3) of the *Criminal Code* which provide for the modification of a probation order after its making. The operation of this section, however, depends upon an application by prosecutor or accused. No such application has been made and the possible operation of that section in these circumstances is therefore not before us.

In addition to the restitution that can be made as part of a probation order, a number of recent changes to the *Code* provide for compensation: see ss. 725-727.

Community Service

See s. 732.1(3)(*f*): now provides for conditions of community service not exceeding 240 hours over 18 months.

In *R. v. Stennes* (1975), 35 C.R.N.S. 123 (B.C. C.A.), the accused was sentenced to a six-month term to be followed by probation for two years with a number of conditions including the condition that he do 40 hours of community work per month. The Court of Appeal noted:

> Counsel for the appellant took the initial objection that the probation order was a nullity under the provisions of the *Criminal Code*, R.S.C. 1970, c. C-34, s. 663(l)(*b*) [am. 1972, c. 13, s. 58], for the reason that the condition which I have mentioned as being that numbered 7, that the appellant do 40 hours of community work per month, was the equivalent of a fine, and that a probation order could be given only in addition to fining or imposing a term of imprisonment, and that as imprisonment had already been imposed in this case no fine could be also imposed.
>
> I find no substance to that argument. In my view a condition in a probation order to do certain work, if appropriate, is not a fine, and I so hold. Accordingly, that submission must fall to the ground. I will have something to say later about the terms of the condition itself.

Later in the judgment, however, the condition was struck out as "inappropriate" with no discussion as to why.

By contrast, in *R. v. Shaw* (1977), 36 C.R.N.S. 358 (Ont. C.A.), the Ontario Court of Appeal approved of conditions of community service projects in respect of two youths convicted of trafficking in marijuana and L.S.D. The Court added:

> Not only do I think that the provisions in the probation orders relating to this matter are valid, but in appropriate cases should be more extensively used.

Intermittent Sentence

See section 732, available for sentences not exceeding 90 days. Note that if an intermittent sentence is imposed, then the Court must order probation. It might be advisable to consider as a term of the probation that the offender attend at the detention centre on time and in a sober condition.

Recognizance to Keep the Peace

See sections 810, 810.1 and 811 of the *Criminal Code*. Along with the authority specified in these sections the Magistrate has a common-law jurisdiction to bind over a person to keep the peace: see *R. v. White; Ex parte Chonan* (1969), 5 C.R.N.S. 30, [1969] 1 C.C.C. 19 (B.C. S.C.).

Imprisonment

Maximum sentences for indictable offences range from life (*e.g.* manslaughter: s. 236), 14 years (*e.g.* incest: s. 155(2)), 10 yrs. (*e.g.* obstructing justice in a judicial proceeding: s. 139(2), five yrs. (*e.g.* for an offence for which no punishment is specially provided: s. 743), and two years (*e.g.* wilful obstruction of a peace officer: s. 129). The maximum is generally six months in the case of offences punishable by summary conviction (*e.g.* assault: s. 266(*b*) and s. 787). In 1994 Parliament increased the maximum penalty for several hybrid offences when proceeded against by way of summary conviction to 18 months: see, *e.g.* assault causing bodily harm (s. 267) and sexual assault (s. 271).

There are a few minimum terms of imprisonment imposed for certain offences (*e.g.* murder, or a second offence of impaired driving: s. 255(1)(*a*)(ii).

Where the accused is convicted of more than one offence and receives more than one prison sentence the Judge has a discretion to declare that the sentences be served concurrently or consecutively (s. 718.3(4)).

Conditional Sentences

See ss. 742-742.7. If a court has decided to impose a sentence of imprisonment of less than two years, these sections, which came into force in September, 1996, permit a court to order that the offender serve the sentence in the community where the court is satisfied that such an order would not endanger the safety of the community. The court is obliged to impose certain conditions and also may impose others. For discussion of the appropriate approach see *R. v. Wust* (2000), 30 C.R. (5th) 73 (S.C.C.). See, generally, Allan Manson, "Finding a Place for Conditional Sentencing" (1997), 3 C.R. (5th) 283; "The Appeal of Conditional Sentences of Imprisonment" (1997), 5 C.R. (5th) 279; and "Conditional Sentences: Courts of Appeal Debate the Principles" (1998), 15 C.R. (5th) 176.

Proceeds of Crime

Parliament has enacted an elaborate scheme to permit the recovery from offenders of the fruits of their criminal activity. See ss. 462.3-462.5. Having defined "enterprise crime offence" to include, amongst others, murder, procuring, extortion, robbery, counterfeit money and fraud, the Code provides:

462.37(1) Subject to this section and sections 462.39 to 462.41, where an offender is convicted or discharged under section 730 of an enterprise crime offence and the Court imposing sentence on the offender, on application of the Attorney General, is satisfied, on a balance of probabilities, that any property is proceeds of crime and that the enterprise crime offence was committed in relation to that property, the Court shall order that the property be forfeited to Her Majesty to be disposed of as the Attorney General directs or otherwise dealt with in accordance with the law.

(2) Where the evidence does not establish to the satisfaction of the Court that the enterprise crime offence of which the offender is convicted or discharged under section 730 was committed in relation to property in respect of which an order of forfeiture would otherwise be made under subsection (1) but the Court is satisfied, beyond a reasonable doubt, that that property is proceeds of crime, the Court may make an order of forfeiture under subsection (1) in relation to that property.

(3) Where a Court is satisfied that an order of forfeiture under subsection (1) should be made in respect of any property of an offender, but that that property or any part thereof or interest therein cannot be made subject to such an order and, in particular,
(a) cannot, on the exercise of due diligence, be located,
(b) has been transferred to a third party,
(c) is located outside Canada,
(d) has been substantially diminished in value or rendered worthless, or
(e) has been commingled with other property that cannot be divided without difficulty,

the Court may, instead of ordering that property or part thereof or interest therein to be forfeited pursuant to subsection (1), order the offender to pay a fine in an amount equal to the value of that property, part or interest.

REPORT OF THE CANADIAN SENTENCING COMMISSION, SENTENCING REFORM. A CANADIAN APPROACH

(1987) pp. 2-10

. . . .

Public Knowledge of Sentencing

The Commission conducted several nation-wide polls to assess public knowledge of sentencing laws and practices in Canada. The results indicated substantial discrepancies between public knowledge and reality.

Table 4.6

Summary of Public Misperceptions Related to Sentencing

Topic	Reality	Public View
1. Maximum Penalties:	Public underestimates severity	
Example: Break and enter	Life Imprisonment	4 years
2. Sentencing Trends:	Public underestimates punitiveness of courts	
Example: Break and enter	Over 50% get a sentence of imprisonment	Fewer than 40% get a sentence of of imprisonment
3. Early Release Rates:	Public overestimates percentage obtaining early release	
Example: Parole release rates	30% of all inmates	Most people estimate over 60%
4. Early Release Rates:	Public overestimates increase of early release rates	
	Release rates have not changed much	More offenders being released now
5 Parole Recidivism:	Public overestimates amount of crime by people obtaining early release	
	About 5% of parolees re-offend while on parole	About 50% of parolees re-offend

Topic	Reality	Public View
6. Crime Rates:	Public overestimates amount of violent crime	
Example: Violent Crime	6% of total reported crime involves violence	$^3/_4$ of public estimate 30%-100% involves violence
7. Homicide Rates:	Public perceives an increase since abolition of death penalty	
Example: Homicide rates since abolition of capital punishment	No change in rates	Rates have increased

2. An Overview of Structural Problems

The Commission found that the problems of sentencing in Canada had more to do with the structure in which sentencing decisions are made than with the people who actually make the decisions. It identified a number of serious problems including the following:

- The almost complete absence of policy from Parliament on the principles that should govern the determination of sentences.

- Maximum penalties that are unrealistically high and which do not always reflect the relative seriousness of offences.

- Mandatory minimum sentences that create injustices by unnecessarily restricting judicial discretion without a accomplishing other functions ascribed to them.

- Parole and early release programs that add uncertainty and an element of indeterminacy to sentences and yet which, at the same time, fail to accomplish the goals set out for them.

- Courts of Appeal that are not structured in such a way as to make adequately comprehensive sentencing policy to provide effective guidance to trial Judges. For example, Courts of Appeal, in formulating sentencing policy, can only respond on a case-by-case basis and only to those few cases brought before them. Indeed, the Courts are understandably reluctant to take on what is essentially a legislative role in setting down explicit policy on sentencing.

- A lack of systematic information about current sentencing practice. For policy-makers and sentencing Judges alike, easily accessible information on sentencing does not exist.

2.1 Lack of Public Confidence in Sentencing

In this context, it is not surprising that the public does not understand sentencing in Canada and yet is also critical of it. It is a system whose structure is in need of change. The public may articulate part of its concern about sentencing in terms of its belief that offenders, in particular violent offenders, are not dealt with harshly enough. However, as the Commission's public opinion surveys show, the public recognizes that the problems are more fundamental than simply a difference of opinion on the appropriate level of penalties.

Victims, too, have expressed some concerns about sentences and the sentencing process. They feel that the criminal justice system generally, is not adequately responsive to their concerns. In the specific area of sentencing, they often feel, for example, that sentences are not predictable and do not reflect the gravity of the offences. When they hear of an offender receiving a custodial sentence, they do not know what portion of that sentence will actually be served in custody. The system is not designed to encourage restitution to victims in all situations where it is appropriate. Admittedly the sentencing process cannot, itself, address the problems of victims in the criminal justice system as a whole. However, in addressing the lack of clarity and predictability in the process and in constructing a framework to encourage the exchange of information between all those involved in and affected by the sentencing process, the recommendations of this Commission will address some of the very real concerns expressed by victims of crime.

2.2 Disparity in Sentencing

The problems with the structures in which sentencing takes place go deeper than public perceptions. There is abundant evidence of unwarranted disparity in sentences including the following:

- The majority of Judges who responded to a Commission survey noted that there was variation in sentencing from Judge to Judge. This was perceived to be largely due to different personal attitudes and/or approaches taken by Judges in sentencing offenders.

- Over 80 percent of almost seven hundred Crown and defence counsel from six provinces who responded to a Commission questionnaire thought that there was unwarranted variation in sentences in their own jurisdiction, and over 90 percent thought there was unwarranted variation across Canada.

- There is evidence that Judges approach similar cases in different ways. These different approaches to cases — based on different views of what principles should be paramount — lead to different sentences being handed down for similar offences committed by similar offenders in similar circumstances.

- There is, for some offences, a fair amount of variation in the sentences handed down across jurisdictions (within and across provinces). This variation follows no discernible pattern.

- Sentencing exercises with Judges who were all given the same written facts to determine a sentence suggest that Judges differ widely in the sentences they would hand down. In addition, the sentences they said they would recommend tended to correspond to their view of the principles that were important in the case.

2.3 Over-Reliance on Imprisonment

Canada does not imprison as high a portion of its population as does the United States. However we do imprison more people than most other western democracies. The *Criminal Code* displays an apparent bias toward the use of incarceration since for most offences the penalty indicated is expressed in terms of a maximum term of imprisonment. A number of difficulties arise if imprisonment is perceived to be the preferred sanction for most offences. Perhaps most significant is that although we regularly impose this most onerous and expensive sanction, it accomplishes very little apart from separating offenders from society for a period of time. In the past few decades many groups and federally appointed committees and commissions given the responsibility of studying various aspects of the criminal justice system have argued that imprisonment should be used only as a last resort and/or that it should be reserved for those convicted of only the most serious offences. However, although much has been said, little has been done to move us in this direction.

2.4 The Courts of Appeal

Over the years, Parliament has provided little guidance to Judges with respect to the determination of sentences. The sentencing Judge must look to the Courts of Appeal for guidance on sentencing. Courts of Appeal are not, however, adequately structured to make policy on sentencing. They are not organized nationally; hence, there is no obvious way of creating a national policy. They do not have the means and resources required to gather all of the necessary information to create policy on appropriate levels of sanctions. They are structured to respond to individual cases that are brought before them rather than to create a comprehensive integrated policy for all criminal offences. Most importantly, Courts of Appeal do not represent the people of Canada as Parliament does; Judges are understandably reluctant to transform their Courts into legislative bodies making public policy with respect to sentencing decisions. They appear to prefer to do what they do best; to guide the interpretation of the will of Parliament in the determination of the appropriate sanction in an individual case.

3. The Need for a Comprehensive and Integrated Set of Proposals

The sentencing structure that is being proposed by this Commission involves a fundamental overhaul of sentencing in Canada. It involves recommendations having to do not only with how the Judge determines a sentence, but also with important components of the criminal justice system that give meaning to the sentence imposed. Thus, the Commission has made recommendations regarding parole and remission recognizing that early release procedures are an integral part of the sentencing process and hence have a profound impact on the meaning of a sentence of imprisonment.

Since the terms of reference and the problems of sentencing are broad, the recommendations made by the Commission are necessarily broad as well. In addition, they are interrelated. Their purpose is to provide a comprehensive structure to make sentencing more equitable, predictable and understandable. This necessarily means that to understand the nature of the Commission's recommendations, one must consider them in the context of the total package. Considering almost any subset of the recommendations in isolation from the rest will distort the overall meaning of those recommendations.

4. The Need for a Canadian Solution

Solutions being proposed in other jurisdictions, though perhaps useful to examine, cannot be imported unchanged into Canada. The structure of sentencing in Canada has many positive features. Ultimately, in developing our approach to sentencing reform in Canada, we endeavoured to preserve the strengths of our sentencing system while directly attacking its weaknesses. Thus the Commission recommends that the ultimate authority for determing the appropriate sentence to impose in an individual case should remain with the trial Judge. Courts of Appeal should continue to have the power and responsibility of reviewing and modifying sentences in individual cases. Parliament, as it does in other areas of national interest, should play a leading role in the formulation of criminal justice policy for the country.

5. Guiding Principles

After examing closely our system of sentencing offenders and identifying its strengths and weaknesses, the Commission was guided, in making its recommendations, by the principles found in the first column below. The second column contains a summary of the current situation.

Guiding Principles	*Current Situation*

Role of Parliament

- The sentencing of criminal offenders should be governed, in the first instance, by principles laid down by Parliament.

Parliament has thus far never stated what principles should guide sentencing.

Purpose

- The fundamental purpose of sentencing is to preserve the authority of and to promote respect for the law through the imposition of just sanctions.

There are at least five main purposes with no explicit system of priorities. In a given case, these purposes may conflict.

Priority

- The paramount principle governing the determination of a sentence is that the sentence be proportionate to the gravity of the offence and the degree of responsibility of the offender for the offence.

As noted above, there is no paramount principle. Judges choose among these purposes and combine them as they see fit. There are no rules determining the priority of these purposes.

Trial Judges

- Within the limits set by Parliament, the sanction imposed on an offender in Canada should ultimately be determined by an impartial and independent person with the best knowledge of the case: the trial Judge.

This is the current situation. The Commission maintained this as an important principle in its recommendation.

Statutory Maximum Penalties

The upper limit of maximum penalties should provide sufficient scope to allow the imposition of appropriate sentences. However, the range available should not be so wide as to provide no guidance.

At the moment, many maximum penalties are so high that they are rarely if ever used. Therefore, at present, the maxima provide little guidance and in many instances give a false impresion of what sentences might be expected.

Guiding Principles	*Current Situation*

Restraint

- In line with the recommendations of numerous Canadian commissions that have reported in the past, sentences of imprisonment should be used more sparingly, especially for those convicted of minor property offences. Sentences of imprisonment should normally be reserved for the most serious offences, particularly those involving violence. People should not be imprisoned because of an inability to pay fines.

Canada presently imprisons more people than do most western democracies. A substantial proportion are imprisoned for minor property offences or for non-payment of fines.

Guidelines

- Within the statutory limits, Judges should be given explicit guidance on the nature and length of the sanction to impose. This guidance should not preclude the Judge from selecting the most appropriate sanction from the full range of sanctions prescribed by Parliament.

Parliament, directly or by implication, provides no guidance to the sentencing Judge in determining the appropriate sentence to impose. Courts of Appeal give some guidance, but because the Supreme Court of Canada does not hear sentence appeals, there is no opportunity for a uniform approach across Canada.

Comprehensibility

- The sentence imposed by the Court should bear a close and predictable relationship to the administration and execution of that sentence. We should move much closer then, to "real time" sentencing. "Real time" sentencng reduces the discrepancy between the sentence as pronounced by the Judge and as administered by correctional authorities.

The sentence pronounced in Court, in many instances, varies substantially with what actually happens to an offender because of the manner in which a sentence is administered and executed. Those sentenced to a term of imprisonment may be granted day release after serving one-sixth of the sentence and full release on parole after serving one-third thereof.

Guiding Principles	*Current Situation*

Equity

- The system to be proposed should, as much as possible, promote equity and enhance clarity and predictablity in sentencing.

There is unwarranted disparity in sentences such that the sentence is determined by factors beyond the seriousness of the case, the blameworthiness of the offender, and the circumstances surrounding the commission of the offence. Sentences are, in most instances, not predictable unless one knows not only the facts of the case but also factors such as the identity of the trial Judge and agreements that might have transpired between defence and Crown counsel. Given the uncertainty and unnecessary complexity of the system, it is not surprising that most people do not understand sentencing.

. . . .

8. The Proposed Reform

8.1 An Overview of the Commission's Main Recommendations

The recommendations made by this Commission are designed to provide the sentencing Judge with additional structure and guidance for the determination of sentences. They are not intended to inhibit the Judge's ability to impose fair and equitable sentences which are responsive to the unique circumstances of individual cases before the court. The net effect on actual sentences would be less dramatic than might otherwise be anticipated from an examination of the individual elements of the overall policy. This is illustrated by examining the Commission's central recommendations:

- A new rationale for sentencing;

- Elimination of all mandatory minimum penalties (other than for murder and high treason);

- Replacement of the current penalty structure for all offences other than murder and high treason with a structure of maximum penalties of 12 years, 9 years, 6 years, 3 years, 1 year or 6 months. In exceptional cases, for the most serious offences which carry a maximum sentence of either 12 or 9 years, provision is made to exceed these maxima;

- Elimination of full parole release (other than for sentences of life imprisonment);

- Provision for a reduction of time served for those inmates who display good behaviour while in prison. The portion that can be remitted would be reduced from one-third to one-quarter of the sentence imposed;

- An increase in the use of community sanctions. The Commission recommends greater use of sanctions which do not imply incarceration (*e.g.* community service orders, compensation to the victim or the community and also fines, which do not involve any segregation of the offender from the community);

- Elimination of "automatic" imprisonment for the fine default to reduce the likelihood that a person who cannot pay a fine will go to jail;

- Creation of a presumption for each offence respecting whether a person should normally be incarcerated or not. The Judge could depart from the presumption by providing reasons for the departure;

- Creation of a "presumption range" for each offence normally requiring incarceration (again the Judge could depart by providing reasons); and

- Creation of a permanent sentencing commission to complete the development of guideline ranges for all offences, to collect and distribute information about current sentencing practice, and to review and, in appropriate cases, to modify (with the assent of the House of Commons) the presumptive sentences in light of current practice and appellate decisions.

R. v. MOSES

11 C.R. (4th) 357 (Y.T. Terr. Ct.)

Stuart Terr. Ct. J.: — The reasons for this sentence will take us on an unusual journey. Unusual, because the process was as influential in moulding the final decision as any substantive factors. Consequently, this judgment examines the process as well as the traditional stuffings of sentences, mitigating and aggravating circumstances.

Many might debate the extent any decision-making process shapes the result, but indisputably process can be as determinative as content. In sentencing, process profoundly influences the result. The process influences, not just what, and how matters are addressed, but who participates and what impact each person has in shaping the final decision.

In this case, by changing the process, the primary issues changed, and consequently, the decision was substantially different from what might have been decided had the usual process been followed.

The justice system rules and procedures provide a comfortable barrier for justice professionals from fully confronting the futility, destruction, and injustice left behind in the wake of circuit Courts. For those who dared in this case to step outside this comfortable barrier, I hope these reasons capture their input and courage.

PART I — PROCESS

A) Overview

Rising crime rates, especially for violent offences, alarming recidivist rates and escalating costs in monetary and human terms have forced societies the world over to search for alternatives to their malfunctioning justice systems. In the western world much of the energy expended in this search has focused on sentencing. While the underlying problems of crime and the gross inadequacies of the justice system stem from much broader, deeper ills within society, significant immediate improvement within the Court process can be achieved by changing the sentencing process.

Currently the search for improving sentencing champions a greater role for victims of crime, reconciliation, restraint in the use of incarceration, and a broadening of sentencing alternatives that calls upon less government expenditure and more community participation. As many studies expose the imprudence of excessive reliance upon punishment as the central objective in sentencing, rehabilitation and reconciliation are properly accorded greater emphasis. All these changes call upon communities to become more actively involved and to assume more responsibility for resolving conflict. To engage meaningful community participation, the sentence decision-making process must be altered to share power with the community, and where appropriate, communities must be empowered to resolve many conflicts now processed through criminal Courts. An important step, towards constructive community involvement must involve significant changes to the sentencing process, before, during and after sentencing.

B) Before Sentencing

The Court circuit flew to Mayo for a special one-day circuit to deal with several charges against Philip Moses.

He was found guilty of carrying a weapon, a baseball bat, for the purpose of committing an assault on Constable Alderston. Philip picked up a baseball bat to confront Constable Alderston who was standing by his vehicle behind an open car door. Despite several warnings from the constable to stop, Philip continued to approach in a menacing and angry manner. Philip did not know that behind the vehicle door, the constable had drawn his revolver. The situation was extremely dangerous. At the last moment, the constable leapt into his vehicle and sped off. By seeking a less dangerous manner of arresting Philip, the constable avoided potentially disastrous consequences. Within the hour, the constable arrested Philip without incident. The prudence, and courage of Constable Alderston averted a violent showdown.

Philip was also found guilty of theft. Philip had stolen clothes from a home within Mayo. Philip pled guilty to a breach of probation.

By evening all trials were completed. A brief adjournment was called to enable counsel and the Court to review pre-sentence reports, psychiatric and alcohol assessments that had been before the Court in 1989. These documents described an incredulous life history.

Philip, a 26-year-old member of the Na-cho Ny'ak Dun First Nation of Mayo, Yukon, is the third youngest in Tommy Moses and Catherine Germaine's family of four sons and five daughters. Tommy Moses, a respected member of the First Nation, works full-time as a heavy equipment operator and spends all of his spare time pursuing a traditional lifestyle through trapping, hunting and fishing. He suffers from the adverse health ramifications of a survivor from long-standing problems of alcohol abuse. Catherine works as a native culture instructor in the Mayo school. A source of strength and stability in the family, she has been sober for eight years. All of Philip's brothers have suffered from substance abuse, and all but one have long criminal records. Philip's sisters survived an early childhood amid extreme alcohol abuse and now raise their own families. Philip has a six-year-old son, whom he rarely sees and plays no part in parenting.

The litany of desperate, destructive circumstances engulfing Philip's early childhood are sadly typical of families caught in the turmoil of alcohol abuse and poverty. Abuse, and neglect within his home launched Philip from age ten until he was 16 into a series of foster homes, group homes, and ultimately into juvenile centres. Along this painful, destructive road of state-imposed care, Philip was physically and sexually abused.

Any hope for a formal education was lost through placements in a series of juvenile facilities. Unable to advance past elementary school, Philip functions at approximately a Grade IV level. Handicapped by extremely poor reading and writing skills, he encounters severe difficulty with basic literacy and other educational courses.

His limited education frustrates attempts to find gainful employment. With virtually no marketable work skills or work experience, without money or a sober home, without a positive personal support system, and with ready access to others addicted to drugs or alcohol, Philip, once out of jail, quickly drifts into the maelstrom of poverty, substance abuse and crime. He commits crimes while impaired by alcohol or drugs, or to support his addictions.

These circumstances explain the short turnaround time from the street back to jail. With such grim prospects on the street, jail continues to be his primary home. His criminal record of 43 convictions has imposed jail sentences totalling almost eight years. Jail, as did long stints in juvenile facilities, destroys his self-image, what little there may be, and induces severe depression and suicidal tendencies.

Since 1980, each in-depth assessment has described Philip as extremely sensitive, lacking the ability to trust, and suffering from numerous personal problems with significant dysfunctional coping skills. In each assessment, the same theme is repeated: Philip needs "extensive personal counselling, needs to bond with an important helping person who can offer one to one counselling". This has never been provided. Most treatment recommendations have not been carried out. Philip's distrust, anger, lack of discipline, ability to disappear into the street, and poor self-image partially explain why prescribed treatment has not been employed to release Philip from his severe personal problems. However, the absence of suitable resources continues to be the primary reason identified treatment needs have not been addressed.

> His life has so far involved a vicious circle of criminal behaviour, alcohol abuse and deteriorating self-esteem and general psychological health which will likely lead to a worsening and perhaps tragic outcome if *major interventions are not employed* (Psychiatric Assessment, September 25, 1989, emphasis added).

Without this intervention, Philip, as predicted by earlier assessments, has grown increasingly dysfunctional, committing crimes more frequently, with greater violence and with less regard for any consequences to himself. He has extremely poor insight into his behaviour and demonstrates neither the judgment nor perspective to adopt a sensible or realistic course of action.

Against this abjectly dark picture, given his extensive criminal record, and a sentence of 15 months imposed at his last appearance in 1989, common practice marked out a simple task for counsel and Judge. How much jail time would be appropriate? Had Mr. Moses now proven by his criminal conduct that a sentence of two years was warranted; a sentence which would send this relatively young aboriginal person out of the territory to a federal penitentiary!

The Court was being asked once more to remove this violent offender from the community, to again demonstrate the power of society to punish those who break "our" laws.

It was late in the evening, everyone was tired. The police plane waited to return Mr. Moses to jail. The charter plane waited to return the Court circuit to Whitehorse. Everyone — including myself — expected the sentencing hearing would be short, directed only to the question of how much time in excess of the last sentence of 15 months would be imposed. Numerous factors which never appear in sentencing decisions but often affect sentencing, pressed the Court to "get on with it".

We didn't.

Somehow the pernicious cycle plaguing the life of Mr. Moses, had to be broken before he tragically destroys himself or someone else.

Insidiously and predictably, Mr. Moses had for ten years travelled from alcohol abuse, to crime, and then to jail. Each time emerging from jail, angrier, more dysfunctional, and more deeply entrenched in a marginal existence that featured alcohol abuse and crime, which inescapably closed the circuit back to jail. His long history with the criminal justice system had proven two unmistakeable conclusions.

First, the criminal justice system had miserably failed the community of Mayo. Born and raised in Mayo, his family in Mayo, Philip instinctively returned to Mayo after each of the previous seven jail sentences. He would again return after any further jail sentences; each time returning, less capable of controlling either his anger or alcohol abuse; more dangerous to the community and to himself. The criminal justice system had not protected, but had endangered the community.

Secondly, the criminal justice system had failed Mr. Moses. After ten years, after expending in excess of a quarter of a million dollars on Mr. Moses, the justice system continues to spew back into the community a person whose prospects, hopes and abilities were dramatically worse than when the system first encountered Philip as a wild, undisciplined youth with significant emotional and general life-skill handicaps. His childhood had destined him for crime, and the criminal justice system had competently nurtured and assured that destiny.

If the criminal justice system had failed, what could the community do? It was hardly the model case to experiment with community alternatives. What could be lost in trying!

Court was adjourned for three weeks. The probation officer was asked to inquire if the First Nation and Philip's family wished to become involved. The local RCMP corporal was asked to enlist other community involvement. Crown and defence counsel were asked to consider what else might be done in addition to incarceration to break the vicious cycle that had inextricably captured Philip.

Another special circuit to Mayo was set for on January 9 to sentence Philip and to thereafter hold an open community meeting to discuss how the community, especially the First Nation might constructively participate in the justice system.

Parts of the plan to involve the community were not pursued. However, the crucial parts were implemented. The probation officer met with the chief and other members of the First Nation. They would assist in searching for a solution. Equally important, the probation officer met with Philip and his family to encourage their participation. A visit to Mayo two days before the sentencing hearing by Crown counsel and the senior Crown, enhanced their knowledge about the community and its concerns. Their time with the local RCMP, the First Nation, the probation officer and others within the community contributed to the collective search for a solution to a difficult case.

· · · ·

If the objective of the sentencing process is now to enhance sentencing options, to afford greater concern to the impact on victims, to shift focus from punishment to rehabilitation, and to meaningfully engage communities in sharing responsibility for sentencing decisions, it may be advantageous for the justice system to examine how Court procedures and the physical arrangements within courtrooms militate against these new objectives. It was in this case.

In this case, a change in the physical arrangement of the courtroom produced a major change in the process.

1) *Physical Setting*

For Court, a circle to seat 30 people was arranged as tightly as numbers allowed. When all seats were occupied, additional seating was provided in an outer circle for persons arriving after the "hearing" had commenced.

Defence sat beside the accused and his family. The Crown sat immediately across the circle from defence counsel to the right of the Judge. Officials and members from the First Nation, the RCMP officers, the probation officer and others were left to find their own "comfortable" place within the circle.

2) *Dynamics of the Circle*

By arranging the Court in a circle without desks or tables, with all participants facing each other, with equal access and equal exposure to each other, the dynamics of the decision-making process were profoundly changed.

Everyone in turn around the circle introduced themselves. Everyone remained seated when speaking. After opening remarks from the Judge, and counsel, the formal process dissolved into an informal, but intense discussion of what might best protect the community and extract Philip from the grip of alcohol and crime.

The tone was tempered by the close proximity of all participants. For the most part, participants referred to each other by name, not by title. While disagreements and arguments were provoked by most topics, posturing, pontification, and the well-worn platitudes, commonly characteristic of courtroom speeches by counsel and Judges were gratefully absent.

The circle setting dramatically changed the roles of all participants, as well as the focus, tone, content and scope of discussions. The following observations denote the more obvious benefits generated by the circle setting.

. . . .

[The Court then reviewed the benefits under a number of headings: (i) Challenges monopoly of professionals (ii) Encourages lay participation (iii) Enhances information (iv) Creative search for new options (v) Promotes a sharing of responsibility (vi) Encouraging the offender's participation (vii) Involving victims in sentencing (viii) Creates constructive environment (ix) Greater understanding of justice system limitations (x) Extending the focus of the criminal justice system (xi) Mobilizing community resources (xii) Merging values: First Nation and western governments. The Court then went on to describe the safeguards which would protect the individual's rights in this new system.]

. . . .

Courage, patience, and tolerance must accompany all participants in the search for a productive partnership between communities and the justice system. The search need not be foolhardy. Many safeguards can be adapted to protect individual rights while opening the process to community involvement. In this experiment with the circle, the following safeguards were used to cushion any adverse impact on individual rights. Within the justice system, a critical assessment must be made about what is truly inviolable and what has by convention been presumed to be. Many conventions have survived long past the justification for their original creation.

(i) *Open Court*

The courtroom remained the same, only the furniture was rearranged. The door was open, the public retained free access to the room.

The long-standing reasons for open Court may not be as persuasive in some sentencing hearings where privacy may be essential to precipitate frank exchanges which reveal extremely sensitive family or personal information. Normally such information, vital to competently employing any sentencing option, is rarely available as participants are understandably reluctant to share intimate circumstances of their life in an open public courtroom, especially in small communities where anonymity is impossible.

In most cases there will be no need to limit access. However, where clear advantages flow from a closed session, the long-standing reasons for open Court must be dusted off and re-examined in light of the advantages derived from acquiring extremely sensitive and personal information from offenders, victims or their families and friends.

(ii) *Transcripts*

The Court reporter remained a part of the circle.

In some cases, there are good reasons to question why a transcript embracing all circle discussions is necessary. Some aspects of the discussion may be best excluded from the transcript, or where the circle is closed to the public, the transcript retained in a confidential manner, available only if required by a Court of Appeal.

To establish appropriate guidelines in assessing the competing values of an open versus a closed process on a case-by-case basis, some of the ancient icons of criminal procedures need an airing and reassessment.

The tradition of a circle — "what comes out in a circle, stays in a circle" — runs counter to the justice tradition requiring both an open Court and transcripts. A more flexible set of rules for exceptions must be fashioned to establish a balance in merging First Nation, community, and justice system values in the circle.

(iii) *Upper limits to sentence*

The circle is designed to explore and develop viable sentencing options drawing upon, whenever possible, community-based resources. The circle is not designed to extract reasons to increase the severity of punishment. Accordingly at the outset of the circle process, Crown and defence counsel were called upon to make their customary sentencing submissions. Based on these submissions, I indicated the upper limit sentence for the offence.

By stating at the outset an upper limit to the sentence based on conventional sentencing principles and remedies, the offender enters the circle without fearing a harsher jail sentence provoked by candour or anger within the circle. This constitutes an important basis to encourage offenders to participate.

The upper limit also provides a basis for the circle to appreciate what will happen in the absence of community alternatives. The utility of the upper limit sentence can be measured against any new information shared in the circle. Any community-based alternative developed by the circle may be substituted for part or all of this sentence.

(iv) *Opportunity for offender to speak*

The *Criminal Code* ensures the offender has an opportunity to speak in his own words before a sentence is imposed. This opportunity is generally offered after all submissions have been made, and the Court has all but formally concluded what the sentence will be. It is generally a perfunctory step in the process, rarely used and generally of little effect.

Defence counsel bears the primary and often exclusive responsibility to represent the offender's interest. How far we have come from the time when lawyers were banned and offenders left to make their own submissions. Somewhere on this journey from exclusive reliance upon the offender to essentially exclusive reliance upon defence counsel, we passed a more fitting balance in the participatory roles of counsel and offender. It may be too cute to suggest Courts currently sentence defence counsel not offenders, but the thought does highlight how much sentencing depends upon the work, competence, knowledge, and eloquence of defence counsel.

The inequities in proceeding without counsel are staggering. Similarly the involvement of communities creates its own inequities within the circle. In a very unequal world, no justice system can create equality, or for that matter render perfect justice. The circle improves the offender's ability to participate, and thereby reduces the obvious inequities in a process that minimizes participation by the very person who is the primary focus of the process. More thought, more innovation must be invested to extract the best from the existing justice process and from the circle to create a viable balance between individual rights and community involvement.

(v) *Crown and defence counsel* .

The traditional and essential functions of Crown and defence counsel are not excluded by the circle.

The Crown at the outset placed before the circle the interests of the state in sentencing the offender. The Crown's participation through questions, and by engaging in the discussions retains the circle's awareness of the larger interests of the state. Aware of community-provided alternatives, having acquired first hand knowledge of a broad spectrum of community concerns and armed with detailed information about the offender, the Crown at the end of the circle discussions can more competently assess how the interests of the state, and the interests of the community are best addressed in sentencing.

Especially on circuit, the Crown is forced to make assumptions about what sentences protect the community. Through the circle, these assumptions are examined by members of the very community Crown submissions are designed to protect.

Defence counsel, knowing that at worst the offender faces a conventional sentence presaged at the outset of the hearing, can constructively use the circle to develop a sentencing plan to advance the immediate and long-term interests of his client. Community support generated by the circle, as it did in this case, creates viable alternatives to jail.

(vi) *Disputed facts*

Any disputed fact must be proven in the customary manner. Proof of a disputed fact can be carried out in the circle by the examination of witnesses under oath. Alternatively, during a break in the circle discussions, Court can be resumed and all the traditional trappings of the courtroom engaged to resolve a disputed fact.

The circle moves along a different road to consensus than the adversarial character of the formal courtroom hearings. The process in a circle can either resolve disputes in a less adversarial manner, or render the disputed fact irrelevant or unimportant by evolving a sentencing disposition principally relevant upon community-based alternatives. However, the formal Court process provides a "safeguard" to be called upon by either counsel at any time a matter in the circle necessitates formal proof.

4) *Summary: The circle*

These changes to the sentencing process are not the makings of a panacea. They are relatively small steps in a very long journey to move the criminal justice system from its destructive impact on people and communities to doing what it should — working closely with communities to prevent crime, protect society, rehabilitate offenders and process conflict in a manner that builds not undermines a sense of community.

Although the circle does not achieve a "truly new direction" in sentencing, it may stimulate discussions at the community level that ultimately generate a different conception of the purpose and function of sentencing. To date decades of discussions on "new directions in sentencing" have been confined to conferences, professional publications, law reform commissions and to the legal community. These discussions are vibrant but bear little fruit. The circle provides the information, insight, and hopefully the motivation for the community to develop and press for "truly new directions".

The circle may not be appropriate for all crimes or all offenders. Experience will explore and test the utility of each new initiative. We must however, continue to search for a less expensive, more purposeful, more humane manner to respond to crime. The current thrust to involve communities in processing and resolving conflict and crime within the community is essential and unavoidable. Costs in monetary and human terms allow no alternative.

Even if funds were unlimited, crime cannot be resolved solely by hiring legions of professionals. This lesson has been repeatedly and expensively learned by many communities who tried to buy their way out of crime.

The greater the reliance upon professionals, the less communities become involved, the faster community well-being deteriorates. The criminal justice system exemplifies the worst case of excessive reliance upon professionals.

A struggle for a safe community must be led by the community. They, not the justice system must be in the front line of defence against crime. All members of the community must appreciate and accept responsibility to carry their share of the burden in establishing and maintaining a safe community. The safety and overall health of each community is directly related to the extent each citizen participates. This is a fact of family well-being as much as it is of community well-being. The 20th century is replete with examples of the demise of communities and families that failed to accord the time and take the responsibility to process conflict in a constructive manner. Conflict will always be a part of community life. Creating constructive processes for dealing with conflict is the primary challenge facing society and the criminal justice system.

The current justice system is a very expensive failure, and in many respects undermines the very objectives it champions. There is an increasing recognition within and without the legal community that something more than mere tinkering must be done to create a criminal justice system that is just and offers genuine protection to the community. The existing system notoriously does neither. Sufficient good ideas exist, and have existed since the 1938 Archambault report to evolve a better process. In the pioneering work that must be done, we must not cling tenaciously to ancient ideas, or regard any existing practices as sacrosanct. We have much to learn and the communities have much to teach us. The communities equally have much to learn. They must begin to appreciate that not only do they have a responsibility to directly participate in preventing crime and processing crime, most importantly they must learn that in many respects they are better suited to successfully achieve the primary objectives of the justice system.

. . . .

By the end of the circle discussion, the search for an appropriate sentence had shifted from punishment to rehabilitation. The resources contributed by Philip's family, his First Nation, and his community created a practical, realistic alternative to incarceration. Without this investment, despite the obvious need for rehabilitation, jail once again would have been the only option.

It is frightening to contemplate how many offenders are routed to jail simply because community and family resources cannot be marshalled to offer a better alternative. Frightening to realize, before the circle discussions, the principal task in sentencing Philip had been to determine whether more jail time than the 15 months imposed in 1989 was warranted.

The new information and additional resources generated by discussions within the circle have created Philip's first reasonable chance to escape a self-destructive lifestyle.

The Crown, while supportive of the need to rehabilitate Philip, stressed the importance of punishing criminal behaviour. The justice system's stock-in-trade has been punishment. While filling our jails at rates among the highest in the western world, we have not succeeded in deterring crime. In repeatedly punishing Philip, we have not succeeded in stopping his criminal activity. There is a growing recognition that no one learns anything by punishment. Whatever constructive purpose punishment continues to serve in the criminal justice system, at this juncture for Philip, nothing can be gained by further punishment. Philip, awaiting trial for these offenses, spent three months in remand, which is equivalent to a sentence of at least six months; that is enough punishment.

The Crown, in challenging the sincerity of Philip's interest in rehabilitation, reported that Philip had remarked immediately after Court in December that "I just want to go to jail, I don't want any of this treatment". Not a surprising reaction to a system whose primary discourse with Philip has been centred around punishment. How could anything called treatment be seen by Philip as anything but further punishment in a new disguise.

This challenge by Crown provoked a riveting response from Philip which successfully removed any of my lingering doubts.

The leaders of the community where Philip will live out his life are willing to risk their safety in a rehabilitative program, his family and First Nation are willing to invest in Philip. After many years of counselling Philip, the local probation officer, a long-time resident of Mayo, believes Philip deserves an opportunity to try and believes he can succeed. Philip recognizes all of this support and spoke eloquently of his motivation to try to change his life. In the face of all of these compelling grounds for a rehabilitation sentence, neither the offences before the Court, nor his criminal record deny taking a risk. What risk could there be? We knew the risks of jail (further offences)! "Neither a trial judge nor an appellate Court should hesitate to take a calculated risk when satisfied by so doing there is a reasonable possibility that the offender may change his life."

The doubts properly raised and fairly expressed by Crown counsel were simply not enough to offset the support of the community for Philip and for the plan that had evolved. The Crown and Judge who do not live in the community and are not familiar with the community must be cautious in opposing, on the basis of a need to "protect the public", a rehabilitative plan developed by the community.

B) The Plan

A suspended sentence, coupled with a two-year probation order provides the legal packaging for the sentencing plan that contains three distinct parts.

The first part commences Philip's rehabilitation by immediately calling upon his family to reintegrate him into their family and lifestyle. Foster homes, juvenile facilities and eight years of jail sentences, removed Philip from any positive interaction with his family and directed his life into an urban context. Consequently, he lost contact with the culture and practices of his family. Philip is required to reside with his family on the trapline located 60 miles outside Mayo. His family will ensure a member of the family will stay with Philip.

The plan's second part sends Philip from the trapline to a two-month residential program for native alcoholics in southern British Columbia. Other members of his First Nation have benefited from this program. His brother may attend with him and in the very least, his family, First Nation and the probation officer will maintain regular contact. Unfortunately as yet, no such program exists in the Yukon. [A local program, reliant upon local resources, constructively engaging local community and family support systems, would significantly increase the likelihood of success at significantly less cost per patient].

The plan's third part brings Philip back to Mayo where his family will provide an alcohol-free home. The First Nation will develop a support program for Philip to upgrade life and employment skills, and provide continuing counselling for substance abuse. The probation officer will add additional support and counselling services. All efforts will be made within the community to help Philip acquire gainful employment.

At each stage, a Court review will be held in the circle to fine-tune the plan and offer whatever further support may be required. The plan depends upon a concerted investment from Philip, his family, his First Nation, his community and from government. Combining all of these resources created for the first time a viable alternative to jail, and incorporates the values and concerns of the First Nation, the justice system, and most importantly, Philip.

PART IV — CONCLUSION

In the justice system, too much is made of "professional objectivity". We are not processing agents solely worried about backlogs and budgets. Crimes expose conflicts that cut to the heart of families and communities. If we insulate ourselves with procedures and rules that afford a comfortable, objective, professional shield from the pain, tragedy and desperateness inherent in all of these conflicts, we will forever fail. We cannot succumb to simply doing "our jobs" passing criminals, victims, and communities from one part of our truncated system to another. Send into our midst, those with the compassion, courage, and perseverance of probation officers such as Sue Davies. Send so many that the objective aloofness, the resignation to highly segregated roles, the ready acceptance of the limitations of our system, are no longer commonplace; but what becomes commonplace is a willingness to deal with human problems, genuine human feelings, and an irrepressible yearning to find "a better way". Sue Davies' persistence may not save Philip from a life of self-destruction, but her persistence and others like her may save the justice system from its persistent destructive impact on offenders, victims, the community, and upon those who work within it.

We must move beyond the self-defeating notion that the justice system can "only do so much". Participation from families like Philip's, from Chiefs like Robert Hager, his councillors and from the community create an opportunity to resolve conflict in a meaningful manner, and prove that through collective efforts that more than "only so much" can be done.

Philip's road to recovery will be tougher than most people appreciate, tougher than I can fathom. How can he ever comprehend a justice system, that after 15 years of degrading, destructive punishment, wants to say, "We were wrong. Now if you succeed with this different plan, we will not punish you anymore". He knows our power, knows our short attention span, and equally our limited tolerance. He handles us and our punishment with anger. He will probably test our new approach, prepared for our predictable response with his predictable anger. We must not be quick to punish his failure, and must persevere until we can convince Philip that our interest is genuinely focused on his rehabilitation; not on his destruction; and that we have far nobler, far more compassionate objectives than punishment.

Without extensive treatment, without long-term one-to-one counselling, without skill upgrading in almost every aspect of his life, and without a durable, persistent, personal support system, Philip hasn't a chance. His first 26 years of life have stolen even the most minimal advantages others enjoy. It is a miracle that despite so much destruction, so much pain, with so little to work with, Philip still clings to the hope he can survive, that he can prevail. Courage and the ability to persevere must be measured in the context of each person's overall life circumstance. Given Philip's personal problems, viciously destructive childhood, criminal record, and severe substance abuse, his very survival manifests a formidable will and prodigious courage to prevail.

As someone said in the circle, "Thank you, Philip for sharing your pain with us, I have learned so much that I did not know before".

Philip, his family, his community, and all of us in the justice system need to say, "Thank you, Sue Davies, for having the courage to reach beyond the sterile, professionally structured role of a probation officer and follow your instincts and compassion. I hope others, as I did, learned and will act upon something I did not know before".

Finally, no one can contend "circuit court's work"; no one can deny that the system squanders money and lives unnecessarily with dubious success in either protecting or improving the community; no one can be content to simply press on; no one can ignore the need to change what circuit Courts do; and equally, no one person, no one agency, no one government can make a change. Yes, change we must. Yes, work together we must. The circle creates a starting point to work constructively with communities and to empower communities to resolve their own problems.

Tragically, Philip's is not a unique story. There are many other victims of the current justice system and will be many more if we irresponsibly believe simply keeping the current machinery of justice in gear defines the parameters of our "professional" responsibility. Unless the system is changed, the community will be victimized by the very system charged with the responsibility of protecting it. We must find a way to change. We must find communities, First Nations, professionals and lay people willing to work together to explore "truly new ways". We will; we have no choice. In making the circle work, the Na-cho Ny'ak Dun First Nation took an important first step. Can we follow?

For commentary, see Manson, "Moses: Involving the Community in Sentencing" (1992), 11 C.R. (4th) 395.

For a report from the point of view of victims criticizing the use of circle sentencing in the case of violent crimes, see *Inuit Women and Justice* (1995), Progress Report Number One.

Sentencing Exercises

Decide on the appropriate sentence in each of the cases. Then compare your disposition with that actually imposed by the Courts (see the full report).

R. v. DOERR

(1974), 20 C.C.C. (2d) 1 (Ont. C.A.)

EVANS J.A. (dissenting): — The Crown applies for leave to appeal and if leave be granted, appeals against the sentence imposed by His Honour Judge Scott at St. Catharines on February 20, 1974, following conviction of the accused on February 14th, pursuant to a plea of guilty to the offence of possession of a narcotic, to wit, *cannabis* marijuana for the purpose of trafficking contrary to s. 4(2) of the *Narcotic Control Act*, R.S.C. 1970, c. N-1.

. . . .

The charge resulted from an incident which occurred on June 12, 1973, when a vehicle, in which the respondent was a passenger, was searched on the Queen Elizabeth Highway and plant-like material, later found upon analysis to be marijuana, was discovered. The respondent admitted ownership and stated that he had paid approximately $1,000 for the marijuana. Shortly after his arrest the respondent made a written statement which he admitted was made voluntarily, in which it was stated that he had purchased the four pounds of marijuana with the intention of selling it. He also stated that he had been selling marijuana for a few weeks prior to his arrest and that he had been a drug-user for three or four years.

The respondent had no criminal record at the time of the commission of this offence but prior to the date upon which he was sentenced he had been convicted and sentenced on three counts of break enter and theft. These offences were committed subsequent in point of time to the drug offence and the sentences imposed on January 31, 1974, for these offences were a suspended sentence in each instance together with probation for a period of 18 months.

. . . .

The respondent was born in 1951, completed high school in 1968 at age 17 and attended Queen's University where he failed to complete his year. He returned home in April and remained there for one year before moving to Toronto. In 1972 he returned to Queen's for summer school and subsequently returned to Welland. His parents were advised that it would be to his benefit to evict him from their home and they did so. The respondent has been involved in the non-medical use of drugs for over three years and his increasing addiction has had an adverse effect upon his mental and physical health. In 1972 he was referred to a psychiatrist, Dr. Burns, who unfortunately was unable to be of much assistance in view of the feeble quality of the respondent's motivation and because he was generally in a psychotic or near-psychotic state from the use of drugs whenever he attended for an appointment. At the same time some group-family therapy was attempted but little progress was made. In November, 1973, following his arrest upon the marijuana charge, he sought treatment at Spera, a drug addiction centre in Niagara Falls and at the Welland Hospital and while we have not been provided with reports from those institutions it appears that he originally made some progress both in his physical condition and his mental attitude. Because of a personality conflict between the respondent and a staff member at Spera, he terminated his treatment at that centre and is at present receiving treatment at Niagara Residential Centre. The probation order which required the respondent to reside at Spera was amended to conform with the change of residence.

In view of this young man's behavioural record and prior lack of motivation, it is obvious that his change in attitude is influenced by the fact he is on probation and no doubt to some extent because his sentence on the narcotic case is under appeal. Prior to arrest on the drug charge and for several months thereafter, he had not shown any inclination to obtain treatment for his drug habit although his family was ready and eager to assist him.

. . . .

When this appeal was argued on June 14th judgment was reserved in order that a post-sentence report might be obtained. That report is now before the Court and indicates that the respondent, following his release on probation on January 31, 1974, resided for six days at the Spera Niagara and then left. He entered the Niagara Residential Centre on March 4, 1974. This centre which is operated by former drug addicts is closing because of lack of financial support and the respondent has arranged to share accommodation with a former counsellor at the centre while the latter attends a community college in the Niagara area.

The respondent is employed as a bell-hop and tour vendor at a Niagara Falls Hotel and has expressed an intention to resume his university career although there is no confirmatory evidence that he will be accepted as a student. He lacks the necessary financial support to continue at university and his parents, quite justifiably, are not prepared to finance him. I am not persuaded that this stated intention is more than a pious hope which presently lacks any realistic basis of fulfilment. His recent work record has been satisfactory and his general attitude has improved; he has not been using drugs for some months and has not associated with drug-users; he does not feel that he requires further treatment but there is no professional evidence to support that view. The recommendation of the probation officer is that a term of imprisonment at this time could have an adverse effect upon the respondent's rehabilitation for drug abuse and criminal behaviour. That recommendation is based to a great extent upon the opinions of the social workers at the Niagara Residential Centre.

R. v. COULTIS AND ZINK

(1974), 18 C.C.C. (2d) 467 (Ont. C.A.)

ARNUP J.A. (orally): — The appellants, Coultis and Zink, were charged that at the Township of Moore, in the County of Lambton, on or about January 30, 1973, they did unlawfully have in their possession for the purpose of trafficking, a narcotic drug, to wit, *cannabis* marijuana, contrary to s. 4(2) of the *Narcotic Control Act*, R.S.C. 1970, c. N-1. They were tried by His Honour Judge Carscallen and a jury. The jury on the first part of the trial, which was in two stages as prescribed by the Act, found that the appellants were in possession of marijuana and subsequently on the second part of the trial found that both appellants were in possession for the purpose of trafficking. The Crown appealed the sentence imposed, and the accused cross-appealed against their convictions.

Briefly, the facts of the matter were that the appellants, having learned that there was a probability that a substantial amount of marijuana had been concealed in a remote area, made their way there in a car driven by Coultis. The evidence as a whole indicates that the leader in the enterprise was Coultis. Unknown to the appellants the R.C.M.P. had received some information of their own and were keeping the area under surveillance. The two appellants went to the area and it was said by the officers that in the course of the accused's journey towards the area in question they were overheard to say that "some hunters must have moved it".

Eventually Coultis saw a trunk, picked it up within sight of Zink and moved it about 15 feet towards Zink and, unknown to him, also towards the police. At that point he opened the trunk and was immediately aware that it in fact contained a large quantity of marijuana. There was evidence from the police that both of the appellants exhibited great excitement and exhilaration, shook hands, and exclaimed, among other things "We're rich! We're rich!" At that point the police made their presence known and the appellants were taken into custody.

. . . .

The question of what is the appropriate sentence is acknowledged to be one of very considerable difficulty. The quantity of marijuana involved was very large, consisting of 19 large "bricks", weighing 22 lbs. in all. If sold to "dealers" in bricks, its value would be from $4,000 to $4,500. If broken down for sale to users its value would be around $7,000.

There is evidence from which it might be inferred that Coultis intended to turn the trunk over to a known "dealer", who was to give him half its value, and that Coultis intended to share equally with Zink.

After their arrest, a search was made of the homes of both accused. In Coultis' bedroom were found three grams of marijuana in a bag, one marijuana cigarette butt, and a document with a list of first names and dollar amounts, said by an R.C.M.P. officer to be similar to several such lists he had seen in his work, showing "people who owe you money". In Zink's bedroom were found two grams of marijuana seeds in a bottle in his dresser.

Pre-sentence reports in considerable detail were made with respect to each of the accused persons. After full representations by counsel for each accused, the trial Judge sentenced Zink "to six months probation" (a sentence not known to the law) and Coultis to a suspended sentence for one year followed by one year's probation. In fact, no terms of probation were then or later prescribed by the trial Judge and no probation orders appear ever to have been issued and accordingly there could not have been compliance with s. 663(4) of the *Criminal Code*.

In my view, the two accused ought not to be given the same sentence. I think it is clear from the background of Coultis, as shown by his pre-sentence report, and considering his leadership in this particular enterprise, that the penalty in his case should be the more severe. So far as Zink is concerned, while he has a prior conviction for possession of LSD, on which he was sentenced to a fine, his pre-sentence report is on the whole a very favourable one. He appears to have achieved completion of grade 12 and to have sought and obtained employment. The police do not regard him as a trafficker, although having "some involvement in the drug scene". We are told that Coultis has now completed grade 12 and intends to go to Fanshaw College in the fall of 1974. Both appellants at the present time are 19 years of age and at the time of the commission of the offence were just under 18 years of age.

R. v. RICHA AND BOU-MOURAD

(1974), 18 C.C.C. (2d) 63 (Ont. C.A.)

SCHROEDER J.A.: — The appellant Richa appeals against his conviction on a charge that he did on or about October 28, 1971, in the City of Ottawa, wilfully traffic in a narcotic, to wit: heroin, contrary to the provision of s. 4(1) of the *Narcotic Control Act*, 1960-61 (Can.), c. 35 [now R.S.C. 1970, c. N-11, following a trial before His Honour Judge J.R. Matheson, and a jury. It was a lengthy trial which commenced on February 20, 1972, and concluded on March 10, 1972.

The accused Richa was charged with three others including the appellant Bou-Mourad, but his co-defendants pleaded guilty at an early stage of the trial and the trial proceeded as against Richa, alone.

. . . .

There was a large amount of heroin involved, three kilos or six pounds, for which the appellants were to receive $90,000 or $30,000 per kilo. That was the price at the wholesale level, but the evidence indicates that at the street level the drug in question had a value of approximately $1,500,000.

It is quite evident that the learned trial Judge concluded that both appellants were operating at an executive level in the organization to which they belonged.

R. v. McGINN

(1989), 49 C.C.C. (3d) 137 (Sask. C.A.)

CAMERON J.A. :—

In its factum, the Crown, without objection from counsel for Mr. McGinn, summarized the facts as follows:

On October 5, 1987, a search warrant was conducted at the residence of William John McGinn at 344 Lillooet St. W. in Moose Jaw, Saskatchewan under the authority of a search warrant obtained pursuant to the *Narcotic Control Act.*

The accused William John McGinn and three other persons were present at the residence during the search.

During the search, the following items were seized:

(1) A gold plated jeweller's scale in its case.

(2) One plastic ziploc bag containing a quarter ounce bag of Cannabis marijuana.

One plastic ziploc bag containing three 1-4 ounce bags of cannabis marijuana. (Total cannabis marijuana was 29.8 grams)

Upon police questioning of the persons in the residence as to who the above items belonged to, the accused stated that the scale and the Cannabis marijuana belonged to him.

The accused was arrested and charged with possession of cannabis marijuana for the purpose of trafficking contrary to s. 4(2) of the *Narcotic Control Act.*

The accused was later interviewed by the police officers and made the following admissions:

He said he had purchased the ounce of Cannabis Marijuana for $250.00

(b) He said that he broke the marijuana down into quarter ounce lots when he got home which he intended to sell for $70.00 a quarter.

Having heard these facts, together with something of the accused and his criminal record, the trial Judge, Mr. Justice MacLean, said this:

Well, I think it is obvious from the amount of drug involved here, that it was very small — one ounce.

I don't think any good purpose would be served by sending this man to jail, intermittent or otherwise. He has been there often enough. I mean I can't see where there would be any deterrent to him.

In my view, a fine and a very lengthy period of probation would be far greater deterrent to seeing to it that he keeps his nose clean in the next couple of years because that way society can be assured that if he's going to do time, he's going to do a nice long time, not a little slap on the wrist for 30 days or 60 days, or something which I would be otherwise inclined to give him.

Mr. McGinn, hopefully you have turned the corner, because you know, this is a minor charge, but my, with this record that you've got, for a 23 year old — 24 year old — that's incredible.

The learned trial Judge then announced the sentence and concluded with the following comments:

Now, all that means is that you will not, in two years, commit another criminal offence, because if you do, you will be brought back; you will be sentenced for breach of probation, and I can guarantee that you are not going to get anything less than 30 days, likely 60 to 90, plus whatever crime you might commit. So you are not getting away scott free; this thing is hanging over your head, and with your record, I am certain the local police will keep an eye on you regularly.

At that, the accused was given a month and a half within which to pay his fine.

. . . .

Mr. McGinn is a single, 24-year-old, seasonal labourer, living in Moose Jaw. And he is no stranger to crime. He has an extensive criminal record, spanning the last several years. This is his record in its entirety:

1980-05-27 Moose Jaw, Sask.	(1) Fail to appear S. 133(2) CC (2 chgs) (2) Breach of recogniza. S. 133(3)(B) CC	(1) 1 mo on each chg consec (2) 1 mo conc.
1980-08-11 Moose Jaw, Sask.	B E & Theft S. 306(1)(B) CC	3 mos.
1980-07-30 Moose Jaw, Sask.	Poss of Stolen Property S. 312 Cc	6 mos consec to sent. serving
1981-08-25 Moose Jaw, Sask.	(1) Mischief (2) Assault Peace officer S. 246(2)(A) Cc	(1) probation for 6 mos. plus restitution (2) $200

1983-09-15(2) Moose Jaw, Sask.	Theft over $200 S. 294(a) CC	$200 I-D 60 days
1983-11-28 Moose Jaw, Sask.	Cause a Disturbance S. 171(1)(A) (II) CC	$200 I-D 60 days & probation for 12 mos.
1983-11-30 Moose Jaw, Sask.	Uttering Forged Document S. 326(1)(A) CC	6 mos. & probation for 3 months restitution of $2000
1983-12-16 Moose Jaw, Sask.	Robbery with violence S. 303 CC	2 yrs less 1 day
1984-05-14 Moose Jaw, Sask.	Forgery S. 325 CC (3 chgs)	6 mos on each chg concs. & Con. with sent. serving
1984-10-12 Moose Jaw, Sask.	Escape Lawful Custody S. 133(1)(a) CC	5 mos cons. to sent serving
1984-03-23 Moose Jaw, Sask.	(1) Assault CBH S. 245.1(1)(B) CC (2) Assault S. 245 CC (3) Drive with more than 80 mgs of alcohol in blood S. 237(B) CC	(1) 6 mos (2) 1 mos conc. (3) $300 I-D 60 days consec. & prohibitedd from driving for 6 mos

R. v. DEMETER AND WHITMORE

(1978), 3 C.R. (3d) S-55, 32 C.C.C. (2d) 379 (Ont. C.A.)

DUBIN J.A. (BLAIR J.A. concurring): — In the early morning hours of Friday, 6th June 1976, Michael Demeter, aged 17, and Daniel Whitmore, aged 16, robbed a pizzeria in Hamilton and took some $265. They both wore ski masks, and Whitmore had an unloaded pellet gun which he pointed at the owner. No other acts of violence accompanied the robbery.

As a result of the police investigation both accused were arrested shortly after the offence had been committed, and the moneys were recovered. They were both extremely co-operative and confessed to their part in the robbery.

Their conduct on this occasion was completely out of character. Their object did not appear to be to obtain moneys in this way but rather was mistakenly viewed by them as some sort of challenge.

At the time of this offence Michael Demeter was residing at home and completed all but two credits in Grade XI. He was quite an outstanding young athlete at school and during the past two summers had been gainfully employed. The psychiatrist found him to be a somewhat defensive individual but with no display of criminal characteristics. A pre-sentence report gave a favourable prognosis as to his being able to respond under probation supervision.

Daniel Whitmore, according to the psychiatrist, would also be a good candidate for probation, which was the view expressed in the pre-sentence report as well. He was in Grade X at the time that this offence was committed, and, while on bail, successfully completed his year at the secondary school which he was attending.

R. v. FINNIS

(1978), 3 C.R. (3d) S-54 (Ont. C.A.)

MARTIN J.A. (orally): — The facts, briefly stated, are these. The appellant and two other men had been drinking in a hotel and flagged a taxi cab. During the course of the drive, the appellant seized the taxi driver around his neck from behind, and with a knife in his hand demanded the taxi driver's money. He subsequently threatened the victim if he told the police, but no physical injury was inflicted in the course of the robbery or the escape afterwards. The appellant and his co-accused were arrested soon after the robbery.

The appellant is 30 years of age and has a record. The record is, however, apart from a conviction for robbery in 1968, not altogether serious or extensive. The appellant successfully completed his period of parole after being released on parole with respect to the sentence of five years. He has not been convicted of any serious offence in the interval between his release on parole and the present offence.

Taxi drivers are vulnerable to robbery and must be protected against conduct such as that of which the appellant was guilty by the imposition of appropriate sentences. Notwithstanding the seriousness of the offence, however, we are all of the view that the sentence imposed is excessive.

The appellant has serious medical and psychiatric problems for which he is receiving treatment. It is in his favour that he pleaded guilty and acknowledged his responsibility for what he did.

R. v. GLASSFORD

(1988) 63 C.R. (3d) 209, 42 C.C.C. (3d) 259 (Ont. C.A.)

BROOKE J.A.: —

[T]he respondent was convicted following a trial on his plea of not guilty on a charge of sexual assault causing bodily harm. The offence took place on 16th August 1986. The trial began on 1st November 1987. The respondent was convicted on 1st December 1987 and sentenced on 22nd January 1988.

The facts are important. Both the complainant and the respondent gave evidence. As to the assault, their accounts were completely different. The complainant's evidence was to the effect that the respondent followed her from a hotel, overtook her, attacked her when she refused to have sexual relations with him, knocked her to the ground, struck her until she was unconscious, partially disrobed her and, when he was finished with her, left her in that state and walked off. She said she fought him as best she could.

The respondent testified that he left the hotel with the complainant, and that she seduced him and engaged in rough play with him. There was no sexual intercourse because he was incapable of completing it. He accounted for his dishevelled appearance by telling others immediately after the event that he had been assaulted by three men as he returned to the hotel.

Both were intoxicated when the assault occurred.

The trial Judge rejected the respondent's testimony. He believed the evidence of the complainant.

In context, the evidence was that the complainant, who was a divorced woman and the mother of two children, was celebrating her 27th birthday. She had been out drinking with her boyfriend and other friends at a hotel. She stayed after her boyfriend had left and continued drinking. She was drunk. She left the hotel about 1:00 a.m. and, while going to the place where she had parked her bicycle, she met three men, who were strangers to her, who were smoking hashish. She joined them. She asked if they knew where there was a party and they took her with them to a hotel, where a party in celebration of a wedding was continuing at rooms which had been rented for that purpose there. The respondent was a member of that group.

One of the group of men, a man named Noble, was attracted to the complainant and took her to the hotel with him. He tried to rent a room, hoping that she would have sexual relations with him, but he could not afford the price of the room. Although drunk, she knew about this and remained with Mr. Noble while she was at the hotel. She sat on the staircase and drank liquor with him from a bottle that he carried. Mr. Noble and the complainant then went to a room that others made available to them. They drank and smoked hashish together. From what had transpired, Mr. Noble was quite aroused and believed that the complainant would have sexual relations with him. He took off his clothes and lay down on the bed with her. She did not take her clothes off. She decided not to have sexual intercourse and that she must leave and go home to her children.

Whether it was while they were on the bed in this state, or earlier, the respondent entered the room and had a conversation with the complainant, suggesting that she have what he termed "kinky sex", meaning a threesome. She refused, and the evidence is that she replied that she would rather have sex one-on-one, which Noble anticipated as meaning that she would have sex with him.

There was evidence that before she left the hotel one Greco came to the room and, while he was there, she said in his presence that she would have oral sex with Mr. Noble.

It was only after she left the hotel that she became aware that the respondent was following her. When he overtook her and requested that she come with him, she refused. He seized her and dragged her towards a garden. She pulled away and started crying for help. But he continued to drag her towards the garden and warned her not to try to get away again. Her evidence was that he said to her: "You are going to fuck me and you are going to like it, because bitches like you like that kind of thing." He pushed her down so that she was on her back, kneeled over her and pulled down her pants. She tried to resist by punching him. He punched her on the side of the face three or four times with is fist closed, until she blacked out. When she regained consciousness, her pants were down and her pantyhose were ripped. She did not know if he had had sexual intercourse with her, and the medical and other evidence was inconclusive.

The police found her at 4:00 a.m. walking on the street, crying and shaken, dirty and dishevelled, her face was swollen and bleeding. She was treated for her injuries at a hospital.

The trial Judge accepted the complainant's version of what had happened.

In his reasons for sentence, he said:

> The accused was drunk as well, and somewhat under the influence of drugs. He went after her upon learning that she had left the hotel, and accosted her in the belief, albeit mistaken, that she might consent to have intercourse with him. When she declined, he forced himself upon her. The assault was not premeditated. Instead, it had an element of impulsiveness, of spontaneity, resulting from a temporary loss of control of himself while under the influence of alcohol and drugs.

> As for the victim, the assault upon her was very traumatic but of short duration, and she recovered from her physical injury in two weeks. There is no evidence before me that she has suffered any lasting emotional or psychological injury.

> As for the accused, he is 22 years of age, with a Grade XII education, and is presently unemployed and in receipt of unemployment insurance. He comes of good family, of parents and of brothers and sisters, eight of them, who are loving and caring. He is the second-youngest of the children, all of whom save him are high achievers, he being interested more in athletics, and particularly in soccer, which he plays and performs well as coach in a public school system. He is disposed to working when work is available, and has performed well in the jobs, some of them menial, that he did have. His present plans are to attend Cambrian College in Sudbury next September for recreation leadership . . .

Compare Patricia Marshall, "Sexual Assault, The *Charter* and Sentencing Reform" (1988), 63 C.R. (3d) 216.

R. v. SANDERCOCK

(1986), 48 C.R. (3d) 154, 22 C.C.C. (3d) 79 (Alta. C.A.)

KERANS J.A.: —

We turn now to the facts in this case. Sandercock was driving his vehicle in a residential area in Calgary. The victim, who was 16, was walking towards her home at 11:15 p.m. He told her that he was lost and asked for directions. After a friendly chat, they went their separate ways. A few moments later he again approached her and asked her to park his car. She agreed to do this, and got behind the wheel. He then forced her to go to a secluded spot and to submit to an act of sexual intercourse. Notwithstanding her protests that she was "too young", he told her: "It's going to be all right; I just want to make out." She cried more than she struggled. He then told her that he loved her, and dropped her off near her home without further incident. As a result, she was able to note his licence number. He had been drinking.

Sandercock is 26. He comes from a good home but began to get into trouble when he came to Alberta from Ontario after high school at age 19. He began to use drugs and alcohol and developed a record for minor offences. He had a good work record.

At the time of this offence, he was on mandatory supervision respecting a sentence of one year's imprisonment for an earlier sexual assault. He says that in that case the victim consented, but he was nevertheless guilty because she was under the age of 14 and he did not know it. As a result of his arrest for this conviction, he served his full term on that matter and also had an additional two months in pre-trial detention.

He pled guilty, but only after the victim here had given evidence at the preliminary inquiry. It is said that he is remorseful and a good candidate for rehabilitation.

The Crown suggests that Sandercock was on the prowl and got the victim into the car on a ruse. On the evidence here, there must be a doubt whether this is so. There must be a doubt whether he was not genuinely lost and the incident at least began innocently.

In the circumstances of this case, it could be said that the victim was imprudent as to her own safety. This does not, however offer the slightest mitigation. Nor is the drunkenness of the accused relevant except in support of the argument that the attack was spontaneous. Nor can Sandercock claim that he previously had good character or that he spared the victim the added pain of offering testimony. In the circumstances, any claim of remorse rings hollowly. The most that can be said for him is that he did offer a plea of guilty and thereby waived some of his constitutional rights in deference to the expeditious administration of justice.

Compare annotation on "tariff" sentencing by Allan Manson (1982), 32 C.R. (3d) 1.

R. v. McDONNELL

[1997] 1 S.C.R. 948, 6 C.R. (5th) 231, 114 C.C.C. (3d) 436

Following a preliminary inquiry, the appellant pleaded guilty to two counts of sexual assault, contrary to s. 271 of the *Criminal Code*. The first offence occurred in 1986 when the appellant was 29 years of age. The complainant was then a 16-year-old ward of the Alberta government and had been placed in the appellant's home by Social Services. Approximately two weeks after her arrival in the appellant's home, the complainant was asleep on the living room couch, lying on her back. The appellant came home intoxicated. He undid the complainant's pants, at which point the complainant turned over on her stomach and tried to press herself into the couch. She testified that she did so in the hope that perhaps he would go away if he thought she were sleeping. He did not. Instead, he took off her jeans and started to kiss her buttock area. She was trying to pretend that she was sleeping. Then he penetrated her vagina with his penis. She described the degree of penetration as being "a little bit" since she had her legs pressed together and he was trying to get them apart. Finally, he said "You're too difficult" and rolled onto the floor. He tried to put the complainant's jeans back on. The complainant waited until she was sure that the appellant was asleep on the floor and then she went downstairs to her room. At no time did the complainant consent to the appellant's actions.

The second offence occurred in 1993 when the appellant was 36 years of age. The complainant was a 14-year-old babysitter for the appellant's family. She had fallen asleep on her stomach on a hide-a-bed while babysitting. She testified that when she had gone to bed, she had been wearing a T-shirt, underwear and had a sleeping bag wrapped around her. When she awoke at 3:30 a.m., her underwear was pulled down and the sleeping bag was around her feet. The appellant was on top of her, rubbing her back under her T-shirt with one hand and rubbing her buttocks with the other. He then reached under her stomach touching her pelvis and vaginal areas. The appellant was trying to turn her over onto her stomach. He did not touch her breasts. She screamed and fled from the residence.

The trial judge did not consider either sexual assault to be a "major sexual assault" within the terminology used by the Alberta Court of Appeal for sentencing. Although the first included penetration, it was only partial. She described the second assault as "less grave", although the victim was "traumatized".

See Allan Manson, "*McDonnell* and the Methodology of Sentencing" (1997), 6 C.R. (5th) 277.

R. v. HILL

(1974), 15 C.C.C. (2d) 145 (Ont. C.A.), affirmed (1975), [1977] 1 S.C.R. 827 at 830, 23 C.C.C. (2d) 321

JESSUP J.A.: — The appellant appeals his sentence of 12 years imposed after his plea of guilty to a charge of rape and his sentence of 12 years concurrent imposed upon his plea of guilty to a charge of causing bodily harm with intent to wound, maim or disfigure. The sentences having been put in issue, the Crown moves for their increase, citing *R. v. Willis*, [1969] 2 C.C.C. 84, 4 C.R.N.S. 325.

. . .

Under circumstances indicating planning and deliberation, the appellant went at night to a home where the 14-year-old virginal complainant was babysitting. After assaulting her with his fists he forcibly stripped her of all her clothes and, although she was menstruating, then raped her. He then forced the complainant, unclothed except for a jacket she threw on, to go outside, with the evident intention of taking her somewhere in his car. When the complainant attempted to run away he overtook her and forced her back into the house. When the complainant then attempted to use the telephone, the appellant knocked her to the floor and with a paring knife stabbed her repeatedly in the face and eyes and about the throat until the knife broke. As a result the complainant may lose the sight of one eye. The appellant then fled the house abandoning the wounded complainant. While the appellant had considerable to drink the evening of the crimes, there is no suggestion that he lacked the requisite intent to commit them.

The appellant has no relevant, previous record. He is aged 26 and is the product of a broken home and a disturbed and unsettled childhood. Overcoming these disadvantages he has been almost continually employed since he was about 15 years. He has applied himself commendably as an apprentice mechanic. He is married and his wife and mother-in-law speak highly of him as a husband and provider.

The reports and evidence available to the learned Provincial Judge at the time of sentencing show that the appellant is not insane, mentally ill or psychotic. However, he suffers from a personality disorder manifested in impulsiveness, low stress tolerance, anger which he does not know how to handle properly and difficulty in knowing his own sexual identity. Dr. Karen Galbraith, a psychologist, and Dr. Peter Rowsell, a psychiatrist, both agreed that he was dangerous to the community. Both were testifying for the appellant.

Dr. Galbraith agreed that the appellant's condition could be treated by psychotherapy. However, she was most guarded as to the expected outcome of such treatment, pointing out that the most important single element for success was the unknown factor of motivation. She offered no prognosis as to when, if ever, the appellant can be safely returned to the community.

Dr. Rowsell was equally guarded in his prognosis. In response to a question by the sentencing Judge he said:

> Q. Doctor, you have agreed that the accused is impulsive, easily frustrated, low stress, with Dr. Galbraith — is that correct?
>
> A. Yes
>
> Q. You said that the consumption of alcohol in a stress situation, particularly with his wife, may be the trigger — is that correct?
>
> A. In my opinion, yes.
>
> Q. Would you consider the explosion rather violent?
>
> A. Yes.
>
> Q. So if the accused drinks, is there a possibility or a probability in a stress situation that he could react in the same way?

A. Yes.

Q. Unless he takes treatment and, perhaps, doesn't drink, or he is inclined to take treatment, from what you know of the accused at this time, would he be a danger to the community?

A. Unfortunately, Your Honour, there's no way yet of dealing with these things. We do, however, know one thing concerning disorders is that for some inexplicable reason I have never been able to fathom, they disappear from psychiatric diagnoses in people over 50. I am not sure quite what this means, but do have the opinon that as a person gets older, the aggressive impulse gradually dies down and it seems to be borne out in a number of these people that because of this they are able to adjust a lot better late in life.

Q. Well, then, Doctor, perhaps, at the present time, is the accused potentially dangerous to the community?

A. Oh, yes.

and:

Q. Dr. Rowsell, in response to a question put to you by His Honour, you indicated that normally any disorderly sort of aggressive tendencies, I understood, disappear at the age of 50. Can you tell us at what age we would begin to notice a change we begin to notice a change in the tendencies? At what age do we being to notice that dissipation?

A. The tendency for aggression to die down appears in the spectrum of middle age which, in my opinion, for clinical purposes is between the ages of 35 and 60, gradual diminishing. I would expect in the case of the accused, assuming that there are no complications, and particularly if he licks his drinking problem, that this might die down probably about the age of 35.

Q. And is that in line with any kind of psychotherapy for the other difficulties?

A. This, in my opinion, is irrespective of the other difficulties.

I take from this evidence that while without treatment the appellant's agressive tendencies would probably begin to abate at about the age of 35, there is no certainty to that point of time so that the appellant may continue to be afflicted by his disorder until he is 60 years.

R. v. INWOOD

(1989), 69 C.R. (3d) 181, 48 C.C.C. (3d) 173 (Ont. C.A.)

HOWLAND C.J.O.: — On 2nd September 1988 the respondent ("Inwood") was convicted of two offences, an assault upon his wife, Tanya Sidorova ("Sidorova"), which caused her bodily harm, and an assault upon his infant son, Michael ("Misha"). While Inwood was charged with assault causing bodily harm on his son, he was convicted only of the lesser and included offence of assault.

. . . .

Inwood met Sidorova in December 1985, while he was on vacation in the Soviet Union. They were married in the Soviet Union on 1st July 1986. A son, Misha, was born on 1st September 1986. About one year later Sidorova and the baby were granted exit permits, primarily as a result of Inwood's efforts. They arrived in Toronto on 4th September 1987 and went to live in Inwood's second floor flat at 293 St. Clair Avenue East. They lived there until 13th September 1987, when Sidorova and Misha left and Inwood was taken into custody.

The incident comprising the assault took place on Sunday, 13th September 1987. It is difficult to be specific as to what happened preceding that date. On Saturday, 12th September 1987, Inwood suddenly became angry when he and Sidorova were window-shopping. He began to shout at her in a car showroom. He abruptly left and went home. When Sidorova and Mish got home he continued to abuse them. He pushed her, with Misha in her arms, out of the kitchen, and told her that she no longer had the right to cook in the kitchen and that Misha did not have the right to be in the same room with him. Sidorova testified that Inwood then lay on the couch and drank alcohol.

On Sunday, September 13th, Sidorova took Misha for a walk. They returned between 11:00 a.m. and noon. Inwood had not been drinking during the morning. While Sidorova was in the kitchen preparing Misha's meal, Inwood ran into the room. Misha began to cry when he saw him. Inwood yelled: "Take away the child; if not, then I'll kill him!" He put his hand over Misha's mouth, picked him up and ran with him to Misha's room. Sidorova ran after them. She alleged that Inwood threw a plastic garbage can at her, called her vulgar names and said he was going to throw her out of the house. She further claimed that he slapped her face and grabbed both her hands, twisting her wrists. She broke free and tried to call the police, but he prevented her from doing so. He told her to get out and said: "When I come back in two hours, I am going to kill you." She urged him to try to settle the problem peacefully. He left the house at 1:00 or 2:00 p.m., after hiding her passport and money. The assault in the morning was not found to be an assault causing bodily harm. The trial Judge did not make any finding of fact as to the physical assault, but simply stated that: "Counsel for the accused argues that [Sidorova] demonstrably exaggerated the attack."

After Inwood left the house, Sidorova called the police. Two officers came. Sidorova related what had transpired and showed them how Inwood pushed her when he left the apartment. The pushing incident was consistent with Inwood's evidence. The police advised her to go to a shelter.

Inwood returned home at 8:40 p.m., and the assaults which are the subject of the convictions occurred between 8:40 p.m. and 8:52 p.m. He testified that he had consumed three-quarters of a bottle of whiskey at the home of a friend. This evidence was confirmed by the friend. Inwood went to the room where Misha was sleeping. When Sidorova heard Misha shrieking, she ran to his room and found Inwood pouring water over him. Inwood ran into the bathroom. Sidorova picked up the baby. Inwood returned and threw water at both of them. While Sidorova held the baby, Inwood beat her about the face, arms and head with his hands.

Sidorova claimed that Inwood prevented her from calling the police, and continued to beat her "heavily" and slapped and punched her. She ran into the living room with Misha in her arms and managed to call the police while Inwood was hitting her. She shielded Misha and then put him behind a little table in the living room. She claimed that Inwood continued to beat her and she fell to the floor, where he kicked her head and she "blacked out" for a few seconds. When she opened her eyes, she saw him drop a vase and throw the flowers at her. He then grabbed her by the hair. She claimed that he struck her with a picture frame, started to choke her on the landing of the stairs and pushed her out the door. She fell onto the porch stairs and ran to the street, where she met John O'Byrne, a social worker with the Domestic Response Team and his partner, P.C. James Mackrell, a plain-clothes officer, who were on their way to the house when they received a request over the police radio to respond to the emergency call. They found Sidorova highly agitated and hysterical. She screamed: "He is killing my baby!" Her sweater was damp and askew, and her hair dishevelled and sticking straight out. She had no shoes on. P.C. McCallum arrived a few moments later. The three men and Sidorova entered the house, which was in darkness. They heard Misha screaming loudly. When they entered his room he was lying face down in his crib, naked and soaking wet. His pyjamas were on the wet mattress. He had red marks on his back, buttocks and thighs, a scratched bump on his forehead and a swollen eye. Inwood told his sister Eileen that when he tried to pick up Misha he fell out of his hands and hit the crown of his head on the bed rails. He also testified that he twice dropped Misha on the floor, the first time by accident and the second time because Misha squirmed out of his hands. Inwood acknowledged having slapped the baby seven or eight times on the back to make him stop crying, and that he stripped him because he believed the slapping noise on the baby's skin would scare Misha and make him stop crying.

Inwood's sister Eileen gave evidence that Inwood telephoned her on 14th April 1988 and admitted assaulting Sidorova. He told her that they had both been celebrating on 13th September 1987 and were both drunk when they arrived home around 4:00 p.m. He stated that there had been an argument, when Sidorova said she was leaving him. According to his sister's evidence, Inwood said:

> She had told me she was leaving me, and I hit her and she fell. I couldn't have hit her that hard . . . so I slapped her and I shoved her a bit. Is that a crime?

Inwood, in his evidence at trial, denied assaulting Sidorova and alleged that her accusations of assaults upon herself and the baby were complete fabrications. He took the position that he was the victim in the relationship.

The trial Judge accepted the testimony of Sidorova over that of Inwood. He considered that a person who was being assaulted might honestly perceive that the attack was worse than it actually was. In his opinion, this did not necessarily destroy Sidorova's credibility as to whether she was assaulted by Inwood. The trial Judge found as a fact that Inwood was fabricating and that Sidorova had exaggerated, as the injuries actually suffered by her were not consistent with the nature and extent of the assault as portrayed by her. He decided that he should consider only those injuries suffered by her which were confirmed by the doctors and the police. Dr. Caspari's evidence of his examination approximately five hours after the assault disclosed tenderness on the left occipital area of her head, a bump on the bridge of her nose, a slight swelling of the nose, a slightly swollen lower lip with lacerations inside, a small bruise at the right elbow, and bruising of the inner upper left arm. Constable McCormick testified that he could still see bruises on Sidorova's arms five days after the incident. Both Dr. Caspari and a physician called by the defence, Dr. Colohon, gave evidence that the injuries to Sidorova's nose were more consistent with contact from the side of the hand or knuckles than with a punch from a closed fist or a slap.

The trial Judge found that the assault on Sidorova caused bodily harm, and that the injuries interfered with her comfort and were more than merely transient and more than merely trifling.

As to the consumption of alcohol by the respondent, the trial Judge said:

> The accused was driven, particularly by the cross-examination, to rely on the amount of whiskey he had drunk as a partial excuse, saying he was a little bit drunk at the time and was fading in and out. That may be, but no witness described him as being falling-down drunk, nor did the accused himself do so.

The trial Judge concluded that the acts of slapping Misha seven or eight times and pouring or throwing water over him were assaults, but did not constitute assaults causing bodily harm. He concluded that the red marks on the child's back were merely transient, and had faded while Misha was seen at the Hospital for Sick Children. He concluded that the bump on Misha's head was not caused by an assault, but presumably resulted from Inwood having dropped the baby by accident.

The trial Judge stated that under s. 43 of the *Criminal Code* a parent is justified in using force by way of correction toward a child who is under his care if the force does not exceed what is reasonable under the circumstances. However, he concluded that slapping and spanking a one-year-old child under the circumstances was force exceeding that which was reasonable. In the trial Judge's opinion, the child was terrified.

Sidorova gave evidence that after the she left the house Inwood wrote her many letters, which were forwarded to her by her friends, in which he expressed remorse at his behaviour toward her and Misha and begged her to return to him. He stated that he was seeking help to control his violent behaviour. In one letter he enclosed a manual "Learning to Live Without Violence: A Handbook for Men". Inwood disputed the suggestion that the letters represented any acknowledgment of his guilt; however, there is no appeal against conviction, only against sentence.

Inwood was 44 at the time of the offences. He was raised and educated in the Toronto area and for a long time had worked in the advertising business. His business had been adversely affected by the publicity surrounding the assault charges. Inwood had been on welfare since April 1988 and had moved to a shared townhouse in Don Mills. He was convicted in March 1988 on eight counts of making false statements in unemployment insurance claims in 1982 and 1983. He was sentenced to a fine of $200 on each count, to be followed by probation for one year on conditions which included a provision requiring the payment of $2,985 by way of restitution. Save for these convictions, he has no other criminal record.

Sidorova had little or no money or clothes or other assets and was also on welfare. She was the sole support for Misha. She had little knowledge of Canada, spoke English poorly, and did not know anyone other than Inwood, who had been her only immigration sponsor. It was conceded at trial that there would be no reconciliation between Sidorova and Inwood. It was also agreed between counsel that the probation order should obtain a condition that the only contact between Sidorova and Inwood should be through counsel, and that the only contact by Inwood with Misha should be through a family court order. Such conditions were not in fact embodied in the probation order imposed by the trial judge.

On the sentence hearing, evidence was called by the Crown of five women with whom Inwood had had a relationship between the years 1969 and 1986. The trial Judge was satisfied beyond a reasonable doubt, not that Inwood had committed any criminal offences respecting them, but that he had the character of a person who was abusive to women, particularly those with whom he had a close relationship. The incidents involved assaultive behaviour, threats of harm, harassment and rage. Alcohol was not a distinctive feature of most of the incidents. The trial Judge clearly recognized that Inwood could not be given a greater sentence because of any acts of abuse against any of these women, as he had not been charged or convicted in respect of such acts. These incidents were simply evidence of his abusive character toward women. He could be sentenced only for the actual assaults committed on Sidorova and Misha.

Counsel for the defence called as a witness Dr. Art Beairsto, a family practitioner who had restricted his practice to family counselling and psychotherapy. He had seen Inwood frequently between the time of the commission of the offences and the sentencing. He stated that Inwood had attended the Addiction Research Foundation between September and December 1987, and had been taking Antabuse. He considered Inwood to be "a classic alcoholic with a short fuse and full of frustration", who had made a very real effort to change himself. He was generally contrite and wanted to see and be with his son. He had been on the verge of suicide several times. Dr. Beairsto felt that a repetition of Inwood's conduct was unlikely as long as he did not drink and remained in therapy. He was not cured, but had made progress.

The trial Judge characterized what had transpired as the functioning of a "sick mind and twisted personality".

Compare *R. v. Brown* (1992), 13 C.R. (4th) 346 (Alta. C.A.).

R. v. STONE

[1997] B.C.J. No. 694, 89 B.C.A.C. 139

The trial judge imposed a prison term of four years, in addition to the 18 months served in custody pending trial. The Crown accepted this as effectively a seven year sentence for the purposes of this appeal. The Crown appealed sentence.

FINCH J.A. (concurring ESSON and DONALD JJ.A.): —

The Crown says a sentence of seven years adequately reflects neither the gravity of the offence nor the criminal responsibility of the offender, and is therefore unreasonable. The Crown says a more appropriate sentence would have been on the order of fifteen years to life imprisonment. The Crown says a seven year sentence is so far outside the range appropriate to the case as to be completely inadequate and demonstrably unfit.

. . . .

The respondent was charged with the second degree murder on 20 March, 1994 of his wife, Donna Stone. After a two week trial in Vancouver by Mr. Justice Brenner and jury, the respondent was convicted of manslaughter on 7 October, 1995. At the commencement of the trial, the respondent admitted killing his wife by stabbing her 47 times. The issue at trial was the respondent's state of mind. There was no evidence that he had consumed any drugs or alcohol prior to the killing. Defence counsel advanced the defence of automatism and, in the alternative, provocation. The trial judge left to the jury the defences of insane automatism and provocation. In returning a verdict of manslaughter, the jury must have found that the respondent intended to kill, but had a reasonable doubt that he did so "in the heat of passion caused by sudden provocation": *Criminal Code*, R.S.C. 1985, c. C-46, s. 232(1).

At the sentence proceedings on 1 December, 1995 defence counsel suggested a sentence of 1 to 2 years in addition to the time already spent in custody; Crown counsel suggested a sentence of 15 years to life imprisonment.

. . . .

The respondent, then aged 42, married Donna Stone, aged 34, on 8 May, 1993 after a brief acquaintance. They lived in Winfield, near Kelowna. Donna Stone was 5'2" tall and weighed 105 pounds. The respondent is 5'4" tall. He owned a fencing business and is the father of two sons, aged 14 and 16, from an earlier marriage. Donna Stone was the mother of two daughters, aged 9 and 16, from a previous marriage and she worked as a waitress at the Kelowna airport. From the very beginning, the marriage seems to have been confrontational and unhappy. A major point of contention was the apparent antipathy of Donna Stone towards the respondent's sons, who lived in Surrey with their mother. In March, 1994, the respondent decided to go to Surrey without telling Donna Stone in order to see his sons for the first time in seven months. At the last minute, Donna Stone discovered his plan and insisted on going with him. The respondent testified that throughout the trip to the Lower Mainland Donna Stone was angry with him and harangued him. He visited his sons for 15 minutes at their home, over the strenuous objections backed up by the threats of Donna Stone, who waited for him in his truck. While in the house he said, "I've had enough. This is it. It's divorce. I'm not going to take it any more." After leaving his sons at around 8:00 p.m. the respondent drove with Donna Stone through New Westminster into Burnaby, where he pulled into a parking lot on Kingsway. He testified that his wife continued to harangue him by telling him that his former wife had been "fucking" all his friends, and that his two sons were not his own. According to his account, she told him in the parking lot that he was a piece of "shit", that she had lied to the police about his abusing her and that they were preparing the paper work to arrest him. She said she was going to get a court order so he would have to leave the house, that she would stay in his house and collect alimony and child support. She said she couldn't stand to listen to him whistle, that every time he touched her she felt sick, that he was a lousy "fuck" with a little penis, and that she was never going to "fuck" him again. The respondent testified that the only thing he said to Donna Stone in the parking lot was when she asked him if he wanted a divorce and he responded, "Yes, we might as well if you won't allow me to see my children." The respondent killed Donna Stone while they were sitting in the front cab of his small pick-up truck. He used a hunting knife that was kept in the front pocket of the driver's door for his chain-link business. She died from loss of blood due to 47 stab wounds to her upper body.

. . . .

Prior to this conviction, he had an unrelated criminal record, which the learned sentencing judge properly ignored: Possession of Stolen Property - June 30, 1969, Suspended Sentence; Driving While Impaired - February 5, 1987, licence suspension. On sentencing, the respondent adduced 15 letters of reference. All spoke highly of the respondent as a kind, generous, hard-working, non-violent person.

The Crown argues that to take provocation into account on sentencing is to duplicate the effect of that defence, of which the respondent already has had the benefit in the reduced verdict of manslaughter.

APPENDIX A

The Canadian Bar Association formed a Task Force in 1990 to comprehensively consider the reform of the General Part of the *Criminal Code*. In its 190-page report, it re-assessed the proposals of the Law Reform Commission Report: *Recodifying Criminal Law* (rev. ed., 1987).

C.B.A. TASK FORCE REPORT
PRINCIPLES OF CRIMINAL LIABILITY (1992)

PART VIII: SUMMARY OF RECOMMENDATIONS

The Canadian Bar Association's *Criminal Code* Recodification Task Force recommends that the General Part of the new *Criminal Code* contain provisions to the following effect:

DECLARATION OF PURPOSE AND PRINCIPLES

WHEREAS the purpose of the criminal law is to ensure the protection and security of all members of Canadian society;

AND WHEREAS that purpose is fulfilled by setting standards which represent the limits of acceptable conduct and by proscribing culpable conduct which falls outside those limits;

AND WHEREAS the criminal law should be used in a manner which least interferes with the rights and freedoms of individuals;

AND WHEREAS the purpose of the *Criminal Code of Canada* is to set out the principles of the criminal law in a single document;

It is declared that the following principles will guide the interpretation and application of the *Criminal Code of Canada*:

(a) no one shall be criminally sanctioned unless that person has the requisite wrongful state of mind;

(b) the criminal law should only be resorted to when other means of social control are inadequate or inappropriate;

(c) persons who commit crimes must bear the responsibility for their actions;

(d) the criminal law is to be administered in a fair and dispassionate manner while recognizing the principles of tolerance, compassion and mercy that are integral values of Canadian society.

Principle of legality

1. No one is criminally liable for conduct that, at the time of its occurrence, was not an offence under this *Code* or under any other Act of the Parliament of Canada.

Criminal liability

2. Except where otherwise specifically provided, no one is criminally liable for an offence unless that person engages in the prohibited conduct, with the required blameworthy state of mind, in the absence of a lawful justification, excuse or other defence.

Prohibited conduct

3. Prohibited conduct consists of an act, omission or state of affairs committed or occurring in specified circumstances or with specified consequences.

Omissions

4. No one is liable for an omission unless:

(a) that persons fails to perform a duty imposed by this Act, or

(b) the omission is itself defined as an offence by this Act.

Causation

5.   (1) A person causes a result when that person's acts or omissions significantly contribute to the result.

(2) A person may significantly contribute to a result even though that person's acts or omissions are not the sole cause or the main cause of the result.

(3) No one causes a result if an independent, intervening cause so overwhelms that person's acts or omissions as to render those acts or omissions as merely part of the history or setting for another independent, intervening cause to take effect.

Conscious involuntary conduct

6.   (1) No one is liable for prohibited conduct which, although conscious, is involuntary.

(2) Prohibited conduct is involuntary if it was not within one's ability physically to control. Without limiting the generality of the foregoing, this includes:

(a) a spasm, twitch or reflex action,

(b) an act or movement physically caused by an external force, and

(c) an omission of failure to act as legally required due to physical impossibility.

(3) This section does not apply to conscious involuntary conduct due to provocation, rage, loss of temper, mental disorder, voluntary intoxication or automatism.

(4) If the involuntary prohibited conduct occurred because of a person's prior, voluntary blameworthy conduct, then that person may be held liable for that prior blameworthy conduct.

Automatism

7.   (1) No one shall be convicted of an offence where the prohibited conduct occurred while that person was in a state of automatism.

(2) For the purposes of this section, automatism means unconscious, involuntary behaviour whereby a person, though capable of action, is not conscious of what he or she is doing, and includes unconscious, involuntary behaviour of a transient nature caused by external factors such as:

(a) a physical blow,

(b) a psychological blow from an extraordinary external event which might reasonably be expected to cause a dissociative state in an average, normal person,

(c) inhalation of toxic fumes, accidental poisoning or involuntary intoxication,

(d) sleepwalking,

(e) a stroke,

(f) hypoglycaemia,

(g) a flu or virus, and

(h) other similar factors.

(3) Subsection (1) does not apply to automatism which is caused by:

(a) mental disorder,

    (b) voluntary intoxication; or

    (c) fault as defined in subsection (5).

(4) For the purpose of this section, automatism is caused by mental disorder when the unconscious, involuntary behaviour arises primarily from an internal, subjective condition or weakness in the accused's own psychological, emotional or organic make-up, including dissociative states caused by the ordinary stresses and disappointments of life.

(5) Notwithstanding subsection (1), automatism is not a defence:

    (a) to an intentional offence if a person voluntarily induces automatism with the intention of causing the prohibited conduct of that offence,

    (b) to a knowledge offence if a person voluntarily induces automatism knowing that it is virtually certain that he or she will commit the prohibited conduct of that offence while in that state of automatism, or

    (c) to a reckless offence if a person voluntarily induces automatism, notwithstanding the fact that the person is aware of a risk that he or she will commit the prohibited conduct of that offence while in that state of automatism, and it is highly unreasonable to take that risk.

Mental elements of an offence

8.   (1) For the purpose of criminal liability, the mental elements of an offence are:

    (a) intent,

    (b) knowledge, and

    (c) recklessness.

Intent

(2) A person acts intentionally with respect to prohibited conduct when the person wants it to exist or occur.

Knowledge

(3) A person acts knowingly with respect to prohibited conduct when the person is virtually certain that it exists or will occur.

Recklessness

    (4) A person acts recklessly with respect to prohibited conduct when, in the circumstances actually known to the person:

        (a) the person is aware of a risk that his or her act or omission will result in the prohibited conduct, and

        (b) it is highly unreasonable to take the risk.

Prescribed state of mind applies to all aspects of prohibited conduct

    (5) When the law defining an offence prescribes the state of mind required for the commission of an offence, without distinguishing among aspects of the prohibited conduct, that state of mind shall apply to all aspects of the prohibited conduct of the offence, unless a contrary intent plainly appears.

Residual rule

    (6) Where the definition of a crime does not explicitly specify the requisite state of mind, it shall be interpreted as requiring proof of intent.

    (7) Where the definition of a crime requires knowledge, a person may be liable if the person acts or omits to act intentionally or knowingly as to one or more aspects of the prohibited conduct in that definition.

Greater culpability requirement satisfies lesser

    (8) Where the definition of a crime requires recklessness, a person may be liable if the person acts, or omits to act, intentionally or knowingly as to one or more aspects of the prohibited conduct in that definition.

Mistaken belief in facts

9. No person is liable for an offence committed through lack of knowledge which is due to mistake or ignorance as to the relevant circumstances; but where on the facts as the person believed them he or she would have committed an included offence, the person shall be liable for committing that included offence.

Caution respecting belief

10. A Court or jury, in determining whether a person had a particular belief in a set of facts, shall have regard to all the evidence including, where appropriate, the presence or absence of reasonable grounds for having that belief.

11. No one is criminally liable for conduct if, through disease or mental disability, the person at the time:

    (a) was incapable of appreciatng the nature or consequences of such conduct, or

    (b) believed what he or she was doing was morally right, or

    (c) was incapable of conforming to the requirements of the law.

Defence of the person

12. (1) Every person is justified in using, in self-defence or in the defence of another, such force as, in the circumstances as that person believes them to be, it is reasonable to use.

Excessive force

    (2) A person who uses excessive force in self-defence or in the defence of another and thereby causes the death of another human being is not guilty of murder, but is guilty of manslaughter.

Defence of property

13. (1) A person is justified in using such force as, in the circumstances which exist or which the person believes to exist, is reasonable:

    (a) to protect property (whether belonging to that person or another) from unlawful appropriaton, destruction or damage, or

    (b) to prevent or terminate a trespass to that person's property.

    (2) In no circumstances is it reasonable, in defence of property, to intend to cause death.

Necessity

14. (1) No one is criminally responsible for acting to avoid harm to oneself or another person or to avoid immediate serious damage to property, if the danger which he or she knows or believes to exist is such that in all the circumstances (including any of his or her personal characteristics that affect its gravity) he or she cannot reasonably be expected to act otherwise.

    (2) Clause (1) does not apply to anyone who has knowingly and without reasonable excuse exposed himself or herself to the danger.

Duress

15. No one is liable for committing a crime in response to a threat of harm to oneself or another person if the threat is one which in all the circumstances

(including any of his or her personal characteristics that affect its gravity) he or she cannot reasonably be expected to resist.

Intoxication

16.   (1) No person is liable for a crime for which, by reason of intoxicaton, the person fails to satisfy the culpability requirements specified by its definition.

(2) Clause (1) does not apply where the voluntary consumption of an intoxicant is a material element of the offence charged.

(3) Notwithstanding clause (1), a person charged with a Schedule 1 offence who would, but for voluntary intoxicaton, be found guilty of that offence shall instead be found guilty of the included offence of criminal intoxication.

(4) A person found guilty under clause (3) is liable to the same punishment as if found guilty of an attempt to commit the offence charged.

Mistake of law

17. No one is liable for a crime committed by reason of mistake or ignorance of law:

a. concerning private or other civil rights relevant to that crime, or

b. resulting from:

i. ignorance of the existence of the law, where the law has not been published or otherwise reasonably made known to the public or persons likely to be affected by it,

ii. reasonable reliance on a judicial decision, or

iii. reasonable reliance on a statement by a Judge, government official or person in authority.

Provocation

18.   (1) An accused is provoked if, as a result of another's act or statement, the accused loses self-control where a person in the accused's situation, under the circumstances as the accused believes them to be, would lose self-control.

(2) An accused who, while provoked:

a. commits murder, shall be convicted of manslaughter, and

b. commits any offence included in the Schedule, shall be convicted of committing that offence under provocation, and shall be liable to half the penalty of the offence charged.

Trivial violations

19. Where the Crown has proved all the essential elements of an offence the Court may, before a finding of guilt is entered, stay the proceedings against the accused with respect to that offence, where the accused satisfies the Court on the balance of probabilities that, having regard to the nature of the conduct and all the attendant circumstances, the violation was too trivial to warrant a finding of guilty, the entering of a conviction or the imposition of a criminal sanction.

Entrapment

20.   (1) Where:

    a. the trier of fact is satisfied that the Crown has proved beyond a reasonable doubt all the essential elements of an offence, and

    b. the Court is satisfied that the accused has established, on the balance of probabilities, that he or she was entrapped into committing that offence,

the Court shall stay the proceedings against the accused respecting that offence.

(2) Without limiting the generality of subsection (1), entrapment includes committing an offence when the authorities:

    a. not having a reasonable suspicion that the accused is already engaged in that particular criminal activity, or not acting in the course of a *bona fide* investigation directed at persons present in an area where it is reasonably suspected that the particular criminal activity is occurring, provide the accused with the opportunity to commit that offence; or

    b. having a reasonable suspicion that the accused is already engaged in that particular criminal activity, or acting in the course of a *bona fide* investigation directed at persons present in an area where it is reasonably suspected that the particular criminal activity is occurring, go beyond providing an opportunity and induce the accused to commit that offence.

Common-law defences

21. No defence, justification or excuse shall be unavailable unless expressly prohibited by this *Code*.

Attempts

22.   (1) Every one who, having an intent to commit an offence, does or omits to do anything for the purpose of carrying out that intention is guilty of

an attempt to commit the offence, even if it was factually or legally impossible under the circumstances to commit the offence.

(2) The question whether an act or omission by a person who has an intent to commit an offence is or is not mere preparation to commit the offence, and too remote to constitute an attempt to commit the offence, is a question of law.

(3) Except where otherwise expressly provided by law, every one who aids or encourages another person to commit an offence is, if that offence is not committed, guilty of an attempt to commit that offence.

Conspiracy

23. (1) Every one is liable for conspiracy who agrees with another person, whether or not they are married to each other, to commit a *Criminal Code* offence which is indictable or which may be proceeded with by indictment.

(2) A person does not conspire unless he or she intends to commit an offence described in clause (1).

(3) A person who abandons a conspiracy to commit an offence described in clause (1), before that offence is attempted or committed, is not liable for the conspiracy.

(4) In determining whether a person abandoned a conspiracy the Court shall consider all relevant circumstances, including whether the person communicated his or her desistance to the other conspirators or to the authorities, or both.

(5) Every one who conspires to commit an offence described in clause (1) is liable, even if it was factually or legally impossible under the circumstances to commit the offence.

(6) Subject to diplomatic and other immunity under law, this *Code* applies to, and the Courts have jurisdiction over:

   a. conduct engaged in outside Canada which constitutes a conspiracy to commit a crime in Canada, where the conduct took place on the high seas or in a state where the crime in question is also a crime in that state, and

   b. conduct engaged in inside Canada which constitutes a conspiracy to commit a crime outside Canada if the crime in question is a crime in Canada and in the place where the crime is to be committed.

Parties

24. Every one is a party to and guilty of an offence who:

      a. actually commits it,

      b. does or omits to do anything knowing that it will aid any person to commit it, or

      c. does or omits to do anything with the intent of encouraging any person to commit it.

Multiple convictions

25. No person shall be convicted twice for the same delict.

APPENDIX B

Text of a General Part Suggested by Don Stuart

The following draft was presented to a conference of academics, judges and lawyers entitled "Making Criminal Law Clear and Just: A Criminal Reports Forum", held in Kingston, Ontario, on November 6-8, 1998. The papers and proceedings of that conference have been published: see Stuart, Delisle and Manson, eds., *Towards a Clear and Just Criminal Law* (Carswell, 1999).

Preamble

Whereas the Criminal Code of Canada has not, since it was first enacted in 1892, comprehensively declared basic principles under which persons can be justly held criminally responsible,

Whereas Criminal Law should be clear and accessible to all,

Whereas the declaration of such principles by the courts has become unduly complex and sometimes inconsistent, and

Whereas the Criminal Code should reflect minimum constitutional standards declared by the courts to be mandated by interpreting the Canadian Charter of Rights and Freedoms,

Parliament hereby enacts a new Part 1 of the Criminal Code entitled Principles of Criminal Responsibility.

Principle of Legality

1.   No one can be found guilty of conduct that is not an offence under this Act or another Act of Parliament.

Principles of Interpretation

2.   In the absence of clear legislative intent to the contrary, the principles in the General Part are to be applied in the interpretation of any offence in the Criminal Code or other Act of Parliament.

3.   Where a provision of the Criminal Code is reasonably capable of two interpretations, the interpretation which is more favourable to the accused must be adopted.

Criminal Responsibility

4. Except where otherwise specifically provided, no one is criminally responsible for an offence unless that person engages in the prohibited conduct with the requisite fault and in the absence of a lawful justification, excuse or other defence.

Prohibited Conduct

5. Prohibited conduct consists of an act committed or omission occurring in specified circumstances and sometimes with specified consequences.

Omissions

6. No one is criminally responsible for an omission unless

    (1)   there is a legal duty declared by the offence definition in the Criminal Code or other Act of the Parliament of Canada, or

    (2)   that person created danger to life or safety of others and rectification was reasonably within that person's control.

Involuntary Conduct

7. (1)   No one is criminally responsible for involuntary conduct.

    (2)   Conduct is involuntary if it was beyond that person's ability to control.

    (3)   This section does not apply to conduct resulting from rage, mental disorder, or where the accused getting into the involuntary state satisfied the fault requirement for the offence charged.

Causation

8. (1)   A person causes a consequence when that person's acts or omissions significantly contribute to the result.

    (2)   A person may significantly contribute to a consequence even though that person's acts or omissions are not the sole or main cause of the consequence.

    (3)   No one causes a consequence if an independent, intervening cause so overwhelms that person's acts or omissions as to render those acts or omissions as merely part of the history or setting for another independent, intervening cause to take effect.

Minimum Fault for Criminal Code Offences

9.   Unless the law creating the offence specifies to the contrary, criminal responsibility under the Criminal Code requires proof of fault in the form of intent, recklessness or criminal negligence.

10.   Unless the law creating the offence specifies to the contrary, recklessness is the fault element required in relation to each element of the offence.

Intention

11.   A person acts "intentionally" with respect to

    (1)   a circumstance where that person hopes or knows that it exists or will exist;

    (2)   a consequence when that person's purpose is to cause it, or that person knows that it would occur in the ordinary course of events if he or she were to succeed in his or her purpose of causing some other consequence.

Recklessness

12.   A person acts "recklessly" with respect to

    (1)   a circumstance when that person is aware of a risk that it exists or will exist;

    (2)   a consequence when that person is aware of a risk that it will occur; and it is, in the circumstances known to that person, unreasonable to take the risk.

Criminal Negligence

13.   A person is "criminally negligent" where a reasonable person in the accused's situation would have been aware of the risk and the failure to avoid it constituted a marked substantial departure from the standard of care a reasonable person would have exercised in the circumstances.

Reasonableness Standard

14.   For the purposes of section 13 and the application of any reasonableness standard under this Criminal Code the trier of fact must take into account the person's awareness, if any, of the circumstances and also factors the person could not have controlled or managed such as race, gender, age and experience, where relevant, but not self-induced intoxication.

Mistake of Fact

15.   (1)   Where the fault requirement is intent or recklessness, to excuse a mistaken belief need not be reasonable although reasonableness is relevant to determining whether the belief existed.

(2)   Where the fault requirement is criminal negligence, to excuse a mistaken belief must be reasonable.

(3)   Where the accused has a mistaken belief within the meaning of subsections (1) or (2) he or she may nevertheless be convicted of an included or attempted offence where the belief constitutes the requisite fault for that offence.

Fault for Offences Under Other Acts of Parliament

16   (1)   Unless Parliament expressly requires intent, recklessness or criminal negligence as a fault requirement or expressly imposes absolute liability, negligence is required for penal liability.

(2)   A person acts "negligently" where he or she departs from the standard of care expected of a reasonable prudent person in the circumstances.

(3)   Before imprisonment can be imposed, intent, recklessness or criminal negligence must be proved.

(4)   Where the Crown has proved the conduct specified in the offence for which the fault requirement is negligence, the accused is presumed to have acted negligently in the absence of evidence to the contrary.

Common Law Defences

17.   No defence, justification or excuse shall be unavailable unless contrary to an express provision of the Criminal Code.

Mistake or Ignorance of Law

18.   Ignorance or mistake of law is not an excuse.

19.   No one is criminally responsible for a mistake or ignorance of law resulting from

(1)   the law not being properly made known to those likely to be affected, or

(2)   reliance on a judicial decision or official advice.

Age Incapacity

20.   No person is criminally responsible for conduct while under the age of twelve years.

Mental Disorder Incapacity

21.   (1)   No person is criminally responsible for conduct while suffering from mental disorder that rendered the person incapable of appreciating the nature and quality of the conduct or of knowing that it was morally wrong.

        (2)   For the purpose of subsection (1), every person is presumed not to suffer from a mental disorder, in the absence of evidence to the contrary.

Self-induced Intoxication

22.   Self-induced intoxication is not a ground of incapacity nor may it be considered in any determination of reasonableness under this Act.

Defence of Person

23.   A person is not criminally responsible for using force against another person if he or she

        (1)   reasonably believes that force is necessary for self-protection or the protection of a third party from unlawful force or the threat thereof; and

        (2)   the degree of force used is reasonable.

Defence of Property

24.   A person is not criminally responsible for using force against another person if he or she

        (1)   reasonably believes that force is necessary to protect property, whether belonging to that person or another, from unlawful appropriation, destruction or damage, or to prevent or terminate a trespass to that person's property; and

        (2)   that force is reasonable.

Duress

25.   A person is not criminally responsible for conduct under threat where

        (1)   that person reasonably believes

(a)   that a threat has been made to cause death or serious personal harm to that person or another if the conduct is not performed;

(b)   that the threat will be carried out immediately if that person does not act or before that person or that other can gain official protection; and

(c)   that there is no other way of preventing the threat being carried out;

(2)   the threat is one which in all the circumstances that person cannot reasonably be expected to resist; and

(3)   the person has not recklessly exposed himself or herself to the risk of threat.

Necessity

26.   A person is not criminally responsible for conduct under necessity where

(1)   that person reasonably believes that it is immediately necessary to avoid serious personal harm to that person or another or serious harm to property;

(2)   in all the circumstances that person cannot reasonably be expected to do otherwise; and

(3)   the person has not recklessly and without reasonable excuse exposed himself or herself to the danger.

Accessories

27.   Every one is an accessory to an offence and liable to the same penalty as a perpetrator who

(1)   does or omits to do anything with intent to procure, assist or encourage another to commit an offence;

(2)   with the fault required for that offence; and

(3)   that other person commits the offence, whether or not that person can be convicted of it.

Corporations

28.   (1)   Corporations may be held criminally responsible for any offence if, on consideration of that corporation's organizational structure and culture, the corporation can be justly held to have

acted with the fault specified for the particular offence, whether this be intention, recklessness or criminal negligence.

(2)   For the purpose of the determination under subsection (1), consideration is to be given to acts of authorization or delegation, corporate goals and practices, past practices, any past offences and the existence and sufficiency of compliance programmes.